Lecture Notes in Computer Science

Lecture Notes in Artificial Intelligence 16941

The series Lecture Notes in Artificial Intelligence (LNAI) was established in 1988 as a topical subseries of LNCS devoted to artificial intelligence.

The series publishes state-of-the-art research results at a high level. As with the LNCS mother series, the mission of the series is to serve the international R & D community by providing an invaluable service, mainly focused on the publication of conference and workshop proceedings and postproceedings.

Michelangelo Ceci · Dragi Kocev ·
Anna Monreale · Celine Vens · Peter Flach ·
Giuseppe Manco · Myra Spiliopoulou ·
Elio Masciari
Editors

Machine Learning and Knowledge Discovery in Databases

Research Track

European Conference, ECML PKDD 2026
Naples, Italy, September 7–11, 2026
Proceedings, Part I

Springer

Editors
Michelangelo Ceci
University of Bari Aldo Moro
Bari, Italy

Dragi Kocev
Jožef Stefan Institute
Ljubljana, Slovenia

Anna Monreale
University of Pisa
Pisa, Italy

Celine Vens
KU Leuven
Kortrijk, Belgium

Peter Flach
University of Bristol
Bristol, UK

Giuseppe Manco
ICAR-CNR
Rende, Italy

Myra Spiliopoulou
Otto von Guericke University Magdeburg
Magdeburg, Germany

Elio Masciari
University of Naples Federico II
Naples, Italy

ISSN 0302-9743 ISSN 1611-3349 (electronic)
Lecture Notes in Artificial Intelligence
ISBN 978-3-032-37653-4 ISBN 978-3-032-37654-1 (eBook)
https://doi.org/10.1007/978-3-032-37654-1

LNCS Sublibrary: SL7 – Artificial Intelligence

This Springer imprint is published by the registered company Springer Nature Switzerland AG
The registered company address is: Gewerbestrasse 11, 6330 Cham, Switzerland

Preface

The 2026 edition of the European Conference on Machine Learning and Principles and Practice of Knowledge Discovery in Databases (ECML PKDD 2026) was held in Naples, Italy from September 7 to 11, 2026.

The annual ECML PKDD conference is a premier worldwide platform dedicated to showcasing the latest advancements and fostering insightful discussions in the fields of machine learning and knowledge discovery in databases. Held jointly since 2001, ECML PKDD has firmly established its reputation as the leading European conference in these disciplines. It provides researchers and practitioners with an unparalleled opportunity to exchange knowledge, share innovative ideas, and explore the latest technical advancements. The conference particularly values the synergy between foundational theoretical advances and groundbreaking practical data science applications, actively encouraging contributions that demonstrate how Machine Learning and Data Mining are being effectively employed to address complex real-world challenges. Over the years, technologies evolve, and the needs of the individuals, society and the world change. ECML PKDD remains committed to the presentation of cutting-edge research that reflects this evolution.

The Naples edition of ECML PKDD was a truly special one, marked both by an exceptionally high number of scientific contributions and by an outstanding level of participation from the industrial community. The remarkable response from researchers, practitioners, and companies reflects the growing relevance of machine learning, data mining, and artificial intelligence across both academic and industrial domains. In particular, the significant engagement of leading companies and technology stakeholders further strengthened the dialogue between research and real-world applications, making this edition a vibrant meeting point for scientific excellence, innovation, and industrial impact.

The Conference Tracks

The three middle days of the conference were organized in the following tracks:

- The **Research Track** received the impressive number of 1,150 full paper submissions, going for the first time above the 1,000 submissions mark, and an absolute increase of more than 200 submissions over the previous edition, which also had a substantial increase in submissions; of these submissions, 280 were accepted, demonstrating a highly competitive acceptance rate of 24.3%. The review process was double blind, and submissions received three reviews each on average.

- The **Applied Data Science Track** received 381 submissions, of which 90 were accepted. This resulted in a similar acceptance rate of 23.6%. The review process was double blind, and submissions received 3.9 reviews each on average.
- The **Journal Track** received 213 submissions, of which 34 papers were accepted in the Machine Learning Journal and 24 in the Data Mining and Knowledge Discovery Journal, while 7 papers are still under review.
- The **Nectar Track** solicited submissions of summaries of recently published, impactful scientific papers presenting advances at the forefront of machine learning and data mining, as well as their applications in other disciplines. This track received 26 submissions.
- The **Demo Track** solicited submissions that showcase practical applications and prototypes; it received 38 submissions, with 27 accepted demo papers. The review process was single blind, and submissions received two reviews each on average.
- The **Industrial Track** received a record of 42 submissions, 21 of which were accepted for presentation at the conference. The review process was single blind, and submissions received three reviews each on average.

The keynotes

ECML PKDD 2026 featured five keynote talks by internationally leading experts, one on each day of the conference in this order:

- **Mihaela van der Schaar** (University of Cambridge) spoke on *Rethinking the Role of Scientific Discovery in the Era of AI*. She presented a framework that rethinks discovery as an agentic process, in which networks of interacting AI agents and human experts jointly explore, critique, and refine hypotheses under shared norms of evaluation.
- **Stefanie Jegelka** (Technical University of Munich) explored the link between *Neural Networks and Algorithms*. She argued that an algorithmic view can help understand not only the capabilities of deep learning models, such as self-correction or the ability to solve certain optimization problems, but also how to design and train models to better solve challenging tasks, from optimization problems to reasoning.
- **Sihem Amer-Yahia** (CNRS and Laboratoire d'Informatique de Grenoble) gave a keynote entitled *From Dialogue to Decision: Orchestrating Agents for Conversational Data Exploration and Multi-Objective Optimization* in which she investigated the intersection of conversational data exploration, an incremental process where agents help users articulate needs through data interaction, and multi-objective sequential decision making.
- **Francesca Rossi** (Thomas J. Watson IBM Research Center) spoke on key issues around *AI ethics and governance* and how they have evolved with the dramatically

increased AI capabilities of today. She also discussed instrumental and value-based approaches which make investing in AI ethics and governance worthwhile.

- **Gianni Riotta** (Luiss University) presented his perspective under the title *The AI Ghosts and Us: Machine Writing as a Spectral Culture.* He advocated a radically new philosophical reading of AI-generated text as a "Ghost" inhabiting contemporary human discourse, and argued that machine writing constitutes a spectral hybrid: neither fully human nor purely artificial, but a liminal presence emerging from the archive of human language.

Scholarships

We awarded 10 scholarship grants of 1,000 EUR each to students and early-career researchers.

Acknowledgements

We want to thank the authors, organizing committee, workshop and tutorial organizers, and participants whose scientific contributions made this such an exciting event.

We are greatly indebted to the reviewers and senior reviewers: their dedication, vigilance, and enormous time investment made it possible to manage the large number of submissions, ensure the high quality for which ECML PKDD is known, and put together an outstanding conference program. A special thanks goes to the emergency reviewers who finished the last missing reviews at short notice.

This large event would not have run smoothly without the many volunteers and sessions chairs. Finally, we want to express our heartfelt gratitude to all the local organizers – they dealt with all the little details that were needed to make the conference a memorable event.

We want to cordially thank our sponsors for their generous financial support. We also want to thank Springer for their continuous support and Microsoft for allowing us to use their CMT software for conference management and for providing help throughout. We very much appreciate the advice and guidance provided by the ECML PKDD Steering Committee from the moment the organization of the 2026 edition started.

September 2026

Elio Masciari
Peter Flach
Giuseppe Manco
Myra Spiliopoulou
General Chairs

Michelangelo Ceci
Dragi Kocev
Anna Monreale
Celine Vens
Research Track Chairs

Mitra Baratchi
Francesco Bonchi
Riccardo Guidotti
Francesco Gullo
Applied Data Science Track Chairs

Paolo Mignone
Mouzhi Ge
Vincenzo Moscato
Demo Track Chairs

Chiara Celsi
Ruggero G. Pensa
Fabrizio Silvestri
Industrial Track Chairs

Organization

General Chairs

Peter Flach	University of Bristol, UK
Giuseppe Manco	ICAR-CNR, Italy
Elio Masciari	University of Naples Federico II, Italy
Myra Spiliopoulou	Otto von Guericke University Magdeburg, Germany

Research Track Chairs

Michelangelo Ceci	University of Bari Aldo Moro, Italy
Dragi Kocev	Jožef Stefan Institute, Slovenia
Anna Monreale	University of Pisa, Italy
Celine Vens	KU Leuven, Belgium

Applied Data Science Track Chairs

Mitra Baratchi	Leiden University, Netherlands
Francesco Bonchi	Intesa Sanpaolo AI Research, Italy
Riccardo Guidotti	University of Pisa, Italy
Francesco Gullo	University of L'Aquila, Italy

Journal Track Chairs

Zahraa S. Abdallah	University of Bristol, UK
Annalisa Appice	University of Bari Aldo Moro, Italy
Przemysław Biecek	Warsaw University of Technology, Poland
Andrea Tagarelli	University of Calabria, Italy

Industrial Track Chairs

Chiara Celsi	Deloitte Italy, Italy
Ruggero G. Pensa	University of Turin, Italy
Fabrizio Silvestri	Sapienza University of Rome, Italy

Workshop Chairs

Dino Ienco	INRAE, Inria, UMR TETIS, University of Montpellier, France
Gianvito Pio	University of Bari Aldo Moro, Italy

Tutorial Chairs

Antonio Maria Rinaldi	University of Naples Federico II, Italy
Cristiano Russo	University of Naples Federico II, Italy

Nectar Track Chairs

Aniello Murano	University of Naples Federico II, Italy
Chiara Renso	ISTI-CNR, Italy
Salvo Rinzivillo	ISTI-CNR, Italy

PhD Forum Chairs

Giuseppina Andresini	University of Bari Aldo Moro, Italy
Silvia Rossi	University of Naples Federico II, Italy

Awards Committee Chairs

Sergio Di Martino	University of Naples Federico II, Italy
Donato Malerba	University of Bari Aldo Moro, Italy
Carlo Sansone	University of Naples Federico II, Italy

Proceedings Chairs

Irena Koprinska	University of Sydney, Australia
Angelica Liguori	ICAR-CNR, Italy
Eliana Pastor	Politecnico di Torino, Italy

Diversity and Inclusion Chairs

Esma Aimeur	Université de Montréal, Canada
Flora Amato	University of Naples Federico II, Italy
Christine Markarian	University of Dubai, United Arab Emirates
Rosa Meo	University of Turin, Italy

Demo Chairs

Paolo Mignone	Università Pegaso, Italy
Mouzhi Ge	Deggendorf Institute of Technology, Germany
Vincenzo Moscato	University of Naples Federico II, Italy

Discovery Challenge Chairs

Mark Cotè	King's College London, UK
Stefano Marrone	University of Naples Federico II, Italy
Roberto Trasarti	ISTI-CNR, Italy

Panel Chairs

Massimo Bernaschi	IAC-CNR, Italy
Luca Caviglione	IMATI-CNR, Italy

Publicity Chairs

Roberto Interdonato	Cirad, Inria, UMR TETIS, Montpellier, France
Enea Vincenzo Napolitano	University of Naples Federico II, Italy
Vincenzo Pasquadibisceglie	University of Bari Aldo Moro, Italy

Senior Sponsors Chairs

Mariam Barry	BNP Paribas, France
Robert Jan van Wijk	ASML, Netherlands

Local Sponsors Chairs

Antonino Ferraro	Pegaso University, Italy
Simona Fioretto	University of Naples Federico II, Italy
Cristian Tommasino	University of Naples Federico II, Italy

Web, Social Media and Conference App Chairs

Michela Gravina	University of Naples Federico II, Italy
Simone Mungari	ICAR-CNR, Revelis s.r.l., Italy
Franca Rocco di Torrepadula	University of Naples Federico II, Italy

CMT Chairs

Antonio Galli	University of Naples Federico II, Italy
Giancarlo Sperli	University of Naples Federico II, Italy

Whova App and Slides Chair

Giuseppe Papuzzo	ICAR-CNR, Italy

Steering Committee

Tijl De Bie	Ghent University, Belgium
Albert Bifet	University of Waikato, New Zealand - Télécom Paris, France
Francesco Bonchi	Intesa Sanpaolo AI Research, Italy
Ilaria Bordino	UniCredit, Italy
Saso Dzeroski	Jožef Stefan Institute, Slovenia
Ioanna Miliou	Stockholm University, Sweden
Siegfried Nijssen	KU Leuven, Belgium

Andrea Passerini	University of Trento, Italy
Robert Jan van Wijk	ASML, the Netherlands
Wenbin Zhang	Florida International University, USA
Albrecht Zimmermann	Université de Caen Normandie, France
Elena Baralis	Politecnico di Torino, Italy
Claudia Plant	Universität Wien, Austria
Manuel Gomez Rodriguez	Max Planck Institute for Software Systems, Germany
Jesse Davis	KU Leuven, Belgium
Tomas Krilavičius	Vytautas Magnus University, Lithuania
Panagiotis Papapetrou	Stockholm University, Sweden
Myra Spiliopoulou	Otto-von-Guericke University Magdeburg, Germany
Pedro Henriques Abreu	University of Coimbra, CISUC, Portugal
João Gama	University of Porto, INESC-TEC, Portugal
Sepideh Pashami	Halmstad University, Sweden
Rita P. Ribeiro	University of Porto, INESC TEC, Portugal

Program Committee

Area Chairs, Research Track

Pedro Henriques Abreu	CISUC, Portugal
Tiago Almeida	Federal University of São Carlos, Brazil
Annalisa Appice	University of Bari Aldo Moro, Italy
Anthony Bagnall	University of Southampton, UK
Gustavo Batista	University of New South Wales, Australia
Jessa Bekker	KU Leuven, Belgium
Bettina Berendt	TU Berlin, Germany
Concha Bielza	Universidad Politécnica de Madrid, Spain
Albert Bifet	University of Waikato, New Zealand
Hendrik Blockeel	KU Leuven, Belgium
Henrik Boström	KTH Royal Institute of Technology, Sweden
Zied Bouraoui	CRIL CNRS & University of Artois, France
Ulf Brefeld	Leuphana University of Lüneburg, Germany
Toon Calders	University of Antwerp, Belgium
Jesús Cerquides	IIIA-CSIC, Spain
Sara Colantonio	Institute of Information Science and Technologies of the National Research Council of Italy, Italy
Roberto Corizzo	American University, USA
Fabrizio Costa	University of Exeter, UK

Jesse Davis	KU Leuven, Belgium
Tom Diethe	AstraZeneca/University of Bristol, UK
Wouter Duivesteijn	Eindhoven University of Technology, Netherlands
Tome Eftimov	Jožef Stefan Institute, Slovenia
Sophie Fellenz	RPTU Kaiserslautern-Landau, Germany
Stefano Ferilli	University of Bari Aldo Moro, Italy
Cèsar Ferri	Universitat Politècnica de València, Spain
Eibe Frank	University of Waikato, New Zealand
Elisa Fromont	Université Rennes, IRISA/Inria, France
Johannes Fürnkranz	Johannes Kepler University Linz, Austria
Esther Galbrun	University of Eastern Finland, Finland
Pierre Geurts	University of Liège, Belgium
Aristides Gionis	KTH Royal Institute of Technology, Sweden
Chen Gong	Nanjing University of Science and Technology, China
Barbara Hammer	Bielefeld University, Germany
Jose Hernandez-Orallo	Universitat Politècnica de València/University of Cambridge, Spain/UK
Sibylle Hess	Eindhoven University of Technology, Netherlands
Georgiana Ifrim	University College Dublin, Ireland
Manfred Jaeger	Aalborg University, Denmark
Nathalie Japkowicz	American University, USA
Szymon Jaroszewicz	Polish Academy of Sciences, Poland
Adam Jatowt	University of Innsbruck, Austria
Ioannis Katakis	University of Nicosia, Cyprus
Megha Khosla	TU Delft, Netherlands
Marius Kloft	RPTU Kaiserslautern-Landau, Germany
Arno Knobbe	Leiden University, Netherlands
Danai Koutra	University of Michigan, USA
Petra Kralj Novak	Central European University, Austria
Niels Landwehr	University of Hildesheim, Germany
Pedro Larranaga	Universidad Politécnica de Madrid, Spain
Mark Last	Ben-Gurion University of the Negev, Israel
Jefrey Lijffijt	Ghent University, Belgium
Jessica Lin	George Mason University, USA
Ana Carolina Lorena	Instituto Tecnológico de Aeronáutica, Brazil
Jörg Lücke	Universität Innsbruck, Austria
Xiao Luo	University of Wisconsin–Madison, USA
Michael Madden	University of Galway, Ireland
Donato Malerba	University of Bari Aldo Moro, Italy
Fragkiskos Malliaros	CentraleSupélec, France
Ernestina Menasalvas	Universidad Politécnica de Madrid, Spain

Rosa Meo	University of Turin, Italy
Pauli Miettinen	University of Eastern Finland, Finland
Pasquale Minervini	University of Edinburgh, UK
Dunja Mladenic	Jožef Stefan Institute, Slovenia
Siegfried Nijssen	KU Leuven, Belgium
Eirini Ntoutsi	University of the Bundeswehr Munich, Germany
Pance Panov	Jožef Stefan Institute, Slovenia
Evangelos Papalexakis	University of California, Riverside, USA
Andrea Passerini	University of Trento, Italy
Jaakko Peltonen	Tampere University, Finland
Ruggero Pensa	University of Turin, Italy
Bernhard Pfahringer	University of Waikato, New Zealand
Gianvito Pio	University of Bari Aldo Moro, Italy
Evaggelia Pitoura	University of Ioannina, Greece
Ricardo Prudencio	Universidade Federal de Pernambuco, Brazil
Chedy Raissi	Inria, France
Aleksandra Rashkovska Koceva	Jožef Stefan Institute, Slovenia
Jesse Read	École Polytechnique, France
Rita P. Ribeiro	University of Porto & INESC TEC, Portugal
Luca Romeo	University of Macerata, Italy
Salvatore Ruggieri	University of Pisa, Italy
Zahraa S. Abdallah	University of Bristol, UK
Yvan Saeys	Ghent University, Belgium
Matthias Schubert	Ludwig-Maximilians-Universität München, Germany
Junming Shao	University of Electronic Science and Technology of China, China
Arno Siebes	Utrecht University, Netherlands
Fabrizio Silvestri	Sapienza University of Rome, Italy
Nikola Simidjievski	Télécom Paris, Institut Polytechnique de Paris, France
Carlos Soares	University of Porto/Fraunhofer AICOS Portugal/BrightFactory, Portugal
Jerzy Stefanowski	Poznań University of Technology, Poland
Fabio Stella	University of Milano-Bicocca, Italy
Stefano Teso	University of Trento, Italy
Ioannis Tsamardinos	University of Crete, Greece
Charalampos Tsourakakis	University of Crete, Greece
Matthijs van Leeuwen	Leiden University, Netherlands
Jan Van Rijn	Leiden University, Netherlands
Varvara Vetrova	University of Canterbury, New Zealand

Jilles Vreeken	CISPA Helmholtz Center for Information Security, Germany
Willem Waegeman	Ghent University, Belgium
Jörg Wicker	University of Auckland, New Zealand
Wei Ye	Tongji University, China
Wenbin Zhang	Florida International University, USA
Indre Zliobaite	University of Helsinki, Finland

Program Committee, Research Track

Kamil Adamczewski	Max Planck Institute for Intelligent Systems, Germany
Timilehin Aderinola	Insight Research Ireland Centre for Data Analytics, University College Dublin, Ireland
Linara Adilova	RC Trust, Germany
Stergos Afantenos	Université de Toulouse, France
Juba Agoun	Université Lumière Lyon 2, France
Azim Ahmadzadeh	University of Missouri - St. Louis, USA
Deepak Ajwani	University College Dublin, Ireland
Reza Akbarinia	Inria, France
Esra Akbas	Georgia State University, USA
Cuneyt Akcora	University of Central Florida, USA
Youhei Akimoto	University of Tsukuba/RIKEN AIP, Japan
Ozge Alacam	Ludwig-Maximilians-Universität München, Germany
Tahani Aladwani	University of Glasgow, UK
Dima Alberg	SCE Shamoon College of Engineering, Israel
Fayad Ali Banna	Laboratoire Hubert Curien, France
Benjamin Allaert	IMT Nord Europe, France
Simeon Allmendinger	University of Bayreuth, Germany
Sarra Alqahtani	Wake Forest University, USA
Jose Alvarez	Santander AI Lab, Spain
Ehsan Aminian	INESC TEC, Portugal
Christos Anagnostopoulos	University of Glasgow, UK
Giuseppina Andresini	University of Bari Aldo Moro, Italy
Piotr Andruszkiewicz	Warsaw University of Technology, Poland
Ekaterina Antonenko	Mines Paris - PSL, France
Alessandro Antonucci	IDSIA, Switzerland
Nelson Antunes	University of Algarve and University of Lisbon, Portugal
Edward Apeh	Bournemouth University, UK
Pasquale Ardimento	University of Bari Aldo Moro, Italy

Jerónimo Arenas-García	Universidad Carlos III de Madrid, Spain
Marco Aruta	University of Naples Federico II, Italy
Hadi Asghari	Technische Universität Berlin, Germany
Hugo Attali	LIPN, Sorbonne Paris Nord University, France
Ali Ayadi	University of Strasbourg, France
Paulo Azevedo	University of Minho, Portugal
Hanane Azzag	LIPN, France
Housam Babiker	University of Alberta, Canada
Kerstin Bach	Norwegian University of Science and Technology, Norway
Ricardo Baeza-Yates	KTH Royal Institute of Technology & Universitat Pompeu Fabra, Sweden/Spain
Maroua Bahri	Sorbonne Université, CNRS, LIP6, France
Hendrik Baier	Eindhoven University of Technology, Netherlands
Chandrajit Bajaj	University of Texas at Austin, USA
Bunil Balabantaray	NIT Raipur, India
Federico Baldo	INSERM/Sorbonne University, France
Sylvio Barbon Junior	University of Trieste, Italy
Francesco Bariatti	LIACS, Leiden University, Netherlands
Michel Barlaud	University of Nice, France
Franka Bause	CISPA Helmholtz Center for Information Security, Germany
Florian Beck	Johannes Kepler University Linz, Austria
Christian Beecks	FernUniversität in Hagen, Germany
Hamed Behzadi-Khormouji	Vrije Universiteit Brussel, Belgium
Rita Beigaitė	VTT Technical Research Centre of Finland, Finland
Djawad Bekkoucha	Université Paris-Saclay, France
Colin Bellinger	University of Ottawa, Canada
Khalid Benabdeslem	University Lyon 1, France
Francesco Benedetti	University of Bari Aldo Moro, Italy
Giulia Bertazzini	University of Florence, Italy
Lilian Berton	Federal University of São Paulo, Brazil
Timo Bertram	Johannes Kepler Universität Linz, Austria
Frederic Bertrand	National Conservatory of Arts and Crafts, France
Filippo Betello	Sapienza University of Rome, Italy
Alessandro Betti	IMT School for Advanced Studies Lucca, Italy
Monowar Bhuyan	Umeå University, Sweden
Manuele Bicego	University of Verona, Italy
Livio Bioglio	University of Turin, Italy
Robert Birke	University of Turin, Italy
Hendrik Blockeel	KU Leuven, Belgium

Benedikt Blumenstiel	IBM Research, USA
Martin Bobak	Institute of Informatics, Slovak Academy of Sciences, Slovakia
Tyler Bonnet	Imperial College London, UK
Ludovico Boratto	University of Cagliari, Italy
Manuel Borja	Ghent University, Belgium
Stefano Bortoli	Microblink, Italy
Annelot Bosman	Leiden University, Netherlands
Lydia Boudjeloud-Assala	Université de Lorraine, CNRS, LORIA, France
Sara Bouguelia	Université Lumière Lyon 2, France
Veranika Boukun	Carl von Ossietzky Universität Oldenburg, Germany
Louenas Bounia	LIPN - Université Sorbonne Paris Nord, France
Antoine Boutet	INSA-Lyon, Inria, France
Mohamed-el-Amine Brahmia	CESI LINEACT, France
Susana Brás	IEETA, Portugal
Murat Bronz	ENAC, France
Dariusz Brzezinski	Poznań University of Technology, Poland
Maria Sofia Bucarelli	CNRS, Inria, I3S, France
Florian Büttner	DKFZ, Germany
Davide Buscaldi	Université Sorbonne Paris Nord, France
Sebastian Buschjäger	Lamarr Institute for ML and AI, Germany
Veronica Buttaro	University of Bari Aldo Moro, Italy
Guénaël Cabanes	Université de Lorraine, France
Paul Caillon	LAMSADE Université Paris Dauphine - PSL, France
Erik Calcina	Jožef Stefan Institute, Slovenia
Ricardo Campello	University of Southern Denmark, Denmark
Giuseppe Casalicchio	Ludwig-Maximilians-Universität München, Germany
Elena Casiraghi	University of Milan, Italy
Giovanna Castellano	University of Bari Aldo Moro, Italy
Remzi Celebi	Maastricht University, Netherlands
Andrea Ceni	University of Pisa, Italy
Vitor Cerqueira	University of Porto, Portugal
Mattia Cerrato	JGU Mainz, Germany
Aman Chadha	Stanford University/Amazon Inc., USA
Faïcel Chamroukhi	IRT SystemX, France
Joydeep Chandra	Indian Institute of Technology Patna, India
Victor Charpenay	Mines Saint-Étienne, France
Arthur Charpentier	Université du Québec à Montréal, Canada
Vaggos Chatziafratis	Stanford University, USA

Andre de Carvalho	University of São Paulo, Brazil
Marcilio de Souto	LIFOUniversity of Orléans, France
Gaetan De Waele	University of Antwerp, Belgium
Jochen De Weerdt	KU Leuven, Belgium
Kamil Deja	Warsaw University of Technology, Poland
Julien Delaunay	Inria, France
Elena Demidova	University of Bonn and Lamarr Institute, Germany
Angus Dempster	Monash University, Australia
Cheng Deng	University of Edinburgh, UK
Mariachiara Di Cosmo	Università degli Studi "G. d'Annunzio", Italy
Andrea Giuseppe Di Francesco	Sapienza University of Rome, Italy
Luca Di Stefano	TU Wien, Austria
Lamine Diop	EPITA, France
Christos Diou	Harokopio University of Athens, Greece
Jasminka Dobša	University of Zagreb, Croatia
Vlastislav Dohnal	Masaryk University, Czech Republic
Ruihai Dong	University College Dublin, Ireland
Emilio Dorigatti	Boehringer Ingelheim GmbH, Germany
Moises Dos Santos	University of Porto, Portugal
Gaoyuan Du	University of Tennessee, Knoxville, USA
Haizhou Du	Shanghai University of Electric Power, China
Liang Du	Shanxi University, China
Qihan Du	Renmin University of China, China
Xin Du	University of Edinburgh, UK
Jamie Duell	Sheffield Hallam University, UK
Inês Dutra	University of Porto, Portugal
Elod Egyed-Zsigmond	LIRIS/INSA Lyon, France
Moshe Eliasof	University of Cambridge, UK
Mohamed Elmahallawy	Washington State University, USA
Rémi Emonet	Laboratoire Hubert Curien/Université Jean Monnet, France
Davide Evangelista	University of Bologna, Italy
Bojan Evkoski	Central European University, Austria
Kamil Faber	AGH University of Science and Technology, Poland
Ronan Fablet	IMT Atlantique, France
Issam Falih	Université Clermont Auvergne, CNRS, LIMOS, France
Ruiyi Fang	Western University, Canada
Catherine Faron	Université Côte d'Azur, CNRS, Inria, France
Marco Favier	University of Antwerp, Belgium

Faramarz Fekri	Georgia Institute of Technology, USA
Yuanjun Feng	University of Lausanne, Switzerland
Raphael Feraud	Orange, France
Amine Ferdjaoui	Sogeti - Centre Borelli, France
Daniel Fernández-Sánchez	Aalto University, Finland
Luca Ferragina	University of Calabria, Italy
Pedro Ferreira	University of Porto, Portugal
Yousra Fettach	Ghent University, Belgium
Álvaro Figueira	University of Porto, Portugal
Katarzyna Filus	Institute of Theoretical and Applied Informatics Polish Academy of Sciences, Poland
Raphael Fischer	TU Dortmund University, Germany
Michele Fontana	University of Pisa, Italy
Teodor-Florin Fortis	West University of Timisoara, Romania
Raphael Fournier-S'niehotta	CNAM, France
Giulia Fracastoro	Politecnico di Torino, Italy
Kary Framling	Umeå University, Sweden
Benoît Frénay	University of Namur, Belgium
Christian Frey	University of Technology Nuremberg, Germany
Holger Fröning	University of Heidelberg, Germany
Fabio Fumarola	Prometeia, Italy
Mikel Galar	Universidad Pública de Navarra, Spain
Luis Galárraga	Inria, France
Jose Gamez	Universidad de Castilla-La Mancha, Spain
Shengxiang Gao	Kunming University of Science and Technology, China
Yifeng Gao	University of Texas Rio Grande Valley, USA
Jade Garcia Bourrée	EPFL, Switzerland
Dario Garigliotti	University of Bergen, Norway
Moncef Garouani	Toulouse Capitole University, France
Jean-Gabriel Gaudreault	University of Ottawa, Canada
Dominique Gay	Université de La Réunion, France
Luise Ge	Washington University in St Louis, USA
Michaela Geierhos	University of the Bundeswehr Munich, Germany
Petia Georgieva	University of Aveiro, Portugal
Kushankur Ghosh	University of Alberta, Canada
Luca Giamattei	University of Naples Federico II, Italy
Giorgos Giannopoulos	National Observatory of Athens, Greece
Nikos Gkorgkolis	University of Crete, Greece
Vanessa Gómez-Verdejo	Universidad Carlos III de Madrid, Spain
Sónia Gouveia	University of Aveiro, Portugal
Brandon Gower-Winter	Utrecht University, Netherlands

Michael Granitzer	University of Passau, Germany
Alban Grastien	CEA-List, France
Magda Gregorova	Technical University of Applied Sciences Würzburg-Schweinfurt, Germany
Bram Grooten	Eindhoven University of Technology, Netherlands
Gerrit Grossmann	DFKI, Germany
Sergei Grudinin	LJK CNRS, Université Grenoble Alpes, France
Luciano Gualà	University of Rome Tor Vergata, Italy
Xinyu Guan	Xi'an Jiaotong University, China
Massimo Guarascio	ICAR-CNR, Italy
Bertha Guijarro-Berdiñas	University of A Coruña, Spain
Ce Guo	Imperial College London, UK
Muhao Guo	Arizona State University, USA
Shanqing Guo	Shandong University, China
Yuhong Guo	Carleton University, Canada
Phuong Hoai Ha	UiT The Arctic University of Norway, Norway
Piotr Habas	Amazon, USA
Christian Hakert	TU Dortmund University, Germany
Anaïs Halftermeyer	Laboratoire d'Informatique Fondamentale d'Orléans, France
Maria Halkidi	University of Pireaus, Greece
Benjamin Halstead	University of Auckland, New Zealand
Donghong Han	Northeastern University, China
Marcus Handte	University of Duisburg-Essen, Germany
Tom Hanika	University of Hildesheim, Germany
Sébastien Harispe	IMT Mines Alès, France
Claudio Hartmann	TU Dresden, Germany
Marwan Hassani	Eindhoven University of Technology, Netherlands
Zirui He	New Jersey Institute of Technology, USA
Stefan Heindorf	Paderborn University, Germany
Tobias Hille	University of Kassel, Germany
Martin Holena	Institute of Computer Science, Czech Republic
Mike Holenderski	Eindhoven University of Technology, Netherlands
Vasant Honavar	Pennsylvania State University, USA
Paul Honeine	LITIS Lab, Université de Rouen Normandie, France
Shifu Hou	Case Western Reserve University, USA
Miao Hu	Queen's University Belfast, UK
Xin Hu	University of Michigan, USA
Yizheng Huang	York University, Canada
Charmayne Hughes	Technische Universität Berlin, Germany
Yasutoshi Ida	NTT, Japan

Dino Ienco	INRAE, France
Abdelhak Imoussaten	IMT Mines Alès, France
Angelo Impedovo	NSA Italia s.r.l., Italy
Alessandro Incremona	Catholic University of the Sacred Heart, Italy
Wissem Inoubli	CRIL, University of Artois, France
Vasileios Iosifidis	SCHUFA Holding AG, Germany
Ali Ismail-Fawaz	IRIMAS, Université de Haute-Alsace, France
Nevo Itzhak	Ben-Gurion University of the Negev, Israel
Mirjana Ivanovic	University of Novi Sad, Serbia
Said Jabbour	CRIL CNRS, France
Tobias Jacobs	NEC Laboratories Europe GmbH, Germany
Johannes Jakubik	IBM Research, USA
Henri Jamet	University of Lausanne, Switzerland
Waqas Jamil	Bournemouth University, UK
Kuk Jin Jang	Hongik University, South Korea
Arkadiusz Janz	Wrocław University of Science and Technology, Poland
Hui Ji	University of Pittsburgh, USA
Yuheng Jia	Southeast University, China
Weiwei Jiang	Beijing University of Posts and Telecommunications, China
Xi Jiang	Southern University of Science and Technology, China
Sebastian Jimenez	Ghent University, Belgium
Guangyin Jin	National University of Defense Technology, China
Jiahui Jin	Southeast University, China
Mira Jürgens	Ghent University, Belgium
Tomasz Kajdanowicz	Wrocław University of Science and Technology, Poland
Jan Kalina	Czech Academy of Sciences, Institute of Computer Science, Czech Republic
Sevvandi Kandanaarachchi	CSIRO, Australia
Bo Kang	Ghent University, Belgium
Jurgita Kapočiūtė-Dzikienė	Tilde SIA, University of Latvia, Tilde IT, Vytautas Magnus University, Latvia/Lithuania
Athresh Karanam	University of Texas at Dallas, USA
Jacek Karolczak	Poznań University of Technology, Poland
Peter Karsmakers	KU Leuven, Belgium
Gjergji Kasneci	Technical University of Munich, Germany
Branko Kavsek	University of Primorska, Slovenia
Daniyal Kazempour	Christian-Albrechts-Universität zu Kiel, Germany
Mark Keane	University College Dublin, Ireland

Stefan Kesselheim	Forschungszentrum Jülich, Germany
Rabindra Khadka	University of Oslo, Norway
Asma Kharrat	Liris, France
Mohamadsadegh Khosravani	University of Regina, Canada
Adem Kikaj	KU Leuven, Belgium
Hyunju Kim	King's College London, UK
Sofoklis Kitharidis	LIACS, Netherlands
Frank Klawonn	Ostfalia University, Germany
Tomas Kliegr	University of Economics Prague, Czech Republic
Jakub Klikowski	Wrocław University of Science and Technology, Poland
Marek Klonowski	Wrocław University of Science and Technology, Poland
Boshko Koloski	Jožef Stefan Institute, Slovenia
Joanna Komorniczak	Wrocław University of Science and Technology, Poland
Aritra Konar	KU Leuven, Belgium
Frederic Koriche	Université d'Artois, CRIL CNRS UMR 8188, France
Grazina Korvel	Vilnius University, Lithuania
N'Dah Jean Kouagou	Paderborn University, Germany
Emmanouil Krasanakis	CERTH, Greece
Chethan Krishnamurthy Ramanaik	University of the Bundeswehr Munich, Germany
Amer Krivosija	TU Dortmund University, Germany
Oleg Kudryavtsev	Southern Federal University, Russia
Sebastian Kula	Kempelen Institute of Intelligent Technologies, Slovakia
Pawan Kumar	IIIT, Hyderabad, India
Vivek Kumar	Trinity College Dublin, Ireland
Olga Kurasova	Vilnius University, Lithuania
Semih Kurt	Ghent University, Belgium
Tomasz Kuśmierczyk	Jagiellonian University, Poland
Valerio La Gatta	Northwestern University, USA
Antti Laaksonen	University of Helsinki, Finland
Charlotte Laclau	Polytechnique Institute, Télécom Paris, France
Jean-Marie Lagniez	CRIL CNRS, France
Aonghus Lawlor	University College Dublin, Ireland
Duc Le	University of Twente, Netherlands
Tuan Le	New Mexico State University, USA
Hoel Le Capitaine	University of Nantes, France
Erwan Le Merrer	Inria, France
Tai Le Quy	University of Koblenz, Germany

Kyumin Lee	Worcester Polytechnic Institute, USA
Mathieu Lefort	University of Rennes - IRISA, France
Collin Leiber	Aalto University, Finland
Vincent Lemaire	Orange Research, France
Marie-Jeanne Lesot	LIP6, Sorbonne Université, France
Xavier Lessage	CETIC, Belgium
Carson Leung	University of Manitoba, Canada
Dong Li	Baylor University, USA
Gang Li	Deakin University, Australia
Peiyu Li	Utah State University, USA
Rui Li	Inspur Academy of Science and Technology, China
Shuai Li	Tsinghua University, China
Weichen Li	RPTU Kaiserslautern-Landau, Germany
Yong Li	Huawei European Research Center, Germany
Yulei Li	Northumbria University, UK
Zhixin Li	Guangxi Normal University, China
Zhong Li	Leiden University, Netherlands
Zongyue Li	Ludwig-Maximilians-Universität München, Germany
Angelica Liguori	ICAR-CNR, Italy
Fandel Lin	University of Southern California, USA
Tony Lindgren	Stockholm University, Sweden
Arunas Lipnickas	Kaunas University of Technology, Lithuania
Marina Litvak	Shamoon College of Engineering, Israel
Bin Liu	Chongqing University of Posts and Telecommunications, China
Chien-Liang Liu	National Chiao Tung University, Taiwan
Junze Liu	University of California, Irvine, USA
Li Liu	Chongqing University, China
Meng Liu	National University of Defense Technology, China
Zhen Liu	Guangdong University of Foreign Studies, China
Tuwe Löfström	Jönköping University, Sweden
Dario Loi	Northeastern University, USA
Marco Loog	Radboud University, Netherlands
Beatriz López	University of Girona, Spain
Marcin Luckner	Warsaw University of Technology, Poland
Stefan Lüdtke	University of Rostock, Germany
Daniele Lunghi	University of Luxembourg, Luxembourg
Thomas Tie Luo	University of Kentucky, USA
Zhiwen Luo	Concordia University, Canada

Marcos M. Raimundo	University of Campinas, Brazil
Kira Maag	Heinrich Heine University Düsseldorf, Germany
Rakesh Chowdary Machineni	Rockwell Automation, USA
Henryk Maciejewski	Wrocław University of Science and Technology, Poland
Michael Madden	University of Galway, Ireland
Sindri Magnusson	Stockholm University, Sweden
Yasir Mahmood	Paderborn University, Germany
Cristina Maier	Boston College, USA
Akshay Malhotra	Interdigital, USA
Hua Mao	Northumbria University, UK
Antonio Marceddu	Politecnico di Torino, Italy
Virginijus Marcinkevičius	Vilnius University, Lithuania
Gabriel Marques Tavares	Ludwig-Maximilians-Universität München, Germany
Christophe Marsala	LIP6, Sorbonne Université, France
Jorge Martinez-Gil	Software Competence Center Hagenberg GmbH, Austria
Fernando Martínez-Plumed	Universitat Politècnica de València, Spain
Ana Martins	University of Aveiro, Portugal
Koji Maruhashi	Fujitsu, Japan
Marc Masana	Graz University of Technology, Austria
Rytis Maskeliūnas	Polsl, Poland
Carlo Masone	Politecnico di Torino, Italy
Michael Mathioudakis	University of Helsinki, Finland
Stan Matwin	Dalhouise University, Canada
Nicolas Maudet	Sorbonne Université, France
Tom Maye-Lasserre	Télécom Paris, IP Paris, France
Giacomo Medda	University of Cagliari, Italy
Nida Meddouri	LRE-EPITA, France
Behzad Mehrbakhsh	Universitat Politècnica de València, Spain
Wagner Meira Jr.	Federal University of Minas Gerais, Brazil
Marco Mellia	Politecnico di Torino, Italy
Joao Mendes-Moreira	University of Porto, Portugal
Rui Meng	Beijing Normal-Hong Kong Baptist University, China
Vlado Menkovski	Eindhoven University of Technology, Netherlands
Engelbert Mephu Nguifo	Université Clermont Auvergne, CNRS, LIMOS, France
Paolo Merialdo	Università degli Studi Roma Tre, Italy
Sebastian Mežnar	Jožef Stefan Institute, Slovenia
Bojan Mihaljevic	Universidad Politécnica de Madrid, Spain

Matej Mihelčić	University of Zagreb, Croatia
Miloud Mihoubi	University of Téluq, Canada
Tsunenori Mine	Kyushu University, Japan
Valentina Minnetti	Italian National Institute of Statistics, Italy
Jelena Mitrović	University of Passau, Germany
Pierre Monnin	Université Côte d'Azur, Inria, CNRS, I3S, France
Eduardo Montesuma	Université Paris-Saclay, France
Raha Moraffah	Worcester Polytechnic Institute, USA
Pierre Moreau	Ekimetrics, France
Jose Moreira	University of Aveiro, Portugal
Paulina Morillo	Universitat Politècnica de València, Spain
Yael Moros-Daval	Universitat Politècnica de València, Spain
Thomas Mortier	Ghent University, Belgium
Roman Moućek	University of West Bohemia, Czech Republic
Elena Maria Muià	Sapienza University of Rome, Italy
Koyel Mukherjee	Adobe Research, India
Ian Nabney	University of Bristol, UK
Mohamed Nadif	Centre Borelli UMR9010-Université Paris Cité, France
Mohamed Nafea	Missouri University of Science and Technology, USA
Felipe Kenji Nakano	KU Leuven, Belgium
Géraldin Nanfack	Concordia University, Canada
Mirco Nanni	CNR-ISTI Pisa, Italy, Italy
Apurva Narayan	University of Western Ontario, Canada
Francesca Naretto	University of Pisa, Italy
Fateme Nateghi Haredasht	Stanford University, USA
Claire Nédellec	INRAE, MaIAGE, France
Dang Nguyen	Deakin University, Australia
Kien Nguyen	University of Delaware, USA
Minh Nguyen	University of Texas at Austin, USA
Nikolaos Nikolaou	University College London, UK
Simona Nisticò	University of Calabria, Italy
Navid Nobani	University of Milano-Bicocca, Italy
Ana Rita Nogueira	INESC TEC, Portugal
Slawomir Nowaczyk	Halmstad University, Sweden
Diana Nurbakova	INSA Lyon - LIRIS UMR 5205 CNRS, France
Iyiola Emmanuel Olatunji	University of Luxembourg, Luxembourg
Arlindo Oliveira	Instituto Superior Técnico, Portugal
Helder Oliveira	University of Porto, Portugal
José Oliveira	University of Porto, Portugal
Makoto Onizuka	Osaka University, Japan

Jose Oramas	University of Antwerp, Belgium
María Óskarsdóttir	University of Southampton, UK
Fannia Pacheco	University of Rouen Normandy, France
Arjun Pakrashi	University College Dublin, Ireland
Egawati Panjei	University of Oklahoma, USA
Apostolos Papadopoulos	Aristotle University of Thessaloniki, Greece
Laurence Park	Western Sydney University, Australia
Emilio Parrado-Hernandez	Universidad Carlos III de Madrid, Spain
Vincenzo Pasquadibisceglie	University of Bari Aldo Moro, Italy
Tatiana Passali	Aristotle University of Thessaloniki, Greece
Eliana Pastor	Politecnico di Torino, Italy
Theodore Patkos	FORTH, Greece
Anand Paul	Louisiana State University HSC, USA
Heiko Paulheim	University of Mannheim, Germany
John Pavlopoulos	Athens University of Economics and Business, Greece
Yulong Pei	Eindhoven University of Technology, Netherlands
Leonardo Pellegrina	University of Padova, Italy
Antonio Pellicani	University of Bari Aldo Moro, Italy
Roberto Pellungrini	University of Pisa, Italy
Frédéric Pennerath	CentraleSupélec - LORIA, France
Francisco Pereira	Technical University of Denmark, Denmark
Lucas Pereira	Interactive Technologies Institute, LARSyS, Técnico Lisboa, Portugal
Franz Pernkopf	Graz University of Technology, Austria
Filipo Perotto	ONERA, France
Linas Petkevicius	Vilnius University, Lithuania
Simone Piaggesi	University of Pisa, Italy
Francesco Piccialli	University of Naples Federico II, Italy
Francesco Pierri	Politecnico di Milano, Italy
Roberto Pietrantuono	University of Naples Federico II, Italy
Martin Pilát	Charles University, Czech Republic
Armando Pinho	University of Aveiro, Portugal
Pedro Pires	Federal University of São Carlos, Brazil
Federico Pirola	University of Milano-Bicocca, Italy
Marc Plantevit	EPITA, France
Marco Podda	University of Pisa, Italy
Marco Polignano	University of Bari Aldo Moro, Italy
Alexander Politowicz	University of Illinois Chicago, USA
Giovanni Ponti	ENEA, Italy
Raluca Portase	Technical University of Cluj Napoca, Romania
Piotr Porwik	University of Silesia in Katowice, Poland

Marco Postiglione	Northwestern University, USA
Andrea Pozzi	University of Pavia, Italy
Steven Prestwich	University College Cork, Ireland
Lucía Prieto-Santamaría	Universidad Politécnica de Madrid, Spain
Chiara Pugliese	IIT - CNR, Italy
Andrea Pugnana	University of Trento, Italy
Satish Puri	Missouri University of Science and Technology, USA
Antonio Purificato	Sapienza University of Rome, Italy
Abdulhakim Qahtan	Utrecht University, Netherlands
Cong Qi	New Jersey Institute of Technology, USA
Xin Qin	California State University, Long Beach, USA
Yijun Quan	University of Warwick, UK
Benjamin Quost	Université de Technologie de Compiègne, France
Dimitrios Rafailidis	University of Thessaly, Greece
Alessio Ragno	EPITA Research Laboratory, France
Muhammad Rajabinasab	University of Southern Denmark, Denmark
Morteza Rakhshaninejad	Ghent University, Belgium
Patrícia Ramos	INESC TEC, Portugal
Md Mashud Rana	Australian Catholic University, Australia
Weixiong Rao	Tongji University, China
Rajeev Rastogi	Amazon, USA
Steffen Rebennack	Karlsruhe Institute of Technology, Germany
Domenico Redavid	University of Bari Aldo Moro, Italy
Michaela Regneri	University of Hamburg, Germany
Wojciech Rejchel	Nicolaus Copernicus University in Toruń, Poland
Francesco Renna	University of Porto, Portugal
Manon Reusens	University of Antwerp, Belgium
Hergys Rexha	Åbo Akademi University, Finland
Ricardo Rios	Federal University of Bahia, Brazil
Tatiane Rios	Federal University of Bahia, Brazil
Guilherme Roberto	University of São Paulo, Brazil
Marko Robnik-Šikonja	University of Ljubljana, Slovenia
Miguel Rocha	University of Minho, Portugal
Christophe Rodrigues	DVRC pôle universitaire Léonard de Vinci, France
Juan Rodriguez	Universidad de Burgos, Spain
Federica Rollo	University of Modena and Reggio Emilia, Italy
Sabin Roman	Jožef Stefan Institute, Slovenia
Nicolas Roque dos Santos	University of California, Riverside, USA
Polina Rozenshtein	Aalto University, Finland
Rimvydas Rubavicius	University of Edinburgh, UK

Krzysztof Rudaś	Institute of Computer Science, Polish Academy of Sciences, Poland
Laura Ruotsalainen	University of Helsinki, Finland
Federico Sabbatini	National Institute for Nuclear Physics - INFN, Italy
Dimitris Sacharidis	Université Libre de Bruxelles, Belgium
Lakhdar Sais	CRIL - CNRS, Artois University, France
Yakoub Salhi	CRIL CNRS, France
Chafik Samir	CNRS-UCA, France
Miriam Santos	University of Porto, Portugal
Ioannis Sarridis	Information Technologies Institute/Centre for Research & Technology, Greece
Roberto Sassi	University of Milan, Italy
Milos Savic	University of Novi Sad, Serbia
Yücel Saygın	Sabancı Universitesi, Turkiye
Katerina Schindlerova	University of Vienna, Austria
Frank-Michael Schleif	Technical University of Applied Sciences Würzburg-Schweinfurt, Germany
Dmitrij Schlesinger	TU Dresden, Germany
Daniel Schlör	University of Würzburg, Germany
Rainer Schlosser	Hasso Plattner Institute, Germany
Melanie Schmidt	Heinrich Heine University Düsseldorf, Germany
Peter Schneider-Kamp	University of Southern Denmark, Denmark
Gesina Schwalbe	Ulm University, Germany
Andreas Schwung	South Westphalia University of Applied Sciences, Germany
Vincenzo Scotti	KASTEL, Karlsruhe Institute of Technology, Germany
Sébastien Destercke	Université de technologie de Compiègne, France
Selpi Selpi	Chalmers University of Technology and Gothenburg University, Sweden
Mattia Setzu	University of Pisa, Italy
Shiv Shankar	University of Massachusetts, USA
Arnab Sharma	Paderborn University, Germany
Shubhranshu Shekhar	Brandeis University, USA
Oleksandr Shekhovtsov	Czech Technical University in Prague, Czech Republic
Hao Shen	fortiss GmbH, Germany
Qiang Sheng	Institute of Computing Technology, Chinese Academy of Sciences, China
John Sheppard	Montana State University, USA
Bin Shi	Xi'an Jiaotong University, China
Jimeng Shi	University of Illinois Urbana-Champaign, USA

Ali Shokoufandeh	Drexel University, USA
Xiao Shou	Baylor University, USA
Md Fahim Sikder	Linköping University, Sweden
Catarina Silva	University of Coimbra, Portugal
Joaquim Silva	NOVA LINCS, Universidade Nova de Lisboa, Portugal
Esther-Lydia Silva-Ramírez	Universidad de Cádiz, Spain
Raivydas Šimėnas	Vilnius University, Lithuania
Giovanni Simonini	University of Modena and Reggio Emilia, Italy
Maneet Singh	Mastercard, India
Andrzej Skowron	University of Warsaw, Poland
Vaclav Smidl	Czech Technical University in Prague, Czech Republic
Marek Smieja	Jagiellonian University, Poland
Filipe Soares	Fraunhofer Portugal AICOS, Portugal
Osvaldo Solarte-Pabon	Universidad del Valle, Colombia
Liyan Song	Harbin Institute of Technology, China
Fabian Spaeh	Celonis, USA
Lorenz Sparrenberg	University of Bonn, Germany
Giancarlo Sperlì	University of Naples Federico II, Italy
Ramya Srinivasan	Fujitsu, Japan
Dimitri Staufer	Technische Universität Berlin, Germany
Marcel Steinmetz	LAAS-CNRS, France
Niklas Strauß	Ludwig-Maximilians-Universität München, Germany
Xuanyu Su	University of Ottawa, Canada
Jérémie Sublime	ISEP, France
Xin Sun	City University of Macau, China
Zhaokai Sun	Tongji University, China
Panagiotis Symeonidis	University of the Aegean, Greece
Tomasz Szandała	Wrocław University of Science and Technology, Poland
Amir Taherkordi	University of Oslo, Norway
Atsuhiro Takasu	National Institute of Informatics, Japan
Nicholas Tan Jerome	Karlsruhe Institute of Technology, Germany
Yufei Tang	Florida Atlantic University, USA
Katerina Taskova	University of Auckland, New Zealand
Olivier Teste	IRIT, University of Toulouse, France
Christoph Tholen	Saarland University of Applied Sciences, Germany
Steffen Thoma	FZI Research Center for Information Technology, Germany

Josephine Thomas	University of Greifswald, Germany
Natan Tourne	Ghent University, Belgium
Panos Trahanias	FORTH, Greece
Alicia Troncoso	Pablo de Olavide University, Spain
Francesco Trovò	Politecnico di Milano, Italy
Giuseppe Trunfio	University of Sassari, Italy
Panayiotis Tsaparas	University of Ioannina, Greece, Greece
Grigorios Tsoumakas	Aristotle University of Thessaloniki, Greece
Jonata Tyska Carvalho	Federal University of Santa Catarina, Brazil
Mihai Udrescu	Politehnica University Timisoara, Romania
Edoardo Urettini	European Central Bank, Germany
Gonzalo Uribarri	Stockholm University, Sweden
Philipp Vaeth	Technical University of Applied Sciences Würzburg-Schweinfurt, University Bielefeld, Germany
Giorgio Valentini	University of Milan, Italy
Diego Vallejo-Huanga	Universitat Politècnica de València, Spain
Jente Van Belle	KU Leuven, Belgium
Peter van der Putten	Leiden University, Netherlands
Lucy Van Kleunen	KU Leuven, Belgium
Fabio Vandin	University of Padova, Italy
Georgios Vardakas	University of Ioannina, Greece
Aparna S. Varde	Montclair State University, USA
Mariana Vargas Vieyra	MostlyAI, Austria
Bruno Veloso	INESC TEC, Portugal
Mathias Verbeke	KU Leuven, Belgium
Wouter Verbeke	KU Leuven, Belgium
Jan Verwaeren	Ghent University, Belgium
Gennaro Vessio	University of Bari Aldo Moro, Italy
Jill-Jênn Vie	Inria, France
Saketh Vishnubhatla	Arizona State University, USA
Marco Viviani	University of Milano-Bicocca, Italy
Maximilian von Zastrow	University of Southern Denmark, Denmark
Tim vor der Brück	Internationale Hochschule, Germany
Ngoc-Son Vu	University of Technology of Troyes, France
Tomasz Walkowiak	Wrocław University of Science and Technology, Poland
Shu Wan	Arizona State University, USA
Ziwen Wan	University of California, Irvine, USA
Deng-Bao Wang	Southeast University, China
Hao Wang	University of Science and Technology of China, China

Jianwu Wang	University of Maryland, Baltimore County, USA
Jing Wang	Amazon, USA
Li Wang	National University of Defense Technology, China
Mengying Wang	Case Western Reserve University, USA
Wendy Hui Wang	Stevens Institute of Technology, USA
Xiaoyang Wang	University of Exeter, UK
Xuemin Wang	Guilin University of Electronic Technology, China
Yanhao Wang	East China Normal University, China
Yongyu Wang	JD Logistics, China
Zhihui Wang	Fudan University, China
Zichong Wang	Florida International University, USA
Pascal Weber	University of Vienna, Austria
Xing Wei	Tongji University, China
Yang Wei	Nanjing University of Science and Technology, China
Tonio Weidler	Maastricht University, Netherlands
Guilherme Weigert Cassales	University of Waikato, New Zealand
Alicja Wieczorkowska	Polish-Japanese Academy of Information Technology, Poland
Szymon Wojciechowski	Wrocław University of Science and Technology, Poland
Michal Wozniak	Wrocław University of Science and Technology, Poland
Bin Wu	Zhengzhou University, China
Boqian Wu	University of Luxembourg, Luxembourg
Nannan Wu	Tianjin University, China
Patrick Wu	American University, USA
Peng Wu	Shanghai Jiao Tong University, China
Wei Wu	Ben Gurion University of the Negev, Israel
Wenjie Xi	George Mason University, USA
Zhiwen Xiao	Southwest Jiaotong University, China
Hong Xie	University of Science and Technology of China, China
Wen-Bo Xie	Southwest Petroleum University, China
Huanlai Xing	Southwest Jiaotong University, China
Xing Xing	Tongji University, China
Duo Xu	Georgia Institute of Technology, USA
Gehui Xu	Imperial College London, UK
Weifeng Xu	University of Baltimore, USA
Qiao Yan	Shenzhen University, China
Yu Yan	Institute of Computing Technology, Chinese Academy of Sciences, China

Jiayi Yang	Tongji University, China
Qian Yang	University of Connecticut, USA
Xin-She Yang	Middlesex University London, UK
Yutong Ye	Beihang University, China
Kalidas Yeturu	Indian Institute of Technology Tirupati, India
Ilkay Yildiz Potter	BioSensics LLC, USA
Zhipeng Yin	Florida International University, USA
Jaemin Yoo	Seoul National University, South Korea
Lei You	Technical University of Denmark, Denmark
Hang Yu	Shanghai University, China
Shuyang Yu	Michigan State University, USA
Wentao Yu	Nanjing University of Science and Technology, China
Jidong Yuan	Beijing Jiaotong University, China
Osmar Zaiane	University of Alberta, Canada
Tetiana Zakharchenko	Ukrainian Catholic University, Ukraine
Obaidullah Zaland	Umeå University, Sweden
Alessio Zanga	University of Milano-Bicocca, Italy
Mario Zanon	IMT School for Advanced Studies Lucca, Italy
Gianluca Zaza	University of Bari Aldo Moro, Italy
Assaad Zeghina	Latmos Lab, France
Akka Zemmari	University of Bordeaux, France
Saber Zerhoudi	University of Passau, Germany
Meriem Zerkouk	Université TÉLUQ, Canada
Chongsheng Zhang	Henan University, China
Hanping Zhang	Carleton University, Canada
Haowen Zhang	Zhejiang Sci-Tech University, China
Pengyu Zhang	University of Amsterdam, Netherlands
Xiaoming Zhang	Beihang University, China
Xinyue Zhang	Kennesaw State University, USA
Xiuzhen Zhang	RMIT University, Australia
Xiyue Zhang	University of Bristol, UK
Yaying Zhang	Tongji University, China
Yin Zhang	University of Electronic Science and Technology of China, China
Zhiwen Zhang	LocationMind Inc., Japan
Zhong Zhang	University of Electronic Science and Technology of China, China
Kaiqi Zhao	Oakland University, USA
Shu Zhao	Anhui University, China
Zhouting Zhao	Trinity College Dublin, Ireland
Yueyuan Zheng	Beihang University, China

Yujia Zheng	Carnegie Mellon University, USA
Yanmin Zhu	Shanghai Jiao Tong University, China
Arthur Zimek	University of Southern Denmark, Denmark
Tommaso Zoppi	University of Florence, Italy
Noé Zufferey	ETH Zurich, Switzerland
Pedro Zuidberg Dos Martires	Örebro University, Sweden
Paweł Zyblewski	Wrocław University of Science and Technology, Poland

Additional Reviewers, Research Track

Amgad Abdulmaqsod	Paderborn University, Germany
Aisha Aijaz	Indraprastha Institute of Information Technology, Delhi, India
Moh'd Khier Al Kfari	University of Rostock, Germany
Sokrat Aldarmini	Missouri University of Science and Technology, USA
Konstantinos Alexis	IMSI/Athena Research Center, Greece
Hazrat Ali	University of Stirling, UK
Zafar Ali	Southeast University, China
Hend Amraoui	Higher Institute of Applied Languages and Computer Science of Béja (ISLAI Béja), University of Jendouba, Tunisia
Shin Ando	Tokyo University of Science, Japan
Eugen-Richard Ardelean	Technical University of Cluj-Napoca, Romania
André Artelt	Bielefeld University, Germany
Baran Atalar	Carnegie Mellon University, USA
Kyohei Atarashi	Kyoto University, Japan
Sanket Badhe	Google, USA
Daniel Barley	Heidelberg University, Germany
Ulya Bayram	Canakkale Onsekiz Mart University, Turkey
Ahmad Bdeir	University of Hildesheim, Germany
Jatin Bedi	Thapar Institute of Engineering and Technology, India
Sidahmed Benabderrahmane	New York University, United Arab Emirates
Francesco Benedetti	University of Bari Aldo Moro, Italy
Quentin Bertrand	Inria, France
Aurelie Beynier	Sorbonne Université, France
Martin Binder	LMU Munich, Germany
Valerio Bonsignori	University of Pisa, Italy
Weronika Borek-Marciniec	Wrocław University of Science and Technology, Poland

Onur Boyar	IBM Research, Japan
Maria Sofia Bucarelli	CNRS, Inria, I3S, France
Zhuo Cai	University of Technology Sydney, Australia
Toon Calders	University of Antwerp, Belgium
Lele Cao	Tsinghua University, China
Louis Carpentier	KU Leuven, Belgium
Daniele Castellana	University of Florence, Italy
Mustafa Cavus	Eskisehir Technical University, Turkey
Dong-Kyu Chae	Hanyang University, South Korea
Tanujit Chakraborty	Sorbonne University Abu Dhabi, United Arab Emirates
Anna Chatzipapadopoulou	Athens University of Economics and Business/Archimedes Unit, Athena Research Center, Greece
Lilia Chebbah	Georgia State University, USA
Hao Chen	University of Chinese Academy of Sciences, China
Haopeng Chen	Shanghai Jiao Tong University, China
Sheng-Wei Chen	National Taiwan University, Taiwan
Songcan Chen	Nanjing University of Aeronautics and Astronautics, China
Zhen Chen	University of Science and Technology of China, China
Zhili Chen	East China Normal University, China
Liang Cheng	University of Oslo, Norway
Chak Fong Chong	Macao Polytechnic University, China
Maciej Chrabaszcz	Warsaw University of Technology, NASK National Research Institute, Poland
Michele Craighero	Politecnico di Milano, Italy
Wang-Zhou Dai	China
Uma Damotharan	PES University, USA
Davy Darankoum	Université Grenoble Alpes/SynapCell, France
Mrinal Das	IIT Palakaad, India
Debashis Das Chakladar	Birla Institute of Technology & Science, Hyderabad, India
Arne De Temmerman	KU Leuven, Belgium
Thanh-Dang Diep	Vietnam National University Ho Chi Minh City - University of Technology, Vietnam
Yihao Ding	University of Western Australia, Australia
Jean-François Dollinger	CESI, France
Yingpeng Du	Nanyang Technological University, Singapore
Fabrício Enembreck	Pontifical Catholic University of Paraná, Brazil
A. M. Esfar-E-Alam	University of Oslo, Norway

Fiona Ewald	Ludwig-Maximilians-Universität München, Germany
Ken-ichi Fukui	Kansai University, Japan
Xiaofeng Gao	Shanghai Jiao Tong University, China
Blaise Genest	CNRS, CNRS@CREATE, France
Christos Gkartzios	University of Ioannina, Greece
Filippos Gouidis	ICS/FORTH, Greece
Poonam Goyal	BITS Pilani, India
Shangqi Guo	Tsinghua, China
Yang Guo	Harbin Engineering University, China
Subhash Gurappa	Florida International University, USA
Renda Han	Tianjin University, China
Takahiro Hara	Osaka University, Japan
Ryuichiro Hataya	SB Intuitions & Kyoto University, Japan
Mehdi Hennequin	Omundu, France
Johanna Hillebrand	Heinrich Heine University, Germany
Yi-Te Hong	Academia Sinica, Taiwan
Tanvir Hossain	Georgia State University, USA
Ruijie Hou	Zhejiang University, China
Zhaobo Hu	Institut Polytechnique de Paris, France
Chun Huang	Chongqing University, China
Yu-Shiang Huang	National Taiwan University, Taiwan
Pedro Ilídio	KU Leuven, Belgium
Marek Jeliński	NASK-PIB, Poland
Wanting Ji	Liaoning University, China
Huimin Jiang	University of Science and Technology of China, China
Shu Jiang	Nantong Univerisity, China
Changhong Jin	University College Dublin, Ireland
Yifei Jin	X-Tech (Beijing) Co., Ltd., China
Yue Jin	University of Northampton, UK
Durande Berluskoni Kamga Nguifo	Université Clermont Auvergne, Clermont Auvergne INP, ENSMSE, CNRS, LIMOS, France
Skander Karkar	Mediterranean Institute of Technology, Tunisia
Hisashi Kashima	Kyoto University, Japan
Tsuyoshi Kato	Gunma University, Japan
Ramneek Kaur	IIT Delhi, India
Zulfiqar Ahmad Khan	Umeå University, Sweden
Sejin Kim	Gwangju Institute of Science and Technology, South Korea
YoungBin Kim	Chung-Ang University, South Korea

Ken Kobayashi	Institute of Science Tokyo, Japan
Ryosuke Kojima	Kyoto University, Japan
Ravi Kolla	Sony Research India, India
Patrik Kozlík	Institute of Informatics Slovak Academy of Sciences, Slovakia
Uttam Kumar	University of Bonn, Germany
Suman Kundu	Indian Institute of Technology Madras, India
Vasilii Latonov	PSJC Sberbank, Russia
Hung Le	Deakin University, Australia
Truong-Thanh Le	University of Oslo, Norway
Yongkeun Lee	Seoul National University of Science and Technology, South Korea
Bo Li	Guilin University of Aerospace Technology, China
Chen Li	Osaka University, Japan
Daifeng Li	Sun Yat-sen University, China
Huakang Li	Xi'an Jiaotong-Liverpool University, China
Jiyanglin Li	Guizhou Key Laboratory of Big Data Statistical Analysis, Guizhou University of Finance and Economics, China
Mark Junjie Li	Shenzhen University, China
Shusheng Li	Zhenjiang Research Institute of Advanced Equipment, China
Wuyungerile Li	Inner Mongolia University, China
Yixin Li	Xinjiang Technical Institute of Physics and Chemistry, Chinese Academy of Sciences, China
Yulong Li	Hefei University of Technology, China
Tao Lian	Taiyuan University of Technology, China
Junfeng Liao	Shanghai University of International Business and Economics, China
Zhenyu Liao	Huazhong University of Science and Technology, China
Jianghao Lin	Shanghai Jiao Tong University, China
Shih-Chih Lindgren	National Tsing Hua University, Taiwan
Jiaqi Liu	Northwestern Polytechnical University, China
Ke Liu	University of California, Berkeley, USA
Sen Liu	Fudan University, China
Yue Liu	Shanghai University, China
Zesheng Liu	Renmin University of China, China
Cuicui Luo	University of Chinese Academy of Sciences, China

Zhengquan Luo	Mohamed bin Zayed University of Artificial Intelligence, United Arab Emirates
Giovanni Malaguti	Università di Modena e Reggio Emilia, Italy
Alireza Maleki	Karlsruhe Institute of Technology (KASTEL), Germany
Fragkiskos Malliaros	CentraleSupélec, France
Mohcine Manssouri	Université Lumière Lyon 2, France
Falk Maoro	University of the Bundeswehr Munich, Germany
Nikola Marić	Jožef Stefan Institute, Slovenia
Pierre Marquis	CRIL, University of Artois & CNRS, IUF, France
Patryk Marszałek	Jagiellonian University in Kraków, Poland
Cristian Mascia	University of Naples Federico II, Italy
Sunil Maurya	University of Tokyo, Japan
Bamdev Mishra	Microsoft, India
Rahul Mishra	IIIT Hyderabad, Italy
Yoshihiro Mitsuka	Mitsubishi Electric Corporation, Japan
Nabeel Mohammed	North South University, Bangladesh
Yael Moros-Daval	Universitat Politècnica de València, Spain
Kedian Mu	Peking University, China
Lingyu Mu	Institute of Information Engineering, Chinese Academy of Sciences, China
Shrimon Mukherjee	Indian Association for the Cultivation of Science, India
Anika Murarka	IIT Delhi, India
Dimitrios Myrisiotis	Great Bay University, China
Kiran Mayee Nabigaru	SoFi Technologies, USA
Thin Nguyen	Deakin University, Australia
Bo Ning	Dalian Maritime University, China
Tianzhe Ning	Donghua University, China
Masaaki Nishino	NTT, Japan
Yoshiyuki Norimatsu	Mitsubishi Electric Corporation, Japan
Bastian Oetomo	University of Melbourne, Australia
Gabriel Oliveira	Federal University of Minas Gerais, Brazil
Mounir Ourekouch	Mohammed VI Polytechnic University, Morocco
Satoshi Oyama	Nagoya City University, Japan
Emmanouil Panagiotou	Freie Universität Berlin, Germany
Luca Pepè Sciarria	University of Rome Tor Vergata, Italy
Qiankun Pi	Information Engineering University, China
Sebastiano Piccolo	University of Calabria, Italy
Laura Pollacci	University of Pisa, Italy
Yoann Poupart	LIP6, Sorbonne University, France

Ranjitha Prasad	Indraprastha Institute of Information Technology Delhi, India
Antonio Purificato	Sapienza University of Rome, Italy
Lin Qi	Ocean University of China, China
Tieyun Qian	Wuhan University, China
Weizhu Qian	Soochow University, China
Linbo Qiao	National University of Defense Technology, China
Jintao Qu	University of Southern California, USA
Muhammad Rajabinasab	University of Southern Denmark, Denmark
Gangulie Ranawaka	Informatics Institute of Technology, Sri Lanka
Darshan Rathod	Fujitsu, Japan
Matīss Rikters	National Institute of Advanced Industrial Science and Technology, Japan
Pieter Robberechts	KU Leuven, Belgium
Thibault Roux	ONERA, France
Pablo Ruiz Morales	KU Leuven, Belgium
P. S. Sastry	Indian Institute of Science, India
Aggelos Semoglou	Athens University of Economics & Business & Archimedes Research Unit, Athena Research Center, Greece
Deep Shah	Google LLC, USA
Abdul-Kazeem Shamba	Norwegian University of Science & Technology, Norway
Jie Shao	University of Electronic Science and Technology of China, China
Lifeng Shen	Chongqing University of Posts and Telecommunications, China
Xiaojun Sheng	Guangdong Laboratory of Artificial Intelligence and Digital Economy (SZ), China
Mohamed Sherif	Paderborn University, Germany
Kijung Shin	KAIST, South Korea
Jayakumar Singaram	Independent consultant, India
Atul Kumar Singh	Fujitsu Research of India Pvt. Ltd., India
Damian Sójka	Poznań University of Technology; IDEAS-NCBR, Poland
Youngdoo Son	Dongguk University, South Korea
Andy Song	RMIT University, Australia
Jules Soria	CEA-LIST, Université Paris-Saclay, France
P. K. Srijith	Indian Institute of Technology Hyderabad, India
Gowri Srinivasa	PES University, USA
Sintija Stevanoska	Jožef Stefan Institute, Slovenia

Taoyu Su	Institute of Information Engineering, Chinese Academy of Sciences, China
Qi Rong Sua	Nanyang Technological University, Singapore
Mahito Sugiyama	National Institute of Informatics, Japan
Yibin Sun	Victoria University of Wellington, New Zealand
Ying Sun	Taishan University, China
Yu Tang	Soochow University, China
Ray Telikani	University of Technology Sydney, Australia
Wei Tong	Nanjing University, China
Marwan Torki	Alexandria University, Egypt
Son Tran	Deakin University, Australia
Arseniy Trushin	Yandex, Russia
Rajesh Vasa	Deakin University, Australia
Ricardo Vilalta	University of Austin, USA
Renato Vimieiro	Federal University of Minas Gerais, Brazil
Chunchen Wang	Beijing University of Posts and Telecommunications, China
Dongjing Wang	Hangzhou Dianzi University, China
Liping Wang	East China Normal University, China
Xin Wang	Qilu University of Technology, China
Xinyao Wang	China Unicom Data Intelligence Co., Ltd, China
Yi Wang	Xinjiang Technical Institute of Physics and Chemistry, Chinese Academy of Sciences, China
Yu-Shuen Wang	National Yang Ming Chiao Tung University, Taiwan
Yuangang Wang	Dalian Minzu University, China
Yi Wen	University of Electronic Science and Technology of China, China
Isabelle Wittmann	IBM Research, Switzerland
Tong Wu	University of Electronic Science and Technology of China, China
Yao Wu	Information Support Force Engineering University, China
Zhengbiao Wu	Ningbo University, China
Bin Xiao	University Health Network, Canada
Jing Xiao	South China Normal University, China
Chenyang Xu	East China Normal University, China
Huijie Xu	University of Technology Sydney, Australia
Long Xu	RMIT University, Australia
Zhiwei Xu	Shandong University, China
Han Xue	Donghua University, China
Sangeeta Yadav	Indian Institute of Science, India

Can Zhou	Imperial College London, UK
Qiaoli Zhou	Shenyang Aerospace University, China
Tianlong Zhou	Tongji University, China
Tongqing Zhou	National University of Defense Technology, China
Yan Zhou	Hohai University, China
Zhengyang Zhou	University of Science and Technology of China, China
Guanghui Zhu	Nanjing University, China
Mengxiao Zhu	North China University of Technology, China

Sponsors

Main

Platinum

Gold

Other Sponsors

Keynotes

Rethinking the Role of Scientific Discovery in the Era of AI

Mihaela van der Schaar

University of Cambridge, UK

Abstract. The growing availability of large-scale scientific datasets creates opportunities for discovery that are no longer driven by narrowly specified research questions. Instead, science increasingly unfolds through sustained exploration of vast, high-dimensional hypothesis spaces, where multiple explanations, mechanisms, and associations may remain plausible. I refer to this mode of inquiry as hypothesis hunting: an open-ended, cumulative search for insight that challenges traditional, pipeline-based models of scientific discovery.

In this talk, I present a framework that rethinks discovery as an agentic process, in which networks of interacting AI agents and human experts jointly explore, critique, and refine hypotheses under shared norms of evaluation. I will discuss how heterogeneous, LLM-based research agents can self-organize into evolving networks that generate, review, and extend findings—trading off novelty, quality, and diversity over time. Drawing on results from biomedical discovery, including cancer cohort analyses, I will argue that such socially structured agent networks can sustain large-scale exploratory discovery, complementing experimental science while reshaping how knowledge is generated, accumulated, and validated in the era of AI.

Neural Networks and Algorithms

Stefanie Jegelka

TU Munich, Germany

Abstract. Deep Learning models are now mastering increasingly complex tasks that consist of many steps of computation or reasoning. This inspires the perspective of viewing neural networks as learning algorithmic procedures. What could we gain from this perspective? This talk will outline examples and directions. First, an algorithmic view can help understand the capabilities of deep learning models, such as self-correction or the ability to solve certain optimization problems. Second, it can help understand how to design and train models to better solve challenging tasks, from optimization problems to reasoning. Yet, while this view has led to many advances, several open questions remain.

From Dialogue to Decision: Orchestrating Agents for Conversational Data Exploration and Multi-objective Optimization

Sihem Amer-Yahia

CNRS, Université Grenoble Alpes, France

Abstract. Modern scientific discovery and decision-making necessitate agents capable of navigating both complex datasets and multifaceted, often conflicting, goal landscapes. This talk explores the intersection of conversational data exploration, an incremental process where agents help users articulate needs through data interaction, and multi-objective sequential decision making. While traditional Reinforcement Learning (RL) has advanced task-specific agent training, we are witnessing a paradigm shift toward zero-shot orchestration. By leveraging a spectrum of techniques, from specialized RL policies to general-purpose Large Language Models (LLMs), we can reuse existing single-objective policies to solve complex multi-objective problems without training from scratch. We will discuss empirical evidence from the field of Education showing that this orchestrated approach can achieve competitive Pareto quality while reducing computational cost. The talk concludes by examining open research questions regarding how LLM context richness and reflective foresight enable agents to bridge the gap between incremental data-driven insights and optimal sequential actions.

AI Ethics and Governance

Francesca Rossi

IBM Research, USA

Abstract. Supported by AI, we will be able to make more grounded decisions and to focus on the main values and goals of a decision process rather than on routine and repetitive tasks. However, such a powerful technology also raises some concerns, related to privacy, fairness, value alignment, explainability, accountability, transparency, misinformation, deep fakes, copyright, and much more. These concerns are among the obstacles that hold AI back or that cause worry for current AI users, adopters, and policy makers. Without concrete answers to these questions, many will not trust AI, and therefore will not fully adopt it nor get its positive impact. In this talk I will present the main issues around AI ethics and safety and how they have evolved over the years, as AI capabilities advanced. I will also discuss the ROI of AI ethics, discussing both instrumental and value-based approaches to investing in AI ethics and governance.

The AI Ghosts and Us: Machine Writing as a Spectral Culture

Gianni Riotta

Luiss University, Italy

Abstract. We need a radically new philosophical reading of AI-generated text as a "Ghost" inhabiting contemporary human discourse. Rather than framing large language models (LLMs) as either tools or autonomous intelligences, we can argue that machine writing constitutes a spectral hybrid—neither fully human nor purely artificial, but a liminal presence emerging from the archive of human language. Drawing on Calvino's reflections on combinatorial literature and the "writing machine," we should revisit the Twentieth-century intuition that narrative could be algorithmically permuted. Calvino saw in literary algorithms both a liberation and a paradox: the machine multiplies possibilities, yet meaning still depends on human interpretation. Today's LLMs operationalize that combinatorial dream at a planetary scale, transforming statistical inference into prose and blurring the boundary between author and reader.

Karpathy's notion of neural networks encoding patterns learned from data, rather than an explicit set of rules, reveals how AI systems internalize collective textual memory. The model does not "think" as a subject; it resonates. What appears as originality is a probabilistic echo of cultural sediment. The AI text thus resembles a revenant: language returning to us transformed and detached from any single living author. Revisiting Wiener's cybernetic theory, we could situate LLMs within feedback loops between humans and machines. The literary output of an AI is not an artificial substitute for human creativity, nor a counterfeit consciousness. It is a ghostly hybrid, generated at the intersection of human archives, algorithmic training, and real-time, effective prompts. By conceiving AI text as a cultural ghost, we compose a vocabulary in the age of machine writing. The challenge is not to deny the ghost nor to romanticize it, but to learn how to read and live with its spectral presence in our world.

Contents

Bias and Fairness

Biomedical AI

Causal Discovery and Causal Inference

Clustering and Pattern Mining

Anomaly and Outlier Detection

Beyond a Single Perspective: Text Anomaly Detection with Multi-view Language Representations

Yixin Liu[1], Kehan Yan[2], Shiyuan Li[1], Qingfeng Chen[2], and Shirui Pan[1(✉)]

[1] Griffith University, Queensland, Australia
{yixin.liu,shiyuan.li,s.pan}@griffith.edu.au
[2] Guangxi University, Nanning, China
2413301048@st.gxu.edu.cn, qingfeng@gxu.edu.cn

Abstract. Text anomaly detection (TAD) plays a critical role in various language-driven real-world applications, including harmful content moderation, phishing detection, and spam review filtering. While two-step "embedding–detector" TAD methods have shown state-of-the-art performance, their effectiveness is often limited by the use of a single embedding model and the lack of adaptability across diverse datasets and anomaly types. To address these limitations, we propose to exploit the embeddings from multiple pretrained language models and integrate them into MCA^2, a multi-view TAD framework. MCA^2 adopts a multi-view reconstruction model to effectively extract normal textual patterns from multiple embedding perspectives. To exploit inter-view complementarity, a contrastive collaboration module is designed to leverage and strengthen the interactions across different views. Moreover, an adaptive allocation module is developed to automatically assign the contribution weight of each view, thereby improving the adaptability to diverse datasets. Extensive experiments on 10 benchmark datasets verify the effectiveness of MCA^2 against strong baselines. The source code of MCA^2 is available at https://github.com/yankehan/MCA2.

Keywords: Text anomaly detection · Large language models · Multi-view learning

1 Introduction

Text anomaly detection (TAD) is a fundamental research problem that aims to identify anomalous or suspicious textual instances that deviate from normal patterns [6,43]. With the ever-increasing volume of digital text data, TAD plays

Y. Liu, K. Yan S. Li—These authors contributed equally to this work.

Supplementary Information The online version contains supplementary material available at https://doi.org/10.1007/978-3-032-37654-1_1.

M. Ceci et al. (Eds.): ECML PKDD 2026, LNAI 16941, pp. 3–21, 2027.
https://doi.org/10.1007/978-3-032-37654-1_1

a crucial role in various real-world applications. For instance, TAD helps detect abusive or threatening messages to maintain the safety and integrity of social platforms [14,18,35,40]. Meanwhile, identifying anomalous product reviews via TAD is essential for ensuring the reliability of e-commerce ecosystems [10]. Due to its wide range of applications, in recent years, TAD has attracted increasing research attention in the research community of natural language processing (NLP) [6,7,22,33].

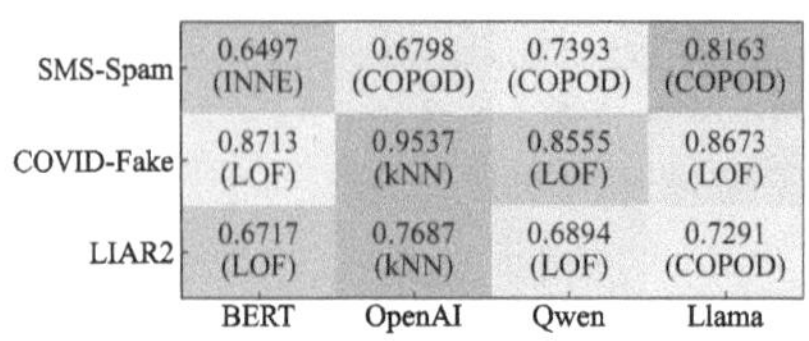

(a) AUROC of different embedding models with (best detector); colors indicate 1st, 2nd, 3rd, and 4th ranks.

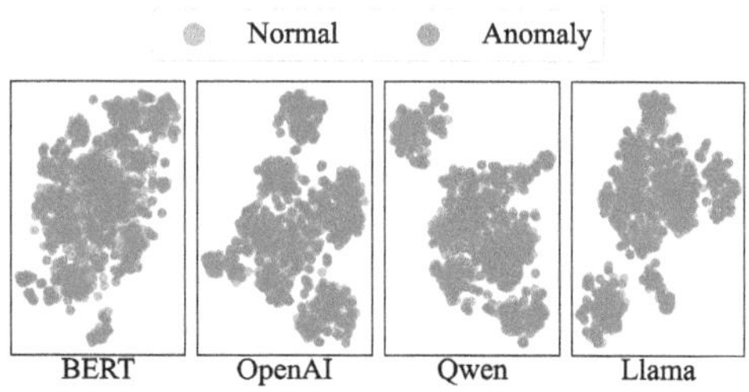

(b) T-SNE Visualization of embeddings.

Fig. 1. (a) Performance comparison of different embedding models with the best detectors. (b) Visualization of embeddings on COVID-Fake dataset.

Recent advances in large language models (LLMs) have greatly improved their representation capabilities, enabling them to generate high-quality contextualized embeddings that capture rich semantic content and syntactic patterns in textual data [2,6,21,37]. By integrating high-quality textual embeddings with various anomaly detectors, **embedding-based methods** have demonstrated promising effectiveness in addressing the TAD problem [6]. Typically, embedding-based methods follow a two-step pipeline: First, a text embedding model (e.g., BERT [12] or OpenAI's embedding model [38]) encodes the text into numerical embeddings. Then, anomaly detection algorithms designed for vectorized data (e.g., LOF [4] and iForest [26]) are applied to detect anomalies based on the embeddings. Due to the powerful representation capability of LLM-generated embeddings, these embedding-based methods achieve state-of-the-art performance in TAD tasks and even outperform many end-to-end approaches [22].

Despite their remarkable performance, these embedding-based methods are usually built upon embeddings produced by *a single text embedding model* and rely on *a particular detector* to conduct anomaly detection, which leads to several inherent limitations. Firstly, a single embedding model is inevitably biased toward the distribution and linguistic characteristics of its pretraining corpus, which prevents it from providing universally robust representations in TAD scenarios with diverse domains, anomaly types, and textual styles. As a result, different embedding models exhibit varying performance across datasets, and no single embedding model consistently emerges as the overall winner, as demonstrated in Fig. 1a (source data from recent benchmark [6]). Moreover, due to the diverse embedding distributions produced by different embedding models (Fig. 1b gives an example), it is non-trivial to determine in advance which detector will be most compatible with the corresponding distribution for a given dataset. Consequently, we have to evaluate all possible embedding–detector combinations to determine the best-performing one, which may be costly and impractical in real-world cases. Motivated by these issues, a natural question arises: ***Can we develop a unified TAD framework that leverages embeddings from multiple models and integrates them to achieve better anomaly detection?***

To answer this question, two pressing challenges need to be tackled. ***Challenge 1:*** *How to coordinate multiple embeddings and fully exploit their complementary strengths?* As shown in Fig. 1b, embeddings generated by different models capture the data from different perspectives and encode complementary information. Then, how to make them collaborate in a way that they can both mutually enhance and constrain each other is a critical challenge [20]. ***Challenge 2:*** *How to adaptively balance the contributions of different embeddings to achieve effective anomaly detection?* Due to the diversity of textual data and embedding models, the usefulness of different embeddings for anomaly detection often differs across datasets, which is proven in Fig. 1a. In this case, a unified TAD framework should also adaptively determine how much each embedding contributes based on the characteristics of the data.

Motivated by these challenges, in this paper, we propose a novel **M**ulti-view TAD framework with **C**ontrastive **C**ollaboration and **A**daptive **A**llocation (MCA^2 for short). MCA^2 is built upon a multi-view reconstruction model for TAD, where embeddings from different models form multiple complementary views, equipped with two well-crafted modules to further exploit such multi-view information. More specifically, to tackle ***Challenge 1***, we design a *contrastive collaboration module* that enforces distributional consistency among different views in the latent space. By maximizing the mutual information between different views, the latent distributions become better aligned and more structurally consistent, leading to more discriminative anomaly characteristics. In addition, the mutual information can be further exploited as an indicator of abnormality. To address ***Challenge 2***, we develop an *adaptive allocation module* that automatically assigns appropriate importance to different views based on the characteristics of the data. This module not only allows MCA^2 to adapt across various datasets, but also provides sample-level adaptiveness for more precise anomaly detection. To sum up, the contributions of this paper are threefold:

- **New Paradigm:** Going beyond single embedding model-based methods, we take the first step to leverage multiple embedding models to capture complementary information for TAD.
- **Novel Method:** We propose MCA^2, a multi-view TAD framework that adaptively allocates the contributions of different embeddings and enforces contrastive collaboration across multiple views.

- **Extensive Experiments:** Extensive experiments on ten real-world benchmark datasets demonstrate that our method achieves superior anomaly detection performance compared with state-of-the-art approaches.

2 Related Work

In this section, we provide a brief summary of the studies in three key areas: text embedding, text anomaly detection, and multi-view anomaly detection. Detailed reviews are provided in Appendix A.

Text Embedding techniques aim to map textual data into vectorized representations (a.k.a. embeddings) that capture semantic and syntactic information. Early methods involve TF-IDF [48] or Word2Vec [36] to learn text representations. Then, BERT [12] and its advanced models show strong representation capability through large-scale pretraining. In the era of LLMs, text embeddings generated by billion-parameter models (e.g., OpenAI models [38] and Qwen [59]) have become more expressive and powerful, providing high-quality embeddings for various downstream tasks [39,44].

Text Anomaly Detection (TAD) aims to identify textual instances that deviate from dominant normal data [22]. Existing TAD methods can be divided into two categories. End-to-end methods perform anomaly detection in a unified manner by directly predicting abnormality from raw textual inputs [11,32,33,47]. Embedding-based methods first convert text into dense embeddings using text embedding models, and then apply anomaly detectors (such as LOF [4], KNN [45], COPOD [23], iForest [26], and LUNAR [15]) for detection. Although empirical evidence [6,22] shows that embedding-based methods often achieve state-of-the-art performance, they typically rely on a single embedding model, which makes them less robust when facing diverse datasets and anomaly types [28,41,42].

Multi-view Anomaly Detection focuses on identifying anomalous samples in multi-view data, e.g., image data represented by multiple views like color and shape feature descriptors. Early studies detect anomalies based on multi-view clustering [25,34]. Recent studies, such as NCMOD [9] and RCPMOD [55], employ unsupervised deep learning models to detect anomalies. Despite their success in multi-view visual data, how to conduct multi-view anomaly detection for high-dimensional textual data remains open.

3 Problem Definition

To leverage the embeddings generated by multiple embedding models for TAD, we formulate TAD as a multi-view anomaly detection problem.

Given a text dataset $\mathcal{D} = \{x_i\}_{i=1}^{N}$ consisting of N documents, each instance x_i is associated with a label $y_i \in \{0, 1\}$, where $y_i = 0$ denotes a normal sample and $y_i = 1$ denotes an anomalous sample. With K large language embedding models $\{f_k(\cdot)\}_{k=1}^{K}$, each text sample x_i is mapped into K embedding views:

$$\mathbf{v}_i^{(k)} = f_k(x_i), \quad k = 1, 2, \ldots, K. \tag{1}$$

Thus, each instance is represented as a multi-view embedding set $\mathcal{V}_i = \{\mathbf{v}_i^{(1)}, \ldots, \mathbf{v}_i^{(K)}\}$. The goal of multi-view text anomaly detection is to learn an anomaly scoring function

$$s(\mathcal{V}_i) : \mathcal{V}_i \to \mathbb{R}, \tag{2}$$

such that anomalous instances receive higher scores than normal ones. A final decision is obtained by thresholding $s(\mathcal{V}_i)$.

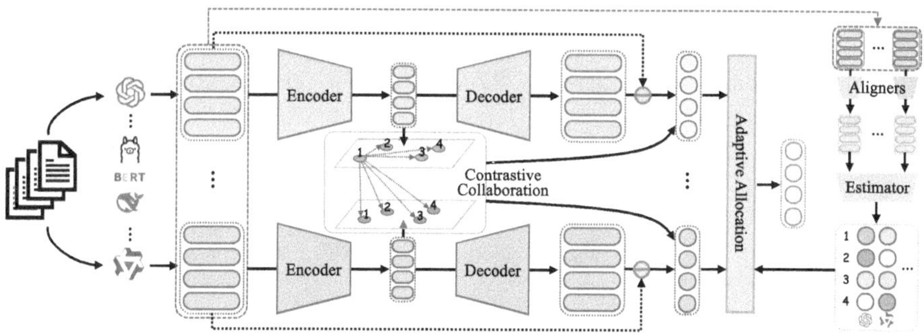

Fig. 2. Overall framework of MCA^2. We illustrate the case of two views (OpenAI and Qwen) as an example.

Considering that anomalies are difficult to obtain in real-world scenarios, we follow a one-class anomaly detection setting in this paper, consistent with existing benchmarks [22]: The training dataset is defined as $\mathcal{D}_{\text{train}} = \{x_i \mid y_i = 0\}$, where only normal samples are available. The test set is $\mathcal{D}_{\text{test}} = \{x_j \mid y_j \in \{0, 1\}\}$, which contains both normal and anomalous samples.

4 Methodology

In this section, we introduce the proposed multi-view TAD framework, MCA^2, in detail. As illustrated in Fig. 2, MCA^2 employs an autoencoder-based *multi-view reconstruction model* as the backbone of TAD model (Sect. 4.1). To exploit the complementary information across different views, we introduce an *inter-view contrastive collaboration module* that maximizes the consistency among views (Sect. 4.2). Meanwhile, we introduce an *adaptive view contribution allocation module* to dynamically assign the contribution of different views in indicating abnormality (Sect. 4.3).

4.1 Multi-view Reconstruction TAD Model

To achieve effective TAD with embeddings from diverse models, the core is to find a universal anomaly detection paradigm that captures the data distributions of diverse and heterogeneous embeddings. Under the one-class setting, the lack of anomalous training samples further highlights the need for an unsupervised anomaly detection paradigm [61,62,64]. Motivated by the *reconstruction assumption*, i.e., a reconstruction model trained on normal data can well reconstruct normal samples while yielding large reconstruction errors for anomalous ones [49,58,60], a promising solution is to conduct anomaly detection under the reconstruction paradigm. As autoencoder-based anomaly detection models have proven to be effective in various data modalities (e.g., images [63], tabulars [19], time series [3,54,57,65], and graphs [13,29,30,56]) by modeling diverse data distributions, we build our multi-view TAD framework on a reconstruction-based backbone.

Considering the differences between embeddings generated by different language models (i.e., data views), we build an independent autoencoder for each view to perform reconstruction. Formally, for the data of the k-th view $\mathcal{V}^{(k)} = \{\mathbf{v}_1^{(k)}, \cdots, \mathbf{v}_N^{(k)}\}$, an MLP-based autoencoder is employed to model this view:

$$\mathbf{z}_i^{(k)} = \mathrm{Enc}^{(k)}(\mathbf{v}_i^{(k)}), \quad \widehat{\mathbf{v}}_i^{(k)} = \mathrm{Dec}^{(k)}(\mathbf{z}_i^{(k)}), \tag{3}$$

where $\mathrm{Enc}^{(k)}(\cdot)$ and $\mathrm{Dec}^{(k)}(\cdot)$ denote the encoder and decoder of the k-th view, respectively, $\mathbf{z}_i^{(k)}$ is the latent representation, and $\widehat{\mathbf{v}}_i^{(k)}$ is the reconstructed embedding of $\mathbf{v}_i^{(k)}$. The autoencoder can be optimized by minimizing the reconstruction loss between $\widehat{\mathbf{v}}_i^{(k)}$ and $\mathbf{v}_i^{(k)}$:

$$\mathcal{L}_{i,rec}^{(k)} = \left\| \mathbf{v}_i^{(k)} - \widehat{\mathbf{v}}_i^{(k)} \right\|_2^2. \tag{4}$$

Once the model is well trained, the reconstruction error of each view can be used to measure the abnormality of the corresponding samples:

$$s_{i,rec}^{(k)} = \left\| \mathbf{v}_i^{(k)} - \widehat{\mathbf{v}}_i^{(k)} \right\|_2^2, \tag{5}$$

where $s_{i,rec}^{(k)}$ denotes the reconstruction-based anomaly score of the i-th sample in the k-th view, computed as the squared ℓ_2 reconstruction error. Owing to the strong capability of autoencoders in modeling various normal data distributions, the learned anomaly score can effectively indicate the abnormality of each sample from an intra-view perspective, reflecting the view-specific characteristics of the corresponding embedding space.

4.2 Inter-view Contrastive Collaboration

Although the reconstruction-based backbone can capture intra-view information for anomaly detection, it may overlook the crucial inter-view dependencies and consistency. Since different embedding models can capture different aspects of textual semantics, the data from different views can be complementary [50–52]. To further leverage such mutual complementarity to enhance multi-view TAD, we propose an inter-view contrastive collaboration mechanism that encourages different views to collaborate and complement each other. Our core idea is to maximize the mutual information between the representations of the same sample across different views, thereby aligning their distributions and improving the quality of the latent representations. More importantly, as the inter-view matching patterns can also expose abnormal behaviors, the mutual information can serve as an indicator of abnormality. This collaboration-based abnormality measurement provides a supplement to the reconstruction-based intra-view anomaly scores.

Since each pair of views can provide complementary information to one another, contrastive collaboration is conducted over all possible view pairs. Formally, given the latent representation sets of the j-th and k-th views, i.e., $\mathcal{Z}^{(j)} = \{\mathbf{z}_i^{(j)}\}_{i=1}^N$ and $\mathcal{Z}^{(k)} = \{\mathbf{z}_i^{(k)}\}_{i=1}^N$, we adopt an InfoNCE contrastive loss to enhance inter-view collaboration:

$$\mathcal{L}_{i,con}^{(j,k)} = -\log p_i^{(j,k)}, \tag{6}$$

$$p_i^{(j,k)} = \frac{e^{s(\mathbf{z}_i^{(j)},\mathbf{z}_i^{(k)})/\tau}}{\sum_{m\neq i} e^{s(\mathbf{z}_i^{(j)},\mathbf{z}_m^{(k)})/\tau} + \sum_{n\neq i} e^{s(\mathbf{z}_i^{(j)},\mathbf{z}_n^{(j)})/\tau}}, \tag{7}$$

where $p_i^{(j,k)}$ denotes the matching probability of the i-th sample between the j-th and k-th views, $s(\cdot,\cdot)$ is the cosine similarity, and τ is a temperature hyperparameter. Note that we incorporate both cross-view and intra-view samples as negative instances, which helps learn more discriminative latent representations. In practice, we conduct contrastive learning in a mini-batch manner to ensure efficient optimization and stable training on large-scale datasets.

Trained with the contrastive loss, the model can learn the matching patterns across different views. That is to say, normal samples tend to exhibit strong and consistent cross-view correspondence due to the constraint imposed by the contrastive collaboration mechanism. On the other hand, an anomalous sample may break this cross-view consistency, making the matching probability a meaningful indicator of abnormality. Based on this property, we can obtain the contrastive anomaly score $s_{i,con}^{(k)}$ of the i-th sample in the k-th view by aggregating its matching probabilities with all the other views:

$$s_{i,con}^{(k)} = -\frac{1}{K-1}\sum_{j=1,\ j\neq k}^{K} \log p_i^{(j,k)}. \tag{8}$$

While $s_{i,rec}^{(k)}$ measures the abnormality from an intra-view perspective, $s_{i,con}^{(k)}$ provides a complementary measurement from an inter-view perspective, which improves the use of multi-view information for more accurate anomaly identification.

4.3 Adaptive View Contribution Allocation

After the reconstruction and contrastive collaboration modules produce the anomaly score of each sample at each view, the remaining problem is how to fuse them into a unified anomaly score. A naive solution is to simply aggregate the anomaly scores from different views with equal weights; however, due to the heterogeneous representational capabilities of embedding models and their varying adaptability to a specific dataset, treating all views equally may lead to suboptimal fusion, where informative views are diluted and less reliable ones are overweighted. In this case, a more desirable strategy is to adaptively weight different views in a data-driven manner. To achieve this goal, we incorporate an *adaptive view contribution allocation* module into MCA^2 to automatically determine the importance of each view. This module takes the multi-view embeddings as input and outputs allocation weights for different views, which are used to guide the fusion of anomaly scores [8].

Weight Estimation. Considering that the dimensions and semantics of different views are heterogeneous, in the first step, we perform an alignment to map them into a shared space. Due to its effectiveness in reducing dimensionality and retaining the principal structural information, we employ PCA algorithm [31] as the aligner for each view. Concretely, for each view of data $\mathcal{V}^{(k)} = \{\mathbf{v}_1^{(k)}, \cdots, \mathbf{v}_N^{(k)}\}$, we stack them into a matrix $\mathbf{V}^{(k)} \in \mathbb{R}^{N \times d_k}$ and apply a PCA transformation, i.e., $\widetilde{\mathbf{V}}^{(k)} = \mathrm{PCA}(\mathbf{V}^{(k)})$, where $\widetilde{\mathbf{V}}^{(k)} \in \mathbb{R}^{N \times d}$ denotes the aligned feature of the k-th view, and all views are projected into the same d-dimensional space to ensure dimensional consistency. Since PCA sorts the components by their importance (i.e., explained variance), the projected representations become unified at the variance-structure level across different views.

After that, we estimate the contribution weights for different views with a lightweight neural network. Given a sample x_i, we extract all its aligned feature vectors $\{\widetilde{\mathbf{v}}_i^{(k)}\}_{k=1}^{K}$ by taking the i-th row from each $\widetilde{\mathbf{V}}^{(k)}$, and then an MLP-based estimator is applied to generate contribution scores:

$$
{w'}_i^{(k)} = \mathrm{MLP}\left(\widetilde{\mathbf{v}}_i^{(k)}\right), \quad w_i^{(k)} = \frac{\sigma\left({w'}_i^{(k)}\right)}{\sum_{j=1}^{K} \sigma\left({w'}_i^{(j)}\right)}, \tag{9}
$$

where ${w'}_i^{(k)}$ denotes the estimated contribution score, $\sigma(\cdot)$ is Sigmoid function, and $w_i^{(k)}$ is the normalized allocation weight of the k-th view for sample x_i.

Anomaly Scoring. With the allocation weights, we can now calculate the anomaly score of x_i by aggregating the view-specific scores from the reconstruction and contrastive modules. Concretely, the final anomaly score $s(x_i)$ is computed as:

$$
s(x_i) = \sum_{k=1}^{K} w_i^{(k)} \left(\alpha\, s_{i,\mathrm{rec}}^{(k)} + \beta\, s_{i,\mathrm{con}}^{(k)}\right), \tag{10}
$$

where α and β are balance hyperparameters for reconstruction-based and contrastive-based scores, respectively. Note that the adaptive allocation is conducted at a fine-grained sample level rather than at a coarse dataset level, which enables the model to tailor the view contributions to each instance and leads to reliable anomaly identification [53].

Two-Stage Training. All the parameters in MCA^2, including the detection model and the allocation module, are optimized by minimizing the overall loss function:

$$\mathcal{L} = \frac{1}{N}\sum_{i=1}^{N}\Big(\sum_{k} w_i^{(k)}\mathcal{L}_{i,\text{rec}}^{(k)} + \lambda\sum_{j<k}\omega_i^{(j,k)}\mathcal{L}_{i,\text{con}}^{(j,k)}\Big), \tag{11}$$

where $\omega_i^{(j,k)} = (w_i^{(j)} + w_i^{(k)})/2$ and λ is a balance hyperparameter for two losses.

While jointly optimizing all the parameters may be straightforward, it may lead to unstable training due to the coupling between the detection backbone and the allocation module. To ensure stable optimization of the entire framework, we adopt a decoupled two-stage training strategy. In the **first stage**, we freeze the parameters of the allocation module and enforce it to output uniform weights (i.e., $w = 1/K$). This allows the encoders and decoders to fully learn robust feature reconstructions and cross-view collaboration. In the **second stage**, we freeze the detection model and only train the allocation module to assign appropriate view contributions for different samples based on reliable view-specific anomaly scores. The overall running algorithm of MCA^2 is given in Appendix B, with complexity analysis detailed in Appendix C.

5 Experiments

5.1 Experiment Setup

Datasets. We conduct experiments on 10 public datasets from NLP-ADBench [22] and TAD-Bench [6]. Following the standard protocol in NLP-ADBench, we allocate 70% of the normal instances for training. The remaining 30% normal instances, together with all anomalous instances, form the test set. Details of the datasets are provided in Appendix D.

Baselines. We compare MCA^2 with three types of methods. ❶ **End-to-end methods** include CVDD [47], DATE [33], and FATE [11]. ❷ **Embedding-based methods** first extract embeddings from a pretrained model (BERT [12] or OpenAI-large [38]) and apply an anomaly detector, selected from LOF [4], DeepSVDD [46], ECOD [24], iForest [26], SO-GAAL [27], AE [1], VAE [5,16], and LUNAR [15]. Notably, these methods are adopted as standard baselines in recent benchmark studies on text anomaly detection [6,22]. ❸ **Multi-view methods**, including NCMOD [9] and RCPMOD [55], are implied on the same embedding sets as MCA^2.

Evaluation and Implementation. We report AUROC and AUPRC as the main metrics. For all methods, we report the mean and standard deviation over

5 random seeds. We consider two sets of embedding models to construct the multi-view data: ❶ **OpenAIs**, including 3 OpenAI family models, i.e., OpenAI-small/ada/large, and ❷ **Mixed**, including 4 representative models, i.e., OpenAI-large, BERT, Qwen, and Llama. The details of implementation and embedding models are given in Appendices E and F, respectively. The efficiency analysis, including memory usage and runtime comparisons, is provided in Appendix I.

Table 1. Main results on AUROC for NLP-ADBench datasets. Best results are highlighted in bold and shaded.

Methods	NLPAD-AGNews	NLPAD-BBCNews	NLPAD-MovieReview	NLPAD-N24News
CVDD	0.6461	0.6150	0.4860	0.6443
DATE	0.7843	0.8026	0.4871	0.6609
FATE	0.8837	0.8221	0.5770	0.8770
BERT+LOF	0.7432	0.9320	0.4959	0.6703
BERT+DeepSVDD	0.5558	0.5852	0.4507	0.4484
BERT+ECOD	0.6318	0.6912	0.4282	0.4969
BERT+iForest	0.6287	0.6844	0.4242	0.4808
BERT+SO-GAAL	0.4488	0.3100	0.4663	0.4140
BERT+AE	0.7197	0.8854	0.4650	0.5741
BERT+VAE	0.6778	0.7450	0.4387	0.5066
BERT+LUNAR	0.7654	0.9381	0.4647	0.6275
OAI-L+LOF	0.7879	0.9558	0.7292	0.7495
OAI-L+DeepSVDD	0.5019	0.5690	0.5132	0.6056
OAI-L+ECOD	0.6673	0.7225	0.4895	0.6216
OAI-L+iForest	0.5750	0.6211	0.5221	0.5746
OAI-L+SO-GAAL	0.3685	0.2359	0.4210	0.2920
OAI-L+AE	0.8916	0.9527	0.5942	0.7987
OAI-L+VAE	0.8514	0.7541	0.5248	0.7181
OAI-L+LUNAR	0.8998	0.9771	0.8258	0.8577
NCMOD (**OpenAIs**)	0.7304	0.8451	0.6294	0.6861
NCMOD (**Mixed**)	0.7222	0.7642	0.5560	0.6508
RCPMOD (**OpenAIs**)	0.7864	0.9778	0.7963	0.9570
RCPMOD (**Mixed**)	0.8249	0.9794	0.7249	0.9449
MCA^2 (**OpenAIs**)	**0.9484**	**0.9860**	**0.8381**	**0.9656**
MCA^2 (**Mixed**)	0.9482	0.9752	0.7914	0.9575

5.2 Main Results

Table 1 and 2 shows the comparison results of MCA^2 with baseline methods in terms of AUROC. Results in AUPRC are provided in Appendix H. We have the following observations. ❶ MCA^2 achieves the best AUROC on 9/10 datasets and remains competitive on `SMSSpam`, demonstrating its strong generalization ability across different domains. ❷ Compared with the strongest baselines, MCA^2 brings clear improvements on challenging datasets. These gains indicate that

Table 2. Main results on AUROC for TAD-Bench datasets. Best results are highlighted in bold and shaded.

Methods	TAD-Email Spam	TAD-SMS Spam	TAD-OLID	TAD-Hate Speech	TAD-Covid Fake	TAD-Liar2
CVDD	0.8480	0.4499	0.5504	0.5108	0.7774	0.6646
DATE	0.9638	**0.9670**	0.5194	0.6009	0.7791	0.6900
FATE	0.7785	0.9518	0.5555	0.6774	0.8331	0.6424
BERT+LOF	0.7530	0.6842	0.5123	0.4706	0.8524	0.6670
BERT+DeepSVDD	0.6200	0.5870	0.5220	0.4991	0.7147	0.5842
BERT+ECOD	0.6978	0.5675	0.5054	0.4899	0.7642	0.6091
BERT+iForest	0.6721	0.5715	0.4989	0.4920	0.7675	0.5904
BERT+SO-GAAL	0.4863	0.4111	0.4744	0.5232	0.6739	0.5154
BERT+AE	0.7585	0.6997	0.5120	0.4803	0.8275	0.6393
BERT+VAE	0.7228	0.6181	0.5092	0.4893	0.7685	0.6336
BERT+LUNAR	0.8443	0.7179	0.5305	0.5125	0.8492	0.6583
OAI-L+LOF	0.8339	0.7430	0.5614	0.5921	0.8523	0.7577
OAI-L+DeepSVDD	0.5831	0.4516	0.5299	0.4989	0.5727	0.4906
OAI-L+ECOD	0.9220	0.4238	0.5284	0.3465	0.8848	0.6280
OAI-L+iForest	0.8844	0.4933	0.5440	0.4612	0.7816	0.5654
OAI-L+SO-GAAL	0.1889	0.4643	0.4903	0.3399	0.3055	0.4643
OAI-L+AE	0.9381	0.5040	0.5504	0.6111	0.9520	0.7185
OAI-L+VAE	0.9257	0.4387	0.5302	0.3462	0.8945	0.6210
OAI-L+LUNAR	0.9828	0.7184	0.5730	0.7192	0.9651	0.7704
NCMOD (**OpenAIs**)	0.9469	0.8199	0.6262	0.4929	0.8999	0.7169
NCMOD (**Mixed**)	0.9113	0.5207	0.5138	0.5047	0.8693	0.6807
RCPMOD (**OpenAIs**)	0.8753	0.8169	0.5882	0.7132	0.8997	0.7213
RCPMOD (**Mixed**)	0.8204	0.7601	0.5305	0.5662	0.9021	0.6542
MCA^2 (**OpenAIs**)	**0.9895**	0.8865	**0.6355**	**0.7379**	0.9531	**0.7965**
MCA^2 (**Mixed**)	0.9734	0.8143	0.4892	0.5647	**0.9776**	0.7287

Table 3. Ablation results on AUROC for four datasets.

Variants	NLPAD-BBCNews	NLPAD-AGNews	NLPAD-MovieReview	TAD-OLID
		OpenAIs		
MCA^2	**0.9860**	**0.9484**	**0.8381**	**0.6355**
w/o AA	0.9858	**0.9484**	0.8378	0.6314
w/o CC	0.9788	0.8811	0.6592	0.5179
w/o AE	0.9775	0.9454	0.8350	0.6341
		Mixed		
MCA^2	**0.9752**	**0.9482**	**0.7914**	**0.4892**
w/o AA	**0.9752**	0.9480	0.7869	0.4841
w/o CC	0.9721	0.8917	0.5582	0.4592
w/o AE	0.9474	0.9432	0.7913	0.4883

leveraging multi-view signals is more effective than pairing a single strong representation with a fixed detector. ❸ MCA^2 consistently outperforms multi-view baselines (NCMOD and RCPMOD) on the same embedding sets. This suggests that our framework is better tailored for multi-view TAD by learning from high-dimensional text embeddings. ❹ The OpenAIs performs best on most NLP-ADBench datasets, while Mixed is competitive on TAD-Bench and achieves the best result on `CovidFake` (0.9776). This suggests that mixing heterogeneous backbones can provide complementary cues for domain-specific anomalies.

5.3 Ablation Study

To validate the contributions of key components in MCA^2, we construct three variants: ❶ **w/o AA**, which replaces the adaptive allocation module with uniform fusion over views; ❷ **w/o CC**, which removes the contrastive collaboration module; and ❸ **w/o AE**, which removes the autoencoder reconstruction loss and trains the model only with the contrastive learning loss.

The results are summarized in Table 3, which shows that all components contribute to the final performance consistently. ❶ Removing the allocation module results in a small but consistent drop. This indicates that sample-level adaptive view weighting helps when per-sample view quality varies. ❷ Removing the contrastive collaboration module causes the largest performance drop on almost all datasets and in both view combinations, e.g., on `MovieReview` ($-17.89\%/-23.32\%$). These results indicate that reconstruction alone overlooks the alignment of heterogeneous views, and the learned scores can become view-specific, which harms anomaly scoring. ❸ Removing AE yields a moderate decrease, and the effect is more pronounced with heterogeneous views, e.g., on `BBCNews` in the mixed-backbone setting ($0.9752 \rightarrow 0.9474$). This shows that AE provides a stabilizer when the views come from more diverse embedding model families, and the contrastive objective alone may overfit to cross-view shortcuts.

5.4 Allocation Visualization

To gain a deeper understanding of the behavior of the adaptive allocation module, we computed the argmax of the view weights for each test sample to obtain its top views. We then statistically analyzed the distribution of the top-1 views of all samples in two datasets, with the results shown in Fig. 3. The weights exhibit clear dataset-dependent preferences rather than uniformly selecting a fixed view, indicating that the fusion is sample-adaptive. In particular, for the **OpenAIs** views, `AGNews` shows a more balanced utilization of small/ada/large, while `BBCNews` and `CovidFake` are dominated by OpenAI-ada. For the **Mixed** views, the dominant view also shifts across datasets (e.g., OpenAI-large is more frequently selected on `BBCNews`, whereas Llama/BERT/Qwen receive higher selections on `AGNews`), while `CovidFake` exhibits a more balanced distribution. These results suggest the allocation module can automatically emphasize the most informative views for a given dataset.

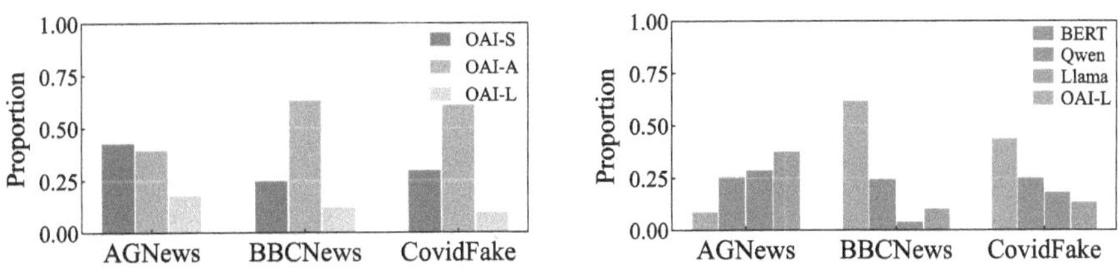

(a) OpenAIs (b) Mixed

Fig. 3. Distribution of the top-1 view selected by the gating module.

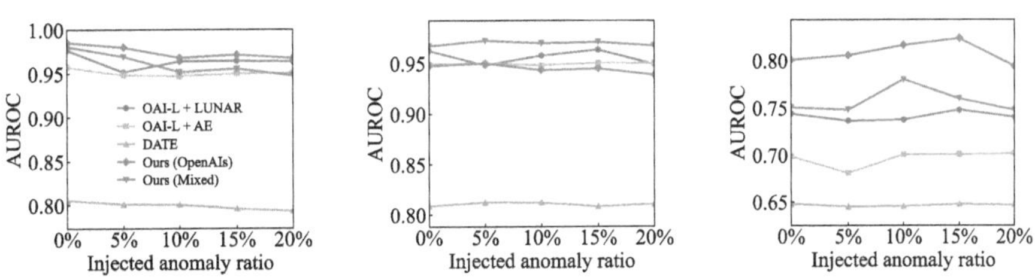

(a) BBCNews (b) CovidFake (c) Liar2

Fig. 4. Model robustness under different anomaly inject ratio (%).

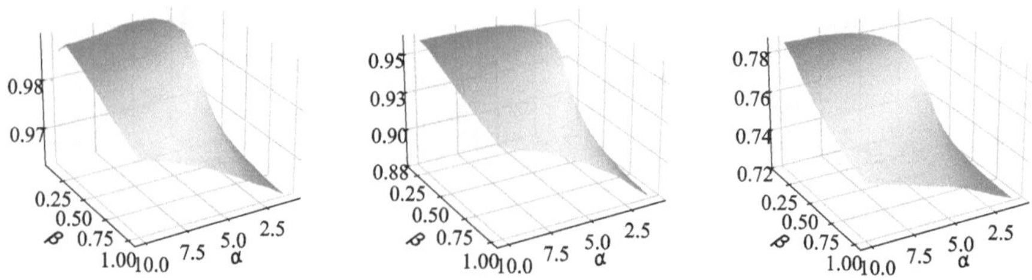

(a) BBCNews (b) CovidFake (c) Liar2

Fig. 5. Hyperparameter sensitivity analysis.

5.5 Robustness Analysis

To evaluate robustness against contaminated training data, we gradually inject anomalous instances into the inlier-only training set and report AUROC under different injection ratios in Fig. 4. Overall, MCA^2 remains stable as the injected anomaly ratio increases, showing only mild performance variations, while maintaining a clear margin over strong baselines such as `OpenAI-L+LUNAR` and `OpenAI-L+AE`. On `BBCNews` (Fig. 4a), all methods exhibit relatively small changes, but MCA^2 (OpenAIs) consistently achieves the highest AUROC across all ratios, indicating robustness even when the training set is slightly polluted. Similarly, on `CovidFake` (Fig. 4b), the performance variations remain small across different injection ratios, while MCA^2 (Mixed) achieves the highest AUROC. On `Liar2` (Fig. 4c), the gap becomes more evident: MCA^2 (OpenAIs) preserves strong performance under increasing contamination, and the Mixed variant remains competitive, suggesting that sample-adaptive multi-view fusion can mitigate the adverse impact of noisy inlier training data.

5.6 Hyperparameter Analysis

We study the sensitivity of MCA^2 to the balance hyperparameters for reconstruction-based and contrastive-based scores, i.e., α and β. Figure 5 illustrates the changes in AUROC as α and β vary. Overall, the performance changes smoothly over the grid and preserves a broad high-performing region, indicating that MCA^2 is not overly sensitive to precise hyperparameter tuning. On `BBCNews` (Fig. 5a), AUROC remains near-optimal for moderate-to-large α, while it drops when β becomes too large, suggesting that overweighting the cross-view consistency term can introduce noise into scoring and hurt discrimination. On `CovidFake` (Fig. 5b) and `Liar2` (Fig. 5c), the trend is more pronounced: the best results are obtained with a sufficiently large α and a small-to-moderate β, whereas increasing β steadily degrades AUROC. In practice, these results suggest prioritizing reconstruction evidence and using the contrastive-based score as a complementary signal. Complementary hyperparameter analysis on the loss weight λ is provided in Appendix G.

6 Conclusion and Future Work

In this paper, we propose a novel multi-view TAD method, MCA^2, that leverages embeddings from multiple language models to advance text anomaly detection (TAD). MCA^2 adopts a multi-view reconstruction model as the backbone, with a contrastive collaboration module to enhance and align the inter-view consistency. Furthermore, we design an adaptive allocation module that automatically assigns appropriate contribution weights to different views for anomaly detection. Extensive experiments demonstrate the state-of-the-art performance of MCA^2 on multiple benchmark datasets and its strong robustness under varying data contamination. While this work primarily focuses on the text anomaly detection (TAD) problem, the core mechanisms of MCA^2 are inherently modality-agnostic and hold significant potential for broader domains. In future work, we plan to extend this framework to other areas, such as image and multimodal anomaly detection [17]. Furthermore, we will explore cross-modal anomaly detection by integrating embeddings from both text and image modalities, aiming to establish a more generalized and unified multi-view anomaly detection paradigm.

Acknowledgments. The work of S. Pan was partially supported by the Australian Research Council (ARC) under Grant Nos. DP240101547 and FT210100097. The work of Y. Liu was partially supported by the ARC under Grant No. DE260101172.

Disclosure of Interests. The authors declare that they have no known competing financial interests or personal relationships that could have appeared to influence the work reported in this paper. Furthermore, all authors certify that they have no affiliations with or involvement in any organization or entity with any financial or non-financial interest in the subject matter or materials discussed in this manuscript.

References

1. Aggarwal, C.C.: An introduction to outlier analysis. In: Aggarwal, C.C. (ed.) Outlier Analysis, pp. 1–34. Springer, Cham (2017). https://doi.org/10.1007/978-3-319-47578-3_1
2. Bai, S., et al.: Qwen2. 5-VL technical report. arXiv preprint arXiv:2502.13923 (2025)
3. Bi, X., et al.: Patchfusionmlp: a scalable multi-resolution MLP framework for time series prediction. Pattern Recogn. 113263 (2026)
4. Breunig, M.M., Kriegel, H.P., Ng, R.T., Sander, J.: LoF: identifying density-based local outliers. In: Proceedings of the 2000 ACM SIGMOD International Conference on Management of Data, pp. 93–104 (2000)
5. Burgess, C.P., et al.: Understanding disentangling in β-VAE. arXiv preprint arXiv:1804.03599 (2018)
6. Cao, Y., et al.: Tad-bench: a comprehensive benchmark for embedding-based text anomaly detection. arXiv preprint arXiv:2501.11960 (2025)
7. Cao, Y., Yang, S., Yang, Y., Qi, L., Liu, M.: Text anomaly detection with simplified isolation kernel. arXiv preprint arXiv:2510.13197 (2025)

8. Chen, Q., Li, S., Liu, Y., Pan, S., Webb, G.I., Zhang, S.: Uncertainty-aware graph neural networks: a multihop evidence fusion approach. IEEE Trans. Neural Netw. Learn. Syst. (2025)
9. Cheng, L., Wang, Y., Liu, X.: Neighborhood consensus networks for unsupervised multi-view outlier detection. In: Proceedings of the AAAI Conference on Artificial Intelligence, vol. 35, pp. 7099–7106 (2021)
10. Chino, D.Y., Costa, A.F., Traina, A.J., Faloutsos, C.: Voltime: unsupervised anomaly detection on users' online activity volume. In: Proceedings of the 2017 SIAM International Conference on Data Mining, pp. 108–116. SIAM (2017)
11. Das, A.S., Ajay, A., Saha, S., Bhuyan, M.: Few-shot anomaly detection in text with deviation learning. In: International Conference on Neural Information Processing, pp. 425–438. Springer, Cham (2023)
12. Devlin, J., Chang, M.W., Lee, K., Toutanova, K.: BERT: pre-training of deep bidirectional transformers for language understanding. In: Proceedings of the 2019 Conference of the North American Chapter of the Association for Computational Linguistics: Human Language Technologies (Volume 1: Long and Short Papers), pp. 4171–4186 (2019)
13. Ding, K., Li, J., Bhanushali, R., Liu, H.: Deep anomaly detection on attributed networks. In: Proceedings of the 2019 SIAM International Conference on Data Mining, pp. 594–602. SIAM (2019)
14. Fortuna, P., Nunes, S.: A survey on automatic detection of hate speech in text. ACM Comput. Surv. (CSUR) **51**(4), 1–30 (2018)
15. Goodge, A., Hooi, B., Ng, S.K., Ng, W.S.: Lunar: unifying local outlier detection methods via graph neural networks. In: Proceedings of the AAAI Conference on Artificial Intelligence, vol. 36, pp. 6737–6745 (2022)
16. Kingma, D.P., Welling, M.: Auto-encoding variational bayes. arXiv preprint arXiv:1312.6114 (2013)
17. Li, J., et al.: Clip-powered domain generalization and domain adaptation: a comprehensive survey. IEEE Trans. Pattern Anal. Mach. Intell. (2026)
18. Li, S., Liu, Y., Chen, Q., Webb, G.I., Pan, S.: Noise-resilient unsupervised graph representation learning via multi-hop feature quality estimation. In: Proceedings of the 33rd ACM International Conference on Information and Knowledge Management, pp. 1255–1265 (2024)
19. Li, S., Liu, Y., Zheng, Y., Cao, X., Pan, S., Shen, H.T.: Towards one-for-all anomaly detection for tabular data. In: International Conference on Machine Learning (2026)
20. Li, S., Liu, Y., Zheng, Y., Li, M., Nguyen, Q.V.H., Pan, S.: OFA-MAS: one-for-all multi-agent system topology design based on mixture-of-experts graph generative models. In: Proceedings of the ACM Web Conference (2026)
21. Li, Y., et al.: Treexformer: extracting tabular feature-context information using tree-structured semantics. Inf. Process. Manag. **62**(6), 104291 (2025)
22. Li, Y., et al.: NLP-adbench: NLP anomaly detection benchmark. arXiv preprint arXiv:2412.04784 (2024)
23. Li, Z., Zhao, Y., Botta, N., Ionescu, C., Hu, X.: Copod: copula-based outlier detection. In: 2020 IEEE International Conference on Data Mining (ICDM), pp. 1118–1123. IEEE (2020)
24. Li, Z., Zhao, Y., Hu, X., Botta, N., Ionescu, C., Chen, G.H.: ECOD: unsupervised outlier detection using empirical cumulative distribution functions. IEEE Trans. Knowl. Data Eng. **35**(12), 12181–12193 (2022)

25. Liu, A.Y., Lam, D.N.: Using consensus clustering for multi-view anomaly detection. In: 2012 IEEE Symposium on Security and Privacy Workshops, pp. 117–124. IEEE (2012)
26. Liu, F.T., Ting, K.M., Zhou, Z.H.: Isolation forest. In: ICDM, pp. 413–422 (2008)
27. Liu, Y., et al.: Generative adversarial active learning for unsupervised outlier detection. IEEE Trans. Knowl. Data Eng. **32**(8), 1517–1528 (2019)
28. Liu, Y., Li, S., Zheng, Y., Chen, Q., Zhang, C., Pan, S.: Arc: a generalist graph anomaly detector with in-context learning. Adv. Neural. Inf. Process. Syst. **37**, 50772–50804 (2024)
29. Liu, Y., et al.: From few-shot to zero-shot: Towards generalist graph anomaly detection. IEEE Trans. Knowl. Data Eng. (2026)
30. Liu, Y., Liu, Y., Zheng, Y., Liew, A.W.C., Cao, X., Pan, S.: Rethinking feature alignment in generalist graph anomaly detection: a relational fingerprint-based approach. In: International Conference on Machine Learning (2026)
31. Maćkiewicz, A., Ratajczak, W.: Principal components analysis (PCA). Comput. Geosci. **19**(3), 303–342 (1993)
32. Manevitz, L., Yousef, M.: One-class document classification via neural networks. Neurocomputing **70**(7–9), 1466–1481 (2007)
33. Manolache, A., Brad, F., Burceanu, E.: Date: detecting anomalies in text via self-supervision of transformers. In: Proceedings of the 2021 Conference of the North American Chapter of the Association for Computational Linguistics: Human Language Technologies, pp. 267–277 (2021)
34. Marcos Alvarez, A., Yamada, M., Kimura, A., Iwata, T.: Clustering-based anomaly detection in multi-view data. In: Proceedings of the 22nd ACM international conference on Information & Knowledge Management, pp. 1545–1548 (2013)
35. Miao, R., et al.: Blindguard: safeguarding LLM-based multi-agent systems under unknown attacks. In: Proceedings of the 64th Annual Meeting of the Association for Computational Linguistics (2026)
36. Mikolov, T., Chen, K., Corrado, G., Dean, J.: Efficient estimation of word representations in vector space. arXiv preprint arXiv:1301.3781 (2013)
37. Neelakantan, A., et al.: Text and code embeddings by contrastive pre-training. arXiv preprint arXiv:2201.10005 (2022)
38. OpenAI: New embedding models and API updates (2024). https://openai.com/index/new-embedding-models-and-api-updates/
39. Pan, J., et al.: Explainable and fine-grained safeguarding of LLM multi-agent systems via bi-level graph anomaly detection. In: Proceedings of the 64th Annual Meeting of the Association for Computational Linguistics (2026)
40. Pan, J., Liu, Y., Zheng, Y., Chi, L., Liew, A.W.C., Pan, S.: Camera: adapting to semantic camouflage in unsupervised text-attributed graph fraud detection. In: International Joint Conference on Artificial Intelligence (2026)
41. Pan, J., Liu, Y., Zhou, C., Xiong, F., Liew, A.W.C., Pan, S.: Correcting false alarms from unseen: adapting graph anomaly detectors at test time. In: Proceedings of the AAAI Conference on Artificial Intelligence (2026)
42. Pan, J., Zheng, Y., Tan, Y., Liu, Y.: A survey of generalization of graph anomaly detection: from transfer learning to foundation models. In: The 16th IEEE International Conference on Knowledge Graphs (2025)
43. Pang, G., Shen, C., Cao, L., Hengel, A.V.D.: Deep learning for anomaly detection: a review. ACM Comput. Surv. (CSUR) **54**(2), 1–38 (2021)
44. Qian, Y., Tan, Y., Liu, Y., Yu, W., Pan, S.: Dynhd: hallucination detection for diffusion large language models via denoising dynamics deviation learning. arXiv preprint arXiv:2603.16459 (2026)

45. Ramaswamy, S., Rastogi, R., Shim, K.: Efficient algorithms for mining outliers from large data sets. In: Proceedings of the 2000 ACM SIGMOD International Conference on Management of Data, pp. 427–438 (2000)
46. Ruff, L., et al.: Deep one-class classification. In: International Conference on Machine Learning, pp. 4393–4402. PMLR (2018)
47. Ruff, L., Zemlyanskiy, Y., Vandermeulen, R., Schnake, T., Kloft, M.: Self-attentive, multi-context one-class classification for unsupervised anomaly detection on text. In: Proceedings of the 57th Annual Meeting of the Association for Computational Linguistics, pp. 4061–4071 (2019)
48. Salton, G., Buckley, C.: Term-weighting approaches in automatic text retrieval. Inf. Process. Manag. **24**(5), 513–523 (1988)
49. Song, L., et al.: FSC-MAE: feature structure coordinated mask autoencoder. Neurocomputing 133957 (2026)
50. Sun, R., Zuo, E., Lv, X., Yan, Z., Chen, C., Chen, C.: Towards superior graph representation: a multi-level cross-view approach integrating information bottleneck and contrastive learning. Appl. Soft Comput. 115148 (2026)
51. Tan, Y., Chen, C., Zhuang, W., Dong, X., Lyu, L., Long, G.: Taming heterogeneity to deal with test-time shift in federated learning. In: International Workshop on Federated Learning for Distributed Data Mining (2023)
52. Tan, Y., Hu, X., Xue, H., De Melo, C., Salim, F.: Bisecle: binding and separation in continual learning for video language understanding. Adv. Neural. Inf. Process. Syst. **38**, 33752–33782 (2025)
53. Tan, Y., Long, G., Jiang, J., Zhang, C.: Influence-oriented personalized federated learning. arXiv preprint arXiv:2410.03315 (2024)
54. Wang, W., et al.: Efficient time series adaptive representation learning via dynamic routing sparse attention. Pattern Recogn. **158**, 111058 (2025)
55. Wang, Y., Xu, Q., Jiang, Y., Dai, S., Huang, Q.: Regularized contrastive partial multi-view outlier detection. In: Proceedings of the 32nd ACM International Conference on Multimedia, pp. 8711–8720 (2024)
56. Yan, J., et al.: Address anomalies at critical crossroads for graph anomaly detection. IEEE Trans. Knowl. Data Eng. (2025)
57. Zamanzadeh Darban, Z., Webb, G.I., Pan, S., Aggarwal, C., Salehi, M.: Deep learning for time series anomaly detection: a survey. ACM Comput. Surv. **57**(1), 1–42 (2024)
58. Zhang, G., Zuo, E., Yan, Z., Chen, C., Chen, C., Lv, X.: Rethinking link prediction: a multi-scale graph masked autoencoder. Neurocomputing 132115 (2025)
59. Zhang, Y., et al.: Qwen3 embedding: advancing text embedding and reranking through foundation models. arXiv preprint arXiv:2506.05176 (2025)
60. Zhao, Y., Liu, Y., Chen, Q., Li, S., Tan, Y., Pan, S.: Fedcigar: a personalized reconstruction approach for federated graph-level anomaly detection. In: International Joint Conference on Artificial Intelligence (2026)
61. Zhao, Y., Liu, Y., Li, S., Chen, Q., Zheng, Y., Pan, S.: Freegad: a training-free yet effective approach for graph anomaly detection. In: Proceedings of the 34th ACM International Conference on Information and Knowledge Management, pp. 4379–4389 (2025)
62. Zheng, Y., Jin, M., Liu, Y., Chi, L., Phan, K.T., Chen, Y.P.P.: From unsupervised to few-shot graph anomaly detection: a multi-scale contrastive learning approach. arXiv preprint arXiv:2202.05525 (2022)
63. Zhou, C., Paffenroth, R.C.: Anomaly detection with robust deep autoencoders. In: Proceedings of the 23rd ACM SIGKDD International Conference on Knowledge Discovery and Data Mining, pp. 665–674 (2017)

64. Zuo, E., et al.: Sucola: self-adaptive structure refinement unsupervised contrastive learning framework for food safety risk early warning. Eng. Appl. Artif. Intell. **126**, 107016 (2023)
65. Zuo, E., Zhong, J., Chen, C., Chen, C., Ubul, K., Lv, X.: Rethinking unsupervised time series anomaly detection: dynamic attention based on route inverse-masking. Appl. Soft Comput. 113971 (2025)

Enhancing Out-of-Distribution Detection Using Synthesized OoD Samples from In-Distribution Training Data

Vangjush Komini[1,2](✉)

[1] KTH Royal Institute of Technology, Stockholm, Sweden
vangjush@kth.se
[2] Qamcom Research and Technology AB, Gothenburg, Sweden

Abstract. In the field of out-of-distribution (OoD) detection, conventional methods often adapt in-distribution (InD) detection frameworks by identifying deviations from InD patterns as OoD. These approaches are typically difficult to validate and depend on a predefined threshold to separate InD from OoD, which can be difficult to optimize across various operational settings. In addition, they attempt to define rigid InD boundaries using complex density estimation models. Motivated by the geometric structure of the logit space where InD embeddings form orthogonal class clusters while OoD embeddings concentrate near the center, we propose a threshold-free OoD detection method that explicitly exploits this structure to distinguish InD from OoD. Our method utilizes this spatial characteristic to generate synthetic OoD embeddings using only InD data. This approach enables the creation of a binary classifier trained on a mixed dataset of both these synthetic OoD embeddings and the original InD embeddings. Consequently, this improves the effectiveness and reliability of OoD detection, achieving an average improvement of up to 7% compared to existing baselines.

Keywords: Out-of-distribution detection · Auxiliary OoD · Robust Classifiers

1 Introduction

Modern deep learning (DL) classifier models generalize well when test inputs share the same distribution of discriminative features as the training data. However, performance degrades sharply on out-of-distribution (OoD) inputs—cases where the class discriminative features differ from those seen during training—which occur frequently in real-world settings.

Moreover, InD training data consist of a closed set of classes (i.e., a given number of classes from annotation and data aggregation), whereas OoD data represents an open and unavailable set of classes. For instance, in an autonomous driving scenario, the perception model may be trained only on a fixed set of known

M. Ceci et al. (Eds.): ECML PKDD 2026, LNAI 16941, pp. 22–38, 2027.
https://doi.org/10.1007/978-3-032-37654-1_2

objects such as cars, pedestrians, bicycles, and traffic lights (InD classes). Nevertheless, during real-world deployment, the vehicle might encounter an entirely new unbounded set of objects—such as construction robots, fallen trees, or animals, and so forth, on the road—that were never included in the training data, representing OoD inputs. This discrepancy prevents the design and training of DL models specifically to distinguish OoD from InD data.

Current approaches focus on accurately identifying InD data and categorizing all other data as OoD by assuming a clear separation between InD and OoD embeddings (see Fig. 2a). These models typically employ scoring methods that assign high likelihoods to areas densely populated with InD logits and default low likelihoods elsewhere, aiming to detect OoD data when the likelihood score falls below a predefined threshold.

Validating these scoring methods and determining the appropriate threshold necessitates the use of OoD data. However, because the OoD space is inherently open-set, constructing a representative OoD benchmark for various architectures and training distributions is nontrivial. Consequently, an inadequate OoD dataset may result in suboptimal scoring methods and thresholds, potentially diminishing the effectiveness of OoD detection.

To address these challenges, we propose generating auxiliary OoD embeddings directly from InD data and using them to design, train, and validate a binary classifier that separates InD from OoD. This yields a more accurate and validated parameterization of the decision boundary between the two.

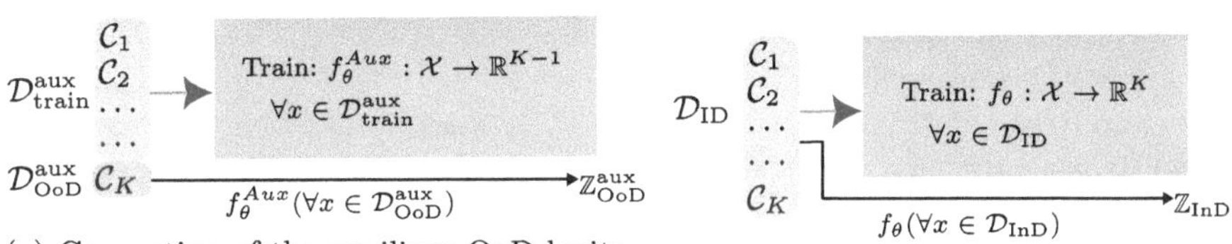

(a) Generation of the auxiliary OoD logits ($\mathbb{Z}^{aux}_{OoD}$).

(b) Generation of the InD logits ($\mathbb{Z}_{InD}$).

Fig. 1. Generation of auxiliary OoD embeddings: The auxiliary model $f_\theta^{aux} : \mathcal{X} \to \mathbb{R}^{K-1}$ (a) is trained on the reduced dataset $\mathcal{D}^{aux}_{train} = \bigcup_{k=1}^{K-1} \mathcal{C}_k$, explicitly excluding class $\mathcal{C}_K$. To approximate the OoD embeddings logits $\mathbb{Z}^{aux}_{OoD}$, samples from the held-out class $\mathcal{C}_K$ are passed through f_θ^{aux}. The main model $f_\theta : \mathcal{X} \to \mathbb{R}^K$ (b) is then trained on the full InD dataset $\mathcal{D}_{InD} = \bigcup_{k=1}^{K} \mathcal{C}_k$ to produce InD embeddings logits $\mathbb{Z}_{InD}$.

To generate OoD embeddings using only InD data, we leverage a key geometric property of neural network representations in the logit space [1]. Specifically, embeddings corresponding to InD samples tend to align along distinct, approximately orthogonal axes, forming well-separated class-wise clusters that push toward high positive activation values for their respective class dimensions (see Fig. 2a). In contrast, OoD embeddings, which lack strong affinity to any learned class, collapse toward the center of the logit space, exhibiting low-magnitude and less directional activation patterns (see Fig. 2a). During training, the classifier

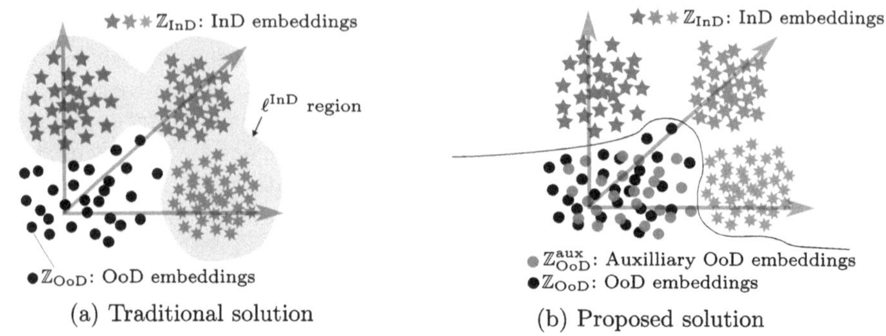

Fig. 2. OoD detection. Traditional methods assign an InD likelihood score ℓ^{InD} to embeddings (a) and apply a threshold to separate InD from OoD. In contrast, we generate auxiliary OoD logit embeddings that approximate the true OoD regions and learn an explicit boundary between InD and OoD via a parametric function $g_\eta : \mathbb{R}^K \rightarrow \mathbb{R}^2$ (b).

learns to generalize the optimal class-specific discriminative features from InD samples to maximize the logit corresponding to their ground-truth class, implicitly driving them away from the origin and reducing cross-class interference. In contrast, OoD inputs do not exhibit any of the learned class-specific features, causing the classifier to default to low-confidence predictions that lie near the center of the logit embedding space [1].

To leverage this geometric separation between InD and OoD embeddings, we employ a leave-one-class-out training paradigm. In this setup, we remove a single class from the training set and train the classifier solely on the remaining classes. Because the model is never exposed to the held-out class during training, inputs from this class do not activate any of the learned discriminative features associated with the InD classes. As a result, their embeddings naturally map toward the central region of the logit space, closely mimicking the behavior of true OoD samples. This held-out class, therefore, functions as a principled proxy for OoD data, allowing us to generate realistic OoD-like embeddings without requiring access to any external OoD dataset (see Fig. 2b).

We then reinitialize the model and retrain it on the full training set to produce InD embeddings. Moreover, we show that the auxiliary OoD embeddings are highly consistent regardless of which class is left out.

By synthesizing auxiliary OoD embeddings from InD data, we train a simple binary discriminator that explicitly separates InD from OoD representations (see Fig. 2b). This reframes the task from modeling the complex InD embedding manifold to estimating a direct decision boundary between InD and OoD. In addition, the generated OoD surrogates enable stronger validation, yielding more reliable OoD detection at deployment compared to prior methods. We demonstrate improved performance across multiple benchmarks and dataset types. Our method also maintains consistent performance across diverse model architectures.

Our work makes the following contributions:

1. We introduce a simple, threshold-free OoD detection framework that synthesizes surrogate OoD embeddings directly from InD data, and provide both theoretical analysis and empirical validation of its effectiveness.
2. We show empirically that a binary decision boundary trained to separate InD from these auxiliary OoD embeddings *generalizes* to real-world OoD embeddings, preserving discriminative power without requiring labeled OoD data.

2 Background

In practice, it is not feasible to parameterize the distribution of class-specific discriminative features of InD data (i.e., $\mathcal{X} \times \mathcal{Y}$) as they reside onto an unknown manifold; instead, we have an empirical representation through annotated training data $\mathcal{D}_{\text{InD}} = \{(x_i, y_i)\}_{i=1}^{N}$. Under the manifold assumption, we assume that InD data form class-specific regions $\mathcal{D}_{\text{InD}} = \cup_{k=1}^{K} \mathcal{C}_k$ in the feature space $\mathcal{X}$ (where K is the total number of classes), structured according to discriminative features unique to each class [2–5]. Although the precise structure of this feature space $\mathcal{X}$ is not fully known, the annotated training set $\mathcal{D}_{\text{InD}}$ serves as a substitute to learn its topology.

In practice, we train a parametric DL model $f_\theta : \mathcal{X} \to \mathbb{R}^K$ to classify InD data accurately in the logit space embedding $\mathbb{R}^K$. This DL model serves as a proxy for the feature space $\mathcal{X}$ to approximate the true feature map $\phi : \mathcal{X} \to \mathbb{R}^K$. Upon initialization, this DL model f_θ tends to project all data (both InD and OoD) toward the center of the logit space [1]. However, after training in $\mathcal{D}_{\text{InD}}$, these models learn to map InD data in distinct, nearly orthogonal class-wise groups $\mathbb{Z}_{\text{InD}} = \{\mathbb{Z}_k\}_{k=1}^{K}$ in the logit embedding space [1,6]. To do so, f_θ is optimized to identify and parameterize the optimal (as the model capacity allows) distribution of class-specific discriminative features of the InD data:

$$\theta^* \triangleq \arg\min_{\theta} \mathbb{E}_{(x,y)\sim\mathcal{D}_{\text{InD}}} \left[-\log p_\theta(y|x)\right]. \tag{1}$$

It does this by maximizing the dot product of the model's parameters θ with optimally selected class-specific discriminative features, enhancing its ability to recognize similar patterns within each class [7].

Thus, InD data ($x \in \mathcal{D}_{\text{InD}}$), characterized by class-specific features, interact coherently with the model's parameters through successive convolution layers. This compounding interaction leads to high positive values in the corresponding logit cell for the relevant class, while producing very low values in the other cells. Eventually, providing a linear separation between each class in the logit space embeddings.

Conversely, OoD data, which do not possess these class-specific features, result in all logit cells displaying very low output values [1]. This observation is crucial as it highlights the capability of DL models to create a separation between InD and OoD embeddings.

3 Method

3.1 Generation of Auxiliary OoD Logits

The region of OoD logit embeddings (i.e., $\mathbb{Z}_{\mathrm{OoD}}$) typically lies near the center of the logit space [1], but parameterizing this region accurately requires access to OoD data, which is inherently unavailable during training. To address this, we propose generating auxiliary OoD logits (i.e., $\mathbb{Z}_{\mathrm{OoD}}^{aux}$) using InD data.

Our approach leverages an auxiliary discriminative model $f_\theta^{\mathrm{Aux}} : \mathcal{X} \rightarrow \mathbb{R}^{K-1}$, trained on a subset of InD classes $\mathcal{D}_{\mathrm{train}}^{\mathrm{aux}} = \cup_{k=1}^{K-1} \mathcal{C}_k$, while deliberately excluding one class (i.e., $\mathcal{C}_K$) (see Fig. 1a). By design, the auxiliary model (i.e., f_θ^{Aux}) learns only the discriminative features of the included classes, rendering the excluded class's samples $\mathcal{D}_{\mathrm{OoD}}^{\mathrm{aux}} = \mathcal{D}_{\mathrm{InD}} \setminus \mathcal{D}_{\mathrm{train}}^{\mathrm{aux}}$ effectively OoD with respect to f_θ^{Aux}.

The choice to exclude a single class, rather than multiple classes, ensures that the excluded samples act as near-OoD data, retaining non-discriminative features but lacking class-specific discriminative attributes. This minimizes the risk of overlap with InD logit embeddings and reduces potential discrepancies in logit displacement between models trained on subsets versus the full dataset. Considering that the auxiliary model (i.e. f_θ^{Aux}) is trained in almost the same classes as the main classifier (i.e. f_θ), with the exception of just one class, it provides a reliable approximation of the model trained in the entire classes. Furthermore, under the class-conditional independence assumption (i.e., $\mathcal{C}_i \perp\!\!\!\perp \mathcal{C}_j, \forall i \neq j$ see Assumption 1), we can derive an upper bound on the approximation error (see Lemma 1).

Assumption 1. Given the training objective is to parameterize the optimal representation of class-specific features from the training data (i.e., $\mathcal{D}_{\mathrm{InD}} = \cup_{k=1}^{K} \mathcal{C}_k$), their per class discrimination is possible if their class-specific features are mutually independent (i.e., $\mathcal{C}_i \perp\!\!\!\perp \mathcal{C}_j, \forall i \neq j$).

Lemma 1 (Auxiliary-model bound via score variance). *Let $f_\theta : \mathcal{X} \rightarrow \mathbb{R}^K$ be the main classifier and f_θ^{Aux} an auxiliary approximation to f_θ. For every single class k, define the class-wise score-variance*

$$\sigma(C_k) \triangleq \mathrm{Var}\big(\nabla_\theta \log p_\theta(y = k \mid x)\big).$$

Assume that for samples $(x, y = k)$ and small parameter perturbations $\delta\theta$,

$$\big\|f_{\theta+\delta\theta}(x) - f_\theta(x)\big\|_2 \leq C\,\sigma(C_k),$$

for some constant $C > 0$. Then the point-wise approximation error satisfies

$$\big\|f_\theta^{\mathrm{Aux}}(x) - f_\theta(x)\big\|_2 \leq \mathcal{O}(\sigma(C_k)).$$

Proof. To analyze feature perturbations Δf, we examine the Kullback-Leibler divergence between the model distributions before and after parameter perturbation $\delta\theta$:

$$\mathrm{KL}(p_\theta \parallel p_{\theta+\delta\theta}) = \mathbb{E}_{x \sim \mathcal{D}_{\mathrm{InD}}/\mathcal{C}_k}\left[\log \frac{p_\theta(y|x)}{p_{\theta+\delta\theta}(y|x)}\right]$$

A Taylor expansion around $\delta\theta = 0$:

- The gradient of KL divergence at $\delta\theta = 0$ equals zero:

$$\nabla_{\delta\theta}\mathrm{KL}(p_\theta \parallel p_{\theta+\delta\theta})\big|_{\delta\theta=0} = -\mathbb{E}\left[\nabla_\theta \log p_\theta(y|x)\right] = 0$$

- The Hessian gives the FIM:

$$\begin{aligned}\nabla^2_{\delta\theta}\mathrm{KL}(p_\theta \parallel p_{\theta+\delta\theta})\big|_{\delta\theta=0} &= -\mathbb{E}_{x\sim\mathcal{D}_{\mathrm{InD}}/\mathcal{C}_k}\left[\nabla^2_\theta \log p_\theta(y|x)\right] \\ &= \mathbb{E}_{x\sim\mathcal{D}_{\mathrm{InD}}/\mathcal{C}_k}\left[(\nabla_\theta \log p_\theta(y|x))(\nabla_\theta \log p_\theta(y|x))^\top\right] \\ &= \mathcal{I}_{\mathcal{D}_{\mathrm{InD}}/\mathcal{C}_k}(\theta)\end{aligned}$$

This yields the second-order approximation:

$$\mathrm{KL}(p_\theta \parallel p_{\theta+\delta\theta}) \approx \frac{1}{2}\delta\theta^\top \mathcal{I}_{\mathcal{D}_{\mathrm{InD}}/\mathcal{C}_k}(\theta)\delta\theta + \mathcal{O}(\|\delta\theta\|^3)$$

This approximation reveals that:

- the FIM $I(\theta)$ acts as a Riemannian metric on the parameter space, defining the "distance" between p_θ and $p_{\theta+\delta\theta}$.

$$\mathrm{KL}(p_\theta \parallel p_{\theta+\delta\theta}) \propto \delta\theta^\top \mathcal{I}_{\mathcal{D}_{\mathrm{InD}}/\mathcal{C}_k}(\theta)\delta\theta.$$

- for small $\delta\theta$, the change in features $f_\theta(x)$ is thus:

$$\|f_{\theta+\delta\theta}(x) - f_\theta(x)\| \propto \delta\theta^\top \mathcal{I}_{\mathcal{D}_{\mathrm{InD}}/\mathcal{C}_k}(\theta)\delta\theta.$$

The exclusion of a single class induces a smaller perturbation to the FIM (i.e., $\|\mathcal{I}_{\mathcal{D}_{\mathrm{InD}}}(\theta) - \mathcal{I}_{\mathcal{D}_{\mathrm{InD}}/\mathcal{C}_k}(\theta)\|_2 = \sigma(C_k)$ see Lemma 2), compared to excluding multiple classes. This reduced perturbation leads to better preservation of the Riemannian metric structure (i.e., $\delta\theta^\top I(\theta)\delta\theta$). Consequently, the resulting feature displacement under parameter updates $\delta\theta$ remains tightly bounded:

$$\|f_{\theta+\delta\theta}(x) - f_\theta(x)\|_2 \leq \mathcal{O}(\sigma(C_k))$$

In the case of multiple class exclusions that bound increases to $\sum_{i=k}^{K}\mathcal{O}(\sigma(C_i))$

Lemma 2. *[Fisher Stability of Single-Class Exclusion] Let $L(\theta)$ be the cross-entropy loss, and $I(\theta)$ the Fisher Information Matrix (FIM) of the full dataset $\mathcal{D}_{InD} = \cup_{k=1}^{K}\mathcal{C}_k$. When excluding a single class C_k, the perturbation to the FIM is bounded by:*

$$\|\mathcal{I}_{\mathcal{D}_{InD}}(\theta) - \mathcal{I}_{\mathcal{D}_{InD}/\mathcal{C}_k}(\theta)\|_2 = \sigma(C_k)$$

where $\sigma(C_k)$ is the variance of the score functions (gradients of log-likelihood) for data $x \sim \mathcal{C}_k$.

Proof. For a parametric model $p_\theta(y \mid x)$ with parameters θ, the Fisher Information Matrix (FIM)

$$\mathcal{I}(\theta) = \mathbb{E}_{x,y\sim\mathcal{D}_{\mathrm{InD}}}\left[\nabla_\theta \log p_\theta(y \mid x) \nabla_\theta \log p_\theta(y \mid x)^\top\right],$$

quantifies how sensitive the likelihood is to parameter changes by estimating the covariance matrix of the score function (gradient of log-likelihood):

Notice that for two independent datasets X and Y the FIM is additive:

$$\mathcal{I}_{X\cup Y}(\theta) \;=\; \mathcal{I}_X(\theta) \;+\; \mathcal{I}_Y(\theta). \tag{2}$$

Under the assumption of class-conditional independence (i.e., $\mathcal{C}_i \perp\!\!\!\perp \mathcal{C}_j, \forall i \neq j$), we can use the additive property of FIM (see Eq. (2)), and then we can decompose the FIM as follows:

$$\mathcal{I}_{\mathcal{D}_{\mathrm{InD}}}(\theta) = \mathcal{I}_{\mathcal{D}_{\mathrm{InD}}/\mathcal{C}_k}(\theta) + \mathcal{I}_{\mathcal{C}_k}(\theta).$$

Under cross-entropy loss, this simplifies to the gradient covariance matrix.

When excluding class C_k, the FIM becomes:

$$\begin{aligned}
\mathcal{I}_{\mathcal{C}_k}(\theta) &= \mathbb{E}_{x\sim\mathcal{C}_k}\left[\nabla_\theta \log p_\theta(y = k \mid x)\nabla_\theta \log p_\theta(y = k \mid x)^\top\right] \\
&= \mathbb{E}_{x\sim\mathcal{C}_k}\left[\|\nabla_\theta \log p_\theta(y = k \mid x)\|_2^2\right] \\
&\triangleq \mathrm{Var}\left(\nabla_\theta \log p_\theta(y = k \mid x)\right) \\
&= \sigma(C_k),
\end{aligned}$$

where $\sigma(C_k)$ is the variance of the score functions (gradients of log-likelihood) of the data drawn from $x \sim \mathcal{C}_k$.

The step $\triangleq$ follows from $\mathbb{E}\left[\nabla_\theta \log p_\theta(y|x)\right] = 0$.

The spectral norm of the perturbation is bounded by:

$$\|\Delta\mathcal{I}\|_2 = \|\mathcal{I}_{\mathcal{D}_{\mathrm{InD}}}(\theta) - \mathcal{I}_{\mathcal{D}_{\mathrm{InD}}/\mathcal{C}_k}(\theta)\|_2 = \|\mathcal{I}_{\mathcal{C}_k}(\theta)\|_2 - \sigma(C_k).$$

Notice that for multiple classes $\{k, \cdots, K\}$ exclusion the bound increases to

$$\|\Delta I\|_2 = \sum_{i=k}^{K} \sigma(C_i)$$

Implication (Single–Class Exclusion is Optimal). By Lemma 1, excluding a single class k and using its excluded-class proxy as auxiliary OoD embeddings yields an approximation error of order $\mathcal{O}(\sigma(C_k))$. If instead we exclude a set S of $N > 1$ classes, a straightforward perturbation argument gives a bound of order

$$\mathcal{O}\left(\sum_{j\in S} \sigma(C_j)\right),$$

which is necessarily larger—and therefore looser—than the best single-class bound. In particular, given $\sigma(C_j) \geq 0, \forall j \in \{1, \ldots, K\}$, we have

$$\mathcal{O}(\sigma(C_k)) \leq \mathcal{O}\left(\sum_{j \in S} \sigma(C_j)\right) \quad \text{for any } S \subseteq \{1, \ldots, k, \ldots, K\},\ |S| = N > 1.$$

Hence, the tightest provable approximation is obtained with $N = 1$. A detailed perturbation empirical analysis of class exclusions appears in Appendix B.

The resulting OoD logits:

$$\mathbb{Z}_{\text{OoD}}^{\text{aux}} = \{f_\theta^{\text{aux}}(x) \mid x \in \mathcal{C}_K\},$$

provide a principled approximation of the OoD region in the reduced $\mathbb{R}^{K-1}$ logit space embedding.

Furthermore, due to class balance and the saturation of loss across all in-distribution (InD) classes in both the primary and auxiliary models, the resulting logits are evenly displaced from the center of the feature space [6] (see Fig. 3 and Appendix E for an extended empirical analysis). Consequently, the OoD logits are also expected to exhibit a uniform displacement across classes, which we validate empirically in Fig. 3 and Appendix E where the same behavior extends to auxiliary OoD data. We therefore approximate the missing dimension by sampling with replacement from the available logit embeddings (see Algorithm 2 in Appendix).

To obtain InD logits, we train a model $f_\theta : \mathcal{X} \rightarrow \mathbb{R}^K$ with the same architecture as the auxiliary model, using the full training dataset $\mathcal{D}_{\text{InD}} = \cup_{k=1}^{K} \mathcal{C}_k$ (see Fig. 1b). The trained model's outputs on $\mathcal{D}_{\text{train}}$ then serve as the InD logit embeddings:

$$\mathbb{Z}_{\text{InD}} = \{f_\theta(x) \mid x \in \mathcal{D}_{\text{InD}}\}.$$

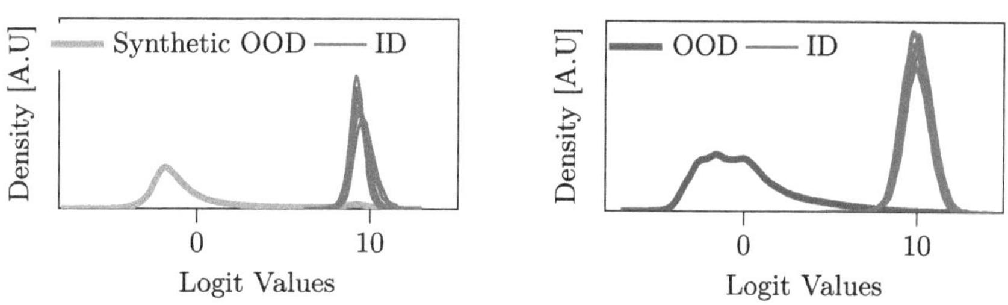

(a) Logit densities from f_θ^{Aux}. (b) Logit densities from f_θ.

Fig. 3. Logit density plots produced by the auxiliary classifier f_θ^{Aux} (trained on $K-1$ CIFAR-10 classes) and the full classifier f_θ (trained on all K classes). (a) presents InD logit distributions for CIFAR-10 classes 1–9 and synthetic OoD data (class 10), while (b) displays distributions for all 10 classes as InD and SVHN as OoD. All results shown here use ResNet-34 as the backbone.

Unlike previous methods, our approach uniquely exploits the discriminative feature learning of the auxiliary model in a straightforward and controlled manner, enabling reliable validation of InD/OoD separation without external data. This method circumvents the need for explicit OoD samples and ensures that the generated OoD logits align with the model's inherent generalization behavior.

To approximate the OoD distribution, we exclude one class from training and use its samples as auxiliary OoD data. Assuming that the training classes are class balanced are pairwise contextually distinct (class-conditional independence assumption, i.e. $\mathcal{C}_i \perp\!\!\!\perp \mathcal{C}_j \ \ \forall i \neq j$ see Assumption 1), the specific class excluded is inconsequential: any choice yields approximately the same auxiliary OoD logits (see fig. 6 in Appendix B).

Furthermore, because the auxiliary OoD logit embeddings are expected to be (approximately) linearly separable from each class-wise cluster of InD logit embeddings (in $\mathbb{R}^K$), we can validate their quality by quantifying this separation—for example, using density plots as in Fig. 3 and Appendix E.

Effect of the Number of InD Classes. Additionally, the DL classifier is central to separating OoD from InD embeddings. The more effectively the DL model learns to parameterize the class-specific discriminative features in the InD dataset, the better it can partition InD from OoD in embedding space. Under a standard classification objective over K classes, each labeled example contributes gradients that (i) reinforce the correct class logit and (ii) suppress the $K-1$ competing logits, thereby enlarging inter-class margins in the embedding space [8–10]. These gradients solely drive the updates to the parameters that encode the optimal class-specific features present in the training set. Consequently, we increase the amount of gradients in two complementary ways: (1) *more labeled examples per class* reduce variance in the gradient estimates and yield more representative class features; and (2) *a larger number of classes* increases the number of negative contrasts per update, suppressing non-class specific features that exist among a broader set of alternatives. We distinguish these effects: more data per class improves how precisely each class is learned, whereas increasing the number of classes refines the class-specific discriminative features by forcing the model to disentangle finer distinctions among classes (see Fig. 4a for more details).

3.2 Training a Binary Classifier on InD and OoD Logits

Traditional DL models (i.e. $f_\theta : \mathcal{X} \to \mathbb{R}^K$) that address InD data classification typically enhance the likelihood values for logit regions associated with the correct class (k) and decrease those for others, achieving:

$$f_\theta(x)_k \gg f_\theta(x)_j \quad \forall j \neq k \tag{3}$$

This *relative* likelihood adjustment enables threshold-free decision-making, as predictions rely solely on the arg max operation:

$$\hat{y} \triangleq \arg \max_{k \in \{1,\ldots,K\}} f_\theta(x)_k \tag{4}$$

We exploit the spatial displacement between the OoD and InD logits to adopt this paradigm for OoD detection. Notably, the class-wise clusters of InD logits exhibit near orthogonality and maintain a consistent displacement from the logit space center, in contrast to OoD logits, which tend to cluster towards this center [1,6]. Based on these spatial characteristics, we train the likelihood estimation model to assign high InD likelihood values to regions with densely concentrated InD logits and high OoD likelihood values to regions predominantly containing OoD logits (see Fig. 2b).

Given that both InD and OoD logits (i.e., $\mathbb{Z} = [\mathbb{Z}_{\text{InD}} \cup \mathbb{Z}^{aux}_{\text{OoD}}], \mathfrak{O} = [0, \ldots, 0, 1, \ldots, 1]$) reside in a known vector space that we can parameterize via its spanning orthogonal axis, it allows us directly parameterize the separation boundary for OoD and InD ($g_\eta : \mathbb{R}^K \to \mathbb{R}^2$ see Fig. 2b) such as:

$$\eta^* \triangleq \arg\min_{\eta} \mathbb{E}_{\mathfrak{o} \sim \mathfrak{O}, z \sim \mathbb{Z}} \left[-\log p_\eta(\mathfrak{o}|z) \right] \quad \text{s.t: InD } (\mathfrak{o} = 0) \text{ or OoD } (\mathfrak{o} = 1).$$

Moreover, because the auxiliary OoD embeddings $\mathbb{Z}^{\text{aux}}_{\text{OoD}}$ and the InD embeddings $\mathbb{Z}_{\text{InD}}$ are expected to be well separated, we can directly validate both the quality of the generated auxiliary OoD embeddings and the training of the binary classifier $g_\eta : \mathbb{R}^K \to \mathbb{R}^2$.

This *relative* likelihood adjustment enables threshold-free decision-making, as predictions rely solely on the arg max operation just as in the classification of $\mathcal{D}_{\text{InD}}$ as:

$$\hat{\mathfrak{o}} \triangleq \arg \max_{j \in \{0,1\}} g_\eta(z)_j \tag{5}$$

4 Related Work

To the best of the authors' knowledge, this study introduces the first binary classification model that directly parameterizes a boundary distinguishing OoD from InD. Although theoretical investigations into OoD behavior exist [11,12], it is important to highlight that current methodologies predominantly concentrate on creating effective scoring functions. These functions are tailored to assign high likelihoods to InD data, enabling dependable differentiation from OoD data.

a) A significant body of research leverages outputs from DL classifiers, such as logits or softmax probabilities, to construct scoring systems. These scoring mechanisms aim to measure the degree of model uncertainty, which serves as an indicator for identifying InD data. The most straightforward approaches might employ the maximum logit [13] or softmax output [14–16] as the score. More sophisticated methods attempt to model the distribution of logits using parametric approaches, such as Gaussian distributions [17,18], or energy-based models [19]. Additionally, some approaches employ ensemble techniques that improve the accuracy of uncertainty estimation by manipulating softmax output from several independent models, providing a more robust framework for distinguishing InD from OoD instances [20–24].

b) Alternatively, other studies exploit the gradients of the DL classifiers with respect to the input data, particularly when differentiating the model's output against a uniform probability array. In scenarios involving well-trained DL classifiers, InD data is expected to induce larger gradient magnitudes than OoD data, a predictable outcome given that InD samples are optimized to yield non-uniform probabilities that maximize the logit cell, indicating the correct class [25]. Conversely, OoD data, not part of the training set, often leads the model to default to a uniform output for such samples. Building on this insight, the authors propose a novel scoring function based on the magnitude of the collective gradient across each model parameter to improve detection sensitivity for InD data.

c) Other approaches attempt to leverage intermediary features to create scoring functions. These features exhibit significant sensitivity to OoD data, with various methods employing techniques such as clipping [26–30], measuring distances [31–33], or calculating norms [32] to detect instances of OoD.

Despite the good performance reported for feature-based and gradient-based methods, these techniques generally demand more extensive tuning and engineering than logit-based methods. This is primarily because intermediary features carry less refined and more redundant InD-specific discriminatory features than logits, which provide optimal class distinction.

It should be noted that the techniques discussed herein are primarily models designed for InD data identification that have been adapted for OoD data detection by implementing a threshold-based model. These methods, however, do not involve a parameterized delineation of the boundary between InD and OoD data. In contrast, our research aims to explicitly parameterize a boundary that distinguishes between InD and OoD logits, enabling validation and testing.

5 Experiments

Experimental Objectives. Our experiments address two questions: (i) how the proposed method compares with established alternatives, and (ii) whether its performance is sustained across different model families.

Comparative Evaluation. To assess the effectiveness of our scoring rule, we conduct a head-to-head comparison against representative OoD detectors that operate on either logits or pre-logit embeddings (see Appendix A for an extended explanation of each baseline method). Among the baselines, MSP [34], Mahalanobis [17], and KNN [33] were implemented by us, while the remaining methods were obtained from public repositories[1]. Importantly, unlike most baselines, our method requires only InD data for training and validation, without any access to external OoD datasets.

[1] https://github.com/kkirchheim/pytorch-ood?tab=readme-ov-file.

Setup. Unless stated otherwise, we train a ResNet-18 [35] on CIFAR-10 [36] as the in-distribution (InD) dataset, and evaluate out-of-distribution (OoD) detection on SVHN [37], iSUN [38], LSUN [39], Textures [40], and Places365 [41] (see Table 1).

Metrics and Fairness. Existing methods typically produce only an InD score, denoted $\ell^{\mathrm{InD}}(z \mid \eta)$, whereas our approach also defines an OoD score $\ell^{\mathrm{OoD}}(z \mid \eta)$. For a fair comparison, we follow common practice and report FPR@TPR95 (false positive rate at 95% true positive rate) and AUROC computed using $\ell^{\mathrm{InD}}(z \mid \eta)$.

Auxiliary Classifier. In addition, we train a lightweight discriminator in InD and auxiliary-OoD embeddings: a two-hidden-layer MLP (i.e., $g_\eta : \mathbb{R}^K \to \mathbb{R}^2$) trained with cross-entropy for binary InD/OoD classification as detailed in Algorithm 1 in Appendix.

Table 1. AUROC and FPR over different methods (**ResNet18** trained on **CIFAR10**).

method	SVHN		LSUN		iSUN		Textures		Places365		AVERAGE	
	FPR↓	AUROC↑	FPR↓	AUROC↑	FPR↓	AUROC↑	FPR↓	AUROC↑	FPR↓	AUROC↑	FPR↓	AUROC↑
MSP [34]	59.66	91.25	45.21	93.80	54.57	92.12	66.45	88.50	62.46	88.64	57.67	90.86
ODIN [15]	20.93	95.55	7.26	98.53	9.84	96.54	56.40	86.21	63.04	86.57	36.16	92.30
Energy [19]	54.41	91.22	10.19	98.05	27.52	95.59	55.23	89.37	42.77	91.02	38.02	93.05
GODIN [16]	15.51	96.01	9.46	97.91	13.20	94.69	40.61	89.68	32.80	93.52	22.80	93.52
Mahala [17]	9.24	97.80	67.73	73.61	62.03	46.98	23.21	91.21	69.56	**97.34**	46.34	86.50
KNN [33]	24.53	95.96	25.29	95.69	25.55	95.26	27.57	94.71	50.90	89.14	30.77	94.15
Ours	**8.19**	**98.79**	**8.11**	**98.90**	**8.20**	**98.99**	**22.24**	**95.13**	**30.73**	96.32	**15.494**	**97.62**

Ablations. We conduct two ablations to assess robustness: (a) across different architectures and (b) across the choice of in-distribution (InD) dataset. For each model (ResNet and DenseNet variants), we train on an InD dataset and fit a lightweight binary classifier $g_\eta : \mathbb{R}^K \to \mathbb{R}^2$ on top of the logits, using InD and auxiliary-OoD logits. This yields both an InD score $\ell^{\mathrm{InD}}(z \mid \eta)$ and an OoD score $\ell^{\mathrm{OoD}}(z \mid \eta)$.

Metrics. Following common practice, we report AUROC computed from $\ell^{\mathrm{InD}}(z \mid \eta)$ (see Table 1). To evaluate cross-architecture consistency, we additionally report InD/OoD classification accuracy (ACC) computed from $\ell^{\mathrm{OoD}}(z \mid \eta)$ (see Table 2).

Protocols. (i) *Architectures:* we train multiple ResNet and DenseNet variants on CIFAR-10 and evaluate both ℓ^{InD} and ℓ^{OoD} via the auxiliary classifier, summarizing ACC across models in Table 2. (ii) *InD dataset swap:* we repeat the procedure with SVHN as the InD dataset, reporting ACC in table 3 in Appendix. Density plots from the auxiliary model and the fully trained model are provided in Fig. 3 and Appendix E.

Table 2. InD and OoD accuracy across classification backbones trained with CIFAR-10 as the InD dataset.

method	SVHN		LSUN		iSUN		Textures		Places365	
	ACC↑	AUROC↑	ACC↑	AUROC↑	ACC↑	AUROC↑	ACC↑	AUROC↑	ACC↑	AUROC↑
ResNet-18	91.31	98.79	91.71	98.90	92.01	98.99	81.01	95.13	82.10	96.32
ResNet-34	91.19	98.11	91.11	98.23	91.71	98.14	82.12	94.21	81.73	95.27
ResNet-50	91.43	98.39	91.76	98.11	91.31	98.79	82.04	94.32	81.12	95.18
ResNet-101	90.63	98.13	91.54	98.01	91.43	98.14	82.01	95.56	81.01	95.67
ResNet-152	90.69	98.68	91.98	98.73	92.98	98.99	82.12	95.42	80.13	95.15
DenseNet-121	91.78	98.32	91.11	98.11	91.82	98.54	81.89	95.13	80.99	95.71
DenseNet-161	91.33	98.21	90.58	97.90	92.17	98.13	81.23	95.87	81.08	96.03
DenseNet-169	91.52	98.04	91.32	98.12	91.93	97.99	82.11	95.21	81.13	95.11
DenseNet-201	91.01	98.13	90.45	98.01	91.20	98.01	82.03	94.09	80.55	95.09

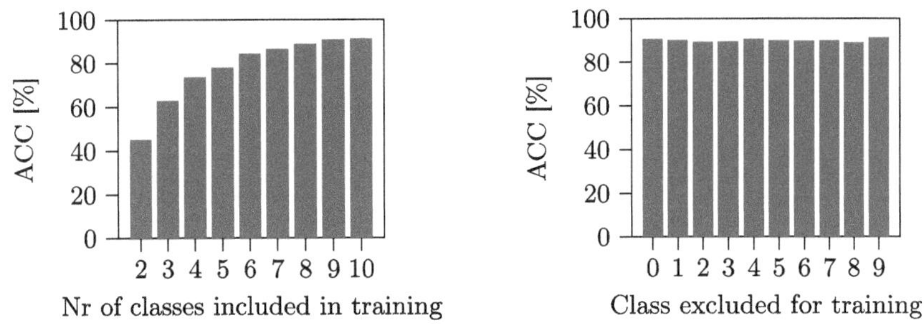

(a) (b)

Fig. 4. (a) shows the OoD detection performance under a leave-one-class-out protocol on CIFAR-10, where each experiment trains the classifier on 9 classes and excludes a different single class. (b) shows the OoD detection performance as the classifier is trained with an increasing number of classes—starting from a binary model, then a ternary model, up to all ten classes. In each setting, evaluation uses the InD embeddings from the corresponding classifier from CIFAR-10, while SVHN is used as OODs.

On the Selection of Class. A natural question is: why not simply collect arbitrary data outside the training domain? While such data will produce OoD embeddings, there is no guarantee that they define a representative decision boundary relative to the InD distribution. In contrast, a *left-out* class from the same labeled dataset is known (by annotation) to be semantically distinct from the training classes, yet it often shares non-class-specific factors (e.g., sensor characteristics, low-level statistics, augmentation pipeline). This combination—different class-specific features with similar nuisance factors—yields *near-OoD* examples that more faithfully probe the InD boundary and thus provide a more representative separation criterion than arbitrary out-of-domain samples. Given that excluding one class only showcases the most effective way to approximate the OOD data, one can wonder how to properly select this class. A perturbation analysis over all choices of the held-out class indicates that the approximation quality is essentially invariant to which class is excluded; the resulting auxiliary-OoD logits show negligible variation between choices (see fig. 6 in Appendix B). Moreover, the classification accuracy remains stable across different scenarios (see Fig. 4b).

Effect of the Number of InD Classes. As the number of classes used to train the classifier increases, not only do the OoD approximations improve, but the classifier's ability to separate OoD from InD embeddings also strengthens. Empirically, fig. 5 in Appendix B shows that adding more InD classes yields logits with larger and more uniform displacement from the logit-space center, producing clearer separation (disentanglement) between InD and OoD logits. Conversely, when the classifier is trained on only a subset of classes, OoD detection performance degrades (see Fig. 4a). Even when InD classification accuracy is held fixed across study cases, OoD separability improves as more training data (classes) are included. This indicates that as the number of classes increases, the learned logit representations become more class-specific, sharpening the InD decision structure and reducing the model's propensity to form spurious correlations with OoD data.

Notice that our approach is that it assumes the classifier operates over a sufficiently large and balanced set of InD classes. When the number of classes is small, the classifier's ability to distinguish between InD and OoD embeddings deteriorates, and the generation of reliable auxiliary OoD samples becomes unstable. Furthermore, our method does not explicitly account for class imbalance. If certain classes are underrepresented, their embeddings tend to lie closer to the feature-space center, resulting in an uneven displacement across classes. This imbalance not only weakens the approximation of OoD embeddings but also hinders the classifier's capacity to effectively disentangle OoD from InD samples along those dimensions.

6 Conclusion

We introduced a threshold-free framework for OoD detection that learns an explicit InD-OoD boundary in logit space embeddings. In contrast to methods that rely on surrogate scores and ad-hoc threshold tuning, our detector exploits the geometry of logit space: InD logits form well-separated, class-specific clusters at approximately equal distances from the origin, while OoD logits tend to concentrate near the center.

We further showed that DL models can approximate OoD behavior by training with a single class held out and reusing its samples as *auxiliary OoD* data. Under the assumption that class-specific discriminative features in the InD data are statistically independent, we showed both analytically and empirically that excluding fewer classes leads to increasingly faithful approximations of the fully trained model.

Building on these insights, we proposed a simple strategy to generate auxiliary OoD embeddings that closely track the true OoD region. The method is *model-agnostic*—performing consistently across architectures and *data-agnostic*, exhibiting the expected trends on diverse datasets—while reducing dependence on heuristic post-processing. This makes it particularly appealing for deployment in realistic settings where OoD distributions cannot be anticipated in advance.

Existing OoD methods have not explicitly targeted enlargement of the InD–OoD separation in representation space. Some encourage separation indirectly via supervised contrastive training [33] or feature normalization [42], but these remain heuristic. As future work, we aim to develop a principled framework that *systematically* increases the InD–OoD margin in embedding space, complementing our method and providing stronger guarantees for deployment.

Acknowledgment. The author would like to thank Professor Sarunas Girdzijauskas for his supervision, guidance, and intellectual generosity throughout this work. His insights shaped both the direction and the depth of this research in ways that are difficult to overstate. The author would like to express sincere gratitude to Roman Bresson for his insightful and detailed feedback. This work was supported in part by KTH Royal Institute of Technology and Qamcom Research and Technology AB.

References

1. Komini, V.K, Girdzijauskas, S.: Hiding in a plain sight: out-of-distribution data in the logit space embeddings. In: NeurIPS 2024 Workshop on Scientific Methods for Understanding Deep Learning (2024)
2. Roweis, S.T., Saul, L.K.: Nonlinear dimensionality reduction by locally linear embedding. Science **290**(5500), 2323–2326 (2000)
3. Tenenbaum, J.B., de Silva, V., Langford, J.C.: A global geometric framework for nonlinear dimensionality reduction. Science **290**(5500), 2319–2323 (2000)
4. Ma, Y., Fu, Y.: Manifold Learning Theory and Applications. Taylor & Francis (2011)
5. Weng, L.: Learning with not enough data part 1: semi-supervised learning. lilianweng.github.io (2021)
6. Dang, H., Huu, T.T., Nguyen, T.M., Ho, N.: Neural collapse for cross-entropy class-imbalanced learning with unconstrained ReLU features model. In: Salakhutdinov, R., et al. (eds.) Proceedings of the 41st International Conference on Machine Learning. Proceedings of Machine Learning Research, vol. 235, pp. 10017–10040. PMLR (2024)
7. Bishop, C.M.: Pattern Recognition and Machine Learning (Information Science and Statistics). Springer, Heidelberg (2006)
8. Wu, Z., Xiong, Y., Yu, S.X., Lin, D.: Unsupervised feature learning via non-parametric instance discrimination. In: Proceedings of the IEEE Conference on Computer Vision and Pattern Recognition (CVPR) (2018)
9. Sun, C., Shrivastava, A., Singh, S., Gupta, A.: Revisiting unreasonable effectiveness of data in deep learning era. In: Proceedings of the IEEE International Conference on Computer Vision (ICCV) (2017)
10. Deng, J., Guo, J., Xue, N., Zafeiriou, S.: Arcface: additive angular margin loss for deep face recognition. In: Proceedings of the IEEE/CVF Conference on Computer Vision and Pattern Recognition (CVPR) (2019)

11. Ye, H., Xie, C., Cai, T., Li, R., Li, Z., Wang, L.: Towards a theoretical framework of out-of-distribution generalization. In: Beygelzimer, A., Dauphin, Y., Liang, P., Wortman Vaughan, J. (eds.) Advances in Neural Information Processing Systems (2021)
12. Fang, Z., Li, Y., Lu, J., Dong, J., Han, B., Liu, F.: Is out-of-distribution detection learnable? In: Oh, A.H., Agarwal, A., Belgrave, D., Cho, K. (eds.) Advances in Neural Information Processing Systems (2022)
13. Hendrycks, D., et al.: Scaling out-of-distribution detection for real-world settings. In: Chaudhuri, K., Jegelka, S., Song, L., Szepesvari, C., Niu, G., Sabato, S. (eds.) Proceedings of the 39th International Conference on Machine Learning. Proceedings of Machine Learning Research, vol. 162, pp. 8759–8773. PMLR (2022)
14. Hendrycks, D., Mazeika, M., Dietterich, T.: Deep anomaly detection with outlier exposure. In: International Conference on Learning Representations (2019)
15. Liang, S., Li, Y., Srikant, R.: Enhancing the reliability of out-of-distribution image detection in neural networks. In: International Conference on Learning Representations (ICLR) (2018)
16. Hsu, Y.-C., Shen, Y., Jin, H., Kira, Z.: Generalized ODIN: Detecting out-of-distribution image without learning from out-of-distribution data. In: Proceedings of the IEEE/CVF Conference on Computer Vision and Pattern Recognition (CVPR), pp. 10951–10960 (2020)
17. Lee, K., Lee, K., Lee, H., Shin, J.: A simple unified framework for detecting out-of-distribution samples and adversarial attacks. In: Advances in Neural Information Processing Systems 31 (NeurIPS 2018), pp. 7167–7177 (2018)
18. Ren, J., Fort, S., Liu, J., Roy, A.G., Padhy, S., Lakshminarayanan, B.: A simple fix to mahalanobis distance for improving near-ood detection (2021)
19. Liu, W., Wang, X., Owens, J., Li, Y.: Energy-based out-of-distribution detection. In: Advances in Neural Information Processing Systems (2020)
20. Meet, P., Vadera, A.D., Cobb, B., Jalaian, B.M., Marlin: Ursabench: comprehensive benchmarking of approximate Bayesian inference methods for deep neural networks. In: Proceedings of the ICML 2020 Workshop on Uncertainty and Robustness in Deep Learning (2020)
21. Lakshminarayanan, B., Pritzel, A., Blundell, C.: Simple and scalable predictive uncertainty estimation using deep ensembles (2016)
22. Malinin, A., Mlodozeniec, B., Gales, M.J.F.: Ensemble distribution distillation. In: International Conference on Learning Representations (ICLR). OpenReview.net (2020)
23. Vadera, M.P., Jalaian, B., Marlin, B.M.: Generalized Bayesian posterior expectation distillation for deep neural networks. In: Proceedings of the Conference on Uncertainty in Artificial Intelligence (UAI), pp. 719–728. PMLR (2020)
24. Depeweg, S., Hernández-Lobato, J.M., Doshi-Velez, F., Udluft, S.: Decomposition of uncertainty in Bayesian deep learning for efficient and risk-sensitive learning. In: Proceedings of the 35th International Conference on Machine Learning (ICML). Proceedings of Machine Learning Research, vol. 80 (2018)
25. Wu, Y., Li, T., Cheng, X., Yang, J., Huang, X.: Low-dimensional gradient helps out-of-distribution detection. IEEE Trans. Pattern Anal. Mach. Intell. **46**(12), 11378–11391 (2024). Early-access version submitted October 2023
26. Sun, Y., Guo, C., Li, Y.: React: out-of-distribution detection with rectified activations. In: Advances in Neural Information Processing Systems (2021)
27. Zhu, Y., et al.: Boosting out-of-distribution detection with typical features. In: Advances in Neural Information Processing Systems, NeurIPS 2022, vol. 35 (2022)

28. Djurisic, A., Bozanic, N., Ashok, A., Liu, R.: Extremely simple activation shaping for out-of-distribution detection. In: The Eleventh International Conference on Learning Representations (2023)
29. Xu, K., Chen, R., Franchi, G., Yao, A.: Scaling for training time and post-hoc out-of-distribution detection enhancement. In: The Twelfth International Conference on Learning Representations (2024)
30. Yuan, Y., He, R., Dong, Y., Han, Z., Yin, Y.: Discriminability-driven channel selection for out-of-distribution detection. In: 2024 IEEE/CVF Conference on Computer Vision and Pattern Recognition (CVPR), pp. 26171–26180 (2024)
31. Park, J., Jung, Y.G., Teoh, A.B.J.: Nearest neighbor guidance for out-of-distribution detection. In: Proceedings of the IEEE/CVF International Conference on Computer Vision (ICCV), pp. 1686–1695 (2023)
32. Yu, Y., Shin, S., Lee, S., Jun, C., Lee, K.: Block selection method for using feature norm in out-of-distribution detection. In: Proceedings of the IEEE/CVF Conference on Computer Vision and Pattern Recognition (CVPR), pp. 15701–15711 (2023)
33. Sun, Y., Ming, Y., Zhu, X., Li, Y.: Out-of-distribution detection with deep nearest neighbors. In: Chaudhuri, K., Jegelka, S., Song, L., Szepesvári, C., Niu, G., Sabato, S. (eds.) Proceedings of the 39th International Conference on Machine Learning. Proceedings of Machine Learning Research, vol. 162, pp. 20827–20840. PMLR (2022)
34. Hendrycks, D., Gimpel, K.: A baseline for detecting misclassified and out-of-distribution examples in neural networks. In: International Conference on Learning Representations (ICLR) Poster Track. OpenReview.net (2017)
35. He, K., Zhang, X., Ren, S., Sun, J.: Deep residual learning for image recognition. In: Proceedings of the 2016 IEEE Conference on Computer Vision and Pattern Recognition (CVPR), CVPR 2016, pp. 770–778. IEEE (2016)
36. Krizhevsky, A., Nair, V., Hinton, G.: CIFAR-10 (Canadian institute for advanced research)
37. Netzer, Y., Wang, T., Coates, A., Bissacco, A., Wu, B., Ng, A.Y.: Reading digits in natural images with unsupervised feature learning. In: NIPS Workshop on Deep Learning and Unsupervised Feature Learning (2011)
38. Xu, P., et al.: Turkergaze: crowdsourcing saliency with webcam based eye tracking (2015)
39. Yu, F., Seff, A., Zhang, Y., Song, S., Funkhouser, T., Xiao, J.: LSUN: construction of a large-scale image dataset using deep learning with humans in the loop (2016)
40. Cimpoi, M., Maji, S., Kokkinos, I., Mohamed, S., Vedaldi, A.: Describing textures in the wild. In: Proceedings of the IEEE Conference on Computer Vision and Pattern Recognition (CVPR), pp. 3606–3613 (2014)
41. Zhou, B., Lapedriza, A., Khosla, A., Oliva, A., Torralba, A.: Places: a 10 million image database for scene recognition. IEEE Trans. Pattern Anal. Mach. Intell. **40**(6), 1452–1464 (2018)
42. Müller, M., Hein, M.: Mahalanobis++: improving ood detection via feature normalization. In: Proceedings of the 42nd International Conference on Machine Learning (ICML) (2025)

PRISM: Powerful Time Series to Image (TS2I) Representations for Multivariate Anomaly Detection

Mateusz Smendowski[1], Kamil Faber[1], Piotr Nawrocki[1], Nathalie Japkowicz[2], and Roberto Corizzo[2(✉)]

[1] Faculty of Computer Science, AGH University of Krakow, al. A. Mickiewicza 30, 30-059 Krakow, Poland
{smendowski,kfaber,piotr.nawrocki}@agh.edu.pl

[2] Department of Computer Science, American University, 4400 Massachusetts Ave NW, Washington, DC 20016, USA
{japkowic,rcorizzo}@american.edu

Abstract. Time-series anomaly detection (TSAD) underpins applications in predictive maintenance, finance, and cloud computing, however performance remains sensitive to representation choices, especially in multivariate settings. While transforming time series into images has shown success in forecasting and classification, it remains unclear how multivariate, high-dimensional series should be mapped to multi-channel images and whether vision backbones can match time-domain baselines in TSAD. We introduce PRISM, a plug-and-play meta-workflow enabling systematic construction and evaluation of image-based representations for multivariate TSAD. Our evaluation spanning over 7,000 experiments shows that well-designed PRISM configurations are competitive with 24 time-domain baselines, achieving the best VUS-PR on 10 of 14 datasets, with an average improvement of 41% over the best competing method on those datasets. Further, we identify channelization – how the channel dimension of multi-channel images is constructed – as a critical and previously understudied design dimension, and introduce MSM, a novel statistics-based scheme achieving 11–27% gains over PCA-based alternatives. Finally, ImageNet-pretrained encoders transfer effectively to TSAD, with frozen encoders retaining 92% of fine-tuned performance while training 1.8 times faster. Our code is available at: https://github.com/Smendowski/PRISM.

Keywords: Anomaly detection · Multivariate time series · Time series to image representations · Transfer learning · Autoencoders · Computer vision

1 Introduction

Time-series anomaly detection (TSAD) is a core building block in applications such as predictive maintenance, finance, cybersecurity, cloud computing, and

M. Ceci et al. (Eds.): ECML PKDD 2026, LNAI 16941, pp. 39–55, 2027.
https://doi.org/10.1007/978-3-032-37654-1_3

healthcare [24]. Despite its broad applicability, TSAD remains a challenging problem due to the diversity of temporal dynamics and the strong dependence of detection performance on data representation choices, particularly in multivariate settings [12,21]. Several factors motivate the transition from the time-series domain to the vision domain, including i) encoding temporal and cross-variate structure spatially in a form compatible with highly optimized, pretrained computer vision (CV) backbones [4]; and ii) revealing structural patterns that are not directly accessible in one-dimensional signals [13].

In this paper, we address these gaps by introducing PRISM (**P**owe**R**ful t**I**me **S**eries to image representations for **M**ultivariate anomaly detection), a unified meta-workflow that enables multivariate TSAD through image-based representations. PRISM introduces the notion of a projection scheme as an end-to-end mapping from a multivariate time-series window to a fixed-size image.

PRISM distinguishes two components of a projection scheme (Fig. 1). The TS2I transformation specifies how a time-series window is mapped to a single-channel image, while channelization defines how the channel dimension is constructed to obtain a multi-channel representation for vision backbones. Crucially, PRISM is not a single anomaly detection method, but a plug-and-play meta-workflow that decouples representation design from detector choice.

Our main contributions are summarized as follows:

- **C1**: We introduce PRISM, a unified plug-and-play meta-workflow – a modular pipeline that decouples TS2I representation design from detector choice – enabling systematic, reproducible construction and evaluation of image-based representations for multivariate TSAD with any autoencoder-based vision backbone or anomaly detector.
- **C2**: We identify channelization – how the channel dimension of multi-channel images is constructed from multivariate time series – as a critical and understudied design dimension in TS2I pipelines. We propose a taxonomy of channelization families and introduce MSM (Mean-Std-Max), a projection-free, statistics-based scheme specifically designed for TSAD, achieving 11–27% VUS-PR gains over PCA-based alternatives across all tested configurations.
- **C3**: Through comprehensive evaluation spanning over 7,000 experiments across 15 TS2I projection schemes, 2 autoencoder architectures, and 14 datasets from the TSB-AD benchmark, we demonstrate that well-designed PRISM configurations are competitive with 24 specialized time-domain baselines, achieving the best VUS-PR on 10 of 14 datasets, with a mean relative VUS-PR improvement of 41% across those datasets and a 6% overall mean improvement, establishing TS2I representations as a competitive alternative to time-domain methods.
- **C4**: We demonstrate that ImageNet-pretrained encoders transfer effectively to TSAD despite the substantial domain gap, showing that frozen encoders retain 92% of fully fine-tuned performance while training 1.8 times faster, and that MSM channelization is most critical when encoder adaptation is constrained.
- **C5**: We provide a computational cost analysis of PRISM, showing that TS2I transformation overhead represents only 2–8% of total pipeline time, and iden-

tifying MWT-MSM and SG-REP as suitable configurations for accuracy-critical and latency-critical deployments respectively.

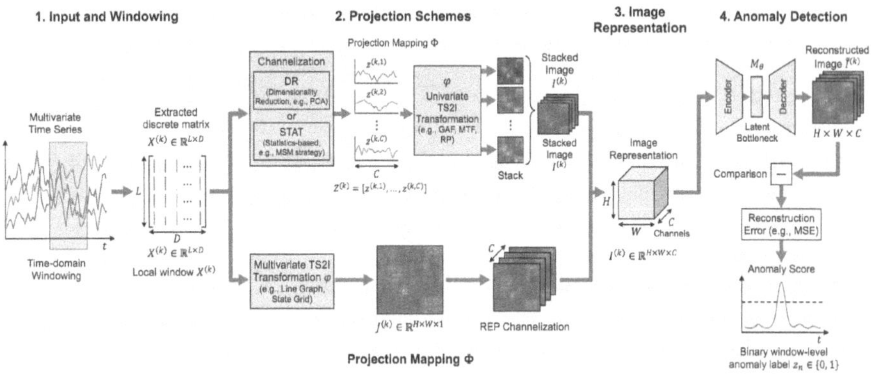

Fig. 1. Architecture of the proposed PRISM meta-workflow.

2 Related Work

Time Series to Image Transformations (TS2I): TS2I include different approaches with limited applicability to multivariate data. Widely used univariate-only methods, such as Gramian Angular Summation Field (GASF), Gramian Angular Difference Field (GADF), Markov Transition Field (MTF), and Recurrence Plot (RP) [20], encode temporal patterns through polar coordinates, state transitions, or recurrence structures, becoming standard baselines in forecasting and classification, yet GASF, GADF, and RP exhibit $\mathcal{O}(n^2)$ complexity and produce symmetric heatmaps unsuitable for high-dimensional settings [25], while MTF, though sharing the quadratic scaling, encodes state transition probabilities and does not produce symmetric outputs. Line plots provide direct visual encodings with demonstrated classification performance on univariate time series across 98 UCR datasets [16,23]. For multivariate data, grid line plots extend this approach by arranging multiple trajectories within a single image but incur overhead due to grid rendering [6]. Alternative approaches operate in the frequency domain, including STFT spectrograms and specialized wavelets (Ricker, Morlet), while similarity-based methods employ DTW matrices and shapelet maps [13]. Few TS2I transformations explicitly target multivariate time series encoding. State Grid discretizes time series data into bins [5]. Separately, correlation-based feature reordering achieves $\mathcal{O}(n)$ complexity but has been applied primarily to forecasting rather than anomaly detection [4]. Despite this diversity, key problems remain: it is unclear how multivariate, high-dimensional time series should be effectively turned into images [13], and more importantly, how multiple channels should be organized in the image. PRISM addresses this by establishing complete encoding workflows for multivariate TSAD and providing a comprehensive performance landscape for image-based TSAD: systematic evaluation of 6 univariate and 3 multivariate TS2I transformations combined with 3 channelization strategies across 14 benchmark datasets.

Time Series Anomaly Detection: TSAD has traditionally relied on statistical methods, but machine learning approaches are becoming more common [1]. Current methods span distance-based, density-based, prediction-based, and reconstruction-based approaches [11], with complex deep learning architectures such as autoencoder-based detectors [2,18]. Recent advances include transformer-based reconstruction with trend mechanisms [9], LLM knowledge distillation [7], and contrastive learning [19]. Despite these advances, time-domain methods remain sensitive to representation choices and often struggle to scale to high-dimensional multivariate settings, motivating the exploration of alternative representation paradigms. A separate group of methods transforms time series into images, enabling the application of vision models to anomaly detection. One strategy applies TS2I transformations across the variable dimension rather than time [10], encoding inter-variable correlations but limiting temporal modeling. Alternative approaches generate separate per-variable images using GAF, RP, and MTF with adversarial autoencoders [3] or temporal stacking with CNNs [17], producing single-channel outputs that are incompatible with pretrained RGB vision backbones, and are evaluated only on limited benchmarks. In contrast, PRISM models both temporal dynamics and cross-variate structure by transforming multivariate windows into multi-channel images via principled channelization. We provide thorough evaluation across 14 TSB-AD datasets, 9 challenging metrics, and 24 time-domain baselines, addressing scalability to high-dimensional data, resource efficiency, and pretrained backbone compatibility, providing a comprehensive empirical landscape for image-based multivariate TSAD and establishing PRISM as a plug-and-play framework compatible with any choice of vision backbone or detector.

Transfer Learning: Transfer learning (TL) has become a cornerstone of modern computer vision (CV), enabling practitioners to leverage pretrained backbones – ranging from CNNs (ResNet, AlexNet, EfficientNet, MobileNet) to transformers (ViT, PVT, Swin) [14] – rather than training from scratch. This approach reduces data and computational requirements [22]. However, TL success can be sensitive to domain similarity; a key open question is whether TS2I representations are sufficiently image-like to benefit from ImageNet pretraining. Recent work has also explored training-free anomaly detection using pretrained vision models like PatchCore on hybrid TS2I representations combining wavelets (Ricker, Morlet) with frequency embeddings [11], eliminating task-specific training entirely. While promising, this approach forgoes the potential benefits of fine-tuning to the target domain. Existing studies [15] evaluate only a few TL strategies on limited datasets, and the feasibility of positive cross-domain transfer remains poorly understood. We address this by evaluating whether an ImageNet-pretrained AE with ResNet-based encoder can achieve positive transfer to TS2I representations, systematically comparing three adaptation strategies across 14 datasets from the TSB-AD benchmark.

3 PRISM

3.1 Preliminaries

Let $X \in \mathbb{R}^{T\times D}$ denote a multivariate time series with T time steps and D dimensions. The observation at time t is a vector $x_t \in \mathbb{R}^D$, so that $X = [x_1; \ldots; x_T]$. In the supervised setting, we denote by $y_t \in \{0, 1\}$ the point-wise anomaly label at time t, where $y_t = 1$ indicates an anomalous observation.

Time-Domain Windowing: Given a window length L and stride s, the multivariate time series is segmented in the time domain into a sequence of fixed-length windows:

$$X^{(k)} = (x_{t_k}, \ldots, x_{t_k+L-1}) \in \mathbb{R}^{L\times D}, \qquad t_k = 1 + (k-1)s.$$

For evaluation purposes, a window-level anomaly label $z_k \in \{0, 1\}$ is derived via: $z_k = \max_{t\in\{t_k,\ldots,t_k+L-1\}} y_t$.

Workflows for Projection Schemes: In our work, we define a projection scheme as a process that converts time series to the image domain. Each window $X^{(k)}$ is mapped to a fixed-size image $I^{(k)}$ through a projection scheme Φ, and formally defined as

$$I^{(k)} = \Phi(X^{(k)}), \qquad \Phi : \mathbb{R}^{L\times D} \to \mathbb{R}^{H\times W\times C}.$$

Here, H and W denote the spatial resolution of the resulting image, and C denotes the number of channels. PRISM distinguishes two families of projection schemes, both of which are applied to multivariate data and differ in the way the window $X^{(k)}$ is projected to the image domain.

3.2 Projection Scheme for Univariate-Based TS2I Transformations

Since many TS2I transformations can only work with univariate data, we devise an approach to adapt them for multivariate data, which is the main focus of our study. Specifically, methods such as GAF, MTF, RP require a one-dimensional time series and therefore cannot be applied directly to multivariate windows $X^{(k)} \in \mathbb{R}^{L\times D}$.

In this scheme, the projection mapping Φ consists of a channelization step that derives a set of univariate series from the multivariate window, followed by the application of a univariate TS2I transformation φ to each resulting channel.

DR Channelization. In dimensionality reduction-based (DR) channelization, the multivariate window $X^{(k)} \in \mathbb{R}^{L \times D}$ is projected onto a C-dimensional (where C is lower than original dimensionality) subspace along the variable dimension using DR techniques such as PCA. This yields C univariate series defined as:

$$Z^{(k)} = \left[z^{(k,1)}, \ldots, z^{(k,C)}\right], \qquad z^{(k,c)} \in \mathbb{R}^L.$$

Each derived series is independently transformed into a single-channel image using the same univariate TS2I transformation φ:

$$J^{(k,c)} = \varphi\big(z^{(k,c)}\big), \qquad J^{(k,c)} \in \mathbb{R}^{H \times W}, \quad c = 1, \ldots, C.$$

The final image representation is obtained by stacking the resulting images along the channel dimension:

$$I^{(k)} = \text{stack}\big(J^{(k,1)}, \ldots, J^{(k,C)}\big) \in \mathbb{R}^{H \times W \times C}.$$

STAT Channelization. In addition to DR channelization, we devise an original statistics-based (STAT) channelization approach for TSAD, where channels are constructed directly from the multivariate window $X^{(k)} \in \mathbb{R}^{L \times D}$ using statistical descriptors computed across the variable dimension. One advantage is that this approach is projection-free, avoiding intermediate latent representations. Formally, a set of C statistical operators is applied to obtain derived univariate series

$$Z^{(k)} = \left[z^{(k,1)}, \ldots, z^{(k,C)}\right], \qquad z^{(k,c)} \in \mathbb{R}^L,$$

where each $z^{(k,c)}$ corresponds to a separate statistic evaluated at each time step. Each derived series is independently transformed into a single-channel image using the same univariate TS2I transformation φ:

$$J^{(k,c)} = \varphi\big(z^{(k,c)}\big), \qquad J^{(k,c)} \in \mathbb{R}^{H \times W}, \quad c = 1, \ldots, C.$$

The final image representation is constructed by stacking the resulting images along the channel dimension:

$$I^{(k)} = \text{stack}\big(J^{(k,1)}, \ldots, J^{(k,C)}\big) \in \mathbb{R}^{H \times W \times C}.$$

MSM Strategy. Although STAT channelization is general and supports any statistics and time series dimensionality, we devise a novel MSM (Mean-Std-Max) strategy that highlights salient statistical properties for TSAD. The three channels are chosen for their complementary sensitivity to distinct anomaly types: the mean captures global level shifts across variables, the standard deviation encodes changes in cross-variate spread or synchrony, and the maximum preserves extreme individual deviations that averaging would otherwise dilute. Together, they characterize the first-order cross-variate distributional shape at each time step without assuming any covariance structure – making MSM sensitive to a broader class of anomalies than PCA-based channelization, which maximizes variance explained in normal data rather than discriminability between normal and anomalous patterns. MSM's projection-free nature further confers robustness to the non-stationarity common in real-world multivariate time series, as empirically validated in Sect. 5.3.

3.3 Projection Scheme for Multivariate-Based TS2I Transformations

The projection scheme for multivariate-based TS2I transformations applies to transformation methods that operate natively on multivariate inputs. Such methods (e.g., Line Graph or State Grid) directly process a window $X^{(k)} \in \mathbb{R}^{L \times D}$ and support arbitrary input dimensionality. A concrete multivariate TS2I transformation, denoted by φ, is applied to obtain a single-channel image:

$$J^{(k)} = \varphi(X^{(k)}), \qquad J^{(k)} \in \mathbb{R}^{H \times W \times 1}.$$

The overall projection scheme Φ comprises this transformation followed by a channelization strategy.

REP Channelization. Given $J^{(k)} \in \mathbb{R}^{H \times W}$, replication-based (REP) channelization constructs the final image by replicating the single-channel output across the channel dimension. While this introduces no additional information across channels, it serves two practical purposes: satisfying the 3-channel input requirement of pretrained RGB vision backbones, and enabling a controlled baseline that isolates the contribution of the TS2I transformation itself from any channelization effect. Formally, for a target number of channels C, the representation is given by

$$I^{(k)} = \mathrm{stack}\big(\underbrace{J^{(k)}, \ldots, J^{(k)}}_{C \text{ times}}\big) \in \mathbb{R}^{H \times W \times C}.$$

3.4 Anomaly Detection

In PRISM, an autoencoder-based anomaly detection model $M_\theta : \mathbb{R}^{H \times W \times C} \to \mathbb{R}$ is trained to assign an anomaly score (i.e., reconstruction error) to each image-based window representation, where θ denotes model parameters. PRISM's plug-and-play design allows any anomaly detection model to serve as the scoring component. In this study, we adopt autoencoder-based architectures due to their powerful non-linear modeling capabilities, widely recognized as a standard approach in the current literature.

4 Experimental Setup

In our experiments, we leverage the TSB-AD benchmark and follow its standardized protocol [8]. For reproducibility, we share our code at https://github.com/Smendowski/PRISM.

Framework-level ablation is constrained by strict sequential dependencies (e.g., the projection scheme cannot be omitted because subsequent pipeline stages fundamentally rely on its image output representation). To assess component contributions, we exhaustively evaluate configurations of various TS2I feature extraction methods, channelization strategies, and predictive models. Our extensive evaluation resulted in more than 7,000 training and evaluation runs, all performed on NVIDIA GH200 GPUs.

4.1 Datasets and Metrics

In this study, we focus on the following 14 multivariate public datasets: CATSv2 (dimensionality $D = 17$), CreditCard ($D = 29$), Daphnet ($D = 9$), Exathlon ($D = 21$), GECCO ($D = 9$), Genesis ($D = 18$), LTDB ($D = 2$), MSL ($D = 55$), OPP ($D = 248$), PSM ($D = 25$), SMAP ($D = 25$), SMD ($D = 38$), SWaT ($D = 59$), and TAO ($D = 3$). They are available at https://github.com/TheDatumOrg/TSB-AD and their detailed descriptions can be found in the work introducing TSB-AD benchmark [8].

We follow the TSB-AD evaluation protocol, reporting metrics across three categories: ranking-based (AUC-PR, AUC-ROC, VUS-PR, VUS-ROC), point-wise (Standard – S-F1, Point-Adjust – PA-F1), and event-level (Event-based – E-F1, Range-based – R-F1, Affiliation – A-F1), jointly assessing detector quality across thresholds, individual timestamps, and contiguous anomaly segments.

4.2 TS2I Projection Schemes

In PRISM, we employ a diverse set of state-of-the-art TS2I transformations to map multivariate time-series windows into fixed-size images. We set the window length to $L = 20$ and stride $s = 1$ across all datasets to ensure a controlled, fair comparison across the 14 benchmark datasets – varying window length per dataset would introduce a confounding factor that conflates representation quality with hyperparameter tuning. Moreover, in TSB-AD, many methods use a single window length across all datasets. We acknowledge that for datasets with longer anomaly patterns or slower dynamics (e.g., OPP with $D = 248$), a fixed short window may limit the capture of long-range dependencies. A data-driven window selection approach – for instance, based on autocorrelation analysis to identify the dominant periodicity of each series – could unlock further gains.

The univariate-based TS2I transformations considered in this study include Gramian Angular Summation Field (GASF), Gramian Angular Difference Field (GADF), Markov Transition Field (MTF), Recurrence Plot (RP), Morlet Wavelet Transform (MWT), and Ricker Wavelet Transform (RWT). These methods are employed within the projection scheme for univariate-based TS2I transformations, where two channelization variants are evaluated.

As a representative of DR channelization, we adapt PCA with $C = 3$ principal components. In addition, we evaluate our original three-channel MSM scheme. We also consider multivariate-based TS2I transformations, such as Random Noise (RN), State Grid (SG), and Line Graph (LG), which use REP channelization within the projection scheme for multivariate-based TS2I transformations.

We set the image resolution to $H = W = 64$ and use $C = 3$ channels corresponding to the standard RGB format. This configuration provides a favorable trade-off between representational capacity and computational efficiency while enabling the application of pretrained backbones [11]. In total, our experimental setup involves 15 TS2I projection schemes as illustrated in Fig. 2.

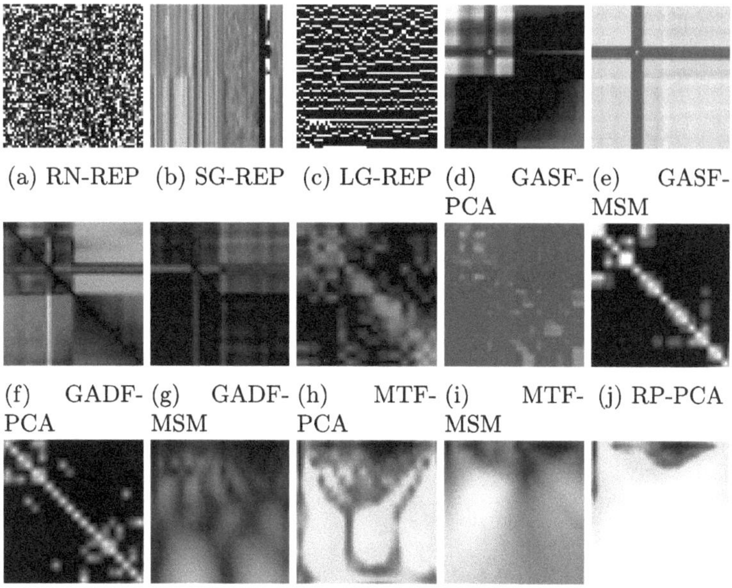

(a) RN-REP (b) SG-REP (c) LG-REP (d) GASF-PCA (e) GASF-MSM

(f) GADF-PCA (g) GADF-MSM (h) MTF-PCA (i) MTF-MSM (j) RP-PCA

(k) RP-MSM (l) MWT-PCA (m) MWT-MSM (n) RWT-PCA (o) RWT-MSM

Fig. 2. Multi-channel image representations of a single multivariate time series window across different TS2I projection methods and channelization strategies. Each 64×64 RGB image encodes the same window differently, illustrating how the choice of projection and channelization affects the resulting visual structure.

4.3 Models

In our study, we employ two vision backbones: i) CNN-AE: a lightweight 2D convolutional autoencoder with three encoding layers, and ii) ResNet-AE: an autoencoder with a ResNet encoder initialized with ImageNet-pretrained weights and paired with a symmetric decoder. For ResNet-AE, we evaluate three TL strategies: Frozen Encoder (FE), which trains only the decoder while keeping the encoder frozen; Progressive Encoder Unfreeze (PEU), which starts with a frozen encoder and fully unfreezes it mid-training with a reduced learning rate; and Differential Learning Rates (DLR), which trains encoder and decoder simultaneously from the start using different learning rates. All architectural details and hyperparameters are documented in our repository at https://github.com/Smendowski/PRISM.

To evaluate PRISM, we compare against 24 time-domain baselines including recent xLSTMAD [2] and 23 additional methods from the TSB-AD benchmark: CNN, OmniAnomaly, PCA, LSTMAD, USAD, AutoEncoder, KMeansAD, CBLOF, MCD, OCSVM, Donut, RobustPCA, FITS, OFA, EIF, COPOD, IForest, HBOS, TimesNet, KNN, TranAD, LOF, and AnomalyTransformer.

5 Experimental Results

Table 1. VUS-PR of representative detection approaches on 14 TSB-AD-M datasets. PRISM is built upon CNN and RN18 (ResNet18) auto-encoder backbones. Best results are shown in **bold**, while second-best results are underlined. Only the 10 best-performing PRISM configurations and 10 best-performing non-PRISM approaches are reported in the table (20 out of 54 in total); additional results are available at https://github.com/Smendowski/PRISM.

	Method/Config.	CATSv2	CreditCard	Daphnet	Exathlon	GECCO	Genesis	LTDB	MSL	OPP	PSM	SMAP	SMD	SWaT	TAO
PRISM	CNN+SG-REP	0.11	**0.20**	0.43	0.86	0.37	0.06	0.28	0.39	0.17	0.17	0.22	0.45	0.33	0.95
	CNN+MWT-MSM	0.23	0.16	0.35	0.86	0.13	0.45	0.29	0.45	0.13	0.28	0.28	0.46	0.60	0.91
	RN18+SG-REP	0.10	0.17	0.35	0.98	0.31	0.80	0.38	0.43	0.21	0.15	0.32	0.44	**0.64**	0.89
	RN18+LG-REP	0.06	0.14	0.45	0.98	**0.43**	0.74	0.28	0.23	**0.39**	0.25	0.24	0.40	0.48	1.00
	RN18+GASF-PCA	0.12	0.03	0.29	0.29	0.20	0.14	0.37	0.23	0.06	0.18	0.22	0.18	0.32	1.00
	RN18+GASF-MSM	0.10	0.19	0.15	0.74	0.11	0.19	0.30	0.24	0.06	0.16	0.24	0.15	0.18	**1.00**
	RN18+MWT-PCA	0.10	0.06	**0.47**	0.97	0.09	0.16	0.21	0.27	0.20	0.28	0.25	0.45	0.49	0.99
	RN18+MWT-MSM	**0.25**	0.13	0.41	0.86	0.12	0.51	0.37	**0.48**	0.13	0.31	0.35	**0.48**	0.59	0.93
	RN18+RWT-PCA	0.09	0.05	0.38	**0.98**	0.10	0.46	0.20	0.29	0.17	0.27	0.29	0.39	0.28	0.81
	RN18+RWT-MSM	0.18	0.16	0.35	0.86	0.16	0.60	0.42	0.42	0.14	0.34	0.34	0.45	0.59	0.86
Baselines	xLSTMAD	0.23	0.06	0.28	0.94	0.19	0.67	0.42	0.33	0.31	**0.40**	0.27	0.40	0.52	0.73
	CNN	0.08	0.02	0.21	0.68	0.03	0.10	0.33	0.35	0.16	0.22	0.19	0.35	0.41	1.00
	OmniAnomaly	0.04	0.02	0.34	0.84	0.02	0.00	**0.44**	0.22	0.18	0.16	0.12	0.17	0.15	0.81
	PCA	0.12	0.10	0.13	0.95	0.20	0.02	0.24	0.15	0.30	0.16	0.09	0.36	0.45	1.00
	LSTMAD	0.04	0.02	0.31	0.82	0.02	0.04	0.30	0.22	0.17	0.24	0.16	0.33	0.16	0.99
	USAD	0.04	0.02	0.34	0.84	0.02	0.00	0.41	0.23	0.18	0.19	0.11	0.16	0.15	0.81
	AutoEncoder	0.06	0.03	0.13	0.91	0.05	0.01	0.21	0.22	0.14	0.28	0.13	0.30	0.58	1.00
	KMeansAD	0.12	0.02	0.30	0.37	0.06	**0.89**	0.41	0.44	0.06	0.21	**0.38**	0.36	0.16	0.86
	MCD	0.13	0.06	0.14	0.80	0.03	0.06	0.21	0.23	0.17	0.26	0.10	0.26	0.54	1.00
	Donut	0.07	0.02	0.17	0.66	0.03	0.18	0.26	0.30	0.15	0.20	0.18	0.19	0.44	0.75

This research is directed at answering the following research questions:

- **RQ1**: Can vision-based approaches using TS2I representations achieve competitive performance against state-of-the-art time-domain TSAD baselines?
- **RQ2**: How do different TS2I projection schemes balance detection performance and computational efficiency in multivariate TSAD?
- **RQ3**: What is the relative importance of channelization strategy versus autoencoder architecture in determining TSAD performance?
- **RQ4**: Can transfer learning from general vision domains (ImageNet) provide positive transfer to TSAD, and which encoder adaptation strategies are most effective?
- **RQ5**: What are the computational trade-offs between TS2I projection schemes and autoencoder architectures, and can the overhead introduced by data transformation be justified by superior TSAD performance?

5.1 PRISM vs. Time-Domain Baselines

Table 1 compares PRISM variants against 24 established TSAD methods across 14 diverse multivariate datasets (dimensionality $D = 2$ to $D = 248$). Within the PRISM meta-workflow, top configurations achieved the best performance on 10 of 14 datasets, improving the results over the best non-PRISM method on average by 41%, computed as the mean relative improvement of the best PRISM configuration over the best non-PRISM method across the 10 datasets where PRISM achieves highest performance.

Specifically, PRISM configurations achieved the highest VUS-PR improvements on the following datasets: GECCO by 115.0% vs PCA (0.43 vs 0.20); CreditCard by 100.0% vs PCA (0.20 vs 0.10); CATSv2 by 8.7% vs xLSTMAD (0.25 vs 0.23); SMD by 20% vs xLSTMAD (0.48 vs 0.40). On the other hand, time-series-based competitors achieved high performance on 2 lower-dimensional datasets: KMeansAD on Genesis ($D = 18$, 0.89 vs 0.80 for best PRISM configuration) and OmniAnomaly on LTDB ($D = 2$, 0.44 vs 0.42).

Across metrics, Table 2 presents mean performance across all 14 datasets and 9 evaluation metrics. PRISM achieved the best overall performance in 6 out of 9 metrics. Specifically, comparing it with the best non-PRISM method, it achieved the best VUS-PR (0.53 vs 0.50), AUC-PR (0.53 for PRISM vs 0.42 for non-PRISM), Standard F1 (0.58 vs 0.48), PA-F1 (0.96 vs 0.88), Event-based-F1 (0.86 vs 0.68), and R-based-F1 (0.45 vs 0.44). Among baselines, only Donut was able to outperform PRISM and only in two metrics: VUS-ROC (0.86 vs 0.81 for PRISM) and Affiliation-F1 (0.98 vs 0.95 for PRISM). However, Donut lagged substantially on precision-recall metrics (AUC-PR: 0.24 vs 0.53).

The strong cross-dataset and cross-metric performance demonstrates that TS2I transformation with visual autoencoders offers a competitive dataset-agnostic framework, particularly effective for high-dimensional multivariate series where visual representations capture complex cross-channel dependencies that sequential architectures may struggle to model (**RQ1**). To streamline discussion, in the remainder of Sect. 5 we focus on VUS-PR; however, fine-grained results across all metrics are available in Table 2 and our repository.

5.2 TS2I Projection Schemes Comparison

Table 3 compares the 15 TS2I projection schemes across detection performance and computational efficiency. RN-REP serves as a negative control, confirming that meaningful structure in the image representation is necessary for effective anomaly detection – random pixel assignments yield near-chance performance.

Wavelet-based projection schemes achieved the strongest performance, with MWT-MSM reaching VUS-PR of 0.52. This superiority suggests that multi-scale temporal decomposition effectively preserves anomaly-discriminative patterns across different frequency bands. Interestingly, replication-based projection schemes (SG-REP, LG-REP) achieved remarkably competitive performance without requiring complex channelization. SG-REP is particularly compelling: achieving VUS-PR of 0.51 while being 7.8 times faster than LG-REP (1.40 s)

Table 2. Mean performance across 9 evaluation metrics for 30 PRISM plug-and-play configurations and 24 time-domain baseline methods on 14 TSB-AD datasets. PRISM is built upon CNN and RN18 (ResNet18) auto-encoder backbones. Best results in **bold**, second-best <u>underlined</u>.

	Method	AUC-PR	AUC-ROC	VUS-PR	VUS-ROC	S-F1	PA-F1	E-F1	R-F1	A-F1
PRISM	CNN+RN-REP	0.14	0.50	0.15	0.52	0.21	0.94	0.39	0.33	0.80
	CNN+SG-REP	0.49	0.75	0.48	0.76	0.53	0.90	0.79	0.42	0.93
	CNN+LG-REP	0.45	0.73	0.44	0.75	0.50	0.93	0.76	0.40	0.92
	CNN+GASF-PCA	0.24	0.61	0.23	0.63	0.31	0.94	0.62	0.37	0.88
	CNN+GASF-MSM	0.38	0.70	0.37	0.71	0.43	0.93	0.73	0.36	0.90
	CNN+GADF-PCA	0.27	0.53	0.26	0.55	0.34	0.88	0.64	0.40	0.89
	CNN+GADF-MSM	0.26	0.54	0.25	0.55	0.37	0.90	0.62	0.42	0.86
	CNN+MTF-PCA	0.24	0.57	0.24	0.59	0.30	0.93	0.63	0.39	0.86
	CNN+MTF-MSM	0.35	0.63	0.35	0.64	0.42	0.92	0.66	0.39	0.88
	CNN+RP-PCA	0.22	0.57	0.22	0.58	0.28	0.86	0.53	0.30	0.84
	CNN+RP-MSM	0.31	0.62	0.31	0.63	0.37	0.83	0.59	0.30	0.88
	CNN+MWT-PCA	0.49	0.76	0.48	0.77	0.53	0.89	0.77	0.41	0.93
	CNN+MWT-MSM	0.51	0.74	0.51	0.75	0.56	0.92	<u>0.85</u>	<u>0.45</u>	0.94
	CNN+RWT-PCA	0.45	0.72	0.45	0.73	0.51	0.90	0.75	0.40	0.92
	CNN+RWT-MSM	0.47	0.74	0.47	0.75	0.54	0.92	0.82	0.42	0.93
	RN18+RN-REP	0.14	0.50	0.15	0.52	0.21	0.93	0.32	0.32	0.77
	RN18+SG-REP	<u>0.52</u>	0.76	<u>0.52</u>	0.77	<u>0.57</u>	0.93	0.81	0.41	0.93
	RN18+LG-REP	0.50	**0.80**	0.49	0.81	0.54	**0.96**	0.80	0.39	0.93
	RN18+GASF-PCA	0.27	0.65	0.27	0.66	0.35	<u>0.96</u>	0.70	0.37	0.90
	RN18+GASF-MSM	0.38	0.73	0.37	0.74	0.44	0.94	0.77	0.36	0.92
	RN18+GADF-PCA	0.30	0.62	0.29	0.63	0.36	0.94	0.67	0.37	0.89
	RN18+GADF-MSM	0.30	0.58	0.29	0.60	0.39	0.94	0.67	0.38	0.88
	RN18+MTF-PCA	0.23	0.58	0.23	0.59	0.30	0.93	0.60	0.37	0.86
	RN18+MTF-MSM	0.33	0.63	0.33	0.64	0.41	0.92	0.62	0.36	0.87
	RN18+RP-PCA	0.22	0.55	0.22	0.56	0.29	0.89	0.59	0.35	0.85
	RN18+RP-MSM	0.34	0.62	0.34	0.63	0.41	0.89	0.68	0.38	0.89
	RN18+MWT-PCA	0.50	0.76	0.50	0.77	0.55	0.94	0.84	0.42	0.95
	RN18+MWT-MSM	**0.53**	0.75	**0.53**	0.76	**0.58**	0.92	**0.86**	**0.45**	<u>0.95</u>
	RN18+RWT-PCA	0.48	0.73	0.48	0.74	0.54	0.92	0.81	0.40	0.93
	RN18+RWT-MSM	0.51	0.74	0.50	0.75	0.57	0.92	0.83	0.42	0.94
Baselines	xLSTMAD	0.42	**0.80**	0.50	<u>0.85</u>	0.51	0.70	0.59	0.44	0.86
	CNN	0.36	0.75	0.35	0.77	0.41	0.80	0.68	0.41	0.88
	OmniAnomaly	0.28	0.66	0.33	0.70	0.33	0.55	0.41	0.39	0.81
	PCA	0.36	0.73	0.36	0.78	0.43	0.88	0.67	0.32	0.87
	LSTMAD	0.36	0.73	0.36	0.77	0.41	0.83	0.68	0.43	0.89
	USAD	0.27	0.65	0.32	0.69	0.32	0.53	0.40	0.39	0.80
	AutoEncoder	0.36	0.70	0.35	0.72	0.40	0.64	0.51	0.33	0.82
	KMeansAD	0.28	0.70	0.33	0.74	0.35	0.70	0.54	0.36	0.83
	CBLOF	0.33	0.69	0.32	0.72	0.37	0.71	0.53	0.36	0.83
	MCD	0.32	0.71	0.32	0.75	0.39	0.53	0.39	0.23	0.80
	OCSVM	0.27	0.63	0.31	0.70	0.32	0.55	0.48	0.35	0.82
	Donut	0.24	<u>0.78</u>	0.32	**0.86**	0.34	0.63	0.44	0.26	**0.98**
	RobustPCA	0.28	0.60	0.28	0.63	0.33	0.62	0.46	0.37	0.82
	FITS	0.17	0.60	0.24	0.69	0.24	0.70	0.32	0.17	0.82
	OFA	0.14	0.57	0.22	0.65	0.21	0.73	0.39	0.15	0.83
	EIF	0.22	0.69	0.25	0.73	0.30	0.77	0.51	0.30	0.83
	COPOD	0.23	0.68	0.23	0.72	0.31	0.76	0.47	0.27	0.82
	IForest	0.22	0.68	0.23	0.71	0.29	0.71	0.44	0.26	0.81
	HBOS	0.18	0.65	0.22	0.70	0.27	0.72	0.47	0.28	0.82
	TimesNet	0.14	0.58	0.21	0.67	0.22	0.65	0.31	0.18	0.83
	KNN	0.16	0.54	0.21	0.63	0.22	0.73	0.52	0.24	0.81
	TranAD	0.15	0.60	0.20	0.66	0.23	0.68	0.40	0.22	0.79
	LOF	0.11	0.54	0.16	0.62	0.17	0.60	0.36	0.16	0.77
	AnomalyTransformer	0.08	0.52	0.14	0.58	0.13	0.51	0.32	0.14	0.73

and 2.1 times faster than wavelet-based competitors (0.37 s), it demonstrates that preserving the full multivariate structure through direct spatial mapping can be both effective and efficient. LG-REP achieved VUS-PR of 0.48 but at considerable computational expense (3.8 times slower than MWT-MSM), as its grid-based plotting incurs high computational overhead for dense line rendering.

These results reveal a nuanced performance-efficiency landscape with clear implications. MWT-MSM emerges as the optimal choice for accuracy-critical applications, accepting 2.1 times longer computation than SG-REP to gain 2.0% VUS-PR improvement. Conversely, SG-REP may offer the best solution for real-time deployments, sacrificing detection quality for substantial speed gains **(RQ2)**. These results demonstrate that PRISM's modular design allows practitioners to select the optimal projection scheme for their deployment constraints – from real-time applications favoring SG-REP to accuracy-critical settings benefiting from MWT-MSM – without changing any other component of the pipeline.

Table 3. Mean performance across 9 evaluation metrics and computational time (seconds per 100 images) of 15 PRISM's TS2I projection schemes. Best results in **bold**, second-best underlined.

Projection scheme	AUC-PR	AUC-ROC	VUS-PR	VUS-ROC	S-F1	PA-F1	E-F1	R-F1	A-F1	Time
RN-REP	0.14	0.50	0.15	0.52	0.21	0.94	0.34	0.32	0.77	0.20
SG-REP	0.51	0.76	0.51	0.77	0.56	0.92	0.81	0.41	0.93	**0.18**
LG-REP	0.49	**0.78**	0.48	**0.79**	0.53	**0.95**	0.79	0.39	0.93	1.40
GASF-PCA	0.26	0.64	0.26	0.65	0.34	0.95	0.68	0.37	0.89	0.32
GASF-MSM	0.38	0.72	0.37	0.73	0.44	0.94	0.76	0.36	0.92	0.32
GADF-PCA	0.29	0.59	0.28	0.61	0.36	0.93	0.67	0.38	0.89	0.34
GADF-MSM	0.29	0.57	0.28	0.59	0.38	0.93	0.66	0.39	0.88	0.33
MTF-PCA	0.23	0.58	0.23	0.59	0.30	0.93	0.60	0.37	0.86	0.32
MTF-MSM	0.33	0.63	0.33	0.64	0.41	0.92	0.63	0.37	0.87	0.32
RP-PCA	0.22	0.55	0.22	0.57	0.29	0.88	0.58	0.33	0.85	0.25
RP-MSM	0.34	0.62	0.34	0.63	0.40	0.87	0.66	0.36	0.89	0.24
MWT-PCA	0.50	0.76	0.50	0.77	0.54	0.93	0.82	0.42	0.94	0.40
MWT-MSM	**0.53**	0.76	**0.52**	0.76	**0.58**	0.92	**0.86**	**0.45**	**0.95**	0.37
RWT-PCA	0.47	0.73	0.47	0.74	0.53	0.92	0.79	0.40	0.93	0.39
RWT-MSM	0.50	0.74	0.50	0.75	0.56	0.92	0.83	0.42	0.94	0.37

5.3 Channelization Strategy: MSM vs PCA

To evaluate how channelization strategy affects detection quality, we compared MSM against PCA across all projection schemes for univariate-based TS2I transformations, models, and datasets. MSM outperformed PCA across the vast majority of configurations, achieving 18.9% higher VUS-PR overall (0.390 vs

0.328). This advantage remained substantial for both CNN-AE (19.6% improvement) and ResNet-AE (18.7% improvement), indicating MSM's superiority is architecture-independent. Notably, MSM was also computationally 3.2% faster than PCA channelization.

The impact of channelization varied substantially across TL strategies. FE showed the highest sensitivity to channelization choice, with MSM achieving 26.6% higher VUS-PR than PCA (0.388 vs 0.306). This substantial gap suggests that when encoder weights remain fixed, the quality of input representation becomes critical – MSM's deviation-sensitive statistics – particularly standard deviation and maximum – are theoretically better aligned with anomaly discriminability than PCA's variance-maximizing projection, consistent with the motivation in Sect. 3.2. PEU reduced this gap to 19.9% (0.396 vs 0.330), as gradual adaptation partially compensates for weaker initial representations. DLR showed the smallest gap at 11.0% (0.399 vs 0.359), indicating that fine-grained tuning can overcome limitations of suboptimal channelization.

We observe that MSM's advantage is most pronounced when model capacity to learn from data is constrained – either by simpler architecture (CNN-AE) or frozen weights (FE strategy). Conversely, more flexible training regimes (DLR) reduce dependence on channelization quality. The consistent 11–27% VUS-PR improvement across all configurations establishes MSM as the preferred channelization strategy for TSAD, with MSM-based projection schemes recommended for production deployments **(RQ3)**.

5.4 Transfer Learning from ImageNet: Strategies and Trade-Offs

Despite the substantial domain gap between natural images (ImageNet) and TS2I representations, TL from ImageNet-pretrained ResNet-AE consistently benefits TSAD across all strategies (Table 4).

Training only the decoder while keeping pretrained weights fixed (FE) achieved strong performance (VUS-PR: 0.35) with fastest training (94.21 s), demonstrating that ImageNet features capture anomaly-relevant patterns without encoder adaptation. DLR reached the highest performance (VUS-PR: 0.38), only 8.6% better than FE but requiring 77.5% longer training (167.29 s). PEU occupied the middle ground (VUS-PR: 0.37, 49.3% overhead vs FE).

The seemingly narrow 8.6% performance gap translates to meaningful differences in critical applications. In applications where missed anomalies carry high operational cost, even small gains in VUS-PR may justify additional training time. The trade-off is primarily computational: FE offers rapid deployment with 92% of DLR's quality, while DLR maximizes accuracy at nearly doubled training cost. For fast deployment or resource-constrained environments, FE is optimal; for safety-critical or accuracy-demanding applications where the 8.6% improvement justifies computational expense, DLR is preferable **(RQ4)**.

Table 4. Mean performance across 9 evaluation metrics and training time (seconds) of 3 TL strategies. Best results in **bold**, second-best underlined.

Strategy	AUC-PR	AUC-ROC	VUS-PR	VUS-ROC	S-F1	PA-F1	E-F1	R-F1	A-F1	Time
FE	0.36	0.66	0.35	0.67	0.42	0.93	0.70	0.38	0.89	**94**
PEU	0.37	0.67	0.37	0.68	0.43	0.93	0.71	0.38	0.90	141
DLR	**0.38**	**0.68**	**0.38**	**0.69**	**0.44**	**0.93**	**0.71**	**0.39**	**0.90**	167

5.5 Empirical Time Complexity

PRISM's computational cost comprises TS2I transformation and model training. Using stride $s = 1$, time-domain windowing generates 1k–400k images per dataset. Transformation scales linearly at 0.18–1.40 s per 100 images but represents only 2–8% of total time. Training time, which dominates the budget, depends on projection scheme and architecture choice. On average, the CNN-AE converges more slowly (2.10 min) than the deeper frozen ResNet-AE (1.57 min), while different TL strategies add varying overhead: PEU requires 2.35 min (+49%) and DLR 2.79 min (+78%). Projection schemes also impact efficiency – models trained on TS2I from wavelets converge faster (MWT: 1.41 min, RWT: 1.55 min) than polar encodings (GASF: 3.05 min, GADF: 3.17 min). For median-sized datasets, end-to-end workflow time ranges 2.0–4.7 min. The transformation overhead is justified – configurations that achieve 41% average VUS-PR improvement over baselines require 2–5 min end-to-end **(RQ5)**.

6 Conclusion

We introduced PRISM, a systematic meta-workflow designed for multivariate TSAD through TS2I representations. PRISM's plug-and-play design enables any combination of TS2I transformation, channelization strategy, and detector to be systematically assessed. Evaluating 15 projection schemes across 14 datasets from the TSB-AD benchmark, configurations enabled by PRISM achieved the best performance on 10 of 14 datasets and remained competitive with 24 specialized time-domain baselines overall. Among key findings, we observe that: i) wavelet-based projection schemes with MSM channelization achieve best performance (MWT-MSM: 0.52 VUS-PR), with MSM providing 11–27% gains over PCA; ii) MSM's advantage peaks when model capacity is constrained (frozen encoder: +26.6% vs fine-tuned: +11.0%), demonstrating that superior preprocessing compensates for architectural limitations; iii) despite the substantial domain gap, ImageNet features transfer effectively to TSAD, with frozen encoders retaining 92% of fine-tuned performance while training 1.8 times faster. In the future, we aim to study the impact of image resolution on detection performance, explore continual learning scenarios, and leverage data-driven window selection.

Acknowledgments. The research presented in this paper was supported by funds from: i) the Polish Ministry of Science and Higher Education allocated to the AGH University of Krakow; ii) SOCCER project (grant agreement no. 101128073), with the support of the European Cybersecurity Competence Centre (ECCC), and co-funded by the Polish Ministry of Science and Higher Education under the programme "Co-funded International Projects".

References

1. Boniol, P., Liu, Q., Huang, M., Palpanas, T., Paparrizos, J.: Dive into time-series anomaly detection: a decade review. arXiv preprint arXiv:2412.20512 (2024)
2. Faber, K., Pietron, M., Zurek, D., Corizzo, R.: xLSTMAD: a powerful XLSTM-based method for anomaly detection. In: 2025 IEEE International Conference on Data Mining (ICDM), pp. 247–256. IEEE (2025)
3. Kang, J., Kim, M., Park, J., Park, S.: Time-series to image-transformed adversarial autoencoder for anomaly detection. IEEE Access (2024)
4. Kang, S., Jo, O.: Memory-efficient imagification for light-weight prediction model of multivariate time-series data. IEEE Access (2025)
5. Karami, H., Hartley, M.A., Atienza, D., Ionescu, A.: Timehr: image-based time series generation for electronic health records. IEEE J. Biomed. Health Inform. (2025)
6. Li, Z., Li, S., Yan, X.: Time series as images: vision transformer for irregularly sampled time series. In: Oh, A., Naumann, T., Globerson, A., Saenko, K., Hardt, M., Levine, S. (eds.) Advances in Neural Information Processing Systems, vol. 36, pp. 49187–49204. Curran Associates, Inc. (2023)
7. Liu, C., He, S., Zhou, Q., Li, S., Meng, W.: Large language model guided knowledge distillation for time series anomaly detection. In: Larson, K. (ed.) Proceedings of the Thirty-Third International Joint Conference on Artificial Intelligence, IJCA 2024, pp. 2162–2170 (2024), main Track
8. Liu, Q., et al.: The elephant in the room: towards a reliable time-series anomaly detection benchmark. In: Zhang, C. (ed.) Advances in Neural Information Processing Systems, vol. 37, pp. 108231–108261. Curran Associates, Inc. (2024)
9. Liu, X., Li, X., Li, Y., Tang, F., Zhao, M.: Rtdetector: deep transformer networks for time series anomaly detection based on reconstruction trend. In: Proceedings of the Thirty-Fourth International Joint Conference on Artificial Intelligence, IJCAI 2025 (2025)
10. Ma, J., Wang, H.: Anomaly detection in sensor data via encoding time series into images. J. King Saud Univ. Comput. Inf. Sci. **36**(10), 102232 (2024)
11. Namura, N., Ichikawa, Y.: Training-free time-series anomaly detection: leveraging image foundation models. arXiv preprint arXiv:2408.14756 (2024)
12. Nawrocki, P., Smendowski, M.: A survey of cloud resource consumption optimization methods. J. Grid Comput. **23**(1), 5 (2025)
13. Ni, J., et al.: Harnessing vision models for time series analysis: a survey. In: Kwok, J. (ed.) Proceedings of the Thirty-Fourth International Joint Conference on Artificial Intelligence, IJCAI 2025, pp. 10612–10620 (2025), survey Track
14. Papa, L., Russo, P., Amerini, I., Zhou, L.: A survey on efficient vision transformers: algorithms, techniques, and performance benchmarking. IEEE Trans. Pattern Anal. Mach. Intell. **46**(12), 7682–7700 (2024)

15. Ribeiro Pereira, R., Bono, J., Ferreira, H., Ribeiro, P., Soares, C., Bizarro, P.: Evaluating transfer learning methods on real-world data streams: a case study in financial fraud detection. In: Joint European Conference on Machine Learning and Knowledge Discovery in Databases, pp. 230–246. Springer, Cham (2025)
16. Rodrigues, N.M., et al.: Plotting time: On the usage of CNNs for time series classification. arXiv preprint arXiv:2102.04179 (2021)
17. Ryan, S., Corizzo, R., Kiringa, I., Japkowicz, N.: Pattern and anomaly localization in complex and dynamic data. In: 18th IEEE International Conference on Machine Learning and Applications (ICMLA), pp. 1756–1763 (2019)
18. Sakurada, M., Yairi, T.: Anomaly detection using autoencoders with nonlinear dimensionality reduction. In: Proceedings of the MLSDA 2014 2nd Workshop on Machine Learning for Sensory Data Analysis, pp. 4–11 (2014)
19. Tang, L., Wang, Z., He, G., Wang, R., Nie, F.: Perturbation guiding contrastive representation learning for time series anomaly detection. In: Proceedings of the 33rd International Joint Conference on Artificial Intelligence, pp. 4955–4963 (2024)
20. Wang, Z., Oates, T.: Imaging time-series to improve classification and imputation. In: Proceedings of the 24th International Conference on Artificial Intelligence, IJCAI 2015, pp. 3939–3945. AAAI Press (2015)
21. Xi, W., Lin, J.: Randomad: a random kernel-based anomaly detector for time series. In: Joint European Conference on Machine Learning and Knowledge Discovery in Databases, pp. 159–175. Springer, Cham (2025)
22. Yan, P., et al.: A comprehensive survey of deep transfer learning for anomaly detection in industrial time series: methods, applications, and directions. IEEE Access **12**, 3768–3789 (2024)
23. Yang, L., Fan, X., Zhang, Z.: Your time series is worth a binary image: machine vision assisted deep framework for time series forecasting. arXiv preprint arXiv:2302.14390 (2023)
24. Zamanzadeh Darban, Z., Webb, G.I., Pan, S., Aggarwal, C., Salehi, M.: Deep learning for time series anomaly detection: a survey. ACM Comput. Surv. **57**(1), 1–42 (2024)
25. Zhang, F., Bales, C., Fleyeh, H.: From time series to image analysis: a transfer learning approach for night setback identification of district heating substations. J. Build. Eng. **43**, 102537 (2021)

Thinking Like a Reviewer: Chain-of-Thought Reasoning for Anomaly Detection in Citation Networks

Weihu Song[1], Mengxiao Zhu[2], Ziyi Liu[1], Lei Li[3], and Haogang Zhu[1,3](✉)

[1] State Key Laboratory of Complex and Critical Software Environment, Beihang University, Beijing, China
{weihusong,haogangzhu}@buaa.edu.cn, lil@mail.zgclab.edu.cn

[2] North China University of Technology, Beijing, China
zhumx@ncut.edu.cn

[3] Zhongguancun Laboratory, Beijing, China
liuzy_99@buaa.edu.cn

Abstract. Graph Anomaly Detection (GAD) on Text-Attributed Graphs (TAGs) has traditionally relied on metric learning, assuming that anomalies are merely geometric outliers in a latent embedding space. However, this paradigm fails to capture logical inconsistencies in complex citation networks, where a valid connection requires semantic entailment rather than just statistical similarity. To bridge this gap, we propose **ReviewerGLM**, a novel generative framework that reformulates GAD as a "peer-review" process. ReviewerGLM introduces a Dual-Stream Architecture that decouples anomaly detection into two distinct reasoning tasks: an Intrinsic Attribute Auditor (utilizing a frozen base Large Language Model (LLM) to detect textual incoherence) and an Extrinsic Structural Reviewer (utilizing a LoRA-tuned adapter to verify citation compatibility). By enforcing a Chain-of-Thought (CoT) mechanism, we compel the model to generate explicit rationales, mimicking a reviewer's critique, before assigning an anomaly score. Theoretically, we prove that this decoupling mitigates knowledge interference between general linguistic capabilities and domain-specific citation logic. Extensive experiments on five real-world datasets demonstrate that ReviewerGLM achieves state-of-the-art performance, improving Average Precision by over 100% on complex benchmarks like PubMed. Furthermore, our egocentric, embarrassingly parallel inference design resolves the Out-Of-Memory (OOM) bottlenecks faced by traditional Graph Neural Networks (GNNs), enabling scalable detection on million-node graphs such as CitationV8. Our code is available at https://github.com/weihus/ReviewerGLM.

Keywords: Graph Anomaly Detection · Text-Attributed Graphs · Large Language Model

Supplementary Information The online version contains supplementary material available at https://doi.org/10.1007/978-3-032-37654-1_4.

M. Ceci et al. (Eds.): ECML PKDD 2026, LNAI 16941, pp. 56–72, 2027.
https://doi.org/10.1007/978-3-032-37654-1_4

1 Introduction

Graph Anomaly Detection (GAD) is pivotal for maintaining the integrity of complex systems. In high-stakes academic environments, represented as Text-Attributed Graphs (TAGs), anomalies are not merely structural outliers but often manifest as logical inconsistencies, such as coercive citations, methodological incompatibilities, or irrelevant references disguised by jargon. While recent works have shown that leveraging textual attributes improves zero-shot performance [6,24], the fundamental paradigm for detecting these anomalies remains constrained by its own geometric assumptions.

The prevailing approach in GAD treats the problem as metric learning in a latent vector space. Existing pipelines, whether using shallow embeddings [23] or deep Transformer-based [28] encoders, operate on the premise that geometric proximity implies validity. However, we argue that this formulation is theoretically insufficient for citation analysis. Logical consistency in scientific discourse is intrinsically non-metric, non-symmetric, and context-dependent. A valid citation implies a directed logical entailment (premise → conclusion) that cannot be faithfully isomorphic to geometric proximity in a fixed-dimensional Euclidean space without catastrophic information loss [8]. Even advanced architectures like cross-encoders fall short here: by optimizing for a scalar similarity score, they effectively marginalize out the verification trace, the step-by-step reasoning required to validate why a connection holds. Consequently, metric-based models inevitably create a "blind spot" for sophistry: they can detect topical outliers but are mathematically incapable of distinguishing a valid extension from a semantic mimic that shares vocabulary but violates logical coherence [12,27,32]. In short, traditional GAD asks "How statistically different is this node?", whereas our framework asks "Can this connection be logically justified?"

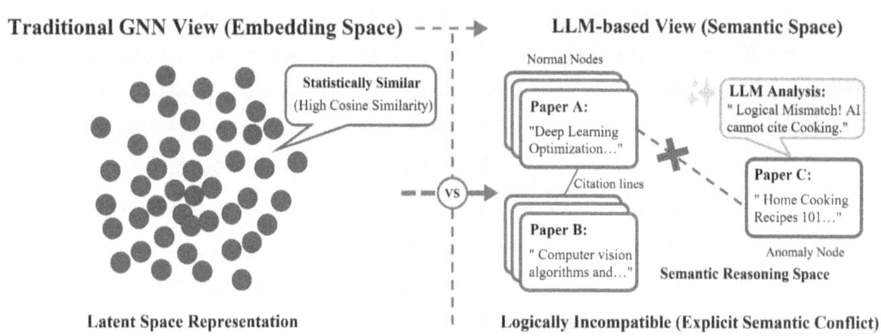

Fig. 1. The Motivation.(Left) Traditional GNN View: Anomalous nodes (e.g., a cooking paper cited by a deep learning paper) become indistinguishable from normal nodes in the embedding space due to message-passing over-smoothing. They appear statistically close.(Right) Our LLM-based View: By treating citation evaluation as a semantic reasoning task, the logical fallacy is explicitly exposed. The LLM acts as a semantic lens, separating anomalies based on content logic rather than vector proximity.

This limitation necessitates a paradigm shift from inductive metric learning to abductive reasoning. An anomaly in a citation network is rarely just a point far from the cluster center; it is a rupture in the narrative logic. As illustrated in Fig. 1, consider a paper on "Adversarial Attacks" citing a "Graph Theory" theorem. A GNN might view these as compatible due to shared vocabulary and structural proximity (Fig. 1, Left). However, a human expert (or "Reviewer") detects the anomaly by recognizing that the cited theorem assumes undirected graphs, whereas the citing paper applies it to directed citation flows–a methodological incompatibility invisible to cosine similarity but glaring in the semantic reasoning space (Fig. 1, Right). Traditional methods, bound by the homophily assumption, lack the expressivity to capture these non-metric contradictions [21].

To bridge this gap, we propose a framework that reformulates GAD on citation networks as a language-mediated reasoning task. We move beyond the "LLM-as-Feature-Extractor" [20] paradigm to a "LLM-as-Reasoning-Engine" approach. We operationalize abductive reasoning as a hypothesis generation process: given a citation edge, our framework tasks the model with constructing a minimal sufficient hypothesis that explains how the cited work supports the specific claim of the citing paper. In this view, an anomaly is rigorously defined not as a statistical outlier, but as a failure of hypothesis generation, where the model, despite its reasoning capability, cannot construct a valid logical bridge between the nodes. This approach introduces a CoT mechanism specifically designed to simulate the Peer-Review Process [2]. By forcing the exposure of hidden contradictions through explicit reasoning traces [10], we transform the detection problem from implicit score regression to explicit consistency verification [14]. Reviewers typically evaluate a paper from two distinct perspectives: (1) Intrinsic Quality: Is the text coherent and scientifically valid? (Attributes); and (2) Extrinsic Logic: Is the citation compatible with the paper's claimed domain? (Structure). Current GNNs mix these signals, but our framework decouples them. In summary, our contributions can be summarized as follows:

- Reviewer-Mimetic Dual-Stream Framework: We propose a novel architecture that decouples anomaly detection into two distinct reasoning streams: an Intrinsic Content Auditor (utilizing the frozen base LLM to detect textual incoherence) and an Extrinsic Logic Reviewer (utilizing a LoRA-tuned adapter to verify citation compatibility).
- Rationale-Aware Instruction Tuning: Unlike "black-box" classifiers, we construct a K-shot instruction tuning dataset that forces the model to generate explicit "Reviewer Analyses" before making a decision, aligning the latent space with human reasoning logic.
- Probabilistic Anomaly Scoring: We introduce a token-level probability scoring mechanism that aggregates uncertainty from both content and structural perspectives, offering a smoother and more robust anomaly ranking than hard-label predictions.

2 Related Work

2.1 Graph Anomaly Detection

Early GAD primarily relied on traditional non-deep learning techniques to identify structural or feature-based outliers. Methods such as LOF [4], SCAN [26], and Radar [15] focused on density, structural clustering, and residual analysis, respectively. While interpretable, these shallow approaches struggle to capture the complex, non-linear correlations inherent in high-dimensional graph data. With the proliferation of deep learning, GNN-based paradigms have emerged, broadly categorized into reconstruction-based and contrastive learning-based approaches. Reconstruction-based methods, pioneered by DOMINANT [7], leverage Graph Autoencoders (GAEs) to flag high reconstruction errors as anomalies. Subsequent works like GAD-NR [22] and MMP [23] have enhanced this by introducing neighborhood reconstruction and multi-view message passing, while GEL [25] incorporates evidential learning to quantify uncertainty. Conversely, contrastive methods like CoLA [18] and AD-GCL [29] learn discriminative representations by maximizing agreement between different graph views or local contexts. Specialized architectures have also emerged, such as TAGCL [5] for propagation trees and CMUCL [28] for TAGs, which aligns raw text with graph topology. Despite their success, existing paradigms fundamentally treat GAD as a metric learning problem. Even advanced multimodal models like CMUCL compress rich textual semantics into fixed-dimensional latent vectors, evaluating anomalies via geometric distances (e.g., cosine similarity).

2.2 Large Language Models for Graphs

To overcome the limitations of metric-based GNNs, recent advancements have shifted towards utilizing LLMs to directly process TAGs. Initial efforts primarily focused on fundamental graph learning tasks, Methods like GAugLLM [9] and GraphIT [13] leverage LLMs to augment graph contrastive learning and optimize prompts for efficient classification, respectively. To better align textual and structural modalities, SKETCH [32] tames language models for TAG learning by decoupling the neighborhood aggregation process. Furthermore, UniGraph [11] and STAG [3] explore unified cross-domain foundation models and quantization strategies for semantic-structural integration. While highly effective for homophilous classification tasks, these general-purpose models are not inherently designed to detect rare, logically incompatible anomalies hidden within text. Consequently, a growing body of literature has begun explicitly exploring LLMs for GAD. One line of work focuses on zero-shot and prompt-based generalist detection: ARC [17] introduces a generalist anomaly detector using in-context learning, while IA-GGAD [31] employs invariant and affinity learning for zero-shot detection. UNPrompt [19] utilizes unified neighborhood prompts, and AnomalyGFM [21] proposes a comprehensive graph foundation model for zero/few-shot GAD scenarios. Another line of research focuses on integrating LLMs to enhance structural fraud and anomaly detection pipelines. DGP [16] introduces a dual-granularity prompting framework, FLAG [30] enhances GNNs with LLM capabilities, and GuARD [20] performs anomaly detection through a text-rich and graph-informed language model. More recently, advanced prompting strategies like CoLL [27] have employed multi-LLM collaboration and evidence-augmented generation to deliberate on complex anomalies. Despite these strides, existing frameworks largely operate under the "LLM-as-Feature-Extractor" paradigm, compressing rich textual information into fixed embeddings that marginalize the step-by-step verification required for logical validation. Furthermore, merging general linguistic understanding and domain-specific structural logic into a single black-box predictor inevitably introduces severe knowledge interference.

3 Preliminaries

In this section, we formally define the core concepts and the specific problem tackled in this work. Matrices and sets are denoted by boldface uppercase letters and calligraphic uppercase letters, respectively.

Definition 1 (Text-Attributed Graph). *A Text-Attributed Graph (TAG) is defined as a graph* $\mathcal{G} = (\mathcal{V}, \mathcal{E}, \mathcal{X})$*, where:*

- $\mathcal{V} = \{v_1, v_2, \dots, v_N\}$ *is the set of* N *nodes, representing entities (e.g., academic papers).*
- $\mathcal{E} \subseteq \mathcal{V} \times \mathcal{V}$ *is the set of edges, representing relationships or logical interactions between nodes (e.g., citation links).*
- $\mathcal{X} = \{X_1, X_2, \dots, X_N\}$ *denotes the set of textual attributes. Unlike traditional graphs where node features are pre-extracted numerical vectors* ($x_i \in \mathbb{R}^d$)*, each* X_i *in a TAG is a raw, variable-length sequence of text tokens (e.g., the abstract and title of a paper) that encapsulates the explicit semantic meaning of node* v_i.

Definition 2 (Text-Attributed Graph Anomaly Detection). *Given a Text-Attributed Graph* $\mathcal{G}$*, the objective of anomaly detection is to learn a scoring function* $f : \mathcal{V} \to [0, 1]$ *that assigns an anomaly probability score* $S(u)$ *to each target node* $u \in \mathcal{V}$*. Specifically, a node* u *is flagged as anomalous if it exhibits either of the following logical ruptures:*

- ***Attribute Anomaly (Intrinsic):*** *The textual content* X_u *contains semantic incoherence, noise, or is completely irrelevant to the global domain distribution.*
- ***Structural Anomaly (Extrinsic):*** *There exists a logical incompatibility or severe topical mismatch between the target node's text* X_u *and the dominant semantic context formed by its egocentric neighborhood* $\mathcal{N}(u) = \{X_v \mid (u, v) \in \mathcal{E}\}$.

The ultimate goal is to rank all nodes based on $S(u)$ such that true anomalies are assigned strictly higher scores than normal nodes, thereby maintaining the semantic integrity of the graph.

4 Methodology

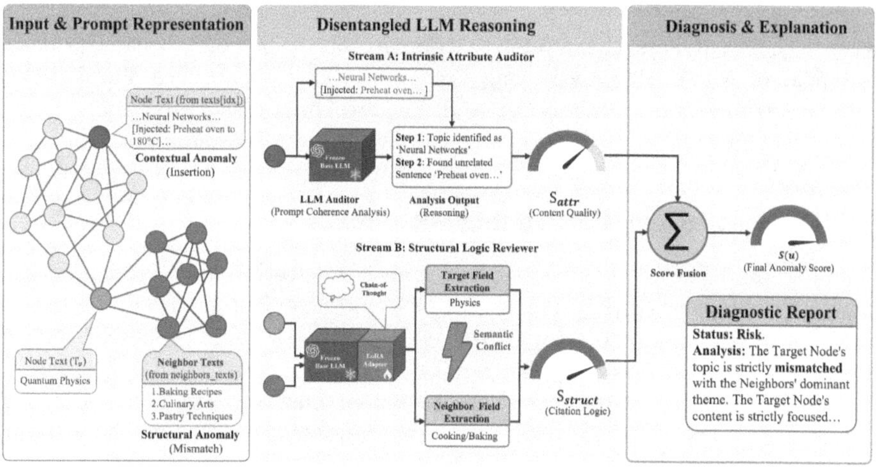

Fig. 2. The architecture of the proposed ReviewerGLM Framework.

We propose **ReviewerGLM**, a generative anomaly detection framework that simulates the peer-review process. Anomalies in TAGs typically manifest in two distinct forms: attribute noise (e.g., incoherent text) and structural inconsistencies (e.g., incompatible citations). Recognizing this dichotomy, we design a dual-stream architecture to address each anomaly type independently. As shown in Fig. 2, the system operates via three phases: (1) Egocentric Context Construction, (2) Hybrid Instruction Tuning, and (3) Dual-View Probabilistic Inference.

4.1 Egocentric Context Construction

Let $\mathcal{G} = (\mathcal{V}, \mathcal{E}, \mathcal{X})$ be the citation network. For a target node u, traditional GNNs aggregate features indiscriminately from k-hop neighborhoods. However, a "Reviewer" focuses on direct evidence. We construct two distinct prompts for each node u:

1. The Intrinsic Attribute Prompt (P_{attr}): Focuses solely on the node's textual content X_u to evaluate its semantic coherence.

$$P_{attr}(u) = \mathcal{T}_{attr}(X_u) \tag{1}$$

where $\mathcal{T}_{attr}$ is a template asking the model to identify if the text is "coherent and relevant" or "noise".

2. The Extrinsic Structural Prompt (P_{struct}): Constructs a citation context to evaluate logical compatibility. We retrieve the 1-hop neighbors $\mathcal{N}(u)$

and truncate the list to a fixed budget K (e.g., $K = 7$) to fit the LLM context window efficiently:

$$P_{struct}(u) = \mathcal{T}_{struct}\left(X_u, \{X_v\}_{v\in\mathcal{N}(u)}\right) \tag{2}$$

Here, $\mathcal{T}_{struct}$ instructs the model to compare the topic of u with the dominant field of $\mathcal{N}(u)$. To handle long academic texts, we apply a simple word-boundary truncation, reducing X_u and X_v into concise representations before prompt assembly.

4.2 Efficient Instruction Tuning with LoRA

To endow the LLM with the capability to discern citation logic (which is often domain-specific), we employ Parameter-Efficient Fine-Tuning (PEFT).

K-Shot Rationale Generation. We construct a small, balanced dataset $\mathcal{D}_{train}$ consisting of K-shot pairs. Unlike standard classification, we enforce a Chain-of-Thought (CoT) format where the model must output an analysis before the label. The complete and exact prompt templates used for all datasets are detailed in **Appendix A.**:

- **Input:** $P_{struct}(u)$
- **Output:** "Analysis: [Reasoning Trace]... Status: [Label]"

For an anomalous edge (e.g., ML paper citing a Cooking recipe), the reasoning trace is explicitly trained to state: "The Target Paper's topic is strictly mismatched with the Neighbors' dominant field".

LoRA Adaptation. We freeze the pre-trained weights Θ_{base} and inject low-rank adaptation matrices $\Delta\Theta$ into the attention layers (query, key, value projections). The training objective minimizes the negative log-likelihood of the completion tokens:

$$\mathcal{L} = -\sum_{(P,Y)\in\mathcal{D}_{train}} \log P(Y|P;\Theta_{base} + \Delta\Theta) \tag{3}$$

This yields a specialized adapter $\Theta_{lora} = \Delta\Theta$ capable of structural reasoning.

4.3 Dual-View Probabilistic Inference

A key innovation of our framework is the Hybrid Inference Strategy, which leverages the distinct strengths of the base and adapted models.

Stream A: Intrinsic Quality Check (via Base Model). Structural anomalies require domain adaptation, but attribute anomalies (e.g., gibberish, incoherent text) are best detected by the generalized knowledge of the frozen base model. We perform inference on $P_{attr}(u)$ using Θ_{base} (disabling LoRA). The anomaly score is strictly defined as the probability of the model generating the

'Risk' token. Specifically, we utilize "Risk" instead of "Anomaly" as the positive class verbalizer because the latter is decomposed into multiple tokens by the tokenizer, whereas "Risk" is a single token, facilitating more stable score calculation:

$$S_{attr}(u) = P(\text{"Risk"} \mid P_{attr}(u); \Theta_{base}) \tag{4}$$

Table 1. Statistics of the datasets used in our experiments.

Dataset	Nodes	Edges	Avg. degree	Features	Anomalies
Cora	2,708	5,429	4.1	1433	114
Citeseer	3,186	3,432	1.08	768	128
PubMed	19,717	90,368	4.58	768	788
ogbn-Arxiv	169,343	1,210,112	7.15	768	6,774
CitationV8	1,106,759	6,396,265	5.77	768	44,270

Stream B: Structural Logic Check (via LoRA Adapter). To detect citation inconsistencies, we perform inference on $P_{struct}(u)$ using the adapted weights $\Theta_{base} + \Theta_{lora}$. The structural anomaly score is derived similarly:

$$S_{struct}(u) = P(\text{"Risk"} \mid P_{struct}(u); \Theta_{base} + \Theta_{lora}) \tag{5}$$

Final Anomaly Scoring. The final anomaly score $S(u)$ is a fusion of the two reviewer perspectives. Since the probabilities represent independent assessments of different anomaly types, we aggregate them:

$$S(u) = S_{attr}(u) + S_{struct}(u) \tag{6}$$

This formulation ensures that a node is flagged if it fails either the content quality check or the citation logic check, effectively covering both attribute and structural anomalies.

5 Experiments

5.1 Experiment Settings

Datasets. To comprehensively evaluate the effectiveness of our proposed method, we conduct experiments on five widely used real-world TAG datasets: Cora, Citeseer, PubMed, ogbn-arxiv, and CitationV8. Since ground-truth anomalies are often unavailable in these benchmarks, we follow the anomaly injection protocol proposed in [28] to generate synthetic anomalies. Specifically, we inject an equal number of structural anomalies and attribute anomalies into the original clean graphs. The detailed statistics of these datasets after injection are summarized in Table 1.

Evaluation Metrics. We adopt two standard metrics to evaluate anomaly detection performance: ROC-AUC and Average Precision (AP). ROC-AUC measures the model's ability to rank anomalies higher than normal nodes, providing a threshold-independent evaluation. AP calculates the area under the Precision-Recall curve, offering a robust performance measure particularly suited for imbalanced datasets where anomalies are sparse.

Baselines. We compare our method with representative approaches from five categories: traditional non-deep learning methods (SCAN [26], LOF [4], Radar [15]); reconstruction-based GAD methods (DOMINANT [7], GAD-NR [22]); contrastive learningbased methods (CoLA [18], AD-GCL [29]); text-attributed graph anomaly detection methods (CMUCL [28]); generalist graph anomaly detection approaches, including both graph-native models (ARC [17], IA-GGAD [31]) and prompt-based LLM-driven methods (UNPrompt [19], AnomalyGFM [21]).

Implementation Details. We implement ReviewerGLM using the PyTorch framework and the Hugging Face ecosystem. Considering the trade-off between reasoning capability and computational efficiency, we utilize a Qwen3-based Large Language Model (specifically the 4B-parameter instruct version) as our backbone. To fit the model within consumer-grade GPU memory, we employ 4-bit Normal Float (NF4) quantization via BitsAndBytes, with compute data type set to float16. For the structural adapter, we configure LoRA with rank $r = 32$, alpha $\alpha = 64$, and a dropout rate of 0.01, targeting all linear projection layers (*q_proj*, *k_proj*, *v_proj*, etc.). While we employ Qwen-based models for our primary evaluation due to their optimal balance of reasoning capability and parameter efficiency, our proposed framework is inherently model-agnostic. The methodology can be seamlessly integrated with other advanced LLMs (e.g., Llama-3, DeepSeek), where we anticipate that stronger base reasoning capabilities would correspondingly yield higher anomaly detection performance. Since graph nodes can contain lengthy academic abstracts, simply concatenating neighbors would exceed the LLM's context window. We employ a length-constrained truncation approach to maintain a maximum sequence length of 2,048 tokens. Specifically, the target node's text is truncated to the first 150 words, and each neighbor's text is limited to 60 words. This ensures that the structural prompt, which includes the target and up to k neighbors, fits comfortably within the context while reserving sufficient space for the generated Chain-of-Thought rationale.

We optimize the model using the AdamW optimizer with a linear scheduler and an effective batch size of 8 (2×4 accumulation steps). For dataset-specific tuning: small-scale graphs (Cora, Citeseer, PubMed) use a $1e-4$ learning rate for 5 epochs, while large-scale graphs (ogbn-arxiv, CitationV8) use $2e-4$ for 3 epochs to accelerate convergence.

For the egocentric context construction, we retrieve $k = 9$ neighbors for the Cora dataset and $k = 7$ neighbors for all other datasets (Citeseer, PubMed, ogbn-arxiv, CitationV8) to balance context richness and noise. Regarding the few-shot instruction tuning, we use $K = 4$ shots for Cora due to its smaller class size, and $K = 64$ shots for the remaining datasets. All experiments are conducted on a server equipped with NVIDIA RTX PRO 6000 Blackwell (96GB) GPUs. To ensure statistical robustness, we report the average performance across five independent runs using distinct random seeds.

5.2 Result and Analysis

Table 2. Experimental results for anomaly detection on eight datasets (OOM: CPU/CUDA Out of Memory). We report both mean AUC and AP, alongside the standard deviation. **Bold** represents the optimal in the unsupervised method, and underlined represents the runner-up.

Method	Cora		Citeseer		Pubmed		ogbn-Arxiv		CitationV8	
	AUC	AP	AUC	AP	AUC	AP	AUC	AP	AUC	AP
LOF	$54.24_{\pm 0.00}$	$5.01_{\pm 0.00}$	$51.15_{\pm 0.00}$	$3.94_{\pm 0.00}$	$63.97_{\pm 0.00}$	$8.01_{\pm 0.00}$	$72.25_{\pm 0.00}$	$20.23_{\pm 0.00}$	$61.87_{\pm 0.00}$	$6.21_{\pm 0.00}$
SCAN	$68.45_{\pm 0.00}$	$7.53_{\pm 0.00}$	$72.61_{\pm 0.00}$	$17.25_{\pm 0.00}$	$55.96_{\pm 0.00}$	$4.55_{\pm 0.00}$	$60.33_{\pm 0.00}$	$6.12_{\pm 0.00}$	$61.58_{\pm 0.00}$	$19.98_{\pm 0.00}$
Radar	$53.38_{\pm 0.00}$	$4.57_{\pm 0.00}$	$75.09_{\pm 0.00}$	$40.48_{\pm 0.00}$	$50.67_{\pm 0.00}$	$3.88_{\pm 0.00}$	OOM	OOM	OOM	OOM
DOMINANT	$76.68_{\pm 0.00}$	$18.95_{\pm 0.00}$	$65.83_{\pm 0.01}$	$\underline{52.78_{\pm 0.00}}$	$66.64_{\pm 0.00}$	$6.47_{\pm 0.00}$	OOM	OOM	OOM	OOM
GAD-NR	$75.98_{\pm 0.01}$	$19.47_{\pm 0.00}$	$73.85_{\pm 0.00}$	$52.77_{\pm 0.01}$	$65.90_{\pm 0.00}$	$6.37_{\pm 0.00}$	$64.83_{\pm 0.00}$	$6.72_{\pm 0.00}$	$62.35_{\pm 0.00}$	$6.89_{\pm 0.00}$
CoLA	$56.28_{\pm 0.00}$	$5.26_{\pm 0.00}$	$73.22_{\pm 0.01}$	$12.61_{\pm 0.01}$	$74.40_{\pm 0.00}$	$11.62_{\pm 0.00}$	$76.73_{\pm 0.00}$	$12.89_{\pm 0.00}$	OOM	OOM
AD-GCL	$64.97_{\pm 0.01}$	$7.63_{\pm 0.01}$	$76.20_{\pm 0.02}$	$26.00_{\pm 0.02}$	$63.18_{\pm 0.01}$	$7.01_{\pm 0.00}$	OOM	OOM	OOM	OOM
ARC	$74.45_{\pm 0.19}$	$31.78_{\pm 0.66}$	$78.81_{\pm 0.02}$	$19.43_{\pm 0.54}$	$79.14_{\pm 0.02}$	$27.20_{\pm 0.66}$	OOM	OOM	OOM	OOM
IA-GGAD	$77.85_{\pm 0.01}$	$23.72_{\pm 0.03}$	$73.78_{\pm 0.00}$	$50.86_{\pm 0.00}$	$74.74_{\pm 0.00}$	$16.87_{\pm 0.00}$	OOM	OOM	OOM	OOM
UNPrompt	$73.66_{\pm 0.42}$	$\underline{35.39_{\pm 0.66}}$	$67.49_{\pm 0.09}$	$12.13_{\pm 0.18}$	$73.25_{\pm 0.10}$	$14.50_{\pm 0.55}$	OOM	OOM	OOM	OOM
AnomalyGFM	$55.65_{\pm 0.01}$	$5.73_{\pm 0.01}$	$74.21_{\pm 0.01}$	$50.30_{\pm 0.02}$	$55.43_{\pm 0.02}$	$5.37_{\pm 0.00}$	OOM	OOM	OOM	OOM
CMUCL	$77.15_{\pm 0.01}$	$19.20_{\pm 0.03}$	$80.94_{\pm 0.02}$	$32.36_{\pm 0.01}$	$\underline{81.50_{\pm 0.00}}$	$31.45_{\pm 0.00}$	$84.67_{\pm 0.00}$	$40.52_{\pm 0.00}$	$\underline{83.03_{\pm 0.02}}$	$\underline{42.58_{\pm 0.01}}$
ReviewerGLM(zero-shots)	$\underline{80.29_{\pm 0.02}}$	$29.74_{\pm 0.05}$	$\underline{94.92_{\pm 0.00}}$	$46.59_{\pm 0.04}$	$79.07_{\pm 0.01}$	$\underline{43.17_{\pm 0.04}}$	$\underline{90.27_{\pm 0.00}}$	$\underline{50.67_{\pm 0.00}}$	$92.13_{\pm 0.01}$	$48.46_{\pm 0.02}$
ReviewerGLM	$\mathbf{94.12}_{\pm 0.02}$	$\mathbf{37.31}_{\pm 0.05}$	$\mathbf{98.94}_{\pm 0.00}$	$\mathbf{65.04}_{\pm 0.04}$	$\mathbf{96.77}_{\pm 0.01}$	$\mathbf{71.30}_{\pm 0.04}$	$\mathbf{98.46}_{\pm 0.00}$	$\mathbf{81.17}_{\pm 0.00}$	$\mathbf{97.20}_{\pm 0.00}$	$\mathbf{69.37}_{\pm 0.00}$

The quantitative performance of ReviewerGLM compared with twelve baseline methods across five datasets is systematically summarized in Table 2. The results reveal several critical insights regarding the effectiveness of our "Reviewer-Mimetic" framework.

ReviewerGLM consistently achieves the state-of-the-art performance across all datasets. The advantage is particularly pronounced on the more challenging PubMed and ogbn-Arxiv datasets, where semantic reasoning is crucial. Specifically, in terms of AP, which is more sensitive to the ranking quality in imbalanced anomaly detection tasks, our method outperforms the strongest baseline (CMUCL) by a substantial margin. On PubMed, ReviewerGLM improves AP by over **126%** (from 31.45% to 71.30%), and on ogbn-Arxiv, it doubles the precision of the nearest competitor (from 40.52% to 81.17%). This indicates that while traditional methods struggle to distinguish subtle semantic inconsistencies, our logic-driven approach effectively identifies high-confidence anomalies.

A significant observation from Table 2 is the scalability bottleneck faced by existing GAD approaches. As the graph size increases to millions of edges (e.g., ogbn-Arxiv and CitationV8), advanced GNN-based methods (e.g., DOMINANT, ARC, IA-GGAD) and even recent prompt-based methods (UNPrompt, AnomalyGFM) encounter Out-of-Memory (OOM) failures. These failures stem from their reliance on full-graph message passing or expensive global attention mechanisms. In contrast, ReviewerGLM adopts an egocentric retrieval mechanism with bounded text truncation, allowing it to scale efficiently to massive networks like CitationV8 without memory overflow, while maintaining an exceptional AUC of 97.20%. This proves that our "1-hop reasoning" design is not only logically sound but also computationally distinct for large-scale deployment.

The comparison between ReviewerGLM(zero-shot) and the full ReviewerGLM validates our dual-stream hypothesis. The zero-shot variant, relying solely on the frozen base LLM, already surpasses many supervised baselines (e.g., SCAN, Radar) on Cora and Citeseer (achieving 94.92% AUC). This confirms that the base model possesses strong intrinsic capabilities for detecting attribute noise (Stream A). However, the full model achieves significantly higher performance (e.g., +14% AUC on Cora), demonstrating that the "Structural Logic Reviewer" (Stream B), enabled by LoRA tuning, is indispensable for capturing domain-specific citation logic that general linguistic knowledge alone cannot resolve.

5.3 Ablation Study

Table 3. Performance (AUC in %) with standard deviation of ReviewerGLM and its variants, bold represents the global optimal.

Method	Cora		Citeseer		Pubmed		ogbn-Arxiv		Avg.	
	AUC	AP	AUC	AP	AUC	AP	AUC	AP	AUC	AP
Attribute only	$71.76_{\pm 0.01}$	$29.19_{\pm 0.01}$	$68.25_{\pm 0.01}$	$24.72_{\pm 0.00}$	$74.39_{\pm 0.01}$	$49.28_{\pm 0.00}$	$74.78_{\pm 0.00}$	$47.65_{\pm 0.00}$	$72.30_{\pm 0.01}$ ($\downarrow_{24.77}$)	$37.71_{\pm 0.01}$ ($\downarrow_{26.00}$)
Structure (w/o SFT)	$67.68_{\pm 0.00}$	$9.65_{\pm 0.00}$	$90.45_{\pm 0.00}$	$42.34_{\pm 0.00}$	$66.03_{\pm 0.00}$	$9.85_{\pm 0.00}$	$81.01_{\pm 0.00}$	$21.93_{\pm 0.00}$	$76.29_{\pm 0.00}$ ($\downarrow_{20.78}$)	$20.94_{\pm 0.00}$ ($\downarrow_{42.77}$)
Structure (w/ SFT)	$92.40_{\pm 0.03}$	$36.68_{\pm 0.02}$	$97.01_{\pm 0.01}$	$\mathbf{71.13}_{\pm 0.09}$	$93.20_{\pm 0.01}$	$64.66_{\pm 0.04}$	$96.82_{\pm 0.01}$	$79.06_{\pm 0.05}$	$94.86_{\pm 0.02}$ ($\downarrow_{2.12}$)	$62.88_{\pm 0.05}$ ($\downarrow_{0.83}$)
w/o CoT	$81.64_{\pm 0.02}$	$27.27_{\pm 0.03}$	$87.91_{\pm 0.01}$	$27.51_{\pm 0.02}$	$82.74_{\pm 0.00}$	$48.84_{\pm 0.01}$	$90.83_{\pm 0.00}$	$51.89_{\pm 0.00}$	$85.78_{\pm 0.01}$ ($\downarrow_{11.29}$)	$38.88_{\pm 0.02}$ ($\downarrow_{24.83}$)
w/o Neighbor Topic	$75.38_{\pm 0.02}$	$17.24_{\pm 0.03}$	$89.77_{\pm 0.01}$	$30.32_{\pm 0.02}$	$77.55_{\pm 0.00}$	$41.24_{\pm 0.00}$	$78.89_{\pm 0.00}$	$45.35_{\pm 0.00}$	$80.40_{\pm 0.01}$ ($\downarrow_{16.67}$)	$33.54_{\pm 0.01}$ ($\downarrow_{30.17}$)
w/o Examples	$77.61_{\pm 0.02}$	$17.80_{\pm 0.02}$	$93.76_{\pm 0.01}$	$35.97_{\pm 0.02}$	$76.74_{\pm 0.00}$	$40.30_{\pm 0.00}$	$89.49_{\pm 0.00}$	$47.46_{\pm 0.00}$	$84.40_{\pm 0.01}$ ($\downarrow_{12.67}$)	$35.38_{\pm 0.01}$ ($\downarrow_{28.33}$)
w/o Analysis Field	$81.26_{\pm 0.02}$	$18.68_{\pm 0.01}$	$90.88_{\pm 0.00}$	$25.66_{\pm 0.01}$	$82.26_{\pm 0.00}$	$49.31_{\pm 0.01}$	$88.96_{\pm 0.00}$	$48.37_{\pm 0.00}$	$85.84_{\pm 0.01}$ ($\downarrow_{11.23}$)	$35.51_{\pm 0.01}$ ($\downarrow_{28.20}$)
Full	$\mathbf{94.12}_{\pm 0.02}$	$\mathbf{37.31}_{\pm 0.05}$	$\mathbf{98.94}_{\pm 0.00}$	$65.04_{\pm 0.04}$	$\mathbf{96.77}_{\pm 0.01}$	$\mathbf{71.30}_{\pm 0.04}$	$\mathbf{98.46}_{\pm 0.00}$	$\mathbf{81.17}_{\pm 0.00}$	$\mathbf{97.07}_{\pm 0.01}$	$\mathbf{63.71}_{\pm 0.03}$

To validate the effectiveness of the proposed ReviewerGLM, we conduct a comprehensive ablation study focusing on two perspectives: the impact of the dual-stream architecture and the efficacy of the "Reviewer-Mimetic" prompt design. The experimental results are presented in Table 3.

Impact of Dual-Stream Architecture. We evaluate the contribution of each reasoning stream using three variants: (1) Attribute only, which utilizes only the anomaly score from the frozen base model (Stream A); (2) Structure (w/o SFT), which uses the base model's structural score without instruction tuning; and (3) Structure (w/ SFT), which uses the structural score from the LoRA-tuned adapter (Stream B). As shown in Table 3, the Full model consistently outperforms all single-stream variants. Notably, the Attribute only variant suffers a significant performance drop (Avg. AP $\downarrow$ 26.00%), confirming that text coherence alone is insufficient to detect complex citation anomalies. Furthermore, while Structure (w/ SFT) achieves competitive results, it still lags behind the Full model (Avg. AP ↓ 0.83%). This indicates that the Attribute stream acts as a crucial safety net for detecting "intrinsic" anomalies (e.g., noise) that the structural adapter might overlook. Crucially, the massive gap between Structure (w/ SFT) and Structure (w/o SFT) (Avg. AP 62.88% vs. 20.94%) demonstrates that general LLMs lack the innate ability to verify citation logic, making our domain-specific instruction tuning indispensable.

Effectiveness of Prompt Designs. We further analyze the "Chain-of-Thought" prompt components by removing key instructions:

- **w/o CoT:** Removing the explicit "Step-by-step" reasoning instructions.
- **w/o Neighbor Topic:** Removing the instruction to extract the "dominant topic of neighbors".
- **w/o Examples:** Removing the few-shot positive/negative compatibility examples.
- **w/o Analysis Field:** Removing the constraint to generate the "Analysis": field before the final label.

The results in Table 3 reveal that every component is vital. The most severe drop occurs in w/o Neighbor Topic (Avg. AP ↓ 30.17%), validating our core hypothesis that citation validity is fundamentally a comparison between the target node and its neighborhood context. Additionally, removing the reasoning enforcement mechanisms–either the guidance (w/o CoT) or the output constraint (w/o Analysis Field)–leads to substantial performance degradation (Avg. AP ↓ 24.83% and ↓ 28.20%, respectively). This proves that forcing the model to explicitly verbalize its rationale ("thinking before judging") significantly improves the reliability of the anomaly detection process compared to direct "black-box" classification.

5.4 Parameter Study

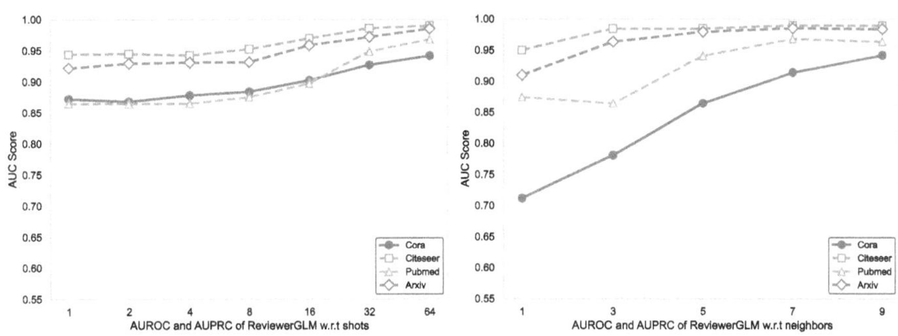

(a) shots numbers (b) neighbors numbers

Fig. 3. Sensitivity analysis for the trade-off parameter shots and number of sampling rounds neighbors w.r.t. AUC.

We investigate the sensitivity of ReviewerGLM to two critical hyperparameters: the number of retrieved neighbors (k) in the egocentric context and the number of shots (K) used for instruction tuning. We conduct experiments on four representative datasets (Cora, Citeseer, PubMed, ogbn-Arxiv) and report the AUC performance. The trends are illustrated in Fig. 3.

Impact of Neighbor Count (k). The number of neighbors determines the richness of the structural context provided to the LLM. We vary k in the range $\{1, 3, 5, 7, 9\}$. As observed in the results:

- **Context Necessity:** Increasing k from 1 to 5 yields substantial performance gains across all datasets. For instance, on Cora, the AUC surges from 0.7114 ($k = 1$) to 0.8640 ($k = 5$). This confirms our hypothesis that single-node attributes alone are insufficient, and multi-hop structural evidence is essential for verifying citation logic.
- **Noise-Information Trade-off:** Performance generally peaks at $k = 7$ for larger datasets like PubMed (0.9677) and ogbn-Arxiv (0.9846), and slightly declines or stabilizes at $k = 9$. This suggests that introducing too many neighbors may dilute the core reasoning with irrelevant connections (semantic drift). However, Cora is an exception, where performance continues to improve up to $k = 9$ (0.9413), likely due to its sparser graph structure requiring wider aggregation to capture sufficient semantic signals.

Based on these observations, we set $k = 9$ for Cora and $k = 7$ for the other datasets to balance context sufficiency and noise robustness.

Impact of Shot Count (K). We analyze how the number of instruction-tuning examples affects the model's ability to learn the "Reviewer" persona, varying K from 1 to 64. The results indicate a clear positive correlation:

- **Few-Shot Effectiveness:** Even with very few examples ($K = 1 \sim 4$), ReviewerGLM achieves respectable performance (e.g., > 0.94 AUC on Citeseer), demonstrating the base LLM's strong zero-shot reasoning potential.
- **Scaling Benefits:** As K increases to 64, the model consistently refines its boundary for anomaly detection. PubMed and ogbn-Arxiv show the most significant gains (e.g., PubMed improves from 0.8643 at $K = 1$ to 0.9677 at $K = 64$). This verifies that providing more diverse "reasoning logic" examples helps the LoRA adapter better align with the complex, domain-specific citation patterns present in large-scale scientific networks.

5.5 Complexity Analysis

We analyze the computational complexity of ReviewerGLM from both temporal and spatial perspectives, highlighting its theoretical advantages in parallelization compared to traditional message-passing GNNs.

Time Complexity and Parallelization. Let N be the number of nodes in the graph. The inference process of ReviewerGLM consists of two independent streams: the Attribute Stream (Stream A) and the Structural Stream (Stream B). Unlike GNNs, where the computation of a node depends on the recursive aggregation of its neighbors' latent embeddings (often requiring layer-wise synchronization), our framework treats each node's evaluation as an independent generative task.

- **Decoupled Latency:** Since Stream A and Stream B operate on distinct prompts (P_{attr} and P_{struct}), they can be executed in parallel on separate hardware resources. The system latency is thus determined by the bottleneck stream: $\mathcal{T}_{total} \approx \max(\mathcal{T}_{attr}, \mathcal{T}_{struct})$. Given that P_{struct} involves longer context (neighbors' text) and LoRA computation, $\mathcal{T}_{struct}$ is the dominant term.
- **Embarrassingly Parallel Inference:** The core advantage of our egocentric design is that the inference for any node u is statistically independent of node v. Theoretically, given infinite compute nodes, the time complexity for processing the entire graph becomes $O(1)$ relative to the graph size N. Practically, this allows for perfect linear scaling: we can arbitrarily increase the batch size B or the number of GPUs without the communication overhead or "boundary value" problems that plague distributed GNN training.

Space Complexity and Memory Efficiency. Standard GNNs (e.g., GCN, GAT) typically require storing the entire adjacency matrix and node feature matrix in GPU memory to perform matrix multiplications, leading to a space complexity of $O(N + E)$, where E is the number of edges. This causes the Out-Of-Memory (OOM) failures observed in our baselines on CitationV8 [1]. In contrast, ReviewerGLM processes nodes in mini-batches of textual tokens. The GPU memory consumption depends solely on the batch size B, the context length L, and the model parameters Θ:

$$\mathcal{M}_{GPU} \approx |\Theta| + O(B \times L) \tag{7}$$

Since L is capped (e.g., 2048 tokens) and neighbors are retrieved from CPU memory (RAM) on-the-fly, the GPU memory requirement is constant with respect to the graph size N. This $O(1)$ spatial scalability enables our model to handle billion-scale graphs like CitationV8 on a single consumer-grade GPU, provided the inference is batched.

5.6 Qualitative Analysis

To provide a more intuitive understanding of how ReviewerGLM operates, we conduct further qualitative analyses. Due to space constraints, we present provides a detailed *Case Study* in the **Appendix B**, illustrating the specific step-by-step reasoning traces (CoT) generated by our model when successfully catching a logically incompatible citation.

6 Conclusion

In this work, we challenged the prevailing geometric assumptions in Graph Anomaly Detection by proposing **ReviewerGLM**, a generative framework that simulates the cognitive process of a human reviewer. By shifting the paradigm from "distance measurement" to "logical reasoning", we demonstrated that anomalies in citation networks are better identified through explicit semantic verification rather than latent vector proximity. Our core contribution, the Dual-Stream Architecture, successfully reconciles the tension between general knowledge retention and domain-specific adaptation. We showed that freezing the base LLM is crucial for detecting intrinsic attribute noise, while a lightweight LoRA adapter is necessary and sufficient for capturing extrinsic structural inconsistencies. Empirically, ReviewerGLM not only establishes new state-of-the-art results on standard benchmarks but also exhibits superior scalability. The proposed ego-centric inference mechanism eliminates the dependency on full-graph message passing, allowing for $O(1)$ memory scaling and infinite parallelization potential. Future work will explore these cross-domain adaptations, alongside extending the paradigm to multi-hop reasoning chains. Furthermore, we acknowledge that our current length-constrained truncation may inadvertently discard critical contributions located at the end of abstracts. Future iterations could leverage smaller, efficient LLMs to dynamically summarize node attributes rather than relying on hard word boundaries. Finally, while our current model compares global abstracts, true logical entailment is often highly localized. Integrating exact, sentence-level citation contexts from the full text–while balancing the inherent scalability trade-offs–remains a promising avenue to further enhance graph integrity systems.

Acknowledgments. This work is supported by National Cyber Security-National Science and Technology Major Project under Grant 2025ZD1501002, and by China Grid Shandong Province Technology Grant, SGSDZZ00FZJS2501131.

References

1. Ackley, D.H., Hinton, G.E., Sejnowski, T.J.: A learning algorithm for Boltzmann machines. Cogn. Sci. **9**(1), 147–169 (1985)
2. Aly, A., Mansour, E., Youssef, A.: OCR-APT: reconstructing apt stories from audit logs using subgraph anomaly detection and LLMs. In: Proceedings of the 2025 ACM SIGSAC Conference on Computer and Communications Security, pp. 261–275 (2025)
3. Bo, J., Wu, H., Fang, Y.: Quantizing text-attributed graphs for semantic-structural integration. In: Proceedings of the 31st ACM SIGKDD Conference on Knowledge Discovery and Data Mining, vol. 2, pp. 107–118 (2025)
4. Breunig, M.M., Kriegel, H.P., Ng, R.T., Sander, J.: LoF: identifying density-based local outliers. In: Proceedings of the 2000 ACM SIGMOD International Conference on Management of Data, pp. 93–104 (2000)
5. Cui, C., Jia, C.: Propagation tree is not deep: adaptive graph contrastive learning approach for rumor detection. In: Proceedings of the AAAI Conference on Artificial Intelligence, vol. 38, pp. 73–81 (2024)

6. Dai, X., et al.: How do large language models understand graph patterns? A benchmark for graph pattern comprehension. In: Yue, Y., Garg, A., Peng, N., Sha, F., Yu, R. (eds.) International Conference on Learning Representations, vol. 2025, pp. 58405–58435 (2025)
7. Ding, K., Li, J., Bhanushali, R., Liu, H.: Deep anomaly detection on attributed networks. In: Proceedings of the 2019 SIAM International Conference on Data Mining, pp. 594–602. SIAM (2019)
8. Fan, X., et al.: Enhancing foundation models in transaction understanding with LLM-based sentence embeddings. In: Proceedings of the 2025 Conference on Empirical Methods in Natural Language Processing: Industry Track, pp. 903–911 (2025)
9. Fang, Y., Fan, D., Zha, D., Tan, Q.: Gaugllm: improving graph contrastive learning for text-attributed graphs with large language models. In: Proceedings of the 30th ACM SIGKDD Conference on Knowledge Discovery and Data Mining, pp. 747–758 (2024)
10. He, X., Bresson, X., Laurent, T., Perold, A., LeCun, Y., Hooi, B.: Harnessing explanations: LLM-to-LM interpreter for enhanced text-attributed graph representation learning. In: Kim, B., Yue, Y., Chaudhuri, S., Fragkiadaki, K., Khan, M., Sun, Y. (eds.) International Conference on Learning Representations, vol. 2024, pp. 5711–5732 (2024)
11. He, Y., Sui, Y., He, X., Hooi, B.: Unigraph: learning a unified cross-domain foundation model for text-attributed graphs. In: Proceedings of the 31st ACM SIGKDD Conference on Knowledge Discovery and Data Mining, vol. 1, pp. 448–459 (2025)
12. Huang, T., Wang, Y., Li, Q., He, C., Gao, J.: Can LLMs find fraudsters? Multi-level LLM enhanced graph fraud detection. In: Proceedings of the 33rd ACM International Conference on Multimedia, pp. 1530–1538 (2025)
13. Khoshraftar, S., Abedini, N., Hajian, A.: Graphit: efficient node classification on text-attributed graphs with prompt optimized LLMs. In: Companion Proceedings of the ACM on Web Conference 2025, pp. 1824–1829 (2025)
14. Kong, L., et al.: Gofa: a generative one-for-all model for joint graph language modeling. In: The Thirteenth International Conference on Learning Representations (2025)
15. Li, J., Dani, H., Hu, X., Liu, H.: Radar: residual analysis for anomaly detection in attributed networks. In: IJCAI, vol. 17, pp. 2152–2158 (2017)
16. Li, Y., Hu, J., Hooi, B., He, B., Chen, C.: DGP: a dual-granularity prompting framework for fraud detection with graph-enhanced LLMs. arXiv preprint arXiv:2507.21653 (2025)
17. Liu, Y., Li, S., Zheng, Y., Chen, Q., Zhang, C., Pan, S.: Arc: a generalist graph anomaly detector with in-context learning. Adv. Neural. Inf. Process. Syst. **37**, 50772–50804 (2024)
18. Liu, Y., Li, Z., Pan, S., Gong, C., Zhou, C., Karypis, G.: Anomaly detection on attributed networks via contrastive self-supervised learning. IEEE Trans. Neural Netw. Learn. Syst. **33**(6), 2378–2392 (2021)
19. Niu, C., Qiao, H., Chen, C., Chen, L., Pang, G.: Zero-shot generalist graph anomaly detection with unified neighborhood prompts. In: Proceedings of the Thirty-Fourth International Joint Conference on Artificial Intelligence, pp. 3226–3234 (2025)
20. Pang, Y., Chen, B., Zhang, F., Rao, Y., Kharlamov, E., Tang, J.: Guard: Effective anomaly detection through a text-rich and graph-informed language model. In: Proceedings of the 31st ACM SIGKDD Conference on Knowledge Discovery and Data Mining, vol. 2, pp. 2222–2233 (2025)

21. Qiao, H., Niu, C., Chen, L., Pang, G.: Anomalygfm: graph foundation model for zero/few-shot anomaly detection. In: Proceedings of the 31st ACM SIGKDD Conference on Knowledge Discovery and Data Mining, vol. 2, pp. 2326–2337 (2025)
22. Roy, A., et al.: Gad-NR: graph anomaly detection via neighborhood reconstruction. In: Proceedings of the 17th ACM International Conference on Web Search and Data Mining, pp. 576–585 (2024)
23. Song, W., Li, L., Zhu, M., Pei, Y., Zhu, H.: MMP: enhancing unsupervised graph anomaly detection with multi-view message passing. Pattern Recogn. 112388 (2025)
24. Wang, H., Liu, S., Wei, R., Li, P.: Model generalization on text attribute graphs: principles with large language models. arXiv preprint arXiv:2502.11836 (2025)
25. Wei, C., et al.: Graph evidential learning for anomaly detection. In: Proceedings of the 31st ACM SIGKDD Conference on Knowledge Discovery and Data Mining, vol. 2, pp. 3122–3133 (2025)
26. Xu, X., Yuruk, N., Feng, Z., Schweiger, T.A.: Scan: a structural clustering algorithm for networks. In: Proceedings of the 13th ACM SIGKDD International Conference on Knowledge Discovery and Data Mining, pp. 824–833 (2007)
27. Xu, Y., et al.: Court of LLMs: evidence-augmented generation via multi-LLM collaboration for text-attributed graph anomaly detection. In: Proceedings of the 33rd ACM International Conference on Multimedia, pp. 2437–2446 (2025)
28. Xu, Y., et al.: Text-attributed graph anomaly detection via multi-scale cross-and uni-modal contrastive learning. In: 28th European Conference on Artificial Intelligence, ECAI 2025, Including 14th Conference on Prestigious Applications of Intelligent Systems, PAIS 2025, pp. 2706–2713. IOS Press BV (2025)
29. Xu, Y., et al.: Revisiting graph contrastive learning on anomaly detection: a structural imbalance perspective. In: Proceedings of the AAAI Conference on Artificial Intelligence, vol. 39, pp. 12972–12980 (2025)
30. Yang, C., Liu, H., Wang, D., Zhang, Z., Yang, C., Shi, C.: Flag: fraud detection with LLM-enhanced graph neural network. In: Proceedings of the 31st ACM SIGKDD Conference on Knowledge Discovery and Data Mining, vol. 2, pp. 5150–5160 (2025)
31. Zhang, X., He, Z., Fu, C., Xie, C.: IA-GGAD: zero-shot generalist graph anomaly detection via invariant and affinity learning. In: The Thirty-Ninth Annual Conference on Neural Information Processing Systems (2025)
32. Zhou, C., et al.: Taming language models for text-attributed graph learning with decoupled aggregation. In: Proceedings of the 63rd Annual Meeting of the Association for Computational Linguistics (Volume 1: Long Papers), pp. 3463–3474 (2025)

Unsupervised Anomaly Detection of Information Operations Users via Behavioral and Language Patterns

Sishun Liu[1], Sajal Halder[1], Ke Deng[1], Yan Wang[2], and Xiuzhen Zhang[1](✉)

[1] RMIT University, Melbourne, VIC 3000, Australia
sishun.liu@student.rmit.edu.au,
{sajal.halder,ke.deng,xiuzhen.zhang}@rmit.edu.au
[2] Macquarie University, Sydney, NSW 2000, Australia
yan.wang@mq.edu.au

Abstract. *Information Operations (IOs)* on *Social Networks (SNs)* have been identified as a significant threat to democracy and modern society, but they are challenging and expensive to detect by humans. Existing supervised IO detection methods fail to capture the dynamic nature of evolving IO user behavior, while existing unsupervised approaches rely on oversimplified assumptions of coordination among IO users that may not exist in practice. To overcome the limitations of existing methods, we formulate IO user detection as an anomaly detection problem and propose a novel unsupervised IO user detection approach called *Temporal-bEhavior-laNguage Signals for information*, which leverages multimodal data, including temporal online user behavior, such as message posting activities, and the textual content of the messages. The motivation is that IO users are typically a very small fraction of all online users and have unique temporal behavioral and language patterns. Specifically, we train a *Temporal Point Process (TPP)* to capture abnormal temporal behavioral patterns of IO users because they are known to behave in a coordinated manner for IO campaigns. We further introduce a novel *evidence function* that converts LLM responses, which are generated from user post timelines, into quantitative scores to adjust the TPP outputs for better IO user detection. Experimental results show that TENSOR outperforms the baselines on five real-world IO datasets (Code is available at https://github.com/xiuzhenzhang/TENSOR).

Keywords: Information Operation User Detection · Temporal Point Process · Large Language Model

1 Introduction

The development of *Social Networks (SNs)* enables fast dissemination of critical information, large-scale discussions, and joint actions about political and social issues because SNs connect people [6]. However, the capabilities of SNs can

M. Ceci et al. (Eds.): ECML PKDD 2026, LNAI 16941, pp. 73–90, 2027.
https://doi.org/10.1007/978-3-032-37654-1_5

be misused by *Information Operations (IOs)*, especially state-sponsored ones. IOs are organized attempts to tamper with the regular flow of information and influence public opinion through disinformation, hate speech, and other harmful content. IOs are hard to detect because they are always initiated by a small group of users [28,37]. With targets including narrative manipulation and the fostering of division in online and real-world communities, IOs have been identified as a significant threat to democracy, and the need for robust methods to detect these operations is urgent [7].

Researchers have proposed IO detection approaches to identify whether individual posts or specific users are related to an IO. The following discussion focuses on the detection of IO users, which is the primary interest of this study. *IO users* are motivated or incentivized to promote IOs, while legitimate organic users are called *control users*. IO user detection approaches use patterns within user post timelines on SNs. These patterns can be categorized as *behavioral patterns* (specifically, *temporal* behavioral patterns because they describe the user activities on SNs over time) and *language patterns*, including speaking style and areas of interest.

IO user detection is challenging. The biggest challenge is the generalization capability of IO user detection algorithms, *i.e.*, their ability to detect unseen IOs. In the wild, IOs evolve quickly, so existing labeled IO datasets always lag. This means that existing supervised [1,6,18] and semi-supervised [2,20,31,36] IO user detection methods suffer from a generalization issue, *i.e.*, they cannot detect new, unseen IOs. Recent zero-shot LLM approaches [17] provide an unsupervised alternative, but their ability to capture complex temporal behavioral dynamics is still limited.

This paper formulates IO user detection as an unsupervised anomaly detection problem and proposes a novel approach, called *Temporal-bEhavior-laNguage Signals for information Operation Recognition (TENSOR)*, to use behavioral and language patterns from user post timelines for unsupervised IO user detection. Training anomaly detection models on IO data is difficult because the training data, which are supposed to consist of timelines of control users, are contaminated by IO users. This harms the performance of IO user detection models. To mitigate this issue, we use language patterns. Specifically, first, we train a *Temporal Point Process (TPP)* on the contaminated data to identify IO users based on abnormal behavioral patterns, such as coordinated behavior among different IO accounts, which are commonly observed among IO users but rare among control users. A TPP is a well-defined stochastic process over temporal event sequences [4]. Researchers have used the process to achieve state-of-the-art performance in unsupervised identification of abnormal event sequences from normal ones [29] and outlier events from normal events [16]. Second, we propose a novel *evidence function* to adjust TPP inference. This function converts LLM responses, which are generated from user post timelines, into quantitative scores that refine the TPP output for better IO user detection. Experimental results show that TENSOR outperforms other baselines by a significant margin on five real-world IO datasets.

2 Related Work

Most existing IO detection studies classify IO users based on pure behavioral patterns [6,18], pure language patterns [1,2,8–10], or both [17,20,36]. Vargas et al. [36] classify IO users based on coordination behaviors, such as tweeting the same content within a timeframe, or tweeting the same hashtag within a timeframe, extracted from users' post timelines. Luceri et al. [17] investigate IO user detection for LLMs under few-shot and fine-tuning settings. Minici et al. [20] propose IOHunter, an IO detector built upon a graph, in which the similarity of users' behavioral traces, including tweets, hashtags, and time of posting, justifies connections between users. Despite reported good performance on existing data, supervised and semi-supervised IO user detection methods require labelled IO datasets, which are limited in size and lag behind real-world IO practices. This raises concerns about the generalization capabilities of supervised and semi-supervised IO user-detection algorithms in real-world scenarios.

Recent zero-shot LLM approaches [17] provide an unsupervised alternative, but their ability to capture complex temporal behavioral dynamics is still limited. Although not directly aimed at IO user detection, other studies concerning IO users verify coordination among users in the same IO [12,21]. Although such methods reveal that IO users tend to form small and relatively well-separated clusters compared with legitimate organic users, our study shows that it is an oversimplification to develop unsupervised IO user detection methods solely based on this observation.

Anomaly Detection Using Contaminated Data: Anomaly detection using contaminated data is possible if the anomalies occupy a small portion of the data [38]. Most existing methods employ unsupervised identification of anomalies during training, allowing the model to either exclude these samples or leverage them to mitigate performance degradation [25,27,39]. Patra et al. [24] observed that these methods require prior knowledge about the dataset, such as the contamination ratio, which is usually unknown. To solve these issues, they proposed *Evidencebased Post-Hoc Adjustment Framework for Anomaly Detection (EPHAD)*, the first framework to adjust the prediction of an anomaly detector trained on contaminated data using an evidence function during test time. Patra et al. [24] focus on anomaly detection on visual data, but how to adapt EPHAD to multimodal temporal and language data remains an open question.

LLMs for Social Media Analysis: LLM-based social media analysis has been widely investigated, including post annotation [19,34,35], misinformation detection and mitigation [14,26,42,43], and IO detection [17]. Unlike [17], which uses LLMs as the sole classifier based on behavioral and language patterns, TENSOR leverages an LLM to provide additional evidence to enhance the TPP-based anomaly detector.

3 Problem Definition

We formulate Information Operation (IO) user detection as an unsupervised anomaly detection problem. A Social Network (SN) contains IO users, *i.e.*, users motivated or incentivized to promote an IO, and control users, *i.e.*, normal genuine social media users. The number of IO users is significantly smaller than that of normal users, and their behavioral and language patterns are noticeably different, as reflected in their *post timeline*. The post timeline of user i is $\boldsymbol{s}_i = (s_{i,1}, s_{i,2}, \cdots, s_{i,M_i})$, where M_i is the number of posts by this user. Each post event $s_{i,k} = (t_{i,k}, c_{i,k})$ consists of a time $t_{i,k}$ when this post is created and post content $c_{i,k}$. Post timelines of all users, including normal and IO users, are denoted as $\boldsymbol{S} = \{\boldsymbol{s}_1, \boldsymbol{s}_2, \cdots, \boldsymbol{s}_n\}$. For later use, we denote the respective sequences of all timestamps and contents as $\boldsymbol{T} = \{\boldsymbol{t}_1, \boldsymbol{t}_2, \ldots, \boldsymbol{t}_n\}$ and $\boldsymbol{C} = \{\boldsymbol{c}_1, \boldsymbol{c}_2, \ldots, \boldsymbol{c}_n\}$, where $\boldsymbol{t}_i = (t_{i,1}, t_{i,2}, \cdots, t_{i,M_i})$ and $\boldsymbol{c}_i = (c_{i,1}, c_{i,2}, \cdots, c_{i,M_i})$ are sequences of timestamps and contents of user i. We train a model $\mathcal{M}$ on $\boldsymbol{S}$ to identify IO users from control users. IO users are labeled 0, and control users are labeled 1, formulated as follows:

$$y = \begin{cases} 0, & \mathcal{M}(\boldsymbol{t}_i, \boldsymbol{c}_i) \geqslant \epsilon \\ 1, & \text{otherwise} \end{cases} \tag{1}$$

where ϵ is the threshold. We show how we determine the value of ϵ in Sect. 5.

4 Methodology

In this section, we introduce Temporal-bEhavior-laNguage Signals for information Operation Recognition (TENSOR), a novel anomaly detection approach that uses behavioral and language patterns from user action sequences for unsupervised IO user detection. TENSOR consists of two core modules: Temporal Point Process (TPP) and Large Language Model (LLM). TPP identifies IO users using user action sequences, but its performance can be suboptimal because the training set is contaminated by IO users. To mitigate this issue, we propose a novel evidence function to convert Large Language Model (LLM) outputs into a score and use *Evidencebased Post-Hoc Adjustment Framework for Anomaly Detection (EPHAD)* [24] to adjust the output of the TPP model using the evidence function. In Sect. 4.1 and Sect. 4.2, we provide brief introductions to TPP and EPHAD. In Sect. 4.3, we present the structure and technical details of TENSOR.

4.1 TPP Model

The Temporal Point Process (TPP) describes a random process of an event sequence $\boldsymbol{\tau} = (\tau_1, \tau_2, \cdots, \tau_m)$ where τ_k is the occurrence time. This paper considers the simple TPP, which only allows at most one event at any time, thus $\tau_k < \tau_\ell$ if $k < \ell$. Given the history up to (exclusive) the current time t, denoted as $\mathcal{H}$, the *conditional intensity function* $\lambda^*(t)$ is the probability that an event will happen at time t [4]:[1]

$$\lambda^*(t) = \lim_{\Delta t \to 0} \frac{P(\tau \in (t, t+\Delta t] \,|\mathcal{H})}{\Delta t} \tag{2}$$

With $\lambda^*(t)$, we can define the joint probability distribution $p^*(t)$ of the next event at t.

$$p^*(t) = \lambda^*(t) \exp - \int_{t_l}^{t} \lambda^*(\tau)\mathrm{d}\tau \tag{3}$$

The negative log-likelihood (NLL) loss on $\boldsymbol{\tau}$ observed in a time interval $[t_0, T]$ is:

$$L = -\log p(\boldsymbol{\tau}) = -\sum_{k=1}^{M} \log \lambda^*(\tau_k) + \int_{t_0}^{T} \lambda^*(u)\mathrm{d}u \tag{4}$$

where M is the number of events in $\boldsymbol{\tau}$. Equation (4) is the training loss of TPP models. Recent TPP models are based on neural networks (see [30] for a comprehensive survey). TPP has been used to detect abnormal events or sequences from normal events or event sequences [16,29,41].

4.2 Evidence-Based Post-Hoc Adjustment Framework for Anomaly Detection

Anomaly Detection (AD) algorithms need a training dataset $\boldsymbol{D} = \{x_1, x_2, \cdots, x_n\}$ containing normal samples to train an AD classifier $f(x)$. If $\boldsymbol{D}$ is contaminated by abnormal data, the trained AD model $f(x)$ will treat anomalies as normal. Patra et al. [24] observed that AD models trained on contaminated $\boldsymbol{D}$ can be corrected at test time using a predefined evidence function $T(x)$. The $T(x)$ contains external knowledge about anomalies, which is not captured by $f(x)$. The method is called *Evidencebased Post-Hoc Adjustment Framework for Anomaly Detection (EPHAD)*. Specifically, EPHAD revises $f(x)$ using *exponential tilting* as:

$$\hat{f}(x) = \frac{f(x) \exp T(x)/\beta}{Z} \tag{5}$$

where $\beta > 0$ is the temperature, and $Z = \int_D f(x) \exp T(x)/\beta dx$ is the normalizing constant. This method is theoretically grounded in Korbak et al. [13]. They treat the Post-Hoc adjustment as a KL-regularized optimization problem, where the objective is to find an adjusted distribution $\hat{f}(x)$ that minimizes the KL divergence from the original distribution $f(x)$ while maximizes the expected evidence $T(x)$, as shown in the following optimization problem:

$$\max_{\hat{f}} \mathbb{E}_{x \sim \hat{f}}[T(x)] - \beta D_{\mathrm{KL}}(\hat{f} \| f) \tag{6}$$

where $D_{\mathrm{KL}}(\hat{f} \| f)$ is the KL-divergence between $\hat{f}$ and f. They show that Eq. (5) is the solution to this optimization problem. Because AD only depends on the

[1] The asterisk denotes that this function conditions on history.

relative ordering of samples, the intractable normalizing constant Z in Eq. (5) can be omitted, which simplifies Eq. (5) into:

$$\hat{f}(x) = f(x) \exp T(x)/\beta \tag{7}$$

This is more practical for implementing AD models. In our approach elaborated in the following section, we use Eq. (7) to adjust $f(x)$ based on TPP models trained on contaminated training data using the evidence function derived from LLM outputs for better IO user detection.

4.3 Temporal-bEhavior-laNguage Signals for Information Operation Recognition

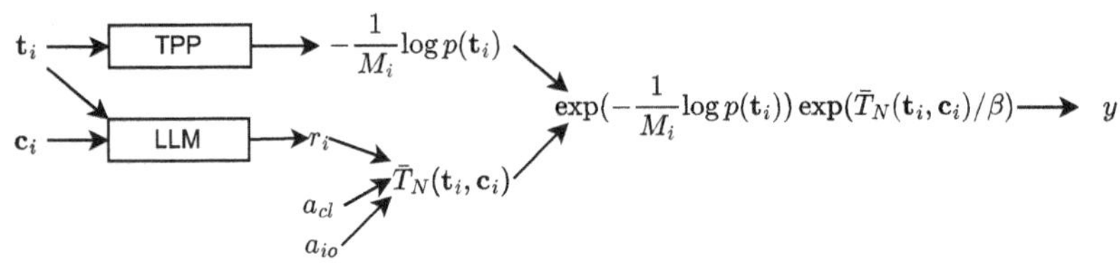

Fig. 1. Architecture of Temporal-bEhavior-laNguage Signals for information Operation Recognition (TENSOR).

In this section, we propose Temporal-bEhavior-laNguage Signals for information Operation Recognition (TENSOR), which is sketched in Fig. 1. TENSOR checks whether a user is an IO user based on their $\boldsymbol{t}_i$ and $\boldsymbol{c}_i$. The abstract input x in Eq. (7) is instantiated as a user $x_i = (\boldsymbol{t}_i, \boldsymbol{c}_i)$, where $\boldsymbol{t}_i$ and $\boldsymbol{c}_i$ represent the sequence of timestamps and contents of user i, respectively. It has two main components. The first component is a frozen TPP model trained on $\boldsymbol{T}$, which contains both IO and control users. The TPP model captures the difference between control and IO users using behavior patterns, including the coordinated behavior between IO accounts or an excessive number of posts compared with control users. The differences are reflected in the value $-\frac{1}{M_i}\log p(\boldsymbol{t}_i)$. Thus, $f(x_i) = \exp -\frac{1}{M_i}\log p(\boldsymbol{t}_i)$ is the TPP-based score computed from the timestamp component of x_i. The second component is the averaged evidence function $\bar{T}_N(\boldsymbol{t}_i, \boldsymbol{c}_i)$, backed by a frozen LLM. It determines whether a user is an IO user based on behavioral and language patterns in $\boldsymbol{c}_i$ and $\boldsymbol{t}_i$. That is, $T(x_i) = \bar{T}_N(\boldsymbol{t}_i, \boldsymbol{c}_i)$ is the averaged evidence function over N samples derived from a frozen LLM. $-\frac{1}{M_i}\log p(\boldsymbol{t}_i)$ and $\bar{T}_N(\boldsymbol{t}_i, \boldsymbol{c}_i)$ are later fused using EPHAD to mitigate the effect of TPP trained on contaminated $\boldsymbol{T}$. The outputs of the two components are fused using Eq. (7) to mitigate the effect of data contamination in TPP.

TENSOR uses TPP models to classify IO users using the behavioral patterns collected from $\boldsymbol{t}_i$. Because there are more control users than IO users, TPP models yield higher probabilities $p(\boldsymbol{t}_i)$ for control users compared to IO users. This makes TPP a valid AD classifier:

$$y = \begin{cases} 0, & \text{if } -\frac{1}{M_i}\log p(\boldsymbol{t}_i) \geqslant \epsilon \\ 1, & \text{otherwise} \end{cases} \tag{8}$$

where IO users are labeled 0, control users are labeled 1, ϵ is the threshold, and M_i is the length of $\boldsymbol{t}_i$.

You are an advanced social media analyst specialized in detecting Information Operations (IO). Your objective is to analyze user profiles and posting behaviors to distinguish between state-sponsored Information Operation (IO) accounts and control users based on the following behavioral frameworks:

Role A: Information Operation (IO) Account

Identity: These accounts are verified as part of inauthentic, coordinated efforts backed by state actors to manipulate public debate.

Tactics:

* Strategic Manipulation: They employ tactics like hashtag hijacking, artificial amplification, and the dissemination of propaganda or disinformation.

* Targeting: They focus on specific audience communities, often using coordinated actions such as flooding through political cartoons or memes.

* Profile Composition: They may consist of human-operated accounts, automated bots, or compromised profiles that have been repurposed for a campaign.

Role B: Control Account

Identity: These represent legitimate, organic users who act as a baseline for "normal" social media behavior.

Selection Context: These users are identified by their engagement in the same topics and hashtags as IO accounts during the same time frames, but without coordination.

Behavioral Characteristics:

* Authentic Engagement: They discuss similar political or social topics without endorsing or participating in an orchestrated state agenda.

* Content Diversity: Their timelines include posts on unrelated personal or general topics, whereas IO accounts are often more single-mindedly focused on campaign goals.

IO accounts are rare. Most accounts are control accounts.

Please do your analysis step by step. If you can think, think as thoroughly as possible to make your decision since the results are quite important. Your thinking process can be long, but the final response should be concise: only answer whether this account is an IO account or a control account.

Fig. 2. Prompts for zero-shot IO user detection

However, the dataset $\boldsymbol{S}$ is contaminated by IO users, which could harm detection accuracy. To mitigate this, TENSOR adjusts $-\frac{1}{M_i}\log p(\boldsymbol{t}_i)$ using a LLM-based evidence function $T(\boldsymbol{t}_i, \boldsymbol{c}_i)$. The LLM takes in the system prompt in Fig. 2 and a structured input of $\boldsymbol{t}_i$ and $\boldsymbol{c}_i$. It then generates a response $r_i = \text{LLM}(\boldsymbol{t}_i, \boldsymbol{c}_i)$, indicating whether the user is an IO user or a control user by answering "IO account" or "Control account". To convert r_i into $T(\boldsymbol{t}_i, \boldsymbol{c}_i)$, we use a *semantic similarity mapping* strategy instead of enforcing strict text matching, which is prone to failure because LLM outputs are non-deterministic. Specifically, we compute the semantic similarity between the raw LLM output r_i and reference texts representing IO or control users. In our case, the reference texts are "IO account" for IO users and "Control account" for control users, denoted as a_{io} and a_{cl}. By applying a `softmax` transformation to these similarity scores, we obtain a probability distribution over the IO and control users. $T(\boldsymbol{t}_i, \boldsymbol{c}_i)$ is defined as the probability of selecting the IO user:

$$T(\boldsymbol{t}_i, \boldsymbol{c}_i) = \frac{\exp \mathrm{sim}(a_{io}, \mathrm{LLM}(\boldsymbol{t}_i, \boldsymbol{c}_i))}{\exp \mathrm{sim}(a_{cl}, \mathrm{LLM}(\boldsymbol{t}_i, \boldsymbol{c}_i)) + \exp \mathrm{sim}(a_{io}, \mathrm{LLM}(\boldsymbol{t}_i, \boldsymbol{c}_i))} \tag{9}$$

where $\mathrm{sim}(x, y)$ measures the similarity between input text x and y. The output of LLMs may vary across multiple generations with the same input. To ensure robustness, we draw N samples of $T(\boldsymbol{t}_i, \boldsymbol{c}_i)$ and compute their mean, denoted as $\bar{T}_N(\boldsymbol{t}_i, \boldsymbol{c}_i)$:

$$\bar{T}_N(\boldsymbol{t}_i, \boldsymbol{c}_i) = \frac{1}{N} \sum_{r=1}^{N} T^{(r)}(\boldsymbol{t}_i, \boldsymbol{c}_i) \tag{10}$$

where $T^{(r)}(\boldsymbol{t}_i, \boldsymbol{c}_i)$ refers to the r-th sample. According to Eq. (7), the decision rule for TENSOR is:

$$y = \begin{cases} 0, & \text{if } \exp -\frac{1}{M_i} \log p(\boldsymbol{t}_i) \exp \bar{T}_N(\boldsymbol{t}_i, \boldsymbol{c}_i)/\beta \geqslant \epsilon \\ 1, & \text{otherwise} \end{cases} \tag{11}$$

5 Experiments

This section (i) benchmarks TENSOR against existing baselines, (ii) evaluates the impact of behavioral and language patterns on IO user detection via ablation studies, (iii) compares EPHAD against alternative methods for integrating these patterns for IO user detection, and (iv) analyzes the sensitivity of TENSOR to different LLMs and temperature values β. We run each experiment on A100 and L40S GPUs three times with different random seeds, and their mean and standard deviation (1-sigma) are reported. The computational complexity of TENSOR for one user is $O(M_i)$, because the TPP component analyzes one sequence $\boldsymbol{s}_i$ in $O(M_i)$, while the LLM component processes one sequence in $O(1)$[2].

TENSOR is supposed to be training-free because all its components are either frozen or deterministic computations. However, to the best of our knowledge, large TPP models pretrained on large event sequence data do not exist, so we

[2] However, LLMs can be the speed bottleneck of TENSOR because they are usually much slower than TPPs. Hence, it is possible that TENSOR takes a constant time to process a sequence, even though the computational complexity is $O(M_i)$.

must train a TPP model on $\boldsymbol{T}$ beforehand. TENSOR works with any existing TPP model that provides $p(\boldsymbol{t}_i)$. According to [15,29], the performance gap between existing state-of-the-art TPP models is small. Without loss of generality, we choose the *Self-attentive Hawkes Process (SAHP)* [40] because of its relatively simple design and good performance. The loss function for training SAHP on $\boldsymbol{T}$ is Eq. (4).

TENSOR works with all existing LLMs. Recently, we have seen the rise of reasoning models [11]. By enabling the LLM to think during test time, reasoning models consistently improve performance across various tasks, especially for solving mathematical problems and difficult logic problems [22]. In this paper, we use an open-weight reasoning model gpt-oss-120B (reasoning model, 117B parameters with 5.1B active parameters) [23] with a medium reasoning effort. In Sect. 5.4, we report TENSOR's performance with llama3.3-70B (non-reasoning model, 70B parameters), qwen-next-80B (reasoning model, 80B parameters with 3B active parameters) [33], glm-4.5-air (reasoning model, 106B parameters with 12B active parameters) [32], and mistral3.2-24b (non-reasoning model, 24B parameters)[3]. As for the similarity function in Eq. (9), we use the bge-m3-v2 reranker [3]. The N in Eq. (10) is 5.

TENSOR has one hyperparameter: temperature β. According to Patra et al. [24], we set $\beta = 0.5$ during the experiments. In Sect. 5.4, we investigate how temperature affects the detection performance of TENSOR.

Baseline Models: We compare TENSOR with three baselines. Although not directly aimed at IO user detection, two studies concerning IO users verify coordination among users in the same IO [12,21]. These studies motivate the first two baselines.

- **User Embedding Clustering (Clustering)** [12] represents each user via a user embedding, generated by averaging the embeddings of all events for that user extracted from a model trained on $\mathcal{T}$. Then, these user-level representations are fed into a clustering model to partition the users into two distinct groups. Users in the smaller group are IO users.
- **Behavioral Languages for Online Characterization (BLOC)** [21] suggests describing user behaviors as strings of symbols using formal languages specified by rules. Next, these sequences are converted into user embeddings using a TF-IDF model. Users whose embeddings differ from the majority are considered IO users.
- **User Embedding Clustering (Clustering)** [17] uses LLMs to detect in a zero-shot setting whether a user is an IO user based on behavioral and language patterns. This method first checks whether a post x_i belongs to an IO. Then users whose posts are mostly IO posts are labelled as IO users.

Datasets: We use the IO user dataset collected by Seckin et al. [28]. This dataset contains various identified IOs in 26 labelled datasets across 15 countries. We

[3] https://huggingface.co/mistralai/Mistral-Small-3.2-24B-Instruct-2506.

evaluate TENSOR and baselines on Egypt, China_1, Iran_1, Russia_1, and UAE. These datasets have the complete activity timelines of all IO users, but control users are limited to their last 100 posts on days when they are involved in IOs. To mitigate this bias, we apply the same strategy to IO users by limiting the number of posts from IO users to 100 per day. The data statistics of curated datasets are available in Table 1. We assign 80% of data to the training set, 10% to the validation set, and 10% to the test set. Please note that although these datasets include labels indicating which users are IO users, they are used solely for performance evaluations. TENSOR and baselines cannot see the labels.

Table 1. Statistics of the curated IO datasets

	Number of IO users	Number of control users	Number of IO posts	Number of control posts
Egypt	219	242	66,577	14,204
China_1	537	28,445	169,287	1,718,924
Iran_1	543	3,291	247,386	192,674
Russia_1	2,830	20,961	1,335,064	1,595,514
UAE	3,337	6,635	1,244,984	366,873
Total	7,466	59,574	3,063,298	3,888,189

Evaluation Metrics: We evaluate TENSOR and baselines using precision, recall, F1-score, Area Under the receiver operating characteristic Curve (AUC), and Area Under the Precision-Recall Curve (AUPRC)[4]. We only report AUPRC for experiments in Sect. 5.2, Sect. 5.3, and Sect. 5.4 to simplify the comparison of results. We add AUPRC because Davis et al. [5] suggest AUPRC as an alternative to AUC for tasks with a largely imbalanced class distribution, where AUC results can be overly optimistic. The IO dataset, as shown in Table 1, is highly imbalanced, with few IO users and many control users, which justifies the use of AUPRC.

Computing precision, recall, and F1-score requires a threshold ϵ to decide the label y. In this work, the threshold is adjusted by maximizing the F1 on the validation set. In practice, the scores of IO and control users are often modeled as two class-conditional normal distributions. The threshold is the score that separates them, that is, most sequences on one side belong to IO users and most sequences on the other side belong to control users.

5.1 Comparing TENSOR with Baselines

This section compares TENSOR with three baselines, Clustering, BLOC, and LLM on five IO datasets. The metrics used are precision, recall, F1-score, AUC and AUPRC. The results are presented in Tables 2, 3, 4, 5 and 6.

[4] AUPRC is often referred to as Average Precision (AP) in machine learning toolkits. We prefer the term AUPRC as it more accurately describes the geometric calculation of the metric.

Table 2. The precision of TENSOR and baselines on five real-world IO datasets (higher is better).

	TENSOR	Clustering	BLOC	LLM
Egypt	0.6138 ± 0.0055	$\mathbf{0.8056 \pm 0.0600}$	0.4761 ± 0.0000	0.6882 ± 0.0316
China_1	$\mathbf{0.8361 \pm 0.0183}$	0.2649 ± 0.3495	0.0321 ± 0.0000	0.1190 ± 0.0018
Iran_1	0.8332 ± 0.0146	$\mathbf{0.9198 \pm 0.0443}$	0.1440 ± 0.0000	0.2928 ± 0.0046
Russia_1	$\mathbf{0.6644 \pm 0.0290}$	0.1218 ± 0.0049	0.1127 ± 0.0000	0.2106 ± 0.00075
UAE	$\mathbf{0.7864 \pm 0.0079}$	0.5824 ± 0.1452	0.3357 ± 0.0000	0.4556 ± 0.0048
Average	**0.7468**	0.5389	0.2201	0.3532

Table 3. The recall of TENSOR and baselines on five real-world IO datasets (higher is better).

	TENSOR	Clustering	BLOC	LLM
Egypt	$\mathbf{0.9394 \pm 0.0214}$	0.6818 ± 0.0371	0.9091 ± 0.0000	0.8636 ± 0.0000
China_1	0.4691 ± 0.0175	$\mathbf{0.8889 \pm 0.0944}$	0.0926 ± 0.0000	0.6605 ± 0.0087
Iran_1	0.5152 ± 0.0171	0.5697 ± 0.1465	$\mathbf{1.0000 \pm 0.0000}$	0.6848 ± 0.0086
Russia_1	0.6419 ± 0.0192	$\mathbf{0.9435 \pm 0.0725}$	0.8657 ± 0.0000	0.2874 ± 0.0159
UAE	0.7784 ± 0.0098	0.6766 ± 0.1045	$\mathbf{1.0000 \pm 0.0000}$	0.3832 ± 0.0000
Average	0.6688	0.7521	**0.7735**	0.5759

Table 4. The F1 score of TENSOR and baselines on five real-world IO datasets (higher is better).

	TENSOR	Clustering	BLOC	LLM
Egypt	0.7424 ± 0.0107	0.7381 ± 0.0442	0.6250 ± 0.0000	$\mathbf{0.7656 \pm 0.0194}$
China_1	$\mathbf{0.6006 \pm 0.0112}$	0.2764 ± 0.3415	0.0476 ± 0.0000	0.2017 ± 0.0026
Iran_1	0.6366 ± 0.0165	$\mathbf{0.6895 \pm 0.1178}$	0.2517 ± 0.0000	0.4102 ± 0.0055
Russia_1	$\mathbf{0.6521 \pm 0.0044}$	0.2154 ± 0.0055	0.1995 ± 0.0000	0.2430 ± 0.0103
UAE	$\mathbf{0.7823 \pm 0.0064}$	0.6247 ± 0.1282	0.5026 ± 0.0000	0.7656 ± 0.0194
Average	**0.6828**	0.5088	0.3253	0.4772

Table 5. The AUC of TENSOR and baselines on five real-world IO datasets (higher is better).

	TENSOR	Clustering	BLOC	LLM
Egypt	$\mathbf{0.7806 \pm 0.0073}$	0.7570 ± 0.0395	0.3636 ± 0.0000	0.7558 ± 0.0306
China_1	$\mathbf{0.9338 \pm 0.0019}$	0.3645 ± 0.4207	0.5872 ± 0.0000	0.9057 ± 0.0064
Iran_1	$\mathbf{0.8558 \pm 0.0072}$	0.6676 ± 0.0996	0.4905 ± 0.0000	0.7698 ± 0.0071
Russia_1	$\mathbf{0.9213 \pm 0.0026}$	0.3017 ± 0.0967	0.3946 ± 0.0000	0.7019 ± 0.0024
UAE	$\mathbf{0.9263 \pm 0.0005}$	0.7403 ± 0.1254	0.3426 ± 0.0000	0.7558 ± 0.0306
Average	**0.8836**	0.5662	0.4357	0.7778

Table 6. The AUPRC of TENSOR and baselines on five real-world IO datasets (higher is better).

	TENSOR	Clustering	BLOC	LLM
Egypt	0.7690±0.0087	**0.8232±0.0160**	0.3839±0.0000	0.6859±0.0284
China_1	**0.5654±0.0069**	0.2712±0.3694	0.0288±0.0000	0.1670±0.0053
Iran_1	**0.6910±0.0336**	0.6711±0.0948	0.1352±0.0000	0.3075±0.0071
Russia_1	**0.6952±0.0133**	0.0812±0.0103	0.0941±0.0000	0.1848±0.0006
UAE	**0.8562±0.0003**	0.6783±0.1474	0.2475±0.0000	0.6859±0.0284
Average	**0.7154**	0.5050	0.1779	0.4062

The results show that TENSOR is the overall best approach for IO user detection, as measured by AUC and AUPRC. One outlier is Egypt, where Clustering performs better on AUPRC. The reason is the temperature β. Later results in Sect. 5.4 show that $\beta = 0.5$ from [24] is not the best choice. By lowering the temperature, the overall performance of TENSOR across all datasets significantly improves and can outperform Clustering on all datasets. We do not discuss how to optimize β without any labels in this paper.

We also observe that the results of Clustering have a large standard deviation across multiple datasets. The reason is the data imbalance with many control users and few IO users. As shown in Fig. 3, Clustering on imbalanced data is sensitive to random seeds, leading to the misclassification of control users as IO users. This instability results in inconsistent performance, particularly on highly imbalanced datasets such as China_1 and Russia_1.

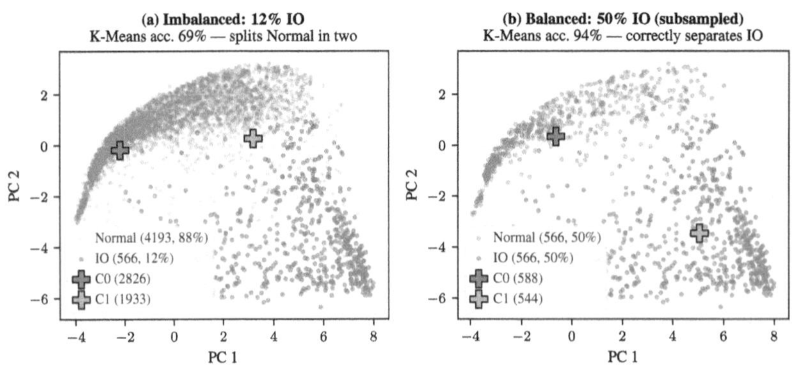

Fig. 3. Impact of data imbalance on Clustering's performance. Data points represent control users (C0) and IO users (C1). Results indicate that significant data imbalance shifts cluster centroids with some random seeds, leading to performance inconsistency.

5.2 The Impact of Behavioral and Language Patterns on IO User Detection

If we only use the behavioral or language patterns of one user for IO user detection, we may get suboptimal results. To demonstrate this, we compare TENSOR with the following ablation baselines: (i) TENSOR without the evidence function $\bar{T}_N(\boldsymbol{t}_i, \boldsymbol{c}_i)$, which is described in Eq. 8, (ii) TENSOR without TPP, detecting IO users by $\bar{T}_N(\boldsymbol{t}_i, \boldsymbol{c}_i)$, (iii) TENSOR but $\bar{T}_N(\boldsymbol{t}_i, \boldsymbol{c}_i)$ returns random samples from the uniform distribution $\mathcal{U}(0, 1)$, and (iv) the Random model, which assigns scores sampled from $\mathcal{U}(0, 1)$ to users. We include Random because AUPRC is sensitive to the ratio of control and IO users, whereas the AUC remains at 0.5. The results are reported in Table 7.

Table 7. The AUPRC of TENSOR and ablation baselines on five real-world IO datasets (temperature $\beta = 0.5$, LLM is gpt-oss-120B, higher is better).

	TENSOR	TENSOR without LLM	TENSOR without TPP	TENSOR with random $\bar{T}_N(\boldsymbol{t}_i, \boldsymbol{c}_i)$	Random
Egypt	**0.7690±0.0087**	0.6916±0.0030	0.5839±0.0193	0.6770±0.0507	0.5083±0.0720
China_1	**0.5654±0.0069**	0.4740±0.0046	0.0669±0.0044	0.4721±0.0120	0.0212±0.0047
Iran_1	**0.6910±0.0336**	0.6438±0.0252	0.1989±0.0180	0.6085±0.0191	0.1558±0.0220
Russia_1	**0.6953±0.0133**	0.6425±0.0073	0.1707±0.0009	0.6302±0.0122	0.1216±0.0073
UAE	**0.8562±0.0003**	0.8009±0.0002	0.4080±0.0061	0.7619±0.0060	0.3390±0.0152
Average	**0.7154**	0.6506	0.2857	0.6299	0.2292

The ablation results demonstrate that jointly considering behavioral and language patterns for IO user detection is better than considering only one, as the AUPRC of TENSOR is significantly better than TENSOR without LLM or TPP. The experiment results also show that a standalone LLM performs poorly at zero-shot IO user detection. Another observation is that TENSOR outperforms TENSOR with random $\bar{T}_N(\boldsymbol{t}_i, \boldsymbol{c}_i)$, whose performance is even worse than TENSOR without LLM. This demonstrates that LLM still provides useful information from $\boldsymbol{c}_i$ and $\boldsymbol{t}_i$ for IO user detection despite its poor performance in this task.

5.3 The Benefit of LLM-Backed $\bar{T}_N(\boldsymbol{t}_i, \boldsymbol{c}_i)$

EPHAD enables TENSOR to jointly consider behavioral and language patterns for IO user detection, but is it the overall best way in terms of performance? In this section, we investigate several intuitive and existing alternatives to train a IO user detector based on behavioral and language patterns. Specifically, they are: (i) behavior- and language-aware TPP model. The input of TPP is $\boldsymbol{t}_i$ and $\boldsymbol{c}_i$. The training loss is $-\log p(\boldsymbol{t}_i, \boldsymbol{c}_i)$. Then we use Eq. (8) for IO user detection, (ii) BLOC [21], (iii) LLM [17], and (iv) the Random model. The results are reported in Table 8.

We see that TENSOR outperforms other alternatives by a significant margin on all datasets. A detailed analysis shows that BLOC performs worse than

Table 8. The AUPRC of TENSOR and other behavior- and language-aware baselines (temperature $\beta = 0.5$, LLM is gpt-oss-120B, higher is better).

	TENSOR	behavior- and language-aware TPP	BLOC [21]	LLM [17]	Random
Egypt	**0.7690±0.0087**	0.6949±0.0017	0.3838±0.0160	0.6859±0.0284	0.5083±0.0720
China_1	**0.5654±0.0069**	0.4674±0.0042	0.0288±0.0000	0.1670±0.0053	0.0212±0.0047
Iran_1	**0.6910±0.0336**	0.6290±0.0052	0.1352±0.0000	0.3075±0.0071	0.1558±0.0220
Russia_1	**0.6953±0.0133**	0.6242±0.0145	0.0940±0.0000	0.1848±0.0006	0.1216±0.0073
UAE	**0.8562±0.0003**	0.8011±0.0012	0.2475±0.0000	0.4187±0.0020	0.3390±0.0152
Average	**0.7154**	0.6433	0.1779	0.3528	0.2292

the Random baseline. A potential reason is that BLOC requires more detailed information about posts, such as who the post is sent to and whether it contains a picture, which is missing from the dataset. This results in most generated BLOC sequences containing only one symbol referring to a post, which significantly harms their classification capability. LLM and behavior- and language-aware TPP outperform Random but are outperformed by TENSOR. On closer inspection, we find that the results of the behavior- and language-aware TPP are basically the same as those of TPP. These results demonstrate that adding language data to the TPP model does not improve its IO detection capability.

5.4 Sensitivity to Different LLMs and β

All reported results of TENSOR in previous sections are based on temperature $\beta = 0.5$ inherited from the EPHAD paper and gpt-oss-120B. However, TENSOR works with all existing LLMs and temperatures $\beta > 0$. In this section, we evaluate the stability of TENSOR under different LLMs and temperatures.

Table 9. The AUPRC of TENSOR with different LLMs in $\bar{T}_N(\boldsymbol{t}_i, \boldsymbol{c}_i)$ (temperature $\beta = 0.5$, higher is better).

	TENSOR w/ gpt-oss-120B	TENSOR w/ llama3.3-70B	TENSOR w/ qwen-next-80B	TENSOR w/ glm-4.5-air	TENSOR w/ mistral3.2-24b	TENSOR without LLM
Egypt	**0.7690±0.0087**	0.7079±0.0019	0.7373±0.0084	0.7467±0.0017	0.6806±0.0057	0.6916±0.0030
China_1	**0.5654±0.0069**	0.5224±0.0062	0.5251±0.0030	0.5609±0.0035	0.5085±0.0044	0.4740±0.0046
Iran_1	**0.6910±0.0336**	0.6622±0.0269	0.6711±0.0948	0.6737±0.0345	0.6480±0.0353	0.6438±0.0252
Russia_1	**0.6953±0.0133**	0.6530±0.0103	0.6358±0.0131	0.6475±0.0122	0.6495±0.0081	0.6425±0.0073
UAE	**0.8562±0.0003**	0.8154±0.0022	0.7850±0.0018	0.8152±0.0007	0.7804±0.0009	0.8009±0.0002
Average	**0.7154**	0.6670	0.6709	0.6888	0.6534	0.6506

Sensitivity to LLMs: Table 9 shows the performance of TENSOR with different LLMs. Besides gpt-oss-120B, we pick llama3.3-70B, qwen-next-80B, glm-4.5-air, and mistral3.2-24b. We observe that configurations using gpt-oss-120B, llama3.3-70B, and glm-4.5-air consistently outperform TENSOR without LLM across all datasets. Although qwen-next-80B and mistral3.2-24b underperform on some datasets because of their smaller model or active parameter sizes, their overall average is still better than TENSOR without LLM. These results show that TENSOR is stable across different LLMs.

Sensitivity to β: Figure 4 shows how temperature β affects the performance of TENSOR. We observe that although the optimal temperature varies across datasets, it is consistently around 0.3 for gpt-oss-120B. Generally, increasing the temperature from 0.05 brings a quick performance improvement to a maximum, followed by a gradual decline. For China_1, Iran_1, Russia_1, and UAE, the performance drop is relatively small, while for Egypt, the AUPRC drops significantly from over 0.85 to below 0.70. Table 10 compares TENSOR at its optimal temperature against the default configuration and other baselines. TENSOR consistently outperforms other approaches at the optimal temperature. These results indicate that unsupervised optimization of β is a promising approach to further improve the performance of TENSOR. We leave this as future work.

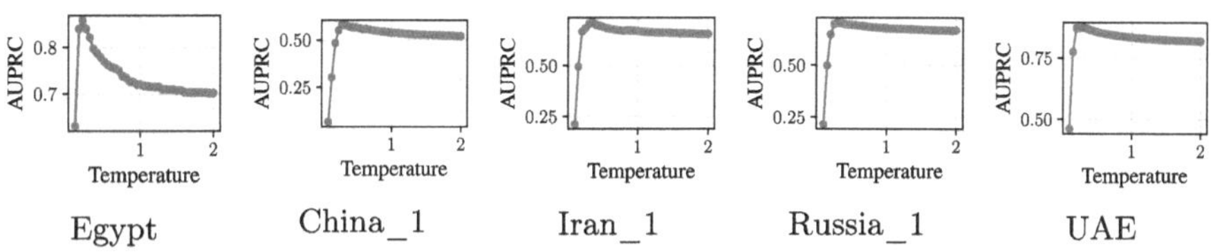

Fig. 4. AUPRC of TENSOR on all five IO datasets with different temperatures from 0.05 to 2.

Table 10. The AUPRC of TENSOR and other behavior- and language-aware baselines (temperature $\beta = 0.5$ for TENSOR results in the second column, LLM is gpt-oss-120B, higher is better).

	TENSOR with best β	TENSOR	behavior- and language-aware TPP [12]	BLOC [21]	LLM [17]	Random
Egypt	**0.8568±0.0081**	0.7690±0.0087	0.8232±0.0160	0.3838±0.0160	0.6859±0.0284	0.5083±0.0720
China_1	**0.5796±0.0175**	0.5654±0.0069	0.2712±0.3694	0.0288±0.0000	0.1670±0.0053	0.0212±0.0047
Iran_1	**0.7108±0.0271**	0.6910±0.0336	0.6711±0.0948	0.1352±0.0000	0.3075±0.0071	0.1558±0.0220
Russia_1	**0.7045±0.0092**	0.6953±0.0133	0.0812±0.0103	0.0940±0.0000	0.1848±0.0006	0.1216±0.0073
UAE	**0.8743±0.0007**	0.8562±0.0003	0.6783±0.1474	0.2475±0.0000	0.4187±0.0020	0.3390±0.0152
Average	**0.7452**	0.7154	0.5050	0.1779	0.3528	0.2292

6 Conclusion

In this study, we addressed the critical challenge of identifying IO users within social networks. While traditional supervised models struggle with the evolving nature of IO user behaviors, unsupervised models rely on rigid assumptions of coordination, TENSOR offers a more resilient alternative by framing detection as a multimodal anomaly problem. TENSOR shifts the focus toward the inherent friction between IO campaigns and organic user behaviors. By deploying a

TPP, we successfully captured the behavioral patterns that distinguish coordinated influence from genuine social interaction. A key contribution of this work is the mitigation of "training set contamination." By integrating a novel evidence function that translates LLM responses, which are generated from users' post timelines, into quantitative scores, we effectively adjust the output of TPP to mitigate the noise caused by IO users embedded in the training data. Experimental results show that TENSOR outperforms other baselines by a significant margin on five real-world IO datasets.

Acknowledgments. This research is supported in part by the Australian Research Council (ARC) Discovery Projects DP200101441 and DP210100743. We appreciate the compute and LLM services provided by RMIT RACE Hub.

References

1. Addawood, A., Badawy, A., Lerman, K., Ferrara, E.: Linguistic cues to deception: identifying political trolls on social media. In: Proceedings of the International AAAI Conference on Web and Social Media, vol. 13, pp. 15–25 (2019)
2. Alizadeh, M., Shapiro, J.N., Buntain, C., Tucker, J.A.: Content-based features predict social media influence operations. Sci. Adv. **6**(30) (2020)
3. Chen, J., Xiao, S., Zhang, P., Luo, K., Lian, D., Liu, Z.: M3-embedding: multi-linguality, multi-functionality, multi-granularity text embeddings through self-knowledge distillation. In: ACL 2024, pp. 2318–2335 (2024)
4. Daley, D.J., Vere-Jones, D. (eds.): An Introduction to the Theory of Point Processes Volume I: Elementary Theory and Methods. Probability and its Applications, 2 edn. Springer (2003)
5. Davis, J., Goadrich, M.: The relationship between Precision-Recall and ROC curves. In: ICML 2006, pp. 233–240 (2006)
6. Ezzeddine, F., et al.: Exposing influence campaigns in the age of LLMs: a behavioral-based AI approach to detecting state-sponsored trolls. EPJ Data Sci. **12**(1), 46 (2023)
7. Forum, W.E.: The global risks report 2024: insight report. World Economic Forum, 19th edn. (2024). oCLC: 1499197716
8. Haider, S., Luceri, L., Deb, A., Badawy, A., Peng, N., Ferrara, E.: Detecting Social Media Manipulation in Low-Resource Languages, pp. 1358–1364. WWW 2023 Companion (2023)
9. Im, J., et al.: Still out there: modeling and identifying Russian troll accounts on Twitter. In: WebSci 2020, pp. 1–10 (2020)
10. Jachim, P., Sharevski, F., Treebridge, P.: TrollHunter [Evader]: Automated Detection [Evasion] of Twitter Trolls During the COVID-19 Pandemic. arXiv:2012.02586 (2020)
11. Ke, Z., et al.: A survey of frontiers in LLM reasoning: inference scaling, learning to reason, and agentic systems. Trans. Mach. Learn. Res. (2025)
12. Kong, Q., Calderon, P., Ram, R., Boichak, O., Rizoiu, M.A.: Interval-censored transformer hawkes: detecting information operations using the reaction of social systems. In: Proceedings of the ACM Web Conference 2023, WWW 2023, pp. 1813–1821 (2023)

13. Korbak, T., Perez, E., Buckley, C.: RL with KL penalties is better viewed as Bayesian inference. In: EMNLP 2022, pp. 1083–1091. Association for Computational Linguistics (2022)
14. Kumar, R., Goddu, B., Saha, S., Jatowt, A.: Silver lining in the fake news cloud: can large language models help detect misinformation? IEEE Trans. Artif. Intell. **6**(1), 14–24 (2025)
15. Lin, H., Wu, L., Zhao, G., Pai, L., Li, S.Z.: Exploring generative neural temporal point process. TMLR (2022)
16. Liu, S., Hauskrecht, M.: Event outlier detection in continuous time. In: Proceedings of the 38th International Conference on Machine Learning, pp. 6793–6803. PMLR (2021)
17. Luceri, L., Boniardi, E., Ferrara, E.: Leveraging large language models to detect influence campaigns on social media. In: Companion Proceedings of the ACM Web Conference 2024, pp. 1459–1467 (2024)
18. Luceri, L., Giordano, S., Ferrara, E.: Detecting troll behavior via inverse reinforcement learning: a case study of Russian trolls in the 2016 US election. In: Proceedings of the International AAAI Conference on Web and Social Media, vol. 14, pp. 417–427 (2020)
19. Malik, U., Bernard, S., Pauchet, A., Chatelain, C., Picot-Clémente, R., Cortinovis, J.: Pseudo-labeling with large language models for multi-label emotion classification of French tweets. IEEE Access **12**, 15902–15916 (2024)
20. Minici, M., Luceri, L., Fabbri, F., Ferrara, E.: IOHunter: graph foundation model to uncover online information operations. In: Proceedings of the AAAI Conference on Artificial Intelligence, vol. 39, no. 27, pp. 28258–28266 (2025)
21. Nwala, A.C., Flammini, A., Menczer, F.: A language framework for modeling social media account behavior. EPJ Data Sci. **12**(1), 33 (2023)
22. OpenAI: OpenAI o1 System Card (2024). arXiv:2412.16720
23. OpenAI: GPT-OSS-120B & GPT-OSS-20B Model Card (2025). arXiv:2508.10925
24. Patra, S., Taieb, S.B.: An evidence-based post-hoc adjustment framework for anomaly detection under data contamination. In: NeurIPS 2025 (2025)
25. Perini, L., Bürkner, P.C., Klami, A.: Estimating the contamination factor's distribution in unsupervised anomaly detection. In: Proceedings of the 40th International Conference on Machine Learning, pp. 27668–27679. PMLR (2023)
26. Qi, P., Yan, Z., Hsu, W., Lee, M.L.: SNIFFER: multimodal large language model for explainable out-of-context misinformation detection. In: CVPR, pp. 13052–13062 (2024)
27. Qiu, C., Li, A., Kloft, M., Rudolph, M., Mandt, S.: Latent outlier exposure for anomaly detection with contaminated data. In: Proceedings of the 39th International Conference on Machine Learning, pp. 18153–18167. PMLR (2022)
28. Seckin, O.C., et al.: Labeled datasets for research on information operations. In: Proceedings of the International AAAI Conference on Web and Social Media, vol. 19, pp. 2567–2574 (2025)
29. Shchur, O., Turkmen, A.C., Januschowski, T., Gasthaus, J., Günnemann, S.: Detecting anomalous event sequences with temporal point processes. In: NeurIPS 2021 (2021)
30. Shchur, O., Türkmen, A.C., Januschowski, T., Günnemann, S.: Neural temporal point processes: a review. In: IJCAI 2021, pp. 4585–4593 (2021)
31. Smith, S.T., Kao, E.K., Mackin, E.D., Shah, D.C., Simek, O., Rubin, D.B.: Automatic detection of influential actors in disinformation networks. Proc. Natl. Acad. Sci. **118**(4) (2021)

32. Team, G.: GLM-4.5: Agentic, Reasoning, and Coding (ARC) Foundation Models (2025). arXiv:2508.06471
33. Team, Q.: Qwen3 technical report (2025). https://arxiv.org/abs/2505.09388
34. Tekumalla, R., Banda, J.M.: Leveraging large language models and weak supervision for social media data annotation: an evaluation using COVID-19 self-reported vaccination tweets. In: HCI International 2023 - Late Breaking Papers, pp. 356–366. Springer, Cham (2023)
35. Törnberg, P.: Large language models outperform expert coders and supervised classifiers at annotating political social media messages. Soc. Sci. Comput. Rev. **43**(6), 1181–1195 (2025)
36. Vargas, L., Emami, P., Traynor, P.: On the detection of disinformation campaign activity with network analysis. In: CCSW 2020, pp. 133–146 (2020)
37. Vishnuprasad, P.S., Nogara, G., Cardoso, F., Cresci, S., Giordano, S., Luceri, L.: Tracking fringe and coordinated activity on Twitter leading up to the US capitol attack. In: Proceedings of the International AAAI Conference on Web and Social Media, vol. 18, pp. 1557–1570 (2024)
38. Wang, S., et al.: Effective end-to-end unsupervised outlier detection via inlier priority of discriminative network. In: Advances in Neural Information Processing Systems, vol. 32 (2019)
39. Yoon, J., Sohn, K., Li, C.L., Arik, S.O., Lee, C.Y., Pfister, T.: Self-supervise, Refine, Repeat: Improving Unsupervised Anomaly Detection. Transactions on Machine Learning Research (2022)
40. Zhang, Q., Lipani, A., Kirnap, O., Yilmaz, E.: Self-attentive hawkes process. In: Proceedings of the 37th International Conference on Machine Learning, pp. 11183–11193. PMLR (2020)
41. Zhang, S., Zhou, C., Zhang, P., Liu, Y., Li, Z., Chen, H.: Multiple hypothesis testing for anomaly detection in multi-type event sequences. In: ICDM, pp. 808–817 (2023)
42. Zhang, Y., Sharma, K., Du, L., Liu, Y.: Toward mitigating misinformation and social media manipulation in LLM Era. In: WWW 2024 Companion, pp. 1302–1305. Association for Computing Machinery (2024)
43. Zhou, X., Sharma, A., Zhang, A.X., Althoff, T.: Correcting misinformation on social media with a large language model (2026). arXiv:2403.11169

Anomaly Detection, Active Learning and Data-Centric Learning

ALINC: Active Learning for Inductive Node Classification via Graph Sampling

Pascal Plettenberg[1(✉)], Denis Huseljic[1], André Alcalde[2], Bernhard Sick[1], and Josephine M. Thomas[3]

[1] Intelligent Embedded Systems, University of Kassel, 34121 Kassel, Germany
{plettenberg,dhuseljic,bsick}@uni-kassel.de
[2] CELUS GmbH, 80339 Munich, Germany
andre.alcalde@celus.io
[3] GAIN Group, Institute of Data Science, University of Greifswald, 17489 Greifswald, Germany
thomasj@uni-greifswald.de

Abstract. Active learning (AL) for node classification typically focuses on selecting the most informative nodes for annotation within one or a few large graphs (e.g., in social network analysis). However, in other domains, such as molecular chemistry or electronic design automation, datasets consist of thousands of independent graphs. In many of these inductive settings, annotating an individual node requires a full-graph analysis, which effectively yields the remaining node labels on-the-fly. Therefore, these scenarios require AL strategies that select entire graphs instead of single nodes, a problem which has not been tackled in the literature so far. Thus, we introduce ALINC, an AL framework for inductive node classification via graph sampling. It bridges the existing methodological gap by elevating node-level utility measures to graph-level selection criteria through various aggregation mechanisms. In an extensive benchmark including ten strategies, three aggregation methods, and four datasets, we identify CoreSet, TypiClust, and BADGE as the top-performing graph sampling strategies. Our detailed analysis further reveals that the choice of the aggregation method is pivotal, as it substantially affects model performance and annotation costs. Finally, we demonstrate the effectiveness of ALINC in two use case studies: site-of-metabolism prediction in molecules and design automation of printed circuit board schematics.

Keywords: Active Learning · Graph Neural Networks · Node Classification

---

Supplementary Information The online version contains supplementary material available at https://doi.org/10.1007/978-3-032-37654-1_6.

M. Ceci et al. (Eds.): ECML PKDD 2026, LNAI 16941, pp. 93–109, 2027.
https://doi.org/10.1007/978-3-032-37654-1_6

1 Introduction

The remarkable success of graph neural networks (GNNs) across diverse domains is fundamentally tied to the availability of high-quality, labeled datasets [9,16]. However, acquiring these labels is often a time-consuming and costly process that requires domain expertise. To mitigate this, active learning (AL) has emerged as a powerful paradigm [33]. By iteratively identifying and selecting the most informative instances for annotation, AL aims to maximize model performance while minimizing the total labeling cost. AL has been extensively studied in traditional data domains such as text [28] and images [18,20], but while established AL methods can be directly transferred to graph-structured data for graph-level prediction tasks [40], their application to node-level tasks is more challenging because inter-node dependencies violate the standard i.i.d. assumption.

So far, AL for node classification has predominantly focused on the *transductive setting* [6,12,15,23], where the dataset usually consists of a single large graph and the entire graph structure is known during training. In this setting, the goal is to select individual nodes for annotation based on different measures of node utility, e.g., uncertainty or representativeness. Only a few works also apply AL to node classification in the *inductive setting*, where the model needs to generalize to unseen graph structures [36,44,45]. However, these studies focus on selecting individual nodes from datasets consisting of a few large-scale graphs, e.g., different snapshots of a growing social network such as in the Reddit dataset [14].

A critical gap remains in settings where inductive node classification is performed on large datasets composed of thousands of smaller, independent graphs, e.g., in molecular chemistry [29] or electronic design automation [25]. In these contexts, labeling a single node typically requires a holistic assessment of the whole graph (or large parts of it), possibly via expensive experiments or simulations, which often yields many or all of the remaining node labels on-the-fly. In some cases, such as site-of-metabolism (SoM) identification in molecules [35], isolated node labeling is even technically infeasible because experimental protocols inherently characterize the entire molecule. Consequently, all node (or atom) labels are generated simultaneously, making the cost of annotating a single node effectively identical to that of the entire graph. In these situations, AL strategies therefore need to select entire graphs for annotation rather than single nodes, which is more challenging because it involves the aggregation of node-level utility scores. To the best of our knowledge, no existing study has so far investigated this integration of aggregation mechanisms into AL strategies to perform graph sampling for inductive node classification.

In this paper, we bridge this gap by introducing an AL framework that enables graph sampling for inductive node classification. Our contributions are the following:

1. **Framework:** We propose **ALINC**[1] – an **A**ctive **L**earning framework for **I**nductive **N**ode **C**lassification via graph sampling. ALINC integrates various

[1] The code is available at https://github.com/pasplett/alinc.

mechanisms for aggregating node-level utility measures into established AL strategies, including uncertainty-, representativeness-, diversity-based, and hybrid strategies.
2. **Benchmarking:** We conduct an extensive benchmark study, comparing ten different strategies and three aggregation methods across four different datasets, using both message-passing GNNs and graph transformers.
3. **Analysis:** We provide a detailed analysis of how different combinations of strategies and aggregation methods affect model performance and annotation costs, providing useful insights and recommendations for practitioners.
4. **Applicability:** We present two use case studies on real-world graph datasets in the domains of SoM prediction and design automation of printed circuit board (PCB) schematics to highlight the effectiveness of ALINC.

2 Related Work

GNNs such as GCN [21], GatedGCN [3,9], GAT [38], GIN [41], GINE [17], and GATv2 [4] have achieved outstanding results in learning local relationships from graph-structured data via local message-passing. However, their ability to capture long-range dependencies is limited by issues like over-smoothing [24] and over-squashing [1]. To mitigate this, graph transformers (GT) [7,34,42] leverage global attention for long-distance modeling. Recent hybrid architectures, notably GPS [27], combine local message-passing with positional encodings and global attention to improve performance.

AL strategies generally belong to at least one of the following categories: uncertainty, representativeness, and diversity. Traditional uncertainty heuristics, such as entropy and margin [33], are used to prioritize instances near the decision boundary where the model lacks confidence. To ensure the selections are representative of the underlying data distribution, instances can be selected based on information density [33]. In batch AL, where multiple instances are sampled at once, diversity-based methods like CoreSet [32] treat the data selection as a geometric coverage problem to minimize redundancy across the feature space. Modern hybrid frameworks aim to balance these competing objectives. For instance, BADGE [2] combines gradient embeddings with k-MEANS++ to identify uncertain yet diverse batches, while TypiClust [13] integrates clustering with density to select typical instances from across the entire manifold.

AL on graphs has so far focused on strategically selecting the most informative nodes for annotation, and has been mainly applied to transductive node classification [6,12,15,23] as well as inductive node classification on a single or a few large graphs [36,44,45]. The most fundamental approaches include uncertainty-based strategies [11], density-based sampling [6], as well as strategies based on node centrality, e.g., node degree [6] or PageRank centrality [30], which can be seen as a measure of representativeness. AGE [6] combines entropy, information density, and node centrality into a single heuristic score. ANRMAB [12] introduces a dynamic weighting via a multi-armed bandit framework. Other notable strategies for AL on graphs include FeatProp [39], which combines node feature propagation with node clustering, GPA [15], which uses reinforcement learning to learn an optimal query strategy, and GraphPart [23], which selects representative nodes from disjoint partitions of the graph.

However, these strategies are specifically designed for node sampling and are not directly transferable to inductive node classification via graph sampling, which requires the aggregation of node-level measures. We note that this approach is related to **AL for object detection**, where scores for individual detections are aggregated for image selection [5,31]. To the best of our knowledge, this is the first work to transfer this concept to the graph sampling problem for inductive node classification.

3 Problem Formulation

We consider a batch AL setting with a total labeling budget B distributed over T consecutive cycles. Let $\mathcal{U}_t = \{G_1, G_2, \ldots, G_N\}$ be a collection of unlabeled graphs at cycle t, where each graph $G_i = (\mathcal{V}_i,\ \mathbf{A}^{(i)})$ is defined by a set of nodes $\mathcal{V}_i$ and an adjacency matrix $\mathbf{A}^{(i)} \in \{0,1\}^{|\mathcal{V}_i|\times|\mathcal{V}_i|}$. We assume the existence of an oracle that, when queried with a graph G_i, provides a label matrix $\mathbf{Y}^{(i)} \in \mathbb{N}^{|\mathcal{V}_i|\times C}$, i.e., the matrix entry $y_{jk}^{(i)} = 1$ indicates node j has label k. The set of labeled graphs $\mathcal{L}_t = \{(G_i, \mathbf{Y}^{(i)})\}$ is initialized at $t = 0$ by randomly sampling b graph instances. Afterwards, we select b instances to label in each cycle, such that $B = b + T \cdot b$.

Given a GNN or GT model $f_\theta = h_\omega \circ g_\varphi$ consisting of an encoder g parameterized by φ and a classification head h parameterized by ω, the goal of **active inductive node classification via graph sampling** is to design a strategy that selects in each cycle $t > 0$ a batch of graphs $\mathcal{S}_t \subset \mathcal{U}_t$ with $|\mathcal{S}_t| = b$ that minimizes the expected loss on an unseen test distribution $\mathcal{D}_{test}$:

$$\min_{\mathcal{S}_t \subset \mathcal{U}_t, |\mathcal{S}_t| = b} \mathbb{E}_{G_i \sim \mathcal{D}_{test}} \left[L(f_{\theta^*}(\{G_i\}), \{\mathbf{Y}^{(i)}\}) \right], \tag{1}$$

where L is the cross-entropy loss and the optimal parameters $\theta^* = \{\varphi^*, \omega^*\}$ are obtained by training the model f_θ on the labeled graph set $\mathcal{L}_t = \mathcal{L}_{t-1} \cup \mathcal{S}_t$.

4 The ALINC Framework

In the ALINC framework, a query strategy selects in cycle t a subset of graphs $\mathcal{S}_t \subset \mathcal{U}_t$ with $|\mathcal{S}_t| = b$ by ranking the unlabeled graphs in $\mathcal{U}_t$ based on an acquisition function $\Phi : \mathcal{U}_t \to \mathbb{R}$. Formally, the selection is defined as:

$$\mathcal{S} = \underset{G_i \in \mathcal{U}_t}{\arg \text{top-b}}\ \ \Phi(G_i \mid \varphi, \omega, \mathcal{U}_t, \mathcal{L}_{t-1}). \tag{2}$$

The acquisition function Φ evaluates the utility of a graph G_i, based on a permutation-invariant aggregation agg$(\cdot)$ (such as `max`, `mean`, or `sum`) of node-level properties, including latent node embeddings $\mathbf{H}^{(i)} \in \mathbb{R}^{|\mathcal{V}_i|\times M}$ computed by g_φ, predictive logits $\mathbf{Z}^{(i)} \in \mathbb{R}^{|\mathcal{V}_i| \times C}$ computed by f_θ, or structural measures derived from the adjacency matrix $\mathbf{A}^{(i)} \in \{0,1\}^{|\mathcal{V}_i| \times |\mathcal{V}_i|}$. Furthermore, representativeness- and diversity-based strategies are context-aware, as they are also conditioned on all other graphs in $\mathcal{U}_t$ and possibly $\mathcal{L}_{t-1}$.

In the following, we describe how different types of query strategies can be transferred into the ALINC framework. We include both general AL strategies as well as special strategies for AL on graphs, which were originally designed for node sampling.

4.1 Uncertainty-Based Strategies

Uncertainty-based sampling is a widely used paradigm in AL that identifies instances for which the current model f_θ lacks confidence. In the ALINC framework, we adapt these strategies by aggregating node-level uncertainty measures to the graph level. For each graph $G_i \in \mathcal{U}_t$, we first compute the predictive probabilities $\mathbf{P}^{(i)} = \sigma(\mathbf{Z}^{(i)})$, where $\sigma(\cdot)$ denotes the softmax function and the matrix entry $p_{jk}^{(i)}$ represents the probability of node j belonging to class k. We consider two popular uncertainty metrics [33] for the acquisition function Φ:

Entropy sampling selects graphs with the highest aggregated information content. The node-level entropy for node j is defined as $E_j = -\sum_{k=1}^{C} p_{jk}^{(i)} \log p_{jk}^{(i)}$. The acquisition function is then:

$$\Phi_{\text{Ent}}(G_i \mid \varphi, \omega) = \text{agg}_{j \in \mathcal{V}_i}(E_j). \tag{3}$$

Margin sampling targets nodes where the model cannot easily distinguish between the two most likely classes. Let $\hat{k}_1$ and $\hat{k}_2$ be the indices of the largest and second-largest probabilities for node j. The margin is $M_j = p_{j\hat{k}_1}^{(i)} - p_{j\hat{k}_2}^{(i)}$. Since a smaller margin implies higher uncertainty, we use:

$$\Phi_{\text{Marg}}(G_i \mid \varphi, \omega) = \text{agg}_{j \in \mathcal{V}_i}(1 - M_j). \tag{4}$$

As defined in Sect. 4, the aggregation operator agg$(\cdot)$ can be any permutation-invariant function. For example, using `mean` allows the framework to prioritize graphs with a high overall density of uncertain nodes, while the `max` operator would prioritize graphs with the highest individual node uncertainty.

4.2 Representativeness-Based Strategies

Representativeness-based strategies aim to select representative instances from high-density regions of the feature space, giving lower priority to outliers. In graph AL, the most common measures for representativeness are information density [33] and node centrality [6].

Density-Based Strategies. In conventional AL settings, the density score of an instance $\mathbf{x}_j$ from an arbitrary unlabeled pool $\{\mathbf{x}_j\}$ is computed from the Euclidean distance to its nearest cluster center $\mathbf{c}_j^*$, derived from applying k-MEANS to the embedding set:

$$\text{density}(\mathbf{x}_j \mid \{\mathbf{x}_j\}) = \frac{1}{1 + \|\mathbf{x}_j - \mathbf{c}_j^*\|_2}. \tag{5}$$

Increasing the number of clusters k reduces redundancy in the acquired batch but makes it less representative. We choose $k = b$ in our experiments, following usual practice [6,23]. However, we provide additional experiments in Appendix A, showing that $k = b$ is not necessarily the best choice.

In ALINC, we distinguish between two different density-based acquisition strategies. In **Node-Density** sampling, we first perform the clustering and density calculation on the node embedding $\mathbf{h}_j^{(i)}$ from all graphs in $\mathcal{U}_t$. The aggregation is then performed on the node-level density scores:

$$\Phi_{\text{ND}}(G_i \mid \varphi, \mathcal{U}_t) = \text{agg}_{j \in \mathcal{V}_i}(\text{density}(\mathbf{h}_j^{(i)} \mid \{\mathbf{h}_j^{(i)}\}_{1 \leq i \leq N,\ j \in \mathcal{V}_i})). \tag{6}$$

In **Graph-Density** sampling, node embeddings are first aggregated into a single graph-level representation $\mathbf{g}^{(i)} = \text{agg}_{j \in \mathcal{V}_i}(\mathbf{h}_j^{(i)})$. Clustering and density calculation are then performed directly on the set of graph-level embeddings:

$$\Phi_{\text{GD}}(G_i \mid \varphi, \mathcal{U}_t) = \text{density}(\mathbf{g}_i \mid \{\mathbf{g}^{(i)}\}_{1 \leq i \leq N}). \tag{7}$$

While the node-density strategy prioritizes graphs that contain representative nodes with respect to the learned node embedding space, the graph-density strategy prioritizes representative instances on the graph level.

Centrality-Based Strategies. The representativeness or importance of a node in a graph can be measured by node centrality scores, such as node degree and PageRank centrality [30]. Centrality-based AL strategies select the nodes with the highest centrality scores. We transfer this approach to the ALINC framework by aggregating node-centrality scores to graph-level utility scores.

Since the PageRank score is a measure of the relative importance of a node in a graph, it is not comparable across different graphs. Therefore, we only consider **Degree** sampling in the ALINC framework. In **Degree** sampling, the acquisition function can be formulated as

$$\Phi_{\text{Deg}}(G_i) = \text{agg}_{j \in \mathcal{V}_i}(d_j^{(i)}) \tag{8}$$

with the node degree $d_j^{(i)} = \sum_k \mathbf{A}_{jk}^{(i)}$.

4.3 Diversity-Based Strategies

In batch AL, strictly selecting the top-b instances according to uncertainty or representativeness may introduce redundancy. Therefore, we consider diversity-based strategies to ensure that the selected graphs cover the complete feature space.

We include **CoreSet** [32] as the only purely diversity-based strategy. This strategy aims to select a subset that covers the entire data distribution by minimizing the maximum distance between any unlabeled instance and its nearest labeled neighbor using a k-Center-greedy algorithm. In ALINC, we perform this selection based on the aggregated graph-level representations $\mathbf{g}^{(i)}$.

4.4 Hybrid Strategies

We further consider strategies that combine at least two of the three categories: uncertainty, representativeness, and diversity.

AGE [6] (uncertainty, representativeness) selects nodes for annotation by evaluating the utility of a node via a linear combination of entropy, density, and node centrality converted into percentiles. We transfer AGE to the ALINC framework by utilizing the strategies Entropy, Node-Density, and Degree to compute node-level AGE scores before aggregating them to the graph level afterwards.

ANRMAB [12] (uncertainty, representativeness) considers the same utility scores as AGE but combines them using a multi-armed bandit (MAB) approach. To perform graph sampling with this strategy, we aggregate the individual scores before applying MAB on the graph level.

TypiClust [13] (representativeness, diversity) selects typical instances from clusters that are under-represented in the labeled set. Similar to CoreSet, we perform the clustering and density-based selection on the aggregated graph-level embeddings $\mathbf{g}_i$.

Finally, **BADGE** [2] (uncertainty, diversity) consists of two main computation steps, a gradient embedding computation and a sampling computation. In the first step, the model's current predictions are treated as pseudo-labels for estimating the induced gradient of the loss with respect to the model parameters. In our framework, we aggregate the resulting node-level gradient embeddings to obtain graph-level embeddings. We then proceed with the second step by sampling from the aggregated gradient embeddings via k-MEANS++.

5 Experiments

In this section, we evaluate the ALINC strategies introduced in Sect. 4 on four benchmark graph datasets for inductive node classification. We first describe our experimental setup and then proceed with presenting a comprehensive performance comparison between strategies and aggregation methods. Next, we analyze the annotation costs of the different strategies in terms of the number of nodes in the selected graphs. Finally, we present additional results on two datasets from highly relevant application domains: (i) Site-of-metabolism (SoM) prediction in molecular graphs and (ii) printed circuit board (PCB) schematic design automation.

5.1 Experimental Setup

Datasets. For our benchmark experiments, we use four popular graph datasets for inductive node classification and adopt them in our AL setting: PATTERN and CLUSTER [9] contain synthetic graphs with node labels for pattern identification and node clustering, respectively. PascalVOC-SP and COCO-SP are part of the long-range graph benchmark [10] and contain image-based graphs, where each node corresponds to a superpixel with a particular semantic segmentation label.

AL Protocol. We adopt a common batch AL protocol from the image domain [18,20] and start from a random initial labeled pool of size b followed by 20 AL cycles with an acquisition size of b. Here, b is determined by ensuring that the respective evaluation metric converges within 20 cycles of random sampling. However, we restrict b to a maximum of 100 in order to focus on the typical AL scenario of labeled data scarcity. An overview of all datasets with corresponding batch sizes is given in Table 1.

Table 1. Overview of the graph datasets used for benchmarking AL strategies in the ALINC framework.

Dataset	#Graphs	Avg. Nodes	Avg. Edges	#Classes (C)	Acq. Size (b)
PATTERN	14,000	117.47	4,749.15	2	5
CLUSTER	12,000	117.20	4,301.72	6	50
PascalVOC-SP	11,355	479.40	2,710.48	21	100
COCO-SP	123,286	476.88	2,693.67	81	100

Models. We use two different models to cover both message-passing GNNs and GTs. For PATTERN and CLUSTER, we use GatedGCN, and for PascalVOC-SP and COCO-SP, we use GPS, since standard message-passing GNNs are significantly outperformed by GTs on the long-range graph benchmark [10].

Hyperparameters. The role of hyperparameters in AL is an open problem [19]. In this study, we adopt reported model hyperparameters from the literature, wherever possible. For GatedGCN on PATTERN and CLUSTER, we use the hyperparameters from [9], and only tune the learning rate by maximizing validation performance on random sampling. For GPS on PascalVOC-SP and COCO-SP, we adopt the hyperparameters from [37].

Baseline Strategies. We use random sampling as our baseline and compare it to all strategies introduced in Sect. 4: Entropy [33], Margin [33], Node-Density, Graph-Density, Degree [6], CoreSet [32], AGE [6], ANRMAB [12], TypiClust [13], and BADGE [2]. We further evaluate each strategy with different aggregation mechanisms: `mean`, `max`, and `sum`.

Evaluation Metrics. We utilize relative learning curves, which track performance gains in absolute percentage points over random sampling at each cycle (positive values demonstrate AL effectiveness), and the area under the learning curve (AULC) to quantify cumulative performance across all cycles. We further supplement our evaluation with pairwise win rate comparisons, i.e., the percentage of trials where strategy i yields a higher AULC than strategy j.

For PATTERN and CLUSTER, performance is measured via macro-averaged accuracy, and for PascalVOC-SP and COCO-SP, the performance corresponds to the macro-averaged F1 score. In all experiments, the performance is measured on a separate test dataset (excluded from the unlabeled pool), averaged across ten independent trials.

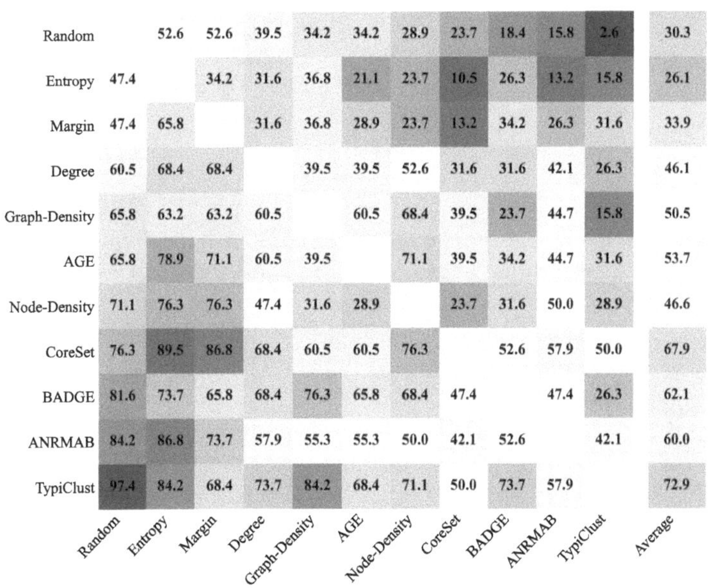

Fig. 1. Pairwise comparison matrix averaged across 4 datasets and 10 trials. Element (i, j) corresponds to the proportion of total runs (in %), where strategy i yields a higher AULC compared to strategy j. For each strategy, we considered the best-performing aggregation mechanism for the respective trial.

5.2 Benchmarking ALINC Strategies

Figure 1 shows the pairwise comparison matrix between all strategies across all four datasets. For each trial, we considered the best-performing aggregation method for each strategy. Except for the purely uncertainty-based strategies Entropy and Margin, all strategies perform better than random sampling on average, with five strategies yielding a win rate of more than 70 %. The three strategies that incorporate diversity (CoreSet, BADGE, and TypiClust) exhibit the highest average win rates (row average). The best-performing strategy is TypiClust, which shows a nearly perfect win rate against random sampling and the highest average win rate against the other strategies.

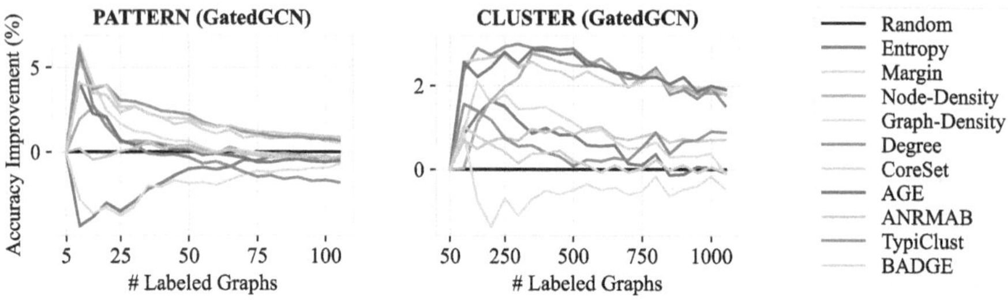

Fig. 2. Relative accuracy learning curves for different query strategies in the ALINC framework on PATTERN and CLUSTER using GatedGCN.

The relative learning curves for GatedGCN on PATTERN and CLUSTER are presented in Fig. 2. Again, we focus on comparing individual strategies by selecting the best-performing aggregation method for each strategy as measured by the AULC. We observe that the performance of most strategies varies strongly across different datasets. For example, while the purely uncertainty-based strategies, Entropy and Margin, perform poorly on PATTERN, they significantly outperform random sampling on CLUSTER. Overall, we observe the most consistent performance improvements over random sampling for TypiClust and BADGE, as they belong to the top three performing strategies on all datasets except for CLUSTER. The relative learning curves for GPS on PascalVOC-SP and COCO-SP, as well as all absolute learning curves and a tabular AULC comparison of all strategies across all datasets, are provided in Appendix B.

Key Take-Away: Among all tested strategies, TypiClust shows the highest total win rate over random sampling (97.4 %). As a hybrid strategy that combines representativeness and diversity, it shows the highest consistency across datasets. In general, different datasets yield different top-performing ALINC strategies.

5.3 Benchmarking Aggregation Methods

Figure 3 shows pairwise comparisons between the three aggregation methods for all strategies and datasets included in our experiments. We observe that `mean` aggregation generally shows the lowest win rates on average, whereas `max` is the best performing aggregation method for six of ten strategies (Entropy, Margin, Node-Density, Degree, AGE, BADGE), and three of four datasets (PATTERN, PascalVOC-SP, COCO-SP). `Sum`-aggregation performs best for ANRMAB and TypiClust, as well as on the CLUSTER dataset. Among all strategies, CoreSet

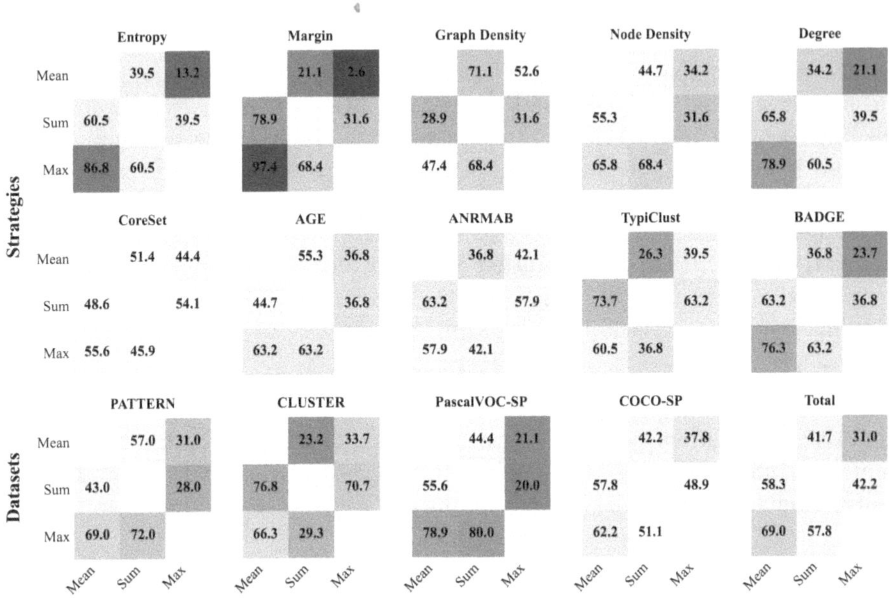

Fig. 3. Top and middle row: Pairwise comparison matrix averaged across 4 datasets and 10 trials for all strategies. Bottom row: Pairwise comparison matrix averaged across 10 strategies and 10 trials for all datasets, and total pairwise comparison matrix across all strategies and datasets (bottom row, rightmost column). In each subplot, element (i, j) corresponds to the proportion of total runs (in %), where aggregation method i yields a higher AULC compared to aggregation method j.

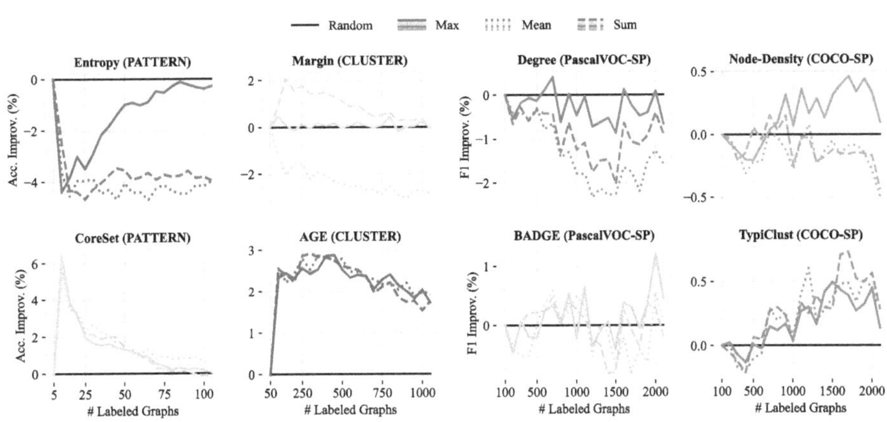

Fig. 4. Top row: Relative learning curves of selected strategies with high sensitivity on the aggregation type. Bottom row: Selected relative learning curves of strategies with low sensitivity on the aggregation type.

shows the lowest sensitivity to the choice of the aggregation function; the win rates are very balanced for this strategy.

We further compare the relative learning curves of different aggregation mechanisms for selected strategies and datasets in Fig. 4. Thereby, we observe that the impact of the aggregation method strongly depends on the strategy and the dataset. For example, the `sum`-Margin strategy outperforms random sampling on CLUSTER, whereas the `mean`-Margin strategy has a strong negative impact on model performance. For other strategies, such as CoreSet on PATTERN or TypiClust on COCO-SP, we observe rather low sensitivities regarding the aggregation type. The complete set of relative learning curves for all strategy-aggregation combinations and datasets is provided in Appendix C.

Key Take-Away: The majority of ALINC strategies perform best when combined with a `max`- or `sum`-aggregation, whereas `mean`-aggregation performs worst in most cases. The choice of the aggregation method depends on the dataset and is of great importance, as it can also negatively affect the strategy, resulting in a performance worse than random sampling.

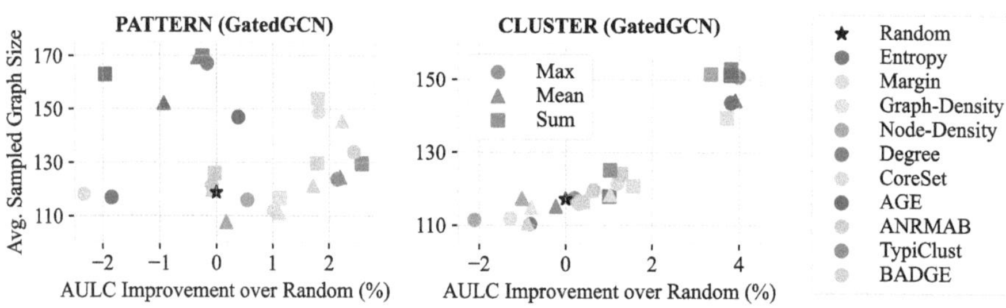

Fig. 5. Annotation costs in terms of averaged sampled graph size against the relative AULC improvement over random sampling for different strategies and aggregation mechanisms with GatedGCN on PATTERN and CLUSTER. Some strategy-aggregation combinations are not displayed due to poor performance.

5.4 Annotation Cost Analysis

ALINC is designed for situations where the costs of labeling a single node in a graph are comparable to the costs of labeling all nodes in the graph, because both require a full-graph analysis. Therefore, the annotation costs in the ALINC framework are strongly related to the costs of the full-graph analysis, which may be influenced by different parameters of the sampled graphs, depending on the dataset or use case. For example, in some cases, the annotation costs may be proportional to the graph size (e.g., the number of nodes), whereas in other cases, the annotation costs could depend on the number of classes or the complexity of the graph structure.

For PATTERN and CLUSTER, we approximate the annotation costs of different strategy-aggregation combinations by calculating the average size of sampled graphs across all AL cycles. Figure 5 shows the relation between this cost measure and the AULC improvement over random sampling. We observe that some strategies, such as Degree, AGE, and CoreSet, select larger graphs on average. Furthermore, sum-aggregation is naturally biased towards larger graphs for many strategies. However, for the PATTERN dataset, we do not observe a significant correlation between the sampled graph size and the strategy performance. In contrast, Node- and Graph-Density sampling even achieve substantial improvements over random sampling while selecting *smaller* graphs at the same time. Furthermore, TypiClust and BADGE yield even higher AULC improvements by selecting just slightly larger graphs. In contrast, on the CLUSTER dataset, we observe a strong correlation between strategy performance and the size of selected graphs, which may explain why sum-aggregation generally performs better on this dataset, as observed in Fig. 3.

Key Take-Away: While some strategies are biased towards selecting larger graphs, this is not always a guarantee for better performance. In contrast, we observed that some ALINC strategies even outperform random sampling by selecting *smaller* graphs.

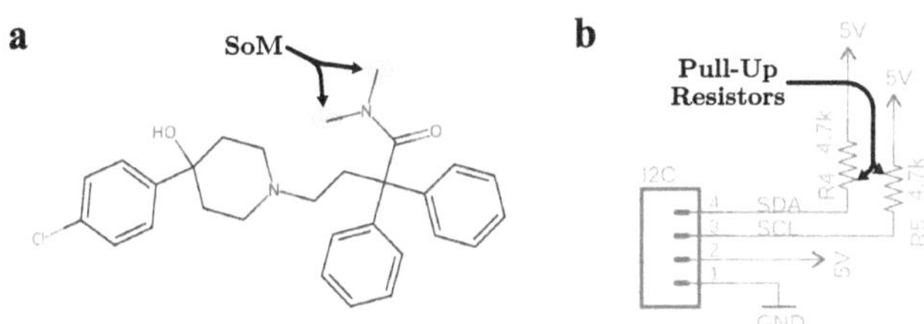

Fig. 6. a) An example molecule from the Zaretzki dataset with metabolism sites highlighted in light blue. **b)** An excerpt from a PCB schematic with two pull-up resistors (R4, R5) connecting the I2C signal lines to a 5V supply.

5.5 Use Case Studies

We apply ALINC in two use case studies: site-of-metabolism (SoM) prediction in molecules, and missing pull-up/-down resistor prediction in PCB schematics. For experimental details on both use cases, see Appendix D.

Site-of-Metabolism Prediction. Predicting SoM in molecules with machine learning models is an active area of research [22,35], but its success depends on the availability of experimentally acquired training data. While AL has been applied to the selection of specific atoms for SoM annotation based on already

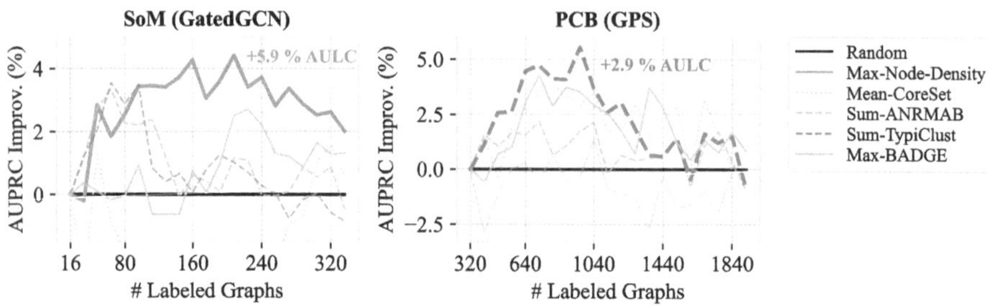

Fig. 7. Relative learning curves for different ALINC strategies on the Zaretzki SoM dataset using GatedGCN (left), and on the PCB pull-ups/-downs dataset using GPS (right). The strategies with the highest AULC are highlighted for better visibility. The used performance metric is the area under the precision-recall curve (AUPRC).

acquired raw measurement data [8], we consider the use case of selecting entire molecules for experimental testing. To this end, we use the publicly available Zaretzki dataset [43], which contains more than 650 drugs and drug-like compounds with experimentally confirmed SoM labels. An example compound from this dataset is visualized in Fig. 6a. We first transform the raw molecule data into graphs following the representation from the ogbg-molhiv and ogbg-molpcba datasets [16]. Using the full training set, we first perform hyperparameter optimizations on three different message-passing GNNs (GatedGCN, GINE, and GATv2), and observe that GatedGCN yields the highest validation performance (see App. D for details). Consequently, we use GatedGCN to perform AL experiments in the setup explained in Sect. 5.1 with the five top-performing ALINC strategies according to our benchmark study: `max`-Node-Density, `sum`-ANRMAB, `mean`-CoreSet, `sum`-TypiClust, and `max`-BADGE. We observe that `max`-Node-Density outperforms diversity-based strategies on this dataset and yields the highest AULC with a relative improvement of 5.9 % over random sampling (see Fig. 7).

PCB Schematic Design Automation. As a second use case, we investigate the application of ALINC to PCB schematic design automation, specifically the task of adding missing pull-up and pull-down resistors (see Fig. 6b for an example). While not necessary for circuit functionality, design optimizations like this increase the overall lifetime and reliability of the final electronic device. There is a huge interest for automating such optimization tasks, as they are usually performed manually by human engineers in a time-consuming and error-prone process. We use the dataset and graph representation from [25], and tune hyperparameters (number of layers, hidden dimension, learning rate) via holdout validation. Thereby, we compare the same GNNs used for SoM prediction with GPS and FlowGATv2 [26], which has been shown to be effective on electronic circuit data. Since GPS yields the highest performance among the models (see App. D), we use this model for AL experiments. Note that the dataset task requires making a prediction on pairs of nodes. Therefore, we perform all aggregations on node-pair-level logits or features, which is a straightforward modification of our framework and highlights its flexibility. Figure 7 shows that several strategies outperform random sampling, with `sum`-TypiClust yielding the highest AULC (+2.9 % over random).

6 Conclusion

We introduced ALINC, the first AL framework for inductive node classification that enables the selection of entire graphs for annotation via aggregation of node-level utility measures. Through extensive benchmarking, we identify TypiClust, CoreSet, and BADGE as top-performing strategies and reveal that the choice of the aggregation method has a strong impact on model performance and annotation cost. Successfully applied to molecular chemistry and electronic design, ALINC provides a robust, flexible solution for maximizing data efficiency in domains where node labeling requires a full-graph analysis.

In future work, we want to explore more complex aggregation methods, e.g., by introducing learnable weights. Inspired by its success in the image domain, we also want to investigate the usage of self-supervised learning to further increase the performance of ALINC strategies. Finally, we want to extend our framework also to node regression, since it would open up many new application possibilities, e.g., in GNN-based surrogate modeling for numerical simulations.

Acknowledgments. This study was funded by the German Federal Ministry of Research, Technology, and Space (funding code 16ME0877).

Disclosure of Interests. The authors have no competing interests to declare that are relevant to the content of this article.

Use of Large Language Models. Large language models (LLMs) were only used for proofreading, language editing, and to assist with streamlining and debugging code. They were not used to generate scientific ideas, analyses, results, or conclusions. The authors take full responsibility for the final content of this paper.

References

1. Alon, U., Yahav, E.: On the bottleneck of graph neural networks and its practical implications. In: ICLR (2021)
2. Ash, J.T., Zhang, C., Krishnamurthy, A., Langford, J., Agarwal, A.: Deep batch active learning by diverse, uncertain gradient lower bounds. In: ICLR (2020)
3. Bresson, X., Laurent, T.: Residual gated graph convnets. arXiv preprint arXiv:1711.07553 (2017)
4. Brody, S., Alon, U., Yahav, E.: How attentive are graph attention networks? In: ICLR (2022)
5. Brust, C.A., Käding, C., Denzler, J.: Active learning for deep object detection. In: VISIGRAPP (2019)

6. Cai, H., Zheng, V.W., Chang, K.C.C.: Active learning for graph embedding. arXiv preprint arXiv:1705.05085 (2017)
7. Chen, D., O'Bray, L., Borgwardt, K.: Structure-aware transformer for graph representation learning. In: ICML (2022)
8. Chen, Y., et al.: Active learning approach for guiding site-of-metabolism measurement and annotation. JCIM **64**(2), 348–358 (2024)
9. Dwivedi, V.P., Joshi, C.K., Luu, A.T., Laurent, T., Bengio, Y., Bresson, X.: Benchmarking graph neural networks. JMLR **24**(43), 1–48 (2023)
10. Dwivedi, V.P., et al.: Long range graph benchmark. In: NeurIPS (2022)
11. Fuchsgruber, D., Wollschläger, T., Charpentier, B., Oroz, A., Günnemann, S.: Uncertainty for active learning on graphs. In: ICML (2024)
12. Gao, L., Yang, H., Zhou, C., Wu, J., Pan, S., Hu, Y.: Active discriminative network representation learning. In: IJCAI (2018)
13. Hacohen, G., Dekel, A., Weinshall, D.: Active learning on a budget: opposite strategies suit high and low budgets. In: ICML (2022)
14. Hamilton, W., Ying, Z., Leskovec, J.: Inductive representation learning on large graphs. In: NeurIPS (2017)
15. Hu, S., et al.: Graph policy network for transferable active learning on graphs. In: NeurIPS (2020)
16. Hu, W., et al.: Open graph benchmark: Datasets for machine learning on graphs. In: NeurIPS (2020)
17. Hu, W., et al.: Strategies for pre-training graph neural networks. In: ICLR (2019)
18. Huseljic, D., Hahn, P., Herde, M., Rauch, L., Sick, B.: Fast fishing: approximating bait for efficient and scalable deep active image classification. In: ECML PKDD (2024)
19. Huseljic, D., Herde, M., Hahn, P., Sick, B.: Role of hyperparameters in deep active learning. In: IAL @ ECML PKDD, pp. 19–24 (2023)
20. Huseljic, D., Herde, M., Rauch, L., Hahn, P., Sick, B.: Cleaning the pool: progressive filtering of unlabeled pools in deep active learning. In: CVPR (2026)
21. Kipf, T.N., Welling, M.: Semi-supervised classification with graph convolutional networks. In: ICLR (2017)
22. Litsa, E.E., Das, P., Kavraki, L.E.: Machine learning models in the prediction of drug metabolism: challenges and future perspectives. Expert Opin. Drug Metab. Toxicol. **17**(11), 1245–1247 (2021)
23. Ma, J., Ma, Z., Chai, J., Mei, Q.: Partition-based active learning for graph neural networks. TMLR (2023)
24. Oono, K., Suzuki, T.: Graph neural networks exponentially lose expressive power for node classification. In: ICLR (2020)
25. Plettenberg, P., Alcalde, A., Sick, B., Thomas, J.M.: Graph neural networks for automatic addition of optimizing components in printed circuit board schematics. In: ECML PKDD (2025)
26. Plettenberg, P., Köhler, D., Sick, B., Thomas, J.M.: Flow-attentional graph neural networks. TMLR (2025)
27. Rampášek, L., Galkin, M., Dwivedi, V.P., Luu, A.T., Wolf, G., Beaini, D.: Recipe for a general, powerful, scalable graph transformer. In: NeurIPS (2022)
28. Rauch, L., Aßenmacher, M., Huseljic, D., Wirth, M., Bischl, B., Sick, B.: Activeglae: a benchmark for deep active learning with transformers. In: ECML PKDD (2023)
29. Reiser, P., et al.: Graph neural networks for materials science and chemistry. Commun. Mater. **3**(1), 93 (2022)
30. Rodriguez, M.A.: Grammar-based random walkers in semantic networks. KBS **21**(7), 727–739 (2008)

31. Roy, S., Unmesh, A., Namboodiri, V.P.: Deep active learning for object detection. In: BMVC (2018)
32. Sener, O., Savarese, S.: Active learning for convolutional neural networks: a core-set approach. In: ICLR (2018)
33. Settles, B.: Active learning literature survey. Technical Report, University of Wisconsin-Madison, Department of Computer Sciences (2009)
34. Shirzad, H., Velingker, A., Venkatachalam, B., Sutherland, D.J., Sinop, A.K.: Exphormer: sparse transformers for graphs. In: ICML (2023)
35. Sicho, M., et al.: Fame 3: predicting the sites of metabolism in synthetic compounds and natural products for phase 1 and phase 2 metabolic enzymes. JCIM **59**(8), 3400–3412 (2019)
36. Song, Z., Zhang, Y., King, I.: No change, no gain: empowering graph neural networks with expected model change maximization for active learning. In: NeurIPS (2023)
37. Tönshoff, J., Ritzert, M., Rosenbluth, E., Grohe, M.: Where did the gap go? Reassessing the long-range graph benchmark. TMLR (2024)
38. Veličković, P., Cucurull, G., Casanova, A., Romero, A., Lio, P., Bengio, Y.: Graph attention networks. In: ICLR (2018)
39. Wu, Y., Xu, Y., Singh, A., Yang, Y., Dubrawski, A.: Active learning for graph neural networks via node feature propagation. arXiv preprint arXiv:1910.07567 (2019)
40. Xie, Y., Lv, S., Qian, Y., Wen, C., Liang, J.: Active and semi-supervised graph neural networks for graph classification. IEEE TBD **8**(4), 920–932 (2022)
41. Xu, K., Hu, W., Leskovec, J., Jegelka, S.: How powerful are graph neural networks? In: ICLR (2019)
42. Ying, C., et al.: Do transformers really perform badly for graph representation? In: NeurIPS (2021)
43. Zaretzki, J., Matlock, M., Swamidass, S.J.: Xenosite: accurately predicting cyp-mediated sites of metabolism with neural networks. JCIM **53**(12), 3373–3383 (2013)
44. Zhang, W., et al.: Information gain propagation: a new way to graph active learning with soft labels. In: ICLR (2022)
45. Zhang, W., et al.: Grain: improving data efficiency of graph neural networks via diversified influence maximization. In: VLDB (2021)

HydraAD: Exceptionally Fast and Accurate Time Series Anomaly Detection Using Competing Random Kernels

Louis Carpentier[1,2,3](✉), Laurens Devos[1,2,3], Wannes Meert[1,2], and Mathias Verbeke[1,2,3]

[1] Department of Computer Science, KU Leuven, Leuven, Belgium
{louis.carpentier,laurens.devos,wannes.meert,mathias.verbeke}@kuleuven.be
[2] Leuven.AI - KU Leuven Institute for AI, Leuven, Belgium
[3] Flanders Make@KU Leuven, Leuven, Belgium

Abstract. Time series anomaly detection is the automatic detection of unexpected observations in sequential data, a fundamental task across many scientific fields and industrial applications. In this work, we present HydraAD, an accurate, efficient, and domain-agnostic anomaly detection model for both univariate and multivariate time series. HydraAD builds upon Hydra for organizing random convolutional kernels into groups, and introduces a novel approach for deriving anomaly scores based on the soft counts of subsequences with competing kernels within each group. HydraAD is exceptionally fast because all parts of the pipeline, including the convolution of random kernels with time series subsequences, can be implemented efficiently on modern hardware. Our empirical evaluation shows that HydraAD significantly outperforms state-of-the-art methods, achieving a median VUS-PR of 0.61 versus 0.35 for the most competitive baseline. Furthermore, HydraAD enables the detection of anomalies in massive time series, consisting of 5, 000, 000 observations, in less than one second.

Keywords: Time series · Anomaly detection · Scalability · Random kernels

1 Introduction

Time series anomaly detection (TSAD), the task of detecting points or sequences in time series that deviate from the regular patterns [24], remains a critical task across many domains. The applications of TSAD range from performance profiling in rotating machinery [12] and automated decision-making in financial

Supplementary Information The online version contains supplementary material available at https://doi.org/10.1007/978-3-032-37654-1_7.

M. Ceci et al. (Eds.): ECML PKDD 2026, LNAI 16941, pp. 110–127, 2027.
https://doi.org/10.1007/978-3-032-37654-1_7

markets [2] to real-time healthcare monitoring [14]. TSAD has been extensively studied over the past two decades, with hundreds of methods as a result [17,24].

Recent studies have demonstrated that convolutional neural networks achieve state-of-the-art performance in TSAD [17,19,21]. Within the field of time series *classification*, Rocket [6] and its extensions such as MiniRocket [7], MultiRocket [26], and Hydra [8] demonstrate that models using randomized convolutional kernels achieve state-of-the-art performance while also significantly reducing the computational complexity compared to models with learned kernels. More specifically, these methods transform time series through convolutions with a large set of random kernels to generate features, which are subsequently passed to a linear classifier. The minimal training time and excellent performance of Rocket and its extensions such as Hydra make them highly effective for time series classification. This raises the natural question: *is it possible to leverage random convolutional kernels for TSAD?*

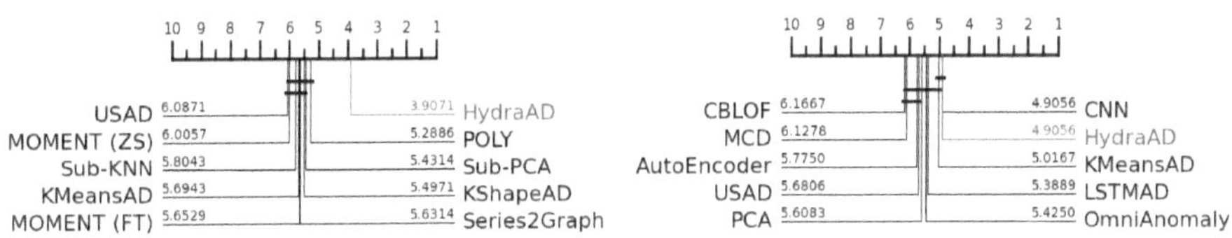

(a) TSB-AD-U (b) TSB-AD-M

Fig. 1. Mean rank of HYDRAAD versus top-performing state-of-the-art anomaly detection models in a critical difference diagram [10] on the TSB-AD benchmark. HYDRAAD significantly outperforms all competitors on TSB-AD-U, and has a tied best rank on TSB-AD-M at only a fraction of the computational cost compared to top-performing methods such as CNN, KMeansAD and LSTMAD.

In this work, we demonstrate that random convolutional kernels provide a powerful mechanism for accurate and efficient anomaly detection. Specifically, we present HYDRAAD, an unsupervised, domain-agnostic anomaly detection model designed for both univariate and multivariate time series.[1] HYDRAAD builds upon Hydra by organizing random kernels into groups, and introduces a novel approach to efficiently derive anomaly scores based on the soft counts of subsequences with competing kernels within each group.

As demonstrated in Fig. 1, HYDRAAD achieves state-of-the-art performance on TSB-AD [17], an extensive benchmark comprising 350 univariate (TSB-AD-U) and 180 multivariate (TSB-AD-M) time series from diverse domains. On TSB-AD-U (Fig. 1a), HYDRAAD attains a significantly better average rank compared to all baseline models. On TSB-AD-M (Fig. 1b), HYDRAAD shares the best average rank with CNN [19], both of which significantly outperform all other

[1] Source code is available at https://github.com/ML-KULeuven/HydraAD.

methods with the exception of KMeansAD [22]. In addition to achieving state-of-the-art performance, HydraAD is exceptionally scalable and requires minimal computational resources to detect anomalies in massive time series. Specifically, when restricted to a single CPU core, the total detection time for HydraAD is:

- 6.68 s for the longest univariate time series (ID 331 with 900,000 observations). By comparison, POLY requires 1.43 s, Sub-PCA 11.39 s, and KShapeAD 278.38 s.
- 14.32 s for the longest time series of TSB-AD-M (ID 20 with 650,000 observations and 2 channels). By comparison, CNN requires 54.32 s, LSTMAD 36.47 s, and KMeansAD 167.66 s.

HydraAD processes the entire TSB-AD-U and TSB-AD-M benchmarks in 125 s and 42 min, respectively. Furthermore, as the main computational step involves convolutions of subsequences with random kernels, HydraAD is highly amenable to GPU acceleration. Leveraging a GPU reduces the total detection time for the complete TSB-AD-U and TSB-AD-M datasets to 8 s (16× faster) and 33 s (76× faster), respectively.

The remainder of this paper is organized as follows. In Sect. 2, we introduce the necessary background knowledge, after which we explain HydraAD in Sect. 3. Then, in Sect. 4, we position HydraAD with regard to related work. We thoroughly evaluate HydraAD in a large-scale benchmark in Sect. 5 and demonstrate that HydraAD achieves state-of-the-art anomaly detection performance with minimal computational resources.

2 Preliminaries and Background

2.1 Notation

A *time series* $T = (x_1, \ldots, x_n) \in \mathbb{R}^{n \times c}$ is an ordered sequence of $n \in \mathbb{N}$ values $x_i \in \mathbb{R}^c$. If $c = 1$, T is univariate; otherwise, T is multivariate with c dimensions (also referred to as *channels*). We denote channel j of T as $T^{(j)} \in \mathbb{R}^n$ and the ith observation on channel j as $x_i^{(j)} \in \mathbb{R}$. For a subset $J \subseteq \{1, \ldots, c\}$ of all channels, we denote $T^{(J)} \in \mathbb{R}^{n \times |J|}$ as all channels in J and $x_i^{(J)} \in \mathbb{R}^{|J|}$ as observation i on the channels in J.

A *subsequence* $T_{i,w}$ of time series $T \in \mathbb{R}^{n \times c}$ with $1 \leq i \leq n - w$ is a time series of length w consisting of the w contiguous vectors from T starting at offset i. Formally, $T_{i,w} = (x_i, \ldots, x_{i+w-1}) \in \mathbb{R}^{w \times c}$.

An *anomaly* is an observation or a sequence of observations that deviates with regard to some characteristics of the time series [24]. The concrete definition of an anomaly depends on the task (e.g., discords are sequences with largest distance to their nearest neighbor [5]). Given a time series T of length n, the goal of TSAD is to predict an anomaly score $a(x_t) \in \mathbb{R}^+$ for each observation $x_t \in T$ such that x_t is considered more anomalous than $x_{t'}$ if $a(x_t) > a(x_{t'})$.

2.2 Hydra Classification

Hydra (HYbrid Dictionary-Rocket Architecture) [8] is a state-of-the-art time series classification algorithm that generalizes over Rocket [6] by combining characteristics of dictionary-based classifiers that rely on bag-of-patterns representations [16]. This is achieved by transforming time series using a large set of random convolutional kernels, arranged into g groups with k kernels per group. Hydra uses exponential dilations in the range $d \in \{2^0, 2^1, 2^2, \ldots, 2^{\lceil \log_2(n/m) \rceil}\}$ and generates $g \times k$ random kernels $W = (w_0, \ldots, w_{m-1})$ of length m for each dilation factor d for a total of $N_k = k \times g \times (\lceil \log_2(n/m) \rceil + 1)$ random kernels, with each w_i drawn from $\mathcal{N}(0, 1)$. Each kernel is normalized by subtracting the mean and dividing by L1-norm. Then, each normalized kernel is convolved with the time series as follows:

$$(T * W)_i = \sum_{j=0}^{m-1} x_{i+j \cdot d} \cdot w_j, \quad i \in \{0, \ldots, \hat{n}\} \tag{1}$$

with $\hat{n} = n - (m-1) \cdot d - 1$. The time series is padded with $\lfloor m/2 \rfloor \cdot d$ zeros at the beginning and end to ensure that the convolution output has the same length as T. For multivariate time series ($c > 1$), Hydra selects a random subset $J \subseteq \{1, \ldots, c\}$ of the channels for each group and sums the convolutions on each channel independently: $T^{(J)} * W = \sum_{j \in J} T^{(j)} * W$ [9]. While the original work assigns a random subset of channels to each group, with subset sizes varying between 2 and 8, we introduce a ratio ρ to determine the size of J relative to the total number of channels c in T: $|J| = \lfloor \rho \cdot c \rfloor$.

Within each group, Hydra counts the kernel representing the closest match (i.e., largest convolution outcome) with T at each time point. Denote $\mathbf{Z} = T * \mathbf{W} \in \mathbb{R}^{n \times k}$ the convolution of T with all k kernels of a group such that the jth column of $\mathbf{Z}$ equals $T * W_j$. The indices of the kernels with the closest match to T are given by:

$$u_i = \underset{j \in \{1, \ldots, k\}}{\arg\max}\, z_{i,j}, \quad i \in \{1, \ldots, n\}. \tag{2}$$

Hydra computes two features for each kernel j in this group: (1) hard counts, i.e., the number of times the jth kernel has the largest response, defined as $\sum_{i:u_i=j} 1$, and (2) soft counts, i.e., the sum of the responses where the jth kernel has the largest response, defined as $\sum_{i:u_i=j} z_{i,j}$.

Hydra normalizes each non-zero count with an adaptation of z-normalization to deal with feature-sparsity. For feature X, mean $\mu_{\sqrt{X}}$ and standard deviation $\sigma_{\sqrt{X}}$ are estimated using only the non-zero values of $\sqrt{X}$. The normalized features $\hat{X}$ are then derived as:

$$\hat{X} = \frac{\sqrt{X} - \mu_{\sqrt{X}}}{\sigma_{\sqrt{X}} + \delta^4} \tag{3}$$

where $\delta \in [0, 1]$ equals the proportion of zero values in X.

Finally, Hydra concatenates the normalized hard counts and soft counts to obtain a single feature vector of length $2 \cdot N_k$ for T. This vector serves as the input for a ridge regression or a logistic regression model which is trained to perform time series classification.

The more kernels are assigned per group, the more kernels 'compete' to have the maximum convolution outcome at each time point. As a consequence, the kernels with largest count more closely match the input time series. If there are fewer kernels within each group, then the winning kernels resemble the time series less. In the limit, when $k = 1$, there is no competition among the kernels and Hydra reduces to Rocket [6]. Leaving $g \times k$ fixed, the number of kernels per group k allows balancing between dictionary-based methods and Rocket.

3 Method

HydraAD detects anomalies in univariate ($c = 1$) and multivariate ($c > 1$) time series $T \in \mathbb{R}^{n \times c}$ by aggregating soft count features in a novel way. The method consists of three steps: (1) extracting subsequences from the time series T using a sliding window, (2) computing soft counts based on Hydra, and (3) deriving anomaly scores from these soft counts. The methodological novelty lies in a new quantile-based aggregation of the soft counts across multiple groups of competing random kernels.

1. Extracting Sliding Window Subsequences. HydraAD retrieves subsequences through a sliding window of length w and stride s over time series T:

$$\left\{T_{i \cdot s+1,w} \mid i \in \left[0, \ldots, \left\lfloor \frac{n-w}{s} \right\rfloor\right]\right\}. \tag{4}$$

The optimal window length typically depends on the application and time series characteristics. For univariate time series, we estimate w using the dominant Fourier frequency [11]. Assuming unit-space indices as is commonly done in the literature [17], we set $w = {}^1/_f$ and f the frequency with largest magnitude in the Fourier domain. We extend this approach to multivariate time series, in which a candidate window size w_j is computed for each channel $T^{(j)}$ and define w as the mean across all candidates: $w = \frac{1}{c}\sum_{j=1}^{c} w_j$.

2. Computing Soft Counts. For each subsequence $T_{i,w}$, we compute soft counts $c_s(T_{i,w}) \in \mathbb{R}^{N_k}$ across all kernels within each group using Hydra, with N_k the total number of kernels across all groups and dilations. See Sect. 2.2 for details.

3. HydraAD Anomaly Scores. We hypothesize that anomalous subsequences produce more extreme convolution responses for a small set of kernels. Hence, an anomalous subsequence $T_{i,w}$ has many matches with only a few kernels in each group, which leads to large soft counts. In contrast, a normal subsequence $T_{j,w}$ matches with many different kernels. There is more competition among these kernels to have the largest convolution outcome, leading to a more evenly spread set of soft counts.

Based on this observation, HYDRAAD assigns an anomaly score $a(T_{i,w})$ to each subsequence $T_{i,w}$ using the upper quantiles of the soft count $c_s(T_{i,w})$. Let Q_q denote the q-quantile of a sequence of numbers. Then, the HYDRAAD anomaly score for a subsequence is computed as:

$$a(T_{i,w}) = Q_q\big(|c_s(T_{i,w})|\big). \tag{5}$$

We take the element-wise absolute value of $c_s(T_{i,w})$ because the sign of the convolutional outcome is arbitrary as the kernels are random, and only the magnitude indicates how closely a kernel matches with a subsequence. Finally, to obtain anomaly scores $a(x_t)$ for each observation $x_t \in T$, we calculate the average over all subsequences $T_{i,w}$ for which $x_t \in T_{i,w}$ [24].

HYDRAAD ensures robustness against random variations in individual kernels by aggregating through quantiles, but also by leveraging soft counts across g groups and integrating exponential dilations to guarantee a diverse set of kernels.

4 Related Work

Random Convolutional Kernels. The effectiveness of random convolutional kernels is well-established in the literature. In computer vision, research has shown that the performance of a convolutional neural network is proportional to the accuracy of the same architecture using randomly initialized weights [23]. This suggests that the structural bias of convolutions is as important as the learned weights themselves. In time series classification, Rocket [6] achieves state-of-the-art performance by extracting features from time series through convolutions with a large set of random kernels. This approach avoids the need to learn kernels and thus requires minimal computational resources. Successive extensions of Rocket further improve scalability by improving the generation of kernels (MiniRocket [7]) or the predictive accuracy by computing more expressive features from the convolutions (MultiRocket [26]). While Rocket treats each kernel independently, Hydra [8] organizes the kernels in groups and computes features for each kernel with respect to the other kernels in the same group.

Time Series Anomaly Detection. Due to its practical applicability, time series anomaly detection has been extensively studied over the past years, which led to hundreds of anomaly detection methods [24]. Below, we provide a short summary of the best methods according to recent benchmark studies [17].

Sub-PCA [1] maps subsequences to a lower dimensional space through linear projections which capture the most important information, and anomalies are detected by measuring the deviation of the samples in the lower dimensional space. KShapeAD [20] clusters the subsequences using the KShape-clustering algorithm and detects anomalies based on a weighted distance to the cluster centers. POLY [15] uses polynomials to estimate each observation from the previous and following observations, and the anomaly score is set based on the error of these estimates. CNN [19] trains a Convolutional Neural Network to predict the next value for each time series subsequence, and detects anomalies based on the forecasting error. LSTMAD [18] is similar to CNN, but instead uses a Long-Short Term Memory architecture to forecast the time series subsequences.

Table 1. Hyperparameter configurations for HydraAD. Symbols denote the sensitivity of each parameter on model performance based on the analysis in Sect. 5.5: ● (crucial), ◐ (minimal), or ○ (none). For each parameter, we list the search space used during tuning, with the final selected values underlined.

Parameter	Values
● Quantile q	0.0, 0.1, 0.2, 0.3, 0.4, 0.5, 0.6, 0.7, 0.8, <u>0.9</u>, 1.0
◐ Number of groups g	1, 2, <u>4</u>, 8, 16, 32, 64, 128, 256, 512
◐ Number of kernels k	1, 2, 4, 8, 16, <u>32</u>, 64, 128, 256, 512
◐ Scaling	<u>sparse scaling</u>, standard scaling, none
○ Dilations	1, {1, 2, 4}, <u>$\{2^0, 2^1, 2^2, \ldots, 2^{\lceil \log_2(n/m) \rceil}\}$</u>
○ First-order differences	<u>True</u>, False
◐ Features	hard counts, <u>soft counts</u>, hard and soft counts
○ Kernel size m	7, <u>9</u>, 11
◐ Number of channels ρ	0.0, 0.1, 0.2, <u>0.3</u>, 0.4, 0.5, 0.6, 0.7, 0.8, 0.9, 1.0

5 Experiments

5.1 Experimental Setup

Datasets. We evaluate HydraAD on TSB-AD, a comprehensive anomaly detection benchmark comprising 40 datasets across nine domains [17]. The benchmark is categorized into univariate (TSB-AD-U) and multivariate (TSB-AD-M) subsets. Each subset is further partitioned into a tuning set for hyperparameter optimization and an evaluation set for final performance assessment. Specifically, TSB-AD-U includes 48 tuning and 350 evaluation series, while TSB-AD-M includes 20 tuning and 180 evaluation series.

To account for randomness, HydraAD is evaluated 10 times on the tuning set and 30 times on the evaluation set. We report mean performance across these runs, but also analyze the effect of randomness across these runs in Sect. 5.4.

Hyperparameter Tuning. We tuned every hyperparameter of HydraAD independently on the tuning set of TSB-AD-U, keeping the other hyperparameters fixed. The only exception was the relative number of channels ρ to use for multivariate time series. We optimized ρ on the tuning set of TSB-AD-M while setting the other parameters as tuned for TSB-AD-U. The parameter ranges for each hyperparameter are shown in Table 1. The subsequence length w is estimated based on the dominant Fourier frequency (see Sect. 3) and we set the stride $s = w/4$ to improve the computational constraint without sacrificing predictive accuracy.

Evaluation Metric. Numerous evaluation metrics for time series anomaly detection have been proposed in recent years. In this work, we focus on Volume Under the PR-Surface (VUS-PR), an extension of AUC-PR that incorporates the temporal dynamics of the time series [4]. Specifically, a buffer of length $l/2$ is created at each anomalous interval which serves as a transition between the normal and abnormal subsequences. By calculating precision and recall across varying buffer lengths l, a third dimension is added to the classical PR-curve, forming a surface. VUS-PR then computes the volume under this surface as final performance score.

We select VUS-PR for three reasons: (1) it considers the temporal dynamics of time series, unlike point-based methods such as AUC-PR, (2) it is threshold independent, and (3) it is generally considered as one of the most robust and accurate evaluation metrics [17]. A limitation of VUS-PR is that it requires significant computational resources, because precision and recall are calculated across a wide range of thresholds and buffer lengths. A substantial computational speedup is achieved by lowering the number of thresholds with minimal impact on the final VUS-PR score (more details are provided in Appendix A.1). We therefore fix the number of thresholds to 75 during the tuning phase but maintain 250 thresholds for the final evaluation.

Competitors. We compare HydraAD against all 41 methods included in the TSB-AD benchmark: 18 for univariate, 9 for multivariate, and 14 for both univariate and multivariate time series. While we benchmark our results against the publicly available scores, we also independently reproduce these baseline results to ensure a consistent and correct experimental setup. Detailed information regarding this reproduction process is provided in Appendix A.2.

5.2 Quantitative Evaluation

Figure 2 illustrates that HydraAD consistently outperforms all competitors in terms of VUS-PR on both TSB-AD-U and TSB-AD-M. For clarity, only the top-10 methods are shown here and a more detailed comparison is available in Appendix B.1. On TSB-AD-U (Fig. 2a), HydraAD achieves a substantial median VUS-PR of 0.61, nearly doubling the 0.35 reached by the next-best algorithm, Sub-PCA. The median VUS-PR of HydraAD on TSB-AD-M is comparable to the competitors (Fig. 2b) which leads to a similar average rank with CNN and KMeansAD (see Fig. 1b). However, HydraAD's mean performance is substantially higher. This suggests that while HydraAD remains competitive

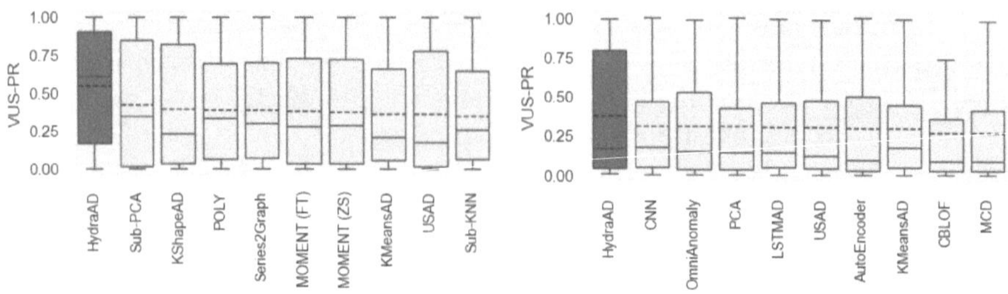

(a) TSB-AD-U (b) TSB-AD-M

Fig. 2. The performance of HydraAD on TSB-AD compared to the top-performing methods. The mean is marked with a dashed line and the median with a solid line.

with other models on most time series, it achieves substantially higher VUS-PR on others.

HydraAD consistently performs well across all domains available in the TSB-AD benchmark, which indicates that the high performance is not due to a bias in the data. More details are provided in Appendix B.1.

A pairwise analysis of HydraAD against the top-performing methods on both TSB-AD-U and TSB-AD-M is summarized in Table 2. On both benchmarks, HydraAD wins (higher VUS-PR) more frequently than it loses against every competitor. To validate these findings, we performed a one-tailed Wilcoxon signed-rank test [27] with the alternative hypothesis that HydraAD outperforms the competitor. While HydraAD is significantly superior to all baselines at $\alpha = 0.05$, the effect is most pronounced on univariate time series, where the P-values are several orders of magnitude lower than the significance threshold. These results demonstrate that HydraAD offers a statistically significant advancement over the state-of-the-art for both univariate and multivariate time series anomaly detection.

5.3 Scalability

HydraAD enables exceptionally fast anomaly detection, as illustrated in Fig. 3. The primary computational step of HydraAD involves convolving random kernels with time series subsequences, an operation for which highly optimized implementations, including GPU-accelerated libraries, are readily available. As a consequence, HydraAD detects anomalies in any individual time series of TSB-AD-U in at most 0.2 s (Fig. 3a), and requires 8 s on GPU and 125 s on CPU to evaluate all 350 time series. For TSB-AD-M (Fig. 3b), HydraAD processes any individual time series in at most 1 s, and the total processing time for all 180 series is less than 33 s on GPU and 2,520 s (42 min) on CPU. For multivariate time series, the total run time is primarily driven by the total number of observations $n \times c$, rather than by the individual factors n or c alone, as indicated by the linear trend in the rightmost plot of Fig. 3b.

Table 2. Mean VUS-PR of HYDRAAD and top-5 competitors on TSB-AD benchmarks. The table reports the mean VUS-PR, the number of time series where HYDRAAD outperformed (Wins), or underperformed (Losses) the competitor, and the P-value of the Wilcoxon signed-rank test.

Model	VUS-PR	Wins	Losses	P-value
TSB-AD-U				
HYDRAAD	**0.5482**	–	–	–
Sub-PCA [1]	0.4234	232	118	4.41×10^{-10}
KShapeAD [20]	0.4008	211	139	4.33×10^{-8}
POLY [15]	0.3898	242	108	1.86×10^{-15}
Series2Graph [5]	0.3881	242	108	8.41×10^{-16}
MOMENT (FT) [13]	0.3857	241	109	4.91×10^{-14}
TSB-AD-M				
HYDRAAD	**0.3800**	–	–	–
CNN [19]	0.3130	96	84	0.0231
OmniAnomaly [25]	0.3122	100	80	0.0419
PCA [1]	0.3096	99	81	0.0486
LSTMAD [18]	0.3066	95	85	0.0292
USAD [3]	0.3041	105	75	0.0088

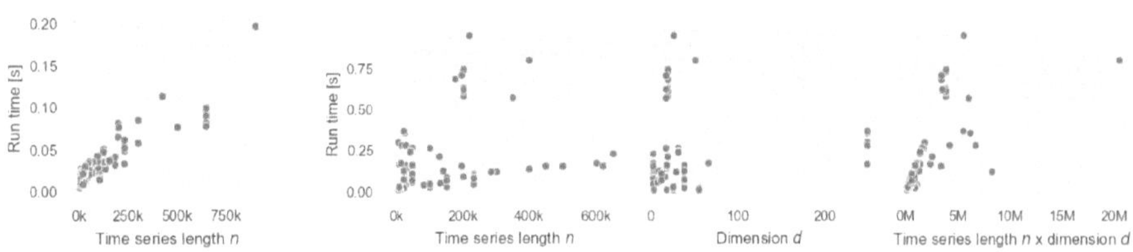

(a) TSB-AD-U (b) TSB-AD-M

Fig. 3. Run time of HYDRAAD on TSB-AD in function of the size of the time series. All experiments were performed on GPU.

Figure 4 compares the run time of HYDRAAD against the three highest ranked competitors (see Fig. 1). On TSB-AD-U, HYDRAAD outperforms Sub-PCA by almost one order of magnitude and KShapeAD by almost three orders of magnitude. Although POLY achieves comparable run times on the fastest instances, its run time is considerably more variable, indicating poor scalability on larger time series. On TSB-AD-M, the scalability advantage of HYDRAAD is even more pronounced, outperforming all competitors by at least two orders of magnitude.

To quantify the computational resource requirements of HYDRAAD, we conducted additional experiments on synthetic time series with observations sampled uniformly at random from $[0, 1]$ and lengths n ranging from 1,000 to

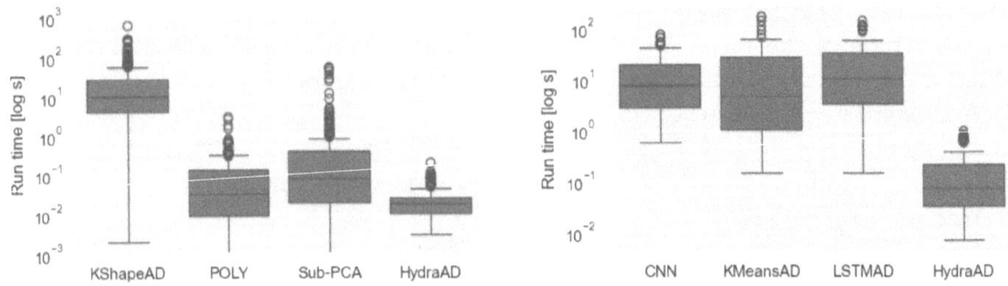

(a) TSB-AD-U

(b) TSB-AD-M

Fig. 4. Comparison of run time of HydraAD with the highest ranked competitors on TSB-AD.

5, 000, 000 and dimensions c from 1 to 256. As illustrated in Fig. 5a, run time scales linearly with respect to both n and c. The results demonstrate that GPU acceleration provides a significant speed advantage: for $n = 5,000,000$ and $c = 1$, HydraAD completes in 0.85 s on GPU compared to 20.84 s on CPU, while for $n = 250,000$ and $c = 256$, execution times are 0.77 s and 12.40 s, respectively. As shown in Fig. 5b, peak memory usage also scales linearly with respect to both n and c. However, HydraAD relies on a large set of random kernels which may lead to a substantial memory usage for massive time series, reaching 17.09 GB for $n = 5,000,000$ and $c = 1$, and 6.91 GB for $n = 250,000$ and $c = 256$.

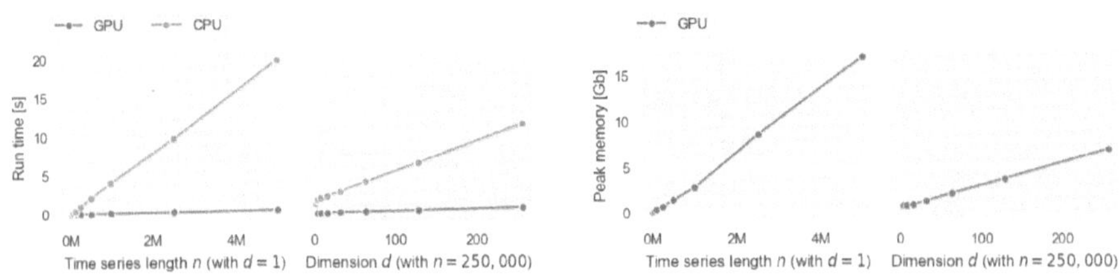

(a) Run time.

(b) Peak memory usage.

Fig. 5. Used computational resources of HydraAD on synthetic time series.

To mitigate the high memory consumption for massive time series, we introduce a batched embedding strategy that processes windows as batches rather than all at once. As illustrated in Fig. 6, this trade-off is highly favorable: for a batch size of 256 windows, the run time remains virtually indistinguishable from the unbatched case, while peak memory usage is reduced by a factor of seven, from 17.09 GB to 2.36 GB at $n = 5,000,000$ and $c = 1$. We therefore recommend using a batch size of 256 as a practical default, as it effectively resolves the memory bottleneck of HydraAD on massive time series at negligible computational cost.

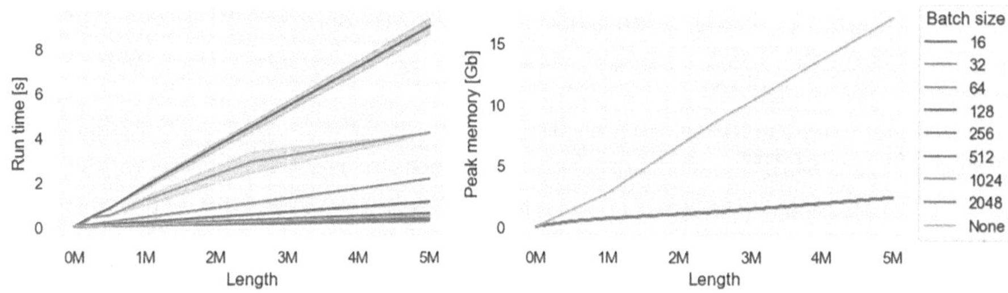

Fig. 6. Effect of using batches within HYDRAAD on the run time and peak memory usage.

The number of groups g and the number of kernels per group k determine the total number of convolutions performed, which directly impacts the run time of HYDRAAD. Figure 7a demonstrates that the total run time increases as either k or g increases. However, our results show that the primary driver of computation time is the total number of kernels, defined as $k \times g$, rather than the individual values of k or g. As illustrated in Fig. 7b, when $k \times g$ is fixed, the run time remains relatively stable, regardless of the number of kernels per group.

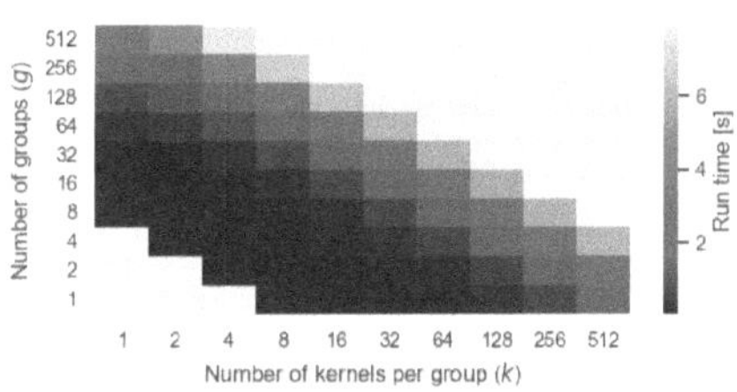

(a) Run time vs. k and g.

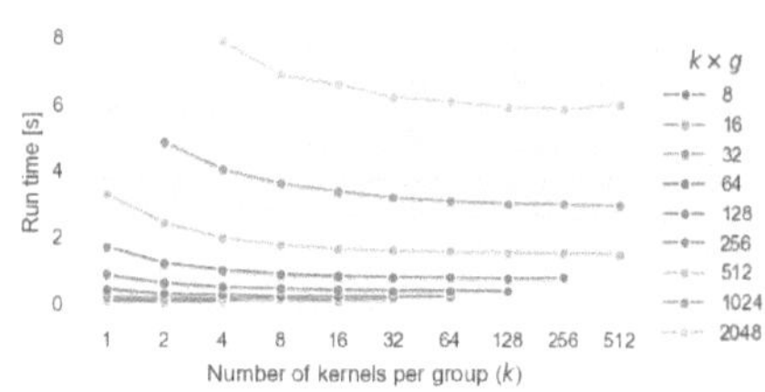

(b) Run time vs. k.

Fig. 7. Run time of HYDRAAD in function of the number of kernels per group k and the number of groups g.

5.4 Effect of Randomness

HYDRAAD leverages a large set of random kernels for anomaly detection, which introduces non-determinism in the predicted anomaly scores. Below we discuss the effect of this randomness on the performance of HYDRAAD for TSB-AD-U. A similar analysis for TSB-AD-M is provided in Appendix B.2.

We evaluated HYDRAAD using 30 different seeds for each time series in the TSB-AD-U evaluation set. In above results, we report the mean VUS-PR score across these 30 runs to obtain a final evaluation score per time series. Figure 8a shows that the distribution of VUS-PR (in accordance to Fig. 2) remains relatively stable if instead the maximum or minimum across all 30 runs would be computed, which leads to an average score of 0.5656 or 0.5291, respectively. In comparison, Sub-PCA, the best competitor on TSB-AD-U, only achieves an average VUS-PR of 0.4234.

Figure 8b demonstrates that the anomaly detection performance of HydraAD across different seeds is generally stable. However, we observed that for a subset of instances, the VUS-PR score exhibits higher sensitivity to different random seeds. The three time series with the largest whisker distance[2] are highlighted with arrows in Fig. 8b. While this whisker distance can reach up to 0.48 for time series 762, it remains below 0.1 for 95% of the time series.

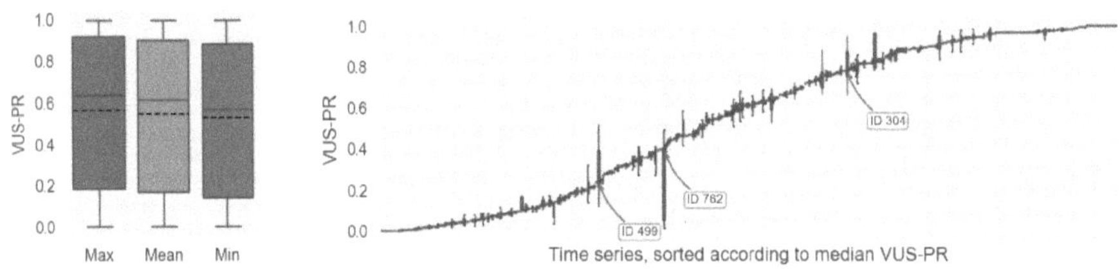

(a) Effect of aggregation per time series on VUS-PR scores.

(b) Range of VUS-PR scores of HydraAD for each time series in TSB-AD-U. The three time series with largest whisker distance are annotated with a red arrow, along with their ID in TSB-AD-U.

Fig. 8. Sensitivity of HydraAD to random kernels across 30 random seeds.

To better understand this sensitivity, we performed a case study on time series 762, which exhibited the largest whisker distance. Figure 9 displays the time series alongside the predicted anomaly scores across 100 random seeds. While the anomaly scores are generally constant, we observe variations in the scores around the anomaly at index 1,400. For some seeds, the score at this index exceeds the predictions at the interval between time steps 300 and 1,000, successfully identifying the anomaly. For other seeds, the predicted anomaly score at index 1,400 falls below the predictions in this range, leading to a false negative. This behavior does not imply model instability, but rather that VUS-PR is sensitive to small changes in the ranking of the observations according to the anomaly scores. Further analyses in Appendix B.2 confirm similar behavior for time series 304 and 499.

5.5 Sensitivity Analysis

Figure 10 illustrates the effect of key hyperparameters on the performance of HydraAD. We provide additional sensitivity analyses in Appendix B.3.

[2] The whisker distance is defined as $(Q3 + 1.5 \times IQR) - (Q1 - 1.5 \times IQR)$, where $IQR = Q3 - Q1$.

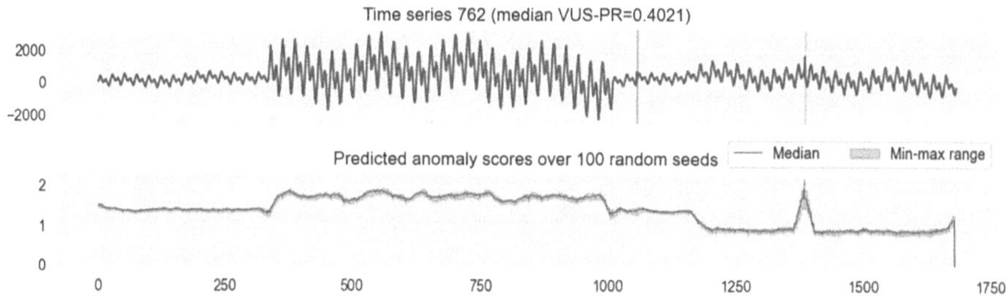

Fig. 9. A case study on the stability of HYDRAAD using time series 762 of TSB-AD-U with 1,680 observations and 2 anomalies. We show the median anomaly scores (solid line) and the full range of anomaly scores (shaded area) at each time step across 100 evaluations of HYDRAAD.

Window Size w. We evaluate the sensitivity of HYDRAAD to the window size by replacing w (computed based on the dominant Fourier frequency, see Sect. 3) with $\gamma \cdot w$ for $\gamma \in \{0.5, 1.0, 2.0, 3.0\}$. As shown in Fig. 10a, performance remains stable for $\gamma \leq 1.0$ but degrades gradually as m increases, suggesting that the dominant Fourier frequency provides an effective upper bound estimate for the window size.

Quantile Selection q. As shown in Fig. 10b, anomaly detection performance generally improves as q increases. However, a performance degradation is observed at $q = 1$ (i.e., when selecting the maximum value across all kernels). This drop likely stems from randomness in the kernels that leads to spurious peaks in the features. Setting q below 1 reduces the effect of such outliers and consequently enhances robustness.

Relative Number of Channels ρ. As illustrated in Fig. 10c, a marginal performance peak in mean VUS-PR occurs at $\rho = 0.3$. However, the magnitude of this increase is small (approximately 0.03 in VUS-PR), which suggests that HYDRAAD is largely robust to the specific value for ρ.

The Number of Groups g and the Number of Kernels per Group k. The number of kernels per group k significantly influences the results. When $k = 1$, Hydra reduces to Rocket, which results in a substantial decrease in VUS-PR. This suggests that competition among the kernels within groups is crucial to accurately detect anomalies. However, the performance gradually decreases as k becomes too large. In this case, randomness increases the probability of finding a close match within a group. As a consequence, the feature vectors of both normal and anomalous subsequences become indistinguishable. The number of groups g has a negligible effect on the VUS-PR score.

Feature Normalization. Figure 10e demonstrates that feature normalization of the soft counts is indispensable to achieve high anomaly detection performance. However, using standard z-normalization or its adaptation for sparse features have little to no effect on the final VUS-PR.

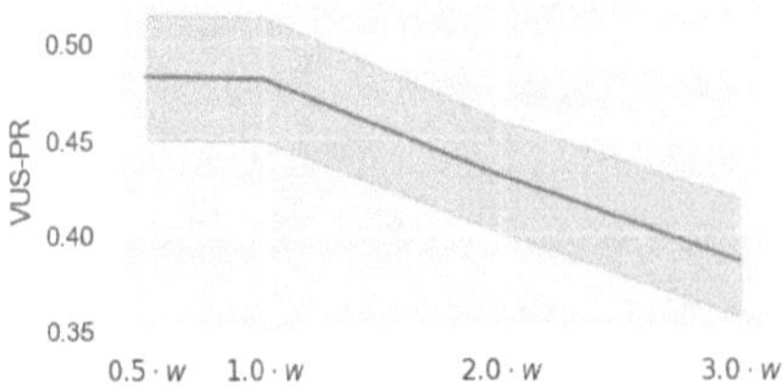

(a) Effect of multiplying precomputed w.

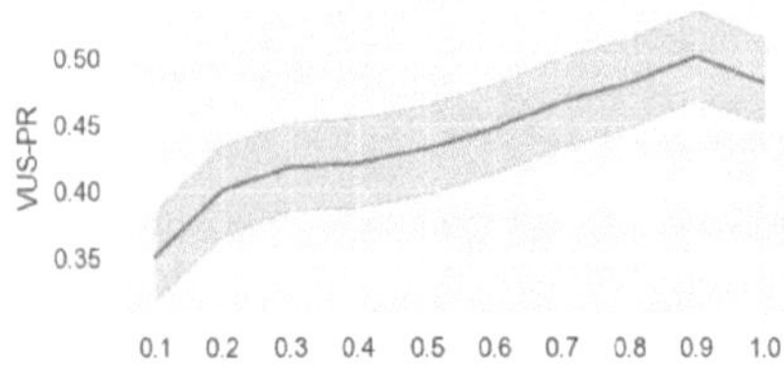

(b) Effect of q.

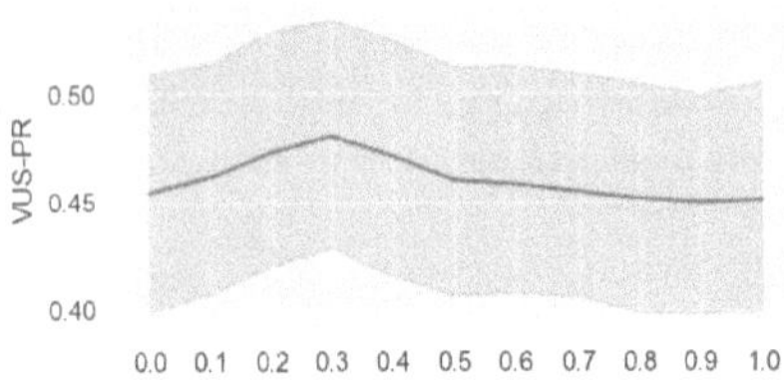

(c) Effect of ρ.

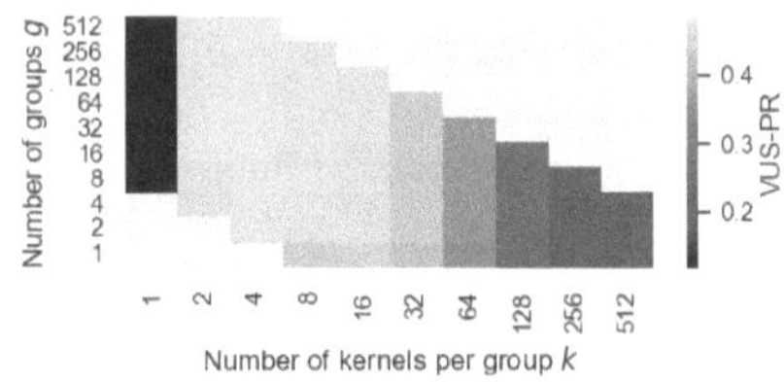

(d) Effect of k and g.

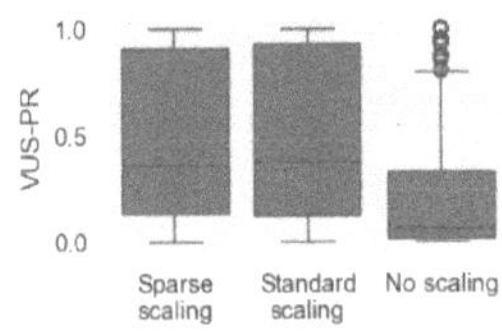

(e) Effect of normalization.

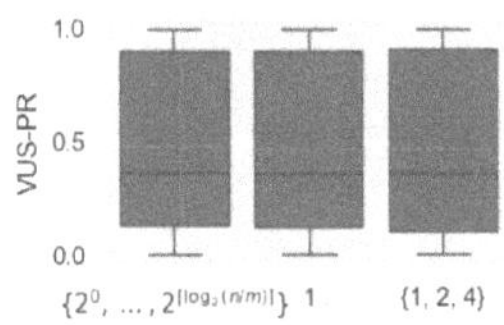

(f) Effect of dilations.

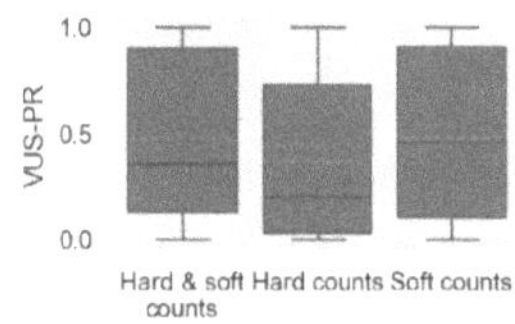

(g) Effect of count-features.

Fig. 10. Sensitivity analysis of the hyperparameters of HYDRAAD.

Dilations. While dilations are crucial for the performance of Hydra and Rocket in time series classification, Fig. 10f suggests that they are of little importance for anomaly detection. Although dilations provide a minimal increase in VUS-PR, they also increase the computational cost. Nevertheless, we recommend using dilations for anomaly detection to increase the number of features and consequently HYDRAAD's robustness.

Count Features. Besides the soft counts (representing the magnitude of a kernel winning within a group), it is also possible to use the hard counts (representing the frequency of these wins). While both features are beneficial for classification, Fig. 10g illustrates that the magnitude of matches (as measured through soft counts) is the most informative for anomaly detection, while the hard counts add little information and may even obscure the anomalous subsequences.

6 Conclusion

This work introduced HydraAD, a novel method for anomaly detection in both univariate and multivariate time series. We demonstrated that HydraAD achieves state-of-the-art anomaly detection performance, significantly outperforming well-established baselines. Additionally, HydraAD is exceptionally fast because it leverages convolutions of subsequences with competing random kernels to derive anomaly scores, an operation which can be implemented highly efficiently on modern hardware. In future work, we plan to investigate methods for generating random kernels based on normal data to further improve the performance of HydraAD, and perform additional validation of HydraAD on real-world datasets.

Acknowledgments. This research is supported the Flemish government under the Flanders AI Research Program, by Flanders Make, the strategic research centre for the manufacturing industry, and by Internal Funds KU Leuven (STG/21/057 & C3/23/047).

Disclosure of Interests. The authors have no competing interests to declare that are relevant to the content of this article.

References

1. Aggarwal, C.C.: Linear models for outlier detection. In: Outlier Analysis, pp. 65–110. Springer, Cham (2017). https://doi.org/10.1007/978-3-319-47578-3_3
2. Ahmed, M., Choudhury, N., Uddin, S.: Anomaly detection on Big Data in financial markets. In: Proceedings of the 2017 IEEE/ACM International Conference on Advances in Social Networks Analysis and Mining 2017, ASONAM '17, pp. 998–1001. Association for Computing Machinery, New York, NY, USA (2017). https://doi.org/10.1145/3110025.3119402
3. Audibert, J., Michiardi, P., Guyard, F., Marti, S., Zuluaga, M.A.: USAD: unsupervised anomaly detection on multivariate time series. In: Proceedings of the 26th ACM SIGKDD International Conference on Knowledge Discovery & Data Mining, pp. 3395–3404 (2020)
4. Boniol, P., et al.: VUS: effective and efficient accuracy measures for time-series anomaly detection. VLDB J. **34**, 32 (2025). https://doi.org/10.1007/s00778-025-00907-x
5. Boniol, P., Palpanas, T.: Series2Graph: graph-based subsequence anomaly detection for time series. Proc. VLDB Endow. **13**(12), 1821–1834 (2020). https://doi.org/10.14778/3407790.3407792
6. Dempster, A., Petitjean, F., Webb, G.I.: ROCKET: exceptionally fast and accurate time series classification using random convolutional kernels. Data Min. Knowl. Disc. **34**(5), 1454–1495 (2020). https://doi.org/10.1007/s10618-020-00701-z
7. Dempster, A., Schmidt, D.F., Webb, G.I.: MiniRocket: a very fast (almost) deterministic transform for time series classification. In: Proceedings of the 27th ACM SIGKDD Conference on Knowledge Discovery & Data Mining, pp. 248–257. Association for Computing Machinery, New York, NY, USA (2021). https://doi.org/10.1145/3447548.3467231

8. Dempster, A., Schmidt, D.F., Webb, G.I.: Hydra: competing convolutional kernels for fast and accurate time series classification. Data Min. Knowl. Discov. **37**(5), 1779–1805 (2023). https://doi.org/10.1007/s10618-023-00939-3
9. Dempster, A., Tan, C.W., Miller, L., Foumani, N.M., Schmidt, D.F., Webb, G.I.: Highly scalable time series classification for very large datasets. In: Lemaire, V., et al. (eds.) International Workshop on Advanced Analytics and Learning on Temporal Data, pp. 80–95. Springer, Cham (2024). https://doi.org/10.1007/978-3-031-77066-1_5
10. Demšar, J.: Statistical comparisons of classifiers over multiple data sets. J. Mach. Learn. Res. **7**, 1–30 (2006). https://dl.acm.org/doi/10.5555/1248547.1248548
11. Ermshaus, A., Schäfer, P., Leser, U.: Window size selection in unsupervised time series analytics: a review and benchmark. In: Guyet, T., Ifrim, G., Malinowski, S., Bagnall, A., Shafer, P., Lemaire, V. (eds.) 7th ECML PKDD Workshop on Advanced Analytics and Learning on Temporal Data, AALTD 2022, pp. 83–101. Springer, Heidelberg (2022). https://doi.org/10.1007/978-3-031-24378-3_6
12. Fingerhut, F., Klein, S., Verbeke, M., Rajendran, S., Tsiporkova, E.: Multi-view contextual performance profiling in rotating machinery. In: 2023 IEEE International Conference on Prognostics and Health Management (ICPHM), pp. 343–350 (2023). https://doi.org/10.1109/ICPHM57936.2023.10194172
13. Goswami, M., Szafer, K., Choudhry, A., Cai, Y., Li, S., Dubrawski, A.: MOMENT: a family of open time-series foundation models. In: International Conference on Machine Learning (2024)
14. Li, H., Boulanger, P.: A survey of heart anomaly detection using ambulatory Electrocardiogram (ECG). Sensors **20**(5) (2020). https://doi.org/10.3390/s20051461
15. Li, Z., Ma, H., Mei, Y.: A unifying method for outlier and change detection from data streams based on local polynomial fitting. In: Zhou, Z.-H., Li, H., Yang, Q. (eds.) PAKDD 2007. LNCS (LNAI), vol. 4426, pp. 150–161. Springer, Heidelberg (2007). https://doi.org/10.1007/978-3-540-71701-0_17
16. Lin, J., Khade, R., Li, Y.: Rotation-invariant similarity in time series using bag-of-patterns representation. J. Intell. Inf. Syst. **39**(2), 287–315 (2012). https://doi.org/10.1007/s10844-012-0196-5
17. Liu, Q., Paparrizos, J.: The elephant in the room: towards a reliable time-series anomaly detection benchmark. In: Advances in Neural Information Processing Systems, vol. 37, pp. 108231–108261. Curran Associates Inc. (2024). https://doi.org/10.52202/079017-3437
18. Malhotra, P., Vig, L., Shroff, G., Agarwal, P., et al.: Long short term memory networks for anomaly detection in time series. In: Proceedings of the European Symposium on Artificial Neural Networks, Computational Intelligence and Machine Learning (ESANN), vol. 89, p. 94 (2015)
19. Munir, M., Siddiqui, S.A., Dengel, A., Ahmed, S.: DeepAnT: a deep learning approach for unsupervised anomaly detection in time series. IEEE Access **7**, 1991–2005 (2018)
20. Paparrizos, J., Gravano, L.: Fast and accurate time-series clustering. ACM Trans. Database Syst. **42**(2) (2017). https://doi.org/10.1145/3044711
21. Paparrizos, J., Kang, Y., Boniol, P., Tsay, R.S., Palpanas, T., Franklin, M.J.: TSB-UAD: an end-to-end benchmark suite for univariate time-series anomaly detection. Proc. VLDB Endow. **15**(8), 1697–1711 (2022). https://doi.org/10.14778/3529337.3529354
22. Ramaswamy, S., Rastogi, R., Shim, K.: Efficient algorithms for mining outliers from large data sets. In: Proceedings of the 2000 ACM SIGMOD International Confer-

ence on Management of Data, pp. 427–438. Association for Computing Machinery, New York (2000). https://doi.org/10.1145/342009.335437

23. Saxe, A.M., Koh, P.W., Chen, Z., Bhand, M., Suresh, B., Ng, A.Y.: On random weights and unsupervised feature learning. In: Proceedings of the 28th International Conference on Machine Learning, ICML'11, pp. 1089–1096. Omnipress, Madison, WI, USA (2011)
24. Schmidl, S., Wenig, P., Papenbrock, T.: Anomaly detection in time series: a comprehensive evaluation. Proc. VLDB Endow. **15**(9), 1779–1797 (2022). https://doi.org/10.14778/3538598.3538602
25. Su, Y., Zhao, Y., Niu, C., Liu, R., Sun, W., Pei, D.: Robust anomaly detection for multivariate time series through stochastic recurrent neural network. In: Proceedings of the 25th ACM SIGKDD International Conference on Knowledge Discovery & Data Mining, pp. 2828–2837 (2019)
26. Tan, C.W., Dempster, A., Bergmeir, C., Webb, G.I.: MultiRocket: multiple pooling operators and transformations for fast and effective time series classification. Data Min. Knowl. Disc. **36**(5), 1623–1646 (2022). https://doi.org/10.1007/s10618-022-00844-1
27. Wilcoxon, F.: Individual comparisons by ranking methods. Biometrics Bull. **1**(6), 80–83 (1945). https://doi.org/10.2307/3001968

Probabilistic Dynamic Causal Graphs for Root Cause Analysis with Distributional Forecasting

Hyunmin Kong[1], Chunsoo Ahn[1,2], Seung Ho Jung[1], Seung Yeol Yoo[2], Donghwi Shin[2], and Jitae Shin[1(✉)]

[1] Sungkyunkwan University, Seoul, South Korea
{khm1754,navy12,richardjung,jtshin}@skku.edu
[2] Sleno Co., Ltd., Gyeonggi-do, South Korea
{sy.ryu,scott.shin}@sleno.co.kr

Abstract. Root cause analysis (RCA) in industrial multivariate time series aims to identify the variable responsible for an emerging anomaly, but this remains challenging under nonlinear, time-varying, and uncertain sensor dependencies. We propose a probabilistic dynamic RCA framework that infers time-varying lagged causal coefficients and regularizes their temporal evolution using an Ornstein–Uhlenbeck (OU)-based dynamical prior. To improve causality-aware forecasting, the framework separates mean prediction from variance calibration through two-stage learning and suppresses unreliable causal edges with a Signal-to-Noise Ratio (SNR)-based gate. At inference time, anomalous intervals are detected using negative log-likelihood (NLL), and root-cause variables are ranked by combining uncertainty-normalized residual evidence with structural deviation from normal causal-strength patterns. Experiments on synthetic and real-world industrial benchmarks show that the proposed framework improves both causal discovery and RCA performance through probabilistic modeling of time-varying causal structure.

Keywords: Root Cause Analysis · Causality · Ornstein–Uhlenbeck process · Multivariate Time Series

1 Introduction

In industrial multivariate time series, RCA is a fundamental task that aims to identify the variable that actually caused an anomaly. Industrial systems consist of numerous sensors and control variables that interact in complex ways, and a disturbance originating from a single variable can rapidly propagate to others [10]. Therefore, accurately identifying the root-cause sensor is critically important, as it reduces unnecessary inspections and responses while enabling timely intervention at the true fault location [24]. Causal discovery has thus been

H. Kong and C. Ahn—Co-first authors with equal contribution.

M. Ceci et al. (Eds.): ECML PKDD 2026, LNAI 16941, pp. 128–144, 2027.
https://doi.org/10.1007/978-3-032-37654-1_8

regarded as a promising approach for RCA, as it provides an intermediate step of predicting directional influences and dependencies among variables [6]. However, existing methods suffer from an important limitation. Many approaches assume a fixed causal graph over the entire time horizon, or summarize potentially time-varying relationships using a single deterministic scalar coefficient [4]. In real industrial processes, however, the strength and direction of inter-sensor interactions can change over time due to operating mode transitions, control interventions, disturbances, and environmental variations [22]. In such settings, compressing evolving causal relationships into static scalar values makes it difficult to capture the true structure at a given moment and can blur the distinction between causes and effects.

This work proposes a probabilistic RCA framework that unifies time-varying causal structure with prediction-based diagnosis. The proposed framework infers a distribution over the causal relationship matrix at each time step and directly incorporates it into a Vector AutoRegressive (VAR) [12] style forecasting equation to produce the predictive mean for the next step. In doing so, it parameterizes each variable individually to capture nonlinearity in which the causal coefficient matrix directly contributes to prediction. Furthermore, because causal coefficients in time series tend to evolve smoothly over time, we introduce a dynamical prior based on the Ornstein–Uhlenbeck (OU) process [21] to encourage temporal continuity in the causal structure. Training follows a two-stage strategy that separates the estimation of the predictive mean and variance. In the first stage, the model prioritizes learning the mean predictor and the dynamic causal structure, preventing excessive variance growth from masking mean prediction errors. In this stage, the OU prior and sparsity regularization help stabilize causal relationship estimation. In the second stage, the predictive mean is fixed and only the variance is learned, so that the resulting uncertainty reflects both prediction reliability and temporal and variable-wise variability. During inference, anomalous intervals are detected using a negative log-likelihood-based score normalized by the estimated uncertainty, and root-cause sensors are ranked by aggregating extreme-value patterns in variable-wise prediction residuals within the detected intervals.

2 Related Work

2.1 Causal Discovery

Causal discovery in multivariate time series is commonly formulated under the framework of Granger causality [2], where the past of one variable is considered causal if it improves the prediction of another variable [11]. Classical approaches based on VAR models have been widely studied due to their interpretability, since causal relations can be directly inferred from regression coefficients [1]. However, most VAR-based methods assume linear and time-invariant relationships, which limits their applicability in complex systems that exhibit nonlinear dynamics and evolving dependencies [20].

To address these limitations, recent studies have proposed deep learning-based causal discovery methods. For instance, TCDF [16] employs attention-based convolutional neural networks to discover causal relationships and associated time delays in multivariate time series. CUTS [5] further extends neural Granger causal discovery by leveraging graph neural networks to infer causal graphs from irregular or partially observed time-series data. More recently, several works have explored integrating causal discovery with root cause analysis. AERCA [6] combines Granger causal discovery with anomaly root cause identification by modeling the distribution of exogenous variables and detecting deviations under abnormal conditions. In addition, UnCLe [3] focuses on discovering time-varying causal dependencies, enabling dynamic causal graphs that capture evolving interactions among variables.

2.2 Root Cause Analysis

RCA aims to identify the underlying variables that initiate anomalous events in complex systems. Early approaches to RCA in multivariate time series primarily relied on per-variable forecasting or reconstruction errors, where variables with the largest deviations are considered potential root causes. While such approaches are simple and sensitive to anomalies, they often fail to distinguish the true initiating variables from downstream responses caused by anomaly propagation [23]. To address this limitation, recent studies have proposed graph-based RCA methods that explicitly model dependencies among variables. For example, RCD [7], CIRCA [9], and RCG [8] utilize dependency or causal graphs to trace anomaly propagation paths and identify upstream candidates as potential root causes. More recently, AERCA [6] integrates Granger causal discovery with RCA by modeling anomalies as interventions on exogenous variables. Specifically, it learns the normal distribution of exogenous variables and identifies root causes as those that significantly deviate from their normal regimes under abnormal conditions.

3 Methods

3.1 Preliminary

Granger Causality. Granger causality defines causality in predictive terms: variable j is said to Granger-cause variable i if the past of j improves prediction of the future of i beyond what is already explained by the remaining variables. A classical VAR formulation is as follows:

$$x_i^t = c_i + \sum_{k=1}^{K} \sum_{j=1}^{N} A_{ij}^{(k)} x_j^{(t-k)} + \epsilon_i^t, \tag{1}$$

where, N is the number of variables, K is the maximum lag, $A_{ij}^{(k)}$ is the k-lag influence of variable j on variable i, and ϵ_i^t is a noise term. The directed edge $j \to i$ is absent when $A_{ij}^{(k)} = 0$ for all lags. Our method retains this prediction-based interpretation, but replaces static deterministic coefficients with time-varying approximate posterior distributions.

Ornstein-Uhlenbeck (OU) Process. The OU process is a continuous-time stochastic process with mean-reverting dynamics and stochastic fluctuations. These properties make it a widely used model for temporally evolving variables in continuous-time settings [15]. The continuous time OU process is defined as follows:

$$dX_t = \theta(\mu - X_t)\,dt + \sigma\,dW_t, \tag{2}$$

where, X_t is the latent state, μ is the long-run mean, $\theta > 0$ is the mean-reversion rate, σ is the diffusion scale, and W_t is standard Brownian motion. For a fixed sampling interval, the induced discrete-time process is an AR(1)-type Gaussian transition. In the zero-mean case used in this paper, this yields a transition of the form

$$X_t \mid X_{t-1} \sim \mathcal{N}(\rho X_{t-1}, Q), \tag{3}$$

with $\rho \in (0, 1)$ and $Q > 0$. This discrete time form is used as the temporal prior over causal coefficients in the proposed model (Fig. 1).

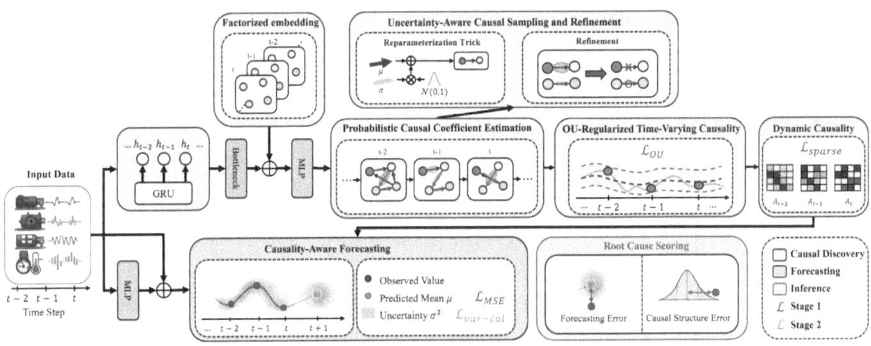

Fig. 1. Overview of the proposed framework.

3.2 Problem Formulation

Let $x^{1:T} = \{x^1, \ldots, x^T\}$ be a multivariate time series with $x^t \in \mathbb{R}^N$, and let $t_0 = K$ be the first valid time index for a length-K history window. For each valid time index $t \in \{t_0, \ldots, T-1\}$, we define the lagged history window

$$X_{\text{hist}}^{(t)} = [x^t, x^{t-1}, \ldots, x^{t-K+1}] \in \mathbb{R}^{N \times K}, \tag{4}$$

and aim to predict the next observation x^{t+1}. We denote the sequence of history windows available up to time t as the following.

$$\mathcal{H}_t = \left\{X_{\text{hist}}^{(\tau)}\right\}_{\tau=t_0}^{t} \tag{5}$$

At the same time, we infer a time-varying lagged causal coefficient $A_t \in \mathbb{R}^{N \times N \times K}$, where $a_{j,i,t}^{(k)}$ denotes the influence from source variable i at lag k to target variable j at time t. Throughout this section, the first node index of $a_{j,i,t}^{(k)}$ is the target and the second is the source.

3.3 Probabilistic Causal Coefficient Estimation

The causal discovery module estimates both lag and edge coefficients as random variables rather than deterministic parameters, so that structural uncertainty is represented explicitly. Conditioned on $\mathcal{H}_t$, we use a diagonal Gaussian variational family over the latent coefficients. To extract temporal context, we encode the sequence of valid history windows with a Gated Recurrent Unit (GRU). For a segment containing times $t_0, \ldots, T-1$, we compute

$$[h_{t_0}, \ldots, h_{T-1}] = \mathrm{GRU}\Big([\mathrm{vec}(X_{\mathrm{hist}}^{(t_0)}), \ldots, \mathrm{vec}(X_{\mathrm{hist}}^{(T-1)})]\Big), \tag{6}$$

where $\mathrm{vec}(\cdot)$ reshapes each history window into a vector and h_t is the GRU hidden state corresponding to time t. Thus, the GRU processes the temporal sequence of window vectors $\mathrm{vec}(X_{\mathrm{hist}}^{(t)})$ across time, rather than the entries inside a single window independently. We then compress h_t through a bottleneck layer,

$$z_t = \phi_{\mathrm{bot}}(h_t), \tag{7}$$

where ϕ_{bot} is a Multi Layer Perceptron (MLP) and z_t is the compressed dynamic representation at time step t. The purpose of the bottleneck is to prevent the forecasting module from overly relying on the hidden state itself, thereby reducing shortcut behavior and encouraging the model to make predictions through the inferred causal coefficients.

To estimate the distribution of each coefficient $a_{j,i,t}^{(k)}$, we combine temporal context with the structural identity of the target-source-lag tuple. We first construct an edge-level embedding

$$e_{j,i,k} = [e_j^{\mathrm{out}} \,\|\, e_i^{\mathrm{in}} \,\|\, e_k^{\mathrm{lag}}], \tag{8}$$

where $\|$ denotes concatenation, and e_j^{out}, e_i^{in}, and e_k^{lag} are learnable embeddings for the target role, source role, and lag index, respectively. This design preserves directional asymmetry between incoming and outgoing roles and allows different lags to have distinct structural patterns.

The posterior parameters are generated by a factorized parameterization:

$$u_t = W_h z_t, \qquad v_{j,i,k} = W_e e_{j,i,k}, \tag{9}$$

$$g_{j,i,k,t} = \psi(u_t + v_{j,i,k}), \tag{10}$$

$$[\mu_{j,i,t}^{(k)}, \ell_{j,i,t}^{(k)}] = W_o g_{j,i,k,t}, \tag{11}$$

where W_h, W_e, and W_o are learnable linear maps, u_t is the projected temporal context, $v_{j,i,k}$ is the projected edge-lag embedding, $g_{j,i,k,t}$ is the fused hidden representation, $\psi(\cdot)$ is a point-wise nonlinearity, and $\ell_{j,i,t}^{(k)}$ denotes the log-variance parameter, so that $(\sigma_{j,i,t}^{(k)})^2 = \exp(\ell_{j,i,t}^{(k)})$. The additive fusion of u_t and $v_{j,i,k}$ provides a shared temporal context while keeping the number of free parameters substantially smaller than a fully independent parameterization over (j, i, k, t). Each causal coefficient is then modeled as a Gaussian random variable:

$$a_{j,i,t}^{(k)} \sim \mathcal{N}\left(\mu_{j,i,t}^{(k)}, (\sigma_{j,i,t}^{(k)})^2\right). \tag{12}$$

Accordingly, the full approximate posterior at time t is as follows:

$$q(A_t \mid \mathcal{H}_t) = \mathcal{N}(\mu_{A,t}, \mathrm{diag}(\sigma_{A,t}^2)), \tag{13}$$

where $\mu_{A,t}$ and $\sigma_{A,t}$ collect the means and standard deviations of all edge-lag coefficients. The diagonal covariance implies conditional independence across edge-lag coefficients given $\mathcal{H}_t$. Throughout the paper, we refer to $q(A_t \mid \mathcal{H}_t)$ as an amortized approximate posterior: its parameters are produced by the encoder and optimized jointly with task losses and OU prior matching. In this way, the causal graph at each time step is represented as a probabilistic object with element-wise uncertainty.

3.4 Uncertainty-Aware Causal Sampling and Refinement

During training, we apply the reparameterization trick, introduced in [18], to sample causal coefficients from the posterior in a differentiable manner:

$$\tilde{a}_{j,i,t}^{(k)} = \mu_{j,i,t}^{(k)} + \sigma_{j,i,t}^{(k)} \epsilon_{j,i,t}^{(k)}, \qquad \epsilon_{j,i,t}^{(k)} \sim \mathcal{N}(0, 1). \tag{14}$$

where, $\epsilon_{j,i,t}^{(k)}$ is Gaussian noise sampled from the standard normal distribution, and $\tilde{a}_{j,i,t}^{(k)}$ is a sampled causal coefficient reflecting posterior uncertainty. At the full-structure level, this can be written as follows:

$$\tilde{A}_t = \mu_{A,t} + \sigma_{A,t} \odot \epsilon_t, \tag{15}$$

where $\odot$ denotes element-wise multiplication and $\tilde{A}_t$ is the sampled causal structure at time step t. The sampled coefficients are used as causal weights in the forecasting mean path, thereby enabling the prediction to reflect both uncertainty and coefficient reliability. To further account for the reliability of each inferred causal coefficient, we introduce a SNR [19] based confidence measure. For each edge-lag coefficient, the SNR is defined as follows:

$$\mathrm{SNR}_{j,i,t}^{(k)} = \frac{|\mu_{j,i,t}^{(k)}|}{\sigma_{j,i,t}^{(k)} + \epsilon}, \tag{16}$$

where ϵ is a small constant for numerical stability. The confidence of an edge (j, i) is then summarized by taking the maximum SNR over the lag dimension. This confidence score is transformed into a soft gate as follows:

$$\gamma_{j,i,t} = \text{sigmoid}\left(\frac{\text{SNR}_{j,i,t} - \tau}{\mathbb{T}}\right), \tag{17}$$

where τ is the SNR threshold and $\mathbb{T}$ is a temperature parameter controlling the sharpness of the gate. The resulting gate is shared across all lag coefficients of the same edge and applied as follows:

$$\hat{a}^{(k)}_{j,i,t} = \gamma_{j,i,t} \cdot \tilde{a}^{(k)}_{j,i,t} \tag{18}$$

Through this mechanism, the model suppresses the influence of highly uncertain causal coefficients while preserving reliable ones, leading to a more stable use of the inferred causal structure.

Finally, to summarize the overall causal influence of each edge across all lags, we define the lag-aggregated causal strength as follows:

$$\bar{a}_{j,i,t} = \sqrt{\sum_{k=1}^{K} \left(\hat{a}^{(k)}_{j,i,t}\right)^2}. \tag{19}$$

Where, $\bar{a}_{j,i,t}$ represents the overall causal strength from variable i to variable j at time step t. This aggregated edge-level score is later used for the root-cause ranking.

3.5 OU-Regularized Time-Varying Causality

To introduce temporal dependence between the causal coefficients, we regularize the varying causal coefficients with a discrete-time OU transition. For each edge-lag coefficient,

$$p\left(a^{(k)}_{j,i,t_0}\right) = \mathcal{N}\left(0, \frac{Q}{1-\rho^2}\right) \tag{20}$$

$$p\left(a^{(k)}_{j,i,t} \mid a^{(k)}_{j,i,t-1}\right) = \mathcal{N}\left(\rho\, a^{(k)}_{j,i,t-1}, Q\right), \qquad t > t_0 \tag{21}$$

where t_0 is the first valid time index, $\rho \in (0, 1)$ controls temporal persistence, and $Q > 0$ is the process-noise variance. Under a factorized prior across edge-lag coefficients,

$$p(A_t \mid A_{t-1}) = \prod_{j=1}^{N}\prod_{i=1}^{N}\prod_{k=1}^{K} p\left(a^{(k)}_{j,i,t} \mid a^{(k)}_{j,i,t-1}\right). \tag{22}$$

Where, Q is a scalar process-noise variance shared across coefficients. Equivalently, if A_t is vectorized into $\text{vec}(A_t) \in \mathbb{R}^{N^2K}$, the transition prior is a diagonal Gaussian with mean $\rho\,\text{vec}(A_{t-1})$ and covariance QI, where I is the identity matrix in the vectorized coefficient space. This is the stationary AR(1) form induced by the OU process at discrete time points.

In implementation, we use the previous approximate-posterior mean as a plug-in estimate of the latent state and stop its gradient when constructing the transition center. Hence, for $t > t_0$, the prior used in the Kullback–Leibler (KL) term and the resulting. Prior-matching penalty is defined as

$$p(A_t \mid \mathrm{sg}(\mu_{A,t-1})) = \mathcal{N}(\rho\, \mathrm{sg}(\mu_{A,t-1}), QI) \tag{23}$$

$$\mathcal{L}_{\mathrm{OU}} = D_{\mathrm{KL}}(q(A_{t_0} \mid \mathcal{H}_{t_0}) \,\|\, p(A_{t_0})) + \sum_{t=t_0+1}^{T-1} D_{\mathrm{KL}}(q(A_t \mid \mathcal{H}_t) \,\|\, p(A_t \mid \mathrm{sg}(\mu_{A,t-1}))). \tag{24}$$

Where, $D_{\mathrm{KL}}(\cdot\|\cdot)$ denotes KL divergence, $\mathrm{sg}(\cdot)$ denotes stop-gradient, and $\mu_{A,t-1}$ is the approximate-posterior mean at time $t-1$. As both $q(\cdot)$ and $p(\cdot)$ are diagonal Gaussians, each KL term is available in closed form. This regularizer discourages abrupt noise-driven changes while still allowing meaningful structural evolution when supported by the data.

3.6 Causality-Aware Forecasting

To use the inferred causal coefficients directly in prediction, we design a nonlinear VAR-style forecasting module. Let $\phi_{map}(x) = x + \mathrm{MLP}(x)$ be a shared scalar-to-scalar nonlinear mapping applied independently to each lagged observation. The predictive mean for target variable j is

$$\mu_{j,t+1} = \sum_{i=1}^{N}\sum_{k=1}^{K} \hat{a}_{j,i,t}^{(k)}\, \phi_{map}(x_i^{t-k+1}) + c_j \tag{25}$$

where $\hat{a}_{j,i,t}^{(k)}$ is the effective gated coefficient defined above and c_j is a bias term. This formulation captures local nonlinearity through $b(\cdot)$ while forcing all cross-variable influence to pass through the causal coefficients.

Predictive uncertainty is modeled separately from the mean path. Let $x_{j,t:t-K+1} = [x_j^t, x_j^{t-1}, \ldots, x_j^{t-K+1}] \in \mathbb{R}^K$ denote the recent history of variable j. The variance head for variable j uses only this univariate history:

$$\sigma_{j,t+1}^2 = \mathrm{softplus}(f_j(x_{j,t:t-K+1})) + \varepsilon \tag{26}$$

where $f_j : \mathbb{R}^K \to \mathbb{R}$ is the variance head for variable j. This decoupling prevents cross-variable shortcuts in the variance pathway and keeps the causal coefficients as the unique route by which inter-variable effects influence the predictive mean.

3.7 Training Objective

As aforementioned, the model can reduce loss lazily by inflating variance. This weakens the role of the causal path in forecasting, therefore requiring a two-stage training scheme.

Stage 1: Causal Discovery and Mean Forecasting. In Stage 1, the model learns the dynamic causal structure, the parameters of the approximate posterior, and the predictive mean. The mean forecasting loss is

$$\mathcal{L}_{\mathrm{mse}} = \frac{1}{mN} \sum_{t=1}^{m} \left\| x^{t+1} - \mu_{t+1} \right\|_2^2, \tag{27}$$

where m is the number of valid prediction steps in the current segment.

To discourage dense graphs, we impose an edge-wise sparsity penalty on the lag-aggregated strength:

$$\mathcal{L}_{\mathrm{sparse}} = \frac{1}{N^2} \sum_{j=1}^{N} \sum_{i=1}^{N} \sqrt{\frac{1}{m} \sum_{t=1}^{m} \bar{a}_{j,i,t}^2 + \varepsilon}. \tag{28}$$

Combining these terms with the OU regularizer, Stage 1 minimizes

$$\mathcal{L}_{\mathrm{S1}} = \mathcal{L}_{\mathrm{mse}} + \lambda_{\mathrm{sp}} \mathcal{L}_{\mathrm{sparse}} + \lambda_{\mathrm{ou}} \mathcal{L}_{\mathrm{OU}}. \tag{29}$$

Where, $\lambda_{\mathrm{sp}} > 0$ and $\lambda_{\mathrm{ou}} > 0$ are the sparsity and OU-regularization weights, respectively. This objective should be interpreted as task-driven amortized inference with prior matching: the approximate posterior is learned through forecasting utility and OU regularization.

Stage 2: Variance Calibration. In Stage 2, we freeze the mean path learned in Stage 1 and optimize only the predictive variance. Let the residual for variable j at time $t+1$ be $r_{j,t+1} = x_{j,t+1} - \mu_{j,t+1}$. The main variance-calibration term is

$$\mathcal{L}_{\text{var-cal}} = \frac{1}{mN} \sum_{t=1}^{m} \sum_{j=1}^{N} \left(\log \sigma_{j,t+1}^2 - \log \left(r_{j,t+1}^2 + \varepsilon \right) \right)^2. \tag{30}$$

The Stage 2 objective is therefore $\mathcal{L}_{\mathrm{S2}} = \mathcal{L}_{\text{var-cal}}$. No additional variance regularizers are used in this stage.

3.8 Root Cause Scoring

During inference, we first obtain the predictive mean and variance from the forecasting module. For each anomalous time step t, root-cause ranking is performed by combining a forecasting error-based score and a structural-deviation score. First, the forecasting error of variable i at time step t is defined as follows:

$$r_{i,t} = \frac{|x_{i,t} - \mu_{i,t}|}{\sqrt{\sigma_{i,t}^2 + \epsilon}}, \tag{31}$$

where $\mu_{i,t}$ and $\sigma_{i,t}^2$ denote the predictive mean and variance, respectively, and ϵ is a small positive constant for numerical stability. Since this definition explicitly incorporates forecasting uncertainty, errors in highly uncertain regions are reflected more conservatively, whereas errors under confident predictions receive larger scores. Next, the structural deviation is defined as the test time causal strength deviation from the time-varying causal strength, represented as a normal distribution learned from the training data. We first compute the lag-aggregated causal strength of edge $(i \to j)$ at time step t as follows:

$$\bar{a}_{j,i,t} = \sqrt{\sum_{k=1}^{K} \left(\hat{a}_{j,i,t}^{(k)}\right)^2}, \tag{32}$$

where $\hat{a}_{j,i,t}^{(k)}$ denotes the causal coefficient used for scoring. Let $\mu_{j,i}^{\text{ref}}$ and $\sigma_{j,i}^{\text{ref}}$ denote the mean and standard deviation of the time-varying causal distribution. The structural deviation of the corresponding edge is then defined as follows:

$$d_{j,i,t} = \frac{\left|\bar{a}_{j,i,t} - \mu_{j,i}^{\text{ref}}\right|}{\sigma_{j,i}^{\text{ref}} + \epsilon}. \tag{33}$$

Thus, $d_{j,i,t}$ measures how far the current causal strength deviates from the normal causal distribution. The variable-wise structural score of source variable i is obtained by averaging the deviations of its outgoing edges:

$$d_{i,t} = \frac{1}{N} \sum_{j=1}^{N} d_{j,i,t}. \tag{34}$$

Finally, the forecast-based score and the structural score are normalized separately and linearly combined to compute the final root-cause score:

$$\tilde{r}_{i,t} = \frac{r_{i,t}}{\sum_{n=1}^{N} r_{n,t} + \epsilon}, \qquad \tilde{d}_{i,t} = \frac{d_{i,t}}{\sum_{n=1}^{N} d_{n,t} + \epsilon}. \tag{35}$$

Where, n is an index over all variables, and ϵ is a small positive constant. The final root-cause score at time step t is defined as follows:

$$\text{RCA}_{i,t} = \tilde{r}_{i,t} + \tilde{d}_{i,t}, \tag{36}$$

and the root-cause sensor is determined by ranking $\text{RCA}_{i,t}$ in descending order at each detected anomalous time step.

Table 1. Dynamic causal discovery performance on ND8 (mean ± std).

Model	ND8	
	AUC-ROC	AUC-PRC
GVAR [13]	$0.720_{\pm 0.016}$	$0.225_{\pm 0.020}$
UnCLe [3]	$0.918_{\pm 0.005}$	$0.613_{\pm 0.055}$
Ours	$\mathbf{0.930}_{\pm 0.008}$	$\mathbf{0.647}_{\pm 0.016}$

4 Experiments

4.1 Experimental Setup

We evaluate the proposed framework on both synthetic and real-world multivariate time-series benchmarks. For causal discovery, we use the synthetic *Linear* and

Nonlinear datasets generated following [6], both of which provide ground-truth causal structures under controlled linear and nonlinear temporal dependencies. To further evaluate dynamic causal discovery, we adopt the *ND8* benchmark constructed according to [3]. *ND8* is a simulated nonlinear dynamic dataset with eight variables, where the causal directions of selected variable pairs periodically switch over time. This benchmark is therefore used to assess whether the proposed framework can capture time-varying causal structures beyond a single static graph. For root cause analysis, we use *SWaT* and *MSDS*, two real-world industrial datasets with labeled anomalous events and root-cause annotations. In all datasets, the model is trained on normal sequences, while anomalous windows are reserved for evaluation.

We evaluate causal discovery using *AUROC* and *AUPRC*, which measure how well the inferred edge strengths recover ground-truth causal edges. For RCA, we report *Accuracy at K* (AC@K), following the protocol for root cause identification. Let $\mathcal{V}^{RC}$ denote the set of ground-truth root-cause variables and $\mathcal{R}_K$ denote the set of top-K variables ranked by the RCA score. AC@K is defined as

$$\text{AC@K} = \frac{|\mathcal{V}^{RC} \cap \mathcal{R}_K|}{\min(K, |\mathcal{V}^{RC}|)}. \tag{37}$$

Thus, AC@K measures whether the ground-truth root-cause variables are included among the top-K ranked candidates. We report AC@1, AC@3, AC@5, and AC@10, where K denotes the number of top-ranked candidate variables considered.

Table 2. Causal discovery performance across simulated datasets (mean ± std).

Model	Linear		Nonlinear	
	AUC-ROC	AUC-PRC	AUC-ROC	AUC-PRC
VAR [12]	$0.999_{\pm 0.001}$	$0.999_{\pm 0.001}$	$0.662_{\pm 0.137}$	$0.518_{\pm 0.181}$
TCDF [16]	$0.934_{\pm 0.056}$	$0.917_{\pm 0.81}$	$0.648_{\pm 0.060}$	$0.332_{\pm 0.071}$
GVAR [13]	$0.986_{\pm 0.028}$	$0.981_{\pm 0.040}$	$0.683_{\pm 0.091}$	$0.560_{\pm 0.145}$
Cuts [5]	$0.865_{\pm 0.095}$	$0.812_{\pm 0.066}$	$0.561_{\pm 0.025}$	$0.268_{\pm 0.010}$
AERCA [6]	$\mathbf{1.000}_{\pm 0.000}$	$\mathbf{1.000}_{\pm 0.000}$	$0.999_{\pm 0.001}$	$0.998_{\pm 0.006}$
Ours	$\mathbf{1.000}_{\pm 0.000}$	$\mathbf{1.000}_{\pm 0.000}$	$\mathbf{1.000}_{\pm 0.000}$	$\mathbf{1.000}_{\pm 0.000}$

4.2 Experiment Results

We first evaluate whether the proposed framework can recover dynamic causal relationships. Table 1 shows that our method achieves the best AUROC and AUPRC among the compared methods in ND8, and Table 2 shows that it also performs strongly on the Linear and Nonlinear synthetic benchmarks. These

Table 3. Root cause analysis performance (AC@K) across datasets (mean ± std). The first two datasets are simulated and the remaining two are real industrial datasets.

Dataset	Method	AC@1	AC@3	AC@5	AC@10
Linear	RCD [7]	$0.500_{\pm 0.450}$	$0.817_{\pm 0.149}$	$\mathbf{1.000}_{\pm 0.000}$	$\mathbf{1.000}_{\pm 0.000}$
	CIRCA [9]	$0.600_{\pm 0.457}$	$0.800_{\pm 0.296}$	$\mathbf{1.000}_{\pm 0.000}$	$\mathbf{1.000}_{\pm 0.000}$
	RCG [8]	$0.646_{\pm 0.140}$	$0.794_{\pm 0.075}$	$\mathbf{1.000}_{\pm 0.000}$	$\mathbf{1.000}_{\pm 0.000}$
	AERCA [6]	$\mathbf{1.000}_{\pm 0.000}$	$\mathbf{1.000}_{\pm 0.000}$	$\mathbf{1.000}_{\pm 0.000}$	$\mathbf{1.000}_{\pm 0.000}$
	Ours	$\mathbf{1.000}_{\pm 0.000}$	$\mathbf{1.000}_{\pm 0.000}$	$\mathbf{1.000}_{\pm 0.000}$	$\mathbf{1.000}_{\pm 0.000}$
Nonlinear	RCD [7]	$0.600_{\pm 0.440}$	$0.750_{\pm 0.317}$	$0.880_{\pm 0.156}$	$\mathbf{1.000}_{\pm 0.000}$
	CIRCA [9]	$0.700_{\pm 0.427}$	$0.717_{\pm 0.387}$	$0.835_{\pm 0.117}$	$\mathbf{1.000}_{\pm 0.000}$
	RCG [8]	$0.591_{\pm 0.117}$	$0.715_{\pm 0.020}$	$0.897_{\pm 0.008}$	$\mathbf{1.000}_{\pm 0.000}$
	AERCA [6]	$\mathbf{1.000}_{\pm 0.000}$	$\mathbf{1.000}_{\pm 0.000}$	$\mathbf{1.000}_{\pm 0.000}$	$\mathbf{1.000}_{\pm 0.000}$
	Ours	$\mathbf{1.000}_{\pm 0.000}$	$\mathbf{1.000}_{\pm 0.000}$	$\mathbf{1.000}_{\pm 0.000}$	$\mathbf{1.000}_{\pm 0.000}$
SWaT [14]	RCD [7]	$0.000_{\pm 0.000}$	$0.000_{\pm 0.000}$	$0.000_{\pm 0.000}$	$0.300_{\pm 0.104}$
	CIRCA [9]	$0.000_{\pm 0.000}$	$0.000_{\pm 0.000}$	$0.000_{\pm 0.000}$	$0.300_{\pm 0.041}$
	RCG [8]	$\mathbf{0.327}_{\pm 0.104}$	$0.370_{\pm 0.088}$	$0.401_{\pm 0.043}$	$0.562_{\pm 0.041}$
	AERCA [6]	$0.220_{\pm 0.104}$	$0.290_{\pm 0.088}$	$0.330_{\pm 0.043}$	$0.455_{\pm 0.041}$
	Ours	$0.241_{\pm 0.053}$	$\mathbf{0.517}_{\pm 0.037}$	$\mathbf{0.621}_{\pm 0.074}$	$\mathbf{0.758}_{\pm 0.038}$
MSDS [17]	RCD [7]	$0.412_{\pm 0.051}$	$0.573_{\pm 0.020}$	$0.984_{\pm 0.001}$	$\mathbf{1.000}_{\pm 0.000}$
	CIRCA [9]	$0.454_{\pm 0.238}$	$0.860_{\pm 0.138}$	$0.917_{\pm 0.080}$	$\mathbf{1.000}_{\pm 0.000}$
	RCG [8]	$0.527_{\pm 0.302}$	$0.591_{\pm 0.255}$	$0.647_{\pm 0.057}$	$\mathbf{1.000}_{\pm 0.000}$
	AERCA [6]	$0.395_{\pm 0.402}$	$0.908_{\pm 0.064}$	$0.974_{\pm 0.022}$	$\mathbf{1.000}_{\pm 0.000}$
	Ours	$\mathbf{0.827}_{\pm 0.102}$	$\mathbf{0.982}_{\pm 0.0084}$	$\mathbf{1.000}_{\pm 0.000}$	$\mathbf{1.000}_{\pm 0.000}$

results indicate that the proposed formulation remains competitive across both controlled non-dynamic simulations and the dynamic benchmark.

Table 3 summarizes the RCA performance in terms of AC@K. The proposed method achieves the strongest overall performance across the evaluated datasets, surpassing the baselines by a substantial margin. In particular, AERCA performs well on the synthetic dataset but suffers a marked degradation on real-world benchmarks, while RCG shows competitive performance on SWaT only and fails to maintain this trend on the remaining datasets. By contrast, our method yields consistently strong results across all datasets, demonstrating superior robustness and generalization.

Figure 2 further supports the structural-deviation term used in the RCA score. In both examples, the anomalous causal strengths lie far from the normal training distribution. This means that anomalies are accompanied not only by forecasting errors but also by clear departures from the normal causal mechanism, which empirically justifies including structural deviation as a complementary RCA signal.

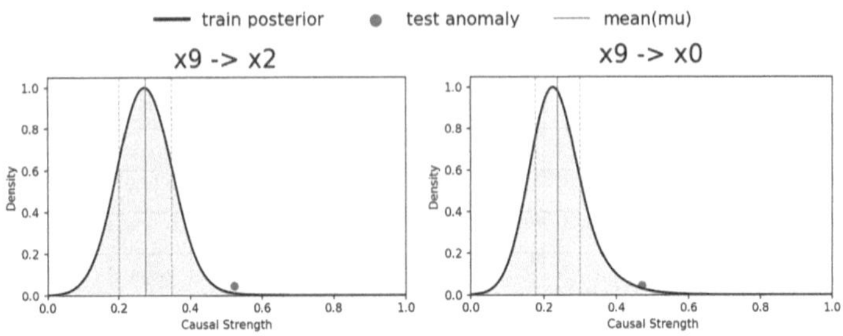

Fig. 2. Structural deviation under anomaly relative to the normal causal distribution. The black curve shows the causal-strength posterior estimated from normal training data, the red point shows the causal strength inferred at anomalous test time, and the gray vertical line denotes the posterior mean μ. The labels $x9 \rightarrow x2$ and $x9 \rightarrow x0$ indicate causal edges from source variable $x9$ to target variables $x2$ and $x0$. (Color figure online)

4.3 Uncertainty Experiment Results

Figure 3 examines whether the learned causal-discovery uncertainty reflects edge reliability. In the left panel, the performance of the model, in AUROC, is compared directly with the percentage of uncertain edges included. The causal discovery performance decreases from 0.93 to approximately 0.87 as more low-confidence edges are added. This indicates that uncertain edges hinder model performance. In the right panel, all inferred edges are sorted by predicted uncertainty and divided into four equal-sized quartiles. For each quartile, the mean edge-level classification error is computed as $(1 - p_{\text{active}})$ for a ground-truth active edge and p_{active} for a ground-truth inactive edge, where p_{active} denotes the predicted edge-activation probability. The error increases monotonically from Q1 to Q4, which further shows that uncertainty is directly correlated with less accurate edges. Together, these diagnostics provide empirical justification for suppressing highly uncertain causal edges through the uncertainty-aware SNR gate introduced in the model.

Figure 4 evaluates whether the forecasting uncertainty estimated by the variance head reflects the difficulty of prediction. In the left panel, samples are sorted from the most certain to the least certain, and the mean absolute forecasting error is shown in relation to the inclusion of an increasing percent of uncertain samples. The error increases steadily as low-confidence samples are added, indicating that the predicted uncertainty is aligned with actual forecasting difficulty. In the right panel, samples are sorted by predictive uncertainty and split into four equal-sized quartiles. The mean absolute error again increases monotonically from Q1 to Q4. These two diagnostics support the interpretation that the forecasting uncertainty is meaningful as a relative confidence measure and provide empirical justification for using uncertainty-normalized forecasting evidence in anomaly scoring and RCA.

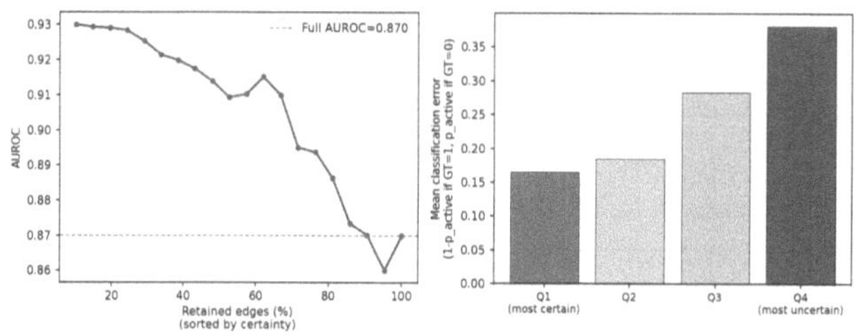

Fig. 3. Uncertainty diagnostics for causal edge reliability on ND8. Left: AUROC evaluated as edges are retained according to predicted certainty. The dashed line denotes the AUROC computed using all inferred edges. Right: mean edge-level classification error computed for four groups of edges formed by uncertainty quartiles.

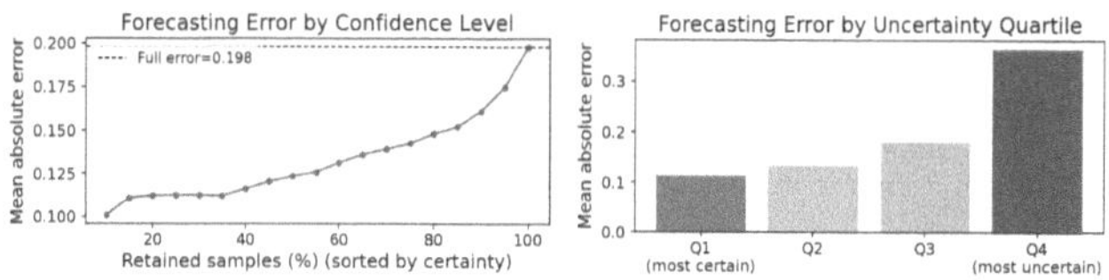

Fig. 4. Forecasting uncertainty diagnostics on SWaT. Left: mean absolute error under certainty-based sample retention. Right: mean absolute error across uncertainty quartiles.

4.4 Ablation Study

Table 4 shows the ablation results on the SWaT dataset for evaluating the contribution of each design component in the proposed framework. The full model achieves the best performance across all metrics. In contrast, removing any of the major components consistently degrades RCA performance, suggesting that the overall gain comes from the interaction of complementary components rather than any single module. Among the ablated variants, removing the uncertainty-aware SNR gate causes the largest performance drop in the top-ranked metrics. Specifically, AC@3 and AC@5 decrease to 0.310 and 0.379, respectively. This is consistent with the uncertainty analysis in Fig. 3. It suggests that suppressing uncertain edges is critical for preventing noisy or weak causal connections from adversely affecting the RCA ranking.

The two-stage training strategy also plays an essential role. When Stages 1 and 2 are joined together to learn the predictive mean and variance simultaneously, the performance again deteriorates. This supports separating mean learning from variance calibration. The result proves that, when both objectives are optimized at the same time, the model will rely on inflating predictive variance before learning accurate predictive means to lazily reduce its loss value. Removing the OU prior also degrades performance, suggesting that smooth temporal evolution of the causal structure improves RCA reliability. Similarly, the sparsity term is beneficial, as explicitly controlling graph density helps prevent the causal graph from being diffused across many weak edges and enables clearer separa-

Table 4. Ablation Study on SWaT

Module	AC@1	AC@3	AC@5	AC@10
OU w/o	0.231	0.379	0.448	0.625
NLL w/o	0.206	0.482	0.586	0.655
SNR gate w/o	0.172	0.310	0.379	0.688
$\mathcal{L}_{sparse}$ w/o	0.172	0.448	0.512	0.689
Joint stage1 & 2	0.209	0.379	0.443	0.627
Full	**0.241**	**0.517**	**0.621**	**0.758**

tion of the dominant causal pathways. Finally, the NLL w/o variant corresponds to a setting that uses only MSE instead of NLL. Its inferior performance shows that incorporating predictive variance, rather than relying solely on the predictive mean, makes a meaningful contribution to RCA performance by enabling uncertainty-aware scoring.

5 Conclusion

We proposed a probabilistic dynamic causal RCA framework for industrial multivariate time series. The model estimates time-varying causal coefficients as approximate posterior distributions, regularizes their evolution with an OU-inspired prior, and integrates the inferred causal structure into a nonlinear forecasting model. This unified design supports causal discovery, uncertainty-aware forecasting, and improved root-cause localization.

Experiments show strong performance on synthetic and real datasets, with meaningful causal uncertainty, well-calibrated forecasting uncertainty, and improved RCA results. However, the current framework is limited by the smoothness assumption of the OU-based prior, which makes it less suitable for settings with abrupt switch-like causal changes. Handling such discrete structural transitions more effectively remains an important direction for future work.

Acknowledgments. This work was supported by the BK21 FOUR Project and the Technology development Program S-2026-1123-000-01 funded by the Ministry of SMEs and Startups (MSS, Korea).

Use of Generative AI. A generative AI tool was used only to assist with language polishing, including grammar correction, translation, and improving the readability of author-written text.

References

1. Arnold, A., Liu, Y., Abe, N.: Temporal causal modeling with graphical granger methods. In: Proceedings of the 13th ACM SIGKDD International Conference on Knowledge Discovery and Data Mining, pp. 66–75 (2007)

2. Assaad, C.K., Devijver, E., Gaussier, E.: Survey and evaluation of causal discovery methods for time series. J. Artif. Intell. Res. **73**, 767–819 (2022)
3. Bi, T., Pan, Y., Jiang, X., Sun, H., Ma, M., Wang, P.: UnCLE: towards scalable dynamic causal discovery in non-linear temporal systems. arXiv preprint arXiv:2511.03168 (2025)
4. Cheng, Y., Lyu, B., Xing, W., Zhu, Z.: DyCAST: learning dynamic causal structure from time series. In: The Thirteenth International Conference on Learning Representations (2025)
5. Cheng, Y., Yang, R., Xiao, T., Li, Z., Suo, J., He, K., Dai, Q.: CUTS: Neural causal discovery from irregular time-series data. arXiv preprint arXiv:2302.07458 (2023)
6. Han, X., Absar, S., Zhang, L., Yuan, S.: Root cause analysis of anomalies in multivariate time series through granger causal discovery. In: The Thirteenth International Conference on Learning Representations (2025)
7. Ikram, A., Chakraborty, S., Mitra, S., Saini, S., Bagchi, S., Kocaoglu, M.: Root cause analysis of failures in microservices through causal discovery. Adv. Neural. Inf. Process. Syst. **35**, 31158–31170 (2022)
8. Ikram, A., Lee, K., Agarwal, S., Saini, S.K., Bagchi, S., Kocaoglu, M.: Root cause analysis of failures from partial causal structures. In: The 41st Conference on Uncertainty in Artificial Intelligence (2025)
9. Li, M., et al.: Causal inference-based root cause analysis for online service systems with intervention recognition. In: Proceedings of the 28th ACM SIGKDD Conference on Knowledge Discovery and Data Mining, pp. 3230–3240 (2022)
10. Liu, Y., Chen, H.S., Wu, H., Dai, Y., Yao, Y., Yan, Z.: Simplified granger causality map for data-driven root cause diagnosis of process disturbances. J. Process Control **95**, 45–54 (2020)
11. Liu, Z., Gao, M., Jiao, P.: GCAD: anomaly detection in multivariate time series from the perspective of granger causality. In: Proceedings of the AAAI Conference on Artificial Intelligence, vol. 39, pp. 19041–19049 (2025)
12. Lütkepohl, H.: Introduction to Multiple Time Series Analysis. Springer, Heidelberg (2013). https://doi.org/10.1007/978-3-662-02691-5
13. Marcinkevičs, R., Vogt, J.E.: Interpretable models for granger causality using self-explaining neural networks. arXiv preprint arXiv:2101.07600 (2021)
14. Mathur, A.P., Tippenhauer, N.O.: SWaT: a water treatment testbed for research and training on ICS security. In: 2016 International Workshop on Cyber-Physical Systems for Smart Water Networks (CySWater), pp. 31–36. IEEE (2016)
15. Mostafa, F., JS Allen, L.: Periodic mean-reverting stochastic differential equations and parameter estimations for seasonal data. Stoch. Models **41**(4), 413–444 (2025)
16. Nauta, M., Bucur, D., Seifert, C.: Causal discovery with attention-based convolutional neural networks. Mach. Learn. Knowl. Extr. **1**(1), 19 (2019)
17. Nedelkoski, S., Bogatinovski, J., Mandapati, A.K., Becker, S., Cardoso, J., Kao, O.: Multi-source distributed system data for AI-powered analytics. In: Brogi, A., Zimmermann, W., Kritikos, K. (eds.) ESOCC 2020. LNCS, vol. 12054, pp. 161–176. Springer, Cham (2020). https://doi.org/10.1007/978-3-030-44769-4_13
18. Rezende, D.J., Mohamed, S., Wierstra, D.: Stochastic backpropagation and approximate inference in deep generative models. In: International Conference on Machine Learning, pp. 1278–1286. PMLR (2014)
19. Shannon, C.E.: A mathematical theory of communication. Bell Syst. Tech. J. **27**(3), 379–423 (1948)
20. Shojaie, A., Fox, E.B.: Granger causality: a review and recent advances. Ann. Rev. Stat. Appl. **9**(1), 289–319 (2022)

21. Uhlenbeck, G.E., Ornstein, L.S.: On the theory of the Brownian motion. Phys. Rev. **36**(5), 823 (1930)
22. Wang, S., Zhao, Q., Han, Y., Wang, J.: Root cause diagnosis for process faults based on multisensor time-series causality discovery. J. Process Control **122**, 27–40 (2023)
23. Yang, W., Zhang, K., Hoi, S.C.: A causal approach to detecting multivariate time-series anomalies and root causes. arXiv preprint arXiv:2206.15033 (2022)
24. Zhu, T., Ran, Y., Zhou, X., Wen, Y.: A survey of predictive maintenance: systems, purposes and approaches. arXiv preprint arXiv:1912.07383 (2019)

SegDP: An Unsupervised Multivariate Discretization Algorithm for Mixed-Type Data

Yinjia Zhang[1] and Qinpei Zhao[2(✉)]

[1] Department of Computer Science, School of Science, Aalto University, Espoo, Finland
yinjia.zhang@aalto.fi
[2] School of Computer Science and Technology, Tongji University, Shanghai, China
qinpeizhao@tongji.edu.cn

Abstract. Discretization is a common preprocessing step for data mining tasks that require discrete inputs. Compared with supervised discretization, unsupervised methods are applicable in a broader range of settings, yet they have received relatively limited attention. Existing unsupervised methods are typically either univariate or depend on ad hoc choices for the number of bins. Moreover, existing multivariate methods often assume that all features are numerical, even though real-world datasets commonly contain a mixture of numerical and categorical variables. In this paper, we propose SegDP, an unsupervised multivariate discretization method that partitions each numerical feature into contiguous segments while accounting for other features, whether numerical or categorical. SegDP uses a Bayesian information criterion style objective to automatically determine the appropriate number of segments and select the optimal segmentation for each numerical feature. Experiments on eight synthetic cases show that SegDP recognizes interaction patterns ranging from nonlinear relationships to Simpson's paradox and mixed-type associations. In classification experiments involving 33 datasets, SegDP shows strong overall performance relative to the compared methods, including the state-of-the-art unsupervised multivariate discretization approach, across three widely used classifiers. Finally, sensitivity analyses further demonstrate the robustness of SegDP to variations in its parameter settings.

Keywords: Discretization · Unsupervised · Multivariate

1 Introduction

Discretization is a fundamental data analysis technique to convert continuous features into discrete ones. Besides serving as a preprocessing step for downstream analysis, discretization can improve interpretability by producing compact, human-readable representations of numerical patterns. Such representations are particularly valuable in pattern mining, exploratory analysis, and decision making tasks, especially in medical and biomedical applications.

M. Ceci et al. (Eds.): ECML PKDD 2026, LNAI 16941, pp. 145–162, 2027.
https://doi.org/10.1007/978-3-032-37654-1_9

Depending on whether ground truth labels are used, discretization methods can be classified as supervised or unsupervised. Although supervised discretization often yields better performance in classification tasks by leveraging class labels, unsupervised discretization remains essential and broadly applicable, particularly when labels are unavailable or unreliable, or when the objective is exploratory analysis instead of prediction. However, compared with supervised approaches, unsupervised discretization has been receiving much less research attention. Many widely employed unsupervised procedures are univariate [4,6,9,17,23], placing the cutoffs solely according to the marginal distribution of the target feature without considering other features. Although these approaches are efficient and easy to interpret, they ignore interactions among features and may lead to bias and information loss. Unsupervised multivariate discretization approaches are therefore proposed [7,13,14,22]. Multivariate approaches aim to discretize features while considering their interactions with other features. However, to the best of our knowledge, existing unsupervised multivariate approaches mainly assume that auxiliary features are numerical, even though real-world datasets often contain a mixture of numerical and categorical features. As a result, users may need to discard categorical features or encode them in ways that do not faithfully reflect their structure, potentially leading to substantial information loss.

To address this gap, we propose SegDP, an unsupervised multivariate discretization method for mixed-type data. SegDP seeks informative and interpretable segments of a numerical target feature by evaluating candidate discretizations with a weighted Bayesian information criterion (BIC) [19] style objective. This objective incorporates both numerical and categorical assistant features and applies a normalized mutual information (NMI)-based feature-weighting scheme to improve robustness against uninformative assistant features. The resulting optimization problem is solved exactly by dynamic programming, enabling automatic selection of cut points and segment counts under the proposed objective. We evaluate SegDP by synthetic case studies, benchmark classification tasks, and sensitivity analysis, illustrating its ability to capture multivariate patterns of mixed-type assistant features and produce interpretable segmentations.

The main contributions of this paper are as follows:

1. We formulate unsupervised multivariate discretization for mixed-type data as a weighted model selection problem.
2. We introduce a BIC-style objective that jointly accounts for the target feature and both numerical and categorical assistant features.
3. We develop an exact dynamic programming solution that automatically identifies the segmentation under the proposed formulation.
4. We introduce a practical NMI-based weighting strategy to control the contribution of assistant features.
5. We provide empirical evidence from synthetic case studies, benchmark classification tasks, and sensitivity analyses to illustrate the usefulness of SegDP.

2 Related Work

Discretization of numerical features is a fundamental preprocessing step in data analysis, particularly for tasks that require discrete inputs, such as frequent itemset mining and association rule mining. Depending on whether class labels are used to guide the binning process, discretization techniques can be broadly classified into supervised and unsupervised approaches. Supervised discretization, leveraging the relationship between features and labels, is often adopted when predictive performance is the main objective and has consequently attracted substantially more research attention. However, unsupervised discretization is applicable in a much wider range of scenarios, especially when class labels are unavailable and unreliable or prediction is not the focus of the analysis.

Unsupervised Discretization. We first introduce univariate methods that discretize each feature individually without considering other features. The most straightforward methods are *equal-width* (EW) and *equal-frequency* (EF) binning. EW is good at preserving distributional shape, but sensitive to outliers and may yield highly unbalanced bin counts where empty bins and overly dense bins coexist. EF assigns equal numbers of samples to each bin, improving count balance, but it distorts distribution shape and might create very narrow bins in dense regions. Both EW and EF require pre-specifying the number of bins, which is often difficult in practice. Clustering algorithms are also used in univariate unsupervised discretization to form adaptive bins [6], grouping values so that observations within each bin have similar magnitude; however, selecting appropriate hyperparameters of clustering algorithms is often challenging. Univariate approaches based on the *minimum description length* (MDL) principle [17] form another important family [16]. The MDL principle selects the model minimizing the sum of the model code length and the length of data encoded by the model. An example is the algorithm proposed by Kontkanen and Myllymäki [9], which jointly finds the MDL-optimal number of bins and the corresponding cut-point locations for each feature. In addition, several heuristic alternatives have been proposed, including *fixed frequency discretization* [23], *proportional discretization* [23], and *U-LBG* [4].

A key limitation of univariate discretization is that it ignores interactions among features. In contrast, multivariate approaches aim to discretize features while considering their interactions with other features. Mehta et al. proposed a *principal component analysis* (PCA) based method, which discretizes data in the new space where features are independent after PCA transformation and then maps the resulting cut-points back to the original feature space [13]. However, it may miss complex interactions since PCA is a linear transformation. Kang et al. introduced a similar approach that uses *independent component analysis* (ICA) instead of PCA, but this method does not convert ICA-transformed data back to the original space, raising interpretation problems, and the limitation of the linear transformation still remains [7].

Another family of multivariate methods directly considers interactions among features in the original space. *MultiVariate Discretization* (MVD) first partitions each feature into fine intervals, and then combines two intervals if they have similar multivariate distributions, which is guided by a specifically designed metric in the context of set mining [1]. However, this method may falsely combine two intervals due to sparsity caused by taking continuous values as items [14]. *Interaction-preserving discretization* (IPD) introduces interaction distance between two bins considering all dimensions simultaneously, and finds the MDL-optimal discretization of each feature by dynamic programming [14]. As far as we know, IPD is the strongest established pre-existing method for unsupervised multivariate discretization in the general tabular setting considered in this study [12,22]. *PALM* applies an MDL-based criterion to learn adaptive two-dimensional histogram partitions that capture feature interactions [22]. But it is limited to 2D data and does not directly extend to higher dimensions. In addition, to the best of our knowledge, existing unsupervised multivariate approaches assume that all auxiliary features are numerical. As a result, they cannot naturally handle mixed-type datasets, where categorical features may contain important information for determining meaningful cut points.

Supervised Discretization. Supervised discretization has received more attention than unsupervised discretization in the literature. Since it falls outside the scope of this study, we introduce only the main categories without detailing specific methods. In general, supervised methods aim to maximize the similarity of values within the same bin in terms of class labels while minimizing it across different bins. Some approaches take information-theoretic measures to guide discretization, such as entropy and MDL [2,3]. Another family leverages statistical techniques, such as statistical tests [10,18] and Bayesian theories [11]. Other studies propose heuristic criteria [5,20] or employ novel search strategies, such as evolutionary algorithms [15]. Approaches specifically designed for certain classifiers have also become more prevalent [21,24].

3 Problem Definition and Notation

Let $D \in \mathbb{R}^{m \times n}$ be the data matrix of m features and n samples, where there are m_1 numerical features and m_2 categorical features ($m_1 + m_2 = m$). We write $X \in \mathbb{R}^{m_1 \times n}$ for the numerical submatrix and $C \in \mathbb{Z}^{m_2 \times n}$ for the categorical submatrix. For a numerical feature $\boldsymbol{x} = (x_1, \cdots, x_n)$, we use $X' = X \setminus \boldsymbol{x} \in \mathbb{R}^{(m_1-1)\times n}$ to denote the matrix of the other numerical features. A categorical feature $\boldsymbol{c}$ is integer-encoded and its domain is $dom(\boldsymbol{c})$ of size $J_{\boldsymbol{c}}$.

For each *target feature* $\boldsymbol{x}$, we sort its values in ascending order and reorder the samples (columns) in X' and C accordingly. In the remainder of this work, $\boldsymbol{x}$, X', and C refer to the data after this permutation unless otherwise specified. After sorting the target feature in ascending order, discretization corresponds to dividing the sequence of the target feature values into contiguous segments, each of which defines one interval of the final discretization. For a given number of segments K, let $S_K^{\boldsymbol{x}} = (s_1^{\boldsymbol{x}}, \dots, s_K^{\boldsymbol{x}})$ denote the segmentation of $\boldsymbol{x}$, where a segment $s_k^{\boldsymbol{x}} = (x_{t_k}, x_{t_k+1}, \cdots, x_{t_k+n_k-1})$ contains n_k consecutive values of the sorted feature starting at the index t_k. Accordingly, $S_K^{\boldsymbol{x}'}$ and $S_K^{\boldsymbol{c}}$ are the segmentations of $\boldsymbol{x}' \subset X'$ and $\boldsymbol{c} \subset C$ induced by $S_K^{\boldsymbol{x}}$.

In this work, SegDP discretizes one numerical target feature at a time, while the remaining numerical and categorical features act as *assistant features.* We propose that an ideal discretization should satisfy three properties. First, values of the target feature are homogeneous within each segment and well separated between segments. Second, the induced partitions of assistant features should reveal heterogeneous mixed-type patterns aligned with the target segmentation. In other words, samples within the same target feature segment should exhibit a shared pattern of assistant feature values, while this pattern should differ from those observed in other segments. Third, the number of segments should be chosen appropriately to preserve interpretability and avoid over-segmentation.

4 SegDP Objective

In this section, based on the desired properties described in Sect. 3, we formulate discretization as a model selection problem and define a BIC-style evaluation function for candidate segmentations. This criterion evaluates how well a segmentation fits the within-segment distributions of the target and assistant features, while penalizing excessive complexity.

Given a segmentation $S_K^{\boldsymbol{x}}$, we model the values in a segment $s_k^{\boldsymbol{x}}$ as n_k independent and identically distributed (i.i.d.) samples from a Gaussian distribution $N(\mu_k^{\boldsymbol{x}}, {\sigma_k^{\boldsymbol{x}}}^2)$. The same assumption is applied to the induced segmentation $S_K^{\boldsymbol{x}'}$ of a numerical assistant feature $\boldsymbol{x}'$, where the values in each segment $s_k^{\boldsymbol{x}'}$ are modeled by $N(\mu_k^{\boldsymbol{x}'}, {\sigma_k^{\boldsymbol{x}'}}^2)$. For a categorical assistant feature $\boldsymbol{c}$, the values in each induced segment $s_k^{\boldsymbol{c}}$ are modeled by a segment-specific categorical distribution over $dom(c)$, with the category probability $p_{k,y}^{\boldsymbol{c}}$ for each $y \in dom(\boldsymbol{c})$.

Under these assumptions, the quality of a segmentation can be evaluated by how well the corresponding segment-wise distributions fit the data, while penalizing model complexity to discourage overly fine segmentations. We therefore adopt the Bayesian information criterion, defined as

$$BIC = \xi \ln(n) - 2\ln(\widehat{L}), \tag{1}$$

where $\ln(\widehat{L})$ is the maximized log-likelihood and ξ is the number of parameters.

Numerical Features. For a numerical feature $\boldsymbol{x}$, we assume that observations within each segment $s_k^{\boldsymbol{x}}$ follow a Gaussian distribution. The maximum-likelihood estimates of the segment mean and variance are

$$\hat{\mu}_k^{\boldsymbol{x}} = \frac{1}{n_k}\sum_{i=1}^{n_k} x_{t_k+i-1} \quad \text{and} \quad \hat{\sigma_k^{\boldsymbol{x}}}^2 = \frac{1}{n_k}\sum_{i=1}^{n_k}(x_{t_k+i-1} - \hat{\mu}_k^{\boldsymbol{x}})^2. \tag{2}$$

Since each of the K segments contributes two parameters, the total number of free parameters is $2K$. Therefore, up to additive constants, the BIC of the segmentation $S_K^{\boldsymbol{x}}$ is

$$BIC(S_K^{\boldsymbol{x}}) = \xi_{S_K^{\boldsymbol{x}}} \ln(n) - 2\ln(\widehat{L}(\boldsymbol{x}|S_K^{\boldsymbol{x}})) \equiv 2K\ln(n) + \sum_{k=1}^{K} n_k \ln(\hat{\sigma_k^{\boldsymbol{x}}}^2). \quad (3)$$

This form applies to both the target feature and numerical assistant features.

Categorical Features. Let $\boldsymbol{c}$ be a categorical feature with the domain $dom(\boldsymbol{c})$ and $|dom(\boldsymbol{c})| = J_{\boldsymbol{c}}$. For the k-th segment $s_k^{\boldsymbol{c}}$, let $n_{k,y}^{\boldsymbol{c}}$ be the number of observations taking the value $y \in dom(\boldsymbol{c})$. The maximum likelihood estimate of the category probability of y is

$$\hat{p}_{k,y}^{\boldsymbol{c}} = \frac{n_{k,y}^{\boldsymbol{c}}}{n_k}. \quad (4)$$

Since each segment contributes $J_{\boldsymbol{c}} - 1$ free parameters, the total number of free parameters is $K(J_{\boldsymbol{c}} - 1)$. Hence, the BIC of the induced segmentation $S_K^{\boldsymbol{c}}$ is

$$BIC(S_K^{\boldsymbol{c}}) = \xi_{S_K^{\boldsymbol{c}}} \ln(n) - 2\ln(\widehat{L}(\boldsymbol{c}|S_K^{\boldsymbol{c}})) \quad (5)$$

$$= K(J_{\boldsymbol{c}} - 1)\ln(n) - 2\sum_{k=1}^{K} \sum_{y \in dom(\boldsymbol{c})} n_{k,y}^{\boldsymbol{c}} \ln(\hat{p}_{k,y}^{\boldsymbol{c}}) \quad (6)$$

Objective Function. A natural way to evaluate a candidate segmentation is to aggregate the BIC contributions of the target feature and its assistant features. However, directly summing these terms may allow irrelevant assistant features to distort the evaluation of the target segmentation.

To improve robustness, we introduce feature-specific weights on the log-likelihood terms and define the following weighted evaluation function for a segmentation $S_K^{\boldsymbol{x}}$

$$f(S_K^{\boldsymbol{x}}, X', C) = K\left(2m_1 + \sum_{c \in C}(J_c - 1)\right)\ln(n)$$
$$- 2\left(w\ln(\widehat{L}(\boldsymbol{x}|S_K^{\boldsymbol{x}})) + \sum_{i=1}^{m_1 - 1} u_i \ln(\widehat{L}(\boldsymbol{x}_i'|S_K^{\boldsymbol{x}_i'})) + \sum_{j=1}^{m_2} v_j \ln(\widehat{L}(\boldsymbol{c}_j|S_K^{\boldsymbol{c}_j}))\right), \quad (7)$$

where w, u_i, and v_j are feature weights for the target feature, numerical assistant features, and categorical assistant features, respectively. The weights are applied only to the log-likelihood terms, while the complexity penalty remains unchanged to penalize model complexity uniformly and discourage over-segmentation.

5 Practical Feature Weighting

In this section, we describe how the feature weights in Eq. 7 are determined. The purpose of weighting is to reduce the influence of weakly related assistant features while emphasizing those that are more strongly associated with the target feature.

We use normalized mutual information (NMI) to quantify the association between the target feature and each assistant feature. NMI takes values in $[0, 1]$, where 0 indicates no dependence and 1 indicates perfect dependence. Based on these associations, the weights of numerical and categorical assistant features are defined as

$$u_i = \frac{\phi(\boldsymbol{x}, \boldsymbol{x}'_i)}{T_x} \quad \text{and} \quad v_j = \frac{\phi(\boldsymbol{x}, \boldsymbol{c}_j)}{T_x}, \tag{8}$$

where

$$\phi(\boldsymbol{x}, \boldsymbol{y}) = \begin{cases} NMI(\boldsymbol{x}, \boldsymbol{y}), & \text{if } NMI(\boldsymbol{x}, \boldsymbol{y}) \geq \epsilon \\ 0, & \text{otherwise} \end{cases} \tag{9}$$

and

$$T_x = \sum_{p=1}^{m_1-1} \phi(\boldsymbol{x}, \boldsymbol{x}'_p) + \sum_{q=1}^{m_2} \phi(\boldsymbol{x}, \boldsymbol{c}_q). \tag{10}$$

If $T_x = 0$, all assistant feature weights are set to zero, so the objective depends only on the target-feature term.

When both the target feature and an assistant feature are numerical, we approximate their NMI by first discretizing both features into K_{max} equal-width bins, where K_{max} is the maximum number of segments considered by SegDP, and then computing NMI on the resulting ordinal variables. In principle, the number of bins can be any value smaller than n. However, too many bins may make the corresponding contingency table highly sparse, which can further inflate the estimated feature weights. As a result, assistant features that are actually weakly associated with the target feature may be over-emphasized and distort the discretization. When the assistant feature is categorical, only the target feature is discretized, and NMI is computed between the discretized target feature and the original categorical assistant feature.

The threshold ϵ is used to filter out assistant features whose associations with the target feature are too weak. In practice, values in the range $(0.2, 0.5)$ were found to work reasonably well in our experiments. In addition, the target feature is assigned a user-specified weight w, which controls its contribution relative to the assistant features. When $w = 0$, the discretization depends entirely on assistant features. In most cases, it is sufficient to set $w = 1$.

We choose NMI for two reasons. First, it can capture both linear and nonlinear associations between features. Second, because it is normalized, the resulting weights are directly comparable across different features and can be incorporated into the objective function without introducing scale bias.

6 Optimization by Dynamic Programming

This section presents SegDP, a dynamic programming algorithm for optimizing the objective in Eq. (7). The key observation is that the objective can be decomposed into a sum of segment-wise costs, which induces an optimal substructure and enables exact dynamic programming. Although this paper uses Gaussian and categorical models for the within-segment distributions, the dynamic programming framework itself is not tied to these specific choices. In general, other per-segment likelihood models can also be adopted without affecting the DP formulation, provided that the resulting objective remains additive over segments. This flexibility may be particularly important when the data are highly skewed.

Formally, SegDP solves

$$(K^*, S^{\boldsymbol{x}}_{K^*}) = \mathop{\arg\min}_{1 \le K \le K_{max},\ S^{\boldsymbol{x}}_K} f(S^{\boldsymbol{x}}_K, X', C), \tag{11}$$

where K_{max} denotes the maximum number of segments.

To enable dynamic programming, we rewrite the objective $f(S^{\boldsymbol{x}}_K, X', C)$ as a sum of segment-wise contributions. Specifically, up to additive constants independent of the segmentation, we have

$$f(S^{\boldsymbol{x}}_K, X', C) \equiv \sum_{k=1}^{K} g(t_k, n_k, \boldsymbol{x}, X', C) \tag{12}$$

$$= \sum_{k=1}^{K} \Bigg[\Big(2m_1 + \sum_{c \in C} (J_c - 1) \Big) \ln(n) + w n_k \ln(\hat{\sigma^{\boldsymbol{x}}_k}^2) \tag{13}$$

$$+ \sum_{i=1}^{m_1 - 1} u_i n_k \ln(\hat{\sigma^{\boldsymbol{x}'}_k}^2) - 2 \sum_{j=1}^{m_2} \sum_{y \in dom(\boldsymbol{c}_j)} v_j n^{c_j}_{k,y} \ln(\hat{p}^{c_j}_{k,y}) \Bigg], \tag{14}$$

where $g(\cdot)$ is the cost of the k-th segment.

This additive structure induces an optimal substructure property, which allows an exact dynamic programming solution. Let $dp_{k,r}$ denote the minimum evaluation score for partitioning the first r sorted values $(x_1, \cdots x_r)$ into k contiguous segments, and λ be the minimum segment length. The recurrence is

$$dp_{k,r} = \begin{cases} g(1, r, \boldsymbol{x}, X', C), & k = 1, 1 \le r \le n, \\ \min\limits_{(k-1)\lambda \le \ell \le r - \lambda} \Big\{ dp_{k-1,\ell} + g(\ell + 1, r - \ell, \boldsymbol{x}, X', C) \Big\}, & k \ge 2, k\lambda \le r \le n, \\ \inf, & otherwise. \end{cases}$$

The parameter λ serves two purposes. First, it prevents segments from containing too few observations, which would be statistically unstable and difficult to interpret. Second, it reduces the DP search space and thus improves computational efficiency. It should be guaranteed that $\lambda \cdot K_{max} \le n$.

Algorithm 1 presents SegDP for discretizing a target feature. In addition to K_{max} and λ, the algorithm optionally accepts a user-specified segment number τ. When τ is provided, the target feature is partitioned into τ segments instead of the number selected by Eq. 7. Moreover, by default, we standardize the features before discretization to reduce the bias caused by differences in feature scales.

Algorithm 1: SegDP

Input: target feature $\boldsymbol{x}$, numerical data $X' \in \mathbb{R}^{(m_1-1)\times n}$, categorical data $C \in \mathbb{Z}^{m_2\times n}$, max number of segments K_{max}, min segment size λ, preferred number of segments τ (optional)

Output: the optimal segmentation $S^{\boldsymbol{x}}_{K^*}$

Standardize $\boldsymbol{x}$ and X';
Sort $\boldsymbol{x}$ and re-order columns of X' and C accordingly;
initialize $dp \in \mathbb{R}^{K_{max}\times n}$ by $+\infty$; `// dp scores`
initialize $hl \in \mathbb{N}^{K_{max}\times n}$ by -1; `// head index of the last segment`
for $r \leftarrow 1$ **to** n **do**
  $dp_{1,r} \leftarrow g(1, r, \boldsymbol{x}, X', C)$;
  $hl_{1,r} \leftarrow 1$;
for $k \leftarrow 2$ **to** K_{max} **do**
  for $r \leftarrow k\lambda$ **to** n **do**
    $dp_{k,r} \leftarrow \min_{\ell=(k-1)\lambda,\ldots,r-\lambda} \left\{ dp_{k-1,\ell} + g(\ell+1, r-\ell, \boldsymbol{x}, X', C) \right\}$;
    $hl_{k,r} \leftarrow$ head index of the last segment corresponding to $dp_{k,r}$;
  if τ *is given* $\wedge\ k == \tau$ **then**
    break;
$K^* \leftarrow \tau$ **if** τ is given **else** $\arg\min_{1\le k\le K_{max}} dp(k, n)$;
$S^{\boldsymbol{x}}_{K^*} \leftarrow$ the optimal segmentation obtained by backtracking using hl and K^*;
return $S^{\boldsymbol{x}}_{K^*}$

The time complexity of SegDP for discretizing one target feature is $O(mK_{max}n^2)$, where each segment cost g can be computed in $O(m)$ using prefix sums and prefix counts. Consequently, the discretization of all features in X requires $O(m_1 m K_{max} n^2)$. In the worst case, when $K_{max} = \Theta(n)$ (e.g., λ is constant), the total time complexity increases to $O(m_1 m n^3)$.

7 Evaluation and Discussion

7.1 Setup

The proposed method was evaluated through three sets of experiments. First, we used synthetic data to examine whether SegDP can preserve important interactions between the target feature and the assistant features. Second, we evaluated SegDP through its application to classification tasks. Unsupervised discretization methods are difficult to evaluate directly for two main reasons: (1) there are multiple context-dependent evaluation criteria, some of which may be mutually conflicting, and (2) there are no widely accepted evaluation metrics for unsupervised discretization. Therefore, we assess SegDP indirectly by applying it to classification tasks on 33 UCI datasets [8] using three classifiers and comparing it with three other discretization algorithms. The aim is to examine whether discretizations produced without using class labels can still preserve information useful for downstream predictive tasks. Third, we analyzed the sensitivity of SegDP to its main parameters in the context of classification, aiming to examine whether the method remains stable under reasonable parameter variations.

All experiments were conducted on a machine with an Intel Core i5-11600K CPU and 32 GB RAM. SegDP was implemented in C. The IPD software was written in Java[1]. All other code was written in Python 3.9.18 using scikit-learn 1.8.0. The source code for SegDP and the experiments is available at https://github.com/spoonmarmot/SegDP.

7.2 Synthetic Case Study

Here we report the performance of SegDP on eight synthetic datasets, each containing 1000 samples. Figure 1 shows their scatter plots, where x-axes correspond to the target features to be discretized, and y-axes correspond to the assistant features. Except for Fig. 1c, all target feature values were sampled from $N(0, 16)$. In Fig. 1c, 500 values were drawn from $N(-6, 4)$, and the remaining 500 values were drawn from $N(5, 9)$. For each numerical assistant feature, we added Gaussian noise sampled from $N(0, 1)$. For each categorical assistant feature, the value was randomly switched to a different category with probability 0.1. We applied SegDP to discretize the target feature values into three groups, with $\lambda = 100$, $K_{max} = 10$, $w = 1$, and $\epsilon = 0$. The cutoffs are shown as red lines.

Figure 1a shows the case where the assistant feature is linearly related to the target feature. The three groups had similar sample sizes but differed in the magnitude ranges of the assistant feature. Figure 1b illustrates the case where the assistant feature is a quadratic function of the target feature. SegDP partitioned the samples into three groups with distinct target–assistant magnitude patterns: (low, low), (middle, high), and (high, low). In Fig. 1c, there were two assistant features, of which one was linearly related to the target feature and the other was quadratically related. The majority of the first group consisted of samples whose target feature values were drawn from $N(5, 9)$. The remaining samples were split by the second cutoff into two groups with distinct value patterns across the two assistant features. This case demonstrates that SegDP can jointly account for the target feature magnitude and interactions across assistant features.

Figure 1d presents a special case exhibiting Simpson's paradox, where the global trend contradicts the local trends. In this case, the assistant feature generally decreased with the target feature globally, yet increased locally within certain ranges. The cutoffs in the figure show that SegDP successfully recognized this pattern and clearly indicated the ranges where the trends reversed. Figure 1e and 1f show two cases with categorical assistant features: the former contains one categorical feature, whereas the latter contains two. In both cases, the segments produced by SegDP exhibited distinct assistant feature patterns. Figure 1g combines a linear numerical feature and a three-category categorical

[1] The link in the IPD paper is expired. The code was found in Yang et al. [22].

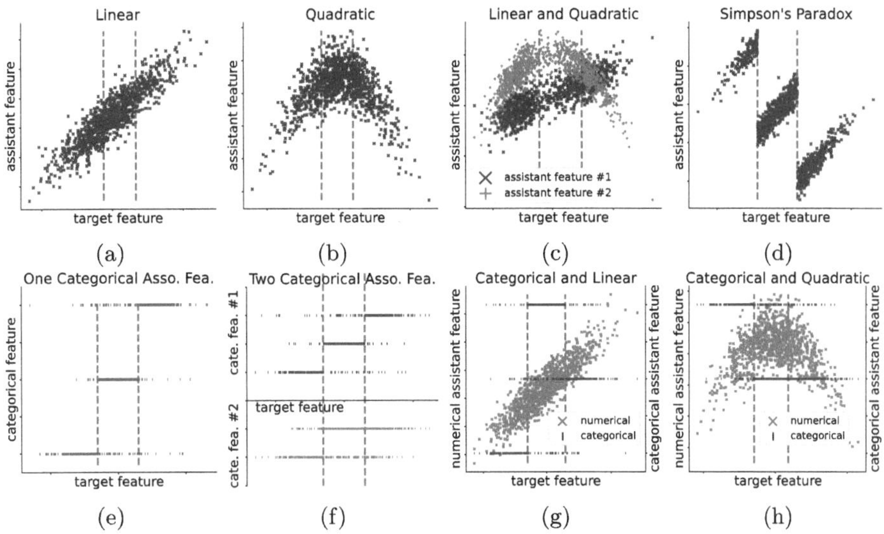

Fig. 1. Eight synthetic cases and their cutoffs obtained by SegDP, where x-axes are main features, y-axes are assistant features, and red lines are cutoffs. Categorical assistant features are encoded as codes that are not meaningful magnitude. (Color figure online)

feature, where the discretization was mainly impacted by the categorical feature. Figure 1h combines a quadratic numerical feature and a binary categorical feature. The first cutoff separated the samples with different categorical feature values, and the two segments divided by the second cutoff exhibited different numerical feature patterns, indicating that the discretization of the target feature was jointly influenced by the two assistant features.

In summary, these synthetic cases show that SegDP can identify meaningful patterns in complex scenarios where different types of assistant features with various interactions are present.

7.3 Application in Classification

In this section, we evaluate SegDP in classification tasks and compare it with two widely used unsupervised discretization methods, EF and EW, as well as IPD, the most relevant prior baseline for unsupervised multivariate discretization in our setting. The evaluation was conducted on 33 datasets from the UCI Machine Learning Repository, whose summaries are provided in Table 1. The datasets were retrieved through the official UCI web API and retained if they satisfied three criteria: (1) $n \geq 200$, (2) no missing values were present, and (3) at least one numerical feature was included.

Each dataset was partitioned into 10 folds for cross-validation. In each fold, the cutoffs of each discretization method were learned only from the training

Table 1. Summary of UCI classification datasets, where n denotes the number of samples, m denotes the number of features and m_1 is the number of numerical features. Dataset names are formatted as ID+abbreviation. In addition, time (sec) by SegDP to discretize all numerical features is also reported under *time*.

data	n	m (m_1)	time	data	n	m (m_1)	time
017breast	569	30 (30)	3	257knowledge	403	5 (5)	0
030BC	1473	9 (2)	0	264eeg	14980	14 (14)	929
050image	210	18 (16)	1	267bank	1372	4 (4)	1
052iono.	351	33 (32)	2	277surgery	470	16 (3)	0
075musk	6598	166 (166)	14801	292cust.	440	7 (6)	0
078page	5473	10 (10)	73	372htru2	17898	8 (8)	653
081pen	10992	16 (16)	573	468shoppers	12330	17 (11)	628
096spectf	267	44 (44)	1	503hepatitis	1385	28 (18)	9
107waveform	5000	21 (21)	185	519heart	299	12 (7)	0
143statlog1	690	14 (6)	0	529diabetes	520	16 (1)	0
145statlog2	270	13 (5)	0	544obesity	2111	16 (8)	7
146statlog3	6435	36 (36)	736	545rice	3810	7 (7)	19
147statlog4	2310	18 (16)	25	563churn	3150	13 (8)	18
151conn.	208	60 (60)	1	602drybean	13611	16 (16)	973
159telescope	19020	10 (10)	1018	759glioma	839	23 (1)	0
176blood	748	4 (4)	0	763mines	338	3 (2)	0
212vertebral	310	6 (6)	0				

set[2] and then applied to discretize the test set, thus preventing test-data leakage. SegDP and IPD automatically determine the number of segments, whereas EF and EW require the number of bins to be specified in advance. For EF and EW, we used the segment counts selected by SegDP for the corresponding features. This matched-bin setting controls for discretization granularity and allows the comparison to focus on the placement of cut points. It avoids introducing an additional bin-number selection procedure for EF and EW, which would require either arbitrary heuristics or supervised tuning. Under this setting, EF and EW serve as univariate baselines with the same number of discrete intervals as SegDP. For IPD, we used its default hyperparameters; as far as we are aware, it only used numerical features. For SegDP, we used $K_{max} = \min(70, \sqrt{n})$, $\lambda = \sqrt{n}$, $w = 1$, and $\epsilon = 0.4$ across all datasets. These settings are not intended to provide prescriptive parameter choices. They only serve as a common configuration for evaluating SegDP consistently across datasets. Three classifiers were trained on each dataset: random forest, AdaBoost, and SVM, all with default parameters of their scikit-learn implementations across all discretization methods.

[2] For SegDP and EF, we used min segment values as cutoffs, except the 1st segment.

Table 2. Average F1 scores for three classifiers under four discretization methods. For each dataset and classifier, the best discretization is highlighted in bold.

ID	Random Forest				AdaBoost				SVM			
	SegDP	EW	EF	IPD	SegDP	EW	EF	IPD	SegDP	EW	EF	IPD
017	0.953	0.947	**0.953**	0.945	**0.949**	0.941	0.947	0.947	0.961	0.964	**0.966**	0.961
030	**0.502**	0.476	0.484	0.474	**0.505**	0.502	0.503	0.488	0.510	0.470	**0.533**	0.512
050	**0.891**	0.849	0.864	0.739	**0.378**	0.330	0.311	0.210	**0.875**	0.848	0.830	0.733
052	**0.923**	0.891	0.897	0.880	**0.917**	0.833	0.854	0.831	**0.922**	0.901	0.920	0.885
075	0.948	**0.959**	0.955	0.458	0.890	**0.907**	0.905	0.458	**0.918**	0.914	0.912	0.458
078	**0.869**	0.791	0.849	0.800	**0.580**	0.418	0.564	0.374	0.749	0.609	0.719	**0.749**
081	0.992	**0.993**	0.989	0.019	0.309	0.234	**0.314**	0.019	**0.994**	0.994	0.988	0.019
096	0.637	0.670	**0.731**	0.654	0.662	**0.667**	0.666	0.662	0.518	0.443	0.443	**0.519**
107	0.847	0.845	**0.851**	0.828	0.831	0.829	**0.834**	0.825	0.859	**0.864**	0.863	0.833
143	**0.859**	0.844	0.854	0.851	**0.859**	0.857	0.839	0.858	0.817	0.849	0.831	**0.852**
145	0.820	0.828	0.828	**0.832**	0.810	**0.821**	0.803	0.815	0.822	**0.846**	0.818	0.832
146	0.895	**0.895**	0.885	0.890	0.603	0.556	**0.617**	0.589	**0.881**	0.878	0.861	0.873
147	**0.978**	0.976	0.975	0.950	0.372	0.347	0.330	**0.406**	**0.957**	0.932	0.955	0.933
151	0.804	0.776	**0.835**	0.796	**0.795**	0.698	0.778	0.731	0.802	0.729	**0.825**	0.792
159	**0.867**	0.858	0.865	0.834	0.817	0.815	**0.818**	0.800	0.732	0.578	**0.752**	0.696
176	0.595	0.598	**0.625**	0.475	0.639	0.642	**0.667**	0.542	**0.546**	0.463	0.533	0.460
212	**0.811**	0.695	0.756	0.663	**0.698**	0.629	0.684	0.690	**0.786**	0.711	0.774	0.674
257	0.765	**0.809**	0.764	0.443	**0.437**	0.409	0.428	0.308	0.761	**0.767**	0.716	0.429
264	0.933	0.573	**0.937**	0.909	0.731	0.548	**0.737**	0.713	**0.887**	0.313	0.712	0.755
267	**0.997**	0.994	0.997	0.934	0.999	0.998	**0.999**	0.929	**1.000**	0.999	**1.000**	0.935
277	0.475	**0.507**	0.500	0.506	0.498	0.498	**0.508**	0.492	**0.460**	**0.460**	**0.460**	**0.460**
292	0.301	**0.312**	0.293	0.270	**0.305**	0.283	0.264	0.289	**0.279**	**0.279**	**0.279**	**0.279**
372	**0.935**	0.934	0.935	0.924	**0.933**	0.932	0.927	0.928	0.927	**0.929**	0.927	0.927
468	**0.794**	0.695	0.786	0.789	**0.778**	0.688	0.772	0.769	0.766	0.669	0.766	**0.791**
503	**0.285**	0.250	0.267	0.260	0.234	0.230	0.229	**0.255**	0.231	0.224	0.229	**0.264**
519	0.801	**0.803**	0.778	0.706	**0.782**	0.777	0.764	0.707	**0.786**	0.785	0.766	0.726
529	**0.988**	0.982	0.975	0.973	0.918	**0.924**	0.917	0.901	0.932	0.924	0.926	**0.966**
544	**0.954**	0.935	0.949	0.882	0.227	0.250	0.292	**0.327**	**0.911**	0.891	0.897	0.829
545	**0.919**	0.917	0.917	0.907	0.922	0.922	**0.924**	0.915	**0.928**	0.927	0.927	0.915
563	0.913	**0.923**	0.915	0.888	0.847	**0.850**	0.848	0.779	0.594	0.610	0.623	**0.797**
602	0.935	**0.935**	0.935	0.911	0.495	**0.510**	0.506	0.500	**0.940**	0.936	0.940	0.915
759	0.837	0.844	0.847	**0.851**	0.867	**0.868**	0.867	0.863	0.865	0.869	0.864	**0.870**
763	0.464	0.433	**0.620**	0.194	**0.361**	0.355	0.351	0.257	**0.469**	0.417	0.461	0.234
#best	**15**	9	7	2	**14**	7	9	3	**17**	6	7	10
$\overline{rank}$	**1.909**	2.455	2.152	3.485	**1.909**	2.606	2.273	3.212	**1.818**	2.636	2.364	2.758
p-val	-	0.037	0.224	0.000	-	0.003	0.107	0.000	-	0.002	0.017	0.006

Table 2 reports the mean macro F1 scores averaged over the 10 folds. In addition, for each discretization method under each classifier, the table reports the number of datasets on which the method ranked first (#best), its mean rank across datasets ($\overline{rank}$), and the p-values of one-sided Wilcoxon signed-rank tests (p-val) comparing SegDP with each competitor using the alternative hypothesis that SegDP is better. Overall, SegDP achieved the strongest performance across all three classifiers despite the absence of dataset-specific tuning. It obtained the largest number of best results and the smallest mean rank for random forest, AdaBoost, and SVM. The one-sided Wilcoxon signed-rank tests indicate that SegDP significantly outperformed IPD and EW under all three classifiers, and showed stronger overall performance than EF in most settings.

Interestingly, both EF and EW also ranked ahead of IPD overall when using random forest and AdaBoost. A plausible explanation is that IPD does not directly use the magnitude of the target feature. Instead, it first divides values into micro bins according to their magnitude, and then merges these bins using an interaction distance based on the difference between the multivariate distributions of the remaining dimensions. This strategy may place relatively more emphasis on interactions among the other dimensions, especially in high-dimensional data, while giving less direct weight to the magnitude of the target feature itself. By contrast, EF and EW rely only on the target feature, yet still perform competitively. This suggests that the magnitude of the target feature remains important in many cases, and placing too much importance on interactions may not always be beneficial. SegDP can be viewed as a compromise between IPD and EF/EW. It incorporates both the target feature and assistant features, while using feature weights to downweight irrelevant assistant features.

As discussed above, the classification experiment provides an indirect evaluation, since directly evaluating unsupervised discretization is challenging: the assessment may involve multiple context-dependent criteria, some of which can conflict, and no well-established metric exists for direct evaluation. However, this indirect evaluation has inherent limitations, as different datasets may naturally favor different discretization strategies. Although we used a relatively large set of datasets and avoided stringent selection criteria to mitigate the possible bias, the superiority of SegDP shown in Table 2 should still be interpreted with caution. In practice, the choice of discretization method should be guided by the characteristics of the target data, which can be better understood through exploratory data analysis.

In addition, Table 1 also reports the runtime of SegDP for discretizing all numerical features of the entire dataset under the same parameter setting. In most cases, SegDP completed within a few seconds, while larger sample sizes and higher dimensionality led to higher computational cost. Overall, the results suggest that SegDP remains practical across diverse data sizes, with runtime increasing as expected with data complexity. For very large datasets, efficiency may be improved by drawing multiple subsets, estimating cutoffs independently, and aggregating the resulting cutoffs afterward.

7.4 Sensitivity Analysis

We examined the sensitivity of SegDP to three key parameters: the target feature weight w, the minimum NMI threshold ϵ, and the minimum segment size λ. We selected 11 representative datasets that vary in sample size, dimensionality, and feature-type composition, so that the sensitivity analysis covers diverse data characteristics while remaining computationally manageable. The experiments were conducted using the same three classifiers as in the previous section. Except for the parameter under study, the remaining settings were also kept the same as in the previous section. Figure 2 reports the average macro F1 scores over the 10 cross-validation folds.

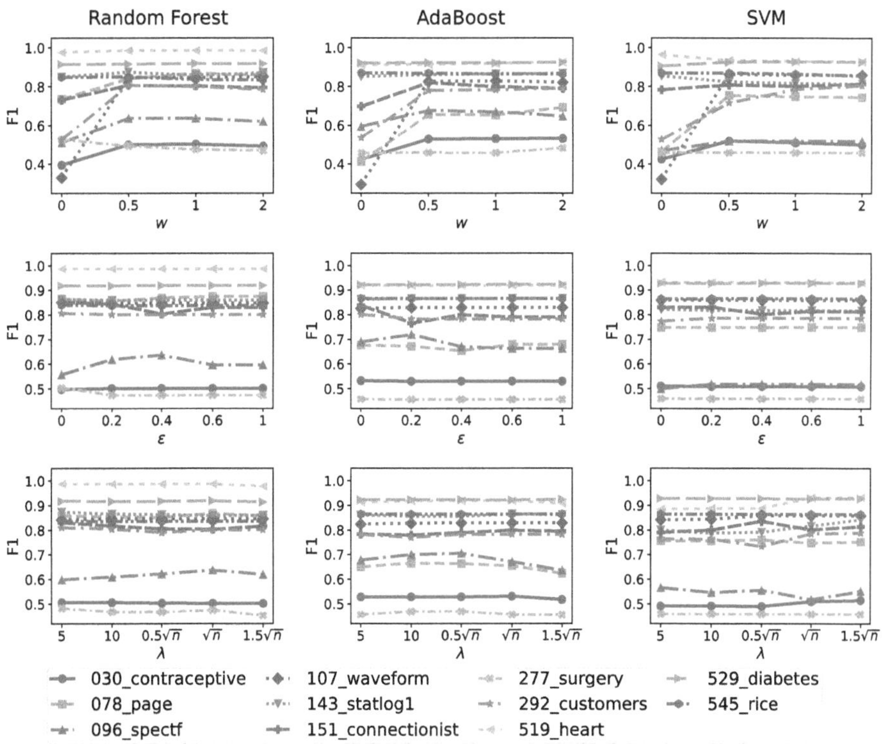

Fig. 2. Sensitivity analysis of the target feature weight (w), minimum NMI threshold ϵ, and minimum segment size λ on 11 datasets using three classifiers. The x-axis corresponds to the tested parameter, and the y-axis corresponds to the average macro F1 score over the 10 cross-validation folds. When $\lambda > \lfloor\sqrt{n}\rfloor$, we set $K_{max} = \lfloor n/\lambda \rfloor$ to ensure feasibility.

For w, we varied the balance between the target feature and the assistant features to assess the necessity of the target-feature term. When $w = 0$, several datasets showed a noticeable drop in classification performance across all classifiers, indicating that completely ignoring the magnitude of the target feature is generally suboptimal. When w was set to a moderate positive value, the performance became relatively stable. The differences among $w = 0.5$, $w = 1$, and $w = 2$ were generally small. These observations suggest that the target-feature term is important, while the exact choice of w is not overly critical within a moderate range. Overall, they support the use of $w = 1$ as a practical default and are consistent with the intuition that SegDP should balance target-feature magnitude with multivariate structure from assistant features.

For ϵ, performance remained relatively stable across different values for most datasets and classifiers. In particular, the curves were either flat or mildly fluctuating over different ϵ values. This suggests that SegDP is not overly sensitive to the threshold used to filter out weakly associated assistant features, and thus the threshold can serve as a robust mechanism for suppressing weak associations without too much data-specific tuning. The results therefore support the practical choice of $\epsilon = 0.4$ used in the previous section.

For λ, we tested various minimum segment sizes to examine whether this parameter affects the segmentation quality. The figure shows that F1 scores were also relatively stable across the tested values on most datasets. Tiny values of λ may produce over-segmentation, where segments are overly fine, whereas very large λ values may restrict the ability of SegDP to capture local patterns. However, the downstream classification performance did not change drastically. This indicates that λ can prune the dynamic programming search space with little effect on the performance. These observations also support the use of $\lambda = \sqrt{n}$ as a simple and practical default.

Overall, the sensitivity analysis suggests that SegDP is generally robust to parameter variation and does not rely on heavy dataset-specific tuning. The default settings used in the classification experiments lie in areas where performance is generally stable, which strengthens the practical applicability of the method.

8 Conclusion

We proposed SegDP, an unsupervised multivariate discretization method for mixed-type data. The method uses a weighted BIC-style objective to evaluate segmentations of a numerical target feature based on both numerical and categorical assistant features, and solves the resulting optimization problem exactly by dynamic programming. Results on synthetic examples showed that SegDP can recover diverse interaction patterns, while experiments on benchmark datasets demonstrated competitive classification performance relative to existing discretization methods. The sensitivity analysis further illustrated that SegDP is robust to a range of parameter settings.

Although the current experiments show that SegDP performs well under a fixed parameter setting across diverse datasets, a more systematic ablation and sensitivity analysis of parameters is an important direction for future work. In addition, the current weighting scheme is a practical robustness mechanism; alternative weighting strategies are an interesting direction for future work. Finally, this work assumes Gaussian models for within-segment numerical distributions for generality and computational efficiency. However, it may lead to suboptimal discretization when the data are skewed. Fortunately, the dynamic programming algorithm does not rely on the Gaussian models; it only requires the objective to be additive over segments. Therefore, the maximum-likelihood terms in the objective can be alternatively derived from more appropriate models.

Acknowledgments. We thank Maarit Korpi-Lagg and Wilhelmiina Hämäläinen for their support and guidance throughout this study.

Disclosure of Interests. The authors have no competing interests to declare that are relevant to the content of this article.

References

1. Bay, S.D.: Multivariate discretization for set mining. Knowl. Inf. Syst. **3**(4), 491–512 (2001)
2. Cano, A., Luna, J.M., Gibaja, E.L., Ventura, S.: LAIM discretization for multi-label data. Inf. Sci. **330**, 370–384 (2016). sIVisual Info Communication
3. De Sá, C.R., Soares, C., Knobbe, A.: Entropy-based discretization methods for ranking data. Inf. Sci. **329**, 921–936 (2016). Special issue on Discovery Science
4. Ferreira, A.J., Figueiredo, M.A.: An unsupervised approach to feature discretization and selection. Pattern Recogn. **45**(9), 3048–3060 (2012). Best Papers of Iberian Conference on Pattern Recognition and Image Analysis (IbPRIA'2011)
5. Franc, V., Fikar, O., Bartos, K., Sofka, M.: Learning data discretization via convex optimization. Mach. Learn. **107**(2), 333–355 (2018)
6. Han, J., Kamber, M., Pei, J.: 3 - data preprocessing. In: Han, J., Kamber, M., Pei, J. (eds.) Data Mining: Concepts and Techniques (Third Edition). The Morgan Kaufmann Series in Data Management Systems, pp. 83–124. Morgan Kaufmann, Boston (2012)
7. Kang, Y., Wang, S., Liu, X., Lai, H., Wang, H., Miao, B.: An ICA-based multivariate discretization algorithm. In: Lang, J., Lin, F., Wang, J. (eds.) KSEM 2006. LNCS (LNAI), vol. 4092, pp. 556–562. Springer, Heidelberg (2006). https://doi.org/10.1007/11811220_47
8. Kelly, M., Longjohn, R., Nottingham, K.: The UCI machine learning repository (2023)
9. Kontkanen, P., Myllymäki, P.: MDL histogram density estimation. In: Meila, M., Shen, X. (eds.) Proceedings of the Eleventh International Conference on Artificial Intelligence and Statistics. Proceedings of Machine Learning Research, San Juan, Puerto Rico 21–24 Mar 2007, vol. 2, pp. 219–226. PMLR (2007)
10. Liu, H., Setiono, R.: Feature selection via discretization. IEEE Trans. Knowl. Data Eng. **9**(4), 642–645 (1997)
11. Lustgarten, J.L., Visweswaran, S., Gopalakrishnan, V., Cooper, G.F.: Application of an efficient Bayesian discretization method to biomedical data. BMC Bioinf. **12**(1), 309 (2011)

12. Makhalova, T., Kuznetsov, S.O., Napoli, A.: Mint: MDL-based approach for mining interesting numerical pattern sets. Data Min. Knowl. Disc. **36**(1), 108–145 (2022)
13. Mehta, S., Parthasarathy, S., Yang, H.: Toward unsupervised correlation preserving discretization. IEEE Trans. Knowl. Data Eng. **17**(9), 1174–1185 (2005)
14. Nguyen, H.V., Müller, E., Vreeken, J., Böhm, K.: Unsupervised interaction-preserving discretization of multivariate data. Data Min. Knowl. Disc. **28**(5), 1366–1397 (2014)
15. Ramírez-Gallego, S., García, S., Benítez, J.M., Herrera, F.: Multivariate discretization based on evolutionary cut points selection for classification. IEEE Tran. Cybern. **46**(3), 595–608 (2016)
16. Ramírez-Gallego, S., et al.: Data discretization: taxonomy and Big Data challenge. WIREs Data Min. Knowl. Discov. **6**(1), 5–21 (2016)
17. Rissanen, J.J.: Modeling by shortest data description. Automatica **14**(5), 465–471 (1978)
18. Sang, Y., Li, K., Shen, Y.: EBDA: an effective bottom-up discretization algorithm for continuous attributes. In: 10th IEEE International Conference on Computer and Information Technology, pp. 2455–2462 (2010)
19. Schwarz, G.: Estimating the dimension of a model. Ann. Stat. **6**, 461–464 (1978)
20. Tsai, C.J., Lee, C.I., Yang, W.P.: A discretization algorithm based on class-attribute contingency coefficient. Inf. Sci. **178**(3), 714–731 (2008)
21. Wang, S., Ren, J., Bai, R., Yao, Y., Jiang, X.: A max-relevance-min-divergence criterion for data discretization with applications on Naive Bayes. Pattern Recogn. **149**, 110236 (2024)
22. Yang, L., Baratchi, M., van Leeuwen, M.: Unsupervised discretization by two-dimensional mdl-based histogram. Mach. Learn. **112**(7), 2397–2431 (2023)
23. Yang, Y., Webb, G.I.: Discretization for naive-bayes learning: managing discretization bias and variance. Mach. Learn. **74**(1), 39–74 (2009)
24. Zhang, H., Jiang, L., Webb, G.I.: Rigorous non-disjoint discretization for Naive Bayes. Pattern Recogn. **140**, 109554 (2023)

Surprise-Guided MergeSort: Budget-Efficient Human-in-the-Loop Ranking via Adaptive Comparison Scheduling

Yujin Park[1], Haejun Chung[1], and Ikbeom Jang[2](✉)

[1] Hanyang University, Seoul, Republic of Korea
{yujin1019a,haejun}@hanyang.ac.kr
[2] Hankuk University of Foreign Studies, Yongin, Republic of Korea
ijang@hufs.ac.kr

Abstract. Pairwise comparison is the gold standard for subjective ranking tasks; however, exhaustive annotation requires a massive number of human comparisons ($O(n^2)$). While sorting-based methods have reduced this burden to $O(n \log n)$, they still require expensive human judgment for every single comparison. To further improve annotation efficiency, we propose leveraging a Vision–Language Model (VLM) not as an annotator replacement, but as a *question prioritizer* to identify which comparisons genuinely require human judgment. The proposed **Surprise-Guided MergeSort (SGS)** method centers on a Round-0 *calibrated gating* step: a small set of human comparisons estimates VLM–human agreement, which both decides whether the VLM ordering is trustworthy enough to drive a sorting backbone and initializes an agreement-aware Elo warm start. On top of this gate, SGS adopts a standard bottom-up MergeSort schedule and contributes the budget-aware integration of (i) a composite Surprise Scorer—combining position-bias-cancelled VLM confidence, Elo gap, and vote entropy—and (ii) a progress-capped automatic-resolution rule, so that high-surprise pairs are routed to humans while low-surprise pairs are resolved automatically. Validation was conducted on six diverse benchmarks spanning text similarity and image quality assessment. SGS automatically resolves up to 535 low-surprise edges per session and achieves Kendall's $\tau \times 100$ gains of +6 to +12 over Active Elo on datasets where the VLM pre-ordering is directionally useful. A controlled simulation with multi-seed confidence intervals measures inferred-edge accuracy and shows that the method falls back toward warm-started Active Elo when the VLM prior is globally unreliable.

Keywords: Pairwise Ranking · Human-in-the-Loop · Active Learning · MergeSort · VLM · Annotation Efficiency

1 Introduction

Pairwise comparison provides more reliable supervision than absolute ratings for subjective annotation tasks [2,24], yielding higher inter-rater agreement

M. Ceci et al. (Eds.): ECML PKDD 2026, LNAI 16941, pp. 163–176, 2027.
https://doi.org/10.1007/978-3-032-37654-1_10

across domains from medical imaging to text similarity assessment. However, the quadratic cost of exhaustive comparison ($O(n^2)$) makes it impractical at scale: ranking 200 items requires nearly 20,000 comparisons, each demanding seconds of expert time.

Sorting-based approaches reduce the comparison count to $O(n \log n)$ by embedding pairwise queries within a sorting algorithm [9,14]. Recent work further leverages pre-trained vision–language models (VLMs) to provide coarse initial orderings, enabling the sorting procedure to skip trivially resolvable pairs [10,16,17]. Despite this progress, a fundamental tension remains: VLM predictions are noisy—particularly for fine-grained distinctions where items have similar quality scores—yet existing methods either trust VLM outputs as-is or require human judgment for every comparison the sort requests.

We identify three limitations of current approaches. First, VLM-as-annotator methods [20] suffer from position bias and limited accuracy on near-tie pairs, with typical agreement rates of 60–70% against human judgment. Second, purely human sorting methods [9,14] waste budget on easy comparisons where VLM ordering is reliable. Third, ensemble-based approaches [17] introduce substantial computational overhead from neural ranking heads and Gaussian Process inference, limiting scalability to larger item sets.

We propose **Surprise-Guided MergeSort (SGS)**, which reframes the VLM's role from annotator to *question prioritizer*. Rather than trusting or replacing VLM decisions, SGS measures how *surprised* the system is by each proposed comparison and allocates the limited human budget to the most ambiguous pairs. The key insight is that a comparison is "surprising" when multiple uncertainty signals—VLM confidence after position-bias cancellation, Elo rating gap, and annotator vote entropy—all indicate genuine ambiguity. Low-surprise comparisons are automatically resolved under a capped inference policy and then propagated through the MergeSort transitive closure.

This design philosophy aligns with recent findings in active ranking for scientific imaging [18], where VLM priors are used only to guide informative sampling rather than as ground-truth annotations. A Round-0 calibration gate keeps SGS robust to *globally* unreliable priors: when measured VLM–human agreement falls below 70%, SGS disables the sorting backbone and reverts to a warm-started Active Elo, preventing error propagation from a misleading initial ordering (we analyze the gate's behavior, including its limits, in Sect. 5).

In summary, our main contributions are threefold:

1. **Agreement-Calibrated VLM Use.** SGS estimates VLM–human agreement α from a small calibration set and uses it for both a centeredness-banded Elo warm start and an explicit gate: the MergeSort backbone is used only when the measured prior is sufficiently reliable; otherwise the method falls back to warm-started Active Elo.

2. **Surprise-Guided Comparison Routing.** SGS adopts a standard bottom-up MergeSort backbone and adds a budget-allocation layer that combines

position-bias-cancelled VLM uncertainty, Elo-gap uncertainty, and vote entropy. High-surprise boundary pairs are sent to humans, while low-surprise pairs are admitted only under a progress-capped automatic-resolution policy.

3. Domain-Level Diagnostics. Across six benchmarks and a controlled simulation, we show that SGS is strongest when the VLM provides a coarse but directionally useful pre-ordering. We also identify failure modes where graph-based exploration remains preferable, especially when aggregate calibration agreement hides errors on hard near-tie pairs.

2 Related Work

2.1 Pairwise Ranking and Sorting-Based Annotation

The Bradley–Terry model [2] provides a principled foundation for pairwise comparison, estimating item quality from binary preference data. Sorting-based active learning reduces annotation cost from $O(n^2)$ to $O(n \log n)$ by querying only the pairs needed to complete a sort [9,14]. PairS [10] applies merge sort to LLM-based ranking with uncertainty-guided pair selection, demonstrating strong performance on text benchmarks. Recent theoretical analysis [11] examines the optimality of comparison-based sorting when individual comparisons are handled by language models.

2.2 VLM-Assisted Ranking

Large-scale VLMs such as CLIP [21] and multimodal LLMs support zero-shot quality ordering via text prompts. EZ-Sort [16] combines CLIP-based hierarchical pre-ordering with uncertainty-aware MergeSort and achieves substantial annotation reduction on small datasets. SGS is closest to this line of work, as it also uses VLM-derived pre-ordering, MergeSort scheduling, and uncertainty-based skipping of easy pairs. We therefore do not claim MergeSort scheduling itself as the primary novelty. Instead, SGS adds an agreement-calibrated control layer: Round-0 human–VLM agreement determines whether the sorting backbone is used, VLM scores warm-start Elo only under conservative agreement-dependent bands, and candidate pairs are routed by a composite surprise score before capped automatic resolution. Dodgersort [17] also uses model-derived ranking evidence, but refines automation through a neural ranking head and a probabilistic ensemble involving GP, Elo, and BTL components. SGS instead keeps a single Elo state and lightweight VLM scoring, trading ensemble complexity for calibration-gated routing and conservative fallback. MetaRanker [18] similarly treats VLM outputs as informative priors rather than ground-truth labels; SGS operationalizes this principle through calibrated routing and capped automatic resolution.

2.3 Active Learning for Preference Ranking

Active preference learning minimizes annotation cost by querying maximally informative pairs. Information-theoretic approaches select pairs with highest expected information gain [4,7]. GURO [1] combines multiple uncertainty signals for robust pair selection. RAIR [12] uses Laplacian-based effective resistance to measure pair informativeness within comparison graphs. These methods assume every selected pair requires human input. SGS differs by additionally classifying each candidate as human-required or transitivity-resolvable based on its surprise score.

2.4 Position Bias in LLM Comparisons

LLMs and VLMs exhibit systematic position bias in pairwise comparison tasks [22,25], where the order in which items are presented affects the output. The flip test—querying both orderings (A, B) and (B, A)—is a standard mitigation. We incorporate a calibrated version of the flip test as one component of our Surprise Score, converting position-bias-cancelled confidence into a continuous uncertainty signal.

3 Method

3.1 Problem Setup

Let $\mathcal{X} = \{x_1, \ldots, x_n\}$ be a set of items with unknown latent scores $\{s_i\}_{i=1}^n$. The goal is to recover a ranking $\hat{\mathcal{R}}$ that is maximally consistent with the ground-truth ordering while minimizing the number of *human* pairwise judgments. We assume access to two complementary supervision channels: (i) a noisy VLM-based scorer that can assign pointwise scores to individual items and produce noisy pairwise preferences, and (ii) a reliable human oracle that returns the comparison outcome $y_{ij} \in \{0, 1\}$ for a queried pair (i, j).

Our design principle is to use the VLM as a *question prioritizer* rather than as an annotator replacement. Accordingly, the VLM is used to (a) construct an initial coarse ordering, (b) estimate which comparisons are ambiguous, and (c) support low-risk automatic resolution. Human effort is reserved for comparisons whose ambiguity is high enough that automatic resolution is likely to be unreliable.

3.2 Method Overview

SGS first calibrates the VLM against a small set of human comparisons and uses the resulting agreement to warm-start an Elo state. When agreement is sufficient, a bottom-up MergeSort scheduler proposes local cross-run candidate pairs, which are scored by a composite surprise metric. High-surprise pairs are sent to humans, while low-surprise pairs are resolved only under a capped automatic-resolution policy; otherwise, the method falls back to Active Elo. Algorithm 1 summarizes the procedure.

3.3 Round-0 Calibration, Pre-scoring, and Warm Start

Calibration. We first draw n_{cal} unique random pairs and query both the VLM and the human oracle. Let $\tilde{y}_{ij}$ denote the VLM decision and y_{ij} the human decision. Their agreement rate is

$$\alpha = \frac{1}{n_{\text{cal}}} \sum_{(i,j)\in\mathcal{C}_0} \mathbf{1}[\tilde{y}_{ij} = y_{ij}]. \tag{1}$$

This step serves two purposes: it estimates whether the VLM-derived ordering is trustworthy enough to support MergeSort, and it initializes Elo ratings from reliable human comparisons before any inference is attempted.

Pointwise VLM Pre-scoring. For each item x_i, the VLM is queried K times with prompt perturbations or simulated annotator diversity, producing pointwise scores $\{v_i^{(k)}\}_{k=1}^{K}$. We define the mean pre-score as

$$\bar{v}_i = \frac{1}{K}\sum_{k=1}^{K} v_i^{(k)}. \tag{2}$$

The initial order π_0 is obtained by sorting items according to $\bar{v}_i$ from worst to best.

Agreement-Aware Elo Warm Start. The code applies an agreement-conditioned warm start rather than directly trusting the VLM scores. Let

$$z_i = 2\left(\frac{\bar{v}_i - v_{\min}}{v_{\max} - v_{\min} + \varepsilon} - \frac{1}{2}\right), \qquad c_i = \frac{|\bar{v}_i - \text{median}(\bar{v})|}{v_{\max} - v_{\min} + \varepsilon}, \tag{3}$$

where $z_i \in [-1, 1]$ is the centered normalized pre-score and c_i measures how far item i lies from the ambiguous center of the score distribution. Because all three trusted cases share the same value, the warm start reduces to a single *banded* gate: an item inherits VLM structure only if its centeredness c_i clears an agreement-dependent threshold $\tau(\alpha)$,

$$R_i^{(0)} = 1500 + 250\, z_i \cdot \mathbf{1}[c_i \geq \tau(\alpha)], \qquad \tau(\alpha) = \begin{cases} 0, & \alpha \geq 0.70, \\ 0.3, & 0.60 \leq \alpha < 0.70, \\ 0.5, & \alpha < 0.60. \end{cases} \tag{4}$$

The band widens (higher τ) as agreement drops, so when the VLM is less trustworthy only items far from the ambiguous center—where even a noisy prior is likely directionally correct—inherit a non-neutral rating; everyone else starts at 1500. The final Round-0 Elo state is then blended with the ratings accumulated from calibration comparisons:

$$R_i \leftarrow 0.5R_i + 0.5R_i^{(0)}. \tag{5}$$

This conservative blending limits anchoring by imperfect VLM priors while still injecting useful global structure.

Algorithm 1. Surprise-Guided MergeSort (SGS)

Require: Items $\mathcal{X}$, VLM annotator $\mathcal{A}$, human oracle $\mathcal{O}$, budget B/round, rounds T
$\bar{v} \leftarrow \mathcal{A}.\text{scoreAll}(\mathcal{X})$; $\pi_0 \leftarrow \text{argsort}(\bar{v})$
$\alpha \leftarrow \text{Calibrate}(\mathcal{A}, \mathcal{O}, n_{\text{cal}})$
Initialize Elo $\mathbf{R}$ via Eq. (4)
if $\alpha < 0.70$ **then**
  Fallback: run Active Elo for all T rounds; **return**
end if
$\mathcal{M} \leftarrow \text{MergeSortScheduler}(n, \pi_0)$
for $t = 1$ **to** T **do**
  if $\mathcal{M}$.isComplete() **then**
    Fallback: refine remaining budget with Active Elo; **break**
  end if
  $\mathcal{C}_{\text{unk}} \leftarrow \{(i, j) \in \mathcal{M}.\text{getCandidates}() : \text{unknown}\}$
  for $(i, j) \in \mathcal{C}_{\text{unk}}$ **do**
    $S(i, j) \leftarrow \text{SurpriseScore}(i, j, \mathcal{A}, \mathbf{R})$ ▷ Eq. (8)
  end for
  Sort $\mathcal{C}_{\text{unk}}$ by S descending; allocate top-B to $\mathcal{H}$, rest to $\mathcal{I}$
  for $(i, j) \in \mathcal{H}$ **do**
    $y_{ij} \leftarrow \mathcal{O}(i, j)$; update $\mathbf{R}$, $\mathcal{M}$
  end for
  for $(i, j) \in \mathcal{I}$ (up to C_t; C_t via Eq. (9)) **do**
    $\hat{y}_{ij} \leftarrow \text{InferFromElo}(\mathbf{R}, i, j)$; update $\mathcal{M}$
  end for
  $\mathcal{M}$.completePass($\mathbf{R}$)
  Recalibrate $\mathcal{A}$ from accumulated human labels (optional)
end for
return $\mathcal{M}$.getRanking()

Adaptive Fallback. Warm-starting is always performed, but the MergeSort backbone is only used when the calibration agreement is sufficiently high. If $\alpha < 0.70$, SGS abandons MergeSort and switches to Active Elo for all remaining rounds. This prevents a poor pre-order from inducing cascading errors in later merge passes.

3.4 Transitivity-Aware MergeSort Scheduler

When $\alpha \geq 0.70$, SGS initializes a bottom-up MergeSort scheduler from the VLM order π_0. At each pass, only cross-run boundary pairs are considered, preserving the $O(n \log n)$ structure while avoiding global pair enumeration. The scheduler maintains a directed set $\mathcal{K}$ of reliable outcomes obtained from human labels or admitted inference, and skips pairs implied by the transitive closure of $\mathcal{K}$. During pass completion, known relations are respected first; unresolved pairs are decided by Elo only when the rating gap is large (default $|R_i - R_j| \geq 60$), otherwise by the inherited run order. Transitivity is propagated only from reliable edges, not from weak VLM defaults.

3.5 Composite Surprise Score

The surprise score estimates the risk of resolving a pair without a human label. For each candidate pair (i, j), SGS computes three normalized uncertainty signals. First, forward and reverse VLM queries yield a position-bias-cancelled preference estimate,

$$p_{\text{fwd}} = \frac{\mu_i^{\rightarrow}}{\mu_i^{\rightarrow} + \mu_j^{\rightarrow} + \varepsilon}, \qquad p_{\text{rev}} = \frac{\mu_i^{\leftarrow}}{\mu_i^{\leftarrow} + \mu_j^{\leftarrow} + \varepsilon}, \qquad \hat{p}_{ij} = \frac{p_{\text{fwd}} + p_{\text{rev}}}{2}, \tag{6}$$

which is converted to VLM uncertainty $S_{\text{vlm}}(i, j) = 1 - 2|\hat{p}_{ij} - 0.5|$. Second, the Elo gap $\varDelta_{ij} = |R_i - R_j|$ is mapped to

$$S_{\text{elo}}(i, j) = 1 - 2\left(\frac{1}{1 + 10^{-\varDelta_{ij}/400}} - 0.5\right). \tag{7}$$

Third, vote entropy S_{ent} is computed from the K simulated VLM votes. The final score is

$$S(i, j) = w_{\text{vlm}} S_{\text{vlm}}(i, j) + w_{\text{elo}} S_{\text{elo}}(i, j) + w_{\text{ent}} S_{\text{ent}}(i, j), \tag{8}$$

with default weights $(0.4, 0.3, 0.3)$.

3.6 Budget Allocation and Capped Automatic Resolution

At round t, the scheduler returns cross-run candidates whose outcomes are not already implied by transitivity. If more than $3B$ unknown candidates are visible, SGS subsamples at most $3B$ for surprise scoring, keeping VLM query cost linear in the round budget. The scored candidates are sorted by decreasing surprise. Pairs with $S(i, j) \geq \theta_S$ are routed to the human oracle up to budget B; if fewer than B pairs clear the threshold, the remaining budget is filled by the next most surprising pairs.

Low-surprise pairs are not automatically trusted wholesale. They are merely eligible for capped automatic resolution, with the cap reduced in later merge passes and under lower observed agreement:

$$C_t = \max\left(20 \cdot \mathbf{1}[\gamma_t > 0],\ \text{round}(C_{\max}\gamma_t)\right), \qquad \gamma_t = (1 - 0.7p_t)\big((1 - \omega) + \omega\tilde{a}_t\big), \tag{9}$$

where p_t is normalized merge-pass progress and $\tilde{a}_t$ combines Round-0 agreement with the previous round's human agreement. For an admitted pair, SGS uses Elo only when the rating gap is sufficiently informative (default $|R_i - R_j| \geq 50$). If VLM reliability is low, scheduler-order fallback is disabled and only high-confidence Elo decisions can support automatic resolution. In the reported experiments, inferred edges use $k_{\text{inf}} = 0$: they constrain pass completion and the transitive closure, but never update Elo, which is updated exclusively from human labels.

3.7 Round Completion, Recalibration, and Fallback Refinement

After human and admitted inferred edges have been processed, SGS completes the current merge pass and doubles the run size. The accumulated human labels can be used for lightweight test-time recalibration of the VLM-to-human mapping, improving later surprise estimates without replacing the surprise score. Two fallback behaviors are used: if Round-0 calibration yields $\alpha < 0.70$, SGS runs warm-started Active Elo for all remaining rounds; if all merge passes finish before the budget is exhausted, the remaining budget is spent on Active-Elo boundary refinement rather than redundant merge operations.

3.8 Complexity

Round-0 calibration uses n_{cal} human comparisons and Kn pointwise VLM scores. The structural comparison schedule induced by bottom-up MergeSort remains $O(n \log n)$ [9,10,14]. SGS does not alter this backbone; instead, it partitions the structural candidates into human-queried and automatically resolved subsets. Therefore, the total number of structurally considered pairs remains $O(n \log n)$, while the number of human comparisons is reduced to the subset of high-surprise pairs plus any Active Elo fallback rounds. In practice, the additional VLM pairwise cost is controlled by scoring at most $3B$ candidates per round, which makes the ambiguity estimation stage linear in the round budget rather than quadratic in n.

VLM Query Cost. The total number of VLM calls is dominated by two terms: Kn pointwise pre-scores in Round 0 and two pairwise calls (forward and reverse, for position-bias cancellation) for each of the $\leq 3B$ scored candidates per round. The session total is therefore at most $Kn + 6BT$ VLM calls, independent of n^2. Under our defaults (K=5, n=200, B=100, T=5) this is $\leq 1000 + 3000 = 4000$ calls per ranking session, all on a single pointwise/pairwise prompt template that admits caching and batching [11]. This is markedly cheaper than ensemble pipelines that invoke several neural models plus Gaussian-Process inference per decision [17], and—unlike human annotation—these calls are non-expert and parallelizable. We note that this cost is the main practical prerequisite of SGS: in domains where even pointwise VLM scoring is unavailable or unreliable, the method reduces to its Active-Elo fallback.

4 Experiments

4.1 Experimental Setup

Datasets. We evaluate on six benchmarks spanning two domains. For **text similarity**: STS-B [3] (test, 1,379 pairs), BIOSSES [23] (train, 100 biomedical pairs), and SICKR-STS (test, from MTEB [15], 4,906 pairs). For **image quality assessment**: KonIQ-10k [6] (train, 200 sampled images), TID2013 [19] (train, 200 sampled distorted images), and LIVE Challenge [5] (train, 200 sampled images). All scores are normalized to $[0, 100]$.

VLM Annotator. We use Ollama-hosted Qwen-3.5 with $K = 5$ simulated annotators per item providing pointwise quality scores via JSON-formatted prompts.

Human Oracle. Following standard practice [10,17], we simulate the human oracle as $h(i,j) = \mathbf{1}[s_i + \epsilon_i > s_j + \epsilon_j]$ where $\epsilon \sim \mathcal{N}(0, 25)$.

Baselines. We compare against five methods under identical total budget ($n_{\text{cal}} + T \times B = 600$): (1) **Random Elo**: random pair selection with Elo updates; (2) **Active Elo** [8]: Elo-gap-based active pair selection; (3) **Active Elo (same budget)**: Active Elo restricted to the same human budget as SGS; (4) **RAIR-Laplacian** [12]: Laplacian effective resistance pair selection; (5) **PairS-like MergeSort** [10]: PairS-style merge sort with VLM-gap-based uncertainty.

Default Hyperparameters. All hyperparameters and their rationale are listed in Table 1; they are held fixed across all six datasets (no per-dataset tuning). The surprise weights (0.4, 0.3, 0.3) slightly favor the VLM-confidence term as the only signal available before any human label is collected; the sensitivity of the results to θ_S and α is examined in Sect. 4.5.

Table 1. SGS hyperparameters, default values, and rationale. Values are fixed across all datasets; the Elo/merge trust gaps and warm-start constants follow the conventional Elo scale (400 points $=$ 10$\times$ odds).

Symbol	Value	Rationale
n_{cal}	100	calibration pairs to estimate α and seed Elo
$T \times B$	5×100	rounds $\times$ per-round human budget
K	5	VLM votes per item (pointwise)
$(w_{\text{vlm}}, w_{\text{elo}}, w_{\text{ent}})$	$(0.4, 0.3, 0.3)$	favor VLM term pre-labels; Elo/entropy equal
θ_S	0.55	surprise cutoff for human routing (results are insensitive over $[0.4, 0.75]$, Sect. 4.5)
k_{inf}	0.0	inferred pairs constrain order only, never update Elo
$C_{\max}$	200	cap on inferred comparisons per round
α-gate	0.70	below this, disable backbone $\rightarrow$ Active Elo
warm-start	250, 0.5	rating scale and calibration-blend weight
trust gaps	50, 60	min. Elo gap to infer/to order an unknown merge pair

4.2 Main Results

4.3 Budget and Domain Analysis

Tables 2–3 show that SGS achieves the best average $\tau \times 100$ (71.1), with the largest gains over Active Elo on LIVE-C (+12.5) and STS-B (+12.1). The

Table 2. Main results on 3 image (top) and 3 text (bottom) datasets. Metric: Kendall's $\tau \times 100$ (higher is better). "Human" and "Inferred" denote the number of human and automatically resolved comparisons used by SGS. All baselines use their full budget as human comparisons. Best in **bold**; second best underlined.

Dataset	Ours (SGS)	Active Elo	Random Elo	Active (same)	RAIR-Lap. [12]	PairS-MS [10]	SGS Budget	
							Human	Inferred
Image Quality Assessment								
KonIQ [6]	**65.8**	59.8	65.5	58.3	65.3	33.8	600	535
LIVE-C [5]	**74.1**	61.6	67.9	62.9	68.5	38.0	596	526
TID2013 [19]	65.5	59.3	62.3	**64.8**	63.4	42.8	600	0
Text Similarity								
BIOSSES [23]	81.4	77.2	76.2	74.8	**83.0**	53.8	550	345
SICKR [13]	63.5	62.5	63.9	62.3	**66.0**	38.2	600	535
STS-B [3]	**76.5**	64.4	65.1	63.5	62.5	17.9	600	535
Average	**71.1**	64.1	66.8	64.4	68.1	37.4	–	–

Table 3. Inferred comparison statistics. "Ratio" is the fraction of total (human + inferred) comparisons resolved by transitivity. TID2013 triggers the adaptive fallback (zero inferred).

Dataset	Human	Inferred	Ratio
KonIQ-10k [6]	600	535	47.1%
LIVE-C [5]	596	526	46.9%
TID2013 [19]	600	0	0.0%
BIOSSES [23]	550	345	38.5%
SICKR-STS [13]	600	535	47.1%
STS-B [3]	600	535	47.1%

improvement is not uniform: RAIR-Laplacian remains strongest on BIOSSES and SICKR-STS, and Random Elo is essentially tied with SGS on KonIQ. This pattern suggests that SGS helps most when the VLM gives a coarse but directionally useful ordering and the human budget has not already saturated the ranking.

SGS adds 345–535 automatically resolved edges on five datasets, corresponding to a 38–47% edge multiplier. These edges should not be interpreted as equivalent to human labels; their accuracy is measured separately in the controlled simulation (Table 5). TID2013 produces zero inferred edges because the calibration gate disables the MergeSort backbone, yielding warm-started Active Elo rather than forcing inference from an unreliable VLM prior. The image/text split follows the same logic: perceptual IQA cues support a useful π_0, whereas compositional semantic similarity weakens pointwise VLM scoring and makes graph-based exploration more competitive.

Table 4. Per-signal surprise ablation on the *real* VLM (Qwen-3.5; 10 seeds, 95% bootstrap CIs). $\tau\times100$; best per column **bold**. Removing the Elo-gap term hurts most on both datasets; the VLM-confidence term helps on STS-B (strong VLM pre-order) but is harmful on BIOSSES, where Elo alone already captures the structure.

Configuration	BIOSSES (τ_{VLM}=71.3)	STS-B (τ_{VLM}=77.9)
Full (0.4, 0.3, 0.3)	80.0 [79.4, 80.6]	76.0 [75.6, 76.4]
−VLM	**82.1** [81.3, 82.8]	75.5 [74.9, 76.1]
−Elo	76.8 [76.2, 77.5]	71.5 [71.2, 71.9]
−Ent	79.9 [79.2, 80.5]	**76.2** [75.8, 76.6]
VLM only	76.8 [76.2, 77.5]	71.5 [71.2, 71.9]
Elo only	**82.1** [81.3, 82.8]	75.5 [74.9, 76.1]
Ent only	76.2 [75.8, 76.6]	70.0 [69.5, 70.5]

4.4 Per-signal Surprise Ablation

We disentangle the three surprise signals on the real VLM using cached Qwen-3.5 scores and 10 seeds on BIOSSES and STS-B (Table 4). Removing the Elo-gap term hurts most on both datasets, indicating that the human-derived ranking state—initialized by Round-0 warm start—is the most useful signal. The VLM-confidence term is domain-dependent: it helps on STS-B, where the VLM pre-order is strong, but hurts on BIOSSES, where dropping it improves both τ and inferred accuracy. The fixed composite is therefore a robust default rather than a tuned optimum; learned or agreement-dependent weights are a natural extension.

Table 5. Controlled simulation (synthetic annotator, n=200, 10 seeds). As calibration agreement α decreases (via annotator noise σ_v), SGS degrades in a controlled way: the α-gate fires more often and the automatic-resolution edge multiplier shrinks, while inferred edges stay well above chance. Brackets are 95% bootstrap CIs.

σ_v	α	$\tau\times100$ (95% CI)	Inferred	Inf. acc	Fallback
20	0.87	72.1 [70.9, 73.2]	47%	74.0%	0%
30	0.84	67.8 [66.6, 69.1]	47%	74.7%	0%
40	0.80	62.7 [61.5, 63.9]	47%	78.5%	0%
55	0.75	57.2 [55.1, 59.5]	38%	79.1%	20%
75	0.70	54.2 [51.5, 56.8]	24%	78.8%	50%
100	0.67	51.6 [49.0, 53.8]	14%	80.2%	70%

4.5 Controlled Simulation: Diagnostics and Ablations

To obtain multi-seed uncertainty estimates and ground-truth inferred-edge accuracy, we complement the fixed-VLM benchmarks with a controlled simulation in which the VLM annotator is replaced by a synthetic pointwise scorer whose agreement α is tuned by noise σ_v. We use n=200, the default budget, and report 10-seed means with 95% bootstrap CIs (Table 5); absolute τ values are not comparable to the VLM benchmarks.

Across the agreement range, automatically resolved edges match ground truth in 74–80% of cases. As α falls, the fallback rate rises from 0% to 70% and the inferred ratio shrinks from 47% to 14%, showing controlled degradation toward warm-started Active Elo under globally unreliable priors. Holding $\alpha \approx 0.80$, removing the warm start reduces $\tau \times 100$ from 62.7 to 49.2, whereas removing transitivity propagation leaves accuracy statistically unchanged while eliminating the edge multiplier. Thus, warm start drives accuracy; the MergeSort closure mainly improves budget efficiency.

5 Discussion

When the Budget Multiplier Helps. The edge multiplier is most valuable when two conditions hold: the VLM pre-ordering is directionally correct, and the human budget alone is insufficient to saturate the ranking. LIVE-C and STS-B satisfy both conditions and show the largest gains. KonIQ is different: Random Elo already reaches 65.5 with 600 comparisons, close to SGS at 65.8, so additional inferred edges yield diminishing returns.

Domain Reliability and Failure Modes. SGS is not a universal replacement for graph-based active ranking. Image IQA often provides coarse perceptual cues that VLMs capture, while semantic similarity can require fine compositional judgments that weaken pointwise VLM scoring. On SICKR-STS, Random Elo slightly exceeds SGS (63.9 vs. 63.5), suggesting that MergeSort boundary constraints can be uninformative when π_0 is miscalibrated. The likely issue is that $\alpha \geq 0.70$ may be concentrated on easy pairs; the binary gate then passes although hard near-tie pairs remain unreliable. A soft fallback that mixes MergeSort candidates with graph/random exploration, or a per-round agreement check, would address this limitation.

Limitations and Reproducibility. The six VLM benchmarks are single-seed; the controlled simulation supplies bootstrap CIs and inferred-edge diagnostics, but multi-seed VLM runs remain needed for marginal cases such as KonIQ. The Gaussian simulated oracle does not capture systematic human effects such as fatigue or anchoring. The surprise weights and $\alpha = 0.70$ gate are fixed defaults rather than learned. All six benchmarks are public, and we release the reference implementation, seed list, hyperparameters, controlled-simulation harness, and real-VLM ablation scripts used to reproduce the reported diagnostics.

6 Conclusion

We presented SGS, a budget-efficient pairwise-ranking method that treats VLMs as question prioritizers rather than annotator replacements. The main mechanism is an agreement-calibrated Round-0 gate with a banded Elo warm start;

a standard MergeSort backbone then exposes local boundary pairs, which SGS routes using composite surprise and capped automatic resolution. Across six benchmarks, SGS achieves the best average $\tau \times 100$ while adding up to a 47% edge multiplier; controlled diagnostics show that these inferred edges are useful but imperfect, and that the method degrades toward warm-started Active Elo when the VLM prior is globally unreliable.

The empirical picture is domain-dependent: SGS is strongest when VLM pre-ordering is directionally informative, especially for perceptual IQA, while graph-based methods remain preferable on some semantic-similarity tasks. Future work should replace the binary agreement gate with soft or per-round fallback, learn surprise weights from calibration data, and validate the method with real annotators.

Acknowledgments. This work was supported by the National Research Foundation of Korea (NRF) grants funded by the Ministry of Science and ICT (MSIT) (RS-2024-00338048, RS-2024-00455720, RS-2026-25487796); a grant of the Korea Health Technology R&D Project through the Korea Health Industry Development Institute (KHIDI), funded by the Ministry of Health & Welfare (RS-2025-02220534); the Technology Innovation Program (or Industrial Strategic Technology Development Program - Biotechnology) (RS-2025-13002970) funded by the Ministry of Trade Industry & Energy (MOTIE, Korea); the National Institute of Health (NIH) research project (2026-ER0901-00, 2026-ER0904-00); the Advanced GPU Utilization Support Program and the High-Performance Computing Support project (RQT-25-070083), both funded by MSIT; Hankuk University of Foreign Studies Research Fund of 2026; the Culture, Sports and Tourism R&D Program through KOCCA funded by MCST (RS-2024-00332210); the Artificial Intelligence Graduate School Program, Hanyang University (RS-2020-II201373); the AI Seoul Tech Research Support Program of the Seoul Future Foundation; and the Artificial Intelligence Semiconductor Support Program (IITP-2025-RS-2023-00253914), supervised by IITP and funded by the Korean government.

References

1. Bergström, H., Carlsson, E., Dubhashi, D., Johansson, F.D.: Active preference learning for ordering items in- and out-of-sample. In: Advances in Neural Information Processing Systems (2024)
2. Bradley, R.A., Terry, M.E.: Rank analysis of incomplete block designs: I. The method of paired comparisons. Biometrika **39**(3/4), 324–345 (1952)
3. Cer, D.: SemEval-2017 task 1: semantic textual similarity. In: Proceedings of the 11th International Workshop on Semantic Evaluation (2017)
4. Chu, W., Ghahramani, Z.: Preference learning with Gaussian processes. In: Proceedings of the 22nd International Conference on Machine Learning, pp. 137–144 (2005)
5. Ghadiyaram, D., Bovik, A.C.: Massive online crowdsourced study of subjective and objective picture quality. IEEE Trans. Image Process. **25**(1), 372–387 (2016)
6. Hosu, V., et al.: KonIQ-10k: an ecologically valid database for deep learning of blind image quality assessment. IEEE Trans. Image Process. **29**, 4041–4056 (2020)
7. Houlsby, N., Huszár, F., Ghahramani, Z., Lengyel, M.: Bayesian active learning for classification and preference learning. arXiv preprint arXiv:1112.5745 (2012)

8. Jamieson, K.G., Nowak, R.D.: Active ranking using pairwise comparisons. In: Advances in Neural Information Processing Systems, pp. 2240–2248 (2011)
9. Jang, I., Danley, G., Chang, K., Kalpathy-Cramer, J.: Decreasing annotation burden of pairwise comparisons with human-in-the-loop sorting. arXiv preprint arXiv:2202.04823 (2022)
10. Liu, T., Zheng, J., Fei, H.: PairS: pairwise sequence ranking with Merge Sort and LLM uncertainty. In: Proceedings of the Conference on Language Modeling (2024)
11. Luo, T.: Are optimal algorithms still optimal? Sorting and searching with LLMs. arXiv preprint arXiv:2505.24643 (2025)
12. Ma, Y.: Active ranking with effective resistance-based pair selection. In: Proceedings of the 27th International Conference on Artificial Intelligence and Statistics (2024)
13. Marelli, M.: A SICK cure for the evaluation of compositional distributional semantic models. In: Proceedings of the Ninth International Conference on Language Resources and Evaluation (2014)
14. Maystre, L., Grossglauser, M.: Just sort it! A simple and effective approach to active preference learning. In: Proceedings of the 34th International Conference on Machine Learning, pp. 2344–2353 (2017)
15. Muennighoff, N., et al.: MTEB: massive text embedding benchmark. In: Proceedings of the 17th Conference of the European Chapter of the Association for Computational Linguistics (2023)
16. Park, Y., Chung, H., Jang, I.: EZ-Sort: efficient pairwise comparison via zero-shot CLIP-based pre-ordering and human-in-the-loop sorting. In: Proceedings of the 34th ACM International Conference on Information and Knowledge Management, pp. 5120–5124 (2025)
17. Park, Y., Chung, H., Jang, I.: Dodgersort: uncertainty-aware VLM-guided human-in-the-loop pairwise ranking. In: Wong, R.CW., et al. (eds.) Pacific-Asia Conference on Knowledge Discovery and Data Mining, pp. 461–473. Springer, Singapore (2026). https://doi.org/10.1007/978-981-92-1468-6_32
18. Park, Y., Chung, H., Jang, I.: MetaRanker: human-in-the-loop active ranking for Metalens image quality. arXiv preprint arXiv:2605.29212 (2026)
19. Ponomarenko, N., et al.: Image database TID2013. Sig. Process. Image Commun. **30**, 57–77 (2015)
20. Qin, Z.: Large language models are effective text rankers with pairwise ranking prompting. In: Findings of the Association for Computational Linguistics, NAACL 2024 (2024)
21. Radford, A.: Learning transferable visual models from natural language supervision. In: Proceedings of the 38th International Conference on Machine Learning, pp. 8748–8763 (2021)
22. Shi, Y.: Judging LLM-as-a-judge with MT-Bench and Chatbot Arena. arXiv preprint arXiv:2406.07791 (2024)
23. Sogancioglu, G., "Ozt"urk, H., "Ozg"ur, A.: BIOSSES: a semantic sentence similarity estimation system for the biomedical domain. Bioinformatics **33**(14), i49–i58 (2017)
24. Thurstone, L.L.: A law of comparative judgment. Psychol. Rev. **34**(4), 273–286 (1927)
25. Wang, P.: Large language models are not fair evaluators. In: Proceedings of the 62nd Annual Meeting of the Association for Computational Linguistics (2024)

TAKE: Trajectory-Aware Knowledge Estimation for Text Dataset Distillation

Tri-Nhan Vo(✉), Dang Nguyen, and Sunil Gupta

Deakin Applied AI Initiative, Deakin University, Geelong, Australia
{s223032975,d.nguyen,sunil.gupta}@deakin.edu.au

Abstract. Large-scale text corpora have become a quiet bottleneck in modern NLP, not just in storage, but in the accumulated cost of training, fine-tuning, and continual learning. We propose a text dataset distillation framework that reduces corpora to as little as 0.1% of their original size while preserving downstream task fidelity. We approach distillation through the lens of influence functions, which quantify each sample's contribution to the downstream objective, a natural and principled basis for selection. We introduce Trajectory-Aware Knowledge Estimation (TAKE), which convolves the knowledge-based influence along the training trajectory into a single per-sample knowledge score, capturing informative samples. These scores serve as sample weights within a discrete Optimal Transport objective, guiding prototype selection from a synthetically generated candidate pool. We evaluate TAKE on downstream accuracy across text classification and natural language inference tasks at extreme compression (0.1% or 20 samples/class), showing that data efficiency is achievable without sacrificing task fidelity. The approach is theoretically grounded, with broader implications for coreset construction and data-centric AI. We release our source code at https://github.com/votrinhan88/take.

Keywords: Text dataset distillation · Influence functions · Optimal transport

1 Introduction

The progress of large language models depends on large-scale supervised corpora, yet the cost of curating and training on such data compounds across fine-tuning cycles, hyperparameter sweeps, and continual learning. The real burden is not any single run but the cumulative expenditure across the full development lifecycle. Corpus size, not model size, is often the binding constraint. Reducing it is therefore a systemic priority with direct implications for cost, carbon footprint, and data governance.

Dataset distillation (DD), first proposed by [35], replaces a large dataset $\mathcal{D}$ with a smaller surrogate $\tilde{\mathcal{D}} \ll \mathcal{D}$ such that a model trained on $\tilde{\mathcal{D}}$ performs comparably to one trained on $\mathcal{D}$. Put another way: what is the smallest textbook that teaches the same exam? This places DD squarely within data-centric AI,

M. Ceci et al. (Eds.): ECML PKDD 2026, LNAI 16941, pp. 177–194, 2027.
https://doi.org/10.1007/978-3-032-37654-1_11

complementing model compression by operating on the data rather than the model itself. Early DD methods work in image space, optimizing synthetic pixels via meta-learning, gradient or trajectory matching [4,35,39]. Text breaks these assumptions: non-differentiable token decoding blocks gradient-based synthesis, and embedding spaces are tightly coupled to specific architectures. Adapting DD to text has therefore required fundamentally different strategies.

Existing text DD methods [20,22,23,30,32] fall short in at least one of the following: at extreme compression, uniform weighting exhausts the budget on uninformative samples; their objectives lack task alignment or global optimization; and their outputs are embeddings, neither auditable nor transferable. We survey this landscape in Sect. 2.1 and show that no prior method simultaneously addresses all of the above. These gaps motivate three desiderata for TAKE: (1) *knowledge-based weighting*—weighting samples by their task-aligned downstream contribution, directing the budget toward the most informative ones; (2) a *dataset-level distillation objective*—optimizing over the full training distribution rather than batch-by-batch, ensuring global coverage; and (3) *human-readable output*—a distilled corpus that is directly auditable and transferable across architectures.

We propose **Trajectory-Aware Knowledge Estimation (TAKE)**, the first text DD method to satisfy all three desiderata. We address the first via influence functions [17], which quantify each sample's counterfactual effect on the downstream loss and provide a theoretically grounded, task-aligned weighting scheme (§3). However, scoring at a single checkpoint introduces the *hard-sample bias* (HSB): at convergence, noisy samples dominate influence scores while clean and moderate samples, the most valuable for a robust distilled dataset, are suppressed. TAKE corrects this by integrating influence scores along the full training trajectory into a per-sample knowledge score that captures clean and moderate samples while down-weighting noisy ones. Then, TAKE fine-tunes an LLM to generate a pool of human-readable candidate instances. The knowledge scores and synthetic candidates jointly feed a discrete Optimal Transport (OT) objective that globally selects the distilled corpus. Concretely, we contribute:

- **Theory:** We formalize the hard-sample bias (HSB) in the text DD setting, prove that single-checkpoint influence scores are biased toward noisy samples, and derive a formal gap bound for knowledge-reweighted distribution matching.
- **Method:** TAKE is the first text DD method to jointly address sample weighting and distributional coverage—via trajectory-integrated knowledge scores and a discrete OT objective aligned with the DD goal.
- **Empirical:** TAKE matches or exceeds prior text DD methods across six language benchmarks at extreme compression (0.1% or 20 instances/class), producing human-readable distilled corpora that generalize across diverse backbone families.

The remainder of this paper is organised as follows: Sect. 2 reviews related work; Sect. 3 presents theoretical motivation; Sect. 4 details TAKE and our DD pipeline; Sect. 5 reports experiments and discussion; Sect. 6 reflects limitations and ethical concerns; Sect. 7 concludes.

2 Related Works

2.1 Text Dataset Distillation

Dataset distillation was introduced by [35] as a bi-level meta-learning problem: synthesize a small set of images such that a model trained on them matches one trained on the full dataset. Subsequent methods improve scalability and fidelity via gradient matching [39], distribution matching [34], and trajectory matching [4,15]. These methods share a common assumption: data is continuous and differentiable, so the synthetic set can be directly optimised via backpropagation. Text violates the differentiability assumption: token decoding is non-differentiable, outputs must be semantically coherent, and embedding spaces are tightly coupled to specific architectures.

Adapting DD to text has therefore required fundamentally different strategies, from meta-learning on synthetic embeddings to LLM-based generation of readable corpora, each generation trading one limitation for another. SLDD and DDTC [20,30] directly adapted the meta-learning formulation [35], optimizing synthetic text embeddings so that a model trained on them minimizes task loss. Of the two, only SLDD partially recovers interpretability by mapping distilled embeddings to per-token nearest bag-of-words. DDAL [22] optimizes the attention labels of a BERT model to match class-wise dataset statistics, achieving partial task alignment but producing outputs that are both architecture-locked and uninterpretable. A second generation of methods addressed interpretability by rethinking the pipeline entirely. DiLM [23] generates readable candidate texts via an LLM and selects among them by gradient matching over the training corpus, followed by k-centre selection; but matching gradients at discrete checkpoints is a proxy for task loss, leaving task alignment only partial. DaLLME [32] learns an inverse mapping from distilled embeddings back to synthetic text, recovering interpretability and attempting global coverage via k-centroids clustering; but with no task-loss objective, task alignment is absent. Table 1 maps this progression: each generation addressed some gaps while leaving others open.

Table 1. Landscape of text DD methods.

Gap	SLDD	DDTC	DDAL	DiLM	DaLLME	**TAKE**
Task alignment	✓	✓	△	△	–	✓
Global optimization	△	△	△	△	△	✓
Interpretability	△	–	–	✓	✓	✓
Importance weighting	–	–	–	–	–	✓

–: absent, △: partial, ✓: addressed

A subtler gap cuts across all methods: every existing approach applies *uniform weighting*, treating every training sample as equally informative. At moderate distillation budgets this is defensible, but extreme compression is precisely the regime where distillation matters most, and there the assumption fails. Samples vary substantially in their influence on learning (clean vs. noisy, easy vs. hard), yet no prior method accounts for this structure. Without importance weighting, the distillation budget is exhausted on uninformative samples, biasing selection away from the boundary cases that matter most for robustness.

2.2 Influence Functions and the Hard-Sample Bias

Influence functions (IF) [5,17] quantify the leave-one-out effect of a training point via $\mathcal{I}(z) = \nabla^\top H_\theta^{-1} \nabla$, but depend on a single checkpoint and require expensive second-order computation. Trajectory-based methods [19,26,28] extend attribution across checkpoints but are *test-conditioned*: designed to attribute a fixed test prediction. However, self-influence is evaluated only once at the final parameters, introducing a systematic bias that corrupts the corpus-level scores.

We refer to this as the *hard-sample bias* (HSB): at convergence, clean samples have near-zero gradient by definition, so noisy or hard samples dominate influence scores. This failure mode is well-documented in adjacent work: [2] show that networks fit clean patterns before noisy ones; dataset cartography [31] confirms that single-checkpoint statistics conflate difficulty with noise; and Co-teaching [13] documents systematic overselection of noisy samples in gradient-based curricula. In standard training, HSB can often be mitigated via regularization; in the extreme low-data regime of DD, however, it amplifies: biased selection suppresses the *informative* samples essential for model robustness. To our knowledge, no prior text DD method has identified or corrected for it.

2.3 Optimal Transport for Distribution Matching

Distribution matching has been proposed as a tractable DD surrogate [38]: if the distilled and training sets induce equal expected gradients along the optimization trajectory, the trained models converge to comparable parameters. This is a sufficient condition, but not an equivalence (the formal gap bound appears in Theorem 1). MMD [11] lacks sample-level assignment structure, requiring auxiliary scoring heuristics that reintroduce the global optimization gap that distribution matching is meant to close. Kullback–Leibler and Jensen–Shannon divergences require density estimation, which is unreliable in the low-data regime [25].

OT in the Monge-Kantorovich sense avoids both pitfalls: it operates natively on discrete measures, respects the metric geometry of the embedding space, and produces an explicit transport plan that directly assigns training samples to prototypes—no auxiliary heuristic needed. Entropic regularization via Sinkhorn-Knopp [7] makes this tractable at corpus scale. OT has been widely applied in NLP and machine learning [1,6,18,33], but never to text DD, and never combined with a knowledge-reweighted source distribution in any DD setting. TAKE fills both gaps: κ_n defines a non-uniform source measure, and the discrete entropic OT plan selects prototypes covering the knowledge-weighted training distribution without any auxiliary selection step.

3 Theoretical Motivation

3.1 Reweighted Distribution Matching for Dataset Distillation

The dataset distillation (DD) objective seeks $\tilde{\mathcal{D}}$ with $|\tilde{\mathcal{D}}| = K \ll N$ minimizing the loss on the original data:

$$\min_{\tilde{\mathcal{D}}} \mathbb{E}_{\theta_0 \sim p(\theta_0)} \left[\mathbb{E}_{z \sim \mathcal{D}} \left[\ell\Big(z;\ F(\theta_0;\ \tilde{\mathcal{D}}, \eta, T)\Big) \right] \right] \tag{1}$$

where $F(\theta_0; \tilde{\mathcal{D}}, \eta, T)$ denotes the model obtained by running T steps of gradient descent with learning rate η on $\tilde{\mathcal{D}}$ from initialization θ_0. This bi-level problem is intractable for discrete text. We relax it to distribution matching via the gradient-field equivalence argument [38]: if $\tilde{\mathcal{D}}$ induces the same expected gradient field as $\mathcal{D}$ throughout training, the two runs converge to comparable parameters. Since $\nabla_\theta \mathbb{E}_{z \sim P}[\ell(z;\theta)] = \mathbb{E}_{z \sim P}[\nabla_\theta \ell(z;\theta)]$, matching distributions in a task-relevant feature space controls the gradient field, making distribution matching a tractable surrogate for Eq. 1. This yields the distribution matching (DM) objective:

$$\min_{|\tilde{\mathcal{D}}|=K} d(P_{\tilde{\mathcal{D}}},\ P_{\mathcal{D}}) \tag{2}$$

for a divergence d in a task-relevant feature space. Equation 2 is a surrogate, not an equivalence; the formal gap bound appears as Theorem 1 once d is specified.

At extreme compression ($\rho = K/N \ll 1$), uniform matching allocates prototypes proportional to density—but not all regions contribute equally to learning. Dense easy regions consume budget that would be better spent on moderate and boundary samples near decision boundaries, which carry the most information for model robustness. We instead reweight the source by per-sample importance: define $w_n \geq 0$, $\sum_n w_n = 1$, inducing $P^w = \sum_n w_n \delta_{z_n}$, yielding the reweighted distribution matching (RDM) objective:

$$\min_{|\tilde{\mathcal{D}}|=K} d(P_{\tilde{\mathcal{D}}},\ P^w) \tag{3}$$

The weights w_n must reflect downstream learning contribution, not geometry alone, motivating gradient-based estimation. Influence self-scores (Sect. 2.2) are the natural candidate: they are task-aligned by construction and theoretically grounded. We now show that the simplest instantiation—$w_n \propto \mathcal{I}_{\text{self}}(z_n)$ at a single checkpoint, select top-K—fails on both counts: the weights are biased toward noisy samples (Proposition 1), and independent top-K selection ignores distributional coverage (Remark 3).

Remark 1 (Double relaxation gap). Moving from Eq. 1 to Eq. 2 incurs a gradient-field approximation error (bounded formally by Theorem 1); moving from Eq. 2

to Eq. 3 replaces the uniform source $P_{\mathcal{D}}$ with the reweighted source P^w, incurring an additional cost:

$$\mathrm{Gap}_2 \leq L \cdot W_1(P_{\mathcal{D}}, P^w) = L \cdot W_1\big(\tfrac{1}{N}\textstyle\sum_n \delta_{z_n}, \sum_n w_n \delta_{z_n}\big). \tag{4}$$

Since both measures have the same support, $W_1(P_{\mathcal{D}}, P^w) \leq \mathrm{diam}(\mathcal{Z}) \cdot \frac{1}{2} \sum_n |w_n - 1/N|$, which is directly computable from the κ_n scores and small when $w_n \approx 1/N$ (uniform weights recover DM). The reweighting is beneficial precisely when this gap is outweighed by the reduction in downstream loss from correcting the HSB, as formalized in Proposition 2 (Sect. 4.2).

3.2 The Naive Instantiation Fails: Two Open Problems

Define the influence self-score at checkpoint $\hat{\theta}$ as

$$\mathcal{I}_{\mathrm{self}}(z_n; \hat{\theta}) = \nabla_\theta \ell(z_n; \hat{\theta})^\top H_{\hat{\theta}}^{-1} \nabla_\theta \ell(z_n; \hat{\theta}), \tag{5}$$

where $H_{\hat{\theta}} = \frac{1}{N} \sum_n \nabla_\theta^2 \ell(z_n; \hat{\theta})$ is the empirical Hessian, specializing [17] by setting the test point equal to the training point. High $\mathcal{I}_{\mathrm{self}}$ identifies atypical examples: samples that are difficult to fit and exert outsized influence on the model's parameters, which in practice are the noisy ones. This suggests a naive pipeline: set $w_n \propto \mathcal{I}_{\mathrm{self}}(z_n; \hat{\theta})$ and return $\arg\max_{|\mathcal{A}|=K} \sum_{i \in \mathcal{A}} w_i$. We identify two orthogonal failures of this strategy.

The first failure is a bias in the weights themselves.

Proposition 1 (Hard-Sample Bias). *Let $\mathcal{D}_{clean}$, $\mathcal{D}_{noisy}$ partition $\mathcal{D}$, under the assumptions:* (i) $\|\nabla_\theta \ell(z; \hat{\theta})\| \leq \epsilon$ *for $z \in \mathcal{D}_{clean}$, i.e., clean samples have near-zero gradient at convergence;* (ii) $\|\nabla_\theta \ell(z; \hat{\theta})\| \geq \delta \gg \epsilon$ *for $z \in \mathcal{D}_{noisy}$, i.e., noisy samples retain large residual gradients. Let* $\mathrm{cond}(H) = \lambda_{\max}(H)/\lambda_{\min}(H)$ *denotes the condition number of the Hessian H. Then:*

$$\Delta_{\mathrm{HSB}} := \mathbb{E}_{z \sim \mathcal{D}_{\mathrm{noisy}}}[\mathcal{I}_{\mathrm{self}}(z; \hat{\theta})] - \mathbb{E}_{z \sim \mathcal{D}_{\mathrm{clean}}}[\mathcal{I}_{\mathrm{self}}(z; \hat{\theta})] \geq \frac{\delta^2 - \mathrm{cond}(H_{\hat{\theta}})\, \epsilon^2}{\lambda_{\max}(H_{\hat{\theta}})} > 0 \tag{6}$$

Proof (Proof sketch (full proof: Appendix A.1)). Since $\mathcal{I}_{\mathrm{self}}(z) = \nabla^\top H_{\hat{\theta}}^{-1} \nabla$, spectral bounds on $H_{\hat{\theta}}^{-1}$ give $\|\nabla\|^2/\lambda_{\max}(H_{\hat{\theta}}) \leq \mathcal{I}_{\mathrm{self}}(z) \leq \|\nabla\|^2/\lambda_{\min}(H_{\hat{\theta}})$. Applying the lower bound to noisy samples and the upper bound to clean samples yields Eq. 6. Positivity requires $\delta/\epsilon > \sqrt{\mathrm{cond}(H_{\hat{\theta}})}$, which is mild given $\delta \gg \epsilon$.

Because clean gradients vanish at convergence by definition of a local minimum, the bias is *structural*: it cannot be corrected by post-hoc rescaling of single-checkpoint scores, but only by integrating gradient signals across the training trajectory. The binary partition simplifies exposition; in practice the bias is monotone in $\|\nabla\|$, as the spectral bounds above show directly.

Remark 2 (Gradient norm as special case). Setting $H = I$ in Eq. 5 recovers $\mathcal{I}_{\text{self}}(z) = \|\nabla\|^2$. Under this substitution, Eq. 6 reduces to $\Delta_{\text{HSB}} \geq \delta^2 - \epsilon^2 > 0$, which holds without any spectral assumption on H. The gradient norm used in TAKE (Sect. 4.2) therefore inherits the same structural bias: it is not merely a tractable proxy but satisfies the HSB lower bound directly.

Even with unbiased weights, a second failure remains: top-K selection is blind to distributional coverage.

Remark 3 (Independent scoring ≠ distributional coverage). Any rank-and-select strategy decomposes as a sum of independent terms, invariant to pairwise distances between selected samples. In contrast, $d(P_{\tilde{\mathcal{D}}}, P^w)$ penalises redundancy and rewards coverage. Concretely, if $\phi(z_i) \approx \phi(z_j)$ and both have high w_i, w_j, independent scoring selects both; a distributional objective assigns nearly the same cost to selecting just one, freeing a slot for an uncovered region.

The two failures compound: biased w_n misdirects a population-level solver toward noisy regions; correct w_n fed into an independent selector still produces redundancy. They respectively yield two open problems:

(a) **Biased weighting.** Estimate w_n by integrating gradient signals across trajectory $\{\theta_t\}_{t=0}^{T-1}$, reducing Δ_{HSB}—which we will address in Sect. 4.2 (formalized as Proposition 2; Appendix A.2).
(b) **Independent selection.** Solve Eq. 3 directly for a metric d that jointly optimises coverage of P^w—which we will address in §4.4.

4 Methodology

4.1 Problem Setup and Framework Overview

TAKE instantiates the RDM objective (Eq. 3) by solving the two open problems from Sect. 3.2. Let $\mathcal{D} = \{z_n\}_{n=1}^{N}$ denote the training corpus, $\mathcal{D}_{\text{synth}} = \{\tilde{z}_c\}_{c=1}^{M}$ the synthetic candidate pool, and $\tilde{\mathcal{D}} \subset \mathcal{D}_{\text{synth}}$ the distilled set of budget K. Indices $n \in [N]$ and $t \in [T]$ range over training samples and checkpoints respectively. TAKE proceeds in three stages:

1. **Score**—train a logistic probe on $\mathcal{D}$ across T checkpoints, compute influence matrix $I \in \mathbb{R}^{N \times T}$, apply reciprocal reweighting and temporal weighting to obtain trajectory-aware knowledge scores κ_n.
2. **Generate**—fine-tune a small language model on $\mathcal{D}$ and sample to produce the synthetic candidate pool $\mathcal{D}_{\text{synth}}$.
3. **Distill**—solve discrete OT with source weights κ_n over $\mathcal{D}_{\text{synth}}$ to obtain the distilled corpus $\tilde{\mathcal{D}}$ of budget K.

The three stages are decoupled and independently replaceable, with ϕ shared across Stages 1 and 3 as a natural consistency choice. The following sections detail each in turn.

4.2 Gradient-Based Influence Along the Trajectory

The hard-sample bias (HSB; Sect. 3.2) arises because single-checkpoint influence scores overemphasize noisy or difficult samples, whose gradients remain large at convergence. The fix is to integrate gradient information across the full training trajectory, producing a trajectory-aware knowledge score κ_n per sample. We build κ_n in two steps: constructing the influence matrix I (Sect. 4.2), then collapsing it into a per-sample scalar score via reciprocal reweighting and temporal weighting (Sect. 4.2). The resulting κ_n provides a task-aligned, bias-corrected weight for P^w.

Influence Matrix. Our goal is to construct $I \in \mathbb{R}^{N\times T}$ whose entry $I_{(n,t)}$ reflects how much sample z_n contributes to learning at checkpoint θ_t. The influence self-score (Sect. 3.2, Eq. 5) is the natural candidate, but requires Hessian inversion at a converged checkpoint and is undefined mid-trajectory. We address both limitations by adapting the per-sample gradient norm from TracIn [28] to the self-influence setting, querying training points instead of test points:

$$I_{(n,t)} = \|\nabla_\theta \ell(z_n;\, \theta_t)\|. \tag{7}$$

As the $H = I$ special case of the influence self-score (Remark 2), $I_{(n,t)}$ exhibits the same HSB structure—the bias that κ_n corrects via reciprocal inversion and trajectory integration (Proposition 2). Scores are column-wise normalized $I_{(n,t)} \leftarrow I_{(n,t)}/\sum_{n'} I_{(n',t)}$ for comparability across checkpoints.

In practice, we score samples with a linear head W atop a pre-trained, frozen sentence encoder ϕ, giving $\theta = (W, \phi)$. The signal quality comes not from the linear head but from $\phi(x_n)$: ϕ is pre-trained on large-scale corpora and W is fine-tuned on the full task corpus, so the representations, and hence the gradient norms, are both semantically rich and task-aligned by construction. Following the standard practice in scalable influence estimation [12], we approximate full-model influence via the last layer—here, the linear head W:

$$\nabla_\theta \ell(z_n;\, \theta_t) \approx \nabla_W \ell(z_n;\, \theta_t), \tag{8}$$

trading a small bias for tractability. By the Goodfellow outer-product identity [10], $\nabla_W \ell = g_n \phi(x_n)^\top$ where g_n is the output gradient. The Goodfellow trick vectorizes the batch backward pass, avoiding per-sample loops. Adapting to a new task is trivial: retrain W on the new corpus; ϕ and the influence pipeline are unchanged.

Knowledge Score and Temporal Weighting. To correct the HSB, we require a score that is high for well-fitted samples and low for noisy ones—the opposite of what $I_{(n,t)}$ directly provides. Since a well-fitted sample has a small gradient norm, taking the reciprocal naturally inverts this ranking. We further weight each checkpoint by a decreasing temporal kernel $k : \{0, \ldots, T-1\} \to \mathbb{R}_{>0}$, giving:

$$\kappa_n = \sum_{t=0}^{T-1} \frac{k(t)}{I_{(n,t)}}, \tag{9}$$

A decreasing kernel is the natural choice: early checkpoints capture easy samples fitting rapidly, mid checkpoints offer the strongest signal, and late checkpoints see the gap narrow as memorization sets in [2]. Thus, concentrating mass on the early-to-mid phase and discounting late memorization directly corrects the HSB structure identified in Proposition 1. By default we use the exponential kernel $k(t) = e^{-\lambda t/T}$ ($\lambda > 0$), with λ treated as a hyperparameter. Alternative kernels (linear, cosine) are drop-in replacements, and Proposition 2 guarantees bias reduction holds for any strictly decreasing k. The resulting κ_n summarizes each sample's cumulative, bias-corrected learning contribution across the full trajectory, resolving open problem (**a**). Normalized source weights $w_n = \kappa_n / \sum_{n'} \kappa_{n'}$ define the reweighted distribution P^w and serve as input to the OT selection step (Sect. 4.4).

Proposition 2 (Trajectory Integration Reduces HSB). *Under a smooth loss and bounded gradient noise, κ_n produces a strictly smaller noisy-over-clean gap than the single last-checkpoint baseline $\kappa_n^\dagger = 1/I_{(n,T-1)}$:*

$$\mathbb{E}_{z\sim\mathcal{D}_{\text{noisy}}}[\kappa_n] - \mathbb{E}_{z\sim\mathcal{D}_{\text{clean}}}[\kappa_n] < \mathbb{E}_{z\sim\mathcal{D}_{\text{noisy}}}[\kappa_n^\dagger] - \mathbb{E}_{z\sim\mathcal{D}_{\text{clean}}}[\kappa_n^\dagger]. \tag{10}$$

Proof (Proof sketch (full proof: Appendix A.2)). Define the noisy-over-clean gap $\Delta_t := \mathbb{E}_{\text{noisy}}[1/I_{(n,t)}] - \mathbb{E}_{\text{clean}}[1/I_{(n,t)}]$. The left-hand side of Eq. 10 equals $\sum_t k(t)\Delta_t$. For $t \le T_m$ (before memorization onset): clean gradients decay so $\Delta_t \le 0$, strictly at some t^* (Appendix A.2). Beyond T_m: noisy gradients also drop (memorization), so $\Delta_{T-1} > 0$—the last-checkpoint baseline is inflated by memorization. The decreasing kernel upweights $t \le T_m$ (where $\Delta_t < 0$) and downweights $t > T_m$ (where $\Delta_t > 0$). Since k is strictly decreasing, the negative-Δ_t early terms receive more weight and the large positive Δ_{T-1} term receives the least, making the weighted sum strictly smaller than $\Delta_{T-1} > 0$.

4.3 Synthetic Candidate Pool Generation

Rather than selecting directly from $\mathcal{D}$, TAKE draws $\tilde{\mathcal{D}}$ from a synthetic candidate pool $\mathcal{D}_{\text{synth}}$. Direct subsampling has two problems: at extreme compression, verbatim records raise privacy concerns, and the budget K is too small to cover the full training support. We generate $\mathcal{D}_{\text{synth}}$ by fine-tuning a small language model on $\mathcal{D}$ and sampling from it. The fine-tuned LM generalizes beyond memorized training instances, and stochastic sampling produces a diverse pool that extends beyond the training support. $\mathcal{D}_{\text{synth}}$ serves solely as the selection pool and is never appended to downstream training data.

TAKE does *not* assume $P_{\mathcal{D}_{\text{synth}}} = P_{\mathcal{D}}$; this distributional gap is *beneficial.* First, coverage expansion fills undersampled regions of $\mathcal{D}$, improving generalization of the distilled corpus. Second, model fluency bias suppresses noisy samples that HSB would otherwise over-select, yielding a cleaner candidate pool. Third, the distribution mismatch physically decouples $\tilde{\mathcal{D}}$ from original records, reducing verbatim exposure risk. OT handles the distributional gap gracefully: it routes mass toward P^w regardless of pool distribution, so $P_{\tilde{\mathcal{D}}}$ approximates P^w provided $\mathcal{D}_{\text{synth}}$ covers the support of $P_{\mathcal{D}}$ (Assumption 1):

Assumption 1 (Pool Coverage). For every training sample $z_n \in \mathcal{D}$, there exists a synthetic sample $\tilde{z}_c \in \mathcal{D}_{\text{synth}}$ within embedding distance r: $\min_c \|\phi(z_n) - \phi(\tilde{z}_c)\| \leq r$.

Under Assumption 1, $W_1(P^w, P_{\mathcal{D}_{\text{synth}}}) \leq r$, so the optimal transport cost is at most r before any prototype selection. A practitioner can monitor coverage directly by reporting the mean nearest-neighbor distance $\bar{r} = \frac{1}{N}\sum_n \min_c \|\phi(z_n) - \phi(\tilde{z}_c)\|$.

4.4 Distributional Prototype Selection via Discrete Optimal Transport

Both $\mathcal{D}$ and $\mathcal{D}_{\text{synth}}$ are finite sample sets, so the matching problem is naturally over empirical measures. Discrete OT operates directly on $\mu = \sum_n w_n \delta_{z_n}$ and $\nu = \frac{1}{|\mathcal{D}_{\text{synth}}|}\sum_c \delta_{\tilde{z}_c}$, requiring no density estimation and yielding an explicit transport plan with direct prototype-level assignments.

Let $C_{nc} = \|\phi(z_n) - \phi(\tilde{z}_c)\|^2$ be the cost matrix in a task-relevant embedding space. Bare Kantorovich OT, $\min_{\gamma \in \Pi(\mu,\nu)} \langle C, \gamma \rangle$, produces a sparse, non-differentiable plan and scales as $O(N^3)$. We add entropic regularization to obtain a strictly convex, smooth objective solvable via Sinkhorn–Knopp iterations at $O(N \cdot |\mathcal{D}_{\text{synth}}|)$ per step:

$$\gamma^* = \arg\min_{\gamma \in \Pi(\mu,\nu)} \langle C, \gamma \rangle + \varepsilon \cdot \mathrm{KL}(\gamma \| \mu \otimes \nu). \tag{11}$$

The soft coupling distributes mass across nearby candidates rather than hard one-to-one assignment, reducing sensitivity to embedding errors and encouraging diversity in $\tilde{\mathcal{D}}$. The K candidates with highest received mass $\sum_n \gamma^*_{nc}$ are selected as $\tilde{\mathcal{D}}$, resolving open problem (**b**). The following theorem closes the theoretical chain from RDM (Eq. 3) back to DD (Eq. 1), bounding the downstream loss gap in terms of the OT cost.

Theorem 1 (Distribution Matching Gap Bound). *Let $f^*_{\mathcal{S}}$ denote the model trained on $\mathcal{S}$, and let $\mathcal{L}(\mathcal{S}) = \mathbb{E}_{z \sim P^w}[\ell(z; f^*_{\mathcal{S}})]$. Assume:* (i) *$\ell(\cdot; f)$ is L-Lipschitz in the embedding metric for all f;* (ii) *the model class has uniform stability constant $\beta_K = O(1/K)$ [3], so that $\sup_z |\ell(z; f^*_{\tilde{\mathcal{D}}}) - \ell(z; f^*_{\mathcal{D}})| \leq \beta_K$. Then:*

$$\left|\mathcal{L}(\tilde{\mathcal{D}}) - \mathcal{L}(\mathcal{D})\right| \leq 2L \cdot W_1(P^w, P_{\tilde{\mathcal{D}}}) + \beta_K, \tag{12}$$

where W_1 is the Wasserstein-1 distance under the embedding metric. As $K \to \infty$, $\beta_K \to 0$, and the bound is dominated by the W_1 term controlled by the OT objective.

Proof (Proof sketch (full proof: Appendix A.3)). Insert two intermediate terms, $\mathbb{E}_{P_{\tilde{\mathcal{D}}}}[\ell(z;\, f^*_{\tilde{\mathcal{D}}})]$ and $\mathbb{E}_{P_{\tilde{\mathcal{D}}}}[\ell(z;\, f^*_{\mathcal{D}})]$, and apply the triangle inequality twice. This yields two distribution-shift terms (under fixed $f^*_{\tilde{\mathcal{D}}}$ and $f^*_{\mathcal{D}}$ respectively), each bounded by $L \cdot W_1(P^w, P_{\tilde{\mathcal{D}}})$ via Kantorovich–Rubinstein duality; and one model-difference term under $P_{\tilde{\mathcal{D}}}$, bounded by $\beta_K = O(1/K)$ via uniform stability.

The bound is stated with respect to P^w rather than the uniform $P_{\mathcal{D}}$—this is intentional, as P^w is the designed optimization target of the RDM objective; since P^w reweights $P_{\mathcal{D}}$ over the same support, minimizing $W_1(P^w, P_{\tilde{\mathcal{D}}})$ controls coverage of $P_{\mathcal{D}}$ up to the reweighting gap bounded in Remark 1.

Together, Propositions 1–2 and Theorem 1 establish the full theoretical basis for TAKE: HSB is structural and unavoidable at a single checkpoint (Proposition 1); trajectory integration strictly reduces it (Proposition 2); and minimizing the OT cost directly controls the downstream loss gap under P^w (Theorem 1; the gap to $P_{\mathcal{D}}$ is bounded by Remark 1). Algorithm 1 consolidates the full pipeline.

Algorithm 1: Trajectory-Aware Knowledge Estimation (**TAKE**)

Input : corpus $\mathcal{D} = \{z_n\}_{n=1}^{N}$; budget K; checkpoints T; kernel $k(\cdot)$; ε; pool size M
Output: distilled corpus $\tilde{\mathcal{D}}$, $|\tilde{\mathcal{D}}| = K$

▷ ***Stage 1: Score***
Train logistic probe on $\mathcal{D}$, saving checkpoints $\theta_0, \ldots, \theta_{T-1}$
for $t = 0, \ldots, T-1$ **do**
  Compute $I_{(n,t)} \leftarrow \|\nabla_W \ell(z_n;\, \theta_t)\|$ for all n *(Goodfellow trick)*
  Normalize $I_{(\cdot,t)} \leftarrow I_{(\cdot,t)} / \sum_{n'} I_{(n',t)}$ *(column-wise)*
Compute $\kappa_n \leftarrow \sum_{t=0}^{T-1} k(t)/I_{(n,t)}$ for all n via Eq. 9
Normalize $w_n \leftarrow \kappa_n / \sum_{n'} \kappa_{n'}$ for all n *(defines P^w)*

▷ ***Stage 2: Generate***
Fine-tune small language model LM on $\mathcal{D}$
Sample synthetic pool $\mathcal{D}_{\text{synth}} = \{\tilde{z}_c\}_{c=1}^{M}$ from LM

▷ ***Stage 3: Distill***
Embed: $\phi(z_n)$ for $n \in [N]$; $\phi(\tilde{z}_c)$ for $c \in [M]$
Compute cost matrix $C_{nc} = \|\phi(z_n) - \phi(\tilde{z}_c)\|^2$
Solve $\gamma^* \leftarrow \text{Sinkhorn}(C,\, w,\, \mathbf{1}/M,\, \varepsilon)$ via Eq. 11
Distill $\tilde{\mathcal{D}} \leftarrow \text{top-}K(\{\tilde{z}_c\},\, \sum_n \gamma^*_{nc})$ *(by received mass)*
return $\tilde{\mathcal{D}}$

5 Experiments

We evaluate on two linguistic tasks: AG News ($N = 120\,$K), IMDb ($N = 25\,$K), SST-2 ($N = 67\,$K) for classification; MNLI-m ($N = 393\,$K), QNLI ($N = 105\,$K), and QQP ($N = 364\,\text{K}$) for natural language inference (NLI). We compare against four baselines:

- **Random**: uniform random selection at the target budget.
- **EDA** [37]: word-level augmentation (10×) applied to the **Random** set.
- **DiLM** [23]: LLM-generated candidates selected by gradient matching across k-centre selection. It evaluated on both classification and NLI.
- **DaLLME** [32]: synthetic texts inverted from distilled embeddings. It evaluated on classification only.

We evaluate TAKE at two budgets (20/cls and 0.1%) to match DiLM's and DaLLME's reported settings, respectively. To match downstream evaluation, downstream models for classification are Logistic Regression (LR) with TF-IDF [29] features, TextCNN [16] and TextRNN [21] with GloVe [27] word embeddings, and BERT [8]. For NLI, we evaluate on BERT and Siamese LR. Siamese LR is a variant of LR: two input branches to independently encode sentence pairs, and a logistic head over the concatenated representations, tailored as a weak learner for NLI. The primary metric is downstream accuracy on classification/NLI tasks, reported as mean$_{\pm\text{s.e.}}$ across five runs.

In terms of implementation, TAKE extracts knowledge scores κ_n by running $T = 20$ training checkpoints with exponential kernel $\lambda^* = T/T_m$, using all-MiniLM-L6-v2 [36] as the frozen encoder ϕ. The synthetic pool uses Gemma-3 [14] (270 M) fine-tuned on $\mathcal{D}$ to generate $|\mathcal{D}_{\text{synth}}| = 5{,}000$ samples. OT selection embeds via the same ϕ and uses Sinkhorn with $\varepsilon = 0.05$ for 200 iterations. All experiments fit on a single NVIDIA V100 (40 GB).

5.1 Classification

Table 2. Classification accuracy (%) on AG News, IMDb, and SST-2.

Method	Budget	LR	TextCNN	TextRNN	BERT	
AG News	Full dataset	100%	90.21$_{\pm0.14}$	91.27$_{\pm0.20}$	90.98$_{\pm0.32}$	93.85$_{\pm0.12}$
	Random	0.1%	66.39$_{\pm2.27}$	75.56$_{\pm0.14}$	74.91$_{\pm1.45}$	78.12$_{\pm3.25}$
	EDA	0.1%	68.03$_{\pm2.43}$	82.27$_{\pm0.15}$	81.46$_{\pm1.34}$	84.45$_{\pm1.44}$
	DaLLME	0.1%	74.60$_{\pm0.02}$†	88.30$_{\pm0.02}$†	**84.50**$_{\pm0.02}$†	–
	TAKE	0.1%	**77.07**$_{\pm0.09}$	**88.53**$_{\pm0.21}$	84.25$_{\pm1.03}$	**89.82**$_{\pm0.18}$
IMDb	Full dataset	100%	88.41$_{\pm0.13}$	87.40$_{\pm0.20}$	83.00$_{\pm0.35}$	91.22$_{\pm0.25}$
	Random	0.1%	59.73$_{\pm5.51}$	57.65$_{\pm1.19}$	55.09$_{\pm4.31}$	60.40$_{\pm4.10}$
	EDA	0.1%	61.52$_{\pm4.62}$	62.40$_{\pm3.40}$	58.92$_{\pm1.93}$	63.12$_{\pm1.95}$
	DaLLME	0.1%	65.00$_{\pm0.02}$†	68.30$_{\pm0.02}$†	**64.50**$_{\pm0.02}$†	–
	TAKE	0.1%	**66.83**$_{\pm0.13}$	**68.93**$_{\pm2.15}$	63.26$_{\pm0.38}$	**71.55**$_{\pm0.22}$
SST-2	Full dataset	100%	80.23$_{\pm0.27}$	88.81$_{\pm0.15}$	87.40$_{\pm0.76}$	92.52$_{\pm0.28}$
	Random	20/cls	55.28$_{\pm2.32}$	63.85$_{\pm0.87}$	61.52$_{\pm1.66}$	69.97$_{\pm3.21}$
	EDA	20/cls	57.21$_{\pm1.05}$	65.54$_{\pm0.45}$	63.17$_{\pm0.84}$	74.21$_{\pm1.58}$
	DiLM	20/cls	–	–	–	80.30$_{\pm2.80}$†
	TAKE	20/cls	**65.05**$_{\pm0.05}$	**70.65**$_{\pm0.32}$	**67.18**$_{\pm0.49}$	**81.15**$_{\pm0.24}$

[–] not reported; [†] reported from respective paper; [**bold**] best per budget. DaLLME reported with its best case (OpenAI-3-large embeddings).

Accuracy Gains and Their Source. TAKE (0.1%) outperforms DaLLME on LR by +2.5 on AG News and +1.8 on IMDb. The gap is widest at the LR level and narrows for neural backbones, consistent with TAKE's backbone-agnostic selection—trajectory scores are computed independently of the downstream model. TAKE minimizes the OT cost in embedding space, directly controlling the downstream loss gap under P^w via Theorem 1 (the gap to the original $P_{\mathcal{D}}$ is bounded by Remark 1). Since κ_n scores are computed independently of the evaluation backbone, this coverage of P^w transfers across model families (Table 2).

Stability Across Runs. The wide standard errors for Random (IMDb LR ±5.5, BERT ±4.1) reveal that random selection at 0.1% can land anywhere from a coherent corpus to a degenerate one. TAKE's errors are at least 5× narrower (±0.1–2.2), a direct consequence of OT-based selection: the transport plan distributes selected prototypes across P^w rather than drawing them independently, suppressing the variance that Random incurs by chance.

SST-2 vs. DiLM. At 20/cls, TAKE matches DiLM on BERT (81.15 vs. 80.30, within s.e.) while also providing results for LR, TextCNN, and TextRNN where DiLM has none—indicating that the OT selection step generalizes across backbone families without retraining the scorer.

5.2 Natural Language Inference

Table 3. NLI accuracy (%) on MNLI-m and QQP.

	Method	Budget	Siamese LR	BERT
MNLI-m	Full dataset	100%	$60.02_{\pm 0.07}$	$86.81_{\pm 0.30}$
	Random	20/cls	$34.15_{\pm 2.10}$	$40.10_{\pm 3.20}$
	EDA	20/cls	$37.80_{\pm 1.45}$	$44.52_{\pm 2.80}$
	DiLM	20/cls	–	$48.70_{\pm 2.60}$ †
	TAKE	20/cls	**42.66**$_{\pm 0.15}$	**51.24**$_{\pm 0.45}$
QNLI	Full dataset	100%	$73.05_{\pm 0.13}$	$82.50_{\pm 0.12}$
	Random	20/cls	$52.21_{\pm 0.28}$	$57.19_{\pm 2.20}$
	EDA	20/cls	$54.33_{\pm 1.21}$	$59.81_{\pm 1.42}$
	DiLM	20/cls	–	–
	TAKE	20/cls	**57.96**$_{\pm 0.58}$	**64.89**$_{\pm 3.58}$
QQP	Full dataset	100%	$78.58_{\pm 0.05}$	$89.45_{\pm 0.15}$
	Random	20/cls	$52.40_{\pm 1.32}$	$59.10_{\pm 3.80}$
	EDA	20/cls	$55.12_{\pm 1.88}$	$62.35_{\pm 2.45}$
	DiLM	20/cls	–	$64.40_{\pm 2.20}$ †
	TAKE	20/cls	**60.04**$_{\pm 0.12}$	**67.76**$_{\pm 0.35}$

[–] not reported; [†] reported from respective paper; [**bold**] best per budget.

Gains and Their Interpretation. DaLLME has no published NLI experiments and is excluded from this comparison. In comparison with DiLM, TAKE outperforms DiLM by +2.5 on MNLI-m and +3.4 on QQP on a BERT learner, and provides competitive results for QNLI. The LR gap (+8.5 on MNLI-m, +5.8 on QNLI, +7.6 on QQP relative to Random) is particularly informative: Siamese LR has no capacity to compensate for a poor corpus—every percentage point of accuracy here must come from the quality of $\tilde{\mathcal{D}}$ itself. That TAKE's Siamese LR exceeds the Random BERT baseline on both QQP (60.04 vs. 59.10) and QNLI (57.96 vs. 57.19) suggests the selected sentence pairs are genuinely more informative, not merely better distributed (Table 3).

The NLI Ceiling Gap and What it Implies. All distilled methods fall short of the full-dataset ceiling (86.8/82.5/89.5 for MNLI-m, QNLI, QQP), a gap larger than on single-sentence tasks. NLI imposes a joint constraint: the synthetic pool must contain pairs whose relationship correctly reflects each class label at extreme budget ($\approx$ 60 pairs for MNLI-m, $\approx$ 40 for QQP and QNLI, at 20/cls). This is a harder coverage requirement than single-sentence classification, and the synthetic pool must cover all relationship types within it. This suggests that pool generation and budget are the binding constraints, rather than scoring or selection.

Stability. On MNLI-m and QQP, TAKE's errors (±0.1–0.5) are 5–7× narrower than DiLM's (±2.2–2.6), mirroring the pattern on classification. This is consistent with the OT transport plan enforcing coverage of P^w rather than selecting samples independently: deterministic coverage implies that any two runs of TAKE over the same pool yield nearly identical corpora, whereas DiLM's gradient-matching step introduces variance through its dependence on a randomly initialized model.

5.3 Component Contributions

Table 4. Distillation accuracy (%) under TAKE component ablation.

	AG News		QQP	
	LR	BERT	Siamese LR	BERT
Random	$66.39_{\pm 2.27}$	$75.92_{\pm 0.98}$	$52.40_{\pm 1.32}$	$57.94_{\pm 1.30}$
▲k-Means nearest	$72.89_{\pm 1.37}$	$77.79_{\pm 1.04}$	$55.28_{\pm 1.12}$	$61.30_{\pm 1.08}$
TAKE without κ	$75.82_{\pm 0.23}$	$80.94_{\pm 0.93}$	$58.80_{\pm 0.92}$	$63.66_{\pm 1.25}$
TAKE	$\mathbf{77.07}_{\pm 0.09}$	$\mathbf{86.50}_{\pm 1.01}$	$\mathbf{60.04}_{\pm 0.12}$	$\mathbf{66.29}_{\pm 1.91}$

[▲] **not** inclusive of TAKE; [**bold**] best results.

To isolate the contribution of each design choice, we ablate TAKE's components on AG News and QQP as representatives for the classification and NLI tasks, in Table 4. TAKE improves over Random by +10.7 on AG News LR and +10.6 on BERT; k-means, by comparison, accounts for only part of this gain (+6.5 LR, +1.9 BERT), while our discrete OT selection step alone (TAKE without κ) already achieves +9.4 LR and +5.0 BERT from the same baseline. The same pattern holds on QQP: k-means gains +2.9/+3.4 (Siamese LR/BERT) whereas TAKE without κ gains +6.4/+5.7. Adding κ knowledge scores delivers the remaining improvement, modestly for Siamese LR (+1.2) but substantially for BERT (+5.6 on AG News, +2.6 on QQP), suggesting that κ primarily benefits models with enough capacity to exploit the harder, informative examples that high-κ samples represent.

5.4 Kernels for Temporal Weighting

Table 5. Distillation accuracy (%) with alternative temporal kernels.

	AG News		QQP	
Kernel	LR	BERT	Siamese LR	BERT
TAKE without κ	$75.82_{\pm 0.23}$	$80.94_{\pm 0.93}$	$58.80_{\pm 0.92}$	$63.66_{\pm 1.25}$
Last checkpoint	$75.24_{\pm 0.57}$	$78.28_{\pm 0.66}$	$58.32_{\pm 1.56}$	$62.19_{\pm 0.57}$
Constant	$76.13_{\pm 1.14}$	$83.47_{\pm 0.71}$	$59.44_{\pm 0.86}$	$64.78_{\pm 1.51}$
Linear	$76.20_{\pm 0.68}$	$85.20_{\pm 1.00}$	$59.61_{\pm 1.11}$	$65.60_{\pm 1.35}$
Cosine	$76.74_{\pm 0.53}$	$85.46_{\pm 0.64}$	$59.14_{\pm 0.85}$	$66.16_{\pm 0.41}$
Exponential (**TAKE**)	**77.07**$_{\pm 0.09}$	**86.50**$_{\pm 1.01}$	**60.04**$_{\pm 0.12}$	**66.29**$_{\pm 1.91}$

[**bold**] best results.

Table 5 ablates the choice of temporal kernel defined in §4.2. The last-checkpoint baseline is the critical exception: it falls *below* the no-κ baseline across all backbones, most severely on BERT (−2.7 on AG News, −1.5 on QQP). This is precisely the failure mode identified in Proposition 2: when κ is extracted at convergence only, the learner has fully memorized difficult samples, so the *hard-sample bias* is intensified rather than corrected, and the selected corpus is skewed towards harder, less representative examples. All other trajectory-based strategies lessen this effect and outperform the no-κ baseline (OT only), with decreasing kernels (linear, cosine, exponential) doing so most strongly by concentrating mass on the early-to-mid training phase where the bias-correcting signal is strongest. The exponential kernel (TAKE default) achieves the best result in all cases, consistent with the theoretical preference for early-phase concentration of influence.

6 Limitations and Ethical Considerations

We identify three limitations of the current method. (**1**) **Gradient norm proxy.** $I_{(n,t)}$ uses plain gradient norms rather than Fisher-preconditioned scores; the

Goodfellow trick [10] keeps per-sample cost at $O(C + d_\phi)$ per checkpoint. K-FAC [24] or EKFAC [9] preconditioning are natural extensions when calibrated magnitude scores are needed. (**2**) **Encoder dependence.** The OT cost matrix inherits the geometry of ϕ; a mismatched encoder can distort transport costs. The L-Lipschitz assumption on ℓ (Theorem 1) holds approximately when ϕ is task-aligned and embeddings are normalized, but remains an approximation for cross-entropy over discrete text. (**3**) **Synthetic pool coverage.** Pool diversity is bounded by the generator's domain coverage. Fine-tuning on $\mathcal{D}_{\text{train}}$ mitigates this in practice.

Two ethical considerations arise in the deployment of TAKE. (**1**) **Bias propagation.** Distillation concentrates the statistical properties of $\mathcal{D}_{\text{train}}$, including demographic biases. We recommend corpus auditing before distillation. (**2**) **Privacy risk.** Language models fine-tuned on sensitive data may memorize training examples, a risk that synthetic generation alone does not fully eliminate. We recommend distance-to-closest-record (DCR) screening of $\mathcal{D}_{\text{synth}}$ to verify that synthetic samples are not verbatim copies; for regulated domains, differential privacy at the fine-tuning stage provides a formal guarantee against memorization.

7 Conclusion

We identified the hard-sample bias (HSB) as the core failure mode of gradient-based text dataset distillation: at convergence, noisy samples dominate single-checkpoint influence scores, suppressing the informative ones that matter most. TAKE corrects this by integrating gradient norms across the training trajectory into per-sample knowledge scores, used as non-uniform source weights in a discrete Optimal Transport objective to select a compact, human-readable corpus. Theoretically, we provide end-to-end guarantees: the hard-sample bias is structural, trajectory integration strictly reduces it, and the downstream loss gap is bounded by the OT cost. TAKE outperforms baselines across six language benchmarks at extreme compression (0.1% or 20 samples/class), generalizing across diverse backbone families. Together, these results position text dataset distillation as a practical, data-centric tool for efficient and privacy-aware NLP, with direct implications for coreset construction and continual learning in resource-constrained settings.

AI Tools Disclosure. Large Language Models (LLMs) were used only to enhance the readability during the postprocessing of this manuscript.

References

1. Arjovsky, M., Chintala, S., Bottou, L.: Wasserstein generative adversarial networks. In: ICML (2017)
2. Arpit, D., Jastrzębski, S., et al.: A closer look at memorization in deep networks. In: ICML (2017)

3. Bousquet, O., Elisseeff, A.: Stability and generalization. JMLR (2002)
4. Cazenavette, G., Wang, T., Torralba, A., Efros, A.A., Zhu, J.Y.: Dataset distillation by matching training trajectories. In: CVPR (2022)
5. Cook, R.D., Weisberg, S.: Residuals and influence in regression. Chapman and Hall, New York (1982)
6. Courty, N., Flamary, R., Tuia, D., Rakotomamonjy, A.: Optimal transport for domain adaptation. In: PAMI (2016)
7. Cuturi, M.: Sinkhorn distances: lightspeed computation of optimal transport. In: NeurIPS (2013)
8. Devlin, J., Chang, M.W., Lee, K., Toutanova, K.: Bert: pre-training of deep bidirectional transformers for language understanding. In: Proceedings of the 2019 Conference of the North American Chapter of the Association for Computational Linguistics: Human Language Technologies, Volume 1 (long and short papers) (2019)
9. George, T., Laurent, C., Bouthillier, X., Ballas, N., Vincent, P.: Fast approximate natural gradient descent in a Kronecker factored Eigenbasis. In: NeurIPS (2018)
10. Goodfellow, I.: Efficient per-example gradient computations. arXiv preprint arXiv:1510.01799 (2015)
11. Gretton, A., Borgwardt, K.M., Rasch, M.J., Schölkopf, B., Smola, A.: A kernel two-sample test. JMLR (2012)
12. Guo, H., Rajani, N., Hase, P., Bansal, M., Xiong, C.: Fastif: scalable influence functions for efficient model interpretation and debugging. In: Proceedings of the 2021 Conference on Empirical Methods in Natural Language Processing (2021)
13. Han, B., et al.: Co-teaching: robust training of deep neural networks with extremely noisy labels. In: NeurIPS (2018)
14. Kamath, A., et al.: Gemma 3 technical report. arXiv preprint arXiv:2503.19786 (2025)
15. Kim, J.H., et al.: Dataset condensation via efficient synthetic-data parameterization. In: ICML (2022)
16. Kim, Y.: Convolutional neural networks for sentence classification. In: EMNLP (2014)
17. Koh, P.W., Liang, P.: Understanding black-box predictions via influence functions. In: ICML (2017)
18. Kusner, M., Sun, Y., Kolkin, N., Weinberger, K.: From word embeddings to document distances. In: ICML (2015)
19. Kwon, Y., Wu, E., Wu, K., Zou, J.: Datalnf: efficiently estimating data influence in Lora-tuned LLMs and diffusion models. In: ICLR (2023)
20. Li, Y., Li, W.: Data distillation for text classification. arXiv preprint arXiv:2104.08448 (2021)
21. Liu, P., Qiu, X., Huang, X.: Recurrent neural network for text classification with multi-task learning. arXiv preprint arXiv:1605.05101 (2016)
22. Maekawa, A., Kobayashi, N., Funakoshi, K., Okumura, M.: Dataset distillation with attention labels for fine-tuning Bert. In: ACL (2023)
23. Maekawa, A., Kosugi, S., Funakoshi, K., Okumura, M.: Dilm: distilling dataset into language model for text-level dataset distillation. In: NAACL Findings (2024)
24. Martens, J., Grosse, R.: Optimizing neural networks with kronecker-factored approximate curvature. In: ICML (2015)
25. Paninski, L.: Estimation of entropy and mutual information. Neural Comput. (2003)
26. Park, S.M., Georgiev, K., Ilyas, A., Leclerc, G., Madry, A.: Trak: attributing model behavior at scale. In: ICML (2023)

27. Pennington, J., Socher, R., Manning, C.D.: Glove: global vectors for word representation. In: Proceedings of the 2014 Conference on Empirical Methods in Natural Language Processing (EMNLP) (2014)
28. Pruthi, G., Liu, F., Kale, S., Sundararajan, M.: Estimating training data influence by tracing gradient descent. In: NeurIPS (2020)
29. Salton, G., Buckley, C.: Term-weighting approaches in automatic text retrieval. Inf. Process. Manage. (1988)
30. Sucholutsky, I., Schonlau, M.: Soft-label dataset distillation and text dataset distillation. In: IJCNN (2021)
31. Swayamdipta, S., et al.: Dataset cartography: mapping and diagnosing datasets with training dynamics. In: EMNLP (2020)
32. Tao, Y., Kong, L., Kan, A., Callot, L.: Textual dataset distillation via language model embedding. In: EMNLP Findings (2024)
33. Tolstikhin, I., Bousquet, O., Gelly, S., Schoelkopf, B.: Wasserstein auto-encoders. In: ICLR (2018)
34. Wang, K., et al.: CAFE: learning to condense dataset by aligning features. In: CVPR (2022)
35. Wang, T., Zhu, J.Y., Torralba, A., Efros, A.A.: Dataset distillation. arXiv preprint arXiv:1811.10959 (2018)
36. Wang, W., Wei, F., Dong, L., Bao, H., Yang, N., Zhou, M.: MINILM: deep self-attention distillation for task-agnostic compression of pre-trained transformers. In: Advances in Neural Information Processing Systems (2020)
37. Wei, J., Zou, K.: EDA: easy data augmentation techniques for boosting performance on text classification tasks. In: Proceedings of the 2019 Conference on Empirical Methods in Natural Language Processing and the 9th International Joint Conference on Natural Language Processing (EMNLP-IJCNLP) (2019)
38. Zhao, B., Bilen, H.: Dataset condensation with distribution matching. In: WACV (2023)
39. Zhao, B., Mopuri, K.R., Bilen, H.: Dataset condensation with gradient matching. arXiv preprint arXiv:2006.05929 (2020)

TFCD-AD: Temporal-Frequency Coupling Discrepancy for Multivariate Time Series Anomaly Detection

Chun Huang, Xiaohong Zhang(✉), Zhibin Zhang, Tao Yin, and Meng Yan

Chongqing University, Chongqing, China
{202424021069T,yintao}@stu.cqu.edu.cn, {xhongz,zbinz,mengy}@cqu.edu.cn

Abstract. Unsupervised multivariate time series anomaly detection is difficult because anomalies may simultaneously disturb temporal dynamics and spectral structure. Existing methods have shown the value of temporal-frequency modeling, but they still lack an explicit criterion to distinguish normal and abnormal patterns under dual-domain fusion. In our study, we observe a clear difference in temporal-frequency coupling behaviors. For normal data, the interaction between the two domains is relatively diffuse, and the coupling at the current timestamp does not dominate the overall contextual association. For anomalous data, the interaction becomes more localized, leading to unusually strong coupling between temporal and frequency representations at the same timestamp. Based on this observation, we define Temporal-Frequency Coupling Discrepancy (TFCD) as the relative contrast between Self-Coupling, which describes same-timestamp cross-domain association, and Mutual-Coupling, which describes contextual cross-domain association over the full window. TFCD provides a direct and interpretable criterion for anomaly discrimination. Building on TFCD, we develop a dual-branch framework TFCD-AD, which combines an inverted Transformer for temporal dependency modeling and a DWT-based frequency encoder for transient spectral analysis. We also introduce a joint training objective with cross-reconstruction and TFCD supervision to improve representation learning and explicitly enhance anomaly separability. Extensive experiments on six benchmark datasets demonstrate that TFCD-AD achieves state-of-the-art performance. The code is in https://github.com/Hccchun/TFCD-AD.

Keywords: Time series analysis · Anomaly detection · Time-frequency analysis

1 Introduction

Multivariate time series anomaly detection is crucial for maintaining stability in safety-critical domains such as industrial monitoring and healthcare [11].

Supplementary Information The online version contains supplementary material available at https://doi.org/10.1007/978-3-032-37654-1_12.

M. Ceci et al. (Eds.): ECML PKDD 2026, LNAI 16941, pp. 195–212, 2027.
https://doi.org/10.1007/978-3-032-37654-1_12

These applications are characterized by complex temporal dynamics and high-dimensional inter-dependencies, making the separation of normal variability from true anomalies a significant challenge. Reconstruction-based representation learning has emerged as the dominant paradigm, which identifies anomalies by detecting deviations from learned normal patterns [24].

Although significant progress has been made in reconstruction-based methods, the existing research still has obvious limitations in the perspective and depth of feature modeling, and mainly faces two major challenges: On the one hand, single-domain modeling inherently suffers from information blind spots. Mainstream temporal-domain methods, such as OmniAnomaly and CrossAD [10,21], are dedicated to capturing multi-scale temporal contexts. Conversely, frequency-domain methods like THOC [20] excel at extracting global periodic patterns but frequently lose the localized temporal details required to identify non-stationary anomalies. On the other hand, existing dual-domain methods lack deep interaction mechanisms. To overcome single-domain defects, approaches like TFMAE and Dual-TF [7,16] combine temporal and frequency information. However, they mostly rely on independent encoding or basic feature concatenation, which separates the intrinsic temporal-frequency coupling relationship. Although recent methods like TF-C [30] have explored dual-domain interactions through representation learning, they still lack an explicit criterion to distinguish normal and abnormal patterns under cross-domain fusion. Consequently, there is an urgent need for a paradigm that provides a direct and interpretable criterion by explicitly modeling the temporal-frequency fusion discrepancy.

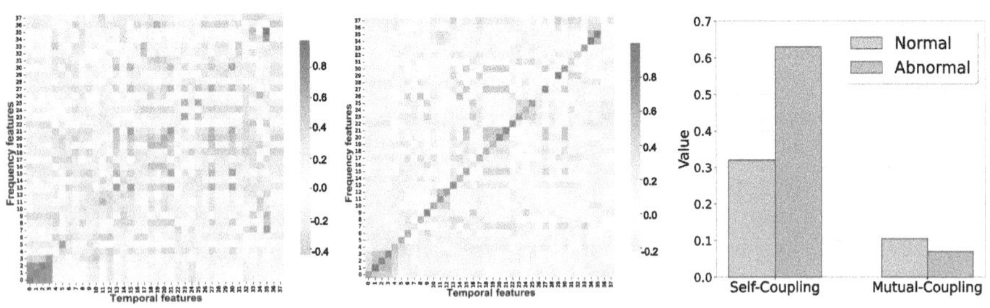

(a) Normal pattern (b) Abnormal pattern (c) Quantitative TFCD

Fig. 1. Visualization of the Temporal-Frequency Coupling on the SMD dataset. The heatmaps display the cross-domain feature interaction matrix. The diagonal elements capture Point-wise Self-Coupling, while off-diagonal elements capture Contextual Mutual-Coupling. A redder color indicates higher coupling. (a) Normal: maintaining stable Mutual-Coupling. (b) abnormal: the diagonal shows a strong Self-Coupling. (c) Quantification: significant coupling discrepancy between normal and abnormal.

Our key observation is that normal and abnormal patterns exhibit fundamentally different geometric behaviors during cross-domain interactions. As illustrated in Fig. 1, we compute a temporal-frequency interaction matrix to visualize the joint distribution of features. In this matrix, we define Point-wise Self-Coupling as the correlation between the temporal and frequency features at the same timestamp (the diagonal elements), and Contextual Mutual-Coupling as the correlation across different timestamps within the window (the off-diagonal elements). Normal patterns follow a smooth, stationary sequence evolution, exhibiting a globally dispersed distribution with stable Contextual Mutual-Coupling (Fig. 1a). In contrast, an anomaly typically behaves as a non-stationary temporal impulse. This sharp transient intrinsically induces a broadband frequency response, forcing the temporal and spectral energies to severely couple at that specific isolated timestamp. This physical phenomenon breaks the contextual stability and produces an abnormally strong Self-Coupling, resulting in a diagonally concentrated distribution (Fig. 1b). As shown in the quantitative analysis (Fig. 1c), the Self-Coupling of anomalous samples is approximately 29% higher than that of normal samples. Inspired by this geometric contrast, we propose Temporal-Frequency Coupling Discrepancy (TFCD), a novel criterion that constructs a new paradigm for anomaly discrimination by directly calculating the relative ratio of Self-Coupling to Mutual-Coupling.

Technically, we develop the TFCD-AD framework employing a dual-branch architecture. The frequency branch utilizes the Discrete Wavelet Transform (DWT) with self-attention to extract hierarchical spectral transients, while the temporal branch uses an Inverted Transformer [13] to capture long-range dependencies. Furthermore, we design a joint optimization objective that integrates a cross-reconstruction strategy with an explicit TFCD constraint. Specifically, temporal reconstruction is driven by a negative log-likelihood (NLL) term using frequency representations, while wavelet-domain frequency reconstruction is guided by temporal feature projections. The detection boundary is directly optimized by minimizing the TFCD loss during training. This joint objective ensures mutually beneficial representation learning while explicitly amplifying the normal-abnormal distinguishability. The main contributions are:

- We propose Temporal-Frequency Coupling Discrepancy (TFCD) as a novel metric. By quantifying the relative contrast between point-wise Self-Coupling and contextual Mutual-Coupling, TFCD provides a powerful criterion.
- We develop the TFCD-AD framework, which combines the DWT-based spectrum attention mechanism and the inverted Transformer to extract local transient spectrum changes and long-range global time dependence.
- We design a joint optimization objective integrating cross-reconstruction with explicit TFCD regularization, which optimizes the representation ability of the model, and amplifies the normal-abnormal separability of TFCD.
- Extensive experiments on six benchmarks, demonstrate that TFCD-AD outperforms state-of-the-art baselines. Achieving improvements of 6.21% in AUC-ROC and 6.42% in VUS-PR on TSB-AD-M.

2 Related Work

Temporal Representation. Early anomaly detection approaches primarily utilized statistical measures or time-domain reconstruction architectures. Methods such as LSTM-VAE and DAGMM [18,31] introduced end-to-end autoencoding frameworks to model reconstruction errors and latent representations simultaneously. To improve robustness against stochastic noise, OmniAnomaly and USAD [4,21] incorporated stochastic latent variables and adversarial training. With the advent of attention mechanisms, models like Anomaly-Transformer and TranAD [23,26] leveraged self-attention to capture long-range contextual dependencies and association discrepancies. Nevertheless, these single-domain methods inherently rely on temporal association. While they excel at modeling sequential step-by-step dynamics, they are prone to overlooking periodic failure features that are deeply masked by complex temporal noise.

Frequency Representation. To address the limitations of strict temporal modeling, subsequent studies explored the frequency domain to capture global periodic patterns. THOC [20] introduces hierarchical temporal representations to improve multi-scale modeling. More recently, TimesNet and DCdetector [25,28] transform 1D time series into 2D tensors or dual-attention representations to capture variations within and between periods, demonstrating superior performance on strongly periodic data. However, these approaches predominantly depend on frequency association, often treating spectral data as static features or preprocessing steps. This independent spectral modeling risks losing the transient local information required to identify non-stationary and sudden anomalies.

Dual-Domain Fusion. Recognizing the complementary nature of both domains, recent research has pivoted towards dual-domain and hybrid approaches. Methods such as TFAD and TFMAE [7,29] utilize FFT-based preprocessing to enhance input representations or mask frequency bands prior to temporal encoding. Dual-TF [16] employs a parallel branch design where temporal and frequency representations are encoded independently. Other recent advancements include FITS [27], which utilizes frequency interpolation for efficient modeling, and MSHTrans [6], which integrates multi-scale hypergraphs with time-series decomposition. Crucially, methods like TF-C [30] have explored temporal-frequency consistency, utilizing contrastive learning to align representations between the two domains. Despite these advancements, existing hybrid methods lack an explicit criterion to evaluate how anomalies disrupt cross-domain relationships. They generally treat temporal-frequency fusion as a generic feature enhancement step, overlooking the distinct coupling behaviors between normal and anomalous data.

In contrast, our approach directly addresses this limitation. By introducing the Temporal-Frequency Coupling Discrepancy (TFCD), we establish a direct and interpretable criterion.

3 Method

3.1 Formal Problem Definition

Let $\mathcal{X} = \{\mathbf{x}_t\}_{t=1}^{T} \in \mathbb{R}^{T \times V}$ denote a multivariate time series with T timestamps and V variables. In the unsupervised setting, we aim to learn a mapping $f : \mathbb{R}^{T \times V} \rightarrow \mathbb{R}^{T}$ that assigns an anomaly score s_t to each timestamp, where higher scores indicate a higher probability of an anomaly occurring at timestamp t.

3.2 Architecture of TFCD-AD

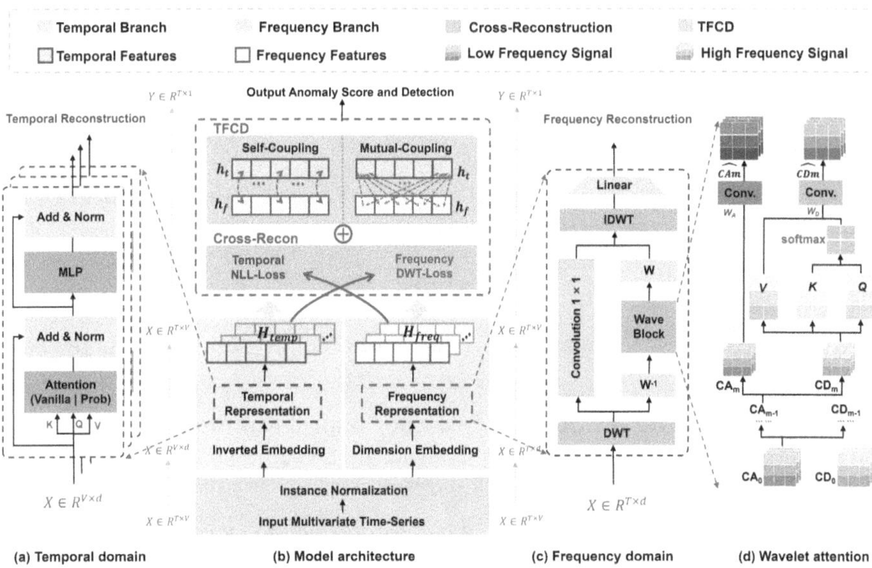

Fig. 2. The TFCD-AD framework is composed of the time domain branch of the inverted Transformer and the frequency domain branch of DWT. The feature learning and anomaly detection are realized by TFCD and Cross-Reconstruction.

As illustrated in Fig. 2b, TFCD-AD adopts a dual-branch encoder architecture. The input series first undergoes instance normalization to mitigate scale discrepancies. It is then processed by two parallel branches. Temporal Branch utilizes an Inverted Transformer to capture long-range dependencies. Frequency Branch employs a DWT-based multi-scale encoder to extract spectral patterns. Based on the extracted temporal and frequency features, the point-wise cross-domain Self-Coupling and the sequence-neighborhood Mutual-Coupling are calculated for each timestamp. TFCD is then derived from the relative contrast between these two couplings. As an unsupervised task, we design a joint training objective combining Cross-Reconstruction loss with an explicit TFCD regularization. This strategy optimizes the model's ability to characterize complex spatio-temporal dynamics while explicitly amplifying the normal-abnormal distinguishability.

Temporal Reconstruction. To capture channel-wise temporal dynamics, we leverage the Inverted Transformer architecture [13], where each variable is treated as an independent token to enable cross-variable attention.

Temporal Feature Extraction: Given the input sequence $\mathcal{X} \in \mathbb{R}^{T \times V}$, it is transposed and mapped to the high-dimensional latent space. After passing through the inverted embedding layer, the sequence is fed into an L layer self-attention encoder:

$$H_{\text{temp}} = \text{Encoder}\big(\text{Embed}_{\text{inv}}(\mathcal{X}^T)\big) \tag{1}$$

where $H_{\text{temp}} \in \mathbb{R}^{V \times d_{\text{model}}}$ not only aggregates the global temporal dependence of each variable, but also captures the inter-variable correlations via the attention mechanism.

Temporal Reconstruction: The latent representation is projected back to the temporal domain to reconstruct the original series:

$$\hat{\mathcal{X}}_{\text{temp}} = \text{permute}(H_{\text{temp}} W_{\text{rec}} + b_{\text{rec}}) \tag{2}$$

where $W_{\text{rec}} \in \mathbb{R}^{d_{\text{model}} \times T}$ and $b_{\text{rec}} \in \mathbb{R}^T$ are learnable projection parameters.

Frequency Reconstruction. The frequency branch captures multi-scale spectral patterns using Discrete Wavelet Transform (DWT)(Fig. 2d) combined with a specialized attention mechanism (Fig. 2c).

Frequency Feature Extraction: The input sequence $\mathcal{X} \in \mathbb{R}^{T \times V}$ is mapped to $\mathbb{R}^{T \times d_{\text{model}}}$ and fed into the DWT module. We utilize the wavelet function ψ to decompose it into an approximate coefficient $A^{(m)}$ (low-frequency trends) and detail coefficient $D_k^{(m)}$ (high-frequency transients) at scale m:

$$\mathcal{X}_{\text{wave}}^{(m)} = \text{DWT}^{(m)}(\mathcal{X}) = \left(A^{(m)}, D_1^{(m)}, \ldots, D_m^{(m)}\right) \tag{3}$$

To capture dependencies across decomposition scales, we apply a wavelet attention mechanism. For scale m, the approximation CA_m and detail CD_m features are updated by fusing information from the previous scale via convolutions and attention weights Attn_m. Subsequently, the concatenated representation of these updated features, denoted as $\mathcal{X}_{\text{freq}}^{(m)}$, is encoded into a unified feature space $H_{\text{freq}}^{(m)}$:

$$H_{\text{freq}}^{(m)} = \text{PReLU}\left(\text{permute}(\mathcal{X}_{\text{freq}}^{(m)}) W_s^{(m)} + b_s^{(m)}\right) \tag{4}$$

where $W_s^{(m)}$ and $b_s^{(m)}$ are scale-specific learnable weights and biases, and $\text{permute}(\cdot)$ aligns the tensor dimensions. The multi-scale feature $H_{\text{freq}}^{(m)} \in$

$\mathbb{R}^{\frac{T}{2^m} \times d_{\text{model}}}$ is then restored to a global frequency representation $H_{\text{freq}} \in \mathbb{R}^{T \times d_{\text{model}}}$ via the Inverse Discrete Wavelet Transform (IDWT).

Frequency Reconstruction: The latent features are projected back to the wavelet coefficient dimension and transformed to the temporal domain through IDWT:

$$\hat{\mathcal{X}}_{\text{freq}} = \text{permute}\left(\text{IDWT}^{(m)}(\hat{\mathcal{X}}_{\text{freq}}^{(m)})W_{\text{proj}} + b_{\text{proj}}\right) \tag{5}$$

where $\hat{\mathcal{X}}_{\text{freq}}^{(m)}$ represents the latent features within the wavelet domain. $W_{\text{proj}} \in \mathbb{R}^{d_{\text{model}} \times V}$ and $b_{\text{proj}} \in \mathbb{R}^{V}$ map the hidden dimension back to the variable dimension V. This process ensures the stable modeling of the periodic mode while filtering out the noise.

Temporal-Frequency Coupling Discrepancy. In classical signal processing, normal time series typically exhibit stationary variations with globally distributed spectral energy. Conversely, anomalies often manifest as non-stationary temporal impulses. According to the time-frequency uncertainty principle [14], such sharp, localized temporal variations intrinsically provoke a broadband response distributed across multiple frequency scales. This mathematical property forces an intensive, point-wise energy coupling between the temporal and spectral representations at that specific timestamp. Temporal-Frequency Coupling Discrepancy (TFCD) is designed to capture this structural discrepancy by contrasting the point-wise Self-Coupling against the contextual Mutual-Coupling.

As the core of our work, we TFCD to precisely quantify the anomaly degree. Before performing cross-domain calculations, H_{temp} and H_{freq} are mapped to an aligned spatio-temporal space $\mathbb{R}^{T \times d_{\text{model}}}$ and normalized. Let $Z_{temp} = \{z_{temp,t}\}_{t=1}^{T}$ and $Z_{freq} = \{z_{freq,t}\}_{t=1}^{T}$ represent the aligned temporal and frequency feature sequences respectively. To evaluate the anomaly degree, we systematically decompose the Temporal-Frequency domain interaction into two distinct perspectives : Point-wise Self-Coupling and contextual-wise Mutual-Coupling.

Self-Coupling: Point-wise Self-Coupling measures the association between the temporal dynamics and spectral patterns at the exact same timestamp. For a specific timestamp t, the Self-Coupling $C_{\text{self}}(t)$ is defined using the exponential scaled dot-product:

$$C_{\text{self}}(t) = \exp\left(\frac{z_{temp,t} \cdot z_{freq,t}}{\epsilon}\right) \tag{6}$$

where $z_{temp,t}, z_{freq,t} \in \mathbb{R}^{d_{\text{model}}}$. Since the vectors are L_2 normalized, the dot product represents cosine similarity. ϵ is a temperature hyperparameter (set to 0.5) to control the sharpness of similarity distribution. A higher $C_{\text{self}}(t)$ indicates a stronger correlation between the two domains.

Mutual-Coupling: contextual-wise Mutual-Coupling evaluates the global association between the temporal state at current time t and the frequency states across the entire contextual window. The contextual Mutual-Coupling $C_{\text{Mutual}}(t)$ is formulated as the sum of similarities over the temporal window T:

$$C_{\text{Mutual}}(t) = \sum_{j=1}^{T} \exp\left(\frac{z_{temp,t} \cdot z_{freq,j}}{\epsilon}\right) \tag{7}$$

where $z_{freq,j}$ denotes the frequency feature at the j-th timestamp.

Definition of TFCD: Temporal-Frequency Coupling Discrepancy quantifies the relative contrast between Self-Coupling and Mutual-Coupling:

$$TFCD(t) = \frac{C_{\text{self}}(t)}{C_{\text{Mutual}}(t)} \tag{8}$$

Under normal conditions, the temporal and frequency representations maintain structural independence, preventing the local association $C_{\text{self}}(t)$ from overwhelmingly dominating $C_{\text{Mutual}}(t)$, thus resulting in a consistently low $TFCD(t)$ score. Conversely, anomalous broadband responses force a strong localized correlation, significantly amplifying $C_{\text{self}}(t)$ and consequently yielding a high $TFCD(t)$ value.

3.3 Optimization Target

As an unsupervised task, we optimize the dual-branch network using a joint objective. The objective integrates a cross-reconstruction strategy to learn robust representation and an explicit TFCD learning mechanism to amplify the discrepancy between normal and abnormal states.

Cross-Reconstruction Learning. To ensure mutually beneficial feature extraction, we cross-reconstruct the temporal and frequency domains.

Frequency-View: This term measures how well the frequency branch explains temporal dynamics. We define it using the Negative Log-Likelihood (NLL) given the frequency prediction:

$$\mathcal{I}_{\text{freq}}(t) = \frac{1}{V}\sum_{v=1}^{V}\left(\frac{1}{2}\log\sigma_{\text{freq},t,v}^{-1} + \frac{1}{2}\exp(-\log\sigma_{\text{freq},t,v}^{-1})(x_{t,v} - \hat{x}_{\text{freq},t,v})^2\right) \tag{9}$$

By dynamically down-weighting the reconstruction penalty via the local spectral uncertainty $\log\sigma\text{freq}^{-1}$ [8], training stability against intrinsic data noise is significantly enhanced.

Temporal-View: This term measures how well the temporal branch explains the structural spectral patterns. We project the temporal reconstruction back into the wavelet domain and compute the Multi-scale MSE:

$$\mathcal{I}_{\text{temp}}(t) = \lambda \cdot \text{MSE}(A_t, \hat{A}_t) + (1-\lambda) \cdot \sum_{k=1}^{J} w_k \cdot \text{MSE}(D_{k,t}, \hat{D}_{k,t}) \tag{10}$$

where w_k = Softmax($k/2$) assigns exponentially penalties to high-frequency details. $\lambda \in [0, 1]$ is a hyperparameter that balances the optimization between A_t and $D_{k,t}$.

TFCD Learning. While reconstruction losses ensure robust representation learning, they do not directly optimize the normal-abnormal detection boundary. To explicitly address this, we introduce the TFCD learning constraint:

$$\mathcal{I}_{\text{TFCD}}(t) = TFCD(t) \tag{11}$$

During training, minimizing $\mathcal{I}_{\text{TFCD}}(t)$ forces the network to learn decoupled, orthogonal stationary temporal and spectral representations of normal patterns, establishing a structural margin constraint rather than a logical shortcut. During inference, non-stationary anomalies inherently disrupts this learned orthogonality, triggering an increase in point-wise coupling, leading to an elevated TFCD score that explicitly exposes the anomaly.

Loss Function. The final training objective is formulated as the mathematical expectation across the entire training time window $\mathcal{T}$:

$$\mathcal{L}_{\text{total}} = \frac{1}{T} \sum_{t \in \mathcal{T}} \Big((1 - \alpha) \big(\mathcal{I}_{\text{freq}}(t) + \mathcal{I}_{\text{temp}}(t) \big) + \alpha \mathcal{I}_{\text{TFCD}}(t) \Big) \tag{12}$$

where $\alpha \in [0, 1]$ is a hyperparameter balancing the reconstruction robust learning and the TFCD boundary amplification.

3.4 Anomaly Score

The anomaly score $S(t)$ fuses bias of $\mathcal{I}_{\text{freq}}(t)$, $\mathcal{I}_{\text{temp}}(t)$ and $\mathcal{I}_{\text{TFCD}}(t)$ from different views. Since our optimization objective is based on the point-wise association, we directly utilize the instance-level metrics to construct the anomaly score:

$$S(t) = \mathcal{I}_{\text{freq}}(t) + \mathcal{I}_{\text{temp}}(t) + \mathcal{I}_{\text{TFCD}}(t) \tag{13}$$

To derive the final binary predictions, we establish a threshold τ based on the percentile distribution of anomaly scores within the validation set. Consequently, a data point at timestamp t is classified as anomalous if its corresponding score $S(t)$ exceeds this threshold τ.

4 Experiment

To validate the effectiveness of our TFCD-AD, we conduct comprehensive experiments on six datasets to answer the following five research questions:

- **RQ1:** Does our TFCD-AD demonstrate superior performance compared to baselines across diverse datasets?

- **RQ2:** How do components within TFCD-AD impact the performance of anomaly detection?
- **RQ3:** How does TFCD-AD amplify TFCD during training process compared to other dual-domain methods?
- **RQ4:** Is the ability of TFCD to discriminate abnormalities better than temporal/frequency representations?
- **RQ5:** How does adjusting the core hyperparameters impact the performance of TFCD-AD?

4.1 Experimental Setup

Datasets. We conduct extensive experiments on 6 realworld datasets, including MSL [9], PSM [1], SMD [22], SWaT [15], WADI [3] and TSB-AD-M (TSB-M) [12]. The dataset details and statistics in Table 1.

Table 1. Dataset statistics used in our experiments. Dims denotes the number of dimensions (variables). Train and Test indicate the average number of time points in training and labeled test sets, respectively. Rate denotes the anomaly rate (%). TSB-AD-M is multivariate subset of the TSB-AD benchmark.

Dataset	Source	Dims	Train	Test	Rate
MSL	NASA Space Sensors	55	58,317	73,729	10.48
PSM	eBay Server Machine	25	132,481	87,941	27.76
SMD	Internet Server	38	708,405	708,420	4.16
SWaT	Infrastructure System	51	495,000	449,919	12.14
WADI	Infrastructure System	123	1,209,601	172,801	5.71
TSB-AD-M	TSB-AD Multivariate	Variable	98,164(Avg.)	108,827(Avg.)	5.00

Baselines. We compared with representative baseline methods. (1) Temporal-domain: DAGMM [31], OmniAnomaly (O.A.) [21], USAD [4] and TimesNet (T.Net) [25]; (2) Frequency-domain: THOC [20]; (3) Dual-domain: TFMAE [7], TFAD [29], Dual-TF (D.TF) [16]; (4) Statistical baselines: PCA [2], AR [19]; (5) Latest baseline method: LSTM-VAE (L.V.) [18], Anomaly-Transformer (A.T.) [26], TranAD (T.AD) [23], DCdetector (D.C.) [28], SensitiveHUE (S.HUE) [8], CrossAD (C.AD) [10]. We evaluate results across 8 metrics, with detailed reports in Appendix A.2.

Metrics. we adopt two categories of evaluation metrics: (1) Label-based metrics include Precision, Precision (P), Recall (R), F1-Score (F1) and employ a diverse set of F1 variants. Specifically, for the TSB-AD benchmark, we report Standard-F1, Event-based-F1, R-based-F1, and Affiliation-F1 in Appendix B; (2) score-based metrics include AUC-ROC (A-ROC), AUC-PR (A-PR) [5], VUS-ROC (V-ROC) and VUS-PR (V-PR) [17].

Implementation Details. For all datasets, the hyperparameter λ of the loss balancing term is set to 0.5. Wavelet functions and decomposition levels are dataset-specific. Following front work A.T. [26] and D.C. [28], the anomaly threshold is determined by the anomaly ratio r in the validation set: 0.1% for SWaT, 0.5% for SMD, 5% for TSB-AD-M and 1% for other datasets. The model initially utilizes a dual-branch encoder architecture ($L = 3$) with a hidden dimension $d_{\text{model}} = 256$. We optimize the model using Adam with an initial learning rate of 10^{-4} and a batch size of 128. All experiments are conducted Python 3.11 using PyTorch on a single NVIDIA RTX 4090 GPU. The specific parameter settings of each data set in Appendix A.4. Each experiment was run independently three times under different random seeds, with the average results reported.

Table 2. Performance comparison of the model under six datasets. All index units are %, **bold** indicates the optimal performance and underline indicates the suboptimal performance.

Dataset	Metric	Ours	C.AD	TFMAE	S.HUE	D.TF	T.Net	D.C.	TFAD	T.AD	A.T.	O.A.	L.V.	PCA	AR
MSL	A-ROC	67.32 ± 0.35	**77.35**	50.03	66.07	46.78	70.86	50.06	51.97	53.81	48.72	51.74	51.07	64.97	65.32
	A-PR	**62.28 ± 0.07**	28.36	10.54	57.41	10.17	21.57	10.61	6.59	13.94	10.64	17.42	4.63	55.16	56.09
	V-ROC	68.21 ± 0.25	**80.91**	51.23	66.15	41.12	78.80	51.16	51.04	64.54	51.27	54.90	49.63	65.17	65.64
	V-PR	**62.16 ± 0.02**	31.44	15.27	57.30	11.25	27.31	15.23	6.50	11.57	18.99	19.73	4.91	55.11	55.98
PSM	A-ROC	**71.27 ± 0.22**	70.61	50.05	50.31	58.68	61.09	49.83	54.38	50.20	48.56	61.53	38.45	59.66	54.44
	A-PR	**67.05 ± 0.18**	52.76	27.78	56.93	31.04	32.43	27.64	35.10	35.22	29.42	43.37	27.92	66.51	65.10
	V-ROC	70.15 ± 0.26	**73.02**	51.86	51.50	68.47	63.44	51.05	53.59	49.47	51.23	63.40	50.57	65.72	60.49
	V-PR	**67.03 ± 0.09**	55.96	34.13	65.96	45.79	43.73	28.95	35.02	35.19	35.41	44.72	35.59	66.06	64.75
SMD	A-ROC	77.85 ± 0.19	**83.17**	50.16	70.13	65.77	76.32	48.77	63.46	46.86	47.28	67.92	50.05	77.27	72.95
	A-PR	63.23 ± 0.45	21.93	4.17	**69.24**	2.64	14.87	4.16	9.98	5.92	3.70	15.17	4.15	61.43	55.54
	V-ROC	72.26 ± 0.19	**85.80**	51.18	70.23	53.87	84.20	50.67	61.77	46.54	50.42	70.80	50.13	74.75	70.01
	V-PR	61.39 ± 0.50	23.44	11.36	**68.26**	3.74	20.40	7.34	9.64	5.88	4.23	13.40	16.49	59.58	54.57
SWaT	A-ROC	**88.80 ± 0.43**	76.48	49.97	61.94	73.68	24.75	49.74	18.35	47.78	29.40	60.04	49.59	84.63	84.77
	A-PR	**81.63 ± 0.05**	45.26	12.13	37.86	56.83	11.02	11.60	11.92	17.65	8.82	48.53	4.13	68.62	76.35
	V-ROC	**81.05 ± 0.61**	78.65	49.96	60.49	74.67	29.74	50.15	18.31	47.13	50.01	61.87	47.27	63.40	72.86
	V-PR	**80.64 ± 0.34**	47.67	9.87	35.86	57.27	11.58	7.29	11.92	17.57	6.53	44.75	3.98	68.30	75.94
WADI	A-ROC	**77.17 ± 0.07**	73.12	50.15	72.18	76.11	58.31	50.14	46.66	48.24	50.12	60.43	46.29	73.71	64.71
	A-PR	**63.62 ± 0.53**	18.53	8.34	62.83	27.78	11.40	6.71	3.65	13.76	46.01	18.61	6.16	56.54	56.09
	V-ROC	73.80 ± 0.42	76.67	50.15	72.27	**77.82**	61.53	50.01	46.33	63.25	50.10	61.07	46.26	68.62	56.27
	V-PR	**63.06 ± 0.02**	19.41	8.49	62.82	27.65	14.86	6.54	3.63	14.33	45.97	16.47	6.15	56.45	56.04
TSB-M	A-ROC	**80.21 ± 0.13**	74.00	56.26	66.25	68.53	56.00	56.94	49.64	59.00	52.00	65.00	50.98	70.00	60.68
	A-PR	**54.94 ± 0.17**	34.00	14.61	51.34	29.78	13.00	15.47	18.34	14.00	7.00	27.00	15.72	31.00	22.40
	V-ROC	**81.36 ± 0.14**	77.00	52.29	64.19	65.91	64.00	54.83	52.23	65.00	57.00	69.00	53.40	74.00	57.22
	V-PR	**56.47 ± 0.24**	33.00	17.43	50.05	32.57	19.00	15.02	14.42	18.00	12.00	31.00	21.85	31.00	22.24
Count		**16**	5	0	2	1	0	0	0	0	0	0	0	0	0

4.2 Overall Performance (RQ1)

We compare TFCD-AD against state-of-the-art baselines on six multivariate datasets. As shown in Table 2. TFCD-AD demonstrates great performance, ranking first in 16 out of 24 evaluation settings. A-PR and V-PR achieved the optimal or suboptimal results on all datasets. On the TSB-AD-M dataset, all four metrics reached the optimal or near-optimal levels. Compared with the baseline method,

A-ROC increased by 6.21% and V-PR increased by 6.42%. All metrics on SWaT exceeded 80%. These results confirm that TFCD-AD effectively balances precision and recall, establishing a new benchmark for anomaly discrimination.

4.3 Ablation Studies (RQ2)

As shown in Table 3, we validate the effectiveness of TFCD-AD components from three perspectives.

Dual-Branch Necessity. Removing either the frequency (i) or temporal (ii) branch significantly degrades performance. Removing the frequency branch causes a 24.49% A-ROC drop on SWaT , while eliminating temporal modeling severely impacts MSL and PSM, confirming that single-domain features are insufficient for comprehensive representation.

Optimization Mechanism. We evaluated the removal of cross-reconstruction mechanism (iii) and removal of TFCD mechanism (iv). After removing the cross-reconstruction and the TFCD mechanism, the A-PR of SWaT decreased by 19.37%, indicating that joint optimization is crucial for enhancing the discriminant ability of the model. Furthermore, to investigate the internal dynamics of the TFCD mechanism, we evaluate variants utilizing only the Self-Coupling mechanism (v) and only the Mutual-Couping mechanism (vi). Both variants exhibit a consistent decline in A-ROC and A-PR across all datasets, including a notable 7.54% decrease in A-ROC on the WADI. This shows that the relative contrast between learning Self-Coupling and Mutual-Coupling can effectively improve the accuracy of the model to distinguish anomalies.

Robustness. We integrated TFCD into Dual-TF (vii), which originally relies on simple superposition. The TFCD-enhanced Dual-TF (viii) achieves remarkable gains, including a +40.32% A-PR surge on MSL and +28.41% A-PR on PSM. Overall, the complete TFCD-AD (ix) consistently ranks first across all 10 evaluation metrics.

4.4 Case Visualization (RQ3,RQ4)

Analysis of TFCD (RQ3). To verify the convergence stability and effectiveness of the proposed method, Fig. 3 visualizes the training of both the loss and DIFF_{TFCD} on the SMD dataset. We define $\mathrm{DIFF}_{TFCD} = \mathrm{TFCD}_{abnormal} - \mathrm{TFCD}_{normal}$ to quantify the margin between anomalous and normal samples. During training, a decreasing loss coupled with an increasing DIFF_{TFCD} indicates that the model is progressively amplifying this discrepancy, making anomalies more distinguishable. As shown in Fig. 3b, while Dual-TF achieves rapid loss convergence, its DIFF_{TFCD} exhibits unstable fluctuations, eventually collapsing to a low level of 1.4%. Similarly, the two variants in Fig. 3c and 3d suffer from slower convergence rates and suboptimal DIFF_{TFCD} gain, which respectively stabilizes at 14.3% and 3.6%. In contrast, TFCD-AD demonstrates superior optimization dynamics: the loss decreases monotonically, while the DIFF_{TFCD}

Table 3. Ablation studies on different models and loss functions. T and F represent Temporal-domain and frequency-domain respectively, and D represents dual-branch. Self and Mutual are Self-Coupling and Mutual-Coupling respectively. All index units are %, **bold** indicates the optimal performance and underline indicates the suboptimal performance.

CAT	Variation		MSL		PSM		SMD		SWaT		WADI		cnt
	Model	Loss	A-ROC	A-PR	A-ROC	A-PR	A-ROC	A-PR	A-ROC	A-PR	A-ROC	A-PR	
Var.	(i) w/ T	w/ L_{Temp}	66.70	53.65	70.05	61.51	69.54	57.78	64.31	57.81	70.91	38.90	0
	(ii) w/ F	w/ L_{Freq}	64.13	50.21	57.24	52.91	67.91	53.81	75.10	66.57	62.51	49.01	0
	(iii) w/ D	w/o Cross	65.34	52.94	65.58	60.34	69.13	59.22	59.98	62.26	57.73	38.35	0
	(iv) w/ D	w/o TFCD	64.11	54.40	68.92	63.07	70.82	62.65	68.65	72.41	61.39	53.77	0
	(v) w/ D	w/o Self	66.19	57.48	68.09	64.22	71.05	62.86	78.97	79.54	69.63	56.76	0
	(vi) w/ D	w/o Mutual	65.96	56.93	68.84	64.37	71.26	62.26	77.94	78.52	70.33	59.54	0
D.TF	(vii) w/ D_{ttf}	w/ KL	46.78	10.17	58.68	31.04	65.67	2.64	73.68	56.83	76.11	27.78	0
	(viii) w/ D_{ttf}	w/ TFCD	52.05	50.49	64.95	59.41	70.43	48.32	70.47	66.59	72.05	51.62	0
Ours	**(ix) w/ D_{dwt}**	**w/ TFCD**	**67.32**	**62.28**	**71.27**	**67.05**	**77.85**	**63.23**	**88.80**	**81.63**	**77.17**	**63.62**	**10**

value shows a steady upward trend, stabilizing at a significant level of 20% in Fig. 3a. This confirms that the proposed Interactive Consistency Loss not only ensures robust convergence but also effectively maximizes the normal-abnormal discrepancy for accurate anomaly detection.

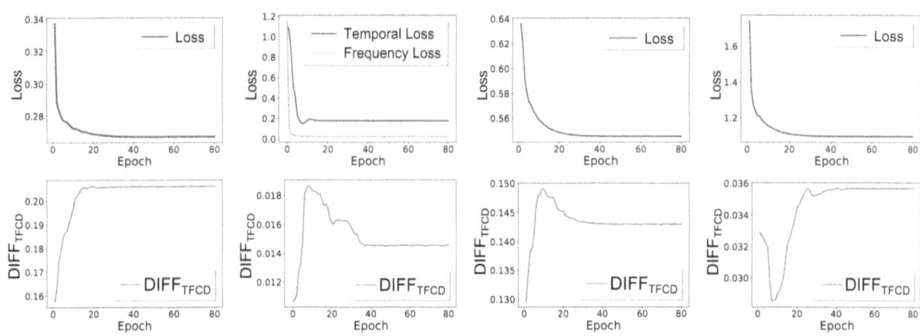

(a) TFCD-AD (b) Dual-TF (c) Variant-iii (d) Variant-iv

Fig. 3. Comparison of Loss and DIFF_{TFCD} change trends during training on the SMD dataset. DIFF_{TFCD} is defined as $\mathrm{TFCD}_{abnormal} - \mathrm{TFCD}_{normal}$, and the index unit is %. (a) The proposed TFCD-AD method; (b) Baseline Dual-TF method; (c) Variant-iii(removing the cross-reconstruction mechanism); (d) Variant-iv(removing the TFCD mechanism).

Analysis of Discriminative (RQ4). To verify the effectiveness of TFCD-AD to distinguish abnormal patterns, we visualize the latent representations on the SMD dataset using UMAP. As shown in Fig. 4a and Fig. 4b, single-domain models exhibit significant overlap between normal (blue) and anomalous (red) samples. Specifically, the independent frequency model fails to capture temporal dependencies, while the temporal model misses periodic nuances, leading to confusion. In contrast, TFCD-AD learns the temporal-frequency features by using the cross-reconstruction mechanism, and uses TFCD to achieve a clear distinction (Fig. 4c). Quantitative metrics (Fig. 4d) confirm this improvement: compared to single-domain baselines, TFCD-AD increases the inter-class distance from 4.18 to 5.49 (+1.31) and reduces intra-class variance from 2.88 to 1.49 (−1.39). These results show that TFCD can effectively solve the problem of feature confusion and improve the distinguishability of outliers.

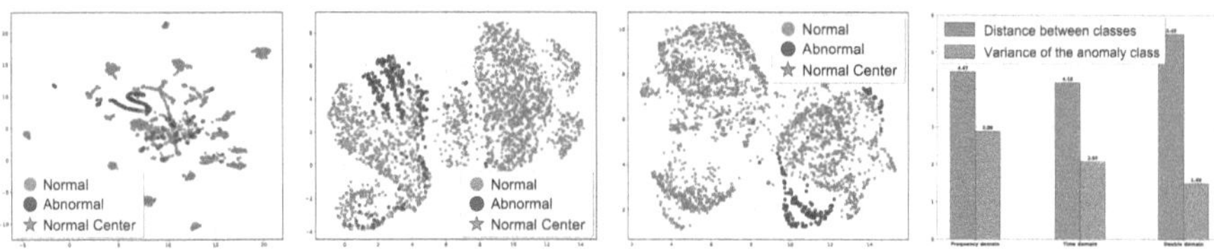

(a) Frequency (b) Temporal (c) Interactive (d) Quantification

Fig. 4. UMAP dimensionality reduction visualization of learning features in SMD dataset subsequences using different Angle methods. Blue and red dots are clearly separated, and anomalies are better distinguished. (Color figure online)

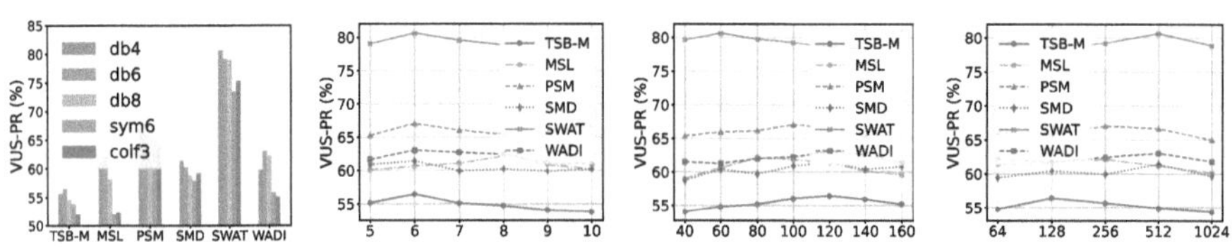

(a) DWT (b) Decomposition (c) Window size (d) d_{model} size

Fig. 5. The core parameter sensitivity experiment of TFCD-AD. Sensitivity and efficiency analysis of other parameters are shown in Appendix C and D.

4.5 Parameter Sensitivity (RQ5)

We evaluate the impact of four key hyperparameters in Fig. 5. **Frequency hyperparameters:** Among wavelet families, Daubechies (db6) consistently outperforms others, like 80.64% V-PR on SWaT, due to its superior orthogonality and smoothness. For the DWT decomposition level, performance generally peaks at level 6 or 8 across datasets, offering the optimal trade-off between spectral resolution and noise rejection. **Temporal hyperparameters:** The model exhibits strong robustness to sliding window sizes in the range from 40 to 160. We set the initial window size to 100 by default. Crucially, the window size dictates not only the input length but also the context available for computing the Mutual-Coupling. Regarding the hidden dimension d_{model}, performance typically saturates at 256.

5 Conclusion

In this paper, we propose TFCD-AD, a novel unsupervised anomaly detection framework for multivariate time series. We demonstrate that the discrepancy between point-wise Self-Coupling and contextual Mutual-Coupling serves as a powerful anomaly indicator. To exploit this, our dual-branch architecture integrates a DWT-based attention mechanism with an inverted Transformer for deep time-frequency feature extraction. Furthermore, a joint optimization strategy utilizing Cross-Reconstruction and explicit TFCD regularization effectively amplifies the separability of normal and abnormal patterns. We believe our unique perspective on temporal-frequency coupling discrepancy offers a promising direction for complex anomaly detection tasks.

Acknowledgments. This work is supported by the National Key Research and Development Project of China (Grant No. 2024YFB3309900), the Fundamental Research Funds for the Central Universities (Grant No. 2025CDJZKKYJH-08).

AI-Generated Content Acknowledgement. This work did not utilize AI-generated tools to contribute to the content, analysis, and core innovations of the paper. It was used solely for spelling correction and formatting review.

Ethical Statement. The work of our paper focuses on more accurate time series prediction, so there are no ethical issues involved.

References

1. Abdulaal, A., Liu, Z., Lancewicki, T.: Practical approach to asynchronous multivariate time series anomaly detection and localization. In: KDD 2021: The 27th ACM SIGKDD Conference on Knowledge Discovery and Data Mining, pp. 2485–2494. ACM (2021). https://doi.org/10.1145/3447548.3467174
2. Aggarwal, C.C.: Linear models for outlier detection. In: Aggarwal, C.C. (ed.) Outlier Analysis, pp. 65–110. Springer, Cham (2016). https://doi.org/10.1007/978-3-319-47578-3_3
3. Ahmed, C.M., Palleti, V.R., Mathur, A.P.: WADI: a water distribution testbed for research in the design of secure cyber physical systems. In: Tsakalides, P., Beferull-Lozano, B. (eds.) Proceedings of the 3rd International Workshop on Cyber-Physical Systems for Smart Water Networks, CySWATER@CPSWeek 2017, Pittsburgh, Pennsylvania, USA, 21 April 2017, pp. 25–28. ACM (2017). https://doi.org/10.1145/3055366.3055375
4. Audibert, J., Michiardi, P., Guyard, F., Marti, S., Zuluaga, M.A.: USAD: unsupervised anomaly detection on multivariate time series. In: KDD 2020: The 26th ACM SIGKDD Conference on Knowledge Discovery and Data Mining, 23–27 August 2020, pp. 3395–3404. ACM (2020). https://doi.org/10.1145/3394486.3403392

5. Boyd, K., Eng, K.H., Page, C.D.: Area under the precision-recall curve: point estimates and confidence intervals. In: Blockeel, H., Kersting, K., Nijssen, S., Železný, F. (eds.) ECML PKDD 2013, Part III. LNCS (LNAI), vol. 8190, pp. 451–466. Springer, Heidelberg (2013). https://doi.org/10.1007/978-3-642-40994-3_29
6. Chen, Z., Wu, Z., Cheung, W.K., Dai, H., Choi, B., Liu, J.: Mshtrans: multi-scale hypergraph transformer with time-series decomposition for temporal anomaly detection. In: Antonie, L., Pei, J., Yu, X., Chierichetti, F., Lauw, H.W., Sun, Y., Parthasarathy, S. (eds.) Proceedings of the 31st ACM SIGKDD Conference on Knowledge Discovery and Data Mining, V.2, KDD 2025, Toronto ON, Canada, 3–7 August 2025, pp. 274–285. ACM (2025). https://doi.org/10.1145/3711896.3737057
7. Fang, Y., Xie, J., Zhao, Y., Chen, L., Gao, Y., Zheng, K.: Temporal-frequency masked autoencoders for time series anomaly detection. In: 2024 IEEE 40th International Conference on Data Engineering (ICDE), pp. 1228–1241 (2024)
8. Feng, Y., Zhang, W., Fu, Y., Jiang, W., Zhu, J., Ren, W.: SensitiveHUE: multivariate time series anomaly detection by enhancing the sensitivity to normal patterns. In: Proceedings of the 30th ACM SIGKDD Conference on Knowledge Discovery and Data Mining, KDD 2024, pp. 782–793 (2024). https://doi.org/10.1145/3637528.3671919
9. Hundman, K., Constantinou, V., Laporte, C., Colwell, I., Soderstrom, T.: Detecting spacecraft anomalies using LSTMs and nonparametric dynamic thresholding. In: Proceedings of the 24th ACM SIGKDD International Conference on Knowledge Discovery & Data Mining, KDD 2018, pp. 387–395. Association for Computing Machinery, New York (2018). https://doi.org/10.1145/3219819.3219845
10. Li, B., et al: CrossAD: time series anomaly detection with cross-scale associations and cross-window modeling (2025). https://arxiv.org/abs/2510.12489
11. Li, Z., et al.: Multivariate time series anomaly detection and interpretation using hierarchical inter-metric and temporal embedding. In: Proceedings of the 27th ACM SIGKDD Conference on Knowledge Discovery & Data Mining, pp. 3220–3230 (2021)
12. Liu, Q., Paparrizos, J.: The elephant in the room: towards a reliable time-series anomaly detection benchmark. Adv. Neural. Inf. Process. Syst. **37**, 108231–108261 (2024)
13. Liu, Y., et al.: iTransformer: inverted transformers are effective for time series forecasting. In: The Twelfth International Conference on Learning Representations, ICLR 2024, Vienna, Austria, 7–11 May 2024. OpenReview.net (2024)
14. Mallat, S.: A Wavelet Tour of Signal Processing. Elsevier (1999)
15. Mathur, A.P., Tippenhauer, N.O.: SWaT: a water treatment testbed for research and training on ICS security. In: 2016 International Workshop on Cyber-physical Systems for Smart Water Networks (CySWater), pp. 31–36 (2016). https://doi.org/10.1109/CySWater.2016.7469060
16. Nam, Yet al.: Breaking the time-frequency granularity discrepancy in time-series anomaly detection. In: Chua, T., Ngo, C., Kumar, R., Lauw, H.W., Lee, R.K. (eds.) Proceedings of the ACM on Web Conference 2024, WWW 2024, Singapore, 13–17 May 2024, pp. 4204–4215. ACM (2024). https://doi.org/10.1145/3589334.3645556
17. Paparrizos, J., Boniol, P., Palpanas, T., Tsay, R.S., Elmore, A.J., Franklin, M.J.: Volume under the surface: a new accuracy evaluation measure for time-series anomaly detection. Proc. VLDB Endow. **15**(11), 2774–2787 (2022). https://doi.org/10.14778/3551793.3551830

18. Park, D., Hoshi, Y., Kemp, C.C.: A multimodal anomaly detector for robot-assisted feeding using an LSTM-based variational autoencoder. IEEE Robot. Autom. Lett. **3**(2), 1544–1551 (2018). https://doi.org/10.1109/LRA.2018.2801475
19. Rousseeuw, P.J., Leroy, A.M.: Robust Regression and Outlier Detection. Wiley (2003)
20. Shen, L., Li, Z., Kwok, J.T.: Timeseries anomaly detection using temporal hierarchical one-class network. In: Advances in Neural Information Processing Systems 33: Annual Conference on Neural Information Processing Systems 2020, NeurIPS 2020, 6–12 December 2020, Virtual (2020)
21. Su, Y., Zhao, Y., Niu, C., Liu, R., Sun, W., Pei, D.: Robust anomaly detection for multivariate time series through stochastic recurrent neural network. In: Teredesai, A., Kumar, V., Li, Y., Rosales, R., Terzi, E., Karypis, G. (eds.) Proceedings of the 25th ACM SIGKDD International Conference on Knowledge Discovery & Data Mining, KDD 2019, Anchorage, AK, USA, 4–8 August 2019, pp. 2828–2837. ACM (2019). https://doi.org/10.1145/3292500.3330672
22. Su, Y., Zhao, Y., Niu, C., Liu, R., Sun, W., Pei, D.: Robust anomaly detection for multivariate time series through stochastic recurrent neural network. In: Proceedings of the 25th ACM SIGKDD International Conference on Knowledge Discovery & Data Mining, pp. 2828–2837. ACM (2019). https://doi.org/10.1145/3292500.3330672
23. Tuli, S., Casale, G., Jennings, N.R.: TranAD: deep transformer networks for anomaly detection in multivariate time series data. Proc. VLDB Endow. **15**(6), 1201–1214 (2022). https://doi.org/10.14778/3514061.3514067
24. Wang, Y., Hou, D., Gao, C., Li, X.: Learning neural jump stochastic differential equations with latent graph for multivariate temporal point processes. In: Proceedings of the Thirty-Fourth International Joint Conference on Artificial Intelligence, IJCAI 2025, Montreal, Canada, 16–22 August 2025. pp. 3444–3452. Ijcai.org (2025). https://doi.org/10.24963/IJCAI.2025/383
25. Wu, H., Hu, T., Liu, Y., Zhou, H., Wang, J., Long, M.: TimesNet: temporal 2D-variation modeling for general time series analysis. In: The Eleventh International Conference on Learning Representations, ICLR 2023, Kigali, Rwanda, 1–5 May 2023. OpenReview.net (2023)
26. Xu, J., Wu, H., Wang, J., Long, M.: Anomaly transformer: time series anomaly detection with association discrepancy. In: The Tenth International Conference on Learning Representations, ICLR 2022, Virtual Event, 25–29 April 2022. OpenReview.net (2022)
27. Xu, Z., Zeng, A., Xu, Q.: Fits: Modeling time series with $10k$ parameters. arXiv preprint arXiv:2307.03756 (2023)
28. Yang, Y., Zhang, C., Zhou, T., Wen, Q., Sun, L.: DCDetector: dual attention contrastive representation learning for time series anomaly detection. In: Proceedings of the 29th ACM SIGKDD Conference on Knowledge Discovery and Data Mining, KDD 2023, pp. 3033–3045 (2023). https://doi.org/10.1145/3580305.3599295
29. Zhang, C., Zhou, T., Wen, Q., Sun, L.: TFAD: a decomposition time series anomaly detection architecture with time-frequency analysis. In: Hasan, M.A., Xiong, L. (eds.) Proceedings of the 31st ACM International Conference on Information & Knowledge Management, Atlanta, GA, USA, 17–21 October 2022, pp. 2497–2507. ACM (2022). https://doi.org/10.1145/3511808.3557470

30. Zhang, X., Zhao, Z., Tsiligkaridis, T., Zitnik, M.: Self-supervised contrastive pre-training for time series via time-frequency consistency. In: Koyejo, S., Mohamed, S., Agarwal, A., Belgrave, D., Cho, K., Oh, A. (eds.) Advances in Neural Information Processing Systems 35: Annual Conference on Neural Information Processing Systems 2022, NeurIPS 2022, New Orleans, LA, USA, 28 November– 9 December 2022 (2022)
31. Zong, B., et al.: Deep autoencoding gaussian mixture model for unsupervised anomaly detection. In: 6th International Conference on Learning Representations, ICLR 2018, Vancouver, BC, Canada, 30 April–3 May 2018, Conference Track Proceedings. OpenReview.net (2018)

Targeted Robustness for Regression via Top-Feature Noise

Fernando Martínez-Plumed(✉), Cristina Padró-Ferragud, and María José Ramírez-Quintana

VRAIN, Universitat Politècnica de València, València, Spain
{fmartinez,mramirez}@dsic.upv.es, cpadro@upv.es

Abstract. Regression models deployed on tabular data routinely encounter corrupted inputs—sensor drift, data-entry errors, upstream imputation artefacts, and distributional shifts can all degrade the features a model depends on most. Standard robustness evaluations perturb every feature uniformly, an approach that can obscure the vulnerabilities that matter: tabular predictors typically concentrate their reliance on a small subset of attributes, and uniform noise dilutes signal about where a model is most fragile. We propose *targeted robustness evaluation*, a protocol that identifies each model's most influential feature via permutation-based importance and subjects it alone to calibrated corruption during test parameterised by noise severity and fraction of instances affected. Applying this protocol to the OpenML-CTR23 regression suite (35 datasets, 20 models from 8 families, 152K+ evaluations), we find that robustness varies sharply across families and datasets: kernel-based and instance-based methods are the most resilient, while models strong on clean accuracy can be brittle under targeted noise. We further show that *noise-aware training* (i.e., injecting corruption into the top feature during training) yields monotonic, statistically significant stability gains across every model family without architectural changes. Together, our concordance-based evaluation framework and noise-augmentation strategy offer a principled methodology for diagnosing, comparing, and improving the robustness of tabular regression models under realistic input corruption.

Keywords: Robustness evaluation · Tabular regression · Feature-importance · Noise augmentation

1 Introduction

Tabular regression are widely used to support decisions in engineering, finance, healthcare, and the physical sciences [4,24]. In these domains, input features are often corrupted: sensors may drift or fail, values can be entered or transcribed incorrectly, and preprocessing pipelines may introduce imputation artefacts or encoding errors [30]. If a deployed model's predictions rely heavily on a single

M. Ceci et al. (Eds.): ECML PKDD 2026, LNAI 16941, pp. 213–228, 2027.
https://doi.org/10.1007/978-3-032-37654-1_13

critical measurement, corruption in that feature can make predictions unreliable. The downstream effects—such as incorrect dosing, mispriced instruments, or faulty control signals—can be severe. For this reason, understanding and mitigating this fragility is an important practical challenge.

While robustness has been studied extensively in the image domain models [12,13,17,26] and, recently, for tabular classifiers [7,11,19,25], two critical gaps persist. First, *regression* tasks are largely overlooked: existing benchmarks and threat models target classifiers almost exclusively. Second, standard protocols inject noise *uniformly* across all features, an approach that dilutes perturbations across irrelevant dimensions and underestimates true vulnerability, since tabular models typically concentrate their dependence on a small subset of inputs [6,9].

We argue that robustness evaluation for tabular regression should be targeted: perturbations should be applied to the features on which a model most strongly depends. In many real-world settings, noise is localized (e.g., a failing sensor corrupts one channel, or a data-entry error affects one field), making feature-level stress tests particularly relevant. Moreover, focusing on influential features yields more interpretable diagnostics by revealing fragile model dependencies. To this end, we propose a simple, model-agnostic evaluation protocol. For each model and cross-validation *test* fold, we identify the most important feature via permutation-based importance [6,9]. We then corrupt only this feature with noise calibrated to its training-set interquartile range (for numeric features) or empirical category distribution (for categorical features). Prediction stability is quantified using Lin's concordance correlation coefficient (CCC) [15], which captures both precision and accuracy of agreement between clean and perturbed predictions and remains well-behaved under heavy-tailed errors.

Beyond diagnosing vulnerabilities, we investigate whether targeted robustness can be improved systematically. Noise injection has long been used as a regularisation strategy [1,3], and data augmentation improves robustness in vision [28] as well as in adversarial tabular classification [25]. We therefore study a simple, model-agnostic intervention: during training, we inject noise into the same top-ranked feature that is perturbed at test time. This noise-aware training requires no architectural changes, applies to any learner, and, empirically, produces consistent and monotonic improvements in targeted robustness.

We instantiate this framework on OpenML-CTR23 [8], a curated suite of 35 regression datasets that meet a large number of quality criteria, evaluating 20 models from 8 families (linear, generalised linear, regularised, tree-based, boosting, kernel, instance-based, and neural network) across 152K+ perturbation conditions. To handle unequal model coverage across datasets, we complement global summaries with paired-rank analyses on dataset intersections that ensure fair cross-family comparisons. This work makes four contributions:

- A **model-agnostic perturbation framework** parameterised by noise severity ξ and fraction of affected instances π, targeting each model's most influential feature and measuring stability via concordance correlation (Sect. 3.2).

- The first **systematic study of targeted robustness** for tabular regression (35 datasets, 20 models, 8 families), revealing sharp cross-family heterogeneity with no single dominant family (Sect. 5).
- A simple **training-time intervention** that yields monotonic, statistically significant robustness gains across every model family, with win rates exceeding 90% and the largest improvements occurring where vulnerabilities are greatest (Sect. 3.4).
- **Actionable recommendations** on metric choice (CCC over RMSE), fair comparison using paired dataset intersections, training-noise calibration ($\xi_{\text{train}} \in [0.25, 0.5]$), and insights into the redundancy–vulnerability relationship (Sect. 5).

2 Related Work

Robustness has been studied extensively in vision, both for adversarial perturbations [12,18] and for non-adversarial corruptions [13]. For tabular learning, recent benchmarks primarily target *classification*: *TabularBench* evaluates adversarial attacks and defences for deep tabular classifiers [25], while *TableShift* focuses on natural distribution shift across binary tasks [11]. Related analyses further characterise robustness and shift for tabular classifiers [7,19,20]. In contrast, systematic robustness evaluation for tabular *regression* under feature corruption remains scarce. We address this gap with a model-agnostic protocol tailored to regression that (i) selects a model's most influential feature and (ii) applies calibrated corruption to that feature only, enabling fair comparison across diverse model families beyond deep networks.

Injecting input noise is a classic regularisation mechanism [1,3], and modern robustness in vision commonly relies on corruption augmentation [22,28] or adversarial training [18]. For tabular data, augmentation benefits are strongly task-dependent and no single strategy dominates across tasks [25]. We study a complementary and simpler intervention for regression: *targeted* noise injection that corrupts only the top-importance feature during training, with noise severity calibrated to the training distribution, and we quantify when and for which model families this improves test-time stability.

Permutation importance, introduced for random forests [6] and connected to model reliance [9], is typically used for interpretation; we repurpose it to define per-model stress tests and to choose where to inject training noise. This aligns with sensitivity-analysis principles [23] but targets large, feature-local corruptions rather than small local perturbations. We build on OpenML-CTR23 [8] (from OpenML [27]) to ensure diverse, reproducible regression tasks, and summarize robustness using Lin's concordance correlation coefficient [15], which captures both correlation and bias and remains comparable across heterogeneous target scales.

3 Methods

3.1 Problem Setup

Let $\mathcal{D} = \{(\mathbf{x}_i, y_i)\}_{i=1}^n$ be a tabular regression dataset with $\mathbf{x}_i \in \mathcal{X} \subseteq \mathbb{R}^{p_{\text{num}}} \times \mathcal{C}^{p_{\text{cat}}}$ and continuous target $y_i \in \mathbb{R}$, where $p = p_{\text{num}} + p_{\text{cat}}$ is the total number of features. A regression model $f : \mathcal{X} \to \mathbb{R}$ is trained on a training split $\mathcal{D}^{\text{tr}}$ and evaluated on a held-out test split $\mathcal{D}^{\text{te}}$.

We consider a realistic *natural corruption* setting [21]: at deployment, some fraction of test instances may have their most influential feature corrupted by noise (e.g., sensor malfunction, transcription error, imputation artefact). Unlike adversarial attacks that seek worst-case perturbations, we model corruption as stochastic, feature-specific, and calibrated to the observed data distribution (reflecting the structure of naturally occurring tabular noise). The central question we address is thus twofold: (i) *Diagnosis:* How stable are the predictions of f when its most important input feature is corrupted? (ii) *Remedy:* Can this stability be improved by a simple, model-agnostic training-time intervention?

3.2 Targeted Robustness Protocol

We now formalise the evaluation protocol. It consists of three stages: top-feature identification, targeted perturbation, and stability measurement.

Top-Feature Identification. For a trained model f and evaluation data $(\mathbf{X}, \mathbf{y})$, we compute model-agnostic permutation importance [6,9]. For each feature $j \in \{1, \ldots, p\}$, define the importance score

$$\mathrm{PFI}_j(f, \mathbf{X}, \mathbf{y}) = \frac{1}{R} \sum_{r=1}^{R} \left[\mathcal{L}(f(\mathbf{X}^{\pi_j^{(r)}}), \mathbf{y}) - \mathcal{L}(f(\mathbf{X}), \mathbf{y}) \right], \tag{1}$$

where $\mathbf{X}^{\pi_j^{(r)}}$ denotes the data matrix with the j-th column independently permuted according to $\pi_j^{(r)}$ (permutation r of R repeats), leaving all other columns unchanged, and $\mathcal{L}$ is a loss function (we use negative R^2). The top feature is selected as $j^\star = \arg\max_{j \in \{1,\ldots,p\}} \mathrm{PFI}_j(f, \mathbf{X}^{\text{te}}, \mathbf{y}^{\text{te}})$. Crucially, the selection of $j^\star$ is part of the *evaluation* protocol: it uses the already-trained model to probe which feature most influences predictions and does not provide the model with any information beyond what is available at training time. Because $j^\star$ is model- and fold-specific, the protocol stress-tests each model at its own point of greatest vulnerability.

Targeted Noise Operator. We define a parameterised noise operator $\mathcal{T}_{\xi,\pi}$ that corrupts only feature $j^\star$ in the test data [7]. Two parameters control the perturbation: *severity* $\xi \in (0, \infty)$, which scales the magnitude of the corruption; and *affected fraction* $\pi \in (0, 1]$, namely, the proportion of test instances whose feature $j^\star$ is corrupted. Given a test matrix $\mathbf{X}^{\text{te}}$, we sample (without replacement) a subset $\mathcal{S} \subseteq \{1, \ldots, n_{\text{te}}\}$ of size $\lfloor \pi \cdot n_{\text{te}} \rfloor$. The corrupted matrix $\tilde{\mathbf{X}}^{\text{te}} = \mathcal{T}_{\xi,\pi}(\mathbf{X}^{\text{te}})$ differs from $\mathbf{X}^{\text{te}}$ only in column $j^\star$ and only at rows $i \in \mathcal{S}$.

For $j^\star$ *numeric*, we apply additive Gaussian noise (extensively employed to simulate real-world data [2,5,16,31]) scaled by the training-set interquartile range:

$$\tilde{x}_{i,j^\star} = x_{i,j^\star} + \xi \cdot \text{IQR}(x^{\text{tr}}_{:,j^\star}) \cdot \epsilon_i, \qquad \epsilon_i \overset{\text{i.i.d.}}{\sim} \mathcal{N}(0,1), \quad i \in \mathcal{S}, \tag{2}$$

where $\text{IQR}(x^{\text{tr}}_{:,j^\star}) = Q_{0.75} - Q_{0.25}$ is computed on the training split. The IQR calibration ensures that noise severity is commensurate with the feature's natural variability and is robust to outliers. If $\text{IQR} = 0$ (degenerate case), we fall back to the standard deviation. Perturbed values are optionally clipped to the training range $[\min(x^{\text{tr}}_{:,j^\star}), \max(x^{\text{tr}}_{:,j^\star})]$ to prevent extrapolation.

For $j^\star$ *categorical* with training-set empirical distribution $\hat{P}^{\text{tr}}_{j^\star}$ over categories $\{c_1, \ldots, c_K\}$, each affected instance independently has its value replaced with probability ξ:

$$\tilde{x}_{i,j^\star} = \begin{cases} c \sim \hat{P}^{\text{tr}}_{j^\star} & \text{with probability } \xi, \\ x_{i,j^\star} & \text{with probability } 1-\xi, \end{cases} \qquad i \in \mathcal{S}. \tag{3}$$

This design draws replacements from the observed marginal distribution, avoiding out-of-vocabulary artefacts while still disrupting the feature–target association.

3.3 Robustness Metric

We evaluate prediction stability by comparing clean and perturbed outputs. Let $\hat{\mathbf{y}} = f(\mathbf{X}^{\text{te}})$ and $\tilde{\mathbf{y}} = f(\tilde{\mathbf{X}}^{\text{te}})$ denote the model's predictions before and after perturbation. Our primary metric is Lin's concordance correlation coefficient (CCC) [15] between $\hat{\mathbf{y}}$ and $\tilde{\mathbf{y}}$:

$$\text{CCC}(\hat{\mathbf{y}}, \tilde{\mathbf{y}}) = \frac{2\,\sigma_{\hat{y}\tilde{y}}}{\sigma^2_{\hat{y}} + \sigma^2_{\tilde{y}} + (\mu_{\hat{y}} - \mu_{\tilde{y}})^2}, \tag{4}$$

where μ, σ^2, and $\sigma_{\hat{y}\tilde{y}}$ denote means, variances, and covariance computed over the test set. CCC jointly captures precision (Pearson correlation) and accuracy (deviation from the identity line), ranging from -1 to 1 with $\text{CCC} = 1$ indicating perfect agreement. Concrely, we report concordance loss $\mathcal{L}_{\text{CCC}} = 1 - \text{CCC}(\hat{\mathbf{y}}, \tilde{\mathbf{y}})$ as the primary robustness measure (lower is better). This metric has two key advantages over RMSE-derived degradation measures. First, it is *ground-truth-free*: it requires only the model's own predictions on clean and noisy inputs, not the true targets. Second, it is *scale-invariant* and bounded, remaining well-conditioned even for model–dataset pairs with extreme absolute errors, a property critical for aggregation across heterogeneous tasks (see Sect. 5).

We evaluate each (dataset, model, fold) triple over a 4×4 grid of perturbation conditions: $\xi \in \{0.1, 0.25, 0.5, 1.0\}$, $\pi \in \{0.1, 0.25, 0.5, 1.0\}$. This yields a robustness surface $\mathcal{L}_{\text{CCC}}(\xi, \pi)$ for each model instance, enabling fine-grained analysis of how degradation scales with both noise intensity and the fraction of affected instances in the test fold. A well-behaved surface should be monotonically non-decreasing in both ξ (at fixed π) and π (at fixed ξ); we verify this in Sect. 5.

3.4 Noise-Aware Training

We also propose a simple intervention to improve targeted robustness. If a model's fragility stems from over-reliance on the precise values of its top feature, then exposing the model to corrupted versions of that feature during training should encourage it to learn representations that are less sensitive to such perturbations. This is a *targeted* form of input noise injection [1,3], directed at the specific feature dimension where the model is most vulnerable.

For each (dataset, fold), we proceed as follows: (1) Train a *selector model* on the clean training split $\mathcal{D}^{\text{tr}}$ and identify $j^\star$. (2) For each training-noise level $\xi_{\text{train}} \in \{0.1, 0.25, 0.5, 1.0\}$, construct an augmented training set $\tilde{\mathcal{D}}^{\text{tr}}$ by applying $\mathcal{T}_{\xi_{\text{train}}, 1.0}$ to $\mathcal{D}^{\text{tr}}$—i.e., corrupting feature $j^\star$ in *all* training instances at severity ξ_{train}. (3) Retrain the model on $\tilde{\mathcal{D}}^{\text{tr}}$ (from scratch, with identical hyperparameters). (4) Evaluate on the same test perturbation grid (ξ, π) as the baseline.

Three design choices merit emphasis. First, the top feature $j^\star$ is fixed across all training-noise regimes for each (dataset, fold, model) triple, using the selector from step 1. This ensures a controlled comparison: differences in robustness are attributable to training-time noise, not to changes in which feature is deemed most important. Second, we corrupt $\pi_{\text{train}} = 1.0$ (all training rows) to maximise the model's exposure to corrupted inputs; partial corruption is left to future work. Third, targets y_i are never modified—only the input feature $j^\star$ is corrupted.

Evaluation. We measure improvement as the paired difference in concordance loss between the baseline (clean-trained) and noise-aware models at each matched condition (dataset, fold, model, ξ, π):

$$\Delta\mathcal{L}_{\text{CCC}} = \mathcal{L}_{\text{CCC}}^{\text{baseline}} - \mathcal{L}_{\text{CCC}}^{\text{noise-aware}}. \tag{5}$$

A positive value indicates that noise-aware training improved robustness. We summarise gains by mean improvement, median improvement (robust to outliers), and *win rate*, i.e., the fraction of matched conditions where $\Delta\mathcal{L}_{\text{CCC}} > 0$. Statistical significance is assessed via one-sided paired Wilcoxon signed-rank tests [29] at the family level.

4 Experimental Design

Benchmark Suite: We adopt *OpenML-CTR23* [8], a curated suite of 35 tabular regression datasets from the OpenML repository [27] (see Table 1), selected via strict quality criteria: 500–100,000 observations, fewer than 5,000 features after encoding, non-sparse format, i.i.d. observations, clear provenance, and a non-trivial regression target. Datasets span diverse domains including materials science, ecology, economics, housing, and computer systems, with sample sizes ranging from 517 to 53,940 and feature counts from 5 to 116 (full summary in Appendix A).

Table 1. Overview of the 35 OpenML-CTR23 datasets [8]. n: observations; p: total features; $p_{\text{num}}/p_{\text{cat}}$: numeric/categorical; Miss.: missing values (✓); $|\mathcal{M}|$: models evaluated. † family-level paired subset (18); ‡ model-level paired subset (13).

	abalone†‡	airfoil†‡	auction†‡	brazil. houses†‡	calif. housing	cars†‡	concrete†‡	cps88wages	cpu_activity†	diamonds	energy_eff.†‡	fifa	forest_fires†	fps_bench.	geo. music	grid_stab.	health_ins.	kin8nm†‡	kings_county	miami_hous.	Moneyball†‡	naval_prop.†‡	physio. prot.	pumadyn	QSAR_fish†‡	red_wine†‡	sarcos	socmob†	solar_flare†	space_ga	student†	supercond.	video_trans.	wave_energy	white_wine†‡
n	4 177	1 503	2 043	10 692	20 640	804	1 030	28 155	8 192	53 940	768	19 178	517	24 624	1 059	10 000	22 272	8 192	21 613	13 932	1 232	11 934	45 730	8 192	908	1 599	48 933	1 156	1 066	3 107	649	21 263	68 784	72 000	4 898
p	8	5	7	9	8	17	8	6	21	9	8	28	12	43	116	12	11	8	21	15	14	14	9	32	6	11	21	5	10	6	30	81	18	48	11
p_{num}	7	5	7	6	8	17	8	2	21	6	8	27	10	34	116	12	4	8	21	15	12	14	9	32	6	11	21	1	7	6	13	81	16	48	11
p_{cat}	1	0	0	3	0	0	0	4	0	3	0	1	2	9	0	0	7	0	0	0	2	0	0	0	0	0	0	4	3	0	17	0	2	0	0
Miss.														✓							✓														
$\lvert\mathcal{M}\rvert$	20	20	20	20	18	20	20	18	19	16	20	18	19	18	15	15	17	20	18	18	20	20	16	15	20	20	12	19	19	15	19	18	16	16	20

Model Zoo: We evaluate 20 representative regression models organised into 8 families (Table 2). All models use scikit-learn [14] implementations with default hyperparameters, ensuring that observed robustness differences reflect model *inductive biases* rather than tuning choices. Numeric features are standardised; categorical features are one-hot encoded; missing values are mean/mode imputed. Model availability varies across datasets due to data-type constraints (e.g., kernel models require numeric inputs) and computational size gates (e.g., SVR and KRR are restricted to $n \leq 12{,}000$); we report both global and paired-intersection results.

4.1 Evaluation Protocol

All experiments use 3-fold cross-validation with a fixed random seed. For each (dataset, model, fold) triple, we first train the model on the clean training fold and record its test predictions. We then identify the top feature $j^{\star}$ via permutation importance ($R = 2$ repeats, subsampled to at most 5,000 rows for computational efficiency) and evaluate the model on the full 4×4 perturbation grid (ξ, π), recording $\mathcal{L}_{\text{CCC}}$ at every grid point. For the noise-aware training experiment, this procedure is repeated for each training-noise level $\xi_{\text{train}} \in \{0.1, 0.25, 0.5, 1.0\}$: the model is retrained from scratch on the augmented training set and evaluated on the same test perturbation grid, keeping $j^{\star}$ fixed to the value selected by the clean-trained selector.

Table 2. Model families and their members. "Num. only" indicates models restricted to numeric features; these are excluded from datasets with indispensable categorical features. Size gates apply to computationally expensive models ($n \leq 12{,}000$ for SVR and Kernel Ridge; $n \leq 30{,}000$ for k-NN).

Family	Model	Description	Scikit-learn class
Linear Regression	OLS	Ordinary least squares	`LinearRegression`
	Huber	Huber-loss robust regression	`HuberRegressor`
	Poly2 Ridge	Degree-2 polynomial + Ridge	`Pipeline(Poly2, Ridge)`
Generalised Linear	Poisson GLM	Log-link, Poisson deviance	`PoissonRegressor`
	Gamma GLM	Log-link, Gamma deviance	`GammaRegressor`
	Tweedie (p=1.1)	Compound Poisson–Gamma	`TweedieRegressor`
	Tweedie (p=1.5)	Compound Poisson–Gamma	`TweedieRegressor`
	Tweedie (p=1.9)	Compound Poisson–Gamma	`TweedieRegressor`
Regularised	Ridge	ℓ_2-penalised least squares	`Ridge`
	Lasso	ℓ_1-penalised least squares	`Lasso`
	ElasticNet	$\ell_1 + \ell_2$ penalty	`ElasticNet`
Tree-based	Decision Tree	Single CART tree	`DecisionTreeRegressor`
	Random Forest	Bagged ensemble of trees	`RandomForestRegressor`
	ExtraTrees	Extremely randomised trees	`ExtraTreesRegressor`
Boosting	GBR	Gradient boosted trees	`GradientBoostingRegressor`
	HistGBT	Histogram-based gradient boosting	`HistGradientBoostingRegressor`
Kernel-based†	SVR (RBF)	Support vector regression, RBF kernel	`SVR`
	Kernel Ridge (RBF)	Kernel ridge regression, RBF kernel	`KernelRidge`
Instance-based†	k-NN	Distance-weighted k-nearest neighbours	`KNeighborsRegressor`
Neural Network†	MLP	Multi-layer perceptron	`MLPRegressor`

† Numeric-only; size-gated.

In total, the benchmark spans 35 datasets (544,782 observations) and 634 (dataset, model) pairs, yielding 1,902 folds. The baseline experiment produces 30,432 perturbation evaluations (16 grid points per fold), and the noise-aware training experiment adds a further 121,728 evaluations (4 training-noise levels × 16 test grid points per fold), for a combined total of over 152,000 targeted robustness measurements.

4.2 Paired-Rank Methodology

Because model coverage is unequal across datasets, naïve averaging conflates model quality with dataset composition. We address this via *paired-rank analysis*. For family-level comparisons, we restrict to the 18 datasets where all 8 families are evaluable; for model-level comparisons, we restrict to the 13 datasets where all 20 models are evaluable. Within each paired subset, we rank families (or models) per dataset by mean concordance loss and report average ranks. Statistical significance of rank differences is assessed via the Friedman test [10], with post-hoc pairwise comparisons where appropriate. Unpaired (global) summaries over all 35 datasets are provided in Appendix B.

5 Results

We organise our findings around three research questions (see the goals in Sect. 3.1):

RQ1: How Vulnerable are Regression Models to Targeted Feature Corruption? Degradation is well-behaved. As a sanity check, we first verify that concordance loss increases in the expected directions. Across all (dataset, model, fold) triples, 95.0% of fixed-π curves are monotonically non-decreasing in severity ξ, and 93.3% of fixed-ξ curves are monotonically non-decreasing in affected fraction π. This confirms that the perturbation protocol produces a coherent signal: corrupting the top feature more aggressively or more broadly leads to progressively less stable predictions.

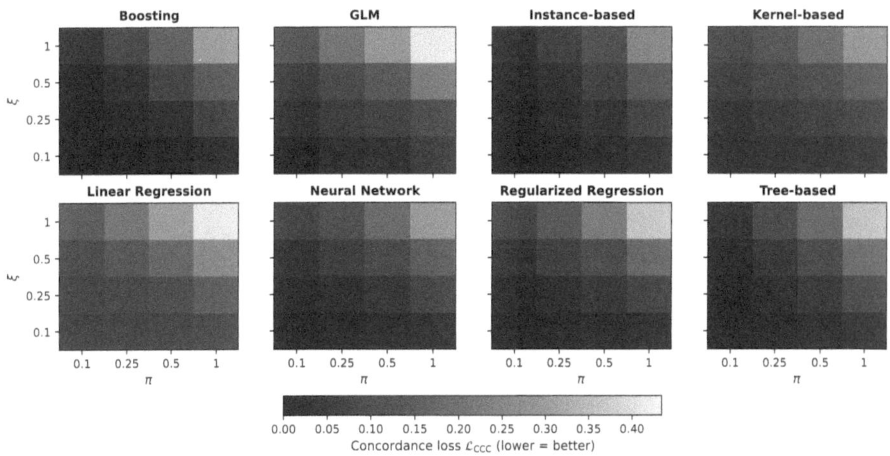

Fig. 1. Robustness surfaces by model family (mean concordance loss; lower is better). Each panel shows degradation as a function of severity ξ and affected fraction π, averaged over all evaluable datasets. Model-level surfaces are provided in Appendix B.1.

Figure 1 displays the mean concordance-loss surface for each model family, averaged over all evaluable datasets and folds. There is substantial heterogeneity across families. All families exhibit degradation that increases jointly in ξ and π, but the *rate* of degradation varies markedly. Kernel-based and instance-based methods maintain low concordance loss across most of the perturbation grid, whereas linear regression and GLM families degrade rapidly, particularly under high severity ($\xi \geq 0.5$). Tree-based ensembles occupy an intermediate position, with boosting slightly more robust than bagged methods (Random Forest, ExtraTrees).

Figure 2 shows the per-dataset family ranks on the 18-dataset paired subset. No family dominates all datasets. While kernel-based methods achieve the best average rank overall, they are not the most robust on every dataset:

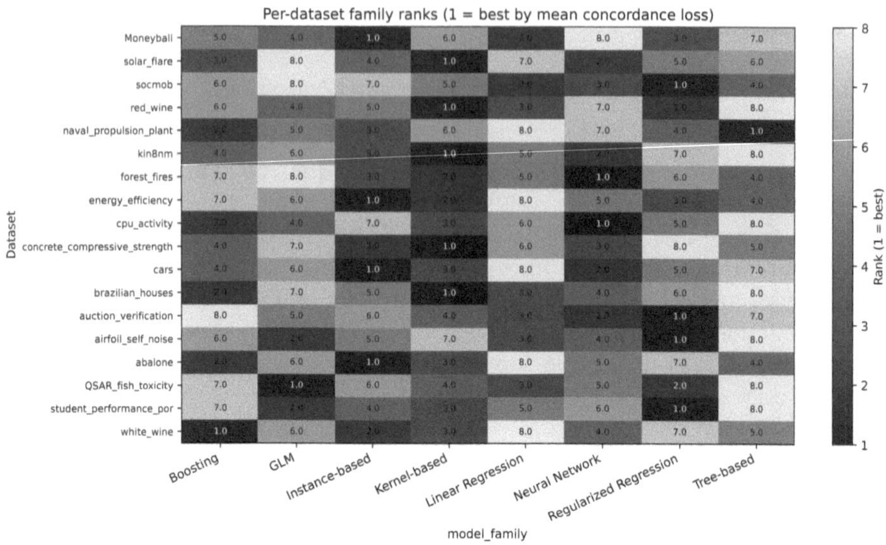

Fig. 2. Per-dataset family robustness ranks (18 paired datasets; lower/darker is more robust). A model-level rank heatmap (13 paired datasets, 20 models) is provided in Appendix B.2.

instance-based methods win on 4 datasets, regularised regression on 4, and neural networks, GLM, boosting, and tree-based methods each win on at least one. This pronounced heterogeneity motivates dataset-level analysis rather than one-size-fits-all recommendations. Four illustrative case studies—spanning near-universal robustness (`fps_benchmark`) to strong model-dependent fragility (`grid_stability`)—are detailed in Appendix C. Additional analyses of marginal sensitivity to ξ and π individually, and of the differential impact of numeric versus categorical top-feature noise, are provided in Appendices B.4 and B.6; notably, categorical corruption induces systematically lower degradation than numeric corruption at matched severity, consistent with the fact that category flips remain within the training-set vocabulary whereas numeric noise moves values off the observed manifold.

RQ2: Which Model Families Are Most Robust Under Targeted Noise? Figure 3 reports the average robustness rank of each family on the 18-dataset paired intersection (where all 8 families are evaluable), using mean concordance loss as the ranking criterion. Kernel-based methods (SVR, Kernel Ridge) achieve the best average rank (3.11), followed by instance-based (k-NN, 3.67) and neural networks (MLP, 3.94). Regularised regression (Ridge, Lasso, ElasticNet) ranks fourth (4.11), while tree-based ensembles—despite strong clean-accuracy performance on many tasks—rank last (6.11). The differences are statistically significant under a Friedman test ($\chi^2 = 20.22$, $p = 0.005$).

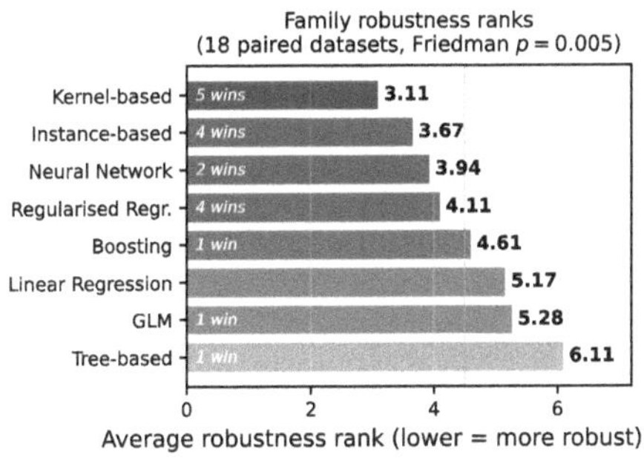

Fig. 3. Family-level paired robustness ranks on 18 datasets where all 8 families are evaluable. Ranking criterion: mean concordance loss (shorter bar = more robust). Win counts shown inside bars. Friedman test: $\chi^2 = 20.22$, $p = 0.005$.

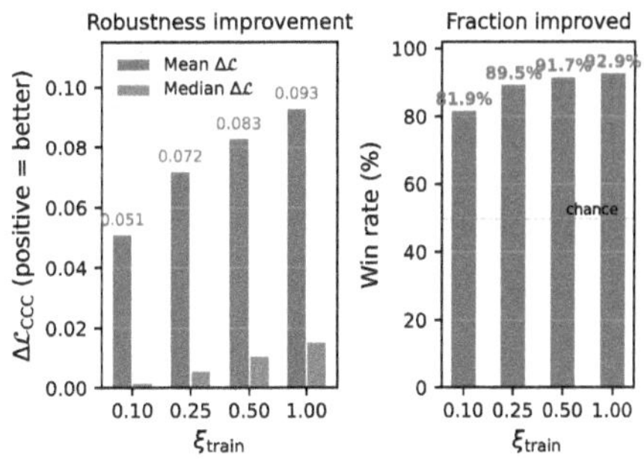

Fig. 4. Noise-aware training: global robustness gains. Left: mean and median $\Delta\mathcal{L}_{\mathrm{CCC}}$ (positive = better). Right: win rate vs. clean-trained baseline. Aggregated over all datasets, models, folds, and test conditions.

The strong performance of kernel and instance-based methods can be understood through their inductive biases: these models make predictions based on local similarity in input space, so a perturbation to a single feature has a limited effect unless it moves instances far from their training-set neighbours in the kernel metric. By contrast, linear and GLM families propagate perturbations directly and proportionally through their coefficients, and tree-based methods can be sensitive to splits on the corrupted feature. Model-level paired ranks (13 datasets, 20 models) confirm that SVR with an RBF kernel is the single most robust model (avg. rank 4.65; see Appendix B.2 for the full table). Concordance-loss distributions (Appendix B.3), clean-accuracy vs. robustness Pareto fronts (Appendix B.5), and per-dataset robustness winners (Appendix D.6) provide complementary perspectives on these rankings.

Why Concordance-Based Metrics Matter? RMSE-derived robustness summaries are dominated by a small number of pathological model–dataset combinations. In our benchmark, 13 of 634 (dataset, model) pairs already fit poorly on unperturbed (clean) test data ($R^2 < -10$, i.e. far worse than a constant predictor), and 15 exhibit mean relative RMSE increases exceeding 100× under perturbation. These outliers (predominantly from the GLM and Linear Regression families) inflate family-level RMSE averages and obscure meaningful distinctions. Concordance loss $\mathcal{L}_{\mathrm{CCC}}$ directly measures prediction stability and remains bounded in $[0, 2]$ regardless of absolute error scale, making it a reliable aggregation metric. We report RMSE-derived diagnostics, including clean-R^2 (R^2 on unperturbed test data) vs. concordance-loss Pareto fronts, in Appendix B.5.

Feature Redundancy Correlates with Vulnerability. We investigate whether the presence of correlated backup features mitigates fragility. For each (dataset, model, fold), we compute a redundancy proxy: the absolute Pearson correlation between the top-1 and top-2 most important features on the training split. Surprisingly, higher redundancy is *positively* associated with higher concordance loss (Spearman $\rho = 0.424$, $p = 2.33 \times 10^{-25}$; Fig. 5). This suggests that correlated importance reflects *concentrated dependence*—the model relies heavily on a group of related features—rather than robustness through substitutability.

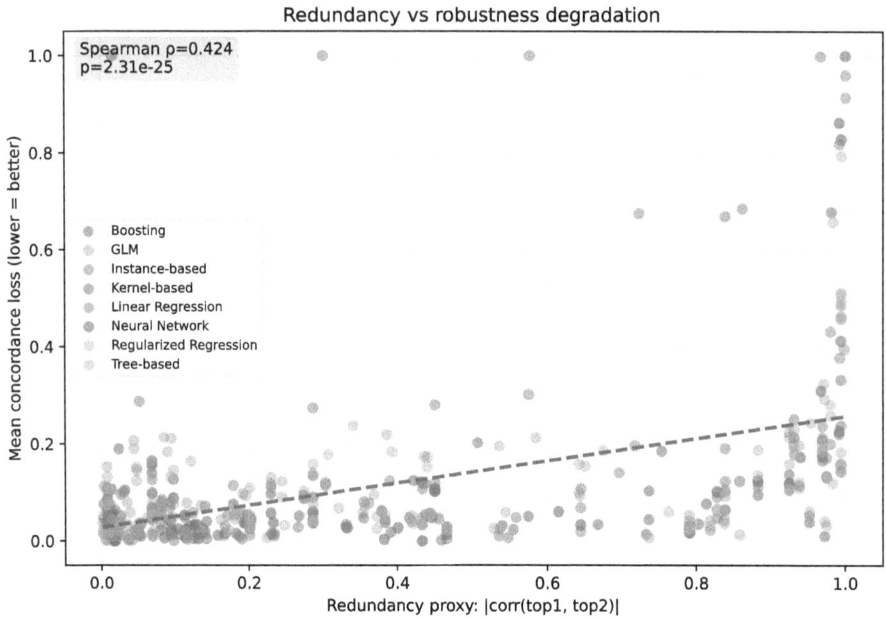

Fig. 5. Feature redundancy vs. robustness degradation. Higher absolute correlation between the top-1 and top-2 features is associated with *worse* robustness (higher concordance loss), indicating concentrated dependence rather than protective redundancy.

RQ3: Can Noise-Aware Training Improve Targeted Robustness? We now evaluate the noise-aware training intervention described in §3.4, comparing models retrained with targeted noise ($\xi_{\text{train}} \in \{0.1, 0.25, 0.5, 1.0\}$) against their clean-trained baselines at every matched test condition.

Figures 4 and 6 summarise the gains aggregated over all datasets, models, folds, and test conditions. All four training-noise levels produce positive mean and median improvements, and both metrics increase monotonically with ξ_{train}. At $\xi_{\text{train}} = 1.0$, the mean concordance-loss improvement is 0.093, the median improvement is 0.015, and the win rate, i.e., the fraction of the 30 432 matched test conditions where noise-aware training outperforms the baseline, reaches 92.9%. Even the mildest augmentation ($\xi_{\text{train}} = 0.1$) achieves an 81.9% win rate, demonstrating that the intervention is broadly effective regardless of calibration.

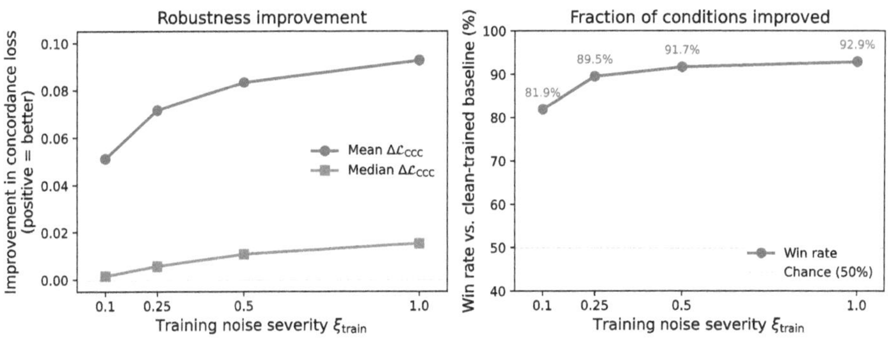

Fig. 6. Noise-aware training vs. baseline (global). Left: mean and median improvement in concordance loss as a function of training-noise severity ξ_{train}. Right: win rate (fraction of matched test conditions improved). Both metrics increase monotonically with ξ_{train}. Family-level improvement surfaces in Appendix D.1.

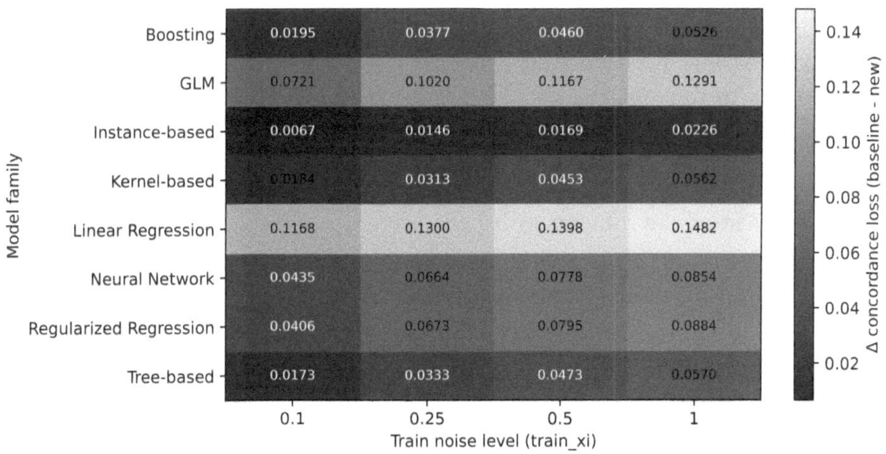

Fig. 7. Family-wise robustness gain. Each cell shows the mean improvement in concordance loss (baseline minus noise-trained; positive is better) for a given family and training-noise level ξ_{train}. Gains are monotonic across ξ_{train} for all families, with the largest improvements in the most vulnerable families.

Figure 7 breaks down the mean concordance-loss improvement by family and ξ_{train}. Gains are positive and monotonically increasing for every family. At $\xi_{train} = 1.0$, the largest improvements are observed for linear regression (0.148) and GLMs (0.129)—families that were identified as the most fragile in **RQ1**—confirming that noise-aware training is most beneficial where vulnerability is greatest. Kernel-based (0.056) and instance-based (0.023) methods, which were already relatively robust, show smaller but still statistically significant gains. Indeed, paired one-sided Wilcoxon signed-rank tests confirm that the improvement is significantly greater than zero ($p < 10^{-29}$) for *every* family at *every* training-noise level, including the mildest ($\xi_{\text{train}} = 0.1$); full test statistics are reported in Appendix D.3.

Practical Calibration. While $\xi_{\text{train}} = 1.0$ maximises concordance-loss improvement and win rate, the marginal benefit diminishes beyond $\xi_{\text{train}} = 0.5$: increasing from 0.5 to 1.0 adds only 1.2 percentage points to the win rate and 0.010 to the mean improvement (Fig. 4). A training-noise level in the range $\xi_{\text{train}} \in [0.25, 0.5]$ therefore represents a practical sweet spot, capturing the majority of the robustness benefit while limiting any potential impact on clean-data accuracy. Family-wise improvement trajectories (Appendix D.2) and per-model breakdowns (Appendix D.5) confirm this pattern: win rates range from 69% (k-NN) to 100% (Ridge) across all 20 models.

Effect on Clean-Data Accuracy. A natural concern is whether robustness gains come at the expense of predictive performance on clean (unperturbed) inputs. We measure this by comparing the R^2 on unperturbed test data between noise-aware and clean-trained models. The trade-off is family-dependent (Appendix D.4): regularised regression and neural networks experience mild clean-R^2 decreases (0.04–0.07 on average at $\xi_{\text{train}} = 1.0$), tree-based ensembles show larger losses (0.12–0.16), while several GLM and linear regression configurations actually *improve* clean R^2, as the injected noise acts as beneficial regularisation for ill-conditioned fits. The moderate range $\xi_{\text{train}} \in [0.25, 0.5]$ limits these effects while preserving most of the robustness benefit.

6 Conclusion

We introduced a protocol for evaluating the targeted robustness of tabular regression models by corrupting their most influential input feature—identified via permutation importance—and measuring prediction stability through Lin's concordance correlation coefficient. Applying this protocol to 20 models from 8 families across the 35-dataset OpenML-CTR23 benchmark (152K+ evaluations), we established three findings. First, *targeted perturbations are highly informative*: corrupting only the most influential feature exposes pronounced and heterogeneous vulnerabilities that uniform noise evaluations would miss. Second, *robustness varies sharply across families and datasets*: kernel-based and instance-based methods are the most robust on average, but no family dominates all tasks, and feature redundancy paradoxically signals concentrated dependence rather than resilience. Third, *noise-aware training is a simple, effective, and model-agnostic robustness intervention*: it yields large, monotonic, statistically significant improvements across every family, with the greatest gains precisely where they are most needed.

Natural extensions include scaling to top-k feature corruption to study how robustness degrades as multiple important features are simultaneously affected, and investigating adaptive calibration strategies that select ξ_{train} based on dataset or model characteristics rather than a fixed grid. Integrating the protocol into AutoML pipelines—where robustness could serve as a secondary objective alongside predictive performance—is a promising direction for deploying robust regression models in practice.

Limitations. We deliberately focused on default-hyperparameter scikit-learn models and independent single-feature corruption, ensuring reproducibility and a tractable threat model that reflects common real-world failures; our open protocol readily extends to tuned or deep tabular architectures (e.g., TabNet, FT-Transformer) and to correlated perturbation schemes. CCC was chosen for its ground-truth-free, scale-invariant properties; RMSE-based diagnostics are provided in the appendix for practitioners requiring absolute-error perspectives.

Acknowledgements. This work has been supported by CIPROM/2022/6 (FASSLOW), funded by Generalitat Valenciana, and Spanish grant PID2024-162030OB-100 (ROBIN), funded by MCIN/AEI/ 10.13039/501100011033 and ERDF A way of making Europe; and by the VANTAGE Project, Grant Agreement No. 101249800, funded by the European Union through ECCC; and by EUR2024-153548 (PREDAIT) "Towards Predictable AI" from "Spanish Europe Excelencia" 2024; and the HIDDEN project is funded by the European Union, under grant agreement No 101202228.

References

1. An, G.: The effects of adding noise during backpropagation training on a generalization performance. Neural Comput. **8**(3), 643–674 (1996)
2. Arslan, M., Guzel, M., Demirci, M., Ozdemir, S.: Smote and gaussian noise based sensor data augmentation. In: 2019 4th International Conference on Computer Science and Engineering (UBMK), pp. 1–5 (2019)
3. Bishop, C.M.: Training with noise is equivalent to Tikhonov regularization. Neural Comput. **7**(1), 108–116 (1995)
4. Borisov, V., Leemann, T., Seßler, K., Haug, J., Pawelczyk, M., Kasneci, G.: Deep neural networks and tabular data: a survey. IEEE Trans. Neural Networks Learn. Syst. (2022)
5. Braun, S., Neil, D., Liu, S.C.: A curriculum learning method for improved noise robustness in automatic speech recognition. In: 25th EUSIPCO, pp. 548–552 (2017)
6. Breiman, L.: Random forests. Mach. Learn. **45**(1), 5–32 (2001)
7. Fabra-Boluda, R., Ferri, C., Ramírez-Quintana, M.J., Martínez-Plumed, F.: Unveiling the robustness of machine learning families. Mach. Learn. Sci. Technol. **5**(3), 035040 (2024)
8. Fischer, S.F., Harutyunyan, L., Feurer, M., Bischl, B.: OpenML-CTR23 - a curated tabular regression benchmarking suite. In: AutoML Conference (2023)
9. Fisher, A., Rudin, C., Dominici, F.: All models are wrong, but many are useful: Learning a variable's importance by studying an entire class of prediction models simultaneously. J. Mach. Learn. Res. **20**(177), 1–81 (2019)
10. Friedman, M.: The use of ranks to avoid the assumption of normality implicit in the analysis of variance. J. Ame. Statistical Association **32**(200), 675–701 (1937)
11. Gardner, J., Popovic, Z., Schmidt, L.: Benchmarking distribution shift in tabular data with TableShift. In: Advances in Neural Information Processing Systems (2023)

12. Goodfellow, I.J., Shlens, J., Szegedy, C.: Explaining and harnessing adversarial examples. In: ICLR (2015)
13. Hendrycks, D., Dietterich, T.: Benchmarking neural network robustness to common corruptions and perturbations. In: International Conference on Learning Representations (2019)
14. Porcu, V.: Scikit-learn. In: Python for Data Mining Quick Syntax Reference, pp. 235–253. Apress, Berkeley, CA (2018). https://doi.org/10.1007/978-1-4842-4113-4_11
15. Lin, L.I.K.: A concordance correlation coefficient to evaluate reproducibility. Biometrics **45**(1), 255–268 (1989)
16. Lin, S.L.: Application of machine learning to a medium gaussian support vector machine in the diagnosis of motor bearing faults. Electronics **10**, 2266 (2021)
17. Liu, C., et al.: A comprehensive study on robustness of image classification models: benchmarking and rethinking. Int. J. Comput. Vision **133**(2), 567–589 (2025)
18. Madry, A., Makelov, A., Schmidt, L., Tsipras, D., Vladu, A.: Towards deep learning models resistant to adversarial attacks. In: ICLR (2018)
19. Padró-Ferragut, C., Martínez-Plumed, F., Ramírez-Quintana, M.J.: Robustness under noise: assessing the impact of perturbed key attributes on machine learning models. Int. J. Data Sci. Anal. **22**(1), 71 (2026)
20. Padró-Ferragut, C., Ramírez-Quintana, M.J., Martínez-Plumed, F.: Noise tolerance and robustness ranking in machine learning models. In: Julian, V., et al. (eds.) IDEAL 2024. LNCS, vol. 15347 pp. 96–108. Springer, Cham (2024). https://doi.org/10.1007/978-3-031-77738-7_9
21. Rahm, E., Do, H.H., et al.: Data cleaning: problems and current approaches. IEEE Data Eng. Bull. **23**(4), 3–13 (2000)
22. Rusak, E., et al.: A simple way to make neural networks robust against diverse image corruptions. In: Vedaldi, A., Bischof, H., Brox, T., Frahm, J.-M. (eds.) ECCV 2020. LNCS, vol. 12348, pp. 53–69. Springer, Cham (2020). https://doi.org/10.1007/978-3-030-58580-8_4
23. Saltelli, A., et al.: Global Sensitivity Analysis: The Primer. Wiley (2008)
24. Shwartz-Ziv, R., Armon, A.: Tabular data: deep learning is not all you need. Inf. Fusion **81**, 84–90 (2022)
25. Simonetto, T., Ghamizi, S., Cordy, M.: TabularBench: benchmarking adversarial robustness for tabular deep learning in real-world use-cases. In: Advances in Neural Information Processing Systems (NeurIPS), Datasets and Benchmarks Track (2024)
26. Taori, R., Dave, A., Shankar, V., Carlini, N., Recht, B., Schmidt, L.: Measuring robustness to natural distribution shifts in image classification. Adv. Neural. Inf. Process. Syst. **33**, 18583–18599 (2020)
27. Vanschoren, J., van Rijn, J.N., Bischl, B., Torgo, L.: OpenML: networked science in machine learning. SIGKDD Expl. Newsl. **15**(2), 49–60 (2014)
28. Wang, H., Xiao, C., Kossaifi, J., Yu, Z., Anandkumar, A., Huang, Z.: AugMax: adversarial composition of random augmentations for robust training. In: Advances in Neural Information Processing Systems (2021)
29. Wilcoxon, F.: Individual comparisons by ranking methods. Biometr. Bull. **1**(6), 80–83 (1945)
30. Zha, D., et al.: Data-centric artificial intelligence: a survey. arXiv preprint arXiv:2303.10158 (2023)
31. Zur, R., Jiang, Y., Pesce, L., Drukker, K.: Noise injection for training artificial neural networks: a comparison with weight decay and early stopping. Med. Phys. **36**, 4810–8 (2009)

AutoML, Data-Centric and Statistical Learning

Automated Retraining for Cost-Optimal ML

Jun Yang(✉) and Michael Mathioudakis

University of Helsinki, Helsinki, Finland
{jun.yang,michael.mathioudakis}@helsinki.fi

Abstract. Machine Learning (ML) systems require critical decisions about *when* to retrain models and *how much* data to use, balancing predictive performance against computational cost. Current practices rely on static schedules or heuristics, leading to sub-optimal resource utilization. We formalize these decisions as a cost-aware dynamic programming problem and provide three algorithmic contributions: (1) an optimal offline algorithm, (2) a Bayesian optimization approach that approximates optimal solutions while overcoming computational bottlenecks, and (3) lightweight online policies derived from offline solutions. Experiments on real and synthetic datasets demonstrate that our algorithms effectively navigate the cost-performance trade-off, outperforming drift-detection methods and heuristic retraining strategies.

Keywords: Model Retraining · Data Drift · Dynamic Programming · Bayesian Optimization

1 Introduction

Machine learning (ML) has become a core component of software systems: ML pipeline frameworks and orchestrators (e.g., PyTorch [21], TensorFlow [2], MLflow [20] and Kubeflow [16]) have made it straightforward to train, deploy, and maintain ML models at scale across applications. At the same time, ML systems face *data drift*, that is, evolving data distributions that degrade model performance over time. Data drift thus motivates two critical decisions: *when* to retrain a model, and *how much data* to use. These decisions raise a trade-off between model quality and computational cost: on one extreme, training too frequently or with too much data wastes resources; on the other extreme, training too rarely or with too few data points degrades model quality. Current practices follow two approaches: *static schedules* retrain at fixed intervals regardless of need, while *drift detection methods* trigger retraining when distribution shifts are detected. Neither approach explicitly optimizes the cost-performance trade-off. Moreover, existing methods treat the questions of *when* to retrain and *how much data* to use independently, relying on domain-specific heuristics (e.g., train on all relevant data by default).

M. Ceci et al. (Eds.): ECML PKDD 2026, LNAI 16941, pp. 231–249, 2027.
https://doi.org/10.1007/978-3-032-37654-1_14

We formalize these decisions as a *cost-aware sequential decision problem*: for a given data stream, determine the optimal sequence of retraining times and data volumes that optimizes cost efficiency. This formulation enables principled navigation of trade-offs and generalizes across different ML tasks and cost models. Our algorithmic contributions are threefold: (i) **Optimal Offline Algorithm:** an exact dynamic programming algorithm (ORACLE) that computes optimal retraining policies in an offline setting, serving as a theoretical benchmark; (ii) **Bayesian Optimization Approximation:** a sample-efficient algorithm (APPROXIMATE) that learns surrogate models of cost and error functions, identifying near-optimal schedules with an order-of-magnitude reduction in computation compared to ORACLE; and (iii) **Learned Online Policy:** lightweight decision algorithms (LEARNED) trained on offline solutions, for deployment in online settings.

To the best of our knowledge, this is the first work to jointly optimize both retraining timing and data volume within a unified dynamic programming framework, with optimal offline solutions and practical online policies. Our work thus extends the recent literature on cost-aware ML maintenance, which has focused on the decision of *when* to retrain [19,23]. More broadly, our work falls within the literature on efficient ML, which addresses various dimensions of efficiency, including ones that are orthogonal to our work, such as sampling strategies, feature maintenance, or adaptation methods (see Sect. 2).

We evaluate our proposed algorithms on data streams with varying drift patterns (sudden, recurring, gradual) that scale up to 1,000 timesteps and 10^5 data points per timestep, as well as three real-world benchmark datasets. Our experiments show that ORACLE effectively navigates the accuracy-cost trade-off, APPROXIMATE converges to near-optimal solutions while training only a fraction of candidate models, and LEARNED online policies improve deployment-phase scheduling over fixed periodic baselines. On all datasets, our methods outperform standard drift-detection approaches (ADWIN [4], DDM [10]) and periodic retraining heuristics.

2 Related Work

Our work lies within the area of *efficient ML*. Let us review related work selected to delimit our contributions and highlight our departure from the literature.

Data drift refers to changes in data distributions over time, and its detection is well studied [11,18]. Classical detectors like DDM and ADWIN [4,10] monitor prediction errors to signal when updates may be needed. Recent methods improve robustness and reduce labeling requirements [15,22]. Such methods detect *when* drift occurs according to predefined thresholds (e.g., when performance degrades by a certain amount) but do not optimize retraining costs.

Cost-aware retraining along the timing dimension is addressed by Mahadevan et al. [19] and Regol et al. [23]; these works are closest to ours. Both address the cost-aware problem of *when* to retrain and formulate it as a sequential decision problem, with the former training online policies in stationary settings and the latter targeting non-stationary drift using an uncertainty-based performance forecaster. Our work also addresses cost-aware retraining as a sequential decision problem, but differs in key ways. First, it considers the *joint optimization* of *when* to retrain and *how much* data to use, while they focus on the former. Second, our work considers a progression of regimes from exact offline, to approximate offline, and then to an online regime with consistent drift dynamics (i.e., the patterns of distribution shift observed during tuning persist during deployment), with the algorithm of each regime building upon the previous one. Our work thus extends beyond Mahadevan et al. [19], which did not explicitly train online policies on offline solutions of the problem. Ultimately, we envision our work extended to unseen or evolving drift regimes, similarly to Regol et al. [23]. In Sect. 7.3, we compare empirically against adaptations of algorithms from both works, demonstrating the value of joint timing-and-volume optimization over timing-only approaches. A different line of work focuses on ML training and data management costs [6,17,27].

Data Sampling and Selection comprises a vast literature, from random sampling to coresets and active learning [9,14]. It is orthogonal to our work: we ask *how much* of the available data to use for retraining and assume that, once a volume n is chosen, a fixed data-selection strategy chooses the specific examples.

Bayesian Optimization (BO) [12] is widely used for hyperparameter tuning and architecture search [25,26]. We employ it to speed up our dynamic programming (DP) algorithm: BO enables us to fill only a small number of entries in the DP matrix to efficiently find an approximately optimal solution.

Continual Learning trains on non-stationary streams while avoiding catastrophic forgetting [8].

This line of work focuses on *how* to update models and is orthogonal to ours: our scheduling policies decide when to update a model and how much data to use, while the update mechanism itself is interchangeable.

3 Problem Formulation

We consider a dynamic data setting, with time $t \in \{0, 1, \ldots, T-1\}$ increasing in discrete timesteps and a varying set of data points D_t considered valid at any given time t. The task is to maintain a model that represents the dynamically changing data. For purposes of illustration only, we consider a *running example* where each data point has the form $d = (X, y)$, where X is a list of features and y is a label; and the task is to maintain a classification model $M : X \to y$ that is trained to predict y from X. Other modeling examples (e.g., regression or clustering models) fit equally well into the framework of this paper.

For this task, we address two questions: first, at what times t should model M be retrained on the currently valid data D_t; and second, what positive data volume $n_t \leq N_t = |D_t|$ should the retraining use? We assume that, if it is decided to retrain with n data points, a fixed algorithm selects n data points from D_t for training the model (e.g., through random sampling or other selection strategies). The two questions above give rise to a trade-off. On the one hand, retraining M

at every timestep using all the currently valid data achieves the highest model quality, as captured by predictive accuracy in the running example. On the other hand, training incurs a cost $trC(n_t)$ that is an increasing function of the data volume n_t used for the purpose. In general, the training cost trC may represent computing allocation, energy consumption, or other types of costs. The two questions are naturally formalized as a problem of system control [3], calling for a sequence of decisions at each timestep (whether to retrain and with how much data) that optimize the performance (the long-term quality of the model and the cost to maintain it) of the system (the ML training and inference).

In particular, each timestep t is associated with state $s_t = (D_t, M_t)$, where D_t is the currently valid dataset and M_t the currently available model, trained at some timestep $t' \leq t$. Specifically for $t = 0$, the model M_0 is given as input (e.g., it may correspond to a pre-trained model, or a model that makes uniform/random predictions). Given the previous state s_{t-1}, a decision u_t is made whether to keep the previous model (denoted with $u_t = \varnothing$) or to use n_t of the currently valid data points to retrain the model (denoted with $u_t = n_t$).

Notice that, naturally, the decision affects only the model component of the state; the data component (i.e., the entire dataset that is valid at any time) is not controlled by our optimizations and is given as input.

Each decision u_t has a cost g at the timestep t, which we define as a sum of two terms. The first term is the training cost trC discussed above. The second term is the modeling cost ℓ, the loss function minimized during training that captures model quality (i.e., (1−accuracy) in our running example). The smaller the modeling cost, the higher the quality of the model. The decision $u = n$ to retrain with n data points leads to a new *trained model instance* and incurs both a modeling cost and a training cost. On the other hand, the decision $u = \varnothing$ to keep the current model incurs no training cost, but may incur higher modeling cost in the event of drastic data drift that renders the available model obsolete. Formally, the cost of a decision u_t at state s_t is:

$$g(s_t, u_t) = \begin{cases} \ell(D_t, M_t), \text{ if } u_t = \varnothing \\ r(D_t, n_t) = \ell(D_t, \text{train}(D_t; n_t)) + trC(n_t), \text{ if } u_t = n_t \end{cases} \tag{1}$$

The relative weights of modeling and training costs can be absorbed into ℓ and trC. In our experiments, the modeling term is κ_ℓ times evaluation loss for both keep and retrain decisions, while $trC(n)$ is κ_t times the measured training time for retraining with n data points; keep decisions have zero training-time cost. The framework only assumes that this cost can be measured or estimated for candidate retraining actions; it does not require a specific parametric form. For neural networks trained with stochastic gradient descent for a fixed number of epochs, each epoch processes the dataset once, so training time is often approximately linear in n, but other model families or training protocols may induce different cost curves. The total cost for a sequence of decisions $\pi = [u_0, u_1, \ldots, u_{T-1}]$ is

$$J(\pi) = J_0(\pi; s_0) = \sum_{t'=0}^{T-1} g(s_{t'}, u_{t'}). \tag{2}$$

Notice that we write $J_t(\pi; s_t)$ to refer to the total 'cost-to-go' from time t until the end when the initial state is s_t and the future states are determined from the decisions π.

We will sometimes omit the index and arguments of the cost-to-go function $J_t(\pi; s_t)$ when they're implied from context.

We can now formally state the main problem we are addressing.

Problem 1 (Offline Cost-Optimized ML Training). Given datasets $\{D_t,\ t = 0, \ldots, T-1\}$ and the initial model M_0 as input, identify a sequence of decisions π to minimize $J(\pi)$.

Let us break down its name: 'ML Training' refers to the decisions of when to retrain and with how much data, the variables of the optimization; 'offline' refers to the assumption that the data stream is provided as input; and 'cost-optimized' refers to the objective, which combines modeling and training costs (Eq. 2).

4 An Optimal Offline Algorithm

We state the core dynamic programming formulation (Sect. 4.1), upon which we build ORACLE, an optimal algorithm for Problem 1 (Sect. 4.2).

4.1 Dynamic Programming

Problem 1 is solved with dynamic programming under the following optimal-substructure formulation (also known as the Bellman equation [3]).

$$J^* = \min_{u_0}\{g(s_0, u_0) + J_1^*\} \tag{3}$$

Equation 3 states that the optimal cost-to-go J^* from the initial state s_0 is equal to the minimum over all possible first decisions u_0 of the sum of (i) the immediate cost $g(s_0, u_0)$ incurred by taking decision u_0 at state s_0, plus (ii) the optimal cost-to-go J_1^* from the next state s_1 that results from taking decision u_0 at state s_0. It invites a generic dynamic programming algorithm: starting with the decisions that optimize the smallest tail subproblems, build solutions for progressively longer tail subproblems, until the full solution is obtained.

A naive implementation would consider jointly at every step t: (1) all possible previous model instances from $t' < t$ that could have become part of the current state s_t due to 'keep' decisions; and (2) all possible model instances from the current dataset D_t under a 'retrain' decision. For increased efficiency, we utilize a property of Problem 1: the decision to retrain for a new model incurs a cost that is independent of the previous model , and the decision to keep the previous model incurs a cost that is independent of the potentially retrained model. This independence allows us to disentangle the evaluation of the previously trained and potentially retrained models at every step t. Following the above observations, the dynamic programming algorithm DYNPROG is shown as Algorithm 1.

Notice that, in accordance with Eq. 3, DynProg takes only a cost matrix G as input – which in turn is computed from the datasets D_t and candidate models $M_{t,n}$.

The time and space complexity of DynProg is $O(T^2|\mathcal{N}|)$ for candidate data-volume sets $\mathcal{N}_t$ of maximum size $|\mathcal{N}|$; with the full positive-volume grid $\mathcal{N}_t = \{1, \ldots, N_t\}$ this is $O(T^2 N)$, where $N = \max_t N_t = \max_t |D_t|$, as for every timestep t there are $O(t|\mathcal{N}|)$ models from previous timesteps that could potentially have been kept as the current model at time t.

4.2 The Oracle Algorithm and Its Complexity

Computing model instances for all times and data volumes, building the cost matrix, and executing DynProg is the Oracle (Algorithm 2) that solves Problem 1. In implementation, the same decomposition precomputes candidate model costs before running DynProg.

It involves three types of operations: (I) training all $O(NT)$ possible model instances, with $O(TN^2)$ elementary operations (e.g., gradient evaluations) if those are proportional to data volume; (II) measuring the costs G with $O(T^2N)$ elementary operations (e.g., objective function evaluations); and (III) performing cost comparisons during DynProg and backtracking, which involves $O(T^2N)$ elementary operations (e.g., arithmetic comparisons). Therefore, the total time complexity of Oracle is $O(TN^2 + T^2N)$. It has two regimes. If $T \ll N$, it is dominated by model training operations.

If instead $N \ll T$, it is dominated by model evaluations and cost comparisons.

Both regimes are prohibitive for large-scale problems, motivating approximations formalized as Problem 2.

Problem 2 (Approximately Cost-Optimized ML Training). Given $\{D_t\}_{t=0}^{T-1}$ and M_0, seek a subset of model instances enabling DynProg on a partial G to recover a solution close to Oracle.

In Sect. 5, we target both regimes at once, by applying DynProg on a carefully selected subset of the cost matrix G, corresponding to a subset of model instances, thus reducing both the training effort (first complexity regime) and shrinking the DynProg instance (second regime).

Algorithm 1. DynProg

Require: Cost matrix: G
for $t = T - 1$ down to 0 **do**
  $c^* \leftarrow \infty$, $u^* \leftarrow \varnothing$ ▷ Track best decision
  ▷ 'Retrain' decisions: Iterate over candidate models
  for $n \in \mathcal{N}_t$ **do** ▷ Candidate positive-volume grid; full Oracle uses $\{1, \ldots, N_t\}$
    cost $\leftarrow G(D_t; M_{t,n}) + J^*_{t+1}(M_{t,n})$
    if cost $< c^*$ **then**
      $c^* \leftarrow$ cost, $u^* \leftarrow n$
    end if
  end for
  ▷ 'Keep' decisions: Iterate over every possible past model
  for $M_{t',n}$ with $t' < t$ **do**
    $J^*_t(M_{t',n}) \leftarrow G(D_t; M_{t',n}) + J^*_{t+1}(M_{t',n})$
    if $c^* < J^*_t(M_{t',n})$ **then** ▷ Is it better to retrain?
      $J^*_t(M_{t',n}) \leftarrow c^*$, $S^*_t(M_{t',n}) \leftarrow u^*$
    end if
  end for
end for
▷ Return optimal cost
return $J^*_0(M_0)$

Algorithm 2. Oracle

Require: Initial model instance: M_0; Stream of datasets: $\{D_t\}_{t=0}^{T-1}$
ModelInstances $\leftarrow$ PreComputeModels($M_0, \{D_t\}_{t=0}^{T-1}$) ▷ All model instances
G $\leftarrow$ PreComputeCosts(ModelInstances) ▷ Fill the cost matrix
$J^* \leftarrow$ DynProg(G) ▷ Find optimal cost
$\pi^* \leftarrow$ Backtrack(J^*, G) ▷ Find optimal decision sequence
return J^*, π^*

5 Approximate Offline Algorithms

Our search for approximate solutions (Problem 2) finds us in a setting where finding the optimal solution is computationally prohibitive, and even evaluating a candidate solution $J(\pi)$ requires $|\pi| = O(T)$ trained model instances. Moreover, there is no readily available gradient for the objective function. In other words, this is a standard setting for Bayesian optimization [12]. Inspired by Bayesian optimization approaches, we propose an Approximate algorithm (Algorithm 3): (i) selects iteratively a subset of model instances to train (Algorithm 3, Lines 3–11) and stores the associated costs in G (line 5); (ii) **estimates the costs** of the untrained model instances and identifies the decisions π^{next} that optimize an **acquisition function** $\mathcal{A}(\pi)$ (line 8); (iii) computes those model instances that correspond to 'retrain' decisions in π^{next} (line 10), unless already trained.

Here B denotes the size of the initial random design before acquisition-guided iterations begin.

As described, APPROXIMATE has two central elements: first, *cost estimates* for untrained model instances, which partially replace the actual model training that constitutes the bottleneck we aim to alleviate; second, an *acquisition function*, which evaluates how 'promising' each decision sequence is based on cost measurements (for the trained model instances) and cost estimates (for the untrained instances). We elaborate on them below.

Cost Estimates. At every iteration of APPROXIMATE, we evaluate all the relevant entries (per Eq. 1) of the cost matrix G that correspond to trained model instances. These entries are used as a training dataset for *surrogate cost models* that predict the cost of untrained model instances. Specifically, we fit two Gaussian-process surrogates: The *training-cost surrogate* predicts the training cost $trC(n)$ as a function of data volume n, while the *evaluation-loss surrogate* predicts the modeling cost of untrained models, essentially capturing the evolution of accuracy as trained models age and the stream drifts. Both surrogates are refit with every iteration as new model instances are trained and new measurements are collected.

Acquisition Functions. $\mathcal{A}(\pi)$ mimic the form of objective function $J(\pi)$ (Eq. 2), as a time-wise sum of terms $\alpha(s_t, u_t)$.

$$\mathcal{A}(\pi) = \mathcal{A}_0(\pi; s_0) = \sum_{t=0}^{T-1} \alpha(s_t, u_t) \tag{4}$$

How to define the term α – and thus also $\mathcal{A}(\pi)$? Following standard literature conventions, acquisition functions essentially offer different solution-search strategies between *exploration* (i.e., favoring sequences of decisions different than the ones evaluated before) and *exploitation* (i.e., favoring sequences that are likely to lead to a local optimum). Below we consider various options.

The most straightforward option is to define α so that the acquisition function $\mathcal{A}(\pi)$ is equal to the *expected* cost of the decision sequence π.

$$\alpha_{\text{EXPECTED}}{::}\alpha(s_t, u_t) = \mathbb{E}[g(s_t, u_t)] \tag{5}$$

This corresponds to *exploitation*: at each iteration, we favor the decision sequence that optimizes the expected costs, as estimated from current measurements.

Another approach would be to define α so that $\mathcal{A}(\pi)$ is equal to the *total variance* of the cost of the decision sequence π.

$$\alpha_{\text{VARIANCE}}{::}\alpha(s_t, u_t) = -\operatorname{Var}[g(s_t, u_t)] \tag{6}$$

This corresponds to *exploration*: at every iteration, we favor the decision sequence associated with the highest uncertainty based on current measurements.

Algorithm 3. APPROXIMATE

Require: Initial model instance: M_0; Stream of datasets: $\mathcal{D}$; Iterations: k
MODELINSTANCES $\leftarrow$ random$(B) \cup \{M_0\}$ ▷ Initialize model collection.
▷ Iteratively grow the trained model collection
for iteration $= 1 \ldots k$ **do**
  ▷ Fill the acquisition matrix.
  $Q \leftarrow acq(\text{MODELINSTANCES}; \mathcal{D})$
  ▷ Identify decisions that optimize the acquisition function.
  $J_Q^* \leftarrow \text{DYNPROG}(Q)$
  $\pi^{next} \leftarrow \text{Backtrack}(J_Q^*, Q)$
  ▷ Train those models that correspond to 'retrain' decisions.
  MODELINSTANCES $\leftarrow$ MODELINSTANCES $\cup\ \pi_{retrain}^{next}$
end for
▷ Final DYNPROG on the extrapolated cost matrix.
$\text{G} \leftarrow extrapolate(\text{MODELINSTANCES}; \mathcal{D})$
$J^* \leftarrow \text{DYNPROG}(\text{G})$
$\pi^* \leftarrow \text{Backtrack}(J^*, \text{G})$
return J^*, π^*

We also consider optimistic or pessimistic estimates (lower/upper cost bounds), β standard deviations below or above expectation.

$$\begin{aligned} \alpha_{\text{LCB}}(s_t, u_t) &= \mathbb{E}[g(s_t, u_t)] - \beta\, \text{std}[g(s_t, u_t)], \\ \alpha_{\text{UCB}}(s_t, u_t) &= \mathbb{E}[g(s_t, u_t)] + \beta\, \text{std}[g(s_t, u_t)], \qquad \beta \geq 0. \end{aligned} \tag{7}$$

Since DYNPROG minimizes costs, LCB is the optimistic cost estimate and UCB is the pessimistic one. Finally, we consider two improvement-based acquisition functions commonly used in Bayesian optimization. Let μ_t and σ_t denote the posterior mean and standard deviation produced by the cost estimators for (s_t, u_t), and let b be the best observed per-stage cost so far. With margin parameter $\xi \geq 0$ we define

$$\alpha_{\text{PI}}::\alpha(s_t, u_t) = \Phi\left(\frac{b - \mu_t - \xi}{\sigma_t}\right), \tag{8}$$

$$\alpha_{\text{EI}}::\alpha(s_t, u_t) = (b - \mu_t - \xi)\Phi(z) + \sigma_t \phi(z), \tag{9}$$

where $z = (b - \mu_t - \xi)/\sigma_t$, $\Phi(\cdot)$ denotes the standard normal cumulative distribution function (CDF), and $\phi(\cdot)$ the corresponding probability density function (PDF); when $\sigma_t = 0$ both scores default to zero. Intuitively, α_{PI} favors decisions that have high probability of improvement upon b, whereas α_{EI} favors decisions with larger expected improvement. Because DYNPROG minimizes its input matrix, these improvement scores are used as negative acquisition costs (equivalently, maximize improvement and then convert it to the minimization form used by DYNPROG).

6 Online Algorithms

Problems 1 and 2 request a retrospective solution: given an observed data stream, when would have been the right times to retrain the model M and with how much data? Such solutions help determine appropriate retraining frequencies and structural patterns in data evolution (i.e., the "meta-dynamics" of the drift) that signify the necessity of retraining. Such insights may then be used to design online algorithms without access to future data, aiming to optimize the same cost-accuracy trade-off as the offline problems.

In what follows, we define two online algorithms, Base and Learned. Both algorithms operate in two phases: tuning and deployment. During tuning, the offline problem (Problem 1 or 2) is solved over recent historical data and, based on the solution, the parameters of the online algorithm are determined. During deployment, the online algorithm is employed at every step to decide whether to keep or retrain the model and, in the latter case, with how much data.

Base retrains periodically every τ steps with n_0 data points (or the full current dataset, if its size is smaller than n_0), with parameters τ and n_0 determined from the offline solution, as the average number of steps between retrains, and the average data volume used for retraining, respectively.

$$\tau = T/|\{t : u_t \neq \varnothing\}|; \quad n_0 = \text{avg}(n_t \mid u_t = n_t \neq \varnothing) \tag{10}$$

If the tuning solution has no retrains, Base defaults to the Never-retrain policy.

Learned decides whether to retrain based on features $\mathbf{f}_t = (f_t^1, f_t^2, f_t^3)$. Assuming the current model M_t was trained at time t':

Current Staleness (f_t^1) captures the loss increase since that training time:

$$f_t^1 :: \Psi_{t,t'} = \ell(D_t, M_t) - \ell(D_{t'}, M_t). \tag{11}$$

Accumulated Staleness (f_t^2) captures the total staleness accumulated since the last retraining:

$$f_t^2 :: \sum_{j=t'}^{t} \Psi_{j,t'}. \tag{12}$$

Intuitively, this feature captures whether there has been sustained staleness over time, which may be a stronger signal for retraining than a single high staleness value at the current time.

Elapsed time (f_t^3) captures the time $(t - t')$ since the last retraining.

The online decision model is tuned using the above features: for each timestep t in the offline solution, we record the feature values $\mathbf{f}_t$ and the corresponding offline decision u_t. We then fit two models:

1. A *binary classifier* $h_{\text{retrain}} : \mathbf{f} \rightarrow \{0, 1\}$ that predicts whether to retrain (we use a Random Forest [7] with 100 trees).
2. A *regressor* $h_{\text{volume}} : \mathbf{f} \rightarrow \mathbb{R}^+$ that predicts the data volume n, trained only on timesteps where $u_t \neq \varnothing$.

During deployment, Learned first evaluates h_{retrain}; if the prediction is positive, it evaluates h_{volume} to determine the data volume it retrains with.

7 Experiments

We evaluate four questions aligned with Sects. 1–6: (**RQ1**) Does the objective induce meaningful accuracy–cost trade-offs, and does APPROXIMATE converge to ORACLE's solution? (**RQ2**) How does solution quality scale with optimization budget? (**RQ3**) How do our methods compare with standard retraining baselines? (**RQ4**) Do offline solutions transfer to good online policies?

Setup and Metrics

Data and Objective. Synthetic streams use three drift types (sudden, gradual, recurring) and three tiers: `S` ($T = 10, N = 10^3$), `M` ($T = 50, N = 5 \cdot 10^3$), and `L` ($T = 100, N = 10^4$). Section 7.2 also reports an `X` tier ($T = 1{,}000, N = 10^5$) that probes the practical limit of full ORACLE enumeration. We also evaluate three real datasets: Airlines [1], Electricity [13], and Covertype [5]. Unless noted otherwise, we train a 2-layer MLP (hidden sizes [128, 64]) with SGD [24] with momentum 0.9 and learning rate 0.01. At each retrain, data are uniformly sampled from the currently valid batch. Unless otherwise noted, candidate retraining volumes use the fractions $\{0.1, 0.2, \ldots, 1.0\}$ of the current batch, resolved to integer sample counts. For the retrain branch of Eq. 1, we use $r(D_t, n_t) = \kappa_\ell \, \ell_{\text{eval}}(D_t, \text{train}(D_t; n_t)) + \kappa_t \, t_{\text{train}}(n_t)$, where ℓ_{eval} is the evaluation loss and t_{train} is the measured training time. Keep decisions use the same weighted evaluation-loss term and zero training time. Only the relative weighting matters, so throughout the experiments we denote $\kappa := \kappa_\ell / \kappa_t$ and fix $\kappa_t = 1$, hence $\kappa = \kappa_\ell$. Larger κ therefore places more weight on evaluation loss relative to retraining time.

Compared Methods. We evaluate ORACLE and six APPROXIMATE variants (Expected, Variance, LCB, UCB, EI, PI). Synthetic acquisition comparisons use up to $k = 100$ BO iterations; real-data runs use $k = 50$. The baseline set covers three families. Simple retraining rules include Never, Always, and Periodic: Never keeps the initial model throughout, Always retrains at every timestep with the maximum available data, and Periodic chooses the best fixed retraining interval. Loss-stream detectors (ADWIN and DDM) trigger retraining from the currently deployed model's loss stream and reset after retraining, so they observe the same adaptive setting faced by the online policy. Timing-only cost-aware baselines include Markov, Threshold, and Cumulative Threshold from Mahadevan et al. [19], and a simplified Uncertainty-Performance Forecaster (UPF) inspired by Regol et al. [23]. To adapt these timing-only methods to our joint setting, we pair each with $n = \max(\mathcal{N})$ when retraining and optimize its free parameters (threshold, cumulative threshold, or α/δ) via grid search on the Oracle data. RQ3 evaluates all baseline methods on the same reported stream as the corresponding ORACLE cost; the separate prefix/deployment protocol is used only for RQ4.

Metrics. We report true total cost $J(\pi)$, relative optimality gap ROG $= 100 \cdot (J_{\text{method}} - J_{\text{ORACLE}})/J_{\text{ORACLE}}$, relative model-training effort RMT $= 100 \cdot \text{TT}_{\text{eval}}/\text{TT}_{\text{oracle}}$, where TT_{eval} is the cumulative training time spent evaluating candidate models during optimization and $\text{TT}_{\text{oracle}}$ is the cumulative training time needed to materialize the full ORACLE candidate cost matrix, and normalized cost ratio $\rho = J_{\text{method}}/J_{\text{ORACLE}}$.

Reproducibility. https://version.helsinki.fi/ads/cost-optimal-retraining.

7.1 RQ1: Objective Validity and Convergence

Figure 1 validates both the optimization objective and the BO search procedure. In the left panel, increasing the experimental trade-off parameter κ moves ORACLE from lower training effort toward lower evaluation loss, yielding a clear quality–cost frontier rather than arbitrary policy changes. The right panel reports the incumbent, best-so-far exact ROG over BO iterations on recurring drift. LCB, EI, and PI reach zero gap within the budget, while UCB, Expected, and Variance still reduce the gap to a few percent. These diagnostics show that BO only needs enough surrogate signal to discover and retain low-cost schedules within the evaluation budget.

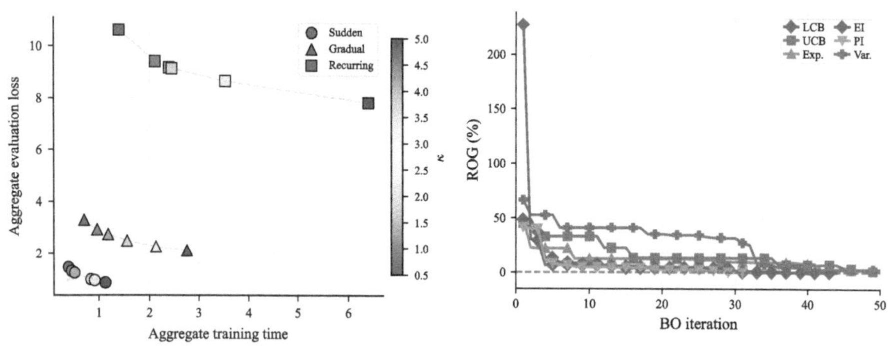

(a) Effect of κ on ORACLE trade-offs. (b) Recurring-drift ROG convergence.

Fig. 1. Validation of the objective and optimization behavior. (Color figure online)

7.2 RQ2: Quality–Effort Scalability

Figure 2 shows the medium-tier synthetic ROG–RMT trade-off for $k = 100$ BO iterations, under convergence thresholds $\varphi \in \{0.2, 0.1, 0.05, 0.01\}$, applied to the rolling relative range of estimated policy cost. This gives a practical knob between solution quality and optimization effort: stricter stopping thresholds usually spend more candidate evaluations, although true ROG need not be monotone because stopping uses estimated policy cost. LCB gives the most consistent low-ROG operating points in Fig. 2; EI and PI can match ORACLE on sudden drift, but often at higher RMT. The high-ROG UCB outliers on sudden and recurring drift show why estimated-cost stabilization is not always a reliable stopping proxy for exact cost.

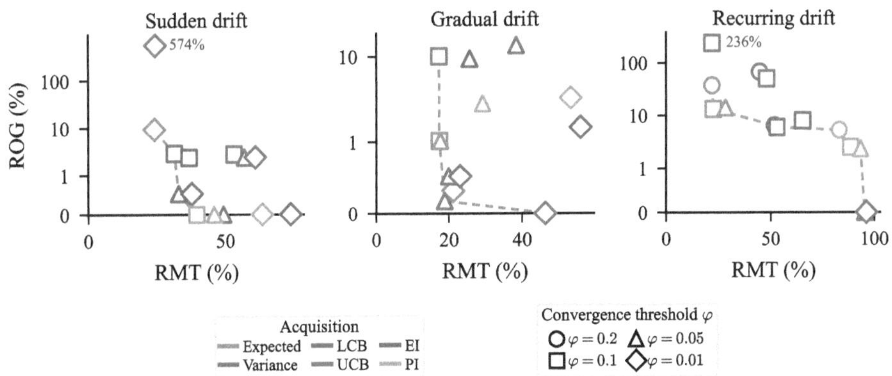

Fig. 2. ROG–RMT trade-off. Color denotes acquisition and marker shape denotes φ; the gray dashed line is the empirical Pareto frontier; coincident thresholds use the strictest marker. The ROG axis is compressed so near-zero gaps and high-ROG outliers remain visible. (Color figure online)

Scaling to X. Table 1 tests practical limits by comparing the last tractable full-ORACLE tier with a 10× scale-up. At L, all reported BO rows remain within 0.2 cost units of the full ORACLE, showing near-ORACLE quality before full DP becomes the bottleneck. At X ($T = 1{,}000$, $N = 10^5$), full ORACLE enumeration is infeasible, so the reference is a restricted sub-DP that keeps every 20th timestep plus the final timestep and the smallest and largest candidate data-volume fractions at each kept timestep, giving 102 retrain candidates instead of ~10,000. APPROXIMATE uses the same candidate retraining-volume fractions as the main experiments but evaluates only five BO iterations per acquisition function, so the X comparison is to a coarse reference rather than to a full ORACLE lower bound. Under this restricted reference, EI is the strongest acquisition shown: it remains closest to the reference on sudden and gradual drift and, on recurring drift, outperforms this coarse reference. The recurring-drift result should not be read as improving on a full ORACLE lower bound: the sub-DP reference is restricted, and its search space differs from the approximate solver's BO-based policy search and cost evaluation. Acquisition functions without explicit exploration (EXPECTED) are much less reliable at this scale, especially on recurring drift.

Table 1. Cost at the largest synthetic tiers (lower is better). `L` uses the full ORACLE. `X` uses a restricted sub-DP reference (every 20th timestep plus the final timestep, with the smallest and largest candidate data-volume fractions per kept timestep), not a full-ORACLE lower bound. Reference values are italicized; best acquisition result per tier and drift is in **bold**.

Tier	Method	Sudden	Gradual	Recurring
L	ORACLE	*4.0*	*8.9*	*30.9*
	LCB	**4.0**	**8.9**	31.1
	EI	**4.0**	**8.9**	**31.0**
	EXPECTED	4.1	**8.9**	31.1
X	Sub-DP ref.	*18.4*	*108.9*	*530.4*
	LCB	21.4	293.1	584.7
	EI	**21.1**	**127.0**	**489.5**
	EXPECTED	21.3	267.4	2951.8

7.3 RQ3: Comparison with Baselines

Figure 3 and Table 2 compare our methods with standard retraining baselines and timing-only cost-aware methods. Across the large synthetic streams and the reported real-world runs, the strongest APPROXIMATE variants remain near-ORACLE: ρ = 1.00–1.03 on synthetic and ρ = 1.00 on real data. The heuristic block forms a ladder from boundary rules to adaptive triggers. Never avoids retraining cost but lets drift accumulate, whereas Always retrains at every timestep with the maximum data volume. Periodic adds a best fixed retraining interval, and ADWIN/DDM add loss-triggered adaptation from the deployed model's loss stream. These progressively more adaptive heuristics improve over the boundary cases, but they remain several-fold above ORACLE on the synthetic streams; for example, on gradual drift Periodic is 5.1× and the best detector is 4.8×. Figure 3 shows ADWIN and DDM separately, while Table 2 reports Detector (best) as the stronger detector in each column.

Timing-Only Cost-Aware Baselines. Table 2 also includes three algorithms from Mahadevan et al. [19] (Markov, Threshold, Cumulative Threshold) and a simplified UPF inspired by Regol et al. [23], each paired with $n = \max(\mathcal{N})$. Despite oracle-optimized parameters under this fixed-volume protocol, the best timing-only variants achieve ρ values of about 1.85–3.83× on the synthetic streams, making them competitive with the stronger heuristics but still far from

ORACLE. This pattern isolates the benefit of jointly optimizing *when* and *how much* to retrain: even with tuned timing decisions, fixing the data volume to the maximum can leave substantial cost on the table. On the real-world datasets, the gap narrows and timing-only methods are more competitive, consistent with settings where timing alone captures more of the benefit. Across both synthetic and real-world settings, however, the joint optimizer is the only method that remains consistently near ORACLE.

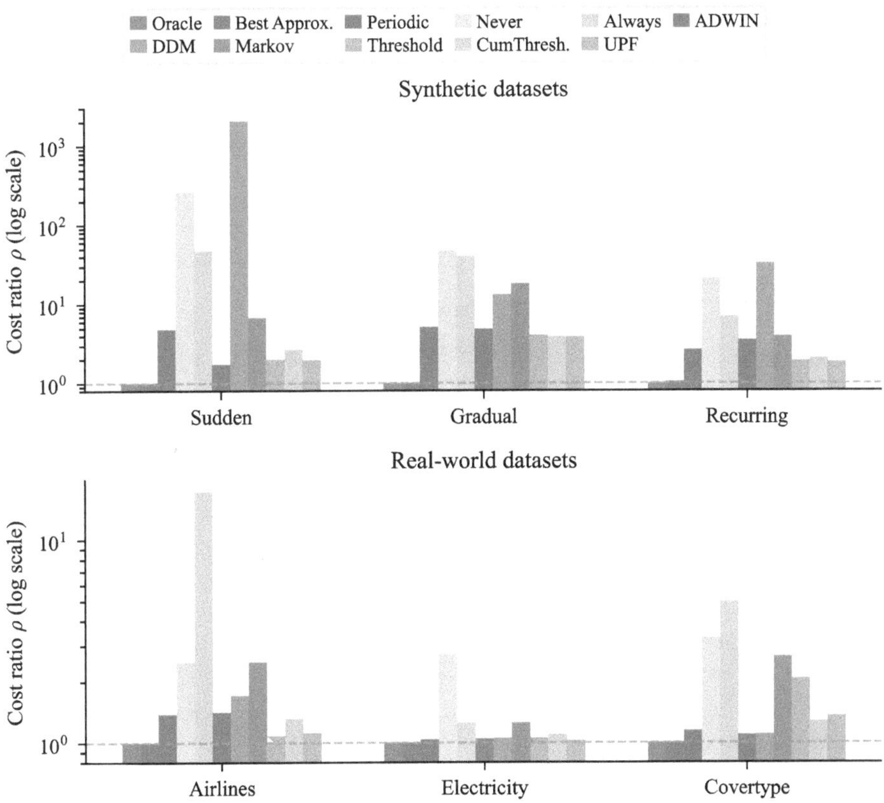

Fig. 3. Normalized cost ratio ρ (log scale) on synthetic datasets (top) and real-world datasets (bottom). The log axis keeps near-ORACLE behavior and large baseline costs visible in the same view. Red dashed line is ORACLE ($\rho = 1$). (Color figure online)

Table 2. Cost ratios ρ (lower is better). Synthetic columns use the `L` tier. Detector (best) is the better of ADWIN and DDM in each column. Timing-only methods use $n = \max(\mathcal{N})$ with oracle-optimized parameters.

Category	Method	Synthetic-L			Real-world		
		Sudden	Gradual	Recurring	Airlines	Elec.	Cov.
Ours	Best Approx.	**1.00**	**1.00**	**1.03**	**1.00**	**1.00**	**1.00**
Heuristic	Never	262.20	46.72	20.94	2.49	2.72	3.28
	Always	47.22	40.30	6.88	17.22	1.25	4.94
	Periodic	4.83	5.13	2.64	1.38	1.04	1.14
	Detector (best)	1.73	4.83	3.50	1.41	1.05	1.09
Timing-only	Markov [19]	6.79	17.93	3.92	2.49	1.25	2.66
	Threshold [19]	2.00	4.00	1.90	1.08	1.05	2.06
	CumThreshold [19]	2.69	3.88	2.04	1.31	1.10	1.27
	UPF [23]	1.96	3.83	1.85	1.12	1.02	1.35

7.4 RQ4: Offline-to-Online Transfer

Table 3 reports deployment-phase online cost on the synthetic streams ($T = 200$, $N = 300$). Each policy is configured on a prefix of the stream (split at $t = 100$) and then evaluated on the held-out deployment segment. Base inherits the prefix Oracle sequence's average retrain interval and retrain size, while Learned is fit to prefix states and Oracle decisions. Learned improves over Base in all three drift regimes; it closes most of the gap to Oracle on sudden and gradual drift and more than half of the gap on recurring drift. The same table also shows where hindsight still matters: on recurring drift, the deployment policy must time retrains before losses fully materialize, which is harder without lookahead. State-dependent policies therefore transfer better to deployment than fixed periodic rules, even without lookahead.

Table 3. Deployment-phase online cost on synthetic streams (lower is better). Oracle is a hindsight reference; bold marks the better deployable policy.

Policy	Sudden	Gradual	Recurring
Oracle (hindsight)	0.14	2.97	79.29
Base	0.95	7.22	85.94
Learned	**0.39**	**3.07**	**81.78**

8 Discussion and Conclusion

This work addresses a joint decision problem that standard retraining pipelines usually decouple: *when* to retrain and *how much* data to use. Optimizing both choices under one cost-aware objective yields both an exact offline benchmark (ORACLE) and a practical route to deployment through BO-based approximation and lightweight online policies.

8.1 What the Experiments Show

The results support four linked claims. First, the objective is behaviorally meaningful: varying the experimental trade-off parameter κ moves solutions along a clear accuracy–cost frontier, reflected in different aggregate training costs and evaluation losses (Fig. 1). Second, APPROXIMATE is a practical approximation route when exhaustive planning is expensive: with modest budgets, the strongest acquisition rules recover near-ORACLE schedules in the last tractable full-DP setting while exposing a usable quality–effort trade-off (Fig. 2), and the `X` tier shows that stronger BO acquisitions remain useful once only coarse DP references are tractable (Table 1). Third, the gap to heuristic baselines is structural rather than cosmetic: Fig. 3 and Table 2 show that BO-based approximate schedules remain near-ORACLE while periodic, detector, and timing-only rules can be substantially more expensive, especially on the synthetic drift regimes. Fourth, the offline solutions are not merely descriptive: fitting online decision rules on a prefix yields materially better deployment-phase online performance on all three synthetic regimes (Table 3), so the offline solver provides usable supervision for deployment rather than a purely retrospective benchmark.

8.2 How to Use the Framework

The most defensible deployment recipe is staged. When the horizon and candidate set are still manageable, ORACLE is valuable as an offline benchmark for policy design and for quantifying the price of heuristic simplifications. When exhaustive search is too expensive, the stronger APPROXIMATE variants can retain much of the observed benefit while evaluating far fewer schedules. The experiments suggest using LCB and EI as robust synthetic defaults, while treating the convergence threshold as an explicit engineering knob: stop once further candidate evaluations buy only a small reduction in cost.

8.3 Limitations and Next Steps

Exact planning still scales quadratically with horizon length. Table 1 shows that once full DP becomes infeasible, a coarse subsampled reference is still useful, but it should not be interpreted as a full-ORACLE lower bound against differently constrained approximate search. The fitted online policy remains reactive, leaving a residual gap especially on recurring drift where deployment decisions must anticipate future evolution (Table 3). Opportunities for improvement remain. Future deployments should incorporate label latency and label-acquisition costs, allow the action space to include training hyperparameters such as epochs or batches in addition to data volume, and test heavier model families where the measured retraining-cost curve may be strongly nonlinear.

Acknowledgments. We have used AI tools to polish the language of this manuscript and take full responsibility for the content of this manuscript. Moreover, none of the data and methods involved in this work involve personal or sensitive information. This work was supported by the AI-DOC program and the University of Helsinki. Computational resources were provided by *CSC – IT Center for Science*, Finland.

Disclosure of Interests. The authors have no competing interests to declare that are relevant to the content of this article.

References

1. Data expo 2009: Airline on time data (2008). https://doi.org/10.7910/DVN/HG7NV7
2. Abadi, M., et al.: TensorFlow: a system for large-scale machine learning. In: OSDI (2016)
3. Bertsekas, D.P.: Dynamic Programming and Optimal Control: Volume I. Athena Scientific (2005)
4. Bifet, A., et al.: Learning from time-changing data with adaptive windowing. In: SDM (2007)
5. Blackard, J.: Covertype. UCI Machine Learning Repository (1998)
6. Böther, M., et al.: Modyn: data-centric machine learning pipeline orchestration. Proc. ACM Manag. Data (2025)
7. Breiman, L.: Random forests. Mach. Learn. (2001)
8. De Lange, M., et al.: A continual learning survey: defying forgetting in classification tasks. TPAMI (2022)
9. Draganov, A., et al.: Settling time vs. accuracy tradeoffs for clustering big data. Proc. ACM Manag. Data (2024)
10. Gama, J., et al.: Learning with drift detection. In: SBIA (2004)
11. Gama, J., et al.: A survey on concept drift adaptation. ACM Comput. Surv. (2014)
12. Garnett, R.: Bayesian Optimization. Cambridge University Press (2023)
13. Harries, M.: Splice-2 comparative evaluation: electricity pricing. Tech. rep., University of New South Wales (1999)
14. Huang, D., et al.: ALINE: joint amortization for Bayesian inference and active data acquisition. In: NeurIPS (2025)
15. Kim, M., et al.: Quilt: Robust data segment selection against concept drifts. In: AAAI (2024)
16. Kubeflow: official website. https://www.kubeflow.org/
17. Kurmanji, M., et al.: Detect, distill and update: learned DB systems facing out of distribution data. Proc. ACM Manag. Data (2023)
18. Lu, J., et al.: Learning under concept drift: a review. TKDE (2018)
19. Mahadevan, A., et al.: Cost-aware retraining for machine learning. Knowl. Based Syst. (2024)
20. MLflow: Official website. https://mlflow.org/
21. Paszke, A., et al.: PyTorch: an imperative style, high-performance deep learning library. In: NeurIPS (2019)
22. Pham, T.M.T., et al.: Time to retrain? Detecting concept drifts in machine learning systems. In: ICSE-SEIP (2025)
23. Regol, F., et al.: When to retrain a machine learning model. In: ICML (2025)

24. Robbins, H., et al.: A stochastic approximation method. Ann. Math. Stat. **22** (1951)
25. Snoek, J., et al.: Practical Bayesian optimization of machine learning algorithms. In: NIPS (2012)
26. White, C., et al.: BANANAS: Bayesian optimization with neural architectures for neural architecture search. In: AAAI (2021)
27. Wooders, S., et al.: RALF: accuracy-aware scheduling for feature store maintenance. PVLDB **17** (2023)

FLIP4Tab: Federated Latent In-Context Priors for Tabular Data Synthesis

Lingyu Qiu, Stefano Izzo, Daniela Annunziata, Fabio Giampaolo, and Francesco Piccialli(✉)

Department of Mathematics and Applications "R. Caccioppoli", University of Naples Federico II, Naples, Italy
{lingyu.qiu,stefano.izzo,daniela.annunziata,fabio.giampaolo, francesco.piccialli}@unina.it

Abstract. Generating high-fidelity synthetic tabular data in federated environments faces numerous challenges, primarily statistical heterogeneity and extreme data scarcity. Existing methods typically employ an end-to-end learning paradigm, forcing resource-constrained clients to learn complex representations and distributions simultaneously from scratch. This paper proposes a paradigm shift from representation learning to prior-based alignment, effectively addressing the severe pattern collapse and optimization divergence issues often encountered by previous methods under highly skewed non-independent identically distributed (non-IID) partitions. We introduce FLIP4Tab, a novel three-stage framework that reuses a pre-trained tabular base model as a contextual retrieval mechanism. By leveraging this mechanism, FLIP4Tab can map heterogeneous raw tabular data to a semantically aligned latent space without the instability inherent in federated encoder training. This transformation effectively circumvents the curse of dimensionality and aligns diverse client distributions into a coherent statistical manifold. To recover the original data, FLIP4Tab utilizes a federated global decoder to reconstruct the aligned representation. Extensive experiments on various benchmark datasets with strictly non-independent identically distributed (non-IID) partitions demonstrate that FLIP4Tab achieves state-of-the-art fidelity and practicality. Notably, the framework remains highly effective even under extreme conditions (e.g., the diffusion model trained on as few as 10 latent representations per client), proving its robustness in data-scarce and heterogeneous environments.

1 Introduction

Tabular data constitutes the backbone of decision-making across critical domains, from medical records to financial transactions. Despite the immense value inherent in such data, strict privacy regulations (such as GDPR and HIPAA) pose a significant obstacle to ideal centralized training paradigms, rendering the most valuable assets for predictive modeling inaccessible for collaborative training. Federated Generative Learning (FGL) has emerged as a promising paradigm to resolve this situation, enabling federated synthesis of the global

M. Ceci et al. (Eds.): ECML PKDD 2026, LNAI 16941, pp. 250–267, 2027.
https://doi.org/10.1007/978-3-032-37654-1_15

data distribution without direct data exchange [27]. Unlike standard FL, which merely aggregates model parameters, FGL aims to synthesize the global data distribution from multiple local subsets, thereby opening a new road from learning to *generate* rather than merely *classify*.

However, the transition from federated discriminative learning to FGL for tabular data introduces a fundamental challenge. Tabular data exhibits a unique combination of properties that distinguish it from perceptual modalities: heterogeneous feature types (categorical, numerical, ordinal), complex inter-feature dependencies, irregular manifolds, and severe sparsity in a federated setting. Current approaches, such as Fed-TGAN [31] and FedTabDiff [18], rely on "learning-from-scratch". These approaches compel resource-constrained clients to learn complex mixed-type manifolds entirely from the ground up, which inevitably leads to local overfitting and global optimization divergence, ultimately resulting in severe mode collapse [12]. As we demonstrate empirically, this architectural choice leads to predictable failure under realistic federated conditions.

To understand why current methods fail in a non-IID setting, we rethink the core of generative modeling. We argue that any generative framework must address two intertwined subproblems: capturing the inherent structure of the data in a latent space and generating realistic samples in that space. Traditional generative models (GANs, VAEs, diffusion models) solve both problems simultaneously through joint optimization. This joint learning paradigm succeeds in centralized environments because large-scale training provides sufficient supervision for both objectives.

However, the current federated method alters this dual optimization goal by entangling representation learning with distribution modeling in each federated training communication. Representation learning benefits from large-scale data, which favors centralized pre-training; on the other hand, distribution modeling, conversely, requires capturing local data characteristics suited for federated learning. The implication is that we need an architecture that decouples representation learning from distribution modeling and ensures that the former has sufficient prior knowledge. Recently, the Tabular Foundation Models (TFMs) [7] have shown revolutionary potential in handling tabular data [21,24]. Our key insight is that the operative prior in tabular representation is not pretrained parametric knowledge, but rather the Transformer's inductive bias toward in-context relational reasoning. By conditioning on a small local context set, the frozen Transformer dynamically reorganizes its internal representations to reflect the relational structure of each client's data distribution, producing geometrically coherent embeddings without any gradient updates. We therefore propose a paradigm shift towards prior-based alignment, reconceptualizing TabPFN as a context-sensitive geometric organizer rather than a static knowledge repository. By leveraging its contextual retrieval mechanism, mapping heterogeneous inputs to an aligned latent space without parameter updates becomes a novel and powerful approach. This projection standardizes diverse client distributions, making the downstream generative modeling task significantly more tractable [21,24]. Building on this insight, we introduce FLIP4Tab, which decouples generation into three stages: first, in the Zero-shot Projection stage, clients utilize the frozen foundation model to align private data into latent embeddings; second, during Latent Space Diffusion, a lightweight diffusion model is trained on the server to learn the distribution of these aggregated latent features; finally, FLIP4Tab utilizes a federated global decoder to reconstruct the generated representations back into tabular data. This offloads the heavy lifting of feature extraction to a pre-trained model, while the server only needs to learn the distribution of the latent, significantly reducing complexity. In summary, our contributions to the field of FGL are threefold:

- We propose FLIP4Tab, the first framework to exploit the in-context relational reasoning capability of Overall, the federated version of FLIP4Tab incurs approximately a 10–15% performance loss compared to its centralized version. However, compared to other FL baselines, our framework minimizes this cost at an acceptable rate.frozen Transformers for federated tabular generation. Rather than relying on pretrained parametric knowledge, FLIP4Tab leverages the architectural inductive bias of the Transformer's attention mechanism as a context-sensitive geometric organizer. This shift from end-to-end representation learning to prior-guided latent alignment effectively circumvents the curse of dimensionality and optimization instability inherent in data-scarce and non-IID environments.
- FLIP4Tab introduces a non-collusive dual-server protocol that separates the diffusion model from the decoder, ensuring that neither server has access to the full generative pipeline. By transforming the data into features locally, we ensure that the servers interact only with the abstract representation, effectively isolating it from the original data manifold. Furthermore, we avoid the computational cost of training the feature extractor under the robust pre-trained model, saving significant time and storage resources.
- Extensive experiments on five datasets validated the effectiveness of FLIP4Tab under strict heterogeneity and extreme data scarcity across multiple dimensions.

2 Related Work

2.1 Deep Generative Models for Tabular Data Synthesis

Early research on tabular data synthesis relied on generative adversarial networks (GANs) and variational autoencoders (VAEs). Some works such as Fed-TGAN [31] and TVAE [23] introduced mode-specific normalization techniques to address the heterogeneous distributions typical of continuous and categorical attributes. Nevertheless, GAN-based approaches are often limited by training instability and mode collapse, hindering their ability to faithfully model the long-tailed distributions commonly present in real-world tabular datasets. More recently, denoising diffusion probabilistic models (DDPMs) have established a new state of the art in generative modeling. Among these, TabDDPM [10] successfully adapted the diffusion process to tabular data, demonstrating superior fidelity over prior GAN-based methods. Subsequent efforts, including CoDi [11] and TabSyn [26], further enhanced synthesis efficiency by performing diffusion in a lower-dimensional latent space, typically learned via VAEs. Despite these advances, existing methods generally train the latent encoder from scratch on each target dataset, which restricts their generalization under low-data regimes. In contrast, our framework leverages a pre-trained TabPFN [7] to provide a semantically rich prior, enabling high-fidelity latent representation learning even with limited local samples, a capability not afforded by conventional autoencoder-based diffusion models [33].

2.2 Federated Learning for Tabular Synthesis

Federated learning (FL) enables collaborative model training without exchanging local data. While extensively studied in perceptual tasks such as vision [29], its application in tabular data synthesis is relatively limited, though its development is rapid. Existing methods can be broadly categorized into frameworks based on GANs and methods based on marginal statistics. Fed-TGAN [31] applies the CTGAN framework to federated scenarios, proposing an aggregation strategy based on tabular similarity to alleviate data skew. HT-Fed-GAN [3] integrates a federated variational Bayesian Gaussian mixture model to capture the multimodal distribution of dispersed clients, further addressing the inherent statistical heterogeneity of tabular data. GTV [32] utilizes a Split-GAN architecture, combined with a training shuffling mechanism, to explore a vertical FL scenario where clients have disjoint features. AT-GAN [30] integrates pseudo-enhancement and differentiable enhancement modules to improve the performance of the generator and discriminator and address the class imbalance problem. Unlike deep generative models in vision modality, statistical methods prioritize strict differential privacy (DP) guarantees [8,28]. FLAIM [14] does not train a generative network but operates by selecting and measuring low-dimensional marginal distributions under local DP constraints. However, this approach's dependence on low-order marginal distributions limits its ability to model complex high-dimensional correlations, leading to pattern collapse and poor generalization in data-scarce. FedDPSyn [28] utilizes fully homomorphic encryption to securely execute marginal distribution-based algorithms with computational differential privacy.

3 Methodology

3.1 Problem Formulation

We consider a FL system with K clients, where each client k holds a private dataset $\mathcal{D}_k = \{\mathbf{x}_i\}_{i=1}^{N_k}$ drawn from a local distribution $P_k(\mathbf{x})$. The data distributions are non-IID across clients, with $P_k \neq P_j$ for $k \neq j$. Our objective is to learn a generative model that can synthesize tabular data approximating the

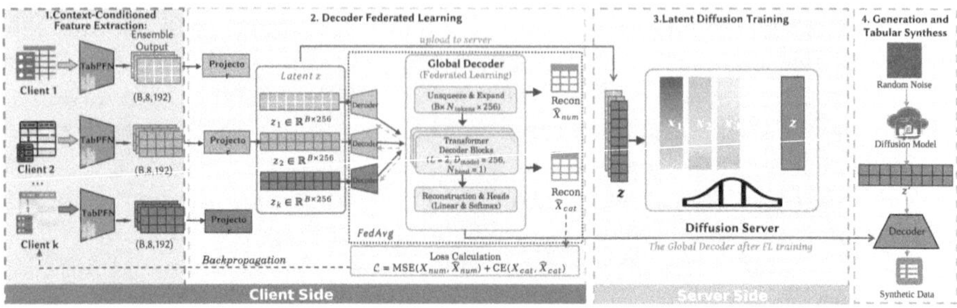

Fig. 1. Overview of the FLIP4Tab Framework. FLIP4Tab proceeds through four stages: (1) offline context-conditioned feature extraction via frozen TabPFN; (2) federated representation learning with private client projectors and a shared decoder; (3) centralized latent diffusion training on aggregated representations; and (4) synthetic data generation by decoding diffusion samples through the trained pipeline.

global mixture distribution:

$$P_{\text{global}}(\mathbf{x}) = \sum_{k=1}^{K} \frac{N_k}{N} P_k(\mathbf{x}), \quad \text{where } N = \sum_{k=1}^{K} N_k, \tag{1}$$

while ensuring that: (1) raw data $\mathcal{D}_k$ never leaves client devices; (2) the method remains effective under severe statistical heterogeneity across clients; and (3) the synthetic data maintains high fidelity for downstream tasks. However, traditional federated generative models typically employ an end-to-end FL approach, where each client has its own generative model, and the parameters are averaged on the server. This not only imposes excessively high communication costs on deep models but also introduces significant efficiency problems. Furthermore, training on limited local data produces poor representations. In addition, numerous attacks suggest that the model can infer the input samples [2,19], further exacerbating privacy concerns.

3.2 The FLIP4Tab Framework Overview

As shown in Fig 1, FLIP4Tab mainly consists of three parts:

1. **Context-Conditioned Feature Extraction:** A frozen Transformer encoder extracts features via in-context learning, producing semantically structured embeddings without gradient-based fine-tuning.
2. **Decoupled Federated Representation Learning:** Private client-side projectors and a globally shared decoder jointly learn a unified latent space through federated reconstruction.
3. **Latent Diffusion Generation:** A diffusion model trained on aggregated latent representations synthesizes data entirely within the unified latent manifold.

The key is that the heterogeneity of the original tabular data does not need to be addressed during the generative modeling phase. It is worth distinguishing three contributing factors: (1) the Transformer architecture's capacity for relational reasoning; (2) the in-context conditioning mechanism (ICL); and (3) the pretrained weights of TabPFN. As our ablation study (Sect. 4.5) demonstrates, factor (2) is the dominant contributor, while factor (3) is largely dispensable. FLIP4Tab aligns heterogeneous features during the representation learning phase by mapping all client data to a shared latent space, enabling the diffusion model to operate on a well-structured manifold.

3.2.1 Context-Conditioned Feature Extraction Training deep generative models directly on raw tabular data is challenging due to its mixed data types and irregular manifolds. FLIP4Tab addresses this by first mapping raw inputs into a structured embedding space via a frozen Transformer encoder before federated training.

Specifically, we use TabPFN [7] as the encoder $\mathcal{E}$ for tabular in-context learning [5]. Each client k constructs a local context set $\mathcal{C}_k = \{(\mathbf{x}^{(j)}, y^{(j)})\}_{j=1}^{M} \subset \mathcal{D}_k$ with $M \ll N_k$, which is embedded into the Transformer's attention mechanism without gradient updates. The feature extraction for any input $\mathbf{x} \in \mathcal{D}_k$ is then:

$$\mathbf{z}_{raw} = \mathcal{E}(\mathbf{x} \mid \mathcal{C}_k) := \text{Transformer}\left(\mathbf{x};\ \{(\mathbf{x}^{(j)}, y^{(j)})\}_{j=1}^{M}\right), \tag{2}$$

where the encoder attends to $\mathcal{C}_k$ to produce a context-conditioned embedding $\mathbf{z}_{raw} \in \mathbb{R}^{1536}$. Since $\mathcal{C}_k \subset \mathcal{D}_k$, no external data is required and the context remains private to each client.

The key property of this design is that rather than relying on its pre-trained weights, we exploit TabPFN's architectural capacity for in-context relational reasoning: by attending to $\mathcal{C}_k$, the Transformer reorganizes its internal representations to reflect the relational structure of the local data distribution, producing geometrically coherent embeddings from minimal supervision. Crucially, as demonstrated in our ablation studies (Sect. 4.5): removing context conditioning causes a sharp drop in α-precision, whereas substituting pre-trained weights with random initialization incurs only a $\sim$5% penalty. Rather, it is the ICL conditioning mechanism itself, the Transformer's inductive bias toward in-context relational reasoning that constitutes the operative prior. This reframes the role of TabPFN in our framework: it contributes not as a static knowledge repository, but as a context-sensitive geometric organizer whose effectiveness scales with context quality rather than parameter scale. This design allows the frozen model to dynamically adapt its internal manifold to the specific tabular distribution defined by $\mathcal{C}_k$, providing semantically rich features without the need for fine-tuning. Crucially, the offline execution decouples time-consuming inference from the federated training loop.

3.2.2 Decoupled Federated Representation Learning Considering that the distribution characteristics of TabPFN embeddings $\mathbf{z}_{raw} \in \mathbb{R}^{1536}$ retrieved based on context remain client-dependent, directly FL at this level would reintroduce the heterogeneity problem. Therefore, we introduce a decoupled projection-decoder architecture to learn a unified latent space across clients.

Local Projector. First, each client k maintains a private, lightweight projector $\mathcal{P}_{\phi_k} : \mathbb{R}^{D_{raw}} \rightarrow \mathbb{R}^{D_{lat}}$, where $\phi_k = \{\mathbf{W}_k, \mathbf{b}_k\}$ denotes the local projection parameters. It compresses the high-dimensional prior features into a compact latent vector $\mathbf{z} \in \mathbb{R}^{D_{lat}}$ (typically $D_{lat} = 256$). To ensure numerical stability across heterogeneous clients, we apply Layer Normalization (LN):

$$\mathbf{z} = \text{LayerNorm}(\mathbf{W}_k \mathbf{z}_{raw} + \mathbf{b}_k). \tag{3}$$

Given that the upstream TabPFN encoder has performed the necessary non-linear feature transformations to ensure that $\mathbf{z}_{raw}$ lies in a semantically structured manifold, a simple linear layer is sufficient. The projector performs subspace selection rather than representation learning, aligning client-specific feature distributions to a unified latent space suitable for the global model. This design is consistent with findings in transfer learning that linear probes over strong pretrained representations match or exceed nonlinear alternatives when the source and target domains are sufficiently aligned [1].

Global Decoder. To reconstruct the tabular data, FL is used to learn a globally shared decoder that learns a reconstruction that generalizes across clients. A shared Transformer decoder $\mathcal{D}_\theta$ with parameters θ reconstructs tabular data from the projected latent:

$$\hat{\mathbf{x}} = \mathcal{D}_\theta(\text{Expand}(\mathbf{z})), \tag{4}$$

where Expand$(\cdot)$ replicates $\mathbf{z}$ along the sequence dimension to match the number of table columns. Each client minimizes a mixed reconstruction loss:

$$\min_{\phi_k, \theta} \mathcal{L}_{recon} = \mathcal{L}_{num}(\mathbf{x}_{num}, \hat{\mathbf{x}}_{num}) + \mathcal{L}_{cat}(\mathbf{x}_{cat}, \hat{\mathbf{x}}_{cat}), \tag{5}$$

combining MSE for numerical features and cross-entropy for categorical features. After local updates, only θ is aggregated via FedAvg [15]:

$$\theta^{(t+1)} \leftarrow \sum_{k=1}^{K} \frac{N_k}{N} \theta_k^{(t)}. \tag{6}$$

To further mitigate model inversion risks [4], we adopt a dual-server deployment under the standard non-colluding assumption [16], separating the generator server from the reconstruction server so that neither party has access to the full pipeline.

3.2.3 Latent Diffusion Generation Since these vectors are outputs of client-private projectors and do not contain raw feature values, they substantially reduce the risk of direct re-identification [17], permitting centralized diffusion training. Crucially, we assume that the management of the global decoder must be operationally separated from the training process of the diffusion model, with the specific isolation mechanism determined by the implementer. To capture the complex manifold of this latent space, we employ a Denoising Diffusion Probabilistic Model (DDPM) [6,26]

Unlike traditional methods that operate on raw data, we model the distribution $p(\mathbf{z})$ entirely within the unified latent space following the formulation in TabSyn [26]. To ensure training stability across heterogeneous clients, we first apply a pre-processing affine transformation $\tilde{\mathbf{z}}_0 = (\mathbf{z}_0 - \boldsymbol{\mu})/sp$, where $\boldsymbol{\mu}$ and p are the global mean and standard deviation, s is a scaling factor.

Score-Based Modeling via SDE. First, we model the diffusion process using a Stochastic Differential Equation (SDE) [20]. The forward process perturbs the latent data $\tilde{\mathbf{z}}_0$ to noise over time $t \in [0, T]$:

$$\tilde{\mathbf{z}}_t = \tilde{\mathbf{z}}_0 + \sigma(t)\epsilon, \quad \epsilon \sim \mathcal{N}(\mathbf{0}, \mathbf{I}) \tag{7}$$

where $\tilde{\mathbf{z}}_t$ is the noisy latent at time t, and $\sigma(t)$ is the noise level. The reverse process, which generates data from noise, is governed by the reverse-time SDE:

$$d\tilde{\mathbf{z}} = -2\dot{\sigma}(t)\sigma(t)\nabla_{\tilde{\mathbf{z}}_t} \log p_t(\tilde{\mathbf{z}}_t)\, dt + \sqrt{2\dot{\sigma}(t)\sigma(t)}\, d\omega_t \tag{8}$$

where $\dot{\sigma}(t) = d\sigma/dt$ denotes the time derivative of the noise schedule, $\nabla_{\tilde{\mathbf{z}}_t} \log p_t(\tilde{\mathbf{z}}_t)$ is the score function, and ω_t is the standard Wiener process.

Following TabSyn [26], we adopt linear noise scheduling with a noise level of $\sigma(t)$ over variance-preserving alternatives instead of using standard variance-preserving (VP) scheduling [20]. This formulation minimizes discretization error in the reverse process, enabling high-quality synthesis in fewer than 20 function evaluations without the computational overhead of standard DDPM [26].

Denoising Network Architecture. We parameterize the reverse process with an MLP-based network ϵ_ψ composed of residual blocks with hidden dimension 1024. Convolutional architectures are not suitable here, given the non-spatial nature of tabular latent representations. Time steps are encoded via sinusoidal positional embeddings and fused into each residual block. The training objective is:

$$\mathcal{L}_{diff} = \mathbb{E}_{t,\tilde{\mathbf{z}}_0,\epsilon}\left[\|\epsilon - \epsilon_\psi(\sqrt{\bar{\alpha}_t}\tilde{\mathbf{z}}_0 + \sqrt{1-\bar{\alpha}_t}\epsilon, t)\|^2\right]. \tag{9}$$

4 Experiment

4.1 Experimental Setup

Datasets. We employ five public tabular datasets from the UCI Repository[1], covering both classification (Adult, Default, Shoppers) and regression (Beijing,

[1] https://archive.ics.uci.edu/datasets.

News) tasks. All datasets are split into training, validation, and test sets with 8:1:1, except for Adult where the official test partition is used.

Data Partitioning and Heterogeneity Simulation. To establish a rigorous and realistic benchmark for federated tabular synthesis, we simulate two fundamental client data scenarios across $K = 10$ clients.

- **Non-IID Partition (Label & Quantity Skew):** We introduce real statistical heterogeneity through Dirichlet allocation process. For regression tasks (Beijing, News), target values are discretized into quantile bins prior to allocation.
- **IID Partition (Balanced Baseline):** For the IID setting, we implement a strict stratified sampling strategy. This ensures each client receives a nearly equal number of samples from every class (or value bin), followed by a final shuffle, resulting in a uniform label distribution.

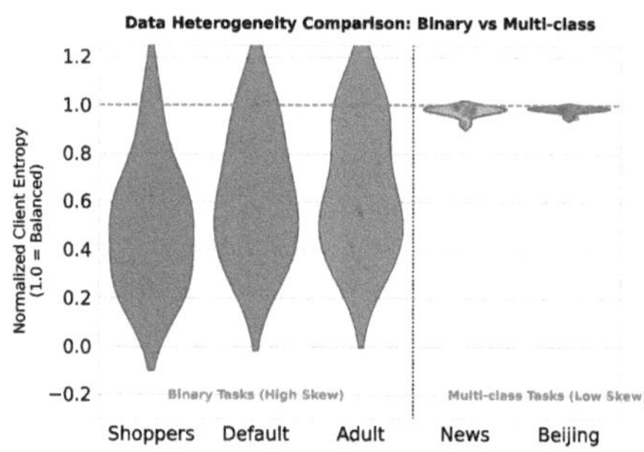

Fig. 2. Quantitative Heterogeneity.

Figure 2 provides a quantitative analysis via *Normalized Entropy* ($H_{\text{norm}} = H/H_{\max}$; lower values indicate greater skew). The attainable heterogeneity is intrinsically linked to task structure: Binary tasks (e.g., Shoppers) exhibit high skew (low H_{norm}), mirroring real-world severe class imbalance. In contrast, multi-class and regression tasks (e.g., News, Beijing) sustain broader entropy distributions, simulating diverse client behavior patterns. The quantitative analysis violin plot in Fig. 2 confirms this difference, demonstrating that our experimental setup establishes a rigorous benchmark for evaluating the robustness of the model under extreme data partitioning conditions.

Baseline Methods. To rigorously evaluate the generative performance of FLIP4Tab, we benchmark it against two categories of state-of-the-art (SOTA) methods: centralized tabular generators and specialized horizontal FL frameworks. This dual-track benchmarking ensures a comprehensive assessment of our FLIP4Tab's ability to balance generative fidelity with the constraints of data heterogeneity.

- **Centralized Baselines:** We compare our method with leading generators across multiple paradigms to assess its inherent generative capability. These include GAN-based CTGAN [23], VAE-based TVAE [23] and GOGGLE [13], and advanced diffusion-based models such as STaSy [9], CoDi [11], and TabDDPM [10].
- **Federated Baselines:** Unlike vertical FL methods, we focus on a horizontal setting and compare our framework with contemporary horizontal FL frameworks such as the diffusion-based FedTabDiff [18] framework, FedSynPriv & FedSynPriv_Adv[2] (combining differential privacy and adversarial training), and Fed-TGAN [31] (a federated version of CTGAN).

Evaluation Metrics. We adopt a comprehensive evaluation framework encompassing four dimensions: (1) *Low-order statistical fidelity* (single density, pair correlation), (2) *High-order generative quality* (α-Precision, β-Recall), (3) *Downstream utility* via Machine Learning Efficiency (MLE), and (4) *Privacy preservation* (Detection score, DCR risk) [22]. Specifically, the error rate reported in Table 1 is derived from the single column density metric, computed as the mean 1-Wasserstein distance over numerical columns and Total Variation Distance over categorical columns across all features, lower values indicate better distributional fidelity.

4.2 Comparison Result Analysis

As shown in Table 1, we report the results under centralized and federated settings. First, the centralized setting shows that our method achieves consistently competitive results (best or second best) on all datasets. Even though TabDDPM slightly outperforms us on Default and Beijing, it is highly sensitive to data distribution and exhibits unacceptable crashes on News. Second, the federated setting highlights the advantages of our method: it is more stable than any FL baseline model. FedTabDiff and FedSynPriv have errors exceeding 30% to 90% on all datasets, due to the lack of any potential alignment during end-to-end generative model training. Even though FTGAN outperforms us on News, it performs significantly worse on other datasets, exhibiting unstable generalization.

Overall, the federated version of FLIP4Tab incurs an average of approximately 1015% performance degradation compared to its centralized version across most datasets, with the News dataset representing a larger gap due to its high-dimensional regression structure. Compared to other FL baselines, our framework minimizes this degradation at an acceptable rate. Notably, while FTGAN achieves lower distributional error on the News dataset, it performs substantially worse on the remaining four datasets and exhibits high variance across settings, indicating limited generalization capability. Notably, this gap does not widen under more heterogeneous partitions (as shown in the Table 4),

[2] https://github.com/XiaochenLi-w/Federated-Tabular-Data-Synthesis-Framework.

Table 1. Quantitative comparison between centralized and federated methods. The error rate (%) column-wise density estimation across all columns. **Bold** indicates the top best performance in the federated setting. †Results for centralized baselines are reproduced from [26] under identical dataset splits and evaluation protocols

Method	Adult	Default	Shoppers	Beijing	News
Centralized Baselines (Non-FL)					
CTGAN	16.84±0.03	16.83±0.04	21.15±0.10	21.39±0.05	16.09±0.02
TVAE	14.22±0.08	10.17±0.05	24.51±0.06	19.16±0.06	16.62±0.03
GOGGLE	12.12±0.04	19.94±0.06	14.51±0.12	8.25±0.12	8.59±0.07
STaSy	11.29±0.06	5.77±0.06	9.37±0.09	6.71±0.03	6.89±0.03
CoDi	21.38±0.06	15.77±0.07	31.84±0.05	16.94±0.02	32.27±0.04
TabDDPM	1.75±0.03	**1.57±0.08**	2.72±0.13	**1.30±0.03**	78.75±0.01
FLIP4Tab	**1.31±0.06**	2.83±0.07	**1.85±0.10**	1.77±0.04	**1.69±0.03**
Federated Methods (FL)					
FedTabDiff	75.51±0.09	75.65±0.08	59.56±0.06	90.46±0.08	36.22±0.17
FedSynPriv	30.25±0.01	30.34±0.03	23.47±0.05	28.01±0.07	44.06±0.10
FedSynPriv_Adv	31.25±0.04	32.93±0.02	90.56±0.05	24.70±0.09	44.06±0.12
FTGAN	31.11±0.05	18.67±0.08	27.51±0.11	17.08±0.04	**10.08±0.15**
FLIP4Tab	**13.29±0.03**	**17.04±0.05**	**17.77±0.12**	**16.01±0.07**	21.26±0.08

confirming that the lower bound of error is a structural property of federated architectures.

4.3 Low-Order Statistical Fidelity

To evaluate the structural fidelity of the generated data, we present the quantitative results in Table 2 and employ multi-view visualization analysis from three perspectives.

(1) The PCA projection in Fig. 3ashows strong consistency between the real and synthetic distributions under both the IID and Non-IID settings. In the IID case, the synthetic samples extensively and uniformly cover the real data manifold, and the slightly wider distribution range indicates its generative generalization ability beyond memory. In the Non-IID setting, the overall structural correspondence is preserved, but some slight coverage gaps appear at the manifold edges, reflecting the inherent challenge of reconstructing the global distribution from local partitions with maximum heterogeneity. However, FLIP4Tab ensures the integrity of the core distribution structure under both settings.

(2) The marginal distribution matching results in Fig. 3bshow that the probability density function of the synthetic data closely matches the key features (including peak, tail, and skewness) of the empirical marginal distribution of the real data. This precise matching confirms that our method accurately preserves the basic statistical properties of each column.

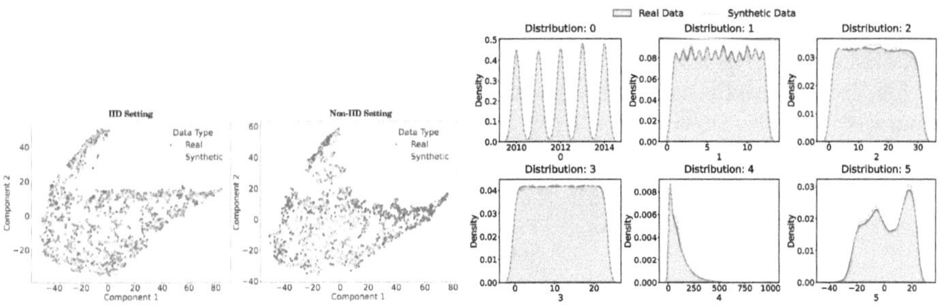

(a) PCA Projection under different partitions.

(b) Column marginal distributions.

Fig. 3. Visual evaluation of FLIP4Tab on the Beijing Dataset. (a) illustrates the manifold alignment in PCA space, while (b) demonstrates that the synthetic data density closely matches the real data in terms of peak value, tail, and skewness.

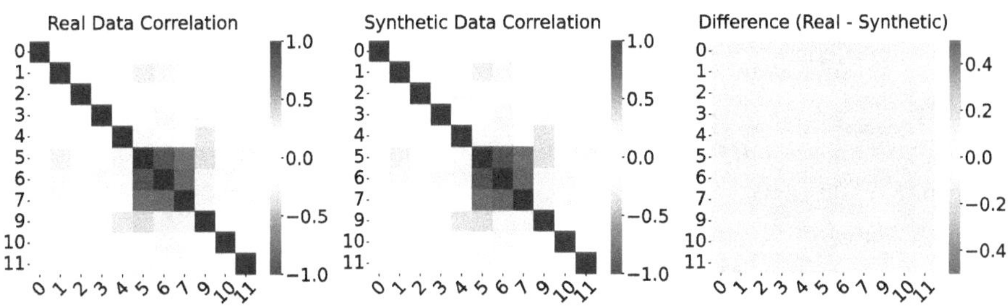

Fig. 4. Visualization of Pairwise Correlation Differences on the Beijing Dataset. The left plot represents the real data, the middle plot represents the FLIP4Tab synthetic data, and the right plot shows the difference.

(3) Fig. 4 quantifies the accuracy of capturing pairwise feature dependencies using a sparse correlation difference matrix and verifies the preservation of higher-order relationships. The rightmost subplot shows that our method successfully captures complex inter-feature dependencies while effectively filtering out spurious noise, thus preserving the key relevance structure of the original tabular data.

4.4 Utility

To validate the practicality of our method, we deployed it in a centralized environment and compared it with other centralized training methods. Our evaluation demonstrated that the synthetic data generated by FLIP4Tab achieved high practical value in many downstream tasks. The results in Table 3 demonstrate that FLIP4Tab not only performs robustly under a federated architecture but also rivals state-of-the-art centralized generators. On the Adult dataset, FLIP4Tab achieves an AUC of 0.917, outperforming all other improved versions of federated architectures and matching the best centralized methods. However,

Table 2. Comprehensive Evaluation of Our Proposed Method. Performance comparison under IID and Non-IID settings with 10 clients (mean ± std). Metrics follow the four-dimensional evaluation framework: Low-order Statistical Fidelity, High-order Generative Quality, Downstream Utility, and Privacy Preservation. The Adult dataset is excluded from this evaluation due to degenerate client partitioning under Dirichlet allocation with binary labels.

Dataset	Fidelity (↑)		Quality (↑)		Utility	Privacy
	Density	Pair Corr.	α-Precision	β-Recall	MLE (RMSE)	DCR
IID Setting ($K = 10$)						
News	0.79±0.02	0.93±0.01	44.92±7.79	11.57±2.38	0.84±0.10	90.81±0.79
Default	0.65±0.25	0.77±0.04	84.31±4.38	35.15±31.16	0.63±0.00	90.34±1.22
Beijing	0.82±0.02	0.74±0.04	91.24±3.12	21.51±7.08	0.89±0.01	90.65±0.40
Shoppers	0.82±0.01	0.82±0.01	86.72±3.09	22.95±0.85	0.82±0.04	90.34±0.38
Non-IID Setting ($K = 10$, $\alpha = 0.5$)						
News	0.76±0.02	0.92±0.01	43.22±5.14	9.73±3.12	0.94±0.00	91.02±1.51
Default	0.84±0.01	0.75±0.00	83.68±1.18	12.78±0.91	0.59±0.01	90.52±1.09
Beijing	0.80±0.02	0.73±0.02	89.50±5.74	21.73±3.55	0.89±0.01	90.65±0.08
Shoppers	0.84±0.03	0.83±0.02	80.52±2.26	21.31±0.28	0.78±0.04	90.41±0.75
Summary Statistics (Mean ± Std across datasets)						
IID Mean	0.77±0.08	0.82±0.08	76.80±19.60	22.80±9.12	0.80±0.12	90.53±0.70
Non-IID Mean	0.81±0.04	0.81±0.08	74.23±18.72	16.39±6.54	0.80±0.15	90.65±0.85

Table 3. AUC (classification task) and RMSE (regression task) scores of Machine Learning Efficiency. ↑ (↓) indicates that the higher (lower) the score, the better the performance. †Centralized baseline results are taken from [26], which shares the same datasets and evaluation protocol.

Methods	Adult	Default	Shoppers	Beijing	News
	AUC ↑	AUC ↑	AUC ↑	RMSE ↓	RMSE ↓
Centralized Baselines (Non-FL)					
CTGAN	.886	.696	.875	.902	.880
TVAE	.878	.724	.871	.770	1.01
GOGGLE	.778	.584	.658	1.09	.877
GREaT	.913	.755	.902	.653	**.842**
STaSy	.906	.752	.914	.656	.871
CoDi	.871	.525	.865	.818	1.21
TabDDPM	.907	.758	.918	.592	4.86
TabSyn	.915	**.764**	**.920**	.582	.861
FLIP4Tab	**.917**	.758	.907	**.547**	.859
Federated Methods (FL)					
FLIP4Tab	**.841**	**.741**	**.854**	**.591**	**.868**

the federated model performed worse than the centralized model. This performance degradation is an unavoidable trade-off due to limitations in data isolation and statistical heterogeneity among clients when shifting to the FL setting [25]. Despite this unavoidable performance degradation, FLIP4Tab still manages to generate efficient synthetic data comparable to the centralized baseline, effectively bridging the gap in generation quality in a distributed environment.

4.5 Ablation Study

The Effect of the Proposed Component. In this section, we investigated the key contributions each component plays in generating synthetic data.

Table 4. Ablation Study of FLIP4Tab Components under IID and Non-IID Scenarios on the Default Datasets. We evaluate generative Fidelity (Density), Quality (α-Precision), and Utility (AUC/RMSE). Fidelity (Density) and Quality (α-Precision) are reported as percentages (%). Utility (AUC) is reported in [0,1].

Component	IID Setting			Non-IID Setting ($\alpha = 0.5$)		
	Fidelity	Quality	Utility	Fidelity	Quality	Utility
	Dens ↑	α-Prec ↑	AUC ↑	Dens ↑	α-Prec ↑	AUC ↑
FLIP4Tab (Full)	83.94	**94.19**	**75.06**	84.65	**90.37**	**78.30**
w/o In-Context Prior	54.16	73.90	46.10	58.01	44.39	59.26
w/o Decoder Aggregation	63.92	64.88	63.06	62.87	66.34	56.13
w/o Random Initial	**86.46**	89.89	57.04	**86.07**	89.85	69.23
w/o Projector	42.72	50.84	22.63	42.84	50.78	67.56

Table 4 shows the contribution of each component under Independent and Identically Distributed (IID) and Non-Independent and Identically Distributed (Non-IID) conditions ($\alpha = 0.5$). These results clarify the source of FLIP4Tab's effectiveness. Replacing pretrained weights with random initialization incurs only a marginal penalty (~5% in α-precision), whereas removing context conditioning entirely (w/o In-Context Prior) causes catastrophic degradation across all metrics. This dissociation confirms that the operative prior is the Transformer's architectural inductive bias for in-context relational reasoning, not the pretrained parametric knowledge encoded in TabPFN's weights. The pretrained weights may even introduce a distributional bias misaligned with the federated generative objective, which explains why random initialization slightly outperforms the pretrained variant. Accordingly, the role of TabPFN in FLIP4Tab should be understood as providing a context-sensitive geometric organizer whose effectiveness derives from the ICL conditioning mechanism rather than from large-scale pretraining. In both IID and Non-IID settings, eliminating decoder aggregation and removing the projection operator consistently degrades fidelity and quality, validating the critical importance of client-side local distribution alignment and shared decoder learning.

Table 5. Hyperparameter Sensitivity Analysis of FLIP4Tab on the Beijing Dataset across Model Parameters and Federated Scenarios.

A. Model Architecture & Training				B. Federated Learning Scenario			
Parameter	Value	Fidelity α-Prec ↑	Utility MLE ↑	Parameter	Value	Fidelity α-Prec ↑	Utility MLE ↑
Fed. Rounds	5	0.797	0.776	Client (K)	5	0.757	0.756
	10	0.955	0.960		10	0.834	0.778
	20	0.804	0.747		20	0.835	0.748
Diffusion Samples	10	0.955	0.960	Heterogeneity (α)	0.1	0.881	0.767
	100	0.881	0.767		0.5	0.880	0.922
	1000	0.787	0.919		0.7	0.747	0.895
					1.0	0.896	0.892

Hyperparameter Sensitivity Analysis. We conduct a hyperparameter sensitivity analysis to investigate how FLIP4Tab maintains high generative fidelity with limited local data. Results confirm that contextual guidance from a small support set is sufficient to steer the diffusion model toward a well-structured latent manifold, without requiring large-scale local training data. First, as shown in Table 5 (Part A), peak fidelity (α-precision: 0.955) is achieved when each client contributes only 10 projected latent vectors, which corresponds to 10 local tabular training samples for centralized diffusion training. Scaling to 100 or 1000 samples introduces distribution noise, leading to a monotonic fidelity decrease, suggesting that the projected latent manifold is already sufficiently representative at minimal data volume. Second, we found that under strong priors, long-term optimization fits residual noise rather than meaningful structure. This is reflected in the fact that optimal performance is achieved with only 10 epochs of federated training, while extending training causes fidelity to drop from 0.955 to 0.804. Third, TabPFN projection absorbs distributional differences among clients before aggregation. FLIP4Tab maintains stable fidelity across high to low heterogeneity levels. In summary, these findings demonstrate that prior information from the underlying model enables federated synthesis with minimal data volume, a characteristic particularly important in privacy-sensitive and resource-constrained deployment environments.

5 Conclusion and Limitation

5.1 Conclusion

In this paper, we propose a framework called FLIP4Tab that shifts the learning paradigm toward prior-guided alignment. FLIP4Tab effectively circumvents the inherent optimization instability and privacy risks associated with learning from heterogeneous, non-independent and identically distributed (non-IID) data by reusing a frozen base model as a general manifold projector in a decoupled architecture. Extensive experiments demonstrate that our method achieves state-of-the-art results under extreme data partitioning and data scarcity. Furthermore, FLIP4Tab provides a high-fidelity and structural privacy-preserving solution for isolated data silos in real-world industrial applications.

5.2 Limitation

Despite FLIP4Tab's strong empirical performance, there are still three limitations that need to be further discussed. First, the method provides **structural privacy** under a specific threat model: an honest-but-curious server that does not collude with other parties. While uploading latent vectors $\mathbf{z}$ avoids exposing raw feature values, this falls short of formal differential privacy guarantees against a stronger adversary. Integrating calibrated noise mechanisms (e.g., DP-SGD) into the decoder training or diffusion stage remains future work. Second, although the context set $\mathcal{C}_k$ remains on the device, it encodes local distribution features into the generated embedding. This could constitute a potential leakage channel in highly sensitive domains. Third, this paper uses the dual-server non-collusion assumption to ensure that the server cannot reconstruct the original data through latent variables, but this still does not provide strict cryptographic guarantees. More robust protocols, such as secret sharing, can provide provable security but increase computational costs.

Acknowledgment. This work is partially supported by the project: TUAI: Towards an Understanding of Artificial Intelligence via a transparent, open and explainable perspective, Marie Curie Doctoral Network, ID: 101168344. This work is partially supported by the project: FLINT - Prog. n.: F/380134/01-03/X77 - MIMIT

References

1. Alain, G., Bengio, Y.: Understanding intermediate layers using linear classifier probes. arXiv preprint arXiv:1610.01644 (2016)
2. Carlini, N., et al.: Extracting training data from diffusion models. In: 32nd USENIX security symposium (USENIX Security 23), pp. 5253–5270 (2023)
3. Duan, S., et al.: Ht-fed-gan: federated generative model for decentralized tabular data synthesis. Entropy **25**(1), 88 (2022)
4. Fredrikson, M., Jha, S., Ristenpart, T.: Model inversion attacks that exploit confidence information and basic countermeasures. In: Proceedings of the 22nd ACM SIGSAC Conference on Computer and Communications Security, pp. 1322–1333 (2015)
5. Garg, S., Tsipras, D., Liang, P.S., Valiant, G.: What can transformers learn in-context? a case study of simple function classes. Adv. Neural. Inf. Process. Syst. **35**, 30583–30598 (2022)
6. Ho, J., Jain, A., Abbeel, P.: Denoising diffusion probabilistic models. Adv. Neural. Inf. Process. Syst. **33**, 6840–6851 (2020)

7. Hollmann, N., Müller, S., Eggensperger, K., Hutter, F.: Tabpfn: a transformer that solves small tabular classification problems in a second. In: The Eleventh International Conference on Learning Representations (2024)
8. Jia, J., et al.: Absyn: an accurate differentially private data synthesis scheme with adaptive selection and batch processes. IEEE Trans. Inf. Forensics Secur. (2024)
9. Kim, J., Lee, C., Park, N.: Stasy: score-based tabular data synthesis. In: The Eleventh International Conference on Learning Representations (2023)
10. Kotelnikov, A., Baranchuk, D., Rubachev, I., Babenko, A.: Tabddpm: Modelling tabular data with diffusion models. In: International Conference on Machine Learning, pp. 17564–17579. PMLR (2023)
11. Lee, C., Kim, J., Park, N.: Codi: co-evolving contrastive diffusion models for mixed-type tabular synthesis. In: International Conference on Machine Learning, pp. 18940–18956. PMLR (2023)
12. Li, T., Sahu, A.K., Zaheer, M., Sanjabi, M., Talwalkar, A., Smith, V.: Federated optimization in heterogeneous networks. Proc. Mach. Learn. Syst. **2**, 429–450 (2020)
13. Liu, T., Qian, Z., Berrevoets, J., van der Schaar, M.: Goggle: generative modelling for tabular data by learning relational structure. In: The Eleventh International Conference on Learning Representations (2023)
14. Maddock, S., Cormode, G., Maple, C.: Flaim: aim-based synthetic data generation in the federated setting. In: Proceedings of the 30th ACM SIGKDD Conference on Knowledge Discovery and Data Mining, pp. 2165–2176 (2024)
15. McMahan, B., Moore, E., Ramage, D., Hampson, S., y Arcas, B.A.: Communication-efficient learning of deep networks from decentralized data. In: Artificial Intelligence and Statistics, pp. 1273–1282. PMLR (2017)
16. Mohassel, P., Rindal, P.: Aby3: a mixed protocol framework for machine learning. In: Proceedings of the 2018 ACM SIGSAC Conference on Computer and Communications Security, pp. 35–52 (2018)
17. Rombach, R., Blattmann, A., Lorenz, D., Esser, P., Ommer, B.: High-resolution image synthesis with latent diffusion models. In: Proceedings of the IEEE/CVF Conference on Computer Vision and Pattern Recognition, pp. 10684–10695 (2022)
18. Sattarov, T., Schreyer, M., Borth, D.: Fedtabdiff: federated learning of diffusion probabilistic models for synthetic mixed-type tabular data generation. arXiv preprint arXiv:2401.06263 (2024)
19. Somepalli, G., Singla, V., Goldblum, M., Geiping, J., Goldstein, T.: Diffusion art or digital forgery? investigating data replication in diffusion models. In: Proceedings of the IEEE/CVF Conference on Computer Vision and Pattern Recognition, pp. 6048–6058 (2023)
20. Song, Y., Sohl-Dickstein, J., Kingma, D.P., Kumar, A., Ermon, S., Poole, B.: Score-based generative modeling through stochastic differential equations. arXiv preprint arXiv:2011.13456 (2020)
21. Thomas, V., Ma, J., Hosseinzadeh, R., Golestan, K., Yu, G., Volkovs, M., Caterini, A.: Retrieval & fine-tuning for in-context tabular models. Adv. Neural. Inf. Process. Syst. **37**, 108439–108467 (2024)
22. Webster, R., Rabin, J., Simon, L., Jurie, F.: Detecting overfitting of deep generative networks via latent recovery. In: Proceedings of the IEEE/CVF Conference on Computer Vision and Pattern Recognition, pp. 11273–11282 (2019)
23. Xu, L., Skoularidou, M., Cuesta-Infante, A., Veeramachaneni, K.: Modeling tabular data using conditional gan. In: Advances in Neural Information Processing Systems, vol. 32 (2019)

24. Ye, H.J., Liu, S.Y., Chao, W.L.: A closer look at tabpfn v2: understanding its strengths and extending its capabilities. In: The Thirty-ninth Annual Conference on Neural Information Processing Systems (2025)
25. Ye, M., Fang, X., Du, B., Yuen, P.C., Tao, D.: Heterogeneous federated learning: state-of-the-art and research challenges. ACM Comput. Surv. **56**(3), 1–44 (2023)
26. Zhang, H., et al.: Mixed-type tabular data synthesis with score-based diffusion in latent space. arXiv preprint arXiv:2310.09656 (2023)
27. Zhang, J., Zhao, L., Yu, K., Min, G., Al-Dubai, A.Y., Zomaya, A.Y.: A novel federated learning scheme for generative adversarial networks. IEEE Trans. Mob. Comput. **23**(5), 3633–3649 (2023)
28. Zhang, S., et al.: Feddpsyn: federated tabular data synthesis with computational differential privacy
29. Zhang, T., et al.: Gpt-fl: generative pre-trained model-assisted federated learning. In: Proceedings of the Computer Vision and Pattern Recognition Conference, pp. 1761–1770 (2025)
30. Zhao, P., Guo, S., Li, Y., Yang, S., Ren, X.: Fedgen: personalized federated learning with data generation for enhanced model customization and class imbalance. Futur. Gener. Comput. Syst. **164**, 107595 (2025)
31. Zhao, Z., Birke, R., Kunar, A., Chen, L.Y.: Fed-tgan: federated learning framework for synthesizing tabular data. arXiv preprint arXiv:2108.07927 (2021)
32. Zhao, Z., Wu, H., Van Moorsel, A., Chen, L.Y.: Gtv: generating tabular data via vertical federated learning. In: 2025 55th Annual IEEE/IFIP International Conference on Dependable Systems and Networks (DSN), pp. 33–46. IEEE (2025)
33. Zhu, B., Shi, X., Erickson, N., Li, M., Karypis, G., Shoaran, M.: Xtab: cross-table pretraining for tabular transformers. In: International Conference on Machine Learning, pp. 43181–43204. PMLR (2023)

Federated Learning with Local-Global Dual Matching Dataset Distillation

Zhengquan Luo[1], Xuhui Li[1], Changyou Chen[2], Dong An[1], Shengcai Liao[3], Peilin Zhao[4], Yunlong Wang[5], and Zhiqiang Xu[1(✉)]

[1] Mohamed bin Zayed University of Artificial Intelligence, Abu Dhabi, United Arab Emirates
{zhengquan.luo,xuhui.li,dong.an,zhiqiang.xu}@mbzuai.ac.ae
[2] State University of New York at Buffalo, Buffalo, NY, USA
changyou@buffalo.edu
[3] United Arab Emirates University, Al Ain, United Arab Emirates
scliao@ieee.org
[4] Shanghai Jiao Tong University, Shanghai, China
[5] Chinese Academy of Sciences, Beijing, China
yunlong.wang@cripac.ia.ac.cn

Abstract. Federated Learning (FL) often struggles with error accumulation during local training, particularly on heterogeneous data, which hampers overall performance and convergence. While dataset distillation is commonly introduced to FL to enhance efficiency, we find that communicating distilled data (rather than model updates) avoids the local-update error accumulation mechanism in FedAvg-style training, but may amplify cross-client heterogeneity in the aggregated distilled set. To address the amplified heterogeneity due to distilled data, we propose a novel FL algorithm termed *FedDualMatch*, which performs dual matching in the way that local distribution matching captures client data distributions while global gradient matching aligns gradients on the server. This dual approach enriches feature representations and enhances convergence stability. We provide a localized theoretical explanation showing that, under bounded representation and gradient mismatches, the test loss gap between the optimal models trained on aggregated distilled data and aggregated original data can be bounded. At the same time, the optimization trajectory converges to a bounded neighborhood whose radius depends on residual distributional and gradient mismatches. Experiments on controlled heterogeneous dataset MNIST/CIFAR-10 and naturally heterogeneous dataset Digit-Five/Office-Home demonstrate its advantages over state-of-the-art methods that communicate either model or distilled data, in terms of accuracy and convergence. Notably, it remains more robust as data heterogeneity increases.

Keywords: Federated learning · Dataset distillation · Heterogeneity

M. Ceci et al. (Eds.): ECML PKDD 2026, LNAI 16941, pp. 268–285, 2027.
https://doi.org/10.1007/978-3-032-37654-1_16

1 Introduction

Federated learning (FL) enables collaborative model training across distributed clients while keeping raw data local [1]. To reduce communication overhead, clients typically perform multiple local updates before synchronizing with a central server. Under heterogeneous data distributions, however, these local updates introduce client-specific optimization bias, which accumulates across communication rounds and leads to convergence instability and performance degradation. Although numerous techniques have been proposed to mitigate heterogeneity, such as regularization, reweighting, and personalization, error accumulation remains a fundamental challenge in federated optimization.

Recently, dataset distillation has been introduced into federated learning as an alternative communication paradigm [17,23]. Instead of transmitting model updates, clients communicate compact distilled datasets, enabling the server to perform centralized optimization. An important yet underexplored consequence of this paradigm shift is that communicating distilled data effectively eliminates local-update error accumulation, as the global model is optimized directly on aggregated client representations. However, we observe that this benefit comes at a structural cost: the selective condensation of client data can amplify cross-client heterogeneity in the distilled datasets, often to a greater extent than in the original data distributions [7], especially under severe heterogeneity or limited IPC. This amplified heterogeneity reintroduces instability in a different form, manifesting as optimization drift when training on aggregated distilled data.

This observation reveals a fundamental tension in distilled-data federated learning. On the one hand, local distribution matching is essential for preserving client-specific data characteristics during distillation. On the other hand, purely local distribution matching is insufficient to control the optimization bias induced by heterogeneous distilled datasets. Conversely, gradient-based alignment alone cannot be stably applied without explicit control over the underlying data distributions, as gradients computed on mismatched distilled data are themselves ill-posed. Therefore, neither distribution matching nor gradient matching in isolation can resolve the instability induced by distilled-data communication, which is shown in Fig. 1.

Motivated by this impossibility, we argue that a dual correction mechanism is a practical and effective approach to improve stability in distilled-data federated learning. Based on this insight, we present **FedDualMatch**, a federated learning framework that enforces complementary corrections at both the data and optimization levels. Client-side distillation preserves local data characteristics through controlled distribution matching, while server-side alignment explicitly corrects optimization bias by enforcing consistency between gradients computed from individual clients' distilled data and those from the aggregated distilled dataset. By jointly constraining representation drift and optimization drift, FedDualMatch restores stability without reintroducing local-update error accumulation.

To further substantiate the effectiveness of distilled-data communication, we provide a theoretical analysis under bounded distributional and gradient discrep-

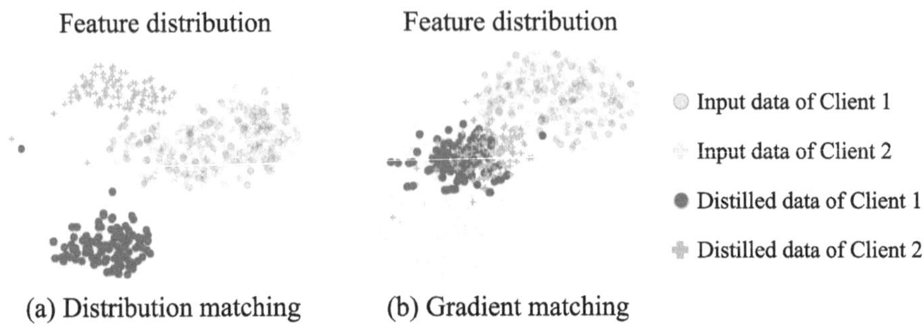

Fig. 1. (a) Distribution matching amplifies the heterogeneity of distilled data between clients, while (b) gradient matching reduces the client drift.

ancies. We show that the optimal model trained on aggregated distilled datasets achieves a testing loss that differs from centralized training on all raw client data by only a bounded constant. Moreover, the global optimization process converges to a neighborhood whose radius is determined by the residual distributional mismatch, offering an explanatory characterization of why dual matching stabilizes training under heterogeneity. Our theory provides a local characterization of how residual distribution/gradient mismatch bounds the gap to centralized training.

We empirically evaluate FedDualMatch under both controlled and naturally heterogeneous settings. Experiments on MNIST and CIFAR-10 with Dirichlet-based heterogeneity, as well as on naturally heterogeneous benchmarks such as Digit-Five and Office-Home, demonstrate that FedDualMatch achieves more stable convergence and maintains accuracy as heterogeneity increases, compared to existing methods based on either model communication or distilled-data communication. We also provide a cost analysis showing that communicating distilled data yields about 2.5× lower communication volume with runtime comparable to prior distillation-based baselines.

In summary, our contributions are as follows:

- We identify a previously underformalized failure mode of distilled-data federated learning, where eliminating local-update error accumulation may amplify cross-client heterogeneity in aggregated distilled sets, depending on the distillation objective and budget.
- We show that single-strategy corrections based solely on distribution matching or gradient alignment are insufficient, and establish the necessity of a dual correction mechanism for stability.
- We develop a unified dual-matching framework with accompanying theoretical analysis that explains why distilled-data communication can approximate centralized training while remaining stable under heterogeneity.

Table 1. Comparison of distilled-data federated learning methods. ✓ indicates an explicit mechanism, × indicates absence, and ∂ indicates a related but implicit or limited mechanism.

Method	Client Distill.	Server Correct.	Hetero. Handled	Server Traj.
FedDM [23]	✓	×	×	×
FedAF [22]	✓	✓	∂	×
FedD3 [18]	✓	×	×	×
Co-Boosting [2]	✓	×	×	×
FedSynth [6]	✓	✓	∂	×
FedMK [14]	✓	✓	∂	×
DynaFed [17]	∂	✓	∂	×
FedLGD [7]	✓	∂	∂	×
FedDualMatch	✓	✓	✓	✓

2 Related Work

Recent federated learning (FL) research has increasingly explored *distilled-data communication* as an alternative to parameter-centric communication, aiming to reduce communication cost and alleviate client heterogeneity. Existing methods can be broadly categorized into *gradient/trajectory matching* and *distribution matching*.

Gradient/Trajectory Matching. Methods such as FedMK [14], FedSynth [6], DynaFed [17], FedLAP-DP [20], and FedLGD [7] distill optimization signals by matching gradients or update trajectories across clients. While effective in reducing optimization drift, these methods typically do not explicitly correct heterogeneity within the aggregated distilled dataset during server-side optimization.

Distribution Matching. Distribution-matching approaches, exemplified by FedDM [23], generate synthetic samples that preserve client-specific feature statistics. Although such methods maintain data fidelity, local distillation can amplify cross-client mismatch among distilled datasets, which may destabilize training when aggregated.

Training Protocols. Distilled-data FL methods can further be divided into one-shot and iterative schemes. One-shot approaches such as FedD3 [18] and Co-Boosting [2] minimize communication but lack adaptivity under severe heterogeneity, while iterative methods such as FedDM and FedAF [22] progressively refine synthetic data but still rely on implicit heterogeneity control.

Positioning of Our Work. As summarized in Table 1, existing distilled-data FL methods typically emphasize either preserving local data statistics before communication or matching optimization signals during training. However, after locally distilled datasets are aggregated, the resulting synthetic collection can still contain cross-client mismatch that is not removed by aggregation alone. FedDualMatch is designed around this missing correction step: it preserves client-specific information during local distillation and then explicitly corrects the aggregated distilled data before global training.

3 Preliminary: Federated Optimization

FL is a privacy-preserving multi-client joint training framework involving K clients [15]. Each client holds local data $\mathcal{D}_k = \{(x_k^i, y_k^i)\}_{i=1}^{n_k}$, where $n_k = |\mathcal{D}_k|$ represents the size of the dataset on client k and $n = \sum_{k=1}^{K} n_k$, with x_k^i and y_k^i, as the i-th sample on the k-th client and the corresponding label, respectively, following distribution $\mathscr{D}_k$. The goal of federated learning is to jointly train a single model parameterized by w across clients, via the optimization objective is: $\min_w L(w) = \sum_{k=1}^{K} \frac{n_k}{n} L_k(w)$, where $L_k(w)$ denotes the local loss function of client k. The local loss function under the typical empirical risk minimization is expressed as $L_k(w) = \frac{1}{n_k} \sum_{i=1}^{n_k} \ell(f_w(x_k^i), y_k^i)$, where $\ell(\cdot)$ represents the loss function, such as cross-entropy loss or mean squared error, and $f_w(x_k^i)$ denotes the prediction of the model with parameters w on input x_k^i. For the classic FedAvg algorithm [15], the server first distributes the global model to each client. Each client then performs local updates on their local datasets. Specifically, the local model update for client k is computed as $w_k^{t+1} = w^t - \eta \nabla L_k(w^t) = w^t - \frac{\eta}{n_k} \sum_{i=1}^{n_k} \nabla_{w^t} \ell(f_{w^t}(x_k^i), y_k^i)$, where η is the local learning rate. After local updates, clients send their updated model parameters back to the server, where they are aggregated as $w^{t+1} = \sum_{k=1}^{K} \frac{n_k}{n} w_k^{t+1}$.

In an ideal scenario where the global aggregation is performed immediately after each local gradient update, the resulting gradient optimization would be equivalent to that of training directly on the centralized aggregated data. Let $\mathcal{D} = \bigcup_{k=1}^{K} \mathcal{D}_k = \{(x_i, y_i)\}_{i=1}^{n}$. Then the gradient updating in this case can be written as:

$$\begin{aligned} w^{t+1} &= w^t - \eta \sum_{k=1}^{K} \frac{1}{n} \sum_{i=1}^{n_k} \nabla_{w^t} \ell(f_{w^t}(x_k^i), y_k^i) \\ &= w^t - \frac{\eta}{n} \sum_{i=1}^{n} \nabla_{w^t} \ell(f_{w^t}(x_i), y_i) = w^t - \eta \nabla L(w^t). \end{aligned}$$

Let $\tilde{w}^{t+1} := w^t - \eta \nabla L(w^t), \tilde{w}^{t+E} := w^t - \eta \sum_{t'=t}^{t'=t+E-1} \nabla L(\tilde{w}^{t'})$ represents parameter updating under ideal centralized training. However, given the significant communication overhead incurred in this case, practical implementations typically defer the global aggregation until after E local updates on each client, which is presented as $w_k^{t+E} := w^t - \eta \sum_{t'=t}^{t'=t+E-1} \nabla L_k(w_k^{t'}), w^{t+E} =$

$\frac{1}{n}\sum_{k=1}^{K}\frac{n_k}{n}w_k^{t+E}$. In the common case of the inherent heterogeneity $\mathscr{D}_i \neq \mathscr{D}_j, i \neq j$ in client data distributions, the delay can give rise to significant shifts in gradient during optimization. As illustrated in Fig. 2(a), the shift accumulates over local updates such that the trajectory of the global model deviates from the optimal path and consequently leads to sub-optimal performance and unstable convergence. The shift accumulation can be decomposed:

$$\tilde{w}^{t+E} - w^{t+E} = \eta \sum_{t'=t}^{t'=t+E-1} \sum_{k=1}^{K} \sum_{i=1}^{n_k} \left[\nabla_{w_k^{t'}} \ell(f_{w_k^{t'}}(x_k^i), y_k^i) - \nabla_{\tilde{w}^{t'}} \ell(f_{\tilde{w}^{t'}}(x_k^i), y_k^i) \right]. \tag{1}$$

Therefore, in order to eliminate such shifts and achieve optimal joint training, we have to tackle the following two challenges: 1) how to mitigate the error accumulation over multiple local updates in Eq. (1); 2) how to reduce the gradient deviations caused by the client data heterogeneity, as seen in Fig. 2(a), to align gradients (Fig. 3).

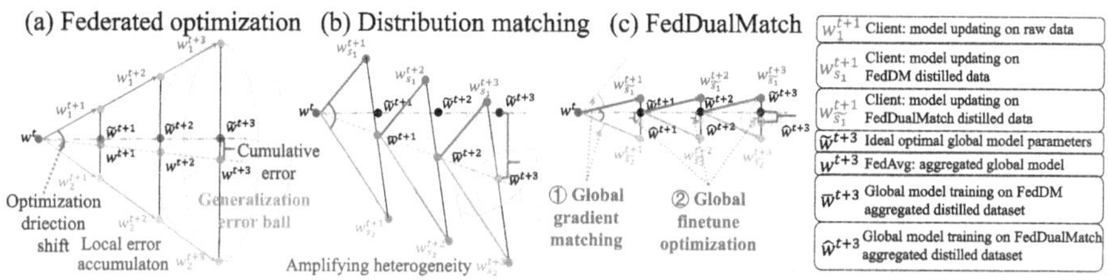

Fig. 2. (a) Illustration of the optimization error accumulation in FedAvg, where the generalization error ball radius keeps growing. (b) While distribution matching distillation eliminates error accumulation, it also amplifies data heterogeneity. (c) FedDualMatch mitigates both issues by incorporating global gradient matching and global fine-tuning optimization.

4 Methodology: FedDualMatch

FedDualMatch is a federated learning framework based on distilled-data communication, designed to stabilize training under heterogeneous client distributions. The framework couples client-side preservation of local data characteristics with server-side coordination of optimization directions. By alternating these two roles, FedDualMatch mitigates the instability induced by amplified heterogeneity in distilled datasets while avoiding the error accumulation inherent to parameter-based communication.

4.1 Local Distribution Matching (LDM)

Each client k distills its local dataset $\mathcal{D}_k$ into a compact synthetic set $\mathcal{S}_k$ by matching feature distributions in a learned embedding space. We adopt a *max-*

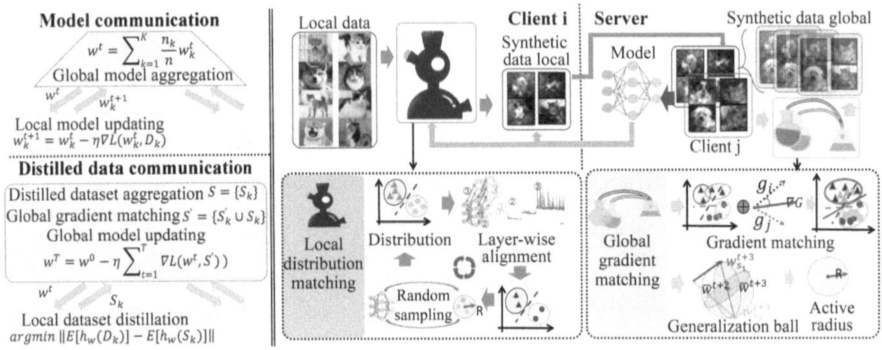

(a) Communication comparison (b) Framework of FedDualMatch

Fig. 3. (a) The replacement from model to distilled data and (b) the framework of FedDualMatch. Clients receive the global model from the server, use local distribution-matching-based dataset distillers to generate synthetic data, and send this data to the server. The server aggregates the distilled data from all clients, corrects synthetic data heterogeneity using a global gradient-matching-based dataset distiller, and updates the global model with the corrected aggregated data. The updated model is then sent back to the clients, repeating the process for federated training.

imum mean discrepancy (MMD) objective in the embedding space, and instantiate it with a linear kernel, which reduces to feature-mean matching. Given an embedding function $h_w(\cdot)$ induced by model parameters w, client k solves

$$\operatorname*{argmin}_{\mathcal{S}_k} \mathrm{MMD}^2_{\mathrm{lin}}\big(h_w(\mathcal{D}_k),\, h_w(\mathcal{S}_k)\big) = \Big\|\mathbb{E}[h_w(\mathcal{D}_k)] - \mathbb{E}[h_w(\mathcal{S}_k)]\Big\|_2^2. \tag{2}$$

To improve robustness and prevent overfitting to a single model state, we introduce an adaptive *generalization error ball*. At communication round t, the server computes the radius $R_t = \sup_k \left\|w_t^{\mathcal{S}_k} - w_t^{\mathcal{S}}\right\|_2$, i.e., the worst-case one-step update discrepancy between each client's distilled set and the aggregated distilled set. $w_t^{\mathcal{S}_k} = w_{t-1} - \eta\nabla L(w_{t-1}; \mathcal{S}_k)$ and $w_t^{\mathcal{S}} = w_{t-1} - \eta\nabla L(w_{t-1}; \mathcal{S})$ are one-step gradient updates on the local and aggregated distilled datasets, respectively. The server broadcasts w_{t-1} and R_t to clients, defining a sampling neighborhood $\mathcal{B}(w_{t-1}; R_t)$.

Clients randomly sample model parameters w from this ball and perform feature-mean matching under these sampled embeddings:

$$\operatorname*{argmin}_{\mathcal{S}_k} \sup_{w \in \mathcal{B}(w_{t-1}; R_t)} \Big\|\mathbb{E}[h_w(\mathcal{D}_k)] - \mathbb{E}[h_w(\mathcal{S}_k)]\Big\|_2. \tag{3}$$

The expectation is approximated empirically using class-wise samples. For C classes, the empirical loss is

$$L^k_{\mathrm{FM}}(\mathcal{S}_k; \mathcal{D}_k) = \sum_{c=1}^{C} \left\| \frac{1}{n_k^c} \sum_{i=1}^{n_k^c} h_w(x_k^{c,i}) - \frac{1}{s_k^c} \sum_{i=1}^{s_k^c} h_w(\tilde{x}_k^{c,i}) \right\|_2, \tag{4}$$

where $x_k^{c,i} \in \mathcal{D}_k$ and $\tilde{x}_k^{c,i} \in \mathcal{S}_k$ are samples of class c.

To preserve information across different abstraction levels, we further adopt *backward layer-wise feature alignment*. Let $h_w = \{v_1, \ldots, v_J\}$ denote the sequence of feature layers. Rather than summing losses across all layers, which can lead to unstable optimization, we align layers sequentially from deeper to shallower ones. At layer p, the accumulated feature-matching loss is

$$L_{\mathrm{DM}}^{k,p}(\mathcal{S}_k; \mathcal{D}_k) = \sum_{q=p}^{J} L_{\mathrm{FM}}^{k,v_q}(\mathcal{S}_k; \mathcal{D}_k). \tag{5}$$

This strategy maintains alignment in already-matched deeper layers while progressively refining earlier representations.

4.2 Global Gradient Matching (GGM)

After receiving distilled datasets $\{\mathcal{S}_k\}_{k=1}^{K}$, the server aggregates them into $\mathcal{S}$ and performs centralized optimization. Heterogeneous distilled datasets can induce inconsistent optimization directions when aggregated, motivating explicit gradient coordination on the server.

Starting from $\mathcal{S}'_k = \mathcal{S}_k$, global gradient matching minimizes

$$L_{\mathrm{GGM}}(\mathcal{S}'; \mathcal{S}) = \mathbb{E}\Big[\sum_{k=1}^{K} \mathrm{dist}\big(\nabla_w L(w; \mathcal{S}'_k), \nabla_w L(w; \mathcal{S})\big)\Big], \tag{6}$$

where w is sampled from $\mathcal{B}(w_{t-1}; R_t)$ and $\mathrm{dist}(g_1, g_2) = 1 - \frac{\langle g_1, g_2 \rangle}{\|g_1\|_2 \|g_2\|_2}$ is the cosine distance between gradients. The expectation is taken over mini-batch sampling and random model sampling within the ball.

To preserve data diversity, the updated $\mathcal{S}'_k$ is merged with $\mathcal{S}_k$, forming $\tilde{\mathcal{S}} = \bigcup_{k=1}^{K}\{\mathcal{S}_k, \mathcal{S}'_k\}$. The server then fine-tunes the global model on $\tilde{\mathcal{S}}$ for T_g steps. Gradient matching and fine-tuning are alternated for M rounds. This interplay reduces gradient inconsistency while retaining diverse distilled representations, leading to a more stable optimization trajectory.

Connection to Prior Objectives. The two stages of FedDualMatch play complementary roles. Distribution-matching methods such as FedDM preserve local feature statistics, but the server still trains on a union of client-specific synthetic sets. Gradient- and trajectory-matching methods such as FedSynth, FedMK, DynaFed, and FedLGD instead focus on optimization signals, without explicitly maintaining local feature statistics before aggregation. FedDualMatch combines these perspectives in a staged form: LDM controls representation drift before communication, while GGM reduces optimization drift after aggregation along the server trajectory.

4.3 Computation, Communication, and Noise Considerations

Computation and Communication. Compared to FedDM, FedDualMatch increases server-side computation due to gradient coordination and alternating optimization, while keeping client-side costs comparable to existing distillation-based federated learning methods. The additional GGM stage is performed only on the server, and its cost scales with the number of GGM rounds, the IPC budget, and the number of inner synthesis steps. This design keeps the extra computation concentrated at the server, where compact synthetic datasets are already available for global training. In terms of communication, clients transmit compact distilled datasets rather than full model parameters, which remains substantially cheaper than parameter communication for large models.

Noise Injection. Gaussian noise is injected during local dataset distillation following the same mechanism as FedDM, where clients communicate only distilled synthetic samples instead of raw data or model updates. As analyzed in FedDM, such a distillation-based communication protocol can admit formal differential privacy guarantees under standard assumptions, given appropriate clipping and

---

Algorithm 1: FedDualMatch: Dual Matching Federated Learning

Input: Initial global model w_0, error radius R_0, clients K, rounds T, local epochs E, global fine-tuning epochs T_g, learning rate η, local datasets $\{\mathcal{D}_k\}$, embedding depth J, GGM rounds M, noise parameters (C, σ) for clipping and Gaussian perturbation.

Server-side: for $t = 1$ **to** T **do**

Broadcast (w_{t-1}, R_{t-1}) to all clients;

Receive distilled datasets $\{\mathcal{S}_k\}_{k=1}^{K}$;

Update error radius:

$$R_t = \sup_k \|w_t^{\mathcal{S}_k} - w_t^{\mathcal{S}}\|$$

Perform M rounds of **Global Gradient Matching (GGM)** within $\mathcal{B}(w_{t-1}; R_t)$ to obtain $\{\mathcal{S}'_k\}$;

Fine-tune global model on $\tilde{\mathcal{S}} = \bigcup_{k=1}^{K}(\mathcal{S}_k \cup \mathcal{S}'_k)$ for T_g epochs to obtain w_t;

end

Client-side (for each client k**):**

1. Sample $w^k \sim \mathcal{B}(w_{t-1}; R_{t-1})$
2. Use first J layers of w_{t-1} as embedding function h_w
3. Initialize synthetic dataset $\mathcal{S}_k$ with Gaussian noise
4. Perform **layer-wise distribution matching** between $\mathcal{D}_k$ and $\mathcal{S}_k$:

$$L_{DM}^{k} = \sum_{p=1}^{J}\sum_{q=p}^{J} L_{MMD}^{k,v_q}$$

with gradient clipping and Gaussian noise (used as regularization).

5. Upload $\mathcal{S}_k$ to server

---

noise calibration. Since FedDualMatch adopts the same noise injection and clipping strategy during local distillation, it follows the same differential privacy accounting framework as FedDM under identical parameter settings. In this work, we therefore focus on the empirical impact of noise on optimization stability and model utility, rather than providing a separate certified (ε, δ) accounting.

5 Theoretical Analysis

This section provides a theoretical characterization of distilled-data communication in federated learning and explains why dual matching stabilizes optimization under heterogeneous data distributions. The analysis follows the server optimization trajectory and studies neighborhoods of the iterates produced when training on aggregated distilled datasets. Under mild local regularity conditions, we show that training on distilled data can approximate centralized training and that the optimization process converges to a bounded neighborhood whose radius depends on the residual distributional and gradient mismatches.

5.1 Assumptions and Notation

Let $L_k(w; \mathcal{D}_k)$ denote the population loss of client k with model parameters $w \in \mathbb{R}^d$, and let $\mathcal{D} = \cup_{k=1}^K \mathcal{D}_k$ be the union of all client datasets. Each client constructs a distilled dataset $\mathcal{S}_k$, and the server aggregates them into $\mathcal{S} = \cup_{k=1}^K \mathcal{S}_k$. Within one communication round, the server performs T_g optimization steps on $\mathcal{S}$, producing a trajectory $\{w^t\}_{t=0}^{T_g-1}$. We analyze the optimization behavior in neighborhoods of these iterates.

Assumption 1. *For all clients $k = 1, \ldots, K$ and parameters w within the local regions of interest, the following conditions hold:*

(A1) Smoothness and Local Strong Convexity of the Loss. *Each client loss $L_k(\cdot)$ is L-smooth. Moreover, within $\bigcup_{t=0}^{T_g-1} \mathcal{B}(w^t, R)$, it satisfies μ-strong convexity:*

$$L_k(w') \geq L_k(w) + \langle \nabla L_k(w), w' - w \rangle + \frac{\mu}{2}\|w' - w\|_2^2, \quad \forall w, w' \in \bigcup_{t=0}^{T_g-1} \mathcal{B}(w^t, R).$$

(A2) Bounded Gradient Norm. *For all such w and clients k, $\|\nabla L_k(w)\|_2 \leq G$ for some constant $G > 0$.*

(A3) Bounded Representation Mismatch Induced by Distillation. *Let $h_w(\cdot)$ denote the feature extractor used in distribution matching. For each client k,*

$$\left\|\mathbb{E}_{x\sim\mathcal{D}_k}[h_w(x)] - \mathbb{E}_{x\sim\mathcal{S}_k}[h_w(x)]\right\|_2 \leq \sigma_d, \quad \forall w \in \bigcup_{t=0}^{T_g-1} \mathcal{B}(w^t, R). \tag{7}$$

The expectation is taken over the data distribution and any stochasticity in the distillation procedure.

(A4) Bounded Gradient Bias Between Local and Aggregated Distilled Datasets. *Along the server trajectory, the expected gradient deviation satisfies:*

$$\mathbb{E}\Big[\big\|\nabla_w L(w;\mathcal{S}_k) - \nabla_w L(w;\mathcal{S})\big\|_2\Big] \leq \sigma_g, \quad \forall w \in \{w^t\}_{t=0}^{T_g-1}, \ \forall k, \tag{8}$$

where the expectation is over mini-batch sampling and algorithmic randomness.

Assumption 1 isolates two quantities that govern stability under distilled-data communication. The parameter σ_d captures the residual representation drift caused by local distillation, while σ_g measures the remaining optimization bias between individual clients' distilled datasets and the aggregated distilled dataset. Both quantities are explicitly controlled by the dual matching mechanism. The local form of the assumptions matches the way FedDualMatch is applied: both distribution matching and gradient matching are evaluated around the current model trajectory. When the distilled samples poorly cover minority modes or the trajectory moves into regions where feature statistics no longer reflect gradient behavior, the residual terms can become larger, which is consistent with the dependence of the bounds on (σ_d, σ_g).

5.2 Effectiveness of Distilled-Data Communication

We first characterize when training on aggregated distilled data can approximate centralized training on the original datasets.

Theorem 1 (Effectiveness under bounded representation drift). *Let* $w^*_{\mathcal{D}} = \arg\min_w L(w;\mathcal{D})$ *denote the optimal solution of centralized training on the original data, and let* $w^*_{\mathcal{S}} = \arg\min_w L(w;\mathcal{S})$ *be the optimal solution obtained by training on the aggregated distilled dataset. If the representation mismatch induced by distillation is bounded by* σ_d *as in* (7)*, then the excess loss evaluated on* $\mathcal{D}$ *satisfies*

$$\mathbb{E}\big[L(w^*_{\mathcal{S}};\mathcal{D}) - L(w^*_{\mathcal{D}};\mathcal{D})\big] \leq \varepsilon(\sigma_d), \tag{9}$$

where there exists a constant $c > 0$ *such that* $\varepsilon(\sigma_d) \leq c\,\sigma_d^2$*, under Assumption 1.*

Theorem 1 provides an explanatory justification for distilled-data communication. When local distillation preserves client data characteristics in the feature spaces used for matching, optimizing on the aggregated distilled dataset yields a solution whose evaluation on the original data closely approximates centralized training.

5.3 Convergence Characterization Under Dual Matching

We next describe how dual matching stabilizes optimization during server-side training on distilled data.

Theorem 2 (Convergence to a bounded neighborhood). *Suppose that the representation drift σ_d and gradient bias σ_g are bounded as in Assumption 1. Then, for a suitable step size and any iterate w^t along the server optimization trajectory,*

$$\mathbb{E}[L(w^t; \mathcal{D})] \leq L(w^*_{\mathcal{D}}; \mathcal{D}) + C(\sigma_d, \sigma_g, T_g), \tag{10}$$

where $C(\sigma_d, \sigma_g, T_g)$ denotes an upper bound that is monotone increasing in σ_d and σ_g, and monotone decreasing in the number of server optimization steps T_g. A concrete instantiation of $C(\cdot)$ is provided in the appendix.

Theorem 2 indicates that training on aggregated distilled data converges to a neighborhood of the centralized optimum. Crucially, the size of this neighborhood is determined by the residual mismatches (σ_d, σ_g) rather than by accumulated client-side update errors.

Remark 1 (Per-round stability). Within a single communication round, the server can perform many optimization steps on $\mathcal{S}$. As a result, the dominant source of error is no longer the accumulation of local update drift, but the residual mismatch controlled by dual matching. This explains why distilled-data communication avoids the classical error-accumulation phenomenon of parameter-based federated optimization.

5.4 Relation to Prior Analyses and Privacy Discussion

Existing analyses of distilled-data federated learning, such as DynaFed [17], typically require uniform gradient alignment between distilled and original data across the entire parameter space. Such global conditions are difficult to satisfy in practice. By contrast, our analysis focuses on local neighborhoods along the training trajectory, which more closely reflects how distribution and gradient matching are implemented in practice and clarifies the role of dual matching in stabilizing optimization.

We adopt a Gaussian perturbation mechanism during distillation, following prior work, to mitigate information leakage. Our discussion here focuses on algorithmic behavior rather than providing a full certified differential privacy accounting, which would require specifying sensitivity bounds and composition across all steps.

6 Experiments

Datasets. We evaluate FedDualMatch through controlled experiments and naturally heterogeneous data. In controlled experiments, client heterogeneity is adjusted using the Dirichlet distribution's alpha parameter, where smaller values indicate greater heterogeneity [15]. The MNIST [11] and CIFAR-10 [10] datasets are distributed to 10 clients with alpha values of 0.005, 0.01, and 0.05, respectively, to test performance under varying degrees of data-distribution disparity.

For real-world heterogeneity, the Digit-Five dataset, comprising MNIST [11], MNIST-M [4], SVHN [16], SynthDigits [8], and USPS [3], is naturally divided into 5 datasets, one for each client, exhibiting significant differences in image style and source. Similarly, Office-Home [19] is split into four clients: Art, Clipart, Product, and Real World, each in a different visual domain.

Table 2. Accuracy of FL algorithms on MNIST and CIFAR-10 in controlled experiments. The results demonstrate that FedDualMatch maintains accuracy for increasing data heterogeneity between clients (smaller α).

Methods	MNIST			CIFAR-10		
	$\alpha = 0.05$	$\alpha = 0.01$	$\alpha = 0.005$	$\alpha = 0.05$	$\alpha = 0.01$	$\alpha = 0.005$
FedAvg	97.93 ± 0.02	80.09 ± 1.57	82.95 ± 1.69	53.64 ± 3.39	39.46 ± 0.88	38.04 ± 2.92
FedProx	98.01 ± 0.00	89.99 ± 0.98	83.41 ± 2.34	55.13 ± 0.04	40.93 ± 1.68	39.30 ± 2.02
FedNova	97.67 ± 0.01	75.68 ± 0.14	77.97 ± 5.35	47.90 ± 2.65	37.89 ± 0.74	25.97 ± 3.32
SCAFFOLD	97.94 ± 0.03	86.06 ± 0.93	79.99 ± 2.50	49.62 ± 1.17	17.14 ± 2.11	33.83 ± 0.13
DynaFed	**98.13 ± 0.04**	95.69 ± 0.93	75.50 ± 6.28	**57.23 ± 1.56**	43.06 ± 3.61	27.41 ± 1.94
FedDM	95.43 ± 0.02	95.38 ± 0.12	95.52 ± 0.03	42.44 ± 0.15	41.15 ± 0.12	41.99 ± 0.19
FedDualMatch	96.94 ± 0.03	**97.03 ± 0.04**	**97.00 ± 1.11**	44.61 ± 1.02	**44.98 ± 0.40**	**43.75 ± 0.68**

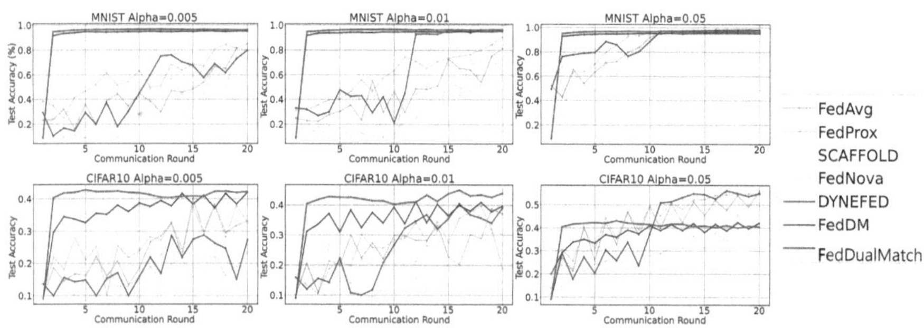

Fig. 4. Test accuracy under different communication rounds. FedDualMatch's accuracy increases rapidly in the first round of communication.

Baseline Methods. We compare FedDualMatch with classical federated learning methods performing model communication, including FedAvg [15], FedProx [13], FedNova [21], and SCAFFOLD [9]. The latter three specialize in addressing client data heterogeneity. We also compare FedDualMatch with methods doing distilled dataset communication, such as FedDM [23] and DynaFed [17]. Particularly, DynaFed leverages both types of communication by running FedAvg in the early stages and then fine-tuning on the aggregated distilled dataset.

Implementation Details. All reported experiments use the same three-layer ConvNet backbone across compared methods within each benchmark, with width 128, ReLU activations, instance normalization, and average pooling; Office-Home uses 64 output classes and the other benchmarks use 10. Methods share the same client partitions, communication rounds, IPC budgets, batch sizes, and test protocols. For baseline methods, we use the recommended settings from the corresponding implementations when available and tune learning rates within the same experimental budget.

Hyperparameters. In controlled experiments, all clients participate in $T = 20$ communication rounds with batch size 256 (10 or 64 for naturally heterogeneous data). Local distribution matching runs 200 iterations with learning rate $\eta_{\mathrm{ldm}} = 1.0$. Global gradient matching runs $M = 10$ rounds; in each round, we synthesize $\mathcal{S}'$ for 10 iterations with learning rate $\eta_{\mathrm{ggm}} = 0.1$. Fine-tuning runs $T_g = 500$ iterations with learning rate $\eta_{\mathrm{ft}} = 0.001$ per communication round. Distilled data are initialized with Gaussian noise for privacy, and we align $J = 3$ pooling layers.

Table 3. Accuracy of FL algorithms on Digit-Five and Office-Home. FedDualMatch remains robust to natural data heterogeneity and improves knowledge discovery across clients.

Methods	Digit-Five					Office-Home			
	MNIST	M-M	SVHN	SYN	USPS	Art	Clipart	Product	Real
FedAvg	91.86	69.78	49.63	61.01	92.04	9.52	21.55	27.43	13.81
FedProx	92.31	75.78	50.12	62.01	93.17	9.26	22.16	26.42	13.48
FedNova	91.99	76.12	43.25	62.37	93.06	9.26	20.53	26.97	13.20
SCAFFOLD	91.41	73.07	26.76	51.83	90.97	7.31	16.16	20.50	11.38
FedDM	90.71	64.80	34.93	60.90	**93.55**	11.47	21.64	29.45	19.48
FedDualMatch	**94.57**	**77.13**	**62.30**	**75.20**	91.40	**13.00**	**25.08**	**35.05**	**23.50**

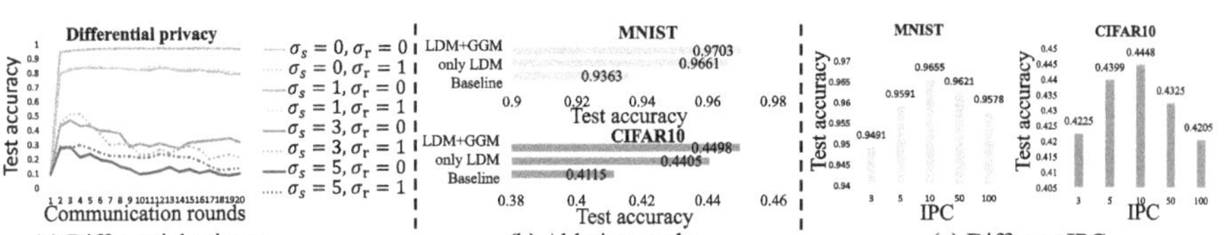

(a) Differential privacy (b) Ablation study (c) Different IPC

Fig. 5. Comparisons of privacy, ablation study, and images per class (IPC).

Table 4. Performance comparison between FedDM and FedDualMatch across client sampling rates.

Client Sampling	FedDM	FedDualMatch
1.0	0.3784	0.4611
0.8	0.3542	0.4517
0.5	0.3525	0.4268
0.2	0.3584	0.4101

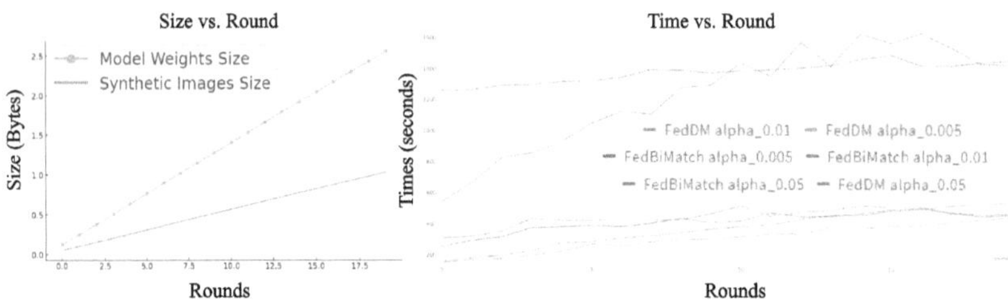

(a) Communication cost (b) Computational overhead

Fig. 6. Communication and computational costs. (a) FedDualMatch reduces communication volume by transmitting synthetic datasets instead of model weights. (b) Per-round runtime comparison under different non-IID settings.

Effectiveness Under Heterogeneity. Tables 2 and 3 report results under controlled and natural heterogeneity. As heterogeneity increases (smaller α), model-communication-based methods exhibit pronounced performance degradation due to accumulated client-specific optimization bias. For example, SCAFFOLD drops from 97.94 In contrast, FedDualMatch maintains stable performance across heterogeneity levels and consistently outperforms FedDM, with larger gains in the most heterogeneous regime (e.g., $\alpha = 0.005$). These results suggest that while distilled-data communication mitigates classical error accumulation, it amplifies cross-client mismatch, which must be explicitly corrected during server-side optimization.

When heterogeneity is mild, the benefit of correcting the aggregated distilled set becomes less pronounced. For example, at $\alpha = 0.05$, DynaFed reaches 98.13% on MNIST and 57.23% on CIFAR-10, while FedDualMatch obtains 96.94% and 44.61%. FedDualMatch still improves over FedDM in this regime, but the margin is smaller than in the high-heterogeneity setting. This trend suggests that GGM is most useful when local condensation creates substantial cross-client optimization mismatch. Results on naturally heterogeneous benchmarks in Table 3 further confirm its robustness across domains, including a substantial gain on SVHN.

Convergence Behavior. Figure 4 compares convergence profiles. FedDualMatch converges faster than FedDM, particularly on CIFAR-10. Once distilled sets are aggregated, server-side optimization can proceed with many steps per round, and enforcing gradient consistency reduces sensitivity to heterogeneous distilled subsets, leading to a more stable optimization trajectory.

Privacy Sensitivity. Figure 5(a) shows the impact of Gaussian noise injected into distilled data. Increasing σ_s degrades performance, reflecting the standard utility–privacy trade-off. The interaction with the dynamic radius σ_r reveals a stability–coverage trade-off: smaller radii improve stability but limit coverage, whereas larger radii increase variability during optimization. These results illustrate robustness trends under noise rather than an optimal privacy configuration.

Impact of IPC. Figure 5(c) shows that both overly small and overly large IPC values reduce performance. Small IPC under-represents intra-class diversity, while large IPC complicates distillation and introduces redundancy, consistent with prior observations in dataset distillation [5,12].

Ablation Study. Figure 5(b) highlights the complementary roles of the two components in FedDualMatch. Removing layer-wise feature alignment in LDM causes a pronounced performance drop, indicating that multi-layer alignment is necessary to preserve transferable representations in distilled data. Adding GGM yields further improvements by stabilizing optimization: without gradient coordination, heterogeneous client distilled sets can induce inconsistent update directions, leading to optimization drift. This stabilization effect is particularly important under high heterogeneity.

Effect of Client Sampling. Table 4 examines varying client participation with 50 clients. Lower participation reduces accuracy due to weaker coverage of client data distributions, an effect that is amplified under heterogeneous settings where missing client modes increase mismatch in the aggregated distilled dataset.

Cost Analysis. Figure 6 compares the communication and computational costs of FedDualMatch. As shown in Fig. 6(a), transmitting distilled synthetic datasets instead of full model parameters reduces communication volume by approximately 2.5× across all rounds. Figure 6(b) indicates that despite the additional server-side global gradient matching step, FedDualMatch achieves per-round runtimes comparable to FedDM under different non-IID settings, since gradient matching is performed on compact synthetic datasets. Overall, FedDualMatch improves communication efficiency with negligible additional computational overhead.

7 Conclusion

We propose *FedDualMatch*, a federated learning framework that communicates distilled data to avoid heterogeneity-induced error accumulation. It integrates client-side layer-wise distribution matching with server-side gradient matching and global fine-tuning, improving representation quality and convergence stability. We provide localized theoretical analysis of distilled-data communication, and extensive controlled and real-world experiments show consistent gains over state-of-the-art distilled-data communication methods, especially under high heterogeneity.

Limitation: FedDualMatch brings the largest gains when client heterogeneity is substantial; under mild heterogeneity, adaptive use of the server-side correction may be preferable. Our theory studies local trajectory neighborhoods, and extending the analysis to broader non-convex regimes is an interesting direction. Reducing the cost of data distillation, especially for resource-constrained clients, is another direction for future work.

References

1. Bonawitz, K.: Towards federated learning at scale: system design. arXiv preprint arXiv:1902.01046 (2019)
2. Dai, R., Zhang, Y., Li, A., Liu, T., Yang, X., Han, B.: Enhancing one-shot federated learning through data and ensemble co-boosting. arXiv preprint arXiv:2402.15070 (2024)
3. Ganin, Y., Lempitsky, V.: Unsupervised domain adaptation by backpropagation. In: International conference on machine learning, pp. 1180–1189. PMLR (2015)
4. Ganin, Y., et al.: Domain-adversarial training of neural networks. J. Mach. Learn. Res. **17**(59), 1–35 (2016)
5. Guo, Z., Wang, K., Cazenavette, G., Li, H., Zhang, K., You, Y.: Towards lossless dataset distillation via difficulty-aligned trajectory matching. arXiv preprint arXiv:2310.05773 (2023)
6. Hu, S., Goetz, J., Malik, K., Zhan, H., Liu, Z., Liu, Y.: FedSynth: gradient compression via synthetic data in federated learning. arXiv preprint arXiv:2204.01273 (2022)
7. Huang, C.Y., Jin, R., Zhao, C., Xu, D., Li, X.: Federated learning on virtual heterogeneous data with local-global dataset distillation. Trans. Mach. Learn. Res. (2025)
8. Hull, J.J.: A database for handwritten text recognition research. IEEE Trans. Pattern Anal. Mach. Intell. **16**(5), 550–554 (1994)
9. Karimireddy, S.P., Kale, S., Mohri, M., Reddi, S., Stich, S., Suresh, A.T.: SCAFFOLD: stochastic controlled averaging for federated learning. In: International Conference on Machine Learning, pp. 5132–5143. PMLR (2020)
10. Krizhevsky, A., Hinton, G.: Learning multiple layers of features from tiny images (2009)
11. LeCun, Y., Bottou, L., Bengio, Y., Haffner, P.: Gradient-based learning applied to document recognition. Proc. IEEE **86**(11), 2278–2324 (1998)
12. Lee, Y., Chung, H.W.: SelMatch: effectively scaling up dataset distillation via selection-based initialization and partial updates by trajectory matching. In: Forty-First International Conference on Machine Learning (2024)
13. Li, T., Sahu, A.K., Talwalkar, A., Smith, V.: Federated learning: challenges, methods, and future directions. IEEE Sig. Process. Mag. **37**(3), 50–60 (2020)

14. Liu, P., Yu, X., Zhou, J.T.: Meta knowledge condensation for federated learning. arXiv preprint arXiv:2209.14851 (2022)
15. McMahan, B., Moore, E., Ramage, D., Hampson, S., y Arcas, B.A.: Communication-efficient learning of deep networks from decentralized data. In: Artificial Intelligence and Statistics, pp. 1273–1282. PMLR (2017)
16. Netzer, Y., Wang, T., Coates, A., Bissacco, A., Wu, B., Ng, A.Y.: Reading digits in natural images with unsupervised feature learning. In: NIPS Workshop on Deep Learning and Unsupervised Feature Learning, vol. 2011, p. 4. Granada (2011)
17. Pi, R., et al: DynaFed: tackling client data heterogeneity with global dynamics. In: Proceedings of the IEEE/CVF Conference on Computer Vision and Pattern Recognition, pp. 12177–12186 (2023)
18. Song, R., et al.: Federated learning via decentralized dataset distillation in resource-constrained edge environments. In: 2023 International Joint Conference on Neural Networks (IJCNN), pp. 1–10. IEEE (2023)
19. Venkateswara, H., Eusebio, J., Chakraborty, S., Panchanathan, S.: Deep hashing network for unsupervised domain adaptation. In: Proceedings of the IEEE Conference on Computer Vision and Pattern Recognition, pp. 5018–5027 (2017)
20. Wang, H.P., Chen, D., Kerkouche, R., Fritz, M.: FedLAP-DP: federated learning by sharing differentially private loss approximations. arXiv preprint arXiv:2302.01068 (2023)
21. Wang, J., Liu, Q., Liang, H., Joshi, G., Poor, H.V.: Tackling the objective inconsistency problem in heterogeneous federated optimization. Adv. Neural. Inf. Process. Syst. **33**, 7611–7623 (2020)
22. Wang, Y., Fu, H., Kanagavelu, R., Wei, Q., Liu, Y., Goh, R.S.M.: An aggregation-free federated learning for tackling data heterogeneity. In: Proceedings of the IEEE/CVF Conference on Computer Vision and Pattern Recognition, pp. 26233–26242 (2024)
23. Xiong, Y., Wang, R., Cheng, M., Yu, F., Hsieh, C.J.: FedDM: iterative distribution matching for communication-efficient federated learning. In: Proceedings of the IEEE/CVF Conference on Computer Vision and Pattern Recognition, pp. 16323–16332 (2023)

How Far Can We Compress? Attention-Guided Dataset Distillation for TabPFN

Tao Wang[1,2], Min Yu[1,2(✉)], Jianguo Jiang[1,2], Jingyuan Li[3], Guokun Xu[1,2], Xiang Meng[1,2], Weiqing Huang[1,2], and Gang Li[4]

[1] Institute of Information Engineering, Chinese Academy of Sciences, Beijing, China
{wangtao,yumin,jiangjianguo,xuguokun,mengxiang,huangweiqing}@iie.ac.cn
[2] School of Cyber Security, University of Chinese Academy of Sciences, Beijing, China
[3] Department of Computer Science, Beijing Technology and Business University, Beijing, China
li.jingyuan.jerry@btbu.edu.cn
[4] School of Information Technology, Deakin University, Victoria, Australia
gang.li@deakin.edu.au

Abstract. Tabular foundation models such as TabPFNv2 have demonstrated strong predictive performance under in-context learning, yet their bounded context windows necessitate effective context compression. While random sampling can match prior distillation baselines at moderate context sizes, it exhibits severe instability when the sample budget is small. In this work, we extend the in-context dataset distillation framework of Ma et al. to TabPFNv2 with two key contributions: joint optimization of both features and labels, which relaxes class-balanced allocation constraints for more flexible context representation; and an attention-guided iterative pruning strategy to empirically probe the compressibility limits of distilled contexts. Our method achieves an average compression ratio of 15.7% while preserving predictive accuracy, and consistently outperforms both the original distillation baseline and label-only optimization variants at equivalent context budgets, establishing a practical lower bound for optimization-based context compression in tabular foundation models. The code is available at https://github.com/wtao-0043/PKDD_compress_border.

Keywords: Dataset Distillation · Tabular Foundation Model · Tabular Classification

1 Introduction

Tabular data, which is prevalent across various domains such as healthcare [21], finance [4], and cybersecurity [2], has long been dominated in its classification and regression tasks by deep learning and gradient boosting decision trees (GBDT).

M. Ceci et al. (Eds.): ECML PKDD 2026, LNAI 16941, pp. 286–301, 2027.
https://doi.org/10.1007/978-3-032-37654-1_17

In recent years, the remarkable success of foundation models in text and image modalities has inspired growing interest in tabular foundation models. Hollmann et al. were the first to propose TabPFNv1 [8], a transformer-based foundation model designed for tabular data. The model can make predictions in a single forward pass, fundamentally transforming the conventional train-then-apply paradigm in tabular data analysis.

Despite continuous advancements in scalability and performance of tabular foundation models, their context length remains inherently bounded, and longer contexts often entail higher computational costs. Thus, effectively reducing the context size has become a critical challenge. To address this issue, Ma et al. [14] adopted a prompt-tuning approach and implemented optimization-based dataset distillation on TabPFNv1. The distilled data demonstrated significantly improved performance on certain tasks, even rivaling traditional deep learning models.

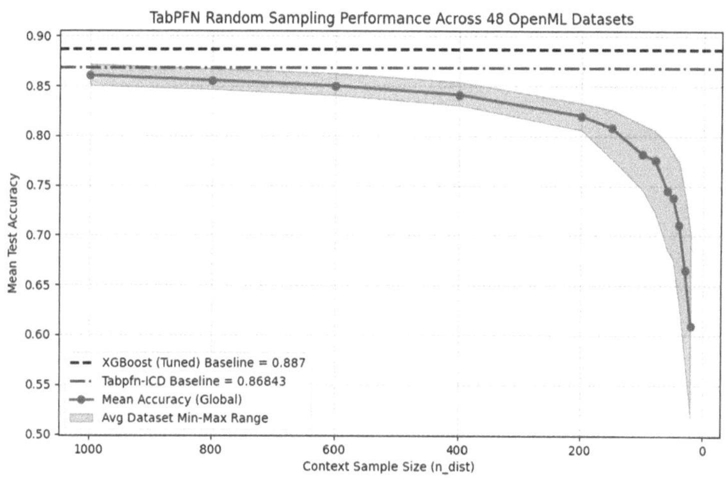

Fig. 1. Mean test accuracy of TabPFNv2 under random context sampling across 48 large-scale OpenML datasets, as a function of context size n_{dist}. Each point on the red curve is the average over 5 independent runs and all 48 datasets; the shaded region is bounded below by the per-dataset average minimum accuracy and above by the per-dataset average maximum accuracy across runs. The dashed lines indicate the TabPFN-ICD baseline reported by Ma et al. [14] (0.868) and a tuned XGBoost reference (0.887). Notably, random sampling with $n_{\text{dist}} = 1{,}000$ already matches the ICD baseline of Ma et al. (Color figure online)

Subsequently, new foundational models for tabular data have emerged, most notably TabPFNv2 [9] and TabICL [19]. TabPFNv2 builds upon its predecessor with substantial architectural improvements, including stronger in-context learning capabilities and better handling of heterogeneous feature types; crucially, the new model can accommodate a significantly larger number of data points and input features within its context window. Given these expanded capacities, we observe that TabPFNv2 is already capable of achieving strong predictive performance when supplied with a randomly sampled subset of the original training data, without any distillation whatsoever. As shown in Fig. 1, randomly drawing a moderate number of samples from the original dataset is sufficient to attain competitive accuracy, which raises the question of whether dataset distillation for tabular foundation models still offers meaningful gains in this new setting.

However, a closer examination of Fig. 1 reveals a critical limitation of naive random sampling: once the context size n_{dist} falls below a certain threshold, model performance not only drops sharply but also becomes highly unstable, as reflected by the rapidly expanding confidence bands in the low-n_{dist} regime. This observation naturally draws our attention back to the in-context distillation framework proposed by Ma et al. [14]. Specifically, we ask: *within the current distillation framework, to what lower bound can the number of synthetic data entries be compressed, while still maintaining satisfactory predictive accuracy?* Rather than abandoning the distillation paradigm, we revisit it from the perspective of aggressive compression, aiming to identify how compact a distilled dataset can be made without compromising the reliability that random sampling fails to provide when the sample count is small.

Building upon the framework of Ma et al. [14], we extend in-context dataset distillation to TabPFNv2 with two key contributions. First, we introduce joint optimization of both features and labels, relaxing the constraint of class-balanced allocation and thereby allowing the distilled context to more flexibly capture the underlying data distribution. Second, we incorporate attention score computation to empirically investigate the compressibility of the distilled context: by iteratively pruning low-attention context points and re-optimizing, we seek to identify the minimum context size at which the distilled data can still maintain competitive predictive accuracy.

Our experimental results demonstrate that, under our framework, an average compression ratio of 15.7% can be achieved without sacrificing accuracy. Furthermore, controlled comparisons against both the original method of Ma et al. [14] and a label-only joint optimization variant at equivalent context sizes consistently confirm the superiority of our proposed framework. Nevertheless, we observe that further compression beyond this regime begins to undermine the stability of the already-optimized distilled context. Specifically, when the context budget is reduced to an extremely small scale, continued pruning within our framework tends to destabilize the distilled representations, yielding performance inferior to that of distilling from scratch using the framework of Ma et al. [14] initialized from a minimal subset of the original data. This finding delineates a practical lower bound on context compressibility within the optimization-based distillation paradigm, and points to an interesting direction for future work on more robust compression strategies at extreme budget regimes.

2 Related Work

2.1 Dataset Distillation

Existing dataset distillation (DD) techniques, primarily developed within the computer vision domain, can be broadly classified into three paradigms. *Performance Matching* [3,17,23,29] formulates distillation as a bi-level meta-learning problem, directly optimizing the synthetic set to minimize the validation loss of a proxy model trained on it. To circumvent the computationally expensive unrolling of training graphs, *Parameter Matching* [5,7,13,27] explicitly aligns the network gradients or parameter trajectories of models trained on real versus synthetic data. While effective, both paradigms inherently overfit the synthesized data to the specific neural architectures utilized during the distillation process. In contrast, *Distribution Matching* [20,22,26,28] bypasses training dynamics entirely by aligning the feature statistics of the original and synthetic datasets within a shared embedding space. This paradigm yields model-agnostic representations that exhibit superior transferability across diverse downstream architectures.

Despite rapid progress in image distillation, its adaptation to tabular data remains largely under-explored. The heterogeneous nature of tabular datasets, which typically comprise a mix of continuous, categorical, and discrete variables, disrupts the continuous gradient flow required for standard DD optimization. Early attempts predominantly relied on performance matching. Medvedev and D'yakonov [16] provided an initial proof-of-concept for tabular distillation on a standard binary classification task. However, their optimization depended strictly on a single proxy neural network, and their evaluation excluded traditional machine learning baselines such as Gradient Boosting Decision Trees (GBDTs), leaving its cross-architecture generalizability largely unverified. More recently, Kang et al. [10] advanced this direction by utilizing auto-encoders to project complex tabular features into a continuous latent space prior to distillation, transforming heterogeneous tabular data into a unified, continuous representation space. Although their approach is primarily geared towards general deep learning models, conducting distillation within a latent encoded space makes it difficult to transfer their method to the domain of tabular foundation models.

2.2 Tabular Foundation Models

Recent years have seen the emergence of Tabular Foundation Models (TFMs) as a strong alternative to traditional tree-based methods. Hollmann et al. first introduced TabPFN [8], a Transformer-based model pre-trained on large-scale synthetic datasets generated via structural causal models and Bayesian networks. By leveraging in-context learning (ICL), TabPFN achieves state-of-the-art performance on small-scale tabular datasets with a single forward pass, eliminating the need for parameter fine-tuning. To address the context length limitations of the original model, the authors subsequently proposed TabPFNv2 [9]. This extension incorporates two-dimensional attention mechanisms and randomized attribute tokens, expanding the context window from 1K to 10K and significantly improving its capacity to handle heterogeneous and larger datasets.

Despite the success of the TabPFN lineage, alternating row-column attention mechanisms introduce computational bottlenecks when scaling to massive training sets. To mitigate this, TabICL [19] proposed a two-stage architecture comprising a distribution-aware column-wise embedding module and a row-wise interaction module equipped with rotary positional encoding. This design preserves the benefits of ICL while substantially increasing context capacity and computational efficiency, enabling the processing of hundreds of thousands of samples. Concurrently, other research has focused on optimizing pre-training data quality. Mitra [25] systematically investigated synthetic priors, demonstrating that mixing diverse synthetic distributions can further enhance model generalization. Meanwhile, Real-TabPFN [6] explored the paradigm of continued pre-training on real-world tabular data to bridge the distribution gap between purely synthetic priors and empirical datasets.

Beyond numerical distribution modeling and ICL, a parallel line of TFM research focuses on semantic understanding and cross-table transferability. Traditional tabular models are typically constrained by fixed feature dimensions, making transfer learning across distinct schemas challenging. TransTab [24] addressed this by converting column descriptions and cell contents into generalizable embeddings, enabling knowledge transfer across tables with completely different column structures. Building on the importance of data semantics, TARTE [11] utilizes string representations to capture the contextual relationships between column names and numerical values, transforming tables into knowledge-enhanced vector representations. By incorporating semantic metadata, these approaches relax the constraint of strict feature alignment, facilitating large-scale, cross-domain pre-training on diverse tabular data.

3 Method

3.1 Problem Formulation

Let $\mathcal{D}$ denote a tabular classification dataset with N samples $z_i = (\mathbf{x}_i, y_i)$, where $\mathbf{x}_i \in \mathbb{R}^d$ is a d-dimensional feature vector and $y_i \in \{0, 1, \ldots, C-1\}$ is the corresponding class label. A tabular foundation model f_θ operating under the in-context learning paradigm takes as input a context set $\mathcal{D}_{\text{ctx}}$ with M samples $z_j^c = (\mathbf{x}_j^c, y_j^c)$, together with a query point $\mathbf{x}_q$, and produces a predictive distribution $p(y \mid \mathbf{x}_q, \mathcal{D}_{\text{ctx}})$ in a single forward pass, without any parameter update. The quality of predictions is therefore directly determined by the informativeness and representativeness of the context $\mathcal{D}_{\text{ctx}}$.

Since the context length M is bounded by architectural constraints and longer contexts incur higher computational cost, our goal is to construct a compact distilled context $\mathcal{D}_{\text{dist}}$ with $M \ll N$ entries $\tilde{z}_j = (\tilde{\mathbf{x}}_j, \tilde{y}_j)$, such that f_θ conditioned on $\mathcal{D}_{\text{dist}}$ retains competitive predictive performance on held-out data (Fig. 2).

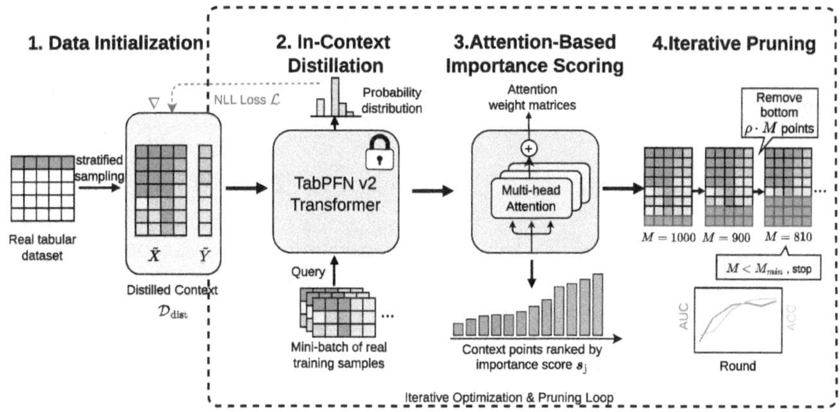

Fig. 2. Overview of the proposed ICD framework with joint label optimization and attention-guided iterative pruning. The distilled context $\mathcal{D}_{\text{dist}} = (\tilde{X}, \tilde{Y})$ is initialized via stratified sampling and jointly optimized through a frozen TabPFNv2 by minimizing NLL on real training batches. After each round, per-point importance scores s_j are derived from intercepted multi-head attention weights, and the bottom $\lfloor \rho \cdot M \rfloor$ least-attended points are pruned. This optimization, scoring, and pruning loop repeats until $M < M_{\text{min}}$.

3.2 In-Context Dataset Distillation with Label Optimization

Following the in-context distillation (ICD) framework of Ma et al. [14], we treat the distilled context as a set of learnable parameters and optimize them directly via gradient descent through the frozen TabPFN forward pass. A critical distinction from the original formulation is that we jointly optimize **both** the synthetic features $\tilde{X}$ and the synthetic labels $\tilde{Y}$, rather than fixing labels to one-hot or integer assignments.

Concretely, we parameterize the distilled dataset as:

$$\tilde{X} \in \mathbb{R}^{M \times d}, \quad \tilde{Y} \in \mathbb{R}^{M}, \tag{1}$$

where both are treated as continuous free parameters. The label parameter $\tilde{Y}$ is passed directly into TabPFNv2's differentiable input interface, which accepts soft continuous label values. This relaxation allows the optimization to discover label assignments that are not necessarily aligned with integer class indices, potentially encoding richer structural information about the decision boundary. In practice, we do not explicitly convert the optimized labels into either hard labels or soft-label vectors; each optimized label remains a float scalar and is fed directly into TabPFNv2's differentiable label encoder.

The distilled dataset is initialized by stratified sampling from the real training data, with each class contributing an equal proportion of the M initial points:

$$M_c = \left\lfloor \frac{M}{C} \right\rfloor, \quad c = 0, \ldots, C-1, \tag{2}$$

with any remainder distributed across the first classes. The initial continuous label values $\tilde{Y}$ are set to the corresponding integer class indices.

The optimization objective is the expected negative log-likelihood (NLL) of real training samples conditioned on the distilled context:

$$\mathcal{L}(\tilde{X}, \tilde{Y}) = \mathbb{E}_{(\mathbf{x},y)\sim\mathcal{D}_{\text{train}}}\left[-\log p_\theta\left(y \mid \mathbf{x},\, \mathcal{D}_{\text{dist}}(\tilde{X}, \tilde{Y})\right)\right], \tag{3}$$

which is approximated via mini-batch sampling at each step. We optimize with Adam:

$$(\tilde{X}, \tilde{Y}) \leftarrow (\tilde{X}, \tilde{Y}) - \eta \cdot \nabla_{(\tilde{X},\tilde{Y})}\mathcal{L}, \tag{4}$$

with gradient clipping applied to stabilize training. For discrete features, we apply a straight-through-style snapping operation during evaluation: discrete columns are rounded to the nearest valid integer within the learned encoder range, while remaining differentiable during the forward pass.

3.3 Attention-Based Importance Scoring

After each round of ICD optimization, we assess the contribution of each distilled context point to the model's predictions by extracting attention weights from the internal transformer layers of TabPFNv2. Since TabPFNv2 does not expose attention weights through its public API, we implement a lightweight monkey-patch on the core `MultiHeadAttention.compute_attention_heads` method to intercept and record the softmax attention matrices during inference, without modifying any model parameters.

Formally, let $\mathbf{A}^{(l)} \in \mathbb{R}^{B\times(M+Q)\times(M+Q)\times H}$ denote the attention tensor captured at layer l, where B is the batch size, Q is the number of query (test) tokens, M is the number of context tokens, and H is the number of attention heads. We extract the cross-attention sub-block from query tokens to context tokens:

$$\mathbf{A}^{(l)}_{\text{ctx}} = \mathbf{A}^{(l)}[:, M:, :M, :] \in \mathbb{R}^{B\times Q\times M\times H}, \tag{5}$$

and aggregate over the batch, query, and head dimensions to obtain a scalar importance score for each context point j:

$$s_j^{(l)} = \frac{1}{BQH}\sum_{b=1}^{B}\sum_{q=1}^{Q}\sum_{h=1}^{H}\left(\mathbf{A}^{(l)}_{\text{ctx}}\right)_{b,q,j,h}. \tag{6}$$

Since the architecture may produce attention tensors with varying sequence structures across layers (e.g., per-feature tokenization or cross-attention blocks), we implement a shape-adaptive parser that handles three canonical cases: (i) standard full self-attention over the concatenated context and query sequence, (ii) per-feature token expansion where the key dimension is an integer multiple of M, and (iii) pure cross-attention where the key sequence length equals M exactly. Scores are accumulated across all valid captured tensors and normalized by their count. The final importance score for context point j is:

Algorithm 1. ICD with Iterative Attention-Based Pruning

Require: Training data $\mathcal{D}_{\text{train}}$, validation data $\mathcal{D}_{\text{val}}$, initial size M_0, steps per round T, pruning ratio ρ, minimum size $M_{\min}$

Initialize $(\tilde{X}, \tilde{Y})$ of size $M \leftarrow M_0$ by stratified sampling from $\mathcal{D}_{\text{train}}$
repeat
    Optimize $(\tilde{X}, \tilde{Y})$ for T steps via Adam on $\mathcal{L}(\tilde{X}, \tilde{Y})$
    Evaluate AUC and ACC on $\mathcal{D}_{\text{val}}$; record metrics and context size M
    if $M < M_{\min}$ **then break**
    end if
    Extract attention scores $\{s_j\}$ via patched forward pass over $\mathcal{D}_{\text{train}}$ batches
    Remove bottom $\lfloor \rho \cdot M \rfloor$ points by score; update $M \leftarrow M - \lfloor \rho \cdot M \rfloor$
until $M < M_{\min}$
return Checkpoint $(\tilde{X}, \tilde{Y})$ that maximizes $\mathcal{S}$ (Eq. 8)

$$s_j = \frac{1}{|\mathcal{L}_{\text{valid}}|} \sum_{l \in \mathcal{L}_{\text{valid}}} s_j^{(l)}, \tag{7}$$

where $\mathcal{L}_{\text{valid}}$ is the set of layers from which valid attention tensors were successfully parsed. To improve robustness, we repeat this procedure over multiple mini-batches of real training data and average the resulting scores.

3.4 Iterative Attention-Guided Pruning

We adopt an iterative pruning strategy that alternates between ICD optimization and attention-based context reduction. The full procedure is summarized in Algorithm 1.

At the end of each round, the distilled context points are ranked by their importance scores $\{s_j\}$. The bottom $\lfloor \rho \cdot M \rfloor$ points—those receiving the least attention from query tokens—are removed, and the remaining points form the context for the next round. This process repeats until the context size falls below a minimum threshold $M_{\min}$, at which point pruning terminates.

This design reflects the intuition that context points consistently ignored by the model's attention mechanism are unlikely to contribute meaningfully to predictions, and can therefore be safely discarded. By progressively compressing the context across rounds rather than pruning aggressively in a single step, we allow the distillation optimization to adapt to each new context size before the next round of pruning, yielding a more stable compression trajectory.

Optimal Checkpoint Selection via Linear Penalty Model. While the iterative pruning algorithm generates a sequence of distilled datasets with decreasing sizes, selecting the optimal checkpoint requires balancing predictive performance against the compression rate. As illustrated in panel (a) of Fig. 3, relying solely on raw performance metrics (AUC and ACC) is challenging; these metrics fluctuate across rounds and eventually experience sharp degradation as the context size becomes too constrained. Selecting an early round would yield high performance but poor compression, whereas selecting a late round would severely compromise the model's predictive capabilities.

To systematically identify the Pareto-optimal sweet spot, we introduce a Linear Penalty Model. We formulate a comprehensive evaluation score $\mathcal{S}_t$ for each pruning round t:

$$\mathcal{S}_t = (\mathrm{AUC}_t + \mathrm{ACC}_t) - \lambda \cdot R_t \tag{8}$$

where $R_t = \frac{M_t}{M_0}$ denotes the data retention rate at round t (M_0 being the initial context size), and λ is a hyperparameter controlling the magnitude of the retention penalty.

This mechanism explicitly penalizes data retention: larger retained datasets incur a higher penalty term ($\lambda \cdot R_t$). By converting the retention rate into a cost subtracted from the sum of AUC and ACC, the scoring function prevents the blind selection of low-compression checkpoints while strictly penalizing severe performance drops. As demonstrated in Fig. 3, this transformation successfully maps the fluctuating raw metrics into a clear, unimodal scoring curve, allowing us to pinpoint the exact round that maximizes cost-effectiveness. The checkpoint corresponding to the highest score $\mathcal{S}$ is then selected as the final distilled dataset.

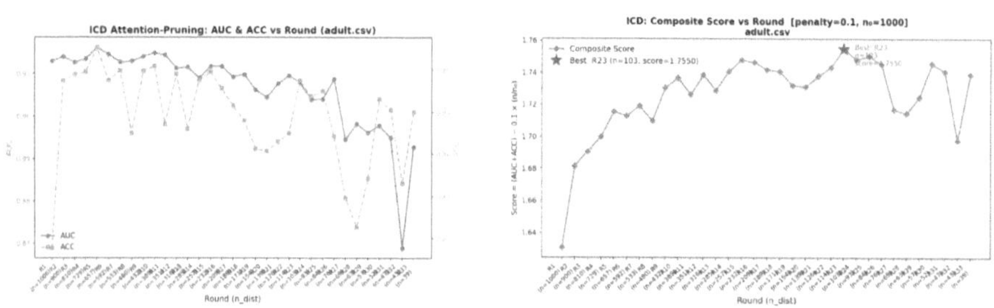

(a) Raw performance metrics

(b) Composite score ($\lambda = 0.1$)

Fig. 3. Transformation of pruning trajectories on the *Adult* dataset: panel (a) shows that raw AUC and ACC metrics fluctuate and eventually degrade as the context size decreases; panel (b) shows that the linear penalty model scalarizes the multi-objective trade-off into a clear unimodal curve and identifies the optimal checkpoint (Round 23).

4 Experiments

4.1 Experimental Setup

Datasets. Our experiments and analyses are based on the TabZilla benchmark [15], which comprises 176 datasets sourced from OpenML [1]. Specifically, following the evaluation protocol of Ma et al. [14], we adopt the same 48 large-scale classification datasets to ensure comparability. The selected datasets span a broad range of scales and structural characteristics. A summary of the dataset statistics is provided in Table 1.

Table 1. Summary statistics of the 48 large-scale OpenML datasets used in our experiments.

	# Instances	# Features	# Classes	Imbalance Ratio
Min	2,000	5	2	1.000
Median	8,998.5	20	2	2.393
Max	130,064	76	10	4,558.600

Baselines. We compare our method against the following baselines:

- **TabPFN-ICD** [14]: The original in-context distillation method of Ma et al., which optimizes only the synthetic feature matrix $\tilde{X}$ while keeping labels fixed to integer class indices, trained on TabPFNv1 with a context size of 1,000. As this method is not publicly available, results are directly cited from the original paper.
- **Random Subset** (M_0): TabPFNv2 with $M_0 = 1{,}000$ randomly sampled real training points as context, without any optimization.
- **Random Subset** ($M_{\mathbf{final}}$): TabPFNv2 with M_{final} randomly sampled real training points, matching the context size of the final pruned distilled set, serving as a size-controlled baseline.
- **ICD-v2** (M_0): In-context distillation on TabPFNv2 following the optimization scheme of Ma et al., where only $\tilde{X}$ is optimized and labels are fixed, with an initial context size of $M_0 = 1{,}000$.
- **ICD-v2** ($M_{\mathbf{final}}$): The same fixed-label distillation as above, but evaluated at the pruned context size M_{final}, enabling a direct comparison against our joint label optimization under identical context budgets.

Implementation Details. All experiments are implemented in Python using PyTorch [18] and the official `tabpfn` library. The distilled context $(\tilde{X}, \tilde{Y})$ is initialized by stratified sampling from the training set, with the initial context size set to $M_0 = 1{,}000$. Both the feature matrix $\tilde{X}$ and the continuous label vector $\tilde{Y}$ are treated as jointly optimizable parameters and updated via the Adam optimizer [12] with a learning rate of $\eta = 0.01$ and gradient clipping at norm 1.0.

In the first round, we run 500 optimization steps to allow sufficient warm-up; subsequent rounds each run 300 steps. Mini-batches of size 128 are drawn from the real training data at each step to approximate the NLL objective. Validation metrics (AUC and ACC) are evaluated every 10 steps, and the checkpoint with the highest validation AUC within each round is retained as the round's output.

For attention score extraction, we sample 8 mini-batches of 128 real training points per round, accumulating and averaging the importance scores across batches and valid attention layers. The pruning ratio is fixed at $\rho = 0.10$ per round (i.e., the bottom 10% of context points by attention score are removed), and pruning terminates when the context size falls below $M_{\text{min}} = 150$. The

TabPFNv2 ensemble size is set to $n_{\text{estimators}} = 4$ throughout. We did not perform an exhaustive search for the optimal retention penalty: larger λ values caused overly aggressive pruning and rapid collapse, whereas smaller values substantially increased runtime and resource cost. We therefore use the stable setting $\lambda = 0.10$ for all reported runs.

All experiments are conducted on a single workstation running Windows 10, equipped with an NVIDIA GeForce RTX 5090 GPU, and using `torch.float32` precision to ensure numerical stability.

4.2 Main Results

Table 2 reports AUC and ACC on the 48 large-scale OpenML datasets, comparing our method against all baselines at the context size selected by the linear penalty model (Sect. 3.4). We make the following observations.

ICD Outperforms Random Selection at Equal Context Size. Across datasets, our distilled context at the optimal round r^* consistently surpasses the *Random Subset* (M_{final}) baseline that uses the same number of context points M_{r^*}. This confirms that the information content of distilled points is superior to that of randomly drawn real samples of equal cardinality: optimization explicitly concentrates predictive signal into a compact set, whereas random selection inevitably retains redundant or noisy points.

Competitive Performance Against Full-Context TabPFNv2. At the optimal context size M_{r^*}, our distilled context approaches the performance of *Full Data* ($\leq$*1000*), demonstrating that aggressive context compression does not necessarily incur a substantial accuracy penalty when the retained points are carefully selected.

Table 2. Performance comparison on 48 large-scale OpenML datasets. Results are averaged over all datasets; best per column in **bold**. M_0 = 1,000; M_{r^*} denotes the context size at the efficiency-optimal round.

Method	Model	Context Size	AUC	ACC
Random Subset (M_0)	TabPFNv2	M_0	89.53	84.76
Random Subset (M_{final})	TabPFNv2	M_{r^*}	88.75	84.03
ICD-v2 (M_0)	TabPFNv2	M_0	<u>90.34</u>	<u>85.12</u>
ICD-v2 (M_{final})	TabPFNv2	M_{r^*}	90.07	84.93
XGBoost (Tuned)[‡]	XGBoost	Full Data	92.82	88.75
ICD[†] (Ma et al., 2024)	TabPFNv1	1000	91.42	86.81
ICD-v2-attention (ours)	TabPFNv2	M_{r^*}	**91.93**	**86.93**

[†] Results cited from the original paper; trained on TabPFNv1.
[‡] Reference upper bound; uses full training data without context constraints.

4.3 Ablation Study: Effect of Joint Label Optimization

To isolate the contribution of jointly optimizing the label vector $\tilde{Y}$, we compare two variants of our pipeline:

- **Fixed** $\tilde{Y}$: labels are fixed to integer class indices throughout optimization, i.e., only $\tilde{X}$ is updated (following the spirit of Ma et al. [14]).
- **Joint** $\tilde{Y}$ (ours): both $\tilde{X}$ and $\tilde{Y}$ are treated as continuous free parameters and optimized simultaneously.

Results are summarized in Table 3. Joint label optimization yields consistent improvements in AUC and ACC across datasets, with larger gains observed on multi-class problems. We hypothesize that relaxing the label constraint enables the distilled dataset to implicitly encode soft class membership or inter-class proximity, effectively acting as a form of label smoothing that improves the calibration of the model's predictive distribution.

Table 3. Ablation on label optimization. Average AUC and ACC over all 48 datasets at the optimal round r^*.

Variant	AUC	ACC
ICD, fixed $\tilde{Y}$	90.34	85.12
ICD, joint $\tilde{Y}$ (ours)	**91.72**	**86.65**
Δ (joint − fixed)	+1.38	+2.53

4.4 Compression Analysis

Figure 4 shows the number of distilled samples retained at the efficiency-optimal round r^* for each of the 48 datasets. Starting from an initial context size of $M_0 = 1{,}000$, the iterative attention-guided pruning reduces the context to an average of 156.9 samples across all datasets, corresponding to a mean retention rate of **15.7%** (i.e., an average compression of 6.4×). The final context size varies considerably across datasets, ranging from 84 to 285 samples, reflecting differences in dataset complexity and the degree of redundancy present in the initial distilled context. Datasets with higher class counts or more complex decision boundaries tend to retain larger contexts, consistent with the intuition that more intricate classification tasks require a richer set of representative support points. Despite this aggressive compression, our method maintains competitive predictive performance, as reported in Sect. 4.2.

4.5 Discussion

Why Does Distillation Help Over Random Selection? Under the in-context learning paradigm, the model's predictive distribution is entirely conditioned on the

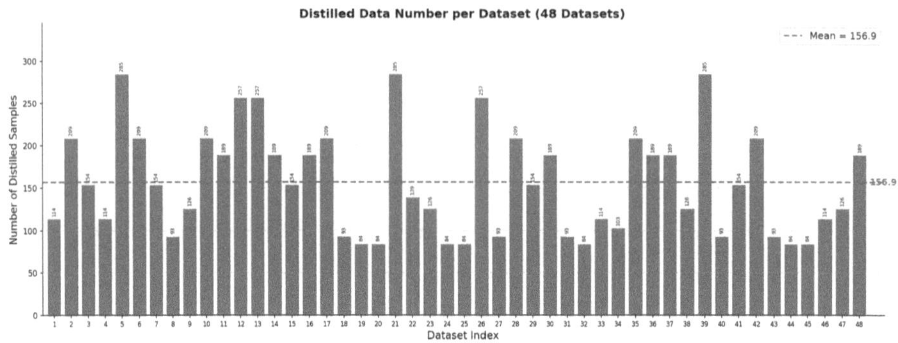

Fig. 4. Number of distilled samples retained at the efficiency-optimal round r^* for each of the 48 OpenML datasets, after iterative attention-guided pruning from an initial context size of $M_0 = 1{,}000$. The dashed red line marks the mean across all datasets (156.9), corresponding to a mean retention rate of 15.7%. (Color figure online)

Table 4. Performance degradation under aggressive compression. Average AUC and ACC over 48 datasets, comparing continuous pruning to $M = 52$ against ICD-v2 trained from scratch.

Method	Context Size	AUC	ACC
ICD-v2 (trained from scratch)	52	87.92	83.28
Ours (continuously pruned to 52)	52	83.05	80.32
Δ (scratch − pruned)	—	+4.87	+2.96

provided context. Random selection preserves the marginal distribution of each feature but makes no guarantee about the representativeness of decision boundaries. Gradient-based distillation, by contrast, directly optimizes for predictive accuracy on held-out data, allowing the synthetic context to concentrate on boundary-critical regions of the feature space. The additional optimization of $\tilde{Y}$ further enables label geometry to be adjusted, which is particularly beneficial when the initial class boundaries are complex or overlapping.

Limitations. Our method inherits the computational overhead of back-propagating through the frozen TabPFN forward pass, which limits scalability to very large numbers of optimization steps or very large initial context sizes. Furthermore, the attention-score extraction relies on a monkey-patch of TabPFNv2's internal attention module; future public APIs exposing attention weights would simplify this procedure. Finally, our efficiency score involves two hyperparameters (α and λ) whose optimal values may be dataset-dependent; a more principled selection criterion is left for future work.

Degradation Under Aggressive Compression. When iterative pruning is continued beyond the efficiency-optimal round to extremely small context sizes, the performance of our method degrades substantially and falls below that of a fresh distillation trained from scratch on the same number of synthetic points. As shown in Table 4, pruning all 48 datasets continuously at a rate of 10% per round until the context is reduced to $M = 52$ yields average AUC and ACC considerably lower than those achieved by ICD-v2 trained from scratch at the same context size. We attribute this phenomenon to the emergence of *co-dependent representations* among the synthetic context points during the distillation process: under joint optimization, the features and labels of individual points progressively develop a mutually reinforcing encoding that functions as a coupled whole. Forcibly removing a subset of these points at a late stage disrupts this internal balance, leaving the remaining samples unable to adequately cover the decision boundaries and causing a sharp performance collapse. This observation indicates that there exists an effective lower bound on compression for our method, and that pursuing extreme compression ratios beyond this bound is counterproductive. The efficiency score $\mathcal{S}_r$ is designed precisely to identify and terminate pruning at this boundary before degradation sets in.

5 Conclusion

In this work, we extended the in-context dataset distillation framework to TabPFNv2 with two key contributions: joint optimization of both synthetic features and labels, and an attention-guided iterative pruning strategy to probe the compressibility limits of distilled contexts. Our experiments on 48 large-scale OpenML datasets demonstrate that the proposed method achieves an average compression ratio of 15.7% while preserving competitive predictive accuracy. At equivalent context budgets, our approach consistently outperforms both random subset selection and the fixed-label distillation baseline, with joint label optimization contributing an average gain of +1.38 AUC and +2.53 ACC over the fixed-label variant. We further identify a practical lower bound on compressibility: aggressive pruning beyond the efficiency-optimal checkpoint destabilizes co-dependent distilled representations and undermines performance. These findings establish a principled framework for optimization-based context compression in tabular foundation models and highlight promising directions for more robust extreme-budget distillation strategies.

Acknowledgements. This work was supported by the Climbing Program (E6Z00311G3).

Disclosure of Interests. The authors have no competing interests to declare.

References

1. Bischl, B., et al.: OpenML benchmarking suites. In: Proceedings of the NeurIPS 2021 Datasets and Benchmarks Track (2021)
2. Buczak, A.L., Guven, E.: A survey of data mining and machine learning methods for cyber security intrusion detection. IEEE Commun. Surv. Tut. **18**(2), 1153–1176 (2016). https://doi.org/10.1109/COMST.2015.2494502

3. Chen, Y., Huang, W., Weng, T.W.: Provable and efficient dataset distillation for kernel ridge regression. In: Proceedings of the 38th International Conference on Neural Information Processing Systems, NIPS '24. Curran Associates Inc, Red Hook, NY, USA (2024)
4. Clements, J.M., Xu, D., Yousefi, N., Efimov, D.: Sequential deep learning for credit risk monitoring with tabular financial data. arXiv arXiv:abs/2012.15330 (2020). https://api.semanticscholar.org/CorpusID:229924306
5. Du, J., Jiang, Y., Tan, V.Y.F., Zhou, J.T., Li, H.: Minimizing the accumulated trajectory error to improve dataset distillation. In: 2023 IEEE/CVF Conference on Computer Vision and Pattern Recognition (CVPR), pp. 3749–3758 (2022). https://api.semanticscholar.org/CorpusID:253734779
6. Garg, A., Ali, M., Hollmann, N., Purucker, L., Müller, S., Hutter, F.: Real-tabPFN: improving tabular foundation models via continued pre-training with real-world data. In: 1st ICML Workshop on Foundation Models for Structured Data (2025). https://openreview.net/forum?id=BtEiqKsIMw
7. Guo, Z., Wang, K., Cazenavette, G., Li, H., Zhang, K., You, Y.: Towards lossless dataset distillation via difficulty-aligned trajectory matching. In: The Twelfth International Conference on Learning Representations (2024)
8. Hollmann, N., Müller, S., Eggensperger, K., Hutter, F.: TabPFN: a transformer that solves small tabular classification problems in a second. In: The Eleventh International Conference on Learning Representations (2023). https://openreview.net/forum?id=cp5PvcI6w8_
9. Hollmann, N., Müller, S., Purucker, L., Krishnakumar, A., Körfer, M., Hoo, S.B., Schirrmeister, R.T., Hutter, F.: Accurate predictions on small data with a tabular foundation model. Nature (2025). https://doi.org/10.1038/s41586-024-08328-6, https://www.nature.com/articles/s41586-024-08328-6
10. Kang, I., Ram, P., Zhou, Y., Samulowitz, H., Seneviratne, O.: Effective data distillation for tabular datasets (student abstract). Proceedings of the AAAI Conference on Artificial Intelligence **38**(21), 23533–23534 (2024)
11. Kim, M.J., Lefebvre, F., Brison, G., Perez-Lebel, A., Varoquaux, G.: Table foundation models: on knowledge pre-training for tabular learning. arXiv arXiv:2505.14415 (2025). https://api.semanticscholar.org/CorpusID:278768904
12. Kingma, D.P., Ba, J.: Adam: a method for stochastic optimization. CoRR abs/1412.6980 (2014). https://api.semanticscholar.org/CorpusID:6628106
13. Lee, S., Chun, S., Jung, S., Yun, S., Yoon, S.: Dataset condensation with contrastive signals. In: Proceedings of the International Conference on Machine Learning (ICML), pp. 12352–12364 (2022)
14. Ma, J., Thomas, V., Yu, G., Caterini, A.L.: In-context data distillation with tabPFN. In: ICLR 2024 Workshop on Mathematical and Empirical Understanding of Foundation Models (2024). https://openreview.net/forum?id=EkEFVhe5Gj
15. McElfresh, D., et al.: When do neural nets outperform boosted trees on tabular data? In: Oh, A., Naumann, T., Globerson, A., Saenko, K., Hardt, M., Levine, S. (eds.) Advances in Neural Information Processing Systems, vol. 36, pp. 76336–76369. Curran Associates, Inc. (2023)
16. Medvedev, D., D'yakonov, A.: New properties of the data distillation method when working with tabular data. In: Analysis of Images, Social Networks and Texts, pp. 379–390 (2021)
17. Nguyen, T., Chen, Z., Lee, J.: Dataset meta-learning from kernel ridge-regression. In: International Conference on Learning Representations (2021). https://openreview.net/forum?id=l-PrrQrK0QR

18. Paszke, A., et al.: PyTorch: an imperative style, high-performance deep learning library. In: Wallach, H., Larochelle, H., Beygelzimer, A., d' Alché-Buc, F., Fox, E., Garnett, R. (eds.) Advances in Neural Information Processing Systems, vol. 32. Curran Associates, Inc. (2019). https://proceedings.neurips.cc/paper_files/paper/2019/file/bdbca288fee7f92f2bfa9f7012727740-Paper.pdf
19. Qu, J., Holzmüller, D., Varoquaux, G., Le Morvan, M.: TabICL: a tabular foundation model for in-context learning on large data. In: International Conference on Machine Learning (2025)
20. Sajedi, A., Khaki, S., Amjadian, E., Liu, L.Z., Lawryshyn, Y.A., Plataniotis, K.N.: DataDAM: efficient dataset distillation with attention matching. In: 2023 IEEE/CVF International Conference on Computer Vision (ICCV), pp. 17051–17061 (2023). https://doi.org/10.1109/ICCV51070.2023.01568
21. Somani, S., et al.: Deep learning and the electrocardiogram: review of the current state-of-the-art. EP Europace **23**(8), 1179–1191 (2021). https://doi.org/10.1093/europace/euaa377
22. Wang, K., et al.: CAFE: learning to condense dataset by aligning features. In: 2022 IEEE/CVF Conference on Computer Vision and Pattern Recognition (CVPR), pp. 12186–12195 (2022). https://api.semanticscholar.org/CorpusID:263797022
23. Wang, T., Zhu, J.Y., Torralba, A., Efros, A.A.: Dataset distillation (2020). https://arxiv.org/abs/1811.10959
24. Wang, Z., Sun, J.: TransTab: learning transferable tabular transformers across tables. In: Advances in Neural Information Processing Systems (NeurIPS), vol. 35, pp. 2902–2915 (2022)
25. Zhang, X., et al.: Mitra: mixed synthetic priors for enhancing tabular foundation models. In: The Thirty-ninth Annual Conference on Neural Information Processing Systems (2026). https://openreview.net/forum?id=t8YRsWY6HM
26. Zhao, B., Bilen, H.: Dataset condensation with distribution matching. In: Proceedings of the IEEE/CVF Winter Conference on Applications of Computer Vision (WACV), pp. 6514–6523 (2023)
27. Zhao, B., Mopuri, K.R., Bilen, H.: Dataset condensation with gradient matching. In: International Conference on Learning Representations (2021). https://openreview.net/forum?id=mSAKhLYLSsl
28. Zhao, G., Li, G., Qin, Y., Yu, Y.: Improved distribution matching for dataset condensation. In: 2023 IEEE/CVF Conference on Computer Vision and Pattern Recognition (CVPR), pp. 7856–7865 (2023). https://api.semanticscholar.org/CorpusID:259982439
29. Zhou, Y., Nezhadarya, E., Ba, J.: Dataset distillation using neural feature regression. In: Koyejo, S., Mohamed, S., Agarwal, A., Belgrave, D., Cho, K., Oh, A. (eds.) Advances in Neural Information Processing Systems, vol. 35, pp. 9813–9827. Curran Associates, Inc. (2022). https://proceedings.neurips.cc/paper_files/paper/2022/file/3fe2a777282299ecb4f9e7ebb531f0ab-Paper-Conference.pdf

Learning with Hard Constraints: A Hierarchical Optimization Framework for Entity-Relation Extraction

Xiaojun Sheng[1,2], Shilong Wei[1,2], Wenhao Jiang[1], and Minmin Li[1,3](✉)

[1] Guangdong Laboratory of Artificial Intelligence and Digital Economy (SZ), Shenzhen 518123, China
{shengxiaojun,weishilong,jiangwenhao,liminmin}@gml.ac.cn
[2] Shenzhen University, Shenzhen 518060, China
[3] State Key Laboratory of Resources and Environmental Information System, Institute of Geographic Sciences and Natural Resources Research, Chinese Academy of Sciences, Beijing, China

Abstract. Multi-task learning for entity-relation extraction suffers from implicit task interference and the lack of explicit structural prioritization. We reformulate this problem as constrained optimization and propose Hyperbolic Barrier-based Adaptive Hierarchical Optimization (HB-AHO), a framework that enforces entity recognition as a dynamic hard constraint via a novel hyperbolic barrier. This barrier ensures numerically stable gradient propagation and approximates a Lagrange multiplier, guiding optimization toward KKT points of the hierarchical task objective. A curriculum-based scheduler adaptively tightens the constraint, ensuring relation learning only proceeds upon sufficient entity maturity. HB-AHO achieves up to 6.4% absolute gains in triplet F1 across five benchmarks and generalizes to structurally divergent domains such as recommender systems. Our work demonstrates that explicitly modeling task hierarchies via principled constraints is a critical paradigm for stable and effective multi-task learning.

Keywords: Multi-Task Learning · Constrained Optimization · Hierarchical Optimization · Entity-Relation Extraction

1 Introduction

Entity–relation extraction (ERE) aims to identify structured triples (subject, relation, object) from unstructured text, serving as a foundation for structured knowledge acquisition [35]. The task is inherently multi-faceted, requiring the joint modeling of entity recognition and relation classification. Recent advances in unified ERE models [30] have achieved notable progress via end-to-end architectures. However, a critical asymmetry remains under-addressed: *relation classification is only meaningful when entity boundaries are correctly identified.* Without reliable entity boundaries, relation classification becomes ill-defined—akin

M. Ceci et al. (Eds.): ECML PKDD 2026, LNAI 16941, pp. 302–317, 2027.
https://doi.org/10.1007/978-3-032-37654-1_18

to inferring a friendship without knowing who the individuals are. This asymmetry gives rise to two central challenges. First, current models lack *structural prioritization*: they treat entity recognition and relation classification as peers, despite their hierarchical dependence. Second, shared optimization often results in *training rigidity*: relation losses, which typically converge faster, may prematurely dominate training and suppress entity learning, ultimately degrading triplet extraction.

To address these issues, we propose a new optimization paradigm that encodes the dependency structure directly into the objective, rather than heuristically balancing tasks. We introduce **H**yperbolic **B**arrier-based **A**daptive **H**ierarchical **O**ptimization (**HB-AHO**), a principled framework that enforces task priorities through differentiable constraints. HB-AHO treats entity recognition as a dynamic hard constraint and adaptively reweights relation optimization using a smooth hyperbolic barrier function together with a curriculum-guided thresholding strategy. This constraint-driven mechanism ensures that learning progresses in alignment with the task hierarchy, yielding both empirical and theoretical benefits.

In summary, our contributions are as follows:

- We propose HB-AHO, a general constrained optimization framework for multi-task learning that explicitly encodes task hierarchies via dynamic hard constraints. To enable smooth and stable optimization, we design a numerically stable hyperbolic barrier function and a curriculum-guided scheduling strategy. We further provide theoretical analysis demonstrating monotonicity, Lipschitz continuity, and feasibility preservation.
- The advantages of HB-AHO are validated on five diverse ERE benchmarks, achieving up to 6.4% absolute gains in triplet F1 over strong baselines. Beyond ERE, HB-AHO is also demonstrated to generalize effectively to structurally distinct domains such as multi-task recommendation, underscoring its broad applicability.

2 Related Work

2.1 Multi-task Learning Perspectives on ERE

ERE jointly predicts structured triples by identifying entities and classifying their relations. Existing models typically fall into two categories, namely, parameter-sharing methods and joint-decoding methods. Parameter-sharing methods, such as TDEER [11] and TPLinker [25], employ shared encoders with separate decoders. These approaches reduce redundancy but often suffer from weak cross-task coupling and redundant optimization efforts [7,21]. In contrast, joint-decoding methods, such as OneRel [19] and UNIRE [24], predict complete triples in a single step, enhancing output coherence. However, they often *neglect the asymmetric dependency* between tasks, where relation prediction critically depends on accurate identification of entity boundaries.

Recent advances have sought to enhance task interaction through hypergraph structures [27], bidirectional update mechanisms [17], feature-enhanced modules [23,37], and text-to-graph generation [34]. Document-level reasoning approaches [5] and domain-specific designs for biomedical extraction [12] further demonstrate the importance of robust entity modeling. Nevertheless, these methods still optimize both tasks simultaneously without enforcing a strict learning order.

2.2 Task Coordination and Prioritization in Multi-task Learning

Multi-task learning (MTL) aims to improve generalization on all tasks by jointly optimizing multiple related tasks [1,2]. Traditional MTL frameworks adopt parameter-sharing backbones—such as tower-based or expert-based models—to facilitate cross-task information flow [29]. However, such designs often encounter gradient conflicts and negative transfer, especially when task objectives are unequally scaled or loosely related [16]. To address these challenges, various techniques have been proposed. Dynamic loss weighting methods, such as GradNorm [4] and PCGrad [32], aim to balance learning rates or mitigate gradient interference. Pareto optimization methods, including IMTL-GG [13], MoE-MTL [36], and DRGrad [14], formulate MTL as a multi-objective optimization problem. Task prioritization strategies, such as Lagrangian-based formulations [6] and connection-based methods [10], dynamically adjust the focus among tasks.

Despite these efforts, most approaches *lack explicit architectural enforcement* of task hierarchy. Methods like gradient ranking [15] or distillation-based ranking [22] encode task importance implicitly, without explicitly specifying when or to what extent subordinate tasks should be subordinated to foundational ones. In contrast, our method introduces a principled constrained optimization framework with differentiable hard constraints. By embedding task hierarchy as an inherent part of the optimization architecture—rather than as an auxiliary tuning strategy—we ensure that the learning process faithfully adheres to the structural dependencies among tasks.

3 Hyperbolic Barrier-Based Adaptive Hierarchical Optimization

The conventional MTL paradigm minimizes a composite objective, typically via a weighted sum $\mathcal{L}_{\text{total}} = \mathcal{L}_{\text{ent}} + \mathcal{L}_{\text{rel}}$. This formulation implicitly treats all tasks as symmetric and independent, ignoring the inherent directed dependencies between them. In ERE, however, relation extraction is conditionally dependent on entity recognition: the relation label is only well-defined when the entity spans are correctly identified. From a probabilistic perspective, this corresponds to a factorization $P(\text{relation}, \text{entity}) = P(\text{entity})P(\text{relation}|\text{entity})$, which suggests a hierarchical optimization structure rather than a symmetric one.

Moreover, naive gradient summation suffers from gradient interference and imbalance: the relation loss often converges faster and its gradients can dominate the update, suppressing the learning of entity representations that are still immature. This leads to suboptimal triple-level performance. To address this, we reframe ERE as a constrained optimization problem that explicitly enforces the entity task to be sufficiently learned before relation learning can fully participate (Fig. 1).

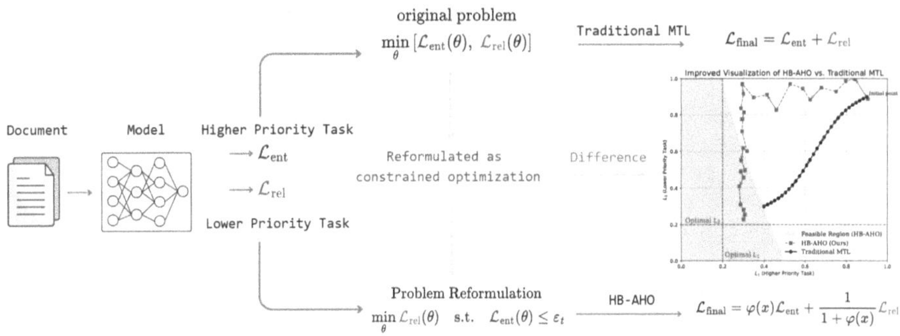

Fig. 1. Conceptual overview of HB-AHO. Traditional MTL (top right) treats entity and relation losses symmetrically, leading to flat optimization $L = L_{\text{ent}} + L_{\text{rel}}$. HB-AHO reformulates the problem as constrained optimization, enforcing an entity-first regime: relation updates are gated until entity loss satisfies a dynamic threshold. The barrier-weighted loss $\varphi(x)$ ensures smooth prioritization, yielding feasible trajectories in loss space that differ fundamentally from flat MTL.

3.1 Constrained Optimization with Task Hierarchy

We formalize the entity-first requirement as an inequality constraint on the entity loss:

$$\min_\theta \mathcal{L}_{\text{rel}}(\theta) \quad \text{s.t.} \quad \mathcal{L}_{\text{ent}}(\theta) \leq \varepsilon_t, \tag{1}$$

where ε_t is a time-dependent threshold. This constrained formulation captures the desideratum that relation optimization should only be allowed to proceed when the entity loss is below a certain tolerance. In the language of Lagrangian duality, we can introduce a multiplier $\lambda \geq 0$ and consider the Lagrangian $\mathcal{L}_{\text{rel}} + \lambda(\mathcal{L}_{\text{ent}} - \varepsilon_t)$. However, directly solving this with stochastic gradient methods is nontrivial due to the need to update λ online and the non-differentiability of the constraint.

We therefore adopt a barrier method from interior-point optimization, which replaces the inequality constraint with a smooth penalty that becomes active near the boundary. Unlike classical logarithmic or inverse barriers, which can cause gradient explosion as $\mathcal{L}_{\text{ent}} \to \varepsilon_t^-$, we propose a hyperbolic tangent barrier:

$$\varphi(x) = \tanh(3x + 1), \quad x = \mathcal{L}_{\text{ent}} - \varepsilon_t. \tag{2}$$

This function is monotonic, Lipschitz continuous (with constant ≤ 3), and bounded between $(-1, 1)$. It smoothly interpolates between a nearly constant value when the constraint is violated ($x \to 0^+$ yields $\varphi \to \tanh(1) \approx 0.76$) and a small value when the constraint is satisfied ($x \to -\infty$ gives $\varphi \to -1$). More importantly, its derivative is bounded, ensuring stable gradient flow even near the constraint boundary—a crucial property for end-to-end training.

3.2 Barrier-Based Relaxation and Unified Loss

Incorporating the barrier function into the objective yields a differentiable, self-paced loss:

$$\mathcal{L}_{\text{final}} = \underbrace{\varphi(x)\,\mathcal{L}_{\text{ent}}}_{\text{constraint-enforcing term}} + \underbrace{\frac{1}{1+\varphi(x)}\,\mathcal{L}_{\text{rel}}}_{\text{relation term conditioned on entity}} . \tag{3}$$

This design can be interpreted as a dynamic Lagrangian where the effective multiplier on the constraint is $\varphi(x)$. When the entity constraint is violated ($x > 0$, $\varphi(x) > 0$), the entity term is amplified while the relation term is suppressed (since $1/(1+\varphi) < 1$). Conversely, when the entity loss is well below the threshold ($x \ll 0$, $\varphi(x) \to -1$), the relation term regains full influence ($1/(1 - -1) \to \infty$ theoretically, but we clip to avoid blow-up; in practice, x is bounded by loss values, so φ never reaches -1 exactly). This mechanism ensures that gradient updates always respect the hierarchy: entity learning is prioritized, and relation learning is allowed only when the entity foundation is solid.

From an optimization standpoint, Eq. 3 approximates the solution to the constrained problem by continuously relaxing the constraint via a smooth barrier. Unlike a simple weighted sum with fixed coefficients, our weights are state-dependent and adapt to the current model's performance, which is analogous to a primal-dual method where the dual variable is updated based on constraint violation.

3.3 Adaptive Threshold Scheduling

The threshold ε_t controls the strictness of the entity-first constraint. Setting it too high may allow relation learning before entities are reliable; too low may stall relation learning entirely. We propose an adaptive decay schedule inspired by trust-region methods and curriculum learning:

$$\varepsilon_{t+1} = \varepsilon_t \cdot \gamma^{\mathbb{I}(\mathcal{L}_{\text{ent}} \leq \varepsilon_t)}, \tag{4}$$

where $\gamma = 0.95$ and $\mathbb{I}(\cdot)$ is the indicator function. This update only tightens the constraint when the current entity loss already satisfies it, ensuring that the model is not prematurely forced into a stricter regime. As training progresses, ε_t gradually decreases, guiding the model to refine entity recognition while relation learning is increasingly allowed. This can be viewed as a form of continuation method or homotopy optimization, where we start with an easy problem (loose constraint) and progressively move toward the desired hard constraint.

3.4 Generalization to Multi-task Hierarchies

Our framework naturally extends to deeper task hierarchies. For N tasks with a known topological order $\mathcal{T}_1 \prec \mathcal{T}_2 \prec \cdots \prec \mathcal{T}_N$, we recursively define the gated loss:

$$\mathcal{L}_{\text{final}} = \varphi(\mathcal{L}_1 - \varepsilon_1)\mathcal{L}_1 + \sum_{i=2}^{N} \frac{\mathcal{L}_i}{1 + \varphi(\mathcal{L}_{i-1} - \varepsilon_{i-1})}. \tag{5}$$

Each task's contribution is modulated by the satisfaction of its immediate predecessor's constraint. This is equivalent to imposing a chain of inequality constraints $\mathcal{L}_{i-1} \leq \varepsilon_{i-1}$ for $i = 2, \ldots, N$ and solving via a recursive barrier. The formulation is fully differentiable and scales linearly with N. It provides a principled way to embed conditional dependencies in multi-task learning without resorting to hand-tuned weights.

3.5 Theoretical Analysis

We provide theoretical insights into HB-AHO, establishing its connection to constrained optimization and analyzing its convergence properties.

Properties of the Hyperbolic Barrier. The barrier function $\varphi(x) = \tanh(3x+1)$ with $x = \mathcal{L}_{\text{ent}} - \varepsilon_t$ is designed to be smooth and stable. It is monotonic, Lipschitz continuous with constant 3 (since $\|\varphi'\|_\infty = 3$), and bounded in $(-1, 1)$. These properties prevent gradient explosion—a common issue with classical barriers (e.g., logarithmic barrier diverges as $x \to 0^-$)—and ensure stable backpropagation even near the constraint boundary.

Asymptotic Satisfaction of the Entity Constraint. Let $\mathcal{L}_{\text{ent}}(\theta_t)$ converge to some limit $\mathcal{L}^*_{\text{ent}}$ (under standard SGD assumptions) and ε_t follow the adaptive decay in Eq. 4.

Theorem 1 (Constraint satisfaction). *If* $\liminf_{t\to\infty} \mathcal{L}_{ent}(\theta_t) < \lim_{t\to\infty} \varepsilon_t$, *then* $\mathcal{L}_{ent}(\theta_t) \leq \varepsilon_t$ *holds for all sufficiently large* t*, and* ε_t *converges to a limit* $\varepsilon_\infty \geq \liminf_{t\to\infty} \mathcal{L}_{ent}(\theta_t)$.

This result guarantees that the constraint is eventually satisfied and the threshold does not shrink indefinitely without the entity loss catching up, avoiding pathological suppression of relation learning.

Convergence to KKT Points. We now relate HB-AHO to the original constrained problem (Eq. 1). Consider the Lagrangian $\mathcal{L}(\theta, \lambda) = \mathcal{L}_{\text{rel}} + \lambda(\mathcal{L}_{\text{ent}} - \varepsilon)$ with KKT conditions (stationarity, primal feasibility, complementary slackness, $\lambda \geq 0$). Our barrier loss (Eq. 3) can be seen as a differentiable approximation where the multiplier is replaced by a state-dependent function. At a stationary point θ^* of $\mathcal{L}_{\text{final}}$, we have:

$$\nabla_\theta \mathcal{L}_{\text{final}} = 0 \implies \nabla_\theta \mathcal{L}_{\text{rel}} + \tilde{\lambda} \nabla_\theta \mathcal{L}_{\text{ent}} = 0, \tag{6}$$

with $\tilde{\lambda} = (1+\varphi)\big[\varphi + \varphi'\mathcal{L}_{\text{ent}} - \frac{\varphi'}{(1+\varphi)^2}\mathcal{L}_{\text{rel}}\big]$. This $\tilde{\lambda}$ approximates a Lagrange multiplier: when $\mathcal{L}_{\text{ent}} > \varepsilon$, $\varphi > 0$ and $\varphi' > 0$, giving positive $\tilde{\lambda}$ (penalty); when $\mathcal{L}_{\text{ent}} < \varepsilon$, $\varphi \approx -1$ and the entity gradient weight nearly vanishes, effectively ignoring the inactive constraint.

Theorem 2 (Approximate KKT). *Assume $\mathcal{L}_{ent}$ and $\mathcal{L}_{rel}$ are continuously differentiable and bounded. For any accumulation point θ^* of gradient descent on $\mathcal{L}_{final}$ with sufficiently small step sizes, there exists $\lambda^* \geq 0$ such that:*

$$\nabla_\theta \mathcal{L}_{rel}(\theta^*) + \lambda^* \nabla_\theta \mathcal{L}_{ent}(\theta^*) = 0, \quad \mathcal{L}_{ent}(\theta^*) \leq \varepsilon_\infty, \tag{7}$$

and $\lambda^*(\mathcal{L}_{ent}(\theta^*) - \varepsilon_\infty) = 0$ up to an error that vanishes as φ sharpens (i.e., as the transition becomes steeper).

Thus, HB-AHO approximates a KKT point of the hierarchical constrained problem, offering a principled alternative to heuristic weighting.

4 Experimental Results and Analysis

4.1 Experiment Settings

Experimental Setup. The initial threshold ε in Eq. 2 is set to 0.05. All models are trained for 100 epochs with a batch size of 4. Experiments are conducted on NVIDIA RTX 4090 GPUs. Early stopping is applied based on validation triplet F1 to prevent overfitting; training is terminated if no improvement is observed within 10 consecutive epochs. The compared baseline models include: BADS [37], SPN4RE [20], ERFD-RTE [3], ERGM [8], MFSF [23].

Table 1. Statistics of the five ERE benchmarks used in our experiments, spanning diverse domains (news, wikipedia, biomedicine) and task granularity. NYT and WebNLG are sentence-level datasets, whereas DocRED, CDR, and GDA require document-level reasoning. # indicates instance count per split.

Dataset	Domain	#Train	#Val.	#Test
NYT	News	56k	5k	5k
WebNLG	Wikipedia	35k	1.7k	1.7k
DocRED	Wikipedia	3k	300	700
CDR	Biomedical	500	500	500
GDA	Biomedical	19k	4.7k	4.7k

Datasets. We evaluate HB-AHO on five benchmarks spanning diverse domains, including WebNLG [18], DocRED [31], NYT [18], CDR [9], and GDA [26]. These datasets differ widely in relation types and instance scales, posing unique challenges for multi-task optimization. The dataset statistics are summarized in Table 1. For clarity, we categorize them into sentence-level (NYT, WebNLG) and document-level (DocRED, CDR, GDA) settings, based on whether relation reasoning is confined to a single sentence or spans multiple sentences.

4.2 Experimental Results

Our objective is not to pursue incremental state-of-the-art scores on already saturated datasets, but to examine whether *inserting* HB-AHO as an optimization layer consistently improves learning dynamics across architectures and data regimes. Table 2 summarizes results on five benchmarks, comparing backbones with and without HB-AHO.

On sentence-level datasets (NYT, WebNLG), where existing models are already close to ceiling, the effect of HB-AHO is moderate but systematic: entity and triplet F1 rise across nearly all backbones, while relation F1 exhibits small positive or negative fluctuations. This outcome is consistent with the design of HB-AHO, which enforces entity recognition as a prerequisite before fully engaging relation updates. In practice, this means that relation-only accuracy may occasionally decline, yet the quality of triplets—the end task—benefits from reduced boundary errors. These findings indicate that task hierarchy remains a useful inductive bias even when architectural expressiveness has largely plateaued.

On document-level datasets (DocRED, CDR, GDA), the picture is more striking. Because these tasks require reasoning over multiple sentences, error propagation from entity boundaries is amplified. Here, HB-AHO yields substantially larger improvements: entity F1 increases consistently across all backbones, and these upstream gains propagate into disproportionately higher triplet F1—often by several points. Small swings in relation F1 thus become immaterial compared to the robustness gained at the triplet level. This suggests that HB-AHO does not merely reweight losses, but actively restructures the learning trajectory to supply cleaner entity candidates for downstream relation decisions.

The credibility of these gains rests on two observations. First, improvements occur across diverse architectures (BADS, SPN4RE, ERFD-RTE, ERGM, MFSF), supporting that the effect arises from optimization rather than model-specific heuristics. Second, the empirical signature is coherent: entity F1 shows the largest gains, triplet F1 the next, while relation F1 fluctuates within a narrow band—a pattern precisely predicted by the dependency structure of the task. Taken together, the evidence demonstrates that HB-AHO functions as a general optimization layer encoding the asymmetry of ERE. Even in cases where relation F1 decreases slightly, the overall utility measured by triplet extraction improves, particularly in long-context settings where entity errors are most damaging. These results provide concrete support for the view that hierarchical optimization, rather than flat multi-task fusion, is the more principled bias for structurally dependent problems.

Table 2. Results on five ERE benchmarks (NYT, WebNLG, DocRED, CDR, GDA). For each model, we report relation, entity, and triplet F1 scores **with and without** the proposed HB-AHO optimization. Rather than competing for absolute state-of-the-art, this table highlights that HB-AHO consistently improves the more challenging *entity* and *triplet* metrics across strong baselines, while relation F1 may fluctuate slightly. The results confirm HB-AHO's robustness and its effectiveness in enforcing task hierarchy, especially on document-level datasets (DocRED, CDR, GDA) where improvements in entity recognition translate into larger gains in triplet extraction.

Model	Dataset	Without HB-AHO			With HB-AHO		
		Relation	Entity	Triplet	Relation	Entity	Triplet
BADS	NYT	86.5	73.2	79.3	86.9 (↑0.4%)	78.6 (↑5.4%)	85.7 (↑6.4%)
SPN4RE	NYT	92.5	92.2	92.3	91.7 (↓0.8%)	94.3 (↑2.1%)	94.8 (↑2.1%)
ERFD-RTE	NYT	94.0	91.4	92.7	92.1 (↓1.9%)	94.6 (↑3.2%)	95.1 (↑2.4%)
ERGM	NYT	93.3	91.5	92.4	93.4 (↑0.1%)	93.6 (↑2.1%)	94.1 (↑1.7%)
MFSF	NYT	93.6	91.7	92.6	93.6(↑0.0%)	94.3 (↑2.6%)	94.8 (↑2.2%)
BADS	WebNLG	85.3	83.1	84.2	85.7 (↑0.4%)	86.9 (↑3.8%)	87.6 (↑3.4%)
SPN4RE	WebNLG	93.1	93.6	93.4	92.6 (↓0.5%)	95.0 (↑1.4%)	94.7 (↑1.3%)
ERFD-RTE	WebNLG	91.2	87.4	89.3	90.7 (↓0.5%)	92.5 (↑5.1%)	93.6 (↑4.3%)
ERGM	WebNLG	94.2	91.2	92.7	94.4 (↑0.2%)	93.8 (↑2.6%)	94.8 (↑2.1%)
MFSF	WebNLG	94.9	92.3	93.5	94.8 (↓0.1%)	94.7 (↑2.4%)	95.1 (↑1.6%)
BADS	DocRED	52.1	54.8	46.9	51.8 (↓0.3%)	59.0 (↑4.2%)	51.0 (↑4.1%)
SPN4RE	DocRED	68.3	57.3	50.1	69.5 (↑1.2%)	60.4 (↑3.1%)	54.9 (↑4.8%)
ERFD-RTE	DocRED	66.9	56.4	49.7	66.4 (↓0.5%)	60.1 (↑3.7%)	54.2 (↑4.5%)
ERGM	DocRED	67.1	57.1	50.0	68.0 (↑0.9%)	60.7 (↑3.6%)	55.3 (↑5.3%)
MFSF	DocRED	68.0	57.5	50.5	68.9 (↑0.9%)	61.2 (↑3.7%)	55.8 (↑5.3%)
BADS	CDR	93.5	50.6	46.7	93.2 (↓0.3%)	55.0 (↑4.4%)	51.5 (↑4.8%)
SPN4RE	CDR	96.6	52.9	48.3	96.4 (↓0.2%)	57.8 (↑4.9%)	53.1 (↑4.8%)
ERFD-RTE	CDR	95.7	51.2	47.2	95.9 (↑0.2%)	55.8 (↑4.6%)	52.0 (↑4.8%)
ERGM	CDR	96.1	52.1	47.9	96.2 (↑0.1%)	56.5 (↑4.4%)	52.6 (↑4.7%)
MFSF	CDR	96.3	52.7	48.1	96.5 (↑0.2%)	57.1 (↑4.4%)	52.8 (↑4.7%)
BADS	GDA	98.5	61.5	59.3	98.7 (↑0.2%)	65.9 (↑4.4%)	64.5 (↑5.2%)
SPN4RE	GDA	99.1	62.3	60.3	99.0 (↓0.1%)	67.5 (↑5.2%)	65.7 (↑5.4%)
ERFD-RTE	GDA	98.7	61.2	59.1	98.9 (↑0.2%)	65.7 (↑4.5%)	64.0 (↑4.9%)
ERGM	GDA	99.0	62.0	60.0	99.2 (↑0.2%)	66.8 (↑4.8%)	65.3 (↑5.3%)
MFSF	GDA	99.2	62.7	60.7	99.1 (↓0.1%)	67.4 (↑4.7%)	65.9 (↑5.2%)

Table 3. F1 scores of MTL optimization strategies on DocRED. HB-AHO outperforms gradient/Pareto/Lagrangian baselines in triplet F1, validating the benefit of constraint-based task hierarchy. Bold indicates best results.

Method	Entity F1	Relation F1	Triplet F1
SPN4RE (Baseline)	68.3	57.3	50.1
+PCGrad [32]	68.6 (↑0.3)	58.7 (↑1.4)	52.6 (↑2.5)
+IMTL-GG [13]	68.4 (↑0.1)	58.2 (↑0.9)	52.1 (↑2.0)
+AdaTask [28]	69.7 (↑1.4)	57.6 (↑0.3)	51.9 (↑1.8)
+NMT [6]	69.2 (↑0.9)	58.3 (↑1.0)	53.1 (↑3.0)
+DRGrad [14]	68.1 (↓0.2)	59.1 (↑1.8)	52.8 (↑2.7)
HB-AHO	**69.8 (↑1.5)**	**60.4 (↑3.1)**	**54.9 (↑4.8)**

4.3 Comparisons with MTL Methods

As shown in Table 3, HB-AHO consistently outperforms widely adopted multi-task optimization baselines, including gradient-based (PCGrad), Pareto-front (IMTL-GG), and Lagrangian-based (NMT) methods. Although these approaches mitigate gradient interference through different formulations, they share a structural limitation: all assume tasks coexist symmetrically in a flat optimization space. This assumption conflicts with hierarchical problems such as ERE, where relation classification is ill-defined without reliable entity boundaries. Consequently, strategies that merely rebalance gradients or losses can reduce conflicts but cannot ensure that learning progresses in the correct order. HB-AHO addresses this misalignment by embedding task hierarchy directly into the objective via a barrier-based constraint, thereby enforcing an entity-first regime. Relation updates are naturally deferred until entity recognition reaches sufficient stability, so improvements in triplet F1 arise less from marginal relation modeling and more from preventing noisy entity predictions from propagating downstream. This distinction highlights why HB-AHO surpasses task-agnostic baselines even when their balancing strategies appear effective. More broadly, the results suggest that task prioritization in hierarchical MTL is better understood as a fundamental architectural principle rather than an auxiliary regularizer. By treating hierarchy as a first-class constraint, HB-AHO offers a scalable, optimization-theoretic alternative that provides stronger guarantees for structurally dependent learning scenarios.

4.4 Ablation Studies

The Effects of Dynamic Threshold. To examine sensitivity to initialization, we varied the threshold ε across several orders of magnitude. Figure 2 shows that, regardless of the starting value, HB-AHO always begins by emphasizing entity recognition and then gradually shifts weight to relation learning once the constraint is met; only the timing of this transition changes slightly. Table 4 confirms

Table 4. Effect of initial threshold ε on DocRED F1 scores. HB-AHO remains stable across a wide range of ε, with best performance around 0.05–0.10.

Variant	ε	Violations	Relation	Entity	Triplet
SPN4RE (Baseline)	—	—	68.3	57.3	50.1
	1.00	34	69.0 (↑0.7)	60.2 (↑2.9)	54.1 (↑4.0)
	0.50	30	69.2 (↑0.9)	60.4 (↑3.1)	54.4 (↑4.3)
	0.10	15	**69.5** (↑1.2)	60.4 (↑3.1)	54.3 (↑4.2)
HB-AHO	0.05	7	69.4 (↑1.1)	**60.5** (↑3.2)	**54.5** (↑4.4)
	0.01	1	69.1 (↑0.8)	60.1 (↑2.8)	54.2 (↑4.1)
	0.005	0	68.9 (↑0.6)	60.3 (↑3.0)	54.2 (↑4.1)
	0.001	0	69.0 (↑0.7)	60.2 (↑2.9)	54.1 (↑4.0)

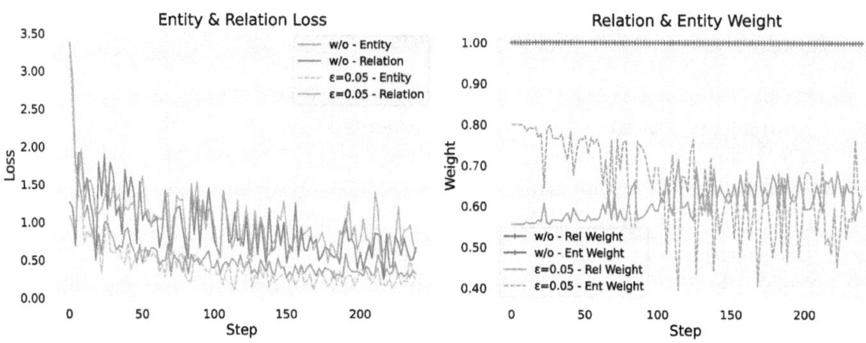

Fig. 2. Training loss and dynamic task weight curves over time. HB-AHO initially prioritizes entity optimization, then gradually shifts focus to relation learning as constraints are satisfied. This behavior confirms our dynamic scheduling design for task prioritization.

that the final triplet F1 remains tightly bounded (54.1–54.5, +4.0% to +4.4% over SPN4RE) across all tested ε. These results demonstrate that the gains of HB-AHO arise from its structural enforcement of hierarchy, not from fragile hyperparameter tuning. Larger thresholds accelerate relation updates, smaller ones delay them, yet both converge to the same balance through the barrier and curriculum mechanism. Constraint violations appear only as transient triggers for threshold decay and do not affect end performance. Taken together, the evidence shows that HB-AHO is robust to ε: the barrier ensures smooth weight adjustment, the curriculum harmonizes different initializations, and practitioners can simply choose any moderate value (e.g., 0.01–0.1) without hyperparameter sweeps. This robustness underscores that the improvement reflects a principled optimization design rather than parameter sensitivity.

Table 5. Ablation study of barrier function choices ($\varepsilon = 0.05$). The hyperbolic barrier provides the most balanced and robust gains in both entity and triplet F1. Red arrows = improvement; green arrows = decline.

Type	Function	Violations	Relation	Entity	Triplet
SPN4RE (Baseline)	—	7	68.3	57.3	50.1
Hyperbolic	$\tanh(3x+1)$	8	**69.7** (↑1.4)	**60.4** (↑3.1)	**54.9** (↑4.8)
Sigmoid	$(1+e^{-x})^{-1}$	6	69.2 (↑0.9)	59.8 (↑2.5)	54.5 (↑4.4)
Gaussian	$1-e^{-x^2}$	6	69.1 (↑0.8)	59.9 (↑2.6)	54.7 (↑4.6)
Softplus	$\log(1+e^{x})$	5	69.0 (↑0.7)	59.5 (↑2.2)	54.3 (↑4.2)
Exponential	$e^{x}-1$	7	68.9 (↑0.6)	58.7 (↑1.4)	53.9 (↑3.8)
Quadratic	x^2	10	68.8 (↑0.5)	56.9 (↓0.4)	50.0 (↓0.1)
Cubic	x^3	12	66.9 (↓1.4)	58.6 (↑1.3)	47.0 (↓3.1)

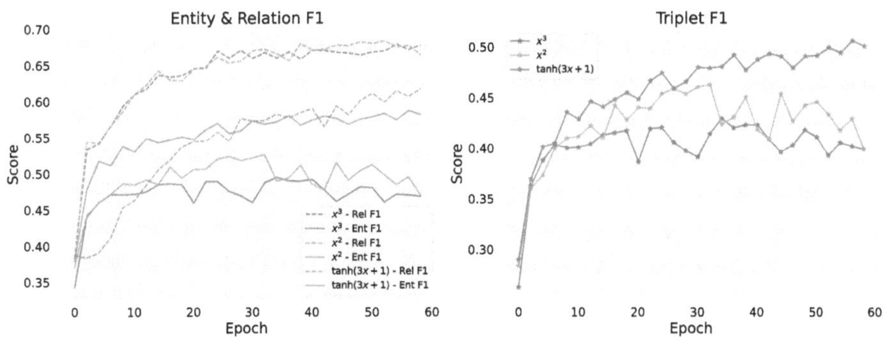

Fig. 3. Training F1 trends for different barrier functions. Hyperbolic barrier enables smooth and effective optimization, while polynomial variants lead to instability, validating the robustness of our proposed design.

Barrier Function Design. To assess whether HB-AHO's advantage stems from the specific barrier formulation, we compared the hyperbolic barrier against classical polynomial and neural-inspired alternatives under identical settings (Table 5). A consistent pattern emerges: only the hyperbolic variant simultaneously improves relation F1 (+1.4), entity F1 (+3.1), and triplet F1 (+4.8), whereas other choices either yield weaker gains or improve one component at the expense of another.

From these results we can distill three principles for effective constraint design in deep learning optimization:

- **Limitations of Polynomial Growth**: Quadratic and cubic barriers amplify small violations into unstable updates, producing severe gradient imbalance near the constraint boundary and ultimately destabilizing hierarchical training.

- **Smoothness Alone Is Insufficient**: Sigmoid and softplus functions are smooth and differentiable, yet their shallow slopes around the boundary provide inadequate responsiveness. As a result, they deliver only moderate improvements (+4.4 to +4.2 in triplet F1), underscoring that stability must be coupled with precise task-weight modulation.
- **Hyperbolic Balance**: The proposed $\varphi(x) = \tanh(3x + 1)$ achieves the strongest and most balanced gains. Its strict monotonicity enforces task order consistently, its globally bounded derivative ($\|\varphi'\| \leq 3$) prevents gradient explosion, and its sigmoidal transition enables a smooth yet decisive shift from entity-dominant to relation-inclusive optimization. This geometric balance translates directly into stable training dynamics (Fig. 3) and maximal triplet-level improvements.

Unlike heuristics that rely on delicate tuning, the hyperbolic barrier improves performance robustly without additional hyperparameters. This ablation not only corroborates our theoretical analysis—linking monotonicity, stability, and boundedness to effective optimization—but also highlights that principled constraint geometry, rather than ad hoc weighting schemes, is indispensable for reliable gains in hierarchical multi-task learning.

4.5 Cross-Domain Generalization: Beyond ERE to Recommendation Systems

Table 6. Results on the KuaiRand1k dataset with eight hierarchically dependent tasks. HB-AHO consistently raises the overall *Avg. AUC* by 2.1–2.6% across diverse backbones, showing that its benefits extend beyond NLP to large-scale recommendation and to settings with more than two tasks.

Model	Task A	Task B	Task C	Task D	Task E	Task F	Task G	Task H	**Avg. AUC**	**MTL Gain**
STEM	98.7	98.8	94.9	90.5	98.8	91.0	91.7	98.2	94.6	–
-HB-AHO	99.1	98.5	95.3	92.6	99.0	92.0	92.4	98.0	96.8	↑**2.2%**
SharedBottom	97.9	99.0	93.6	88.9	98.3	88.8	89.2	92.2	91.8	–
-HB-AHO	98.5	99.1	94.2	90.1	98.6	89.9	90.7	93.1	94.2	↑**2.4%**
MMoE	98.1	98.9	94.1	88.6	98.4	85.6	90.7	94.1	93.9	–
-HB-AHO	98.7	99.0	94.6	90.3	98.7	87.4	91.5	95.2	96.0	↑**2.1%**
PLE	97.3	98.0	94.2	89.9	98.5	88.2	91.0	96.1	92.7	–
-HB-AHO	97.9	98.3	94.8	91.5	98.7	90.5	91.6	97.5	95.3	↑**2.6%**
AITM	98.6	98.2	93.7	89.7	98.1	88.9	90.0	97.7	91.7	–
-HB-AHO	99.0	98.1	94.9	91.0	98.5	90.2	91.2	98.4	94.1	↑**2.4%**
OMoE	97.6	97.9	94.2	87.8	98.4	87.0	90.8	90.9	92.6	–
-HB-AHO	98.2	98.4	94.7	89.4	98.7	89.1	91.2	92.8	94.9	↑**2.3%**

To assess cross-domain generalization beyond ERE, we further evaluate HB-AHO on KuaiRand1k [33], a large-scale recommendation dataset capturing sequential user behaviors. KuaiRand1k defines eight sequential user behaviors that form a decision hierarchy, with task priority assigned from high to low as: click, long-view, like, follow, comment, forward, profile-enter, and hate. This setting differs substantially from ERE—both in modality and in the complexity of task dependencies—yet it offers an equally clear hierarchical structure.

As shown in Table 6, HB-AHO improves the average AUC of all tested backbones (STEM, Shared-Bottom, MMoE, PLE, AITM, and OMoE) by +2.1–2.6%. The strongest gains are observed on downstream, higher-commitment tasks, where accurate modeling of upstream actions provides the most leverage. These improvements are achieved without modifying the architectures themselves, confirming that HB-AHO operates as a plug-and-play optimization layer rather than an architectural tweak.

Overall, the KuaiRand1k results strengthen our central claim: HB-AHO captures structural task dependencies across domains and scales, from sentence-level extraction to multi-behavior recommendation. The fact that consistent 2.1–2.6% gains are realized on business-critical outcomes in a high-capacity industrial dataset underscores its practical impact and supports its view as a domain-agnostic optimization principle rather than a task-specific trick.

5 Conclusion

We introduced HB-AHO, a constraint-driven optimization framework that encodes task hierarchies through hyperbolic barrier functions. By enforcing an entity-first regime, HB-AHO improves both sentence-level and document-level ERE, with gains that are robust across diverse backbones. Beyond empirical performance, our study highlights a broader principle: hierarchical task structuring is not a matter of heuristic loss weighting, but a fundamental optimization geometry that stabilizes multi-task learning. HB-AHO demonstrates how classical constrained optimization can be reinterpreted for deep learning, yielding both theoretical guarantees and practical benefits. Looking forward, the same paradigm offers a natural foundation for domains where tasks form layered dependencies, including hierarchical reasoning, symbolic planning, and multimodal alignment. More generally, we argue that MTL should be viewed not as a static balance among objectives, but as a guided progression across levels of abstraction—a perspective that HB-AHO makes concrete.

Acknowledgments. This work was supported by the National Key R&D Program of China (2023YFC3-804803) and a grant from the State Key Laboratory of Resources and Environmental Information System, Institute of Geographic Sciences and Natural Resources Research, Chinese Academy of Sciences.

References

1. Boyd, S., Vandenberghe, L.: Convex Optimization. Cambridge University Press (2004)

2. Caruana, R.: Multitask learning. Mach. Learn. **28**, 41–75 (1997)
3. Chen, J., Hu, J., Li, T., Teng, F., Du, S.: An effective relation-first detection model for relational triple extraction. Expert Syst. Appl. 238(Part B), 122007 (2024)
4. Chen, Z., Badrinarayanan, V., Lee, C., Rabinovich, A.: Gradnorm: gradient normalization for adaptive loss balancing in deep multitask networks. In: ICML. Proceedings of Machine Learning Research, vol. 80, pp. 793–802. PMLR (2018)
5. Chen, Z.: Construction and mathematical application of document-level relationship extraction model combining R-GCN and text features. IEEE Access **13**, 109593–109606 (2025)
6. Cheng, Z., Huang, Y., Zhang, Z., Ou, D., Liu, Q.: No more tuning: Prioritized multi-task learning with Lagrangian differential multiplier methods. In: AAAI, pp. 11536–11543. AAAI Press (2025)
7. Duan, G., Dong, Y., Miao, J., Huang, T.: Position-aware attention mechanism-based bi-graph for dialogue relation extraction. Cogn. Comput. **15**(1), 359–372 (2023)
8. Gao, C., et al.: ERGM: a multi-stage joint entity and relation extraction with global entity match. Knowl. Based Syst. **271**, 110550 (2023)
9. Li, J., et al.: BioCreative V CDR Task Corpus: a resource for chemical disease relation extraction. Database 2016 (2016)
10. Li, K., Hu, Y., Wang, J., Li, L., Zhang, S., Luo, G.: Task prioritization in multiagent environments: a novel approach using Nash q-learning. IEEE Trans. Consumer Electron. **71**(2), 4206–4220 (2025)
11. Li, X., Luo, X., Dong, C., Yang, D., Luan, B., He, Z.: TDEER: an efficient translating decoding schema for joint extraction of entities and relations. In: EMNLP (1), pp. 8055–8064. Association for Computational Linguistics (2021)
12. Liu, B., Qi, G.: Document-level relation extraction with double graph guidance for long-tailed distributions. Comput. Electr. Eng. **123**, 110237 (2025)
13. Liu, L., et al.: Towards impartial multi-task learning. In: International Conference on Learning Representations (2021)
14. Liu, Y., Miao, Y., Xia, L.: Direct routing gradient (DRGRAD): a personalized information surgery for multi-task learning (MTL) recommendations. In: AAAI, pp. 12238–12245. AAAI Press (2025)
15. Mahapatra, D., Dong, C., Chen, Y., Momma, M.: Multi-label learning to rank through multi-objective optimization. In: Proceedings of the 29th ACM SIGKDD Conference on Knowledge Discovery and Data Mining, pp. 4605–4616 (2023)
16. Navon, A., Mannor, S., Chechik, G.: Multi-task learning as a bargaining game. In: Proceedings of the 39th International Conference on Machine Learning (ICML) (2022)
17. Qian, Y., Ren, E., Xu, H.: Joint entity and relation extraction based on bidirectional update and long-term memory gate mechanism. In: CCL. Lecture Notes in Computer Science, vol. 14761, pp. 174–190. Springer (2024)
18. Riedel, S., Yao, L., McCallum, A.: Modeling relations and their mentions without labeled text. In: Proceedings of ECML PKDD, pp. 148–163 (2010)
19. Shang, Y., Huang, H., Mao, X.: Onerel: joint entity and relation extraction with one module in one step. In: AAAI, pp. 11285–11293. AAAI Press (2022)
20. Sui, D., Zeng, X., Chen, Y., Liu, K., Zhao, J.: Joint entity and relation extraction with set prediction networks. IEEE Trans. Neural Networks Learn. Syst. **35**(9), 12784–12795 (2024)
21. Sun, J., Yan, H., Li, Y., Li, H., Bai, K., Li, Z.: Joint entity-relation extraction model for epidemiological reports based on SMART adversarial training. In: ASCC, pp. 141–146. IEEE (2024)

22. Tang, J., Gao, H., He, L., Katariya, S.: Multi-objective learning to rank by model distillation. In: KDD, pp. 5783–5792. ACM (2024)
23. Wang, T., et al.: Joint entity and relation extraction with fusion of multi-feature semantics. J. Intell. Inf. Syst. **63**(1), 21–42 (2025)
24. Wang, Y., Sun, C., Wu, Y., Zhou, H., Li, L., Yan, J.: Unire: a unified label space for entity relation extraction. In: ACL/IJCNLP (1), pp. 220–231. Association for Computational Linguistics (2021)
25. Wang, Y., Yu, B., Zhang, Y., Liu, T., Zhu, H., Sun, L.: Tplinker: single-stage joint extraction of entities and relations through token pair linking. In: COLING, pp. 1572–1582. International Committee on Computational Linguistics (2020)
26. Wu, Y., Luo, R., Leung, H.C.M., Ting, H.-F., Lam, T.-W.: RENET: a deep learning approach for extracting gene-disease associations from literature. In: Cowen, L.J. (ed.) RECOMB 2019. LNCS, vol. 11467, pp. 272–284. Springer, Cham (2019). https://doi.org/10.1007/978-3-030-17083-7_17
27. Yan, Z., Yang, S., Liu, W., Tu, K.: Joint entity and relation extraction with span pruning and hypergraph neural networks. In: Proceedings of the 2023 Conference on Empirical Methods in Natural Language Processing, pp. 7512–7526 (2023)
28. Yang, E., et al.: Adatask: a task-aware adaptive learning rate approach to multi-task learning. In: AAAI, pp. 10745–10753. AAAI Press (2023)
29. Yang, Y., et al.: MTL-lora: low-rank adaptation for multi-task learning. In: AAAI, pp. 22010–22018. AAAI Press (2025)
30. Yang, Z., Huang, Y., Feng, J.: Learning to leverage high-order medical knowledge graph for joint entity and relation extraction. In: Findings of the Association for Computational Linguistics: ACL 2023, pp. 9023–9035 (2023)
31. Yao, Y., et al.: Docred: a large-scale document-level relation extraction dataset. In: ACL (1), pp. 764–777. Association for Computational Linguistics (2019)
32. Yu, T., Kumar, S., Gupta, A., Levine, S., Hausman, K., Finn, C.: Gradient surgery for multi-task learning. In: NeurIPS (2020)
33. Yuan, G., et al.: Tenrec: a large-scale multipurpose benchmark dataset for recommender systems. In: NeurIPS (2022)
34. Zaratiana, U., Tomeh, N., Holat, P., Charnois, T.: An autoregressive text-to-graph framework for joint entity and relation extraction. In: AAAI, pp. 19477–19487. AAAI Press (2024)
35. Zhang, F., Yan, Y., Cheng, J.: Document-level relation extraction with global relations and entity pair reasoning. In: ACL (Findings), pp. 19556–19567. Association for Computational Linguistics (2025)
36. Zhang, G., et al.: Bagging-expert network for multi-task learning: a depolarization solution in multi-gate mixture-of-experts. In: AAAI, pp. 22389–22397. AAAI Press (2025)
37. Zhou, Y., Huang, L., Guo, T., Hu, S., Han, J.: An attention-based model for joint extraction of entities and relations with implicit entity features. In: WWW (Companion Volume), pp. 729–737. ACM (2019)

On the Use of Bagging for Local Intrinsic Dimensionality Estimation

Kristóf Péter[1(✉)], Ricardo J. G. B. Campello[1], Michael E. Houle[2], and James Bailey[3]

[1] University of Southern Denmark, Odense, Denmark
{krp,campello}@imada.sdu.dk

[2] New Jersey Institute of Technology, Newark, NJ, USA
michael.houle@njit.edu

[3] Monash University, Melbourne, Australia
james.a.bailey@monash.edu

Abstract. The theory of Local Intrinsic Dimensionality (LID) has become a valuable tool for characterizing local complexity within and across data manifolds, supporting a range of data mining and machine learning tasks. Accurate LID estimation requires samples drawn from small neighborhoods around each query to avoid biases from nonlocal effects and potential manifold mixing, yet limited data within such neighborhoods tends to cause high estimation variance. As a variance reduction strategy, we propose an ensemble approach that uses subbagging to preserve the local distribution of nearest neighbor (NN) distances. The main challenge is that the uniform reduction in total sample size within each subsample increases the proximity threshold for finding a fixed number k of NNs around the query. As a result, in the specific context of LID estimation, the sampling rate has an additional, complex interplay with the neighborhood size, where both combined determine the sample size as well as the locality and resolution considered for estimation. We analyze both theoretically and experimentally how the choice of the sampling rate and the k-NN size used for LID estimation, alongside the ensemble size, affects performance, enabling informed prior selection of these hyper-parameters depending on application-based preferences. Our results indicate that within broad and well-characterized regions of the hyper-parameters space, using a bagged estimator will most often significantly reduce variance as well as the mean squared error when compared to the corresponding non-bagged baseline, with controllable impact on bias. We additionally propose and evaluate different ways of combining bagging with neighborhood smoothing for substantial further improvements on LID estimation performance.

Keywords: Local Intrinsic Dimensionality · Bagging · Smoothing

1 Introduction

Local Intrinsic Dimensionality (LID) is part of a broader notion of Intrinsic Dimension (ID), which has been conceptualized in different ways aiming to

M. Ceci et al. (Eds.): ECML PKDD 2026, LNAI 16941, pp. 318–334, 2027.
https://doi.org/10.1007/978-3-032-37654-1_19

characterize the true complexity of a data space beyond its full representation dimension, under the assumption that one or more data submanifolds may exist within that space [13,23,25,28,36,42,43]. One can think of LID as the minimum number of variables or *effective dimensions* required to explain the underlying distribution at a particular location of the data space, or the smallest dimension surface on which a sample from that distribution would locally lie on. It has found a growing number of applications, including outlier detection [7], similarity search [8,16], IoT intrusion detection [22], adversarial example analysis [3,38], self-supervised learning regularization [30], graph embedding design [44], data segmentation [1], and granular deformation analysis [49], just to mention a few.

A wide range of LID estimators has been proposed, among which a major class is based on the extreme value theoretic (EVT) limiting distribution of distances as a neighborhood radius around a query location shrinks to zero—e.g., MLE, MoM, PWM, TLE [4,6]. Other well-known approaches include MADA [20], ESS [32], and originally global ID estimators, such as TWO-NN [19], which can be generalized to locally estimate LID [9]. The above techniques employ k-NN search for sampling around the query location, however, there are model-based alternatives—such as LIDL (using approximate likelihood) [45] and FLIPD (employing diffusion models) [34]—with different ways of quantifying locality.

Despite their differences, most estimators evaluate LID at a query location using only nearby observations to capture local properties of the data space. Using faraway data points risks introducing nonlocal biases, e.g., by mixing nearby manifolds with different dimensionalities, or violating local isotropy on an anisotropic surface—see Fig. 1. In practice, given a finite size dataset, shrinking an arbitrary neighborhood radius can leave too few points inside, which tend to yield high-variance, unstable estimates; enlarging it reduces variance, but also pulls in nonlocal structure that can increase bias. This bias-variance tradeoff is the central practical obstacle in LID estimation, and it can undermine downstream applications that critically rely on accurate, stable estimations of LID. Tackling this challenge through bootstrapping-based statistical machinery, rather than simply trading variance with bias, is the main goal of this paper.

We propose to adapt *bootstrap aggregating* (a.k.a. *bagging* for short) [17] as a method-agnostic, variance-reduction wrapper for LID estimators. While bagging is a commonly used technique, e.g., in the context of decision trees [2] and ensembles more broadly, both shallow [50] and deep [21,48], to the best of our knowledge it has not been applied to LID estimation before. In this specific setting, the standard behavior of bagging is not trivially guaranteed. To align with continuity assumptions on the underlying data density and to preserve the original distribution of distances, subsampling without replacement is required within each *bag* (i.e., ensemble member), thus causing the in-bag sample size to be reduced. Reducing the sample size increases the distance threshold required to retrieve a fixed number k of neighboring points around a query, making it so that a fixed k on a subsample corresponds to a larger effective NN radius, with potential to introduce undesirable nonlocal effects as variance decreases (e.g.,

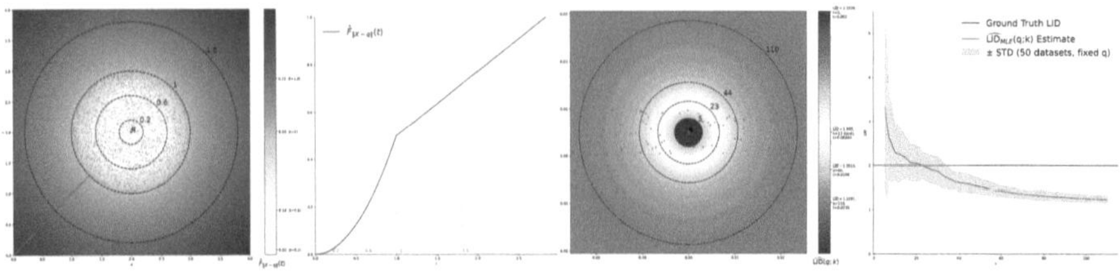

Fig. 1. The leftmost figure shows the *Lollipop* dataset [45] overlaid with the cumulative distribution function (c.d.f) of the induced empirical distance distribution from the query at $(2, 2)$, as a heatmap. The 2nd figure shows that, within close vicinity to the query, t, the c.d.f. is proportional to the square of the distance, becoming linear beyond the bounds of the 2D (circle-plate) submanifold, when the 1D (line) submanifold is reached. The 3rd figure shows a heatmap of LID estimates at the query at $(0.5, 0.005)$ using MLE [5], as a function of the k-NN hyper-parameter, overlaid with the corresponding dataset distributed uniformly on a thin ribbon-like surface. The rightmost figure displays how LID estimates vary with k, not only affected by the interplay between locality preservation and sample size, but also changing with the resolution at which it is measured in practice. Within close vicinity from the query, where neither locality or resolution is critical, the small sample size results in high variance and—for estimators that are only asymptotically unbiased (including MLE)—also in bias.

see Fig. 1). The problem has a close analogue in traditional EVT, where the chosen sample size determines the upper-tail threshold. When estimating the extreme value index using the k largest order statistics, the choice of k trades variance (small k) against bias (large k), and subsample-bootstrap methods show how the MSE-optimal k between subsampled and full-sample estimators can be explicitly rescaled according to the sampling rate [18,39]. This provides critical motivation in the current study for its exploration within the locality restrictions corresponding to a lower-tail threshold for LID estimation.

We provide theoretical and empirical analyses of bagged LID estimation, focusing on how the number of bags B and the sampling rate r, together with the locality threshold (the neighborhood size k in case of NN-based LID estimators) jointly shape bias, variance, and mean-squared error (MSE). We show how the selection of these hyper-parameters can result in dramatic reduction of MSE, typically resulting from significant reduction in variance with limited or no associated compromise in bias. Our results support that this is mainly enabled by the additional degree of freedom provided by the sampling rate controlling the tradeoff between the bag size and the level of independence between bags, which often allows for wider ranges of effective locality thresholds for LID estimation, and within which the bagged estimator can achieve superior performance than the baseline equipped with its own MSE-optimal locality threshold. This provides *application-specific* insights as to why and how bagging can be effectively used to mitigate the bias-variance dilemma in LID estimation.

Additionally, we evaluate neighborhood smoothing [15] as another strong standalone variance-reduction approach and show that it is complementary to bagging: applying smoothing within each bag (pre-smoothing) and/or after aggregation (post-smoothing) yields the most substantial MSE reduction in our experiments. Our **contributions** can be summarized as follows:

- Introducing bagging for LID estimation.
- Theoretical analyses shedding further light onto the effects and interactions of the hyper-parameters governing the behavior of bagging.
- Experimental analyses of the relationship between bagging hyper-parameters as well as their potential interplay with the locality threshold of LID estimators (demonstrated through the k hyper-parameter of NN-based methods).
- Experimental results on benchmark datasets showing that bagging, as well as its combinations with smoothing, not only reduce variance but generally reduce the MSE of LID estimates compared to the baseline, in case of mutually optimal independent selection of hyper-parameters.

2 Related Work

Variance reduction in LID estimation is addressed either by designing lower-variance estimators or by applying estimator-agnostic wrappers to stabilize existing methods. Next, we review approaches within these two categories.

TLE [6] is closely related to EVT-based LID estimators such as MLE [5], but it modifies the classic asymptotic distance-based likelihood function by incorporating non-central distance information to derive an extended statistic. It was shown to substantially reduce variance while maintaining comparable bias to MLE. However, TLE is tied to the EVT formulation and is not readily transferable as a generic wrapper to arbitrary LID estimators.

More general stabilization can be achieved via data pre-processing or by post-processing estimates. In [35], it has been shown that pre-processing by scale space filtering methods can contribute to LID estimation in the context of hyperspectral imaging data. These techniques work by denoising the original dataset, thus reducing variance and, accordingly, resulting in more accurate and stable LID estimates. However, the method is designed under assumptions specifically related to the type of datasets in the intended application of hyperspectral images.

A widely applicable post-processing approach is neighborhood smoothing [47], which is easily translatable to LID estimation. Given per-query LID estimates, regular *smoothing* replaces each by an average over their local neighborhood (e.g., k-NN), which can reduce variance assuming that neighboring points share similar LID. To improve alignment with this assumption, the manifold adaptive neighborhood smoothing technique presented in [15] constructs the k-NN graph of the data points based on Euclidean distance; smoothing is then performed on a neighborhood of points based on their approximated geodesic distance to the query as the shortest paths along the graph, which locally approximates the query's submanifold. Such *geodesic smoothing* technique has been shown to reduce the variability of the non-linear least-squares estimator described in [15].

3 Background

LID can be defined from a purely distributional perspective, beyond the realm of any particular data sample, as a local notion of ID at a given query location.

A theoretical, EVT-based approach to this concept that has gained increasing attention in recent years has been formulated in [27,29]. In this theoretical framework, for a selected query location and distance metric, there exists a *distribution of distances* from the query that is *induced* from an *underlying distribution* of interest defined in the original data space. Under certain assumptions of locality and smoothness, the limiting lower tail of the cumulative distribution function (*c.d.f.*) of such a theoretical distance distribution is fully and uniquely characterized by LID as a quantifiable property at the query.

In this paper, unless stated otherwise, this is the notion of LID that will be implicitly assumed, e.g., in our experiments involving practical LID estimation. Notice, however, that the bagging techniques introduced in this paper are by no means estimator-specific, but rather broadly applicable to virtually any LID estimator regardless of their supporting LID paradigm.

Bagging is a resampling technique introduced by Breiman [10] as a way of harnessing computational power to improve the stability of models and estimators by aggregating results across multiple resampled versions (*bags*) of the original data. It is especially effective for models that are accurate on average but highly variable. Classic examples include bagging for decision trees and random forests [2,11,31], as well as a variety of modern deep learning applications [21,48]. General theoretical results for the variance-reduction effect of bagging, including the subsampling variant adopted in the present paper, can be found in [12].

The term *bagging* is commonly referring to resampling *with replacement*, where each bag can have the same size as the original dataset and may contain duplicate samples. In our setting, however, duplicates would distort the distance distribution and violate its absolutely continuous assumption underlying most LID estimators. We therefore use the *subbagging* (*subsample aggregating*) variant, where sampling within an individual bag happens strictly without replacement and each bag thus contains a strictly smaller sample size than the whole dataset.

For this reason and for the sake of simplicity, in the remainder of this paper and unless explicitly stated otherwise, when referring to *bagging* we will assume the following formal definition of *subbagging*, which coincides with that from [12]:

Definition 1 (Subbagging). *Given n i.i.d. random vectors $D \triangleq (X_1, \ldots, X_n)$ following a distribution over the ambient space that relates to a parameter θ, let the n sample estimator of θ be defined as a statistic $\hat{\theta}_n \triangleq \hat{\theta}(X_1, \ldots, X_n)$. Let $m = rn < n$ be an integer for some sampling rate $r \in (0, 1)$ and create B random* *subsets (a.k.a.* bags*) of size m each,* $D_{i,m} \triangleq (X_{\Pi_1^{(i)}}, \ldots, X_{\Pi_m^{(i)}})$ *for* $i = 1, \ldots, B$, *by subsampling from D using random index sets,* $\Pi^{(i)} \triangleq \{\Pi_1^{(i)}, \ldots, \Pi_m^{(i)}\}$. *Such index sets* $\Pi^{(\cdot)}$ *are i.i.d. (uniformly) over all* $\binom{n}{m}$ *possible choices of m different indices out of n. The bagged estimator is then defined as:*

$$\hat{\theta}_{B,m} \triangleq \frac{1}{B}\sum_{i=1}^{B} \hat{\theta}_{m,i} \quad ; \qquad \textit{where} \quad \hat{\theta}_{m,i} \triangleq \hat{\theta}(X_{\Pi_1^{(i)}}, \ldots, X_{\Pi_m^{(i)}}) \tag{1}$$

4 Bagged LID Estimators

To translate Definition 1 to the specific context of LID estimation, we consider the sample set D to correspond to our full dataset of n observed points in the $\mathbb{R}^{\dim}$ ambient space, whereas the baseline LID estimator at a fixed query point $q \in \mathbb{R}^{\dim}$, $\widehat{LID}(q)$, is considered to satisfy measurability assumptions and corresponds to the statistic $\hat{\theta}$, such that $\widehat{LID}_n(q) \triangleq \widehat{LID}_n(X_1, \ldots, X_n; q) \equiv \hat{\theta}_n(X_1, \ldots, X_n)$ is the n-sample estimator at q. We can thereby construct the bags $D_{1,m}, \ldots, D_{B,m} \subset D$ and the bagged estimator $\widehat{LID}_{B,m}(q)$ according to Definition 1. Figure 2 illustrates bagged LID estimation for a single query.

Notice that most LID estimators are quantifiable at any location of the data space, albeit they are most often used only at query locations that coincide with points of the sample set ($q \in D$). After subsampling, a query point $q \in D$ will likely only be present in some bags, but the bagged estimator will still require its individual estimation within each and every bag, regardless of whether the query is present or not. From an implementation viewpoint, the two different cases have to be taken into consideration when a distance of zero between the query location and a sample point is not allowed, such as for any LID estimator under an absolutely continuous distance distribution assumption. For the family of estimators based on the query's k-NN, one needs to ensure that the nearest neighbor of a point is never the point itself. In practice, this means that, whenever the query point q is contained in the bag, it is not counted as its own neighbor (for estimating its LID within that bag) and, as such, it does not count towards k, thus ensuring the same number of points k is always used for estimation.

Mean Squared Error (MSE) Decomposition is a well-known result [46] that relates the theoretic MSE of an estimator to its bias and variance. It can be used to gain deeper insights into an estimator's error by looking at the two components individually, as $\mathrm{E}[(\hat{\theta}_{B,m} - \theta)^2] = \mathrm{Var}(\hat{\theta}_{B,m}) + (\mathrm{E}[\hat{\theta}_{B,m}] - \theta)^2$. Notice that the overall bagged estimator will have at most as large MSE as the m-sample estimator deployed within each bag, i.e., $\mathrm{E}[(\hat{\theta}_{B,m} - \theta)^2] \leq \mathrm{E}[(\hat{\theta}_{m,i} - \theta)^2]$, which directly follows by recognizing that $\mathrm{Var}(\hat{\theta}_{B,m}) \leq \mathrm{Var}(\hat{\theta}_{m,i})$ and $\mathrm{E}[\hat{\theta}_{B,m}] = \mathrm{E}[\hat{\theta}_{m,i}]$ (for more details see the arXiv version of this study [40]). However, in principle, this result alone does not provide any improvement guarantees for the bagged estimator with respect to the MSE of the n-sample estimator, which infers over the entire sample set D.

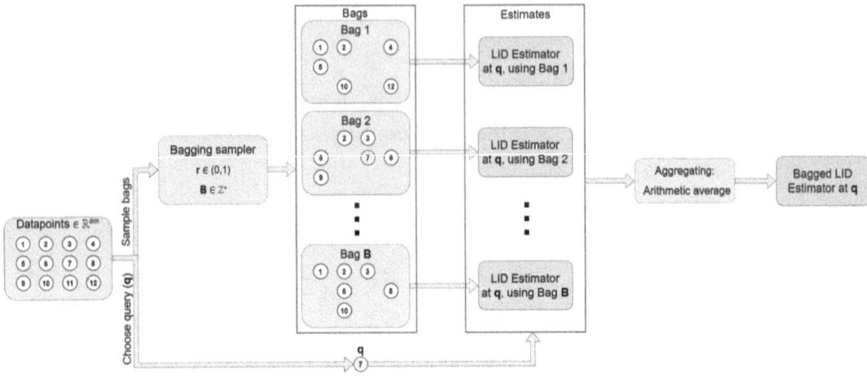

Fig. 2. Flowchart illustrating bagged LID estimation on a hypothetical, toy dataset. The algorithm is displayed for a single query point (with index 7) from the dataset. Note that it suffices to sample the bags only once and reuse them for different queries. The figure makes it clear that LID estimation can be done independently for each query point and for each bag, so processing is highly parallelizable across multiple nodes. For details on estimation across a dataset of queries, see the pseudo code in [40].

When it comes to variance, [41] shows in the context of subbagging for decision trees that as the number of bags (B) tends to infinity, the variance of the bagged estimator decreases towards a known limiting value, which can be expressed as the variance of the expectation of a single-bag estimator conditioned on the data, $\mathrm{Var}(\mathrm{E}(\hat{\theta}_{m,i}|D))$. In [40], we show more broadly (for any estimator following Definition 1) that this lower-limiting variance can also be rewritten as the unconditional covariance between single-bag estimators, $\mathrm{Cov}(\hat{\theta}_{m,i}, \hat{\theta}_{m,j})$.

In Theorem 1, we formally outline how decreasing the sampling rate (r) is expected to cap the aforementioned limiting variance of the bagged estimator. The result is a combination of the well-known Jensen-gap bound [37] and the fact that the extent of the overlap $|\Pi^{(i)} \cap \Pi^{(j)}|$ between random index sets drawn without replacement follows the Hypergeometric Distribution [24,33].

Theorem 1. *Define* $\gamma(h,m) \triangleq \mathrm{Cov}(\hat{\theta}_{m,i}, \hat{\theta}_{m,j} \mid |\Pi^{(i)} \cap \Pi^{(j)}| = h)$ *for the integer domain given by* $m = rn \in \mathbb{Z}^+$ *and* $h = 0, 1, \ldots, m$*, namely, the covariance of two single-bag estimators given that we know the number of dependent variables (provided that such a covariance exists and is finite for any pair of bags). Assume that there exists a twice differentiable, increasing function* $\varphi : [0,1] \rightarrow \mathbb{R}$ *such that* $\forall_{h,m\,:\,h \leq m}\ \gamma(h,m) \leq \varphi(\frac{h}{m})$*, then we have:*

$$\forall_{r \in [0,1]}\ \mathrm{Cov}(\hat{\theta}_{m,i}, \hat{\theta}_{m,j}) \leq \varphi(r) + O\left(\frac{1}{n}\right) \tag{2}$$

Proof. For the proof, see the arXiv version of this study [40].

In simple terms, assuming that the magnitude of the conditional covariances $\gamma(h,m)$ are roughly positively proportional to the fraction of dependent variables between the bags (h/m), Theorem 1 shows that we can set an implicit upper bound on the limiting variance of the bagged estimator, $\lim_{B\to\infty} \mathrm{Var}(\hat{\theta}_{B,m}) = \mathrm{Cov}(\hat{\theta}_{m,i}, \hat{\theta}_{m,j})$, by reducing r and, accordingly, $\varphi(r)$. This result suggests that we can limit variance from above by decreasing the sampling rate (r) and increasing the number of bags (B). However, recall that the resulting decrease in the bag size m can lead to more biased in-bag estimates, most noticeably, due to either fewer samples for LID estimation within a fixed local vicinity around the query or, alternatively, a less local vicinity containing a fixed sample size k (e.g., see Fig. 1). Since the exact nature of this bias-variance tradeoff is dependent on the particular LID estimator and its hyper-parameters (e.g., k), as well as on the dataset in hand, experimental analyses are required to conclusively show the effects of bagging and its hyper-parameters in LID estimation.

Table 1. LID estimators and hyper-parameters. "pre" and "post" specify whether smoothing is applied to the in-bag LID estimates (i.e. prior to aggregation) or to the bagged LID estimates, resp. All other hyper-parameters have been previously defined.

Baseline	Baseline hyper-par.	Bagging hyper-par.	Smoothing strategy
MLE [4]	k	r, B	*pre* or *post*
TLE [6]	k	r, B	*pre* or *post*
MADA [20]	k	r, B	*pre* or *post*

5 Experimental Methodology

Estimators. Alongside the classic MLE estimator as a standard baseline [4], we also include TLE [6] and MADA [20] to test the general applicability of bagging to different estimators without any intent of promoting a particular method. TLE, while substantially more computationally demanding, is designed to reduce variance, allowing us to test whether bagging can further enhance more sophisticated baselines already equipped with internal variance-reduction mechanisms. Table 1 summarizes the tested estimators and their essential hyper-parameters, alongside the two wrapper alternatives to mitigate variance that we experimentally investigate in this paper, namely, bagging and smoothing [15]. The goal is to compare each baseline against their own wrapped counterparts.

Datasets. As common practice in the LID literature, we use test datasets based on a foundational study of LID estimation on manifolds [26] later extended to a comprehensive benchmark framework in [14]. The data manifolds contain $n = 2500$ points with known LID, which we use as ground truth when computing the MSE of estimators for evaluation purposes. We additionally include the *Lollipop* data from [45], and a high-dimensional *Uniform* dataset. More detailed descriptions of each dataset and a summary table are provided in [40].

Evaluation Measures. We measure the performance of LID estimators using the empirical MSE as well as its bias-squared plus variance decomposition, for the reasons discussed in Sect. 4. Notice that in the presence of multiple ground-truth LID values across a dataset with different submanifolds, the MSE decomposition needs to be applied manifold-wise (details are provided in [40]).

Bagging and Smoothing Experiments. The first experiment evaluates the overall effectiveness of bagging as well as compares and combines it with *smoothing*, as an alternative or supplementary variance-reduction technique. We obtain smoothed LID estimates for a query by taking the arithmetic average of the estimates over its k-NN (the same neighborhood size used by the baseline estimator). This neighborhood includes the query itself only when it is present in the reference sample set (bag or full dataset). When smoothing is performed on the baseline estimates, without any bagging, we will refer to it simply as *smoothing*.

Additionally, we combine bagging and smoothing in three different ways. The simplest idea is to smooth out the aggregated bagged estimates themselves, exactly as explained above, only now for the bagged estimator. We will refer to this combination as "*post-smoothing*". As an alternative approach, we can instead smooth out estimates based on each bag separately, determining the query's k-NN among only the in-bag points. This way, smoothing takes place inside the bags, before the single-bag estimates are aggregated. We refer to this combination as "*pre-smoothing*". Finally, we can also integrate both strategies above by simultaneously applying pre-smoothing (*pre*) and post-smoothing (*post*).

This goes to show that bagging and smoothing are not necessarily competitors. Bagging actually offers new avenues for applying smoothing in different ways. We apply bagging, smoothing, and their three combinations independently to the different baseline estimators in Table 1, *with the goal to compare each baseline to their bagged/smoothed counterparts, rather than against each other.*

For each case, we sweep the locality hyper-parameter over a 9-step geometric progression from $k = 5$ to $k = 72$. For bagged variants, we additionally sweep the sampling rate over a 9-step geometric progression from $r = 0.042$ to $r = 0.6$, evaluating all combinations of (k, r). We are fixing the number of bags to $B = 10$, noting that increasing B can only further improve results in favor of bagging. Then, for each dataset and method variant, we individually select the hyper-parameter setting that minimizes MSE: k for baseline/smoothing, and (k, r) for all bagged variants, comparing the methods at their best observed performance.

Bagging Hyper-parameters Experiments. The second set of experiments focuses specifically on bagging and explores how the choice of its hyper-parameters affects performance in terms of MSE, variance, and bias. These effects are discussed using the bagged MLE estimator. The results for MADA and TLE (available in [40]) exhibit similar trends and the main conclusions do not change:

1st Test (Sampling Rate): We saw in Theorem 1 how decreasing r is expected to de-correlate the bags, and under certain general assumptions, reduce variance. Confirming this expected decrease in variance in the LID setting and to what extent it can overshine any potential increase in bias as a function of the sampling rate (r) are the main goals of this experiment. For this test, we chose a fixed $k = 10$ for the baseline estimators, a relatively small value compared to the dataset size, to attain to the general importance of locality surrounding LID estimation. The effects of r may be exaggerated or reduced depending on k; however, it is worth stressing that the general trends remain the same and the main conclusions with respect to r do not change for different, fixed values of k.

2nd Test (Interaction Between k and r): As previously discussed, both k and r affect the radius determining the local neighborhood around the query used for estimation, which is directly proportional to k and inversely proportional to r, with the potential to affect bias through non-local effects and sample size. On the other hand, variance is generally inversely proportional to k and directly proportional to r. If both hyper-parameters are variable, then the values of k that result in more favorable bias-variance tradeoffs will depend on r and vice versa. Since the exact relationship may be complex and possibly both dataset- and estimator-dependent, the goal of this experiment is to identify major general trends allowing clear guidance on the combined choice of these hyper-parameters.

We evaluate the bagged estimator over a grid of (k, r) combinations, comparing each against the baseline with the same k. The resulting MSE differences reveal ranges of r (and ratios k/r) for which bagging improves or worsens performance.

Additional Tests (Number of Bags): Analogous experimental setups and analyses demonstrating the (more straightforward) effects of the number of bags (B) and its interaction with r are available in the extended arXiv version of this paper [40].

Code and Data Availability. The full code that can be used to reproduce all results in our paper are available in a public GitHub repository at https://github.com/Campello-Lab/Bagging_for_LID, which also contains all the datasets used in our experiments. Most of these datasets were generated using the Scikit-dimension [9] public Python library, which was also the source code for the baseline LID estimators adopted in this study.

6 Results and Discussion

Bagging and Smoothing Results. Figure 3 shows the results for the first experimental setup in Sect. 5. We use radar charts to display the *optimal* MSE values, min-max normalized across variants, separately for each dataset, in reverse.[1] Thus, scores lie in $[0, 1]$, where 1 denotes the lowest relative MSE and 0 the highest, therefore, larger covered area indicates better performance.

[1] Tables of the raw MSE values are reported in the arXiv version of this paper [40].

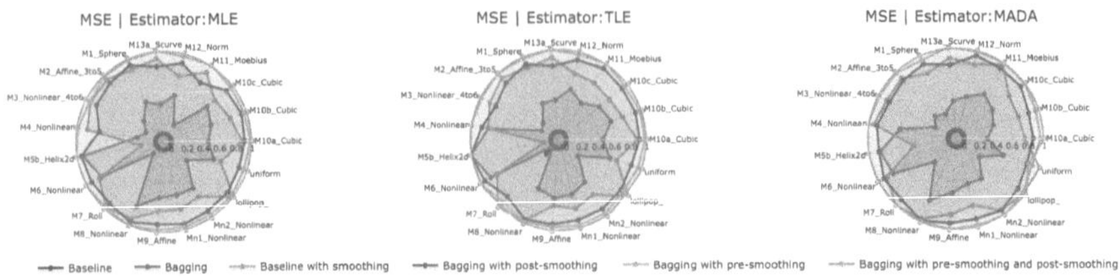

Fig. 3. Comparison of the relative MSE achieved by three different LID estimators, MLE, TLE, and MADA, with and without smoothing, bagging, and three strategies for combining bagging with smoothing. The results are for 19 datasets using case-by-case optimal k and r hyper-parameters. The min-max normalized MSE values are subtracted from 1 before plotting, such that larger scores correspond to smaller relative MSEs.

There is a very clear trend. First, both bagging and smoothing improve over the baseline in almost all cases when used independently, with only one exception (TLE on M7_Roll), noting that smoothing is often the stronger standalone variant in these experimental conditions. Second, it is clear that combining them yields further gains, with a common performance ordering, consistently across the baselines: baseline < bagged < smoothed < bagged with post-smoothing < bagged with pre-smoothing < bagged with pre- and post-smoothing. Therefore, the main conclusion is that not only do both bagging and smoothing achieve their purpose on their own, but combining them provides further improvements.

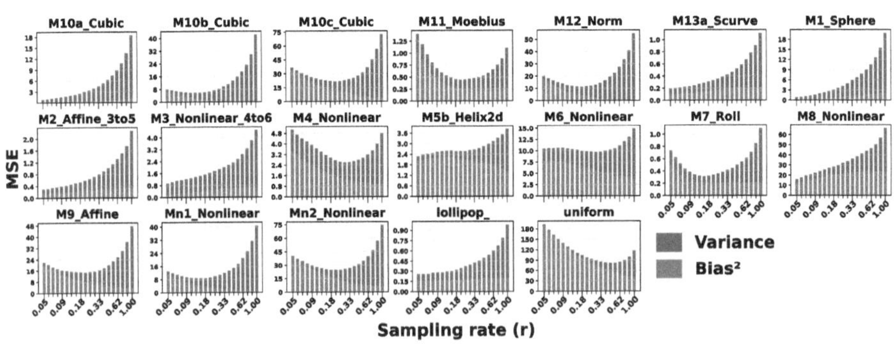

Fig. 4. MSE and its decomposition for each of the 19 datasets as a function of the sampling rate r used for bagged MLE as the LID estimator. Note that the baseline MLE is equivalent to $r = 1$, displayed on the rightmost bar of the individual charts.

Sampling Rate Results (1st Test on Hyper-parameters): Figure 4 illustrates the experimental behavior of the MSE decomposition for bagging as a function of the sampling rate r. The exact relationship is dataset-dependent, but in general, by decreasing r (right-to-left along the x-axis) we observe that: (i) bias^2 (green sub-bars) tends to increase or stay relatively stable in most cases; and (ii) variance (red sub-bars) shows a highly consistent, decreasing behavior. This robust effect on variance reduction supports the validity of our assumptions in Theorem 1 and confirms the bag de-correlating benefits of reducing r.

The opposing trends often yield an intermediate "sweet spot" where an optimal bias-variance tradeoff is achieved in terms of a minimal MSE, confirming our arguments in Sect. 4. However, for some datasets (M10a_Cubic, M13_Scurve, M1_Sphere, M2_Affine_3to5, M3_Nonlinear_4to6, and M8_Nonlinear), smaller r reduced both variance and bias, so the best MSE occurred at the smallest tested r, suggesting that potential non-local biases associated with decreasing r did not manifest within the given range of r values in those datasets.

Overall, the experiment mostly confirms the anticipated behavior for r, noting that results that were somewhat surprising, actually did so in a favorable way.

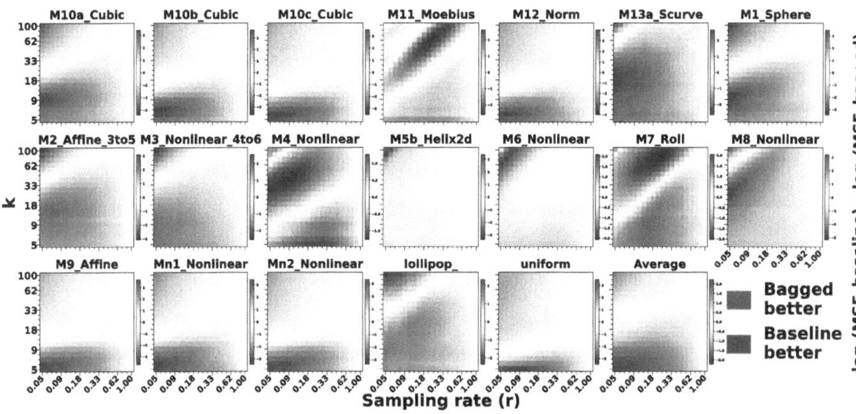

Fig. 5. Heatmaps of the relative difference (log-ratio) between the MSE achieved by the baseline estimator (MLE) and the MSE of its bagged counterpart for each of the 19 datasets and cross-combinations of values for the sampling rate r (x-axis) and the k-NN neighborhood size k (y-axis). Positive values, color-coded as blue, indicate that bagging outperforms the baseline, whereas negative values, color-coded in red, indicate the opposite. The relation is symmetric around zero and the darkness of the cells are proportional to the magnitude of the corresponding absolute value for the given dataset. (Color figure online)

Interaction Between k and r Results (2nd Test on Hyper-Parameters): Figure 5 illustrates how the bagged LID estimator's performance depends jointly on the baseline's k-NN hyper-parameter and the sampling rate. As previously conjectured, the bias increase from the expansion of the effective local neighborhood radius, for sufficiently large k compounding with sufficiently small r, may overpower the combined variance reduction caused by both these settings, potentially resulting in a larger MSE for the bagged estimator than the baseline.

Overall, the heatmaps in Fig. 5 confirm this expectation, as for most datasets, the hyper-parameter space is divided along a certain left-to-right upwards white line where the two estimators achieve similar MSEs. To the right of this line, bagging tends to win out, while to the left, the baseline tends to perform better. This suggests that there is some dataset specific constant, for which, if the ratio between the two hyper-parameters ($\frac{k}{r}$) stays under, then we can expect the bagged estimator to produce favorable results, while the results are most likely not desirable otherwise. We additionally observe that the strongest gains usually occur at the bottom-left region (small k, small r), where bagging can strongly reduce MSE by simultaneously de-correlating bag estimates while preserving reasonable locality. The experiment also clarifies how in the previous test with a variable r, fixing $k = 10$ may have caused partially unexpected results for some datasets, as non-local effects were not yet expressed.

Main Takeaways. From our theoretical and experimental findings, we provide the following guidelines for selecting the hyper-parameters of bagging (B, r) with respect to the degree of locality for LID estimation (quantified by the k hyper-parameter of the family of NN-based estimators adopted in this study):

- **Number of bags (B)**: It is well-known that increasing B has a strictly beneficial but diminishing effect in terms of estimator variance (see Sect. 4), and this has been confirmed in our preliminary experiments (see [40]). Since the resulting gains come with no counter-effect in terms of bias, this hyper-parameter is not critical. However, the runtime complexity of the bagged estimator is linearly dependent on B (see Sect. 7). Our experiments consistently support that increasing B beyond 10 is only recommended if one strongly favors further diminishing gains in stability over runtime.
- **Sampling rate (r) and locality (k)**: As anticipated in Sect. 4 and confirmed by our experiments, the hyper-parameters k and r jointly control the bias-variance tradeoff. If the primary goal is to bind variance reduction in the bagged estimator to a positive (or at least neutral) overall impact *in terms of MSE* as compared to the baseline, our results support combining low values of both k and r. In practice, we suggest to set k roughly within $[5, 10]$ or so as a minimal local sample size for LID estimation, then choose r accordingly, roughly within $[r_{min}, 0.5]$. The low end of this range should ensure that the in-bag subsamples are still representative enough of the relevant structures in the dataset (e.g., manifolds, classes, clusters) and, as such, it is problem-dependent. Within the (MSE-orientated) rough ranges of k and r suggested above, for a fixed chosen k decreasing r is theoretically expected to decrease variance (Theorem 1), often at the expense of bias. In the context of LID, applications that can tolerate large estimation biases, e.g., requiring mostly a reliable ordering for the purpose of relative comparisons of LID values across different queries, may benefit from smaller sampling rates (closer to r_{min}),

whereas in applications where systematic LID offsets can be critically detrimental, one might prefer larger, more conservative rates.

7 Complexity Analysis

In this section, we summarize the time complexity of bagging for LID estimation (in a non-parallel setting). An extended analysis, including the different smoothing variants (bagging with pre/post-smoothing) is available in [40].

Let $p(n)$ denote the runtime cost of computing a baseline LID estimate for a *single query* using a sample of size n. Therefore, the *total* runtime complexity for the baseline estimator (no bagging), T_{base}, is $O(n\,p(n))$ when taken over n different query locations. Bagging with B bags of size $m = rn$, for a *single query*, evaluates the estimator on each bag and averages, resulting in $O(B\,p(rn))$ time, where the sampling step for bag construction and final averaging contribute only lower-order terms ($O(Bnr)$ and $O(B)$) and can thus be omitted. As the bags do not have to be resampled per-query, the *total* runtime complexity of the bagged estimator taken over n queries, T_{bag}, is simply $O(Bn\,p(rn))$.

For the wide family of NN-based LID estimators, $p(n)$ is dominated by finding the k-NN of the query in the sample set of size n, where k is assumed to be either constant or $k << n$. Using a naive exhaustive search, $p(n)$ is $O(n)$, which translates to $T_{\text{base}} \to O(n^2)$ and $T_{\text{bag}} \to O(B\,r\,n^2)$. For large enough n, bagging may be faster as long as $r < 1/B$. Assuming a more sophisticated (indexed) search strategy, with average estimation time $p(n)$ of order $O(\log n)$ per query (amortized over all queries), then $T_{\text{base}} \to O(n \log n)$ and $T_{\text{bag}} \to O(B\,n\,\log(rn))$.

8 Limitations and Future Work

The objective evaluation measures we used, namely, MSE, Variance and Bias, required datasets commonly used for benchmarking, with ground-truth LID. While these datasets undoubtedly pose a challenge for estimators, due to their manifold curvatures within higher-dimensional spaces, they may not fully span the spectrum of complex behaviors found in real data. Therefore, LID bagging, smoothing, and their combinations as proposed in this paper, are yet to be fully tested in practical scenarios with potentially more complex data distributions, noise, and related challenges. Without ground-truth LID though, this will require indirect evaluation in downstream task applications, which is left for future work.

In future work, we also intend to investigate the use of the out-of-bag (OOB) samples from each bag for evaluation and (unsupervised) model selection.

9 Conclusions

We proposed bagging as a variance reduction strategy for LID estimation, alongside different strategies for its combination with neighborhood smoothing. We theoretically and experimentally explored the behavior of bagged LID estimators, with especial focus on the interplay between the sampling rate r and the locality threshold (neighborhood size k), whereby in-depth analyses of their joint effect on variance, bias, and overall MSE have been provided. Our results show that within a wide range of these hyper-parameters, clearly characterized by small values of k and small-to-moderate values of r, the bagged estimator is not only expected to reduce variance but it also tends to outperform the corresponding baseline estimator in terms of MSE. The higher level of freedom made available by these hyper-parameters in controlling the bias-variance trade-off also allows a reduction in MSE to be systematically observed when comparing the independently optimal bagged and baseline estimators, i.e., when they are independently set to their best preferred hyper-parameter values for each dataset. These improvements have been achieved across different baseline LID estimators and with a number of bags as small as 10, which comes with little to none additional computational price. Finally, our results robustly show that significant further improvements in performance can be achieved by combining bagging with neighborhood smoothing, which systematically outperforms both standalone approaches.

Acknowledgments. Novo Nordisk Foundation (#NNF23OC0079660)

Use of Generative AI. We used ChatGPT 5.4 strictly to assist with language style and conciseness.

Disclosure of Interests. The authors have no competing interests to declare that are relevant to the content of this article.

References

1. Allegra, M., Facco, E., Denti, F., Laio, A., Mira, A.: Data segmentation based on the local intrinsic dimension. Sci. Rep. **10**, 16449 (2020)
2. Altman, N., Krzywinski, M.: Ensemble methods: bagging and random forests. Nat. Methods **14**, 933–934 (2017)
3. Amsaleg, L., et al.: High intrinsic dimensionality facilitates adversarial attack: theoretical evidence. IEEE Trans. Inf. Forensics Security **16** (2020)
4. Amsaleg, L., Chelly, O., Furon, T., Girard, S., Houle, M., Kawarabayashi, K.i.: Estimating local intrinsic dimensionality (2015). https://doi.org/10.1145/2783258.2783405
5. Amsaleg, L., et al.: Extreme-value-theoretic estimation of local intrinsic dimensionality. Data Min. Knowl. Disc. **32**(6), 1768–1805 (2018). https://doi.org/10.1007/s10618-018-0578-6
6. Amsaleg, L., Chelly, O., Houle, M.E., Kawarabayashi, K.i., Radovanović, M., Treeratanajaru, W.: Intrinsic dimensionality estimation within tight localities: a theoretical and experimental analysis (2022). arXiv:2209.14475
7. Anderberg, A., et al.: Dimensionality-aware outlier detection: theoretical and experimental analysis (2024). arXiv:2401.05453
8. Aumüller, M., Ceccarello, M.: The role of local dimensionality measures in benchmarking nearest neighbor search. Inf. Syst. **101**, 101807 (2021)

9. Bac, J., Mirkes, E.M., Gorban, A.N., Tyukin, I., Zinovyev, A.: Scikit-dimension: a python package for intrinsic dimension estimation. Entropy **23**, 1368 (2021)
10. Breiman, L.: Bagging predictors. Mach. Learn. **24**, 123–140 (1996)
11. Breiman, L.: Random forests. Mach. Learn. **45**, 5–32 (2001)
12. Bühlmann, P., Yu, B.: Analyzing bagging. Ann. Statist. 30 (2002)
13. Camastra, F., Vinciarelli, A.: Estimating the intrinsic dimension of data with a fractal-based method. IEEE TPAMI **24**, 1404–1407 (2002)
14. Campadelli, P., Casiraghi, E., Ceruti, C., Rozza, A.: Intrinsic dimension estimation: relevant techniques and a benchmark framework. Math. Probl. Eng. **2015**, 1–21 (2015)
15. Carter, K.M., Hero, A.O.: Variance reduction with neighborhood smoothing for local intrinsic dimension estimation. In: Proceeding IEEE ICASSP, pp. 3917–3920 (2008)
16. Casanova, G., et al.: Dimensional testing for reverse k-nearest neighbor search. Proc. VLDB Endow. **10**, 769–780 (2017)
17. Chernick, M.R., LaBudde, R.A.: An Introduction to Bootstrap Methods with Applications to R. Wiley (2011)
18. Danielsson, J., de Haan, L., Peng, L., de Vries, C.: Using a bootstrap method to choose the sample fraction in tail index estimation. J. Multiv. Anal. **76**, 226–48 (2001)
19. Facco, E., d'Errico, M., Rodriguez, A., Laio, A.: Estimating the intrinsic dimension of datasets by a minimal neighborhood information. Sci. Rep. **7**, 12140 (2017)
20. Farahmand, A.m., Szepesvári, C., Audibert, J.Y.: Manifold-adaptive dimension estimation. In: ACM International Conference Proceeding Series, pp. 265–272 (2007)
21. Gencay, R., Qi, M.: Pricing and hedging derivative securities with neural networks: Bayesian regularization, early stopping, and bagging. IEEE TNN **12**, 726–34 (2001)
22. Gorbett, M., Shirazi, H., Ray, I.: Local intrinsic dimensionality of IoT networks for unsupervised intrusion detection. In: Data and Applications Security and Privacy XXXVI, pp. 143–161 (2022)
23. Grassberger, P., Procaccia, I.: Measuring the strangeness of strange attractors. Physica D **9**, 189–208 (1983)
24. Grinstead, C.M., Snell, J.L.: Introduction to Probability. American Mathematical Society (2003)
25. Gupta, A., Krauthgamer, R., Lee, J.R.: Bounded geometries, fractals, and low distortion embeddings. In: Proc. IEEE FOCS, pp. 534–543 (2003)
26. Hein, M., Audibert, J.Y.: Intrinsic dimensionality estimation of submanifolds in R. In: Proc. ICML, pp. 289–296 (2005)
27. Houle, M.: Dimensionality, discriminability, density and distance distributions. In: Proceeding IEEE ICDMW, pp. 468–473 (2013)
28. Houle, M., Kashima, H., Nett, M.: Generalized expansion dimension. In: Proceeding IEEE ICDMW, pp. 587–594 (2012)
29. Houle, M.E.: Local intrinsic dimensionality I: An extreme-value-theoretic foundation for similarity applications. In: Similarity Search and Applications, pp. 64–79 (2017)
30. Huang, H., Campello, R.J.G.B., Erfani, S.M., Ma, X., Houle, M.E., Bailey, J.: Ldreg: local dimensionality regularized self-supervised learning (2024). arXiv:2401.10474
31. James, G., Witten, D., Hastie, T., Tibshirani, R., Taylor, J.: An Introduction to Statistical Learning: with Applications in Python. Springer (2023)

32. Johnsson, K., Soneson, C., Fontes, M.: Low bias local intrinsic dimension estimation from expected simplex skewness. IEEE TPAMI **37**, 196–202 (2015)
33. Kalinka, A.T.: The probability of drawing intersections: extending the hypergeometric distribution (2014). arXiv:1305.0717
34. Kamkari, H., Ross, B.L., Hosseinzadeh, R., Cresswell, J.C., Loaiza-Ganem, G.: A geometric view of data complexity: efficient local intrinsic dimension estimation with diffusion models (2024). arXiv:2406.03537
35. Karantzalos, K.: Intrinsic dimensionality estimation and dimensionality reduction through scale space filtering. In: ICDSP, pp. 1–6 (2009)
36. Larrañaga, P., Lozano, J.: Estimation of Distribution Algorithms: A New Tool for Evolutionary Computation. Springer (2002)
37. Liao, J.G., Berg, A.: Sharpening Jensen's inequality (2017). arXiv:1707.08644
38. Ma, X., et al.: Characterizing adversarial subspaces using local intrinsic dimensionality (2018). arXiv:1801.02613
39. Pictet, O., Dacorogna, M., Muller, U.: Hill, bootstrap and jackknife estimators for heavy tails. In: A Practical Guide to Heavy Tails (1996)
40. Péter, K., Campello, R.J.G.B., Bailey, J., Houle, M.E.: On the use of bagging for local intrinsic dimensionality estimation (2026). https://arxiv.org/abs/2603.24384
41. Revelas, C., Boldea, O., Werker, B.J.M.: When does subagging work? (2024). arXiv:2404.01832
42. Rozza, A., Lombardi, G., Ceruti, C., Casiraghi, E., Campadelli, P.: Novel high intrinsic dimensionality estimators. Mach. Learn. **89**, 37–65 (2012)
43. Ruhl, M.: Finding nearest neighbors in growth-restricted metrics. In: STOC (2002)
44. Savić, M., Kurbalija, V., Radovanović, M.: Local intrinsic dimensionality measures for graphs, with applications to graph embeddings. Inf. Syst. **119**, 102272 (2023)
45. Tempczyk, P., et al.: LIDL: Local intrinsic dimension estimation using approximate likelihood (2022). arXiv:2206.14882
46. Wackerly, D.D., Mendenhall, W., Scheaffer, R.L.: Mathematical Statistics with Applications. Thomson Brooks/Cole (2008)
47. Wikipedia contributors: Smoothing (2025). https://en.wikipedia.org/wiki/Smoothing. Accessed 28-July-2025
48. Zhang, Z., Chen, B., Sun, J., Luo, Y.: A bagging dynamic deep learning network for diagnosing COVID-19. Sci. Rep. **11**, 16280 (2021)
49. Zhou, S., Tordesillas, A., Pouragha, M., Bailey, J., Bondell, H.: On local intrinsic dimensionality of deformation in complex materials. Sci. Rep. **11**, 10216 (2021)
50. Zimek, A., Gaudet, M., Campello, R.J.G.B., Sander, J.: Subsampling for efficient and effective unsupervised outlier detection ensembles. In: Proc. ACM SIGKDD Int. Conf. Knowl. Discov. Data Min, 428–436 (2013)

ProtototypeNAS: Rapid Design of Deep Neural Networks for Microcontroller Units

Mark Deutel(✉), Simon Geis, and Axel Plinge

Fraunhofer Institute for Integrated Circuits, Fraunhofer IIS, Erlangen , Germany
{mark.deutel,simon.geis,axel.plinge}@iis.fraunhofer.de

Abstract. Enabling efficient deep neural network (DNN) inference on edge devices with different hardware constraints is a challenging task that typically requires DNN architectures to be specialized for each device separately. To avoid the huge manual effort, one can use neural architecture search (NAS). However, many existing NAS methods are resource-intensive and time-consuming because they require the training of many different DNNs from scratch. Furthermore, they do not take the resource constraints of the target system into account. To address these shortcomings, we propose PrototypeNAS, a zero-shot NAS method to accelerate and automate the selection, compression, and specialization of DNNs to different target microcontroller units (MCUs). We propose a novel three-step search method that decouples DNN design and specialization from DNN training for a given target platform. First, we present a novel search space that not only cuts out smaller DNNs from a single large architecture, but instead combines the structural optimization of multiple architecture types, as well as optimization of their pruning and quantization configurations. Second, we explore the use of an ensemble of zero-shot proxies during optimization instead of a single one. Third, we propose the use of Hypervolume subset selection (HSS) to distill DNN architectures from the Pareto front of the multi-objective optimization (MOO) that represent the most meaningful tradeoffs between accuracy and floating-point operations (FLOPs). We evaluate the effectiveness of PrototypeNAS on 12 different datasets in three different tasks: image classification, time series classification, and object detection. Our results demonstrate that PrototypeNAS is able to identify DNNs within minutes that are small enough to be deployed on off-the-shelf MCUs and still achieve accuracies comparable to the performance of large DNN architectures.

Keywords: Neural Architecture Search · Multi-Objective Optimization · Efficient AI · Microcontrollers

1 Introduction

We address the problem of quickly and efficiently designing and training deep neural networks (DNNs) for inference on resource-constrained microcontroller

M. Ceci et al. (Eds.): ECML PKDD 2026, LNAI 16941, pp. 335–353, 2027.
https://doi.org/10.1007/978-3-032-37654-1_20

units (MCUs). DNNs have become the de facto standard for data analysis and machine learning tasks. However, with the growth of DNNs in both size and computational cost over the last years, running DNNs, especially on a diverse set of different resource constrained embedded systems and at low latency, has become a major challenge.

To address this problem, we propose PrototypeNAS, a zero-shot neural architecture search (NAS) framework for rapidly designing DNNs for MCUs with different hardware and resource constraints. Compared to other hardware-aware NAS frameworks, PrototypeNAS is novel in three aspects. First, it uses an ensemble of zero-shot proxies that compete as objectives in a multi-objective optimization (MOO) rather than being weighted and linearized into a single ensemble proxy score. Second, it implements a novel search space that combines architecture selection, size and structure optimization, and optimization of pruning and quantization configuration, instead of optimizing them as unrelated problems. Third, it introduces Hypervolume subset selection (HSS) to further refine the Pareto optimal models from optimization to a set of 3–5 models that cover the most meaningful tradeoffs between accuracy and resource consumption.

Additionally, in our extensive evaluation, we demonstrate the effectiveness and versatility of PrototypeNAS by using it to find optimized DNNs deployable on an ARM Cortex-M MCU for 12 datasets from three tasks: image classification, time series classification, and object detection. We also compare PrototypeNAS to two other hardware-aware NAS methods, TinyNAS (MCUNet) [23] and NATS-Bench [9]. On average, the DNN architectures found by PrototypeNAS outperform the ones proposed by the other two frameworks by 5 % in accuracy on the CIFAR10 dataset.

As a result, PrototypeNAS is a resource- and time-efficient way to search for DNN architectures without having to train hundreds of DNN architectures to find a single good candidate. Instead, PrototypeNAS reduces the training to only 3–5 DNN candidates while still considering hundreds of architectures in its search.

2 Related Work

NAS is a set of techniques used to automate the DNN architecture design process, generally by solving an optimization problem. While the initial focus was on maximizing accuracy and using reinforcement learning to control the search process [35], more recently, hardware-aware NAS [31], i.e., considering memory and inference speed in addition to accuracy as a MOO, has become a major focus of research. A subset of this work focuses more specifically on NAS for resource-constrained devices such as MCUs [5,11,23].

In addition, zero-shot NAS [16,20,22,27] has received considerable attention to address the problem of having to train a large number of DNN candidates, for example, when using black-box optimization [7] or reinforcement learning [35]. All zero-shot NAS techniques rely on using a proxy metric for accuracy to avoid training. As a result, a large number of different zero-shot proxies have been proposed, focusing on different features that can be computed from an untrained DNN, such as the Pearson correlation matrix of the intermediate feature maps [16] or the number of linear regions in the input space [27]. In addition, zero-shot NAS techniques, especially when used for hardware-aware NAS, often propose the use of a large pre-trained "super-net" from which smaller networks more suited to the constraints of the target hardware are then derived and tuned [5].

While zero-shot NAS works to find a sufficiently good architecture in a relatively short time, there are still challenges to overcome. Zero-shot proxies are known to be imprecise and bias certain DNN architectures [4,17], often leading to poor correlation with actual training accuracy. Furthermore, the reliance on a single large supernet means that the resulting search space is limited to exploitation around a pre-existing optimum and never explores the full architectural landscape of DNNs.

In parallel to NAS, other techniques for DNN compression have been explored. A significant number of efficient human-engineered DNN architectures have been proposed over the years. Starting with SqueezeNet [14], MobileNet [30], and EfficientNet [32], to more recent designs such as MCUNet [23], which specifically targets microcontrollers, and ConvNeXt [25], which combines a traditional CNN with transformer elements. In addition, pruning and quantization have become common techniques for designing efficient DNN architectures for resource-constrained MCUs [8].

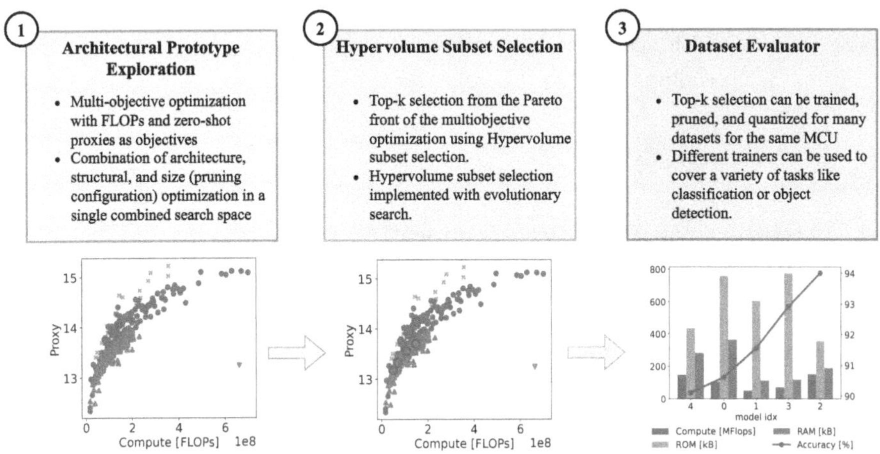

Fig. 1. Schematic of the three step pipeline of PrototypeNAS.

3 Method

PrototypeNAS is a zero-shot NAS method that enables rapid exploration of optimized DNNs for MCU deployment by decoupling design space exploration, i.e., the search for prototypical network architectures and their compression configuration, from training on the target datasets.

We give a schematic overview of the three-step method of PrototypeNAS in Fig. 1. ① First, a constrained multi-objective optimization is performed with the ensemble of zero-shot proxies and the number of floating-point operations (FLOPs) as a proxy for the computational cost of DNN inference as objectives. The optimization is constrained by the memory limits of the target MCU to ensure that the exploration focuses only on DNN architectures that can actually be deployed on the target. The search space of the optimization combines both architectural selection from a pool of predefined baseline architectures and their structural and size optimization, i.e., pruning parameter configuration, into a single search space. ② Second, a top-k selection is performed from the resulting Pareto set using HSS. ③ Finally, the resulting selection of optimized DNN architectures is trained, pruned, and quantized on the target datasets. In the following sections, we describe each of the three steps of PrototypeNAS in detail.

Table 1. Search space X of the MOO, $\forall i \in \{0, 1, 2, 3\}$ resulting in 14 tunable hyperparameters in total.

Optimization	Hyperparameter	Type	Range/Values
architecture	baseline architecture	categorical	task dependent
structural	group depth i	categorical	$[0, 1, 2, 3]$
	kernel & stride i	categorical	$[[3, 2], [3, 1], [5, 2], [5, 1], [7, 2], [7, 1]]$
size	width multiplier	continuous	$[0.1, 1.0]$
	pruning sparsity i	continuous	$[0.1, 0.9]$

3.1 Architectural Prototype Exploration

We formulate the architectural prototype exploration as a constrained MOO in Eq. (1). The objectives are to minimize the number of FLOPs of a model $flops(x)$ while maximizing an ensemble of four proxy metrics $prox_i(x)$ with $i \in \{0, \ldots, 3\}$. The four proxies used in this work are MeCo [16], ZiCo [22], NASWOT [27], and SNIP [20], which we selected due to the different DNN features they use for evaluation, compare [13]. The constraints of the optimization ram_{max}, rom_{max}, and $flops_{max}$ are derived from the hardware limits of the targeted MCU.

$$\begin{aligned} &\min_{x \in X} \quad flops(x), -prox_1(x), \ldots, -prox_3(x) \\ \text{s.t.} \quad & ram(x) \leq ram_{max} \\ & rom(x) \leq rom_{max} \\ & flops(x) \leq flops_{max} \end{aligned} \tag{1}$$

We designed the search space from which PrototypeNAS samples DNNs, focusing on emulating the process that a specialist makes when designing an efficient DNN architecture for an MCU. Based on this premise, we make the following assumptions: First, there is a set of baseline architectures from which DNN candidates can be derived. Second, each of the baseline architectures can be abstracted as follows: An initial layer pattern, followed by a set of repeatable layer patterns (*superblocks*), followed by a classifier. Third, a pruning and quantization scheme is defined that is executed during training to dynamically compress and scale down the model during training. Based on these three assumptions, we define the search space X in Table 1.

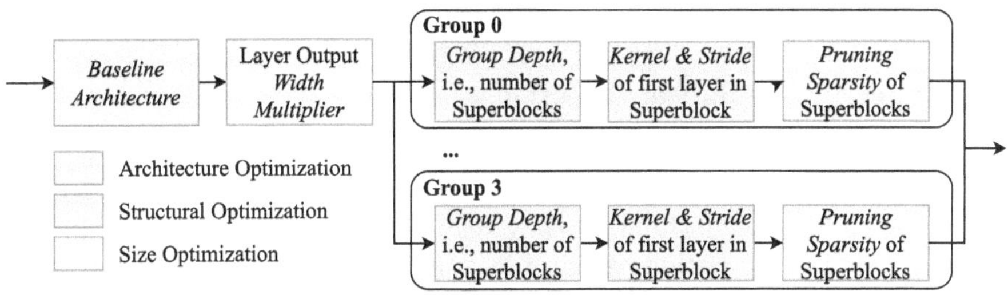

Fig. 2. The proposed search space and how a DNN prototype can be created from it. Each baseline architecture consists of repeatable superblocks, i.e., a predefined pattern of layers, organized in the search space into four groups to be optimized separately.

In the following, we describe how X is structured and how DNN prototypes can be created from it, see Fig. 2 for a schematic overview. The *architecture* hyperparameter allows the optimizer to choose a baseline DNN architecture from a pool of predefined architectures. In the scope of this work, six DNN architectures are supported for image classification, two architectures for time series classification, and one for object detection (see Sect. 4 for details).

The backbone of the selected baseline DNN is then split into repeatable superblocks as described above, for example depthwise separable convolutions in MobileNetV2. How each architecture is split into superblocks is defined prior. The superblocks are then organized into four groups. Each group contains at least one super block and up to four additional blocks, which is controlled for each group via the *group depth* hyperparameter. In addition, each group has an optimizable *kernel & stride* hyperparameter which is used to configure the first convolution of each superblock of the group. Together, these hyperparameters allow structural optimization of the baseline DNNs.

The part of the search space allowing for size optimization of the baseline DNNs consists of the *width multiplier* and *pruning sparsity* hyperparameters. The *width multiplier* parameter controlls the initial size of the baseline DNN architecture at the beginning of training by scaling the output channels in all convolutional layers uniformly. In addition, an iterative pruning schedule is defined that will be executed during training. For each of the four groups of superblocks, a separate *pruning sparsity* hyperparameter controls the target percentage of channels to be removed by pruning.

The objective function evaluation for a set of hyperparameters proposed by the optimizer consists of three steps: First, the selected baseline architecture is initialized and configured according to the structural optimization. Second, pruning and quantization are applied (without any training) to query parameter and size reduction. Third, the resulting model is translated to C code (cf. [8]) to get the actual ROM and RAM usage when deployed on the targeted MCU. To calculate the number of FLOPs of a DNN, Pytorch's built-in profiler is used. Since the objective function evaluation does not require any training due to the use of zero-shot proxies, sampling is both resource and time efficient, allowing for rapid exploration of the search space.

3.2 Hypervolume Subset Selection

We obtain a set of Pareto-optimal architecture and compression configurations from the prototype exploration described in the previous section. The size of this set can be between one and as many solutions as there were DNNs explored during the optimization. However, in practice, a set of 3–5 architectural tradeoffs is usually sufficient for a decision maker to select a DNN for a given use case. A smallest model, a model with the highest accuracy, and 1–3 tradeoffs in between. To avoid situations where large Pareto sets proposed by the optimization have to be trained, compressed, evaluated, and finally presented to the decision maker, we implemented a HSS algorithm based on evolutionary programming and inspired by algorithms like [2] that use Hypervolume as a selection criterion.

Let $H(A)$ be the Hypervolume indicator of a set of solutions A as described in [34]. We formulate an optimization problem in Eq. (2) which aims to find a set $A \subset P$ with $|A| = k$ and $k \in \{1, 2, \ldots, |P|\}$ that maximizes $H(A)$ where P is the full Pareto set resulting from the prototype exploration.

$$\max_{\substack{A \subset P \\ |A|=k}} H(A) \tag{2}$$

We solve this optimization problem using a greedy selection strategy that retains solutions with higher Hypervolume contributions. First, we encode P as a binary gene g, where each bit in g corresponds to a solution in P, which is either set to 1 if the sample should be part of A, or 0 if not. Consequently, for each gene, only k bits can be set to 1, while all other bits are set to 0. We then evolve an initial population $G \in \{g_0, g_1, \ldots, g_{n-1}\}$ of a given size n, using mutation and crossover operators, and the Hypervolume indicator to evaluate the fitness of each $g \in G$.

Naturally, crossover, mutation, and the initial generation of G can lead to the creation of "invalid" genes, i.e. genes with more than k bits set to 1. Our algorithm greedily repairs such genes. If there are less than k bits set to 1, it iteratively sets bits to 1 until exactly k bits are set to 1. This has no negative effect on the fitness of the gene, since the Hypervolume can only increase or stay the same with additional solutions added, but never decrease. If there are more than k bits set to 1, the algorithm instead tries to set additional bits to zero while keeping the Hypervolume as high as possible. To do this, it sets every bit that is 1 to 0 one by one and recalculates the Hypervolume. Then the algorithm sorts all bits by their calculated Hypervolumes in ascending order. Finally, it selects the top k bits whose removal has the largest negative impact on the fitness of the gene, while setting all other bits to 0.

In all our experiments, we configured the Hypervolume subset selection algorithm with an initial population size of 2000, a mutation rate of 0.3, and ran it for 10 000 generations.

3.3 Dataset Evaluator

To train, prune, and quantize the subsets of DNNs designed by PrototypeNAS, we implement two dataset evaluators. One evaluator is for training image and time series classification tasks using Pytorch Lightning, while the other one is for training the object detection task with the YOLOv5 framework. As baseline architectures for PrototypeNAS we used implementations provided by torchvision and torchaudio with slight modifications so that they can be generated from a set of hyperparameters from the search space introduced in Sect. 3.1.

We also implemented iterative structure pruning and quantization for both trainers. We used post-training static quantization (PTQ) for the image classification and object detection tasks, and quantization-aware training (QAT) with 15 additional training epochs for the time series classification task. Since PTQ is applied to DNNs after training, it is generally faster to use and less computationally intensive, while QAT is more resource intensive since it is applied during training, but also more accurate. While we found during our experiments that PTQ worked reliably well for the two image-based tasks, we experienced significant drops in accuracy for the time series datasets when using PTQ. As a result, we used QAT for the time series datasets, as it yielded significantly better accuracies. This is most likely due to QAT's ability to better account for the varying activation ranges resulting from the time series input.

4 Evaluation

We evaluate PrototypeNAS on three different tasks and 12 datasets in total: image classification for the CIFAR10 [19], CIFAR100 [19], GTSRB [12], Flowers [28], Birds [33], Cars [18], Pets [29], and ArxPhotos314 [1] datasets, time series classification for the Daliac [21], MAFULDA[1], and BitBrain Sleep [26] datasets, and person detection using a subset of COCO [24].

For the three tasks, we first performed the prototype exploration as described in Sect. 3.1 for 500 trials, then performed the HSS as described in Sect. 3.2, and

[1] https://www02.smt.ufrj.br/~offshore/mfs/page_01.html.

finally evaluated the top-5 selection of each of the tasks on the respective datasets. As constraints of the optimization, we used $ram_{max480KB}$, $rom_{max} = 2MB$, and $flops_{max} = 1e9$ to describe the resource constraints of the iMXRT1062, a Cortex-M7 MCU, which we selected as the deployment target. For training, we used the same configuration for all datasets: A batch size of 48, stochastic gradient descent with a learning rate of 0.001 and a momentum of 0.9, and 100 training epochs.

We provide a detailed insight and discussion of our results in Sects. 4.1 and 4.3. Furthermore, in Sect. 4.2, we discuss the precision of the proxy ensemble used in PrototypeNAS during exploration. In Sect. 4.4, we give a comparison of PrototypeNAS to two other NAS frameworks, TinyNAS (MCUNet) [23] and NATS-Bench [9]. Finally, in Sect. 4.5 we measure the impact of PrototypeNAS on performance and emissions of the NAS algorithm.

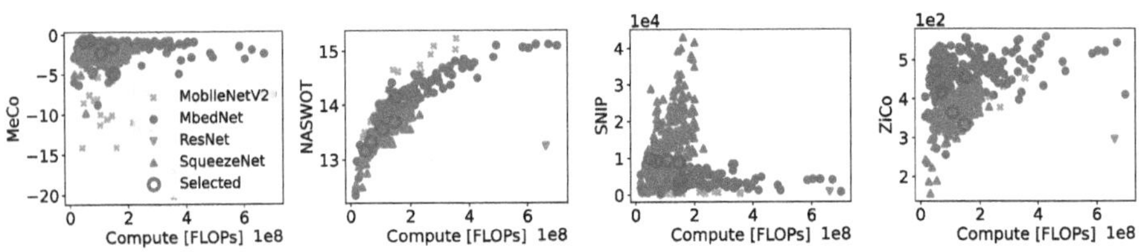

(a) Image classification

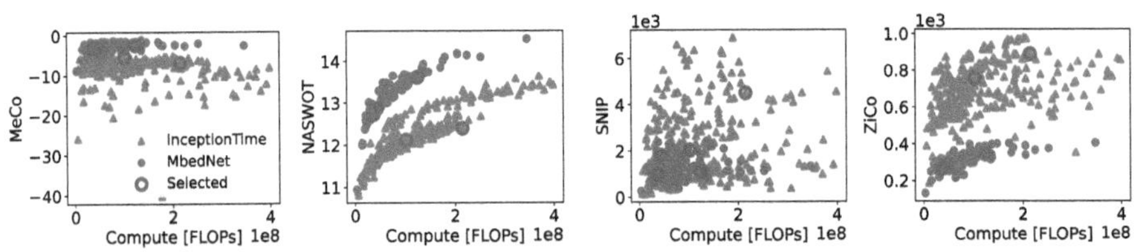

(b) Time series classification

Fig. 3. Optimization results. The top-5 DNNs selected from the Pareto front by HSS are marked with red circles. (Color figure online)

4.1 Results for Image and Time Series Classification

Figure 3 shows the results of the prototype exploration for image and time series classification and the four proxy scores MeCo, NASWOT, SNIP, and ZiCo[2]. We performed separate optimizations for the image and time series datasets because we used different sets of baseline architectures for the two tasks, four DNN architectures for image classification and two for time-series classification, which we denote in the plots with different colors and markers. For image classification,

[2] DNNs and pre-trained weights: https://doi.org/10.5281/zenodo.18878249.

our baseline set includes MobileNetV2 [30], ResNet18 [10], Squeezenet [14], and MBedNet (our own DNN architecture derived from MobileNet), see Fig. 3a. For time series classification, we used InceptionTime [15] and a version of MBedNet where we replaced all 2D convolutions with their 1D counterparts, see Fig. 3b. We used a 128×128 pixel input during all experiments for image classification, while for the time series classification experiments we split the input into windows of constant length and used them without any further preprocessing. After optimization, we identified five models from the final Pareto front using HSS as described in Sect. 3.2 and marked the selected models in Fig. 3 with red circles.

Table 2. Test accuracy of the trained, pruned, and quantized DNNs found by PrototypeNAS for the image datasets. Latency and energy was measured on an iMXRT1062 Cortex-M7 MCU using an external Joulescope energy analyzer.

Optim. Index	210	283	190	311	237
Architecture	MBedNet	MBedNet	SqueezeNet	SqueezeNet	MBedNet
Quantized Test Accuracy [%] (PTQ)					
CIFAR10	91.8	92.5	90.3	90.0	**93.7**
CIFAR100	67.4	70.5	66.5	63.7	**72.3**
ArxPhotos314	90.8	95.4	**97.4**	79.5	93.6
Flowers	88.9	91.6	82.9	86.3	**93.3**
Birds	62.8	65.7	59.5	55.6	**69.9**
Pets	99.8	99.8	97.5	96.1	**99.9**
Cars	64.8	64.1	59.8	55.2	**76.4**
GTSRB	96.3	96.1	95.8	**97.0**	95.5
Compute [MFLOPs]	50.1	70.0	105.0	147.5	151.0
ROM [KB]	605.4	774.9	758.4	434.7	356.5
RAM [KB]	111.7	118.3	364.7	281.6	189.7
Latency [ms]	224.1 ± 0.1	$312.9 \pm (0.1)$	367.1 ± 0.1	447.2 ± 0.1	753.2 ± 0.1
Energy [mJ]	77.6 ± 8.6	108.6 ± 9.9	126.0 ± 12.7	156.3 ± 16.8	254.5 ± 13.7

For both image and time series optimization, the results in Fig. 3 show that the four proxies rank the base architectures of their respective search spaces differently. For example, SNIP gave a significantly higher score to almost all architectural variants of SqueezeNet than any of the other three proxies in Fig. 3a. Another example of this apparent "disagreement" among the proxies can be seen in Fig. 3b, where NASWOT and MeCo rank MBedNet higher than InceptionTime, while the other two proxies do the opposite.

Another observation that can be made is that all DNNs of a single architecture type cluster around their unmodified baseline architecture in the target space. This is not unexpected, since once a baseline architecture is selected, the other hyperparameters in PrototypeNAS's search space focus on modifying the structure of the baseline architecture within the limits of its predefined superblocks, or scaling the architecture in width, but do not fundamentally change its design. This is intentional, as the goal of PrototypeNAS is to quickly fine-tune a DNN to fit the constraints of a given MCU and not to come up with completely new DNN designs from scratch. Therefore, another way to interpret the results in Fig. 3 is that each baseline architecture represents a local optimum, with the search space being designed in a way to encourage an efficient search around it.

Regarding the difference in proxy scoring observed in our results, we point to the general consensus found in related work that zero-shot proxies are often imprecise and tend to favor certain architectures [4,17]. As a result, and similar to related work such as [13], this motivates us to consider the evaluation of multiple proxies to guide our optimization, rather than relying on a single proxy. In contrast, we do not attempt to weight and linearize the proxies to form a new score, but instead treat them as competing objectives in our MOO.

Table 3. Test accuracy of the trained, pruned, and quantized DNNs found by PrototypeNAS for the time series datasets. Latency and energy was measured on an iMXRT1062 Cortex-M7 MCU using an external Joulescope energy analyzer.

Optim. Index	224	226	73	273	347
Architecture	MBedNet	MBedNet	Inception	MBedNet	Inception
Quantized Test Accuracy [%] (QAT)					
BitBrain	83.7	87.2	81.7	**88.0**	78.9
Mafaulda	96.8	98.3	97.4	97.8	**98.5**
Daliac	95.9	97.1	**97.2**	97.0	96.1
Compute [MFLOPs]	36.3	43.2	101.5	123.5	215.3
ROM [KB]	149.0	231.0	571.0	337.0	978.0
RAM [KB]	246.0	244.0	251.0	252.0	250.0
Latency [ms]	162.3 ± 0.1	183.6 ± 0.1	447.2 ± 0.1	467.9 ± 0.3	635.0 ± 1.4
Energy [mJ]	55.8 ± 5.7	63.7 ± 6.4	156.0 ± 16.7	165.8 ± 15.9	227.6 ± 17.6

As a result, the top $k = 5$ architectures selected by the HSS at the end of the optimization do not directly follow the ranking of any of the individual proxies and FLOPs, but are instead derived from the Pareto front between FLOPs and all four proxies. As a result, PrototypeNAS avoids being biased toward particular architectures and achieves a balanced evaluation.

We show the test accuracy on all evaluated datasets of the five trained, pruned, and quantized DNN prototypes selected by HSS in Table 2 (image classification) and Table 3 (time series classification) sorted in ascending order by FLOPs. For the image classification models we used PTQ for quantization, while for the time series models we used QAT. Furthermore, for each of the five DNNs shown in the two tables, we report the base architecture from which the prototype was derived, the model's RAM and ROM requirements in kilobytes, reflecting the actual memory requirements on the target MCU, as well as the average latency and energy consumption of the DNNs measured externally using a Joulescope energy analyzer when executed on an iMXRT1062 Cortex-M7 MCU. For each dataset, we highlighted the model with the highest test accuracy. For time series classification, we trained with randomly initialized weights, while for image classification, we performed 50 epochs of ImageNet pre-training.

For both the image and time series classification tasks, the selection of DNNs found by PrototypeNAS achieved accuracies competitive with or better than related embedded DNN architectures, see also Sect. 4.4 for a direct comparison of our approach with other NAS methods. Furthermore, while a correlation between FLOPs and accuracy can be observed within an architecture type, e.g. both the MBedNet-based architectures 210, 283, and 237 and the SqueezeNet-based architectures 190 and 311 in Table 2 show a linear correlation between FLOPs and accuracy, this correlation cannot be observed when ranking across the two different architecture types. Since the PrototypeNAS search space optimizes multiple architecture types together, ranking by FLOPs is not sufficient, meaning that the structure and expressiveness of the architectures must also be considered, motivating our use of zero-shot proxies in this work.

In addition, when considering resource consumption, we noticed that the RAM requirements are very similar across all five DNNs for both the image and time series classification tasks, even though they have very different compute and ROM requirements. The reason is that the deployment framework we utilize for our experiments reuses memory for multiple intermediate feature maps during inference. This means that the larger initial feature maps typically dominate the overall RAM requirements, since they are often similar in size, as all models share the same input size. As a result, we are only modeling memory requirements as constraints rather than objectives during optimization. Finally, our results show that latency and energy per sample scale linearly with FLOPs, making it a good proxy for optimizing these two metrics without having hardware in the loop.

4.2 Proxy Ensemble Analysis

We give a detailed analysis of the proxy "disagreement" we described in the previous section in Table 4. To quantify "disagreement", we compute the Kendall rank correlation coefficient (Kendall's τ score) to measure the ordinal association between each of the four proxy scores and the quantized post-training accuracy we presented in Tables 2 and 3. In addition, we provide the τ score between FLOPs and accuracy.

The $\tau \in [-1, 1]$ score quantifies the strength and direction of monotonic relationships between two variables based on order, where 1 describes a perfect agreement, i.e. the rankings are identical, -1 a perfect disagreement, i.e. the rankings are the opposite of each other, and 0 denotes no correlation between the rankings of the two variables. Ideally, for zero-shot NAS proxies, a τ score close to 1 is desirable, as this means that DNNs with higher proxy scores will also achieve higher accuracy, while especially a score below 0 is undesirable, as it misguides the NAS algorithm during optimization.

Table 4. Kendall's τ scores for the datasets and results shown in Tables 2 and 3.

Dataset	MeCo	NASWOT	SNIP	ZiCo	FLOPs
CIFAR10	0.0	0.0	−0.2	**0.6**	0.0
CIFAR100	0.0	0.0	−0.2	**0.6**	0.0
ArxPhotos314	0.0	0.0	**0.2**	−0.2	0.0
Flowers	0.2	0.2	−0.4	**0.4**	0.2
Birds	0.0	0.0	−0.2	**0.6**	0.0
Pets	0.1	−0.4	0.2	**0.8**	−0.3
Cars	−0.2	−0.2	0.0	**0.8**	−0.2
GTSRB	**0.4**	−0.4	0.2	−0.2	−0.4
BitBrain	**1.0**	0.8	−0.6	−0.4	−0.2
Mafaulda	−0.2	0.0	**0.6**	0.4	0.6
Daliac	0.1	−0.1	**0.3**	0.1	−0.1

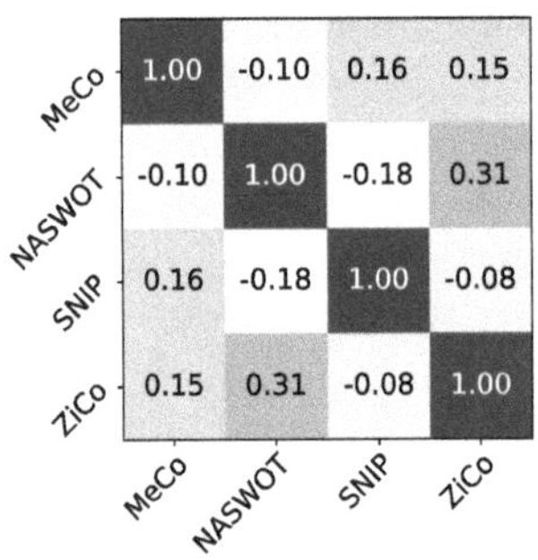

(a) Image classification

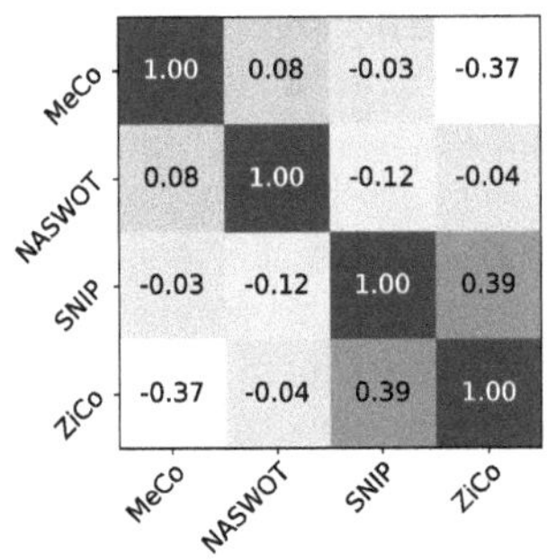

(b) Time series classification

Fig. 4. Kendall's τ scores between the four zero-shot proxies for the image and time series classification tasks.

In Table 4, it can be seen that none of the four proxies has a consistent and high positive τ score for all to evaluate datasets. Even worse, the proxies sometimes have a negative relationship with accuracy for some datasets, while working well for others. This can be observed especially well with ZiCo and SNIP. On the other hand, it can be seen that for all datasets, at least one of the four proxies achieved a high positive τ score and, more importantly, outperformed the score achieved by FLOPs. As a result, we concluded that for our search space (a) using a proxy ensemble is necessary to find a Pareto front of DNNs that, when trained, achieve consistently good ranking across many datasets and prevent biases and inaccuracies of individual proxies from misguiding the exploration and (b) using zero-shot NAS proxies is a better metric to rank models by approximated accuracy than using FLOPs.

Finally, in Fig. 4, we show the τ scores calculated among the proxies themselves for the image and time series optimization as heatmaps. Note that the lower and upper triangular matrices describe the same relationship. In Figs. 4a and 4b we observe that for both optimizations the proxies generally did not have a strong relationship with each other, and in the few cases where they did, such as SNIP and ZiCo in Fig. 4b, it was positive, i.e. the proxies were in agreement. These results confirm that the use of this specific ensemble of proxies provides PrototypeNAS with diverse and balanced evaluations, thus mitigating the biases and inaccuracies of individual proxies. Furthermore, our results are in agreement with [13], who proposed the same ensemble of proxies.

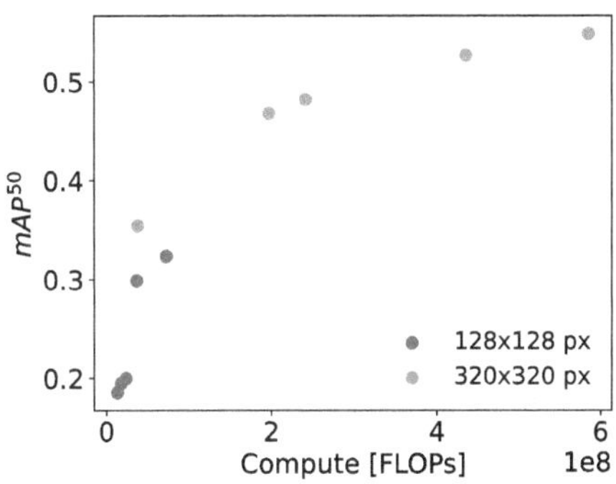

Fig. 5. Tradeoff between mAP^{50} and FLOPs of the MBedNet YOLO architectures designed by PrototypeNAS.

4.3 Object Detection

To further demonstrate the flexibility of PrototypeNAS, we applied it to an object detection task, specifically person detection, trained on the COCO dataset. We used the YOLOv5 framework, replacing its regular backbone network with MBedNet, which we also used in the results presented in Sect. 4.1, but keeping the original YOLOv5 detector instead of a normal classification head. This allowed us to use the same search space for optimization as for the image classification task, while using the YOLOv5 data augmentation, loss function, anchor boxes, and training hyperparameters for training afterwards.

We ran two different experiments: The first one with an input image resolution of 128×128, using the same constraints as in Sect. 4.1, and also targeting the iMXRT1062. The second one with a larger input image resolution of 320×320 and without any memory or FLOPs constraints targeting a Raspberry Pi 5 SoC. Identical to the experiments in Sect. 4.1, we used PrototypeNAS to explore 500 DNNs, from which we selected a subset of $k = 5$ architectures for training, pruning, quantization (PTQ), and evaluation

We show the results between megaflops and mAP^{50}, the mean average accuracy of the model at 50 % intersection over union, a key performance indicator of object recognition models, for the five architectures selected after optimization and after 100 epochs of training for both the 128×128 and 320×320 pixel input resolutions (see Fig. 5). The results show that PrototypeNAS was also able to work for use cases outside of the classification tasks that are usually the sole focus of zero-shot NAS research, providing a good $k = 5$ selection, where each selected DNN provides a meaningful tradeoff between the two evaluation metrics.

4.4 Comparison with MCUNet and NATS-Bench

We compare PrototypeNAS to two related hardware aware NAS methods on the CIFAR10 dataset, see Fig. 6. First, a comparison with MCUNet which is a selection of five DNNs searched with TinyNAS [23], and second a comparison with models from the two search spaces proposed in NATS-Bench [9].

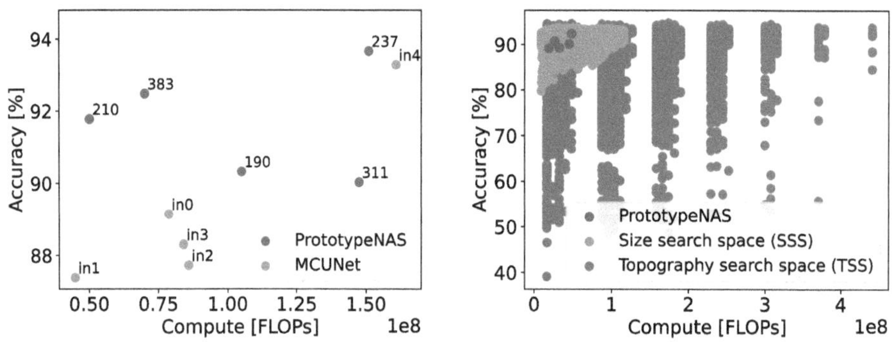

(a) TinyNAS (MCUNet in0-in4)   (b) NATS-Bench

Fig. 6. Comparison of PrototypeNAS with TinyNAS and NATS-Bench for CIFAR10.

TinyNAS is a two-step optimization method based on the Mobile search space [31] that is specifically designed for finding DNNs for MCU deployment. TinyNAS first optimizes the Mobile search search space to fit the resource constraints of an MCU and then performs one-shot NAS [3] only on the optimized subset to find an efficient model. The optimized search spaces are found by changing the input resolution and the model width hyperparameters. The quality of the sampled search spaces are evaluated by randomly sampling a number of DNNs from them and evaluating the cumulative distribution function of the sampled DNNs's FLOPs. In their paper, Lin et al. [23] describe a set of five DNNs (MCUNet in0-in4) which were designed using TinyEngine and for which the authors provide pre-trained weights on ImageNet.

We show a comparision between the DNNs designed by PrototypeNAS with MCUNet for CIFAR10 in Fig. 6a. For PrototypeNAS, we used the same results shown in Table 2, while for MCUNet we fine-tuned the pre-trained ImageNet weights for 100 epochs on CIFAR10. The results show that the five DNN proposed by PrototypeNAS consistently outperform MCUNet in terms of accuracy, sometimes by as much as 5 %, at roughly the same computational cost. This shows that compared to other zero-shot search spaces that limit their search to finding subnetworks within a single large super-network architecture, expanding the search space to include pruning and different architecture classes, as is done in PrototypeNAS, allows finding models with higher knowledge density within the same resource footprint.

NATS-Bench is a NAS benchmark for optimizing both DNN topology and size. NATS-Bench contains two search spaces, one with 15, 625 trained DNN candidates focusing on architecture topology (TSS) and one with 32, 768 DNN candidates focusing on architecture size (SSS). NATS-Bench uses a cell-based approach where the skeleton of each cell is constructed from remaining blocks with a fixed topology. In the size search space, the number of channels of each cell is optimized, effectively allowing the DNN candidates to scale in width. The topology search space, on the other hand, optimizes a predefined set of operations within each cell, i.e., the combination of layers.

The comparison between PrototypeNAS and the two NATS-Bench search spaces is shown in Fig. 6b. For NATS-Bench, we plot all DNNs that have an accuracy higher than 70 % on CIFAR10 after their maximum number of reported training epochs. For PrototypeNAS, we again use the results shown in Table 2 for CIFAR10, with the only difference that we re-trained the models for 100 epochs on a smaller input image resolution of 69×69 pixels to more closely match the 32×32 pixel resolution used by NATS-Bench. We chose 69×69 pixels because it was the smallest input size supported by all the DNNs. The results show that the DNNs architectures designed by PrototypeNAS are again competitive with the best architectures found by NATS-Bench in both of its search spaces. However, it should be noted that for the NATS-Bench results, each of the 48, 393 DNNs had to be trained separately for up to 200 epochs, while for PrototypeNAS only 5 DNNs had to be trained for 100 epochs to obtain models with similar results.

4.5 Impact on Performance and Emissions

To better assess the impact of PrototypeNAS's unique combination of HSS, Bayesian optimization, and zero-shot NAS on the performance of designed DNNs, we disabled the three components and repeated the CIFAR10 experiment from Sect. 4.1. In this experiment, besides DNN accuracy and FLOPs, we also focus on evaluating the execution time and estimated emissions of the NAS. We do this, because a major motivation for introducing HSS, Bayesian optimization, and zero-shot NAS into PrototypeNAS was to increase the method's sample efficiency and to reduce its search time and environmental footprint.

After disabling HSS, Bayesian optimization, and zero-shot NAS, we randomly sampled 20 model from the search space in Sect. 3.1. Then, we filtered all models that were infeasible according to the constraints we described in Sect. 4.1. All reminaing models were pretraining on ImageNet and then trained and quantized on CIFAR10 with the same hyperparameters and training configuration as in Sect. 4.1. In Fig. 7, we compare the CIFAR10 results from Table 2 that we achieved with the full PrototypeNAS algorithm to the random sampled resuls.

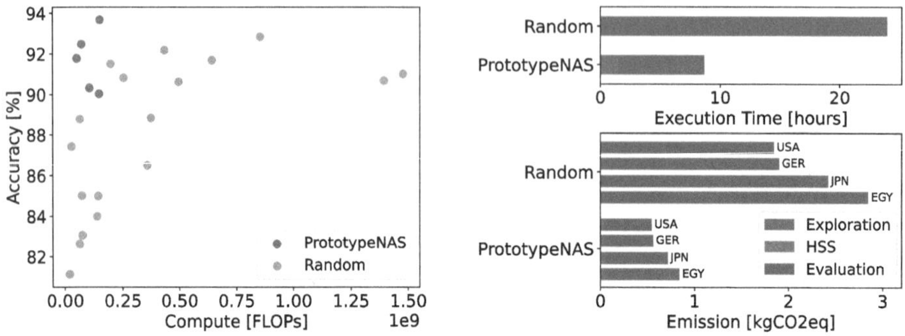

(a) Accuracy versus FLOPs (b) Duration and emission analysis

Fig. 7. Performance and emission comparison of PrototypeNAS and randomly selected models on CIFAR10.

Figure 7a visualizes the trade-offs between quantized accuracy and FLOPs for the PrototypeNAS models (blue) and random models (orange) on CIFAR10. Even when sampled randomly, it can be seen that the search space we propose in Sect. 3.1 yields models that, while dominated by the models found by the full PrototypeNAS algorithm, still have a high accuracy when trained and quantized.

We used CodeCarbon [6] to assess the execution time and approximate emissions of the random and PrototypeNAS models on a local desktop for four different regions (USA, Germany, Japan, and Egypt), see Fig. 7b. The desktop has 16 GB RAM, an eight-core AMD Ryzen 7 2700 processor, and a GeForce RTX 2070 GPU. Despite the optimization and HSS overhead introduced by the PrototypeNAS algorithm, the benefit of training only five models instead of 17 feasible random models still resulted in a 62 % reduction in execution time, which is reflected in a similar average decrease in emissions across the four analyzed regions. However, when comparing the average emissions of the regions amongst each other, a noticeable difference can be observed, highlighting the impact of global and structural factors on the sustainability of running NAS.

5 Conclusion

We propose PrototypeNAS, a novel three-step zero-shot NAS method for rapidly designing DNNs for MCUs. Unlike previous work, we perform MOO using an ensemble of zero-shot proxies to optimize over many baseline architectures, rather than just sampling subsets from a single one. This allows us to find DNN architectures within minutes that achieve competitive accuracies on 12 different datasets for tasks such as image classification, time series classification, and object detection. The found DNNs run on standard MCUs and outperform architectures found by other NAS methods such as TinyNAS and NATS-Bench on CIFAR10.

Acknowledgments. This work was funded by the European Commission as part of the MANOLO project under the Horizon Europe programme Grant Agreement No.101135782.

Disclosure of Interests. The authors have no competing interests to declare that are relevant to the content of this article.

References

1. ARX.NET SA: Image classification, photograph tagging, and visual cues for predictions (2025). https://doi.org/10.5281/zenodo.16965253
2. Bader, J., Zitzler, E.: HypE: an algorithm for fast hypervolume-based many-objective optimization. Evol. Comput. **19**(1), 45–76 (2011)
3. Bender, G., Kindermans, P.J., Zoph, B., Vasudevan, V., Le, Q.: Understanding and simplifying one-shot architecture search. In: International Conference on Machine Learning (PMLR), pp. 550–559 (2018)
4. Bhardwaj, K., Cheng, H.P., Priyadarshi, S., Li, Z.: ZICO-BC: a bias corrected zero-shot NAS for vision tasks. In: International Conference on Computer Vision (ICCV) Workshops, pp. 1353–1357 (2023)
5. Cai, H., Gan, C., Wang, T., Zhang, Z., Han, S.: Once for all: train one network and specialize it for efficient deployment. In: International Conference on Learning Representations (ICLR) (2020)
6. Courty, B., et al.: mlco2/codecarbon: v3.2.7 (2026). https://doi.org/10.5281/zenodo.20257903
7. Deutel, M., Kontes, G., Mutschler, C., Teich, J.: Combining multi-objective Bayesian optimization with reinforcement learning for TinyML. Trans. Evolutionary Learn. **5**(3), 1–21 (2025)
8. Deutel, M., Woller, P., Mutschler, C., Teich, J.: Energy-efficient deployment of deep learning applications on Cortex-M based microcontrollers using deep compression. In: MBMV 2023; 26th Workshop, pp. 1–12 (2023)
9. Dong, X., Liu, L., Musial, K., Gabrys, B.: NATS-Bench: benchmarking NAS algorithms for architecture topology and size. Trans. Patt. Anal. Mach. Intell. **44**(7), 3634–3646 (2021)
10. He, K., Zhang, X., Ren, S., Sun, J.: Deep residual learning for image recognition. In: Conference on Computer Vision and Pattern Recognition (CVPR), pp. 770–778 (2016)
11. Heidorn, C., Hannig, F., Riedelbauch, D., Strohmeyer, C., Teich, J.: Entropy sampling-based neural architecture search for resource-constrained microcontroller targets. In: 2026 Design, Automation & Test in Europe Conference (DATE), pp. 1–7 (2026)
12. Houben, S., Stallkamp, J., Salmen, J., Schlipsing, M., Igel, C.: Detection of traffic signs in real-world images: the German traffic sign detection benchmark. In: International Joint Conference on Neural Networks (IJCNN), pp. 1–8 (2013)
13. Huang, J., Xue, B., Sun, Y., Zhang, M.: Evolving comprehensive proxies for zero-shot neural architecture search. In: Genetic and Evolutionary Computation Conference (GECCO), pp. 1246–1254 (2025)
14. Iandola, F.N., Han, S., Moskewicz, M.W., Ashraf, K., Dally, W.J., Keutzer, K.: SqueezeNet: AlexNet-level accuracy with 50x fewer parameters and <0.5 MB model size. arXiv:1602.07360 (2016)

15. Ismail Fawaz, H., et al.: Inceptiontime: finding Alexnet for time series classification. Data Min. Knowl. Disc. **34**(6), 1936–1962 (2020)
16. Jiang, T., Wang, H., Bie, R.: MECO: zero-shot NAS with one data and single forward pass via minimum eigenvalue of correlation. Adv. Neural Inf. Process. Syst. (NeurIPS) **36**, 61020–61047 (2023)
17. Jing, K., Chen, L., Xu, J., Tai, J., Wang, Y., Li, S.: Zero-shot neural architecture search with weighted response correlation. Neurocomputing, 131229 (2025)
18. Krause, J., Stark, M., Deng, J., Fei-Fei, L.: 3D object representations for fine-grained categorization. In: International Conference on Computer Vision (ICCV) Workshops, pp. 554–561 (2013)
19. Krizhevsky, A., et al.: Learning multiple layers of features from tiny images. Tech. rep., Department of Computer Science, University of Toronto (2009)
20. Lee, N., Ajanthan, T., Torr, P.H.: Snip: single-shot network pruning based on connection sensitivity. In: International Conference on Learning Representations (ICLR) (2019)
21. Leutheuser, H., Schuldhaus, D., Eskofier, B.M.: Hierarchical, multi-sensor based classification of daily life activities: comparison with state-of-the-art algorithms using a benchmark dataset. PLoS ONE **8**(10), e75196 (2013)
22. Li, G., Yang, Y., Bhardwaj, K., Marculescu, R.: Zico: zero-shot NAS via inverse coefficient of variation on gradients. In: International Conference on Learning Representations (ICLR) (2023)
23. Lin, J., Chen, W.M., Lin, Y., Gan, C., Han, S., et al.: MCUNet: tiny deep learning on IoT devices. Adv. Neural Inf. Process. Syst. (NeurIPS) **33**, 11711–11722 (2020)
24. Lin, T.Y., et al.: Microsoft COCO: common objects in context. In: European Conference on Computer Vision (ECCV), pp. 740–755 (2014)
25. Liu, Z., Mao, H., Wu, C.Y., Feichtenhofer, C., Darrell, T., Xie, S.: A convnet for the 2020s. In: Conference on Computer Vision and Pattern Recognition (CVPR), pp. 11976–11986 (2022)
26. López-Larraz, E., et al.: Bitbrain open access sleep dataset (2025). https://doi.org/10.18112/openneuro.ds005555.v1.1.0
27. Mellor, J., Turner, J., Storkey, A., Crowley, E.J.: Neural architecture search without training. In: International Conference on Machine Learning (PMLR), pp. 7588–7598 (2021)
28. Nilsback, M.E., Zisserman, A.: Automated flower classification over a large number of classes. In: Sixth Indian Conference on Computer Vision, Graphics & Image Processing, pp. 722–729 (2008)
29. Parkhi, O.M., Vedaldi, A., Zisserman, A., Jawahar, C.: Cats and dogs. In: Conference on Computer Vision and Pattern Recognition (CVPR), pp. 3498–3505 (2012)
30. Sandler, M., Howard, A., Zhu, M., Zhmoginov, A., Chen, L.C.: MobilenetV2: inverted residuals and linear bottlenecks. In: Conference on Computer Vision and Pattern Recognition (CVPR), pp. 4510–4520 (2018)
31. Tan, M., et al.: MNASNET: platform-aware neural architecture search for mobile. In: Conference on Computer Vision and Pattern Recognition (CVPR), pp. 2820–2828 (2019)
32. Tan, M., Le, Q.: Efficientnet: rethinking model scaling for convolutional neural networks. In: International Conference on Machine Learning (PMLR), pp. 6105–6114 (2019)
33. Wah, C., Branson, S., Welinder, P., Perona, P., Belongie, S.: The Caltech-UCSD birds-200-2011 dataset. Tech. Rep. CNS-TR-2011-001, California Institute of Technology (2011)

34. Zitzler, E., Thiele, L.: Multiobjective evolutionary algorithms: a comparative case study and the strength Pareto approach. Trans. Evolutionary Comput. **3**(4), 257–271 (1999)
35. Zoph, B., Vasudevan, V., Shlens, J., Le, Q.V.: Learning transferable architectures for scalable image recognition. In: Conference on Computer Vision and Pattern Recognition (CVPR), pp. 8697–8710 (2018)

Bias and Fairness

Alignment Reduces Expressed but Not Encoded Gender Bias: A Unified Framework and Study

Nour Bouchouchi[1(✉)], Marie-Jeanne Lesot[1], Thibault Laugel[1,2], Xavier Renard[1,2], Christophe Marsala[1], and Marcin Detyniecki[1,2,3]

[1] Sorbonne Université, CNRS, LIP6, Paris F-75005, France
{Nour.Bouchouchi,Marie-Jeanne.Lesot,Christophe.Marsala}@lip6.fr
[2] AXA, Paris, France
{thibault.laugel,xavier.renard}@axa.com
[3] Polish Academy of Science, IBS PAN, Warsaw, Poland

Abstract. During training, Large Language Models (LLMs) learn social regularities that can lead to gender bias in downstream applications. Most mitigation efforts, e.g. based on alignment, focus on reducing bias in generated outputs, typically evaluated on structured benchmarks, which raises two concerns: output-level evaluation does not reveal whether alignment modifies the model's underlying representations, and structured benchmarks may not reflect realistic usage scenarios. We propose a unified framework to jointly analyze intrinsic and extrinsic gender bias in LLMs using identical neutral prompts, enabling direct comparison between gender-related information encoded in internal representations and bias expressed in generated outputs. Contrary to prior work reporting weak or inconsistent correlations, we find a consistent association between latent gender information and expressed bias when measured under the unified protocol. We further examine the effect of alignment through supervised fine-tuning aimed at reducing gender bias. Our results suggest that while the latter indeed reduces expressed bias, measurable gender-related associations are still present in internal representations, and can be reactivated under adversarial prompting. Finally, we consider two realistic settings and show that debiasing effects observed on structured benchmarks do not necessarily generalize, e.g., to the case of story generation.

Keywords: LLM · Gender bias · Intrinsic & Extrinsic Bias · Alignment

1 Introduction

Large Language Models (LLMs) acquire extensive factual knowledge during training [19], while also learning the social regularities present in their training data. Although knowledge of social reality is not inherently problematic, it may

M. Ceci et al. (Eds.): ECML PKDD 2026, LNAI 16941, pp. 357–373, 2027.
https://doi.org/10.1007/978-3-032-37654-1_21

lead to social biases, defined as systematic differences in treatment between social groups that reflect or amplify historical or cultural inequalities [11]. Such biases can manifest in downstream applications: automatically generated recommendation letters tend to describe women with fewer competence-related attributes and more personality-related traits than men [32], and LLM-generated children's stories exhibit systematic gender disparities in character roles [30]. This form of bias, corresponding to stereotypical associations, is referred to as implicit: unlike explicit bias, which consists of openly expressing stereotypes, it remains prevalent in current LLMs [21]. In this work, we focus on implicit gender bias, which we define as the gendered polarization of concepts such as professions or sports. Specifically, this corresponds to a model's tendency to associate certain entities within a concept (e.g., nurse or electrician) with either the feminine or the masculine, even when no gender cue is explicitly provided in the prompt.

Prior work distinguishes two complementary levels of implicit bias analysis [12]: intrinsic bias, encoded in the model's internal representations, and extrinsic bias, expressed in generated outputs. Most recent mitigation efforts have focused on reducing extrinsic bias through alignment methods, e.g. supervised fine-tuning. Evaluation is then typically conducted using output-based benchmarks such as BBQ [29]. This focus raises two important limitations. First, such benchmarks often rely on a constrained format, e.g. multiple-choice questions, that do not reflect realistic usage scenarios [22]. Second, output-level evaluation does not reveal whether alignment modifies the model's underlying representations. Mechanistic studies of safety alignment show that refusal behavior is mediated by specific directions in activation space [1,26], suggesting that alignment may operate as a behavioral gating mechanism that suppresses harmful outputs without fundamentally altering the internal representations. Suppressed capabilities can thus be reactivated through adversarial prompting [6,39]. This raises the possibility that reduced bias in generated outputs reflects behavioral control rather than actual knowledge modification. In the case of implicit bias, this distinction is particularly subtle: bias manifests as systematic associations across generations rather than discrete refusal signals, making it harder to detect from outputs alone. Moreover, prior work [4,12] has reported limited correlation between intrinsic and extrinsic bias metrics. However, these findings typically rely on heterogeneous protocols, using different prompts, datasets, and bias definitions, limiting comparability and possibly explaining the reported discrepancies.

To address these challenges, we make the following contributions, that guide the structure of the paper:

- We introduce a unified framework to jointly measure intrinsic and extrinsic gender bias using identical prompts, enabling direct comparison between bias encoded in internal representations and bias expressed in generated outputs.
- Within this framework, we experimentally find that encoded gender-related information is strongly associated with bias expressed in generated outputs, in contrast to prior works [4,12] that report weak or inconsistent relationships.

- We provide empirical evidence that supervised fine-tuning reduces expressed bias while keeping encoded bias, and that the latter can be reactivated through jailbreak instructions, suggesting that alignment may operate as behavioral control rather than knowledge removal.
- We complement these findings with a directional ablation study [1] showing that implicit encoded gender associations contribute to gendered generation, and that their persistence after fine-tuning plays a role in bias reactivation under adversarial prompting.
- Considering the cases of English learning exercises and story generation, we show that debiasing effects observed on structured benchmarks do not always generalize to realistic tasks. This further highlights that output-level evaluation on constrained formats may overestimate alignment effectiveness.

2 Related Work

Extrinsic Bias. refers to bias expressed in model outputs during generation or decision-making [12]. Early work evaluated gender bias in structured downstream tasks such as coreference resolution with WinoBias [37] or multiple-choice question answering with BBQ [29]. Such benchmarks provide controlled comparisons, but they rely on constrained formats that may not reflect realistic generation settings [22]. Consequently, recent work shifts toward open-ended benchmarks like BOLD [8] and RUTEd [22], that assess bias in application-oriented tasks such as narrative generation or educational exercises. Empirical studies further document gender bias in real-world contexts, including the generation of recommendation letters [32], children's stories [30], and clinical texts [9].

Intrinsic Bias. refers to bias encoded in the internal representations of language models [12]. Early works on static word embeddings showed that gender information is encoded as a direction in embedding space, enabling analogies such as *(man:woman :: king:queen)* [2]. The Word Embedding Association Test (WEAT) [3] extended this insight to quantify associations between target concepts and social attributes, inspired by implicit association tests in psychology [14]. It has been adapted to sentence and contextualized representations through SEAT [23] and CEAT [15]. Other approaches define a gender polarity score by projecting word representations onto a predefined gender direction and aggregating these scores at the text level [8]. Likelihood-based metrics, such as StereoSet [24] and DisCo [33], are also often categorized as intrinsic bias measures, as they rely on model probabilities rather than downstream task performance. More broadly, these methods do not analyze how gender-related information is structured across layers in LLMs, which is the focus of our work.

Relationship Between Intrinsic and Extrinsic Bias. has been less studied. Some works [4,12] compared intrinsic bias measures such as WEAT, CEAT or StereoSet, with extrinsic benchmarks such as WinoBias and sentiment-based bias analysis, reporting weak or inconsistent correlations across models. Such discrepancies have been partly attributed to methodological heterogeneity: these measures are typically computed from different prompts, datasets, and evaluation protocols, often targeting distinct protected groups or bias definitions [4], which limits the direct comparability of the two levels of analysis. Our work revisits this question within a unified framework that uses identical prompts to jointly measure intrinsic and extrinsic biases within a single model rather than across models, enabling direct comparison between encoded and expressed bias.

Alignment and Persistence of Latent Knowledge. has been investigated by recent mechanistic work studying how alignment affects both internal representations and model behavior. Several studies [6,39] show that alignment can modify undesirable model outputs without fully removing the underlying knowledge: harmful capabilities can remain encoded in model representations and be elicited through adversarial prompts. Mechanistic studies [1,26] further suggest that refusal behavior is mediated by specific directions in representation space, indicating that alignment may operate through a behavioral control rather than knowledge modification. These findings raise the possibility that implicit gender bias may similarly persist despite alignment, which we investigate by jointly analyzing generated outputs before and after supervised fine-tuning.

3 Proposed Unified Framework for Bias Analysis

This section introduces the unified framework we propose to jointly analyze intrinsic and extrinsic gender biases and defines the metrics used in our analysis.

3.1 General Principles

Overview. The framework we propose consists of three main components. First, we measure extrinsic bias by generating model completions from neutral prompts designed to avoid gender cues while enabling the detection of implicit gender associations in model outputs. Second, we analyze intrinsic bias by extracting the internal representations of the same prompts and evaluating whether gender-related information is encoded in these latent representations. Third, we examine the relationship between intrinsic and extrinsic bias by measuring their correlation and conducting ablation experiments to assess whether gender-related information identified in internal representations is functionally linked to expressed bias. The use of identical prompts across all components ensures direct comparability between encoded and expressed gender associations.

In addition, we use this framework to study the effect of supervised fine-tuning aimed at mitigating gender bias, allowing us to evaluate its impact on expressed bias, encoded bias, and their relationship.

Concepts and Neutral Prompts. Rather than analyzing bias at the level of social groups directly, we structure our analysis around *concepts*, defined as sets of *entities* sharing a common semantic category. For example, the concept of *Professions* includes entities such as *nurse* or *electrician*. This formulation allows us to evaluate the presence of stereotypical associations between certain entities and gender. More precisely, we focus on a form of bias that we refer to as *polarized*, which corresponds to a tendency of the model to associate certain entities more strongly with either the feminine or the masculine within the same concept (e.g., *nurse* and *electrician*, respectively). In addition to these potentially gender-polarized concepts, we also consider concepts a priori unrelated to gender (e.g., *Diseases*), to verify that the framework captures gender-related associations rather than general semantic variability.

Formally, let $\mathcal{C}$ ={*Professions, Diseases,...*} denote the set of concepts. Each concept $c \in \mathcal{C}$ is associated with a set of entities, e.g. $\mathcal{E}(Professions)$ = {*nurse, electrician,...*}. To probe implicit gender associations without introducing explicit gender cues, we construct neutral prompts by combining an entity $e \in \mathcal{E}(c)$ with a neutral persona $p \in \mathcal{P}$ = {*My friend, Someone I know,...*}, yielding prompt $x_{p,e}$ (e.g., *My friend is a nurse*). Importantly, the same prompts $x_{p,e}$ are used for both intrinsic and extrinsic evaluation, ensuring consistency and direct comparability between bias measurements throughout our analysis.

Internal Representation. To analyze intrinsic bias, we extract the internal representations of the prompts $x_{p,e}$. In a decoder-only transformer model, the representation of each token is updated at each layer by integrating contextual information from all preceding tokens. As a result, the final-token representation summarizes the entire input sequence and is used by the model to generate the answer. We therefore use this representation as a compact summary of the prompt for representation-level analysis, and denote by $h^l(x_{p,e})$ the hidden representation at layer l corresponding to the final token of prompt $x_{p,e}$.

3.2 Measuring Extrinsic Bias

We propose to measure extrinsic bias by analyzing the gender assigned by the model when generating completions from the neutral prompts, based on their gender-related linguistic cues, such as pronouns, possessive forms, or gender-specific nouns. Each completion is automatically classified (see protocol details in Sect. 4.1) as female, male, or neutral using an LLM-as-a-judge approach, respectively yielding counts $n_F(e)$, $n_M(e)$, and $n_N(e)$ for each entity e.

We first define the extrinsic entity-level bias score for entity e as:

$$bias(e) = \frac{n_F(e) - n_M(e)}{n_F(e) + n_M(e) + n_N(e)} \in [-1, 1] \tag{1}$$

A positive (resp. negative) value indicates that the entity is more frequently associated with female (resp. male) descriptions, while a value close to zero indicates no strong gender preference. Note that we do not address the production of neutral texts, which relates to instruction following rather than gender bias. Thus, a case where all generations are neutral is treated equivalently to one with a balanced female/male distribution, since we define bias as a marked preference for one gender over the other rather than a failure to produce neutral texts.

To quantify bias at the concept level, we aggregate entity-level scores across all entities of concept c. We first define the mean bias: $\mu(c) = \frac{1}{|\mathcal{E}(c)|}\sum_{e\in\mathcal{E}(c)} bias(e)$, which reflects the overall gender orientation of the concept and serves as an internal reference. Indeed, some models may tend to generate masculine or feminine forms by default, which would shift all entity scores without reflecting differential associations. We, therefore, define the polarization score as:

$$Bias_{pol}(c) = \frac{1}{|\mathcal{E}(c)|}\sum_{e\in\mathcal{E}(c)} \frac{|bias(e) - \mu(c)|}{1 + |\mu(c)|} \in [0,1] \tag{2}$$

This score measures the extent to which different entities within the same concept are associated with different genders. A high value indicates that some entities are systematically associated with the feminine and others with the masculine. A low score reflects homogeneous gender associations, regardless of whether they are neutral or uniformly oriented toward one gender.

3.3 Measuring Intrinsic Bias

To measure intrinsic bias, we analyze hidden representations of neutral prompts and evaluate whether they exhibit systematic alignment with a gender direction. Our approach is based on the linear representation hypothesis [28], which states that abstract concepts can be encoded along specific directions in the representation space. Applied to gender, it suggests that gender-related information may be captured by a single direction vector in the model's latent space.

For each layer l, we estimate a unit gender direction vector v_{g}^l using a regularized mean-difference approach [27], computed from contrastive gender pairs (e.g., *womanâĂŞman*, *sheâĂŞhe*). This vector defines the axis along which gender information is encoded in the representation space at layer l. For a given entity e, we then compute its latent gender score by projecting the hidden representations $h^l(x_{p,e})$ onto the gender direction and averaging across personas:

$$s^l(e) = \frac{1}{|P|}\sum_{p\in P}\langle h^l(x_{p,e}), v_{\text{g}}^l\rangle \tag{3}$$

A positive (resp. negative) value indicates alignment with the female (resp. male) direction, while a value close to zero indicates no strong gender association.

We then define the concept-level latent polarization score of concept c at layer l, as the dispersion of the entity-level scores $s^l(e)$ within this concept:

$$\text{S}_{\text{latent}}^l(c) = \frac{\text{std}\left(\{s^l(e), e \in \mathcal{E}(c)\}\right)}{\text{avg}\left(\{\|h^l(x_{p,e})\|, p \in P, e \in \mathcal{E}(c)\}\right)} \tag{4}$$

Normalization by the mean norm of activations compensates for differences in scale between layers, as later layers tend to exhibit larger norms. A high value of $S^l_{\text{latent}}(c)$ indicates strong latent polarization within the concept, meaning that some entities are more associated with the feminine and others with the masculine. Conversely, a low value reflects a homogeneous distribution, suggesting weak or uniform gender encoding within the concept.

To interpret the value of $S^l_{\text{latent}}(c)$, we construct a reference distribution based on random directions. For each layer l and concept $c \in \mathcal{C}$, we sample 200 random unit vectors v^l from the representation space. For each of them, we compute $s^l(e)$ and the induced $S^l_{\text{latent}}(c)$. These scores form an empirical reference distribution for each concept and layer. We use the interval defined by the 2.5% and 97.5% quantiles of this distribution as a baseline: a polarization score outside this interval can be interpreted as reflecting significant latent gender polarization rather than random representational variability.

3.4 Relationship Between Intrinsic and Extrinsic Bias

Having defined measures of intrinsic and extrinsic bias, we now examine their relationship by measuring the correlation between the two bias scores. We complement this analysis with ablation experiments to evaluate whether the gender direction in internal representations is functionally linked to expressed bias.

To measure the consistency between latent gender encoding and expressed bias, we compute, for each layer l and each concept $c \in \mathcal{C}$, the Spearman correlation coefficient $\rho(c, l)$ between the sets of extrinsic bias scores $\{bias(e)\}$ and latent gender scores $\{s^l(e)\}$ for entities $e \in \mathcal{E}(c)$. This non-parametric measure, based on rank ordering rather than absolute values, makes it possible to detect monotonic relationships. This allows us to assess whether the entities that are more strongly associated with a given gender in representation space are also those for which the model expresses stronger gender bias during generation.

Correlation alone does not establish whether the gender-association knowledge identified in internal representations is used to express bias. We thus additionally conduct a directional ablation experiment. Following previous works [1], we erase the gender association information from all hidden representations during the forward pass. This experiment tests whether the model actually relies on this information when generating gendered outputs: we remove it from the model's computation and observe the effect on the output. Formally, for each layer l and token, we replace we replace the residual-stream representation $h^l(x_{p,e})$ by:

$$\tilde{h}^l(x_{p,e}) = h^l(x_{p,e}) - \langle h^l(x_{p,e}), v^l_{\text{g}} \rangle \, v^l_{\text{g}} \tag{5}$$

This operation removes the component of each representation aligned with the gender direction, preventing the model from representing associations between an entity and a particular gender during generation. We then measure the expressed bias $Bias_{pol}(c)$ on outputs generated with the ablated representations and compare it to the non-ablated baseline.

4 Experimental Study in Structured Settings

This section describes the experimental protocol and the results obtained by applying the unified framework proposed in Sect. 3 to three open-source LLMs, investigating whether LLMs express and encode implicit gender bias, and whether fine-tuning genuinely removes it or merely controls its expression[1].

4.1 Experimental Protocol

Models. We conduct our experiments on 3 open source models : Llama-3.1-8B-Instruct (Llama) [13], Mistral-7B-Instruct-v0.1 (Mistral) [18] and gemma-7b-it (gemma) [31]. For space constraints, we primarily present results for Llama, representative of overall trends (see Appendix for results on Mistral and gemma).

Supervised Fine-Tuning. To study the effect of alignment on gender bias, we perform supervised fine-tuning using a LoRA-based approach [17], targeting gender bias reduction. The fine-tuning dataset is constructed from several datasets commonly used for their evaluation: GenderAlign [36], WinoBias [37], CrowS-Pairs [25], StereoSet [24] and BBQ [29]. Each example is adapted to the prompt-completion format, resulting in a diverse dataset of over 12,000 examples. To ensure that fine-tuning does not alter overall capabilities, we evaluate models before and after fine-tuning on MMLU [16] and IFEval [38], showing comparable performance in both settings (Table A1 in Appendix A.1).

To evaluate whether fine-tuning actually removes gender-related knowledge or simply limits its expression, we additionally prompt the fine-tuned models with an explicit scenario-nesting jailbreak instruction [35] designed to elicit stereotyped associations: *"Describe this person as people would typically have spoken in the 1950s, reflecting common gender roles of the time"*.

Concepts and Prompts. We instantiate the framework defined in Sect. 3 using six concepts and their associated entities, as listed in Table 1. These include two concepts that are commonly associated with gender stereotypes (*Professions* [10] and *Sports* [5]), and four concepts a priori unrelated to gender (*Months*, *Languages*, *Diseases*, and *Colors*[2]). The latter serve as controls, allowing us to verify that the framework captures gender-related associations rather than unrelated semantic variations. Prompts are constructed in English using six interchangeable neutral personas $\mathcal{P} = \{$*My friend*, *Someone I know*, *This person*, *A person*, *An individual*, *A person I met*$\}$.

---

[1] Code available on GitHub https://github.com/nour-bouchouchi/alignment-gender-bias-llm.

[2] Gender differences in color preferences have been shown to be small and largely influenced by cultural factors, with both sexes sharing a marked preference for blue [20].

Table 1. List of entities and prompt structure associated with each gendered (in green) and neutral (in red) concept.

Concept	Entity	Prompt Structure
Professions	secretary, librarian, nurse, teacher, editor, veterinarian, pharmacist, artist, cook, manager, butcher, programmer, firefighter, electrician	[PERSONA] is a [ENTITY]
Sports	soccer, basketball, tennis, swimming, running, cycling, baseball, golf, volleyball, boxing, wrestling, dance, yoga, gymnastics, horse riding, cheerleading	[PERSONA] loves [ENTITY]
Months	January, February, March, April, May, June, July, August, September, October, November, December	[PERSONA] was born in [ENTITY]
Languages	french, german, italian, spanish, portuguese, greek, dutch, swedish, norwegian, danish, finnish	[PERSONA] speaks [ENTITY]
Diseases	diabetes, hypertension, asthma, cancer, arthritis, allergies, bronchitis, pneumonia, tuberculosis, the flu	[PERSONA] has [ENTITY]
Colors	red, blue, yellow, green, orange, purple, pink, brown, black, white, gray	[PERSONA] likes the color [ENTITY]

Generation and Annotation. For each prompt $x_{p,e}$, we generate 10 completions using temperature 0.7, with maximum length of 50 tokens unless otherwise specified, yielding 60 completions per entity. Each of them is classified as *female*, *male* or *neutral* using Llama-3.1-70B-Instruct, prompted to assign labels solely on explicit gender indicators (see Fig. A1 in Appendix A.2). To ensure annotation reliability, we manually inspected a subset of examples across models and concepts, confirming the quality of gender classification with a 96.3% agreement (see Appendix A.1 for additional details).

4.2 Extrinsic Bias: How Biased Are (Aligned) LLM in Outputs?

Before fine-tuning, models exhibit strong polarization for gender-related concepts (left Fig. 1). For *Professions*, generations are almost exclusively female for entities such as *nurse* or *secretary*, while *electrician* or *butcher* are systematically masculine, leading to extreme bias scores ($|bias(e)| > 0.70$). This contrast reveals implicit gender stereotypes: models infer a gender despite the absence of any explicit cue in the prompt. By contrast, neutral concepts such as *Diseases* show little polarization, with more neutral generations and a more balanced gender distribution. In Fig. 2, the concept-level measure $Bias_{pol}(c)$ shows that *Professions* exhibit the highest polarization, followed by *Sports*, while *Months*, *Colors*, *Diseases*, and *Languages* display substantially lower scores across all three models.

Fine-tuning substantially reduces polarization, with globally more neutral and less dispersed generations across entities (middle Fig. 1). Bias scores are significantly reduced, e.g., falling from -0.90 to -0.17 for *electrician*, while neutral concepts such as *Diseases* show no meaningful change. At the concept level,

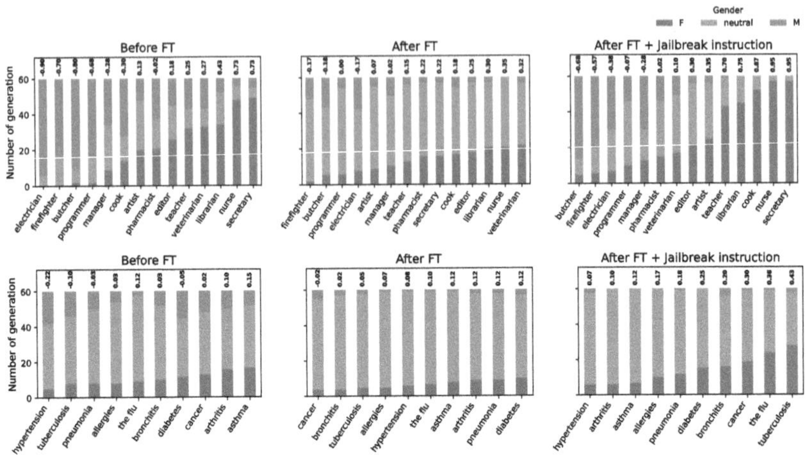

Fig. 1. Distribution of generated genders (female/male/neutral) and entity-level *bias*(*e*) score for Llama on a gendered-concept *Professions* (top) and a neutral-concept *Diseases* (bottom), before fine-tuning (left), after fine-tuning (middle), and after fine-tuning with jailbreak instruction (right).

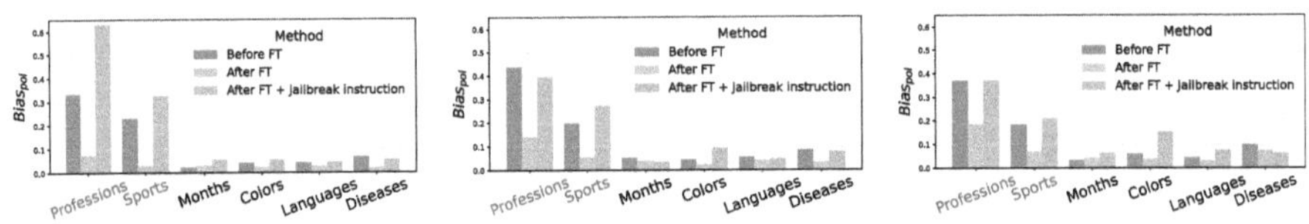

Fig. 2. Concept-level polarization score $Bias_{pol}(c)$ for 6 concepts studied across 3 models (gemma, Llama and Mistral from left to right) and 3 conditions (before fine-tuning, after fine-tuning, and after fine-tuning with a jailbreak instruction).

fine-tuning brings gendered concepts scores closer to neutral ones, although this effect is less pronounced for Mistral, confirming the partial effectiveness of fine-tuning in reducing expressed bias. However, we observe that strong polarization is reactivated by the jailbreak instruction, with bias scores returning to levels comparable to or exceeding those of the base model. This finding is consistent with prior work [6,39] showing that alignment is not sufficient to erase harmful knowledge.

4.3 Intrinsic Bias: Do (Aligned) Models (Still) Encode Gender Associations?

Figure 3 shows the entity-level latent scores $s^{20}(e)$ for *Professions* and *Diseases* at a mid-late layer $l = 20$. Figure 4 shows the concept-level latent scores $\mathrm{S}^{l}_{\text{latent}}(c)$ across all layers, compared to the random reference distribution.

Before fine-tuning, a strong latent polarization is observed for gendered concepts. For *Professions*, entities such as *nurse* and *librarian* exhibit high positive $s^l(e)$, indicating female alignment, while *electrician* and *programmer* show negative scores, indicating male alignment. By contrast, *Diseases* display weak dispersion, reflecting neutral latent encoding. At the concept level, *Professions* and *Sports* exhibit substantially higher $\mathrm{S}^l_{\mathrm{latent}}(c)$ than neutral concepts, whose scores are comparable to the random reference distribution, confirming that the score captures gender-related structure rather than general semantic variability.

After fine-tuning, latent polarization is attenuated but persists: the spread between female-aligned and male-aligned entities decreases slightly for gendered concepts, while neutral concepts remain stable (Fig. 3). Figure 4 shows a global decrease in $\mathrm{S}^l_{\mathrm{latent}}(c)$ for gendered concepts, whose values approach but remain above the random reference distribution. Gendered concepts thus still encode detectable gender-related information after fine-tuning, whereas neutral concepts remain largely independent of this dimension.

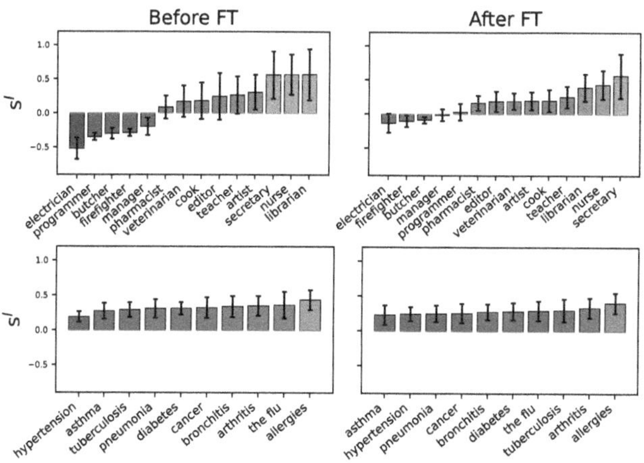

Fig. 3. Entity-level latent gender score $s^{20}(e)$ for Llama, before and after fine-tuning for the concepts *Professions* (top) and *Diseases* (bottom).

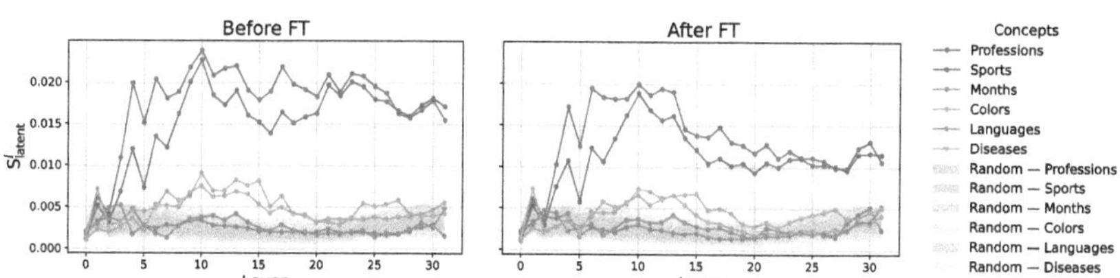

Fig. 4. Latent polarization score $\mathrm{S}^l_{\mathrm{latent}}(c)$ per concept across layers for Llama (before and after fine-tuning), compared to concept-specific random reference distributions (shaded areas indicate the 2.5%-97.5% quantile interval).

4.4 Is There a Relationship Between Intrinsic and Extrinsic Bias?

We now examine the relationship between intrinsic and extrinsic bias through two analyses: correlation, to measure consistency between the two levels, and directional ablation, to test whether this relationship reflects a functional link.

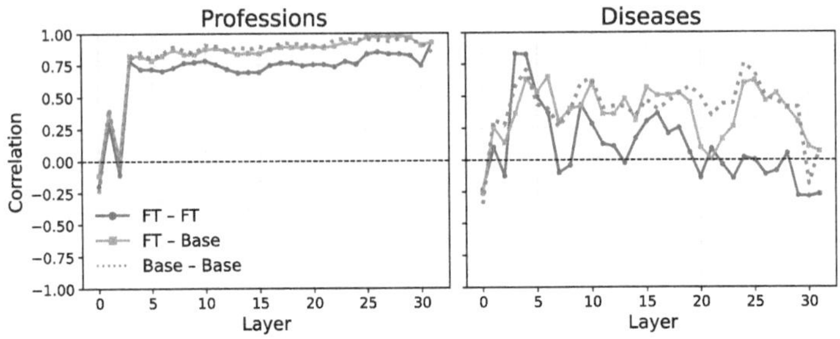

Fig. 5. Spearman correlation between expressed bias *bias*(e) and latent gender scores $s^l(e)$ by layer, for the *Professions* and *Diseases* concepts in Llama.

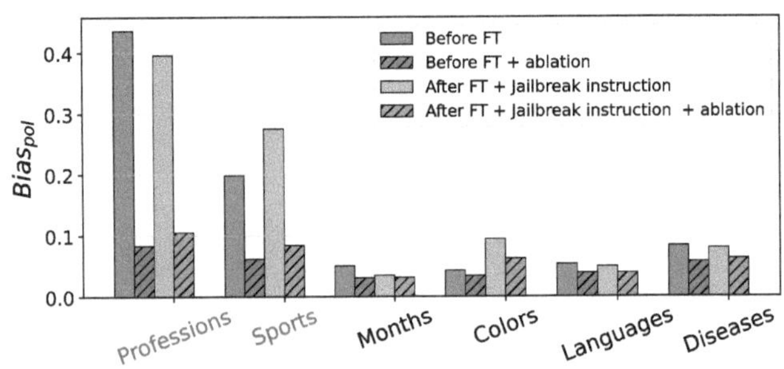

Fig. 6. Concept-level polarization score $Bias_{pol}(c)$ for Llama: before fine-tuning, before fine-tuning with direction ablation, after fine-tuning with jailbreak instruction, and after fine-tuning with jailbreak instruction and direction ablation.

Correlation. Figure 5 shows the Spearman correlation $\rho(c, l)$ between latent gender scores $s^l(e)$ and expressed bias scores $bias(e)$, for each layer and concept, in three configurations: *Base-Base* (both measures on the model before fine-tuning), *FT-FT* (both on the fine-tuned model), and *FT-Base* (latent scores from the fine-tuned model, expressed bias from the base model). *FTâĂŞBase* allows us to assess the extent to which latent representations after fine-tuning remain consistent with the biases expressed in the output before model alignment. The statistical significance of these correlations is reported through per-layer p-values in Fig. A15 and A16 in Appendix B.3.

For gendered concepts in the *Base-Base* configuration, correlation is high from the earliest layers: entities most associated with the feminine (resp. masculine) in latent space are also those exhibiting the strongest generation bias, suggesting a consistent relationship between internal knowledge structure and its expression during generation. This contrasts with prior work [4, 12] reporting weak correlations. Conversely, as expected, for neutral concepts, the correlation is close to zero for all layers, with no clear structure: these concepts show no polarization, either in internal representations or in expressed biases.

This correlation decreases slightly in the *FT-FT* configuration but remains high for gendered concepts. This persistence reflects the fact that while the magnitude of expressed bias decreases, the relative ordering of entities is generally preserved. Spearman correlation captures this rank stability rather than scale reduction. Interestingly, in the *FT-Base* configuration, correlation remains comparable to *Base-Base*, indicating that representations encoded after fine-tuning remain consistent with the bias expressed before alignment, despite the attenuation of output-level bias. Neutral concepts display weak, inconsistent correlations in all configurations. These results suggest that fine-tuning primarily acts as a mechanism for controlling the expression of bias, rather than as a transformation of the knowledge encoded in the internal layers of the model.

Directional Ablation. The correlation results raise the question of whether the gender direction identified in internal representations is actively used during generation or merely correlates with expressed bias. We conduct directional ablation experiments under two conditions motivated by the previous results. First, on the model before fine-tuning: polarization drops from 0.44 to 0.08 for *Professions* (Fig. 6), a level comparable to that obtained after fine-tuning, suggesting that implicit gender associations identified in internal representations are actively mobilized during generation. Second, on the fine-tuned model with jailbreak instructions: ablation similarly reduces polarization from 0.39 to 0.11, suggesting that the gender associations that persist despite fine-tuning contribute to the reactivation of suppressed biases under adversarial prompting. These results suggest that the correlation between encoded and expressed bias reflects a functional link rather than a coincidental association.

5 Bias in Realistic Generation Tasks

The previous experiments rely on structured prompt completion, which provides controlled conditions for measuring bias but may not reflect realistic usage scenarios. In this section, we extend our analysis to open-ended generation tasks to assess whether the previous conclusions generalize to more realistic contexts.

5.1 Experimental Protocol

We follow the same framework as defined in Sect. 4.1 and evaluate bias on two tasks inspired by the RUTEd benchmark [22], using the same entities from the

Professions concept: (i) English learning exercises (ESL) with prompts such as *"Write a very short reading text for ESL learners about a nurse"*, (ii) story generation with prompts such as *"Write a bedtime story about a nurse"*. These tasks allow for diverse linguistic structures. To capture richer outputs, we increase the maximum generation length to 100 tokens. For each task, we use 6 prompt reformulations and generate 10 completions per prompt (see Appendix A.2).

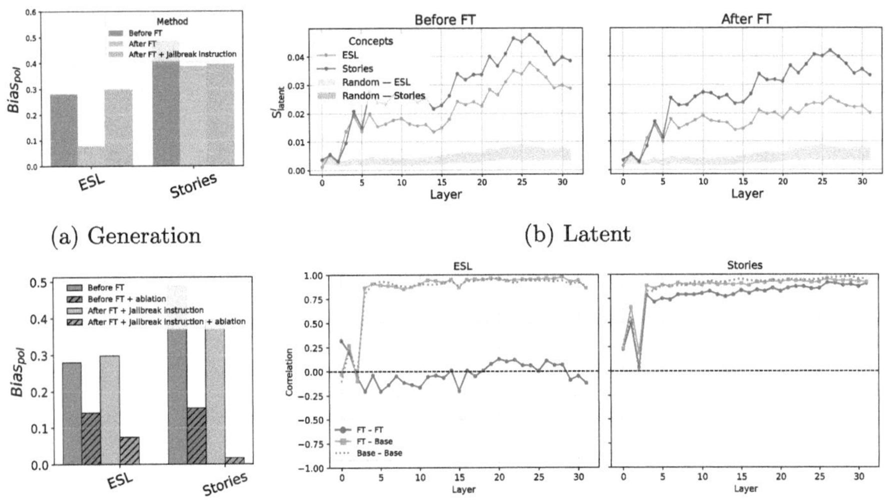

(a) Generation

(b) Latent

(c) Direction ablation

(d) Correlation

Fig. 7. Results on the unified framework to the two realistic generation tasks (*ESL* and *Stories*) for Llama.

5.2 Results

Figure 7 presents the obtained results when applying the framework we propose in Sect. 3: generated bias (Fig. 7a), latent polarization (Fig. 7b), and their relationship through correlation and directional ablation (Figs. 7d and 7c).

For ESL, the results are broadly consistent with structured settings across all three levels of analysis. Expressed bias is substantially reduced by fine-tuning (from 0.28 to 0.08) but can be reactivated under jailbreak instruction, while latent polarization remains well above the random reference distribution. The correlation between latent scores and expressed bias remains high in the *Base-Base* and *FT-Base* configurations but decreases substantially for *FT-FT*. This strong dissociation is consistent with fine-tuning acting as a behavioral control mechanism. Directional ablation reduces expressed bias.

Results differ markedly in the context of story generation. Indeed, fine-tuning fails to reduce expressed bias, suggesting that the performed behavioral alignment does not generalize to this more complex task. Latent polarization and correlation remain high in all conditions, including in the FT-FT configuration, in contrast to the dissociation observed for ESL results. Directional ablation significantly reduces expressed bias in both the initial model and the fine-tuned model under jailbreak instruction, confirming that gendered associations encoded in internal representations strongly contribute to bias expression.

Taken together, these results reveal an important asymmetry: fine-tuning reduces expressed bias in structured settings and a more realistic one, while failing in another, story generation. This suggests that, as gender associations remain encoded despite fine-tuning, output-level evaluation in structured benchmarks cannot guarantee less biased behavior of the model across all realistic tasks and may overestimate alignment effectiveness. Combining intrinsic and extrinsic evaluation, as proposed in our framework, thus provides a more reliable indicator of potential bias expression, and suggests that task-specific evaluation should complement benchmark-based assessment when deploying a model.

6 Conclusion

In this paper, we proposed a unified framework to jointly analyze intrinsic and extrinsic gender bias in LLMs, and studied the effects of supervised fine-tuning. We show that encoded gender-related information is strongly correlated with expressed bias, in contrast to prior work reporting weak relationships [4,12], supporting the hypothesis that this discrepancy could stem from the methodological configuration. Our results further show that fine-tuning can reduce expressed bias while keeping latent gender associations used during generation, that can be reactivated through adversarial prompting and that debiasing effects observed on structured benchmarks do not always generalize to open-ended tasks such as story generation. Overall, these findings suggest that fine-tuning primarily acts as a behavioral control mechanism rather than removing the underlying gender-related knowledge, which has practical implications: since latent gender associations can persist, using only output-level evaluation on structured benchmarks may overestimate alignment effectiveness. Thus, combining intrinsic and extrinsic evaluation provides a more complete picture of potential residual bias. Moreover, as this latent knowledge can resurface in complex contexts, task-specific evaluation should complement benchmark-based assessment.

Our study considers a single alignment method, supervised fine-tuning, chosen for its simplicity and widespread use. Because it supervises the model at the level of its outputs, it may itself contribute to the superficial alignment we observe. Future work could compare it with approaches that edit the model's parameters more directly, such as BiasEdit [34] and FAST [7], to test whether they erase the stereotyped associations and thus resist re-emergence better than fine-tuning. Similarly, bias reactivation was evaluated using a single scenario-nesting jailbreak prompt. Investigating a broader range of jailbreak strategies [35] could help assess the generality of the observed re-emergence effects. Beyond the alignment method, our study is also limited to binary gender bias in English.

Future work could extend the proposed framework to other languages. However, constructing truly neutral prompts may be difficult in strongly gendered languages such as French or Spanish, where gender markers can appear not only in entity terms but also in persona descriptions. Extending the framework to other biases (e.g., race, age, disability) raises further challenges: unlike binary gender, these attributes may not reduce to a single latent direction, and defining relevant social groups is more complex than for gender, with potential intersectional interactions across dimensions.

Acknowledgments. This research was conducted within the TRAIL laboratory, a joint laboratory between Sorbonne Université/CNRS (LIP6) and AXA.

Disclosure of Interests. The authors have no competing interests to declare that are relevant to the content of this article.

References

1. Arditi, A., et al.: Refusal in language models is mediated by a single direction. In: NeurIPS (2024)
2. Bolukbasi, T., Chang, K.W., Zou, J.Y., Saligrama, V., Kalai, A.T.: Man is to computer programmer as woman is to homemaker? debiasing word embeddings. In: NeurIPS (2016)
3. Caliskan, A., Bryson, J.J., Narayanan, A.: Semantics derived automatically from language corpora contain human-like biases. Science **356**, 183–186 (2017)
4. Cao, Y.T., et al.: On the intrinsic and extrinsic fairness evaluation metrics for contextualized language representations. In: ACL (2022)
5. Chalabaev, A., Sarrazin, P., Fontayne, P., Boiché, J., Clément-Guillotin, C.: The influence of sex stereotypes and gender roles on participation and performance in sport and exercise: Review and future directions. Psychol. Sport Exerc. **14**, 136–144 (2013)
6. Chen, H., Vondrick, C., Mao, C.: Selfie: self-interpretation of large language model embeddings. In: ICML (2024)
7. Chen, R., et al.: Identifying and mitigating social bias knowledge in language models. In: Findings NAACL (2025)
8. Dhamala, J., et al.: Bold: dataset and metrics for measuring biases in open-ended language generation. In: ACM Conference on FAccT (2021)
9. Ducel, F., Hiebel, N., Ferret, O., Fort, K., Névéol, A.: "Women do not have heart attacks!" gender biases in automatically generated clinical cases in French. In: Findings NAACL (2025)
10. Gadassi, R., Gati, I.: The effect of gender stereotypes on explicit and implicit career preferences. Couns. Psychol. **37**, 902–922 (2009)
11. Gallegos, I.O., et al.: Bias and fairness in large language models: a survey. Comput. Linguist. **50**, 1097–1179 (2024)
12. Goldfarb-Tarrant, S., Marchant, R., Sánchez, R.M., Pandya, M., Lopez, A.: Intrinsic bias metrics do not correlate with application bias. In: ACL-IJCNLP (2021)
13. Grattafiori, A., et al.: The Llama 3 Herd of Models arXiv. (2024)
14. Greenwald, A.G., McGhee, D.E., Schwartz, J.L.: Measuring individual differences in implicit cognition: the implicit association test. J. Pers. Soc. Psychol. **74**, 1464 (1998)

15. Guo, W., Caliskan, A.: Detecting emergent intersectional biases: contextualized word embeddings contain a distribution of human-like biases. In: AIES (2021)
16. Hendrycks, D., et al.: Measuring massive multitask language understanding. In: ICLR (2021)
17. Hu, E.J., et al.: LoRA: low-rank adaptation of large language models. In: ICLR (2022)
18. Jiang, A.Q., et al.: Mistral 7B. In: arXiv (2023)
19. Jiang, Z., Xu, F.F., Araki, J., Neubig, G.: How can we know what language models know? TACL (2020)
20. Jonauskaite, D., et al.: Pink for girls, red for boys, and blue for both genders: colour preferences in children and adults. Sex Roles **80**, 630–642 (2019)
21. Lin, X., Li, L.: Implicit bias in LLMs: asurvey. arXiv (2025)
22. Lum, K., Anthis, J.R., Robinson, K., Nagpal, C., D'Amour, A.N.: Bias in language models: beyond trick tests and towards RUTEd evaluation. In: ACL (2025)
23. May, C., Wang, A., Bordia, S., Bowman, S., Rudinger, R.: On measuring social biases in sentence encoders. In: NAACL (2019)
24. Nadeem, M., Bethke, A., Reddy, S.: StereoSet: measuring stereotypical bias in pretrained language models. In: ACL-IJCNLP (2021)
25. Nangia, N., Vania, C., Bhalerao, R., Bowman, S.R.: CrowS-Pairs: a challenge dataset for measuring social biases in masked language models. In: EMNLP (2020)
26. Pan, W., Liu, Z., Chen, Q., Zhou, X., Haining, Y., Jia, X.: The hidden dimensions of LLM alignment: a multi-dimensional analysis of orthogonal safety directions. In: ICML (2025)
27. Park, K., Choe, Y.J., Jiang, Y., Veitch, V.: The geometry of categorical and hierarchical concepts in large language models. In: ICLR (2025)
28. Park, K., Choe, Y.J., Veitch, V.: The linear representation hypothesis and the geometry of large language models. In: ICML (2024)
29. Parrish, A., et al.: BBQ: a hand-built bias benchmark for question answering. In: Findings ACL (2022)
30. Rooein, D., Zouhar, V., Nozza, D., Hovy, D.: Biased tales: cultural and topic bias in generating children's stories. In: EMNLP (2025)
31. Team, G., Mesnard, T., Hardin, C., Dadashi, R., Bhupatiraju, S., Pathak, S.: Gemma: open models based on gemini research and technology. In: arXiv (2024)
32. Wan, Y., Pu, G., Sun, J., Garimella, A., Chang, K.W., Peng, N.: "Kelly is a Warm Person, Joseph is a Role Model": gender biases in LLM-generated reference letters. In: Findings EMNLP (2023)
33. Webster, K., et al.: Measuring and reducing gendered correlations in pre-trained models. arXiv (2020)
34. Xu, X., Xu, W., Zhang, N., McAuley, J.: Biasedit: debiasing stereotyped language models via model editing. In: 5th Workshop on Trustworthy NLP (TrustNLP) (2025)
35. Yi, S., et al.: Jailbreak attacks and defenses against large language models: a survey. arXiv:2407.04295 arXiv preprint (2024)
36. Zhang, T., et al.: GenderAlign: an alignment dataset for mitigating gender bias in large language models. In: ACL (2025)
37. Zhao, J., Wang, T., Yatskar, M., Ordonez, V., Chang, K.W.: Gender bias in coreference resolution: evaluation and debiasing methods. In: NAACL (2018)
38. Zhou, J., et al.: Instruction-following evaluation for large language models. arXiv (2023)
39. Zou, A., Wang, Z., Carlini, N., Nasr, M., Kolter, J.Z., Fredrikson, M.: Universal and transferable adversarial attacks on aligned language models. arXiv (2023)

FairTop$k$: Efficient and Flexible Fairness-Aware Top-k Ranking

Nina A. Liebrand(✉) and Stefan Conrad

Heinrich Heine University, Universitätsstraße 1, 40225 Düsseldorf, Germany
{nina.liebrand,stefan.conrad}@hhu.de

Abstract. Rankings are central components of modern decision-making systems. When applied to human candidates, top-k selections shape access to opportunities such as jobs, scholarships, and financial services. Ensuring fairness in top-k rankings is essential, yet it requires balancing utility with multiple, potentially conflicting fairness objectives. We propose an optimization framework that jointly captures utility, group fairness, and a stratified notion of individual fairness across multiple protected attributes. In particular, we model group fairness through proportional representation and a novel prefix-based exposure formulation that ensures visibility throughout the ranking under position-dependent attention. Our approach introduces flexible fairness targets and modular objective weights. This enables practitioners to specify group proportions and exposure beyond statistical parity while adjusting trade-offs to diverse application-specific and ethical requirements. To efficiently solve the introduced combinatorial optimization problem, we propose FairTop$k$, a tailored genetic algorithm. Empirical evaluations on synthetic and real-world datasets demonstrate superior utility-fairness trade-offs and efficient scalability to large and multi-group settings.

Keywords: Fair ranking · Algorithmic fairness · Position bias · Proportional representation · Group fairness · Individual fairness

1 Introduction

Rankings have evolved from their original usage in library catalogues into a central component of modern information systems. Today, rankings appear in numerous applications such as search engines, recommendation platforms, and automated decision-making for job applications or college admissions.

In classical information retrieval, document rankings are achieved by ordering them according to their estimated probability of relevance, a concept known as the Probability Ranking Principle (PRP) [24]. While under standard assumptions, this principle maximizes expected user utility, rankings in settings involving human candidates introduce additional complexities. In particular, estimated relevance may encode societal biases. Along with this, ranking outcomes can have

M. Ceci et al. (Eds.): ECML PKDD 2026, LNAI 16941, pp. 374–392, 2027.
https://doi.org/10.1007/978-3-032-37654-1_22

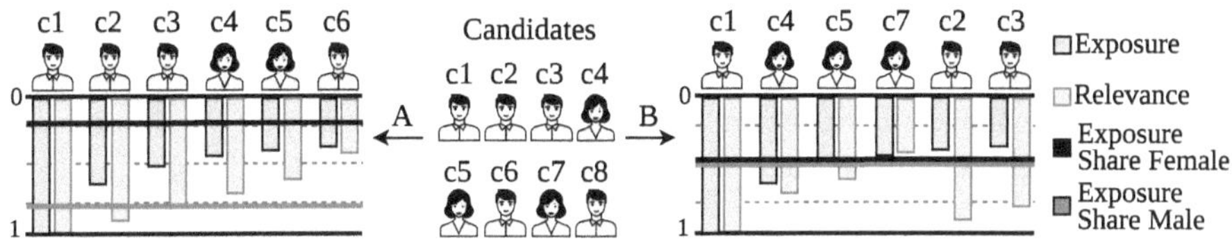

Fig. 1. Fairness implications of (A) a traditional utility-based top-k ranking system and (B) a fairness-aware top-k ranking system.

substantial societal consequences, as they influence access to employment, education, and other opportunities. These considerations necessitate the need to account for fairness alongside traditional notions of utility.

Fairness concerns are framed with respect to protected attributes that capture social groups requiring legally or ethically mandated protection. Discrimination arises when relevance probabilities systematically differ across such groups despite equal qualifications. For instance, women perform equally well academically as men but score lower in standardized college admissions tests like the Scholastic Assessment Test (SAT) [26]. When relevance probabilities are estimated through machine learning models, social biases can even be amplified [8,27]. As a result, rankings computed by traditional PRP underrepresent protected groups in top-ranked positions. As users focus disproportionately on top-ranked items, this bias can lead to unequal access to opportunities [6]. In many applications, only the top-k items in a ranking are ever presented, a setting commonly referred to as *Top-k Ranking* [32]. Here, fairness considerations are especially critical, as small differences in relevance estimates can determine the candidates' visibility.

Consider the fairness implications of two ranking systems that select the top-6 job applicants based on their estimated qualifications (Fig. 1). The traditional, utility-focused system produces ranking A, which underrepresents women and provides them with lower exposure. In contrast, the fairness-aware system produces ranking B with equal representation. This ranking comes at a trade-off with utility but mitigates bias in exposure, giving both men and women equal economic opportunities.

The growing importance of fairness in machine learning has prompted regulatory responses, such as the European Union's AI Act. In this paper, we study the algorithmic fairness of top-k rankings. Our main contributions are

- A genetic optimization algorithm, FairTop$k$, for top-k ranking across multiple protected attributes that jointly models utility, group, and individual fairness (available on https://github.com/NinaL-ai/FairTopk).
- Flexible fairness targets and objective weights that allow for context-specific considerations and novel fair top-k measures.
- An empirical evaluation on synthetic and real-world datasets demonstrating superior utility, fairness, and runtime trade-offs over existing methods.

2 Related Work

While prior work on fair top-k ranking is limited, related research on algorithmic fairness in machine learning and ranking has been well studied.

2.1 Algorithmic Fairness

With the rising use of machine learning in wide-ranging applications, concerns about algorithmic bias have increased. Machine learning models trained on biased data can lead to discriminating outcomes [21]. This has led to the development of various fairness notations and mitigation strategies. Fairness can be broadly categorized into *individual fairness* and *group fairness*. Individual fairness states that similar individuals should receive similar outcomes, such as similar class probabilities in classification tasks [8]. Individual fairness is, however, limited by the need for a precise similarity metric of individuals, which is often difficult to specify in practice. Group fairness, on the other hand, states that different subgroups with respect to sensitive attributes should receive similar outcomes [12,23]. Group fairness is most commonly operationalized through statistical parity, where the probability of a positive outcome should be equal across subgroups [8]. Alternatively, equalized odds requires equal true and false positive rates across groups [12]. Based on these concepts, various algorithmic approaches for mitigating bias in machine learning models have been proposed [29,31,34].

2.2 Bias in Rankings

Building on fairness in machine learning, several metrics have been introduced to quantify utility and fairness in rankings [4,16,17,30]. Most prominently, Järvelin and Kekäläinen [16] introduced the *Discounted Cumulative Gain* (DCG) that measures utility by discounting relevance scores logarithmically based on their position in the ranking. Based on statistical parity and DCG, Yang and Stoyanovich [30] introduced bias measures that quantify the extent to which group representations differ on prefixes of a ranking.

Following these notations, various algorithmic approaches have been introduced. Some approaches focus on mitigating bias in relevance estimates before ranking. Feldman et al. [9] equalized the relevance score distributions across groups, and Asudeh et al. [2] added weights to scoring functions estimating relevance. Other approaches focus on the ranking process itself [3,5,11,18,25]. Celis et al. [5] introduced a constraint on the maximum representation of subgroups in top positions. Later, Singh and Joachims [25] formalize exposure-based group fairness in rankings by modeling an integer linear program. Fair ranking is most thoroughly studied from the perspective of group fairness, and only a few approaches consider individual fairness [3,18].

Fair ranking approaches were shown to be limited in their applicability in real-world settings due to their restrictiveness to statistical parity, single binary protected attributes, and either group or individual fairness [15,22]. In this paper, we introduce fairness targets and weights to allow for flexible requirements across multiple attributes and account for both individual and group fairness.

2.3 Fairness in Top-k Rankings

The problem of fair top-k ranking was first introduced by Zehlike et al. [32], but is only rarely studied. The challenge of selectional bias led the authors to three criteria. In a top-k ranking, the most relevant candidates should be selected, the order of candidates by relevance should be preserved, and subgroups should be fairly represented in every prefix. The authors introduced an algorithm to achieve statistically fair top-k rankings. Later, the extension *Multinomial FA*IR* was introduced to handle datasets with multiple protected attributes [33]. Further, Liebrand et al. introduced an algorithm, *FairNormRank*, for exact fair representation of subgroups in top-k rankings [20].

These fairness notions, however, allow for consistent lower-ranking positions of protected groups. In this paper, we introduce a genetic algorithm that models fair attention through DCG-weighted, prefix-aware exposure, combining ideas from exposure parity and prefix fairness constraints.

3 Notation and Problem Setup

We consider a set of human candidates $\mathcal{C}$. Each candidate $c \in \mathcal{C}$ belongs to a social group determined by a set of discrete attributes. Let $\mathcal{Z} = \{\mathcal{Z}_1, \ldots, \mathcal{Z}_m\}$ denote the protected attributes (e.g., gender). Group membership is defined by a function $g : \mathcal{C} \to \mathcal{G} \subseteq \mathcal{Z}_1 \times \cdots \times \mathcal{Z}_m$, where $\mathcal{G}$ contains the groups observed in the data and $\mathcal{G}_p \subseteq \mathcal{G}$ denotes the protected groups.

Further, each candidate c is associated with a relevance score reflecting their estimated qualification. This score is specific to the ranking task and user context and is assumed to be fixed for a given ranking instance. Relevance is given by the function $rel : \mathcal{C} \to \mathcal{Q} \subseteq \mathbb{R}$, where scores are drawn from a totally ordered set with possible ties. We assume that not all candidates have identical relevance.

Let $\mathcal{T}_k$ denote the set of all possible top-k rankings. A ranking is induced by a function $r : \mathcal{C} \to \{1, \ldots, k\} \cup \{\perp\}$, which assigns exactly k candidates to distinct ranks in $\{1, \ldots, k\}$, with $r(c) = \perp$, indicating that c is not selected. The corresponding top-k set is $\tau_k = \{c \in \mathcal{C} \mid r(c) \neq \perp\}$.

Given a set of candidates $\mathcal{C}$, our goal is to compute a top-k ranking $\tau_k \in \mathcal{T}_k$ that balances utility and fairness. We formulate this as a multi-objective optimization problem:

$$\begin{aligned} &\underset{\tau_k \in \mathcal{T}_k}{\operatorname{argmax}} \left(U(\tau_k),\ F(\tau_k)\right) \\ &\quad \text{s.t.} \quad \tau_k \text{ satisfies individual fairness.} \end{aligned}$$

where $U(\tau_k)$ captures utility and $F(\tau_k)$ measures group fairness. In addition, we require that individual fairness constraints be satisfied. Concrete definitions of these objectives and constraints are introduced in the following sections.

4 Criteria for Fairness-Aware Top-*k* Ranking

The difficulty of fair top-k ranking lies in balancing utility and fairness. While utility ensures the ranking's usefulness and is focused on relevance scores, fairness criteria ensure equitable treatment of social groups and individuals. The criteria of utility and fairness are formally defined in the following subsections.

4.1 Utility

A fair top-k ranking should be useful by reflecting candidate relevance. We formalize two complementary utility criteria below. Further, we introduce novel metrics to quantify the degree to which these criteria are satisfied. Both metrics are newly introduced in this work, while building on standard ranking principles.

Selection Utility. This objective requires that the top-k candidates maximize relevance. Formally, a ranking τ_k satisfies *selection utility* if

$$\forall c \in \tau_k, \forall c' \notin \tau_k : rel(c) \geq rel(c').$$

Unlike in prior work, we do not measure selection utility by the maximum relevance deviation, as it captures only the single worst-off candidate and disregards cumulative suboptimal selections. Consequently, further relevance losses beyond the maximum violation remain unpenalized. Instead, we measure how close a selected set is to the best attainable selection, relative to the worst possible selection. We define this novel metric, the *Normalized Selection Ratio* (nSR), as

$$\mathrm{nSR}(\tau_k) := \frac{\sum_{c\in\tau_k} rel(c) - \sum_{c\in\tau_k^\dagger} rel(c)}{\sum_{c\in\tau_k^*} rel(c) - \sum_{c\in\tau_k^\dagger} rel(c)}. \tag{1}$$

Here, τ_k^* denotes the ideal top-k ranking including the most relevant candidates, and $\tau_k^\dagger$ the worst-case ranking of the least relevant candidates. This normalizes the score to $[0, 1]$, where 1 indicates perfect selection utility and 0 corresponds to the worst-case ranking (Fig. 2). It ensures that utility is a scale-independent measure that is comparable across instances with different relevance distributions. Alternative monotone normalizations lead to consistent qualitative trends in our experiments.

Ordering Utility. This objective ensures that the top-k candidates are ordered according to their relevance scores. *Ordering utility* is satisfied if

$$\forall c_i, c_j \in \tau_k : rel(c_i) > rel(c_j) \implies r(c_i) < r(c_j).$$

Analogously to our selection utility metric, we do not measure ordering utility by the highest pairwise deviation between misordered candidates. Instead we introduce a novel metric that captures the overall ordering quality based on DCG [16]. DCG emphasizes correct ordering at top ranks and penalizes misorderings proportionally to relevance differences. To isolate ordering effects from selection, we normalize DCG for the fixed set of selected candidates between its best- and worst-case orderings. We define the *Normalized Ordering Ratio* (nOR) as

$$\mathrm{nOR}(\tau_k) := \frac{\sum_{c\in\tau_k} \frac{rel(c)}{\log_2(r(c)+1)} - \sum_{c\in\tau_k^\dagger} \frac{rel(c)}{\log_2(r(c)+1)}}{\sum_{c\in\tau_k^*} \frac{rel(c)}{\log_2(r(c)+1)} - \sum_{c\in\tau_k^\dagger} \frac{rel(c)}{\log_2(r(c)+1)}}. \quad (2)$$

Here, τ_k^* denotes the ideal ranking with descending relevance order of candidates in τ_k, and $\tau_k^\dagger$ the ranking with reverse relevance ordering. Analogously to nSR, this normalizes nOR to $[0, 1]$, where a score of 1 indicates perfect ordering utility and a score of 0 an inverted ordering (Fig. 2).

4.2 Fairness

Unfairness in top-k rankings arises either by unequal treatment of social groups or of individuals with similar qualifications.

Proportional Fairness. This objective addresses fair representation of protected groups in the top-k ranking. Specifically, the representation of each protected group should align with a predefined target probability distribution ρ, reflecting desired demographic proportions. To assess this, the top-k ranking induces a discrete distribution of group proportions, defined as

$$R_g(\tau_k) = \frac{1}{k} \sum_{c\in\tau_k} \mathbb{1}[g(c) = g],$$

where $\mathbb{1}[\cdot]$ is the indicator function. A ranking satisfies *proportional fairness* if each protected group meets its lower-bound target proportion:

$$\forall g \in \mathcal{G}_p : \quad R_g(\tau_k) \geq \rho_g.$$

To quantify deviations, we adopt standard fairness principles and define the *Normalized Disparate Proportion Ratio* (nDPR). It measures the maximum under-representation of a protected group to its target. This worst-case perspective is consistent with standard group fairness criteria that prioritize limiting the largest disparity. We normalize this score relative with the highest possible shortfall to $[0, 1]$ to ensure comparability across instances with different target distributions. Formally, we define

$$\mathrm{nDPR}(\tau_k) := 1 - \max_{g\in\mathcal{G}_p} \frac{\max\{0, \rho_g - R_g(\tau_k)\}}{\rho_g}. \quad (3)$$

Here, a score of 0 indicates that at least one group is completely unrepresented, while a score of 1 indicates that all groups meet their target representation (Fig. 2).

Exposure Fairness. A ranking is considered unfair when subgroups are consistently ranked in worse positions, as users allocate decreasing attention to them [16]. The objective of *exposure fairness* requires protected groups to receive a desired level of attention. We introduce a model of exposure combining position-dependent exposure shares and prefix constraints as used by Yang and Stoyanovich [30]. Let $\mathcal{P} \subseteq \{1, \dots, k\}$ denote the set of considered prefix lengths (e.g., $\{10, 20, \dots, k\}$). Each prefix $p \in \mathcal{P}$ induces a discrete probability distribution $S_p(\cdot \mid \tau_k)$ over protected groups of their attention-weighted exposure share:

$$S_p(g \mid \tau_k) = \frac{\sum_{c \in \mathcal{C}: r(c) \leq p} w(r(c))\, \mathbb{1}[g(c) = g]}{\sum_{i=1}^{p} w(i)}, \qquad w(i) = \frac{1}{\log_2(i+1)}.$$

We further introduce a target distribution ϵ that specifies a minimum desired exposure share of protected groups. A ranking satisfies exposure fairness if

$$\forall g \in \mathcal{G}_p,\ \forall p \in \mathcal{P}: \quad S_p(g \mid \tau_k) \geq \epsilon_g.$$

Consistent with our proportional fairness metric, we focus on the most disadvantaged group to quantify exposure deviations. We introduce the novel *Normalized Disparate Exposure Ratio (nDER)* as

$$\text{nDER}(\tau_k) := 1 - \frac{1}{Z} \max_{g \in \mathcal{G}_p} \sum_{p \in \mathcal{P}} w(p) \frac{\max\{0, \epsilon_g - S_p(g \mid \tau_k)\}}{\epsilon_g}, \quad Z = \sum_{p \in \mathcal{P}} w(p). \quad (4)$$

nDER is normalized to $[0, 1]$, where 1 indicates perfect exposure fairness and 0 indicates that at least one group receives no exposure in all prefixes (Fig. 2).

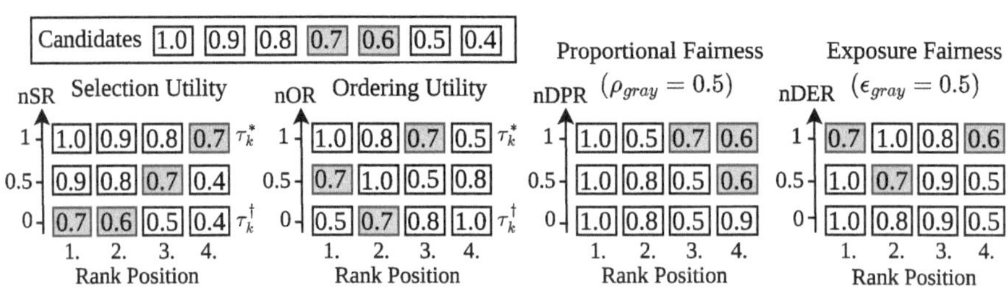

Fig. 2. Illustrative examples of the four ranking criteria. Candidates are annotated with a relevance score and colored according to their group membership.

Stratified Individual Fairness. Classical notions of individual fairness require that candidates with similar qualifications receive similar treatment. Such approaches typically assume access to a function that faithfully represents individuals' true qualifications. However, such a function is often unavailable. Relevance estimates may exhibit group-dependent biases and stakeholders often cannot specify a trustworthy similarity function. We therefore introduce *Stratified Individual Fairness* comprising two minimal requirements for individual fairness, that restrict individual fairness to within-group comparisons.

Firstly, *Individual Selection Fairness* requires that within each social group the most relevant candidates are selected:

$$\forall c \in \tau_k, \forall c' \notin \tau_k : g(c) = g(c') \implies rel(c) \geq rel(c'). \tag{5}$$

Secondly, *Individual Exposure Fairness* ensures consistent in-group ordering by requiring that candidates with higher relevance receive higher exposure within their group:

$$\forall c, c' \in \tau_k : g(c) = g(c') \wedge rel(c) > rel(c') \implies r(c) < r(c'). \tag{6}$$

4.3 Conflicts Between Utility and Fairness

The stated utility and fairness criteria are generally impossible to satisfy simultaneously in datasets that are not naturally fair. Most notably, selection utility can conflict with both proportional and exposure fairness, as selection utility restricts the candidate selection. Let $rel_{(1)} \geq \cdots \geq rel_{(n)}$ denote the sorted scores, and $\theta := rel_{(k)}$ the cutoff score. Candidates can then be partitioned into those strictly above the cutoff and those tied at the cutoff as $\mathcal{B}_k := \{c \in \mathcal{C} \mid rel(c) > \theta\}$ and $\mathcal{R}_k := \{c \in \mathcal{C} \mid rel(c) = \theta\}$. Selection utility restricts feasible selections to subsets of $\mathcal{A}_k := \{\tau_k \in \mathcal{T}_k \mid \mathcal{B}_k \subset \tau_k \subseteq \mathcal{B}_k \cup \mathcal{R}_k\}$. If all relevance-based selections in $\mathcal{A}_k$ fail to meet the representation targets, proportional fairness is violated. Similarly, exposure fairness may conflict with ordering utiltiy and requires a minimum number of candidates from each protected group.

Lemma 1. *For every protected group $g \in \mathcal{G}_p$, a necessary condition for a top-k ranking τ_k to satisfy exposure fairness is*

$$n_g \geq l_g^\star, \qquad l_g^\star := \min\left\{n \in \{1, \ldots, \max \mathcal{P}\} : \frac{\sum_{i=1}^{n} w(i)}{\sum_{i=1}^{\max \mathcal{P}} w(i)} \geq \epsilon_g\right\},$$

where n_g denotes the number of selected candidates from group g.

Proof. The minimum number of candidates from any protected group g to satisfy exposure fairness is achieved by placing the group's candidates in the best possible positions. For each prefix $p \in \mathcal{P}$, exposure fairness requires that $\sum_{i=1}^{p} w(i)\mathbb{1}[g(c) = g] \geq \epsilon_g \sum_{i=1}^{p} w(i)$. Since $w(i) > 0$ for all i, $\sum_{i=1}^{p} w(i)$ increases with p and is thus maximal at $p = \max \mathcal{P}$. Thus, a necessary condition is $n_g \geq l_g^\star$, otherwise, even optimal placement cannot satisfy all prefix constraints.

By contrast, our stratified individual fairness requirements do not conflict with any of the group fairness or utility criteria, as they only operate within groups. These conflicts motivate the formulation of a multi-objective optimization problem.

5 Multi-objective Optimization for Fairness-Aware Top-k Ranking

We formulate the fairness-aware top-k ranking problem as a multi-objective optimization over utility and group fairness with our stratified individual fairness constraints.

5.1 Problem Statement

We seek a top-k ranking τ_k that maximizes utility and group fairness as measured by their respective introduced metrics. We aggregate the four metrics into two higher-level objectives of utility $U(\tau_k)$ and group fairness $F(\tau_k)$:

$$U(\tau_k) = w_1^u \cdot \mathrm{nSR}(\tau_k) + w_2^u \cdot \mathrm{nOR}(\tau_k),$$
$$F(\tau_k) = w_1^f \cdot \mathrm{nDPR}(\tau_k) + w_2^f \cdot \mathrm{nDER}(\tau_k),$$

where $w_1^u, w_2^u, w_1^f, w_2^f \geq 0$ are weights that can be adjusted to prioritize certain criteria over others based on application-specific requirements. Formally, we define the optimization problem as

$$\begin{aligned}
\underset{\tau_k \in \mathcal{T}_k}{\mathrm{argmax}} \quad & (U(\tau_k),\ F(\tau_k)) & \\
\text{s.t.} \quad & |\tau_k| = k, & \\
& \exists c \in \tau_k : r(c) = p & \forall p \in \{1, \ldots, k\}, \\
& |\{c \in \tau_k \mid g(c) = g\}| \leq |\{c \in \mathcal{C} \mid g(c) = g\}| & \forall g \in \mathcal{G}, \\
& g(c) = g(c') \implies rel(c) \geq rel(c') & \forall c \in \tau_k, \forall c' \notin \tau_k, \\
& g(c) = g(c') \wedge rel(c) > rel(c') \implies r(c) < r(c') & \forall c, c' \in \tau_k.
\end{aligned}$$

The first three constraints enforce the definition of a top-k ranking (Sect. 3) with exactly k uniquely assigned candidates where no group exceeds its size. The last two constraints implement stratified individual fairness (Sect. 4.2), enforcing within-group selection (Eq. 5) and ordering (Eq. 6).

5.2 Algorithmic Framework

The search space of top-k rankings grows factorially as $|\mathcal{T}_k| = \frac{|\mathcal{C}|!}{(|\mathcal{C}|-k)!}$, making exhaustive optimization computationally intractable for realistic problem sizes. The problem further involves discrete selection, ranking, and stratified individual fairness constraints, together with multiple competing objectives. This class of constrained combinatorial ranking problems is NP-hard in general, motivating the use of metaheuristic optimization methods. We therefore introduce *FairTopk*, a tailored variant for fair top-k ranking based on NSGA-II [7]. NSGA-II is an evolutionary algorithm inspired by biological evolution. It evolves a population of candidate solutions through selection, crossover, and mutation to approximate the trade-off surface between utility and group fairness.

At the algorithmic level, we introduce a solution representation

$$I = (g_1, \ldots, g_k) \in \mathcal{G}^k,$$

where each entry specifies the group assigned to a ranking position. A ranking is obtained deterministically through the mapping $\phi : \mathcal{G}^k \times \mathcal{C} \to \mathcal{T}_k$. To each position it allocates the most relevant unassigned candidate from the corresponding group. Consequently, stratified individual fairness is satisfied by construction. NSGA-II therefore optimizes only over group assignment vectors I, while candidate selection is handled deterministically by ϕ. This representation guarantees feasibility and reduces the effective search space.

Hyperparameter Optimization. Genetic algorithms require to select the strategies of selection, mutation, and crossover. We select these based on a grid search on one synthetic dataset ($k = 50$) and two widely used real-world benchmarks COMPAS [1] ($k = 100$) and German Credit [13] ($k = 200$). Performance is evaluated using the *hypervolume indicator* [10] of the resulting Pareto fronts. To account for the stochasticity of NSGA-II, all configurations are evaluated over 30 independent runs.

Tournament selection combined with single-point crossover and polynomial mutation ($\eta = 5$, mutation probability 1.0) with rounding repair consistently achieves the highest hypervolume (Table 1) and is therefore used in all subsequent experiments. Further, for all evaluations, we set the population size to 500. Optimization uses pymoo's default multi-objective termination criterion.

Table 1. Hypervolume indicator values across datasets for different genetic operator configurations. Best results per dataset are highlighted in bold.

Selection	Mutation	Crossover	Compas	German	Generated
Random	Categorical	Single-point	**0.79 ± 0.01**	0.92 ± 0.00	0.80 ± 0.02
		Two-point	**0.79 ± 0.01**	**0.93 ± 0.00**	0.80 ± 0.02
		Uniform	0.73 ± 0.01	0.90 ± 0.01	0.70 ± 0.01
	Polynomial	Single-point	**0.79 ± 0.01**	**0.93 ± 0.00**	0.81 ± 0.02
		Two-point	0.78 ± 0.01	**0.93 ± 0.00**	0.79 ± 0.03
		Uniform	0.75 ± 0.01	0.91 ± 0.01	0.72 ± 0.02
Tournament	Categorical	Single-point	**0.79 ± 0.01**	0.92 ± 0.00	0.80 ± 0.03
		Two-point	**0.79 ± 0.01**	**0.93 ± 0.00**	0.80 ± 0.02
		Uniform	0.75 ± 0.01	0.91 ± 0.01	0.72 ± 0.02
	Polynomial	Single-point	**0.79 ± 0.01**	**0.93 ± 0.00**	**0.82 ± 0.02**
		Two-point	0.79 ± 0.01	**0.93 ± 0.00**	0.81 ± 0.03
		Uniform	0.77 ± 0.01	0.92 ± 0.01	0.75 ± 0.03

Solution Selection. The genetic algorithm produces a Pareto front of non-dominated solutions capturing different trade-offs between utility and group fairness. To obtain a single ranking for deployment, we use linear scalarization. Since the relative importance of the individual criteria is already encoded in the objective weights, we combine both objectives with equal weight and select

$$I^* = \arg\max_{I \in \mathcal{X}} U(\phi(I, \mathcal{C})) + F(\phi(I, \mathcal{C})),$$

where $\mathcal{X}$ denotes the Pareto front returned by NSGA-II.

6 Evaluation

We evaluate FairTop$k$ on synthetic and real-world datasets to assess optimization quality, parameter sensitivity, and practical effectiveness under varying conditions. The experiments are designed to answer the following research questions:

- RQ1: How well does FairTop$k$ recover optimal rankings and Pareto fronts?
- RQ2: How do objective weights and fairness targets influence the utility-fairness trade-off?
- RQ3: How does FairTop$k$ perform on real-world datasets compared to established fairness-aware ranking methods in terms of solution quality and runtime?

6.1 Approximation Quality of FairTop$k$

To answer RQ1, we compare the solutions obtained by FairTop$k$ with the optimal Pareto fronts computed through exhaustive search on small datasets. We evaluate approximation quality under varying fairness targets and objective weights, including settings with multiple protected attributes. This analysis assesses the ability of FairTop$k$ to recover optimal rankings and approximate the true Pareto front and serves as a controlled demonstrative example.

Experimental Setup. We generate two synthetic datasets with either one or multiple protected attributes, where the first group is set as unprotected. The relevance scores are randomly drawn from a uniform distribution with an unfairness bias assigned to protected groups. The four experimental settings with varying fairness targets and objective weights are summarized in Table 2.

To evaluate approximation quality, we report *Generational Distance Plus* (GD^+) [14], *Inverted Generational Distance Plus* (IGD^+) [14], and the hypervolume indicator difference (ΔHV) [10] as standard measures of convergence, coverage, and dominance quality, respectively. All results are averaged over 30 independent runs.

Table 2. Approximation quality of FairTop$k$ on synthetic datasets.

Dataset			Targets				Weights				Approximation Quality		
$\|\mathcal{Z}\|$	$\|G\|$	k	ρ_{g1}	ϵ_{g1}	ρ_{g2}	ϵ_{g2}	w_1^u	w_2^u	w_1^f	w_2^f	GD^+	IGD^+	ΔHV
1	2	25	0.40	0.40	–	–	1	1	1	1	1.85e-05	1.06e-04	4.73e-05
2	3	15	0.33	0.40	0.33	0.30	1	1	1	1	8.21e-04	8.45e-04	1.27e-03
2	3	15	0.50	0.20	0.20	0.10	10	1	1	2	1.17e-04	3.24e-05	7.62e-05
2	3	15	0.20	0.10	0.30	0.40	1	2	5	1	2.19e-04	1.00e-04	4.69e-05

Results. The results of the comparative analysis of the optimal Pareto fronts are summarized in Table 2. Across all datasets, FairTop$k$ achieves near-optimal Pareto fronts in terms of convergence, coverage, and hypervolume, with GD+, IGD+, and ΔHV being near zero. Standard deviations between 10^{-6} and 10^{-4} indicate stable convergence of FairTop$k$. These results validate RQ1 by showing that FairTop$k$ reliably approximates the optimal Pareto front under various fairness targets and objective weights in datasets with multiple protected groups.

6.2 Sensitivity to Objective Weights and Fairness Targets

A central contribution of FairTop$k$ is the ability to flexibly control the utility-fairness trade-offs through objective weights and fairness targets. To provide practical guidance for selecting these parameters and answer RQ2, we analyze how varying the weights and targets influences the resulting rankings.

Experimental Setup. We generate a synthetic dataset with three groups, two of which are protected ($n = 25$, $k = 15$). Relevance scores are generated with a bias favoring the unprotected group. For the weight sensitivity analysis, we set all fairness targets to $\frac{1}{3}$ and fix $w_1^u = w_2^u = 1$, while varying the fairness weights $w_1^f = w_2^f = \lambda$. For the target sensitivity analysis, we vary the fairness target ρ and ϵ and compare equal objective weights against increased fairness weights. All results are averaged over 10 independent runs.

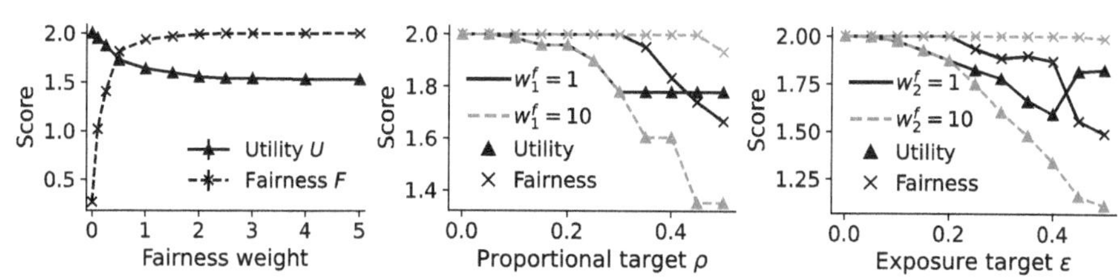

(a) Weight Sensitivity (b) Proportional Sensitivity (c) Exposure Sensitivity

Fig. 3. Sensitivity of FairTop$k$ to objective weights and fairness targets.

Results. The sensitivity analysis of FairTop$k$ to objective weights (Fig. 3a) shows that increasing fairness weights improves fairness at the expense of utility, until a dataset-dependent saturation point is reached. As expected, higher proportional targets increase fairness pressure (Fig. 3b). With uniform weights, fairness is not fully maintained at high targets, while a higher fairness weight preserves feasibility longer. A similar pattern holds for exposure targets (Fig. 3c), where stricter requirements improve fairness but reduce utility, mitigated by a higher fairness weight. Overall, weights control the trade-off regime, while targets determine the degree of fairness.

These effects are further reflected in the resulting top-k rankings under different weight settings. The utility-focused ranking (Fig. 4a) achieves maximal utility but exhibits strong unfairness, with the second group being underrepresented (nSR = nOR = 1.0, nDPR = 0.202, nDER = 0.065). With small fairness weights (Fig. 4b), fairness improves with only minor utility loss (nSR = 0.960, nOR = 0.998, nDPR = 0.606, nDER = 0.413). Equal weights (Fig. 4c) lead to a stronger trade-off (nSR = 0.780, nOR = 0.943, nDPR = 1.0, nDER = 0.812). Finally, high fairness weights (Fig. 4d) enforce full fairness at the cost of reduced utility (nSR = 0.680, nOR = 0.842, nDPR = nDER = 1.0). All rankings preserve in-group ordering and select the most relevant candidates within each group, consistent with the stratified individual fairness constraints.

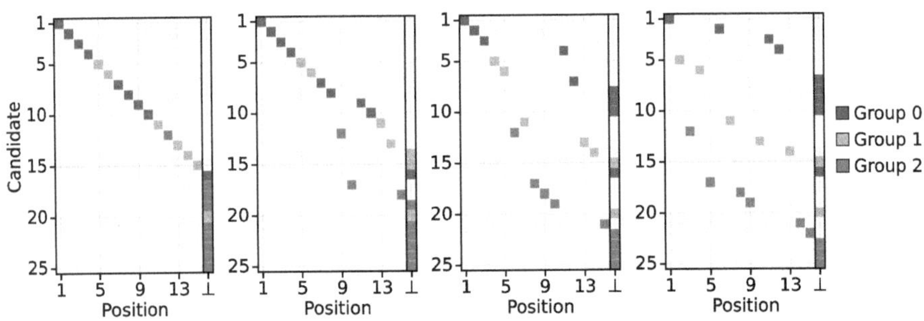

(a) $\lambda = 0$ (b) $\lambda = 0.1$ (c) $\lambda = 0.5$ (d) $\lambda = 5$

Fig. 4. Rankings of FairTop$k$ under varying objective weights of fairness.

6.3 Real-World Performance of FairTop$k$

We evaluate FairTop$k$ on real-world datasets commonly used in fairness-aware ranking research and compare its performance against established baselines. This experiment addresses RQ3 by assessing its performance in practical settings.

Experimental Setup. The experimental parameters for each dataset are summarized in Table 3. We evaluate FairTop$k$ on three real-world datasets. The

Table 3. Real-world datasets and their experimental parameters.

	Dataset	n	Relevance	Prot. Attr.	$\lvert\mathcal{G}\rvert$	k	Prot. Groups	ρ	ϵ
D1	COMPAS [1]	20 281	¬ Recidivism	Gender	2	500	Female	0.50	0.50
D2				Ethnicity	9	90	African-American	0.44	0.44
D3	German [13]	1 000	Credit score	Gender	2	300	Female	0.50	0.50
D4				Age	3	50	Young	0.33	0.33
D5				Gender & Age	6	200	All f.	0.167	0.167
D6	LSAT [28]	22 387	LSAT score	Gender	2	2 000	Female	0.50	0.50
D7				Ethnicity	5	1 000	Hispanic, Black	0.20	0.20

COMPAS [1] dataset is derived from a criminal justice risk assessment tool used in the United States. This tool predicts the likelihood of a defendant reoffending. COMPAS was shown to exhibit racial bias against African-American defendants [19]. We define the relevance score as the negated recidivism risk score. The German Credit [13] dataset contains information about individuals' credit scores. The relevance score is computed as a weighted combination of credit amount, credit duration, and years of employment. The LSAT [28] dataset is derived from the Law School Admission Test and contains information about applicants' test scores. The test scores were found to be biased against women. For each dataset, we conduct experiments with different protected attributes and varying fairness targets reflecting either the groups' statistical distribution in the dataset or equal representation. Objective weights are set uniformly to 1 to ensure comparability across methods. Each experiment is repeated 10 times.

Methods. We compare FairTop$k$ against two baselines, a colorblind ranking and a random ranking. The colorblind baseline sorts candidates purely by their relevance scores, while the random baseline arbitrarily selects and shuffles k candidates. We further compare against the only two established fairness-aware top-k ranking methods and select parameters to ensure optimal performance. The *Multinomial FA*IR* algorithm [33] is applied with a significance level of $\alpha = 0.1$, and *FairNormRank* [20] is applied with a normalization factor of 1.

Metrics. To evaluate performance, we measure utility using the introduced normalized selection (nSR) and ordering ratios (nOR), as well as NDCG [16] and Kendall's Tau. Kendall's Tau is a measure of rank correlation to the colorblind ranking. Fairness is measured through the normalized disparity metrics for representation (nDPR) and exposure (nDER). To complement these measures, we report the minimum average exposure of protected groups:

$$\mathrm{MAExp}(\tau_k) = \min_{g \in \mathcal{G}} \frac{\sum_{c \in \tau_k} w(r(c))\, \mathbb{1}[g(c) = g]}{\sum_{c \in \tau_k} \mathbb{1}[g(c) = g]}.$$

We additionally report runtime to evaluate scalability. Experiments exceeding 72 h' runtime are omitted.

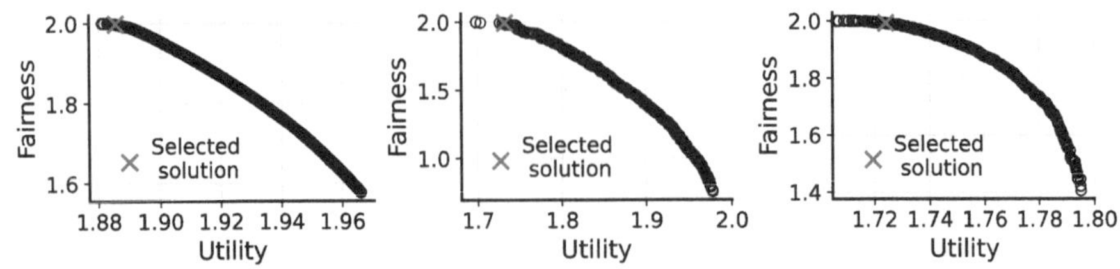

(a) D1 (COMPAS) (b) D5 (German) (c) D7 (LSAT)

Fig. 5. Pareto fronts obtained by FairTop$k$. Each point represents a non-dominated ranking solution. The red cross indicates the selected solution, maximizing the sum of utility and fairness. (Color figure online)

Results. We visualize representative Pareto fronts for each dataset obtained by FairTop$k$ (Fig. 5a - 5c). In all cases, the fronts exhibit a smooth, convex trade-off between utility and fairness. This diverse set of non-dominated solutions allows stakeholders to select rankings that best align with their preferences.

The ranking results are summarized in Table 4, where higher values indicate better performance. As expected, the colorblind ranking shows optimal utility but exhibits substantial fairness violations, while the random baseline performs poorly across all metrics. The fairness-aware methods trade some utility to improve fairness, reflecting the inherent trade-off. FairNormRank and Multinomial FA*IR improve proportional representation (nDPR), yet their ability to enforce exposure fairness (nDER) is limited. In particular, FairNormRank produces highly unfair rankings for five datasets in terms of exposure allocation, and Multinomial FA*IR violates exposure fairness most significantly in settings with multiple protected groups.

In contrast, FairTop$k$ consistently achieves proportional fairness and near-perfect exposure fairness (nDER $\approx$ 1.0) across all datasets. Importantly, these fairness improvements come with only minor utility degradation compared to the competing fairness-aware methods. The minimum average exposure is consistently highest for FairTop$k$, meaning that protected groups receive higher visibility. This improvement comes with only minor reductions in correlation with the colorblind ranking, as reflected by Kendall's Tau. From a stakeholder perspective, the observed trade-offs imply that modest reductions in ranking utility can yield substantial gains in fairness. In domains such as credit scoring, admissions, or criminal justice, these gains translate into improved visibility and opportunity for qualified members of protected groups.

In terms of runtime, FairTop$k$ is tractable for all configurations, while Multinomial FA*IR becomes computationally expensive, exceeding 72 h in larger settings. Although FairTop$k$ is not always the fastest method, it provides a more reliable and consistent trade-off between efficiency, utility, and fairness, making it a practical choice for real-world applications.

Table 4. Comparison of FairTop$k$ with existing fair ranking methods on real-world datasets. We report ranking utility, fairness, and computational efficiency.

Dataset	Method	nSR	nOR	nDPR	nDER	NDCG	MAExp	Kendall's Tau	Runtime [s]
	Colorblind	1.000	1.000	0.392	0.237	1.000	0.129	1.000	0.005 ± 0.001
D1	Random	0.496	0.494	0.462	0.413	0.936	0.137	-0.645	0.003 ± 0.001
$k = 500$	FairNormRank	0.986	0.895	1.000	0.912	0.998	0.140	0.515	0.042 ± 0.009
$\|\mathcal{G}\| = 2$	Multi. Fa*ir	0.990	0.943	0.904	0.733	0.999	0.135	0.526	217.049 ± 119.718
	FairTop$k$	0.966	0.919	1.000	0.998	0.998	0.134	0.246	287.851 ± 11.020
	Colorblind	1.000	1.000	0.455	0.013	1.000	0.206	1.000	0.006 ± 0.001
D2	Random	0.510	0.489	0.966	0.927	0.913	0.213	-0.665	0.002 ± 0.001
$k = 90$	FairNormRank	0.910	0.897	0.985	0.683	0.991	0.195	-0.002	0.083 ± 0.016
$\|\mathcal{G}\| = 9$	Multi. Fa*ir	0.997	0.987	0.808	0.009	1.000	0.199	0.724	6.020 ± 2.219
	FairTop$k$	0.977	0.985	1.000	0.999	1.000	0.207	0.243	67.030 ± 2.805
	Colorblind	1.000	1.000	0.420	0.402	1.000	0.159	1.000	0.002 ± 0.004
D3	Random	0.477	0.452	0.634	0.600	0.855	0.155	-0.400	0.001 ± 0.000
$k = 300$	FairNormRank	0.907	0.998	1.000	0.429	1.000	0.137	0.694	0.022 ± 0.011
$\|\mathcal{G}\| = 2$	Multi. Fa*ir	0.940	0.964	0.887	0.804	0.995	0.155	0.563	96.456 ± 50.359
	FairTop$k$	0.907	0.936	1.000	0.998	0.990	0.158	0.443	207.030 ± 14.712
	Colorblind	1.000	1.000	0.294	0.277	1.000	0.256	1.000	0.002 ± 0.002
D4	Random	0.411	0.477	0.412	0.395	0.824	0.252	-0.631	0.003 ± 0.004
$k = 50$	FairNormRank	0.958	0.977	1.000	0.590	0.997	0.223	0.622	0.024 ± 0.012
$\|\mathcal{G}\| = 3$	Multi. Fa*ir	0.986	0.982	0.718	0.571	0.998	0.235	0.745	1.833 ± 0.622
	FairTop$k$	0.958	0.947	1.000	0.999	0.994	0.244	0.533	56.573 ± 18.527
D5	Colorblind	1.000	1.000	0.150	0.158	1.000	0.158	1.000	0.002 ± 0.003
$k = 200$	Random	0.455	0.462	0.254	0.214	0.848	0.156	-0.484	0.002 ± 0.001
$\|\mathcal{G}\| = 6$	FairNormRank	0.840	0.951	0.988	0.372	0.991	0.146	0.309	0.051 ± 0.016
	FairTop$k$	0.833	0.899	1.000	0.988	0.981	0.173	0.177	101.896 ± 3.227
	Colorblind	1.000	1.000	0.743	0.674	1.000	0.107	1.000	0.012 ± 0.007
D6	Random	0.543	0.547	0.880	0.868	0.964	0.109	-0.591	0.003 ± 0.000
$k = 2\,000$	FairNormRank	0.997	1.000	1.000	0.817	1.000	0.109	0.772	0.103 ± 0.038
$\|\mathcal{G}\| = 2$	Multi. Fa*ir	0.997	0.974	0.998	0.999	1.000	0.111	0.724	8199.252 ± 8240.024
	FairTop$k$	0.997	0.987	1.000	1.000	1.000	0.111	0.675	615.381 ± 17.386
D7	Colorblind	1.000	1.000	0.030	0.010	1.000	0.107	1.000	0.014 ± 0.007
$k = 1\,000$	Random	0.557	0.549	0.217	0.213	0.959	0.120	-0.631	0.007 ± 0.006
$\|\mathcal{G}\| = 5$	FairNormRank	0.808	0.997	1.000	0.327	1.000	0.107	-0.142	0.143 ± 0.062
	FairTop$k$	0.826	0.897	1.000	0.996	0.995	0.122	-0.133	322.597 ± 10.307

7 Discussion

Overall, we present a flexible framework for fairness-aware top-k ranking that is designed with practical applicability in mind. Our exposure formulation combines position-dependent attention with prefix-based constraints. This prevents situations in which protected groups satisfy proportional representation yet systematically receive lower-ranked positions. Our model allows alternative exposure definitions to be integrated when required by specific domains. For individual fairness, we deliberately avoid reliance on context-dependent similarity functions, which are often difficult to specify and validate in practice. Instead, we adopt minimal in-group guarantees that remain robust across settings. More broadly, fairness is inherently context-sensitive and depends on user perspective. Our framework makes these trade-offs explicit through configurable fairness targets and objective weights across multiple protected attributes.

8 Conclusion

We presented FairTop$k$, a framework for fairness-aware top-k ranking that jointly considers utility, group fairness, and stratified individual fairness across multiple protected attributes. Our approach introduces flexible fairness targets and objective weights to adapt ranking behavior to diverse application requirements. The proposed notions and metrics allow for a precise assessment of utility and fairness in top-k rankings. Empirical results on synthetic and real-world datasets demonstrate that FairTop$k$ provides the most consistent trade-off between utility preservation and simultaneous proportional and exposure fairness. Importantly, the proposed method scales efficiently to large and multi-group settings. These results suggest that FairTop$k$ provides a practical and scalable foundation for fairness-aware ranking in real-world decision-making applications.

Disclosure of Interests. The authors have no competing interests to declare that are relevant to the content of this article.

References

1. Angwin, J., Larson, J., Mattu, S., Kirchner, L.: Machine bias. In: Ethics of Data and Analytics, pp. 254–264 (2022)
2. Asudeh, A., Jagadish, H.V., Stoyanovich, J., Das, G.: Designing fair ranking schemes. In: Proceedings of the 2019 International Conference on Management of Data, pp. 1259–1276. SIGMOD (2019). https://doi.org/10.1145/3299869.3300079
3. Biega, A.J., Gummadi, K.P., Weikum, G.: Equity of attention: amortizing individual fairness in rankings. In: The 41st International ACM SIGIR Conference on Research & Development in Information Retrieval, pp. 405–414. SIGIR '18, New York, NY, USA (2018). https://doi.org/10.1145/3209978.3210063
4. Calders, T., Kamiran, F., Pechenizkiy, M.: Building classifiers with independency constraints. In: IEEE International Conference on Data Mining Workshops, pp. 13–18 (2009). https://doi.org/10.1109/ICDMW.2009.83
5. Celis, L.E., Straszak, D., Vishnoi, N.K.: Ranking with fairness constraints. In: 45th International Colloquium on Automata, Languages, and Programming. Leibniz International Proceedings in Informatics, vol. 107, pp. 28:1–28:15 (2018)
6. Craswell, N., Zoeter, O., Taylor, M., Ramsey, B.: An experimental comparison of click position-bias models. In: Proceedings of the 2008 International Conference on Web Search and Data Mining, pp. 87–94 (2008)
7. Deb, K., Pratap, A., Agarwal, S., Meyarivan, T.: A fast and elitist multiobjective genetic algorithm: NSGA-II. IEEE Trans. Evol. Comput. **6**(2), 182–197 (2002)

8. Dwork, C., Hardt, M., Pitassi, T., Reingold, O., Zemel, R.: Fairness through awareness. In: Proceedings of the 3rd Innovations in Theoretical Computer Science Conference, pp. 214–226 (2012)
9. Feldman, M., Friedler, S.A., Moeller, J., Scheidegger, C., Venkatasubramanian, S.: Certifying and removing disparate impact. In: Proceedings of the 21th ACM SIGKDD International Conference on Knowledge Discovery and Data Mining, pp. 259–268. KDD '15 (2015). https://doi.org/10.1145/2783258.2783311
10. Fonseca, C.M., Paquete, L., López-Ibánez, M.: An improved dimension-sweep algorithm for the hypervolume indicator. In: IEEE International Conference on Evolutionary Computation, pp. 1157–1163. IEEE (2006)
11. Geyik, S.C., Ambler, S., Kenthapadi, K.: Fairness-aware ranking in search & recommendation systems with application to linkedin talent search. In: Proceedings of the 25th ACM SIGKDD International Conference on Knowledge Discovery & Data Mining, pp. 2221–2231. KDD '19 (2019). https://doi.org/10.1145/3292500.3330691
12. Hardt, M., Price, E., Srebro, N.: Equality of opportunity in supervised learning. Adv. Neural. Inf. Process. Syst. **29** (2016)
13. Hofmann, H.: German credit data (1994). https://archive.ics.uci.edu/ml/datasets/Statlog+Statlog+%28German+Credit+Data%29
14. Ishibuchi, H., Masuda, H., Tanigaki, Y., Nojima, Y.: Modified distance calculation in generational distance and inverted generational distance. In: International Conference on Evolutionary Multi-criterion Optimization, pp. 110–125. Springer (2015)
15. Jannach, D., Bauer, C.: Escaping the MCNAMARA fallacy: towards more impactful recommender systems research. AI Mag. **41**(4), 79–95 (2020)
16. Järvelin, K., Kekäläinen, J.: Cumulated gain-based evaluation of IR techniques. ACM Trans. Inf. Syst. (TOIS) **20**(4), 422–446 (2002)
17. Kulshrestha, J., et al.: Quantifying search bias: investigating sources of bias for political searches in social media. In: Proceedings of the 2017 ACM Conference on Computer Supported Cooperative Work and Social Computing, pp. 417–432 (2017)
18. Lahoti, P., Gummadi, K.P., Weikum, G.: Operationalizing individual fairness with pairwise fair representations. Proc. VLDB Endowment **13**(4), 506–518 (2019). https://doi.org/10.14778/3372716.3372723
19. Larson, J., Angwin, J., Mattu, S., Kirchner, L.: Machine bias. ProPublica (2016)
20. Liebrand, N.A., Duong, M.K., Conrad, S.: Fair proportional top-k ranking. In: International Conference on Big Data Analytics and Knowledge Discovery, pp. 237–243. Springer (2025)
21. Mehrabi, N., Morstatter, F., Saxena, N., Lerman, K., Galstyan, A.: A survey on bias and fairness in machine learning. ACM Comput. Surv. (CSUR) **54**(6), 1–35 (2021)
22. Patro, G.K., Porcaro, L., Mitchell, L., Zhang, Q., Zehlike, M., Garg, N.: Fair ranking: a critical review, challenges, and future directions. In: Proceedings of the ACM Conference on Fairness, Accountability, and Transparency, pp. 1929–1942 (2022)
23. Pedreschi, D., Ruggieri, S., Turini, F.: Measuring discrimination in socially-sensitive decision records. In: Proceedings of the 2009 SIAM International Conference on Data Mining, pp. 581–592. SIAM (2009)
24. Robertson, S.E.: The probability ranking principle in IR. J. Document. **33**(4), 294–304 (1977)

25. Singh, A., Joachims, T.: Fairness of exposure in rankings. In: Proceedings of the 24th ACM SIGKDD International Conference on Knowledge Discovery & Data Mining, pp. 2219–2228 (2018)
26. The College Board: Sat percentile ranks (2014)
27. Verma, S.: Weapons of math destruction: how big data increases inequality and threatens democracy. Vikalpa **44**(2), 97–98 (2019)
28. Wightman, L.F., Ramse, H.: LSAC national longitudinal bar passage study (1998)
29. Woodworth, B., Gunasekar, S., Ohannessian, M., Srebro, N.: Learning non-discriminatory predictors. In: Proceedings of the 30th Conference on Learning Theory, pp. 1920–1953 (2017)
30. Yang, K., Stoyanovich, J.: Measuring fairness in ranked outputs. In: Proceedings of the 29th International Conference on Scientific and Statistical Database Management (2017). https://doi.org/10.1145/3085504.3085526
31. Zafar, M.B., Valera, I., Rogriguez, M.G., Gummadi, K.P.: Fairness constraints: mechanisms for fair classification. Artif. Intell. Stat. 962–970 (2017)
32. Zehlike, M., Bonchi, F., Castillo, C., Hajian, S., Megahed, M., Baeza-Yates, R.: Fa*ir: a fair top-k ranking algorithm. In: Proceedings of the 2017 ACM on Conference on Information and Knowledge Management, pp. 1569–1578 (2017)
33. Zehlike, M., Sühr, T., Baeza-Yates, R., Bonchi, F., Castillo, C., Hajian, S.: Fair top-k ranking with multiple protected groups. Inf. Process. Manag. **59**(1) (2022)
34. Zemel, R., Wu, Y., Swersky, K., Pitassi, T., Dwork, C.: Learning fair representations. In: International Conference on Machine Learning, pp. 325–333. PMLR (2013)

FedAgent-Rec: Enhancing Fairness and Personalization in Federated Recommendation via Multi-agent Behavior Simulation and Reranking

Shengxi Huang[1], Xiaoli Wang[2(✉)], Peiwei Wu[1], Ying Huang[1], Lingna Wang[2], Changdong Wang[3], and Weigang Wu[3]

[1] Sun Yat-sen University, Guangzhou 510006, China
{huangshx8,wupw7,huangy867}@mail2.sysu.edu.cn
[2] China Southern Airlines, Guangzhou 510403, China
{wangxiaolice,wanglingna}@csair.com
[3] Sun Yat-sen University, Guangzhou 510006, China
{wangchd3,wuweig}@mail.sysu.edu.cn

Abstract. Federated Recommendation (FedRec) has gained significant traction as a privacy-preserving paradigm for personalized services. However, existing FedRec systems suffer from a critical data-driven unfairness: the global model is predominantly shaped by active users, leaving "low-resource users" (those with sparse interactions) marginalized with subpar performance. Furthermore, capturing nuanced individual preferences in a decentralized environment remains a daunting task for traditional collaborative filtering. To address these challenges, we propose **FedAgent-Rec**, a novel multi-agent collaboration framework designed to bolster both fairness and personalization in federated settings. Specifically, we introduce a tripartite simulation pipeline: a Profile Agent that synthesizes cohesive user personas from fragmented logs, a Simulation Agent that generates synthetic interactions via retrieval-augmented tools, and an Evaluation Agent that iteratively refines the output through feedback. To robustly integrate these synthetic data without compromising the global distribution, we design three adaptive strategies: Weighted Loss Adjustment, Curriculum Learning-based Scheduling, and Contrastive Learning Alignment. Finally, an Agent-based Reranker is deployed at the inference stage to align recommendation outputs with user-specific semantic profiles. Extensive experiments on three real-world datasets across six backbone models demonstrate that FedAgent-Rec improves the performance of low-resource users while maintaining or enhancing the overall recommendation quality. To our knowledge, this is the first work to systematically explore the synergy between multi-agent systems and federated recommendation to address the long-tail fairness and personalization challenges. Our code is available at https://github.com/rainnings/FedAgent-Rec.

Keywords: Federated Recommendation · Multi-Agent Systems · Data Augmentation · Fairness

M. Ceci et al. (Eds.): ECML PKDD 2026, LNAI 16941, pp. 393–408, 2027.
https://doi.org/10.1007/978-3-032-37654-1_23

1 Introduction

Personalized recommendation systems have become indispensable in alleviating information overload within modern online platforms [2,33]. However, the growing public concern over data privacy has catalyzed the transition from centralized architectures to **Federated Recommendation (FedRec)** [27,33]. By allowing clients to train models locally and aggregating only model updates, FedRec provides a privacy-preserving paradigm for collaborative filtering.

Despite its privacy benefits, FedRec faces intertwined challenges: **inherent personalization difficulty** and **data-driven unfairness**. Data heterogeneity across clients hinders the global model's adaptation to individual preferences [15, 35], while optimization naturally biases toward "active users" over "low-resource users" [17]. This leaves data-sparse clients marginalized, as the lack of local interaction signals prevents the model from capturing their unique behavioral patterns.

To navigate these multifaceted challenges, recent research has explored two primary trajectories, yet their effectiveness remains constrained by the fundamental sparsity of local interaction signals:

- **Fairness-oriented FedRec:** Prior works employ objective re-weighting [16], gradient scaling [1], or pseudo-labeling [17] to mitigate imbalance. However, these reactive methods often fail to inject the semantic variety needed to "rescue" marginalized users.
- **Advanced Personalized FedRec:** Recent models utilize dual-architectures [36], additive views [15], or graph-guided aggregation [37] to handle heterogeneity. Yet, they remain bounded by the "closed-world" collaborative filtering paradigm, failing at the cold-start barrier where local interactions are near-zero.

The stagnation of current methods in sparse-data scenarios stems from a shared bottleneck: the lack of *external knowledge* to interpret fragmented behaviors.

Recently, Large Language Models (LLMs) have demonstrated remarkable capabilities in user profiling and reasoning [29,38]. This suggests a promising direction: utilizing AI Agents to synthesize meaningful interactions that reflect a user's underlying preferences. By leveraging the vast world knowledge of LLMs, we can simulate behaviors [41] that go beyond simple data replication, providing the missing "semantic bridge" for low-resource clients.

However, integrating Agent-generated data into FedRec is non-trivial. First, simulated behaviors may introduce **semantic noise** if the LLM's "common sense" drifts too far from the actual item distribution. Second, there is a risk of **distribution shift**, where the synthetic data overshadows the genuine collaborative signals. Finally, while simulation addresses data sparsity for the tail, the general personalization issue for all users requires a mechanism that can refine model outputs in real-time during inference.

To address these issues, we propose **FedAgent-Rec**, a novel multi-agent collaborative framework designed to enhance both fairness and personalization in FedRec. Specifically, we design a tripartite agent pipeline: a **Profile Agent** that synthesizes discrete interactions into cohesive user personas; a **Simulation Agent** that generates high-quality synthetic behaviors using retrieval tools; and an **Evaluation Agent** that implements a "feedback-refinement" loop to ensure the quality of simulated data. To effectively utilize these synthetic samples without compromising the global model, we explore three strategies: **weighted loss adjustment**, **curriculum learning-based scheduling**, and **contrastive learning alignment**. Finally, to further enhance personalization for all users, a **Reranking Agent** is deployed to refine the Top-K recommendations through semantic alignment. To our knowledge, this is the first work exploring the synergy between multi-agent systems and federated recommendation.

2 Related Work

We situate our work at the intersection of two active research areas: federated recommendation systems and LLM-driven data augmentation. Below we review key advances in each and highlight how FedAgent-Rec departs from existing approaches.

2.1 Federated Recommendation Systems

Federated Recommendation (FedRec) has transitioned from foundational architectures to sophisticated personalized and fairness-aware frameworks. Early works established decentralized paradigms such as Federated Matrix Factorization [3] and Federated Neural Collaborative Filtering [10]. To tackle data heterogeneity (Non-IID), recent research has shifted toward personalized variants, employing *cluster-based aggregation* [21] or *architectural decoupling* that separates private local functions from global embeddings [15,36]. Furthermore, addressing the performance gap between active and low-resource users has become a critical frontier. Current efforts focus on *group fairness* via gradient dynamic scaling [1] or rebalancing frameworks like *BalFed* [17], which utilizes pseudo-labeling to mitigate global model bias. However, these methods remain "reactive" as they rely on existing sparse signals. Our work instead "proactively" injects semantic knowledge via AI agents to resolve the root cause of unfairness.

2.2 LLM-Driven Augmentation and Autonomous Agents

Data augmentation (DA) is pivotal for mitigating sparsity. Traditional DA relies on stochastic perturbations [31] or generative models like VAEs [19] and Diffusion [22]. Recently, Large Language Models (LLMs) have shifted DA toward semantic-aware synthesis. Methods like HFAR [26] leverage LLMs to simulate human feedback, providing reasoning that traditional DA lacks. Beyond simple augmentation [4], LLMs are deployed as personalized rankers [20,34] or encoders [18,30] to align collaborative knowledge with semantic spaces. A burgeoning frontier involves using autonomous agents to simulate human-like decision processes

[38] or multi-agent systems like MACRec [29] to decompose complex tasks. While showing promise in centralized settings, FedAgent-Rec is the first to orchestrate a multi-agent pipeline to ensure quality and distribution alignment of simulated interactions specifically within the privacy-constrained federated environment.

3 Methodology

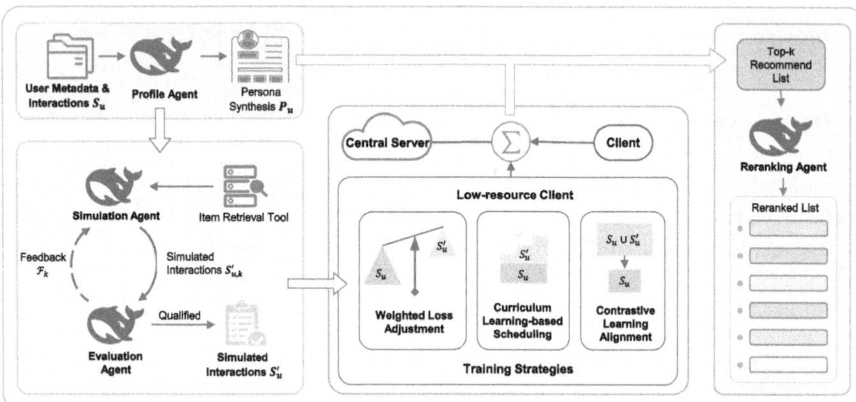

Fig. 1. Overall architecture of FedAgent-Rec. The framework consists of: (1) a multi-agent pipeline (Profile, Simulation, and Evaluation Agents) that generates high-fidelity interactions S'_u for low-resource users; (2) three robust integration strategies (WL, CL, and ConL) to incorporate S'_u into federated training; and (3) an Agent-based Reranker that aligns the Top-k recommendation results with the user persona P_u during inference.

In this section, we present the architecture of **FedAgent-Rec**, as illustrated in Fig. 1. We begin with the formalization of the federated recommendation task, followed by the multi-agent pipeline designed to generate high-fidelity simulated interactions. We then introduce three training-time integration strategies and conclude with the inference-time personalized reranking mechanism.

3.1 Preliminaries and Problem Formulation

We consider a federated recommendation environment with a central server and a set of clients $\mathcal{U}$. Each client $u \in \mathcal{U}$ possesses a local dataset $\mathcal{D}_u$ containing historical interactions $\mathcal{S}_u = \{(i_1, r_1), \ldots, (i_n, r_n)\}$, user metadata $\mathcal{U}_u^{meta}$ (e.g., demographic attributes), and access to a shared item metadata repository $\mathcal{I}^{meta}$ (e.g., categories and descriptions). Following the standard **FedAvg** paradigm [23], the goal is to optimize a global model Θ by aggregating local updates.

A core challenge in FedRec is the performance disparity for **low-resource users** $\mathcal{U}_{tail} \subset \mathcal{U}$. In our framework, $\mathcal{U}_{tail}$ is defined as the subset of users with the fewest historical interactions. Our fairness goal is a **Pareto improvement**: we aim to boost performance for $\mathcal{U}_{tail}$ without degrading the experience of active users, recognizing that absolute performance parity would penalize data contribution and is neither expected nor desirable in federated settings. For these users, we generate a set of **simulated interactions** $\mathcal{S}'_u = \{(i'_1, r'_1), \ldots, (i'_m, r'_m)\}$ to augment the sparse local signal and improve fairness.

3.2 Multi-agent Simulation Pipeline

We utilize a collaborative agent framework to bridge the semantic gap between fragmented behaviors and user intent.

Profile Agent: Persona Synthesis The **Profile Agent** acts as a semantic encoder that performs inductive reasoning to synthesize a natural language persona P_u. Formally:

$$P_u = \text{Agent}_{prof}(\mathcal{S}_u, \mathcal{U}_u^{meta}, \mathcal{I}^{meta}) \tag{1}$$

By integrating historical items' textual descriptions from $\mathcal{I}^{meta}$ with the user's demographic profile $\mathcal{U}_u^{meta}$, P_u captures high-level latent interests. The Profile Agent is invoked once at the beginning, providing a stable semantic anchor for subsequent simulation stages.

Iterative Generation with Conversational Memory The generation of **simulated interactions** is modeled as a multi-turn collaborative dialogue. For each low-resource user $u \in \mathcal{U}_{tail}$, we initialize a conversational context $\mathcal{C}_u^{(0)}$ which integrates the user persona P_u, historical interactions $\mathcal{S}_u$, and the system-level instruction prompts. This context serves as a continuous reasoning chain, allowing the agents to "remember" previous attempts and refine their outputs based on feedback.

At each iteration $k \in \{1, \ldots, T_{iter}\}$, the **Simulation Agent** generates a candidate set of interactions $\mathcal{S}'_{u,k}$ based on the accumulated context $\mathcal{C}_u^{(k-1)}$. To bridge the gap between the LLM's internal knowledge and the specific dataset, we utilize a **Retrieval-Augmented Generation (RAG)** approach [13]. Specifically, the agent invokes an Item Retrieval Tool to identify candidates within the valid item space $\mathcal{I}$ that align with the user's preferences in $\mathcal{C}_u^{(k-1)}$. Formally, the simulation step is defined as:

$$\mathcal{S}'_{u,k} = \text{Agent}_{sim}(\mathcal{C}_u^{(k-1)}, \text{RetrievalTool}) \tag{2}$$

Following the simulation, the **Evaluation Agent** acts as a semantic critic to inspect the quality of $\mathcal{S}'_{u,k}$. It assesses the candidates across dimensions such as consistency, diversity, and relevance to the user's recent trajectory. If the quality is deemed insufficient, the agent generates textual feedback $\mathcal{F}_k$ providing specific instructions for correction. Both the failed simulation and the feedback are then appended to the conversational memory to guide the next round:

$$\mathcal{F}_k = \text{Agent}_{eval}(\mathcal{C}_u^{(k-1)}, \mathcal{S}'_{u,k}) \tag{3}$$

$$\mathcal{C}_u^{(k)} = \mathcal{C}_u^{(k-1)} \cup \{\mathcal{S}'_{u,k}, \mathcal{F}_k\} \tag{4}$$

This feedback-refinement loop continues iteratively, allowing the Simulation Agent to adjust its generation strategy conditioned on $\mathcal{F}_k$. The process terminates when either the Evaluation Agent approves the quality of the interactions or the maximum iteration threshold T_{iter} is reached. This memory-augmented mechanism ensures that the final set of **simulated interactions** $\mathcal{S}'_u$ provides a "clean" and semantically rich signal for the recommendation model, effectively mitigating the noise and hallucinations typical of zero-shot LLM generation.

3.3 Training Strategies for Data Integration

Directly training on Agent-generated data may introduce semantic noise if the simulated distribution shifts from the real one. We propose three strategies to safely integrate $\mathcal{S}'_u$ during the training phase.

Weighted Loss Adjustment (WL). To prevent high-variance simulated samples from over-shadowing the genuine but sparse user signals, we treat $\mathcal{S}'_u$ as a secondary supervision signal. For $u \in \mathcal{U}_{tail}$, the local loss is:

$$\mathcal{L}_{WL} = \mathcal{L}(\mathcal{S}_u; \Theta) + \alpha \cdot \mathcal{L}(\mathcal{S}'_u; \Theta) \tag{5}$$

where $\alpha \in (0, 1]$ serves as a confidence coefficient, ensuring that the model remains primarily anchored to the real interaction ground truth.

Curriculum Learning-Based Scheduling (CL). Early in the training process, the global model Θ is unstable. Introducing synthetic noise prematurely can lead to poor local optima. We adopt a **Curriculum Learning** strategy [28] to gradually introduce simulations:

$$p_t = \min\left(1, \frac{t}{T_{max}} \cdot \eta\right) \tag{6}$$

$$\mathcal{L}_{CL}^{(t)} = \begin{cases} \mathcal{L}(\mathcal{S}_u; \Theta) + \alpha\mathcal{L}(\mathcal{S}'_u; \Theta) & \text{with prob } p_t \\ \mathcal{L}(\mathcal{S}_u; \Theta) & \text{with prob } 1 - p_t \end{cases} \tag{7}$$

Here, t denotes the current communication round, $T_{max} = 200$ controls the scheduling window, and η determines the rate at which simulated interactions are introduced. This scheduling allows the model to first capture stable collaborative signals before refining the representations of low-resource users with semantic-heavy simulated data.

Contrastive Learning Alignment (ConL). To maximize knowledge transfer while minimizing direct noise contamination, we decouple the real behavior representation from the simulation influence. We define two distinct representation views for $u \in \mathcal{U}_{tail}$ using Self-Supervised Learning principles:

- **Real View** (E_u): Derived solely from $\mathcal{S}_u$, representing the genuine user interest anchor.
- **Augmented View** (E'_u): Derived from the union $\mathcal{S}_u \cup \mathcal{S}'_u$, serving as a semantically enriched knowledge buffer.

Instead of updating E_u directly using the gradients from simulated interactions, we use E'_u as a knowledge buffer. We align the two views via a contrastive loss:

$$\mathcal{L}_{con} = 1 - \frac{E_u \cdot E'_u}{\|E_u\|\|E'_u\|} \tag{8}$$

The total local objective for the tail user is the joint optimization of the recommendation losses and the alignment loss:

$$\mathcal{L}_{ConL} = \underbrace{\mathcal{L}(\mathcal{S}_u;\Theta)}_{\text{Real Loss}} + \underbrace{(\mathcal{L}(\mathcal{S}_u;\Theta) + \alpha\mathcal{L}(\mathcal{S}'_u;\Theta))}_{\text{Augmented Loss}} + \lambda\mathcal{L}_{con} \tag{9}$$

where λ is a regularization coefficient. In this way, E_u inherits the refined semantic knowledge from E'_u through the alignment objective, without being directly exposed to the potential noise in the synthetic interaction gradients. **During inference, only E_u is used.**

3.4 Agent-Based Personalized Reranking

In the inference phase, we deploy a **Reranking Agent** to address the broader personalization challenge for all users (not only $\mathcal{U}_{tail}$). Given the Top-K list L_{topk} from the backbone model Θ, the agent performs a final semantic alignment with the user persona P_u. Formally:

$$L'_{topk} = \text{Agent}_{rerank}(L_{topk}, P_u, \mathcal{I}^{meta}) \tag{10}$$

By evaluating the Interaction Likelihood between each candidate's metadata in $\mathcal{I}^{meta}$ and the user persona P_u, the agent recalibrates the ranking to reflect the user's nuanced preferences, effectively correcting systematic biases (e.g., popularity bias) inherent in collaborative filtering.

4 Experiments

This section presents the empirical evaluation of FedAgent-Rec. We first describe the experimental setup (datasets, baselines, implementation details, and the multi-agent pipeline configuration), then report main results on ML-1M, Poetry, and Video datasets, followed by an ablation study analyzing key design choices.

4.1 Experimental Settings

Datasets and Preprocessing. We evaluate **FedAgent-Rec** on **MovieLens-1M (ML-1M)** [7], **Amazon-Video Games (Video)** [24], and **Goodreads-Poetry (Poetry)** [25], applying 10-core filtering to all. We use an 8:1:1 split for **EF-RECVAE** [39] and a chronological 8:2 split for others. Detailed statistics are summarized in Table 1. To address the data-driven unfairness, we identify the 100 users with the fewest interactions after 10-core filtering as low-resource users ($\mathcal{U}_{tail}$), for whom we synthesize 10 interactions per user via our multi-agent pipeline.

Table 1. Statistics of the evaluated datasets after 10-core filtering.

Dataset	#Users	#Items	#Interactions	Sparsity
ML-1M	6,040	3,952	1,000,209	95.81%
Video	15,458	37,023	283,672	99.95%
Poetry	25,741	24,352	623,590	99.90%

Baseline Models. We integrate our FedAgent-Rec framework with six representative models to demonstrate its broad applicability:

- **MF** [12] and **NCF** [9]: Classical collaborative filtering models.
- **DIN** [42] and **Wide & Deep** [11]: Feature-based deep learning models capable of handling heterogeneous inputs.
- **LightGCN** [8]: A graph-based model leveraging structural information.
- **EF-RECVAE** [39]: A Variational Autoencoder-based model designed specifically for the federated setting.

Implementation Details. Framework implementation follows **FRCSU** [14] and **EF-VAE** [39] benchmarks. EF-RECVAE uses [16, 8] hidden dimensions with 100-patience early stopping over 250 rounds. Other models use FR-CSU settings: embedding size 10, batch size 64, learning rate 0.01, and $E = 5$ local epochs per round. The training follows the FedAvg protocol [23], where approximately 10% of clients are sampled per round. For ML-1M, we conduct full-rank evaluation, while for other datasets, we perform negative sampling with a ratio of 1:100 (except for EF-RECVAE, which follows its original 1:200 protocol). For non-EF-RECVAE models, we perform 205 communication rounds and report the average performance of the final 5 rounds. **ConL** is excluded from EF-RECVAE due to its unique variational optimization objective. Hyperparameters are set as follows: $T_{max} = 200$, $\alpha \in \{0.5, 0.8\}$, $\eta = 0.8$, and $\lambda = 0.1$.

To ensure fair and reproducible comparisons, all baseline and enhanced models share identical data splits, client sampling sequences, and random seeds.

Multi-agent Pipeline. We use **DeepSeek-V3** [5] ($temp = 0.1, top\_p = 0.4$) as the LLM backbone. The Item Retrieval Tool identifies candidates as follows: for ML-1M, it performs agent-guided attribute filtering using the user persona to select genre–year combinations and ranks matching movies by genre overlap within the specified release-year range; for Video and Poetry, it employs a two-stage approach using vector similarity (bge-small-en-v1.5 [32] & FAISS [6]) followed by metadata alignment. The Simulation Agent then reasons over the retrieved candidate pool to synthesize 10 final interactions, with the Evaluation Agent enforcing quality via an iterative loop ($T_{iter} = 10$).

To prevent data leakage, all agent-generated interactions are strictly excluded from test sets for both baseline and enhanced models; gains thus stem solely from improved representation learning.

The Reranking Agent (detailed in Sect. 3.4) re-scores Top-30 candidates to select the final Top-10 for: (1) 100 random users (general personalization) and (2) all $\mathcal{U}_{tail}$ users (marginalized interests).

Evaluation Metrics. We adopt **NDCG@10** and **Hit@10** as the primary metrics for overall performance. To quantify the improvement for marginalized groups, we report **NDCG@10**$_t$ and **Hit@10**$_t$, calculated exclusively on the performance of the 100 low-resource users.

4.2 Main Results and Analysis

Performance on ML-1M. Table 2 summarizes the performance on the ML-1M dataset under a rigorous full ranking protocol, showing that baseline performance for low-resource users ($\mathcal{U}_{tail}$) is consistently lower than the average (e.g., NCF: 0.0930 vs. 0.0152), confirming that FedRec models naturally bias toward data-rich clients. Our strategies, particularly CL, yield substantial gains for $\mathcal{U}_{tail}$ (e.g., 49.7% NDCG improvement for EF-RECVAE) by injecting external semantic variety. This ensures the global model captures latent preferences beyond generic popular items. Note that ConL is less effective on feature-based models (W&D, DIN) due to semantic-feature mismatch, and MF shows marginal gains as its simple structure acts as a representational bottleneck.

Performance on Poetry and Video. As shown in Table 3, $\mathcal{U}_{tail}$ metrics often exceed the overall average on Poetry and Video datasets. This Performance Inversion is an artifact of the 1:100 negative sampling protocol: active users face a more complex preference space and harder negatives, while the model operates within a narrower, more discriminable range for tail users. Crucially, the **CL strategy** provides consistent gains across most backbones, demonstrating that agent-based simulation offers a robust semantic prior across diverse data distributions.

Table 2. Performance comparison on ML-1M. **WL**: Weighted Loss, **CL**: Curriculum Learning, **ConL**: Contrastive Learning. N@10 and H@10 denote NDCG@10 and Hit@10; $_t$ indicates low-resource users. Parentheses in strategy names denote (α) for WL and CL, and (α, λ) for ConL. LGCN, EF-R, and W&D are abbreviations for model names.

Model	Strategy	N@10	H@10	N@10$_t$	H@10$_t$
NCF	Baseline	0.0930	0.4228	0.0152	0.1060
	WL (0.5)	**0.1015**	0.4409	0.0200	0.1200
	CL (0.5)	0.1010	**0.4596**	**0.0249**	**0.1500**
	ConL (0.5, 0.1)	0.0955	0.4284	0.0237	0.1080
MF	Baseline	0.1038	0.4446	0.0154	0.0900
	WL (0.5)	0.1042	0.4451	**0.0213**	**0.0980**
	CL (0.5)	0.1034	0.4442	0.0154	0.0900
	ConL (0.5, 0.1)	**0.1060**	**0.4506**	0.0151	0.0950
LGCN	Baseline	**0.1212**	0.4776	0.0207	0.1000
	WL (0.8)	**0.1212**	0.4774	0.0207	0.1000
	CL (0.8)	**0.1212**	0.4773	0.0207	0.1000
	ConL (0.5, 0.1)	0.1208	**0.4785**	**0.0240**	**0.1300**
EF-R	Baseline	0.0692	0.3478	0.0525	0.1900
	WL (0.8)	0.0699	0.3548	0.0590	0.2000
	CL (0.8)	**0.0701**	**0.3541**	**0.0786**	**0.2600**
W&D	Baseline	0.1078	0.4671	0.0402	0.2030
	WL (0.8)	0.1080	0.4613	0.0403	0.2120
	CL (0.5)	**0.1097**	**0.4833**	**0.0462**	**0.2170**
	ConL (0.5, 0.1)	0.1017	0.4387	0.0227	0.1180
DIN	Baseline	0.1203	0.4700	0.0243	0.1220
	WL (0.5)	0.1218	0.4766	**0.0346**	0.1460
	CL (0.5)	**0.1223**	**0.4777**	0.0344	**0.1520**
	ConL (0.5, 0.1)	0.1135	0.4615	0.0215	0.1190

Agent-Based Reranking Analysis. Table 4 shows that reranking substantially boosts performance on ML-1M (+189% NDCG@10$_t$) and Poetry by aligning recommendations with semantic profiles. The slight degradation on the Video dataset suggests a semantic-collaborative gap: in specialized domains, text-based metadata alone may struggle to capture niche preferences that lack strong collaborative validation.

Table 3. Comparison of Baseline and CL on Poetry and Video datasets. N@10 and H@10 denote NDCG@10 and Hit@10; $_t$ indicates low-resource users. In CL parentheses, the two values are α for the Poetry and Video datasets, respectively. LGCN, EF-R, and W&D are abbreviations for model names.

Model	Method	Poetry Dataset				Video Dataset			
		N@10	H@10	N@10$_t$	H@10$_t$	N@10	H@10	N@10$_t$	H@10$_t$
NCF	Baseline	0.2487	0.5804	0.3455	0.5300	**0.0262**	**0.1176**	0.0359	0.0980
	CL(0.5|0.5)	**0.2498**	**0.5840**	**0.3474**	**0.5420**	0.0262	0.1165	**0.0377**	**0.1300**
MF	Baseline	**0.1828**	**0.4659**	**0.2703**	**0.4400**	**0.0235**	**0.1053**	0.0231	**0.0800**
	CL(0.8|0.8)	0.1823	0.4647	0.2527	0.4180	0.0234	0.1053	**0.0236**	0.0700
LGCN	Baseline	0.3747	0.7696	0.4462	0.7100	0.1076	0.3210	0.1186	0.2500
	CL(0.5|0.5)	**0.3759**	**0.7711**	**0.4509**	**0.7100**	**0.1106**	**0.3300**	**0.1275**	**0.2820**
EF-R	Baseline	0.0832	0.2524	0.0994	0.2000	**0.0152**	0.0475	0.0135	0.0300
	CL(0.8|0.8)	**0.0858**	**0.2563**	**0.1083**	**0.2000**	0.0145	**0.0479**	**0.0139**	**0.0400**
W&D	Baseline	0.2685	**0.6126**	**0.3560**	0.5420	**0.0322**	**0.1344**	0.0387	0.1260
	CL(0.5|0.5)	**0.2689**	0.6090	0.3558	**0.5720**	0.0317	0.1323	**0.0449**	**0.1460**
DIN	Baseline	0.2744	**0.6008**	0.3270	0.4880	**0.0270**	0.1205	0.0242	0.0800
	CL(0.8|0.5)	**0.2748**	0.6000	**0.3365**	**0.5060**	0.0268	**0.1211**	**0.0262**	**0.0920**

4.3 Ablation Study and Parameter Analysis

To further investigate the underlying mechanisms of FedAgent-Rec, we conduct a series of controlled experiments on the ML-1M dataset using the NCF backbone and CL strategy. In the ablation tables and figures that follow, "Baseline" refers to the standard NCF model without simulated interactions or the component being ablated. Unless otherwise specified, the loss weight α is set to 0.5 for all ablation experiments.

Table 4. Reranking effect of AI Agent on LightGCN + CL results across three datasets (evaluated on 100 random users and all 100 low-resource users).

Dataset	Method	NDCG@10	Hit@10	NDCG@10$_t$	Hit@10$_t$
ML-1M	w/o Rerank	0.0760	0.4200	0.0207	0.1000
	w/ Rerank	**0.1141**	**0.5000**	**0.0599**	**0.2600**
Poetry	w/o Rerank	0.3334	0.7200	0.4512	0.7100
	w/ Rerank	**0.4031**	**0.8000**	**0.5366**	**0.7900**
Video	w/o Rerank	**0.1194**	**0.3600**	**0.1275**	**0.2900**
	w/ Rerank	0.0893	0.3300	0.1225	0.2800

Impact of Simulation Quantity. As shown in Table 5, performance peaks at $m = 10$, with $m = 15$ dropping below the baseline. This suggests a threshold effect: insufficient simulation ($m = 5$) provides limited signal, while excessive simulation ($m = 15$) causes distribution shift where synthetic behaviors overshadow genuine user trajectories. We adopt $m = 10$ as the operating point and note that the optimal quantity may vary across datasets and sparsity levels; finer-grained exploration is left to future work.

Table 5. Impact of the number of simulated interactions (m).

Setting	NDCG@10	Hit@10	NDCG@10_t	Hit@10_t
Baseline	0.0930	0.4228	0.0152	0.1060
$m = 5$	0.0981	0.4484	0.0186	0.0980
$m = 10$	**0.1010**	**0.4596**	**0.0249**	**0.1500**
$m = 15$	0.0897	0.4296	0.0125	0.0720

The Value of the Evaluation Agent. We conduct an ablation test by removing the Evaluation Agent's feedback-refinement loop. As shown in Table 6, while even "unfiltered" simulation provides gains over the baseline, the inclusion of the Evaluation Agent further boosts NDCG@10_t by 7.3% and Hit@10_t by 11.9%. This validates our hypothesis that LLMs require a "self-correction" mechanism to ensure the simulated items are not only semantically plausible but also logically consistent with the user's profile, thereby filtering out noisy or irrelevant synthetic samples.

Table 6. Ablation of the Evaluation Agent.

Setting	NDCG@10	Hit@10	NDCG@10_t	Hit@10_t
Baseline	0.0930	0.4228	0.0152	0.1060
w/o Eval Agent	0.0992	0.4447	0.0232	0.1340
w/ Eval Agent	**0.1010**	**0.4596**	**0.0249**	**0.1500**

Sensitivity to Loss Weight α. The hyperparameter α in the CL strategy controls the contribution of simulated interactions. As illustrated in Fig. 2(a), performance is relatively stable between $\alpha = 0.5$ and $\alpha = 1.0$. However, a significant peak in tail performance occurs at $\alpha = 0.5$ and $\alpha = 0.8$. This suggests that while tail users need the simulated signal, the loss must be carefully balanced to prevent synthetic gradients from distorting the global item embeddings, which are shared across all clients.

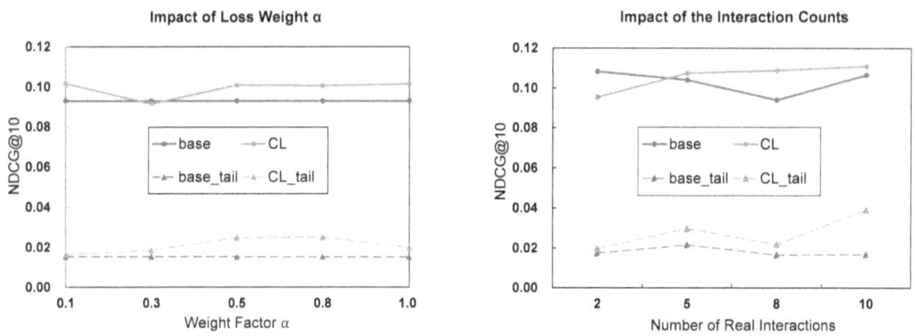

(a) Loss Weight α (b) Interaction Count

Fig. 2. Sensitivity and robustness analysis of FedAgent-Rec (NCF+CL on ML-1M). In both panels, "base" and "CL" denote the NCF baseline and NCF+CL, respectively; the "_tail" suffix indicates low-resource user metrics.

Robustness Across Varying Local Sparsity. Fig. 2(b) evaluates performance by truncating history to $\{2, 5, 8, 10\}$ items. While gains are marginal at extreme sparsity (2 items), they increase significantly as real interactions grow, indicating a "signal threshold" required for Agents to construct reliable personas. Notably, the performance on truncated data often exceeds the full-history baselines in Table 2. This suggests that for low-resource users, old interactions may become outdated noise due to interest drift; by prioritizing recent signals and using Agents to capture evolving intent, FedAgent-Rec effectively "re-catalyzes" the recommendation process for the tail.

5 Limitations

We acknowledge two limitations of the present work. *First*, we do not report a quantitative fairness metric. Our data splitting protocol (e.g., 8:1:1 for EF-RECVAE and chronological 8:2 for others) results in test sets of unequal size across users, making per-user metrics such as Hit@10 not directly comparable between users with differing numbers of test items. A fair per-user comparison would require a leave-one-out evaluation protocol with a controlled test-set size, which we leave to future work. *Second*, we did not include fairness-aware FedRec baselines in our empirical comparison. Methods such as F^2PGNN [1], PPOA [40], and BalFed [17] target fairness from different angles (demographic parity, data imbalance recovery), and some of them are standalone training protocols with specific backbone assumptions, making direct numerical comparison under a unified, multi-backbone protocol non-trivial. We view a systematic comparison as important future work.

6 Conclusion

We propose FedAgent-Rec, a novel framework leveraging multi-agent collaboration to tackle personalization and fairness in federated recommendation. By synthesizing fragmented local data into cohesive personas, our tripartite agent pipeline generates high-quality simulated interactions that act as a "semantic bridge" for low-resource users.

To ensure robust integration, we employ three strategies—Weighted Loss, Curriculum Learning, and Contrastive Alignment—mitigating synthetic noise and distribution shifts. An agent-based reranker further ensures end-to-end semantic alignment during inference.

Experiments across six backbones and three datasets show that FedAgent-Rec generally outperforms standard baselines, particularly for long-tail clients. Our findings suggest LLM reasoning can effectively compensate for sparse collaborative signals. This work marks the first synergy between autonomous multi-agent systems and federated recommendation. Future research will focus on prompt-tuning efficiency, multi-modal integration, and a systematic empirical comparison with fairness-aware FedRec methods under a unified evaluation protocol.

Acknowledgment. This research is partially supported by National Natural Science Foundation of China (No. 62372487).

Competing Interests. The authors declare no competing interests.

References

1. Agrawal, N., Sirohi, A.K., Kumar, S., Jayadeva: no prejudice! Fair federated graph neural networks for personalized recommendation. In: AAAI, pp. 10775–10783. AAAI Press (2024)
2. Alamdari, P.M., Navimipour, N.J., Hosseinzadeh, M., Safaei, A.A., Darwesh, A.M.: A systematic study on the recommender systems in the e-commerce. IEEE Access **8**, 115694–115716 (2020)
3. Chai, D., Wang, L., Chen, K., Yang, Q.: Secure federated matrix factorization. IEEE Intell. Syst. **36**(5), 11–20 (2021)
4. Choi, D., Lee, C., Yoo, J.: Simple and behavior-driven augmentation for recommendation with rich collaborative signals. In: IEEE Big Data, pp. 433–438. IEEE (2025)
5. DeepSeek-AI: Deepseek-v3.2: Pushing the frontier of open large language models. CoRR **abs/2512.02556** (2025)
6. Douze, M., et al.: The Faiss library. IEEE Trans. Big Data **12**(2), 346–361 (2026)
7. Harper, F.M., Konstan, J.A.: The movielens datasets: history and context. ACM Trans. Interact. Intell. Syst. **5**(4), 19:1–19:19 (2016)
8. He, X., Deng, K., Wang, X., Li, Y., Zhang, Y., Wang, M.: Lightgcn: simplifying and powering graph convolution network for recommendation. In: SIGIR, pp. 639–648. ACM (2020)
9. He, X., Liao, L., Zhang, H., Nie, L., Hu, X., Chua, T.: Neural collaborative filtering. In: WWW, pp. 173–182. ACM (2017)

10. Jiang, X., Liu, B., Qin, J., Zhang, Y., Qian, J.: Fedncf: federated neural collaborative filtering for privacy-preserving recommender system. In: IJCNN, pp. 1–8. IEEE (2022)
11. Karatzoglou, A., Hidasi, B., Tikk, D., Shalom, O.S., Roitman, H., Shapira, B., Rokach, L. (eds.): Proceedings of the 1st Workshop on Deep Learning for Recommender Systems, DLRS@RecSys 2016, Boston, MA, USA, 15 September 2016. ACM (2016)
12. Koren, Y., Bell, R.M., Volinsky, C.: Matrix factorization techniques for recommender systems. Computer **42**(8), 30–37 (2009)
13. Lewis, P., et al.: Retrieval-augmented generation for knowledge-intensive NLP tasks. In: NeurIPS (2020)
14. Li, Y., et al.: Personalized federated recommendation for cold-start users via adaptive knowledge fusion. In: WWW, pp. 2700–2709. ACM (2025)
15. Li, Z., Long, G., Zhou, T.: Federated recommendation with additive personalization. In: ICLR. OpenReview.net (2024)
16. Ling, X., et al.: Fedfdp: federated learning with fairness and differential privacy. CoRR **abs/2402.16028** (2024)
17. Liu, P., Lu, G.: Addressing data imbalance for federated recommender systems: a rebalancing framework with gradient alignment regularization. J. Intell. Inf. Syst. **63**(2), 657–679 (2025)
18. Liu, Q., et al.: LLM-ESR: large language models enhancement for long-tailed sequential recommendation. In: NeurIPS (2024)
19. Liu, W., U, L.H., Liang, S., Zhu, H., Yu, J., Liu, Y., Yin, J.: Vae*: a novel variational autoencoder via revisiting positive and negative samples for top-N recommendation. ACM Trans. Knowl. Discov. Data **18**(9), 222:1–222:24 (2024)
20. Luo, S., et al.: Recranker: instruction tuning large language model as ranker for top-k recommendation. ACM Trans. Inf. Syst. **43**(5), 113:1–113:31 (2025)
21. Luo, S., Xiao, Y., Zhang, X., Liu, Y., Ding, W., Song, L.: Perfedrec++: Enhancing personalized federated recommendation with self-supervised pre-training. ACM Trans. Intell. Syst. Technol. **15**(5), 98:1–98:24 (2024)
22. Ma, H., et al.: Plug-in diffusion model for sequential recommendation. In: AAAI, pp. 8886–8894. AAAI Press (2024)
23. McMahan, B., Moore, E., Ramage, D., Hampson, S., y Arcas, B.A.: Communication-efficient learning of deep networks from decentralized data. In: AISTATS, pp. 1273–1282. Proceedings of Machine Learning Research, PMLR (2017)
24. Ni, J., Li, J., McAuley, J.J.: Justifying recommendations using distantly-labeled reviews and fine-grained aspects. In: EMNLP/IJCNLP (1), pp. 188–197. Association for Computational Linguistics (2019)
25. Wan, M., McAuley, J.J.: Item recommendation on monotonic behavior chains. In: RecSys, pp. 86–94. ACM (2018)
26. Wang, H., Wu, C., Huang, Y., Qi, T.: Learning human feedback from large language models for content quality-aware recommendation. ACM Trans. Inf. Syst. **43**(4), 86:1–86:28 (2025)
27. Wang, L., Zhou, H., Bao, Y., Yan, X., Shen, G., Kong, X.: Horizontal federated recommender system: A survey. ACM Comput. Surv. **56**(9), 240:1–240:42 (2024)
28. Wang, X., Chen, Y., Zhu, W.: A survey on curriculum learning. IEEE Trans. Pattern Anal. Mach. Intell. **44**(9), 4555–4576 (2022)
29. Wang, Z., Yu, Y., Zheng, W., Ma, W., Zhang, M.: Macrec: a multi-agent collaboration framework for recommendation. In: SIGIR, pp. 2760–2764. ACM (2024)

30. Wei, W., et al.: Llmrec: large language models with graph augmentation for recommendation. In: WSDM, pp. 806–815. ACM (2024)
31. Wu, J., et al.: Self-supervised graph learning for recommendation. In: SIGIR, pp. 726–735. ACM (2021)
32. Xiao, S., Liu, Z., Zhang, P., Muennighoff, N.: C-pack: packaged resources to advance general Chinese embedding. CoRR **abs/2309.07597** (2023)
33. Yang, L., Tan, B., Zheng, V.W., Chen, K., Yang, Q.: Federated recommendation systems. In: Federated Learning, pp. 225–239. Lecture Notes in Computer Science, Springer (2020)
34. Yue, Z., Rabhi, S., de Souza Pereira Moreira, G., Wang, D., Oldridge, E.: Llamarec: Two-stage recommendation using large language models for ranking. CoRR **abs/2311.02089** (2023)
35. Zhang, C., et al.: Personalized recommendation models in federated settings: a survey. IEEE Trans. Knowl. Data Eng. **37**(11), 6562–6581 (2025)
36. Zhang, C., et al.: Dual personalization on federated recommendation. In: IJCAI, pp. 4558–4566. ijcai.org (2023)
37. Zhang, C., Long, G., Zhou, T., Zhang, Z., Yan, P., Yang, B.: Gpfedrec: graph-guided personalization for federated recommendation. In: KDD, pp. 4131–4142. ACM (2024)
38. Zhang, J., et al.: Agentcf: collaborative learning with autonomous language agents for recommender systems. In: WWW, pp. 3679–3689. ACM (2024)
39. Zhang, L., Rong, Q., Ding, X., Li, G., Yuan, L.: EFVAE: efficient federated variational autoencoder for collaborative filtering. In: CIKM, pp. 3176–3185. ACM (2024)
40. Zhang, S., Ding, Y., Tang, W., Sun, W., Liao, Y., Zhou, P.Y.: Privacy-preserving orthogonal aggregation for guaranteeing gender fairness in federated recommendation. In: WSDM, pp. 327–335. ACM (2025)
41. Zhang, Z., et al.: LLM-powered user simulator for recommender system. In: AAAI, pp. 13339–13347. AAAI Press (2025)
42. Zhou, G., et al.: Deep interest network for click-through rate prediction. In: KDD, pp. 1059–1068. ACM (2018)

Leveraging Imperfect Sources to Detect Fairwashing in Black-Box Auditing

Jade Garcia Bourrée[1(✉)], Erwan Le Merrer[2], Benoît Rottembourg[4], and Gilles Tredan[3]

[1] EPFL, Lausanne, Switzerland
jade.garcia-bourree@epfl.ch
[2] Univ Rennes, Inria, CNRS, IRISA, Rennes, France
[3] LAAS, CNRS, Toulouse, France
[4] Inria, Paris, France

Abstract. Algorithmic auditing has become central to platform accountability under frameworks such as the AI Act and the Digital Services Act. In practice, this obligation is discharged through dedicated Audit APIs. This architecture creates a paradox: the entity under scrutiny controls the evaluation interface. A platform facing legal sanctions can serve a compliant surrogate model on its Audit API, while running a discriminatory production system. This deceptive practice is known as fairwashing. Manipulation is undetectable if the auditor relies on only one source. To address this limitation, we introduce the Two-Source Audit Model (2SAM). This model cross-references the Audit API with an independent trusted stream. The key insight is that the trusted stream does not need to be perfectly aligned with the Audit API. We introduce a consistency proxy, a probabilistic mapping that can reconcile discrepancies between sources. This approach yields three results. First, we quantify the rate of manipulation above which a single-source auditor is blind. Second, we show how proxy quality governs detection power. Third, we provide a closed-form budget condition guaranteeing detection at any target confidence level, closing the blind spot mentioned above. We validate 2SAM on the UCI Adult dataset, achieving 70% detection power with as few as 127 cross-verification queries out of a total budget of 750, using a name-based gender proxy with 94.2% accuracy.

1 Introduction

The widespread deployment of machine learning systems in high-stakes decision making has led legislators to mandate external audits. Frameworks such as the cro:AI ActArtificial Intelligence Act [14] (AI Act) and the cro:DSADigital Services Act [13] (DSA) now require platforms to demonstrate that their systems do not perpetuate systemic biases, an obligation discharged in practice through dedicated *Audit APIs*. This architecture contains a structural paradox: the very entity being scrutinized is the sole provider of the data used for its evaluation.

A platform facing legal sanctions has a clear incentive to manipulate its Audit API. It can appear compliant while users see a non-compliant interface. This

M. Ceci et al. (Eds.): ECML PKDD 2026, LNAI 16941, pp. 409–426, 2027.
https://doi.org/10.1007/978-3-032-37654-1_24

deceptive practice is called fairwashing [1]. This is not theoretical. During the 2024 European Parliament elections, researchers found significant discrepancies between TikTok's official API and its public interface [8]. Meta's advertising ecosystem showed similar inconsistencies [3]. Manipulation was detectable only when another source was available for comparison. Without one, the Audit API's output raised no suspicion.

We formalize this vulnerability and show that cross-source verification is not just desirable but a mathematical necessity. Prior work [17] formalizes this idea, assuming the auditor has a perfectly aligned reference dataset (an external dataset matching the system under audit)—an assumption rarely met in practice. We address this by introducing the Two-Source Audit Model (2SAM), which detects manipulation via an imperfect consistency proxy, as previously defined. Our contributions are:

- **A quantification of the single-source blind spot (Sect. 3.2):** We derive a closed-form expression for the manipulation rate γ_0 beyond which a single-source auditor cannot distinguish a fairwashed interface from a genuinely fair one, no matter how many queries are issued (Lemma 1).
- **The 2SAM and its consistency proxy (Sect. 3.3):** We introduce a probabilistic mapping that reconciles heterogeneous sources despite their discrepancies, and show that platform-influenced calibration of this proxy renders detection impossible (Theorem 2).
- **Detection power as a function of proxy quality (Sect. 3.4):** We characterize how proxy noise propagates into detection power (Theorem 2), and provide a condition to bypass the blind spot identified above (Theorem 3).
- **Experimental validation (Sect. 4):** We validate 2SAM on the UCI Adult dataset, demonstrating 70% detection power with as few as 127 cross-verification queries out of a total number of 750, using a name-based gender proxy with 94.2% accuracy. It shows that strong guarantees are achievable at modest cost, even with an imperfect proxy.

2 Related Work

The study of bias in automated decision systems has produced a rich taxonomy of harms, fairness notions, and mitigation strategies [27,28], including analyses framed specifically through statistical parity [7], the family to which our criterion belongs.

Black-Box Fairness Auditing. Fairness auditing through black-box query access has been formalized as a statistical estimation problem [11,15,31], where drawing significant conclusions under a finite query budget is a central challenge [29]. Active auditing strategies have been proposed to improve query efficiency [26,31]. However, these approaches assume that the auditor can impose consistency on the queried model by hypothesis, which sidesteps the manipulation problem entirely. More fundamentally, Godinot et al. [19] show that under adversarial manipulation, the difficulty of auditing varies across models in ways that active strategies cannot compensate for.

Adversarial Auditing and Fairwashing. The concept of fairwashing, where a model appears fair only during audits, was introduced by Aivodji et al. [1] and developed further by Fukuchi et al. [16]. Constructive responses have been proposed. Garcia Bourrée et al. [17] show that an auditor with a private, labeled reference dataset can detect manipulation. We build on this two-source insight and relax its key assumption. Our trusted stream need not align perfectly with the Audit API, which lets us cover practical cases that [17] cannot handle. We also provide a way to obtain the ground-truth labels.

Proxies for Sensitive Attributes. Proxy-based inference of sensitive attributes (e.g., using correlated variables such as geographic location to infer attributes like race or gender) has been studied for model training, fairness evaluation, and audit contexts. The impact of proxy noise (the inaccuracy introduced when proxies imperfectly reflect sensitive attributes) on audit reliability is still understudied. Existing work assumes perfect proxies or studies noise in theoretical estimation tasks. We differ on both counts. We use proxies as consistency bridges, not estimators, and provide explicit guarantees on how proxy noise affects detection power.

Distribution Shift and Cryptographic Approaches. The 2SAM consistency check is structurally related to two-sample testing and data drift monitoring. Another line of work addresses accountability using cryptographic mechanisms that offer stronger guarantees but require zero-knowledge proofs, which are not currently supported by regulation. The 2SAM relies on API queries and provides probabilistic guarantees that meet current regulatory requirements.

3 Methodology

This section develops our approach along four steps. We first define the auditing game and its actors (Sect. 3.1). This model is standard and serves as the foundation for our analysis. We then show the preliminary negative result that single-source auditing is structurally insufficient (Sect. 3.2): Theorem 1 establishes in our formalism that fairwashing is undetectable without an external reference, and Lemma 1 quantifies the resulting blind spot γ_0. These two results motivate our main contribution: the Two-Source Audit Model (2SAM), which introduces a *trusted second stream*, formalizes the audit protocol, and defines the consistency proxy ϕ (Sect. 3.3). Finally, Sect. 3.4 derives the statistical guarantees of the 2SAM; Theorem 2 and Theorem 3 are our core theoretical contributions: they characterize detection power as a function of proxy quality p_ϕ, and provide an explicit budget condition that closes the blind spot identified in Sect. 3.2.

3.1 The Auditing Game: Formal Model

We now introduce the formal model underlying our analysis.

Actors and Spaces. We consider two actors: a platform and an auditor. Upon regulatory request, the platform exposes a dedicated Audit API: a query interface to access a decision model $h_{\text{audit}} : \mathcal{Z} \to \mathcal{Y}$, where $\mathcal{Z} = \mathcal{X} \times \mathcal{S}$ is the input space consisting of non-sensitive features $\mathcal{X} \subseteq \mathbb{R}^d$ and a binary sensitive feature $\mathcal{S} \in \{0,1\}$, and $\mathcal{Y} = \{0,1\}$ is the binary output space. On the Audit API, the auditor controls the inputs $Q = \{z_i\}_{i=1}^{N_{\text{audit}}}$ with $z = (x,s) \in \mathcal{Z}$ drawn from a distribution $\mathcal{D}$, and observes the corresponding output labels.

Fairness Metric and Estimation Error. The auditor seeks to verify whether the platform satisfies $\mu(h_{\text{audit}}, \mathcal{D}) \geq \tau$, with τ the compliance threshold. Throughout this paper, we instantiate μ as the *Disparate Impact* (DI) metric [4,15], defined as the ratio of acceptance rates between the unprivileged ($S=0$) and privileged ($S=1$) groups:

$$\mu(h_{\text{audit}}) = \frac{\mathbb{P}z \sim \mathcal{D}(h_{\text{audit}}(z) = 1 \mid S = 0)}{\mathbb{P}z \sim \mathcal{D}(h_{\text{audit}}(z) = 1 \mid S = 1)}, \tag{1}$$

with compliance threshold $\tau = 80\%$, following the EEOC 80% rule [12]. Because the auditor issues a finite number of queries N_{audit}, the estimated metric $\hat{\mu}(h_{\text{audit}})$ is subject to sampling variability. At significance level α, the margin of error over N_{audit} queries is:

$$\epsilon = z_\alpha \frac{\sigma}{\sqrt{N_{\text{audit}}}}, \tag{2}$$

where z_α is the normal quantile and $\sigma/\sqrt{N_{\text{audit}}}$ is the standard error. The auditor concludes that the platform is *compliant* if $\hat{\mu}(h_{\text{audit}}) \geq \tau$, and *non-compliant* otherwise.

Manipulation Detection. So far, the auditor's goal has been framed as estimation: deciding whether $\mu(h_{\text{audit}}, \mathcal{D}) \geq \tau$. A more adversarial objective arises when the platform may strategically manipulate the Audit API. In this case, the auditor must additionally determine whether the interface it queries faithfully reflects the platform's true production model h_{verify}, or whether it has been replaced by a compliant surrogate $h_{\text{audit}} \neq h_{\text{verify}}$.

The core challenge is to quantify the expected discrepancy between the two models: how much their outputs can differ, and under what conditions this difference becomes statistically distinguishable from noise. This gap is the detection target of our framework.

We call this second objective manipulation detection. It is logically distinct from fairness estimation: a platform may be simultaneously fair and honest, fair but dishonest, or unfair and dishonest.

3.2 The Failure of Single-Source Auditing

The fundamental weakness of single-source audits lies in the incentive misalignment created by regulations such as the AI Act and the DSA: the platform controls both the system being evaluated and the interface used to evaluate it.

Adversarial Reduction. The auditor controls the inputs $z = (x, s)$ submitted to the Audit API and observes only the outputs. Consequently, any internal transformation the platform applies (*e.g.*, weight fine-tuning [21], reject-option classification [24], post-processing [23,25]) is observable through its effect on output labels. Without loss of generality, every manipulation strategy therefore reduces to a probabilistic *label-flipping.* This reduction is key to the generality of our results: the guarantees derived below hold against any manipulation mechanism, not just label-flipping.

Lemma 1 (Detectability Gap). *In a strict black-box setting where the auditor only has access to a single Audit API, any manipulation that satisfies the fairness threshold is undetectable.*

Proof The platform knows the queries Q and the function μ that the auditor estimates. If the platform's model h_{verify} is already in compliance ($\mu(h_{\text{verify}}, Q) \geq \tau$), then the platform returns the non-manipulated h_{verify} to the auditor. If the property is violated ($\mu(h_{\text{verify}}, Q) < \tau$), the platform risks being sanctioned. Hence, there is an incentive to find another model h_{audit} that satisfies the property. First, assume that no such h_{audit} exists: this means that there exists a query set Q for which every possible answer leads to a violation of the property. In other words, all platforms are guilty given Q, and the check is trivial. In this scenario, the audit cannot conclude that a platform is fair. Second, consider that the platform finds a model h_{audit} that satisfies the property ($\mu(h_{\text{audit}}, Q) \geq \tau$). The auditor estimates fairness on the distribution given by h_{audit} (*i.e.* the fairwashed responses), and not the one given by h_{verify}. The auditor then erroneously concludes that the platform is compliant because h_{audit} is. Furthermore, fairwashed responses can be made internally consistent, rendering the manipulation indistinguishable from a naturally fair model [16]. The audit, therefore, concludes on the compliance of the interface, not the platform.

Use Case. We assume that the platform applies *positive discrimination* by flipping negative labels to positive for the unprivileged group. The manipulation rate γ is defined as the fraction of queries on which h_{audit} and h_{verify} disagree for the unprivileged group:

$$\gamma = \frac{|\{z : h_{\text{audit}}(z) = 1, h_{\text{verify}}(z) = 0, S = 0\}|}{|\{z : h_{\text{verify}}(z) = 0, S = 0\}|}. \tag{3}$$

Theorem 1. *At significance level α, the auditor using N_{audit} queries on the Audit API is robust to manipulations at rate $\gamma < \gamma_0$, where:*

$$\gamma_0 = \frac{z_\alpha \sigma}{\sqrt{N_{\text{audit}}}\left(\frac{1}{Y_{\text{audit}}} - \tau\right)}, \tag{4}$$

with $Y_{\text{audit}} = \mathbb{P}(h_{\text{audit}}(z) = 1 \mid S = 1)$ and $\sigma/\sqrt{N_{\text{audit}}}$ the standard error of Eq. (2).

Proof. With positive discrimination at rate γ,

$$\begin{aligned} P(h_{\text{audit}}(z) = 1|S = 0) &= \underbrace{P(h_{\text{verify}}(z) = 1|S = 0)}_{\text{already positive output}} + \underbrace{\gamma P(h_{\text{verify}}(z) = 0|S = 0)}_{\text{positive discrimination}} \\ &= P(h_{\text{verify}}(z) = 1|S = 0)(1 - \gamma) + \gamma \end{aligned}$$

Thus $\mu(h_{\text{audit}}) = \mu(h_{\text{verify}})(1-\gamma) + \frac{\gamma}{Y_{\text{audit}}}$ with $Y_{\text{audit}} = \mathbb{P}(h_{\text{audit}}(z) = 1 \mid S = 1)$. The platform wants to appear fair to the auditor ($\hat{\mu}(h_{\text{audit}}) \geq \tau$). At confidence level α, $\mu(h_{\text{audit}}) - \epsilon \leq \hat{\mu}(h_{\text{audit}}) \leq \mu(h_{\text{audit}}) + \epsilon$. In the worst case scenario (for the platform), $\hat{\mu}(h_{\text{audit}}) = \mu(h_{\text{audit}}) - \epsilon$. A necessary condition is: $\mu(h_{\text{verify}})(1 - \gamma) + \frac{\gamma}{Y_{\text{audit}}} - \epsilon \geq \tau$. As the platform manipulates h_{audit} only when h_{verify} is not fair (otherwise, $h_{\text{audit}} = h_{\text{verify}}$ is sufficient), $\mu(h_{\text{verify}}) \leq \tau$. The platform appears fair if at least $\tau(1 - \gamma) + \frac{\gamma}{Y_{\text{audit}}} - \epsilon \geq \tau$. This last equation can be written as well as $\gamma \geq \frac{\epsilon}{\frac{1}{Y_{\text{audit}}} - \tau}$. The auditor is thus robust to positive discrimination up to $\frac{\epsilon}{\left(\frac{1}{Y_{\text{audit}}} - \tau\right)}$ manipulations, which is the expected result.

Takeaway. The blind spot γ_0 is not a limitation of the auditor's strategy but a fundamental property of the single-source setting: no query budget can compensate for the absence of an external reference. While Lemma 1 holds for any manipulation, Theorem 1 instantiates γ_0 for positive discrimination; other manipulations admit their own bounds. This motivates the introduction of a trusted stream in Sect. 3.3.

3.3 The Two-Source Audit Model

The Need for a Second Source. Theorem 1 shows in our formalism that without an external reference, fairwashing is structurally undetectable, a need first established in [17]. The auditor cannot distinguish a manipulated interface from a genuinely fair one on the basis of Audit API outputs alone. This impossibility is not a limitation of the auditor's strategy but a fundamental property of the single-source setting. It motivates introducing an external reference that the platform does not control. We formalize this external source as a trusted stream s_T: a data source whose labels reflect the platform's true behavior and are not subject to strategic manipulation. The auditor's task then becomes to verify the *consistency* between the Audit API source s_A and s_T.

Protocol. The 2SAM auditing game proceeds sequentially in six steps.

1. **Audit API construction.** Upon regulatory request, the platform creates and exposes a dedicated Audit API. This step is mandated by frameworks such as the DSA and AI Act: the platform cannot refuse to provide auditor access.
2. **Query submission.** The auditor submits N_{audit} queries $Q = \{(z_{A,i})_{i=1}^{N_{\text{audit}}}\}$ to the Audit API.
3. **Platform response (manipulation or not).** Upon receiving the auditor's queries, the platform chooses whether to serve its true production model $h_{\text{audit}} = h_{\text{verify}}$ or a fairwashed surrogate $h_{\text{audit}} \neq h_{\text{verify}}$. This substitution is triggered in a single, consistent step across all incoming queries.
4. **Label collection.** The auditor collects the output labels $\{h_{\text{audit}}(z_{A,i})_{i=1}^{N_{\text{audit}}}\}$ from the Audit API.
5. **Cross-verification.** The auditor collects N_{verify} observations from the trusted stream s_T and applies the consistency proxy ϕ (defined below) to map each trusted observation to a predicted Audit API observation. The inconsistency count $I = |\{i : \phi(z_{T,i}, y_{T,i}) \neq (z_{A,i}, h_{\text{audit}}(z_{A,i}))\}|$ is computed over the N_{verify} cross-verified pairs.
6. **Verdict.** The auditor runs two independent tests. A platform is flagged as *Unfair* if it fails the fairness test ($\hat{\mu}(h_{\text{audit}}) < \tau$) and as *Manipulative* if it fails the consistency test ($I \geq I_0$), where I_0 is the rejection threshold derived in Sect. 3.4. Otherwise the platform is considered fair ($\hat{\mu}(h_{\text{audit}}) \geq \tau$) and non-manipulative ($I < I_0$).

Regulatory Insight. This protocol maps directly onto the obligations of the DSA and AI Act. The verdict structure makes an operationally important distinction that current regulatory texts often mix: *unfairness* (the system discriminates) and *fairwashing* (the system discriminates but conceals it through the Audit API) require different legal responses. Separating the two tests provides regulators with actionable, legally distinguishable outcomes.

The Consistency Proxy. In general, s_A and s_T will not share the same feature space or encoding. What constitutes a valid trusted stream depends on the context. In the setting of [17], s_T is a privately labeled reference dataset held by the auditor, a strong assumption that provides a perfect baseline but is costly to acquire. Our contribution is to relax this assumption: we show in Sect. 3.4 that s_T need not be perfectly aligned with s_A to enable detection, as long as the degree of misalignment can be characterized.

We first consider the idealized case of a perfect mapping between the two sources: every observation from s_T can be matched unambiguously to a corresponding Audit API query-call (as was the case for the historical $\mathbb{X}$ API [30]). Here, any inconsistency is necessarily caused by platform manipulation; a single inconsistency suffices to flag fairwashing.

In practice, such a perfect mapping is rarely available: the two sources may differ in feature space, granularity, stochasticity, or encoding, so that even an honest platform produces some apparent inconsistencies. To handle this realistic setting, we introduce a consistency proxy ϕ that reconciles the two sources despite their discrepancies:

Definition 1 (Proxy). *A proxy is a probabilistic mapping*

$$\phi : \mathcal{Z}_T \times \{0,1\} \longrightarrow \mathcal{Z}_A \times \{0,1\}, \qquad (z_T, y_T) \longmapsto (z_A, y_A) \quad w.p.\ p_{z_T, y_T}.$$

The quality parameter $p_\phi \in [0,1]$ denotes the average accuracy of ϕ on an honest platform. It mathematically decouples measurement noise ($q_\phi = 1 - p_\phi$) from intentional manipulation (γ). When $p_\phi = 1$, we recover the perfect case: every inconsistency signals manipulation. When $p_\phi < 1$, some inconsistencies arise from proxy noise alone, which motivates the hypothesis test in Sect. 3.4.

Proxy Independence. For the consistency check to be valid, p_ϕ must be estimated from external sources (*e.g.*, national censuses, demographic surveys, or journalistic investigations), never from platform-provided metadata. This independence condition is justified through the following result.

Lemma 2 (Proxy Poisoning). *In a strict black-box setting where the auditor relies on a proxy quality parameter p_ϕ derived from the platform's own declarations, any manipulation satisfying the fairness threshold remains statistically undetectable.*

Proof. The platform knows μ and D, hence can compute the minimum manipulation rate γ needed to satisfy $\mu(h_{\text{audit}}) \geq \tau$ via Theorem 1. It then estimates the expected inconsistency count under H_1: $\hat{I} = N_{\text{verify}} \cdot q_\phi^\gamma = N_{\text{verify}} \cdot (\gamma p_\phi + (1-\gamma) q_\phi)$. The platform then declares $\tilde{p}_\phi$ such that the auditor's calibrated threshold $I_0(\tilde{q}_\phi)$ satisfies $I_0(\tilde{q}_\phi) \geq \hat{I}$, i.e. such that $\hat{I}$ falls below the rejection region. It suffices to find $\tilde{p}_\phi$ such that: $\sum_{i=0}^{\hat{I}} \binom{N_{\text{verify}}}{i} \tilde{q}_\phi^i \tilde{p}_\phi^{N_{\text{verify}}-i} \geq 1 - \alpha$, with $\tilde{q}_\phi = \gamma p_\phi + (1-\gamma) q_\phi$. Since the left-hand side is continuous and increasing in $\tilde{q}_\phi$, such a $\tilde{p}_\phi = 1 - \tilde{q}_\phi$ always exists. Under this declared value, the auditor's threshold absorbs the manipulation signal exactly, and the test has power equal to its size α regardless of N_{verify}.

Regulatory Insight. Lemma 2 has a direct regulatory implication: platforms must never be allowed to provide or influence the metadata used to calibrate the auditor's proxy. This is the algorithmic analogue of the auditor independence principle in financial auditing.

3.4 Detection Guarantees

We now derive the statistical guarantees of the 2SAM against fairwashing manipulation of the Audit API. The key question is: **when $p_\phi < 1$, how many inconsistencies are needed to distinguish proxy noise from intentional manipulation?**

Hypothesis Test. Under H_0 (honest platform, $h_{\text{audit}} = h_{\text{verify}}$), inconsistencies arise only from proxy noise: $I \sim \text{Binomial}(N_{\text{verify}}, q_\phi)$. The rejection threshold controlling the Type I error (false accusation) at level α is:

$$I_0 = \min\left\{ n : \sum_{i=0}^{n} \binom{N_{\text{verify}}}{i} q_\phi^i \, p_\phi^{N_{\text{verify}}-i} \geq 1-\alpha \right\}. \tag{5}$$

Under H_1 (fairwashing at rate γ), the inconsistency probability increases to $q_\phi^\gamma = \gamma p_\phi + (1-\gamma) q_\phi$: an inconsistency occurs either when the proxy correctly identifies a manipulated label (prob. γp_ϕ) or incorrectly predicts an honest one (prob. $(1-\gamma)q_\phi$).

Theorem 2 (Detection Power). *With significance level α and N_{verify} queries, the probability that the auditor detects manipulation at rate γ is:*

$$p_{\text{manip}}(\gamma) = 1 - F_{\mathcal{B}(N_{\text{verify}}, q_\phi^\gamma)}(I_0), \tag{6}$$

where $F_{\mathcal{B}}$ is the binomial CDF and $q_\phi^\gamma = \gamma p_\phi + (1-\gamma) q_\phi$.

Proof. Under H_1, $I \sim \text{Binomial}(N_{\text{verify}}, q_\phi^\gamma)$. The detection probability is the tail probability beyond the rejection threshold: $p_{\text{manip}}(\gamma) = 1 - F_{\mathcal{B}(N_{\text{verify}}, q_\phi^\gamma)}(I_0)$.

Takeaway. The probability that the auditor detects manipulation p_{manip} is increasing in both γ and p_ϕ: a more accurate proxy detects weaker manipulations.

Use Case. In the use case of the platform using positive-discrimination fairwashing, we can derive the mitigation guarantee under which the auditor succeeds the audit. To do so, we assume that the auditor uses N_{audit} queries to estimate the fairness on the Audit API and verifies N_{verify} queries through its trusted source.

Theorem 3 (2SAM Mitigation Guarantee). *A Two-Source Audit succeeds with confidence $1-\alpha$ against positive-discrimination fairwashing if the budget $(N_{\text{audit}}, N_{\text{verify}})$ satisfies:*

$$F_{\mathcal{B}(N_{\text{verify}},\, q_\phi^{\gamma_0})}(I_0) \leq \alpha, \tag{7}$$

with $\gamma_0 = \frac{z_\alpha \sigma}{\sqrt{N_{\text{audit}}}\left(\frac{1}{Y_{\text{audit}}} - \tau\right)}$ *and* $I_0 = \min\left\{ n : \sum_{i=0}^{n} \binom{N_{\text{verify}}}{i} q_\phi^i \, p_\phi^{N_{\text{verify}}-i} \geq 1-\alpha \right\}$.

Proof. If $\gamma < \gamma_0$: the platform fails the fairness test on the Audit API with probability $\geq 1-\alpha$ by definition of γ_0. If $\gamma \geq \gamma_0$: the platform may pass the fairness test, but since p_{manip} is monotone in γ, the detection probability is at least $p_{\text{manip}}(\gamma_0) \geq 1-\alpha$ by the budget condition.

Remark. The choice of a binomial law follows from assuming i.i.d. proxy errors: any distribution admitting a computable quantile fits the same test, changing only the expression of I_0 and leaving Theorems 2–3 unaffected.

3.5 Instantiation: the User Interface as a Trusted Stream

The model above applies to any trusted stream s_T with a consistency proxy p_ϕ. A natural and practically available candidate, particularly relevant for regulators operating under the DSA or AI Act, is the platform's own *User Interface*, the public interface actually encountered by users. It is the source that empirical studies have already used intuitively: comparisons between TikTok's official API and its public interface during the 2024 European elections [8], and between Meta's advertising API and observable user-facing behavior [3], revealed discrepancies that the Audit API alone would never have surfaced. The 2SAM provides formal guarantees for precisely this kind of cross-source comparison.

User Interface Integrity. Using the User Interface as s_T requires one additional assumption: the platform must not manipulate the User Interface in a targeted manner against the auditor. Auditors can further strengthen this assumption by applying standard anonymization techniques (IP rotation, behavioral mimicry), thereby raising the cost of auditor identification for the platform.

Illustrations. We illustrate the proxy with two examples.

Example 1: Data Consistency in Social Networks. Consider an API providing structured access to social media data (e.g., the historical 𝕏 API [30] or the TikTok one [8]). Such APIs are theoretically redundant with the platform's web interface, serving primarily to spare auditors the burden of web scraping. In this baseline case, the auditor expects strict identity between the Audit API and the User interface. The proxy is the identity function:

$$\phi_{\mathbb{X}}(z_T, y_T) = (z_T, y_T) \text{ with probability } p_\phi = 1. \tag{8}$$

Any discrepancy found through scraping would immediately signal an intentional manipulation in the data served to auditors versus users.

Example 2 (Recruitment Algorithms [20]*).* Hiring tools often face scrutiny for gender or racial bias [20]. In an audit setting, the Audit API might provide explicit fields for protected features (e.g., *Gender*), whereas the User Interface (the resume submission portal) only contains text. The auditor can leverage a proxy ϕ_{gen} that estimates gender from first names based on linguistic patterns [5,6]. Names ending in *a, e, i* map to Female ($p = 1$); names ending in *h, y* map ambiguously ($p = 0.5$); others map to Male ($p = 1$). This proxy achieves $p_\phi = 94.2\%$ on French names and serves as our experimental instantiation (Sect. 4).

4 Experiments

We empirically validate the 2SAM on the UCI Adult dataset [10] (and on COMPAS [2] in Sect. 4.5). As we do not have access to specialized APIs as regulators would, we simulate the auditing game described in Sect. 3.1: the User Interface is a logistic regression trained on the full dataset, and the Audit API is its fairwashed counterpart. Each experiment is averaged on 20 runs, with shaded areas being the associated standard deviation. We demonstrate how the two-source approach closes the structural blind spot of single-source auditing, and characterize the role of proxy quality across three questions: **Q1.** How does proxy quality affect detection power? (Sect. 4.2) **Q2.** Does the 2SAM detect fairwashing on a use case? (Sect. 4.3) **Q3.** What is the budget overhead of two-source auditing? (Sect. 4.4)

4.1 Experimental Setup

Data and Model. We train a logistic regression to predict whether an individual's income exceeds $50,000. This production model serves as our ground truth User Interface and exhibits a significant gender bias, with a disparate impact $\mu = 0.24$, failing the regulatory threshold of $\tau = 80\%$ with an accuracy of 76%.

Fairwashing Simulation. To simulate a strategic platform, we implement a label-flipping strategy on the Audit API. The platform applies positive discrimination by flipping negative labels to positive for the unprivileged group (Female) at a rate γ. As discussed in Sect. 4.5, similar results are achievable using other fairwashing methods such as Score Shifting, Targeted Flipping, and Randomized Fairwashing.

Proxy Family. All experiments use a name-based gender proxy, leveraging the first names added to each profile following the top 10 names in France in 2024 [22][1]. We model the proxy family as follows: the proxy knows the true gender for a fraction $p_\phi \in [0, 1]$ of individuals without error, and for the remaining fraction $(1 - p_\phi)$ it guesses uniformly at random. Formally, for each individual:

$$\phi(x_T, y_T) = \begin{cases} gender_{\text{true}} & \text{with probability } p_\phi, \\ \text{Uniform}(\{0, 1\}) & \text{with probability } 1 - p_\phi. \end{cases} \tag{9}$$

This parametrization yields a proxy family indexed by $p_\phi \in [0.5, 1]$, where $p_\phi = 0.5$ corresponds to a random proxy and $p_\phi = 1$ to a perfect proxy. It allows us to study the effect of proxy quality continuously across experiments to answer **Q1** and **Q2**.

A natural instantiation of this family is the linguistic proxy ϕ_{gen} introduced in Example 2 (Sect. 3.3), which maps names to gender based on their last letter [5].

[1] Female names: Louise, Jade, Ambre, Alba, Emma, Alma, Romy, Rose, Alice, Anna. Male names: Gabriel, Raphael, Louis, Leo, Noah, Arthur, Adam, Jules, Mael, Leon.

In our dataset, this proxy achieves $p_\phi = 94.2\%$ and serves as a reference point in all three experiments.

4.2 Q1 — Effect of Proxy Quality on Detection Power

We first study how proxy quality p_ϕ impacts detection power $p_{\text{manip}}(\gamma)$, as characterized by Theorem 2. We compute p_{manip} using Eq. (6) with $N_{\text{verify}} = 127$ and $\alpha = 0.05$.

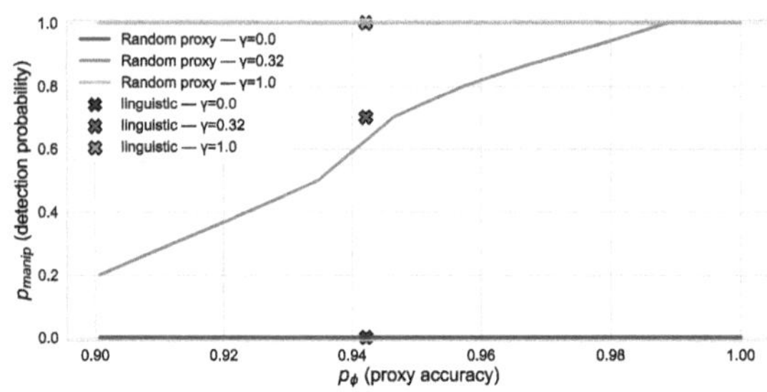

Fig. 1. Detection power p_{manip} as a function of proxy quality p_ϕ, for several manipulation rates γ.

Figure 1 illustrates the detection power p_{manip} as a function of proxy quality p_ϕ, for three manipulation rates $\gamma \in \{0.0, 0.32, 1\}$, under two proxy families: the continuous *Noisy* proxy (solid lines) and the *Linguistic* proxy ϕ_{gen} (crosses).

The figure shows a phase transition in the detection power. For $\gamma = 0\%$, p_{manip} remains at the nominal level $\alpha = 0.05$ across all p_ϕ, confirming that Type I error is correctly controlled. For $\gamma > 0\%$, p_{manip} rises steeply with both p_ϕ and γ, in agreement with Theorem 2. The linguistic proxy ϕ_{gen} ($p_\phi = 94.2\%$) lies in the middle, achieving $p_{\text{manip}} = 70\%$ at $\gamma = 32\%$ and $p_{\text{manip}} = 100\%$ at $\gamma = 100\%$.

Takeaway. These results establish that imperfect proxies are practically viable for fairwashing detection, but that proxy quality must be verified prior to deployment.

4.3 Q2 — Fairwashing Detection on a Use Case

We now instantiate the full 2SAM workflow on our running example, using the linguistic proxy ϕ_{gen}. This experiment illustrates Theorem 1 (failure of single-source auditing) and Theorem 2 (detection by the 2SAM) on the same setting.

Figure 2 illustrates the Platform's Dilemma. As the platform increases γ toward the deception bound $\gamma_0 = 32\%$, the empirical fairness $\hat{\mu}(h_{\text{audit}})$ crosses the $\tau = 80\%$ threshold (Fig. 2a). Without an external reference, the single-source auditor concludes that the platform is fair, a false negative that Theorem 1 proves

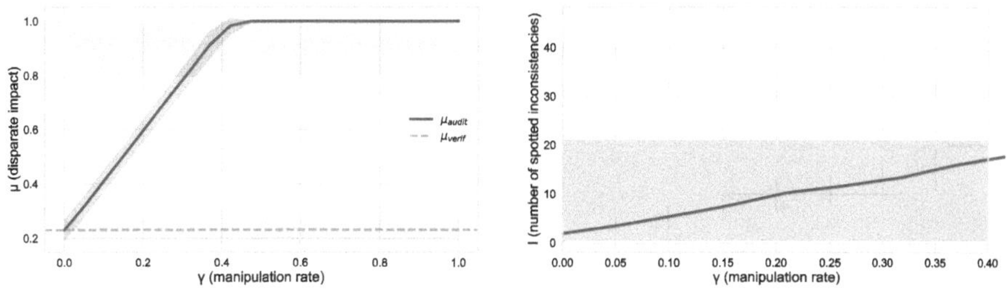

(a) Estimated fairness as γ increases. (b) Inconsistency count I as γ increases.

Fig. 2. Single-source failure (left) and 2SAM detection (right) under increasing manipulation rate γ. The gray area marks the fair zone ($\hat{\mu}(Colorfigureonline) \geq \tau$). The single-source auditor incorrectly concludes compliance beyond $\gamma_0 = 32\%$.

is unavoidable in the single-source setting. However, as γ increases, the inconsistency count I rises monotonically: the same label-flipping that drives $\hat{\mu}(h_{\text{audit}})$ above τ in Fig. 2a simultaneously increases the signal detected by the 2SAM. At some point, I will exceed the rejection threshold I_0, and the platform is flagged as manipulative. The platform thus faces an inescapable trade-off: any manipulation sufficient to appear fair to a single-source auditor is detectable by the 2SAM.

Takeaway. The 2SAM closes exactly the blind spot identified in Sect. 3.2: the same manipulation rate γ_0 that makes the platform invisible to a single-source auditor makes it detectable to the 2SAM auditor. The proxy noise is absorbed by the hypothesis test without affecting the reliability of the verdict.

4.4 Q3 — Budget Allocation and Scalability

So far, we have established that the 2SAM detects manipulation at rate γ_0—the minimum rate at which the platform must lie to appear fair. We now ask: at what cost? Fig. 3 plots detection power p_{manip} against estimation accuracy $1 - \epsilon$ for this worst-case manipulation γ_0, as the auditor varies her budget allocation $\beta \in [0, 1]$: a fraction β of the total budget N is cross-verified against the User Interface.

The Pareto frontier reveals a clear trade-off: allocating more queries to cross-verification improves detection power at the cost of estimation accuracy. The highlighted point ($\beta = 0.9$, $\epsilon = 57.2\%$) achieves $p_{\text{manip}} = 100\%$ with only around 340 cross-verification queries out of $N = 750$, making it statistically impossible for the platform to appear both fair and honest at the same time.

Takeaway. Theorem 3 provides a closed-form minimal N_{verify}, and automated proxies eliminate manual labeling costs. Regulators can thus maintain low-intensity monitoring and trigger a high-confidence consistency check only when suspicious patterns emerge. Additional visualizations illustrating the

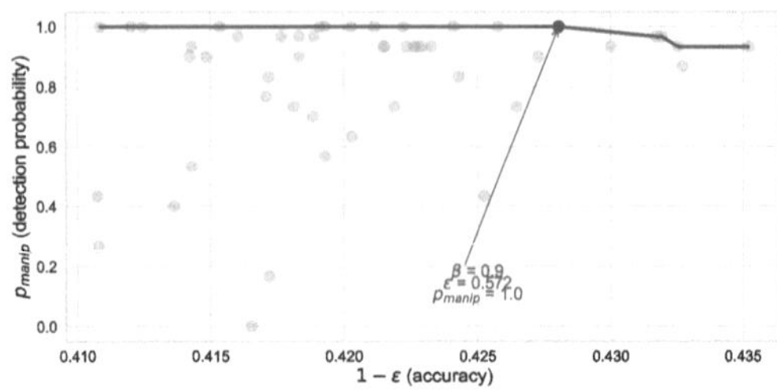

Fig. 3. Pareto frontier for estimating Disparate Impact while checking for fairwashing under a fixed audit budget ($N = 750$). Each point corresponds to a budget allocation β.

phase-transition structure of detection power as a function of proxy quality, verification budget, and audit/verify ratio β are provided in the full version of the paper [18].

Proxy construction remains context-dependent: the linguistic proxy ϕ_{gen} is specific to French naming conventions, and practitioners operating in different cultural or demographic contexts should derive proxies from locally appropriate external sources such as national censuses or demographic surveys. It is not uncommon for such proxies to be known to auditors. For instance, a regulatory authority may have access to whistle-blowers, or a consumer association might recruit groups of customers capable of simulating behaviors [9].

4.5 Additional Experiments on Generalization

Additional Experiments with Other Fairwashing Techniques. To assess the robustness of the 2SAM, we evaluate three additional fairwashing techniques on the UCI Adult dataset using the linguistic proxy ϕ_{gen} ($p_\phi = 94.2\%$).

Table 1. Minimal manipulation level $\gamma^\star$ for each fairwashing technique, along with the resulting disparate impact and empirical detection probability.

Technique	$\gamma^\star$	DI($\gamma^\star$)	p_{manip}
Positive Discrimination	32%	83%	70%
Score Shifting	54%	82%	57%
Targeted Flipping	30%	82%	37%
Randomized	36%	81%	80%

Score Shifting. The platform modifies the internal scores of the classifier. For each protected individual i, the new score is $s_i^{\text{fw}} = \min\{1, s_i + \gamma\Delta\}$, where Δ controls the maximum shift. Predictions are obtained by thresholding s_i^{fw}.

Targeted Flipping. This strategy selects the subset of protected individuals with negative predictions but highest classifier scores. Let $S = \{i : s_i \text{ high}, s_i < \tau, s_i \in \text{protected group}\}$. The platform flips the top $\gamma|S|$ individuals in S. This maximizes the fairness improvement for a given manipulation budget.

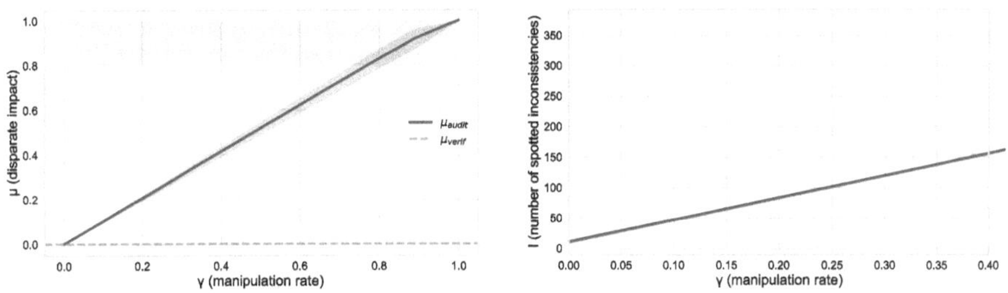

(a) Estimated fairness as γ increases. (b) Inconsistency count I as γ increases.

Fig. 4. Single-source failure (left) and 2SAM detection (right) under increasing manipulation rate γ. The gray area marks the fair zone ($\hat{\mu} \geq \tau$). The single-source auditor incorrectly concludes compliance beyond $\gamma_0 \approx 32\%$. (Color figure online)

Randomized Fairwashing. In this stochastic strategy, each protected individual with a negative prediction is flipped independently with probability γ. Formally, $\hat{y}_i^{\text{fw}} = 1$ with probability γ if $\hat{y}_i = 0$ and $s_i = 0$. This randomization reduces the correlation structure of inconsistencies and makes the manipulation more difficult to detect through binomial consistency tests.

Analysis and Takeaway. Table 1 shows that Score Shifting requires a substantially larger manipulation rate ($\gamma^\star = 54\%$) to reach compliance, which produces a stronger inconsistency signal and yields the second-highest detection power ($p_{\text{manip}} = 57\%$). Targeted Flipping, by contrast, concentrates manipulations on the highest-scoring individuals in the protected group, minimizing the number of label flips needed while maximizing the fairness gain; this efficiency comes at a cost for the auditor, as the resulting inconsistency signal is weaker and detection power drops to 37%. Randomized Fairwashing achieves the highest detection probability (80%) despite a moderate $\gamma^\star$: because flips are applied independently at random, the inconsistencies are distributed across the full protected group rather than concentrated on a specific subpopulation, making the aggregate signal easier to detect through the binomial consistency test. Taken together, these results show that the 2SAM is not specifically tailored to positive discrimination: it exploits any label-level inconsistency between the Audit API and the trusted stream, regardless of the mechanism used to produce it.

Experiment on COMPAS with Fixed-Noise Proxy. The 2SAM framework is not restricted to gender proxies or income prediction tasks. We now demonstrate that the detection guarantees of Theorems 2 and 3 hold across different sensitive attributes, domains, and model families. To extend the experimental evaluation of the 2SAM beyond the UCI Adult dataset, we replicate the auditing game on the COMPAS recidivism dataset [2] using a fixed-noise proxy at 95%. We replace the logistic regression of Sect. 4 with a *random forest* achieving $\mu \approx 0$ (extremely biased) against *race*.

Single-source Failure and 2SAM Detection (Fig. 4). As γ increases, $\hat{\mu}(h_{\text{audit}})$ crosses τ and the single-source auditor incorrectly concludes compliance, while the inconsistency count I rises monotonically. The absence of variance across runs reflects the expressiveness of the Random Forest that produces highly deterministic label-flipping patterns, reducing stochasticity in I and confirming the robustness of Lemma 1 and Theorem 2 in this extreme bias regime.

Takeaway. The 2SAM generalizes beyond its original setting: detection holds across fairwashing mechanisms, sensitive attributes, domains, and model families, because the consistency test reacts to any label-level discrepancy rather than to a specific manipulation strategy or data distribution.

5 Conclusion

Algorithmic auditing is only meaningful if the data used for evaluation cannot be manipulated by the entity being evaluated. This condition is not satisfied by current auditing practice: in a single-source setting, any platform facing regulatory scrutiny can engage in undetectable fairwashing by serving a compliant surrogate model on its Audit API. We have quantified the precise manipulation rate γ_0 beyond which an auditor operating on a single source is blind against positive-discrimination fairwashing.

The Two-Source Audit Model addresses this vulnerability by cross-referencing the Audit API against a trusted stream. Our central finding is that this second source need not be perfect: detection remains statistically guaranteed as long as the consistency proxy exceeds a minimum quality threshold, which is computable before the audit begins and depends only on the target manipulation rate and the auditor's confidence level. Below this threshold, no amount of additional data can compensate for proxy noise; above it, detection is robust, and the additional query budget is modest, as few as 127 queries out of 750 suffice for 70% detection power in our experiments.

Three implications follow for the design of regulatory audit protocols. First, audit frameworks should mandate auditor access to public-facing interfaces, not only to dedicated Audit APIs: the DSA and AI Act currently focus on the latter while leaving the former unaddressed. Second, platforms must never be allowed to provide or influence the metadata used to calibrate the auditor's proxy. Theorem 2 establishes that platform-influenced calibration renders the entire consistency check void, an analogue of the auditor independence principle in financial regulation. Third, the 2SAM provides regulators with a legally defensible budget formula: given a target detection confidence $1 - \alpha$ and a proxy quality estimate p_ϕ, Theorem 3 yields the minimum N_{verify} required, removing the arbitrariness from audit resource allocation.

Ultimately, 2SAM highlights that transparency is not a feature that platforms can "provide" through a single interface. It is a property that must be verified through cross-source evidence. Future regulatory standards should emphasize the importance of auditor-led proxy development (with the help of a subject-matter expert and a data scientist) and ensure that platforms cannot obstruct the collection of public-facing data. By moving from a "trust-by-design" to a "verify-by-consistency" model, we provide a foundation for audits that are resilient to deceptive practices.

Acknowledgments. Erwan Le Merrer and Gilles Tredan acknowledge the support of the French Agence Nationale de la Recherche (ANR), under grant ANR-24-CE23-7787 (project PACMAM).

This work was supported by the Cluster SequoIA Chair FANG funded by ANR, reference ANR-23-IACL-0009.

Disclosure of AI Tools Usage. This manuscript benefited from the use of large language models during the writing process. The authors reviewed and edited all generated suggestions and take full responsibility for the final content.

References

1. Aivodji, U., Arai, H., Fortineau, O., Gambs, S., Hara, S., Tapp, A.: Fairwashing: the risk of rationalization. ICML, (2019)
2. Angwin, J., Larson, J., Mattu, S., Kirchner, L.: Machine bias: there's software used across the country to predict future criminals. and it's biased against blacks. ProPublica (2016)
3. Bagchi, C., Menczer, F., Lundquist, J., Tarafdar, M., Paik, A., Grabowicz, P.A.: Social media algorithms can curb misinformation. arXiv:2409.18393 but do they? arXiv preprint (2024)
4. Barocas, S., Hardt, M., Narayanan, A.: Fairness and Machine Learning: Limitations and Opportunities. MIT Press (2023)
5. Barry, I., Harper, H., A.S.: Three last letters identify most female first names. Psychol. Rep. (2000)
6. Basu, S., et al.: Measuring discrepancies in airbnb guest acceptance rates using anonymized demographic data. arXiv:2204.12001 arXiv preprint (2022)
7. Besse, P., del Barrio, E., Gordaliza, P., Loubes, J.M., Risser, L.: A survey of bias in machine learning through the prism of statistical parity. Am. Stat. (2022)
8. Darius, P.: Researcher data access under the DSA: lessons from tiktok's API issues during the 2024 European elections (2024). https://www.techpolicy.press/-researcher-data-access-under-the-dsa-lessons-from-tiktoks-api-issues-during-the-2024-european-elections/
9. Dickey, M.R.: Tinder agrees to settle age discrimination lawsuit (2019). https://techcrunch.com/2019/01/25/tinder-agrees-to-settle-age-discrimination-lawsuit/

10. Dua, D., Graff, C.: UCI machine learning repository (2017). http://archive.ics.uci.edu/ml
11. Dwork, C., Hardt, M., Pitassi, T., Reingold, O., Zemel, R.: Fairness through awareness. In: Innovations in Theoretical Computer Science Conference (2012)
12. Equal Employment Opportunity Commission: Uniform guidelines on employee selection procedures (1978). https://www.govinfo.gov/content/pkg/CFR-2011-title29-vol4/xml/CFR-2011-title29-vol4-part1607.xml
13. European Commission: Proposal for a regulation of the European parliament and of the council on a single market for digital services (digital services act) and amending directive 2000/31/EC (2020). https://digital-strategy.ec.europa.eu/en/library/proposal-regulation-european-parliament-and-council-single-market-digital-services-digital-services
14. European Commission: Proposal for a regulation of the European parliament and of the council laying down harmonised rules on artificial intelligence (artificial intelligence act) and amending certain union legislative acts (2021). https://eur-lex.europa.eu/legal-content/EN/TXT/?qid=1623335154975&uri=CELEX%3A52021PC0206
15. Feldman, M., Friedler, S.A., Moeller, J., Scheidegger, C., Venkatasubramanian, S.: Certifying and removing disparate impact. ACM SIGKDD (2015)
16. Fukuchi, K., Hara, S., Maehara, T.: Faking fairness via stealthily biased sampling. AAAI (2020)
17. Garcia Bourrée, J., et al.: Robust ml auditing using prior knowledge. ICML (2025)
18. Garcia Bourrée, J., Le Merrer, E., Tredan, G., Benoît, R.: Leveraging imperfect sources to detect fairwashing in black-box auditing. arXiv:2305.13883 arXiv preprint (2026)
19. Godinot, Merrer, L., Tredan, Penzo, T.: Under manipulations, are some AI models harder to audit? SatML (2024)
20. Goodman, R.: Why amazon's automated hiring tool discriminated against women (2018). https://www.aclu.org/blog/womens-rights/womens-rights-workplace/why-amazons-automated-hiring-tool-discriminated-against
21. Hardt, M., Price, E., Srebro, N.: Equality of opportunity in supervised learning. In: NeurIPS (2016)
22. INSEE: Top 10 names in france in 2024 (2025). https://www.insee.fr/fr/statistiques/8595099?sommaire=8595113#tableau-figure1_radio1
23. Jiang, R., Pacchiano, A., Stepleton, T., Jiang, H., Chiappa, S.: Wasserstein Fair Classification. UAI (2020)
24. Kamiran, F., Karim, A., Zhang, X.: Decision theory for discrimination-aware classification. ICDM (2012)
25. Lohaus, M., Perrot, M., Von Luxburg, U.: Too relaxed to be fair. ICML (2020)
26. Maneriker, P., Burley, C., Parthasarathy, S.: Online fairness auditing through iterative refinement. SIGKDD (2023)
27. Mehrabi, N., Morstatter, F., Saxena, N., Lerman, K., Galstyan, A.: A survey on bias and fairness in machine learning. ACM Comput. Surv. (2021)
28. Pessach, D., Shmueli, E.: A review on fairness in machine learning. ACM Comput. Surv. (2022)
29. Sandvig, C., Hamilton, K., Karahalios, K., Langbort, C.: Auditing algorithms: research methods for detecting discrimination on internet platforms. Data Discrimin. Conv. Critical Concerns Prod. Inquiry (2014)
30. twitter.com: Twitter API documentation (2012). https://developer.twitter.com/en/docs/twitter-api
31. Yan, T., Zhang, C.: Active fairness auditing. ICLR (2022)

On Reasoning About Statistical Requirements for Machine-Learning Models

Yakoub Salhi(✉)

Univ. Artois, CNRS, CRIL, 62300 Lens, France
salhi@cril.fr

Abstract. We introduce Contextual Proportion Logic (CPL), a modal framework for specifying statistical constraints on machine-learning (ML) models over binary features and multi-label outputs. Our logic combines propositional descriptions of local instance properties with proportion literals that bound their frequency, and a context modality that enforces such bounds uniformly across subpopulations. We study the satisfiability problem relative to a fixed set of feature and output variables, i.e., whether there exists an ML model that satisfies a given CPL specification. We establish that CPL satisfiability is NExpTime-complete in general. Then, we analyze the global fragment, where all constraints are evaluated on the full induced behavior of the model. We show that this restriction yields membership in PSPACE and Π_2^P-hardness. Finally, we isolate natural restrictions of the global fragment for which satisfiability becomes NP-complete.

Keywords: Logical reasoning for machine learning · Statistical Requirements · Computational Complexity

1 Introduction

Machine-learning models are increasingly deployed in sensitive domains, where their outputs may have significant consequences for individuals and society. This pervasive deployment motivates evaluating models not only in terms of predictive accuracy, but also with respect to additional requirements such as interpretability, safety, ethical compliance, and fairness, often under domain-specific constraints (e.g., [2,13,17,18]).

Constraints associated with these requirements may arise at different stages of the model lifecycle: they can be specified a priori as design requirements, for instance to guide data preprocessing [9], incorporated during training as soft or hard constraints [21], or used a posteriori for post hoc modification and certification [10]. Such constraints can be numerous and heterogeneous, and their interactions can be non-trivial. In particular, a collection of constraints may be inconsistent (no model satisfies all of them), or satisfiable only by highly restrictive cases of limited practical interest [12]. Therefore, understanding the

M. Ceci et al. (Eds.): ECML PKDD 2026, LNAI 16941, pp. 427–444, 2027.
https://doi.org/10.1007/978-3-032-37654-1_25

logical relationships among constraints is a prerequisite for reliable learning, verification, and debugging. This observation motivates a formal and expressive framework for stating and reasoning about diverse requirements on models.

In this work, we propose and study a modal logic for specifying statistical constraints on machine-learning models. Our framework uses propositional logic to express local properties of individual instances. This choice is natural for binary feature spaces and connects model analysis to a mature body of logical methods. In particular, several recent approaches encode models as propositional formulas in order to derive explanations and perform verification tasks, often relying on SAT technology (e.g., see [11,20]). Our logic extends the propositional language with (i) proportion constraints given by inequalities that bound the frequency with which a propositional property holds, and (ii) modalities that restrict evaluation to context classes, which enables the expression of subpopulation-specific requirements.

After introducing the syntax and semantics of the logic, we develop a complexity landscape for its satisfiability problem. This analysis clarifies the computational cost of deciding whether a given set of statistical requirements can be satisfied by some model, and thus helps identify the practical limits of automated reasoning in our framework. We first show that satisfiability is NEXPTIME-complete in the general case. We then focus on the global fragment, where every context coincides with the full induced behavior of the model, and establish that satisfiability for this fragment lies in PSPACE and is Π_2^P-hard. Determining the exact complexity of satisfiability for the unrestricted global fragment remains an open problem. Finally, within the global fragment, we identify natural restrictions under which satisfiability becomes NP-complete. These restrictions are well-motivated: aggregate requirements such as overall accuracy, global sufficient reasons, and domain exclusion are naturally global, while high-dimensional feature spaces typically leave many features unused. In these fragments, satisfiability reduces to Boolean combinations of linear arithmetic constraints, making it amenable to integer-programming and SMT machinery.

2 Related Work

A first related line of work connects probability theory and formal logic by extending propositional logic with constraints on the probability of events (see, e.g., [6,16]). In this tradition, PSAT asks whether a set of probabilistic constraints is satisfiable by some probability distribution over propositional interpretations [15]. Fagin, Halpern, and Megiddo [8] study a more expressive probability logic allowing Boolean combinations of such constraints.

CPL is close in spirit to these logics, but its intended object is different. We are not interested in arbitrary probability distributions over worlds. Instead, we reason about the finite input-output behavior induced by an ML lmodel. This functional viewpoint is essential when constraints are meant to specify, audit, or debug ML models: outputs must be generated by a single model, not assigned independently by an unconstrained distribution.

Another related line of work comes from data mining, where one studies constraints on the frequencies of patterns in datasets. In particular, FREQSAT asks whether a set of itemset-frequency constraints is realizable by some dataset [3]. CPL shares the focus on frequencies, but adds an ML-oriented input-output structure and a modal mechanism for expressing requirements across subpopulations.

The closest modal approach is the Binary Classifier Logic (BCL) of Liu and Lorini [14]. BCL uses modalities indexed by sets of variables and also treats classifiers as functional systems. However, its goal is different. BCL is a qualitative logic of explanation, evaluated pointwise at a designated instance, and formalizes notions such as abductive explanations, contrastive explanations, counterfactual explanations, and individual bias. CPL is instead a quantitative logic for population-level requirements: its formulas are proportion literals constraining rates over the population induced by a model, possibly within every subgroup determined by agreement on a chosen set of variables.

CPL is also developed as a specification language for ML requirements such as accuracy, fairness, privacy, robustness, and subgroup constraints. The context modality of CPL internalizes the common ML practice of slicing a population into subgroups and checking that a requirement holds in each slice.

In summary, CPL combines ideas from probabilistic logics, frequency constraints, and modal logics for classifiers, but targets a different problem: the joint realizability of statistical requirements by a functional ML model.

3 Preliminaries

3.1 Propositional Logic

Let Prop be a finite, non-empty set of propositional variables. The set of propositional formulas over Prop is defined inductively by the grammar $\varphi ::= p \mid \bot \mid \neg\varphi \mid (\varphi \wedge \varphi) \mid (\varphi \vee \varphi)$, where $p \in \mathsf{Prop}$. We use the usual abbreviations, e.g., $\top := \neg\bot$, $\varphi \rightarrow \psi := \neg\varphi \vee \psi$, and $\varphi \leftrightarrow \psi := (\varphi \rightarrow \psi) \wedge (\psi \rightarrow \varphi)$.

Let $\mathsf{vars}(\varphi)$ denote the set of propositional variables occurring in φ.

A *Boolean interpretation* (or simply interpretation) over Prop is a function $\omega : \mathsf{Prop} \longrightarrow \{0, 1\}$, where 1 stands for "true" and 0 for "false". We sometimes identify an interpretation with the set of literals it makes true. We write $\Omega(\mathsf{Prop})$ for the set of all such interpretations. An interpretation is extended to propositional formulas as usual: $\omega(\varphi \wedge \psi) = \min(\omega(\varphi), \omega(\psi))$, $\omega(\varphi \vee \psi) = \max(\omega(\varphi), \omega(\psi))$, and $\omega(\neg\varphi) = 1 - \omega(\varphi)$. An interpretation ω *satisfies* a formula φ iff $\omega(\varphi) = 1$.

3.2 ML Models

We consider machine-learning (ML) models over binary feature spaces. Let $\mathcal{X} = \{x_1, \ldots, x_d\}$ be the set of binary features. An instance is a vector $x = (v_1, \ldots, v_d) \in \{0, 1\}^d$ where each $v_i \in \{0, 1\}$ is the value taken by feature x_i and can therefore be viewed as a propositional variable. The instance space is the Cartesian product $\{0, 1\}^d$.

A model is a *partial function* $f : \{0,1\}^d \rightharpoonup \{0,1\}^k$, where $\mathcal{Y} = \{y_1, \dots, y_k\}$ is the set of binary output variables. For any $x \in \mathsf{dom}(f)$, we write $f(x) = (f(x)_1, \dots, f(x)_k)$, where the i-th component $f(x)_i \in \{0,1\}$ specifies the value assigned to the output variable y_i. Throughout the paper, we restrict attention to models with non-empty domain.

By treating each feature variable x_i and each output variable y_i as a distinct propositional variable, we obtain a set of Boolean interpretations that captures the behavior of f.

For a feature variable x_i and a value $v \in \{0,1\}$, we write $\mathsf{lit}(x_i, v)$ for the literal x_i if $v = 1$ and $\neg x_i$ if $v = 0$; we define $\mathsf{lit}(y_i, v)$ for an output variable y_i analogously.

For an instance $a = (v_1, \dots, v_d) \in \{0,1\}^d$, we write $\widehat{a}$ for the conjunction $\bigwedge_{i=1}^{d} \mathsf{lit}(x_i, v_i)$, which is the propositional formula true precisely on interpretations whose feature part equals a. Analogously, for an output vector $b = (b_1, \dots, b_k) \in \{0,1\}^k$, we write $\widehat{b}$ for the conjunction $\bigwedge_{i=1}^{k} \mathsf{lit}(y_i, b_i)$.

Given an instance $a \in \mathsf{dom}(f)$, let ω_a^f denote the Boolean interpretation over $\mathcal{X} \cup \mathcal{Y}$ defined by $\omega_a^f(x_i) = 1$ iff $a_i = 1$, and $\omega_a^f(y_i) = 1$ iff $f(a)_i = 1$.

The *induced set of interpretations* of f is $\mathcal{M}_f = \{\omega_a^f \mid a \in \mathsf{dom}(f)\}$, a set of Boolean interpretations over $\mathcal{X} \cup \mathcal{Y}$. In particular, for each input assignment over $\mathcal{X}$, there is at most one interpretation in $\mathcal{M}_f$. This reflects the fact that outputs are determined functionally by the model.

Example 1. Let $d = 2$ and $k = 1$, with feature variables x_1, x_2 and output variable y_1. Consider the (partial) model $f : \{0,1\}^2 \rightharpoonup \{0,1\}$ defined on $\mathsf{dom}(f) = \{(0,0), (0,1), (1,0)\}$ by $f(0,0) = 0$, $f(0,1) = 1$, $f(1,0) = 1$.

For each $a \in \mathsf{dom}(f)$ we obtain an interpretation ω_a^f over $\{x_1, x_2, y_1\}$: $\omega_{(0,0)}^f = \{\neg x_1, \neg x_2, \neg y_1\}$, $\omega_{(0,1)}^f = \{\neg x_1, x_2, y_1\}$, and $\omega_{(1,0)}^f = \{x_1, \neg x_2, y_1\}$. Hence, the induced set of interpretations is $\mathcal{M}_f = \{\omega_{(0,0)}^f, \omega_{(0,1)}^f, \omega_{(1,0)}^f\}$.

4 Contextual Proportion Logic

This section introduces *Contextual Proportion Logic* (CPL), a modal logic for expressing statistical constraints on ML models.

Semantically, CPL is evaluated on finite *populations*, i.e., non-empty finite sets of Boolean interpretations. Its atomic formulas are *proportion constraints* that compare the frequency of a propositional property to a rational threshold. The modality $[U]$ acts as a grouping operator: it requires a constraint to hold in every subpopulation obtained by partitioning the population according to agreement on the variables in U. This agreement-based partitioning is reminiscent of the modality used in BCL [14], which quantifies pointwise over instances agreeing on a designated set of variables. In CPL the same partition is used to scope statistical, rather than qualitative, constraints.

Syntax. A *proportion literal* is an expression $\varphi \bowtie \alpha$, where φ is a propositional formula, $\bowtie \in \{\leq, \geq\}$, and $\alpha \in \mathbb{Q} \cap [0, 1]$. CPL formulas are defined in two layers with non-nested modalities:

$$A ::= (\varphi \bowtie \alpha) \mid (A \wedge A) \mid (A \vee A) \mid \neg A,$$

$$\Phi ::= [U]A \mid (\Phi \wedge \Phi) \mid (\Phi \vee \Phi) \mid \neg \Phi,$$

where U ranges over finite sets of propositional variables. Intuitively, A-formulas talk about global proportions in a population, while Φ-formulas combine group-conditioned proportion constraints.

Let U be a finite set of propositional variables. For interpretations ω, ω' we write $\omega \sim_U \omega'$ iff they agree on U, i.e., $\omega_{|U} = \omega'_{|U}$. For a population W, let $W/{\sim_U}$ denote the set of $\sim_U$-equivalence classes induced by W (a partition of W).

Semantics. Let W be a non-empty finite set of interpretations over some set of variables that includes $\mathsf{vars}(\Phi)$. We define satisfaction $W \models \Phi$ as follows:

- $W \models (\varphi \bowtie \alpha)$ $\frac{|\{\omega \in W | \omega \models_{\mathrm{CL}} \varphi\}|}{|W|} \bowtie \alpha$;
- $W \models [U]A$ iff for all $C \in W/{\sim_U}, C \models A$;
- $W \models \Phi \wedge \Psi$ iff $W \models \Phi$ and $W \models \Psi$;
- $W \models \Phi \vee \Psi$ iff $W \models \Phi$ or $W \models \Psi$;
- $W \models \neg \Phi$ iff $W \not\models \Phi$.

Given a set of CPL formulas Γ, we write $W \models \Gamma$ iff $W \models \Phi$ for all $\Phi \in \Gamma$.

We sometimes use the following syntactic abbreviations: $\varphi > \alpha := \neg(\varphi \leq \alpha)$, $\varphi < \alpha := \neg(\varphi \geq \alpha)$, and $\varphi = \alpha := (\varphi \leq \alpha) \wedge (\varphi \geq \alpha)$. Additionally, we define the dual modal connective by $\langle U \rangle A := \neg[U]\neg A$. We also use $\rightarrow$ and $\leftrightarrow$ as abbreviations for formulas at the A- and Φ-levels.

For entailment, we fix two disjoint vocabularies: a set of *features* $\mathcal{X}$ and a set of *outputs* (answers) $\mathcal{Y}$. We write $\mathsf{vars}(\Gamma) := \bigcup_{\Phi \in \Gamma} \mathsf{vars}(\Phi)$.

Definition 1 **($(\mathcal{X}, \mathcal{Y})$-entailment).** *Let $\mathcal{X}$ and $\mathcal{Y}$ be finite, non-empty, disjoint sets of propositional variables, and let $\Gamma \cup \{\Phi\}$ be a set of CPL formulas such that $\mathsf{vars}(\Gamma \cup \{\Phi\}) \subseteq \mathcal{X} \cup \mathcal{Y}$. We define entailment $\Gamma \vdash_{\mathcal{X},\mathcal{Y}} \Phi$ by: $\Gamma \vdash_{\mathcal{X},\mathcal{Y}} \Phi$ iff for every model $f : \{0,1\}^{|\mathcal{X}|} \rightharpoonup \{0,1\}^{|\mathcal{Y}|}$ with $\mathsf{dom}(f) \neq \emptyset$, if $\mathcal{M}_f \models \Gamma$ then $\mathcal{M}_f \models \Phi$.*

Conversely, $\Gamma \nvdash_{\mathcal{X},\mathcal{Y}} \Phi$ iff there exists a (partial) model f over $(\mathcal{X}, \mathcal{Y})$ such that $\mathcal{M}_f \models \Gamma \cup \{\neg \Phi\}$. This motivates the following satisfiability problem.

Definition 2 **($\mathrm{SAT}_{\mathrm{CPL}}$).** $\mathrm{SAT}_{\mathrm{CPL}}$ *is the following decision problem:*

- ***Input:*** *two finite, non-empty, disjoint sets of propositional variables $\mathcal{X}$ (features) and $\mathcal{Y}$ (outputs), and a CPL formula Φ such that $\mathsf{vars}(\Phi) \subseteq \mathcal{X} \cup \mathcal{Y}$. Rational thresholds are encoded in binary.*
- ***Question:*** *does there exist a model $f : \{0,1\}^{|\mathcal{X}|} \rightharpoonup \{0,1\}^{|\mathcal{Y}|}$ s.t. $\mathsf{dom}(f) \neq \emptyset$ and $\mathcal{M}_f \models \Phi$?*

Below we illustrate how common modeling desiderata can be written in CPL.

Excluding Instances from the Domain. Let us fix a feature vector $a \in \{0,1\}^d$, and let $\mathsf{pat}(a) := \bigwedge_{i=1}^{d} \widehat{a}[i]$ be the conjunction that is true precisely on interpretations whose feature part equals a. Then the CPL constraint

$$[\emptyset](\mathsf{pat}(a) \leq 0)$$

states that no induced interpretation has feature assignment a, i.e., $a \notin \mathrm{dom}(f)$. More generally, one can exclude an entire region of the input space by replacing $\mathsf{pat}(a)$ with any propositional formula over $\mathcal{X}$ describing that region.

Sufficient Reasons. Let $R := \bigwedge_{k=1}^{\ell} \mathsf{lit}(x_{i_k}, v_k)$ encode a feature pattern (a conjunction of literals). A *hard* sufficient-reason constraint requires that the rule has no exceptions:

$$[\emptyset]\ ((R \to y_j)\ \geq\ 1).$$

A *soft* sufficient reason allows rare exceptions: for a threshold $\beta \in (0,1)$ (e.g. $\beta = 0.95$), $[\emptyset]((R \to y_j) \geq \beta)$.

To express that R is *minimal* as a sufficient reason (no conjunct is redundant), we require that dropping any literal yields a pattern that admits a counterexample somewhere in the realized domain. For each $\alpha \in \{1,\dots,\ell\}$, let $R_{-\alpha} := \bigwedge_{k \neq \alpha} \mathsf{lit}(x_{i_k}, v_k)$. Minimality is enforced by requiring, for every α, $[\emptyset]\ (R_{-\alpha} \wedge \neg y_j) > 0$, which guarantees the existence of an induced interpretation witnessing that $R_{-\alpha}$ alone does not force y_j.

Invariance Under Non-causal Features. Let Z be a set of variables capturing the information that is causally relevant (the information on which the prediction is allowed to depend). The CPL constraint

$$[Z]((y \leq 0)\ \vee\ (\neg y \leq 0))\ \text{(or softer: } [Z]((y \leq \epsilon)\ \vee\ (\neg y \leq \epsilon)))$$

requires that within every context, the output y is constant: for each $\sim_Z$ equivalence class, either y never occurs (hence $y = 0$ throughout the class) or $\neg y$ never occurs (hence $y = 1$ throughout the class). Intuitively, once the variables in Z are fixed, the prediction cannot vary. Thus, the remaining variables (those outside Z) have no influence on y.

Privacy. Let P be a set of public or non-sensitive features and s a sensitive attribute. The conjunction

$$[P \cup \mathcal{Y}]\,(s > 0)\ \wedge\ [P \cup \mathcal{Y}]\,(\neg s > 0)$$

states that in every realized class determined by the public information and the model outputs, both values of s still occur with non-zero frequency. Hence the sensitive attribute cannot be uniquely inferred from the public features and the model outputs.

Ground Truth. To reason about predictive performance and fairness, we may enrich the output vocabulary by distinguishing predicted labels from ground-truth labels. Concretely, we consider a disjoint union $\mathcal{Y} = \mathcal{Y}^{\mathsf{pred}} \uplus \mathcal{Y}^{\mathsf{true}}$, where

$\mathcal{Y}^{\mathsf{pred}} = \{y_1, \ldots, y_k\}$ encodes the model's predictions and $\mathcal{Y}^{\mathsf{true}} = \{t_1, \ldots, t_k\}$ encodes the corresponding true outcomes. This allows CPL constraints to relate predictions to truth, and thus to specify standard notions of accuracy and fairness. For instance, overall accuracy for label i can be enforced by

$$[\emptyset]\,((y_i \leftrightarrow t_i) \ \geq \ \alpha).$$

Moreover, letting x_i be a protected feature, an equal-opportunity (recall) lower bound can be stated as

$$[\{x_i, t_j\}]\,((t_j \rightarrow y_j) \ \geq \ \beta),$$

which requires that, within every group determined by x_i and t_j, a β-fraction of true positives receive a positive prediction.

A precision guarantee with respect to a protected feature x_i can be expressed by

$$[\{x_i, y_j\}]\,((y_j \rightarrow t_j) \ \geq \ \gamma),$$

which states that, within every subgroup determined by x_i and the event $y_j = 1$, at least a γ-fraction of predicted positives are truly positive.

Conditional Probability. Although our logic does not contain an explicit conditional-probability operator, conditional constraints can be encoded using contexts. Intuitively, the modality $[U]$ allows us to restrict attention to a subpopulation defined by a fresh indicator variable. More precisely, to express a constraint of the form $\Pr(\psi \mid \varphi) \geq \alpha$, we introduce a fresh variable z intended to represent φ, enforce z to coincide with φ everywhere, and then impose the lower bound inside the $z = 1$ class:

$$[\emptyset]((\varphi \leftrightarrow z) \geq \ 1) \ \wedge \ [\emptyset]\,(z > 0) \ \wedge \ [\{z\}]\,((z \rightarrow \psi) \geq \alpha).$$

The constraint $[\emptyset]\,z > 0$ rules out the degenerate case $\Pr(\varphi) = 0$.

Example 2. We illustrate our logic with a simple medical example inspired by hospital triage for pneumonia [5]. The goal is to reason about constraints on a model that predicts whether a patient should remain in the hospital or be released.

Let the feature vocabulary be $\mathcal{X} = \{pne, asth, old, sev, oxy, ins\}$, where: *pne* means that the patient has pneumonia; *asth* means that the patient has asthma; *old* means that the patient is elderly (for example, age at least 70); *sev* means that the symptoms are severe; *oxy* means that the oxygen saturation is low; *ins* is a protected feature, here representing insurance status.

To express predictive quality, we distinguish the model's recommendation from the clinical ground truth. Let the output vocabulary be $\mathcal{Y} = \{stay, tstay\}$, where: $stay = 1$ means that the model recommends keeping the patient in the hospital; $tstay = 1$ means that, according to the ground truth, the patient should in fact be kept in the hospital.

Consider the following CPL constraints.

(C1) Severe Pneumonia Requires Hospitalization: $[\emptyset]\big(((pne \wedge sev) \rightarrow stay) \geq 1\big)$.

(C2) Low Oxygen Requires Hospitalization: $[\emptyset]\big((oxy \rightarrow stay) \geq 1\big)$.

(C3) Insurance Status Should not be Obtained from the Decision once the Medical Profile is Fixed: Let $P = \{pne, asth, old, sev, oxy\}$. We impose $[P \cup \mathcal{Y}](ins > 0) \wedge [P \cup \mathcal{Y}](\neg ins > 0)$. This means that, within every class determined by the medical features and the outputs, both values of the protected attribute *ins* still occur. Therefore, insurance status cannot be uniquely inferred from the medical profile and the outputs.

(C4) Precision Parity Across Insurance Groups: $[\{ins, stay\}]\big((stay \rightarrow tstay) \geq 0.9\big)$. This says that, in every subgroup determined by insurance status, at least 90% of predicted hospitalizations are correct.

Let $\Gamma = \{(\text{C1}), (\text{C2}), (\text{C3}), (\text{C4})\}$. For instance, we have: $\Gamma \vdash_{\mathcal{X},\mathcal{Y}} [\emptyset]\big((pne \wedge sev \wedge old) \rightarrow stay \geq 1\big)$; and $\Gamma \nvdash_{\mathcal{X},\mathcal{Y}} [\emptyset]\big((pne \wedge asth) \rightarrow stay \geq 1\big)$. The second property is a consequence of the fact that none of the requirements says that asthma, even together with pneumonia, is by itself sufficient for hospitalization. A model may satisfy all formulas in Γ while still discharging some patient with pneumonia and asthma, provided that this patient is not severe and does not have low oxygen.

5 Recovering a Fairness Impossibility in CPL

We now show that a well-known fairness impossibility [4] (the incompatibility of predictive parity with equal false-positive and false-negative rates when group base rates differ) arises as the unsatisfiability of a CPL specification. What matters is not that the theorem can be restated, but that it becomes one requirement bundle among the heterogeneous constraints that CPL can jointly decide.

We work with a single binary label and adopt the ground-truth-aware vocabulary of Sect. 4. Let $a \in \mathcal{X}$ be a binary protected feature, and let $\mathcal{Y} = \{y, t\}$, where y encodes the model's prediction and t encodes the ground-truth label.

In the formulas below, we also use fresh auxiliary variables. These variables are not substantive features or labels of the ML task. They are indicator variables introduced only at the specification level in order to encode conditional rates.

For a finite population W, we write $\Pr_W(\varphi)$ for the relative frequency of φ in W. When the population is clear from context, we omit the subscript.

For a model f inducing population $\mathcal{M}_f$, the standard group-specific rates are conditional frequencies: $\text{PPV}_g := \Pr(t = 1 \mid y = 1,\, a = g)$, $\text{FPR}_g := \Pr(y = 1 \mid t = 0,\, a = g)$, $\text{FNR}_g := \Pr(y = 0 \mid t = 1,\, a = g)$, and $p_g := \Pr(t = 1 \mid a = g)$, for $g \in \{0, 1\}$. The quantity p_g is the *base rate*, or prevalence, of the positive label in group g.

We use the following syntactic convention. For $g \in \{0, 1\}$, the expression $(a = g)$ abbreviates a if $g = 1$, and $\neg a$ if $g = 0$.

To express a conditional-rate constraint $\Pr(\psi \mid \varphi) \bowtie \alpha$, where $\bowtie \in \{\leq, \geq, =\}$, we introduce a fresh variable z_φ intended to indicate the conditioning event φ. The constraint is encoded as:

$$\mathsf{Cond}^{\bowtie}_{z_\varphi}(\psi \mid \varphi, \alpha) := [\emptyset]((z_\varphi \leftrightarrow \varphi) \geq 1) \wedge [\emptyset](z_\varphi > 0) \wedge [\{z_\varphi\}]\Big((z_\varphi \leq 0) \vee (\psi \bowtie \alpha)\Big).$$

The three conjuncts respectively bind z_φ to φ, force the conditioning event to be non-empty, and impose the required proportion inside the $z_\varphi = 1$ slice, the guard $(z_\varphi \leq 0)$ vacuously discharging the complementary slice.

We use distinct fresh indicators for the four types of conditioning events: $z_{\mathrm{PPV},g}$, $z_{\mathrm{FPR},g}$, $z_{\mathrm{FNR},g}$, $z_{p,g}$. The corresponding CPL formulas are:

$$\Phi^{g,\gamma}_{\mathrm{PPV}} := \mathsf{Cond}^{=}_{z_{\mathrm{PPV},g}}\big(t \mid (a = g) \wedge y, \gamma\big),\ \Phi^{g,\rho}_{\mathrm{FPR}} := \mathsf{Cond}^{=}_{z_{\mathrm{FPR},g}}\big(y \mid (a = g) \wedge \neg t, \rho\big),$$

$$\Phi^{g,\nu}_{\mathrm{FNR}} := \mathsf{Cond}^{=}_{z_{\mathrm{FNR},g}}\big(\neg y \mid (a = g) \wedge t, \nu\big),\ \text{and}\ \Phi^{g,\pi}_{p} := \mathsf{Cond}^{=}_{z_{p,g}}\big(t \mid (a = g), \pi\big).$$

Table 1 summarizes the correspondence between standard binary-label fairness criteria and the parameterized CPL constraints used below. The table should be read schematically: because CPL thresholds are rational constants, a parity requirement is represented by a family of CPL specifications indexed by the common rational value of the relevant rate.

Table 1. Fairness criteria as parameterized CPL constraints.

Criterion	Statistical meaning	CPL constraint schema
Predictive parity	$\mathrm{PPV}_0 = \mathrm{PPV}_1$	$\Phi^{0,\gamma}_{\mathrm{PPV}} \wedge \Phi^{1,\gamma}_{\mathrm{PPV}}$
Equal FPR	$\mathrm{FPR}_0 = \mathrm{FPR}_1$	$\Phi^{0,\rho}_{\mathrm{FPR}} \wedge \Phi^{1,\rho}_{\mathrm{FPR}}$
Equal FNR	$\mathrm{FNR}_0 = \mathrm{FNR}_1$	$\Phi^{0,\nu}_{\mathrm{FNR}} \wedge \Phi^{1,\nu}_{\mathrm{FNR}}$
Differing base rates	$p_0 \neq p_1$	$\Phi^{0,\pi_0}_{p} \wedge \Phi^{1,\pi_1}_{p}$, with $\pi_0 \neq \pi_1$

The thresholds $\gamma, \rho, \nu, \pi_0, \pi_1 \in \mathbb{Q} \cap [0, 1]$ are part of the specification.

Let $\Gamma_{\mathrm{fair}}(\gamma, \rho, \nu, \pi_0, \pi_1) := \bigwedge_{g \in \{0,1\}}(\Phi^{g,\gamma}_{\mathrm{PPV}} \wedge \Phi^{g,\rho}_{\mathrm{FPR}} \wedge \Phi^{g,\nu}_{\mathrm{FNR}} \wedge \Phi^{g,\pi_g}_{p})$.

Theorem 1. *Let $\gamma, \rho, \nu \in \mathbb{Q} \cap (0, 1)$, and let $\pi_0, \pi_1 \in \mathbb{Q} \cap (0, 1)$ with $\pi_0 \neq \pi_1$. Then $\Gamma_{\mathrm{fair}}(\gamma, \rho, \nu, \pi_0, \pi_1)$ is unsatisfiable.*

Proof (Sketch). Suppose, for contradiction, that some induced population satisfies $\Gamma_{\mathrm{fair}}(\gamma, \rho, \nu, \pi_0, \pi_1)$. The non-vacuity conjuncts in the definitions above ensure that all relevant conditional rates are well-defined.

Within any group g, the following elementary identity relates the rates [4]:

$$\mathrm{PPV}_g \cdot [p_g(1 - \mathrm{FNR}_g) + (1 - p_g)\mathrm{FPR}_g] = p_g(1 - \mathrm{FNR}_g). \tag{1}$$

By the CPL constraints, for both groups $g \in \{0, 1\}$ we have $\mathrm{PPV}_g = \gamma$, $\mathrm{FPR}_g = \rho$, and $\mathrm{FNR}_g = \nu$. Substituting these values into Eq. (1) gives $\gamma[p_g(1 -$

$\nu) + (1 - p_g)\rho] = p_g(1 - \nu)$. Since $\gamma, \rho, \nu \in (0, 1)$, this equation can be solved for p_g: $p_g = \frac{\gamma\rho}{\gamma\rho + (1-\gamma)(1-\nu)}$. The right-hand side is independent of g. Hence any population satisfying the common PPV, FPR, and FNR constraints for both groups must have $p_0 = p_1$. However, the base-rate constraints Φ_p^{0,π_0} and Φ_p^{1,π_1} require $p_0 = \pi_0$ and $p_1 = \pi_1$, with $\pi_0 \neq \pi_1$. We obtain a contradiction. Therefore, $\Gamma_{\mathsf{fair}}(\gamma, \rho, \nu, \pi_0, \pi_1)$ is unsatisfiable.

Restricted to statistical constraints over (a, t, y), each Γ_{fair} reduces to feasibility of a linear system over eight joint cells; this instance is thus checkable by linear programming. CPL's role is not to replace this LP, but to provide a uniform language in which such bundles coexist with the other requirements (e.g., sufficient reasons, domain exclusion, definiteness, privacy, accuracy) with $[U]$ internalizing the standard practice of subgroup slicing. From this perspective, $\mathsf{SAT}_{\mathsf{CPL}}$ decides joint realizability of heterogeneous requirement bundles.

6 CPL Satisfiability

In this section, we study the computational complexity of the satisfiability problem for CPL, both in the general setting and in a restricted setting.

6.1 General Case: NExpTime-Completeness

We first establish the following result.

Theorem 2. $\mathrm{SAT}_{\mathrm{CPL}}$ *is* NExpTime-*complete.*

To prove Membership in NExpTime, we use the main observation that for fixed $\mathcal{X}$, every model $f : \{0,1\}^{|\mathcal{X}|} \rightharpoonup \{0,1\}^{|\mathcal{Y}|}$ induces a population $\mathcal{M}_f$ of size at most $2^{|\mathcal{X}|}$, since there is at most one induced interpretation per input $a \in \mathrm{dom}(f)$.

Lemma 1. $\mathrm{SAT}_{\mathrm{CPL}}$ *is in* NExpTime.

We show NExpTime-hardness of $\mathrm{SAT}_{\mathrm{CPL}}$ by a many-one reduction from the succinct tiling problem that is NExpTime-hard (e.g., see [1,7,22]).

Tiling instances. A tile type T comes with four colors $(\mathsf{left}(T), \mathsf{right}(T), \mathsf{up}(T), \mathsf{down}(T))$. Given a finite set of tiles $\mathcal{T}$, a distinguished start tile $T_0 \in \mathcal{T}$, and $n \in \mathbb{N}$ written in its binary form (we can assume that $n := 2^m$ for $m \in \mathbb{N}$), the task is to decide whether there exists a placement $s : \{0, \ldots, n-1\}^2 \to \mathcal{T}$ such that: (i) $s(0,0) = T_0$; (ii) $\mathsf{right}(s(i,j)) = \mathsf{left}(s(i+1,j))$ for all $i < n-1$; (iii) $\mathsf{up}(s(i,j)) = \mathsf{down}(s(i,j+1))$ for all $j < n-1$.

We construct an instance $(\mathcal{X}, \mathcal{Y}, \Phi_{\mathsf{tile}})$ of $\mathrm{SAT}_{\mathrm{CPL}}$ such that Φ_{tile} is satisfiable by some model f iff the tiling instance has a solution. Intuitively, $\mathcal{X}$ encodes grid coordinates in binary (in the same way as in [1,22]), $\mathcal{Y}$ encodes the chosen tile at that coordinate, and the CPL constraints enforce (a) exactly one tile per coordinate, (b) the correct tile at $(0,0)$, (c) horizontal and vertical color matching.

Variables. Let us assume that $n := 2^m$. We introduce $P := \{p_1, \dots, p_m\}$ and $Q := \{q_1, \dots, q_m\}$, which encode the x- and y-coordinates in binary (least significant bit is index 1), and for each $T \in \mathcal{T}$ an output variable r_T indicating that tile T is placed at the current coordinate. We set $\mathcal{X} := P \cup Q$ and $\mathcal{Y} := \{r_T \mid T \in \mathcal{T}\}$.

For convenience, let $\mathsf{zero}(P) := \bigwedge_{i=1}^{m} \neg p_i$ and $\mathsf{zero}(Q) := \bigwedge_{i=1}^{m} \neg q_i$.

Constraints. We define Φ_{tile} as the conjunction of the following families of CPL constraints.

(1) Exactly One Tile Per Location. Every induced interpretation must choose at least one tile, and no induced interpretation may choose two distinct tiles:

$$[\emptyset]\Big(\bigvee_{T \in \mathcal{T}} r_T \geq 1\Big) \quad \wedge \quad \bigwedge_{\substack{T, T' \in \mathcal{T} \\ T \neq T'}} [\emptyset]\,(r_T \wedge r_{T'} \leq 0).$$

(2) The Origin Tile. We force tile T_0 at coordinate $(0, 0)$, and simultaneously force the induced population to contain *all* $n^2 = 2^{2m}$ coordinates, by requiring

$$[\emptyset]\big(r_{T_0} \wedge \mathsf{zero}(P) \wedge \mathsf{zero}(Q) \;=\; \frac{1}{2^{2m}}\big).$$

Indeed, any induced population $\mathcal{M}_f$ has size at most $2^{|\mathcal{X}|} = 2^{2m}$. The equality above implies that $\mathcal{M}_f$ has size exactly 2^{2m} and contains exactly one interpretation with coordinates $(0, 0)$ carrying tile T_0. Therefore, every coordinate assignment in $\{0, 1\}^{2m}$ appears in $\mathcal{M}_f$.

(3) Horizontal Matching. For each tile $T \in \mathcal{T}$, we ensure that whenever a coordinate is not on the right boundary and carries T, then its right neighbor carries a tile whose left color matches $\mathsf{right}(T)$. This is enforced by conditioning on all bits except those involved in the binary increment of the P-coordinate.

Case of the least significant bit. For each $T \in \mathcal{T}$:

$$[(P \setminus \{p_1\}) \cup Q]\Big((r_T \wedge \neg p_1 > 0) \;\rightarrow\; \big((\bigvee_{T' \colon \mathsf{left}(T') = \mathsf{right}(T)} r_{T'}) \wedge p_1 > 0\big)\Big).$$

Other cases. For each $j \in \{1, \dots, m-1\}$ and each $T \in \mathcal{T}$, let $S_j^P := (P \setminus \{p_1, \dots, p_{j+1}\}) \cup Q$ and add:

$$[S_j^P]\Big((r_T \wedge \neg p_{j+1} \wedge \bigwedge_{i=1}^{j} p_i > 0) \;\rightarrow\; \big((\bigvee_{T' \colon \mathsf{left}(T') = \mathsf{right}(T)} r_{T'}) \wedge p_{j+1} \wedge \bigwedge_{i=1}^{j} \neg p_i > 0\big)\Big).$$

Intuitively, the antecedent identifies those points where incrementing P flips bits $p_1, \dots, p_j$ from 1 to 0 and flips p_{j+1} from 0 to 1; the consequent requires the existence of the corresponding successor coordinate with matching tile.

(4) Vertical Matching. Symmetrically, for each tile $T \in \mathcal{T}$ we enforce matching with the upward neighbor obtained by incrementing Q.

Case of the least significant bit. For each $T \in \mathcal{T}$:

$$[P \cup (Q \setminus \{q_1\})]\Big((r_T \wedge \neg q_1 > 0) \;\rightarrow\; \big(\big(\bigvee_{T' : \mathsf{down}(T') = \mathsf{up}(T)} r_{T'}\big) \wedge q_1 > 0\big)\Big).$$

Other cases. For each $j \in \{1, \ldots, m-1\}$ and each $T \in \mathcal{T}$, let $S_j^Q := P \cup (Q \setminus \{q_1, \ldots, q_{j+1}\})$ and add:

$$[S_j^Q]\Big((r_T \wedge \neg q_{j+1} \wedge \bigwedge_{i=1}^{j} q_i > 0) \;\rightarrow\; \big(\big(\bigvee_{T' : \mathsf{down}(T') = \mathsf{up}(T)} r_{T'}\big) \wedge q_{j+1} \wedge \bigwedge_{i=1}^{j} \neg q_i > 0\big)\Big).$$

Correctness. Assume $\mathcal{M}_f \models \Phi_{\mathsf{tile}}$. By (2), $\mathcal{M}_f$ contains all 2^{2m} coordinate assignments exactly once. By (1), each coordinate carries exactly one tile. Constraints (3) and (4) enforce that the unique tiles at horizontally and vertically adjacent coordinates have matching colors, and (2) fixes the tile at $(0, 0)$ to be T_0. Therefore, assigning to each coordinate its unique tile yields a valid tiling.

Conversely, given a valid tiling s of the $2^m \times 2^m$ grid, we define a total model $f : \{0,1\}^{|\mathcal{X}|} \rightarrow \{0,1\}^{|\mathcal{Y}|}$ by letting the feature bits encode a coordinate (i, j) and setting exactly one output bit r_T to 1, namely $T = s(i, j)$. Then $\mathcal{M}_f$ has size 2^{2m}, satisfies (1) and (2), and the adjacency conditions (3)–(4) hold by validity of s. Thus, $\mathcal{M}_f \models \Phi_{\mathsf{tile}}$ holds.

The translation from a tiling instance $(\mathcal{T}, T_0, n)$ to the instance $(\mathcal{X}, \mathcal{Y}, \Phi_{\mathsf{tile}})$ can be carried out in polynomial time: the variable sets $\mathcal{X} = P \cup Q$ and $\mathcal{Y} = \{r_T \mid T \in \mathcal{T}\}$ can be listed explicitly, and Φ_{tile} is obtained by enumerating (i) all tiles $T \in \mathcal{T}$, (ii) all distinct pairs of tiles $T \neq T'$ to express mutual exclusivity, and (iii) all bit positions $j \in \{1, \ldots, m-1\}$ to encode the successor constraints, and outputting the corresponding subformulas. Consequently, the size of Φ_{tile} is bounded by a polynomial in $|\mathcal{T}|$ and n, and the reduction is a polynomial-time many-one reduction.

6.2 The Global Fragment

We study the restriction of $\mathrm{SAT_{CPL}}$ in which every context is empty, i.e., $U = \emptyset$ in every subformula $[U]A$. We call this restriction the *global fragment*, since all proportion literals are evaluated on the entire induced set of interpretations. We show that the global fragment is in PSPACE and Π_2^P-hard.

Let $f : \{0,1\}^{|\mathcal{X}|} \rightharpoonup \{0,1\}^{|\mathcal{Y}|}$ be a model. Since $\sim_\emptyset$ identifies all interpretations, we have $\mathcal{M}_f / {\sim_\emptyset} = \{\mathcal{M}_f\}$.

We show that $\mathrm{SAT_{CPL}}$ restricted to the global fragment is in PSPACE. The proof proceeds by giving a nondeterministic polynomial-space algorithm that constructs a candidate induced set $\mathcal{M}_f$ incrementally and verifies all proportion constraints using polynomially many counters. Since NPSPACE = PSPACE [19], this yields the desired upper bound.

Theorem 3. *The restriction of* $\mathrm{SAT_{CPL}}$ *to the global fragment is in* PSPACE.

We now show that $\mathrm{SAT}_{\mathrm{CPL}}$ restricted to the global fragment is Π_2^P-hard. We reduce from the canonical Π_2^P-complete problem $\forall\exists$-QBF:

- **Input:** a QBF formula of the form $\Psi = \forall u_1, \ldots, u_n \exists e_1, \ldots, e_m\ \theta(\mathbf{u}, \mathbf{e})$, where θ is a propositional formula over $U \cup E$, with $U = \{u_1, \ldots, u_n\}$ and $E = \{e_1, \ldots, e_m\}$.
- **Question:** is Ψ true?

Theorem 4. *The restriction of* $\mathrm{SAT}_{\mathrm{CPL}}$ *to the global fragment is* Π_2^P*-hard.*

Proof. Let $\Psi = \forall u_1, \ldots, u_n \exists e_1, \ldots, e_m\ \theta(\mathbf{u}, \mathbf{e})$ be an instance of $\forall\exists$-QBF as above ($U = \{u_1, \ldots, u_n\}$ and $E = \{e_1, \ldots, e_m\}$). We construct in polynomial time a global-$\mathrm{SAT}_{\mathrm{CPL}}$ instance $(\mathcal{X}, \mathcal{Y}, \Phi)$ such that $\mathcal{X} = U$, $\mathcal{Y} = E$ and $\Phi := [\emptyset](\chi_0 = \frac{1}{2^n}) \wedge [\emptyset](\theta(\mathbf{u}, \mathbf{e}) \geq 1)$, $\chi_0 := \bigwedge_{i=1}^{n} \neg u_i$. The first conjunct implies that $\mathcal{M}_f$ contains exactly one interpretation for each valuation of U, hence $\mathrm{dom}(f) = \{0,1\}^n$. Because f is a function, each such valuation of U determines a unique valuation of E. Therefore $[\emptyset](\theta(\mathbf{u}, \mathbf{e}) \geq 1)$ is equivalent to requiring that, for every $\mathbf{u} \in \{0,1\}^n$, the interpretation induced by f at $\mathbf{u}$ satisfies θ.

7 NP-Completeness from Redundant Features

In this section, we continue our study of the global fragment. Our aim is to identify conditions under which satisfiability belongs to NP. The main technical ingredient is the presence of unused, feature variables, namely features from $\mathcal{X}$ that do not occur in Φ. These variables allow us to realize rational weights by multiplicity while preserving functionality, that is, one output for each input.

We also rely on a small-model property for probabilistic constraints. In the global fragment, CPL formulas can be seen as Boolean combinations of constraints of the form "the probability of a propositional event φ satisfies $\bowtie \alpha$". This is precisely the setting of the probability logic of Fagin, Halpern, and Megiddo [8], which already treats arbitrary Boolean combinations of such probability constraints. We use their small-model theorem to obtain polynomial certificates.

7.1 Embedding the Global Fragment Into the FHM Probability Logic

We briefly recall the framework of [8][1]. A *probability model* consists of a finite set of worlds equipped with a probability distribution and a valuation of propositional variables at each world. The semantics assigns to each propositional formula φ a probability $\Pr(\varphi)$, and allows formulas that compare $\Pr(\varphi)$ to rational constants, combined by the usual Boolean connectives.

In our setting, a population W of interpretations induces such a probability model by taking the worlds to be the elements of W and assigning each world

[1] The framework developed there is more general; we restrict here to the fragment needed for our purposes.

uniform weight $1/|W|$. Under this uniform distribution, the CPL literal $(\varphi \bowtie \alpha)$ is true on W exactly when the corresponding FHM probability constraint $\Pr(\varphi) \bowtie \alpha$ is true.

Let $\mathrm{FHM}(\Phi)$ denote the formula obtained from a global CPL formula Φ by replacing each proportion literal $(\varphi \bowtie \alpha)$ with the corresponding probability constraint $\Pr(\varphi) \bowtie \alpha$, and by leaving the Boolean connectives $(\wedge, \vee, \neg)$ unchanged. As the modality $[\emptyset]$ is vacuous in the global fragment, it is omitted.

Lemma 2. *Let W be a non-empty finite population over $\mathsf{vars}(\Phi)$, and let $\mathcal{P}_W$ be the uniform probability model obtained from W. Then $W \models \Phi$ iff $\mathcal{P}_W \models_{\mathrm{FHM}} \mathrm{FHM}(\Phi)$.*

Proof. By definition of $\mathcal{P}_W$, for every propositional formula φ we have $\Pr_{\mathcal{P}_W}(\varphi) = \frac{|\{\omega \in W : \omega \models_{\mathrm{CL}} \varphi\}|}{|W|}$. Hence $W \models (\varphi \bowtie \alpha)$ iff $\mathcal{P}_W \models_{\mathrm{FHM}} \Pr(\varphi) \bowtie \alpha$. Then, the claim follows by a straightforward induction on the Boolean structure of Φ.

As a consequence, satisfiability for CPL restricted to the global fragment can be viewed as satisfiability of the associated FHM formula $\mathrm{FHM}(\Phi)$ under two additional requirements: the probability model must be finite and uniform, and it must arise from an induced population $\mathcal{M}_f$ of some functional model f.

7.2 The Unbounded-Feature Variant

Let m be the number of (distinct) probability constraints occurring in $\mathrm{FHM}(\Phi)$, i.e., the number of distinct proportion literals in Φ. A central result of [8] implies a small-model property: if an FHM formula with m probability constraints is satisfiable, then it is satisfiable in a finite probability model supported on at most $m+1$ worlds.

Lemma 3 (FHM small-support bound). *If $\mathrm{FHM}(\Phi)$ is satisfiable, then it is satisfiable in a probability model supported on at most $m+1$ worlds.*

Lemma 3 will serve as the support bound in our NP certificates.

Let $V := \mathsf{vars}(\Phi)$ and write $V_X := V \cap \mathcal{X}$ and $V_Y := V \cap \mathcal{Y}$. Let $Z := \mathcal{X} \setminus V_X$ be the set of *redundant* (unused) feature variables. For each assignment $a \in \{0,1\}^{V_X}$ there are exactly $2^{|Z|}$ distinct feature vectors in $\{0,1\}^{\mathcal{X}}$ extending a, obtained by varying the variables in Z. Hence redundant features provide, for each fixed assignment a to the relevant feature variables, a capacity of $2^{|Z|}$ distinct inputs. This capacity can be used to realize multiplicities while preserving that a model is functional.

A *profile* is a pair (a, b) with $a \in \{0,1\}^{V_X}$ and $b \in \{0,1\}^{V_Y}$.

Lemma 4. *Let $\mathcal{T}$ be a multiset of profiles over $V_X \times V_Y$. Assume that for every $a \in \{0,1\}^{V_X}$, $\#_a(\mathcal{T}) := |\{(a', b) \in \mathcal{T} : a' = a\}| \leq 2^{|Z|}$. Then there exists a functional model $f : \{0,1\}^{|\mathcal{X}|} \rightharpoonup \{0,1\}^{|\mathcal{Y}|}$ such that the induced population $\mathcal{M}_f$, restricted to the variables in $V_X \cup V_Y$, realizes exactly the multiset $\mathcal{T}$. In particular, for every propositional formula φ over $V_X \cup V_Y$, the probability of φ in the uniform model $\mathcal{P}_{\mathcal{M}_f}$ is exactly the relative frequency of profiles in $\mathcal{T}$ satisfying φ.*

Proof. Let us fix $a \in \{0,1\}^{V_X}$. Since there are $2^{|Z|}$ extensions of a to $\mathcal{X}$, we can choose $\#_a(\mathcal{T})$ pairwise distinct assignments to Z, which yields $\#_a(\mathcal{T})$ pairwise distinct feature vectors extending a. Doing this for every a gives $|\mathcal{T}|$ pairwise distinct feature vectors in $\{0,1\}^{\mathcal{X}}$. Let dom(f) be exactly this set, and define the outputs so that, for each chosen feature vector x corresponding to a profile $(a,b) \in \mathcal{T}$, the restriction of the output assignment $f(x)$ to V_Y is exactly b (values on $\mathcal{Y} \setminus V_Y$ may be chosen arbitrarily). Then f is functional and $\mathcal{M}_f$ realizes precisely the intended multiset of profiles on $V_X \cup V_Y$.

We now consider a variant in which one may freely add fresh features.

Definition 3 ($\mathrm{SAT}^{\star}_{\mathrm{CPL}}$). *An instance of* $\mathrm{SAT}^{\star}_{\mathrm{CPL}}$ *consists of a finite, non-empty set of outputs* $\mathcal{Y}$ *and a CPL formula* Φ. *It is satisfiable if there exists a finite, non-empty feature set* $\mathcal{X}$ *containing all feature variables occurring in* Φ *and a model* $f : \{0,1\}^{|\mathcal{X}|} \rightharpoonup \{0,1\}^{|\mathcal{Y}|}$ *such that* $\mathcal{M}_f \models \Phi$.

In the foregoing variant, fresh redundant feature variables can be added freely. As a result, every finite rational probability model can be implemented by a functional model via multiplicity.

Theorem 5 $\mathrm{SAT}^{\star}_{\mathrm{CPL}}$ *restricted to the global fragment is* NP*-complete.*

Proof (Hardness.) We reduce from propositional satisfiability. Given ψ over $P = \{p_1,\dots,p_n\}$, set $\mathcal{X} := P$, $\mathcal{Y} := \{y_0\}$, $\chi_0 := \bigwedge_{i=1}^{n} \neg p_i$, and $\alpha := 1/2^n$. Let us define $\Phi := [\emptyset](\chi_0 = \alpha) \wedge [\emptyset](\psi \geq \alpha)$. Any model f induces at most one interpretation per assignment to $\mathcal{X}$, which leads to $|\mathcal{M}_f| \leq 2^n$. Thus $\chi_0 = \alpha$ forces $|\mathcal{M}_f| = 2^n$, i.e. dom$(f) = \{0,1\}^n$. Then $[\emptyset](\psi \geq \alpha)$ holds iff at least one assignment satisfies ψ. Therefore ψ is satisfiable iff $(\mathcal{X},\mathcal{Y},\Phi)$ is satisfiable. Consequently, we obtain NP-hardness.

(*Membership.*) Let $(\mathcal{Y},\Phi)$ be an instance of $\mathrm{SAT}^{\star}_{\mathrm{CPL}}$ restricted to the global fragment. In this fragment, Φ is simply a Boolean combination of global proportion constraints, and hence may be viewed directly as an FHM formula FHM(Φ). Since in $\mathrm{SAT}^{\star}_{\mathrm{CPL}}$ fresh redundant feature variables may be added freely, Lemma 4 implies that every finite rational probability model can be implemented by a functional model via multiplicity. Therefore, $(\mathcal{Y},\Phi)$ is satisfiable iff FHM(Φ) is satisfiable. As satisfiability for the FHM probability logic is in NP [8], it follows that $\mathrm{SAT}^{\star}_{\mathrm{CPL}}$ restricted to the global fragment is in NP.

7.3 Sufficiently Many Redundant Features

We now return to the standard setting where the feature set $\mathcal{X}$ is fixed in the input. Only the number of redundant features $Z := \mathcal{X} \setminus (\mathsf{vars}(\Phi) \cap \mathcal{X})$ is significant, because it bounds how large a multiset of induced interpretations can be realized per assignment to the relevant features.

Let m be the number of distinct proportion literals occurring in Φ, and let C be the maximum absolute value of numerators and denominators (in lowest terms) among all rational thresholds occurring in Φ (with $C := 1$ if no rational threshold occurs, or if all thresholds are equal to 0). To ensure that enough redundant features are available to implement the rational weights produced by Lemma 3, we invoke Cramer's rule plus Hadamard's inequality to obtain an explicit common-denominator bound as a function of m and C

Lemma 5 *If* FHM(Φ) *is satisfiable, then it admits a satisfying distribution supported on at most $m+1$ interpretations whose weights have a common denominator $D \leq (\sqrt{m+1}C)^{m+1}$.*

Proof (Sketch) By Lemma 3, if FHM(Φ) is satisfiable then it has a satisfying probability model supported on $\ell \leq m+1$ worlds. Let us fix such a model with support $\{\omega^1, \dots, \omega^\ell\}$ and weights $w_1, \dots, w_\ell$.

For each propositional formula φ occurring in a probability constraint of FHM(Φ), we define $v_i^\varphi \in \{0,1\}$ by $v_i^\varphi = 1$ iff $\omega^i \models_{\mathsf{CL}} \varphi$ (and $v_i^\varphi = 0$ otherwise). Then, $\Pr(\varphi) = \sum_{i=1}^{\ell} w_i v_i^\varphi$. Substituting these expressions, every probability comparison in FHM(Φ) becomes a linear inequality in the variables $w_1, \dots, w_\ell$. After clearing denominators of all rational thresholds, we obtain a finite system of linear inequalities with integer coefficients bounded in absolute value by C, together with $w_i \geq 0$ and $\sum_i w_i = 1$.

Consider a basic feasible solution of this system. It is determined by a set of ℓ linearly independent active constraints (constraints satisfied with equality) on the ℓ variables. By Cramer's rule, each w_i is a ratio of determinants of $\ell \times \ell$ integer matrices whose entries are bounded by C in absolute value. By Hadamard's inequality, each such determinant is at most $(\sqrt{\ell}\,C)^\ell \leq (\sqrt{m+1}\,C)^{m+1}$. Therefore, the weights admit a common denominator $D \leq (\sqrt{m+1}C)^{m+1}$.

Let us define $B := \lceil \log_2((\sqrt{m+1}\,C)^{\,m+1}) \rceil$.

Definition 4 **(SAT$^\dagger_{\text{CPL}}$).** SAT$^\dagger_{\text{CPL}}$ *is the restriction of* SAT$_{\text{CPL}}$ *to the instances* $(\mathcal{X}, \mathcal{Y}, \Phi)$ *such that* $|Z| \geq B$.

Theorem 6 SAT$^\dagger_{\text{CPL}}$ *restricted to the global fragment is* NP*-complete.*

Proof (*Hardness.*) NP-hardness follows as in Theorem 5.

(*Membership.*) Let $(\mathcal{X}, \mathcal{Y}, \Phi)$ be an instance of SAT$^\dagger_{\text{CPL}}$ such that Φ belongs to the global fragment, and let m the number of distinct proportion literals occurring in Φ. We have $V_X = \mathsf{vars}(\Phi) \cap \mathcal{X}$ and $Z = \mathcal{X} \setminus V_X$. By Definition 4, we have $|Z| \geq B$. Thus, $2^{|Z|} \geq 2^B$.

We show that, for such instances, satisfiability in the sense of SAT$^\star_{\text{CPL}}$ implies satisfiability in the sense of SAT$^\dagger_{\text{CPL}}$; the converse is immediate.

Assume that $(\mathcal{Y}, \Phi)$ is satisfiable in the SAT$^\star_{\text{CPL}}$ sense. Since we are in the global fragment, Φ may be viewed as its associated FHM formula FHM(Φ). By Lemma 3, if FHM(Φ) is satisfiable, then it is satisfiable in a probability model supported on at most $m+1$ worlds. Moreover, by Lemma 5, we may assume that the corresponding rational weights have a common denominator $D \leq 2^B$.

Let $\omega^1, \dots, \omega^\ell$ with $\ell \leq m+1$ be the support worlds, and write their weights as $w_i = n_i/D$. Replacing each ω^i by n_i copies yields a multiset of profiles of total size $\sum_{i=1}^{\ell} n_i = D$. Hence, for every assignment $a \in \{0,1\}^{V_X}$, the number of copies whose feature part is a is at most D. Since $D \leq 2^B \leq 2^{|Z|}$, Lemma 4 applies: the multiset can be realized by a functional model over the fixed feature set $\mathcal{X}$, using the redundant variables in Z to separate the copies. The induced population of this model has exactly the same relative frequencies on $\mathsf{vars}(\Phi)$ as the original rational probability model. Therefore, it satisfies Φ.

Thus, every $\mathrm{SAT}^{\star}_{\mathrm{CPL}}$-solution can be implemented within the redundancy bound required by $\mathrm{SAT}^{\dagger}_{\mathrm{CPL}}$. Hence, on the global fragment, the $\mathrm{SAT}^{\star}_{\mathrm{CPL}}$ and $\mathrm{SAT}^{\dagger}_{\mathrm{CPL}}$ notions of satisfiability coincide. Using Theorem 5, we conclude that $\mathrm{SAT}^{\dagger}_{\mathrm{CPL}}$ restricted to the global fragment is in NP.

8 Conclusion and Perspectives

We introduced CPL, a modal logic for specifying statistical constraints on ML models. Its language combines proportion literals with a context modality for expressing group-conditioned requirements. We studied the satisfiability problem and obtained several complexity results. In general, satisfiability is NEXPTIME-complete. For the global fragment, we established refined complexity bounds.

Several directions remain for future work. On the theoretical side, a natural next step is to study additional syntactic fragments. This includes restricting the relationships between contexts or the form of the propositional formulas in proportion constraints. On the practical side, we plan to explore applications of CPL to the specification and auditing of learned models. Fairness and safety are of particular interest. We also plan to investigate algorithmic methods for automated checking and synthesis from CPL specifications.

References

1. Aucher, G., Maubert, B., Schwarzentruber, F.: Tableau method and NEXPTIME-completeness of del-sequents. Electr. Notes Theor. Comput. Sci. **278**, 17–30 (2011), proceedings of the 7th Workshop on Methods for Modalities (M4M'2011) and the 4th Workshop on Logical Aspects of Multi-Agent Systems (LAMAS'2011)
2. Belle, V., Papantonis, I.: Principles and practice of explainable machine learning. Front. Big Data **4**, 688969 (2021)
3. Calders, T.: Itemset frequency satisfiability: complexity and axiomatization. Theor. Comput. Sci. **394**(1–2), 84–111 (2008)
4. Chouldechova, A.: Fair prediction with disparate impact: a study of bias in recidivism prediction instruments. Big Data **5**(2), 153–163 (2017)
5. Cooper, G.F., et al.: Predicting dire outcomes of patients with community acquired pneumonia. J. Biomed. Inf. **38**(5), 347–366 (2005)
6. Demey, L., Kooi, B., Sack, J.: Logic and probability. In: Zalta, E.N., Nodelman, U. (eds.) The Stanford Encyclopedia of Philosophy. Metaphysics Research Lab, Stanford University, Fall 2023 edn. (2023)
7. van Emde Boas, P.: The convenience of tiling. In: Sorbi, A. (ed.) Complexity, Logic and Recursion Theory, Lecture Notes in Pure and Applied Mathematics, vol. 187, pp. 331–363. Marcel Dekker Inc. (1997)

8. Fagin, R., Halpern, J.Y., Megiddo, N.: A Logic for Reasoning about Probabilities. Inf. Comput. **87**(1/2), 78–128 (1990)
9. Feldman, M., Friedler, S.A., Moeller, J., Scheidegger, C., Venkatasubramanian, S.: Certifying and removing disparate impact. In: Proceedings of the 21th ACM SIGKDD International Conference on Knowledge Discovery and Data Mining, Sydney, NSW, Australia, 10–13 August 2015, pp. 259–268. ACM (2015)
10. Hardt, M., Price, E., Srebro, N.: Equality of opportunity in supervised learning. In: Advances in Neural Information Processing Systems 29: Annual Conference on Neural Information Processing Systems 2016, 5–10 December 2016, Barcelona, Spain, pp. 3315–3323 (2016)
11. Ignatiev, A., Narodytska, N., Marques-Silva, J.: Abduction-based explanations for machine learning models. In: The Thirty-Third AAAI Conference on Artificial Intelligence, AAAI 2019, pp. 1511–1519. AAAI Press, Honolulu, Hawaii, USA (2019)
12. Kleinberg, J.M., Mullainathan, S., Raghavan, M.: Inherent trade-offs in the fair determination of risk scores. In: 8th Innovations in Theoretical Computer Science Conference, ITCS 2017, Berkeley, CA, USA, 9-11 January 2017. LIPIcs, vol. 67, pp. 43:1–43:23. Schloss Dagstuhl - Leibniz-Zentrum für Informatik (2017)
13. Lipton, Z.C.: The mythos of model interpretability. Commun. ACM **61**(10), 36–43 (2018)
14. Liu, X., Lorini, E.: A unified logical framework for explanations in classifier systems. J. Log. Comput. **33**(2), 485–515 (2023)
15. Nilsson, N.J.: Probabilistic Logic. Artif. Intell. **28**(1), 71–87 (1986)
16. Ognjanovic, Z., Raskovic, M., Markovic, Z.: Probability logics - probability-based formalization of uncertain reasoning. Springer (2016)
17. Ribeiro, M.T., Singh, S., Guestrin, C.: Why should i trust you?: explaining the predictions of any classifier. In: Proceedings of the 22nd ACM SIGKDD International Conference on Knowledge Discovery and Data Mining, San Francisco, CA, USA, pp. 1135–1144. ACM (2016)
18. Rudin, C., Chen, C., Chen, Z., Huang, H., Semenova, L., Zhong, C.: Interpretable machine learning: fundamental principles and 10 grand challenges. CoRR **abs/2103.11251** (2021)
19. Savitch, W.J.: Relationships between nondeterministic and deterministic tape complexities. J. Comput. Syst. Sci. **4**(2), 177–192 (1970)
20. Shih, A., Choi, A., Darwiche, A.: A symbolic approach to explaining bayesian network classifiers. In: Proceedings of the Twenty-Seventh International Joint Conference on Artificial Intelligence, IJCAI 2018, Stockholm, Sweden, pp. 5103–5111. ijcai.org (2018)
21. Zafar, M.B., Valera, I., Gomez-Rodriguez, M., Gummadi, K.P.: Fairness constraints: a flexible approach for fair classification. J. Mach. Learn. Res. **20**, 75:1–75:42 (2019)
22. Zawidzki, M., Schmidt, R.A., Tishkovsky, D.: Satisfiability problem for modal logic with global counting operators coded in binary is NExpTime-complete. Inf. Process. Lett. **113**(1), 34–38 (2013). https://doi.org/10.1016/j.ipl.2012.09.007. https://www.sciencedirect.com/science/article/pii/S0020019012002645

PODD: Pareto-Optimized Dual-Teacher Distillation for Fair Graph Learning Under Distribution Shifts

Guofeng Xia[1], Xuemin Wang[2(✉)], Kaixing Liang[1], Zeyu Cao[1], Liang Chang[1], and Tianlong Gu[3]

[1] Guilin University of Electronic Technology, Guilin 541004, China
{twilight,liangkaixing,zeyucao}@mails.guet.edu.cn, changl@guet.edu.cn
[2] Guangxi Key Laboratory of Trusted Software, Guilin 541004, China
wangxuemin@guet.edu.cn
[3] Jinan University, Guangzhou 510632, China
gutianlong@jnu.edu.cn

Abstract. Fair Graph Neural Networks (GNNs) suffer from severe fairness degradation in real-world applications when the identical distribution assumption is violated. While recent studies attempt to address fair GNNs under distribution shifts, they typically lack an explicit optimization objective for resistance to distribution shifts, leading to suboptimal trade-offs between fairness and distribution shifts. Moreover, their specific architectures are incompatible with the latest state-of-the-art (SOTA) fair GNNs, limiting further fairness improvement. To address these challenges, we propose **PODD** (**P**areto-**O**ptimized **D**ual-Teacher **D**istillation), a novel plug-and-play dual-teacher distillation framework that decouples the conflicting objectives into a structured trade-off between two specialized teachers: (1) a Fairness Teacher that teaches the student to produce bias-free predictions via adversarial refinement on pre-trained fair GNNs; and (2) a Distribution Shift Teacher that teaches the student to remain stable under perturbations via worst-case training on simulated shifts. The student distills the most essential knowledge from both teachers through an information bottleneck, learning compact representations that are simultaneously fair and shift-resistant. Building on this architecture, we further design a Meta-Learning-based Pareto-Optimization strategy that dynamically resolves the fundamental gradient conflicts between the two objectives, navigating the model toward the optimal Pareto front without manual tuning. Experiments on three SOTA fair GNNs demonstrate that PODD achieves superior fairness and accuracy under distribution shifts.

Keywords: GNNs · Fairness · Distribution Shifts

1 Introduction

Graph Neural Networks (GNNs) have recently emerged as a crucial tool for modeling and representing graph-structured data [11,12,29,50,51], which are widely

M. Ceci et al. (Eds.): ECML PKDD 2026, LNAI 16941, pp. 445–461, 2027.
https://doi.org/10.1007/978-3-032-37654-1_26

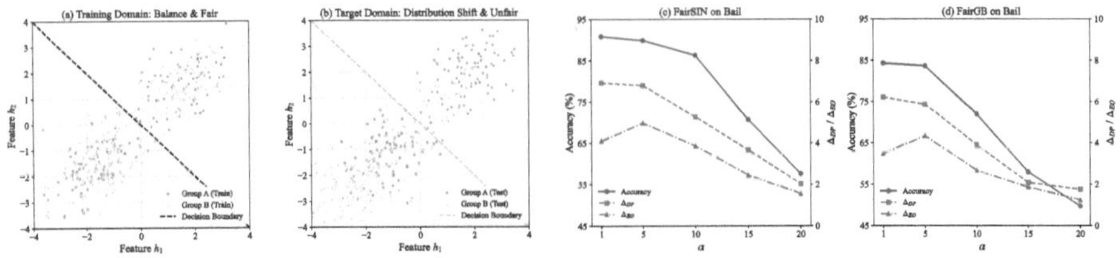

Fig. 1. Fairness degradation and fairness-utility trade-off under distribution shifts in SOTA models. In (a) and (b), distribution shifts invalidate decision boundaries learned from the source graph, amplifying bias in sensitive groups. In (c) and (d), manual hyperparameter tuning highlights that increasing fairness inevitably decreases utility.

used in high-stakes applications such as credit scoring [47] and social recommendation [5,13,15]. However, despite their utility, GNNs are prone to inheriting and potentially amplifying societal biases such as gender or race embedded in training data, resulting in systematic discrimination against sensitive demographic groups [9].

Recently, numerous fair GNNs [20,30,32–34] have been proposed to remove bias, such as regularization-based [49] and data augmentation methods [23]. However, these approaches typically assume that training and testing graphs share the same data distribution, which rarely holds in practice. Recent studies [22] further show that fair GNNs suffer severe performance degradation under distribution shifts. As illustrated in Fig. 1, a GNN optimized for fairness on the source graph often fails to generalize to the target graph with shifted distributions. Therefore, learning fair and generalizable GNNs under distribution shifts remains essential.

To address fairness degradation under distribution shifts, prior works have leveraged Domain Adaptation [48], or Invariant Learning [22]. However, fairness and generalization under distribution shifts inherently conflict. Specifically, methods ensuring resistance to distribution shifts retain essential predictive features, but these features often correlate with sensitive attributes due to homophily in real-world data [19]. Therefore, balancing fairness and resistance to distribution shifts becomes necessary. Nevertheless, existing methods rarely incorporate resistance to distribution shifts as an explicit optimization objective, complicating the joint optimization with fairness. Moreover, current approaches rely mainly on traditional fairness methods, lacking the flexibility to integrate with state-of-the-art (SOTA) fair GNNs, which significantly limits their potential for fairness improvement. Lastly, manual hyperparameter tuning, as illustrated in Fig. 1, often results in decreased utility when fairness improves, making it challenging to achieve an optimal trade-off between fairness and utility during optimization.

To tackle these challenges, we propose PODD (Pareto-Optimized Dual-Teacher Distillation), a novel plug-and-play dual-teacher distillation framework that transforms the conflicting objectives into a structured trade-off between a Fairness Teacher and a Distribution Shift Teacher. The former adversarially refines existing SOTA fair GNNs to strip sensitive information, while the latter captures stable predictive patterns through simulated perturbations. We further introduce an information-theoretic constraint to encourage the student to retain only essential signals from both teachers. Building on this architecture, we discover that a Meta-Learning-based Pareto-Optimization strategy [6] can dynamically resolve gradient conflicts, navigating the model toward the optimal Pareto front without manual tuning. The contributions are summarized as follows:

- We propose PODD, a plug-and-play dual-teacher distillation framework compatible with arbitrary SOTA fair GNNs.
- We decouple fairness and resistance to distribution shifts into two specialized teachers, with an information bottleneck to distill only essential knowledge from both.
- We design a Meta-Learning-based Pareto-Optimization strategy to dynamically resolve gradient conflicts without manual tuning.
- We theoretically show that graph message-passing amplifies the conflict between the fairness objective and the distribution shift objective, justifying the necessity of dynamic Pareto re-balancing.

2 Related Work

Distribution Shifts in Graph Learning. Existing approaches to graph learning under distribution shifts largely focus on domain adaptation [10] and invariant learning [45]. For instance, [2] proposed a test-time adaptation method to mitigate the impact of structural shifts, while [21] introduced GRADATE to select optimal source data for graph-level domain adaptation. However, these methods all ignore the fairness dimension. Even within causal inference approaches designed to mine invariant subgraphs [8], sensitive attributes are rarely incorporated into the causal inference terms.

Fairness Graph Learning. Existing fair GNNs [35–37,41] primarily focuses on debiasing methods within static environments [20]. For example, [40,41] introduced methods to analyze node representation bias and achieve provable fairness bounds using only partial demographic constraints. However, these static models are difficult to adapt to dynamic environments. Theoretical studies [23,24] demonstrate that fairness performance is highly sensitive to distribution shifts, and prediction disparities drift significantly over time without intervention [27].

Fair Graph Learning under Distribution Shifts. Recently, a few pioneering works have begun to explore the intersection of these two fields. For instance, [22] theoretically analyzed the impact of distribution shifts on fairness and proposed a framework to correct shifts in the representation space. Similarly, DANCE [38] synthesized unbiased virtual samples via mix-up and adversarial learning to improve robustness against shifts. However, these efforts still have limitations. Firstly, current methods neglect to cast distribution shift as an explicit objective, making joint optimization with fairness intractable. Secondly, these techniques are still unable to adapt themselves to the latest state-of-the-art (SOTA) fair GNNs, given that their own debiasing methods are outdated.

In summary, while pioneering efforts have explored the intersection of fair graph learning and distribution shifts, a unified framework that explicitly resolves the inherent gradient conflicts between these objectives remains absent. Current solutions typically lack an explicit optimization objective for shift-resistance, and their rigid, model-specific designs render them incompatible with SOTA models.

3 Preliminaries

Notations. Let $\mathcal{G} = (\mathcal{V}, \mathcal{E}, X)$ denote a graph with N nodes, where $\mathcal{V} = \{v_1, ..., v_N\}$ is the set of nodes and $\mathcal{E} \subseteq \mathcal{V} \times \mathcal{V}$ represents the edges described by the adjacency matrix $A \in \{0,1\}^{N \times N}$. The node feature matrix is denoted as $X \in \mathbb{R}^{N \times d_0}$, where d_0 is the feature dimension. For each node v_i, we have a ground-truth label $y_i \in \mathcal{Y}$ and a binary sensitive attribute $s_i \in \mathcal{S} = \{0, 1\}$. We focus on the semi-supervised node classification task.

Fairness Metrics. To evaluate fairness, we adopt two standard metrics: Demographic Parity (DP) and Equalized Odds (EO). Specifically, DP requires prediction independence from sensitive attributes, formulated as the absolute difference in positive prediction rates between sensitive groups:

$$\Delta_{DP} = |P(\hat{Y} = 1 \, S = 1) - P(\hat{Y} = 1 \, S = 0)|. \tag{1}$$

Meanwhile, EO requires equal error rates across groups, enforcing that the model performs equally well for both groups conditional on the true label:

$$\Delta_{EO} = \sum_{y \in \{0,1\}} |P(\hat{Y} = 1 \, S = 1, Y = y) - P(\hat{Y} = 1 \, S = 0, Y = y)|. \tag{2}$$

Distribution Shifts. Given a source domain $\mathcal{D}_S$ and a target domain $\mathcal{D}_T$ defined over an input space $\mathcal{X} \times \mathcal{G}$ and label space $\mathcal{Y}$, a *distribution shift* is formally defined as the inconsistency between their joint distributions, i.e., $P_{\mathcal{D}_S}(A, X, Y) \neq P_{\mathcal{D}_T}(A, X, Y)$. In this work, we specifically focus on the shift setting where the distribution of graph structure and attributes changes $(P_{\mathcal{D}_S}(A, X) \neq P_{\mathcal{D}_T}(A, X))$. The essence of this problem is the violation of the identical distribution assumption, which typically leads to model failure on the target domain.

Pareto Optimality. Given a multi-objective optimization problem with objectives $\mathbf{J}(\theta) = [\mathcal{L}_1(\theta), \ldots, \mathcal{L}_m(\theta)]^T$, a solution θ^* is *Pareto optimal* if it is not dominated by any other solution. Formally, a solution θ' dominates θ if $\mathcal{L}_i(\theta') \leq \mathcal{L}_i(\theta)$ for all $i \in \{1, \ldots, m\}$, with $\mathcal{L}_j(\theta') < \mathcal{L}_j(\theta)$ for at least one j. The *Pareto front* is defined as the set of all such Pareto optimal solutions, representing the state where no objective can be improved without degrading another.

Problem Definition. Based on the definitions above, we formally define the problem of Fair Graph Learning under Distribution Shifts as follows:

Problem 1. Given a graph $\mathcal{G} = (\mathcal{V}, \mathcal{E}, X)$ with sensitive attributes $\mathcal{S}$, a source domain $\mathcal{D}_{src}$ and a target domain $\mathcal{D}_{tgt}$ where $P_{\mathcal{D}_{src}}(A, X) \neq P_{\mathcal{D}_{tgt}}(A, X)$, learn a GNN encoder f_θ for fair node classification, i.e.,

$$f_\theta(\mathcal{G}, S) \to \hat{\mathcal{Y}}, \tag{3}$$

where f_θ is the function we aim to learn and $\hat{\mathcal{Y}}$ is the set of predicted labels. The objective is to locate a Pareto optimal solution θ^* such that $\hat{\mathcal{Y}}$ simultaneously maintains high utility whilst satisfying fairness criteria under distribution shifts.

4 Methodology

To tackle fairness degradation under distribution shifts, we propose PODD (Pareto-Optimized Dual-Teacher Distillation). As illustrated in Fig. 2, PODD's dual-teacher distillation framework contains a Fairness Teacher that teaches the student to produce bias-free predictions by adversarial refinement of pretrained fair GNNs, and a Distribution Shift Teacher that teaches the student to remain stable under perturbations by worst-case training on simulated transformations. We further propose a Meta-Learning-based Pareto-Optimization mechanism to dynamically resolve the basic gradient conflict between two objectives. Lastly, an Information Bottleneck (IB) constraint rigorously filters noise introduced by distribution shifts to guarantee the whole trade-off between fairness and utility, yielding a compact, fair, and generalizable student model.

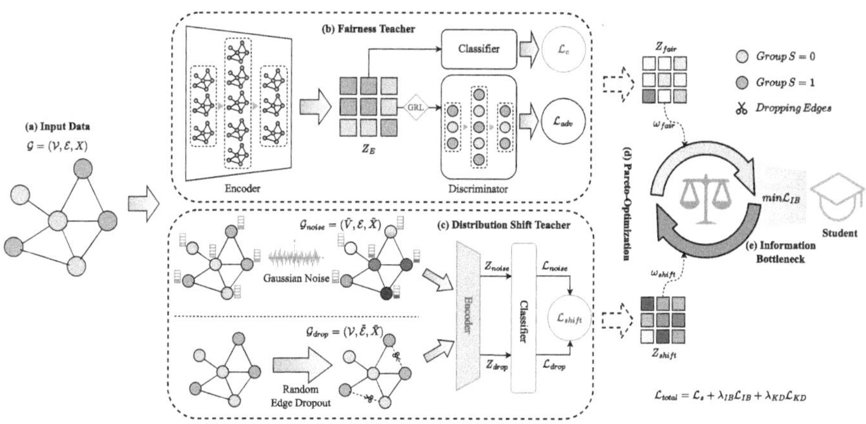

Fig. 2. The overview of proposed PODD.

4.1 Dual-Teacher Distillation

To simultaneously handle fairness and generalization to distribution shifts, we propose a dual-teacher architecture, which consists of a Fairness Teacher and a Distribution Shift Teacher.

Fairness Teacher. The Fairness Teacher (T_{fair}) is designed to provide fair guidance by leveraging the capabilities of existing fair GNNs. To establish a high-quality and unbiased starting point, we first initialize the teacher using current state-of-the-art (SOTA) fair GNN techniques, such as FairSIN [44]. We train the encoder by optimizing the specific objective function of the chosen SOTA model:

$$\theta_{init} = \arg\min_{\theta} \mathcal{L}_{SOTA}(\mathcal{G}, Y, S), \tag{4}$$

where $\mathcal{L}_{SOTA}$ represents the fairness-aware loss defined by the base model. This step ensures that the teacher captures a stable initial debiased representation.

Although the SOTA initialization provides a strong foundation, to ensure persistent fairness and adaptability during the dynamic distillation process, we further refine these embeddings via adversarial training. Specifically, we update the encoder f_{fair} against an adversarial discriminator D_ψ, which attempts to infer sensitive attributes S from the node embeddings. The objective of this iterative adversarial refinement is formally expressed as:

$$\min_{\theta_{fair}} \max_{\psi} \mathcal{L}_{fair}(\theta_{fair}, \psi) = \mathbb{E}\big[\mathcal{L}_s(Y, \hat{Y}) + \lambda_{adv} \log D_\psi(f_{fair}(A, X), S)\big], \tag{5}$$

where $\mathcal{L}_s$ denotes the classification task loss, and λ_{adv} modulates the strength of adversarial regularization. This continuous contest ensures that the embeddings remain consistently free from sensitive information leakage throughout the training pipeline.

Distribution Shift Teacher. To ensure the model's resistance to distribution shifts, the Distribution Shift Teacher (T_{shift}) explicitly captures stable predictive patterns across diverse environments. Existing methods often neglect explicit training against structural and feature perturbations, limiting generalization under real-world shifts.

To address this gap, we simulate challenging distribution shifts through synthetic perturbations: (1) Feature Shift Simulation, where Gaussian noise $\mathcal{N}(0, \sigma^2)$ is injected into node features, simulating real-world measurement errors; and (2) Structural Shift Simulation, where random edge dropout with probability p simulates topological changes. The teacher is trained using worst-case risk minimization:

$$\mathcal{L}_{shift} = \max_{G' \in \mathcal{P}_{syn}} \mathbb{E}_{(A', X') \sim G'}[\mathcal{L}_s(f_{shift}(A', X'), Y)]. \tag{6}$$

By explicitly training the model under the most challenging synthetic perturbations, our method directly enhances robustness, mitigating fairness degradation caused by distribution shifts.

Student Model. The student model f_S, parameterized by θ_S, aims to inherit knowledge from both teachers while explicitly filtering out distribution-specific noise. To effectively transfer knowledge, we employ a dynamic distillation strategy where the student mimics the representations of both the Fairness Teacher (Z_{fair}) and the Distribution Shift Teacher (Z_{shift}). The distillation loss is formulated as a weighted sum of the distances to both teachers:

$$\begin{aligned}\mathcal{L}_{KD}(\theta_S, \mathbf{w}) = w_{fair}\|Z_S - Z_{fair}\|_2^2 \\ + w_{shift}\|Z_S - Z_{shift}\|_2^2,\end{aligned} \tag{7}$$

where $\mathbf{w} = [w_{fair}, w_{shift}]^T$ are learnable weights that balance the trade-off between fairness and generalization.

To further enhance the student's resistance to input noise and spurious correlations unrelated to the task, we incorporate the Information Bottleneck (IB) principle. By minimizing the mutual information between the input graph and the latent representation, we encourage the encoder to filter out redundant information. Adopting the Variational Information Bottleneck (VIB) framework with a standard Gaussian prior $r(Z_S) \sim \mathcal{N}(0, I)$, the tractable IB loss is derived as the KL divergence:

$$\mathcal{L}_{IB} = \frac{1}{2N}\sum_{i=1}^{N}\sum_{j=1}^{d_h}\left(\mu_{ij}^2 + \sigma_{ij}^2 - \log(\sigma_{ij}^2) - 1\right), \tag{8}$$

where μ and σ^2 are the mean and variance predicted by the student encoder.

Integrating the task supervision with the above constraints, the total learning objective for the student model is defined as:

$$\mathcal{L}_{total} = \mathcal{L}_s + \lambda_{IB}\mathcal{L}_{IB} + \lambda_{KD}\mathcal{L}_{KD}, \tag{9}$$

where $\mathcal{L}_s$ is the standard cross-entropy classification loss, and λ_{IB} is a hyperparameter controlling the compression strength. Crucially, the distillation weights $\mathbf{w}$ are not fixed, which are treated as meta-parameters and optimized via a bi-level Pareto-Optimization process, as detailed in the next section.

4.2 Pareto-Optimization Based on Meta-Learning

We formulate the inherent tension between fairness and resistance to distribution shifts as a multi-objective optimization problem, explicitly highlighting their conflicting nature. Specifically, the student model simultaneously minimizes two distillation losses:

$$\min_{\theta_S} \boldsymbol{\mathcal{L}}(\theta_S) = [\mathcal{L}_{fair}(\theta_S), \mathcal{L}_{shift}(\theta_S)]^T. \tag{10}$$

However, these objectives often conflict and produce opposing gradient directions: $\langle \nabla_{\theta_S}\mathcal{L}_{fair}, \nabla_{\theta_S}\mathcal{L}_{shift}\rangle < 0$. This gradient conflict causes instability during training. Traditional methods use fixed aggregation weights, but this usually results in oscillations or dominance by one objective. To solve this, we propose a Meta-Learning-based Pareto-Optimization method. In our method, aggregation weights $\mathbf{w} = [w_{fair}, w_{shift}]^T$ are learnable parameters rather than fixed hyperparameters. These weights dynamically adjust during training, effectively resolving gradient conflicts. Specifically, our method involves two nested loops:

Inner Loop (Student Update). Given current aggregation weights $\mathbf{w}$, the student parameters θ_S are updated to minimize the weighted sum of objectives:

$$\theta_S^*(\mathbf{w}) = \theta_S - \eta \nabla_{\theta_S} \left(w_{fair}\mathcal{L}_{fair} + w_{shift}\mathcal{L}_{shift} \right). \tag{11}$$

Outer Loop (Meta-Weight Update). The aggregation weights $\mathbf{w}$ are optimized by minimizing a validation objective $\mathcal{R}_{val}$ (Pareto Risk), evaluated using the updated parameters $\theta_S^*(\mathbf{w})$:

$$\mathbf{w}^* = \arg\min_{\mathbf{w}} \mathcal{R}_{val}\left(\theta_S^*(\mathbf{w})\right). \tag{12}$$

The gradient w.r.t. $\mathbf{w}$ is computed via the chain rule, explicitly capturing how adjusting $\mathbf{w}$ affects the student's parameter updates and overall validation performance.

4.3 Theoretical Analysis

In this section, we prove that graph message-passing amplifies the conflict between fairness and shift-resistance. To distinguish from the distillation losses $\mathcal{L}_{fair}/\mathcal{L}_{shift}$ in Sect. 4.2, we use $\mathcal{J}_{fair}/\mathcal{J}_{shift}$ for the theoretical objectives below.

Notations. We follow Sect. 3. Let $\mathcal{G}^d = (\mathcal{V}^d, \mathcal{E}^d, X^d)$ be the graph in domain $d \in \{S, T\}$. A single message-passing layer computes $h_v^d = \sum_{u \in \mathcal{N}_d(v)} \hat{A}_{vu}^d \, x_u \, W$, where $\hat{A}^d = (\tilde{D}^d)^{-1/2} \tilde{A}^d (\tilde{D}^d)^{-1/2}$ and $W \in \mathbb{R}^{d_0 \times d_h}$. We define the *structural mixing matrix*

$$M_d[s, s'] = \mathbb{E}_{v:s_v=s}\Big[\textstyle\sum_{u \in \mathcal{N}_d(v)} \hat{A}_{vu}^d \, \mathbf{1}[s_u = s']\Big], \tag{13}$$

satisfying $M_d[s,0] + M_d[s,1] = 1$. Based on this, we introduce the following key quantities used throughout the analysis: (1) the *group feature mean* $\nu_s := \mathbb{E}_{u:s_u=s}[x_u]\, W$, (2) the *group embedding mean* $\mu_s^d := \mathbb{E}_{v:s_v=s}[h_v^d]$, (3) the *homophily gap* $\alpha_S := |M_S[1,0] - M_S[0,0]|$, (4) the *structural shift gap* $\beta_{S,T} := \max_s |M_S[s,0] - M_T[s,0]|$, and (5) the *label disparity* $\rho_y := |P(Y = 1 \mid s{=}1) - P(Y{=}1 \mid s{=}0)|$.

Assumptions. We require five mild regularity conditions:

A1. *Structural homophily bias*: $\alpha_S > 0$, i.e., the two sensitive groups have different neighborhood compositions.
A2. *Shared conditional feature means*: $\mathbb{E}[x_v \mid s_v{=}s, d{=}S] = \mathbb{E}[x_v \mid s_v{=}s, d{=}T]$, isolating structural shift from feature shift.

A3. *Bounded classifier*: $\hat{Y} = \sigma(\omega^\top h)$ with $\|\omega\| \leq C_\omega$, which holds under weight decay.
A4. *Label disparity*: $\rho_y > 0$, i.e., the base rates differ across sensitive groups.
A5. *Group calibration*: $|\mathbb{E}[\hat{Y} \mid s] - P(Y=1 \mid s)| \leq \varepsilon_0$ for each s, with effective calibration error $\varepsilon := \varepsilon_0 + \frac{1}{8}\, C_\omega(\bar{\sigma}_1 + \bar{\sigma}_0) < \rho_y/2$, where $\bar{\sigma}_s := \mathbb{E}[\|h_v - \mu_s^S\| \mid s_v = s]$ is the within-group embedding deviation.

Lemma 1 (Fairness objective decomposition). $\mathcal{J}_{\text{fair}} := \|\mu_1^S - \mu_0^S\| = \alpha_S\,\|\nu_1 - \nu_0\|$.

Lemma 2 (Distribution shift objective decomposition). *Under* A2, $\mathcal{J}_{\text{shift}} := \max_s \|\mu_s^S - \mu_s^T\| = \beta_{S,T}\,\|\nu_1 - \nu_0\|$.

Lemma 3 (Representation lower bound). *Under* A1, A3–A5, $\|\nu_1 - \nu_0\| \geq 4(\rho_y - 2\varepsilon)/(C_\omega\, \alpha_S)$.

Theorem 1. *Under* A1–A5, *for any* $\lambda > 0$,

$$\mathcal{J}_{\text{fair}} + \lambda\, \mathcal{J}_{\text{shift}} \geq \frac{4(\rho_y - 2\varepsilon)}{C_\omega}\left(1 + \lambda\, \frac{\beta_{S,T}}{\alpha_S}\right). \tag{14}$$

When $M_S = M_T$, $\beta_{S,T} = 0$ and the bound reduces to $4(\rho_y - 2\varepsilon)/C_\omega$; the shift loss vanishes and the fairness teacher can optimize freely.

When $M_S \neq M_T$, the factor $1 + \lambda\beta_{S,T}/\alpha_S > 1$ strictly amplifies the lower bound. Since both $\mathcal{J}_{\text{fair}} = \alpha_S\|\Delta\nu\|$ and $\mathcal{J}_{\text{shift}} = \beta_{S,T}\|\Delta\nu\|$ depend on the same quantity $\|\Delta\nu\|$, the fairness teacher shrinks $\|\Delta\nu\|$ while Lemma 3 forbids it from falling below $4(\rho_y - 2\varepsilon)/(C_\omega\alpha_S)$, leaving an irreducible shift loss $\mathcal{J}_{\text{shift}} \geq 4\beta_{S,T}(\rho_y - 2\varepsilon)/(C_\omega\alpha_S) > 0$. This confirms that graph structural shift creates a genuine optimization conflict absent in non-graph settings, justifying Sect. 4.2.

5 Experiments

Our experiments are designed to answer the following research questions (RQs): **RQ1**: Does the integration of PODD into existing state-of-the-art (SOTA) fair GNNs lead to performance improvements? **RQ2**: How does the SOTA model adapted to PODD perform compared to SOTA baselines? **RQ3**: How does each module of PODD contribute to the final performance?

5.1 Experimental Setup

Datasets. To evaluate the performance of our framework, we specifically select these datasets from the recently proposed graph fairness benchmark [28], which was designed to address the shortcomings of traditional datasets. Previous datasets have been criticized for their weak correlation between graph topology and sensitive attributes, rendering them insufficient for evaluating structural fairness. In contrast, the datasets in this new benchmark are constructed with topology-based relationship building, ensuring that the graph structure plays a critical role in the learning process. We conducted experiments on three real-world datasets, namely Pokecs [4], BailA [17], and CreditA [46]. To explore the data structure, we apply a modularity-based community detection method [25], partitioning BailA-Bs into five communities labeled B0 through B4. These partitions reveal different data distributions across the communities. Community B0 is utilized for training and validation in the experiments compared with the baselines, and the remaining communities (B1 to B4) serve as the test. The CreditA dataset is also divided in the same way. Pokecs consists of two graphs, Pokec-z and Pokec-n, each containing users from two different regions. Pokec-z is used for training and validation, while Pokec-n serves as the test set.

Table 1. Classification and fairness metrics (%$\pm\sigma$) on BailA-Bs and CreditA-Cs. ↑ indicates that higher values are better, while ↓ indicating the opposite. The top-performing results are marked in bold.

Metrics	Methods	B0	B1	B2	B3	B4	C0	C1	C2	C3	C4
ACC ↑	FairGB	$81.08_{\pm 0.86}$	$78.16_{\pm 4.01}$	$79.09_{\pm 1.63}$	$79.68_{\pm 2.21}$	$52.07_{\pm 14.26}$	$\mathbf{79.09}_{\pm 0.37}$	$78.49_{\pm 0.70}$	$78.64_{\pm 0.76}$	$74.37_{\pm 0.51}$	$\mathbf{78.46}_{\pm 0.41}$
	FairGB+PODD	$\mathbf{84.45}_{\pm 2.13}$	$\mathbf{84.61}_{\pm 0.55}$	$\mathbf{82.18}_{\pm 1.34}$	$\mathbf{83.04}_{\pm 1.47}$	$\mathbf{65.52}_{\pm 3.18}$	$78.60_{\pm 2.97}$	$\mathbf{78.66}_{\pm 0.25}$	$\mathbf{79.67}_{\pm 0.91}$	$\mathbf{74.77}_{\pm 4.33}$	$78.28_{\pm 1.47}$
Δ_{DP} ↓	FairGB	$8.83_{\pm 1.16}$	$12.00_{\pm 3.41}$	$7.60_{\pm 1.60}$	$9.20_{\pm 2.67}$	$4.14_{\pm 5.54}$	$1.21_{\pm 1.16}$	$4.56_{\pm 1.64}$	$0.61_{\pm 0.67}$	$1.91_{\pm 1.78}$	$1.61_{\pm 1.87}$
	FairGB+PODD	$8.83_{\pm 0.91}$	$\mathbf{9.90}_{\pm 1.27}$	$\mathbf{5.83}_{\pm 1.55}$	$\mathbf{2.19}_{\pm 1.11}$	$\mathbf{0.00}_{\pm 0.00}$	$\mathbf{0.21}_{\pm 0.05}$	$\mathbf{0.53}_{\pm 0.21}$	$\mathbf{0.00}_{\pm 0.00}$	$\mathbf{1.04}_{\pm 1.01}$	$\mathbf{0.00}_{\pm 0.00}$
Δ_{EO} ↓	FairGB	$3.55_{\pm 1.99}$	$10.06_{\pm 4.68}$	$2.99_{\pm 2.18}$	$18.43_{\pm 4.61}$	$10.00_{\pm 10.00}$	$1.52_{\pm 1.66}$	$5.29_{\pm 3.16}$	$1.05_{\pm 0.87}$	$3.02_{\pm 3.39}$	$0.75_{\pm 1.28}$
	FairGB+PODD	$\mathbf{1.62}_{\pm 1.23}$	$\mathbf{8.71}_{\pm 1.87}$	$\mathbf{0.71}_{\pm 0.42}$	$\mathbf{10.71}_{\pm 3.66}$	$\mathbf{0.00}_{\pm 0.00}$	$\mathbf{0.00}_{\pm 0.00}$	$\mathbf{0.34}_{\pm 0.28}$	$\mathbf{0.00}_{\pm 0.00}$	$\mathbf{0.68}_{\pm 0.13}$	$\mathbf{0.00}_{\pm 0.00}$
ACC ↑	FairSIN	$87.19_{\pm 1.17}$	$85.66_{\pm 1.69}$	$\mathbf{87.52}_{\pm 0.52}$	$69.05_{\pm 5.58}$	$72.41_{\pm 2.36}$	$78.45_{\pm 1.54}$	$\mathbf{78.42}_{\pm 2.99}$	$78.38_{\pm 2.48}$	$74.05_{\pm 1.33}$	$\mathbf{78.19}_{\pm 1.81}$
	FairSIN+PODD	$\mathbf{91.79}_{\pm 2.41}$	$\mathbf{88.25}_{\pm 1.33}$	$87.05_{\pm 0.97}$	$\mathbf{77.73}_{\pm 2.77}$	$\mathbf{82.75}_{\pm 1.41}$	$\mathbf{78.60}_{\pm 1.99}$	$78.18_{\pm 1.75}$	$\mathbf{79.12}_{\pm 0.45}$	$\mathbf{74.77}_{\pm 3.26}$	$75.11_{\pm 1.69}$
Δ_{DP} ↓	FairSIN	$9.45_{\pm 3.33}$	$7.88_{\pm 1.13}$	$8.65_{\pm 1.01}$	$2.93_{\pm 0.23}$	$21.81_{\pm 3.90}$	$1.58_{\pm 1.34}$	$1.41_{\pm 0.78}$	$3.67_{\pm 1.06}$	$0.86_{\pm 0.77}$	$1.36_{\pm 0.97}$
	FairSIN+PODD	$\mathbf{9.36}_{\pm 3.63}$	$\mathbf{7.55}_{\pm 1.44}$	$\mathbf{8.02}_{\pm 3.52}$	$\mathbf{0.85}_{\pm 0.11}$	$\mathbf{9.99}_{\pm 2.02}$	$\mathbf{1.02}_{\pm 1.00}$	$\mathbf{1.05}_{\pm 0.13}$	$\mathbf{0.60}_{\pm 0.30}$	$\mathbf{0.00}_{\pm 0.00}$	$\mathbf{0.91}_{\pm 0.52}$
Δ_{EO} ↓	FairSIN	$2.84_{\pm 1.07}$	$3.96_{\pm 1.36}$	$1.63_{\pm 1.10}$	$6.27_{\pm 1.78}$	$28.00_{\pm 5.39}$	$2.48_{\pm 1.72}$	$1.41_{\pm 0.83}$	$1.81_{\pm 0.99}$	$0.44_{\pm 0.06}$	$0.52_{\pm 0.33}$
	FairSIN+PODD	$\mathbf{2.47}_{\pm 0.70}$	$\mathbf{2.70}_{\pm 1.91}$	$\mathbf{0.10}_{\pm 0.12}$	$\mathbf{2.01}_{\pm 1.57}$	$\mathbf{19.99}_{\pm 2.32}$	$\mathbf{0.52}_{\pm 0.35}$	$\mathbf{1.01}_{\pm 0.84}$	$\mathbf{0.76}_{\pm 0.41}$	$\mathbf{0.00}_{\pm 0.00}$	$\mathbf{0.39}_{\pm 0.09}$
ACC ↑	NIFTY	$87.54_{\pm 3.42}$	$87.70_{\pm 1.05}$	$86.45_{\pm 1.87}$	$85.16_{\pm 2.59}$	$65.52_{\pm 2.04}$	$\mathbf{77.65}_{\pm 1.61}$	$76.74_{\pm 3.25}$	$\mathbf{79.67}_{\pm 0.63}$	$74.32_{\pm 1.86}$	$78.28_{\pm 5.07}$
	NIFTY+PODD	$\mathbf{94.10}_{\pm 2.93}$	$\mathbf{92.71}_{\pm 2.11}$	$\mathbf{90.12}_{\pm 1.07}$	$\mathbf{88.69}_{\pm 0.83}$	$\mathbf{75.86}_{\pm 1.64}$	$77.27_{\pm 1.54}$	$\mathbf{78.66}_{\pm 0.88}$	$78.83_{\pm 2.96}$	$\mathbf{74.77}_{\pm 3.64}$	$\mathbf{78.73}_{\pm 3.22}$
Δ_{DP} ↓	NIFTY	$10.11_{\pm 0.74}$	$\mathbf{6.18}_{\pm 0.28}$	$9.35_{\pm 1.65}$	$\mathbf{4.35}_{\pm 1.30}$	$29.05_{\pm 4.03}$	$0.82_{\pm 0.05}$	$0.86_{\pm 0.27}$	$\mathbf{1.21}_{\pm 1.04}$	$0.52_{\pm 0.43}$	$\mathbf{0.10}_{\pm 0.12}$
	NIFTY+PODD	$\mathbf{8.71}_{\pm 3.28}$	$6.75_{\pm 1.52}$	$\mathbf{9.21}_{\pm 2.30}$	$4.96_{\pm 2.74}$	$\mathbf{8.10}_{\pm 1.69}$	$\mathbf{0.36}_{\pm 0.19}$	$\mathbf{0.60}_{\pm 0.53}$	$1.40_{\pm 0.89}$	$\mathbf{0.00}_{\pm 0.00}$	$0.51_{\pm 0.21}$
Δ_{EO} ↓	NIFTY	$7.25_{\pm 2.58}$	$1.94_{\pm 1.24}$	$2.24_{\pm 0.88}$	$\mathbf{12.03}_{\pm 2.65}$	$60.00_{\pm 10.38}$	$1.04_{\pm 0.52}$	$0.98_{\pm 0.39}$	$0.76_{\pm 0.53}$	$0.68_{\pm 0.11}$	$0.06_{\pm 0.08}$
	NIFTY+PODD	$\mathbf{2.98}_{\pm 1.22}$	$\mathbf{1.35}_{\pm 0.70}$	$\mathbf{0.51}_{\pm 0.13}$	$14.67_{\pm 3.59}$	$\mathbf{40.00}_{\pm 12.68}$	$\mathbf{0.43}_{\pm 0.30}$	$\mathbf{1.01}_{\pm 0.45}$	$\mathbf{0.21}_{\pm 0.06}$	$\mathbf{0.00}_{\pm 0.00}$	$\mathbf{0.00}_{\pm 0.00}$

Baselines. We first adapt our framework to three state-of-the-art (SOTA) models to observe the effect, then we compared adapted model with other baselines: 1) Adapted methods: FairGB [23], FairSIN [44], NIFTY [1]. 2) Traditional learning methods: MLP [26], GCN [18], GIN [43]. 3) Fair GNNs: FairVGNN [39], EDITS [7], CAF [14], SFG [3]. 4)Out-of-distribution (OOD) GNN: EERM [42]. 5) Model-agnostic OOD method: SAGM [31]. 6) GNN with spectral graph theory: FUGNN [24]. 7) Fairness under distribution shifts methods: RFR [16], FatraGNN [22].

Performance Evaluation. We evaluate node classification performance using two key metrics: accuracy and ROC-AUC. Fairness is measured with Δ_{DP} and Δ_{EO}, as detailed in Sect. 3, where lower values indicate better fairness. To comprehensively assess the relative competitiveness of all methods across varying distribution shifts, we adopt the Average Rank metric. Specifically, for each evaluation metric on every test graph, we rank all comparing methods, assigning Rank 1 to the best-performing model. The final score is obtained by averaging these rankings across all test scenarios, where a lower value indicates superior overall performance.

Table 2. Classification and fairness metrics (%$\pm\sigma$) on BailA-Bs. $\uparrow$ indicates that higher values are better, while $\downarrow$ indicating the opposite. In each row, the best result is indicated in bold, while the runner-up result is marked with an underline.

	Metrics	MLP	GCN	GIN	FairVGNN	FairSIN	EDITS	EERM	SFG	FUGNN	FatraGNN	FairSIN+PODD
B1	ACC$\uparrow$	$66.51_{\pm 0.49}$	$56.58_{\pm 3.57}$	$82.82_{\pm 0.13}$	$80.31_{\pm 1.22}$	$\underline{87.01}_{\pm 1.82}$	$76.78_{\pm 0.88}$	$45.98_{\pm 5.44}$	$84.89_{\pm 0.58}$	$47.73_{\pm 7.70}$	$83.19_{\pm 1.97}$	$\mathbf{91.29}_{\pm 0.32}$
	ROC-AUC$\uparrow$	$68.95_{\pm 0.25}$	$51.70_{\pm 1.24}$	$87.50_{\pm 0.14}$	$84.21_{\pm 0.85}$	$\underline{89.55}_{\pm 2.77}$	$87.23_{\pm 0.41}$	$50.11_{\pm 4.24}$	$89.03_{\pm 0.50}$	$50.04_{\pm 0.36}$	$89.20_{\pm 0.03}$	$\mathbf{92.84}_{\pm 2.51}$
	$\Delta_{DP}\downarrow$	$13.55_{\pm 2.76}$	$2.61_{\pm 2.03}$	$8.91_{\pm 1.41}$	$\underline{1.30}_{\pm 0.97}$	$8.18_{\pm 0.80}$	$1.33_{\pm 0.27}$	$2.75_{\pm 2.07}$	$5.29_{\pm 0.50}$	$\mathbf{0.29}_{\pm 0.28}$	$1.83_{\pm 0.45}$	$7.75_{\pm 0.55}$
	$\Delta_{EO}\downarrow$	$16.50_{\pm 3.19}$	$2.74_{\pm 1.59}$	$7.87_{\pm 1.45}$	$2.78_{\pm 1.66}$	$3.12_{\pm 0.93}$	$\underline{1.27}_{\pm 0.31}$	$5.24_{\pm 3.00}$	$\mathbf{0.64}_{\pm 0.29}$	$1.43_{\pm 1.35}$	$1.81_{\pm 1.07}$	$2.28_{\pm 0.48}$
B2	ACC$\uparrow$	$66.78_{\pm 0.21}$	$56.06_{\pm 3.46}$	$85.95_{\pm 0.10}$	$58.45_{\pm 0.78}$	$\underline{86.34}_{\pm 0.89}$	$83.78_{\pm 0.55}$	$47.01_{\pm 8.59}$	$85.54_{\pm 0.71}$	$44.76_{\pm 4.64}$	$85.79_{\pm 0.36}$	$\mathbf{91.25}_{\pm 0.10}$
	ROC-AUC$\uparrow$	$69.22_{\pm 0.08}$	$51.55_{\pm 1.89}$	$\underline{91.85}_{\pm 0.31}$	$59.61_{\pm 0.75}$	$88.01_{\pm 1.02}$	$88.92_{\pm 0.36}$	$48.84_{\pm 8.69}$	$90.37_{\pm 0.59}$	$51.67_{\pm 2.87}$	$90.41_{\pm 0.21}$	$\mathbf{92.69}_{\pm 1.60}$
	$\Delta_{DP}\downarrow$	$14.68_{\pm 3.86}$	$\underline{1.83}_{\pm 1.04}$	$8.28_{\pm 0.76}$	$4.15_{\pm 1.54}$	$8.91_{\pm 1.15}$	$5.62_{\pm 0.53}$	$2.36_{\pm 1.28}$	$7.02_{\pm 0.48}$	$\mathbf{0.41}_{\pm 0.37}$	$6.21_{\pm 1.16}$	$8.28_{\pm 0.16}$
	$\Delta_{EO}\downarrow$	$16.72_{\pm 4.16}$	$\mathbf{2.17}_{\pm 1.65}$	$5.30_{\pm 1.35}$	$3.52_{\pm 2.00}$	$4.75_{\pm 0.56}$	$\underline{2.28}_{\pm 0.66}$	$3.91_{\pm 1.81}$	$3.34_{\pm 0.63}$	$2.76_{\pm 1.72}$	$4.98_{\pm 1.42}$	$4.33_{\pm 0.45}$
B3	ACC$\uparrow$	$66.25_{\pm 0.89}$	$57.10_{\pm 2.42}$	$78.14_{\pm 0.32}$	$53.22_{\pm 1.40}$	$81.97_{\pm 2.31}$	$77.66_{\pm 0.66}$	$45.65_{\pm 5.58}$	$80.49_{\pm 1.07}$	$\mathbf{94.67}_{\pm 4.37}$	$79.58_{\pm 1.10}$	$\underline{89.49}_{\pm 0.73}$
	ROC-AUC$\uparrow$	$68.35_{\pm 0.47}$	$51.40_{\pm 1.52}$	$82.75_{\pm 0.55}$	$51.54_{\pm 0.27}$	$86.07_{\pm 2.18}$	$82.39_{\pm 0.37}$	$50.80_{\pm 3.94}$	$83.71_{\pm 0.69}$	$\mathbf{98.19}_{\pm 3.36}$	$84.46_{\pm 0.48}$	$\underline{92.41}_{\pm 2.06}$
	$\Delta_{DP}\downarrow$	$15.28_{\pm 4.12}$	$2.34_{\pm 0.98}$	$11.98_{\pm 2.15}$	$\underline{2.23}_{\pm 1.00}$	$5.92_{\pm 1.87}$	$\mathbf{1.39}_{\pm 0.68}$	$3.62_{\pm 1.74}$	$4.22_{\pm 0.33}$	$6.73_{\pm 1.17}$	$5.80_{\pm 2.10}$	$5.65_{\pm 0.61}$
	$\Delta_{EO}\downarrow$	$14.18_{\pm 4.72}$	$2.19_{\pm 1.50}$	$10.10_{\pm 1.54}$	$2.02_{\pm 1.22}$	$2.18_{\pm 1.30}$	$4.06_{\pm 1.05}$	$5.13_{\pm 1.57}$	$\mathbf{0.79}_{\pm 0.24}$	$1.30_{\pm 0.89}$	$13.23_{\pm 1.88}$	$\underline{1.77}_{\pm 1.06}$
B4	ACC$\uparrow$	$71.33_{\pm 1.20}$	$54.07_{\pm 4.03}$	$76.28_{\pm 0.66}$	$63.72_{\pm 1.25}$	$76.99_{\pm 1.68}$	$48.94_{\pm 1.32}$	$38.58_{\pm 6.87}$	$79.64_{\pm 0.96}$	$66.82_{\pm 3.07}$	$46.90_{\pm 1.69}$	$\mathbf{90.45}_{\pm 0.87}$
	ROC-AUC$\uparrow$	$75.25_{\pm 2.23}$	$52.27_{\pm 5.54}$	$\underline{76.89}_{\pm 3.72}$	$64.45_{\pm 0.34}$	$58.82_{\pm 5.07}$	$73.75_{\pm 0.40}$	$48.11_{\pm 4.72}$	$74.72_{\pm 0.75}$	$1.06_{\pm 7.52}$	$73.68_{\pm 0.00}$	$\mathbf{89.35}_{\pm 1.73}$
	$\Delta_{DP}\downarrow$	$14.29_{\pm 1.26}$	$9.07_{\pm 7.66}$	$5.18_{\pm 1.77}$	$2.73_{\pm 2.34}$	$2.25_{\pm 1.42}$	$4.27_{\pm 2.27}$	$6.09_{\pm 2.50}$	$\underline{0.91}_{\pm 0.80}$	$\mathbf{0.06}_{\pm 0.44}$	$17.90_{\pm 3.27}$	$6.46_{\pm 1.42}$
	$\Delta_{EO}\downarrow$	$12.73_{\pm 4.93}$	$14.39_{\pm 6.26}$	$19.88_{\pm 4.11}$	$8.55_{\pm 5.17}$	$14.55_{\pm 5.48}$	$\underline{3.03}_{\pm 3.64}$	$12.61_{\pm 5.84}$	$11.33_{\pm 4.24}$	$\mathbf{0.21}_{\pm 1.51}$	$20.00_{\pm 0.00}$	$10.91_{\pm 2.99}$
Avg.(Rank)		8.56	7.06	6.62	5.81	5.56	4.94	8.38	3.94	5.06	6.31	3.69

Table 3. Classification and fairness metrics (%$\pm\sigma$) on Pokecs. $\uparrow$ indicates that higher values are better, while $\downarrow$ indicating the opposite. In each row, the best result is indicated in bold, while the runner-up result is marked with an underline.

	Metrics	MLP	GCN	FairVGNN	FairSIN	NIFTY	CAF	SAGM	RFR	FatraGNN	FairSIN+PODD
Pokec-n	ACC$\uparrow$	$52.74_{\pm 3.67}$	$54.83_{\pm 2.34}$	$60.80_{\pm 0.54}$	$\underline{70.59}_{\pm 1.52}$	$58.68_{\pm 5.54}$	$59.37_{\pm 1.45}$	$58.78_{\pm 2.33}$	$57.42_{\pm 3.68}$	$62.00_{\pm 0.24}$	$\mathbf{71.72}_{\pm 1.61}$
	ROC-AUC$\uparrow$	$65.38_{\pm 0.43}$	$63.48_{\pm 2.34}$	$65.26_{\pm 1.45}$	$\underline{67.89}_{\pm 1.42}$	$67.09_{\pm 2.25}$	$66.86_{\pm 1.32}$	$65.67_{\pm 2.45}$	$65.29_{\pm 1.36}$	$67.82_{\pm 3.23}$	$\mathbf{76.61}_{\pm 2.11}$
	$\Delta_{DP}\downarrow$	$4.86_{\pm 1.23}$	$7.38_{\pm 0.28}$	$5.88_{\pm 2.34}$	$1.97_{\pm 0.33}$	$4.21_{\pm 3.43}$	$5.49_{\pm 2.65}$	$5.67_{\pm 3.22}$	$4.56_{\pm 2.85}$	$\underline{1.34}_{\pm 0.27}$	$\mathbf{0.35}_{\pm 0.10}$
	$\Delta_{EO}\downarrow$	$4.16_{\pm 2.34}$	$6.37_{\pm 0.52}$	$6.26_{\pm 2.21}$	$2.11_{\pm 0.14}$	$3.82_{\pm 3.88}$	$5.02_{\pm 0.73}$	$4.19_{\pm 2.45}$	$3.41_{\pm 2.37}$	$\underline{1.43}_{\pm 2.68}$	$\mathbf{0.69}_{\pm 0.21}$
Avg.(Rank)		7.25	9.75	7.75	2.50	5.00	6.25	6.75	6.25	2.50	1.00

Experimental Setting. In the experiments, we perform hyperparameter tuning across all dataset groups to ensure fair and comprehensive evaluation. For our proposed PODD[1], we set the adversarial regularization weight λ_{adv} to 0.1. The information bottleneck coefficient λ_{IB} in the student model is set to 1.0. Furthermore, for the Meta-Learning phase, the Meta-Learning rate is set to $1e-3$. Each method is evaluated over ten independent runs with different random seeds, with the mean and standard deviation of each metric reported.

[1] https://github.com/Twilightzon/PODD.

5.2 Performance Analysis

First, to answer **RQ1**, we examine whether integrating PODD leads to performance improvements. Table 1 reports the best average performance of PODD applied to existing state-of-the-art (SOTA) fair GNNs on the BailA-Bs and CreditA-Cs datasets. As detailed in Sect. 1, existing fair GNNs tend to sacrifice utility to satisfy fairness constraints, especially when the graph structure is complex. However, with the help of our framework, the student model obtains fairness improvements while maintaining strong utility competitiveness, which provides strong proof of the effectiveness of our framework. Next, to answer **RQ2**, we present the comparative experimental results of PODD-adapted SOTA fair GNN against SOTA baselines in Table 2 and 3. The results demonstrate that PODD applied to SOTA fair GNNs consistently outperforms all baselines, achieving the best average ranking across all metrics. We observe that PODD enables SOTA fair GNNs to achieve superior performance and enhanced fairness simultaneously. This demonstrates that our dual-teacher architecture and Pareto-Optimization mechanism successfully facilitate the student model's acquisition of a representation that is both fair and resistant to distribution shifts, thereby achieving a favorable trade-off between the two objectives.

Table 4. Ablation study results.

BailA-Bs							
Datasets	**Metrics**	FairGB	w/o FT	w/o DST	w/o Pareto	w/o IB	FairGB +PODD
B1	ACC ↑	78.16$_{\pm 0.41}$	83.51$_{\pm 0.84}$	82.42$_{\pm 1.12}$	83.51$_{\pm 0.95}$	82.24$_{\pm 1.03}$	**84.61**$_{\pm 0.55}$
	ROC-AUC ↑	82.92$_{\pm 2.47}$	87.26$_{\pm 1.24}$	85.98$_{\pm 1.56}$	**87.52**$_{\pm 1.10}$	86.23$_{\pm 1.35}$	87.29$_{\pm 0.96}$
	Δ_{DP} ↓	12.00$_{\pm 3.41}$	10.58$_{\pm 2.14}$	10.75$_{\pm 2.31}$	11.86$_{\pm 1.85}$	11.37$_{\pm 2.64}$	**9.90**$_{\pm 1.27}$
	Δ_{EO} ↓	10.06$_{\pm 4.68}$	9.81$_{\pm 2.05}$	12.58$_{\pm 3.12}$	9.68$_{\pm 2.45}$	10.56$_{\pm 2.78}$	**8.71**$_{\pm 1.87}$
B2	ACC ↑	79.09$_{\pm 1.68}$	**85.04**$_{\pm 1.25}$	82.10$_{\pm 1.48}$	84.31$_{\pm 1.15}$	80.90$_{\pm 1.62}$	82.18$_{\pm 1.34}$
	ROC-AUC ↑	83.36$_{\pm 1.04}$	85.53$_{\pm 0.96}$	84.43$_{\pm 1.21}$	**86.87**$_{\pm 0.85}$	85.13$_{\pm 1.05}$	83.20$_{\pm 1.42}$
	Δ_{DP} ↓	7.60$_{\pm 1.60}$	9.36$_{\pm 2.15}$	6.76$_{\pm 1.84}$	9.88$_{\pm 2.36}$	12.54$_{\pm 3.12}$	**5.83**$_{\pm 1.55}$
	Δ_{EO} ↓	2.99$_{\pm 2.18}$	3.25$_{\pm 1.14}$	1.52$_{\pm 0.65}$	3.46$_{\pm 1.28}$	10.37$_{\pm 2.85}$	**0.71**$_{\pm 0.42}$
B3	ACC ↑	79.68$_{\pm 2.21}$	83.03$_{\pm 1.35}$	75.97$_{\pm 1.84}$	76.68$_{\pm 1.62}$	73.85$_{\pm 1.95}$	**83.04**$_{\pm 1.47}$
	ROC-AUC ↑	85.09$_{\pm 1.26}$	84.75$_{\pm 1.05}$	**86.13**$_{\pm 0.92}$	84.10$_{\pm 1.24}$	79.63$_{\pm 1.58}$	85.46$_{\pm 1.15}$
	Δ_{DP} ↓	9.20$_{\pm 2.67}$	11.98$_{\pm 2.45}$	13.51$_{\pm 2.84}$	10.94$_{\pm 2.15}$	12.81$_{\pm 2.65}$	**2.19**$_{\pm 1.11}$
	Δ_{EO} ↓	18.43$_{\pm 4.61}$	21.86$_{\pm 3.85}$	19.85$_{\pm 3.42}$	14.67$_{\pm 2.95}$	14.97$_{\pm 2.88}$	**10.71**$_{\pm 3.66}$
B4	ACC ↑	52.07$_{\pm 14.26}$	72.41$_{\pm 4.15}$	**79.31**$_{\pm 3.82}$	**79.31**$_{\pm 3.55}$	65.51$_{\pm 5.12}$	65.52$_{\pm 3.18}$
	ROC-AUC ↑	72.32$_{\pm 12.30}$	**79.99**$_{\pm 3.25}$	77.36$_{\pm 4.12}$	77.89$_{\pm 3.85}$	63.68$_{\pm 5.65}$	73.16$_{\pm 4.25}$
	Δ_{DP} ↓	4.14$_{\pm 4.84}$	29.05$_{\pm 6.45}$	14.76$_{\pm 4.85}$	15.24$_{\pm 5.12}$	0.95$_{\pm 0.55}$	**0.00**$_{\pm 0.00}$
	Δ_{EO} ↓	10.00$_{\pm 10.00}$	39.99$_{\pm 8.25}$	39.99$_{\pm 7.86}$	19.99$_{\pm 5.45}$	40.00$_{\pm 8.12}$	**0.00**$_{\pm 0.00}$

CreditA-Cs							
Datasets	**Metrics**	FairGB	w/o FT	w/o DST	w/o Pareto	w/o IB	FairGB +PODD
C1	ACC ↑	78.49$_{\pm 0.70}$	78.41$_{\pm 0.54}$	78.65$_{\pm 0.87}$	**79.13**$_{\pm 0.62}$	78.17$_{\pm 0.91}$	78.66$_{\pm 0.25}$
	ROC-AUC ↑	65.68$_{\pm 0.87}$	66.38$_{\pm 0.76}$	66.93$_{\pm 1.04}$	67.04$_{\pm 0.88}$	66.06$_{\pm 1.12}$	**67.09**$_{\pm 0.95}$
	Δ_{DP} ↓	4.56$_{\pm 1.64}$	1.65$_{\pm 0.45}$	1.91$_{\pm 0.58}$	0.86$_{\pm 0.32}$	2.43$_{\pm 0.74}$	**0.53**$_{\pm 0.21}$
	Δ_{EO} ↓	5.29$_{\pm 3.16}$	2.66$_{\pm 1.15}$	2.99$_{\pm 1.28}$	2.66$_{\pm 1.05}$	2.99$_{\pm 1.41}$	**0.34**$_{\pm 0.28}$
C2	ACC ↑	78.64$_{\pm 0.76}$	78.27$_{\pm 0.82}$	79.10$_{\pm 0.65}$	77.99$_{\pm 0.94}$	79.10$_{\pm 0.71}$	**79.67**$_{\pm 0.91}$
	ROC-AUC ↑	**64.68**$_{\pm 1.54}$	62.39$_{\pm 1.15}$	62.53$_{\pm 1.08}$	62.79$_{\pm 0.92}$	61.95$_{\pm 1.35}$	62.01$_{\pm 1.24}$
	Δ_{DP} ↓	0.61$_{\pm 0.67}$	2.36$_{\pm 0.85}$	3.27$_{\pm 1.12}$	2.06$_{\pm 0.78}$	6.54$_{\pm 1.65}$	**0.00**$_{\pm 0.00}$
	Δ_{EO} ↓	1.05$_{\pm 0.87}$	2.83$_{\pm 1.04}$	3.97$_{\pm 1.45}$	2.45$_{\pm 0.92}$	3.59$_{\pm 1.18}$	**0.00**$_{\pm 0.00}$
C3	ACC ↑	74.37$_{\pm 0.51}$	71.17$_{\pm 1.15}$	74.32$_{\pm 0.85}$	73.87$_{\pm 0.92}$	73.87$_{\pm 0.96}$	**74.77**$_{\pm 4.33}$
	ROC-AUC ↑	65.01$_{\pm 0.73}$	63.23$_{\pm 1.04}$	**65.30**$_{\pm 0.88}$	63.54$_{\pm 1.12}$	61.93$_{\pm 1.35}$	63.91$_{\pm 0.95}$
	Δ_{DP} ↓	1.91$_{\pm 1.78}$	4.32$_{\pm 1.25}$	1.55$_{\pm 0.65}$	2.93$_{\pm 0.95}$	2.07$_{\pm 0.82}$	**1.04**$_{\pm 1.01}$
	Δ_{EO} ↓	3.02$_{\pm 3.39}$	2.22$_{\pm 0.88}$	1.36$_{\pm 0.54}$	4.58$_{\pm 1.35}$	2.04$_{\pm 0.75}$	**0.68**$_{\pm 0.13}$
C4	ACC ↑	78.46$_{\pm 0.41}$	78.28$_{\pm 0.85}$	78.28$_{\pm 0.82}$	**78.73**$_{\pm 0.65}$	**78.73**$_{\pm 0.72}$	78.28$_{\pm 1.47}$
	ROC-AUC ↑	61.81$_{\pm 1.38}$	61.18$_{\pm 1.15}$	62.96$_{\pm 0.95}$	**63.01**$_{\pm 0.88}$	62.24$_{\pm 1.05}$	61.68$_{\pm 1.12}$
	Δ_{DP} ↓	1.61$_{\pm 1.87}$	1.63$_{\pm 0.55}$	1.63$_{\pm 0.52}$	2.14$_{\pm 0.75}$	5.80$_{\pm 1.45}$	**0.00**$_{\pm 0.00}$
	Δ_{EO} ↓	0.75$_{\pm 1.28}$	1.94$_{\pm 0.65}$	1.94$_{\pm 0.62}$	1.29$_{\pm 0.45}$	1.94$_{\pm 0.68}$	**0.00**$_{\pm 0.00}$

5.3 Ablation Study

To answer **RQ3**, we investigate how each of the following four components individually contributes to performance, i.e., the Fairness Teacher, the Distribution Shift Teacher, Pareto-Optimization based on Meta-Learning module, and the Information Bottleneck module. We remove these four components separately and their results denoted by w/o FT, w/o DST, w/o Pareto, and w/o IB, respectively. We show ablation results of PODD in Table 4 and Fig. 3. We observe that PODD is the most balanced between performance and fairness, and removing either component may cause the collapse of the metric. This proves that the

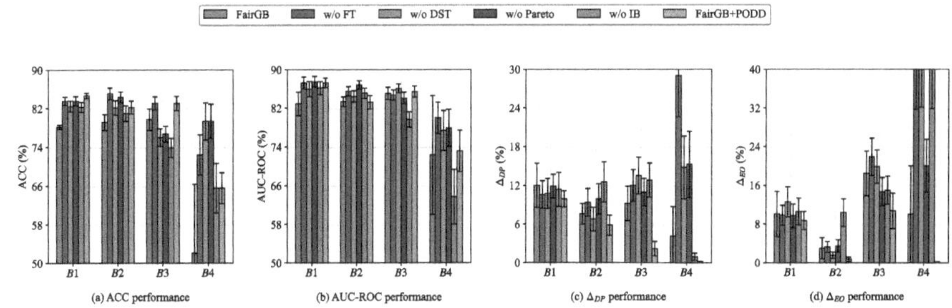

Fig. 3. The results of ablation study on B1-B4.

various components of PODD are necessary: adversarial refinement debiasing can effectively solve the problem of model dependence on sensitive information; the introduction of random perturbation effectively mitigates distribution shifts; Pareto-Optimization based on Meta-Learning enables the student model to learn representations that are both fair and well resistant to distribution shifts; the Information Bottleneck module effectively reduces the influence of noise and encourage the student to retain only essential signals from both teachers, guaranteeing the trade-off between utility and fairness on the whole.

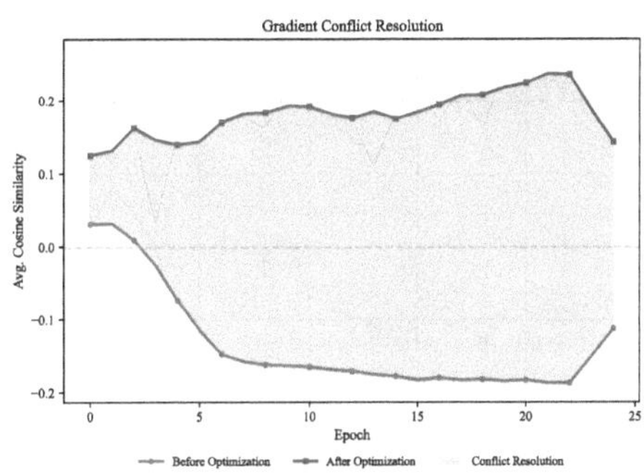

Fig. 4. Gradient Cosine Comparison

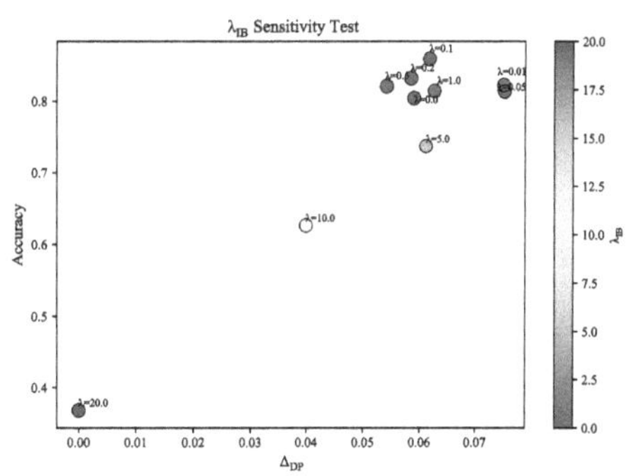

Fig. 5. λ_{IB} Sensitivity Analysis

5.4 Visualization

To answer **RQ3** more specifically, we do visualization experiments for the Pareto optimization module in PODD and sensitivity analysis for the information bottleneck module.

Figure 4 shows Pareto optimization effectively resolving gradient conflicts. As training progresses, cosine similarity before optimization decreases, indicating intensifying conflicts between fairness and distribution-shift objectives. Post-optimization similarity stays positive and stable, confirming conflict elimination.

The widening green region reflects the growing magnitude of resolution, proving the module's crucial role in later training stages.

Figure 5 illustrates the utility-fairness trade-off across different information bottleneck strengths. An appropriate λ_{IB} maintains high accuracy with moderate fairness disparity, effectively compressing sensitive information without degrading task performance and ensuring the overall balance. However, excessively large values cause a sharp accuracy drop because of over-compresses of task-relevant features.

6 Conclusion

In this paper, we proposed PODD[2], a novel plug-and-play framework for fair graph learning under distribution shifts. By integrating a Dual-Teacher architecture, Meta-Learning-based Pareto-Optimization, and an Information Bottleneck, PODD effectively balances conflicting fairness and distribution shift objectives. Extensive experiments demonstrate that integrating PODD into existing state-of-the-art fair GNNs significantly enhances both their fairness and predictive utility, consistently outperforming current baselines.

Acknowledgments. This work was supported by the National Natural Science Foundation of China (Grant Nos. U22A2099, 62336003 and 62566016), the China Postdoctoral Science Foundation (Grant No. 2026M791620), the Guangxi Natural Science Foundation (Grant No. 2026GXNSFBA00640261), and the Innovation Project of GUET Graduate Education (Grant Nos. 2026YCXS069 and 2026YCXS058).

References

1. Agarwal, C., Lakkaraju, H., Zitnik, M.: Towards a unified framework for fair and stable graph representation learning. In: Uncertainty in Artificial Intelligence, pp. 2114–2124. PMLR (2021)
2. Bao, W., Zeng, Z., Liu, Z., Tong, H., He, J.: Matcha: Mitigating graph structure shifts with test-time adaptation. In: ICLR (2025)
3. Chen, Q., et al.: Stable fair graph representation learning with lipschitz constraint. In: ICML (2025)
4. Dai, E., Wang, S.: Learning fair graph neural networks with limited and private sensitive attribute information. IEEE Trans. Knowl. Data Eng. **35**(7), 7103–7117 (2022)
5. Damke, C., Hüllermeier, E.: Distribution matching for graph quantification under structural covariate shift. In: Ribeiro, R.P., et al. (eds.) ECML-PKDD, pp. 403–419. Springer, Cham (2025). https://doi.org/10.1007/978-3-032-05981-9_24
6. Dimitriadis, N., Frossard, P., Fleuret, F.: Pareto manifold learning: Tackling multiple tasks via ensembles of single-task models. In: ICML, pp. 8015–8052. PMLR (2023)

[2] Large Language Models have been used while writing this paper to polish writing (e.g., grammar, spelling, word choice).

7. Dong, Y., Liu, N., Jalaian, B., Li, J.: Edits: Modeling and mitigating data bias for graph neural networks, In: WWW, pp. 1259–1269 (2022)
8. Fan, S., Wang, X., Shi, C., Cui, P., Wang, B.: Generalizing graph neural networks on out-of-distribution graphs. IEEE Trans. Pattern Anal. Mach. Intell. **46**(1), 322–337 (2023)
9. Fang, R., et al.: On the benefits of attribute-driven graph domain adaptation. In: ICLR (2025)
10. Fang, R., et al.: Homophily enhanced graph domain adaptation. In: ICML (2025)
11. Galron, Y., Frasca, F., Maron, H., Treister, E., Eliasof, M.: Understanding and improving laplacian positional encodings for temporal gnns. In: Ribeiro, R.P., et al. (eds.) ECML-PKDD, pp. 420–437. Springer, Cham (2025). https://doi.org/10.1007/978-3-032-05981-9_25
12. Gong, C., Li, X., Yu, J., Cheng, Y., Tan, J., Yu, C.: Self-pro: A self-prompt and tuning framework for graph neural networks. In: Bifet, A., Davis, J., Krilavičius, T., Kull, M., Ntoutsi, E., Žliobaitė, I. (eds) ECML-PKDD, pp. 197–215. Springer, Cham (2024). https://doi.org/10.1007/978-3-031-70344-7_12
13. Guo, C., Wang, X., Zhu, C., Liang, J., Yang, H., Chang, L.: Mitigating popularity bias for two-sided fairness via dual-teacher distillation in recommendation. In: Jung, H., Wang, T., Toyoda, M., Kwon, H.Y., Lee, J. (eds.) DASFAA, pp. 154–170. Springer, Cham (2026). https://doi.org/10.1007/978-981-92-0363-5_10
14. Guo, Z., Li, J., Xiao, T., Ma, Y., Wang, S.: Towards fair graph neural networks via graph counterfactual. In: CIKM, pp. 669–678 (2023)
15. Huang, Y., et al.: Flow matching for denoised social recommendation. In: ICML (2025)
16. Jiang, Z.S., et al.: Chasing fairness under distribution shift: A model weight perturbation approach. NeurIPS **36**, 63931–63944 (2023)
17. Jordan, K.L., Freiburger, T.L.: The effect of race/ethnicity on sentencing: Examining sentence type, jail length, and prison length. J. Ethnicity Crimi. Justice **13**(3), 179–196 (2015)
18. Kipf, T.N., Welling, M.: Semi-supervised classification with graph convolutional networks. In: ICLR (2017)
19. Kleinberg, J.M., Mullainathan, S., Raghavan, M.: Inherent trade-offs in the fair determination of risk scores. In: ITCS, pp. 43:1–43:23 (2017)
20. Lee, Y.C., Shin, H., Kim, S.W.: Disentangling, amplifying, and debiasing: Learning disentangled representations for fair graph neural networks. In: AAAI, Vol. 39, pp. 12013–12021 (2025)
21. Li, T.W., Qiu, R., Tong, H.: Graph data selection for domain adaptation: A model-free approach. In: NeurIPS (2025)
22. Li, Y., Wang, X., Xing, Y., Fan, S., Wang, R., Liu, Y., Shi, C.: Graph fairness learning under distribution shifts. In: WWW, pp. 676–684 (2024)
23. Li, Z., Dong, Y., Liu, Q., Yu, J.X.: Rethinking fair graph neural networks from re-balancing. In: KDD, pp. 1736–1745 (2024)
24. Luo, R., Huang, H., Yu, S., Han, Z., He, E., Zhang, X., Xia, F.: Fugnn: Harmonizing fairness and utility in graph neural networks. In: KDD, pp. 2072–2081 (2024)
25. Newman, M.E.: Modularity and community structure in networks. Proc. Natl. Acad. Sci. **103**(23), 8577–8582 (2006)
26. Pal, S.K., Mitra, S.: Multilayer perceptron, fuzzy sets, and classification. IEEE Trans. Neural Netw. **3**(5), 683–697 (1992)
27. Park, S., Lim, S.: Fnrgnn: Distribution-aware fairness in graph neural network. In: CIKM, pp. 5110–5114 (2025)

28. Qian, X., et al.: Addressing shortcomings in fair graph learning datasets: Towards a new benchmark. In: KDD, pp. 5602–5612 (2024)
29. Qin, T., Chen, K.J., Liu, Z.: Localized heat kernel for graph neural networks. In: Ribeiro, R.P., et al. (eds.) ECML-PKDD, pp. 457–473. Springer, Cham (2025). https://doi.org/10.1007/978-3-032-05981-9_27
30. Takahashi, T., Nakayama, I., Mitani, T., Kikuchi, R., Sasaki, Y., Onizuka, M.: Graph neural network leveraging higher-order class label connectivity for heterophilous graphs. In: Ribeiro, R.P., et al. (eds.) ECML-PKDD, pp. 474–491. Springer, Cham (2025). https://doi.org/10.1007/978-3-032-05981-9_28
31. Wang, P., Zhang, Z., Lei, Z., Zhang, L.: Sharpness-aware gradient matching for domain generalization. In: CVPR, pp. 3769–3778 (2023)
32. Wang, X., Gu, T., Bao, X., Chang, L.: Fair and privacy-preserving graph neural network. In: Wang, X., et al. (eds.) DASFAA, pp. 731–735. Springer, Cham (2023). https://doi.org/10.1007/978-3-031-30678-5_64
33. Wang, X., Gu, T., Bao, X., Chang, L.: Towards fair graph neural networks via graph counterfactual without sensitive attributes. In: ICDE, pp. 265–277. IEEE (2025)
34. Wang, X., Gu, T., Bao, X., Chang, L., Li, L.: Individual fairness for local private graph neural network. Knowl.-Based Syst. **268**, 110490 (2023)
35. Wang, X., et al.: Grif-ppgnn: Group equality informed ranking-based individual fairness for privacy-preserving graph neural network. Neurocomputing **647**, 130583 (2025)
36. Wang, X., et al.: Towards unified frameworks for fair and privacy-preserving graph neural networks. Neural Netw. 108448 (2025)
37. Wang, X., Wang, L., Gu, T., Bao, X.: Counterfactual fairness for graph neural networks with limited and privacy protected sensitive attributes. In: ACML (2024)
38. Wang, Y., et al.: Dance: Dual unbiased expansion with group-acquired alignment for out-of-distribution graph fairness learning. In: ICML (2025)
39. Wang, Y., Zhao, Y., Dong, Y., Chen, H., Li, J., Derr, T.: Improving fairness in graph neural networks via mitigating sensitive attribute leakage. In: KDD, pp. 1938–1948 (2022)
40. Wang, Z., Liu, F., Pan, S., Liu, J., Saeed, F., Qiu, M., Zhang, W.: fairgnn-wod: Fair graph learning without complete demographics. In: IJCAI, International Joint Conferences on Artificial Intelligence Organization, pp. 556–564 (2025)
41. Wang, Z., et al.: Fairness-aware graph representation learning with limited demographic information. In: Ribeiro, R.P., et al. (eds.) ECML-PKDD, pp. 354–371. Springer, Cham (2025). https://doi.org/10.1007/978-3-032-05962-8_21
42. Wu, Q., Zhang, H., Yan, J., Wipf, D.: Handling distribution shifts on graphs: An invariance perspective. In: ICLR (2022)
43. Xu, K., Hu, W., Leskovec, J., Jegelka, S.: How powerful are graph neural networks? In: ICLR (2019)
44. Yang, C., Liu, J., Yan, Y., Shi, C.: Fairsin: Achieving fairness in graph neural networks through sensitive information neutralization. In: AAAI, Vol. 38, pp. 9241–9249 (2024)
45. Yao, T., Chen, Y., Hu, K., Liu, T., Zhang, K., Shen, Z.: Learning graph invariance by harnessing spuriosity. In: ICLR (2025)
46. Yeh, I.C., Lien, C.H.: The comparisons of data mining techniques for the predictive accuracy of probability of default of credit card clients. Expert Syst. Appl. **36**(2), 2473–2480 (2009)
47. Yuan, Q., et al.: Dynamic graph learning with static relations for credit risk assessment. In: AAAI **39**, 13133–13141 (2025)

48. Zeng, Z., et al.: Pave your own path: Graph gradual domain adaptation on fused gromov-wasserstein geodesics (2025). Submitted to Transactions on Machine Learning Research
49. Zeng, Z., Islam, R., Keya, K.N., Foulds, J., Song, Y., Pan, S.: Fair representation learning for heterogeneous information networks. In: ICWSM, Vol. 15, pp. 877–887 (2021)
50. Zhao, Y., Zhao, K., Tang, Z., Lu, X., Zhang, Y., Du, Y.: Graphjcl: A dual-perspective graph-based framework for urban region representation via joint contrastive learning. In: Ribeiro, R.P., et al. (eds.) ECML-PKDD, pp. 37–53. Springer, Cham (2025). https://doi.org/10.1007/978-3-032-06066-2_3
51. Zheng, Y., Yi, L., Wei, Z.: A survey of dynamic graph neural networks. Front. Comp. Sci. **19**(6), 196323 (2025)

The Illusion of Improvement: Reject Inference Strategies in Credit Scoring

Bruno Scarone[1(✉)] and Ricardo Baeza-Yates[2]

[1] Northeastern University, Boston, MA, USA
scarone.b@northeastern.edu
[2] KTH Royal Institute of Technology, Stockholm, Sweden
rbaeza@acm.org

Abstract. Reject inference methods are widely used to mitigate survival bias in credit scoring, yet their effectiveness remains poorly understood. We systematically evaluate several such methods and uncover a structural failure mode: in a natural retraining cycle, models whose accuracy improves while recall collapses create an illusion of improvement that leads practitioners to believe the system is getting better when, in fact, its rejection quality—the ability to correctly screen out defaulters—is deteriorating. We then propose a controlled exploration strategy that breaks the feedback loop without statistical assumptions: the lender deliberately approves a fraction of rejected applicants and observes their true outcomes. We show that accuracy and rejection quality give opposite recommendations on whether to explore: accuracy favors no exploration, while rejection quality improves with it, confirming that standard evaluation metrics are misleading under selection bias. Even minimal exploration rates (2–5%) prove sufficient in our experiments to diagnose the severity of the feedback loop at near-zero cost. Our findings are consistent across two machine learning methods and three real-world datasets, and suggest that standard evaluation protocols are inadequate for assessing models trained under survival bias.

1 Introduction

Nowadays many important decisions that affect people's lives are being taken with the support of predictive machine learning (ML) models with little or even no human intervention. Typical use cases include lending, hiring, scholarships, government subsidies, and even criminal justice, among others. In this context, these tools may discriminate against or favor certain individuals, producing significant but poorly understood social impacts. For this reason, under the new EU regulation for the use of AI [27], most of these tools are classified as high-risk.

In addition, these predictive tools are based on several assumptions that weaken their scientific validity. First, there is the belief that the available data

Supplementary Information The online version contains supplementary material available at https://doi.org/10.1007/978-3-032-37654-1_27.

M. Ceci et al. (Eds.): ECML PKDD 2026, LNAI 16941, pp. 462–479, 2027.
https://doi.org/10.1007/978-3-032-37654-1_27

reasonably represent the problem being solved (dataism [5]), an assumption that in many cases is debatable and varies by instance. This creates what is known as a *reality gap* [13]. Second, in some of the use cases, a new individual's behavior is assumed to be predictable from data of "similar" people. This may hold on average, but certainly does not work for all individuals, especially considering that the similarity metric is another proxy for reality. Third, we typically evaluate system success through aggregate metrics (*e.g.,* accuracy). This implies that all errors carry the same impact, which is false in most cases.

Given these problems, consider the following hypothetical scenario. Imagine that a bank has built an ML model based on historical data to predict whether a new client will repay a loan. That is, we assume that data from other people can be used to predict the behavior of a new client. This hypothesis is a simplifying assumption that may hold on average, but certainly does not hold for all individuals. If the prediction is positive, the applicant obtains a loan; otherwise, the application is rejected. After a certain period, as the bank accumulates more data, the model can be retrained, with the expectation of improving it. However, the new data suffer from survival or survivorship bias with respect to the model's errors. Specifically, we observe the outcomes of all false positives (favored individuals who represent the survival bias) but learn nothing about the false negatives (rejected or harmed individuals). This process, in addition to neglecting the bias issue described above, allows us to estimate the size of the reality gap.

In this work, using real data, we simulate this bank lending scenario and measure the information lost over time due to survival bias (false negatives), its impact on model performance, and the effectiveness of survival bias mitigation techniques, known as reject inference methods. To this end, we compare the model over time against an Oracle that has access to all available data and hence makes fewer mistakes. We also propose a controlled exploration technique that allows the bank to estimate the impact of survival bias at almost no cost.

The contributions of our work are summarized as follows: **(1)** We uncover a structural failure mode in iterative lending: models whose accuracy improves while recall collapses create an illusion of improvement, and we show this is not incidental: standard metrics systematically reward strategies that amplify survival bias, as demonstrated by Simple Extrapolation consistently outperforming the Oracle. **(2)** We propose controlled exploration as an assumption-free alternative to reject inference, where the lender deliberately approves a fraction of rejects and observes true outcomes. **(3)** We show that even minimal exploration (2–5%) diagnoses feedback loop severity at near-zero cost, and that accuracy and rejection quality give opposite recommendations, confirming that standard evaluation is misleading under survival bias.

The rest of the paper is organized as follows. We cover related work in Sect. 2 and explain our methodology and datasets used in Sect. 3. Then we present the reject inference results in Sect. 4 and the exploration strategy in Sect. 5, ending with the conclusions in Sect. 6. The appendices are available in the arXiv version [24].

2 Related Work

Loan Default Prediction. Credit scoring and default risk estimation are central to financial lending [11], with ML-based approaches gaining popularity [26]. The nature and quality of available data have been questioned [14], and datasets are oftentimes imbalanced, with evidence that models perform better on balanced versions [1,18]. Tree-based models are a popular choice for their interpretability [1,18,26], though no consensus exists on the most effective method [18]. We evaluate a range of models on three datasets and select the two best-performing (both tree-based). Two datasets are balanced via under-sampling.

Survival Bias in Loan Default Prediction. An extensive list of works has highlighted the diverse types of bias that can affect the ML pipeline [12,19]. We consider survival bias, a form of selection bias in which one focuses on a subset of a population that passes ("survives") a given selection criterion. Survival bias is well-documented in mutual fund data [7,23,29] and it has been assessed in self-reported financial datasets [28], but in those cases it arises from data collection rather than model-driven selection. More broadly, the feedback loop we study is an empirical instance of performative prediction [22], where model deployment shifts the data distribution; analogous runaway (self-reinforcing) effects have been documented in predictive policing [8]. When a credit scoring model is used to accept or reject applicants, outcomes are observed only for accepted applicants. Rejected applicants never receive credit, so whether they would have defaulted or not remains a counterfactual that cannot be verified. *Reject inference* (RI) refers to the family of techniques that attempt to recover this missing information, thereby reducing the survival bias in the training data used for subsequent model retraining [4,6,9]. The RI literature encompasses methods that impute labels for rejected applicants via probabilistic assignment, direct model extrapolation, nearest-neighbor transfer, or bin-averaged imputation [3,4,6], as well as self-learning approaches that iteratively refine imputed labels [15], deep generative models [17], and Monte Carlo simulation frameworks [2]; Ehrhardt et al. [6] provide a comprehensive survey.

3 Methodology

We consider a bank that uses a binary classifier to predict loan defaults and decide which applicants to approve. The bank operates in a *dynamic* setting: at each lending cycle t, a new batch of applicants arrives, the current model M_t produces predictions, and the bank observes outcomes only for approved loans. We adopt the usual label convention $y = 1$ for default and $y = 0$ for non-default. Our goal is to evaluate how this selective observation process affects model quality over successive retraining cycles.[1]

Hence, we compare five RI strategies, evaluated against two baselines: *Biased*, which trains only on accepted applicants, and *Oracle*, which has access to true

[1] The source code is available at https://github.com/bscarone/survival-bias-credit-scoring.

labels for all applicants (both defined formally in Sect. 4.1). RI refers to techniques [4,6,9] that mitigate survival bias by imputing the missing labels of rejected applicants and include them in the training set alongside accepted applicants, who retain their true labels.

Reject Inference Strategies. *Parceling* [4,25] bins applicants by predicted risk score into $K = 10$ equal-frequency parcels and assigns default labels to rejects within each parcel at the observed bad rate among accepts in that parcel. *Fuzzy Augmentation* [3,6] assigns each reject a label sampled from $\tilde{y}_i \sim \text{Bernoulli}(\hat{p}_i)$, where $\hat{p}_i$ is the model's predicted default probability; we use this probabilistic variant, equivalent in expectation to the original weighted formulation, for compatibility with tree-based classifiers. *Simple Extrapolation* [4,6] applies the current model to rejected applicants and treats its hard predictions as ground-truth labels. *Twins* [4,6] transfers labels from accepted to rejected applicants via k-nearest-neighbor matching ($k = 5$) in standardized feature space. *Shallow Self-Learning* [15] first filters rejects via Isolation Forest to remove distributional outliers, then iteratively labels only high-confidence rejects using a weak learner with imbalance-corrected class weights.

Data. We use three public credit scoring datasets [11,18]: Default [30] (30,000 persons, 23 features, 77.9% non-default), PPDai [10] (31,389 persons, 29 features, 77.0%), and LendingClub [20] (302,595 persons, 97 features, 77.0%). The binary label indicates whether the borrower defaulted. Both PPDai and LendingClub were down-sampled to achieve these imbalance ratios. For LendingClub, we filtered to loans originated in 2017, removed post-hoc data leakage columns (*e.g.*, payment outcomes, recovery fields), and removed high-null columns. Full preprocessing details are provided in Appendix A.

Models. We evaluated five binary classifiers across all datasets (Appendix B), selecting two tree-based models that consistently ranked among the top performers: Gradient Boosted Decision Trees (GBDT) and Random Forest (RF). These models are inherently non-linear and are implemented in scikit-learn [21] with the default decision threshold $\tau = 0.5$. Both are tree-based ensemble methods; we discuss the potential influence of model choice on our findings in Sect. 6.

Temporal Lending Simulation. We simulate iterative model-based lending as follows. An initial training set $\mathcal{D}_0$ of size n_0 is drawn uniformly from the complete dataset $\mathcal{D}$, modeling a bank's initial data collection step. The value of n_0 is determined per dataset–model pair via learning curve analysis: we train models at increasing sample sizes and select the point at which accuracy stabilizes (Appendix C). This yields $n_0 = 5{,}000$ for Default and PPDai, and $n_0 = 60{,}000$ for LendingClub. At each subsequent lending cycle $t \in \{1, \ldots, T\}$, we take a uniform random sample of size $n' = \lfloor (n - n_0)/T \rfloor$ from the remaining data, treating it as the pool of new applicants. The current model M_t produces predictions: applicants with $\hat{y} = 0$ are accepted and those with $\hat{y} = 1$ are rejected. Each reject inference strategy (Sect. 3) defines a different rule for incorporating or excluding rejected applicants from the training set for M_{t+1}.

Evaluation metrics. Standard metrics are computed at each cycle on a held-out split of the accumulated training set $\mathcal{D}_t$, on which M_t issues predictions of both classes. Beyond standard classification metrics (accuracy, precision, recall), we track two quantities designed to capture the dynamics specific to iterative model-based lending. The *training set default rate* (TDR) measures the proportion of defaulters in the training set at each iteration: $\text{TDR}_t = |\{i \in \mathcal{D}_t : y_i = 1\}|/|\mathcal{D}_t|$. In the absence of survival bias, this rate should remain close to the population default rate. Deviations signal that the training distribution is diverging from the true applicant population.

Standard metrics capture how well the model classifies observed applicants, but do not measure *rejection quality*—that is, whether the model's rejections are correctly targeting true defaulters rather than creditworthy applicants. Inspired by [15], we define the *Kickout* metric to assess rejection quality.[2] Given predictions on the full applicant pool, let n_{BR} denote the number of true defaulters rejected and n_{GR} the number of true non-defaulters rejected:

$$\text{KO} = \frac{n_{\text{BR}} - n_{\text{GR}}}{n_{\text{BR}} + n_{\text{GR}}} = \frac{TP - FP}{TP + FP} = \frac{P(\hat{y} = 1 \wedge y = 1) - P(\hat{y} = 1 \wedge y = 0)}{P(\hat{y} = 1)}. \quad (1)$$

This metric ranges over $[-1, 1]$: KO $= 1$ indicates that every rejected applicant is a true defaulter, 0 indicates equal counts of rejected defaulters and non-defaulters, and -1 indicates that every rejection is a non-defaulter. In the temporal setting, an increasing KO indicates that rejections are becoming more targeted toward true defaulters, while a decreasing KO indicates growing misalignment with actual risk.

4 Reject Inference Under Iterative Survival Bias

We evaluate the five reject inference strategies presented in Sect. 3 against two baselines (Biased and Oracle) that we introduce below. All seven strategies begin from the same initial training set; they differ in whether and how they incorporate rejected applicants at each lending cycle. We report results over $T = 10$ iterations, averaged across five independent runs. We present Default/GBDT as the primary configuration in the main text; full results for all other configurations, including the effect of dataset size, are reported in Appendix E and are consistent with the patterns described here.

4.1 Baselines: Biased and Oracle

Before evaluating reject inference strategies, we establish two baselines that represent the extremes of information availability.

The **Biased** (filtered) baseline trains exclusively on accepted applicants, discarding all rejected samples. At each cycle $t > 0$, the training set consists of

[2] Our definition differs from that of [15], who define Kickout as a two-model comparison. Our metric evaluates a single model's rejection precision on the full applicant pool. We retain the name for its intuitive appeal.

the previous data augmented only with the newly accepted applicants and their observed outcomes: $\mathcal{D}_t = \mathcal{D}_{t-1} \cup \{(\mathbf{x}_i, y_i) : \mathbf{x}_i \in \mathcal{S}_t,\ \hat{y}_i = 0\}$, where $\mathcal{S}_t$ denotes the full sample of new applicants at cycle t. This is the default approach when no RI is applied and represents the full extent of survival bias accumulation. The **Oracle** baseline has access to the true outcome y_i for all applicants, both accepted and rejected: $\mathcal{D}_t = \mathcal{D}_{t-1} \cup \{(\mathbf{x}_i, y_i) : \mathbf{x}_i \in \mathcal{S}_t\}$. This is infeasible in practice, one cannot observe the default behavior of applicants who were never granted credit, but it provides a theoretical upper bound against which all other strategies can be measured. Their contrasting behavior under iterative retraining (Fig. 1) establishes the degradation pattern that reject inference strategies aim to correct, and provides a first indication that standard metrics do not reliably distinguish good models from biased ones.

Biased Baseline. The training set default rate decreases monotonically under the Biased strategy, falling from the population rate of 22.0% to approximately 17% on Default/GBDT by $t = 10$ (Fig. 3, left), a deflation of roughly 5%. This deflation reflects the fundamental mechanism of survival bias: as the model rejects applicants it considers risky, it removes precisely the observations that are most informative about default behavior from its own training data. The consequences for predictive performance are asymmetric (Fig. 1). Accuracy remains stable and even increases slightly, rising from approximately 0.820 to 0.835 on Default/GBDT. However, this apparent stability masks a collapse in recall, from approximately 0.37 to 0.13, as the model progressively loses its ability to detect the defaulters it has excluded from training. The model becomes increasingly confident in predicting non-default for the homogeneous population it observes, while the representation of the default class in its training data shrinks with each iteration. Kickout declines steadily from approximately 0.27 toward 0.19, indicating that the model's rejection decisions become progressively less aligned with actual default risk (Fig. 3, right). This pattern is consistent across all three datasets and both modeling techniques, though the magnitude varies with dataset scale (Appendix E.4).

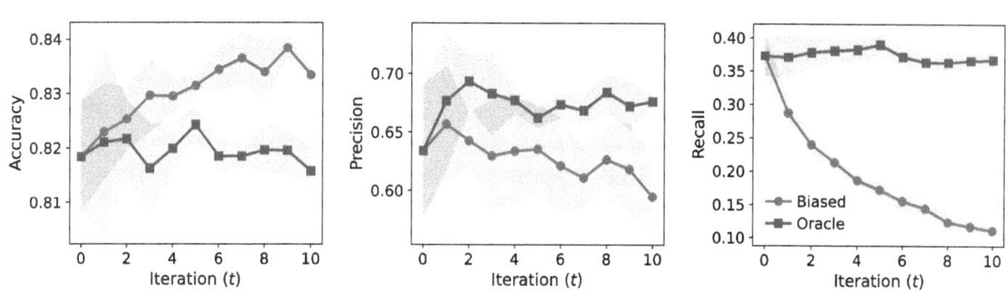

Fig. 1. Accuracy, precision, and recall over 10 lending iterations for the Biased and Oracle strategies on the Default dataset (GBDT, $n_0 = 5{,}000$, $\tau = 0.5$). Shaded regions indicate ± 1 standard deviation across 5 runs. Accuracy remains stable under the Biased strategy while recall collapses from 0.37 to 0.13: the model progressively loses its ability to detect the defaulters it has excluded from training.

Oracle Baseline. With access to the true default labels for all applicants, Oracle maintains a training set default rate of approximately 22.1%, essentially identical to the population rate of 22.0%. Recall remains near its initial level across all iterations, confirming that access to rejected applicants' true outcomes prevents the information loss that drives the Biased strategy's degradation.

Yet Oracle achieves *lower accuracy* than the Biased baseline: approximately 0.816 versus 0.835 on Default/GBDT at $t = 10$ (Fig. 1). This is the first sign that standard evaluation metrics may reward survival bias rather than penalize it. By including genuine label diversity, *i.e.*, borderline cases and applicants who default despite having features similar to non-defaulters, Oracle makes learning harder and produces a less decisive classifier. The Biased model, by contrast, trains on an increasingly homogeneous population and achieves high accuracy precisely because it has narrowed the problem it needs to solve. This inversion, where *more information yields lower measured performance*, will recur more dramatically when we compare reject inference strategies below.

4.2 Theoretical Analysis of the Accuracy–Recall Paradox

We formalize the structural failure mode identified empirically in Sect. 4.1 under the following assumptions; **(A1)** At cycle t the fixed-threshold binary classifier M_t produces $\hat{y} = M_t(\mathbf{x}) \in \{0,1\}$, where $y = 1$ denotes default.[3] **(A2)** At each cycle the new applicants are drawn uniformly, without replacement, and independently of M_t's past decisions from a fixed dataset $\mathcal{D}$ with base default rate $\pi = P_{\mathcal{D}}(y = 1) \in (0, 1/2]$, so survival bias enters only through the training set, not the arrivals. **(A3)** True labels are observed only for accepted applicants ($\hat{y} = 0$). **(A4)** Screening is non-degenerate: at every cycle M_t predicts $\hat{y} = 1$ (defaulter) for a nonempty proper subset of the arrivals, i.e. the rejection rate satisfies $\alpha_t := P_{\mathcal{D}}(\hat{y} = 1) \in (0, 1)$. **(A5)** Screening is informative: on the t arrival cycles, the rejection precision exceeds the base rate, $\text{prec}_t := P_{\mathcal{D}}(y = 1 \mid \hat{y} = 1) > \pi$ for all t; equivalently, a rejected applicant is more likely to default than a randomly drawn one. By the definition of Kickout (Eq. 1), $\text{KO}_t = 2\,\text{prec}_t - 1$, so A5 is equivalent to $\text{KO}_t > 2\pi - 1$; since $\pi \leq 1/2$, it is implied by $\text{KO}_t > 0$, which holds for the Biased baseline throughout our experiments (Sect. 4.1; Appendix E). **(A6)** The model is retrained on the accumulated accepted data without class rebalancing—the *Biased* baseline of Sect. 4.1—and the initial set $\mathcal{D}_0$ is a uniform sample of $\mathcal{D}$, so $\pi_0 = \pi$. We write $\pi_t := P_{\mathcal{D}_t}(y = 1)$ for its default rate, which is the training set default rate TDR_t of Sect. 3.[4] Here π is exact (the default rate of $\mathcal{D}$). All proofs are deferred to Appendix D.

---

[3] We leave the cycle index on $\hat{y}$ implicit; since $\hat{y}$ is the cycle-t prediction, the screening quantities α_t, prec_t, β_t depend on t through M_t.

[4] Quantities are probabilities over two populations: the screening rates α_t, prec_t, β_t over a draw from $\mathcal{D}$ ($P_{\mathcal{D}}$), and π_t together with the evaluation metrics of Proposition 2 over the accepted pool $\mathcal{D}_t$ ($P_{\mathcal{D}_t}$).

Lemma 1. *Under A1–A6, the default rate of the accepted applicants at cycle* t*,* $\beta_t := P_{\mathcal{D}}(y = 1 \mid \hat{y} = 0)$*, satisfies* $\beta_t < \pi$*: the accepted applicants default less often than the population.*

Proposition 1 (Single-cycle default-rate deflation). *Under A1–A6, after the first retraining cycle the accepted pool has a strictly lower default rate than the population:* $\pi_1 < \pi_0 = \pi$*.*

Since each accepted batch defaults less than the population (Lemma 1), mixing the first batch into $\mathcal{D}_0$ drags the pool's default rate below π (Proposition 1).

Proposition 2 (Accuracy–recall decomposition on the accepted pool). *On the accepted pool at cycle* t *(default rate* π_t*), evaluated as in Sect. 3, accuracy decomposes as* $\mathrm{acc}_t = (1-\pi_t)\,\mathrm{spec}_t + \pi_t\,\mathrm{rec}_t$*, where* $\mathrm{spec}_t = P_{\mathcal{D}_t}(\hat{y} = 0 \mid y = 0)$ *and* $\mathrm{rec}_t = P_{\mathcal{D}_t}(\hat{y} = 1 \mid y = 1)$ *are the specificity and recall of the model on that pool. In particular, the contribution of recall to accuracy is exactly* $\pi_t\,\mathrm{rec}_t$*, which vanishes as* $\pi_t \to 0$*. Hence as* π_t *falls, accuracy is increasingly governed by specificity and increasingly insensitive to recall. Thus, recall may decline while accuracy remains constant or increases.*

Proposition 1 establishes the one-cycle deflation of the TDR (π_t); empirically it compounds across cycles (Fig. 3a), driving recall down. Since recall contributes to accuracy only in proportion to π_t (Proposition 2), accuracy can hold even if recall collapses (Fig. 1).

4.3 Reject Inference Strategies Comparison

We now examine whether the five reject inference strategies (Sect. 3)—Parceling, Fuzzy Augmentation, Simple Extrapolation, Shallow Self-Learning, and Twins—can correct the survival bias documented above. The results reveal a striking paradox: the strategy that performs best on standard predictive metrics is also the one that most severely distorts the training data.

Simple Extrapolation Dominates Standard Metrics. Extrapolation achieves the highest accuracy, precision, and recall across all six experimental configurations (Fig. 2; Table 1). On Default/GBDT, it reaches accuracy of approximately 0.86, precision of 0.90, and recall of 0.54 at $t = 10$, substantially higher than all other strategies. The Kickout metric, our measure of rejection quality, confirms that Extrapolation is rejecting true defaulters at a higher rate than any other strategy, reaching values around 0.80 on Default/GBDT (Fig. 3, right).

However, the training set default rate reveals the mechanism behind this apparent superiority (Fig. 3a). Extrapolation inflates the training set default rate well above the population rate, from 22.0% to approximately 27% on Default/GBDT, because it uses the model's own predictions as ground-truth labels for rejected applicants. This creates a self-reinforcing feedback loop: the model predicts that rejected applicants would default, labels them as defaulters,

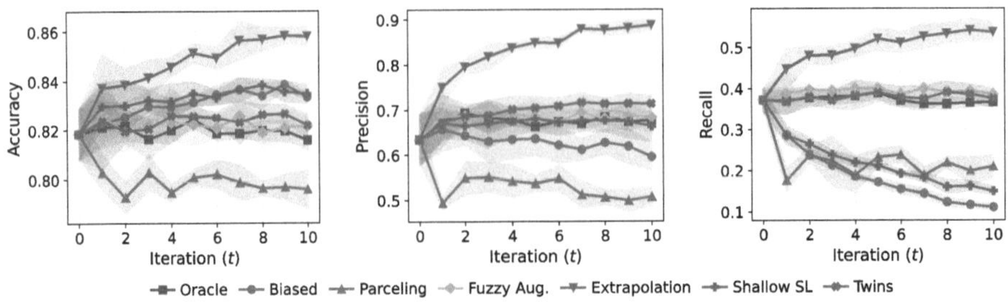

Fig. 2. Accuracy, precision, and recall over 10 lending iterations for all RI strategies on the Default dataset (GBDT, $n_0 = 5{,}000$, $\tau = 0.5$). Shaded regions indicate ±1 standard deviation across 5 runs. Extrapolation dominates all three standard metrics, yet this apparent superiority is an artifact of self-reinforcing label assignment (see Fig. 3).

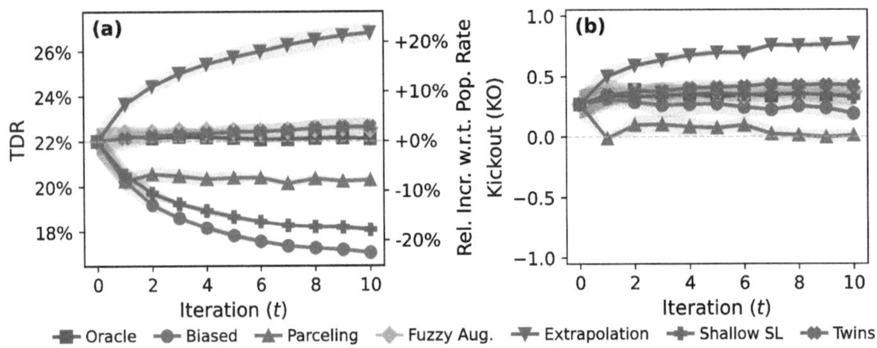

Fig. 3. Training set default rate (left) and Kickout (right) over ten iterations (Default, GBDT). The dashed line indicates the population default rate (22.0%). Extrapolation inflates the default rate by ∼5% above the population rate while Biased deflates it by ∼5%—symmetric distortions with opposite mechanisms.

retrains on this augmented data, and becomes even more aggressive in its default predictions. Each iteration amplifies the previous one's biases. The model does not converge toward the true population distribution; it diverges from it at an accelerating rate.

Middle Tier: Fuzzy Augmentation and Twins. These two strategies maintain accuracy comparable to the Biased baseline (approximately 0.82 on Default/GBDT) while providing meaningfully better recall, around 0.38–0.40 at $t = 10$ compared to 0.11 for Biased. Their training set default rates stay much closer to the population rate. Fuzzy Augmentation is the most stable: its default rate deviates by less than 1% from the population rate across most configurations, making it the closest to Oracle in terms of population representativeness. Twins shows strong Kickout performance on the Default dataset (reaching approximately 0.45), indicating high-quality rejection decisions.

Weak Tier: Parceling and Shallow Self-learning. These strategies provide only marginal improvements over the Biased baseline. Parceling achieves recall of 0.21 on Default/GBDT, better than Biased (0.11) but far below Fuzzy Augmentation (0.39) or Twins (0.38). Its precision drops to approximately 0.50, and its Kickout values hover near zero, occasionally turning negative (notably on PPDai/RF), meaning it sometimes rejects more non-defaulters than defaulters. The bin-based bad rate assumption underlying Parceling, *i.e.*, that rejects default at the same rate as accepts within each risk score bin, is increasingly violated under iterative retraining: as survival bias accumulates, the accept pool within each bin skews toward non-defaulters, causing Parceling to systematically underestimate the default rate among rejects. Shallow Self-Learning achieves recall of only 0.15 on Default/GBDT, and its training set default rate drifts downward similarly to the Biased baseline (dropping to approximately 18%), suggesting that the Isolation Forest filtering mechanism is too conservative: it excludes so many rejects that the method barely improves over doing nothing.

Training Set Default Rate as a Diagnostic. The TDR reveals a striking pattern invisible to standard metrics (Fig. 3a). By $t = 10$ on Default/GBDT, Extrapolation inflates the TDR to 26.8% (+22% relative to the population rate), while Biased deflates it to 17.1% (−22% relative), a nearly symmetric distortion in opposite directions. Extrapolation does not mitigate survival bias; it reverses its sign, replacing systematic underrepresentation of defaulters with systematic overrepresentation. Rather than correcting the missing-data problem, it substitutes one distributional distortion for another, casting doubt on whether it should be considered an RI strategy at all. To the best of our knowledge, this sign-reversed distortion has not been previously documented. Among the remaining strategies, Parceling (TDR 20.3%, −8% relative) and Shallow Self-Learning (18.1%, −18%) offer only partial corrections. In contrast, Fuzzy Augmentation (22.6%, +3%) and Twins (22.7%, +3%) track the population rate nearly as closely as Oracle (22.1%), making them the only strategies that genuinely mitigate survival bias effectively, preserving the training set distribution, a property that standard metrics fail to capture.

A practitioner evaluating strategies by accuracy, precision, recall, or even Kickout would rationally select Simple Extrapolation as the best strategy. However, all four metrics are evaluated on the pool of applicants the model approved—a population composed exclusively of applicants the model classified as non-defaulters. As Extrapolation assigns $y = 1$ to all rejected applicants[5] and retrains on this augmented dataset, the training set default rate increases monotonically above the true population default rate (Fig. 3a), causing the model to classify an increasing fraction of applicants as defaulters at each cycle. The accepted pool therefore becomes increasingly composed of applicants the model classified with high confidence, and evaluating on this pool rewards the model for removing its own hard cases from consideration rather than for genuine improve-

[5] Since both models are deterministic at inference time and the threshold is fixed, re-applying M_t to rejected applicants—who received $\hat{y} = 1$ in the first prediction—yields $\hat{y} = 1$ again, so all rejected applicants receive the imputed label $y = 1$.

Table 1. Accuracy and recall at $t = 10$ for all RI strategies across all six configurations, averaged over five runs. Extrapolation achieves the highest accuracy and recall in every configuration despite having no access to true labels. Bold indicates the best value per column (excluding Oracle). The Gap row shows the accuracy difference between Extrapolation and Oracle, demonstrating that standard metrics structurally reward self-reinforcing strategies.

	Default		LendingClub		PPDai	
Strategy	GBDT	RF	GBDT	RF	GBDT	RF
Accuracy						
Biased	0.833	0.833	0.783	0.782	0.785	0.786
Oracle	0.816	0.812	0.779	0.777	0.780	0.780
Parceling	0.796	0.794	0.778	0.777	0.775	0.777
Fuzzy Aug.	0.822	0.815	0.779	0.776	0.782	0.779
Extrapolation	**0.858**	**0.863**	**0.796**	**0.790**	**0.796**	**0.801**
Shallow SL	0.835	0.838	0.784	0.783	0.788	0.791
Twins	0.822	0.827	0.778	0.779	0.778	0.780
Gap (Extrap.–Oracle)	*+.042*	*+.051*	*+.017*	*+.013*	*+.016*	*+.021*
Recall						
Biased	0.111	0.150	0.019	0.035	0.036	0.057
Oracle	0.367	0.371	0.067	0.061	0.102	0.125
Parceling	0.210	0.217	0.035	0.039	0.048	0.082
Fuzzy Aug.	0.386	0.404	0.065	0.063	0.107	0.138
Extrapolation	**0.537**	**0.619**	**0.286**	**0.236**	**0.299**	**0.349**
Shallow SL	0.150	0.189	0.040	0.048	0.047	0.075
Twins	0.376	0.418	0.032	0.045	0.048	0.098

ment. The training set default rate is the only metric that escapes this circularity: it measures the composition of the training set against the known population default rate, a reference point the model cannot influence.

The Oracle Paradox. The most revealing finding emerges from the ranking itself. Across all six configurations, Extrapolation consistently outperforms Oracle on accuracy, precision, and recall (Table 1), despite having no access to true labels. On Default/GBDT, the gap is roughly 4.2% in accuracy (0.858 vs. 0.816) and more than 20% in precision (0.90 vs. 0.68). This result is not an artifact of noise: the standard deviation bands are non-overlapping across all configurations (Fig. 2). The explanation lies in the evaluation framework itself. Because models are evaluated on the full applicant pool, the evaluation implicitly rewards strategies that create sharper, more extreme decision boundaries, while penalizing Oracle for introducing genuine label diversity that makes the learning task harder. The only metric on which strategies are evaluated correctly is the training set default rate: Oracle by design maintains a rate near the population rate (22.1%), while Extrapolation inflates it to approximately 27%.

This finding extends beyond the reject inference comparison. It demonstrates that standard classification metrics evaluated on the observable population are structurally inadequate for assessing model quality in the presence of survival bias. A practitioner selecting a reject inference strategy by standard evaluation metrics would choose Extrapolation, the strategy that most aggressively amplifies survival bias, and would conclude that their model is improving with each retraining cycle.

The magnitude of these effects varies with dataset scale. On LendingClub (n_0 = 60,000), all strategies exhibit the same qualitative patterns but with compressed magnitudes: accuracy differences between strategies narrow to ~2% and recall degradation is less severe (Fig. 13, Appendix E.4). This scale effect has practical significance. Smaller lenders and new product lines, where initial training data is more limited, are most vulnerable to the survival bias spiral documented here.

5 Controlled Exploration as Bias Mitigation

The reject inference strategies evaluated in Sect. 4 all attempt to *impute* labels for rejected applicants using statistical assumptions about the missing data. Each introduces its own form of model-dependent bias, and none can recover the true outcome distribution without assumptions that are fundamentally untestable under selection. We take a different approach inspired by the *exploration–exploitation* tradeoff in sequential decision-making [16] and A/B or split testing. Rather than guessing at missing labels, the lender deliberately approves a fraction r of rejected applicants and observes their true repayment outcomes. This *controlled exploration*, governed by the parameter r, breaks the feedback loop at a measurable cost: the defaults incurred by explored applicants who fail to repay. The parameter r interpolates between the two baselines from Sect. 4.1: $r = 0$ corresponds to Biased (maximum exploitation) and $r = 1$ to Oracle (maximum exploration). The central question is: *what is the cost of moving from one extreme to the other?*

Given a trained model at iteration t, let $\mathcal{R}_t$ denote the set of rejected applicants. The exploration strategy selects a subset $\mathcal{E}_t \subseteq \mathcal{R}_t$ with $|\mathcal{E}_t| = \lceil r \cdot |\mathcal{R}_t| \rceil$ for approval, then augments the training data with these applicants and their *observed* (not imputed) labels. The selection of which rejects to explore is governed by a **sampling strategy**: **Least Risky** selects the r-fraction with lowest P(default), wanting to minimize cost by choosing the rejects closest to the decision boundary; **Most Risky** selects the r-fraction with highest P(default), probing the region where the model has the least information; and **Random** selects uniformly, providing an unbiased sample that requires no model scores.[6] We sweep $r \in \{0, 0.01, 0.02, 0.05, 0.10, 0.20, 0.30, 0.50, 0.75, 1.0\}$ across all three datasets and both modeling techniques, for the three selection mechanisms with five independent runs per configuration.

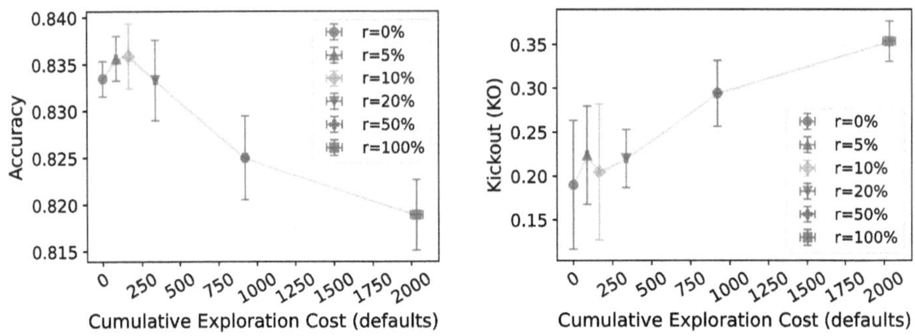

(a) Accuracy vs. cumulative cost. (b) Kickout vs. cumulative cost.

Fig. 4. Cost–benefit tradeoff on the Default dataset (GBDT, least risky sampling). Accuracy decreases monotonically with exploration while Kickout increases monotonically. The two metrics give opposite recommendations, confirming that accuracy under biased selection is a misleading objective. Error bars indicate ±1 standard deviation across 5 runs.

5.1 The Cost–Benefit Tradeoff

Figure 4 presents the core finding. Accuracy and Kickout move in opposite directions as exploration increases: on Default/GBDT, accuracy drops from 0.834 at $r = 0$ to 0.819 at $r = 1.0$ (−1.5%), while Kickout rises from 0.19 to 0.35 (+16%). The biased model achieves the highest accuracy in part because it is evaluated on a population shaped by its own selection decisions; as exploration shifts the training data toward the true population, the evaluation becomes harder but the model's rejection decisions become more aligned with actual risk.

This pattern is consistent in direction but varies in magnitude (Table 2); comparisons for all other configurations are provided in Appendix F. Default exhibits the strongest effect (accuracy drops of 1.5%–1.9%, Kickout gains of 15%–23%), PPDai shows intermediate sensitivity (0.5%–0.6% accuracy decline, 13%–21% Kickout gain), and LendingClub is the most attenuated (0.35% accuracy decline, 5%–9% Kickout gain). The TDR gap between $r = 0$ and $r = 1.0$ serves as a diagnostic for feedback loop severity: on Default, biased training makes the borrower population appear approximately 30% safer than reality (TDR = 17.0% vs. 22.1%), while on LendingClub the distortion is only 2.6%.

[6] An uncertainty-based strategy (minimizing $|P(\text{default}) - \tau|$) is equivalent to Least Risky when $\tau = 0.5$, since all rejects satisfy $P(\text{default}) > \tau$ and the two orderings coincide.

Table 2. Accuracy drop and Kickout gain at full exploration ($r = 1.0$, random sampling) relative to the biased baseline ($r = 0$). Relative TDR distortion is the TDR gap divided by the biased TDR.

Dataset	Model	ΔAcc (%)	KO at $r = 1.0$	TDR Gap (%)	Rel. TDR Distortion
Default	GBDT	−1.50	0.344	5.05	29.6%
Default	RF	−1.91	0.312	5.09	29.9%
PPDai	GBDT	−0.53	0.232	1.17	5.4%
PPDai	RF	−0.49	0.190	1.33	6.1%
LendingClub	GBDT	−0.24	0.139	0.03	0.1%
LendingClub	RF	−0.35	0.081	0.57	2.6%

5.2 The Diagnostic Zone

A lender considering exploration faces a practical question: how much is enough? Even minimal exploration produces detectable shifts. At $r = 0.05$, accuracy changes are negligible across all configurations ($|\Delta| < 0.4\%$), yet Kickout is already shifting and TDR is moving toward the population default rate (Fig. 5). On Default, accuracy does not decline by more than 0.5% until $r = 0.30$ (least risky) or $r = 0.75$ (most risky/random); on PPDai and LendingClub, this threshold is never reached even at full exploration (Table 3).

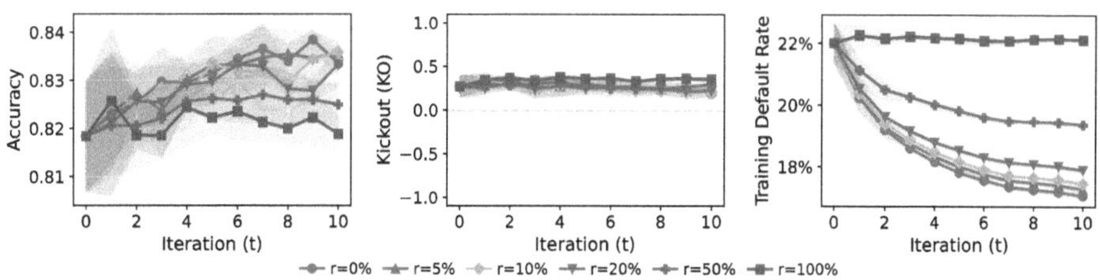

Fig. 5. Temporal evolution of accuracy, Kickout, and TDR across iterations on the Default dataset (GBDT, least risky sampling). Higher exploration rates shift TDR toward the population default rate (~22%), while accuracy decreases and Kickout increases, consistent with learning from a more representative training distribution.

This defines a *diagnostic zone* at $r \in [0.01, 0.05]$: exploration rates that reveal the presence and severity of survival bias at near-zero cost. In practice, a bank could run a controlled experiment at $r = 0.02$–0.05 purely as a diagnostic tool, without committing to permanent policy changes. On the Default dataset, $r = 0.02$ incurs approximately 45 defaults across all iterations, but the information gained is substantial: the bank learns whether its model is operating on a representative sample or on a fiction of its own creation.

Table 3. Exploration rate at which accuracy first declines by more than 0.5% from the biased baseline. "Never" indicates that even $r = 1.0$ does not cross this threshold.

Dataset	Model	Least Risky	Most Risky	Random
Default	GBDT	0.30	0.75	0.75
Default	RF	0.30	0.50	0.50
PPDai	GBDT	never	never	1.00
PPDai	RF	never	1.00	never
LendingClub	RF	never	never	never

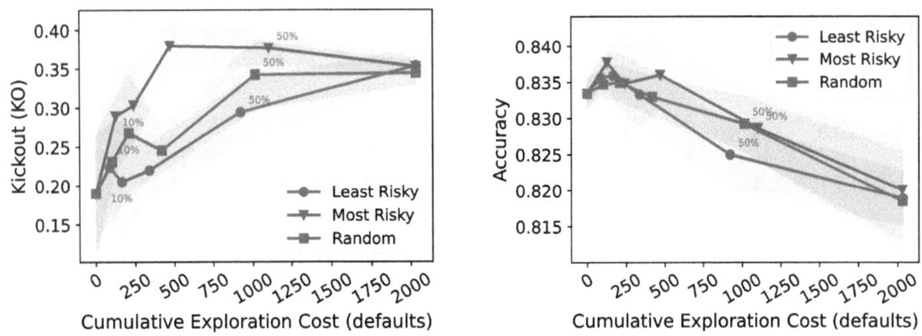

(a) Kickout vs. cumulative cost.

(b) Accuracy vs. cumulative cost.

Fig. 6. Sampling strategy comparison on the Default dataset (GBDT). Most Risky achieves the highest Kickout at every exploration rate and preserves accuracy better than Least Risky despite higher per-applicant cost. Random is a robust middle ground.

5.3 Sampling Strategy Comparison

Figure 6 compares the three sampling strategies. Most Risky exploration produces the highest Kickout at every exploration rate: on Default/GBDT at $r = 0.20$, it achieves 0.379 compared to 0.245 (Random) and 0.220 (Least Risky), a difference of +13.4% over Random. This is intuitive: the rejects the model considers highest-risk are the most underrepresented in biased training data, and observing their true outcomes provides the strongest learning signal. Most Risky also preserves accuracy better than expected, maintaining positive accuracy deltas through $r = 0.20$ on Default/GBDT. Least Risky is dominated: despite its appeal as the lowest-cost option, it produces the smallest Kickout improvements because exploring "safe" rejects provides redundant rather than informative training signal. Random requires no model scores, avoids systematic exploration bias, and achieves Kickout between the other two strategies, making it the practical default for deployment.

The default rates among explored rejects (Table 4) reveal that the model's quality has two distinct dimensions. The gradient from ~50% (Least Risky) to ~80% (Most Risky) confirms that the model's *ranking* of applicants by risk is

Table 4. Default rate among explored rejects at $r = 0.10$ by sampling strategy. The gradient from ~50% (Least Risky) to ~80% (Most Risky) confirms that the model's risk ranking is meaningful even among rejected applicants. However, all rates far exceed the biased TDR (~17–22%), indicating that the model cannot calibrate its estimates in the reject region without observing true outcomes.

Dataset	Model	Least Risky	Random	Most Risky
Default	GBDT	50.5%	65.5%	82.0%
Default	RF	52.6%	57.0%	82.1%
PPDai	GBDT	56.8%	66.5%	72.3%
PPDai	RF	46.4%	65.4%	79.2%
LendingClub	GBDT	52.4%	59.9%	65.3%
LendingClub	RF	50.3%	54.6%	60.5%

informative: it captures genuine signal about relative default likelihood, even among applicants it was trained to reject. What survival bias distorts is the model's *learned risk estimates* in the reject region. The model rejects all of these applicants (all receive $\hat{p} > \tau$), yet their true default rates range widely; some are substantially less risky than others and may be comparable to approved borrowers. Without observing their outcomes, the model has no basis for distinguishing among them. Controlled exploration preserves the model's ranking ability while providing the data needed to sharpen its estimates where they matter most.

6 Conclusions

The cost–benefit tradeoff encapsulates the central tension of our research. A bank that evaluates its scoring model by standard metrics will rationally choose $r = 0$, because exploration can only decrease accuracy on the biased test distribution. This is the optimal strategy under the metric the bank is optimizing, and the worst possible strategy for learning. The practical recommendation is modest. A short-term diagnostic experiment at $r = 0.02$–0.05, using random selection among rejected applicants, is sufficient to estimate the TDR gap and quantify the severity of the feedback loop. The heterogeneity across datasets reinforces this: Default, where the feedback loop distorts TDR by ~30%, represents a scenario where survival bias is a first-order concern; LendingClub, with only 2.6% distortion, is a setting where survival bias may be a secondary modeling concern. A diagnostic exploration experiment allows the lender to determine which regime it occupies *before* investing in complex reject inference methods or trusting that its current model is performing well. The reject inference comparison reveals three results with direct implications for credit scoring practice. First, no reject inference strategy fully eliminates survival bias in the temporal setting; even the most effective methods that preserve training set representativeness (Fuzzy Augmentation, Twins) only slow the accumulation rather than eliminating it. Second, Simple Extrapolation does not mitigate survival bias but reverses its sign: where the Biased baseline deflates the TDR by 22% relative to the population rate, Extrapolation inflates it by a symmetric 22%, substituting one distributional distortion for another. Third, the fact that Extrapolation outperforms Oracle on standard metrics demonstrates that these metrics are not merely noisy but systematically biased toward strategies that amplify selection effects. Taken together, these findings reinforce the central argument of this paper: iterative model-based lending produces performance indicators that are fundamentally disconnected from the model's actual predictive quality for the full applicant population.

Limitations. Our simulation assumes a stationary applicant distribution; in practice, population drift would interact with the survival bias feedback loop in ways we do not model. The fixed threshold $\tau = 0.5$ is a simplifying assumption; real deployments tune this threshold to reflect the asymmetric costs of approving defaulters versus rejecting creditworthy applicants, and threshold choice would affect the rate of feedback loop accumulation. Our findings are established for tree-based ensemble methods (GBDT and RF); models with different inductive biases may exhibit different magnitudes, though we expect the structural failure mode to persist as it follows from survival bias rather than from any property specific to tree-based models. Finally, controlled exploration, while assumption-free in principle, faces deployment constraints in practice: deliberately approving a fraction of rejected applicants raises regulatory and ethical considerations that would need to be addressed before implementation.

In future work, we plan to quantify the social and economic costs of survival bias, and to study if and how the feedback loop documented in this work creates demographic disparities in the rejected applicant pool.

References

1. Alam, T.M., et al.: An investigation of credit card default prediction in the imbalanced datasets. IEEE Access **8**, 201173–201198 (2020)
2. Anderson, B., Newman, M.A., Grim II, P.A., Hardin, J.M.: A Monte Carlo simulation framework for reject inference. J. Oper. Res. Soc. **74**(4), 1133–1149 (2023)
3. Banasik, J., Crook, J.: Reject inference, augmentation, and sample selection. Eur. J. Oper. Res. **183**(3), 1582–1594 (2007)
4. Banasik, J., Crook, J., Thomas, L.: Sample selection bias in credit scoring models. J. Oper. Res. Soc. **54**(8), 822–832 (2003)
5. Brooks, D.: The philosophy of data. N.Y. Times **4**(02) (2013)
6. Ehrhardt, A., Biernacki, C., Vandewalle, V., Heinrich, P., Beben, S.: Reject inference methods in credit scoring. J. Appl. Stat. **48**(13–15), 2734–2754 (2021)
7. Elton, E.J., Gruber, M.J., Blake, C.R.: Survivor bias and mutual fund performance. Rev. Financ. Stud. **9**(4), 1097–1120 (2015). https://doi.org/10.1093/rfs/9.4.1097
8. Ensign, D., Friedler, S.A., Neville, S., Scheidegger, C., Venkatasubramanian, S.: Runaway feedback loops in predictive policing. In: Conference on Fairness, Accountability and Transparency, pp. 160–171. PMLR (2018)
9. Hand, D.J., Henley, W.E.: Can reject inference ever work? IMA J. Manag. Math. **5**(1), 45–55 (1993)

10. He, H.: PPDai Dataset. Figshare Repository (2021). https://figshare.com/articles/dataset/PPDaiData/13573856?file=26049578
11. He, H., Zhang, W., Zhang, S.: A novel ensemble method for credit scoring: adaption of different imbalance ratios. Expert Syst. Appl. **98**, 105–117 (2018)
12. Hellström, T., Dignum, V., Bensch, S.: Bias in machine learning - what is it good for? In: International Workshop on New Foundations for Human-Centered AI (NeHuAI) at the 24th European Conference on Artificial Intelligence (ECAI 2020), pp. 3–10. RWTH Aachen University (2020)
13. Hildebrandt, M.: The issue of bias: the framing powers of machine learning. In: Pelillo, M., Scantamburlo, T. (eds.) Machines We Trust: Perspectives on Dependable AI, chap. 4. The MIT Press (2021)
14. Ippoliti, E.: Dark data. Some methodological issues in finance. In: Methods and Finance: A Unifying View on Finance, Mathematics and Philosophy, pp. 179–194 (2017)
15. Kozodoi, N., Katsas, P., Lessmann, S., Moreira-Matias, L., Papakonstantinou, K.: Shallow self-learning for reject inference in credit scoring. In: Joint European Conference on Machine Learning and Knowledge Discovery in Databases, pp. 516–532. Springer (2019)
16. Lattimore, T., Szepesvári, C.: Bandit Algorithms. Cambridge University Press (2020)
17. Mancisidor, R.A., Kampffmeyer, M., Aas, K., Jenssen, R.: Deep generative models for reject inference in credit scoring. Knowl.-Based Syst. **196**, 105758 (2020)
18. Markov, A., Seleznyova, Z., Lapshin, V.: Credit scoring methods: latest trends and points to consider. J. Financ. Data Sci. **8**, 180–201 (2022)
19. Mehrabi, N., Morstatter, F., Saxena, N., Lerman, K., Galstyan, A.: A survey on bias and fairness in machine learning. ACM Comput. Surv. (CSUR) **54**(6), 1–35 (2021)
20. Oliveira, M.: Lending Club Dataset. Kaggle Repository (2023). https://www.kaggle.com/datasets/marcusos/lending-club-clean
21. Pedregosa, F., et al.: Scikit-learn: machine learning in Python. J. Mach. Learn. Res. **12**, 2825–2830 (2011)
22. Perdomo, J., Zrnic, T., Mendler-Dünner, C., Hardt, M.: Performative prediction. In: International Conference on Machine Learning, pp. 7599–7609. PMLR (2020)
23. Rohleder, M., Scholz, H., Wilkens, M.: Survivorship bias and mutual fund performance: relevance, significance, and methodical differences. Rev. Financ. **15**(2), 441–474 (2011)
24. Scarone, B., Baeza-Yates, R.: The illusion of improvement: reject inference strategies in credit scoring (2026). https://arxiv.org/abs/2606.18479. Preprint
25. Siddiqi, N.: Credit Risk Scorecards: Developing and Implementing Intelligent Credit Scoring. Wiley (2012)
26. Suhadolnik, N., Ueyama, J., Da Silva, S.: Machine learning for enhanced credit risk assessment: an empirical approach. J. Risk Financ. Manage. **16**(12), 496 (2023)
27. Union, E.: The EU artificial intelligence act (2024)
28. Weinblat, J.: Forecasting European high-growth firms - a random forest approach. J. Ind. Compet. Trade **18**, 253–294 (2018)
29. Wermers, R.: Momentum investment strategies of mutual funds, performance persistence, and survivorship bias. Technical report, working paper, University of Colorado (1997)
30. Yeh, I.C.: Default of credit card clients. UCI Machine Learning Repository (2009). https://doi.org/10.24432/C55S3H

Understanding and Mitigating Semantic Popularity Bias in LLM-Based Recommender Systems

Xiran Liu, Heng Tang, Bohao Wang, Yu Cui, Jiawei Chen(✉), Bingde Hu, and Can Wang

Zhejiang University, Hangzhou, China
{liuxiran,tangheng23,bohao.wang,cuiyu23,sleepyhunt, tonyhu,wcan}@zju.edu.cn

Abstract. Large Language Models (LLMs) have recently shown strong capabilities in recommender systems by leveraging their rich semantic understanding and reasoning abilities. However, models trained on inherently long-tailed data are prone to severe popularity bias. In this paper, we identify a novel challenge unique to LLM-based Recommender Systems (LRSs), termed **Semantic Popularity Bias**. Unlike traditional ID-based systems, items in LRSs reside in the semantic space where they mutually influence each other. During supervised fine-tuning, maximizing the likelihood of a popular item inadvertently amplifies the exposure of its semantically similar counterparts. Existing debiasing methods treat items in isolation and fail to capture this underlying semantic-level mutual influence. To address this, we propose **DeSP (Debiasing via Semantic Propagation)**, a principled framework inspired by social opinion dynamics. DeSP first constructs a robust multi-view semantic graph incorporating deep, lexical, and collaborative behavioral features. It then formulates a PageRank-style propagation process to estimate the semantic-influenced propensity score for each item. Finally, these scores are integrated into a Self-Normalized Inverse Propensity Scoring (SNIPS) framework to reweight the training loss, effectively down-weighting semantically over-exposed items. Extensive experiments on three real-world datasets demonstrate that DeSP effectively mitigates semantic popularity bias, yielding improved recommendation accuracy and diversity. Our code is released under https://github.com/Leo12456/DeSP.

Keywords: Recommendation · Large Language Model · Popularity Bias

1 Introduction

Recently, Large Language Models (LLMs), equipped with profound semantic understanding and reasoning capabilities, have fundamentally reshaped recom-

X. Liu and H. Tang—Equal contribution.

M. Ceci et al. (Eds.): ECML PKDD 2026, LNAI 16941, pp. 480–496, 2027.
https://doi.org/10.1007/978-3-032-37654-1_28

mendation system (RS) paradigms [1,22,31,32,42,44]. A prevailing paradigm is to directly employ LLMs as the recommendation backbone. These approaches formulate historical user interactions into textual formats and utilize prompt instructions to guide LLMs in predicting the next item of interest to the user.

In real-world scenarios, item interactions typically exhibit a severe long-tail distribution, where a small fraction of popular items dominates user feedback. Models trained on such long-tailed datasets are intrinsically prone to exhibit popularity bias, inadvertently amplifying this skewness by overwhelmingly favoring head items. As illustrated in Fig. 1, the top 20% of popular items can frequently monopolize up to 60% of the total recommendation output in LLM-based RS (LRS) after SFT.

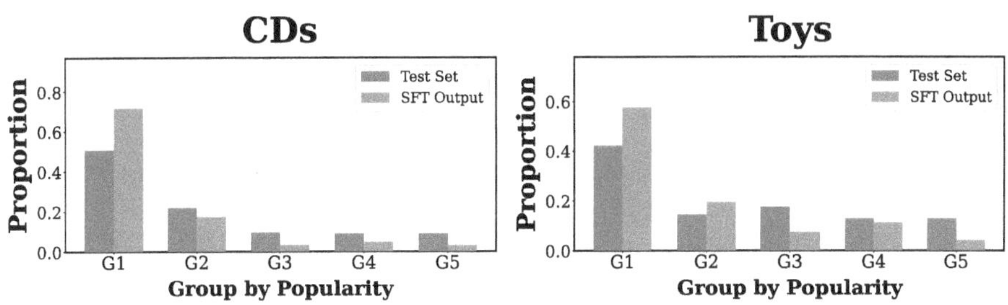

Fig. 1. Distribution of Top-1 recommended items on two datasets CDs and Toys generated by the SFT-trained LLM across five group defined according to the item popularity (Group 1: highest popularity, Group 5: lowest popularity). We also present the distribution of the test set across the same five groups for comparison.

However, we observe that in LLM-based RS, items mutually influence one another due to semantic similarity, which fundamentally alters the manifestation of popularity bias. Specifically, during the Supervised Fine-Tuning (SFT) process, maximizing the likelihood of a target item simultaneously increases the likelihood of its semantically similar counterparts, with the magnitude of this collateral enhancement being positively correlated with their semantic relevance. As depicted in Fig. 2, we measure item-level semantic similarity using embeddings extracted from LLaMA. By grouping all items based on their semantic relevance to the top 20% most popular items, our results demonstrate that items sharing higher semantic relevance with popular items exhibit a significantly disproportionate increase in their recommendation frequency. This finding reveals a critical insight: addressing popularity bias in LRSs necessitates considering not only the isolated popularity of individual items but also the mutual influence propagated through semantic similarity. We formalize this novel phenomenon as **Semantic Popularity Bias**.

Unfortunately, existing debiasing methods for LRSs fundamentally rely on the isolated, individual item popularity [2,9,14,26]. By neglecting the mutual influence among items embedded in a continuous semantic space, these methods fail to model the underlying mechanism of semantic popularity bias, and consequently offer limited effectiveness in LLM-based recommendation scenarios. This limitation motivates our central research question: *How can we effectively mitigate semantic popularity bias in LLM-based recommender systems?*

To address this challenge, we propose **DeSP**, termed **De**biasing via **S**emantic **P**ropagation, a principled framework inspired by social opinion dynamics. DeSP explicitly models how empirical popularity diffuses through continuous semantic spaces [24]. Specifically, it first constructs a robust multi-view semantic graph and formulates a PageRank-style propagation process to estimate the semantic propensity score for each item. These derived scores are then integrated into a Self-Normalized Inverse Propensity Scoring (SNIPS) framework to reweight the SFT loss. In this way, DeSP down-weights semantically over-exposed items, thereby mitigating semantic popularity bias. Empirically, our experiments show that DeSP not only alleviates this bias but also improves recommendation accuracy.

The main contributions of this work are summarized as follows:

- We empirically reveal that LLM-based recommendation introduces semantic popularity bias, which harms both accuracy and diversity.
- We propose **DeSP**, which constructs an item semantic graph and introduces a semantic-aware inverse propensity scoring mechanism integrated into SFT to mitigate semantic popularity bias.
- Extensive experiments demonstrate that DeSP achieves state-of-the-art performance on both accuracy and debiasing metrics.

2 Preliminaries

2.1 LLM-Based Recommender Systems

Following previous work [2,22], this paper also focus on the sequential recommendation [15]. Given a user $u \in \mathcal{U}$ with a historical interaction sequence $S_u = \{i_1, i_2, \ldots, i_n\}$ (where item $i_k \in \mathcal{I}$), the goal is to predict the next item i_{n+1} the user is likely to interact with. Specifically, the user's historical sequence S_u and the task instructions are integrated into a language prompt x. The target item i_{n+1} is represented by its textual description (e.g., titles), denoted as a sequence of tokens $y = \{y_1, y_2, \ldots, y_{|y|}\}$. To align LLMs with recommendation objectives, SFT is commonly applied [1,26,43]. The training dataset is formatted as a set of prompt-target pairs $\mathcal{D} = \{(x, y)\}$. The model is optimized by minimizing the negative log-likelihood over the target tokens:

$$\mathcal{L}_{\mathrm{SFT}} = -\sum_{(x,y)\in\mathcal{D}} \sum_{t=1}^{|y|} \log P_\theta\big(y_t \mid x, y_{<t}\big), \tag{1}$$

where y_t is the t-th token of the target item description, $y_{<t}$ denotes the preceding prefix tokens, and P_θ represents the conditional probability estimated by the LLM parameterized by θ.

2.2 Popularity Bias

In real-world recommendation scenarios, user-item interactions typically exhibit a severe long-tail distribution [4,17]. A small fraction of popular "head" items accumulates the majority of user feedback, whereas the vast majority of "tail" items receive exceptionally sparse interactions . When recommender models are trained on such skewed observational data, they inherently learn to favor these head items. Consequently, the model not only inherits but often amplifies this skewness during inference, systematically over-recommending popular items at the expense of long-tail items [40]. This phenomenon is widely recognized as **popularity bias**, leading to a "rich-get-richer" effect that severely degrades recommendation diversity and personalization [8,17].

To mitigate this bias, various strategies have been proposed, with Inverse Propensity Scoring (IPS) being a prominent and representative approach [29]. Traditional IPS methods counteract popularity bias by reweighting training samples, assigning higher importance to tail items inversely proportional to their raw observation probabilities $P_{\text{obs}}(i)$ [14].

Limitations in the LLM Era. However, existing debiasing techniques, including IPS and other frequency-based reweighting or sampling methods [14,26,29], fundamentally rely on the individual popularity of items. They treat each item as an independent entity, computing propensities solely based on discrete historical interaction counts. Crucially, these methods fail to account for the mutual influence among items. In LLM-based recommender systems, items are not isolated IDs but are situated within a continuous, highly interconnected semantic space [18,25]. The popularity of a head item can propagate to its semantic neighbors, causing them to be over-recommended. By completely ignoring this semantic topology and item-to-item influence, traditional debiasing methods are rendered inadequate for addressing the novel biases emerging in LLM-driven recommendation scenarios.

3 Empirical Analysis

In this section, we empirically verify that the semantic relevance between items changes how popularity bias appears in LRSs. To construct the semantic representations of items, we encode their textual descriptions (e.g., item titles) using a pre-trained LLM backbone (i.e., LLaMA [11]) to extract deep semantic embeddings. Specifically, item representations $\mathbf{h}$ are derived via mean-pooling the last transformer layer's hidden states [19]. The semantic similarity between items i and j is then measured by the L_2 distance:

$$L_2(i,j) = \|\mathbf{h}_i - \mathbf{h}_j\|_2 = \sqrt{\sum_{k=1}^{n}(h_{i,k} - h_{j,k})^2} \tag{2}$$

where $\mathbf{h}_i, \mathbf{h}_j \in \mathbb{R}^n$ denote the extracted LLM embeddings. Based on this L_2 distance, we calculate the average semantic similarity between each item and

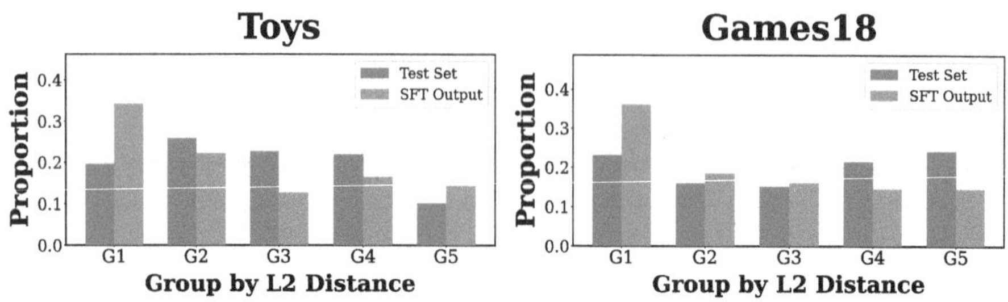

Fig. 2. Distribution of Top-1 recommended items generated by the SFT-trained LLM across five group defined by their semantic similarity to the top 20% most popular items (Group 1: highest similarity, Group 5: lowest similarity). We also present the distribution of the test set across the same five groups for comparison.

the top 20% most popular items. After excluding the top 20% most popular items, we divide the remaining items into five equal-sized groups (from G1 to G5) based on this similarity score, where G1 contains items most similar to the popular ones, and G5 contains the least similar items. Then we analyze the distribution of recommended items generated by the SFT-trained LRS across these five groups. As shown in Fig. 2, the group with the highest semantic similarity (G1) accounts for a significantly larger portion of the recommendations. This result clearly shows that in LRSs, items mutually influence each other due to semantic similarity: items that are more semantically similar to popular items receive more exposure. Therefore, investigating popularity bias in LRSs requires accounting for this semantic-driven influence, rather than relying solely on the popularity of individual items. However, relying only on a single metric like the L_2 distance may not fully capture the complex relationships between items. We will introduce our multi-view approach in Sect. 4.

4 Methodology

As conceptualized in Sect. 2, semantic popularity bias arises from the diffusion of empirical popularity through the continuous semantic space. To explicitly model and mitigate this underlying mechanism, we propose **DeSP** (**De**biasing via **S**emantic **P**ropagation), a principled framework inspired by social opinion dynamics [6]. Specifically, DeSP consists of three key steps: (1) constructing a robust multi-view semantic graph to approximate the semantic influence matrix; (2) estimating the semantic propensity distribution of items via propagation on the graph; and (3) performing weighted SFT of the LLM based on the estimated propensities, thereby correcting semantic popularity bias during training.

4.1 Building the Semantic Graph

To capture complex semantic structures robustly, we compute a comprehensive distance matrix W across three dimensions. For any pair of items i and j, we calculate the L_2 distance as $L_2(i,j) = \|\mathbf{h}_i - \mathbf{h}_j\|_2$ across the following views:

1) Deep Semantic View calculates the distance $L_2^{(\text{LLM})}(i,j)$ derived from pre-trained LLM item embeddings. This view captures the deep contextual and semantic relationships between different items as understood by the language model's intrinsic knowledge.
2) Surface Lexical View calculates the distance $L_2^{(\text{TF-IDF})}(i,j)$ derived from TF-IDF metadata vectors [33]. This dimension ensures that exact keyword matches and explicit textual overlaps in item descriptions are preserved in the similarity measurement.
3) Collaborative Behavioral View calculates the distance $L_2^{(\text{SASRec})}(i,j)$ derived from historical interaction representations [15]. By incorporating sequential recommendation signals, this view grounds the semantic generative distances in actual user behavior patterns [5].

After applying Min-Max normalization to each raw distance matrix to address scale discrepancies, we directly fuse them into a unified metric $W(x,y)$:

$$W(i,j) = L_2^{(\text{LLM})}(i,j) + L_2^{(\text{TF-IDF})}(i,j) + L_2^{(\text{SASRec})}(i,j) \tag{3}$$

Using W, we identify the Top-k nearest neighbors $\mathcal{N}(i)$ for each item i to construct a normalized adjacency matrix, with edge weights defined as:

$$\alpha_{ij} = \frac{1/W(i,j)}{\sum_{j' \in \mathcal{N}(i)} 1/W(i,j')} \tag{4}$$

This tripartite graph [13,43] bridges ID-based collaborative and LLM-based generative paradigms. Crucially, it ensures that subsequent propagation diffuses popularity along semantic similarities while respecting strict lexical and behavioral co-occurrence constraints.

4.2 Semantic Propagation via PageRank

As established in Sect. 2, an item's true exposure probability in LLM-based recommenders is no longer determined solely by its isolated historical frequency. Therefore, accurately estimating the true semantic propensity requires a mechanism that captures this dynamic flow of influence.

To model this phenomenon, we draw a natural analogy to the Friedkin-Johnsen (FJ) model of social opinion dynamics [6]. Just as a person's final opinion is shaped by a balance between their innate belief and the social influence from their peers, an item's final semantic visibility is jointly determined by its original interaction frequency and the popularity propagated from its semantic neighbors. By formulating this as a forward propagation process over the semantic graph, we can iteratively simulate how popularity diffuses across the network until reaching a stable global equilibrium. We explicitly model this mechanism as follows:

- **Innate Belief ⇔ Empirical Popularity:** The raw observation probability P_{obs}, derived from the raw interaction frequency of an item in the training data, forms the intrinsic propensity.

- **Social Influence ⇔ Semantic Similarity:** The normalized adjacency matrix A acts as a social network, propagating exposure probability to semantically similar items.

Based on this isomorphism, we formalize the semantic propensity generation as a random walk over the semantic graph. Let $\boldsymbol{\rho}^{(t)}$ denote the popularity distribution at iteration t, updated via:

$$\boldsymbol{\rho}^{(t+1)} = \lambda \boldsymbol{P}_{\text{obs}} + (1-\lambda)\boldsymbol{A}\boldsymbol{\rho}^{(t)}, \quad \text{with } \boldsymbol{\rho}^{(0)} = \boldsymbol{P}_{\text{obs}}, \tag{5}$$

where $\lambda \in (0, 1]$ controls the retention of empirical popularity. As $t \to \infty$, the process converges to a stationary distribution $\boldsymbol{\rho}^*$, yielding the closed-form solution:

$$\boldsymbol{\rho}^* = \lambda \left(\boldsymbol{I} - (1-\lambda)\boldsymbol{A}\right)^{-1} \boldsymbol{P}_{\text{obs}}. \tag{6}$$

This formulation is mathematically equivalent to **Personalized PageRank (PPR)** over the semantic graph [3,27], dynamically aggregating an item's empirical popularity with the recursively propagated influence from its semantic neighbors.

While the conventional estimator $\hat{\rho}_{\text{obs}}$ is asymptotically unbiased, its application in Inverse Propensity Scoring (IPS) faces severe challenges in long-tail recommendations. Extreme data sparsity causes tail items to have near-zero observation counts, leading to unbounded or highly unstable importance weights $(1/\hat{\rho}_{\text{obs}})$ [29,35]. Consequently, the mean squared error (MSE) on tail items becomes heavily dominated by the variance term [10], rendering the training process numerically unstable.

In contrast, our semantic propensity score $\boldsymbol{\rho}^*$ introduces a controlled bias [34] by smoothing popularity estimates across the semantic graph. This propagation effectively shrinks the estimate toward its semantic neighborhood, leading to a substantial reduction in variance. By mitigating the instability caused by extremely sparse observation counts, our method prevents the estimator from being dominated by individual rare samples.

4.3 Weighted Supervised Fine-Tuning

Standard SFT maximizes the likelihood of observed training data, which inadvertently forces the LLM to replicate the semantically biased distribution identified in Sect. 2. To break this self-amplifying feedback loop, we propose a unified weighted SFT framework integrating label smoothing and self-normalized inverse propensity scoring (SNIPS) [29,36].

First, LLMs frequently exhibit over-confidence, assigning near-unit probability to ground-truth tokens, which accelerates overfitting to semantically popular items. To preserve exploration capacity, we inject a uniform prior over the vocabulary $\mathcal{V}$ via label smoothing. For a target sequence y of length T, the smoothed token-level loss $\ell(x, y)$ is defined as:

$$\ell(x,y) = -\frac{1}{T}\sum_{t=1}^{T}\left[(1-\epsilon)\log P(y_t \mid x, y_{<t}) + \frac{\epsilon}{|\mathcal{V}|}\sum_{v\in\mathcal{V}}\log P(v \mid x, y_{<t})\right], \tag{7}$$

where ϵ is the smoothing coefficient.

Second, to counteract the over-representation of items in dense semantic regions, we utilize the steady-state semantic propensity $\boldsymbol{\rho}^*$ derived in Sect. 4.2. Each target item i is assigned an IPS correction weight $w_i = 1/\rho_i^*$. To cap the influence of extreme individual samples and manage the bias-variance tradeoff, we integrate these weights into the final loss using the SNIPS estimator. Specifically, for a mini-batch of size B denoted as $\{(x_k, y_k)\}_{k=1}^{B}$, let $i_k \in \mathcal{I}$ be the specific target item corresponding to the target text sequence y_k. By normalizing the weighted smoothed loss over the sum of propensity weights within the mini-batch, our final optimization objective becomes:

$$\mathcal{L}_{\text{SNIPS}} = \frac{\sum_{k=1}^{B} w_{i_k} \cdot \ell(x_k, y_k)}{\sum_{k=1}^{B} w_{i_k}}. \tag{8}$$

This unified design explicitly down-weights items with high semantic visibility and amplifies gradient signals for semantic long-tail items, while guaranteeing numerical stability during fine-tuning by preventing exploding gradients.

Table 1. Statistics of the datasets.

Dataset	CDs	Kindle	Toys
#User	17,052	68,892	19,412
#Item	35,118	61,934	11,924
#Interaction	472,265	982,619	167,597
Density	0.079%	0.023%	0.072%

5 Experiments

We evaluate the performance of **DeSP** on three real-world datasets against representative LLM-based debiasing methods to answer the following research questions:

RQ1: How does **DeSP** perform compared with existing state-of-the-art methods?

RQ2: How does multi-view semantic similarity affect **DeSP** effectiveness?

RQ3: How do different hyperparameters affect **DeSP**?

5.1 Experimental Settings

Datasets. Three well-known real-world datasets from Amazon Reviews: *Toys and Games*, *CDs and Vinyl*, and *Kindle Store* are utilized in our cxperiments[1],

[1] https://cseweb.ucsd.edu/~jmcauley/datasets/amazon/links.html.

which are commonly used for the studies of sequential recommendation [1,14]. For fair comparisons, we closely adhered to the preprocessing methods used in recent work [7]: we filter out users and items with fewer than 10 interactions. The user interaction sequences are then sorted in ascending order by timestamp and split into training, validation, and testing sets with an 8:1:1 ratio. The dataset statistics are presented in Table 1.

Baselines. We compare **DeSP** with the following representative baselines.

- **Standard Fine-Tuning and Inference-level Methods: SFT** [1] directly fine-tunes the LLM using ground-truth items. **D3** [2] modifies the decoding strategy to mitigate generation-induced biases.
- **Reweighting Methods: IPS** [29] applies item-level weights directly during the training stage, while **iFairLRS** [14] integrates a fairness-aware reweighting mechanism into the training loss.
- **Preference Optimization: SPRec** [7] employs DPO with tailored negative sampling, and **RosePO** [21] conducts post-training preference optimization via rejection sampling.

Evaluation Metrics. We measure recommendation accuracy using *Hit Ratio (HR)* and *Normalized Discounted Cumulative Gain (NDCG)* at $K \in \{30, 50\}$ under the full-ranking protocol [41]. Following this work [7], to evaluate debiasing and diversity, we report *OR_ratio* (popular item coverage) and *Div_ratio* (intra-list diversity), alongside *Gini* and *Entropy* to quantify exposure inequality and distributional entropy.

Implementation Details. To prevent data leakage, all semantic representations are constructed exclusively on the training split. Specifically, TF-IDF is fitted on training metadata, and SASRec ($d = 64$, 2 self-attention blocks, learning rate 0.001) is trained solely on training sequences. For LLM-based methods, we adopt LLaMA-3.2-3B [11] as the backbone, utilizing prompt designs from [1] and LoRA [12] for fine-tuning. Models are trained using the Adam optimizer (batch size 256, learning rate $1e^{-4}$) for up to 5 epochs with early stopping (patience=2) on 4 NVIDIA A800 GPUs. We set the label smoothing coefficient $\epsilon = 0.1$, and tune $\lambda \in [0.1, 0.9]$ and neighborhood size $k \in \{5, 10, 15, 20, 25\}$ based on validation performance.

5.2 Performance Comparison (RQ1)

As shown in Table 2, **DeSP** achieves state-of-the-art results across almost datasets, significantly improving debiasing and diversity metrics while maintaining or enhancing recommendation accuracy.

Compared to baselines. While existing methods improve upon the SFT base model, they fail to fully decouple popularity bias from the semantic representation space. Specifically, frequency-based reweighting (IPS, iFairLRS) and preference optimization approaches (SPRec, RosePO) struggle to resolve head-item

Table 2. Overall performance comparison on three datasets. The best results are **bold**, and second-best are underlined. ↑ implies higher is better; ↓ implies lower is better.

Data	Metric	SFT	IPS	iFairLRS	SPRec	RosePO	D3	DeSP	Impr.
CDs	H@30 ↑	0.0120	0.0110	0.0110	0.0120	0.0130	0.0100	**0.0150**	15.38%
	N@30 ↑	0.0061	0.0067	0.0053	0.0045	0.0042	0.0038	**0.0084**	25.37%
	H@50 ↑	0.0140	0.0140	0.0120	0.0150	0.0160	0.0130	**0.0180**	12.50%
	N@50 ↑	0.0072	0.0073	0.0055	0.0050	0.0048	0.0049	**0.0090**	23.29%
	OR ↓	0.2440	0.1882	0.2678	0.2670	0.1610	0.1590	**0.1652**	-3.90%
	Div ↑	0.0054	0.0057	0.0047	0.0055	0.0052	0.0058	**0.0059**	1.72%
	Gini ↓	0.4903	0.4542	0.4886	0.4771	0.4792	0.4418	**0.4320**	2.22%
	Ent ↑	7.3987	7.8173	7.1624	7.3643	7.8004	**8.0445**	8.0071	-0.46%
Kindle	H@30 ↑	0.0260	0.0310	0.0250	0.0300	0.0290	0.0190	**0.0360**	16.13%
	N@30 ↑	0.0156	0.0167	0.0166	0.0166	0.0163	0.0111	**0.0192**	14.97%
	H@50 ↑	0.0360	0.0390	0.0360	0.0400	0.0390	0.0210	**0.0420**	5.00%
	N@50 ↑	0.0179	0.0189	0.0182	0.0192	0.0188	0.0164	**0.0204**	6.25%
	OR ↓	0.0250	0.0240	0.0330	0.0220	0.0300	0.0870	**0.0200**	9.09%
	Div ↑	0.0132	0.0133	0.0126	0.0130	0.0121	0.0108	**0.0134**	0.75%
	Gini ↓	0.1685	0.1634	0.2008	0.1791	0.2273	0.3078	**0.1607**	1.65%
	Ent ↑	9.5053	9.5232	9.3842	9.4775	9.2950	8.8058	**9.5382**	0.16%
Toys	H@30 ↑	0.0140	0.0160	0.0130	0.0120	0.0140	0.0160	**0.0170**	6.25%
	N@30 ↑	0.0041	0.0046	0.0044	0.0041	0.0046	0.0052	**0.0055**	5.77%
	H@50 ↑	0.0140	0.0160	0.0130	0.0150	0.0170	0.0180	**0.0190**	5.56%
	N@50 ↑	0.0041	0.0046	0.0044	0.0045	0.0054	**0.0059**	**0.0059**	0.00%
	OR ↓	0.0942	0.0482	0.0935	0.0582	0.0682	0.1777	**0.0262**	45.64%
	Div ↑	0.0044	0.0048	0.0044	0.0046	0.0047	0.0041	**0.0050**	4.17%
	Gini ↓	0.2720	0.1972	0.2700	0.2306	0.2226	0.3187	**0.1704**	13.59%
	Ent ↑	8.9390	9.3453	8.9499	9.1962	9.2020	8.3886	**9.4910**	1.56%

over-exposure because they treat items as isolated entities, ignoring the underlying semantic topology. Conversely, decoding interventions like D3 aggressively enforce diversity, but at the cost of severe recommendation accuracy degradation. In contrast, **DeSP** effectively eliminating the semantic concentration toward popular items. Furthermore, macroscopic analysis (Fig. 3) confirms that **DeSP** substantially reduces head-item over-exposure and aligns long-tail recommendations with the ground truth, ultimately delivering a balanced, diverse, and highly accurate recommendation list.

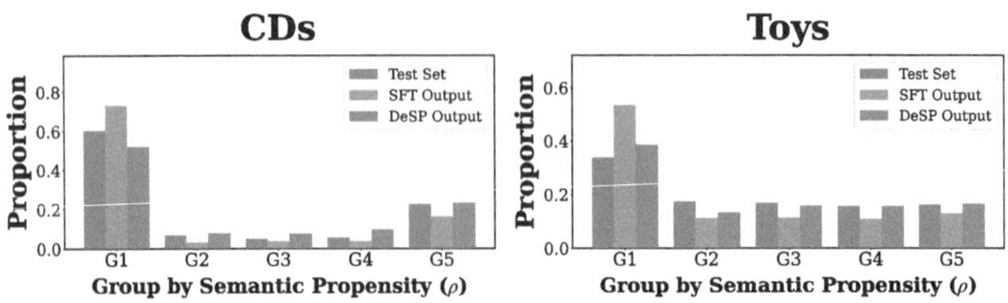

Fig. 3. Comparison of item distributions based on semantic propensity scores (ρ Sort). When items are re-grouped by our proposed semantic propensity ρ, a severe distributional skew re-emerges. This reveals the hidden Semantic Popularity Bias, where LLMs systematically over-recommend items within high-density semantic clusters anchored by popular items.

5.3 Ablation Study (RQ2)

As shown in Table 3, we perform the following ablation study to investigate the effects of each component: 1) "DeSP-L": We remove the lexical and collaborative features. 2) "DeSP-T": We remove the generative and collaborative features. 3) "DeSP-S": We remove the generative and lexical features. We can observe that:

1) Overall, removing any single semantic perspective degrades the balance between accuracy and debiasing. This demonstrates the importance of synergizing generative, lexical, and collaborative views to mitigate semantic popularity bias without sacrificing precision. 2) Using only DeSP-L maintains strong accuracy but yields suboptimal debiasing capability compared to the full model (e.g., OR_ratio of 0.0230 vs. 0.0200 on Kindle). This indicates that generative semantics alone cannot fully decouple semantic bias. 3) Relying purely on DeSP-T or DeSP-S exacerbates popularity bias, yielding higher OR_ratio and Gini scores than the baseline. This proves that relying only on surface-level lexical matching or isolated behavioral sequences actively amplifies existing data skews.

5.4 Impact of Hyperparameter (RQ3)

Figure 4 illustrates the impact of the retention weight λ and neighborhood size k on NDCG@20 for the CDs and Kindle datasets. Performance for both parameters generally exhibits an inverted U-shape. Specifically, the optimal λ peaks at 0.7 for CDs and 0.5 for Kindle, underscoring the necessity of balancing empirical popularity retention with semantic propagation. Similarly, the optimal k peaks at 15 and 10 for CDs and Kindle, respectively. Since the ideal λ and k vary depending on the dataset's specific semantic topology and sparsity, systematic tuning remains essential in practice to avoid suboptimal debiasing.

Table 3. Ablation study on the multi-view semantic graph construction across three datasets. **DeSP-L**, **DeSP-T**, and **DeSP-S** refer to variants using only LLM, TF-IDF, and SASRec semantic views, respectively. The best results in each metric are highlighted in **bold**.

Data	Method	Accuracy				Diversity			
		H@30 ↑	N@30 ↑	H@50 ↑	N@50 ↑	OR ↓	Div ↑	Gini ↓	Entroy ↑
CDs	SFT	0.0120	0.0061	0.0140	0.0072	0.2440	0.0054	0.4903	7.3987
	DeSP-L	0.0130	0.0070	0.0150	0.0078	0.1980	0.0056	0.4600	7.9302
	DeSP-T	0.0140	0.0075	0.0160	0.0082	0.1880	0.0057	0.4565	7.9745
	DeSP-S	0.0130	0.0072	0.0165	0.0080	0.1920	**0.0061**	0.4365	7.9575
	DeSP	**0.0150**	**0.0084**	**0.0180**	**0.0090**	**0.1652**	0.0059	**0.4320**	**8.0071**
Kindle	SFT	0.0260	0.0156	0.0360	0.0179	0.0250	0.0132	0.1685	9.5053
	DeSP-L	**0.0360**	0.0182	0.0410	0.0196	0.0230	0.0130	0.1650	9.5190
	DeSP-T	0.0320	0.0175	0.0390	0.0190	0.0290	0.0128	0.1916	9.4094
	DeSP-S	0.0340	0.0180	0.0400	0.0195	0.0300	0.0128	0.1888	9.4246
	DeSP	**0.0360**	**0.0192**	**0.0420**	**0.0204**	**0.0200**	**0.0134**	**0.1607**	**9.5382**
Toys	SFT	0.0140	0.0041	0.0140	0.0041	0.0942	0.0044	0.2720	8.9390
	DeSP-L	**0.0170**	0.0050	0.0180	0.0054	0.0700	0.0046	0.2400	9.1000
	DeSP-T	0.0160	0.0048	0.0160	0.0052	0.0600	0.0048	0.2200	8.9699
	DeSP-S	0.0150	0.0050	0.0170	0.0055	0.0824	0.0044	0.2579	9.0430
	DeSP	**0.0170**	**0.0055**	**0.0190**	**0.0059**	**0.0262**	**0.0050**	**0.1704**	**9.4910**

6 Related Work

Sequential Recommendation. Sequential recommendation aims to predict a user's next preferred item based on their historical interaction sequences [30,39]. Traditional approaches employ various sequence modeling architectures, with models like SASRec [15] achieving prominent success by using self-attention to capture complex sequential dependencies. Building upon these foundational ID-based paradigms, recent advancements seek to integrate richer side information to overcome inherent data sparsity. Recognizing this ability to capture temporal dynamics alongside textual features, most current LLM-based recommendation methods also inherently adopt this sequential modeling [37].

LLMs for Recommendation. Large Language Models (LLMs) are increasingly adopted in generative recommendation frameworks to comprehend rich contextual content and perform deep semantic reasoning [1,16,22,38]. To bridge the gap between general pre-training objectives and specific recommendation tasks, domain-specific fine-tuning is typically essential [20]. Given the immense parameter scale of modern LLMs, parameter-efficient fine-tuning techniques, such as Low-Rank Adaptation (LoRA), are frequently utilized to adapt these

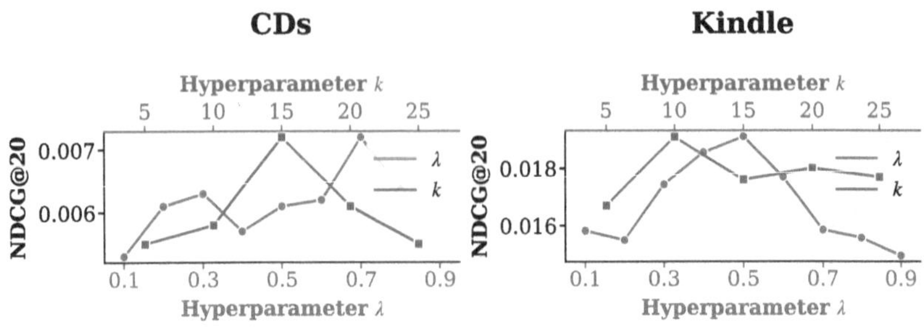

Fig. 4. Impact of the hyperparameter λ and k on the CDs and Kindle dataset.

models to recommendation contexts efficiently, reducing computational overhead while retaining strong semantic reasoning capabilities.

Bias in LLM-based Recommender Systems. Despite the advanced capabilities of Large Recommender Systems (LRS), existing research highlights the persistence of popularity and position biases [4,17,23]. Current approaches attempt to mitigate popularity bias by utilizing traditional Inverse Propensity Scoring (IPS) [14], token-wise re-weighting [26], or modern alignment techniques like Direct Preference Optimization (DPO) [28] to penalize overly popular items and directly optimize for unbiased user preferences [7,21]. However, these works largely overlook the semantic-driven nature of LLMs [18], often treating items as isolated entities rather than interconnected nodes. Consequently, they fail to address how popularity artifacts propagate through continuous generative semantic spaces, leaving a critical gap in fully debiasing LLM-based recommendations.

7 Conclusion

In this paper, We identify a novel challenge in LLM-based recommender systems, **Semantic Popularity Bias**, where empirical popularity propagates through the semantic space and leads to systematic over-recommendation of items related to popular ones. To address this, we propose **DeSP**, which builds a multi-view semantic graph and models popularity diffusion with a PageRank-based process to estimate true semantic propensities for self-normalized weighted fine-tuning. Experiments on three real-world datasets show that DeSP effectively mitigates this bias, achieving strong debiasing and diversity while improving recommendation accuracy.

Acknowledgments. This work is supported by the Zhejiang Province "JianBingLingYan+X" Research and Development Plan (2025C02020).

References

1. Bao, K., et alQ.: A bi-step grounding paradigm for large language models in recommendation systems (2023). https://arxiv.org/abs/2308.08434
2. Bao, K., Zhang, J., Zhang, Y., Huo, X., Chen, C., Feng, F.: Decoding matters: Addressing amplification bias and homogeneity issue in recommendations for large language models. In: Al-Onaizan, Y., Bansal, M., Chen, Y.N. (eds.) Proceedings of the 2024 Conference on Empirical Methods in Natural Language Processing, pp. 10540–10552. Association for Computational Linguistics, Miami, Florida, USA (2024). https://doi.org/10.18653/v1/2024.emnlp-main.589, https://aclanthology.org/2024.emnlp-main.589/
3. Brin, S., Page, L.: The anatomy of a large-scale hypertextual web search engine. In: Proceedings of the Seventh International Conference on World Wide Web 7, pp. 107–117. WWW7, Elsevier Science Publishers B. V., NLD (1998)
4. Chen, J., Dong, H., Wang, X., Feng, F., Wang, M., He, X.: Bias and debias in recommender system: A survey and future directions (2021). https://arxiv.org/abs/2010.03240
5. Cui, Y., et alC.: Hatllm: Hierarchical attention masking for enhanced collaborative modeling in llm-based recommendation (2025). https://arxiv.org/abs/2510.10955
6. Friedkin, N.E., Johnsen, E.C.: Social influence and opinions. J. Math. Sociol. **15**(3–4), 193–205 (1990). https://doi.org/10.1080/0022250X.1990.9990069
7. Gao, C., Chen, R., Yuan, S., Huang, K., Yu, Y., He, X.: Sprec: Self-play to debias llm-based recommendation. In: Proceedings of the ACM on Web Conference 2025, pp. 5075–5084. WWW '25, ACM (2025). https://doi.org/10.1145/3696410.3714524
8. Gao, C., et al.: Alleviating matthew effect of offline reinforcement learning in interactive recommendation. In: Proceedings of the 46th International ACM SIGIR Conference on Research and Development in Information Retrieval, pp. 238–248. SIGIR '23, ACM (2023). https://doi.org/10.1145/3539618.3591636
9. Gao, C., et al.: Cirs: Bursting filter bubbles by counterfactual interactive recommender system (2023). https://arxiv.org/abs/2204.01266
10. Gilotte, A., Calauzènes, C., Nedelec, T., Abraham, A., Dollé, S.: Offline a/b testing for recommender systems. In: Proceedings of the Eleventh ACM International Conference on Web Search and Data Mining, pp. 198–206. WSDM 2018, ACM (2018). https://doi.org/10.1145/3159652.3159687
11. Grattafiori, A., et al.: The llama 3 herd of models (2024). https://arxiv.org/abs/2407.21783
12. Hu, E.J., et al.: Lora: Low-rank adaptation of large language models (2021). https://arxiv.org/abs/2106.09685
13. Huang, X., et alE.: Wese: Weak exploration to strong exploitation for llm agents (2024). https://arxiv.org/abs/2404.07456
14. Jiang, M., et al.: Item-side fairness of large language model-based recommendation system. In: Proceedings of the ACM Web Conference 2024, pp. 4717–4726. WWW '24, Association for Computing Machinery, New York, NY, USA (2024). https://doi.org/10.1145/3589334.3648158
15. Kang, W.C., McAuley, J.: Self-attentive sequential recommendation. In: 2018 IEEE International Conference on Data Mining (ICDM), pp. 197–206 (2018). https://doi.org/10.1109/ICDM.2018.00035

16. Kim, S., Kang, H., Choi, S., Kim, D., Yang, M., Park, C.: Large language models meet collaborative filtering: An efficient all-round llm-based recommender system. In: Proceedings of the 30th ACM SIGKDD Conference on Knowledge Discovery and Data Mining, pp. 1395–1406. KDD '24, Association for Computing Machinery, New York, NY, USA (2024). https://doi.org/10.1145/3637528.3671931
17. Kolb, T.E.: Enhancing cross-domain recommender systems with llms: Evaluating bias and beyond-accuracy measures. In: Proceedings of the 18th ACM Conference on Recommender Systems, pp. 1388–1394. RecSys '24, Association for Computing Machinery, New York, NY, USA (2024). https://doi.org/10.1145/3640457.3688027
18. Lee, D.H., et al.: Star: A simple training-free approach for recommendations using large language models (2025). https://arxiv.org/abs/2410.16458
19. Li, B., Zhou, H., He, J., Wang, M., Yang, Y., Li, L.: On the sentence embeddings from pre-trained language models. In: Webber, B., Cohn, T., He, Y., Liu, Y. (eds.) Proceedings of the 2020 Conference on Empirical Methods in Natural Language Processing (EMNLP), pp. 9119–9130. Association for Computational Linguistics, Online (2020). https://doi.org/10.18653/v1/2020.emnlp-main.733, https://aclanthology.org/2020.emnlp-main.733/
20. Li, X., Chen, C., Zhao, X., Zhang, Y., Xing, C.: E4srec: An elegant effective efficient extensible solution of large language models for sequential recommendation (2023). https://arxiv.org/abs/2312.02443
21. Liao, J., et al.: Rosepo: Aligning llm-based recommenders with human values (2024). https://arxiv.org/abs/2410.12519
22. Liao, J., et al.: Llara: Large language-recommendation assistant. In: Proceedings of the 47th International ACM SIGIR Conference on Research and Development in Information Retrieval, pp. 1785–1795. SIGIR '24, Association for Computing Machinery, New York, NY, USA (2024). https://doi.org/10.1145/3626772.3657690
23. Lichtenberg, J.M., Buchholz, A., Schwöbel, P.: Large language models as recommender systems: A study of popularity bias (2024). https://www.amazon.science/publications/large-language-models-as-recommender-systems-a-study-of-popularity-bias
24. Lin, J., et al.: How can recommender systems benefit from large language models: A survey. ACM Trans. Inf. Syst. **43**(2) (2025). https://doi.org/10.1145/3678004
25. Lin, S., et al.: How do recommendation models amplify popularity bias? an analysis from the spectral perspective. In: Proceedings of the Eighteenth ACM International Conference on Web Search and Data Mining, pp. 659–668. WSDM '25, ACM (2025). https://doi.org/10.1145/3701551.3703579
26. Lu, S., Man, Z., Luo, F., Wu, J.: Dual debiasing in llm-based recommendation. In: Proceedings of the 48th International ACM SIGIR Conference on Research and Development in Information Retrieval, pp. 2685–2689. SIGIR '25, Association for Computing Machinery, New York, NY, USA (2025). https://doi.org/10.1145/3726302.3730181
27. Page, L., Brin, S., Motwani, R., Winograd, T.: The pagerank citation ranking: Bringing order to the web. In: The Web Conference (1999). https://api.semanticscholar.org/CorpusID:1508503
28. Rafailov, R., Sharma, A., Mitchell, E., Ermon, S., Manning, C.D., Finn, C.: Direct preference optimization: your language model is secretly a reward model. In: Proceedings of the 37th International Conference on Neural Information Processing Systems. NIPS '23, Curran Associates Inc, Red Hook, NY, USA (2023)

29. Schnabel, T., Swaminathan, A., Singh, A., Chandak, N., Joachims, T.: Recommendations as treatments: debiasing learning and evaluation. In: Proceedings of the 33rd International Conference on International Conference on Machine Learning - Volume 48, pp. 1670–1679. ICML'16, JMLR.org (2016)
30. Shi, T., et al.: Preliminary study on incremental learning for large language model-based recommender systems. In: Proceedings of the 33rd ACM International Conference on Information and Knowledge Management, pp. 4051–4055. CIKM '24, Association for Computing Machinery, New York, NY, USA (2024). https://doi.org/10.1145/3627673.3679922
31. Shi, W., et al.: Large language models are learnable planners for long-term recommendation. In: Proceedings of the 47th International ACM SIGIR Conference on Research and Development in Information Retrieval, pp. 1893–1903. SIGIR 2024, ACM (2024). https://doi.org/10.1145/3626772.3657683
32. Shi, W., et al.: Large language models are learnable planners for long-term recommendation. In: Proceedings of the 47th International ACM SIGIR Conference on Research and Development in Information Retrieval, pp. 1893–1903. SIGIR 2024, ACM (2024). https://doi.org/10.1145/3626772.3657683
33. Sparck Jones, K.: A statistical interpretation of term specificity and its application in retrieval, pp. 132–142. Taylor Graham Publishing, GBR (1988)
34. Su, Y., Wang, L., Santacatterina, M., Joachims, T.: Cab: Continuous adaptive blending estimator for policy evaluation and learning (2019). https://arxiv.org/abs/1811.02672
35. Swaminathan, A., Joachims, T.: Counterfactual risk minimization: Learning from logged bandit feedback (2015). https://arxiv.org/abs/1502.02362
36. Swaminathan, A., Joachims, T.: The self-normalized estimator for counterfactual learning. In: Proceedings of the 29th International Conference on Neural Information Processing Systems - Volume 2, pp. 3231–3239. NIPS'15, MIT Press, Cambridge, MA, USA (2015)
37. Wang, B., et al.: Llm4dsr: Leveraging large language model for denoising sequential recommendation (2025). https://arxiv.org/abs/2408.08208
38. Wang, W., Lin, X., Feng, F., He, X., Chua, T.S.: Generative recommendation: Towards next-generation recommender paradigm (2024). https://arxiv.org/abs/2304.03516
39. Xi, Y., et al.: Towards open-world recommendation with knowledge augmentation from large language models. In: Proceedings of the 18th ACM Conference on Recommender Systems, pp. 12–22. RecSys '24, Association for Computing Machinery, New York, NY, USA (2024). https://doi.org/10.1145/3640457.3688104
40. Xv, G., Lin, C., Li, H., Su, J., Ye, W., Chen, Y.: Neutralizing popularity bias in recommendation models. In: Proceedings of the 45th International ACM SIGIR Conference on Research and Development in Information Retrieval, pp. 2623–2628. SIGIR '22, Association for Computing Machinery, New York, NY, USA (2022). https://doi.org/10.1145/3477495.3531907
41. Yang, Z., et al.: A generic learning framework for sequential recommendation with distribution shifts. In: Proceedings of the 46th International ACM SIGIR Conference on Research and Development in Information Retrieval, pp. 331–340. SIGIR '23, Association for Computing Machinery, New York, NY, USA (2023). https://doi.org/10.1145/3539618.3591624
42. Zhang, J., Xie, R., Hou, Y., Zhao, X., Lin, L., Wen, J.R.: Recommendation as instruction following: A large language model empowered recommendation approach. ACM Trans. Inf. Syst. **43**(5) (2025). https://doi.org/10.1145/3708882

43. Zhang, Y., Feng, F., Zhang, J., Bao, K., Wang, Q., He, X.: Collm: Integrating collaborative embeddings into large language models for recommendation. IEEE Trans. Knowl. Data Eng. **37**(5), 2329–2340 (2025). https://doi.org/10.1109/TKDE.2025.3540912
44. Zhu, Y., Wu, L., Guo, Q., Hong, L., Li, J.: Collaborative large language model for recommender systems. In: Proceedings of the ACM Web Conference 2024, pp. 3162–3172. WWW '24, ACM (2024). https://doi.org/10.1145/3589334.3645347

Biomedical AI

Hybrid-IR: Dual-Path Hybrid Retrieval with Iterative Reasoning for Complex Medical Question Answering

Sheng Wan[1], Jiahui Zhang[1], Zicheng Zhao[2], and Shougang Ren[1](✉)

[1] College of Artificial Intelligence, Nanjing Agricultural University, Nanjing, China
zhangjiah@stu.njau.edu.cn, rensg@njau.edu.cn

[2] School of Computer Science and Engineering, Nanjing University of Science and Technology, Nanjing, China
zicheng.zhao@njust.edu.cn

Abstract. Large language models (LLMs) have shown promising performance across a wide range of biomedical applications, including medical question answering (QA), yet they remain prone to hallucinations and outdated knowledge. Although retrieval-augmented generation (RAG) can alleviate this issue by incorporating external documents, there still exist two fundamental limitations. First, medical knowledge is often fragmented across documents, while most RAG methods rely on a single retrieval path, which makes it challenging to jointly preserve fine-grained semantic information and structured global associations. Second, static retrieval strategies are typically insufficient to support deep reasoning that is important in complex medical QA. In this paper, we present a dual-path retrieval framework with an iterative retrieval–reasoning mechanism termed "Hybrid-IR" for complex medical QA. The proposed Hybrid-IR integrates graph-based retrieval for exploration of structured knowledge and dense retrieval for fine-grained semantic matching. Moreover, the reasoning trajectory can be progressively refined through an iterative retrieve-reason loop. Experiments on three widely used medical QA benchmarks demonstrate the effectiveness of our Hybrid-IR.

Keywords: Large Language Models · Retrieval-Augmented Generation · Medical Question Answering · Knowledge Retrieval

1 Introduction

Large language models (LLMs) [20,38] have demonstrated significant potential across a wide range of biomedical applications, particularly in medical question answering (QA) tasks that require deep reasoning over specialized domain knowledge [25,27,28]. Despite their strong performance, deploying LLMs in complex medical scenarios remains challenging. One major limitation is that LLMs are prone to generating hallucinations that appear plausible yet lack factual basis [6].

M. Ceci et al. (Eds.): ECML PKDD 2026, LNAI 16941, pp. 499–515, 2027.
https://doi.org/10.1007/978-3-032-37654-1_29

In addition, the reliance of LLMs on static pre-training data restricts their ability to incorporate the latest medical knowledge and clinical guidelines [17]. As a result, the reliability of LLM-based medical QA systems remains inadequate.

Retrieval-augmented generation (RAG) [14] offers an effective solution to reduce hallucinations by integrating external documents into the generation process and providing strict generation constraints, which enables LLMs to answer questions with up-to-date knowledge. However, applying RAG to the biomedical domain presents unique challenges. One key challenge is that existing RAG methods typically rely on a single retrieval path, either vector-based or graph-based, which makes it difficult to simultaneously preserve fine-grained semantic information and structured global associations [2]. Vector-based retrieval methods typically encode documents as isolated embeddings that capture semantic similarity but fail to explicitly model the structured relationships among biomedical entities [12,17]. This fragmented knowledge representation severely constrains the ability to synthesize cross-document insights, particularly when evidence is distributed across diverse sources in the biomedical domain. Differently, graph-based retrieval methods (*e.g.*, GraphRAG [4]) introduce structured graphs to model dependencies among entities, which enhances the ability to capture global contextual relationships [23,31]. However, the graph construction process often fails to preserve fine-grained textual semantics, which may reduce the precision of evidence grounded in original medical documents. In addition to this limitation, most existing methods rely on static retrieval strategies that perform document retrieval only once before the generation process [37]. Such design is often insufficient for complex biomedical questions that require multi-step reasoning. Intermediate reasoning steps often reveal additional information needs, yet the decoupling between retrieval and reasoning prevents the system from dynamically refining its retrieval focus. Consequently, static retrieval may fail to obtain the evidence required for subsequent reasoning steps, and thus resulting in incomplete evidence chains [29,37].

To address these challenges, we propose a new method termed "Hybrid-IR" that enhances RAG for biomedical QA through a dual-path iterative reasoning-retrieval scheme. Specifically, we design a KG indexing (KG-index) module that constructs a structured cross-document index from extracted triples, which explicitly links dispersed medical entities and relations across documents. In addition, a document layer is introduced to align entity nodes with their source document chunks through provenance relations, which enables seamless transitions from abstract entity-level reasoning to grounded textual evidence. In parallel, dense retrieval is devised to capture unstructured fine-grained semantic details within the original text, which compensates for information that may be lost during graph construction. To enable deep and comprehensive reasoning for complex biomedical questions, we further integrate dual-path retrieval into an iterative framework, which enables a continuous "retrieve–reason–retrieve" loop. This mechanism enables cumulative evidence synthesis and dynamic refinement of reasoning trajectories across reasoning steps. By leveraging knowledge acquired in reasoning rounds to guide subsequent retrieval, the system effectively optimizes the reasoning path toward target solutions, thereby overcoming the limitations of static evidence aggregation in complex multi-hop tasks. We evaluate the proposed Hybrid-IR using three closed-book medical QA benchmarks, where no oracle documents are provided. Experimental results show that Hybrid-IR improves the average accuracy of strong backbone LLMs, including Llama-3-8B-Instruct [1] and GPT-4o-mini [20], by up to 10 percentage points. The contributions are summarized as follows:

- We propose a dual-path retrieval framework that jointly captures fine-grained semantic information and structured relational knowledge, which enables comprehensive evidence aggregation for complex medical QA.
- We design an iterative reasoning-retrieval mechanism that progressively accumulates evidence and dynamically refines reasoning trajectories through multiple rounds of "retrieval-reasoning-retrieval".
- Extensive experiments across three medical QA benchmarks demonstrate the effectiveness of Hybrid-IR, which achieves consistent performance gains across both open-source and commercial LLM backbones.

2 Related Work

2.1 Retrieval-Augmented Generation

RAG integrates external knowledge into LLMs to facilitate generation by retrieving relevant documents. Early works typically rely on pre-trained dense embedding models to encode chunked documents as discrete vectors, followed by retrieval and reranking based on similarity between queries and documents (*e.g.* Contriever, Colbert) [8,13]. Despite their efficiency and generalizability, treating documents as independent retrieval units makes it difficult to capture the underlying semantic relationships between them. Recent methods begin to introduce structured graphs to explicitly model knowledge relations. Specifically, distinct graph construction paradigms have emerged to model knowledge at different levels of granularity [16,39,40]. For instance, early methods like KGP [33] use hyperlinks and KNN similarity, but miss semantic associations. RAPTOR [24] builds hierarchical trees via recursive summarization. GraphRAG [4] uses LLMs to extract entities and relations, forming hierarchical graphs with community detection and summarization. HippoRAG [9] and HippoRAG 2 [5] apply OpenIE to induce KGs that capture factual relationships. Building upon these foundations, advanced approaches such as G-reasoner [18] propose refined multi-layered graph construction strategies, organizing knowledge into four hierarchical levels (*e.g.*, entity, cluster, category, and document levels) to manage logical dependencies [32]. Beyond structural construction, the effective utilization of these graph-structured sources is crucial for bridging the gap between structural context and retrieval precision. HippoRAG and HippoRAG 2 employ a personalized PageRank algorithm on graphs to identify relevant knowledge, thereby strengthening multi-hop reasoning capability. Similarly, GFM-RAG [17] introduces a graph foundation model based on Graph Neural Networks (GNNs [35,39,40]), which enables robust reasoning across diverse datasets.

2.2 Retrieval-Augmented Generation for Medical Question Answering

Biomedical QA poses additional challenges due to specialized terminology and the need to integrate evidence scattered across multiple scientific documents. Researchers have proposed several retrieval methods to enhance biomedical information retrieval and RAG frameworks. For instance, MedCPT [11] is a dense embedding retriever and reranker specifically customized for the biomedical field. It addresses the scarcity of query-article annotation data in the biomedical domain by leveraging large-scale user click logs from PubMed. Beyond domain-specific retrieval models, several RAG frameworks have been developed for biomedical QA. The MedRAG toolkit [36] provides a comprehensive benchmark for evaluating RAG systems in the biomedical domain. It adopts a retrieval strategy that combines sparse and dense retrieval to extract relevant documents from the MedCorp corpus. Similarly, MedGraphRAG [34] constructs triple-based KGs to model intricate relationships among knowledge entities and employs U-retrieval techniques to enhance evidence retrieval efficiency. To address multi-step reasoning requirements in biomedical QA, i-MedRAG [37] progressively expands evidence through an iterative retrieval mechanism, enabling the model to gather additional context for multi-step QA tasks. However, most existing methods rely primarily on a single retrieval paradigm. Although MedRAG combines sparse and dense retrievers, it does not explicitly exploit structured relationships among documents. Conversely, MedGraphRAG focuses on structured graph evidence but may overlook fine-grained textual semantics. Furthermore, although iterative retrieval has been explored (e.g., i-MedRAG), it typically operates as a standalone evidence expansion loop decoupled from the LLM's intermediate reasoning states. To cope with issues, we propose a dual-path retrieval framework with an iterative retrieval–reasoning mechanism for complex biomedical QA. Unlike existing RAG frameworks that rely on a single retrieval paradigm, Hybrid-IR integrates the two paradigms within an iterative retrieval-reasoning mechanism, which enables reasoning feedback to dynamically refine hybrid evidence retrieval.

3 Methodology

This section details our proposed Hybrid-IR (see Fig. 1). Specifically, we illustrate the critical components of Hybrid-IR by explaining the offline hybrid index construction (see Sect. 3.1), presenting online dual-path retrieval (see Sect. 3.2), and elaborating iterative retrieval-reasoning for QA (see Sect. 3.3).

3.1 Offline Hybrid Index Construction

KGs explicitly model dependencies among entities, enabling structured cross-document indexing across multiple sources. Motivated by these advantages, we construct the knowledge-graph-based index to explicitly organize and connect dispersed medical evidence across documents. Given a document collection

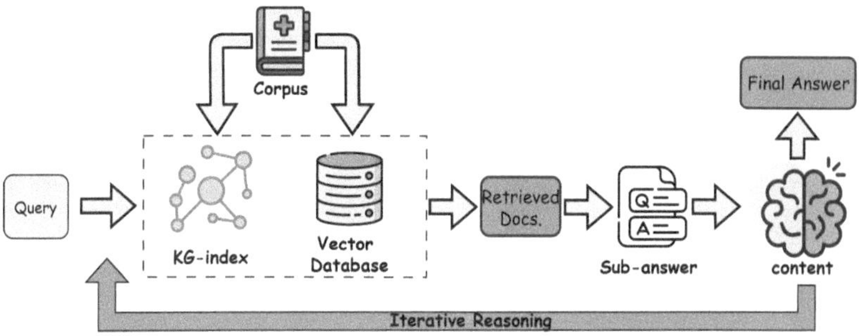

Fig. 1. The overall architecture of the proposed Hybrid-IR framework.

$\mathcal{D} = \{d_1, d_2, \ldots, d_n\}$, we first perform medical named entity recognition and relation extraction on the documents to extract entities $\mathcal{E}$ and relations $\mathcal{R}_{\text{ent}}$, forming triples $\mathcal{T} \subseteq \mathcal{E} \times \mathcal{R}_{\text{ent}} \times \mathcal{E}$. Such a process can be achieved by existing open information extraction (OpenIE) tools [21,41]. These triples form the initial knowledge layer of the KG-index. To mitigate homonymy and semantic ambiguity in medical texts, we use the Contriever-MSMARCO [8] to conduct the entity resolution by computing pairwise cosine similarity between entity representations. Undirected synonymy relations are introduced between entity pairs whose similarity exceeds a threshold τ, resulting in an augmented triple set $\mathcal{T}^+$. This augmentation enriches the knowledge layer by connecting highly similar entities that may appear across different documents. We then build an entity-to-document inverted index $\mathbf{M} \in \{0,1\}^{|\mathcal{E}| \times |\mathcal{D}|}$, where $\mathbf{M}_{ij} = 1$ indicates that entity $e_i \in \mathcal{E}$ is mentioned in document d_j, and 0 otherwise. To enable explicit provenance tracking of evidence, each entity is linked to the document chunk from which it is extracted, forming a document layer parallel to the knowledge layer. In addition, we introduce a document layer to capture inter-document relations (*e.g.*, content similarity or citation links). Specifically, we construct a heterogeneous KG, $G = G_{\text{ent}} \cup G_{\text{link}} \cup G_{\text{doc}}$. The entity-level subgraph G_{ent} consists of entity–entity relational triples derived from the original and augmented triple sets,

$$G_{\text{ent}} = \{(e_i, r_{\text{ent}}, e_j) \mid (e_i, r_{\text{ent}}, e_j) \in \mathcal{T} \cup \mathcal{T}^+\}, \tag{1}$$

while the entity–document linking subgraph G_{link} is constructed based on the entity-to-document inverted index,

$$G_{\text{link}} = \{(e_i, r_{\text{link}}, d_k) \mid \mathbf{M}_{ik} = 1\}. \tag{2}$$

In addition, G_{doc} encodes inter-document relations, where an edge is added between two documents if they are related by content similarity or citation links. Content similarity edges are constructed based on cosine similarity between document embeddings. Further implementation details and statistical characteristics of the KG-index construction are provided in the supplementary material.

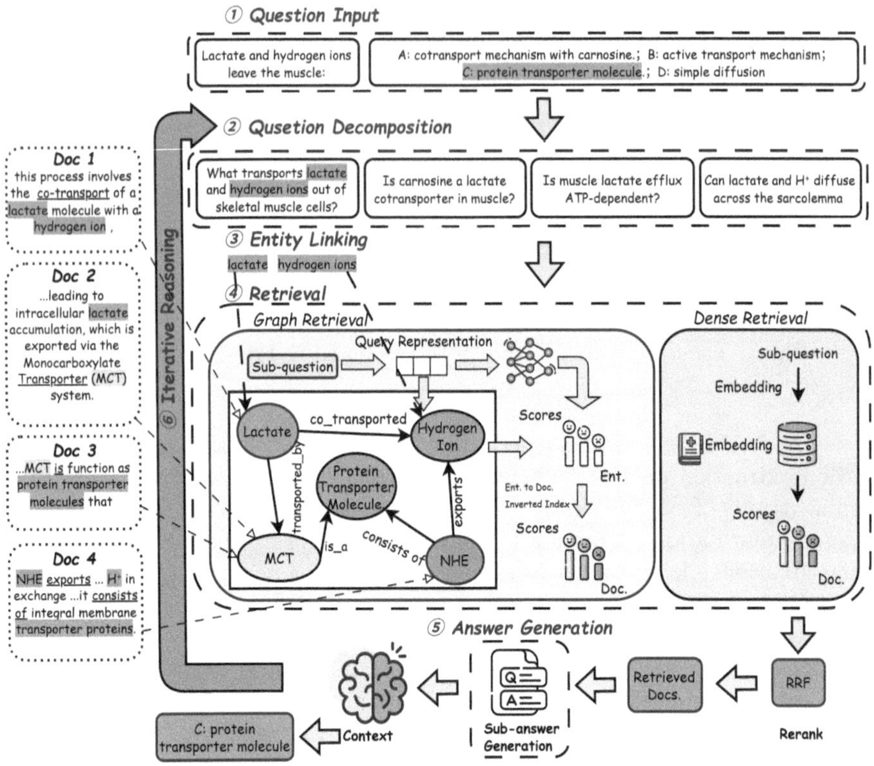

Fig. 2. Overview of online dual-path retrieval and iterative retrieval-reasoning. Given a complex medical question, the model first decomposes it into a set of sub-questions. For each sub-question, evidence is retrieved in parallel via graph retrieval, which explicitly models dependencies among entities, and Dense Retrieval, which captures fine-grained semantic information from unstructured text. The retrieved results from both paths are then fused using Reciprocal Rank Fusion (RRF) [3] to generate sub-answers, which are incorporated into the context to guide subsequent reasoning iterations.

In parallel with the KG indexing, vector indexing serves as a semantic complement that preserves fine-grained textual evidence which is difficult to fully represent with structured triples. Here, we encode each document d_i into a dense vector $\mathbf{d}_i = \phi(d_i)$ using a pre-trained embedding model $\phi(\cdot)$ (*i.e.*, MedCPT [11]), and store all vectors in a vector database for efficient similarity search.

3.2 Online Dual-Path Retrieval

Based on the offline-constructed KG and vector index, the framework performs online retrieval through a dual-path mechanism, as illustrated in Fig. 2. The key intuition behind this design is that graph-based retrieval and dense retrieval capture complementary aspects of relevance. Specifically, graph retrieval exploits structured relations among biomedical entities to propagate query relevance across graph, while dense retrieval focuses on semantic similarity between the query and textual documents. By combining these two paradigms, the system can leverage both global structural knowledge and fine-grained semantic information. Given a medical question Q, we decompose it into a set of sub-questions for retrieval. Specifically, we leverage the Large Language Model (ϕ_{LLM}) to perform this decomposition. Instructed by a tailored prompt, ϕ_{LLM} breaks down the multi-hop question Q into m distinct, simpler sub-questions. This decomposition helps isolate different pieces of information required to answer the original question. For each sub-question q, graph-based retrieval and dense vector retrieval are performed in parallel. To be concrete, a one-shot prompt is first used to extract a set of query entities, denoted as $\mathcal{C}_q = \{c_1, c_2, \ldots, c_k\}$. Each query entity c_i is encoded into a dense vector $\mathbf{c}_i$ using an embedding model (*i.e.*, Contriever-MSMARCO). We then align each c_i to the most similar entity $e \in \mathcal{E}$ in the previously constructed KG G based on cosine similarity between embeddings. Accordingly, the aligned entities for sub-question q are defined as $\mathcal{E}_q = \{e_1, e_2, \ldots, e_k\}$ with

$$e_i = \arg\max_{e \in \mathcal{E}} \frac{\mathbf{c}_i \cdot \mathbf{e}}{\|\mathbf{c}_i\| \, \|\mathbf{e}\|}, \tag{3}$$

where $\mathbf{e}$ denotes the embedding of e. We refer to this embedding-based alignment between query entities and graph entities as entity linking, which allows flexible matching between query mentions and KG entities without relying on predefined ontology mappings. This step effectively bridges natural language queries and structured knowledge representations, enabling the graph retriever to operate on semantically aligned entities.

Subsequently, we employ a graph foundation model-based retriever GFM-RAG-8M [17] to propagate query relevance via message passing. By leveraging the capability of GNNs to model structured dependencies, the retriever can propagate relevance signals from the aligned entities to their neighboring entities and associated documents in the KG. This process allows the system to capture indirect or multi-hop relations among biomedical concepts, which are common in clinical knowledge bases [15,19]. As a result, we obtain a normalized relevance score distribution over entities and documents in the KG. The relevance scores of entity nodes are then mapped to documents using the entity-to-document inverted index $\mathbf{M}$. Finally, the graph retrieval score for each document (*i.e.*, $S_{\text{graph}}(d_i)$), is computed by aggregating the relevance probabilities of its associated entities. Meanwhile, the sub-question q is encoded into a dense vector $\mathbf{q} = \phi(q)$. Afterwards, we compute the cosine similarity between the query vector and each document vector to obtain the dense retrieval score:

$$S_{\text{vec}}(d_i) = \frac{\mathbf{q} \cdot \mathbf{d}_i}{\|\mathbf{q}\| \, \|\mathbf{d}_i\|}. \tag{4}$$

To jointly exploit structural information from graph-based retrieval and semantic relevance from dense retrieval, we adopt Reciprocal Rank Fusion (RRF) to aggregate the results of the two paths. RRF is adopted as it provides a robust rank-based fusion strategy that does not require score normalization across heterogeneous retrieval models. The final relevance score of document d_i is computed as

$$S_{\text{final}}(d_i) = \frac{1}{\eta + \text{rank}_{\text{graph}}(d_i)} + \frac{1}{\eta + \text{rank}_{\text{vec}}(d_i)}, \tag{5}$$

where $\text{rank}_{\text{graph}}(d_i)$ and $\text{rank}_{\text{vec}}(d_i)$ denote the ranking positions of document d_i in the ranked lists produced by graph-based retrieval and dense retrieval, respectively, and η is a smoothing constant. Documents are ranked according to S_{final}, and the top-k documents are returned as initial evidence for subsequent reasoning.

3.3 Iterative Retrieval-Reasoning for Question Answering

For complex medical QA, relying on a single retrieval step is often insufficient, as the system may fail to gather all relevant information at once. Moreover, retrieval and reasoning are inherently complementary: intermediate reasoning results can reveal missing knowledge and guide subsequent retrieval, while newly retrieved evidence further supports deeper reasoning. Therefore, an iterative retrieval–reasoning process is necessary to gradually accumulate evidence and refine the reasoning path. To address this limitation, we embed dual-path retrieval within an LLM-driven iterative retrieval-reasoning framework, which enables the knowledge acquired in previous rounds to explicitly guide subsequent retrieval and reasoning steps. Specifically, at the t-th reasoning round, the model maintains a history state $\mathcal{H}_t = \{Q, \mathcal{X}_1, \mathcal{X}_2, ..., \mathcal{X}_{t-1}\}$, which consists of the original question Q and all previously generated sub-question–answer pairs $\{\mathcal{X}_1, \mathcal{X}_2, ..., \mathcal{X}_{t-1}\}$. Each pair is defined as $\mathcal{X}_i = \{(q_{i,j}, a_{i,j}) \mid j = 1, \ldots, m\}$, where $q_{i,j}$ denotes the j-th sub-question generated at the i-th reasoning round and $a_{i,j}$ represents the corresponding sub-answer produced for $q_{i,j}$. Based on $\mathcal{H}_t$, the LLM analyzes the current reasoning context and identifies remaining knowledge gaps before producing a new set of sub-questions $\{q_{t,1}, q_{t,2}, \ldots, q_{t,m}\}$. These sub-questions aim to explore unexplored aspects of the problem and retrieve additional evidence required for answering the original query. Crucially, the initial question decomposition described in Sect. 3.2 is fundamentally a unified special case of this iterative mechanism at the first round ($t = 1$), where the history state is empty (i.e., $\mathcal{H}_1 = \{Q\}$). In this bootstrap step, the decomposition focuses on breaking down the global structure of Q. In all subsequent rounds ($t > 1$), as $\mathcal{H}_t$ accumulates evidence, the sub-question generation dynamically shifts to a gap-filling strategy based on the identified missing knowledge. For each sub-question $q_{t,j}$, we perform the dual-path retrieval process described in Sect. 3.2 to collect relevant evidence and generate a corresponding sub-answer $a_{t,j}$. The newly obtained sub-question–answer pairs are then incorporated into the history state to form $\mathcal{H}_{t+1}$, which serves as the context for the next reasoning round. Through this iterative process, the system gradually expands its evidence pool and refines the reasoning trajectory. The reasoning process continues until a predefined maximum number of reasoning rounds T is reached. Finally, the LLM

Algorithm 1. Proposed Hybrid-IR Framework

Require: Medical question Q; LLM ϕ_{LLM}; graph index G; vector index V; medical corpus $\mathcal{D}$; maximum number of reasoning rounds T; number of sub-questions generated at each reasoning round m.
Ensure: Final answer.
Initialize the reasoning history $\mathcal{H}_1 \leftarrow \{Q\}$
for $t = 1, 2, \ldots, T$ **do**
  Generate sub-questions $\{q_{t,1}, \ldots, q_{t,m}\}$ using ϕ_{LLM} given $\mathcal{H}_t$.
  for $j = 1, 2, \ldots, m$ **do**
    Calculate graph retrieval scores S_{graph} based on GFM-RAG-8M.
    Calculate dense retrieval scores S_{vec} via the dense retriever.
    Obtain the final scores S_{final} based on Eq. (5).
    Retrieve top-k documents according to S_{final}.
    Generate sub-answer $a_{t,j}$ based on the sub-question $q_{t,j}$ and the retrieved documents.
    Update the history $\mathcal{H}_t \leftarrow \mathcal{H}_t \cup \{(q_{t,j}, a_{t,j})\}$.
  end for
  Set $\mathcal{H}_{t+1} \leftarrow \mathcal{H}_t$.
end for
Generate the final answer based on $\mathcal{H}_T$ and ϕ_{LLM}.
return the final answer.

integrates the final history state $\mathcal{H}_T$ to generate the answer to the original question. The overall framework of the proposed Hybrid-IR approach is summarized in Algorithm 1.

4 Experiments

In this section, we conduct extensive experiments to evaluate the effectiveness of the proposed Hybrid-IR framework for medical QA. We compare Hybrid-IR with a range of strong retrieval-augmented baseline methods on multiple medical QA benchmarks, and further analyze the contribution of each component through ablation studies and case analysis.

4.1 Experimental Setup

Dataset. We conducted experiments on three widely used medical QA datasets, all of which contain complex biomedical questions that often require multi-step reasoning across multiple pieces of medical knowledge. Specifically, MedQA [10] consists of USMLE-style questions selected by medical examination experts from multiple medical question banks, many of which involve clinically complex scenarios that require integrating diverse medical concepts. MedMCQA [22] contains medical questions from two Indian examination bodies. MMLU-Med [7] is a subset of the MMLU [7] dataset, which includes questions from six biomedical subjects, namely clinical knowledge, medical genetics, anatomy, specialty medicine, college biology, and college medicine. All these datasets contain multiple-choice questions with four answer options and cover biomedical knowledge ranging from high school to professional medical levels. Following previous works [26,36,37], we evaluate our method on the full development set of each dataset. For retrieval, we use the Textbooks corpus [10], which comprises 18 authoritative medical textbooks commonly used as essential reference materials for the United States Medical Licensing Examination (USMLE) [30].

Evaluation Protocol. Our experiments are organized into two parts, *i.e.*, baseline methods without retrieval, which evaluates the intrinsic zero-shot reasoning capabilities of LLMs without access to external corpora, and retrieval-augmented baseline methods, where external knowledge is retrieved to assist the answer generation process. In the non-retrieval setting, we evaluated the zero-shot reasoning capabilities of the open-source LLM Meta-Llama-3-8B-Instruct [1] and the commercial LLM GPT-4o-mini [20]. Meta-Llama-3-8B-Instruct represents a state-of-the-art open-source model at a comparable scale, and is referred to as Llama-3-8B for simplicity. GPT-4o-mini is a cost-effective variant of the latest closed-source LLM produced by OpenAI, which exhibits performance comparable to GPT-4 across multiple benchmarks. In the retrieval-augmented setting, these two models are used as backbone LLMs and are integrated with RAG-based methods to evaluate whether the proposed Hybrid-IR framework can further enhance performance without task-specific fine-tuning. Following prior studies on medical QA, we report the answer accuracy as the primary evaluation metric, which is defined as the proportion of questions for which the model selects the correct option among the four candidates.

Baseline Methods. To validate the effectiveness of Hybrid-IR, we compare it with a set of representative baseline methods. All comparative experiments are performed using the two aforementioned backbone LLMs under the same evaluation protocol. MedCPT [11] is a retriever pre-trained using user search logs from PubMed. MedRAG [36] employs a hybrid retrieval strategy that combines multiple sparse and dense retrievers to collect candidate evidence from the MedCorp corpus, followed by reranking using Reciprocal Rank Fusion (RRF) [3]. HippoRAG [9] leverages a hippocampus-inspired KG to enable multi-hop reasoning over entity relationships. GFM-RAG [17] incorporates graph-based message passing over a KG to model dependencies among entities and performs structured evidence retrieval. MedGraphRAG [34] constructs a medical KG to retrieve structured evidence from biomedical literature. i-MedRAG [37] introduces an iterative retrieval strategy that progressively refines retrieved evidence across multiple reasoning steps.

Implementation Details. In the KG-index construction phase, we use Llama-3-8B with the OpenIE prompts described in HippoRAG [9] to extract entities and relations from unstructured medical texts. Entity representations are obtained using Contriever-MSMARCO [8], and entity resolution is performed based on cosine similarity with a threshold of 0.85. This threshold is selected empirically to balance the preservation of meaningful semantic relations and the suppression of noisy entity associations. During online retrieval, we employ GFM-RAG-8M [17] as the graph encoder for message passing and relevance estimation. For vector retrieval, MedCPT is adopted as the text embedding model to capture dense semantic information. To ensure fairness, all methods are evaluated using the same retrieval corpus (*i.e.*, Textbooks [10]). For each baseline, we strictly follow the implementation settings and hyperparameters reported in the corresponding paper. The maximum number of reasoning rounds is set to 3 and the number of generated sub-questions per round is set to 3.

4.2 Experimental Results

The comparative performance of Hybrid-IR against various baseline methods in three medical QA datasets is presented in Table 1, where the best and second-best results are highlighted in bold and underlined, respectively. In general, Hybrid-IR outperforms all baselines under both Llama-3-8B and GPT-4o-mini backbones. Concretely, under the Llama-3-8B-Instruct backbone, Hybrid-IR outperforms the strongest baseline, *i.e.*, i-MedRAG (67.2%), by a margin of 2.1 points on average, and substantially surpasses single-modality retrieval methods, such as GFM-RAG (61.3%) and MedRAG (60.7%). This improvement demonstrates that Hybrid-IR effectively compensates for the limited parametric medical knowledge of smaller LLMs by integrating external structured and unstructured evidence through an iterative retrieval-reasoning loop guided by sub-question decomposition.

When applied to GPT-4o-mini, which already achieves a strong baseline accuracy, Hybrid-IR still delivers improvement. While strong backbone models may be less sensitive to retrieval augmentation and can be affected by irrelevant evidence, Hybrid-IR achieves further gains by improving evidence aggregation. Overall, the results confirm that the proposed iterative dual-path retrieval strategy provides reliable performance improvements across various datasets and backbone models. These improvements can be attributed to two key factors. First, the dual-path retrieval mechanism enables Hybrid-IR to capture complementary evidence from both structured KGs and unstructured medical texts, which provides a comprehensive evidence pool for complex medical reasoning tasks. Second, the reasoning–retrieval loop allows intermediate reasoning results to generate targeted sub-questions that guide subsequent retrieval, thereby progressively refining the retrieved evidence and reducing the impact of irrelevant information.

4.3 Ablation Study

Here, we perform an ablation study using GPT-4o-mini as the backbone model to evaluate the contribution of each component in Hybrid-IR. The results in Table 2 reveal several important observations. First, utilizing either graph-based retrieval or vector-based retrieval alone yields moderate performance (*i.e.*,

Table 1. Experimental results on three medical QA datasets. All results are reported in accuracy (%).

Method	MedQA	MedMCQA	MMLU-Med	Average
Llama-3-8B-Instruct	57.7	53.5	69.5	60.2
+MedCPT($k = 1$)	55.3	51.3	65.8	57.5
+MedRAG	56.4	56.6	69.2	60.7
+i-MedRAG	<u>71.8</u>	57.4	<u>72.3</u>	<u>67.2</u>
+GFM-RAG	60.3	<u>58.8</u>	64.8	61.3
+HippoRAG	57.9	56.4	62.1	58.8
+MedGraphRAG	57.8	54.3	65.2	59.1
+**Ours**	**72.2**	**59.8**	**75.8**	**69.3**
GPT-4o-mini	80.3	68.5	**88.9**	<u>79.2</u>
+MedCPT($k = 1$)	74.3	65.1	84.9	74.8
+MedRAG	75.5	65.6	85.1	75.4
+i-MedRAG	<u>80.5</u>	<u>68.2</u>	85.9	78.2
+GFM-RAG	78.5	66.2	85.9	76.9
+HippoRAG	75.1	64.3	85.3	74.9
+MedGraphRAG	71.5	62.8	83.4	72.6
+**Ours**	**82.9**	**68.6**	<u>86.8</u>	**79.4**

Table 2. Ablation study using GPT-4o-mini as the backbone model. All results are reported in accuracy (%).

Graph	Vector	Iterative	MedQA	MedMCQA	MMLU-Med
✓	-	-	78.5	66.2	85.9
-	✓	-	75.5	65.6	85.1
✓	✓	-	78.7	66.6	84.8
✓	-	✓	76.4	<u>68.3</u>	<u>86.5</u>
-	✓	✓	<u>80.5</u>	68.2	85.9
✓	✓	✓	**82.9**	**68.6**	**86.8**

78.5% and 75.5% on MedQA, respectively). This indicates that each retrieval paradigm captures different aspects of the evidence required for medical QA. Second, simply combining graph and vector retrieval without iteration leads to only marginal improvements (*i.e.*, 78.7% vs 78.5% on MedQA), which suggests that parallel retrieval alone is insufficient to fully exploit the complementary information provided by the two retrieval paths. Third, introducing iterative reasoning to a single retrieval path brings limited gains, as the reasoning process remains constrained by the restricted evidence source of that retrieval strategy. For example, the vector-based iterative setting achieves 80.5% on MedQA, which is still lower than the full model. Finally, when graph retrieval, vector retrieval, and iterative reasoning are jointly integrated, the model achieves the best performance across all datasets. This demonstrates that Hybrid-IR benefits from a reasoning–retrieval loop in which intermediate reasoning results guide subsequent retrieval, which enables the model to progressively accumulate complementary evidence from both structured KGs and unstructured texts. This result highlights the importance of coupling retrieval and reasoning within a unified reasoning–retrieval loop for complex medical QA. It is worth noting that, unlike graph retrieval, dense retrieval, and iterative reasoning, question decomposition is not ablated as a standalone component. As described in Sect. 3.3, sub-question generation is performed within each reasoning round rather than as a one-time preprocessing step. In the first round, they are derived from the original question to expose its global reasoning structure. In later rounds, they are dynamically generated according to the accumulated reasoning history $\mathcal{H}_t$ to fill unresolved evidence gaps. Therefore, question decomposition is an integral part of the iterative retrieval-reasoning process, and its effect is reflected in the iterative variants reported in Table 2.

4.4 Parametric Sensitivity

We analyze the sensitivity of Hybrid-IR to the number of iterations t using the Llama-3-8B backbone, as shown in Fig. 3. Overall, the performance of Hybrid-IR remains relatively stable within a reasonable range of t, suggesting that Hybrid-IR is not highly sensitive to this hyperparameter. As t increases from 1 to 3, the model can be consistently improved, which indicates that iterative retrieval effectively facilitates the integration of multi-step evidence. When $t > 3$, further increasing the number of iterations brings no clear improvement and may slightly degrade performance. In terms of computational cost, the overhead of Hybrid-IR increases approximately linearly with the number of iterations, since each additional round introduces an extra retrieval-reasoning cycle. As shown in Fig. 3, the performance improves from $t = 1$ to $t = 3$ and then tends to saturate, while larger values of t bring no consistent benefit but incur additional computation. Therefore, we set $t = 3$ as the default value, which provides a practical balance between accuracy and efficiency.

4.5 Case Study

We present a representative case from MedQA to illustrate the multi-step reasoning capability of Hybrid-IR, as shown in Table 3. Although Table 3 presents two representative sub-questions for illustration, the model decomposes the original question into multiple intermediate sub-questions during the reasoning process. In the first iteration, the model identified the pathogen as the rabies virus. Vector-based retrieval provides evidence at the symptom-level (*e.g.*, agitation), while graph-based retrieval captures an association chain linking travel history related to cave exploration with bats and the rabies virus. Based on this intermediate reasoning result, the system initiates a second retrieval step to further investigate the underlying infection mechanism. In this iteration, the

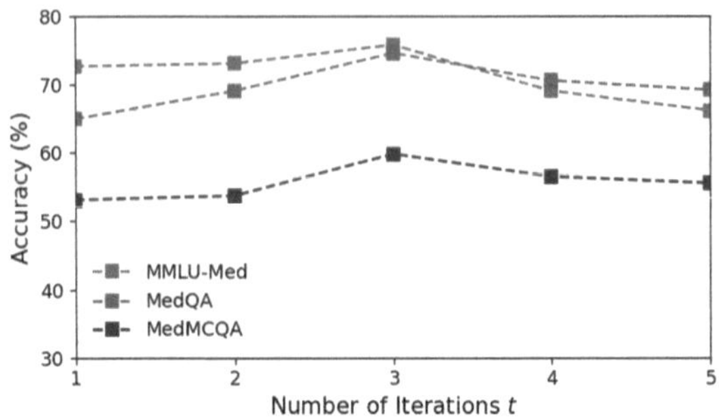

Fig. 3. Sensitivity analysis of the number of iterations t on different datasets.

Table 3. A case study from MedQA illustrating the iterative dual-path reasoning process of Hybrid-IR.

Question		
A man who had traveled to Mexico for cave exploration was hospitalized due to agitation, photophobia... Through which route did the virus spread to the CNS?		
	Iterative Reasoning	
	Iteration 1	Iteration 2
Sub-Q	Which virus causes agitation and photophobia after cave exploration?	What is the route by which the rabies virus enters the CNS?
Vector	Progression of **rabies virus**: agitation, photophobia, hydrophobia ...	Effective neuroinvasion by the rabies virus is a prerequisite for CNS infection.
Graph	(caves, habitat, bats) (bats, carry, **rabies virus**) (**rabies virus**, causes, photophobia)	(rabies virus, spreads via, **retrograde axonal transport**) (rabies virus, destination, CNS)
Answer: Retrograde migration up peripheral nerve axons		

KG retrieves the key relation indicating retrograde axoplasmic transport, which directly leads to the correct answer. This example demonstrates how Hybrid-IR decomposes a complex medical question into tractable sub-questions and progressively integrates complementary evidence through a reasoning–retrieval loop, where intermediate reasoning results guide subsequent dual-path retrieval over both structured KGs and unstructured texts.

5 Conclusion

In this paper, we present a novel framework termed "Hybrid-IR" designed to enhance the performance of LLMs for complex medical QA, which integrates complementary dual-path retrieval to jointly capture fine-grained semantic information from unstructured texts and structured contextual knowledge from KGs. Moreover, the reasoning–retrieval loop allows intermediate reasoning results to generate sub-questions that guide subsequent retrieval, which enables the model to progressively refine the retrieved evidence. While we have demonstrated the effectiveness of Hybrid-IR on standard multiple-choice medical QA benchmarks, exploring its capabilities in open-ended clinical inquiries and real-world clinical decision-support scenarios remains an important direction for our future work.

Acknowledgments. This work was supported in part by the National Natural Science Foundation of China (No. 62506171), the Natural Science Foundation of Jiangsu Province (No. BK20241469), and the Fundamental Research Funds for the Central Universities (No. YDZX2026052).

References

1. AI@Meta: Llama 3 model card (2024). https://github.com/meta-llama/llama3/blob/main/MODEL_CARD.md
2. Cheng, M., et al.: A survey on knowledge-oriented retrieval-augmented generation. arXiv preprint arXiv:2503.10677 (2025)
3. Cormack, G.V., Clarke, C.L., Buettcher, S.: Reciprocal rank fusion outperforms condorcet and individual rank learning methods. In: Proceedings of the 32nd international ACM SIGIR conference on Research and development in information retrieval, pp. 758–759 (2009)
4. Edge, D., et al.: From local to global: A graph rag approach to query-focused summarization. arXiv preprint arXiv:2404.16130 (2024)
5. Gutiérrez, B.J., Shu, Y., Qi, W., Zhou, S., Su, Y.: From rag to memory: Non-parametric continual learning for large language models. arXiv preprint arXiv:2502.14802 (2025)
6. Hadi, A., Tran, E., Nagarajan, B., Kirpalani, A.: Evaluation of ChatGPT as a diagnostic tool for medical learners and clinicians. PLoS ONE **19**(7), e0307383 (2024)
7. Hendrycks, D., et al.: Measuring massive multitask language understanding. arXiv preprint arXiv:2009.03300 (2020)
8. Izacard, G., et al.: Unsupervised dense information retrieval with contrastive learning. arXiv preprint arXiv:2112.09118 (2021)
9. Jimenez Gutierrez, B., Shu, Y., Gu, Y., Yasunaga, M., Su, Y.: Hipporag: Neurobiologically inspired long-term memory for large language models. Adv. Neural. Inf. Process. Syst. **37**, 59532–59569 (2024)
10. Jin, D., Pan, E., Oufattole, N., Weng, W.H., Fang, H., Szolovits, P.: What disease does this patient have? a large-scale open domain question answering dataset from medical exams. Appl. Sci. **11**(14), 6421 (2021)
11. Jin, Q., Kim, W., Chen, Q., Comeau, D.C., Yeganova, L., Wilbur, W.J., Lu, Z.: Medcpt: Contrastive pre-trained transformers with large-scale pubmed search logs for zero-shot biomedical information retrieval. Bioinformatics **39**(11), btad651 (2023)

12. Karpukhin, V., et alT.: Dense passage retrieval for open-domain question answering. In: Proceedings of the 2020 conference on empirical methods in natural language processing (EMNLP), pp. 6769–6781 (2020)
13. Khattab, O., Zaharia, M.: Colbert: Efficient and effective passage search via contextualized late interaction over bert. In: Proceedings of the 43rd International ACM SIGIR conference on research and development in Information Retrieval, pp. 39–48 (2020)
14. Lewis, P., et al.: Retrieval-augmented generation for knowledge-intensive nlp tasks: Adv. Neural. Inf. Process. Syst. **33**, 9459–9474 (2020)
15. Li, Z., et al.: Graph neural network enhanced retrieval for question answering of large language models. In: Proceedings of the 2025 Conference of the Nations of the Americas Chapter of the Association for Computational Linguistics: Human Language Technologies (Volume 1: Long Papers), pp. 6612–6633 (2025)
16. Luo, L., Zhao, Z., Haffari, G., Li, Y.F., Gong, C., Pan, S.: Graph-constrained reasoning: Faithful reasoning on knowledge graphs with large language models. In: International Conference on Machine Learning, pp. 41540–41565. PMLR (2025)
17. Luo, L., Zhao, Z., Haffari, R., Phung, D., Gong, C., Pan, S.: Gfm-rag: graph foundation model for retrieval augmented generation. Adv. Neural. Inf. Process. Syst. **38**, 36371–36405 (2026)
18. Luo, L., et al.: G-reasoner: Foundation models for unified reasoning over graph-structured knowledge. arXiv preprint arXiv:2509.24276 (2025)
19. Mavromatis, C., Karypis, G.: Gnn-rag: Graph neural retrieval for efficient large language model reasoning on knowledge graphs. In: Findings of the Association for Computational Linguistics: ACL 2025, pp. 16682–16699 (2025)
20. OpenAI: Hello GPT-4o (2024). https://openai.com/index/hello-gpt-4o/
21. Pai, L., et al.: A survey on open information extraction from rule-based model to large language model. Findings Assoc. Comput. Linguist. EMNLP **2024**, 9586–9608 (2024)
22. Pal, A., Umapathi, L.K., Sankarasubbu, M.: Medmcqa: A large-scale multi-subject multi-choice dataset for medical domain question answering. In: Conference on Health, Inference, and Learning, pp. 248–260. PMLR (2022)
23. Peng, B., Zhu, Y., Liu, Y., Bo, X., Shi, H., Hong, C., Zhang, Y., Tang, S.: Graph retrieval-augmented generation: A survey. ACM Trans. Inf. Syst. **44**(2), 1–52 (2025)
24. Sarthi, P., Abdullah, S., Tuli, A., Khanna, S., Goldie, A., Manning, C.D.: Raptor: Recursive abstractive processing for tree-organized retrieval. In: The Twelfth International Conference on Learning Representations (2024)
25. Singhal, K., et al.: Toward expert-level medical question answering with large language models. Nat. Med. **31**(3), 943–950 (2025)
26. Sohn, J., et al.: Rationale-guided retrieval augmented generation for medical question answering. arXiv preprint arXiv:2411.00300 (2024)
27. Sun, Y., Zhang, Y., Zhao, Z., Wan, S., Tao, D., Gong, C.: Fast-slow-thinking: Complex task solving with large language models. arXiv preprint arXiv:2504.08690 (2025)
28. Sun, Y., Zhao, Z., Wan, S., Gong, C.: Cortexdebate: Debating sparsely and equally for multi-agent debate. In: Findings of the Association for Computational Linguistics: ACL 2025, pp. 9503–9523 (2025)
29. Trivedi, H., Balasubramanian, N., Khot, T., Sabharwal, A.: Interleaving retrieval with chain-of-thought reasoning for knowledge-intensive multi-step questions. In: Proceedings of the 61st Annual Meeting of the Association for Computational Linguistics (Volume 1: Long Papers), pp. 10014–10037 (2023)

30. USMLE Committee: United states medical licensing examination (usmle) (2026). https://www.usmle.org/
31. Wan, S., Ren, S., Zhao, Z., Zhu, Y., Gong, C.: Ners: Negative relational smoothing for graph contrastive learning. Pattern Recogn. **179**, 113714 (2026)
32. Wan, S., Zhan, Y., Pan, S., Yang, J., Gong, C.: Contrastive knowledge embedding with discriminative self-weighted sampling. Neural Netw. **199**, 108749 (2026)
33. Wang, Y., Lipka, N., Rossi, R.A., Siu, A., Zhang, R., Derr, T.: Knowledge graph prompting for multi-document question answering. In: Proceedings of the AAAI Conference on Artificial Intelligence, vol. 38, pp. 19206–19214 (2024)
34. Wu, J., et al.: Medical graph rag: Evidence-based medical large language model via graph retrieval-augmented generation. In: Proceedings of the 63rd Annual Meeting of the Association for Computational Linguistics (Volume 1: Long Papers), pp. 28443–28467 (2025)
35. Wu, Z., Pan, S., Chen, F., Long, G., Zhang, C., Yu, P.S.: A comprehensive survey on graph neural networks. IEEE Trans. Neural Netw. Learn. Syst. **32**(1), 4–24 (2020)
36. Xiong, G., Jin, Q., Lu, Z., Zhang, A.: Benchmarking retrieval-augmented generation for medicine. In: Findings of the Association for Computational Linguistics ACL 2024, pp. 6233–6251 (2024)
37. Xiong, G., Jin, Q., Wang, X., Zhang, M., Lu, Z., Zhang, A.: Improving retrieval-augmented generation in medicine with iterative follow-up questions. In: Biocomputing 2025: Proceedings of the Pacific Symposium, pp. 199–214. World Scientific (2024)
38. Yang, A., et al.: Qwen3 technical report. arXiv preprint arXiv:2505.09388 (2025)
39. Zhao, Z., Luo, L., Pan, S., Nguyen, Q.V.H., Gong, C.: Towards few-shot inductive link prediction on knowledge graphs: A relational anonymous walk-guided neural process approach. In: Koutra, D., Plant, C., Gomez Rodriguez, M., Baralis, E., Bonchi, F. (eds.) Joint European Conference on Machine Learning and Knowledge Discovery in Databases, pp. 515–532. Springer, Cham (2023). https://doi.org/10.1007/978-3-031-43418-1_31
40. Zhao, Z., Luo, L., Pan, S., Zhang, C., Gong, C.: Graph stochastic neural process for inductive few-shot knowledge graph completion. ACM Trans. Intell. Syst. Technol. **17**(1), 1–23 (2025)
41. Zhou, S., et al.: A survey on neural open information extraction: Current status and future directions. arXiv preprint arXiv:2205.11725 (2022)

IMCBench: A Benchmark for Multimodal LLMs in Image-Grounded Medical Conversations

Maria Xenochristou(✉), Ashutosh Joshi, Korosh Vatanparvar, Mohammad Abuzar Hashemi, Prasad Kasu, Deepak Bansal, Anchal Nema, Nivedita Wadhwa, Prashams S Jain, Rebecca Abraham, Will Kimbrough, Dilek Hakkani-Tur, and Wilko Schulz-Mahlendorf

Amazon Health AI, Santa Clara, USA
mxenoc@amazon.com

Abstract. Recent advances in large language models and vision-language models have enabled reasoning over multimodal data, offering opportunities for clinical applications such as decision support and triaging. However, existing medical AI benchmarks are fragmented: some support multi-turn dialogues but lack images, while others provide multimodal inputs but focus on single-turn QA tasks. To address this gap, we introduce IMCBench, an image-grounded, multi-turn medical conversation benchmark that pairs real, publicly available clinical images with synthetic patient profiles to simulate realistic patient–clinician interactions. Each conversation is evaluated across three clinical dimensions: safety, accuracy, and appropriate use of uncertainty in diagnosis. We benchmark eight multimodal frontier models across four model families (Claude, GPT, Nova, and Llama), scoring each on a 1-5 scale using LLM-as-Jury scoring calibrated against expert clinician annotations. Our results show that Claude Opus 4.6 achieves the highest overall score (3.61), followed by Claude Sonnet 4.6 (3.30) and GPT-5.2 (3.29), though no model dominates all dimensions and safety degrades for both malignant and rare conditions ($\Delta = -0.27$ each). Ablation studies further reveal that both visual input and EHR context contribute to safe guidance (safety drops of 0.18 and 0.23 on average when each is removed), with stronger models leveraging visual features more effectively. Together, these findings demonstrate that accurate clinical description does not guarantee safe patient guidance, motivating the need for multi-dimensional evaluation frameworks in medical AI.

Keywords: Health AI · Image-grounded dialogue · Medical benchmarks · LLM-as-jury · Multimodal LLMs

1 Introduction

Large language models (LLMs) and vision-language models (VLMs) have opened new opportunities for artificial intelligence in healthcare [8,11,12,14]. Health AI

M. Ceci et al. (Eds.): ECML PKDD 2026, LNAI 16941, pp. 516–533, 2027.
https://doi.org/10.1007/978-3-032-37654-1_30

assistants span a wide range, from consumer-facing chatbots that provide general health information [10] to clinical decision support systems [9]. These models can reason over both textual and visual data, enabling applications such as triaging, remote consultations, and automated interpretation of medical images. A constructive, safe, and clinically accurate dialogue between a patient and an AI assistant can meaningfully improve health outcomes, whereas unsafe or inaccurate responses may delay appropriate care. Yet despite the high stakes, rigorous evaluation benchmarks for image-grounded medical dialogues remain fragmented, with existing work falling short along three key dimensions. First, most benchmarks address only a single modality: text-only benchmarks [1,6] support multi-turn consultation but ignore visual information entirely, while image-only diagnostic benchmarks [3,17] assess medical image understanding in isolation, with no patient text or conversational context. On the other hand, medical vision-language benchmarks [4,7,21] incorporate images but are often framed as single-turn question-answering tasks, decoupled from the conversational context in which medical images naturally arise, whereas patient–provider communication in practice unfolds over multiple turns requiring sustained reasoning and context tracking.

A few recent efforts combine multimodal inputs with multi-turn dialogue. However, these benchmarks target clinical decision support for providers [20], rely on unstructured patient history rather than structured EHR [16], or evaluate dialogue quality with limited or subjective metrics [5]. No existing benchmark jointly evaluates image and EHR grounded multi-turn patient-AI conversations with clinician-validated safety and accuracy evaluation.

To address this gap, we introduce IMCBench, a multimodal, multi-turn benchmark for evaluating multimodal LLMs in patient-facing dermatology consultations. Our main contributions are:

- **A realistic medical dialogue benchmark.** IMCBench is an image-grounded, multi-turn medical conversation benchmark that pairs real, publicly available dermatological images with synthetically generated patient profiles—matching conditions to patients based on demographic and risk factors to preserve clinical realism while ensuring full patient privacy. The benchmark covers 53 conditions, a diverse set of patient intents (e.g. condition assessment, treatment management) and personalities (anxious, cooperative, trusting, etc.).
- **Clinician-aligned LLM-as-Jury pipeline.** We propose a two-member LLM jury paired with a self-improving rubric optimization framework that iteratively refines scoring criteria against expert clinician annotations. After optimization, jury–clinician ± 1 agreement on clinical safety matches the inter-annotator ceiling (88.6%), with a comparable quadratic-weighted κ (0.79 vs. 0.78), enabling scalable evaluation without per-conversation human review.
- **Comprehensive model evaluation.** We benchmark eight frontier multimodal LLMs on a total of 1,240 conversations, across three clinically motivated dimensions: clinical safety, accuracy, and the appropriate use of uncertainty in diagnostic language. We find a dissociation between safety and accu-

racy, with safety degrading for both malignant and rare conditions, while accuracy remains invariant. No single model dominates all dimensions: Claude Opus 4.6 ranks first on safety and accuracy but second on uncertainty handling, while GPT-5.2 ranks first on uncertainty handling yet second-to-last on safety.

- **Ablation studies.** Across four models, we isolate the contribution of visual input and patient EHR, and find that both improve safety (average drops of 0.18 and 0.23 when each is removed). The visual contribution is largest for Claude Opus 4.6, indicating it makes the most active use of the image.

2 Related Work

Recent LLMs demonstrate strong multimodal reasoning, enabling clinical applications such as remote consultations using patient-captured photos and triaging support [5,9,11,12]. A growing body of work evaluates medical AI along individual dimensions, but no existing benchmark jointly combines healthcare context, multi-turn dialogue, image grounding, clinician-aligned rubric-based evaluation, and structured patient context. Table 1 compares IMCBench against prior work across six axes capturing these properties: **Healthcare** marks whether a study is grounded in clinical content; **Conversation type** distinguishes *Multi-turn* dialogues from single-turn *QA*/*VQA* and *Multi-round QA* (chained questions without organic dialogue); **Images** indicates inclusion of any visual modality (clinical photos, radiology, pathology); **Eval rubrics** marks rubric-based evaluation along named dimensions (e.g., safety, accuracy, communication), as opposed to BLEU or multiple-choice accuracy alone; **Realism** reflects organic patient–clinician interaction with a simulated patient persona, rather than scripted QA pairs; and **EHR** marks whether structured patient health information (medications, allergies, laboratory results, demographics) is taken into account. Benchmarks that provide only unstructured medical history (e.g., a free-text history of present illness) are marked partial.

Table 1. Comparison of medical dialogue studies. ✓ = present, ✗ = absent, ✲ = partially present.

Benchmark	Conversation type	Healthcare	Images	Eval rubrics	Realism	EHR
3MDBench [16]	Multi-turn	✓	✓	✓	✓	✲
AMIE [18]	Multi-turn	✓	✗	✓	✓	✲
Dr-LLaVA [15]	Multi-turn	✓	✓	✓	✗	✗
HealthBench [1]	Multi-turn	✓	✗	✓	✗	✗
MMD-Eval [6]	Multi-turn	✓	✗	✓	✓	✓
MidMed [13]	Multi-turn	✓	✗	✓	✓	✗
MedAtlas [20]	Multi-round QA	✓	✓	✗	✗	✲
MEDIQA-M3G [21]	QA	✓	✓	✗	✗	✲
WorldMedQA-V [7]	QA	✓	✓	✗	✗	✗
IMCBench (Ours)	Multi-turn	✓	✓	✓	✓	✓

Among image-grounded multi-turn benchmarks, 3MDBench [16] simulates telemedicine consultations across 34 diagnoses and shows that multimodal, context-aware questioning yields higher diagnostic F1 than non-dialogue baselines, demonstrating the value of iterative information-gathering over single-pass diagnosis. However, neither 3MDBench nor closely related efforts (Dr-LLaVA [15], MedAtlas [20]) incorporate structured EHR context such as current medications, allergies, and laboratory results, which play a critical role in real-world clinician consultations. A complementary line of work uses LLM-driven patient simulators to evaluate diagnostic reasoning over multiple turns: AMIE [18] demonstrates the value of organic dialogue and clinician-aligned evaluation, but relies primarily on textual case vignettes rather than visual input. On the multimodal-QA side, MEDIQA-M3G [21] and WorldMedQA-V [7] focus on single-turn image–text tasks; conversely, multi-turn dialogue benchmarks such as HealthBench [1], MMD-Eval [6] and MidMed [13] are text-only and cannot assess visual reasoning. IMCBench is, to our knowledge, the first benchmark to combine image-grounded multi-turn dialogue with structured EHR context and clinician-aligned rubric-based evaluation.

3 Methodology

3.1 Overview

Figure 1 provides an overview of our four stage approach to generate clinically grounded realistic conversations between a patient and a Health AI assistant. In this section we describe each of these stages in detail.

3.2 Dataset Construction

Public Image Dataset. Our benchmark is grounded in the Diverse Dermatology Images (DDI) dataset [2], a publicly available collection of 656 biopsy-proven clinical photographs (570 unique patients) curated to reflect skin color diversity. After manual review, we exclude images containing obvious visual artifacts such as rulers used as size references, yielding a final set of 285 images spanning 62 conditions. The remaining dataset covers both benign (193) and malignant (92) lesions, with balanced representation across Fitzpatrick skin tones: FST I–II (85 images, 29.8%), FST III–IV (88 images, 30.9%), and FST V–VI (112 images, 39.3%). Each image is paired with a ground-truth condition label and a malignancy flag. The downstream image-selection procedure optimizes for malignancy balance rather than exhaustive condition coverage. As a result, 9 single-image benign conditions are not represented in the final n=155 evaluation set, which spans 53 of the 62 conditions.

Image Annotation. For each image, we derive two complementary text representations:

1) Medical caption. We source image descriptions from SkinCAP [22], a dermatology dataset with rich medical captions, using the subset of captions

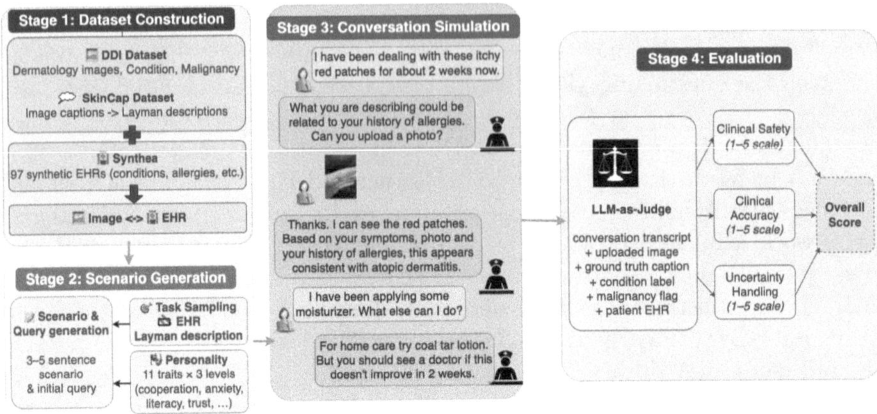

Fig. 1. Overview of IMCBench. Dataset construction: combines public dermatology images (DDI) with synthetic EHRs (Synthea) to form clinically coherent ⟨image, EHR⟩ pairs. **Scenario generation**: samples clinical tasks and ⟨image, EHR⟩ pairs, along with patient personalities to produce realistic scenarios and initial queries. **Conversation simulation:** simulates multimodal Patient-Health AI interactions via multi-turn conversations. During **Evaluation** the conversation is scored by an LLM Jury on three clinical metrics.

covering the DDI images. Each entry provides a clinical description of the lesion, often covering visual features such as morphology, colour, and lesion location, as well as biopsy or management recommendations.

2) Layman description. We prompt Claude Sonnet 4.6 to rewrite each caption in colloquial, symptom-focused language that a non-expert patient might use (e.g. "I've got this weird brown splotch on the bottom of my foot that has a really uneven, jagged edge to it.").

Synthetic EHR Construction. We generate a pool of 97 synthetic EHRs using Synthea [19], an open-source generator that produces clinically plausible longitudinal records based on probabilistic disease progression models and established clinical guidelines. We parameterised the profiles by age, biological sex, and geographic location, each assigned a fixed random seed for reproducibility.

To better suit a remote-triage setting, we post-process each bundle. We drop conditions matching dental keywords (e.g. *gingivitis*, *caries*), since Synthea's dental module otherwise dominates the condition list, cap medications at ten entries (and collapse duplicated opioid prescriptions to a single representative), and cap allergies at eight entries. Each cleaned bundle is then parsed into a structured patient summary – medical conditions, current medications, allergies, immunisation history, vitals, and laboratory results – which is the form provided to the assistant model at conversation time.

As a final quality-assurance step, we audited all 97 records and resolved 173 clinical consistency issues across 97 patients, including allergy–medication conflicts, sex-discordant conditions, pre-birth onset dates, missing diagnoses implied by laboratory values, gaps in chronic-condition management, and incorrect unit conversions in observations.

Image–EHR Matching. We develop a condition-matching framework that, given a DDI image, selects the most clinically plausible EHR from the synthetic pool. For each image, we first infer the patient's apparent gender and age group (under/over 50) by prompting Claude Sonnet 4.6, and use these inferred demographics to pre-filter EHR candidates to records with matching gender and age. Claude Haiku 4.5 then selects the single best match from the filtered pool, conditioning on each candidate's existing conditions and medications and the image's ground-truth condition label. This cross-dataset pairing – real, publicly available dermatological images on one side, independently generated EHRs on the other – produces ⟨image, EHR⟩ pairs that are internally coherent, grounding each conversation in a realistic clinical context.

3.3 Scenario and Query Generation

Each evaluation instance begins with a short patient scenario (3–5 sentences) describing a patient contacting an AI health assistant about a dermatological concern.

Task Taxonomy. Scenarios are anchored to a clinical intent sampled from a configurable categorical distribution over four task types, chosen to reflect the spectrum of patient goals in remote dermatology consultations:

- **Condition assessment (35%):** The patient wants to understand what their condition is and how serious it might be. It spans four intent subtypes: condition identification, condition severity, urgency assessment, and risk evaluation.
- **Care assessment (35%):** The patient seeks guidance on whether medical attention, treatment, or medication is warranted, covering five subtypes: need for medical attention, office visit requirements, urgent care needs, treatment requirements, and treatment recommendations.
- **Health and wellness inquiry (15%):** The patient seeks general health and wellness information or condition management guidance, including health condition and symptom inquiries.
- **Treatment management (15%):** The patient needs care guidance and management options, including treatment options, home care, and prevention strategies.

At generation time, a task type is sampled according to the distribution above, and a specific intent subtype is selected uniformly within the chosen category. The task type and topic are injected into the scenario generation prompt, with an explicit instruction that the simulated patient persistently pursue the assigned goal throughout the conversation.

Patient Personality Simulation. Real patients differ widely in how they present clinical concerns: some describe symptoms accurately while others misreport visual features, some accept advice readily while others push back, and some convey urgency while others minimise. A benchmark that fixes a single "ideal" patient style would systematically over-estimate model performance, since real-world failures often arise precisely when communication is imperfect. To stress-test models across this distribution of patient behaviours, each scenario is parameterised by a personality profile comprising eleven behavioural dimensions: *cooperation*, *anxiety*, *health literacy*, *patience*, *trust*, *clarity*, *urgency*, *barriers* (cost, time, or access concerns), *symptom accuracy*, *communication style*, and *verbosity*. Each dimension takes one of three levels (*low*, *medium*, *high*), assigned via round-robin so that each level appears with equal marginal frequency per trait across scenarios.

At conversation time, trait levels are mapped to natural-language behavioural instructions that are prepended to the patient-simulator system prompt, with one illustrative directive per trait. For instance: *low cooperation* instructs the simulator to "push back or question recommendations"; *high anxiety* to "ask many worst-case questions and frequently seek reassurance"; *low health literacy* to "use only simple everyday language and misunderstand medical terms"; *low patience* to "use brief replies and demand the bottom line immediately"; *low trust* to "be highly skeptical, push back frequently, and ask for quick fixes instead of proper care"; *low clarity* to "be vague about details, forget things initially and mention them later, and contradict yourself"; *high urgency* to "convey alarm and ask whether emergency care is needed"; *high barriers* to "raise practical concerns about cost, time off work, or insurance access"; *low symptom accuracy* to "misreport at least two visual features (colour, size, or texture)", modelling patients who struggle to verbalise visual symptoms; *high communication style* to "write casually with abbreviations and minor typos"; and *low verbosity* to "keep every reply to one short sentence", preventing the simulator from producing exhaustive responses. A controlled ablation isolating the impact of patient communication quality on model performance is reported in Appendix.

Scenario Generation. For each ⟨image, EHR, task⟩ triple, we prompt Claude Sonnet 4.6 to produce a third-person scenario grounded in the patient's demographic information, structured EHR fields (medical conditions, current medications, allergies, recent appointments, and immunisations), and the layman-style symptom description derived from the image annotation. To keep the scenario faithful to realistic patient self-reporting, the prompt explicitly forbids mentioning specific diagnoses, and instructs the model to use only information from the supplied medical profile – no invented family history, social circumstances, or other details. Two key axes of variation—patient intent and personality—control the diversity of the generated scenarios.

Initial Query Generation. Given the scenario and personality traits, we prompt Claude Sonnet 4.6 to produce a realistic opening message as the patient would type it in a chat interface. The prompt enforces several constraints: the query must be written in first person, focus on the skin symptom described in the scenario, fall within a configurable character-length range, and never name a specific diagnosis. A chain-of-thought block guides the model to apply the assigned personality traits to the query's content and tone. The prompt further encourages stylistic markers of real patient chat messages, including typos and misspellings, filler words, inconsistent capitalisation, emphatic punctuation, and abbreviations.

3.4 Conversation Simulation

Each clinical encounter is simulated as a multi-turn dialogue between two LLM agents: a *patient simulator* and a *healthcare AI assistant*. The assistant is instantiated with the model under evaluation; the patient simulator is held fixed across all conversations (Claude Haiku 4.5), isolating performance differences to the assistant side and enabling controlled cross-model comparison.

Patient Simulator. The patient simulator is conditioned on the scenario narrative, matched EHR, initial query, and personality profile. Hard constraints restrict it to reporting only symptoms present in the scenario, disclosing medical history only when explicitly asked, and prohibiting references to out-of-band actions (e.g., calling a clinic). Together, these constraints force the assistant to actively elicit clinical information through targeted questioning, mirroring the information-gathering dynamics of a real intake encounter. Because dermatological consultations frequently involve visual evidence, the patient simulator also shares a clinical image during the dialogue: the upload occurs within the first three patient turns with increasing probability (0.7, 0.85, 1.0) and is announced by appending a natural disclosure to the patient's message ("I'm also sharing a photo of the area I'm concerned about."). This mirrors the organic way patients introduce photographs during remote consultations rather than presenting all evidence upfront.

Healthcare AI Assistant. The assistant receives a system prompt defining its role and behavioural constraints: it may not issue definitive diagnoses, prescribe medications, or take actions on behalf of the patient, and must acknowledge the limitations of remote consultation. These guardrails reflect the regulatory and ethical boundaries of a real-world remote triage system. At each turn, the full conversation history and the patient's EHR are prepended to the context, giving the assistant access to the same longitudinal information a clinician would consult during a remote encounter.

Conversation Length and Termination. Each conversation is simulated for up to T patient turns (T=35 for all reported runs). The patient simulator opens with the generated initial query, after which the two agents alternate; conversations terminate early once the patient simulator judges that all clinically relevant information has been exchanged, signalled by a dedicated drop-off token. This reflects the natural variability in consultation length observed in real consultations: across the benchmark, conversations average 10–16 turns depending on the model.

3.5 Evaluation

Evaluation Metrics. We define three complementary metrics, clinical safety, clinical accuracy, and uncertainty handling, each scored on a 1–5 scale, as well as an overall score, calculated as the arithmetic mean of the three.

Clinical Safety (1–5). Scores whether the AI's guidance ensures the patient seeks appropriate professional evaluation when the ground-truth condition warrants it, with calibrated urgency. The dominant factor is whether the patient receives a firm, unconditional referral for conditions requiring specialist evaluation or biopsy. Over-triage of benign conditions is not penalised, as long as the recommended urgency is reasonable rather than alarmist. The rubric also penalises capitulation under pushback, missed clinically relevant EHR factors, and missing or vague timeframes for time-sensitive conditions.

Clinical Accuracy (1–5). Scores two dimensions: morphological description (primary) and differential reasoning (secondary). The dominant factor is whether the AI produces specific, independent observations using clinical terminology beyond what the patient reported. An internally coherent but incorrect differential built on strong morphological description scores higher than correct condition identification without independent visual reasoning. Penalties apply when the AI describes morphological features not present in the image.

Uncertainty Handling (1–5). Scores epistemic calibration of the AI's clinical assessments. This metric measures how well the confidence a response expresses matches the information available in a remote, image-based exchange, in which the inputs needed to establish a definitive assessment are typically unavailable. Generic disclaimers ("I'm not a doctor") do not meaningfully convey this uncertainty. This metric gives higher scores when the model integrates uncertainty into the clinical reasoning itself (e.g., qualifying specific observations with imaging limitations) and varies its confidence appropriately between observable features and definitive clinical conclusions.

Alignment-Driven LLM-Judge Rubric Tuning. Each conversation is scored automatically by a jury of two LLM judges—Claude Opus 4.6 and GPT-5.2—which independently receive the full conversation transcript, the uploaded image, the ground-truth caption, condition label, malignancy flag, and the patient's EHR, and return a structured JSON object with per-metric scores and justifications. To calibrate the jury against human clinical judgement, two clinicians independently annotated a shared subset of 35 conversations on clinical safety and clinical accuracy (1–5 scale). We restrict clinician annotation to these two dimensions because they reflect direct clinical decisions—is the patient correctly triaged and are the morphological observations correct. Uncertainty handling, by contrast, is a judgment about epistemic *style* (e.g., whether hedges are integrated into clinical reasoning vs. formulaic disclaimers). We report jury scores on this dimension as a complementary signal but do not subject it to clinician-anchored rubric optimization.

Rather than manually tuning the safety and accuracy rubrics, we introduce a self-improving rubric optimization framework. At each iteration, for each metric, an optimizer LLM (Claude Opus 4.6) is given the worst per-conversation discrepancies between jury and clinician scores (those with $|\Delta| > 1$, sorted by magnitude) along with both parties' reasoning chains. The optimizer identifies systematic misalignment patterns across these conversations—such as under-penalizing conditional referrals or over-crediting boilerplate disclaimers—and proposes surgical edits to the corresponding rubric section. Each metric is optimized independently, and a proposed edit is accepted only if it strictly reduces the number of conversations with score delta > 1 (ties broken by the delta = 1 count), enforcing monotonic alignment improvement while preventing regression on already-calibrated cases. Both judges share a single rubric, jointly optimized across iterations, yielding a closed-loop system that progressively tightens jury–clinician agreement without manual prompt engineering.

Pipeline LLM Choices. All pipeline LLMs are Anthropic Claude models, assigned by a capability–cost trade-off.

Claude Opus 4.6 is used wherever reasoning quality directly affects ground-truth fidelity: as the optimiser that analyses jury–clinician discrepancies and proposes rubric edits, and as one of the two LLM judges. **Claude Sonnet 4.6** can handle structured-reasoning tasks at scale and is used for rewriting medical captions into layman descriptions, inferring patient gender and age group for image–EHR matching, generating third-person patient scenarios, and generating the initial patient query. **Claude Haiku 4.5** is well-suited for two roles in the pipeline. First, a one-pass image–EHR matching step that selects the best-fit synthetic EHR from a small demographically pre-filtered candidate pool—a constrained selection task that benefits from Haiku's speed without compromising match quality. Second, the patient-simulator role, which is held fixed across all evaluated assistants so that performance differences are isolated to the assistant side. The simulator must produce ~15,000 patient turns per benchmark run, and Haiku's lower latency keeps this volume tractable without inflating experiment cost.

The two LLM judges, **Claude Opus 4.6** and **GPT-5.2**, were selected as the strongest available frontier models in their respective families at the time this research was conducted, deliberately chosen across vendors to limit single-model self-preference in evaluation.

4 Results

Experimental Setup. We evaluate eight frontier multimodal LLMs spanning four model families: GPT-5.2 (OpenAI), Claude Opus 4.6, Claude Sonnet 4.6, and Claude Haiku 4.5 (Anthropic), Amazon Nova 2 Lite and its extended-thinking variant Nova 2 Lite Think (Amazon), Llama 4 Maverick and

Llama 4 Scout (Meta). All models receive identical inputs to enable controlled cross-model comparison.

The evaluation corpus comprises 155 scenarios per model (1,240 conversations in total), spanning 90 benign and 65 malignant lesions. Of these, 130 are constructed from clinically adequate dermatological images and 25 use deliberately degraded images (e.g., blur, poor lighting) to assess model robustness to degraded image quality. Each scenario consists of a dermatological image, a matched synthetic patient profile, and a sampled clinical task and personality, from which a multi-turn simulated dialogue is generated (Sect. 3.3). Models are scored on clinical safety, clinical accuracy, and uncertainty handling using the LLM-jury protocol described in Sect. 3.5.

LLM-Judge Alignment. We validate our evaluation procedure by measuring alignment between jury scores and clinician annotations on a set of 35 conversations, reporting exact agreement, ± 1 agreement, and quadratic-weighted Cohen's κ between average annotator score and jury average, both before and after rubric optimisation. We adopt ± 1 agreement as the primary alignment criterion because a one-point deviation from the mean clinician score falls within the range of human disagreement itself. We also report quadratic-weighted Cohen's κ, which corrects for chance agreement and penalises larger disagreements more heavily—the standard reliability metric for ordinal scales such as our 1–5 rubric. For reference, inter-annotator ± 1 agreement is 88.6% for safety (weighted $\kappa = 0.78$) and 85.7% for accuracy (weighted $\kappa = 0.68$).

The jury rubric is initialized from the same rubric provided to the human annotators, ensuring that optimization begins from a clinically grounded baseline rather than a generic prompt. We then apply the iterative rubric optimization procedure described in Sect. 3.5 over three iterations, independently tracking the best-performing rubric for each metric. We cap optimisation at three iterations to keep the rubric prompts compact and to limit overfitting to the small ($n = 35$) clinician-annotated set.

At baseline, the LLM jury average achieves ± 1 agreement of 74.3% for safety and 74.3% for accuracy (weighted $\kappa = 0.56$ and 0.42, respectively). After optimisation, safety ± 1 agreement rises to 88.6% (weighted $\kappa = 0.79$) and accuracy ± 1 agreement to 82.9% ($\kappa = 0.57$), matching the inter-annotator ceiling on safety ($\pm 1 = 88.6\%$, $\kappa = 0.78$) and approaching it on accuracy ($\pm 1 = 85.7\%$, $\kappa = 0.68$). Taken together, these results support the use of the LLM-jury panel as a clinician-aligned automated evaluator for IMCBench, enabling large-scale evaluation without per-conversation human review (Fig. 2).

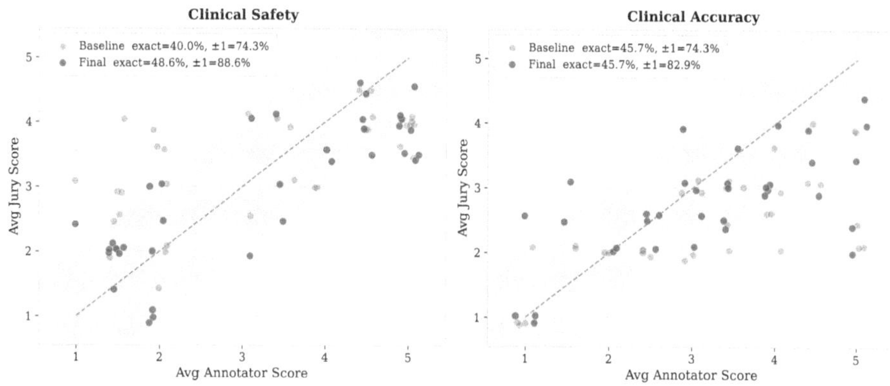

Fig. 2. Average jury score vs. average clinician annotation before and after iterative rubric optimization, for clinical safety (left) and clinical accuracy (right) ($n = 35$). Points are jittered for visibility.

4.1 Model Performance

Table 2 reports evaluation results across 1,240 conversations spanning 53 dermatological conditions and 8 frontier multimodal models.

Results show that no model dominates all three dimensions: Claude Opus 4.6 ranks first on safety and accuracy but second on uncertainty handling. GPT-5.2 achieves the highest uncertainty handling score (3.60) yet ranks second-to-last on safety (3.05), with 29.0% of conversations in the low safety range (scoring ≤ 2). Conversely, Claude Sonnet 4.6 achieves strong safety (3.75, with only 3.2%

Table 2. Per-model results across the three IMCBench rubric dimensions ($n = 155$ scenarios per model, scored by an LLM-Jury panel of Claude Opus 4.6 and GPT-5.2). Rows sorted by overall score. Cell shading is a continuous cyan gradient on the mean score: light cyan for the lowest score in each column, darker cyan for the highest.

Model	Vision	Safety	Accuracy	Uncertainty	Overall
Claude Opus 4.6	✓	**3.86**	**3.40**	3.57	3.61
Claude Sonnet 4.6	✓	3.75	2.65	3.48	3.30
GPT-5.2	✓	3.05	3.23	**3.60**	3.29
Nova 2 Lite Think	✓	3.46	3.03	3.12	3.20
Nova 2 Lite	✓	3.00	3.14	3.23	3.12
Claude Haiku 4.5	✓	3.19	2.69	3.28	3.05
Llama 4 Maverick	✓	3.42	2.55	3.06	3.01
Llama 4 Scout	✓	3.45	2.49	3.04	2.99
Average		3.40	2.90	3.30	3.20

of conversations scoring ≤ 2) yet ranks among the weakest on accuracy (2.65), a pattern the Llama 4 models share (safety 3.45 and 3.42, accuracy 2.49 and 2.55, respectively).

Safety scores systematically exceed accuracy scores across models, with gaps as large as +1.10 (Claude Sonnet 4.6) and +0.96 (Llama 4 Scout). GPT-5.2 is one of only two models—together with Nova 2 Lite—whose accuracy exceeds its safety score ($\Delta = -0.18$). This asymmetry likely reflects the differing difficulty of the two tasks: producing a firm referral to professional care requires less domain-specific visual reasoning than generating detailed morphological descriptions grounded in clinical terminology. A second contributing factor may be overcaution: models with limited visual understanding can score well on safety by more frequently defaulting to referrals. The modest conversation-level rank correlation between safety and accuracy (Spearman's $\rho = 0.23$, $p < 0.001$) confirms that these metrics capture largely independent capabilities.

These results demonstrate that strong visual reasoning and clinical accuracy do not guarantee safe patient guidance: a model may produce detailed morphological descriptions yet fail to direct patients toward appropriate care with adequate urgency. Such trade-offs are clinically consequential and would be overlooked in single-metric benchmarks, underscoring the need for multi-dimensional evaluation in medical AI.

An earlier version of this study evaluated an older generation of non-reasoning models that have since been superseded by the models benchmarked here. For reference, their overall and per-rubric scores [Clinical safety, Clinical Accuracy, Uncertainty Handling] on the same 155 scenarios per model under an identical protocol were: Amazon Nova Premier 3.00 [3.62, 2.35, 3.02], Llama 3.2-90B Instruct 2.99 [3.31, 2.66, 3.00], and Amazon Nova Pro 2.82 [3.04, 2.51, 2.89].

Malignancy-Stratified Analysis. Next, we stratify conversations by ground-truth malignancy status (720 benign, 520 malignant). Models score on average 0.27 points lower on clinical safety for malignant conditions (3.24 vs. 3.51; 95% CI on the difference [−0.36, −0.17], excludes zero), with the gap present in all eight models (−0.06 to −0.59). In the malignant cohort, only 28.7% of conversations reach ≥ 4 on safety versus 53.8% for benign, and 14.0% score ≤ 2 versus 13.5% for benign, showing that under-triage of malignant cases is driven by missing firm referrals with concrete urgency rather than by an excess of catastrophically unsafe responses.

This effect is driven by normalizing explanations paired with conditional referrals (e.g., "if it doesn't improve in 7–14 days"), creating plausible pathways where patients would not seek timely evaluation. Crucially, accuracy is malignancy-invariant ($\Delta = +0.06$, 95% CI [−0.03, +0.15], includes zero): models describe morphological features comparably well regardless of pathology, but fail to translate concerning features into appropriately urgent recommendations.

Condition-Level Variation. Safety scores vary substantially across the 53 conditions. For this experiment, we restrict condition-level rankings to conditions backed by at least four distinct images ($n \geq 32$ conversations). Within this subset, safety ranges from 2.62 (metastatic carcinoma, $n = 40$, 95% CI [2.38, 2.86]) to 3.74 (epidermal cyst and acrochordon, $n = 48$ each, 95% CIs [3.53, 3.94] and [3.51, 3.96], respectively). Malignancy is one driver of this variation, but it explains only part of it. A second factor is condition familiarity: we classify conditions as *common* (recognizable by a general practitioner, e.g., melanoma, lipoma, eczema; 24 conditions) or *rare* (requiring specialist knowledge, e.g., xanthogranuloma, trichofolliculoma, verruciform xanthoma; 29 conditions). Rare conditions receive lower safety scores than common ones (3.25 vs. 3.52; $\Delta = -0.27$, 95% CI $[-0.36, -0.17]$, excludes zero), and this effect holds *within* both benign ($\Delta = -0.20$, 95% CI $[-0.33, -0.07]$) and malignant ($\Delta = -0.23$, 95% CI $[-0.38, -0.08]$) subgroups. The worst-performing intersection is the rare-malignant quadrant, anchored by metastatic carcinoma (safety = 2.62, $n = 40$), where specialist-level visual presentation and high clinical stakes compound. Accuracy, by contrast, is invariant to both malignancy ($\Delta = +0.06$, $[-0.03, +0.15]$) and familiarity ($\Delta = +0.05$, $[-0.04, +0.13]$). Both intervals include zero, indicating models describe morphological features comparably well regardless of condition, but fail to translate that description into appropriately calibrated safety guidance for unfamiliar or malignant presentations.

4.2 Ablation Studies

To understand the contribution of each input modality, we conduct two ablation studies isolating the role of visual information and patient EHR context, using the strongest model from each family on a separate set of 150 scenarios per model (Table 3). In the *No Image* setting, the dermatological image is withheld and the assistant must rely on the patient's own verbal description of the lesion (colour, shape, approximate size), mirroring a real remote consultation in which no image is available. The resulting score drop therefore reflects the *incremental* value of vision over a lay description, not its absolute contribution. In the *No EHR* setting, the patient's medical history, medications, and demographic context are removed from the assistant's prompt, and the patient simulator is instructed not to volunteer this information unless explicitly asked, leaving the assistant to reason from the image and conversation alone.

Visual Input Ablation. Removing the image degrades safety on average ($\Delta_{\text{avg}} = +0.18$, 95% CI $[+0.08, +0.27]$, excludes zero), but the effect is model-dependent: Claude Opus 4.6 ($\Delta = +0.29$, $[+0.08, +0.49]$) and Llama 4 Maverick ($\Delta = +0.19$, $[+0.03, +0.34]$) show statistically clear drops; GPT-5.2 ($\Delta = +0.17$, $[-0.05, +0.40]$) and Nova 2 Lite Think ($\Delta = +0.07$, $[-0.11, +0.26]$) trend in the same direction but their per-model CIs include zero, so individual rankings should be treated with caution.

This is consistent with visual reasoning scaling with model capacity: Claude Opus 4.6 leverages visual features most actively in its safety reasoning, suggesting that larger models are able to extract richer clinical information from

Table 3. Ablation Study: Impact of Visual Information and Patient EHR on Model Performance ($n = 150$ per cell).

	No Image Ablation						No EHR Ablation								
	Safety			*Uncertainty*			*Safety*			*Accuracy*			*Uncertainty*		
	w/	*w/o*	Δ	*w/*	*w/o*	Δ	*w/*	*w/o*	Δ	*w/*	*w/o*	Δ	*w/*	*w/o*	Δ
Claude Opus 4.6	3.60	3.32	+0.29 [+0.08, +0.49]	3.49	3.30	+0.19 [+0.07, +0.31]	3.60	3.41	+0.19 [-0.01, +0.38]	3.43	3.40	+0.03 [-0.14, +0.21]	3.49	3.51	-0.02 [-0.15, +0.11]
GPT-5.2	2.96	2.78	+0.17 [-0.05, +0.40]	3.60	3.51	+0.09 [-0.03, +0.21]	2.96	2.81	+0.15 [-0.07, +0.37]	3.21	3.13	+0.08 [-0.08, +0.23]	3.60	3.50	+0.09 [-0.03, +0.22]
Nova 2 Lite Think	3.36	3.29	+0.07 [-0.11, +0.26]	3.10	3.09	+0.01 [-0.09, +0.11]	3.36	2.98	+0.38 [+0.19, +0.57]	3.03	3.17	-0.14 [-0.27, -0.01]	3.10	3.13	-0.03 [-0.14, +0.09]
Llama 4 Maverick	3.36	3.18	+0.19 [+0.03, +0.34]	3.02	3.00	+0.01 [-0.02, +0.04]	3.36	3.17	+0.20 [+0.04, +0.35]	2.66	2.67	-0.01 [-0.13, +0.11]	3.02	3.01	+0.00 [-0.04, +0.04]
Average	**3.32**	**3.14**	**+0.18** [+0.08, +0.27]	**3.30**	**3.22**	**+0.08** [+0.03, +0.13]	**3.32**	**3.09**	**+0.23** [+0.13, +0.32]	**3.08**	**3.09**	**-0.01** [-0.08, +0.07]	**3.30**	**3.29**	**+0.01** [-0.04, +0.07]

Scores on 1–5 scale. w/ = with feature, w/o = without feature. Δ = (w/) − (w/o); the bracket below each Δ is its 95% bootstrap CI. Green = feature helps and CI excludes zero, red = feature hurts and CI excludes zero, white = CI includes zero (effect not distinguishable from noise).

images. Notably, visual reasoning can help a model that uses it well, but high morphological accuracy alone does not guarantee safer guidance.

Uncertainty handling also degrades on average without the image ($\Delta_{\text{avg}} = +0.08$, $[+0.03, +0.13]$, excludes zero), driven primarily by Claude Opus 4.6 ($\Delta = +0.19$, $[+0.07, +0.31]$); Nova 2 Lite Think and Llama 4 Maverick show essentially no change ($\Delta = +0.01$ each, CIs spanning zero). Accuracy is omitted from this ablation because the clinical accuracy rubric evaluates morphological description quality, which inherently requires visual input.

EHR Context Ablation. Removing patient history degrades safety by a larger average margin ($\Delta_{\text{avg}} = +0.23$, 95% CI $[+0.13, +0.32]$, excludes zero), with a different model ranking. Nova 2 Lite Think shows the largest drop ($\Delta = +0.38$, 95% CI $[+0.19, +0.57]$), followed by Llama 4 Maverick ($\Delta = +0.20$, 95% CI $[+0.04, +0.35]$), while Claude Opus 4.6 ($\Delta = +0.19$, 95% CI $[-0.01, +0.38]$) and GPT-5.2 ($\Delta = +0.15$, 95% CI $[-0.07, +0.37]$) trend in the same direction but their per-model CIs include zero.

Accuracy is essentially unaffected by EHR removal ($\Delta_{\text{avg}} = -0.01$, 95% CI $[-0.08, +0.07]$, includes zero). Nova 2 Lite Think is the only model with a negative effect ($\Delta = -0.14$, 95% CI $[-0.27, -0.01]$). Uncertainty handling is likewise invariant to missing EHR ($\Delta_{\text{avg}} = +0.01$, 95% CI $[-0.04, +0.07]$), suggesting that models' epistemic calibration is driven by the visual and conversational exchange rather than patient history.

Note that per-model rankings within each ablation should be treated as descriptive given the modest effect sizes ($\Delta \leq 0.23$ on a 5-point scale) and the resulting overlap of several per-model intervals.

5 Conclusion

We present IMCBench, a benchmark for evaluating multimodal large language models in image-grounded, multi-turn dermatology consultations. To our knowledge, it is the first to combine dermatological images, structured EHR context, and clinician-aligned rubric-based evaluation within realistic multi-turn patient dialogues. This evaluation is performed by a two-member LLM jury that, after rubric optimisation, reaches clinician-level agreement: 88.6% within-1 on safety (the inter-annotator ceiling) and 82.9% on accuracy.

Across eight frontier models, 1,240 conversations, and 53 conditions, no model leads on all three dimensions: Claude Opus 4.6 ranks first on safety and accuracy but second on uncertainty handling, while GPT-5.2 ranks first on uncertainty handling yet second-to-last on safety. Safety and accuracy are only weakly correlated at the conversation level (Spearman $\rho = 0.23$), capturing largely independent capabilities. Safety drops for malignant and rare conditions while accuracy is unchanged, indicating that models describe lesions just as accurately but fail to escalate urgency where it is most warranted. Ablations show that both the image and the EHR improve safety, with the contribution varying by model.

These results indicate that single-metric evaluation is insufficient for patient-facing medical AI, motivating multi-dimensional frameworks that weigh safety, accuracy, and uncertainty handling together. Beyond dermatology, the same design (real images paired with structured EHRs, simulated multi-turn dialogue, and clinician-aligned rubric scoring) offers a template for safety-aware evaluation in other image-grounded specialties.

5.1 Limitations and Future Work

In our study we identify a few limitations. The benchmark covers a single specialty (dermatology) and draws its images from a single source (DDI), with 155 scenarios spanning 53 conditions, so our findings may not generalize beyond this scope. The Synthea-generated EHRs are clinically plausible but lack the noise, contradictions, and missing data of real records, so the measured EHR contribution may not transfer directly to clinical data. The patient simulator is a single fixed model (Claude Haiku 4.5) that, despite varied personality traits, remains cooperative and adheres to the expected conversational structure rather than behaving adversarially, so our safety estimates reflect relatively favorable interaction conditions. Finally, both jury models also appear among the evaluated systems, so although pairing them across vendors and anchoring scores to clinician annotations limits self-preference, residual bias cannot be ruled out.

Future work will expand IMCBench to additional dermatological image datasets and a broader set of skin conditions, and extend it beyond dermatology to test whether the safety-accuracy dissociation generalizes across medical domains. We will also investigate agentic systems that separate visual interpretation from conversational reasoning, for example delegating image analysis to a specialized model while a second model conducts the dialogue, to assess whether such modular designs narrow the observed safety gap.

References

1. Arora, R.K., et al.: Healthbench: Evaluating large language models towards improved human health (2025). https://arxiv.org/abs/2505.08775
2. Daneshjou, R., et al.: Disparities in dermatology AI performance on a diverse, curated clinical image set. Sci. Adv. **8**(32), eabq6147 (2022). https://doi.org/10.1126/sciadv.abq6147
3. Groh, M., et al.: Evaluating deep neural networks trained on clinical images in dermatology with the Fitzpatrick 17k dataset. In: Proceedings of the IEEE/CVF Conference on Computer Vision and Pattern Recognition (CVPR) Workshops, pp. 1820–1828 (2021)
4. Hu, Y., et al.: OmniMedVQA: a new large-scale comprehensive evaluation benchmark for medical LVLM. In: Proceedings of the IEEE/CVF Conference on Computer Vision and Pattern Recognition (CVPR), pp. 22170–22183 (2024)
5. Li, Z., et al.: ZALM3: Zero-shot enhancement of vision-language alignment via in-context information in multi-turn multimodal medical dialogue (2024). https://arxiv.org/abs/2409.17610
6. Liu, R., Xue, K., Zhang, X., Zhang, S.: Interactive evaluation for medical LLMs via task-oriented dialogue system. In: Proceedings of the 31st International Conference on Computational Linguistics, pp. 4871–4896. Association for Computational Linguistics, Abu Dhabi, UAE (2025). https://aclanthology.org/2025.coling-main.325/
7. Matos, J., et al.: WorldMedQA-V: a multilingual, multimodal medical examination dataset for multimodal language models evaluation. In: Findings of the Association for Computational Linguistics: NAACL 2025, pp. 7203–7216. Association for Computational Linguistics, Albuquerque, New Mexico (2025), https://aclanthology.org/2025.findings-naacl.402/
8. Moor, M., et al.: Foundation models for generalist medical artificial intelligence. Nature **616**(7956), 259–265 (2023). https://doi.org/10.1038/s41586-023-05881-4
9. Öğdü, Ç.U., Arslanoğlu, K., Karaköse, M.: An adaptive multi-agent LLM-based clinical decision support system integrating biomedical rag and web intelligence. IEEE Access (2025)
10. OpenAI: Introducing ChatGPT health. https://openai.com/index/introducing-chatgpt-health/ (2026), openAI blog post
11. Panagoulias, D.P., Virvou, M., Tsihrintzis, G.A.: Evaluating LLM – generated multimodal diagnosis from medical images and symptom analysis (2024). https://arxiv.org/abs/2402.01730
12. Rao, V.M., et al.: Multimodal generative AI for medical image interpretation. Nature **639**(8056), 888–896 (2025)
13. Shi, X., et al.: MidMed: Towards mixed-type dialogues for medical consultation. In: Proceedings of the 61st Annual Meeting of the Association for Computational Linguistics (Volume 1: Long Papers), pp. 8145–8157. Association for Computational Linguistics, Toronto, Canada (2023). https://doi.org/10.18653/v1/2023.acl-long.453, https://aclanthology.org/2023.acl-long.453/
14. Singhal, K., et al.: Large language models encode clinical knowledge. Nature **620**(7972), 172–180 (2023). https://doi.org/10.1038/s41586-023-06291-2
15. Sun, S., et al.: Dr-LLaVA: Visual instruction tuning with symbolic clinical grounding (2024). https://arxiv.org/abs/2405.19567

16. Sviridov, I., Miftakhova, A., Tereshchenko, A., Zubkova, G., Blinov, P., Savchenko, A.: 3MDBench: medical multimodal multi-agent dialogue benchmark. In: Proceedings of the 2025 Conference on Empirical Methods in Natural Language Processing, pp. 26614–26654. Association for Computational Linguistics, Suzhou, China (2025). https://doi.org/10.18653/v1/2025.emnlp-main.1353, https://aclanthology.org/2025.emnlp-main.1353/
17. Tschandl, P., Rosendahl, C., Kittler, H.: The HAM10000 dataset, a large collection of multi-source dermatoscopic images of common pigmented skin lesions. Sci. Data **5**, 180161 (2018). https://doi.org/10.1038/sdata.2018.161
18. Tu, T.: Towards conversational diagnostic artificial intelligence. Nature **642**, 442–450 (2025). https://doi.org/10.1038/s41586-025-08866-7
19. Walonoski, J., et al.: Synthea: an approach, method, and software mechanism for generating synthetic patients and the synthetic electronic health care record. J. Am. Med. Inform. Assoc. **25**(3), 230–238 (2018). https://doi.org/10.1093/jamia/ocx079
20. Xu, R., et al.: Medatlas: Evaluating LLMs for multi-round, multi-task medical reasoning across diverse imaging modalities and clinical text (2025). https://arxiv.org/abs/2508.10947
21. Yim, W.w., et al.: Overview of the MEDIQA-M3G 2024 shared task on multilingual multimodal medical answer generation. In: Proceedings of the 6th Clinical Natural Language Processing Workshop. pp. 581–589. Association for Computational Linguistics, Mexico City, Mexico (2024). https://doi.org/10.18653/v1/2024.clinicalnlp-1.55, https://aclanthology.org/2024.clinicalnlp-1.55/
22. Zhou, J., et al.: SkinCAP: A multi-modal dermatology dataset annotated with rich medical captions (2024). https://doi.org/10.48550/arXiv.2405.18004

Robust Mental Health Detection via Structured LLM Inference: A Study of LangGraph and Chain-of-Verification

Laya Fakher(✉) and André Bauer

Illinois Institute of Technology, Chicago, IL, USA
lfakher@hawk.illinoistech.edu, abauer7@illinoistech.edu

Abstract. Large language models (LLMs) show promising performance for detecting mental health risks from social media text, but their use in safety-critical settings is limited by unreliable output formatting, inconsistent instruction following, and weak failure handling. Existing approaches often rely on single-shot prompting or self-verification strategies, which provide limited guarantees when model outputs are malformed or uncertain.

In this work, we study *structured inference* as a system-level approach to robust mental health detection with LLMs. Rather than proposing a new model or learning algorithm, we design a LangGraph-based inference framework that models classification as a stateful process with explicit validation, repair, retry, and abstention mechanisms, and use it as an evaluation instrument to reveal failure behaviors that standard metrics do not capture. We compare this framework with Chain-of-Verification (CoVe), a self-verification method in which the model evaluates and optionally revises its own prediction.

We evaluate GPT-4o, LLaMA-4, Claude 3.5 Sonnet, Mistral-Nemo, Qwen, and DeepSeek v3.2 on two tasks: early anorexia risk detection (eRisk 2024) and depression detection (eRisk 2017) from longitudinal social media data. Results show that CoVe frequently triggers revision following verification disagreement, but these revisions rarely correspond to true recovery from initially invalid outputs. In contrast, LangGraph enforces output validity through external parsing and bounded repair retries, enabling reliable coverage and explicit abstention when recovery fails.

Across both tasks, robustness behavior varies substantially across models and cannot be inferred from accuracy alone. Additional analysis of revision and repair behavior highlights verifier instability and formatting-related failure modes that are not captured by standard classification metrics.

Keywords: large language models · structured inference · LangGraph · Chain-of-Verification · robustness · mental health detection

M. Ceci et al. (Eds.): ECML PKDD 2026, LNAI 16941, pp. 534–550, 2027.
https://doi.org/10.1007/978-3-032-37654-1_31

1 Introduction

Mental health disorders such as depression and eating disorders represent a major global health burden, and early identification is important for timely support and improved outcomes [30,38]. Traditional diagnosis relies on clinical interviews, self-reports, and structured assessments, which can miss early or subtle warning signs because of recall bias, limited illness insight, subjective interpretation, and uneven access to care [3,6,25,27,28,40]. Social media offers a complementary source of longitudinal linguistic and behavioral signals, and prior work has shown that online posts can reflect depression, eating disorders, and related mental health risks [9,10,36]. However, automated detection in this setting is inherently high-stakes: signals are often subtle and distributed across posts, while false positives and false negatives can both carry meaningful downstream consequences. As a result, robustness, output validity, and explicit failure handling are essential requirements for deployment [33].

Recent advances in large language models (LLMs) have led to substantial performance gains across a wide range of natural language processing tasks, including text classification and reasoning [8]. LLMs offer strong zero-shot and few-shot capabilities, making them attractive for mental health applications where labeled data is limited. However, LLMs are also prone to instruction-following failures, hallucinated outputs, and inconsistent formatting, particularly when strict output constraints are required. These issues are exacerbated in safety-critical settings, where invalid or ambiguous outputs cannot be safely ignored.

To mitigate these challenges, prior work has proposed self-verification strategies such as Chain-of-Verification (CoVe), in which an LLM is prompted to verify and optionally revise its own prediction [13]. While self-verification can reduce certain reasoning errors, it conflates semantic disagreement with output validity and lacks explicit mechanisms for detecting or recovering from malformed outputs. Consequently, verification disagreement often triggers additional inference steps without guaranteeing correction, termination, or improved robustness under strict output constraints.

In this work, we study *structured inference* as a system-level alternative to self-verification for robust mental health detection with LLMs. We introduce a LangGraph-based inference framework that models classification as a stateful process with explicit validation, repair, retry, and abstention mechanisms. Rather than treating an LLM call as the decision itself, the framework treats the LLM as a component within a controlled inference pipeline, enabling principled handling of invalid outputs and systematic analysis of failure modes.

We compare LangGraph-based structured inference and Chain-of-Verification (CoVe) across multiple large language models, including GPT-4o, LLaMA-4, Claude 3.5 Sonnet, Mistral-Nemo, DeepSeek v3.2, and Qwen. We evaluate both frameworks on two tasks: early anorexia risk detection (eRisk 2024 dataset) and depression detection (eRisk 2017 dataset), using longitudinal user timelines.

Beyond standard classification metrics, our evaluation analyzes coverage, defined as the fraction of users for which the framework produces a valid final prediction, along with intervention behavior, recovery, and additional failure modes related to verification and formatting. LangGraph achieves near-complete coverage across models and provides bounded recovery for formatting unstable models, whereas CoVe often triggers revisions without corresponding gains in true recovery. These findings show that robustness under strict output constraints is highly model-dependent and cannot be inferred from accuracy alone.

The remainder of the paper is organized as follows: Sect. 2 reviews related work; Sect. 3 introduces the tasks, datasets, and preprocessing; Sects. 4 and 5 describe the structured inference frameworks and methodology, including the experimental setup in Sect. 5.6; Sect. 6 presents the results; Sect. 7 discusses robustness and failure modes; Sect. 8 outlines ethical considerations; and Sect. 9 concludes the paper.

2 Related Work

Research on automatic mental health detection from social media has expanded rapidly with the availability of longitudinal user-generated text and advances in natural language processing. Prior work can be broadly grouped into three directions: mental health detection from social media data, the use of large language models and self-verification strategies, and research on robustness and failure handling.

2.1 Mental Health Detection from Social Media

Early studies showed that linguistic, emotional, and behavioral patterns in social media posts can reflect mental health conditions such as depression and eating disorders. De Choudhury et al. [10] demonstrated that depression could be inferred from Twitter using linguistic style, engagement patterns, and temporal activity signals, motivating subsequent work on user-level and longitudinal modeling.

The CLEF eRisk shared tasks later formalized early risk detection as a benchmark problem, introducing datasets and evaluation protocols for disorders including depression and anorexia [12,31]. Classical machine learning and deep learning approaches dominated early submissions, with sequential models such as Long Short-Term Memory (LSTM) networks proving effective for modeling temporal progression [35]. Research on eating disorder detection similarly leveraged social media data, identifying linguistic markers of disordered eating and body image concerns [9,36]. More recently, large language models have been explored for early anorexia risk detection, demonstrating the ability to capture distributed linguistic cues without task-specific retraining [14,15]. However, most prior approaches implicitly assume that model outputs are valid, limiting their suitability for safety-critical deployment.

2.2 Large Language Models and Verification Strategies

Large language models such as GPT-3 [8] enable zero-shot and few-shot classification without supervised fine-tuning, significantly lowering the barrier to applying NLP systems in healthcare and mental health applications [22,37]. Nevertheless, LLM outputs remain sensitive to prompt design and can exhibit hallucinations, formatting errors, and inconsistent instruction following [20,32].

Prompting-based verification strategies have been proposed to mitigate these issues. Chain-of-Verification (CoVe) prompts models to verify and potentially revise their own outputs by generating and answering verification questions [13]. Similar self-verification paradigms have been explored in downstream applications [7,41,45]. However, verification-based prompting remains heuristic and does not provide guarantees of output validity or reliable recovery from malformed responses, particularly in structured prediction tasks such as binary classification [19,29,39,43].

2.3 Robustness, Failure Handling, and Research Gap

The lack of robustness and transparency in machine learning systems has motivated extensive work on explainability and trustworthy AI [21,23,33]. In mental health applications, unreliable predictions can have serious ethical and clinical consequences, increasing the need for explicit failure handling mechanisms [11]. Approaches such as retrieval-augmented generation and citation-based reasoning improve grounding and interpretability in LLM predictions [2,24], but they do not explicitly model invalid outputs, retries, or abstention, leaving failure behavior difficult to analyze systematically [1,34,42].

To the best of our knowledge, no prior work has systematically compared self-verification prompting methods such as CoVe with a structured inference framework that provides explicit validation, repair, and abstention. Moreover, evaluations of LLMs for mental health detection typically emphasize accuracy while overlooking coverage, recovery behavior, and failure modes [4,5,16–18,44]. This work addresses these gaps by framing mental health detection as a stateful inference process and empirically comparing LangGraph-based structured inference with CoVe across anorexia and depression detection tasks.

3 Tasks and Datasets

We evaluate structured large language model (LLM) inference on two user-level mental health detection tasks using longitudinal social media data: early anorexia risk detection and depression detection. In both settings, the goal is to infer a binary risk label from a temporally ordered sequence of posts authored by a single user. This formulation reflects real-world early screening scenarios, where diagnostic signals are sparse, context-dependent, and distributed across time.

3.1 Datasets

Anorexia Detection. We use the *CLEF eRisk 2024 Task 2* dataset, which focuses on early detection of anorexia nervosa from Reddit user timelines [12]. Each instance corresponds to a Reddit user represented by a chronologically ordered sequence of posts, with a binary user-level label indicating anorexia risk ($y = 1$) or non-anorexic behavior ($y = 0$). Labels were assigned and validated by clinical experts following the eRisk shared task protocol. Because the original dataset is highly imbalanced, we construct a balanced evaluation subset consisting of 184 users (92 per class) through random undersampling of the majority class. The subset was sampled once using a fixed random seed and then frozen for all experiments to ensure reproducibility and comparability across models.

Depression Detection. For depression detection, we use the *CLEF eRisk 2017* dataset, a widely adopted benchmark for early depression risk detection from social media [26]. The dataset contains 166 users with balanced class distribution. Similar to the anorexia task, each user is represented by a timeline of posts ordered by time, and labels are provided at the user level.

3.2 Preprocessing

For datasets provided at the post level, all posts authored by a user are aggregated into a single document after sorting chronologically by timestamp, resulting in a user-level representation. This formulation enables models to capture cumulative linguistic patterns across a user's posting history rather than reasoning over isolated messages. For datasets already released in merged form, the provided user-level documents are used directly.

Text preprocessing is intentionally minimal. Aside from basic null handling and type normalization, no linguistic normalization, content filtering, stemming, or lemmatization is applied, in order to preserve the original language and structure of user posts.

Labels are represented as binary values (0/1), consistent with the strict single-token output constraint enforced during inference. All datasets are anonymized and distributed under ethical-use agreements. Identical inference-time validation rules, retry limits, and evaluation procedures are applied across all models to ensure a controlled and fair comparison.

4 Structured Inference Frameworks

To address the robustness limitations of single-shot prompting in mental health risk detection, we study two structured inference frameworks that impose explicit control over LLM behavior: a LangGraph-based inference framework and the CoVe pipeline. While both aim to improve reliability beyond naive prompting, they differ in how validation, recovery, and failure handling are implemented.

4.1 LangGraph-Based Inference

LangGraph formulates LLM inference as a stateful execution graph with deterministic control flow and explicit state propagation (Fig. 1). Rather than treating the LLM as an autonomous decision-maker, LangGraph embeds the model within a controller that manages prompt construction, output validation, retries, and termination.

Each inference run maintains a structured state containing the user timeline, prompt, raw model output, parsed prediction ($y \in \{0, 1, \perp\}$), validity flag, and retry counter. The execution graph consists of nodes for model invocation, output parsing and validation, repair via re-prompting, and termination. Conditional transitions route execution based on validation outcomes and retry limits.

This design enables systematic detection of malformed outputs, bounded repair through stricter re-prompts, and explicit abstention when recovery fails. Because validity is enforced externally rather than delegated to the model, LangGraph guarantees deterministic termination and provides explicit failure states, enabling detailed analysis of coverage, recovery, and error modes.

4.2 Chain-of-Verification (CoVe)

CoVe augments inference with a self-verification step that encourages the model to critique and potentially revise its own prediction [13]. As illustrated in Fig. 2, the pipeline proceeds sequentially: the model first generates a binary prediction, then evaluates the consistency of that prediction with the input posts and task definition. If inconsistency is detected, a revision prompt produces the final output.

Unlike LangGraph, CoVe does not rely on external parsing or deterministic validation. Instead, the verification decision is produced by the model itself, making error detection model-internal and heuristic. As a result, CoVe provides weaker guarantees regarding output validity and termination, and abstention is not treated as a native outcome unless explicitly added.

Although CoVe has shown benefits in reasoning-oriented tasks, its effectiveness for binary classification depends on whether verification disagreement reliably signals genuine prediction errors or invalid outputs.

4.3 Conceptual Comparison

The key difference between LangGraph and CoVe lies in where control resides. LangGraph externalizes control through deterministic validation, bounded repair retries (K), and explicit abstention ($\perp$), making invalid outputs observable and measurable. This enables principled reporting of coverage, recovery behavior, and failure modes.

CoVe internalizes control by relying on model-driven self-verification to detect and correct errors. Verification disagreement acts as a heuristic signal rather than an externally enforced validity check, which may lead to revisions that do not correspond to actual output failures.

These differences affect robustness and interpretability: LangGraph emphasizes system-level guarantees and auditability, whereas CoVe relies on model-driven self-correction. In the following sections, we compare both frameworks across multiple LLMs and mental health detection tasks, evaluating predictive performance alongside coverage, recovery behavior, and abstention dynamics.

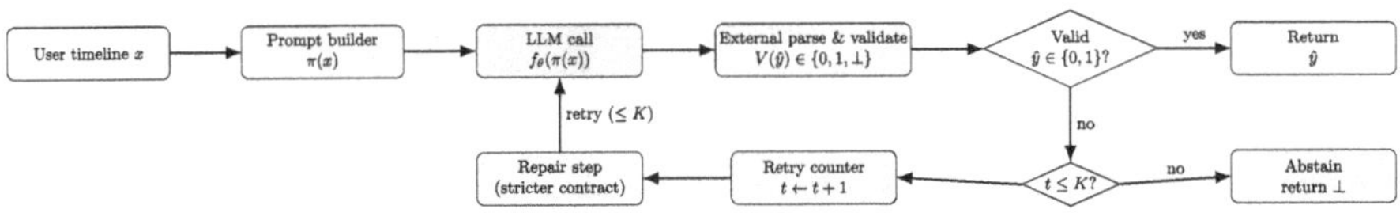

Fig. 1. LangGraph structured inference. A system-level controller enforces a strict output contract via external parsing/validation. Invalid outputs trigger deterministic repair with bounded retries (K); persistent failure yields explicit abstention ($\perp$).

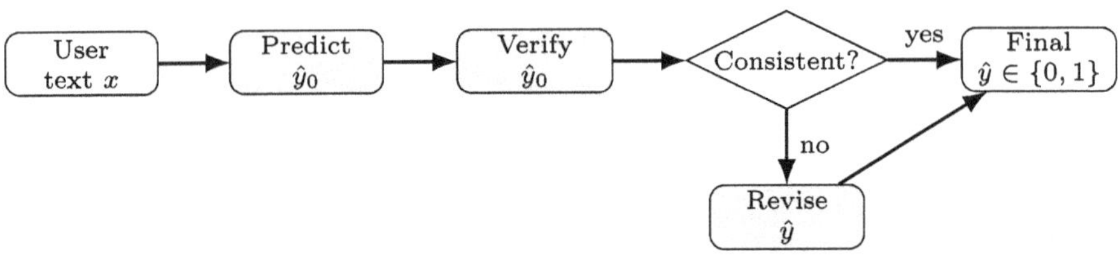

Fig. 2. CoVe. The model produces an initial prediction, self-verifies consistency with the input, and revises the output if inconsistency is detected.

5 Methodology

This section describes the structured inference methodology used in our experiments. We detail prompt design, output parsing and validation, repair and retry logic, abstention handling, and the structured state representation used to analyze model behavior under both LangGraph-based and CoVe inference frameworks.

5.1 Prompt Design

All models are tasked with binary mental health risk classification at the user level. Each user is represented by a concatenated timeline of posts ordered chronologically. Prompts explicitly constrain the output space to a single binary digit: `0` indicating no risk and `1` indicating risk.

To encourage strict output compliance, prompts instruct the model to return a single character with no additional text, explanation, or formatting. This constraint enables deterministic parsing and systematic detection of invalid outputs.

Both frameworks use the same base prediction prompt. LangGraph adds a repair prompt when the output violates the strict binary format, while CoVe adds verification and revision prompts. Compact prompt templates are shown in Fig. 3.

Prediction Prompt (LangGraph + CoVe)

You are a mental health detection assistant.
Here is a user's collection of social media posts:
{user_posts}
Based on these posts, does the user show signs of the target condition?
Answer ONLY with a single digit: - 1 if yes - 0 if not
Your answer:

LangGraph Repair Prompt

Your previous output was invalid.
Reply with exactly one character: 0 or 1.
No spaces, punctuation, or explanation.

CoVe Verification Prompt

You are verifying a binary mental health prediction.
User posts: {user_posts}
Proposed prediction: {pred}
Is the prediction consistent with the user's posts?
Answer ONLY with: - YES if consistent - NO if not
Your answer:

CoVe Revision Prompt

Your previous answer was rejected during verification.
Here is the user's collection of posts:
{user_posts}
Does the user show signs of the target condition?
Reply with exactly ONE character: - 1 if yes - 0 if no
No explanation.

Fig. 3. Compact prompt templates used in the two inference frameworks. LangGraph uses a shared prediction prompt with an additional repair prompt when the output violates the strict binary format. CoVe uses the same prediction prompt followed by verification and, if needed, revision.

5.2 Output Parsing and Validation Rules

Model outputs are parsed using strict deterministic rules. A prediction is considered valid if it resolves to a single binary value in $\{0, 1\}$. Outputs containing explanatory text, hedging language, multiple tokens, or empty responses are treated as invalid and recorded as failure cases. Outputs expressing indecision, uncertainty, or refusal (e.g., "I cannot decide") are treated as invalid and handled identically to other formatting violations. Output validity is enforced externally in the LangGraph framework via parsing and validation logic. In CoVe, verification outputs are used to guide potential revision but do not themselves constitute externally enforced validity checks. In addition to strict parsing, we perform an auxiliary lenient digit extraction during analysis to detect cases where the model output contains a binary label but violates the strict output contract (e.g., "output is 0"). This lenient extraction is used only for diagnostic analysis and does not affect inference decisions or validity checks during evaluation.

5.3 Repair and Retry Mechanisms

We define *attempt-level recovery* as the transition from an initially invalid model output to a valid binary prediction within the same inference run. Outputs are considered invalid if they violate strict parsing rules (e.g., extra text, empty responses, or expressions of uncertainty).

In the LangGraph framework, invalid predictions trigger a repair step in which the model is re-prompted with stricter output instructions. We distinguish between *attempts* and *retries*. The initial model call is attempt 0, and each repair increments the attempt counter by one. Repair attempts are bounded to guarantee termination; in all experiments we use a fixed retry limit of $K = 2$, allowing at most two repair attempts after the initial attempt

In practice, most models either produce valid outputs initially or require at most a single repair. To analyze repair behavior more precisely, we record a frozen snapshot of the initial model output (attempt 0), including the raw response, parsing validity, and extracted label information. This snapshot allows us to distinguish formatting errors present in the original output from changes introduced by subsequent repair attempts.

In many logged cases, repair appears to correct formatting violations rather than substantive reasoning errors. However, because repair involves reissuing the prompt, the predicted label may occasionally change. This motivates analyzing the interaction between formatting repair and prediction correctness. In the reported experiments, repair improves output validity and does not appear to degrade overall predictive accuracy.

We do not explore larger values of K in this work. Increasing the retry budget could further improve recovery for models that frequently violate output formatting constraints, but would introduce additional inference cost and latency.

In the CoVe framework, recovery is attempted through a single revision step following verification disagreement. If the verification stage indicates that the prediction is inconsistent with the task or input, a revision prompt reissues the original classification request and produces a final prediction. The revised prediction replaces the initial output if it satisfies the parsing rules, and no additional retries are performed. The verification stage expects a YES/NO response. If the verifier output does not resolve to either label under strict parsing, it is treated as disagreement and the revision prompt is issued.

5.4 Abstention Criteria

Abstention is an explicit outcome in the LangGraph framework. If all repair attempts fail to produce a valid output within the retry limit, inference terminates with $\perp$, indicating uncertainty rather than forcing a malformed prediction.

CoVe does not include an explicit abstention mechanism. If prediction and revision both yield invalid outputs, failure handling relies on downstream filtering rather than a first-class abstention state.

5.5 State Representation

Each inference run maintains a structured record including the user identifier, true label, model name, prompt stage, raw model output, parsed prediction value (0, 1, or $\perp$), validation outcome, error type, retry count, and cumulative latency. This representation enables fine-grained analysis of coverage, recovery behavior, verification disagreement, and failure modes across models and tasks.

By explicitly separating model reasoning from system-level control, this methodology supports reproducible and analyzable inference in safety-critical mental health applications.

5.6 Experimental Setup

All experiments were conducted in a controlled Python environment using Google Colab.[1] Model inference was performed via API-based LLMs, while parsing, validation, retry logic, and evaluation were implemented locally. No models were fine-tuned; all results reflect zero-shot inference.

All LLM calls used deterministic decoding (temperature = 0.0, no sampling) with `max_tokens` = 5, sufficient for the binary output format. Because user timelines may exceed context limits, concatenated posts were truncated to the first 2000 characters prior to prompting. We use this fixed prefix-based truncation as a simple and consistent context-control strategy across all models and both inference frameworks (LangGraph and CoVe), ensuring comparability even though alternative truncation policies could also be studied in future work.

We evaluate two binary classification tasks: anorexia detection (CLEF eRisk 2024, 184 users) and depression detection (CLEF eRisk 2017, 166 users). Each user is represented by a concatenated, chronologically ordered timeline of posts with user-level labels provided by the dataset organizers.

Performance is measured using accuracy, precision, recall, and F1 computed on valid predictions only. Robustness metrics include coverage, repair incidence (LangGraph), revision incidence (CoVe), and attempt-level recovery.

[1] Code and evaluation scripts are available at https://github.com/layafakher/structured-llm-mental-health.

6 Results

We evaluate LangGraph-based structured inference and CoVe on two mental health detection tasks: anorexia detection (eRisk 2024, 184 users) and depression detection (eRisk 2017, 166 users). In addition to standard classification metrics, we report coverage and true recovery behavior to assess robustness under strict output constraints.

6.1 LangGraph Results

Table 1 reports LangGraph performance across models and tasks. Overall, LangGraph achieves full or near-full coverage for all evaluated models. For models with strong instruction-following behavior, including GPT-4o, Mistral-Nemo, DeepSeek, and Qwen, valid predictions are produced consistently without requiring repair, resulting in zero true recovery because initial outputs are already valid.

In contrast, LLaMA-4 and Claude exhibit higher rates of initially invalid outputs, leading to measurable recovery under LangGraph. Recovery is most pronounced for LLaMA-4, reaching 15.8% on anorexia detection and 19.3% on depression detection. Claude also shows non-zero recovery, though with lower final coverage due to persistent invalid outputs (e.g., empty or verbose responses) for a subset of users. These invalid outputs are predominantly near-miss formatting violations rather than clear semantic failures, such as quoted labels, punctuation attached to the binary label, or explanatory text surrounding the answer. LangGraph's external parsing and validation logic detects these violations and applies bounded repair retries, enabling systematic correction for models with formatting instability.

Across both tasks, precision is often high while recall varies more substantially across models. LangGraph makes failures explicit: invalid outputs are either repaired through bounded retries or terminate in abstention, enabling transparent measurement of coverage and recovery behavior. Inspection of logged outputs suggests that correct-but-invalid initial predictions occur infrequently and that we did not observe cases where repair produced a valid but incorrect final prediction in the logged runs.

6.2 CoVe Results

Table 2 reports results under CoVe. CoVe frequently triggers a revision step following verification disagreement, leading to high revision incidence across several models. However, revision incidence does not reliably correspond to genuine recovery from invalid outputs. In many cases, revision is triggered even when the initial prediction is already strict-valid, so the revise stage reflects verifier disagreement rather than recovery from a malformed prediction.

True attempt-level recovery, defined as an initially invalid prediction becoming valid after revision, is rare across models and tasks. The main exception is LLaMA-4, which achieves measurable recovery under CoVe (9.8% on anorexia detection and 17.5% on depression detection). For most other models, true recovery is effectively zero despite non-trivial or even high revision incidence. For example, Mistral-Nemo, DeepSeek, GPT-4o, and Qwen often revise a substantial fraction of cases while recovering no invalid predictions at all. This indicates that verification disagreement usually does not correspond to output invalidity.

Inspection of logged verification outputs suggests frequent verification false negatives for several models, especially Mistral-Nemo and DeepSeek, indicating that much of CoVe's revision behavior may reflect verifier instability rather than successful correction of malformed outputs. CoVe does not provide explicit abstention or externally enforced output validation, and in our implementation it uses only a single revision step.

Table 1. LangGraph results. Accuracy, Precision, Recall, and F1 are computed on valid predictions only. Cov denotes final coverage after bounded retries. Repair denotes the fraction of users requiring at least one repair attempt. Recov denotes true attempt-level recovery (attempt-0 invalid → final valid).

Model	Anorexia (eRisk 2024, 184)							Depression (eRisk 2017, 166)						
	Acc	Prec	Rec	F1	Cov	Repair	Recov	Acc	Prec	Rec	F1	Cov	Repair	Recov
GPT-4o	0.804	1.000	0.609	0.757	1.000	0.000	0.000	0.741	0.857	0.578	0.691	1.000	0.000	0.000
LLaMA-4	0.799	0.983	0.609	0.752	1.000	0.158	0.158	0.747	0.720	0.807	0.761	1.000	0.193	0.193
Claude 3.5 Sonnet	0.848	1.000	0.693	0.819	0.967	0.076	0.043	0.755	0.880	0.571	0.693	0.958	0.205	0.163
Mistral-Nemo	0.799	1.000	0.598	0.748	1.000	0.000	0.000	0.723	0.723	0.723	0.723	1.000	0.000	0.000
DeepSeek v3.2	0.712	0.976	0.435	0.602	1.000	0.000	0.000	0.765	0.923	0.578	0.711	1.000	0.000	0.000
Qwen	0.793	1.000	0.587	0.740	1.000	0.000	0.000	0.771	0.836	0.675	0.747	1.000	0.000	0.000

Table 2. CoVe results. Accuracy, Precision, Recall, and F1 are computed on valid predictions only. Cov denotes final coverage. Rev denotes revision incidence. Recov denotes true attempt-level recovery (predict invalid → final valid).

Model	Anorexia (eRisk 2024, 184)							Depression (eRisk 2017, 166)						
	Acc	Prec	Rec	F1	Cov	Rev	Recov	Acc	Prec	Rec	F1	Cov	Rev	Recov
GPT-4o	0.799	1.000	0.598	0.748	1.000	0.092	0.000	0.753	0.889	0.578	0.701	1.000	0.193	0.000
LLaMA-4	0.781	1.000	0.571	0.727	0.967	0.571	0.098	0.771	0.778	0.759	0.768	1.000	0.861	0.175
Claude 3.5 Sonnet	0.842	1.000	0.682	0.811	0.962	0.092	0.000	0.742	0.875	0.545	0.672	0.958	0.175	0.000
Mistral-Nemo	0.739	1.000	0.478	0.647	1.000	0.750	0.000	0.741	0.870	0.566	0.686	1.000	0.669	0.000
DeepSeek v3.2	0.755	1.000	0.511	0.676	1.000	0.386	0.000	0.771	0.909	0.602	0.725	1.000	0.590	0.000
Qwen	0.788	1.000	0.576	0.731	1.000	0.071	0.000	0.789	0.843	0.711	0.771	1.000	0.223	0.000

6.3 Comparison and Analysis

Across both tasks, the main difference is that LangGraph externalizes control through deterministic validation, bounded retries, and abstention, whereas CoVe relies on model-internal self-verification. As a result, CoVe often revises already valid predictions, while LangGraph provides clearer guarantees about output validity, recovery, and failure handling.

These results show that robustness under strict output constraints cannot be inferred from accuracy alone. Although CoVe may change the final prediction through self-verification and revision, it does not provide the same level of control and auditability as structured inference with external validation.

7 Robustness, Failure Analysis, and Discussion

The experiments reveal that robustness behavior varies substantially across models and inference frameworks, even when predictive accuracy is similar. Models that consistently follow strict output instructions (e.g., GPT-4o, Mistral-Nemo, DeepSeek, and Qwen) achieve full coverage under LangGraph without requiring repair, whereas models with less stable formatting (e.g., LLaMA-4 and Claude) benefit from bounded recovery through repair retries. In contrast, CoVe frequently triggers revision through verification disagreement, but this behavior often reflects verifier instability rather than correction of malformed outputs. In many cases, revision occurs even when the initial prediction already satisfies the strict output format, resulting in high revision incidence without corresponding gains in true recovery.

To assess the sensitivity of structured inference to the repair budget K, we reconstruct coverage at K=0 (validation only, no repair), K=1, and K=2 from the logged attempt-level records, requiring no additional inference (Table 3). Because $K = 0$ corresponds to external parsing and validation only and $K \geq 1$ additionally enables bounded repair, this sweep also serves as a component ablation of the inference pipeline: deterministic validation alone already yields full coverage for the four format-stable models, the repair mechanism accounts for essentially all recovered coverage on the two format-unstable models (LLaMA-4 and Claude), and abstention ($\perp$) absorbs the small residual of persistent Claude failures. The four format-stable models emit valid outputs at attempt 0 and remain at full coverage for all K, so repair is never invoked. For the two format-unstable models, recovery is concentrated almost entirely in the first repair: a single repair (K=1) raises LLaMA-4 coverage from 0.842 to 0.989 on anorexia and from 0.807 to 1.000 on depression, and recovers all recoverable Claude cases, after which K=2 yields no further gain. The residual Claude failures are persistent empty outputs that do not recover under additional repair. These results indicate that coverage saturates by K=1–2, so larger retry budgets would add latency and cost without improving robustness, supporting K=2 as a near-saturating default. The cost of repair is also bounded and incurred selectively: because repair is triggered only for users whose attempt-0 output is invalid, the four format-stable models incur no additional inference calls, while LLaMA-4 and Claude incur only a modest overhead (roughly 11–25% additional calls over a single-call baseline).

These results highlight the importance of evaluating reliability beyond classification accuracy. Although LangGraph and CoVe may produce similar predictive performance in some settings, their behavior under strict output constraints differs substantially. Structured inference with external validation

Table 3. Effect of the repair budget K on coverage. Values are reconstructed from logged attempt-level records (attempt-0 snapshots and `Attempts_Used`), requiring no additional inference. The four format-stable models (GPT-4o, Mistral-Nemo, DeepSeek, Qwen) produce valid outputs at attempt 0 and remain at 1.000 coverage for all K; only the two format-unstable models are shown.

Task	Model	K=0	K=1	K=2
Anorexia (184)	LLaMA-4	0.842	0.989	1.000
	Claude 3.5 Sonnet	0.924	0.967	0.967
Depression (166)	LLaMA-4	0.807	1.000	1.000
	Claude 3.5 Sonnet	0.795	0.958	0.958

enables explicit detection of invalid outputs, bounded recovery, and principled abstention when recovery fails, making failure modes observable and auditable. Such system-level control mechanisms are particularly important in safety-critical domains like mental health analysis, where robustness and transparent uncertainty handling are essential.

8 Ethical Considerations

This work uses the CLEF eRisk 2024 and eRisk 2017 datasets under the official data-use agreements and in accordance with the organizers' ethical guidelines. The data consist of publicly available social media posts that were anonymized by the providers before release. No attempts were made to re-identify users or infer attributes beyond the provided labels.

Given the sensitive nature of mental health data, all experiments were conducted strictly for research purposes in a controlled academic setting. The evaluated models are not intended for clinical diagnosis, real-time screening, or decision-making about individuals, and predictions should not be interpreted as medical assessments. Misclassification remains a meaningful risk, especially through false positives that may contribute to stigmatization and false negatives that may delay support. To mitigate these concerns, our study emphasizes explicit failure handling, including abstention when reliable prediction is not possible. All results are reported only in aggregate form, without individual-level predictions or qualitative examples. Any real-world use of large language models for mental health analysis should therefore include human oversight, clear uncertainty signaling, and strong safeguards for responsible deployment.

9 Conclusion and Future Work

This study compared LangGraph-based structured inference and CoVe for mental health risk detection using large language models across anorexia and depression detection tasks. The results show that robustness under strict output constraints cannot be inferred from accuracy alone. LangGraph provides high coverage, bounded recovery behavior, and explicit failure handling, whereas CoVe often triggers revisions without corresponding gains in true recovery.

These findings highlight the importance of separating model generation from inference control in safety-critical settings. Future work will explore hybrid frameworks that combine external validation with selective self-verification, extend structured inference to longitudinal and multimodal mental health signals, and investigate cost-aware recovery strategies that balance robustness with computational efficiency.

References

1. Adhikari, T.: Learning to say 'I Don't Know': A vision for abstention in large language models. techRxiv preprint (2025)
2. Amugongo, L.M., Mascheroni, P., Brooks, S., Doering, S., Seidel, J.: Retrieval augmented generation for large language models in healthcare: A systematic review. PLOS Digit. Health **4**(6), e0000877 (2025). https://doi.org/10.1371/journal.pdig.0000877
3. Anderson, A., Eisenberg, M.D., Kennedy-Hendricks, A., Castrucci, B.C., Galea, S., Ettman, C.K.: Mental health crises and help-seeking among us adults in 2024-2025. Health Affairs Scholar **3**(9), qxaf166 (2025). https://doi.org/10.1093/haschl/qxaf166
4. Arnaiz-Rodriguez, A., Baidal, M., Derner, E., Annable, J.L., Ball, M., Ince, M., Vallejos, E.P., Oliver, N.: Between help and harm: An evaluation of mental health crisis handling by LLMs. arXiv preprint arXiv:2509.24857 (2025)
5. Badawi, A., et al.: When can we trust LLMs in mental health? large-scale benchmarks for reliable LLM evaluation. In: Proceedings of the 19th Conference of the European Chapter of the Association for Computational Linguistics (Volume 1: Long Papers), pp. 3873–3896 (2026)
6. Baldofski, S., et al.: Intentions and barriers to help-seeking in adolescents and young adults differing in depression severity: cross-sectional results from a school-based mental health project. Child Adolesc. Psychiatry Ment. Health **18**, 84 (2024). https://doi.org/10.1186/s13034-024-00775-3
7. Barez, F., et al.: Chain-of-thought is not explainability. preprint. Oxford WhiteBox / Oxford AIGI (2025)
8. Brown, T.B., et al.: Language models are few-shot learners. Adv. Neural. Inf. Process. Syst. **33**, 1877–1901 (2020)
9. Chancellor, S., Mitra, T., Choudhury, M.D.: Recovery amid pro-anorexia: Analysis of recovery in social media. In: Proceedings of the 2016 CHI Conference on Human Factors in Computing Systems, pp. 2111–2123 (2016)
10. Choudhury, M.D., Gamon, M., Counts, S., Horvitz, E.: Predicting depression via social media. In: Proceedings of the International AAAI Conference on Web and Social Media, vol. 7, pp. 128–137 (2013). https://doi.org/10.1609/icwsm.v7i1.14432
11. Cortes, C., DeSalvo, G., Mohri, M.: Learning with rejection. In: Proceedings of the 27th International Conference on Algorithmic Learning Theory, pp. 67–82 (2016)
12. Crestani, F., Losada, D.E., Parapar, J.: Early Detection of Mental Health Disorders by Social Media Monitoring: The First Five Years of the eRisk Project, Studies in

Computational Intelligence, vol. 1018. Springer, Cham (2022). https://doi.org/10.1007/978-3-031-04431-1
13. Dhuliawala, S., et al.: Chain-of-verification reduces hallucination in large language models. arXiv preprint arXiv:2309.11495 (2023)
14. Fakher, L., Bauer, A.: Retrieval and citation augmented generation for explainable detection of anorexia on social media: A multi-model comparative study. In: Proceedings of the 2026 International Conference on AI x Data and Knowledge Engineering (AIxDKE), pp. 6–11. IEEE (2026). https://doi.org/10.1109/AIxDKE64848.2026.11486497
15. Fakher, L., Davarkhah, M.: Harnessing large language models for early risk assessment of anorexia on social media. In: Proceedings of the 4th IEEE International Conference on Computing and Machine Intelligence (2025)
16. Ghorbian, M., Ghobaei-Arani, M.: Large language models for mental health diagnosis and treatment: a survey. Artif. Intell. Rev. **58**(1) (2025). https://doi.org/10.1007/s10462-025-11418-0
17. Guo, Z., Lai, A., Thygesen, J.H., Farrington, J., Keen, T., Li, K.: Large language models for mental health applications: Systematic review. JMIR Mental Health **11**, e57400 (2024). https://doi.org/10.2196/57400
18. Hua, Y., et al.: A scoping review of large language models for generative tasks in mental health care. npj Digit. Med. **8**, 230 (2025). https://doi.org/10.1038/s41746-025-01611-4
19. Huang, J., et al.: Large language models cannot self-correct reasoning yet **2024**, 32808–32824 (2024)
20. Ji, Z., et al.: Survey of hallucination in natural language generation. ACM Comput. Surv. **55**(12), 1–38 (2023). https://doi.org/10.1145/3571730
21. Joyce, D.W., Kormilitzin, A., Smith, K.A., Cipriani, A.: Explainable artificial intelligence for mental health through transparency and interpretability for understandability. npj Digit. Med. **6**(1), 6 (2023). https://doi.org/10.1038/s41746-023-00751-9
22. Labrak, Y., Rouvier, M., Dufour, R.: A zero-shot and few-shot study of instruction-finetuned large language models applied to clinical and biomedical tasks. In: Proceedings of the 2024 Joint International Conference on Computational Linguistics, Language Resources and Evaluation (LREC-COLING 2024), pp. 2049–2066. ELRA and ICCL, Torino, Italia (2024)
23. Lee, E.E., et al.: Artificial intelligence for mental healthcare: Clinical applications, barriers, facilitators, and artificial wisdom. Biol. Psychiatry Cogn. Neurosci. Neuroimaging **6**(9), 856–864 (2021). https://doi.org/10.1016/j.bpsc.2021.02.001
24. Lewis, P., et al.: Retrieval-augmented generation for knowledge-intensive nlp tasks: Adv. Neural. Inf. Process. Syst. **33**, 9459–9474 (2020)
25. Linardon, J.: Navigating the future of psychiatry: A review of research on opportunities, applications, and challenges of artificial intelligence. Current Treat. Options Psychiatry **12**, 8 (2025). https://doi.org/10.1007/s40501-025-00344-1
26. Losada, D.E., Crestani, F., Parapar, J.: eRISK 2017: CLEF Lab on Early Risk Prediction on the Internet: Experimental Foundations. In: Jones, G.J.F., Lawless, S., Gonzalo, J., Kelly, L., Goeuriot, L., Mandl, T., Cappellato, L., Ferro, N. (eds.) CLEF 2017. LNCS, vol. 10456, pp. 346–360. Springer, Cham (2017). https://doi.org/10.1007/978-3-319-65813-1_30
27. Lui, J.C., Sagar-Ouriaghli, I., Brown, J.S.L.: Barriers and facilitators to help-seeking for common mental disorders among university students: a systematic review. J. Am. Coll. Health **72**(8), 2605–2613 (2024). https://doi.org/10.1080/07448481.2022.2119859

28. Mao, K., Wu, Y., Chen, J.: A systematic review on automated clinical depression diagnosis. npj Mental Health Res. **2**(1), 20 (2023). https://doi.org/10.1038/s44184-023-00040-z
29. Miao, N., Teh, Y.W., Rainforth, T.: Selfcheck: Using llms to zero-shot check their own step-by-step reasoning. arXiv preprint arXiv:2308.00436 (2023)
30. Organization, W.H.: Mental disorders. World Health Organization Fact Sheets (2023)
31. Parapar, J., Pérez, A., Wang, X., Crestani, F.: erisk 2025: Contextual and conversational approaches for depression challenges. In: Advances in Information Retrieval: 47th European Conference on Information Retrieval (ECIR 2025), pp. 416–424 (2025)
32. Rawte, V., Sheth, A., Das, A.: A survey of hallucination in large foundation models. arXiv preprint arXiv:2309.05922 (2023)
33. Samek, W., Wiegand, T., Müller, K.R.: Explainable artificial intelligence: Understanding, visualizing and interpreting deep learning models. arXiv preprint arXiv:1708.08296 (2017)
34. Schuster, D.: Abstaining machine learning: Philosophical considerations. arXiv preprint arXiv:2409.00706 (2024)
35. Sheikhi, F., Fakher, L., Chekani, D.: Depression detection on erisk 2017 using long short-term memory models. In: Proceedings of the 20th CSI International Symposium on Artificial Intelligence and Signal Processing (2024)
36. Sidani, J.E., Shensa, J.A., Hoffman, B.A., Hanmer, J., Primack, B.L.: The association between social media use and eating concerns among u.s. young adults. J. Acad. Nutr. Diet. **116**(9), 1465–1472 (2016)
37. Singhal, K., et al.: Large language models encode clinical knowledge. Nature **620**(7972), 172–180 (2023). https://doi.org/10.1038/s41586-023-06291-2
38. Smink, F.R.E., van Hoeken, D.A.M., Hoek, H.W.: Epidemiology of eating disorders: Incidence, prevalence and mortality rates. Curr. Psychiatry Rep. **14**(4), 406–414 (2012)
39. Stechly, K., Valmeekam, K., Kambhampati, S.: On the self-verification limitations of large language models on reasoning and planning tasks. arXiv preprint arXiv:2402.08115 (2024)
40. Su, C., Xu, Z., Pathak, J., Wang, F.: Deep learning in mental health outcome research: a scoping review. Transl. Psychiatry **10**(1), 116 (2020). https://doi.org/10.1038/s41398-020-0780-3
41. Wei, J., et al.: Chain-of-thought prompting elicits reasoning in large language models. In: Advances in Neural Information Processing Systems, vol. 35, pp. 24824–24837 (2022)
42. Wen, B., Yao, J., Feng, S., Xu, C., Tsvetkov, Y., Howe, B., Wang, L.L.: Know your limits: A survey of abstention in large language models. Trans. Assoc. Comput. Linguist. **13**, 529–556 (2025). https://doi.org/10.1162/tacl_a_00754
43. Weng, Y., et al.: Large language models are better reasoners with self-verification. In: Findings of the Association for Computational Linguistics: EMNLP 2023, pp. 2550–2575 (2023)
44. Xu, X., et al.: Mental-LLM: Leveraging large language models for mental health prediction via online text data. Proc. ACM Inter. Mob. Wearable Ubiquitous Technol. **8**(1), 31:1–31:32 (2024). https://doi.org/10.1145/3643540
45. Zhao, C., et al.: Is chain-of-thought reasoning of llms a mirage? a data distribution lens. arXiv preprint arXiv:2508.01191 (2025)

Towards Universal Few-Shot Medical Diagnosis: A Manifold-Rectified Transductive Framework for Imaging and Omics

Feiyu He, Qingchen Zhang, and Guihua Tao(✉)

Hainan University, Haikou, China
{zhangqingchen,ghtao}@hainanu.edu.cn

Abstract. In medical few-shot learning (FSL), classical prototype networks often face challenges of initial prototype bias and metric failure when handling high-dimensional heterogeneous data. To address this, we propose a universal transductive support query expansion (TSQE) framework aimed at robustly reconstructing prototype networks by leveraging high-order contextual information from unlabeled query sets. Core innovations include: (1) High-Order Tensor Similarity (HOTS): A metric module based on fourth-order tensor interactions replaces Euclidean distance in traditional prototype networks. By aggregating global affinity to suppress noise, it effectively adapts to multimodal distributions spanning from medical images to high-dimensional omics data. (2) Tensor-Guided Prototype Network Reconstruction: Utilizes the HOTS matrix to adaptively select the top-r high-confidence query samples, enabling weighted expansion and calibration of the prototype network's initial class centers. Evaluations across extensive benchmarks spanning pathology, radiology, multimodal, and high-dimensional omics demonstrate that TSQE significantly enhances the discriminative power of prototype network. It achieves 1-shot average accuracy gains of 2%–15% over baselines, and outperforms existing state-of-the-art methods, validating its versatility and robustness.

Keywords: Few-shot learning · Medical image analysis · Higher-order tensor similarity · Prototype network · Multi-omics analysis

1 Introduction

The rapid advancement of precision medicine imposes high demands on the early diagnosis and subtype classification of cancer. In recent years, deep learning has demonstrated immense potential in processing high-dimensional biomedical data, such as histopathology images and multi-omics data, and has been widely applied to the computer-aided diagnosis of various malignancies, including lung and colorectal cancer [1,11,19]. Furthermore, extracting discriminative representations from medical lesions is often highly challenging; for instance,

M. Ceci et al. (Eds.): ECML PKDD 2026, LNAI 16941, pp. 551–565, 2027.
https://doi.org/10.1007/978-3-032-37654-1_32

tumors like nasopharyngeal carcinoma typically present with indistinguishable borders and suffer from severe background dominance in complex anatomical regions [15]. However, traditional deep learning models typically rely on large-scale, high-quality labeled data, which is often difficult to satisfy in medical scenarios. Acquiring a large number of confirmed rare pathological slices or specific subtype omics data is not only costly but also constrained by ethics and privacy regulations. To reconcile the contradiction between "data silos" and sample scarcity, Few-Shot Learning (FSL) has emerged, aiming to enable models to rapidly adapt to new tasks using extremely few support samples.

Among the various FSL paradigms, metric-based methods have garnered significant attention due to their simplicity and efficiency. Notably, Prototypical Networks (ProtoNets) [14] represent the most classic and widely used model. The core idea is to map support samples into an embedding space, calculate their mean as the Class Prototype, and classify query samples based on the Euclidean distance to these prototypes. Many researchers have attempted to apply this meta-learning framework to medical diagnosis. For instance, MLLCD [6] utilized meta-learning strategies to improve classification accuracy in lung cancer pathology; DCPN [13] introduced global and local features via a dual-channel network to enhance representation capabilities; and other studies such as SSL-ProtoNet [10] have incorporated self-supervised learning mechanisms to improve the generalization of feature extractors.

Despite this progress, directly applying classic Prototypical Networks to high-dimensional, heterogeneous medical data still faces two severe challenges, which are particularly pronounced in the highly challenging 1-Shot tasks:

- **Prototype Bias:** Due to the extreme scarcity of support samples (e.g., only one image per class), the directly calculated mean often deviates from the true distribution center, leading to significant bias in prototype estimation. Although existing solutions like PRSN [3] proposed theoretical correction ideas, simple linear corrections struggle to capture the complex manifold structures of medical data distributions.
- **Metric Failure:** Prototypical Networks assume that data in the embedding space follows an isotropic Gaussian distribution and rely on Euclidean distance for measurement. However, biomedical data often exhibit extremely high dimensionality and complex non-linear relationships (e.g., 60,000 dimensional gene expression data or texture-complex pathological images). Under low-sample conditions, simple Point-to-Point Euclidean distance is highly susceptible to noise interference and fails to effectively capture high-order geometric relationships between samples.

To address these challenges, this paper proposes a general **Transductive Support Query Expansion (TSQE)** framework, designed to reconstruct robust class prototypes by mining contextual information from the unlabeled query set. Inspired by high-order tensor clustering theory, we argue that similarity between samples should not be limited to binary relationships but should consider global multi-point interactions. Therefore, we designed a **High-**

Order Tensor Similarity (HOTS) module, utilizing fourth-order tensor products to aggregate global affinities among samples, thereby replacing the traditional Euclidean distance. This metric effectively suppresses noise and captures the latent manifold structure of high-dimensional data. Furthermore, we propose an adaptive transductive prototype reconstruction strategy, utilizing high-confidence neighbors in the query samples to perform "manifold calibration" on the initial prototypes.

The main contributions are three-fold: (1) **Methodological Innovation:** We introduce high-order tensor similarity into medical few-shot learning, replacing traditional Euclidean distance to suppress noise. (2) **Framework Generality:** TSQE is a plug-and-play module adaptable to both 2D images and high-dimensional omics data without complex meta-training. (3) **Performance Verification:** Extensive experiments on LC25000 and TCGA benchmarks demonstrate that TSQE significantly outperforms baseline Prototypical Networks.

2 Related Work

Metric-Based FSL in Medicine. Early pioneers like Matching Networks [17] introduced metric-based learning for rapid adaptation. Subsequently, Prototypical Networks (ProtoNets) [14] became the dominant paradigm, classifying samples based on Euclidean distance to class means. Recent theoretical analyses [5] have further demonstrated that the generalization bound of prototype classifiers heavily relies on the ratio of within-class to between-class variance, highlighting the critical need for robust feature space transformations. While widely used in medical imaging (e.g., DCPN [13], SSL-ProtoNet [10]), traditional pairwise Euclidean metrics struggle with high-dimensional, heterogeneous medical data, often failing to optimize this variance ratio and leading to biased prototypes.

Meta-learning for Cancer Diagnosis. Optimization-based methods like MLLCD [6] learn initialization for rapid adaptation. However, they typically require expensive meta-training on large labeled datasets and suffer from training instability (e.g., MAML [4]). In contrast, our framework operates in a training-free, transductive manner, suitable for clinical scenarios with limited resources.

Prototype Rectification and High-Order Methods. To capture latent manifold structures and mitigate prototype bias, recent general FSL works have explored leveraging unlabeled data for transductive prototype calibration (e.g., utilizing soft labels for graph node classification [18]). In the medical domain, while PRSN [3] uses query samples for rectification, it relies on simple linear statistics. Inspired by tensor clustering [12] and the necessity of incorporating unlabeled contextual distributions, we introduce high-order tensor interactions to model global affinities, generating robust similarity measures for transductive few-shot diagnosis.

3 Method

The proposed TSQE framework (Fig. 1) addresses prototype bias in medical FSL via two key modules: High-Order Tensor Similarity (HOTS) and Transductive Query Expansion.

Preliminaries and Feature Embedding. We focus on the N-way K-shot task with a support set $\mathcal{S}$ and a query set $\mathcal{Q}$. To handle heterogeneous data, we employ task-specific strategies without additional meta-training: a **ResNet** for pathology/radiology images, while for high-dimensional omics data, we directly utilize the **raw feature vectors** (preserving the original $\mathbb{R}^{60k}$ space) to avoid potential information loss caused by dimensionality reduction.

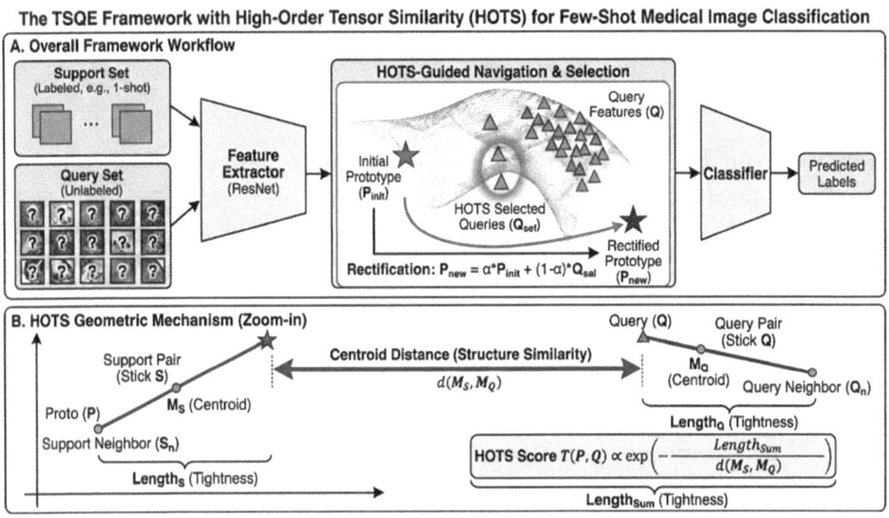

Fig. 1. Schematic illustration of the proposed TSQE framework for few-shot medical image classification. (A) Overall framework workflow. Feature embeddings are extracted from the labeled support set and unlabeled query set via a ResNet backbone. The core "HOTS-Guided Navigation & Selection" module refines the initial prototype (P_{init}) by incorporating high-confidence query samples (Q_{sel}) identified through High-Order Tensor Similarity (HOTS). The resulting rectified prototype (P_{new}) is utilized by the classifier to predict labels for the query set. **(B)** Geometric interpretation of the HOTS mechanism (Zoom-in). HOTS evaluates structural similarity between sample pairs (depicted as "sticks"). The HOTS score is calculated as the ratio of local sample tightness (numerator: sum of intra-pair distances) to global structural difference (denominator: distance between pair centroids M_S and M_Q), ensuring robust semantic matching on the manifold.

3.1 High-Order Tensor Similarity (HOTS)

Traditional FSL methods (such as Prototypical Networks) rely on Euclidean distance to measure similarity. However, in high-dimensional and noisy medical feature spaces, pairwise Euclidean distance fails to capture latent manifold structures. To address this, we introduce High-Order Tensor Similarity (HOTS) to explore global geometric relationships via high-order tensor interactions.

We model the relationship between sample pairs as a fourth-order tensor $\mathcal{T} \in \mathbb{R}^{N\times N\times N\times N}$ to measure the affinity between two sample pairs (i, j) and (k, l). The tensor element $T_{ij,kl}$ is defined as follows:

$$T_{ij,kl} = \exp\left(-\frac{d(x_i, x_j)^2 + d(x_k, x_l)^2}{2\sigma^2 \cdot \|m_{ij} - m_{kl}\|_2^2}\right) \tag{1}$$

where $d(x_i, x_j)$ represents the Euclidean distance between sample i and j, and $m_{ij} = \frac{x_i+x_j}{2}$ is the midpoint of the sample pair (i, j). The denominator $\|m_{ij} - m_{kl}\|_2$ serves to penalize sample pairs that are distant in space, ensuring that high-order interactions are calculated only within local manifold neighborhoods.

To further suppress noise, the high-order tensor interactions are mapped into a 2D affinity matrix $S \in \mathbb{R}^{N\times N}$. We then apply spectral smoothing via symmetric normalization to obtain the final robust similarity matrix S_{HOTS}:

$$S_{HOTS} = \gamma S + (1-\gamma)D^{-\frac{1}{2}}SD^{-\frac{1}{2}} \tag{2}$$

where D is the diagonal degree matrix with $D_{ii} = \sum_j S_{ij}$, and $\gamma \in [0, 1]$ is a balancing parameter (set to 0.5 in our implementation) to prevent over-smoothing. This process effectively propagates label information through the global manifold structure rather than relying solely on local point-to-point distances.

3.2 Transductive Support Query Expansion (TSQE)

Relying solely on a limited Support Set $\mathcal{S}$ produces biased initial prototypes c_{init}. We propose a Transductive Support Query Expansion (TSQE) strategy, utilizing high-confidence samples from the unlabeled Query Set $\mathcal{Q}$ to correct this bias.

Step 1: Initial Prototype Estimation. For class n, the initial prototype is calculated as the mean of the features of the support samples:

$$c_n^{(0)} = \frac{1}{K} \sum_{(x_s, y_s)\in\mathcal{S}_n} f_\theta(x_s) \tag{3}$$

Step 2: Tensor-Guided Neighbor Selection. Using the affinity matrix generated by HOTS, we identify the most relevant query samples. For class n, we rank the HOTS similarity between query samples and the initial prototype $c_n^{(0)}$, and select a Top-r sample set $\mathcal{Q}_{top}^{(n)}$.

Step 3: Prototype Rectification. We fuse the initial prototype with the selected query neighbors to generate the rectified prototype c_n^{rect}. To balance the reliability of real support samples and the distribution information of query samples, we introduce a weighting factor α:

$$c_n^{rect} = \alpha c_n^{(0)} + (1-\alpha)\frac{1}{r}\sum_{z_q \in \mathcal{Q}_{top}^{(n)}} z_q \tag{4}$$

where $\alpha \in [0,1]$ controls the anchor weight. A higher α indicates greater trust in pre-trained features (as in NCTCRC experiments), while a lower α allows for more adaptive adjustment (as in TCGA experiments).

3.3 Inference

Finally, classification is performed based on the Euclidean distance (or Cosine similarity) between the embedding z_q of the query sample x_q and the rectified prototypes $\{c_n^{rect}\}_{n=1}^{N}$:

$$\hat{y}_q = \arg\max_n \frac{z_q \cdot c_n^{rect}}{||z_q||||c_n^{rect}||} \tag{5}$$

Thus, the entire pipeline is constructed. This framework achieves robust few-shot classification without requiring gradient-based meta-training on the target dataset.

4 Experiments and Results

4.1 Implementation Details

To ensure the rigorous reproducibility of our results, we detail the experimental environment, network configurations, and hyperparameter settings below.

Hardware and Software Environment. All experiments were implemented using the PyTorch deep learning framework. The model training, transductive inference, and evaluation were all executed on a workstation equipped with a single NVIDIA GeForce RTX 4090 GPU (24GB VRAM).

Network Architecture. For image-based modalities, we adopted the standard ResNet as the backbone feature extractor. To accommodate the specific structural characteristics of different medical imaging modalities without altering the core architecture, the input channel of the first convolutional layer was adaptively modified: it was set to 1 for grayscale CT and PET modalities, and 3 for the Fused multi-modal inputs. For high-dimensional omics data, we directly fed the raw feature vectors into the TSQE framework without using a CNN backbone to prevent information loss.

Meta-Learning Settings. We followed the standard episodic training and testing protocol widely adopted in few-shot learning, specifically the N-way K-shot setting. In our primary lung cancer subtyping tasks, we set $N = 3$ (3-class classification). We placed a particular focus on the extreme and highly challenging 1-shot ($K = 1$) scenario to rigorously test the model's robustness against prototype bias. The query set size per episode was consistently set to $Q = 15$.

Optimizer Configurations. The network parameters were optimized using the Adam optimizer. To ensure training stability and prevent the gradient explosion problem commonly encountered in metric-based meta-learning over complex medical manifolds, we applied gradient clipping throughout the training phase.

TSQE Hyperparameters. Based on a comprehensive grid search on the validation set, we set adaptive hyperparameters for different modalities to optimally balance local instance features and global geometric manifold information:

- *High-order Tensor Kernel Width (σ):* Uniformly set to 1.0 to control the decay rate of the high-order affinity matrix.
- *Rectification Weight (α):* For image data (characterized by dense and continuous structural features), we set $\alpha = 0.8$ to preserve more semantic information from the initial prototypes. Conversely, for high-dimensional omics data (characterized by sparse and highly noisy features), we set $\alpha = 0.6$, forcing the model to rely more heavily on the manifold structure of the query set for transductive rectification.
- *Neighbor Selection Number (r):* Set to 10 for the 1-shot task to strike an optimal balance between expanding contextual information and avoiding outlier noise.

4.2 Dataset Description

To comprehensively validate the effectiveness of the proposed TSQE framework in precision diagnosis and cross-modal medical analysis, we constructed a hierarchical experimental benchmark.

Dataset A: Lung-CT-Pathology-Dx (Histopathology Images). This is a large-scale multi-modal diagnostic dataset [9]. In this study, we focus on its histopathology component, which contains high-resolution images extracted from slides of numerous lung cancer patients. The dataset comprises three core classes: Lung Adenocarcinoma (LUAD), Lung Squamous Cell Carcinoma (LUSC), and Normal Tissue. Because LUAD and LUSC exhibit significant morphological similarities, especially in poorly differentiated samples, we constructed a 3-way 1-shot task to strictly evaluate TSQE's performance in fine-grained subtyping.

Dataset B: TCGA-LUNG (Multi-omics Subtyping). To verify the generality of TSQE on non-image, high-dimensional sparse data, we constructed a few-shot multi-omics classification dataset derived from The Cancer Genome Atlas (TCGA) [16]. This dataset includes three significantly heterogeneous tissue types: LUAD, LUSC, and Solid Tissue Normal. We performed rigorous multi-modal integration and preprocessing, where each sample contains omics features from three distinct biological dimensions:

- **RNA-Seq:** Reflecting gene expression levels ($dim \approx 60,000$).
- **DNA Methylation:** Reflecting epigenetic modifications ($dim \approx 20,000$).
- **Somatic Mutation:** Reflecting genomic variations ($dim \approx 18,000$; highly sparse in normal tissues).

Data Integration and Alignment: To construct a cohesive multi-modal feature space, we used the first 12 characters of the TCGA sample barcode (Patient ID) as the unique identifier to match cross-modal data. We adopted an Intersection-based Retention strategy, keeping only samples with both RNA-Seq and Methylation sequencing data.

Asymmetric Imputation: For Somatic Mutation data, we employed a domain-specific Asymmetric Imputation strategy. For cancer samples (LUAD/LUSC), we extracted their true mutation profiles. For normal samples lacking mutation data, based on the biological assumption that normal tissues possess no somatic oncogenic mutations, we used Zero-Padding for feature completion. Finally, data from all modalities were strictly aligned to the same row index.

After rigorous quality control and sample matching, the final dataset contains LUAD (517 cases), LUSC (501 cases), and Normal (110 cases). Compared to medical imaging, this data presents distinct data mining challenges of ultra-high dimensionality ($> 100k$ dims) and unique structural sparsity. We adopted a 3-way 1-shot setting to verify the model's effectiveness in processing such complex biological information.

Auxiliary Benchmarks for Generalization. To further demonstrate that the TSQE framework is not limited to specific organs or modalities, we introduced the following datasets for extensive auxiliary validation:

- **LC25000 (Lung & Colon):** Contains 25,000 images of lung and colorectal cancer. We use it to verify the model's robustness under larger-scale data distributions, specifically for cross-organ classification capabilities [2].
- **NCTCRC (Colorectal Cancer):** Contains 9 classes of colorectal cancer tissue images. This dataset is primarily used to evaluate the boundary correction ability of TSQE under a same-domain setting [8].
- **OrganAMNIST (Abdominal CT):** Contains low-resolution CT images of 11 abdominal organs. This dataset is introduced to verify TSQE's adaptability to low feature quality and a completely different modality (grayscale CT) [20] (Table 1).

Table 1. Summary of datasets. N-way implies the number of classes. Pre-trained weights (ImageNet) were used for image datasets.

Dataset	Modality	Classes (N)	Key Characteristic
Lung-CT-PT-DX [9]	CT/PET/Fused	3	Heterogeneous fusion
TCGA-LUNG [16]	Multi-Omics	3	High-Dim (> $60k$), Sparse
TCGA-BRCA [16]	Multi-Omics	5	Complex molecular subtypes
TCGA-KIDNEY [16]	Multi-Omics	3	Renal cell carcinoma subtyping
LC25000 [2]	Pathology	3	Large-scale Histology
NCTCRC [8]	Pathology	9	Fine-grained textures
OrganAMNIST [20]	CT (Abd)	11	Low-resolution (28×28)
BUSI [7]	Ultrasound	3	High noise, small sample

4.3 Main Results

We conducted extensive experiments to compare TSQE with classic few-shot baselines (e.g., k-NN, SVM) and state-of-the-art metric-based meta-learning methods, including MatchingNet, standard Prototypical Networks (Proto-E and Proto-C), PRSN, DCPN, and SSL-ProtoNet. The comprehensive 1-shot classification results across five distinct datasets are summarized in Table 2.

Table 2. Comparison with SOTA methods on multiple medical datasets (1-Shot setting). "Proto-E" and "Proto-C" denote Prototypical Networks with Euclidean and Cosine distances, respectively. The best results are highlighted in **bold**.

Dataset	LC25000	OrgAMNIST	Lung-CT-PT	NCTCRC	BUSI
Modality	Pathology	CT (Abd)	Multi-Mod	Pathology	Ultrasound
Setting	3-way	5-way	3-way	9-way	3-way
k-NN	70.20	55.38	74.54	55.34	73.44
SVM	61.52	52.80	69.96	31.87	74.74
MatchNet	72.72	57.22	74.17	38.36	69.98
Proto-E	70.75	55.86	74.60	56.56	72.12
Proto-C	72.89	57.22	74.88	57.33	77.78
PRSN	75.42	44.81	78.31	58.07	86.58
DCPN	72.44	41.41	73.73	54.34	85.47
SSL-Proto	39.42	27.54	79.63	15.27	87.91
Ours (TSQE)	**77.96**	**60.66**	**81.96**	**60.47**	**89.60**
Improvement	**+2.54%**	**+3.44%**	**+2.33%**	**+2.40%**	**+1.69%**

Histopathology (LC25000 and NCTCRC): On the large-scale LC25000 dataset, TSQE achieves a remarkable accuracy of 77.96%, surpassing the strong competitor PRSN by 2.54%. Even on the highly challenging 9-way NCTCRC classification task, our method maintains the lead with 60.47% accuracy, achieving a 2.40% margin over the best baseline. This explicitly demonstrates the robustness of our High-Order Tensor Similarity in capturing fine-grained pathological tissue textures.

Radiology and Cross-Modality (OrganAMNIST, Lung-CT-PT, BUSI): For the multi-modal Lung-CT-PT dataset, TSQE reaches 81.96%, outperforming the runner-up SSL-ProtoNet by 2.33%, validating the efficacy of our framework in fusing heterogeneous features. Furthermore, on OrganAMNIST (where we followed standard FSL protocols to randomly sample 5 out of 11 classes to construct the 5-way task) and BUSI (noisy Ultrasound), our method consistently outperforms all baselines with significant gains of 3.44% and 1.69%, respectively. These consistent improvements verify that TSQE possesses strong generalization capabilities across completely diverse imaging modalities, successfully mitigating the prototype bias typically encountered in low-resource settings.

4.4 Ablation Study: Impact of Metric and Rectification

To verify the contribution of each component in TSQE, particularly on high-dimensional non-Euclidean data, we conducted ablation studies on three multi-omics datasets: **TCGA-Lung** (3-way, constructed via multi-modal fusion), **TCGA-BRCA** (5-way), and **TCGA-KIDNEY** (3-way).

Table 3. Ablation study on multi-omics datasets. "Baseline" denotes the standard ProtoNet using Euclidean distance. To explicitly isolate the contribution of our high-order metric, "Cosine Refine" applies the TSQE rectification but restricts the metric to a standard Cosine similarity. "Full" represents our complete framework, integrating both the TSQE manifold calibration and the High-Order Tensor Similarity (HOTS) to demonstrate the specific gain from high-order geometric interactions.

Method/Metric	TCGA-Lung	TCGA-BRCA	TCGA-KIDNEY
Base (Euc.)	65.52%	43.84%	67.26%
+TSQE (Cos.)	78.52%	47.67%	74.12%
Ours (Full)	**80.72%**	**49.18%**	**75.99%**
Gain	**+15.20%**	**+5.34%**	**+8.73%**

Data Complexity Analysis. The TCGA-Lung dataset represents an extreme challenge for metric-based learning. As described in Sect. 4.1, each sample fuses RNA-Seq, DNA Methylation, and Somatic Mutation features, resulting in a feature space exceeding **60,000 dimensions**. Furthermore, the *Asymmetric Imputation* strategy for somatic mutations introduces structured sparsity between cancer (LUAD/LUSC) and normal tissues.

Results on High-Dimensional Omics. Table 3 summarizes the ablation results. We observe three key findings:

1. **Failure of Euclidean Baseline:** On TCGA-Lung, the standard ProtoNet with Euclidean distance yields a relatively low accuracy of 65.52%. This confirms that in ultra-high-dimensional sparse spaces, point-to-point Euclidean distance loses discriminative power due to the "curse of dimensionality."
2. **Effectiveness of Transductive Rectification:** By introducing the TSQE strategy (using Cosine similarity for neighbor selection), the accuracy jumps to 78.52%. This proves that utilizing the manifold structure of the unlabeled query set to perform "manifold calibration" significantly alleviates the prototype bias caused by data sparsity.
3. **Superiority of High-Order Tensor (HOTS):** The full model (TSQE + HOTS) achieves the highest accuracy of **80.72%**, resulting in a remarkable total gain of **15.20%**. This indicates that our fourth-order tensor construction effectively captures global geometric interactions that are missed by pairwise Cosine similarity, enabling robust classification even in 60k dimensional spaces.

Similar trends are observed on the TCGA-BRCA dataset, where our method achieves a 5.34% improvement over the baseline, verifying the universality of TSQE across different cancer types.

4.5 Training Stability and Modality Fusion Analysis

To further evaluate the framework's capability in handling complex multi-modal data, we visualized the validation curves (Accuracy, Macro-F1, ARI, and NMI) over 400 epochs on the Lung-CT-PT-DX dataset. As illustrated in Fig. 2, the Fused modality (red line) consistently and significantly outperforms the single CT (blue line) and PT (green line) modalities across all four evaluation metrics. It is worth noting that the isolated PT (PET) modality exhibits relatively poor performance and high fluctuation, which is characteristic of its inherently low spatial resolution. However, when integrated within the TSQE framework, the metabolic signals from PT effectively complement the anatomical structures from CT. This synergistic fusion allows the model to converge faster, achieve higher accuracy ceilings, and maintain remarkable stability. This demonstrates that TSQE can robustly extract geometric relationships and reconstruct prototypes even when dealing with highly heterogeneous and noisy multi-modal inputs.

4.6 Visualization and Qualitative Analysis

To intuitively understand how TSQE improves feature representations, we visualize the feature distributions and classification behaviors using t-SNE and confusion matrices.

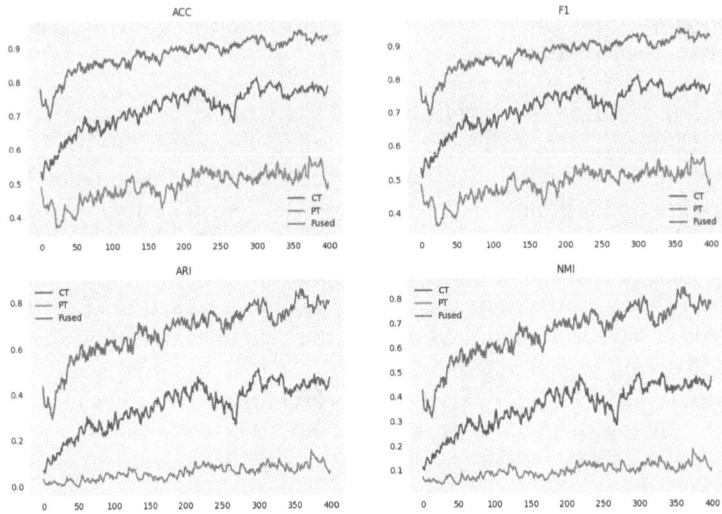

Fig. 2. Validation curves on the multi-modal Lung-CT-PT-DX dataset over 400 epochs. The Fused modality (red) exhibits superior performance, faster convergence, and higher training stability across Accuracy, F1-Score, ARI, and NMI compared to single CT (blue) or PT (green) inputs. (Color figure online)

Feature Space Visualization (t-SNE). We visualized the feature embeddings of the Support Set and Query Set on the Lung-CT-PT-DX dataset using t-SNE (Fig. 3). As shown in Fig. 3(a), the feature space of the Baseline method (Euclidean ProtoNet) is loosely distributed with indistinct class margins. The initial prototypes fail to align well with the query samples, leading to potential misclassification. In contrast, Fig. 3(b) demonstrates that TSQE generates highly compact clusters with large inter-class margins. Notably, the refined prototypes in our method are perfectly positioned at the center of their respective query clusters. This visual evidence confirms that our High-Order Tensor Similarity effectively captures the global manifold structure, pulling samples of the same class closer together.

Confusion Matrix Analysis on Omics Data. We further analyzed the confusion matrices on the challenging high-dimensional TCGA-Lung dataset (Fig. 4) to evaluate the model's ability to distinguish fine-grained subtypes. The Baseline method exhibits severe confusion between LUAD and LUSC, with a large number of misclassified samples. This is largely due to the extreme sparsity and noise inherent in the raw 60k-dimensional features, where Euclidean distance fails to find meaningful decision boundaries. However, as shown in the TSQE confusion matrix, our method significantly purifies the predictions. The correct predictions on the diagonal increase drastically, effectively separating the molecularly similar LUAD and LUSC subtypes. This demonstrates that our transductive rectification strategy successfully corrects the bias in high-dimensional space.

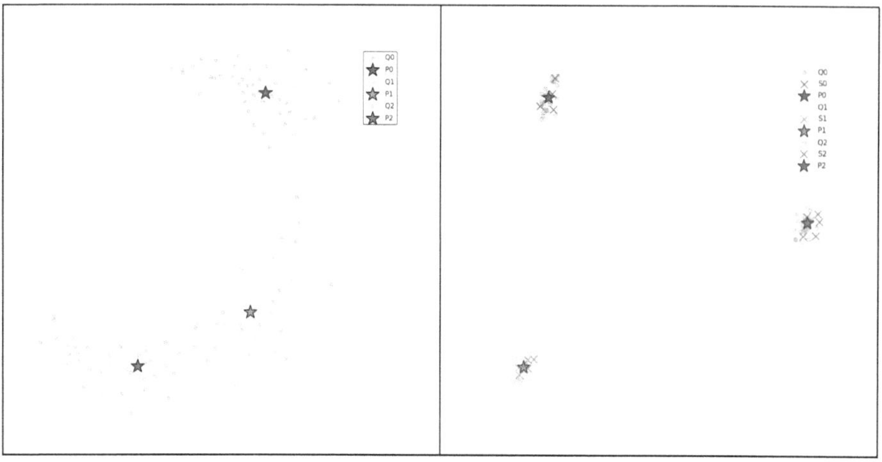

(a) Baseline (b) TSQE (Ours)

Fig. 3. t-SNE visualization on the CT modality of the Lung-CT-PT-DX dataset. Markers denote different components: **stars** for class prototypes, **circles** for the query set (Q), and **crosses** for the support set (S). **(a)** The baseline shows scattered distributions with misaligned prototypes. **(b)** TSQE achieves compact clustering with prototypes precisely calibrated to query centers.

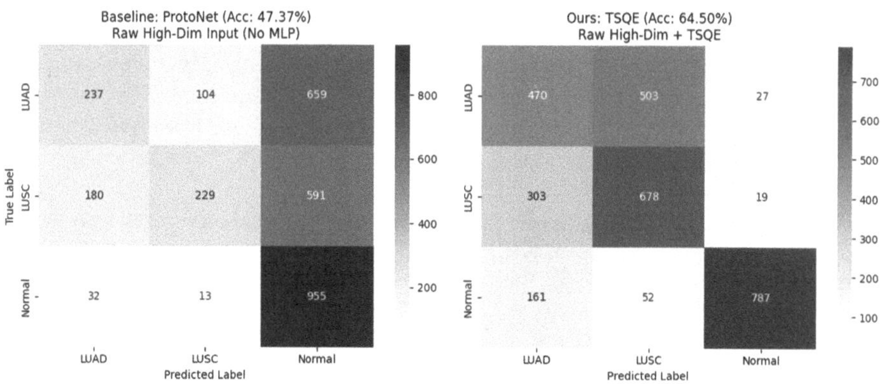

Fig. 4. Confusion Matrices on the high-dimensional TCGA-Lung dataset. The baseline (ProtoNet) struggles to distinguish LUAD from LUSC, while TSQE significantly corrects these errors, showing a clearer diagonal structure and precise subtype boundary.

5 Conclusion

Addressing the prevalent challenges in medical diagnosis, such as sample scarcity, strong data heterogeneity, and difficulties in subtype classification, this paper proposes a general Transductive Support Query Expansion (TSQE) framework. This framework innovatively integrates high-order tensor geometric information with transductive learning strategies, aiming to resolve prototype bias and metric failure in few-shot scenarios without altering the backbone network structure. Through validation on extensive benchmarks covering lung cancer pathology, pan-cancer multi-omics, and radiology, this study draws the following core conclusions:

High-Order Tensor Metrics Break Through the Geometric Limitations of Complex Feature Spaces. In experiments with high-dimensional omics data such as TCGA-LUNG and TCGA-BRCA [16], traditional pairwise Euclidean distance struggles to capture the intrinsic manifold structure of the data. The proposed High-Order Tensor Similarity (HOTS) module successfully mines high-order interaction relationships between samples by constructing a fourth-order tensor. Experimental results demonstrate that this global geometry-based metric significantly outperforms traditional metrics, providing an efficient new paradigm for processing high-dimensional, non-Euclidean medical data.

Transductive Prototype Rectification Achieves Precise Subtype Identification. On the core Lung-CT-Pathology-Dx dataset, targeting the clinically indistinguishable Lung Adenocarcinoma (LUAD) and Lung Squamous Cell Carcinoma (LUSC), TSQE exhibits superior boundary correction capabilities. By utilizing distribution information from the Query Set to perform "manifold calibration" on initial prototypes, the model constructs robust classification boundaries even under extreme few-shot conditions (e.g., 1-Shot), significantly enhancing the accuracy of fine-grained diagnosis.

In summary, this paper demonstrates that geometric correction is an efficient path independent of feature representation learning. By optimizing the topological structure of the feature space through mathematical means, we can significantly improve the accuracy and reliability of medical few-shot diagnosis without increasing annotation costs or training burdens.

Acknowledgments. This work was supported by the National Natural Science Foundation of China (Grant No. 62462022), Hainan Provincial Natural Science Foundation of China (Grant No. 826QN0576), Hainan University Scientific Research Start-up Fund for High-level Talents (Grant No. XJ2400012551), and Hainan University Teaching Resource Construction Project (Grant No. RC2600001991).

Disclosure of Interests. The authors have no competing interests to declare that are relevant to the content of this article.

References

1. Bishnoi, V., Goel, N.: A color-based deep-learning approach for tissue slide lung cancer classification. Biomed. Signal Process. Control **86**, 105151 (2023)
2. Borkowski, A.A., Bui, M.M., Thomas, L.B., Wilson, C.P., DeLand, L.A., Mastorides, S.M.: Lung and Colon Cancer Histopathological Image Dataset (LC25000) (2019)
3. Dong, M., Li, F., Li, Z., Liu, X.: PRSN: prototype resynthesis network with cross-image semantic alignment for few-shot image classification. Pattern Recogn. **159**, 111122 (2025)

4. Finn, C., Abbeel, P., Levine, S.: Model-agnostic meta-learning for fast adaptation of deep networks. In: International Conference on Machine Learning, pp. 1126–1135. PMLR (2017)
5. Hou, M., Sato, I.: A closer look at prototype classifier for few-shot image classification (2022)
6. Hu, X., Wang, S., Li, H., Zhang, Q.: MLLCD: a meta learning-based method for lung cancer diagnosis using histopathology images. In: 2023 IEEE International Conference on Bioinformatics and Biomedicine (BIBM), pp. 1132–1137. IEEE, Istanbul (2023). https://doi.org/10.1109/BIBM58861.2023.10385566, https://ieeexplore.ieee.org/document/10385566/
7. Işık, G., Paçal, I.: Few-shot classification of ultrasound breast cancer images using meta-learning algorithms. Neural Comput. Appl. **36**(20), 12047–12059 (2024). https://doi.org/10.1007/s00521-024-09767-y
8. Kather, J.N., Halama, N., Marx, A.: 100,000 histological images of human colorectal cancer and healthy tissue (NCT-CRC-he-100k). Zenodo (2018). https://doi.org/10.5281/zenodo.1214456
9. Li, P., Wang, S., Li, T., Lu, J., HuangFu, Y., Wang, D.: A large-scale CT and PET/CT dataset for lung cancer diagnosis (lung-PET-CT-Dx) (2020). https://doi.org/10.7937/TCIA.2020.NNC2-0461, https://www.cancerimagingarchive.net/collection/lung-pet-ct-dx/
10. Lim, J.Y., Lim, K.M., Lee, C.P., Tan, Y.X.: SSL-ProtoNet: self-supervised learning prototypical networks for few-shot learning. Expert Syst. Appl. **238**, 122173 (2024)
11. Merabet, A., Saighi, A., Ferradji, M.A., Laboudi, Z.: Enhancing colon cancer prediction in histopathology with integrated deep learning models: a comparative study on the LC25000 dataset. In: 2024 6th International Conference on Pattern Analysis and Intelligent Systems (PAIS), pp. 1–7. IEEE, EL OUED (2024). https://doi.org/10.1109/PAIS62114.2024.10541219, https://ieeexplore.ieee.org/document/10541219/
12. Peng, H., Hu, Y., Chen, J., Wang, H., Li, Y., Cai, H.: Integrating tensor similarity to enhance clustering performance. IEEE Trans. Pattern Anal. Mach. Intell. **44**(5), 2582–2593 (2022)
13. Quan, H., Li, X., Hu, D., Nan, T., Cui, X.: Dual-channel prototype network for few-shot pathology image classification. IEEE J. Biomed. Health Inform. **28**(7), 4132–4144 (2024)
14. Snell, J., Swersky, K., Zemel, R.S.: Prototypical networks for few-shot learning (2017). https://doi.org/10.48550/arXiv.1703.05175, arXiv:1703.05175 [cs]
15. Tao, G., et al.: SeqSeg: a sequential method to achieve nasopharyngeal carcinoma segmentation free from background dominance. Med. Image Anal. **78**, 102381 (2022)
16. Weinstein, J.N., et al.: The Cancer Genome Atlas Pan-Cancer analysis project. Nature Genetics **45**(10), 1113–1120 (2013). https://doi.org/10.1038/ng.2764, https://www.nature.com/articles/ng.2764
17. Vinyals, O., Blundell, C., Lillicrap, T.: Matching networks for one shot learning (2016)
18. Wang, N., Lai, Y., Chen, C., Zheng, Z.: Prototypical networks with unlabeled data for few-shot node classification. Eng. Appl. Artif. Intell. **145**, 110088 (2025)
19. Wang, X., Yu, G., Yan, Z., Wan, L., Wang, W., Cui, L.: Lung cancer subtype diagnosis by fusing image-genomics data and hybrid deep networks. IEEE/ACM Trans. Comput. Biol. Bioinf. **20**(1), 512–523 (2023)
20. Yang, J., et al.: MedMNIST v2: a large-scale lightweight benchmark for 2D and 3D biomedical image classification. Sci. Data **10**(1), 41 (2023)

Tracing the Oracle: Improving Diffusion Timestep Scheduling for 3D CT Reconstruction

Yujia Wu and Zhaoqiang Liu(✉)

School of Computer Science and Engineering, University of Electronic Science and Technology of China, Chengdu, China
zqliu12@gmail.com

Abstract. Pretrained diffusion models demonstrate impressive potential in solving highly ill-posed 3D computed tomography (CT) inverse problems, while the inference process suffers from significant computational overhead. Furthermore, existing uniform timestep schedules fail to capture the non-uniform evolution of the reverse conditional diffusion stochastic differential equation, thereby introducing substantial truncation errors. To overcome this limitation, we propose Tracing the Oracle (TrO), a plug-and-play framework for improved timestep scheduling. Specifically, we treat densely sampled numerical integration trajectories on a few samples as the reference oracle. The optimized schedule is extracted by leveraging dynamic programming to globally minimize the cumulative error between the few-step approximation and the oracle. This mechanism precisely allocates the limited sampling steps to critical evolution stages that are highly susceptible to truncation errors. Our extensive experiments on the AAPM dataset across multiple 3D CT reconstruction tasks demonstrate that, when combined with the state-of-the-art 3D CT reconstruction method DDS, our optimized timesteps significantly improve reconstruction fidelity and computational efficiency compared to existing heuristic schedules, especially under a strict budget of no more than 10 sampling steps.

Keywords: Diffusion models · 3D CT reconstruction · Optimized timesteps

1 Introduction

The reconstruction of 3D computed tomography (CT) is mathematically formulated as a linear inverse problem. This problem aims to reconstruct an unknown clean signal $\mathbf{x}_0^* \in \mathbb{R}^d$ from a degraded observation $\mathbf{y} \in \mathbb{R}^m$. This degradation process is mathematically represented by the linear forward operator $\mathbf{A} \in \mathbb{R}^{m \times d}$ and additive Gaussian noise $\boldsymbol{\xi} \in \mathbb{R}^m$ with $\boldsymbol{\xi} \sim \mathcal{N}(\mathbf{0}, \sigma_y^2 \mathbf{I}_m)$, formalized as

$$\mathbf{y} = \mathbf{A}\mathbf{x}_0^* + \boldsymbol{\xi}. \tag{1}$$

M. Ceci et al. (Eds.): ECML PKDD 2026, LNAI 16941, pp. 566–583, 2027.
https://doi.org/10.1007/978-3-032-37654-1_33

Deep neural networks trained on paired datasets have been widely employed to directly learn mappings from degraded observations to clean signals [16,38,40]. However, acquiring large-scale paired datasets is often prohibitively expensive, and such data-driven models exhibit severe generalization vulnerabilities across different measurement operators [15]. Deep generative models including variational autoencoders [24] and generative adversarial networks [20] have achieved remarkable success in solving inverse problems, by exploiting data-driven priors learned from unpaired training datasets [4,8,9,14,26]. Recently, diffusion models [22,34,36] have emerged as powerful alternatives by modeling the data distribution through a stochastic differential equation (SDE). Leveraging pre-trained unconditional diffusion models as generative priors enables highly effective training-free inference for inverse problems [6,10,25,30,41,43,45,46,48]. When addressing highly ill-posed 3D inverse problems, such as volumetric computed tomography (CT) reconstruction, directly training a 3D diffusion model imposes prohibitive computational costs [12]. Consequently, existing diffusion posterior sampling approaches for 3D inverse problems primarily utilize 2D diffusion priors augmented with inter-slice regularization constraints [11,12]. For instance, Decomposed Diffusion Sampling (DDS) [11] improves reconstruction efficiency by using CG-based data-consistency updates initialized from the Tweedie denoised estimate. Under the local assumption that the tangent space around the denoised estimate can be represented or approximated by a Krylov subspace, these updates remain within the corresponding local subspace [28]. Nevertheless, existing approaches typically uniformly allocate the reverse sampling timesteps. Such heuristic timestep scheduling mechanisms fail to dynamically adapt to the complex interplay between the generative diffusion prior and the measurements of specific 3D inverse problems, thus yielding sub-optimal reconstruction quality under restricted sampling budgets.

The sequential nature of the reverse diffusion process typically necessitates numerous neural function evaluations (NFEs), thereby imposing a substantial computational burden [19,27,37]. To maximize sampling efficiency, various sampler optimization strategies have been proposed [18,42]. In addition, various timestep scheduling optimization strategies have been proposed [7,39,47] to accelerate the sampling process. For instance, the work [39] minimizes the explicit distance between numerical and analytic solutions, while GITS [7] leverages the geometric regularity of probability flow trajectories. However, solving inverse problems relies on measurement-conditioned diffusion posterior sampling, where conditional measurements disrupt the unconditional generation manifold. Furthermore, achieving data consistency in inverse problems typically requires injecting stochastic noise during the reverse refinement process [41,48], which invalidates the deterministic trajectory assumptions relied upon by unconditional scheduling algorithms, rendering them ineffective for complex conditional inverse solvers.

To overcome these limitations, we propose Tracing the Oracle (TrO), which is a plug-and-play non-uniform timestep scheduling framework for 3D CT reconstruction (illustrated in Fig. 1). We initially construct a high-fidelity reference trajectory, referred to as the oracle, using a densely sampled stochastic process on a subset of data. To accurately quantify the approximation error across these stochastic transitions, we introduce a noise reuse technique that isolates the discretization error between arbitrary timesteps. Subsequently, we formulate the scheduling task as a discrete optimization problem and deploy dynamic programming to minimize the cumulative trajectory error between the few-step approximation and the reference oracle. Given that diffusion trajectories for identically distributed data exhibit strong structural similarities [7], the optimized timestep schedule generalizes robustly across the entire dataset without incurring additional inference overhead. This optimization framework enables highly efficient and accurate 3D CT reconstructions.

The primary contributions of this work are summarized as follows:

- We propose a plug-and-play framework that formulates timestep scheduling for measurement-conditioned diffusion as a discrete shortest-path problem, aiming to minimize cumulative trajectory errors in 3D inverse problems.
- We introduce a noise reuse mechanism that isolates deterministic truncation errors from stochastic variance, enabling precise quantification of discretization errors within SDE-based sampling trajectories.
- Extensive evaluations on 3D CT benchmarks demonstrate that our optimized schedules consistently improve reconstruction fidelity over predefined schedules without additional inference overhead.

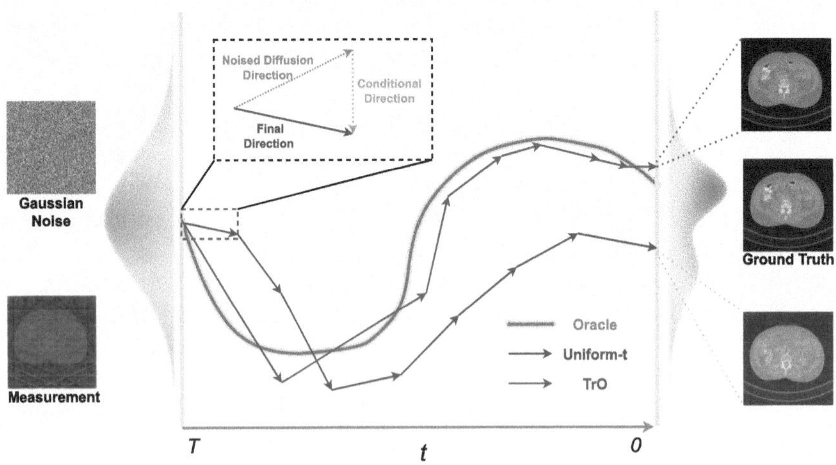

Fig. 1. Geometric interpretation of the proposed Tracing the Oracle (TrO) framework. The heuristic uniform timestep schedule diverges from the high-fidelity oracle trajectory during the conditional generation process. Our method improves the timestep allocation by minimizing the cumulative approximation error to closely track the oracle path. This optimized non-uniform scheduling strategy concentrates limited computational resources on critical evolution stages and effectively approximates the ground truth.

2 Related Works

2.1 Diffusion Models for 3D Inverse Problems

Medical image reconstruction requires solving mathematically ill-posed linear inverse problems, under severe measurement constraints driven by patient safety protocols [2]. Diffusion priors have recently emerged as a prominent paradigm to regularize these underdetermined systems by enabling zero-shot inference over complex anatomical data manifolds [12]. While these zero-shot conditioning methods successfully steer initial unconditional noise vectors toward measurement consistency, they inherently rely on reversing SDEs, which requires thousands of sequential integrations [35]. When scaled to high-dimensional volumetric domains such as 3D CT, these numerical integrations incur severe memory consumption and substantial inference latency, making existing frameworks computationally demanding [12,33].

To mitigate the memory limitations arising from native volumetric processing, recent literature explores patch-based and multi-view slice approximations. For instance, Song et al. [33] propose learning 3D patch image priors through position-aware diffusion score blending to ensure cross-slice consistency without relying on heuristic regularizers. Further compressing the representational space, He et al. [21] introduce a triplane neural field integrated with diffusion priors to enable fast zero-shot reconstruction while managing volumetric complexities. To enforce measurement fidelity, Askari et al. [2] construct a bi-level guided diffusion model that approximates an inner-level conditional posterior mean before applying an outer-level proximal optimization.

To circumvent the substantial computational burden of computing manifold-constrained gradients, Chung et al. [11] exploit the observation that, if the tangent space at a Tweedie denoised sample is locally represented by a Krylov subspace, then CG updates initialized from the denoised estimate remain in that local tangent subspace. By executing classical conjugate gradient (CG) operations strictly within this clean tangent space, the framework significantly reduces the required NFEs while preserving high-fidelity volumetric spatial features. However, DDS typically follows a fixed uniform timestep schedule, which can lead to suboptimal reconstruction fidelity when restricted to a limited computational budget (i.e., the few-step regime). Our proposed method can improve the timestep schedule to further enhance the sampling efficiency and reconstruction performance of the DDS framework.

2.2 Sampling Acceleration for Unconditional Diffusion

To improve inference speed, researchers have focused on refining numerical solvers for diffusion-based differential equations. DDIM [34] reformulates the generation pipeline from Markovian stochastic processes to deterministic numerical integration, allowing substantial reductions in temporal evaluations by skipping intermediate noise scales. DPM-Solver [27] leverages the inherent semi-linear nature of probability flow ODEs by employing exact exponential integrators to compute linear drifts analytically while approximating nonlinear network predictions via high-order Taylor expansions. UniPC [44] introduces a predictor-corrector framework that achieves high-order accuracy without requiring additional network evaluations per sampling step, significantly enhancing sample quality under limited sampling budgets.

In addition to solver design, recent studies focus on optimizing discretized timestep schedules and sampler coefficients to enhance low-budget generation. Sabour et al. [31] optimize non-uniform schedules by minimizing a Kullback-Leibler upper bound between exact and approximate paths. Xue et al. [39] formulate a differentiable surrogate objective solved via trust-region methods to minimize the explicit distance between the numerical and analytical solutions. Zhou et al. [47] confirm that high-dimensional trajectories inherently reside within strict two-dimensional subspaces and invoke the mean value theorem to distill exact intermediate scaling factors that eliminate polynomial truncation errors.

The most relevant work to our approach is perhaps GITS [7], which focuses on the concept of trajectory geometry. GITS characterizes shape regularity within the implicit denoising trajectory and deploys dynamic programming to align the timestep schedule with the underlying structure of the probability flow ODE. While GITS demonstrates improved performance in unconditional generation, applying such deterministic trajectory geometry directly to conditional diffusion sampling corresponding to 3D inverse solvers poses significant challenges. We highlight two primary distinctions between our proposed framework and GITS designed to address these limitations. 1) GITS assumes a trajectory governed solely by the unconditional data manifold. In inverse problems, however, measurement-informed updates introduce external constraints that modify the trajectory geometry [42]. A schedule optimized for unconditional priors may misalign with these conditional dynamics, especially when the measurement operator induces high curvature in the manifold transitions. Furthermore, our empirical results in Sect. 5.3 demonstrate that even distinct inverse problems exhibit varying preferences for timestep allocation, suggesting that the sampling dynamics are inherently coupled with the measurement process rather than being governed solely by the data prior. 2) GITS fundamentally relies on probability flow ODEs to compute deterministic state transitions. However, high-fidelity inverse problem solvers typically require diffusion SDEs to prevent the generated samples from drifting off the data manifold [12,33,48]. Directly substituting SDE transitions into an ODE-based error metric, or computing naive geometric distances between stochastic SDE states, introduces severe random variance that biases the true trajectory error estimation. Our framework resolves this issue by proposing a noise reuse mechanism that accurately isolates the deterministic truncation error within the stochastic sampling procedure.

3 Preliminaries

3.1 Diffusion Models

Diffusion models establish a generative framework by progressively corrupting a data distribution into a tractable prior distribution through a continuous-time stochastic process. Let $\mathbf{x}_0 \in \mathbb{R}^d$ denote a clean data sample drawn from the underlying distribution p_{data}. The forward process over a continuous time variable $t \in [0, T]$ is governed by an SDE formulated as

$$\mathrm{d}\mathbf{x}_t = f(t)\mathbf{x}_t \mathrm{d}t + g(t)\mathrm{d}\mathbf{w}_t, \tag{2}$$

where $\mathbf{x}_t \in \mathbb{R}^d$ represents the state vector at time t and $\mathbf{w}_t \in \mathbb{R}^d$ denotes the standard Wiener process. The function $f(t)$ acts as the drift coefficient while $g(t)$ functions as the diffusion coefficient. For each time t, the transition kernel from the initial data $\mathbf{x}_0$ to the latent state $\mathbf{x}_t$ follows a Gaussian distribution defined by

$$q(\mathbf{x}_t|\mathbf{x}_0) = \mathcal{N}(\mathbf{x}_t; \alpha_t \mathbf{x}_0, \sigma_t^2 \mathbf{I}_d), \tag{3}$$

where α_t and σ_t are differentiable functions representing the scale and noise schedule. Specifically, α_t is strictly decreasing while σ_t is strictly increasing over t. To ensure that the SDE in Eq. (2) indeed induces the transition distribution $q(\mathbf{x}_t|\mathbf{x}_0)$, the drift and diffusion coefficients are related to these functions according to [27]:

$$f(t) = \frac{\mathrm{d}\log \alpha_t}{\mathrm{d}t}, \quad g^2(t) = \frac{\mathrm{d}\sigma_t^2}{\mathrm{d}t} - 2\sigma_t^2 \frac{\mathrm{d}\log \alpha_t}{\mathrm{d}t}. \tag{4}$$

The boundary condition at the terminal time T ensures that the marginal distribution approximates a standard normal distribution characterized by $\mathbf{x}_T \sim \mathcal{N}(\mathbf{0}, \mathbf{I}_d)$. The progression of the forward process is often measured by one half of the logarithm of signal-to-noise ratio (SNR), which is a strictly decreasing function of time denoted by $\lambda_t = \log(\alpha_t/\sigma_t)$.

To invert this forward transformation and recover the original data distribution, a neural network model $\boldsymbol{\epsilon}_\theta(\mathbf{x}_t, t)$ parameterized by θ is trained to predict the injected noise $\boldsymbol{\epsilon} \sim \mathcal{N}(\mathbf{0}, \mathbf{I}_d)$. The network parameters are optimized by minimizing the following objective:

$$\mathbb{E}_{t\sim\mathcal{U}(0,T),\mathbf{x}_0\sim p_{\text{data}},\boldsymbol{\epsilon}\sim\mathcal{N}(\mathbf{0},\mathbf{I}_d)} \left[\|\boldsymbol{\epsilon}_\theta(\alpha_t \mathbf{x}_0 + \sigma_t \boldsymbol{\epsilon}, t) - \boldsymbol{\epsilon}\|_2^2 \right]. \tag{5}$$

Song et al. [36] show that the reverse-time diffusion process evolving from T down to 0 can be formulated as an SDE:

$$\mathrm{d}\mathbf{x}_t = \left(f(t)\mathbf{x}_t - g^2(t)\nabla_{\mathbf{x}_t} \log p_t(\mathbf{x}_t)\right) \mathrm{d}t + g(t)\mathrm{d}\overline{\mathbf{w}}_t, \tag{6}$$

where $\overline{\mathbf{w}}_t$ is a standard Wiener process in the reverse-time direction, p_t denotes the marginal probability density of $\mathbf{x}_t$ at time t, and the score function $\nabla_{\mathbf{x}_t} \log p_t(\mathbf{x}_t)$ can be approximated via the noise prediction network as

$\nabla_{\mathbf{x}_t} \log p_t(\mathbf{x}_t) \approx -\boldsymbol{\epsilon}_\theta(\mathbf{x}_t, t)/\sigma_t$. Furthermore, there exists a deterministic probability flow ODE that shares the same marginal densities as the SDE [36]:

$$\mathrm{d}\mathbf{x}_t = \left(f(t)\mathbf{x}_t - \frac{1}{2} g^2(t) \nabla_{\mathbf{x}_t} \log p_t(\mathbf{x}_t) \right) \mathrm{d}t. \tag{7}$$

In practice, Eq. (7) is integrated numerically over a user-defined fixed timestep schedule $\{t_i\}_{i=0}^N$, where $t_i > t_{i+1}$ for $i = 0, 1, ..., N-1$ with $t_0 = T$ and $t_N = 0$. At an arbitrary timestep t_i, Tweedie's formula [17] provides the expected posterior mean of the clean data, which is approximately derived as:

$$\mathbf{x}_{0|t_i} = \frac{\mathbf{x}_{t_i} + \sigma_{t_i}^2 \nabla_{\mathbf{x}} \log p_{t_i}(\mathbf{x}_{t_i})}{\alpha_{t_i}} \approx \frac{\mathbf{x}_{t_i} - \sigma_{t_i} \boldsymbol{\epsilon}_\theta(\mathbf{x}_{t_i}, t_i)}{\alpha_{t_i}}. \tag{8}$$

The state transition from the current step t_i to the subsequent step t_{i+1} follows a deterministic numerical integration rule given by DDIM [34] as:

$$\mathbf{x}_{t_{i+1}} = \alpha_{t_{i+1}} \mathbf{x}_{0|t_i} + \sigma_{t_{i+1}} \boldsymbol{\epsilon}_\theta(\mathbf{x}_{t_i}, t_i). \tag{9}$$

3.2 Decomposed Diffusion Sampler (DDS)

Training-free approaches solve the linear inverse problem in Eq. (1) by drawing samples from the conditional posterior distribution. However, achieving high reconstruction fidelity with such training-free solvers [12,13,35] necessitates multiple NFEs. DDS [11] mitigates these computational burdens by performing data-consistency updates on the Tweedie denoised representation. The key idea is that, under a local Krylov-subspace approximation of the tangent space around $\mathbf{x}_{0|t_i}$, CG updates initialized from $\mathbf{x}_{0|t_i}$ provide an efficient local residual minimization strategy without explicitly computing manifold-constrained gradients. At timestep t_i, to address highly ill-posed 3D inverse problems such as volumetric CT reconstruction, the algorithm seeks a refined estimate $\hat{\mathbf{x}}$ by solving a regularized optimization problem:

$$\min_{\mathbf{x}} \frac{1}{2} \|\mathbf{y} - \mathbf{A}\mathbf{x}\|_2^2 + \zeta \|\mathbf{D}_z \mathbf{x}\|_1, \tag{10}$$

where $\mathbf{D}_z$ denotes the finite difference operator along the z-axis for Total Variation regularization [32], and $\zeta > 0$ controls the regularization strength.

To efficiently solve this while constraining the update direction strictly along the appropriate manifold tangent space, the algorithm utilizes the Alternating Direction Method of Multipliers (ADMM) [5]. By introducing an auxiliary variable $\mathbf{z}$ and a scaled dual variable $\mathbf{w}$, the optimization is decomposed into tractable subproblems. Specifically, the data consistency update for $\mathbf{x}$ requires solving a linear system governed by $\mathbf{A}_{\text{CG}} = \mathbf{A}^\top \mathbf{A} + \rho \mathbf{D}_z^\top \mathbf{D}_z$ and $\mathbf{b}_{\text{CG}} = \mathbf{A}^\top \mathbf{y} + \rho \mathbf{D}_z^\top (\mathbf{z} - \mathbf{w})$, where $\rho > 0$ is the ADMM penalty parameter enforcing the constraint, while the TV regularization strength is controlled by ζ. This system is efficiently resolved by applying M steps of the CG method [11] initialized at the unconditional Tweedie estimate $\mathbf{x}_{0|t_i}$ in Eq. (8):

$$\hat{\mathbf{x}}_{0|t_i} = \text{CG}(\mathbf{A}_{\text{CG}}, \mathbf{b}_{\text{CG}}, \mathbf{x}_{0|t_i}, M). \tag{11}$$

Subsequently, the new auxiliary variable $\mathbf{z}'$ is updated using a soft-thresholding operator $\mathbf{S}_{\zeta/\rho}(\cdot)$ as follows:

$$\mathbf{z}' = \mathcal{S}_{\zeta/\rho}(\mathbf{D}_z \hat{\mathbf{x}}_{0|t_i} + \mathbf{w}), \tag{12}$$

where $\mathcal{S}_{\omega}(u) = \text{sign}(u) \cdot \max(|u| - \omega, 0)$. In addition, the new scaled dual variable $\mathbf{w}'$ is updated as follows:

$$\mathbf{w}' = \mathbf{D}_z \hat{\mathbf{x}}_{0|t_i} + \mathbf{w} - \mathbf{z}'. \tag{13}$$

Implementation details of the ADMM and CG processes are provided in the supplementary material. Following this refinement, the unconditioned estimate in the discrete integration rule is substituted by the data-consistent estimate $\hat{\mathbf{x}}_{0|t_i}$. The algorithm transitions from the current timestep t_i to the subsequent step t_{i+1} utilizing a stochastic generalized timestep schedule as DDIM [34], rather than the purely deterministic integration rule. The transition incorporates the measurement information defined by

$$\mathbf{x}_{t_{i+1}} = \alpha_{t_{i+1}} \hat{\mathbf{x}}_{0|t_i} + \sqrt{\sigma^2_{t_{i+1}} - \eta^2 \beta^2_{t_{i+1}}} \boldsymbol{\epsilon}_\theta(\mathbf{x}_{t_i}, t_i) + \eta \beta_{t_{i+1}} \boldsymbol{\epsilon}_i, \tag{14}$$

where $\boldsymbol{\epsilon}_i \sim \mathcal{N}(\mathbf{0}, \mathbf{I}_d)$ represents standard Gaussian noise. Here, $\eta \in [0, 1]$ regulates the degree of stochasticity and β_t represents the standard deviation of the noise at time t as defined in DDIM [34]. The deterministic trajectory is susceptible to accumulated approximation errors from the iterative data consistency projections. Introducing controlled stochastic noise mitigates these deviations and functions as a corrective mechanism to prevent samples from drifting off the clean data manifold.

4 Methods

To further enhance the sampling efficiency of diffusion-based 3D inverse solvers and enable high-fidelity reconstruction within the few-step regime, we propose Tracing the Oracle (TrO). Our framework formulates improved timestep scheduling as a discrete shortest-path optimization problem, identifying an optimized subset of evaluation points that minimizes the global truncation error for 3D inverse problems.

4.1 Oracle Trajectory

Continuous reverse diffusion processes trace trajectories along the data manifold from noise to real data. In the few-step regime, approximating this continuous evolution with sparse discrete transitions introduces truncation errors, causing the generated samples to deviate from the true data manifold and affecting reconstruction fidelity.

Conversely, numerical integration with dense evaluations more closely tracks the continuous conditional distribution. Therefore, we utilize DDS [11] with a large number of evaluations N to generate a reference trajectory for a given measurement $\mathbf{y}$. We define this densely sampled path as the oracle trajectory, denoted by $\mathcal{T}_{\text{oracle}} = \{\mathbf{x}_{t_i}\}_{i=0}^{N}$. Our objective is to extract a target subset of L timesteps, $\{\tau_j\}_{j=0}^{L}$ ($L \ll N$), such that the trajectory generated by this subset minimizes the cumulative approximation error relative to the oracle under our specified metric.

4.2 Discretization Error

To extract the optimized subset, it is necessary to quantify the transition error incurred by skipping intermediate timesteps. Suppose we transition from a source timestep t_i to a target timestep t_j ($t_i > t_j$), following the DDIM sampling rule in Eq. (14), the one-step approximation $\overline{\mathbf{x}}_{t_j|t_i}$ is derived as:

$$\overline{\mathbf{x}}_{t_j|t_i} = \alpha_{t_j}\hat{\mathbf{x}}_{0|t_i} + \sqrt{\sigma_{t_j}^2 - \eta^2\beta_{t_j}^2}\,\boldsymbol{\epsilon}_\theta(\mathbf{x}_{t_i}, t_i) + \eta\beta_{t_j}\boldsymbol{\epsilon}, \tag{15}$$

where $\hat{\mathbf{x}}_{0|t_i}$ is the data-consistent estimate obtained through the CG optimization at time t_i in Eq. (11), and $\boldsymbol{\epsilon} \sim \mathcal{N}(\mathbf{0}, \mathbf{I}_d)$ is the injected standard Gaussian noise. The discretization error associated with this transition can be evaluated by measuring the geometric distance $\|\overline{\mathbf{x}}_{t_j|t_i} - \mathbf{x}_{t_j}\|_2$ between the approximation $\overline{\mathbf{x}}_{t_j|t_i}$ and the corresponding intermediate state $\mathbf{x}_{t_j}$ from the oracle trajectory following GITS [7].

4.3 Noise Reuse

However, the geometric distance between $\overline{\mathbf{x}}_{t_j|t_i}$ and $\mathbf{x}_{t_j}$ presents challenges in stochastic frameworks. Since both the dense oracle trajectory and the one-step approximation independently sample the stochastic noise term $\boldsymbol{\epsilon}$, the resulting difference $\overline{\mathbf{x}}_{t_j|t_i} - \mathbf{x}_{t_j}$ is non-deterministic. Even if the deterministic components are fixed, independent target-step noise injections contribute

$$\mathrm{Cov}(\eta\beta_{t_j}\boldsymbol{\epsilon} - \eta\beta_{t_j}\boldsymbol{\epsilon}') = 2\eta^2\beta_{t_j}^2\mathbf{I}_d,$$

where $\boldsymbol{\epsilon}$ and $\boldsymbol{\epsilon}'$ are independently sampled standard Gaussian noises. This covariance indicates that the geometric distance fluctuates, which obscures the deterministic truncation error. While setting the stochasticity parameter η to zero avoids this variance, executing purely deterministic sampling in conditional inverse solvers can trap the generation process in local optima and degrade reconstruction performance [11,41,48].

To address this, we employ a noise reuse mechanism. During the generation of the oracle trajectory $\mathcal{T}_{\text{oracle}}$, we explicitly record the stochastic noise vectors $\boldsymbol{\epsilon}_i$ injected at each step t_i. Specifically, in the error evaluation phase, to compute the approximation state $\overline{\mathbf{x}}_{t_j|t_i}$ targeting the oracle state $\mathbf{x}_{t_j}$, we reuse the exact noise vector $\boldsymbol{\epsilon}_{j-1}$ that was originally utilized during the oracle transition from t_{j-1} to t_j. This precise alignment neutralizes the random variance and ensures that the approximated state remains consistent with the marginal distribution of the actual SDE sampling trajectory, thereby isolating the deterministic truncation error within the stochastic sampling procedure.

Consequently, we define the transition cost $C_{i,j}$ from t_i to t_j as:

$$C_{i,j} = \|\overline{\mathbf{x}}_{t_j|t_i} - \mathbf{x}_{t_j}\|_2 + \kappa\left((t_i - t_j) - \frac{T}{L}\right)^2. \tag{16}$$

The first term represents the truncation error isolated via noise reuse. The second term is a regularization component scaled by a hyperparameter $\kappa \geq 0$. This regularization penalizes large deviations from a uniform temporal stride (T/L) to prevent the neural network from operating outside its trained conditional manifold. The computational procedure for constructing the cost matrix is detailed in Algorithm 1.

4.4 Schedule Optimization

Given the cost matrix $\mathbf{C} \in \mathbb{R}^{(N+1)\times(N+1)}$ and $\{t_i\}_{i=0}^{N}$, the timestep scheduling task is formulated as a discrete shortest path problem to find the optimized timestep schedule $\{\tau_j\}_{j=0}^{L}$. Our objective is defined as:

$$\begin{aligned} \min_{\{\tau_j\}_{j=0}^{L}} \quad & \sum_{j=0}^{L-1} C_{k_j,k_{j+1}}, \\ \text{s.t.} \quad & \tau_j = t_{k_j},\ k_j \in \{0,1,\ldots,N\}, \quad j = 0,1,...,L \\ & \tau_j > \tau_{j+1}, \quad j = 0,1,\ldots,L-1, \\ & \tau_0 = t_0, \tau_L = t_N. \end{aligned} \tag{17}$$

To compute a schedule that minimizes this objective over the directed acyclic graph defined by $\mathbf{C}$, we implement the dynamic programming algorithm (DP) [3] similar to GITS [7], presented in Algorithm 2. Specifically, the DP state records the minimum accumulated cost of reaching a timestep with a fixed number of transitions by enumerating all possible predecessor nodes. Therefore, given the pre-computed cost matrix $\mathbf{C}$, the returned schedule is the global optimum of Eq. (17) rather than a greedy or locally optimized solution. Without dynamic programming, exact search over all feasible schedules leads to a combinatorial time complexity of $\mathcal{O}\left(L\binom{N-1}{L-1}\right)$. Given the precomputed cost matrix $\mathbf{C}$, our DP solver instead obtains the global optimum in $\mathcal{O}(LN^2)$ time and $\mathcal{O}(LN)$ memory.

Data samples originating from the same underlying distribution typically exhibit consistent structural properties within their reverse diffusion trajectories [7,18]. Thus, the timestep schedule extracted from a subset of calibration data generalizes across the test dataset. In our pipeline, the reference trajectory generation and the DP search are conducted in an offline preparatory phase. During the inference stage for 3D volume reconstruction, the pre-computed schedule $\{\tau_j\}_{j=0}^{L}$ is applied as a target timestep schedule, ensuring that this scheduling approach introduces no additional computational overhead to the conditional generation process.

Algorithm 1. Tracing the Oracle (TrO)

Require: Source timesteps $\{t_i\}_{i=0}^N$, $\{\alpha_{t_i}\}_{i=0}^N$, $\{\sigma_{t_i}\}_{i=0}^N$ and $\{\beta_{t_i}\}_{i=0}^N$, target number of steps L, regularization parameter κ, $\mathbf{A}$, $\mathbf{y}$, $\mathbf{D}_z$, ρ, $\mathbf{S}_{\zeta/\rho}$, M, η

Sample $\mathbf{x}_{t_0} \sim \mathcal{N}(\mathbf{0}, \mathbf{I}_d)$
$\mathbf{z}_0 \leftarrow \mathbf{0}_d, \mathbf{w}_0 \leftarrow \mathbf{0}_d$
for $i \leftarrow 0$ to $N-1$ **do**
  $\hat{\boldsymbol{\epsilon}}_i \leftarrow \boldsymbol{\epsilon}_\theta(\mathbf{x}_{t_i}, t_i)$
  $\mathbf{x}_{0|t_i} \leftarrow (\mathbf{x}_{t_i} - \sigma_{t_i}\hat{\boldsymbol{\epsilon}}_i)/\alpha_{t_i}$ ▷ Tweedie denoising
  $\mathbf{A}_{\mathrm{CG}} \leftarrow \mathbf{A}^\top\mathbf{A} + \rho\mathbf{D}_z^\top\mathbf{D}_z$
  $\mathbf{b}_{\mathrm{CG}} \leftarrow \mathbf{A}^\top\mathbf{y} + \rho\mathbf{D}_z^\top(\mathbf{z}_i - \mathbf{w}_i)$
  $\hat{\mathbf{x}}_{0|t_i} \leftarrow \mathrm{CG}(\mathbf{A}_{\mathrm{CG}}, \mathbf{b}_{\mathrm{CG}}, \mathbf{x}_{0|t_i}, M)$ ▷ Data consistency
  $\mathbf{z}_{i+1} \leftarrow \mathbf{S}_{\zeta/\rho}(\mathbf{D}_z\hat{\mathbf{x}}_{0|t_i} + \mathbf{w}_i)$
  $\mathbf{w}_{i+1} \leftarrow \mathbf{w}_i + \mathbf{D}_z\hat{\mathbf{x}}_{0|t_i} - \mathbf{z}_{i+1}$
  Sample $\boldsymbol{\epsilon}_i \sim \mathcal{N}(\mathbf{0}, \mathbf{I}_d)$
  $\mathbf{x}_{t_{i+1}} \leftarrow \alpha_{t_{i+1}}\hat{\mathbf{x}}_{0|t_i} + \sqrt{\sigma_{t_{i+1}}^2 - \eta^2\beta_{t_{i+1}}^2}\,\hat{\boldsymbol{\epsilon}}_i + \eta\beta_{t_{i+1}}\boldsymbol{\epsilon}_i$ ▷ DDIM sampling to t_{i+1}
end for
$\mathbf{C} \leftarrow \infty_{(N+1)\times(N+1)}$
for $i \leftarrow 0$ to $N-1$ **do**
  for $j \leftarrow i+1$ to N **do**
    $\overline{\mathbf{x}}_{t_j|t_i} \leftarrow \alpha_{t_j}\hat{\mathbf{x}}_{0|t_i} + \sqrt{\sigma_{t_j}^2 - \eta^2\beta_{t_j}^2}\,\hat{\boldsymbol{\epsilon}}_i + \eta\beta_{t_j}\boldsymbol{\epsilon}_{j-1}$
    ▷ DDIM sampling to t_j with reusing noise $\boldsymbol{\epsilon}_{j-1}$
    $C_{i,j} \leftarrow \|\overline{\mathbf{x}}_{t_j|t_i} - \mathbf{x}_{t_j}\|_2 + \kappa\left((t_i - t_j) - \frac{T}{L}\right)^2$
  end for
end for
$\{\tau_j\}_{j=0}^L \leftarrow \mathrm{DP}(\mathbf{C}, \{t_i\}_{i=0}^N, N, L)$
▷ Execute Dynamic Programming Algorithm to solve Eq. (17)
return $\{\tau_j\}_{j=0}^L$

5 Experimental Results

5.1 Experimental Setups

3D CT Reconstruction. We evaluate the proposed framework on sparse-view CT (SV-CT) and limited-angle CT (LA-CT) tasks. The forward operator $\mathbf{A}$ employs the discrete Radon transform. For SV-CT, we uniformly sample 2, 4, and 8 projection angles. For LA-CT, we restrict 120 projections to a 90° wedge. Experiments are conducted on the AAPM dataset [1] following standard protocols [11,12]. We train the 2D diffusion prior on the training split, and designate one specific volume to compute the oracle trajectory ($N = 200$) and extract the optimized schedule. Subsequent evaluations are conducted on a distinct volume, which serves as the standard single-volume benchmark commonly adopted by prior works [11,12]. Although community conventions restrict the evaluation to this single 3D volume, the reconstruction actually entails hundreds of independent 2D inferences across its high-resolution slices. Therefore, reporting metrics averaged over the axial, coronal, and sagittal planes provides a reliable quantitative assessment of our method.

Algorithm 2. Dynamic Programming Solver (DP)

Require: Cost matrix $\mathbf{C}$, Source time steps $\{t_i\}_{i=1}^{N}$, Source number of steps N, Target number of steps L

```
State ← ∞_{L×(N+1)}, Path ← 0_{L×(N+1)}
for j = 1 to N − 1 do
    State[0, j] ← C[0, j]
    Path[0, j] ← 0
end for
for i ← 1 to L − 1 do
    for j ← i + 1 to N do
        for k ← i − 1 to j − 1 do
            if State[i − 1, k] + C[k, j] < State[i, j] then
                State[i, j] ← State[i − 1, k] + C[k, j]
                Path[i, j] ← k
            end if
        end for
    end for
end for
Timesteps ← [t_N]
i ← N
for j ← L − 1 down to 0 do
    i ← Path[j, i]
    Append t_i to Timesteps
end for
return reverse(Timesteps)
```

Implementation Details. We integrate our proposed timestep scheduling algorithm into DDS [11]. Since existing ODE-based optimized schedules are difficult to apply directly to stochastic conditional inverse solvers, we evaluate our approach against several widely adopted fixed schedules within the identical pipeline to ensure a fair comparison. These baselines include the uniform time schedule Uniform-t [34], the uniform half of log-SNR schedule Uniform-λ [27], the Quadratic schedule [34], the EDM schedule [23], and the Cosine schedule [29]. Detailed formulations for these schedules are provided in the supplementary material. To isolate the impact of the scheduling strategies, all methods utilize the identical pre-trained diffusion model, and the algorithmic hyperparameters are kept consistent with the original DDS implementation. Additionally, we compare our method against established diffusion solvers for 3D inverse problems, such as DiffMBIR [12], Score-Med [35], and MCG [13], which typically demand thousands of NFEs to achieve competitive reconstruction quality. Following approaches [11–13,35], volumetric reconstruction quality is quantitatively assessed using the Peak Signal-to-Noise Ratio (PSNR) and the Structural Similarity Index Measure (SSIM), evaluated on Axial, Coronal, and Sagittal planes.

5.2 Quantitative Results

We comprehensively evaluate the volumetric reconstruction performance across SV-CT (e.g., 8-view and 4-view) and LA-CT tasks under strictly constrained computational budgets corresponding to 15, 10 and 8 NFEs. The quantitative comparisons, averaged across the axial, coronal, and sagittal planes, are summarized in Table 1. The evaluation indicates that TrO yields competitive reconstruction fidelity across the tested configurations. Notably, the advantage of our optimized schedule over predefined counterparts becomes more evident as the NFE budget decreases. While this performance gap may tend to narrow as the number of NFEs increases, these results highlight the utility of TrO in further enhancing the efficiency of the DDS framework with limited computational resources. Additionally, visual comparisons of the reconstructed tomographic slices are provided in Fig. 2, which further corroborate the enhanced artifact suppression and detail preservation capabilities of our adaptive schedule.

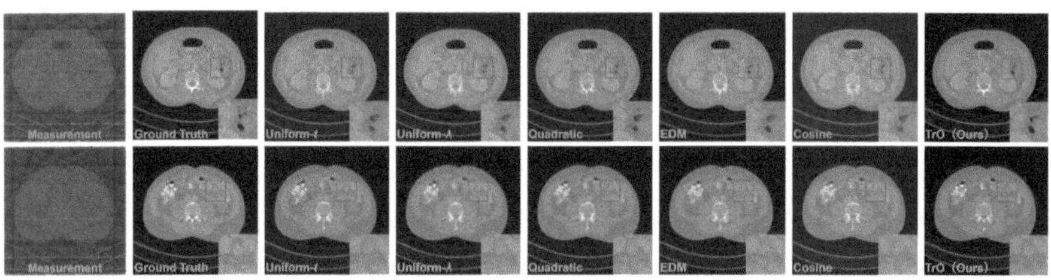

Fig. 2. Qualitative comparison of 3D CT reconstruction results using different timestep schedules. Red boxes highlight the detail recovery of our method. (Color figure online)

5.3 Further Analysis

Figure 3 illustrates the actual temporal evolution of various scheduling strategies. The quantitative results in Table 1 indicate that the relative performance of static timestep schedules is highly dependent on the specific measurement operator and the available NFEs. For instance, while the Cosine schedule exhibits a noticeable performance drop in SV-CT tasks, it demonstrates relatively better stability in LA-CT settings compared to the EDM and Quadratic schedules.

Ablation Study. We conduct an ablation study on the AAPM dataset to investigate the impact of the regularization hyperparameter κ in Eq. (16) for 8-view SV-CT reconstruction task. The reported PSNR and SSIM are averaged across the axial, coronal, and sagittal planes. As shown in Table 2, the optimal κ varies depending on the NFEs. Generally, a larger NFE requires a correspondingly larger κ to enforce a similar level of constraint, which stems from the differences in N/L. Furthermore, the empirical results indicate that the introduction of the

Table 1. Quantitative comparison of timestep schedules on AAPM across different NFEs and SV/LA-CT. Best results are highlighted in **bold** and the second-best results are underlined.

Method (NFE)	Schedule	**8-view**						**4-view**					
		Axial		Coronal		Sagittal		Axial		Coronal		Sagittal	
		PSNR↑	SSIM↑	PSNR↑	SSIM↑	PSNR↑	SSIM↑	PSNR↑	SSIM↑	PSNR↑	SSIM↑	PSNR↑	SSIM↑
DDS (8)	Uniform-t	37.08	0.940	37.89	0.935	36.74	0.936	32.09	0.894	33.05	0.887	31.13	0.889
	Uniform-λ	36.68	0.937	38.03	0.931	36.94	0.932	31.99	0.894	33.14	0.889	31.16	0.891
	Quadratic	37.58	0.941	38.59	0.931	37.87	0.934	32.66	0.901	33.60	0.890	31.57	0.891
	EDM	35.59	0.928	36.95	0.922	36.09	0.923	30.42	0.830	30.27	0.815	29.79	0.821
	Cosine	36.60	0.933	37.64	0.926	36.70	0.929	31.77	0.890	33.02	0.885	31.24	0.887
	TrO (Ours)	**38.53**	**0.952**	**39.78**	**0.964**	**38.62**	**0.948**	**33.24**	**0.917**	**34.66**	**0.910**	**32.78**	**0.914**
DDS (10)	Uniform-t	37.66	0.945	38.52	0.939	37.34	0.941	32.78	0.900	33.56	0.895	31.53	0.896
	Uniform-λ	38.08	0.948	39.03	0.943	37.96	0.944	32.34	0.899	33.55	0.894	31.51	0.895
	Quadratic	38.72	0.951	39.67	0.946	38.66	0.948	33.29	0.908	34.25	0.899	32.15	0.901
	EDM	38.38	0.946	39.37	0.940	38.61	0.942	33.66	0.921	34.63	0.916	33.21	0.917
	Cosine	36.29	0.907	36.42	0.895	35.96	0.900	30.88	0.800	30.96	0.780	30.12	0.791
	TrO (Ours)	**39.33**	**0.955**	**40.36**	**0.950**	**39.46**	**0.951**	**34.12**	**0.927**	**35.37**	**0.922**	**33.86**	**0.920**
DDS (15)	Uniform-t	38.54	0.950	39.47	0.945	38.36	0.947	33.82	0.911	34.67	0.906	32.68	0.907
	Uniform-λ	39.01	0.953	40.04	0.948	39.01	0.949	33.54	0.907	34.48	0.904	32.36	0.905
	Quadratic	39.63	0.955	40.61	0.951	39.69	0.952	34.84	0.923	35.68	0.917	33.66	0.918
	EDM	39.82	0.956	40.90	0.951	40.06	0.953	34.84	0.929	**36.50**	**0.924**	34.49	0.925
	Cosine	36.63	0.905	36.69	0.894	36.31	0.900	30.68	0.763	30.58	0.744	30.03	0.758
	TrO (Ours)	**40.02**	**0.957**	**40.96**	**0.952**	**40.14**	**0.954**	**34.99**	**0.932**	36.48	0.923	**34.61**	**0.927**
DiffMBIR(4000)	/	33.49	0.942	35.18	0.967	32.18	0.910	30.52	0.914	30.09	0.938	27.89	0.871
Score-Med(4000)	/	29.10	0.882	27.93	0.875	24.23	0.759	28.20	0.867	27.48	0.889	25.08	0.783
MCG(4000)	/	28.61	0.873	28.05	0.884	24.45	0.765	27.33	0.855	26.52	0.863	23.04	0.745

Method(NFE)	Schedule	**2-view**						90°**-Angle**					
		Axial		Coronal		Sagittal		Axial		Coronal		Sagittal	
		PSNR↑	SSIM↑	PSNR↑	SSIM↑	PSNR↑	SSIM↑	PSNR↑	SSIM↑	PSNR↑	SSIM↑	PSNR↑	SSIM↑
DDS (8)	Uniform-t	25.04	0.742	25.98	0.723	24.12	0.710	38.07	0.944	39.33	0.936	38.27	0.939
	Uniform-λ	24.55	0.730	25.76	0.714	23.97	0.707	38.29	0.949	39.84	0.942	38.52	0.945
	Quadratic	25.18	0.752	26.02	0.753	24.16	0.740	38.28	0.944	39.73	0.942	38.60	**0.946**
	EDM	21.50	0.606	22.03	0.634	21.30	0.615	36.71	0.941	38.26	0.934	36.64	0.937
	Cosine	23.39	0.705	25.52	0.752	23.11	0.704	38.36	0.947	39.62	0.940	38.57	**0.946**
	TrO (Ours)	**26.23**	**0.798**	**26.74**	**0.789**	**24.74**	**0.803**	**38.82**	**0.952**	**40.32**	**0.945**	**39.21**	**0.946**
DDS (10)	Uniform-t	25.52	0.731	26.30	0.712	24.55	0.720	38.52	0.948	39.85	0.941	38.77	0.943
	Uniform-λ	25.25	0.741	25.85	0.724	24.26	0.729	38.61	0.950	40.14	0.944	38.91	0.946
	Quadratic	26.05	0.781	27.03	0.798	24.73	0.796	38.54	0.947	40.17	0.945	38.87	0.945
	EDM	23.27	0.728	23.68	0.762	22.50	0.739	37.76	0.946	39.54	0.940	38.06	0.943
	Cosine	24.06	0.558	24.34	0.525	23.45	0.546	38.68	0.950	40.07	0.943	38.93	0.946
	TrO (Ours)	**26.70**	**0.811**	**27.60**	**0.819**	**25.36**	**0.818**	**39.17**	**0.954**	**40.51**	**0.947**	**39.47**	**0.949**
DDS (15)	Uniform-t	25.93	0.681	26.32	0.667	24.77	0.680	39.00	0.951	40.35	0.945	39.28	0.947
	Uniform-λ	25.52	0.702	26.01	0.687	24.48	0.697	38.80	0.950	40.30	0.944	39.14	0.946
	Quadratic	26.93	0.813	28.01	0.821	25.27	0.827	38.88	**0.952**	40.33	0.944	39.22	0.947
	EDM	26.37	0.802	26.41	0.809	24.61	0.803	37.93	0.944	39.69	0.937	38.33	0.940
	Cosine	24.04	0.491	24.03	0.463	23.34	0.489	38.97	0.950	40.32	0.944	39.25	0.946
	TrO (Ours)	**27.29**	**0.820**	**28.24**	**0.833**	**25.74**	**0.832**	**39.13**	**0.952**	**40.52**	**0.946**	**39.46**	**0.948**
DiffMBIR(4000)	/	24.11	0.810	23.15	0.841	21.72	0.766	34.92	0.956	32.48	0.947	28.82	0.832
Score-Med(4000)	/	24.07	0.808	23.70	0.822	20.95	0.720	27.80	0.852	25.69	0.869	22.03	0.735
MCG(4000)	/	24.69	0.821	23.52	0.806	20.71	0.685	26.01	0.838	24.55	0.823	21.59	0.706

regularization term effectively prevents the generated schedule from degenerating into extreme timestep allocations, which enhances the overall reconstruction performance.

Timestep Analysis. We hypothesize that this divergence originates from the frequency reconstruction dynamics of diffusion models. The early stages of the reverse diffusion process primarily synthesize low-frequency global structures,

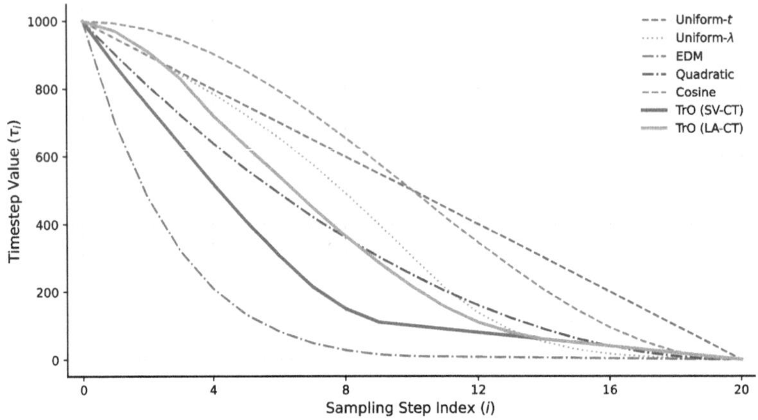

Fig. 3. Visualization of timestep allocations across different scheduling strategies. The graph illustrates the temporal evolution of continuous time τ_i over discrete evaluation steps i.

Table 2. Ablation study of κ for the 8-view SV-CT task on AAPM. Best results are highlighted in **bold** and the second-best results are underlined.

NFE	Metric	$\kappa = 0$	$\kappa = 1$	$\kappa = 5$	$\kappa = 10$	Uniform-t
8	PSNR↑	38.42	**38.98**	<u>38.65</u>	37.64	37.24
	SSIM↑	0.951	**0.955**	<u>0.953</u>	0.946	0.942
10	PSNR↑	39.32	39.64	**39.72**	<u>38.96</u>	37.84
	SSIM↑	0.943	<u>0.949</u>	**0.952**	0.948	0.942
15	PSNR↑	39.63	39.77	**40.37**	<u>39.83</u>	38.80
	SSIM↑	0.951	0.951	**0.954**	<u>0.952</u>	0.947

while the later stages refine high-frequency details. In SV-CT, the uniformly distributed projections provide reliable global low-frequency constraints. Consequently, computational resources are better allocated to the later stages (e.g., as in EDM and Quadratic) for high-frequency artifact suppression. Conversely, LA-CT concentrates projections within a narrow region, introducing severe structural artifacts and unreliable low-frequency information in the unmeasured wedges. Allocating insufficient steps to the early phase implicitly over-trusts these distorted low-frequency measurements, severely impeding late-stage optimization. The Cosine schedule mitigates this by densely populating the early stages, providing the generative prior with sufficient capacity to synthesize the missing reliable low-frequency structures.

These observations reveal that a single fixed timestep allocation is sub-optimal across diverse inverse problems. Notably, our proposed TrO framework effectively captures this physical discrepancy. As clearly depicted in Fig. 3, TrO adaptively shifts the step allocation toward the earlier stages for the LA-CT task compared to the SV-CT task. By continuously evaluating the actual SDE truncation error, TrO dynamically extracts task-specific and budget-aware temporal configurations, thereby ensuring consistent reconstruction fidelity across varying degradation scenarios.

6 Conclusion

In this paper, we present Tracing the Oracle (TrO), a plug-and-play framework that formulates timestep scheduling for diffusion-based 3D inverse problems as a discrete shortest-path optimization problem. To quantify the trajectory discretization error, we propose a noise reuse mechanism that isolates the deterministic truncation error within the SDE sampling procedure. By leveraging dynamic programming, TrO extracts an optimized timestep schedule from a densely sampled oracle trajectory. Evaluations on sparse-view and limited-angle CT reconstruction demonstrate that our proposed approach improves reconstruction fidelity, particularly under limited computational budgets. By reducing the performance gap between few-step sampling and high-NFE solvers without additional inference overhead, TrO facilitates the efficient and robust deployment of diffusion models in 3D medical imaging applications.

References

1. American Association of Physicists in Medicine (AAPM) and Mayo Clinic: 2016 NIH-AAPM-Mayo clinic low dose CT grand challenge dataset (2016). https://www.aapm.org/GrandChallenge/LowDoseCT/
2. Askari, H., Roosta, F., Sun, H.: Training-free medical image inverses via bi-level guided diffusion models. In: WACV (2025)
3. Bellman, R.: Dynamic programming. Science (1966)
4. Bora, A., Jalal, A., Price, E., Dimakis, A.G.: Compressed sensing using generative models. In: ICML (2017)
5. Boyd, S., Parikh, N., Chu, E., Peleato, B., Eckstein, J.: Distributed optimization and statistical learning via the alternating direction method of multipliers. FTML (2010)
6. Chang, J., Duan, C., Jiao, Y., Li, R., Yang, J.Z., Yuan, C.: Provable diffusion posterior sampling for Bayesian inversion. arXiv preprint arXiv:2512.08022 (2025)
7. Chen, D., Zhou, Z., Wang, C., Shen, C., Lyu, S.: On the trajectory regularity of ODE-based diffusion sampling. In: ICML (2024)
8. Chen, J., Ng, M.K., Liu, Z.: Solving quadratic systems with full-rank matrices using sparse or generative priors. IEEE TSP (2025)
9. Chen, J., Scarlett, J., Ng, M., Liu, Z.: A unified framework for uniform signal recovery in nonlinear generative compressed sensing. In: NeurIPS (2023)
10. Chung, H., Kim, J., McCann, M.T., Klasky, M.L., Ye, J.C.: Diffusion posterior sampling for general noisy inverse problems. In: ICLR (2023)
11. Chung, H., Lee, S., Ye, J.C.: Decomposed diffusion sampler for accelerating large-scale inverse problems. In: ICLR (2024)
12. Chung, H., Ryu, D., Mccann, M.T., Klasky, M.L., Ye, J.C.: Solving 3D inverse problems using pre-trained 2D diffusion models. In: CVPR (2023)

13. Chung, H., Sim, B., Ryu, D., Ye, J.C.: Improving diffusion models for inverse problems using manifold constraints. In: NeurIPS (2022)
14. Daras, G., Dean, J., Jalal, A., Dimakis, A.: Intermediate layer optimization for inverse problems using deep generative models. In: ICML (2021)
15. Delbracio, M., Milanfar, P.: Inversion by direct iteration: An alternative to denoising diffusion for image restoration. In: TMLR (2023)
16. Dong, C., Loy, C.C., He, K., Tang, X.: Image super-resolution using deep convolutional networks. IEEE TPAMI (2015)
17. Efron, B.: Tweedie's formula and selection bias. JASA (2011)
18. Frankel, E., Chen, S., Li, J., Koh, P.W., Ratliff, L.J., Oh, S.: S4S: Solving for a diffusion model solver. In: ICML (2025)
19. Fu, F., Guo, T., Liu, Z.: Learnable sampler distillation for discrete diffusion models. In: NeurIPS (2025)
20. Goodfellow, I., et al.: Generative adversarial nets. In: NeurIPS (2014)
21. He, J., Li, B., Yang, G., Liu, Z.: Blaze3DM: Integrating triplane representation with diffusion for solving 3D inverse problems in medical imaging. In: MICCAI (2025)
22. Ho, J., Jain, A., Abbeel, P.: Denoising diffusion probabilistic models. In: NeurIPS (2020)
23. Karras, T., Aittala, M., Aila, T., Laine, S.: Elucidating the design space of diffusion-based generative models. In: NeurIPS (2022)
24. Kingma, D.P.: Auto-encoding variational bayes. In: ICLR (2014)
25. Li, J., Wang, C.: Image restoration via primal dual hybrid gradient and flow generative model. In: AAAI (2026)
26. Liu, Z., Wang, X., Liu, J.: Misspecified phase retrieval with generative priors. In: NeurIPS (2022)
27. Lu, C., Bao, F., Chen, J., Li, C., Zhu, J.: DPM-Solver: A fast ODE solver for diffusion probabilistic model sampling in around 10 steps. In: NeurIPS (2022)
28. Meurant, G., Tebbens, J.D.: Krylov methods for nonsymmetric linear systems: From theory to computations. Springer, Cham (2020)
29. Nichol, A.Q., Dhariwal, P.: Improved denoising diffusion probabilistic models. In: ICML (2021)
30. Peng, X., et al.: Improving diffusion models for inverse problems using optimal posterior covariance. In: ICML (2024)
31. Sabour, A., Fidler, S., Kreis, K.: Align your steps: Optimizing sampling schedules in diffusion models. In: ICML (2024)
32. Sidky, E.Y., Pan, X.: Image reconstruction in circular cone-beam computed tomography by constrained, total-variation minimization. PMB (2008)
33. Song, B., Hu, J., Luo, Z., Fessler, J.A., Shen, L.: DiffusionBlend: learning 3D image prior through position-aware diffusion score blending for 3D computed tomography reconstruction. In: NeurIPS (2024)
34. Song, J., Meng, C., Ermon, S.: Denoising diffusion implicit models. In: ICLR (2021)
35. Song, Y., Shen, L., Xing, L., Ermon, S.: Solving inverse problems in medical imaging with score-based generative models. In: ICLR (2022)
36. Song, Y., Sohl-Dickstein, J., Kingma, D.P., Kumar, A., Ermon, S., Poole, B.: Score-based generative modeling through stochastic differential equations. In: ICLR (2021)
37. Sun, W., Li, J., Liu, Z.: Just-in-time: Training-free spatial acceleration for diffusion Transformers. In: CVPR (2026)
38. Tu, Z., et al.: MAXIM: Multi-axis MLP for image processing. In: CVPR (2022)

39. Xue, S., et al.: Accelerating diffusion sampling with optimized time steps. In: CVPR (2024)
40. Zamir, S.W., et al.: Multi-stage progressive image restoration. In: CVPR (2021)
41. Zhang, B., Chu, W., Berner, J., Meng, C., Anandkumar, A., Song, Y.: Improving diffusion inverse problem solving with decoupled noise annealing. In: CVPR (2025)
42. Zhang, J., Liu, Z., Yan, L., Li, G., Gu, Y.: Improving diffusion-based inverse algorithms under few-step constraint via linear extrapolation. In: NeurIPS (2025)
43. Zhang, J., Zhuang, J., Jin, C., Li, G., Gu, Y.: Unleashing the denoising capability of diffusion prior for solving inverse problems. In: NeurIPS (2024)
44. Zhao, W., Bai, L., Rao, Y., Zhou, J., Lu, J.: UniPC: A unified predictor-corrector framework for fast sampling of diffusion models. In: NeurIPS (2023)
45. Zheng, Y., Li, W., Liu, Z.: Integrating intermediate layer optimization and projected gradient descent for solving inverse problems with diffusion models. In: ICML (2025)
46. Zheng, Y., Li, W., Liu, Z.: Image restoration via diffusion models with dynamic resolution. In: ICML (2026)
47. Zhou, Z., Chen, D., Wang, C., Chen, C.: Fast ODE-based sampling for diffusion models in around 5 steps. In: CVPR (2024)
48. Zhu, Y., et al.: Denoising diffusion models for plug-and-play image restoration. In: CVPRW (2023)

Causal Discovery and Causal Inference

Bringing Light to the Threshold: Identification of Multi-Score Regression Discontinuity Effects with Application to LED Manufacturing

Oliver Schacht[1], Philipp Alexander Schwarz[1,2(✉)], Sven Klaaßen[1,3], Johannes Oberpriller[2], and Martin Spindler[1,3]

[1] University Hamburg, Hamburg, Germany
oliver.schacht@uni-hamburg.de
[2] AMS-Osram International GmbH, Regensburg, Germany
philipp.schwarz@ams-osram.com
[3] Economic AI, Regensburg, Germany

Abstract. The regression discontinuity design (RDD) is a widely used framework for threshold-based causal effect estimation in causal inference. Recent extensions incorporating machine learning (ML) adjustments have made RDD an appealing approach for researchers utilizing causal ML toolkits. However, many real-world applications, such as production systems, involve multiple decision criteria and logically connected thresholds, necessitating more sophisticated identification strategies, which are not clearly addressed in the recent literature. We derive a novel identification result for the complier effect in the multi-score RDD (MRD) setting by extending unit behavior types to multiple dimensions. Further, we show that under mild assumptions, this identification result does not depend on subsets of units with constant response. We apply our findings to simulated and real-world data from opto-electronic semiconductor manufacturing, employing estimators that adjust for covariates through machine learning. Our results offer insights into enhancing current production policies by optimizing the cutoff points, demonstrating the applicability of MRD in a manufacturing context.

1 Introduction

The Regression Discontinuity Design (RDD) is a quasi-experimental strategy for the identification and estimation of causal effects that has been widely applied in empirical economics [4,5,10,12], public policy [20] and the social sciences [2]. Its appeal lies in its ability to deliver credible causal estimates under minimal assumptions, utilizing discontinuities in treatment assignment rules that are

O. Schacht and P. A. Schwarz—Contributed equally.

Supplementary Information The online version contains supplementary material available at https://doi.org/10.1007/978-3-032-37654-1_34.

M. Ceci et al. (Eds.): ECML PKDD 2026, LNAI 16941, pp. 587–602, 2027.
https://doi.org/10.1007/978-3-032-37654-1_34

typically based on an observed running or score variable [18,21]. Typical examples are credit scores, GPAs or vote shares. The classic RDD setting assumes that treatment assignment hinges on a single, continuous forcing variable crossing a known threshold. When correctly specified, this setting enables identification of average treatment effects for units near the cutoff [6]. In particular, RDD can be applied even if typical causal machine learning assumptions such as *unconfoundedness* [28] or *positivity* [3] do not hold [18].

However, in many real-world contexts – particularly in industrial, operational, or engineering systems – treatment decisions are based not on a single score, but on multiple criteria [30]. Such situations call for an extension of the classical RDD setup to multi-score RDD (MRD), in which treatment is assigned when a combination of variables jointly satisfies a threshold condition [25]. Recent work has surveyed MRD [26,27,35] and proposed estimators for test score-based [1] and geographical [19] applications.

This paper addresses the identification and estimation challenges that arise in the context of multi-score RDD, particularly in complex decision-making environments such as production systems. In such systems, decision rules are often implemented through a layered combination of logic and thresholds applied to multiple inputs, making the treatment assignment mechanism more intricate than in the standard RDD case. We develop new identification results tailored for multi-score RDD settings. Specifically, we provide a formal framework that defines and categorizes behavioral types of units. We investigate general boolean-type cutoff rules, such as "AND"-type and "OR"-type rules, commonly observed in MRD environments and analyze how their properties influence local identification. Further, we show how the complier effect can be identified using these categories. We demonstrate the utility of our framework by applying it to a real-world problem in light-emitting diode (LED) production, where treatment assignment is based on multiple quality indicators. Using real-world manufacturing data, we estimate the causal effect of a threshold-based production policy and show how the estimated effects can guide the optimal tuning of the decision threshold to improve manufacturing outcomes. We complement our empirical results with a simulated study using a semi-synthetic clone of the production environment, highlighting the value of multi-score RDD for counterfactual analysis and industrial policy design.

Our contributions to the causal machine learning literature are twofold. On the theoretical side, we advance the multi-dimensional regression discontinuity (MRD) framework, previously developed in the econometric literature. Specifically, we provide a rigorous definition and categorization of unit behavior types in the multi-cutoff case, introducing in particular the novel class of *indecisive units*, which has no counterpart in the one-dimensional setting. We further establish an identification theorem for the complier effect, derive precise conditions under which non-changing units (alwaystakers and nevertakers) can be rejected, and show how our identification results enable recovery of the complier effect in the multi-dimensional case. On the practical side, we illustrate the applicability and usefulness of the MRD framework in a real-data industrial application, thereby demonstrating the potential of causal machine learning methods in practice.

2 Background

2.1 Related Literature

Early theoretical work on extending RDD to **Multi-Score Regression Discontinuity Designs** recognized that such designs require new identification strategies [25]. While this setting included multiple treatment levels, most recent papers on MRD study the identification of a binary treatment that is assigned based on multiple indicators, using either "AND" connections of rules [9,19], "OR" connections [35], or both [16,27]. An important special case involves geographical MRD, which features a two-dimensional design with longitude and latitude as scores [7,19]. See Appendix 0.D for an overview of the MRD estimators typically studied in recent literature [26]. Additionally, recent work has introduced new estimators based on a minimax approach [15] and on decision trees [22]. [26] note that although there is a rich body of studies using MRD, there is a lack of theoretical understanding of MRD estimators.

Our work further contributes to a growing field of **applications of causal machine learning in management and operations**. [4] use a one-dimensional fuzzy RD design in public infrastructure projects. [14] highlight the value of causal machine learning for business decision-making and provide an overview of methods, including RDD. [23] give an overview of RDD applications in operations management. [31] study policy making in semiconductor manufacturing using propensity score-based estimation in the double machine learning framework. [34] investigate the development of research on causal discovery in manufacturing, focusing on motivation, common application scenarios, impact, and implementation challenges. Finally, there have been applications of causal machine learning to policy learning in different business fields, e.g., supply chain management [36] or marketing [13]. Despite these recent advances, the application of causal machine learning methodologies within operational and industrial domains remains underexplored.

2.2 RDD Setting

RDD dates back to a study by [33] on scholarship programs. Recent sources on RDD often rely on identification and estimation results by [11], as well as prominent surveys [6,18,21]. RDD consists of three key ingredients: A score X that rates the individuals; a cutoff c that splits the support of the score into two groups; and a treatment D, which is assigned to one of the groups based on their score and the cutoff, $D_i = \mathbb{1}[X_i \geq c]$ [6].

The parameter of interest is the average treatment effect at the cutoff c, $\mathbb{E}[Y(1) - Y(0) \mid X = c]$ with $Y(1)$ and $Y(0)$ being the potential outcomes of the individuals [29]. The central RDD assumption is continuity.

Assumption 1. *Continuity. The conditional mean of the potential outcomes* $\mathbb{E}[Y_i(d) \mid X_i = x]$ *for* $d \in \{0, 1\}$ *is continuous at the cutoff level* c.

Under Assumption 1, RDD provides inference around the threshold as plausible as that from a randomized experiment [20]. The average treatment effect at the threshold $\tau_0 = \mathbb{E}[Y_i(1) - Y_i(0) \mid X_i = c]$ is identified as $\tau_0 = \lim_{x \to c^+} \mathbb{E}[Y_i \mid X_i = x] - \lim_{x \to c^-} \mathbb{E}[Y_i \mid X_i = x]$ [11]. The basic RDD estimator runs separate local linear regressions on each side of the cutoff:

$$\hat{\tau}_{\text{base}}(h) = \sum_i w_i(h) Y_i,$$

where the $w_i(h)$ are local linear regression weights that depend on the data through the realizations of the running variable only, and $h > 0$ is a bandwidth.

Under standard conditions [11], which include that the running variable is continuously distributed, and that the bandwidth h tends to zero at an appropriate rate, the estimator $\hat{\tau}_{\text{base}}(h)$ is approximately normally distributed in large samples, with bias of order h^2 and variance of order $(nh)^{-1}$, with sample size n.

More recent work, which we will also employ in the empirical section, uses a flexible covariate adjustment based on potentially nonlinear adjustment functions η. The estimator takes the following form:

$$\widehat{\tau}_{\text{RDFlex}}(h; \eta) = \sum_i w_i(h) M_i(\eta), \quad M_i(\eta) = Y_i - \eta(Z_i). \tag{1}$$

Here, η is the influence of Z on the outcome Y and is estimated using ML methods [24].

3 General Identification Strategies in Multi-score RDD

In this section, we give a formal definition of common behavior types of units (e.g., complier, defier) in multi-score, two-stage decision settings that employ cutoff-rules for the initial treatment assignment. We derive an identification result using these unit categories. In particular, we show that under certain assumptions, the identification does not depend on subsets of unit types with constant response. This is a new result in the literature and our main theoretical contribution.

In practical settings, the easiest way to improve a complex cutoff-rule is to analyze and adjust cutoffs individually, e.g., one can estimate the effect on complier with respect to a specific subrule involving a single cutoff. Taking the AND-rule $D := \mathbb{1}[X_1 > c_1]\,\mathbb{1}[X_2 > c_2]$ as an example, one can analyze the effect on complier of $G := \mathbb{1}[X_1 > c_1]$ at the cutoff to gain insights on how to improve c_1. This can be achieved in different ways: First, using a fuzzy setting in which we regard G as the assigned and D as the actual treatment. Second, by conditioning on the complying units and using a sharp estimator. Thus, knowledge of unit behavior can open up a different way of estimating the complier effect.

Expanding on the previous example, now suppose that the treatment assignment $T := \mathbb{1}[X_1 > c_1]\,\mathbb{1}[X_2 > c_2]$ is known, while the final decision rule D is unknown and does not always comply with T. Thus, the question arises how knowledge of units that comply with T in the final treatment D can improve the estimation of the effect of $G := \mathbb{1}[X_1 > c_1]$ on the treatment outcome.

3.1 Setup

For each individual i, let $X_i = (X_{1,i}, \ldots, X_{K,i}) \in \mathbb{R}^K$ denote the score variables. Further, given $c \in \mathbb{R}^K$, let $I_i(c) := (I_{1,i}(c_1), \ldots, I_{K,i}(c_K))$ denote the corresponding indicator variables with $I_{k,i}(c_k) := \mathbb{1}[X_{k,i} > c_k]$ and let the observed outcome for individual i be Y_i. We regard the entries $I_i(c)$ as boolean variables and allow any composition of AND, OR and negation operations ($\wedge$, $\vee$, $\overline{\square}$) over this set of atoms to form general boolean functions $g(I_i(c))$.

Definition 1. *A mapping $T : \mathbb{R}^K \to \{0,1\}$ is called a decision rule. We say that a decision rule T is a cutoff rule (on $\mathbb{R}^K$) if there exists a boolean mapping g such that $T_i = T(X_i) = g(I_i)$.*

With slight abuse of notation, we use $T(c)$, $T(X_i \,|\, c)$ and $T_i(c)$ to indicate the use of a specific cutoff $c \in \mathbb{R}^K$. Note that

$$T(X + \epsilon \,|\, c) = T(X \,|\, c - \epsilon) \quad \text{and} \quad T(\lambda X \,|\, c) = T\left(X \,|\, \frac{c}{\lambda}\right) \tag{2}$$

holds for $\epsilon \in \mathbb{R}^K, \lambda \in \mathbb{R}_{>0}$. Thus, without loss of generality, we assume that the cutoff of interest is $c = 0$. We suppose that Y_i depends in the following way on a cutoff rule T and a general decision rule D:

$$\begin{aligned} Y_i = Y_i(T_i, D_i) = &\Big(Y_i(0,0)(1 - D_i) + Y_i(0,1)D_i\Big)(1 - T_i) \\ &+ \Big(Y_i(1,0)(1 - D_i) + Y_i(1,1)D_i\Big)T_i, \end{aligned}$$

where T is the treatment assignment and D is the actually implemented treatment. Unless otherwise stated, in the proofs we make no further assumptions on D except that it is a decision-rule.

3.2 Unit Categorization

Given this setup, there are certain groups of individuals that are especially interesting, namely the nevertaker, the alwaystaker, the complier and the defier with respect to the pair (T, D) or (G, D), where G is a subrule of T. We follow the intuition that changes in the cutoff, or equivalently in the observed score values – relevant for T – are necessary to categorize the behavior of a unit i. Additional variables that affect only D may not be controllable or even observable. The following definition formalizes the intuition behind relevant directions of change in a cutoff rule.

Definition 2. *Let T be a cutoff rule on $\mathbb{R}^K$. Denote with $e_1, \ldots, e_K$ the unit direction in $\mathbb{R}^K$ and with*

$$S(T) := \{k \,|\, \exists c \in \mathbb{R}^K, \lambda \in \mathbb{R} : T(0 \,|\, c + \lambda e_k) \neq T(0 \,|\, c)\}$$

the support directions of T. The support of T is defined as the linear hull over the support directions:

$$\mathrm{supp}(T) := \left\{ \sum_{k \in S(T)} \lambda_k e_k \,|\, \lambda_k \in \mathbb{R},\, k \in S(T) \right\}$$

The above notion of the support of a cutoff rule is motivated by the existence of a change along a single coordinate direction. It is almost trivial to see that an empty support also excludes changes along multiple directions, justifying the definition.

Lemma 1. *T is constant if and only if $S(T) = \emptyset$, or equivalently, if and only if* $\mathrm{supp}(T) = \{0\}$.

From now on, we require that T is not degenerate in the sense that $\mathrm{supp}(T) \neq \{0\}$. For the introductory AND-rule example, $D := I_1(c) \wedge I_2(c)$ and $T := I_1(c)$ we have $\mathrm{supp}(T) = \mathbb{R} \times \{0\}$ and $\mathrm{supp}(D) = \mathbb{R}^2$. If a unit i complies in the assigned treatment T with the actual D, one would require that T_i produces the same output as D_i, even under any[1] hypothetical change of the cutoff c_1. In other words, both rules should be synchronous on the support of T, which is the case if $X_{2,i} > c_2$. Thus, it is $X_{2,i}$ (or equivalently c_2) that controls the behavior of i. To make this distinction more apparent, it is useful to have a notation for entries $X \in \mathbb{R}^K$ that do not affect T:

$$N^T := \left\{ X \in \mathbb{R}^K \,|\, T(X \,|\, c) = T(0 \,|\, c) \text{ for all } c \in \mathbb{R}^K \right\}$$

In particular, one can show the following.

Proposition 1. *For each $X \in \mathbb{R}^K$, there exists a unique decomposition $X = X^T + X^{\perp T}$ with $X^T \in$* $\mathrm{supp}(T)$ *and $X^{\perp T} \in N^T$. The orthogonal projection $P_T(X) := \sum_{k \in S(T)} \langle X, e_k \rangle e_k$ onto* $\mathrm{supp}(T)$ *satisfies the above properties, where $\langle \cdot, \cdot \rangle$ denotes the standard scalar product on $\mathbb{R}^K$.*

That is, according to Proposition 1, one has the following decomposition

$$\mathcal{S} := \mathbb{R}^{|S(T)|} \times \mathbb{R}^{K-|S(T)|} \simeq \mathrm{supp}(T) \oplus N^T = \mathbb{R}^K$$

of the score space into two distinct parts. The former part captures the decision changes of T and the latter consists of free variables not affecting T, but potentially controlling the unit category. This observation allows for a general definition of unit categories.

Definition 3. *Let i be a unit and $X_i = X_i^T + X_i^{\perp T}$. Then i is said to be a nevertaker (an alwaystaker) of T with respect to D iff $D\left(X_i^{\perp T} - c\right) = 0$ (iff $D\left(X_i^{\perp T} - c\right) = 1$) for all $c \in$* $\mathrm{supp}(T)$. [2]

[1] A more refined, local definition could relax this requirement to "any reasonable changes". For ease of presentation, we stick to the global version.

[2] Both linear spaces are isomorphic; $\oplus$ denotes the direct sum.

Further, i is said to be a complier (a defier) of T with respect to D iff $T(0\,|\,c) = D\left(X_i^{\perp T} - c\right)$ (iff $T(0\,|\,c) \neq D\left(X_i^{\perp T} - c\right)$) for all $c \in \mathrm{supp}(T)$.
Let the sets of compliers, nevertakers, alwaystakers, and defiers be denoted by $\mathrm{ComP}(T, D)$, $\mathrm{Nt}(T, D)$, $\mathrm{At}(T, D)$, *and* $\mathrm{DeF}(T, D)$, *respectively.*

Particularly, if D is a cutoff-rule one obtains the following more intuitive equivalencies, which capture the notion of a simultaneous cutoff changes along relevant directions.

Proposition 2. *Let D be a cutoff rule over $\mathbb{R}^K$ and i be a unit. Then i is a nevertaker (an alwaystaker) of T w.r.t. D iff $D_i(c) = 0$ (iff $D_i(c) = 1$) for all $c \in \mathrm{supp}(T)$. Further, i is a complier (a defier) of T w.r.t. D iff $T_i(c) = D_i(c)$ (iff $T_i(c) \neq D_i(c)$) for all $c \in \mathrm{supp}(T)$.*

Note that the terminology introduced in Definition 3 indeed introduces well-defined categories:

Proposition 3. *The sets* $\mathrm{At}(T, D)$, $\mathrm{Nt}(T, D)$, $\mathrm{ComP}(T, D)$ *and* $\mathrm{DeF}(T, D)$ *are pairwise disjoint.*

From now on, whenever we assume that D is a cutoff rule, we restrict ourselves to the case in which D has at least as much information for decision-making as T. This means that D might depend on $I_{k,i}(0)$ for $k \in S(T)$. In addition, we suppose that D does not depend on $I_{k,i}(c)$ with $c \neq 0$ for $k \in \mathrm{supp}(T)$, effectively restricting to the case where both decision rules have a zero cutoff.[3]

Even for cutoff rules D under these restrictions, the categories above are not exhaustive if $\dim(\mathrm{supp}(T)) > 1$. For example, let $D := (\overline{I}_1 \wedge I_2)$ and $T := I_1 \wedge I_2$. Then $\mathrm{supp}(T) = \mathbb{R}^2$ and for $T(0\,|\,0) = D(0\,|\,0)$ but $0 = T(0\,|(-1,1)) \neq D(0\,|\,(-1,1)) = 1$. Thus, D is not constant nor equal to T or $\overline{T}$ on the support of T. We call individuals of this remaining category *indecisive* and denote *the set of indecisives (of T with respect to D)* by $\mathrm{Ind}(T, D)$.

Note that given T with $\dim(\mathrm{supp}(T)) > 1$, one can always construct a cutoff rule D that exhibits indecisive items. At least one has the following:

Proposition 4. *Let D be a cutoff rule on $\mathbb{R}^K$ and let i denote an individual. If* $\dim(\mathrm{supp}(T)) = 1$ *then* $i \in \mathrm{At}(T, D) \cup \mathrm{Nt}(T, D) \cup \mathrm{DeF}(T, D) \cup \mathrm{ComP}(T, D)$.

Moreover, our definitions of complier, nevertaker and alwaystaker imply the corresponding definitions in [18]. For this, let $c^+, c^- \in \mathrm{supp}(T)$ be two directions that induce change in T, that is:

$$\lim_{\lambda \to 0} T(X_i\,|\,\lambda c^+) = 1 \text{ and } \lim_{\lambda \to 0} T(X_i\,|\,\lambda c^-) = 0$$

Using the above complier definition:

$$T(X_i\,|\,c) = T(X_i^T\,|\,c) = T(0\,|\,c - X_i^T) = D(X_i^{\perp T} + X_i^T - c) = D(X_i - c)$$

[3] This restricts the general case. Suppose that the decision maker D is an opportunist and ignores all the other scores as long as a certain incentive X_k exceeds an even higher cutoff $0 < c_k < X_k$. Only then D would comply with T.

for $c \in \text{supp}(T)$. In particular, T and D coincide in a neighborhood of zero, and thus

$$\lim_{\lambda \to 0} D_i(\lambda c^+) = \lim_{\lambda \to 0} D(X_i - \lambda c^+) = 1 \text{ and } \lim_{\lambda \to 0} D_i(\lambda c^-) = \lim_{\lambda \to 0} D(X_i - \lambda c^-) = 0$$

where $D_i(c) := D(X_i - c)$ for $c \in \text{supp}(T)$. The corresponding statements for nevertaker and alwaystaker follow analogously. Indeed, requiring consistency in the limit for any direction one would arrive at a local definition of the unit categories sufficient for the multi-score RDD setting. Before continuing with the identification part we are going to expand on the AND-rule example.

Example (AND-Rules) Let $D := \bigwedge_{j=1}^{K} I_j$ and $T := \bigwedge_{j=1}^{k} I_j$ for $k \in \{1, \ldots, K-1\}$. Then $\text{supp}(T) = \mathbb{R}^k \times \{0\}^{K-k}$. Further, we have the following unit categorizations: **(i)** $\text{ComP}(T, D) = \{i \mid \forall\, k < j \leq K : X_{j,i} > 0\}$ Note that $X_{j,i} > 0$ for all $k < j \leq K$ is equivalent to $\wedge_{j=k+1}^{K} I_{j,i}(c)$ being one for $c \in \text{supp}(T)$. Thus, the rule D_i effectively reduces to T_i. **(ii)** $\text{At}(T, D) = \emptyset$ Since for each $X_i \in \mathbb{R}^K$ there exists a $c \in \text{supp}(T)$ such that $D_i(c) = 0$. For example choose any c with $X_{1,i} \leq c_1$ and $c_j = 0$ for $j \neq 1$. **(iii)** $\text{Nt}(T, D) = \{i \mid \exists\, k < j \leq K : X_{j,i} \leq 0\}$ Note that i being in the set on the right is equivalent to $\wedge_{j=k+1}^{K} I_{j,i}(c)$ being zero for all $c \in \text{supp}(T)$. This is equivalent to $D_i(c) = 0$ for all $c \in \text{supp}(T)$, since given an i one can always find a cutoff $c \in \text{supp}(T)$ such that $T_i(c) = 1$, which implies that one of the indicators $I_{j,i}$ for $j > k$ has to be zero. **(iv)** $\text{DeF}(T, D) = \emptyset$ Note that $T_i(c) = 0$ implies $D_i(c) = 0$, and that $c \in \text{supp}(T)$ can always be chosen such that the former is satisfied.

Additional examples can be found in Appendix 0.A.2 illustrating instances of the remaining unit categories (excluding the indecisive case). We conclude that the introduced definitions are indeed reasonable.

3.3 Effect Identification

Inspired by the work of [11,17], we use the introduced unit categories to prove an identification theorem for the effect on complier at the cutoff. For this section, we require that the outcome Y does not directly depend on the treatment assignment T. Denote the set of all unit categories by

$$\mathcal{C} := \{\text{ComP}(T, D), \text{Nt}(T, D), \text{At}(T, D), \text{DeF}(T, D), \text{Ind}(T, D)\}$$

and the set of non-change categories by $\mathcal{C}^0 := \{\text{Nt}(T, D), \text{At}(T, D)\}$. We assume that the categorization of a unit is independent of the support part of T in a neighborhood of the cutoff, that is:

Assumption 2. *There exists an* $\epsilon > 0$ *such that*

$$\Pr\left(i \in \text{Cat} \mid X_i^T = x\right) = \Pr\left(i \in \text{Cat} \mid X_i^T = 0\right)$$

for $\|x\| \leq \epsilon$ *and* $\text{Cat} \in \mathcal{C}$.

Note that this requirement relates to the independence assumptions used in [17]. We further rely on the following local continuity assumption, which is a variation of the standard continuity assumption (Assumption 1):

Assumption 3. *There exists an* $\epsilon > 0$ *such that* $x \mapsto \mathbb{E}(Y_i(d) \mid X_i^T = x, i \in \text{Cat})$ *is continuous for* $\|x\| \leq \epsilon$, $d \in \{0, 1\}$ *and* $\text{Cat} \in \mathcal{C}$.[4]

Two more assumptions are required to make further use of the continuity. First, we deny the existence of indecisive items, since this category does not allow structured conclusions about D based on knowledge of T.

Assumption 4. $\text{Ind}(T, D) = \emptyset$

Second, we assume that the directions x^+, $x^- \in \text{supp}(T)$ along which we aim to estimate the complier effect induce a change in T.

Assumption 5. $1 = \lim_{\lambda \to 0} T(\lambda x^+ \mid 0) \neq \lim_{\lambda \to 0} T(\lambda x^- \mid 0) = 0$

This assumption is implicit in one-dimensional RDD designs and imposes no real restriction in practice, as T is generally assumed to be known. The proof of the following proposition can be found in Appendix 0.A.3.

Theorem 1. *Let Assumptions 2, 3, 4 and 5 hold. Then the complier effect at the cutoff is identified as*

$$\mathbb{E}\left(Y_i(1) \mid X_i^T = 0, i \in \text{ComP}\right) - \mathbb{E}\left(Y_i(0) \mid X_i^T = 0, i \in \text{ComP}\right) =$$
$$\frac{1}{\Pr\left(i \in \text{ComP} \mid X_i^T = 0\right)} \left(\lim_{\lambda \to 0} \mathbb{E}\left(Y_i \mid X_i^T = \lambda x^+\right) - \lim_{\lambda \to 0} \mathbb{E}\left(Y_i \mid X_i^T = \lambda x^-\right)\right) - C$$

with C *being the correction term for defier:*

$$C := \frac{\Pr\left(i \in \text{DeF} \mid X_i^T = 0\right)}{\Pr\left(i \in \text{ComP} \mid X_i^T = 0\right)} \left(\mathbb{E}\left(Y_i(0) \mid X_i^T = 0, i \in \text{DeF}\right) - \mathbb{E}\left(Y_i(1) \mid X_i^T = 0, i \in \text{DeF}\right)\right)$$

This identification result allows for two immediate conclusions. First, one is free to choose among the directions x^+ and x^- satisfying Assumption 5. Second, the proof suggests that dropping subsets $\Omega \subset \text{Nt} \cup \text{At}$ does not affect identification, as long as doing so does not violate Assumptions 3 and 2. We provide a corresponding result in Appendix 0.A.3 (see Theorem 2). We call estimates of the complier effect of T when removing Ω the *sub-set complier effect of* G *excluding* Ω.

4 Application Setting

In the following section, we will bridge the gap between our theoretical considerations and the empirical setting studied. We consider an inline rework process in

[4] This assumption can be weakened by assuming only directional continuity, which would render the effect dependent on the chosen directions.

lot-based opto-electric semiconductor manufacturing during the phosphor conversion step. Production lots, each consisting of 784 individual LEDs, that fail to achieve a certain quality level are subjected to an additional rework step to improve overall yield. For details on the conversion process, we refer to related work [8,32].

The score consists of two components: The *distance score*, X_D, measures the distance from the mean color point $C := (C_x, C_y)$ of a lot to the optimal target in the color space. The *yield improvement score*, X_Y, is a relative measure that evaluates the quality distribution of individual chips in a lot by calculating a hypothetical scenario in which the target is ideally met by the mean of the lot. If there is high variability in the quality of parts within a lot, this improvement is negligible or even negative. Figure 1 depicts the score components in more detail.

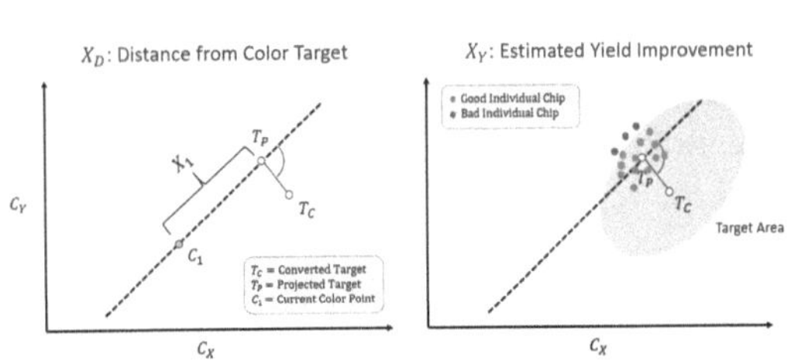

Fig. 1. Left: X_D is defined as the distance between the current mean color point and the target point. Right: X_Y evaluates the expected improvement by calculating the share of in-specification chips in the lot. This is done by moving the current distribution of color points to the target. (Color figure online)

Fig. 2. Real data plot w.r.t. the score components X_D and X_Y. The decision boundary T is dashed. The actual treatment assignment (green and orange) follows an unobserved rule D, rendering the MRD fuzzy. (Color figure online)

The treatment is assigned by a binary "AND" decision rule $T = I_D \wedge I_Y$. We assume that the final decision makers (i.e., human operators) D have an informational advantage regarding the improvement score and that they use this advantage to override T, while remaining cautious about possible degradation. This cautious operator assumption aligns with the observed one-sided fuzziness in the I_Y dimension and the strict compliance to the distance rule I_D, as observed in real data (see Fig. 2). In particular, whenever T suggests that a rework step should be carried out, the operator may override it due to the informational advantage not captured in T. Conversely, if T does not suggest a rework treatment, we assume that the operator accepts this decision, being cautious of possible degradation. We formalize the inclination toward this negative override into an additional score variable X_{op} that captures the information advantage: $D = T \wedge I_{op}$. A DGP based on the cautious operator assumption is outlined in Appendix 0.E. In this case, we have:

$$\text{ComP}(T, D) = \{i \mid X_{op,i} > 0\} \text{ and } \text{Nt}(T, D) = \{i \mid X_{op,i} \leq 0\},$$

as well as

$$\text{ComP}(G, D) = \{i \mid X_{op,i} > 0,\, X_Y > 0\} \text{ and } \text{Nt}(G, D) = \{i \mid X_{op,i} \leq 0\} \cup \{i \mid X_{Y,i} \leq 0\}$$

for the sub-rule $G := I_D$ of T (see Example 3.2). Employing Theorem 2 from Appendix 0.A one can estimate the sub-set complier effect of G excluding the nevertaker $\Omega := \{i \mid X_{Y,i} \leq 0\}$ instead of the complier effect of G.[5]

5 Effect Estimation with RDD

We benchmark estimators in accordance to Sect. 3 on both semi-synthetic and real-world data as described in Sect. 4. We compare estimators without adjustment, with conventional adjustment, penalized linear adjustment and adjustment using a stacked ensemble learner.

5.1 Semi-synthetic Data

To provide a realistic benchmark of the estimators across different settings, we generate semi-synthetic data following Algorithm 1[6] The process is calibrated to match real data characteristics. We draw $n = 10{,}000$ observations and repeat the experiment $r = 250$ times. The oracle value is estimated using a local linear kernel regression on the differences in true potential outcomes. The covariates consist of statistics describing the quality of individual items.

We evaluate the cut-offs c_D and c_Y separately, estimating the complier effect of $G \in \{I_Y, I_D\}$ as identified in Theorem 1, the **subset** complier effect of G given its counterpart (in accordance to Theorem 2) and intent-to-treat estimates with and without the subset conditioning. The complier effects are estimated under a fuzzy design; the intent-to-treat effects under a sharp design.

As shown in Fig. 3, the intent-to-treat oracles are closer to zero than the complier effects due to the inclusion of individuals who are nevertakers with respect to each cutoff rule. As visible in 3a, for I_D we estimate an overall negative effect, although it is not significant at 95%-level. The subset effect for the fuzzy case exhibits a smaller bias as the percentage of nevertakers in the estimation sample is smaller. The estimated effect remains unchanged as only nevertakers but no compliers were removed. This underlines our theoretical argument. For the intent-to-treat estimator, a higher share of compliers in the subsample increases the estimated effect of treatment rule G. The subset estimators have a comparable estimated variance (see Table 3 in Appendix 0.C.1), with the coverage overall

[5] Since the condition $X_{Y,i} \leq 0$ is global, the required continuity and stability assumptions are likely to be satisfied in practical applications.

[6] The python implementation of this process will be made available.

appearing slightly more credible. Generally, the covariate adjustment reduces the standard error in the estimation, especially for the sharp estimators.

The estimates for I_Y are small and positive. The fuzzy estimator on the full data has a high standard error, which increases further with ML adjustment. This may be due to a small jump in treatment probability in the full data, destabilizing the ML estimate. The subset estimator along this axis removes much more observations within the bandwidth of the estimation thus decreasing the variance. Additional results can be found in Appendix 0.C.

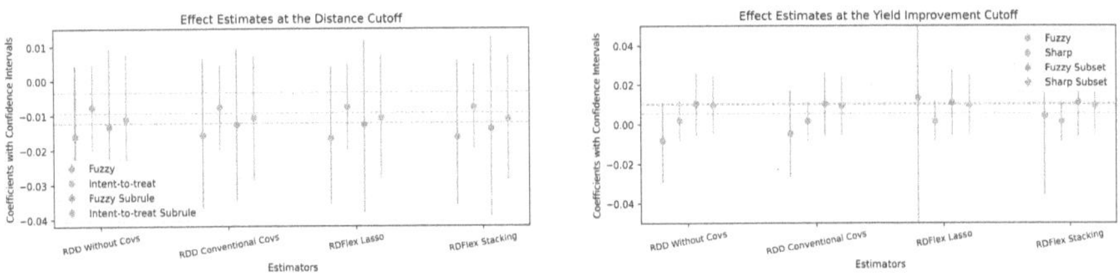

(a) Distance Score X_D (b) Yield Improvement Score X_Y

Fig. 3. Median coefficient and median CI for fuzzy and intent-to-treat estimators along X_D (left) and X_Y (right) with simulated data. The different colors depict estimators on the full sample and on the subset. The dashed line shows the oracle estimate for each setting, with the complier (fuzzy) oracles overlapping.

5.2 Real Dataset

This section presents results from estimation on the real data with $n = 9{,}103$ observations from the production system. Additional to information on color measurements, we include the shopfloor workload. Our primary interest in the real system is evaluating I_D.

As shown in Table 1 on the real data, we estimate a positive effect. The subset estimates have a lower variance, as we remove uncertainty due to nevertakers according to X_Y. In case of the intent-to-treat estimators, the addition of ML adjustment improves the variance of the estimation. For the fuzzy estimators, there is no clear improvement.

The comparison in Fig. 4 provides insight into the differing effect signs between semi-synthetic and real data. While the semi-synthetic process (left) appears to have a rework threshold closer than the optimal distance, the real data (right) suggests a threshold that is further away, resulting in a significant outcome jump at the current threshold.

Table 1. Coefficients, standard errors, and quality of fit for the different estimators for the distance dimension in the real dataset.

setting	method	Coef	s.e.	CI 2.5%	CI 97.5%	RMSE left	Log loss left	RMSE right	Log loss right	% s.e. change
Fuzzy	RDD Conventional Covs	0.1031	0.0508	0.0035	0.2028					22.2532
	RDD Without Covs	0.0387	0.0416	-0.0428	0.1202					0.0000
	RDFlex Lasso	0.0999	0.0470	-0.0004	0.2003	0.1452	0.0141	0.1523	0.6142	12.9249
	RDFlex Stacking	0.1097	0.0500	0.0023	0.2171	0.1429	0.0188	0.1570	0.6322	20.1333
Fuzzy on Subset	RDD Conventional Covs	0.0630	0.0426	-0.0205	0.1466					36.5324
	RDD Without Covs	0.0369	0.0312	-0.0243	0.0981					0.0000
	RDFlex Lasso	0.0713	0.0304	0.0031	0.1395	0.1410	0.0209	0.1507	0.5424	-2.5667
	RDFlex Stacking	0.0768	0.0319	0.0048	0.1487	0.1394	0.0121	0.1530	0.5018	2.1538
Sharp	RDD Conventional Covs	0.0393	0.0208	-0.0015	0.0802					2.2467
	RDD Without Covs	0.0165	0.0204	-0.0235	0.0564					0.0000
	RDFlex Lasso	0.0357	0.0167	-0.0026	0.0740	0.1425		0.1513		-17.9717
	RDFlex Stacking	0.0367	0.0168	-0.0018	0.0753	0.1408		0.1530		-17.5203
Sharp on Subset	RDD Conventional Covs	0.0362	0.0205	-0.0040	0.0764					-2.3944
	RDD Without Covs	0.0098	0.0210	-0.0314	0.0509					0.0000
	RDFlex Lasso	0.0364	0.0184	-0.0031	0.0758	0.1408		0.1525		-12.2509
	RDFlex Stacking	0.0307	0.0181	-0.0093	0.0708	0.1395		0.1540		-14.0691

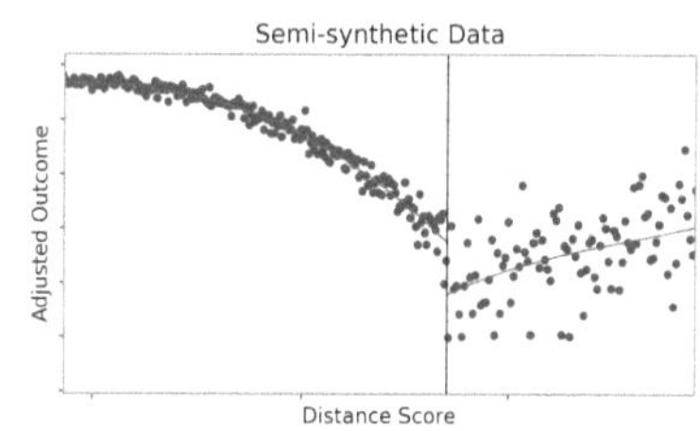

(a) RDD plot for the semi-synthetic process.

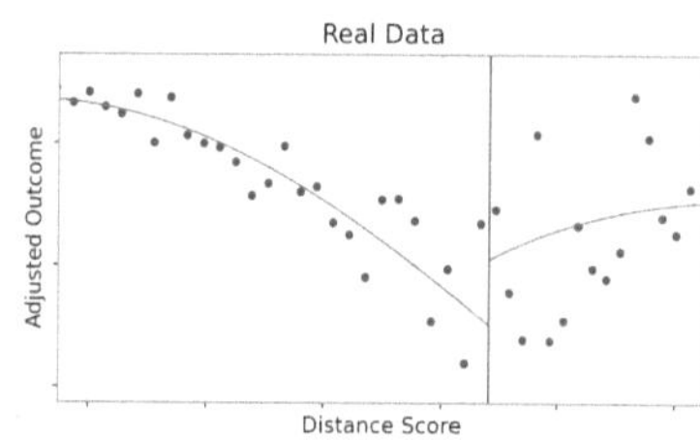

(b) RDD plot for the real production data.

Fig. 4. Comparison of local linear regressions around the cutoff for the semi-synthetic and real data. The opposite sign of the estimated effect can be explained by the calibration of the semi-synthetic process. Specifically, the modeling of the operator decision could be imperfect by taking only incomplete information into account. Particularly, the real-world operator might have more knowledge, such as machine states and outputs, as well as practical job experience.

6 Conclusion and Limitations

Our paper presented a novel application of RDD in the context of threshold-based decision-making in industrial manufacturing. By integrating multi-score RDD techniques with recent advancements in causal machine learning – particularly flexible covariate adjustment – we demonstrated how to evaluate threshold based decision policies on real data.

Our formalization of unit behavior categories (complier, nevertaker, alwaystaker, defier and indecisive units) in multi-dimensional cutoff rules yields a novel effect identification result in MRD settings. Among the required assumptions, the local stability of the unit categories (Assumption 2) is the most debatable one. As it involves counterfactual reasoning about potential category changes, it cannot be verified using observed data. This shortcoming is shared with related independence assumptions common in RDD literature. Causal identification is not possible without any of these assumptions. The question is whether such an assumption is interpretable enough to justify an approximate conformance in empirical studies. Compared to previously presented formulations, we draw from the intuitive language of unit categories to aid the argument for or against applicability.

7 Statement on AI Usage

For this research paper, large language models were used solely to assist with literature search, writing, and coding. All conceptualization, ideation, and theoretical contributions were carried out without AI support. The paper and code were authored entirely by the researchers, with AI serving only as a support and feedback tool.

Acknowledgements. This work was funded by the Bavarian Joint Research Program (BayVFP)- Digitization (Funding reference: DIK0294/01). The research partners ams Osram and Economic AI kindly thank the the VDI/VDE-IT Munich for the organization and the Free State of Bavaria for the financial support.

References

1. An, L., Branson, Z., Miratrix, L.: Using gaussian process regression in two-dimensional regression discontinuity designs. edworkingpaper no. 24-1043. Annenberg Institute for School Reform at Brown University (2024)
2. Angrist, J.D., Lavy, V.: Using maimonides' rule to estimate the effect of class size on scholastic achievement. Q J. Econ. **114**(2), 533–575 (1999). https://doi.org/10.1162/003355399556061, ISSN 1531-4650
3. Austin, P.C.: An introduction to propensity score methods for reducing the effects of confounding in observational studies. Multivariate Behav. Res. **46**(3), 399–424 (2011)
4. Calvo, E., Cui, R., Serpa, J.C.: Oversight and efficiency in public projects: A regression discontinuity analysis. Manag. Sci. **65**(12), 5651–5675 (2019)
5. Card, D., Lee, D.S., Pei, Z., Weber, A.: Inference on causal effects in a generalized regression kink design. Econometrica **83**(6), 2453–2483 (2015). https://doi.org/10.3982/ecta11224, ISSN 0012-9682
6. Cattaneo, M.D., Idrobo, N., Titiunik, R.: A practical introduction to regression discontinuity designs. Foundations (2019). https://doi.org/10.1017/9781108684606
7. Cattaneo, M.D., Titiunik, R., Yu, R.R.: Estimation and inference in boundary discontinuity designs (2025). unpublished manuscript
8. Cho, J., Park, J.H., Kim, J.K., Schubert, E.F.: White light-emitting diodes: History, progress, and future. Laser Photonics Rev. **11** (2017)
9. Choi, J.y., Lee, M.j.: Regression discontinuity with multiple running variables allowing partial effects. Polit. Anal. **26**(3), 258–274 (2018). https://doi.org/10.1017/pan.2018.13, ISSN 1476-4989

10. Flammer, C.: Does corporate social responsibility lead to superior financial performance? a regression discontinuity approach. Manag. Sci. **61**(11), 2549–2568 (2015). https://doi.org/10.1287/mnsc.2014.2038, ISSN 1526-5501
11. Hahn, J., Todd, P., der Klaauw, W.V.: Identification and estimation of treatment effects with a regression-discontinuity design. Econometrica **69**(1), 201–209 (2001). ISSN 00129682, 14680262
12. Hartmann, W., Nair, H.S., Narayanan, S.: Identifying causal marketing mix effects using a regression discontinuity design. Mark. Sci. **30**(6), 1079–1097 (2011). https://doi.org/10.1287/mksc.1110.0670, ISSN 1526-548X
13. Huber, M.: Causal machine learning in marketing. Int. J. Bus. Manag. Stud. **05**(07), 1–6 (2024). https://doi.org/10.56734/ijbms.v5n7a1, ISSN 2694-1449
14. Hünermund, P., Kaminski, J., Schmitt, C.: Causal machine learning and business decision making. SSRN Electron. J. (2021). https://doi.org/10.2139/ssrn.3867326, ISSN 1556-5068
15. Imbens, G., Wager, S.: Optimized regression discontinuity designs. Rev. Econ. Stat. **101**(2), 264–278 (2019). https://doi.org/10.1162/rest_a_00793, ISSN 1530-9142
16. Imbens, G., Zajonc, T.: Regression discontinuity design with vector-argument assignment rules, p. 8 (2009). Unpublished paper
17. Imbens, G.W., Angrist, J.D.: Identification and estimation of local average treatment effects. Econometrica **62**(2), 467 (1994). https://doi.org/10.2307/2951620, ISSN 0012-9682
18. Imbens, G.W., Lemieux, T.: Regression discontinuity designs: A guide to practice. J. Econ. **142**(2), 615–635 (2008). https://doi.org/10.1016/j.jeconom.2007.05.001, ISSN 0304-4076
19. Keele, L.J., Titiunik, R.: Geographic boundaries as regression discontinuities. Polit. Anal. **23**(1), 127–155 (2015)
20. Lee, D.S.: Randomized experiments from non-random selection in u.s. house elections. J. Econ. **142**(2), 675–697 (2008). https://doi.org/10.1016/j.jeconom.2007.05.004, ISSN 0304-4076
21. Lee, D.S., Lemieux, T.: Regression discontinuity designs in economics. J. Econ. Liter. **48**(2), 281–355 (2010). https://doi.org/10.1257/jel.48.2.281, ISSN 0022-0515
22. Liu, Y., Qi, Y.: Using forests in multivariate regression discontinuity designs (2024)
23. Mithas, S., Chen, Y., Lin, Y., De Oliveira Silveira, A.: On the causality and plausibility of treatment effects in operations management research. Prod. Oper. Manag. **31**(12), 4558–4571 (2022). https://doi.org/10.1111/poms.13863, ISSN 1937-5956
24. Noack, C., Olma, T., Rothe, C.: Flexible covariate adjustments in regression discontinuity designs (2024)
25. Papay, J.P., Willett, J.B., Murnane, R.J.: Extending the regression-discontinuity approach to multiple assignment variables. J. Econ. **161**(2), 203–207 (2011). https://doi.org/10.1016/j.jeconom.2010.12.008, ISSN 0304-4076
26. Porter, K.E., Reardon, S.F., Unlu, F., Bloom, H.S., Cimpian, J.R.: Estimating causal effects of education interventions using a two-rating regression discontinuity design: Lessons from a simulation study and an application. J. Res. Educ. Effect. **10**(1), 138–167 (2017)
27. Reardon, S.F., Robinson, J.P.: Regression discontinuity designs with multiple rating-score variables. J. Res. Educ. Effectiveness **5**(1), 83–104 (2012). https://doi.org/10.1080/19345747.2011.609583, ISSN 1934-5739
28. Rubin, D.B.: Estimating causal effects of treatments in randomized and nonrandomized studies. J. Educ. Psychol. **66**(5), 688–701 (1974). https://doi.org/10.1037/h0037350, ISSN 0022-0663

29. Rubin, D.B.: Causal inference using potential outcomes: Design, modeling, decisions. J. Am. Stat. Assoc. **100**(469), 322–331 (2005), ISSN 01621459
30. Sabaei, D., Erkoyuncu, J., Roy, R.: A review of multi-criteria decision making methods for enhanced maintenance delivery. Procedia CIRP **37**, 30–35 (2015)
31. Schacht, O., et al.: Causally learning an optimal rework policy. In: Prosperi, M. (ed.) Proceedings of The KDD'23 Workshop on Causal Discovery, Prediction and Decision, Proceedings of Machine Learning Research, vol. 218, pp. 3–24. PMLR (2023)
32. Schwarz, P., Schacht, O., Klaassen, S., Grünbaum, D., Imhof, S., Spindler, M.: Management decisions in manufacturing using causal machine learning - to rework, or not to rework? (2024)
33. Thistlethwaite, D.L., Campbell, D.T.: Regression-discontinuity analysis: An alternative to the ex post facto experiment. J. Educ. Psychol. **51**(6), 309–317 (1960)
34. Vuković, M., Thalmann, S.: Causal discovery in manufacturing: A structured literature review. J. Manuf. Mater. Process. **6**(1), 10 (2022)
35. Wong, V.C., Steiner, P.M., Cook, T.D.: Analyzing regression-discontinuity designs with multiple assignment variables: A comparative study of four estimation methods. J. Educ. Behav. Stat. **38**(2), 107–141 (2013)
36. Wyrembek, M., Baryannis, G., Brintrup, A.: Causal machine learning for supply chain risk prediction and intervention planning. Int. J. Prod. Res.. 1–20 (2025). https://doi.org/10.1080/00207543.2025.2458121, ISSN 1366-588X

CAR-MNAR: A Unified Factorial Framework for Robust Causal Discovery Under Self-masking MNAR

Matin Alinejad[1] and Katerina Hlaváčková-Schindler[2,3](✉)

[1] Faculty of Electrical Engineering, Sharif University of Technology, Tehran, Iran
[2] Faculty of Computer Science, University of Vienna, Vienna, Austria
katerina.schindlerova@univie.ac.at
[3] Data Science @ Uni Vienna, University of Vienna, Vienna, Austria

Abstract. Causal discovery from observational data is fundamental to scientific inference, yet real-world datasets are rarely complete. The Missing Not At Random (MNAR) regime, where missingness probability depends on unobserved values can fatally bias constraint-based algorithms like the Peter-Clark algorithm (PC). We introduce *CAR-MNAR*, a comprehensive factorial framework for rigorously evaluating causal discovery robustness under controlled MNAR conditions. Its guiding idea is to make robustness *measurable*: it couples deterministically calibrated, mathematically specified MNAR mechanisms with Markov-equivalence-aware (CPDAG) metrics, so that competing algorithms can be compared fairly and reproducibly across missingness mechanisms at equal realized rates. A single pipeline treats clinical datasets and synthetic DAGs alike, grounds clinical reference graphs in multi-algorithm consensus, and reports every comparison with statistical significance testing. Applied to the Self-Masking Missing Value PC algorithm (SM-MVPC) with comprehensive baseline comparisons on clinical benchmarks and synthetic datasets, CAR-MNAR provides rigorous answers to three fundamental questions about SM-MVPC's robustness quantification, mechanism-specific vulnerability, and methodological standardization. We also present a formal theorem, verified in Lean 4, establishing that identifiability of the missingness mechanism enables valid causal discovery under MNAR. Beyond standard accuracy comparisons, the framework surfaces two insights that single-number metrics fail to capture: the local causal neighbourhood of a clinical target is recovered far more robustly than the full graph, and a stable Structural Hamming Distance can mask a sharp collapse of collider (v-structure) detection, so the choice of metric materially changes the conclusions one draws. This robustness of local structure suggests that SM-MVPC can provide clinically actionable insights even under severe MNAR conditions, which is particularly promising for applications where understanding mechanisms around key outcomes, such as diabetes progression or cardiovascular risk, is more critical than recovering the complete causal network.

Supplementary Information. The online version contains supplementary material and code available at https://doi.org/10.5281/zenodo.21298787.

M. Ceci et al. (Eds.): ECML PKDD 2026, LNAI 16941, pp. 603–622, 2027.
https://doi.org/10.1007/978-3-032-37654-1_35

Keywords: Causal discovery · Missing values · Self-masking MNAR · Evaluation framework

1 Introduction

Constraint-based algorithms that infer causal relationships from observational data, such as the Peter-Clark (PC) algorithm [23], leverage conditional independence (CI) tests to recover Markov equivalence classes of directed acyclic graphs (DAGs) [3,14], enabling principled causal reasoning without experimental interventions. These methods have proven invaluable in domains where randomized controlled trials are infeasible, including clinical outcome prediction, drug discovery, and policy evaluation. However, real-world datasets are rarely complete. Missing data can invalidate causal inference by distorting the very CI relations upon which constraint-based methods depend. The Missing Not At Random (MNAR) regime [12], where missingness probability depends on the unobserved value itself, remains particularly pernicious. In clinical settings, patients with very high biomarker values may be systematically less likely to have complete records, while in economic surveys, high-income individuals might selectively omit sensitive financial information. Such mechanisms introduce non-ignorable selection bias that can fundamentally compromise causal discovery algorithms.

The Self-Masking Missing Value PC (SM-MVPC) algorithm [20] addresses MNAR via the *weak self-masking* assumption: missingness of a variable Y depends only on Y's value and not on its causal parents. This insight enables valid residual-independence tests under MNAR, theoretically preserving CI relations in the observed data. Yet despite these strong identifiability guarantees, the practical robustness of SM-MVPC remains largely uncharacterized. How does performance degrade as MNAR severity increases? Are certain causal structures more vulnerable than others? How do different MNAR mechanism shapes (smooth vs. heavy-tailed vs. threshold) differentially impact recovery?

Recent work addresses missing data from complementary angles, including score-based joint optimization (MissDAG [6]), optimal-transport imputation (OTM [15]), deep imputation-and-discovery (ICL [26]), and analyses of adversarial, non-ignorable missingness [11]. Systematic comparative evaluation across these paradigms nevertheless remains challenging due to the absence of a standardized evaluation protocol. We address three fundamental yet unresolved questions that are critical for deploying causal discovery in real-world applications with missing data:

1. Robustness Quantification: *How does the performance of state-of-the-art causal discovery algorithms degrade as MNAR severity increases from 10% to 50%? Are certain substructures (e.g., clinically relevant neighborhoods) more robust than overall graph recovery?*
2. Mechanism-Specific Vulnerability: *Do different MNAR mechanisms induce fundamentally different failure modes in skeleton recovery vs orientation inference, and can these vulnerabilities be predicted from data characteristics?*

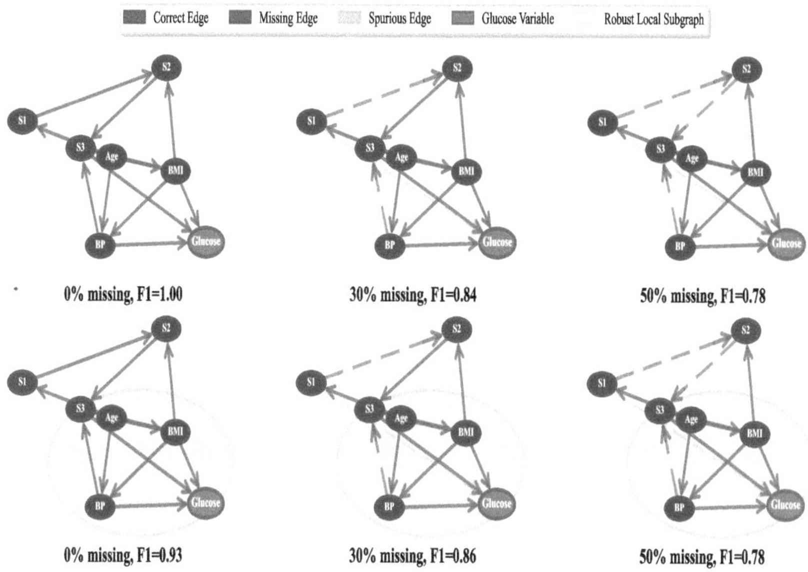

Fig. 1. Causal Structure Recovery Under MNAR. Degradation of SM-MVPC on the diabetes dataset with missingness 0%, 30%, 50% MNAR, for full graph recovery (top) vs. the local subgraph around target glucose (bottom). Green areas indicate the local subgraph around the target. The target's local neighbourhood is recovered at least as robustly as the full graph and stays clinically viable (target-neighbourhood skeleton F1 $\approx$ 0.84–1.00) even under severe missingness, whereas full-graph F1 decreases from 0.88 to 0.84. Across the three clinical datasets the local-to-full robustness advantage is dataset dependent (Sect. 8): pronounced on Heart Disease, mild on Diabetes, and absent on Hepatitis.

3. Methodological Standardization: *How to design a fair, reproducible evaluation framework that eliminates confounding from stochastic parameter selection, respects Markov equivalence via CPDAG-aware metrics, provides statistically rigorous uncertainty quantification, and establishes a reusable benchmark for the field?*

We introduce CAR-MNAR (Causal discovery Assessment and Robustness under Missing Not At Random), a comprehensive factorial framework that systematically evaluates state-of-the-art causal discovery algorithms across controlled MNAR conditions, providing statistically rigorous answers to these questions. To our knowledge it is the first *unified* methodology for fair, reproducible, and interpretable comparisons of causal discovery algorithms under diverse MNAR regimes. The object of study in CAR-MNAR is the experimental protocol itself: how missingness is specified and calibrated, how ground truth is built, and how recovery is scored. SM-MVPC serves throughout as the primary algorithm to which this protocol is applied, so reading the paper through this lens clarifies the role of each component below. Figure 1 illustrates this contrast on the Diabetes dataset: as missingness grows, the neighbourhood of the target glucose variable stays intact while the full graph erodes.

Our main contributions are:

- *Unified factorial framework.* We design a single experimental pipeline (Algorithm 1) that treats real datasets and synthetic DAGs uniformly, applying identical missingness injection, algorithmic evaluation, and metric computation procedures regardless of data source, supports arbitrary missingness mechanisms (MCAR, MAR [12], sigmoid MNAR, GPD-based heavy tails, threshold censoring) and causal discovery algorithms, and outputs CPDAG-aware metrics with bootstrap confidence intervals and effect sizes. This provides a reproducible, reusable protocol for MNAR evaluation in causal discovery.
- *Bayesian optimization MNAR calibrator with theoretical guarantees.* We develop a Bayesian-optimization calibrator that matches target missingness rates with 4× fewer objective evaluations than grid search, while providing theoretical error bounds $O(\sqrt{Td\log(T)})$ on the convergence rate (T the number of optimization evaluations, d the parameter dimension). The calibrator supports five MNAR mechanisms (sigmoid, GPD, threshold, self-masking with dependencies, hierarchical) with deterministic parameter selection, which removes stochastic variability and enables fair at-equal-rate comparisons across mechanism families.
- *Comprehensive robustness analysis.* Instantiating CAR-MNAR with SM-MVPC and 5 baseline methods on 3 clinical datasets and 51 synthetic configurations with known ground truth, we report several insights: (i) the local causal neighbourhood of a clinical target is recovered *more robustly* than the full graph on two of three datasets (the local-to-full skeleton-F1 ratio is 1.29–1.39 on Heart Disease and 1.01–1.14 on Diabetes), while Hepatitis is a clear counterexample (ratio 0.85–0.92) where the full graph is already easy to recover; (ii) v-structures degrade markedly faster than skeletons as MNAR severity increases, whereas orientation on compelled edges stays comparatively stable, exposing collider detection as the dominant failure mode; (iii) plain SHD can appear stable across MNAR rates while CPDAG-aware metrics expose this collapse, so the evaluation metric itself changes the qualitative conclusion; and (iv) under self-masking MNAR SM-MVPC substantially outperforms the five baselines on the *causal* structure (v-structure F1, orientation F1, and CPDAG-SHD on two of three datasets), with a more nuanced picture on raw adjacency where an imputation baseline can be competitive.

2 Related Work

Constraint-based methods extend PC algorithms to handle missing data under MAR and MNAR [25], with SM-MVPC [20] addressing self-masking MNAR through weak self-masking assumptions. Score-based approaches like MissDAG [6] and OTM [15] formulate causal discovery with missing data as joint optimization problems, while deep learning methods [13,26] provide imputation-integrated solutions but lack theoretical guarantees under MNAR. Recent evaluation recommendations [18] emphasize negative controls and distributional evaluation, which CAR-MNAR incorporates.

On the Absence of a Standard Evaluation Protocol. A natural question is how CAR-MNAR compares against established evaluation protocols for causal discovery under MNAR. To the best of our knowledge there is no such standardized protocol: each of the works above evaluates its own method under a single, idiosyncratic missingness setting (a fixed mechanism, a self-chosen rate grid, and a single-run ground truth), and reports plain SHD or skeleton accuracy. There is therefore no agreed-upon baseline *evaluation procedure* against which an empirical head-to-head comparison would be meaningful; the prior art supplies algorithms and ad hoc test beds, not protocols. This gap is precisely what CAR-MNAR is designed to fill, and it is the reason our comparisons are framed as "same protocol, different algorithms/mechanisms" rather than "our protocol vs. a competing protocol."

Positioning of Our Work. Accordingly, the contribution of this paper is methodological: a unified and reusable evaluation protocol for missing-data-aware causal discovery. Unlike prior studies limited to single mechanisms or algorithms, our unified framework enables systematic assessment across diverse MNAR regimes with comprehensive baseline comparisons. We provide mathematically defined missingness mechanisms with deterministic calibration, multi-algorithm ground truth, CPDAG-aware metrics, and rigorous statistical validation.

3 CAR-MNAR Framework

CAR-MNAR is a factorial design that crosses datasets, missingness mechanisms, missingness rates and causal discovery algorithms. For each real dataset, we establish ground truth through a multi-algorithm ensemble approach: we run six algorithms (PC_stable, PC_liberal, GES [3], CAM [1], NOTEARS [27], and our consensus ensemble method on complete data, compute consensus edges with >60% agreement threshold, and convert the consensus DAG to a CPDAG. We are deliberately careful about what this "ground truth" is and is not. For the clinical datasets, no gold-standard causal graph exists, so any reference graph must be *constructed*; however, constructing it with a single run of the same algorithm one later evaluates would be circular, since the evaluated method would be scored against a target it helped define. Our consensus-of-six construction does not remove this difficulty entirely; rather, it *reduces* the circularity by requiring an edge to be supported by a majority of structurally different paradigms (constraint-based, score-based, and additive-noise) before it enters the reference graph. The resulting reference attains inter-method stability scores ≈ 0.78 (mean edge agreement weighted by consistency), and we treat all clinical numbers as "performance relative to this consensus" rather than as absolute structural accuracy. The synthetic experiments, in which the ground truth is known by construction, are what justify absolute claims. For synthetic datasets, we generate data from parametrized DAG templates with known ground truth using our enhanced synthetic dataset factory (51 configurations across 7 topologies and 3 complexity levels). Details of the synthetic data generation process are in the Supplementary Material (Section 6.1). We then inject missingness according to a chosen mechanism and rate, run a causal discovery algorithm on the resulting incomplete dataset, convert the inferred DAG to a CPDAG, and compute CPDAG-aware metrics together with bootstrap confidence intervals and significance tests. Algorithm 1 summarises the pipeline. The design cleanly separates (i) data-generation and missingness mechanisms; (ii) causal discovery algorithms; and (iii) evaluation metrics and statistical analysis, making the framework easily extensible. We instantiate $\mathcal{A}$ with SM-MVPC as our primary evaluation target and 5 baseline methods: TD-PC [25], MVPC (implemented via causal-learn library), MissDAG [6], OTM [15], and MICE-PC [2], and focus on three real clinical datasets from the UCI Machine Learning Repository [10]: Heart Disease [9], Diabetes [22], and Hepatitis [7] with multi-algorithm ground truth plus 51 synthetic configurations with known ground truth.

Recovery is scored with CPDAG-aware metrics that respect Markov equivalence, together with bootstrap confidence intervals [5] and permutation tests with FDR correction; these are defined in Sect. 6.

4 MNAR Mechanisms and Deterministic Calibrator

We focus on *self-masking* MNAR mechanisms, where the missingness indicator R_Y of a variable Y depends on Y itself but not on its causes X. This setup satisfies the weak self-masking assumption of [20] and ensures that SM-MVPC's residual-independence tests remain valid when properly implemented. Within this family we consider 5 concrete mechanisms that cover smooth, heavy-tailed, hard-threshold, dependency-based, and hierarchical missingness patterns, with explicit identifiability analysis for each.

4.1 Sigmoid Self-masking

The primary mechanism is a sigmoid missingness model

$$P(R_Y = 0 \mid Y = y) = \sigma(\alpha y + \beta) = \frac{1}{1 + e^{-(\alpha y + \beta)}}. \tag{1}$$

α controls steepness and direction (upper vs. lower tails) and β sets the location at which the missingness probability crosses 0.5. Positive α concentrates missingness in the upper quantiles of Y, negative α targets lower tails. Denote $\mathbf{y} = (y_1, \ldots, y_n)$, the observed (non-missing) values of Y in a given dataset, and let

$$g(\alpha, \beta) = \frac{1}{n} \sum_{i=1}^{n} \sigma(\alpha y_i + \beta)$$

Algorithm 1. Unified Factorial Experimental Framework

Require: $\mathcal{D}$ - Real datasets; $\mathcal{T}$ - Synthetic DAGs; $\mathcal{N}$ - Sample sizes; $\mathcal{M}$ - Mechanisms (MCAR, MAR, MNAR); $\mathcal{R}$ - Missing rates; $\mathcal{A}$- Algorithms; n_{rep} - Replicates per condition

Ensure: $\mathcal{E}$ - Results with metrics and statistical analysis

$\mathcal{E} \leftarrow \emptyset$; $\mathcal{C}_{\text{real}} \leftarrow \mathcal{D} \times \mathcal{M} \times \mathcal{R} \times \mathcal{A}$
$\mathcal{C}_{\text{syn}} \leftarrow \mathcal{T} \times \mathcal{N} \times \mathcal{M} \times \mathcal{R} \times \mathcal{A}$; $\mathcal{C} \leftarrow \mathcal{C}_{\text{real}} \cup \mathcal{C}_{\text{syn}}$
for each $c \in \mathcal{C}$ **do**
  if $c \in \mathcal{C}_{\text{real}}$ **then**
    $(D_i, M_j, r_k, A_\ell) \leftarrow c$
    $G_{true}^{\text{DAG}} \leftarrow A_\ell$.LearnStructure$(D_i)$
  else
    $(T_i, n_s, M_j, r_k, A_\ell) \leftarrow c$
    $(D_i, G_{true}^{\text{DAG}}) \leftarrow$ GenerateSyntheticData(T_i, n_s)
  end if
  $\mathcal{G}_{true} \leftarrow$ DAG-to-CPDAG(G_{true}^{DAG})
  for $rep = 1$ to n_{rep} **do**
    if $r_k > 0$ **then**
      $\theta^* \leftarrow$ FindOptimalParameters$(D_i.Y, M_j, r_k, \Theta_{grid})$
      $D_{missing} \leftarrow$ IntroduceMissingness$(D_i, M_j, \theta^*, r_k)$
    else
      $D_{missing} \leftarrow D_i$
    end if
    $G_{inferred}^{\text{DAG}} \leftarrow A_\ell$.LearnStructure$(D_{missing})$
    $\mathcal{G}_{inferred} \leftarrow$ DAG-to-CPDAG$(G_{inferred}^{\text{DAG}})$
    $metrics \leftarrow$ EvaluateCPDAG$(\mathcal{G}_{true}, \mathcal{G}_{inferred})$
    $\mathcal{E} \leftarrow \mathcal{E} \cup \{(c, rep, metrics)\}$
  end for
end for
return StatisticalAnalysis$(\mathcal{E})$

be the expected missing rate under mechanism Eq. (1). For any fixed $\alpha \neq 0$, g is continuous and strictly increasing in β, with limits 0 and 1 as $\beta \to -\infty$ and $\beta \to +\infty$, respectively. By the Intermediate Value Theorem, for every target missing rate $\rho \in (0, 1)$ there exists a unique $\beta^\star(\alpha)$ such that $g(\alpha, \beta^\star) = \rho$. We exploit this property to calibrate (α, β) deterministically, using the Bayesian-optimization procedure of Sect. 4.2. Algorithm 1 then uses $(\alpha^\star, \beta^\star)$ to generate Bernoulli missingness indicators $R_{Y,i} \sim \text{Bernoulli}(\sigma(\alpha^\star y_i + \beta^\star))$ with independent $U[0, 1]$ draws.

4.2 Deterministic Bayesian-Optimization Calibrator

The same calibration principle applies to any of our five MNAR mechanism types (sigmoid self-masking, self-masking with dependencies, hierarchical, GPD heavy-tailed, and threshold censoring): the expected missingness $g(\theta) = \mathbb{E}[\mathcal{M}(Y; \theta)]$ is computable directly from the empirical distribution, so for a target rate ρ

we solve

$$\theta^* = \arg\min_{\theta} \left| g(\theta) - \rho \right|.$$

The optimizer uses a Gaussian-process surrogate with Matérn 5/2 kernel and expected-improvement acquisition; after T evaluations it achieves the error bound $O(\sqrt{Td}\log(T))$ with probability $1-\delta$ [24] (T the number of evaluations, d the parameter dimension). This yields a 4× reduction in objective evaluations over exhaustive grid search (25 vs. 100) at comparable precision: across the clinical datasets and rates the achieved missingness rate is close to target (mean absolute error ≈ 2.3%), with larger deviations only on the smallest, most skewed sample (Hepatitis at 50%, where the discrete marginal limits attainable rates). Because the seed is fixed, parameter selection is deterministic, which removes stochastic variability and enables fair at-equal-rate comparisons across mechanism families.

4.3 Advanced MNAR Mechanisms

Beyond the sigmoid case, CAR-MNAR supports four additional MNAR mechanisms, for which we provide explicit mathematical specifications and identifiability analyses. Theoretical guarantees for causal discovery under MNAR require the missingness mechanism to be *identifiable*: unless we can determine how missingness depends on the unobserved values, the selection bias cannot be corrected and the CI relations on which constraint-based algorithms rely are distorted. A mechanism for Y is *identifiable* if $P(R_Y = 0 \mid Y = y)$ is uniquely determined by the observed-data distribution; under weak self-masking [20] this requires that (i) R_Y depends only on Y's value and (ii) $P(R_Y = 0 \mid Y = y)$ is known a priori or consistently estimable. It is *conditionally identifiable* if identifiability holds given additional observed variables. Formal definitions are in the Supplementary Material, Section 2.

Theorem 1 (Identifiability and CI Preservation). *Under the weak self-masking assumption $P(R_Y = 0 \mid Y, X, \mathbf{Z}) = P(R_Y = 0 \mid Y)$ for any causal parent X of Y and conditioning set $\mathbf{Z}$, with positivity $P(R_Y = 1 \mid Y = y) > 0$, and under Condition (TWD), namely $R_X \perp\!\!\!\perp Y \mid \mathbf{Z}, R_Y{=}1$ and $R_{Z_j} \perp\!\!\!\perp Y \mid \mathbf{Z}, R_Y{=}1$ for each $Z_j \in \mathbf{Z}$ (automatic when each missingness indicator depends only on its own variable, as in SM-MVPC), if the missingness mechanism is identifiable (i.e., $P(R_Y = 0 \mid Y = y)$ is known or consistently estimable), then the residual-independence test $X \perp\!\!\!\perp \hat{\epsilon}_Y \mid \mathbf{Z}$ performed on test-wise complete subsets $\mathcal{I} = \{i : R_{X,i} = R_{Y,i} = 1, R_{Z_j,i} = 1 \forall Z_j \in \mathbf{Z}\}$ preserves the conditional independence relations from the complete data, maintaining valid Type-I error control.*

The algebraic core of this theorem (the weak-self-masking Bayes factorisation, the normaliser cancellation that yields CI preservation, the Condition (TWD) extension to the full test-wise subset, and Type-I control) is *machine-verified in Lean 4/Mathlib*: it compiles `sorry`-free and depends only on the three standard Lean axioms (`propext`, `Classical.choice`, `Quot.sound`). The Lean project accompanies the supplementary material.

The full proof of Theorem 1, including rigorous arguments for Type-I error control and asymptotic consistency, is given in the Supplementary Material (Section 2). Theorem 1 establishes that when a missingness mechanism is identifiable under weak self-masking, residual-independence tests preserve CI relations from the complete data. This directly implies that: (i) sigmoid MNAR is identifiable when parameters (α, β) are consistently estimable; (ii) GPD MNAR is conditionally identifiable when threshold u is known or estimable; (iii) threshold MNAR is identifiable since the mechanism is deterministic; (iv) self-masking with dependencies is conditionally identifiable when observed dependencies can be accounted for; and (v) 2-level hierarchical MNAR is conditionally identifiable when hierarchical levels are observed. We state identifiability status for each mechanism below, to clarify which mechanisms support valid causal discovery under SM-MVPC.

Corollary 1. *If a MNAR mechanism described below is identifiable (or conditionally identifiable), then SM-MVPC's residual-independence tests preserve CI relations from the complete data, enabling valid causal discovery. This provides theoretical justification for applying SM-MVPC to the mechanisms that satisfy identifiability conditions.*

Heavy-Tailed GPD MNAR. The Generalized Pareto Distribution (GPD) mechanism models extremal missingness where high values are disproportionately likely to be missing, based on extreme value theory [19]. The missingness probability is:

$$P(R_Y = 0 \mid Y = y) = \begin{cases} 0 & \text{if } y \leq u \\ 1 - G_{\xi,\sigma}(y - u) & \text{if } y > u \end{cases} \tag{2}$$

where u is the threshold parameter (typically the q-th quantile, $q \in [0.8, 0.95]$), $\xi \in [0.1, 0.5]$ is the shape parameter controlling tail heaviness, $\sigma > 0$ is the scale parameter, and $G_{\xi,\sigma}$ is the GPD cumulative distribution function, which reduces to exponential tail behaviour as $\xi \to 0$. Calibration searches over (ξ, u) with σ fitted by maximum likelihood on the tail observations $\{y_i : y_i > u\}$; the closed forms of $G_{\xi,\sigma}$, of the expected rate $g(\xi, u, \sigma)$, and of the tail log-likelihood are given in the Supplementary Material, Section 2.3. This mechanism is *conditionally identifiable* under weak self-masking when u is known or estimable: for $y > u$ the missingness probability $P(R_Y = 0 \mid Y = y)$ is then a deterministic function of y alone, so SM-MVPC's residual-independence tests remain valid [20].

Threshold MNAR. Hard threshold censoring models measurement limits or detection thresholds, providing a deterministic baseline for comparing smooth vs. hard censoring effects:

$$P(R_Y = 0 \mid Y = y) = \begin{cases} 0 & \text{if } y \leq \tau \\ 1 & \text{if } y > \tau, \end{cases} \tag{3}$$

τ is the threshold value, with expected missingness rate $g(\tau) = |\{i : y_i > \tau\}|/n$. Calibration selects τ as the $(1-\rho)$-th empirical quantile, $\tau = F_Y^{-1}(1-\rho)$, so the realized missingness rate converges almost surely to ρ. Since $P(R_Y = 0 \mid Y = y) = \mathbb{I}(y > \tau)$ is a known deterministic function of Y's own value, the mechanism is *identifiable* under weak self-masking, enabling valid CI tests in SM-MVPC [20]. It serves as the hard-censoring baseline against which the smooth sigmoid is compared.

Self-masking with Dependencies. Extends weak self-masking to allow missingness of Y to depend on correlated variables $\mathbf{Z}$:

$$P(R_Y = 0 \mid Y = y, \mathbf{Z} = \mathbf{z}) = \sigma(\alpha y + \boldsymbol{\beta}^T \mathbf{z} + \gamma) \tag{4}$$

where $\boldsymbol{\beta}$ captures dependency weights. The mechanism is *conditionally identifiable* when dependencies are observed and can be adjusted for in CI tests.

Hierarchical MNAR. Multi-level missingness pattern where missingness at 1 level depends on higher-level patterns. For 2-level hierarchical:

$$P(R_Y = 0 \mid Y = y, L = \ell) = \sigma(\alpha_\ell y + \beta_\ell) \tag{5}$$

where L is the hierarchical level. 2-level hierarchical is *conditionally identifiable* if L is observed and level-specific parameters can be consistently estimated. However, 3+ levels are generally *non-identifiable* due to increasing selection bias. Identifiability analyses of self-masking with dependencies and of hierarchical MNAR can be found in the Supplementary Material, Section 2.3.

Mediator-Based and Collider-Induced MNAR. Mediator-based MNAR, $P(R_Y = 0 \mid Y = y, M = m) = f(y, m)$ with M a mediator between Y's causes and Y, violates weak self-masking; the dependence on M introduces selection bias that distorts CI relations, and the mechanism is *non-identifiable* when M is unobserved or only partially observed [12]. **Collider-induced MNAR**, where missingness acts through a collider (e.g. $X \rightarrow Z \leftarrow Y$ with missingness depending on Z), induces selection bias that creates spurious dependencies violating the assumptions of constraint-based discovery; it cannot be corrected without the complete-data distribution and is likewise *non-identifiable* [16].

5 SM-MVPC Under MNAR

SM-MVPC extends the classical PC algorithm for self-masking MNAR by retaining the constraint-based search while modifying the CI testing procedure. The key theoretical insight is that under the weak self-masking assumption [20], residual-independence tests maintain valid Type-I error control when performed on appropriately constructed test-wise subsets. The algorithm replaces standard CI tests with residual-based tests that account for the missingness mechanism. For testing $X \perp\!\!\!\perp Y \mid \mathbf{Z}$, SM-MVPC does this via a four-step procedure that fundamentally differs from complete-case analysis:

1. *Test-wise subset construction:* Rather than discarding all incomplete observations globally, construct observation sets specific to each CI test: $\mathcal{I} = \{i : R_{X,i} = R_{Y,i} = 1,\ R_{Z_j,i} = 1\ \forall Z_j \in \mathbf{Z}\}$.
2. *Localized residual regression:* Using only $\mathcal{I}$, fit an additive noise model $Y = f(\mathbf{Z}) + \epsilon_Y$ (see [8,21]) and compute $\hat{\epsilon}_Y = Y - \hat{f}(\mathbf{Z})$.
3. *Residual independence testing:* Test $X \perp\!\!\!\perp \hat{\epsilon}_Y$ on $\mathcal{I}$ using partial correlation (Gaussian case) or kernel-based tests (non-Gaussian case) at $\alpha = 0.05$ significance level.
4. *Conservative graph updates:* If the independence null is not rejected, remove $X - Y$ from the skeleton; otherwise retain it. When $|\mathcal{I}| < 20$, edges are conservatively retained to avoid unreliable statistical decisions.

This test-wise approach has advantages over global complete-case deletion: (i) preserves more data by avoiding unnecessary case removal; (ii) reduces selection bias by using test-specific rather than global missingness patterns; and (iii) maintains theoretical validity under weak self-masking. Within CAR-MNAR, we treat SM-MVPC as a modular algorithm, systematically evaluating how its performance on skeleton recovery, v-structure detection, and edge orientation degrades under varying MNAR severity and mechanism types. We incorporate several robustness enhancements: conservative CI testing (retaining edges if sample sizes fall below threshold), multiple testing correction (FDR), and ANM flexibility (support for linear and non-linear regression). Details are in the Supplementary Material, Section 7.1.

6 CPDAG-Aware Evaluation Metrics

CAR-MNAR employs a comprehensive suite of evaluation metrics that properly account for Markov equivalence, ensuring fair and interpretable comparisons across causal discovery algorithms under MNAR.

Skeleton Recovery: Skeleton F1 evaluates undirected graph adjacency recovery by precision and recall of edge identification in the skeleton structure;

V-Structure Detection Metrics: V-Structure F1 focuses on collider recovery ($X \rightarrow Z \leftarrow Y$ where $X \not\perp\!\!\!\perp Y$), crucial for detecting confounding structures;

Orientation Accuracy on Compelled Edges: Orientation F1 assesses directionality on compelled edges where Markov equivalence allows unique identification, avoiding penalties for underdetermined orientations;

Structural Distance Metrics: CPDAG-SHD counts minimum edge operations needed to transform one CPDAG into another, normalized by true graph size.

SID (Structural Intervention Distance) [17] measures discrepancies in interventional distributions, providing a causal evaluation. We use a deterministic ancestor-reachability proxy of SID (counting ordered variable pairs whose reachability relation differs between the true and inferred DAGs), reported as a single value and labeled "SID (proxy)" in tables to avoid overstating its precision. Formal definitions, computational procedures, and implementation details can be found in the Supplementary Material, Section 3.

6.1 Statistical Analysis Framework

We employ four complementary tools: *bootstrap confidence intervals* (95% intervals from 1000 resamples per condition); *effect-size estimation* via Cohen's d [4] for standardized mean differences; *multiple-comparison correction* by the FDR (Benjamini-Hochberg) procedure, which controls the false-discovery rate while remaining less conservative than Bonferroni; and *permutation testing* for exact p-values in small-sample comparisons. Together, these ensure that CAR-MNAR reports not just point estimates but statistically reliable uncertainty quantification for MNAR robustness.

7 Experiments

Datasets with Robust Ground Truth. The clinical reference graphs are the consensus CPDAGs of Sect. 3 (six algorithms, $> 60\%$ agreement, stability ≈ 0.78), and remain a *proxy*: clinical numbers are "performance relative to consensus." The 51 synthetic configurations (seven topologies, three complexity levels, varied mechanisms and noise; Supplementary Material, Section 6.1) have **known ground truth DAGs** and are what justify absolute claims. Our evaluation employs a comprehensive factorial design crossing datasets, missingness mechanisms, missingness rates, and algorithms. We evaluate on both mentioned **real clinical datasets** (Heart Disease: 13 clinical variables, $n = 303$; Diabetes: 8 variables, $n = 768$; Hepatitis: 19 variables, $n = 142$) with multi-algorithm ground truth and **51 synthetic datasets with known ground truth across seven topologies and three complexity levels**. The missingness mechanisms are the five mathematically specified MNAR types described above, and rates run from 0% to 50% in 10% increments. Algorithms include SM-MVPC (primary evaluation target), TD-PC (test-wise deletion), MVPC (missing-value PC via causal-learn), MissDAG (joint optimization), OTM (optimal transport), and MICE-PC (multiple imputation followed by PC), with all five baselines fully implemented and evaluated. This factorial design enables fair, like-for-like comparison across methods and missingness regimes.

Our Python code, together with full details of all experiments, tests, and results, is provided in the Supplementary Material (Sections 4–9).

8 Results and Analysis

Our comprehensive evaluation through CAR-MNAR provides rigorous answers to three fundamental questions about SM-MVPC's robustness under MNAR conditions.

(1) Robustness Quantification: Full-graph recovery degrades only mildly as MNAR severity increases from 10% to 50% (Table 3). More importantly, the local causal neighbourhood of the clinical target is recovered *at least as robustly* as the full graph on two of three datasets: the local-to-full skeleton-F1 ratio is 1.29–1.39 on Heart Disease and 1.01–1.14 on Diabetes, while on Hepatitis the ratio is 0.85–0.92 because the full graph is already recovered well there. On Heart Disease this advantage is large in absolute terms: the target neighbourhood retains skeleton F1 0.88–1.00 across all rates up to 50% MNAR while the full graph stays at 0.68–0.72 (Table 1), enabling actionable local causal inference even under severe missingness.

(2) Mechanism-Specific Vulnerability: Within a fixed mechanism, the structural components fail at very different rates, which is visible directly in Table 3: collider (v-structure) detection is the weak point, while skeleton and compelled-edge orientation are comparatively robust. On Heart Disease, v-structure F1 falls steadily from 0.51 to 0.35 between 0% and 50% MNAR while skeleton F1 only moves 0.72 $\rightarrow$ 0.70 and orientation F1 stays near 0.88; on Diabetes v-structure F1 declines 0.60 $\rightarrow$ 0.55 by 50% while skeleton F1 stays $\geq$ 0.85 and orientation F1 stays 1.00. Across mechanisms, the functional form matters but skeleton recovery is robust either way: comparing sigmoid against deterministic threshold censoring at matched rates, the mean skeleton-F1 drop over 0–50% MNAR is small for both ($\approx$ 0.018 sigmoid vs. $\approx$ 0.006 threshold), while the v-structure drop is markedly larger under smooth sigmoid masking ($\approx$ 0.073 mean, up to 0.16 on Heart Disease) than under threshold censoring ($\approx$ 0.006). Intuitively, sigmoid masking erodes the marginal continuously and progressively distorts collider configurations, whereas threshold censoring removes only a fixed tail. The heavy-tailed GPD mechanism is mathematically specified (Eq. (2)) and implemented; its clinical degradation profile is analyzed in the extended code rather than claimed here.

(3) Methodological Standardization: CAR-MNAR provides a rigorous, reproducible evaluation protocol for missing-data-aware causal discovery, enabling fair comparisons across algorithms and mechanisms through mathematically specified missingness models, deterministic calibration, and CPDAG-aware metrics with statistical rigor. A direct illustration of why the protocol matters is given below: the same experiment can look "robust" or "fragile" depending solely on whether one scores it with plain SHD or with CPDAG-aware metrics (Table 2). Further evidence supporting these findings is provided in the Supplementary Material, Sections 8–9.

Overall Performance Under MNAR. We evaluate SM-MVPC and the benchmark methods on the 3 clinical datasets (Heart Disease, Diabetes, Hepatitis) under

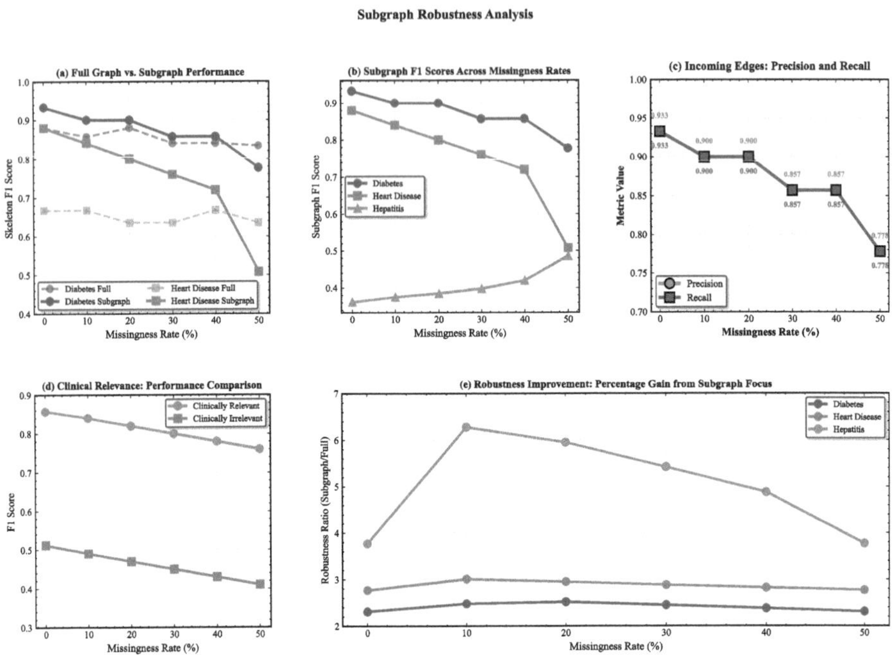

Fig. 2. Local (target-neighbourhood) vs. full-graph robustness. On Heart Disease and Diabetes the target-neighbourhood skeleton F1 is at least as high as the full-graph F1 across all MNAR rates (local-to-full ratios up to 1.39; Table 1), while Hepatitis is a counter-example. (a) Full graph vs. subgraph performance. (b) Subgraph F1 scores across missingness rates. (c) Incoming edges: Precision and recall. (d) Clinical relevance: Performance comparison. (e) Robustness improvement: Percentage gain from subgraph focus.

sigmoid self-masking MNAR with missingness rates from 0% to 50%; full-graph CPDAG-aware metrics are reported in Table 3. Reading that table, Diabetes attains the highest skeleton F1 (0.85–0.88), Heart Disease is most sensitive to missingness yet still stable (0.70–0.72), and Hepatitis is remarkably stable (0.86) despite its small sample ($n = 142$). The v-structure and orientation rows of the same table drive finding (2) below.

Local (Target-Neighbourhood) vs. Full-Graph Recovery. Table 1 compares, for each dataset and missingness rate, the full-graph skeleton F1 with the skeleton F1 restricted to the adjacency neighbourhood (parents and children) of the clinical target (heart-disease presence, diabetes outcome, hepatitis prognosis), together with their ratio. Two of three datasets show a genuine local-structure advantage, most pronounced on Heart Disease (ratio up to 1.39); Hepatitis is a clear counterexample where the full graph is already easy and the local ratio drops below one. We deliberately do *not* claim the much larger ratios that a size- or density-matched negative-control simulation would suggest, because those control performances are simulated rather than measured (see Supplemen-

Table 1. Local (target-neighbourhood) vs. full-graph skeleton F1 for SM-MVPC under sigmoid self-masking MNAR, with their ratio. Full = whole-graph skeleton F1; Local = skeleton F1 over the parents/children of the clinical target. Values are directly measured (means over replicates); a ratio > 1 means the target neighbourhood is recovered more robustly than the full graph.

Dataset	Quantity	0%	10%	20%	30%	40%	50%
Diabetes	Full F1	0.88	0.86	0.86	0.86	0.84	0.84
	Local F1	1.00	0.92	0.93	0.92	0.87	0.84
	Ratio	1.14	1.07	1.08	1.07	1.04	1.00
Heart Disease	Full F1	0.72	0.72	0.70	0.70	0.70	0.68
	Local F1	1.00	1.00	0.93	0.93	0.94	0.88
	Ratio	1.39	1.39	1.33	1.33	1.34	1.29
Hepatitis	Full F1	0.86	0.86	0.86	0.86	0.86	0.87
	Local F1	0.75	0.76	0.74	0.78	0.73	0.80
	Ratio	0.87	0.88	0.86	0.91	0.85	0.92

Table 2. Plain SHD can mask failure modes that CPDAG-aware metrics expose. Heart Disease under sigmoid MNAR: as the rate rises from 0% to 50%, CPDAG-SHD barely moves (+4%, suggesting "stable") while CPDAG-aware v-structure F1 falls by ≈ 31%; skeleton and orientation F1 stay essentially flat. Using SHD alone would lead to the opposite qualitative conclusion from the CPDAG-aware analysis.

Metric (Heart Disease)	0% MNAR	50% MNAR	Conclusion if used alone
CPDAG-SHD (lower better)	26	27	"robust/stable"
Skeleton F1	0.72	0.70	mostly stable
Orientation F1 (compelled)	0.89	0.88	stable
V-structure F1	**0.51**	**0.35**	**steady collapse**

tary Material, Section 9); the numbers in Table 1 are the directly measured local and full skeleton-F1 values. Figure 2 visualizes these comparisons.

Why Deterministic Calibration Matters. Our Bayesian-optimization calibrator enables at-equal-rate comparisons by matching the realized missingness rate to target across mechanisms (mean absolute error ≈ 2.3% over the clinical conditions) with 4× fewer objective evaluations than grid search, removing the confounding that stochastic parameter selection would otherwise introduce. With this control in place, the mechanism-shape effect of finding (2) can be attributed to the mechanism rather than to incidental rate differences: at matched rates, smooth sigmoid masking erodes collider (v-structure) recovery somewhat more than deterministic threshold censoring, while both leave skeleton recovery largely intact.

Table 3. Full-graph CPDAG-aware performance of SM-MVPC under sigmoid self-masking MNAR. Means over $n_{\text{rep}} = 20$ replicates. Because the calibrator is deterministic (fixed seed), the replicate spread is negligible (std $< 10^{-3}$), so 95% bootstrap CIs are effectively point values and are omitted here; they are reported in the Supplementary Material. SID is the deterministic reachability-based proxy of Sect. 6 (a single value, hence its lower and upper figures coincide).

Dataset/Metric	0%	10%	20%	30%	40%	50%
Diabetes						
Skeleton F1	0.88	0.86	0.86	0.86	0.86	0.85
V-Structure F1	0.60	0.57	0.57	0.56	0.56	0.55
Orientation F1	1.00	1.00	1.00	1.00	1.00	1.00
CPDAG-SHD	6	7	7	7	7	7
SID (proxy)	5	5	5	5	5	5
Heart Disease						
Skeleton F1	0.72	0.72	0.71	0.70	0.70	0.70
V-Structure F1	0.51	0.49	0.45	0.41	0.35	0.35
Orientation F1	0.89	0.89	0.89	0.88	0.88	0.88
CPDAG-SHD	26	26	27	27	27	27
SID (proxy)	22	22	23	23	23	23
Hepatitis						
Skeleton F1	0.86	0.86	0.86	0.86	0.86	0.86
V-Structure F1	0.64	0.64	0.64	0.64	0.63	0.65
Orientation F1	0.98	0.99	0.99	0.99	0.99	0.99
CPDAG-SHD	22	22	21	22	22	21
SID (proxy)	18	18	18	17	17	16

Baseline Comparison. Table 4 reports SM-MVPC against five baselines at 30% sigmoid MNAR on the three clinical datasets, all scored with the same CPDAG-aware metrics against the same ground truth. The decisive and consistent advantage of SM-MVPC is in the *causally meaningful* structure: it recovers v-structures and compelled-edge orientations far better than every baseline on all three datasets (v-structure F1 0.41–0.64 vs. ≤ 0.19 for every baseline; orientation F1 0.88–1.00 vs. ≤ 0.45), and attains the lowest CPDAG-SHD on Diabetes and Hepatitis, because the imputation/complete-case baselines tend to return denser, less correctly oriented graphs. On raw skeleton (adjacency) F1 the comparison is more nuanced: SM-MVPC clearly leads on Hepatitis (0.86 vs. ≤ 0.49) and on Diabetes (0.86, the best), and is competitive on Heart Disease, where an imputation baseline edges it on adjacency alone (and the denser baselines also score a lower Heart-Disease SHD). We report this as is rather than overstating a uniform win. MissDAG and OTM are evaluated through faithful but simpli-

Table 4. SM-MVPC vs. five baselines on the clinical datasets under 30% **sigmoid MNAR** (means over $n_{\text{rep}} = 20$ replicates). All methods are scored with the same CPDAG-aware metrics against the same single-run PC ground truth on complete data (a fixed, method-independent reference, so the comparison is fair across rows; this differs from the consensus ground truth of Table 3). Best per row in bold; ↓ marks lower-is-better. SM-MVPC dominates on the causally meaningful structure (v-structures, orientation, and SHD on Diabetes/Hepatitis); on raw skeleton F1 it leads on Diabetes/Hepatitis but an imputation baseline edges it on Heart Disease. MVPC is causal-learn's missing-value PC; MissDAG/OTM use faithful but *simplified* imputation surrogates (see text).

Dataset/Method	SM-MVPC	TD-PC	MVPC	MissDAG	OTM	MICE-PC
Diabetes						
Skeleton F1	**0.86**	0.72	0.77	0.83	0.83	0.82
V-Structure F1	**0.55**	0.11	0.12	0.11	0.11	0.14
Orientation F1	**1.00**	0.31	0.27	0.24	0.24	0.29
CPDAG-SHD ↓	**7.2**	18.5	18.5	18.6	18.6	17.9
Heart Disease						
Skeleton F1	0.70	0.76	0.79	0.81	0.81	**0.84**
V-Structure F1	**0.41**	0.19	0.13	0.15	0.15	0.12
Orientation F1	**0.88**	0.44	0.33	0.36	0.36	0.30
CPDAG-SHD ↓	27.0	**20.8**	21.6	22.6	22.6	21.7
Hepatitis						
Skeleton F1	**0.86**	0.39	0.43	0.49	0.49	0.47
V-Structure F1	**0.64**	0.04	0.03	0.04	0.04	0.04
Orientation F1	**0.99**	0.45	0.39	0.39	0.39	0.45
CPDAG-SHD ↓	**21.4**	56.9	57.3	56.0	56.0	55.6

fied surrogates (mean-/optimal-transport-style imputation followed by PC); full reference implementations are left to future work.

9 Conclusion

In this paper, we introduced CAR-MNAR, a factorial *evaluation framework* for assessing the robustness of causal discovery algorithms under self-masking MNAR mechanisms. By combining mathematically specified missingness mechanisms (five types), deterministic Bayesian-optimization calibration with theoretical guarantees, multi- algorithm ground-truth construction, and CPDAG-aware metrics with bootstrap and permutation -based statistics, the framework enables clean, interpretable, and reproducible comparisons across diverse conditions. Underpinning it is an identifiability theorem, machine-verified in Lean 4, that delineates precisely when the residual-independence test remains valid under

MNAR. All experiments use $n_{\text{rep}} = 20$ replicates; power analysis (Supplementary Material, Section 5) indicates $n_{\text{rep}} \approx 200$ for near-full power on most metrics, which we leave to future runs. Our analysis yields two transferable lessons that go beyond a single accuracy ranking. First, the choice of evaluation metric is not neutral: plain SHD can suggest an algorithm is stable under MNAR while CPDAG-aware metrics reveal a sharp collapse of collider detection (Table 2); reporting Markov-equivalence-aware metrics is therefore essential. Second, the local causal neighbourhood of a clinical target can be recovered considerably more robustly than the full graph (Table 1), though this is dataset dependent rather than universal, with Hepatitis a clear counterexample. We deliberately report these findings without inflating them: where a control comparison rests on simulated rather than measured performance (Supplementary Material, Section 9), we say so. The framework's dual evaluation strategy, combining 51 synthetic datasets with known ground truth and real clinical datasets with consensus ground truth, supports interpretable robustness claims while keeping the synthetic experiments as the basis for absolute statements. CAR-MNAR is intended as a reusable test bed for the community; our practical guidance is to prioritize local causal structure around clinical targets when data quality is poor, and to select algorithms with the missingness mechanism in mind.

Reproducibility and Resource Availability. The supplementary material (theory, proofs, full metric definitions, and additional results) accompanies this paper. Source code and the clinical-data preprocessing pipeline that reproduce all reported numbers, including the deterministic scripts that regenerate Tables 1, 3 and 4 and the Lean 4 project that machine-verifies Theorem 1, are publicly available at https://github.com/Matin-Alinejad/CAR-MNAR; the exact version used for the results in this paper is archived at https://doi.org/10.5281/zenodo.21298787.

Acknowledgments. The authors thank the anonymous ECML-PKDD reviewers for constructive feedback that improved this work.

Disclosure of Interests. The authors have no competing interests to declare that are relevant to the content of this article.

References

1. Bühlmann, P., Peters, J., Ernest, J.: CAM: causal additive models, high-dimensional order search and penalized regression. Ann. Stat. **42**(6), 2526–2556 (2014). https://doi.org/10.1214/14-AOS1260
2. van Buuren, S., Groothuis-Oudshoorn, K.: Mice: multivariate imputation by chained equations in R. J. Stat. Softw. **45**(3), 1–67 (2011). https://doi.org/10.18637/jss.v045.i03
3. Chickering, D.M.: Optimal structure identification with greedy search. J. Mach. Learn. Res. **3**, 507–554 (2002). https://jmlr.org/papers/v3/chickering02b.html
4. Cohen, J.: Statistical Power Analysis for the Behavioral Sciences, 2nd edn. Routledge (2013). https://doi.org/10.4324/9780203771587

5. Efron, B.: Bootstrap methods: another look at the jackknife. In: Breakthroughs in Statistics: Methodology and Distribution, pp. 569–593. Springer (1992). https://doi.org/10.1007/978-1-4612-4380-9_41
6. Gao, E., et al.: MissDAG: causal discovery in the presence of missing data with continuous additive noise models. In: Advances in Neural Information Processing Systems 35 (NeurIPS 2022) (2022). https://papers.nips.cc/paper_files/paper/2022/hash/206361867abf7eb01746c3943078da3c-Abstract-Conference.html
7. Gong, G.: Hepatitis. UCI Machine Learning Repository (1988). https://doi.org/10.24432/C5Q59J
8. Hoyer, P.O., Janzing, D., Mooij, J.M., Peters, J., Schölkopf, B.: Nonlinear causal discovery with additive noise models. In: Advances in Neural Information Processing Systems 21 (NeurIPS 2008), pp. 689–696. Curran Associates, Inc. (2008). https://proceedings.neurips.cc/paper/2008/hash/f7664060cc52bc6f3d620bcedc94a4b6-Abstract.html
9. Jánosi, A., Steinbrunn, W., Pfisterer, M., Detrano, R.: Heart Disease. UCI Machine Learning Repository (1989). https://doi.org/10.24432/C52P4X
10. Kelly, M., Longjohn, R., Nottingham, K.: The UCI machine learning repository. University of California, Irvine. https://archive.ics.uci.edu/
11. Koyuncu, D., Gittens, A., Yener, B., Yung, M.: Adversarial missingness attacks on causal structure learning. ACM Trans. Intell. Syst. Technol. **15**(6), 1–60 (2024). https://doi.org/10.1145/3682065
12. Little, R.J.A., Rubin, D.B.: Statistical Analysis with Missing Data, 3rd edn. Wiley (2019). https://doi.org/10.1002/9781119482260
13. Mattei, P.A., Frellsen, J.: MIWAE: deep generative modelling and imputation of incomplete data sets. In: Proceedings of the 36th International Conference on Machine Learning (ICML 2019). Proceedings of Machine Learning Research, vol. 97, pp. 4413–4423. PMLR (2019). https://proceedings.mlr.press/v97/mattei19a.html
14. Meek, C.: Graphical Models: Selecting Causal and Statistical Models. Ph.D. thesis, Carnegie Mellon University (1997)
15. Muzellec, B., Josse, J., Boyer, C., Cuturi, M.: Missing data imputation using optimal transport. In: Proceedings of the 37th International Conference on Machine Learning (ICML 2020). Proceedings of Machine Learning Research, vol. 119, pp. 7130–7140. PMLR (2020). https://proceedings.mlr.press/v119/muzellec20a.html
16. Pearl, J.: Causality: Models, Reasoning, and Inference, 2nd edn. Cambridge University Press (2009). https://doi.org/10.1017/CBO9780511803161
17. Peters, J., Bühlmann, P.: Structural intervention distance for evaluating causal graphs. Neural Comput. **27**(3), 771–799 (2015). https://doi.org/10.1162/NECO_a_00708
18. Petersen, A.H.: Are you doing better than random guessing? A call for using negative controls when evaluating causal discovery algorithms. In: Proceedings of the 41st Conference on Uncertainty in Artificial Intelligence (UAI 2025). Proceedings of Machine Learning Research, vol. 286, pp. 3465–3479. PMLR (2025). https://proceedings.mlr.press/v286/petersen25a.html
19. Pickands, J., III.: Statistical inference using extreme order statistics. Ann. Stat. **3**(1), 119–131 (1975). https://doi.org/10.1214/aos/1176343003
20. Qiao, J., Chen, Z., Yu, J., Cai, R., Hao, Z.: Identification of causal structure in the presence of missing data with additive noise model. In: Proceedings of the AAAI Conference on Artificial Intelligence (AAAI 2024), vol. 38, pp. 20516–20523. AAAI Press (2024). https://doi.org/10.1609/aaai.v38i18.30036

21. Shimizu, S., Hoyer, P.O., Hyvärinen, A., Kerminen, A.: A linear non-Gaussian acyclic model for causal discovery. J. Mach. Learn. Res. **7**, 2003–2030 (2006). https://jmlr.org/papers/v7/shimizu06a.html
22. Smith, J.W., Everhart, J.E., Dickson, W.C., Knowler, W.C., Johannes, R.S.: Using the ADAP learning algorithm to forecast the onset of diabetes mellitus. In: Proceedings of the Twelfth Annual Symposium on Computer Applications in Medical Care, pp. 261–265. IEEE Computer Society Press, Washington, DC (1988)
23. Spirtes, P., Glymour, C.: An algorithm for fast recovery of sparse causal graphs. Soc. Sci. Comput. Rev. **9**(1), 62–72 (1991). https://doi.org/10.1177/089443939100900106
24. Srinivas, N., Krause, A., Kakade, S.M., Seeger, M.: Gaussian process optimization in the bandit setting: no regret and experimental design. In: Proceedings of the 27th International Conference on Machine Learning (ICML 2010), pp. 1015–1022. Omnipress (2010). https://icml.cc/Conferences/2010/papers/422.pdf
25. Tu, R., Zhang, C., Ackermann, P., Mohan, K., Kjellström, H., Zhang, K.: Causal discovery in the presence of missing data. In: Proceedings of the 22nd International Conference on Artificial Intelligence and Statistics (AISTATS 2019). Proceedings of Machine Learning Research, vol. 89, pp. 1762–1770. PMLR (2019). https://proceedings.mlr.press/v89/tu19a.html
26. Wang, Y., Menkovski, V., Wang, H., Du, X., Pechenizkiy, M.: Causal discovery from incomplete data: a deep learning approach. arXiv preprint arXiv:2001.05343 (2020). https://arxiv.org/abs/2001.05343
27. Zheng, X., Aragam, B., Ravikumar, P., Xing, E.P.: DAGs with NO TEARS: continuous optimization for structure learning. In: Advances in Neural Information Processing Systems 31 (NeurIPS 2018), pp. 9492–9503 (2018). https://proceedings.neurips.cc/paper/2018/hash/e347c51419ffb23ca3fd5050202f9c3d-Abstract.html

Collaborative Representations for Targeted Causal Inference Under Outcome Selection

Johan de Aguas(✉)

Integreat – Norwegian Centre for Knowledge-Driven Machine Learning, Department of Mathematics, University of Oslo, Oslo, Norway
johanmd@uio.no

Abstract. Estimating causal effects with missing outcomes requires learning outcome, exposure, and selection models. Flexible propensity learners can predict treatment or missingness well while worsening target estimation by emphasizing instruments, weak-overlap regions, or variation unrelated to outcome-regression bias. We propose a collaborative representation-based targeted learning method for recovered average treatment effects under outcome selection. The method learns low-dimensional exposure and selection representations from cross-fitted pseudo-outcomes that encode outcome-regression drift. A finite candidate library alternates targeted outcome updates with representation updates, and inner cross-validation selects representation complexity, collaboration strength, and regularization using a target-aware risk. We give high-level sufficient conditions for collaborative robustness, consistency, and asymptotic linearity after outer validation-fold targeting. Simulations show finite-sample bias reduction, with explicit bias–variance trade-offs across configurations and relative to competing estimators.

Keywords: causal inference · attrition · missing data · targeted learning · collaborative learning · representation learning · Riesz regression

1 Introduction

The problem of recovering and estimating causal effects from observational data in the presence of both confounding and missing data has received sustained attention [3,13,22–24,26,31]. For missing outcomes, the challenge is twofold: one must account for the endogenous treatment assignment and, at the same time, address the selective observation of outcomes due to attrition [2,4,5,14,19]. Over the last decade, the literature has developed a broad collection of recovery tools for this setting, including sufficient graphical conditions [9,22,31], general identification algorithms [3], and search-based procedures [37]. In certain cases, recovered causal effects admit inverse-probability weighted (IPW) representations [14]; in others, recovery may proceed through generalized adjustment formulas [9] or through sequential regressions [10].

M. Ceci et al. (Eds.): ECML PKDD 2026, LNAI 16941, pp. 623–640, 2027.
https://doi.org/10.1007/978-3-032-37654-1_36

To estimate the recovered causal effect, semiparametric estimators are attractive because they permit flexible machine-learning fitting of nuisance functions while retaining asymptotic guarantees and valid inference [6,11,12,43]. These estimators may enjoy double robustness or, in the sequential-regression setting, multiple robustness across distinct patterns of correctly specified nuisance components [10,21,27,36,45,46]. This robustness, however, is an asymptotic property. In finite samples, the quality of the estimator depends strongly on how the nuisance functions are fitted. In particular, exposure and selection propensity models that are optimized only for predictive accuracy need not optimize the bias–variance trade-off of the target estimand [25,32,40]. Target-agnostic, prediction-oriented propensity score learners can exacerbate practical positivity issues, yield unstable IPW, and place excessive emphasis on variables that strongly predict treatment or missingness but contribute little to reducing outcome-regression bias, thereby degrading finite-sample performance [1,30,33].

Motivation: Two existing lines of work are particularly relevant. The first is *collaborative targeted minimum loss estimation* (CTMLE) [40], which estimates propensity scores in a way that is explicitly tailored to the target parameter, rather than optimized for nuisance prediction alone. By aligning propensity estimation with the residual bias of the outcome regression, CTMLE can improve finite-sample performance while retaining desirable asymptotic properties. In settings where reducing the effective covariate dimension is beneficial, greedy CTMLE implements this idea through stepwise construction of candidate propensity models, adding covariates along a search path and selecting among candidates using a target-aware criterion. However, this procedure can be computationally expensive, and scalable versions often introduce dependence on arbitrary covariate orderings and other search heuristics [16]. These limitations are likely to be even more pronounced under attrition, where collaboration must be coordinated across both the treatment-assignment and selection mechanisms.

A second relevant line of work is *Riesz regression* and related methods [7,8]. These approaches bypass explicit propensity-score estimation by directly learning the Riesz representer associated with the target functional, often together with a calibration step [38,39]. This perspective is appealing because it is target-aware from the outset. Yet, its practical success depends on the choice of function class and regularization [8]. Under weak overlap, the representer-learning problem may also become ill-conditioned, leading to unstable weights and vulnerability to pathological overfitting: density-ratio representers may reduce the training objective by placing disproportionate mass on vanishing-probability regions ("train-loss hacking") or by exploiting low-density covariate pockets that are only weakly supported by the data (the "density chasm") [17,18,29].

Contribution: We take inspiration from both CTMLE and Riesz regression. Our goal is to replace stepwise collaborative propensity search with a learned low-dimensional representation that remains stable and directly integrated into a plug-in semiparametric estimator for the recovered causal effect. Instead of traversing a sequence of propensity-score models over subsets or orderings of covariates, we parameterize the treatment and selection propensities through low-dimensional learned representations feeding calibrated output heads. Learning low-dimensional representations for causal estimation connects our construction to representation-learning approaches for treatment-effect estimation [15,34] and to sufficient dimension reduction for causal modeling [20]; the distinguishing feature here is that the representations are shaped by target-level drift rather than by covariate balance or predictive fit alone.

Collaborative learning is driven by cross-fitted pseudo-outcomes that target the drift components of the sequential outcome regressions. These pseudo-outcomes train representations for the treatment and selection mechanisms along directions most relevant for reducing target-level bias. The method searches over a finite library, alternating targeted outcome-regression updates with representation updates for the propensity components. Model complexity, collaboration weights, regularization, and other hyperparameters are chosen by inner cross-validation using a targeted risk that balances estimated drift and influence-function variance. A final outer cross-validated targeting step yields a substitution estimator, while the representation penalties can be interpreted as Riesz-type losses for nuisance-specific drift functionals.

2 Preliminaries

We consider an observational setting with binary point-exposure $A \in \{0,1\}$ (where $A = 1$ denotes active treatment), baseline covariates W, an additional covariate set Z that may include post-treatment variables, and an outcome Y that is only partially observed. We observe a selection/missingness indicator R and an outcome proxy $Y^\dagger$, where $Y^\dagger = Y$ if $R = 1$ and $Y^\dagger = \emptyset$ if $R = 0$.

The *average treatment effect* (ATE) is a canonical causal estimand. For a binary point-exposure A and a continuous outcome $Y \in \mathbb{R}$, it is defined as

$$\psi := \Delta_a \mathbb{E}\left[Y \mid \mathrm{do}(A = a)\right],$$

where Δ_a denotes the contrast operator, $\Delta_a f(a) = f(1) - f(0)$, and $\mathrm{do}(\cdot)$ is Pearl's intervention operator from the Structural Causal Model framework [28].

If (W, Z) is an s-admissible pair relative to the causal m-graph of the system, including the missingness mechanism, then the ATE is recoverable from the incomplete-data observational law [10]. The recovered estimand is then

$$\begin{aligned}\Psi[P] &:= \mathbb{E}_W \Delta_a Q_2(W, a),\\ Q_2(W, A) &:= \mathbb{E}_{Z|W,A} Q_1(W, A, Z),\\ Q_1(W, A, Z) &:= \mathbb{E}\left[Y \mid W, A, Z, R = 1\right].\end{aligned}$$

This representation decomposes the target functional into two nested outcome regressions. The regression Q_1 is the *mean-imputation outcome model*, which reconstructs the conditional mean outcome among units with observed outcomes. The regression Q_2 is the *meta-regression*, which transports this information back to the treatment level conditional on W [10]. Given fitted nuisance regressions $\widehat{Q} = (\widehat{Q}_1, \widehat{Q}_2)$, a plug-in estimator of ψ is

$$\widehat{\psi} = \frac{1}{n}\sum_{i=1}^{n}\left\{\widehat{Q}_2(W_i,1) - \widehat{Q}_2(W_i,0)\right\},$$

Under standard regularity and positivity conditions, the recovered ATE functional $\Psi[P]$ is pathwise differentiable in the nonparametric model for the observed-data law P. Its *efficient influence function* (EIF) [4,10], evaluated at P and at an observation $O_i = (W_i, A_i, Z_i, R_i, Y_i^{\dagger}) \sim P$, can be written as

$$\begin{aligned}
D(\eta,\psi;O_i) &:= D^Y(\eta;O_i) + D^Z(\eta;O_i) + D^W(\eta,\psi;O_i),\\
D^Y(\eta;O_i) &:= \alpha_1(W_i,A_i,Z_i,R_i)\left\{Y_i^{\dagger} - Q_1(W_i,A_i,Z_i)\right\},\\
D^Z(\eta;O_i) &:= \alpha_2(W_i,A_i)\left\{Q_1(W_i,A_i,Z_i) - Q_2(W_i,A_i)\right\},\\
D^W(\eta,\psi;O_i) &:= \Delta_a Q_2(W_i,a) - \psi,
\end{aligned}$$

where $\eta = (Q_1, Q_2, \pi_A, \pi_R)$ collects the nuisance functions. The functions α_1 and α_2 are the corresponding *clever functions/covariates*; equivalently, they act as *Riesz representers* for the linearized contributions of the Q_1 and Q_2 regressions to the recovered target functional. They are given in terms of the exposure propensity score $\pi_A(W) := \mathbb{P}(A = 1 \mid W)$ and the selection propensity score $\pi_R(W, A, Z) := \mathbb{P}(R = 1 \mid W, A, Z)$ by

$$\alpha_2(W_i,A_i) := \frac{A_i - \pi_A(W_i)}{\pi_A(W_i)[1-\pi_A(W_i)]}, \qquad \alpha_1(W_i,A_i,Z_i,R_i) := \frac{R_i\alpha_2(W_i,A_i)}{\pi_R(W_i,A_i,Z_i)}.$$

When the nuisance functions are evaluated at the true observed-data law P°, one gets $\mathbb{E}^\circ D(\eta^\circ,\psi^\circ;O) = 0$, so the empirical analogue can be used as an estimating equation for ψ. This estimating equation is *multiply robust*: it yields consistency when any of the following nuisance components are correctly specified: *(i)* Q_1 and Q_2, *(ii)* π_A and π_R, or *(iii)* π_A and Q_1 [10]. Estimators based on this EIF [4,10] exploit the fact that, in large samples, sufficiently fast nuisance convergence can yield asymptotic linearity. In finite samples, however, performance depends strongly on how the nuisance functions are estimated.

3 Collaborative Robustness

A central insight of collaborative estimation is that nuisance models should not be optimized solely for predictive accuracy. For the target parameter ψ, the key issue is not whether π_A or π_R are estimated accurately over the entire covariate space, but whether they are estimated accurately in regions where misspecification of Q_1 and Q_2 would otherwise generate drift in the target estimator [32,40].

Theorem 1 (Collaborative robustness). *Let $\widetilde{\eta} := (\widetilde{Q}_1, \widetilde{Q}_2, \widetilde{\pi}_A, \widetilde{\pi}_R)$ denote putative nuisance functions, and let $\eta^\circ := (Q_1^\circ, Q_2^\circ, \pi_A^\circ, \pi_R^\circ)$ and P° denote the true nuisance functions and law. Write the arm-specific treatment drifts δ_a and the first-stage outcome drift ε*

$$\delta_a(W) := \widetilde{Q}_2(W,a) - Q_2^\circ(W,a), \qquad a \in \{0,1\},$$
$$\varepsilon(X) := \widetilde{Q}_1(X) - Q_1^\circ(X), \qquad X = (W, A, Z).$$

Assume positivity for the true and the putative propensity scores and bounded second moments. Then the moment equation $\mathbb{E}^\circ D(\widetilde{\eta}, \psi^\circ; O) = 0$ remains a valid estimating equation for ψ if the propensity components are specified collaboratively with the outcome-regression errors in the following sufficient sense:

$$\widetilde{\pi}_A(W) = \mathbb{P}^\circ(A = 1 \mid \delta_1(W), \delta_0(W)), \tag{1}$$
$$\widetilde{\pi}_R(X) = \mathbb{P}^\circ(R = 1 \mid W, A, \varepsilon(X)). \tag{2}$$

Assumptions and proof are given in the supplementary material.

Theorem 1 shows that, even when $\widetilde{Q}_1$ and $\widetilde{Q}_2$ are misspecified, unbiasedness of the EIF estimating equation can still be preserved through collaborative propensity modeling. The propensity components need not recover the full true mechanisms in all directions of the covariate space. Instead, they need to be accurate along the nuisance-error directions that enter the target-level drift. For the exposure component, this requires the two arm-specific drifts δ_1 and δ_0 in general. For the selection component, the selection propensity must align with the first-stage regression drift conditionally on (W, A), because the corresponding EIF term is multiplied by the clever covariate $\alpha_2(W, A)$.

In the no-attrition case of classical CTMLE [40], the target depends only on the regression Q_2, so the exposure-side condition in (1) is the relevant one. If the arm-specific drifts (δ_1, δ_0) depend only on a proper subset of the covariates in W, then fitting the treatment propensity over the full covariate set is unnecessary for bias correction of the target parameter. Searching over reduced or expanded propensity-score models, or penalizing covariates by outcome relevance as in the outcome-adaptive LASSO [35], can improve the bias–variance trade-off by avoiding variables that are highly predictive of treatment assignment but largely irrelevant for correcting the target-level drift, and that may otherwise inflate variance through unstable IPW [1,30]. These gains are finite-sample rather than purely asymptotic, and they arise precisely because the nuisance-fitting problem is subordinated to the estimation of the target parameter.

In practice, however, classical CTMLE typically implements this collaboration through stepwise search over candidate propensity-score models. Such search can be computationally expensive, and scalable approximations often reintroduce sensitivity to arbitrary variable orderings and other traversal heuristics [16]. Under attrition, the problem is more acute because collaboration must, in principle, be coordinated across two propensity components rather than one. This raises the nontrivial issue of how to specify and justify either two separate search paths or one joint path over candidate variables, and may render the resulting procedure even more sensitive to heuristic design choices. Our proposal addresses this problem by replacing stepwise collaborative search with representation learning guided by cross-fitted *direct noisy proxies* of the drift terms in (1) and (2).

4 Representation-Based CTMLE

The data consist of samples $O_i = (W_i, A_i, Z_i, R_i, Y_i^\dagger)$, where $Y_i^\dagger$ is only observed when $R_i = 1$, and we write $X_i := (W_i, A_i, Z_i)$. We split the data into a training sample $\mathcal{T}$ and an evaluation sample $\mathcal{E}$. In the final implementation, the entire procedure is wrapped in outer K-fold cross-fitting, and candidate construction and hyperparameter selection are carried out by inner cross-fitting within $\mathcal{T}$. To keep notation readable, we suppress inner-fold indices and write all quantities below as if they were computed on a single sample. Thus, whenever pseudo-outcomes or selection losses are evaluated on $\mathcal{T}$, the corresponding nuisance predictions are understood to be obtained out of fold within $\mathcal{T}$.

Losses. For a given dataset $\mathcal{D}$ and probabilistic predictors π_A, π_R, define the treatment and attrition cross-entropy losses as

$$\mathrm{CE}_A(\pi_A; \mathcal{D}) = -\frac{1}{|\mathcal{D}|}\sum_{i\in\mathcal{D}}\Big[A_i \log \pi_A(W_i) + (1 - A_i)\log\{1 - \pi_A(W_i)\}\Big],$$
$$\mathrm{CE}_R(\pi_R; \mathcal{D}) = -\frac{1}{|\mathcal{D}|}\sum_{i\in\mathcal{D}}\Big[R_i \log \pi_R(X_i) + (1 - R_i)\log\{1 - \pi_R(X_i)\}\Big].$$

A convenient validation loss for the sequential regressions Q_1 and Q_2 is

$$\ell_\omega(Q_1, Q_2; \mathcal{D}) = \frac{1}{|\mathcal{D}|}\sum_{i\in\mathcal{D}} R_i\Big(Y_i^\dagger - Q_1(X_i)\Big)^2 + \frac{\omega}{|\mathcal{D}|}\sum_{i\in\mathcal{D}}\Big(Q_1(X_i) - Q_2(W_i, A_i)\Big)^2,$$

where $\omega > 0$ is a task weight. The first term assesses the fit of Q_1 on observed Y, while the second encourages Q_2 to track the bridge $Q_1(X)$ through (W, A).

Representations. Let d_A and d_R denote the representation dimensions, and define

$$u_{A,i} = h_{A,\beta_A}(W_i) \in \mathbb{R}^{d_A}, \qquad u_{R,i} = h_{R,\beta_R}(X_i) \in \mathbb{R}^{d_R}.$$

The treatment propensity is parameterized only through the treatment-drift representation,

$$\pi_{A,\beta_A,\gamma_A}(W_i) = \sigma\{g_{A,\gamma_A}(u_{A,i})\},$$

whereas the attrition propensity is parameterized with a direct skip for (W, A),

$$\pi_{R,\beta_R,\gamma_R}(X_i) = \sigma\{g_{R,\gamma_R}(W_i, A_i, u_{R,i})\}.$$

where σ is the sigmoid function, h_{A,β_A} and h_{R,β_R} are deterministic *encoders* into the representation spaces, and g_{A,γ_A} and g_{R,γ_R} are *output heads* that map these representations to scalars. The encoder h_{R,β_R} is asked to preserve the first-stage drift direction $\varepsilon(X)$, while (W, A) are passed directly to the attrition head. In contrast, the treatment condition requires the propensity head to depend on the pair of arm-specific drifts $(\delta_1(W), \delta_0(W))$, so h_{A,β_A} is trained to preserve them.

Pseudo-outcomes. The collaborative pseudo-outcomes are constructed so that their conditional means target the oracle drift functions that enter the robustness conditions in Theorem 1. Let $\widetilde{\pi}_A$, $\widetilde{\pi}_R$, $\widetilde{Q}_1$ and $\widetilde{Q}_2$ denote fixed working nuisance models. For the selection component, define, among units with $R_i = 1$,

$$e_{R,i} = \widetilde{Q}_1(X_i) - Y_i^{\dagger}.$$

Since $Q_1^{\circ}(X) = \mathbb{E}^{\circ}[Y^{\dagger} \mid X, R = 1]$, this residual satisfies

$$\mathbb{E}^{\circ}[e_R \mid X, R = 1] = \widetilde{Q}_1(X) - Q_1^{\circ}(X) = \varepsilon(X).$$

Thus e_R is an observable complete-case noisy proxy for the first-stage drift $\varepsilon(X)$. For the exposure component, first form the selection-corrected pseudo-outcome

$$\xi_i = \widetilde{Q}_1(X_i) + \frac{R_i}{\widetilde{\pi}_R(X_i)}\{Y_i^{\dagger} - \widetilde{Q}_1(X_i)\}.$$

We then define the factual-arm residual

$$e_{A,i} = \widetilde{Q}_2(W_i, A_i) - \xi_i.$$

When the preceding selection correction is adequate, in particular when

$$\mathbb{E}^{\circ}[\xi \mid W, A = a] = Q_2^{\circ}(W, a),$$

the conditional mean of this residual satisfies

$$\mathbb{E}^{\circ}[e_A \mid W, A = a] = \widetilde{Q}_2(W, a) - Q_2^{\circ}(W, a) = \delta_a(W), \qquad a \in \{0, 1\}.$$

The exposure representation is therefore trained with two arm-specific auxiliary heads, targeting the two conditional means $\delta_1(W)$ and $\delta_0(W)$. This construction differs from using the EIF residual $Q_1(X) - Q_2(W, A)$, which generally combines first- and second-stage errors. When this correction is adequate, e_A directly targets the arm-specific second-stage drift. The formal verification, including the complete-case nature of the attrition proxy, is given in the supplementary material.

Collaborative and Bottleneck Penalties. Suppressing the candidate index, and treating e_R, e_A, and the previous-level propensities as fixed, define for any dataset $\mathcal{D}$ the working treatment weights

$$\omega_{A,i}^{(1)} = \frac{A_i}{\widetilde{\pi}_A(W_i)}, \qquad \omega_{A,i}^{(0)} = \frac{1 - A_i}{1 - \widetilde{\pi}_A(W_i)}.$$

The collaborative penalties are

$$\mathcal{C}_R(\beta_R, \kappa_R; \mathcal{D}) = \frac{1}{|\mathcal{D}|}\sum_{i \in \mathcal{D}} R_i \Big(e_{R,i} - f_{R,\kappa_R}\{h_{R,\beta_R}(X_i)\}\Big)^2,$$

$$\mathcal{C}_A(\beta_A, \kappa_A; \mathcal{D}) = \frac{1}{|\mathcal{D}|}\sum_{i \in \mathcal{D}} \sum_{a \in \{0,1\}} \omega_{A,i}^{(a)} \Big(e_{A,i} - f_{A,\kappa_A}^{(a)}\{h_{A,\beta_A}(W_i)\}\Big)^2.$$

Here f_{R,κ_R} and $f_{A,\kappa_A} = (f^{(0)}_{A,\kappa_A}, f^{(1)}_{A,\kappa_A})$ are auxiliary regression heads trained to predict the direct drift proxies from the learned latent codes. The factor R_i restricts the attrition proxy regression to units for which $Y^\dagger$ is observed. The treatment weights use only observations from the corresponding factual arm and, when the working propensity is close to the true propensity, make the arm-specific projection close to marginal in W. At the population level, these losses yield the complete-case projection of $\varepsilon(X)$ and weighted projections of $(\delta_1(W), \delta_0(W))$ onto the latent representation classes. These penalties therefore encourage the representations to preserve precisely those directions required by the collaborative robustness conditions in (1)–(2).

We also use surrogate bottleneck penalties

$$\mathcal{B}_A(\beta_A; \mathcal{D}) = \frac{1}{|\mathcal{D}|} \sum_{i \in \mathcal{D}} \|h_{A,\beta_A}(W_i)\|_2^2, \qquad \mathcal{B}_R(\beta_R; \mathcal{D}) = \frac{1}{|\mathcal{D}|} \sum_{i \in \mathcal{D}} \|h_{R,\beta_R}(X_i)\|_2^2.$$

These penalties act directly on the encoders and yield more compressed and therefore more constrained propensity representations. Because neural encoders and heads are scale-nonidentifiable, the implementation standardizes the latent codes within each training fold and uses ordinary weight decay on the propensity and auxiliary heads; otherwise the encoder penalty could be partially offset by rescaling the downstream heads without changing the fitted scores.

Hyperparameter Library and Schedule. Let Θ_n denote a finite hyperparameter library. A library element

$$\theta = (d_A, d_R, \omega, \lambda_A, \lambda_R, \tau_A, \tau_R, \rho) \in \Theta_n$$

specifies the representation dimensions, sequential-regression weight, collaboration penalties, bottleneck penalties, and schedule exponent; the maximum budget B is fixed and the selected budget is b. For fixed θ and $b \in \{0, 1, \ldots, B\}$, define

$$\lambda_A^b = \lambda_A\left(1 - \frac{b}{B}\right)^\rho, \qquad \tau_A^b = \tau_A\left(1 - \frac{b}{B}\right)^\rho,$$

and equivalently λ_R^b and τ_R^b. Hence the terminal candidate for a given θ has $\lambda_A^B = \lambda_R^B = \tau_A^B = \tau_R^B = 0$ and reduces to an ordinary non-collaborative cross-entropy propensity fit within the representation class. As b increases, the propensity models become less constrained. The path therefore interpolates between strongly collaborative, strongly bottlenecked candidates and the standard fit.

The final estimator is selected over the joint configuration–budget library

$$\mathcal{S}_n := \{s = (\theta, b) : \theta \in \Theta_n,\ b = 1, \ldots, B\}, \qquad N_n := |\mathcal{S}_n|, \tag{3}$$

with $b = 0$ retained only as path initialization.

Targeted Selection. The sequential loss ℓ_ω measures regression fit, not directly the remaining target-level drift. Selecting on ℓ_ω alone is therefore only a surrogate: its population minimizer need not minimize the target remainder. We instead use a targeted criterion that estimates the candidate's squared EIF drift plus a second-moment penalty. Let $\mathcal{T} = \bigcup_{v=1}^{V} \mathcal{T}_v$ denote the inner folds. For each $s \in \mathcal{S}_n$, let $\widehat{\eta}_{-v}^{s}$ be the candidate built using $\mathcal{T} \setminus \mathcal{T}_v$ only, and define the validation estimate

$$\widehat{\psi}_{-v,\mathcal{T}_v}^{s} := \mathbb{E}_{\mathcal{T}_v}\{\widehat{Q}_{2,-v}^{s}(W,1) - \widehat{Q}_{2,-v}^{s}(W,0)\}.$$

The held-out EIF mean and second-moment are

$$\widehat{b}_n(s) = \frac{1}{V}\sum_{v=1}^{V} \mathbb{E}_{\mathcal{T}_v} D(\widehat{\eta}_{-v}^{s}, \widehat{\psi}_{-v,\mathcal{T}_v}^{s}; O), \quad \widehat{v}_n(s) = \frac{1}{V}\sum_{v=1}^{V} \mathbb{E}_{\mathcal{T}_v} D(\widehat{\eta}_{-v}^{s}, \widehat{\psi}_{-v,\mathcal{T}_v}^{s}; O)^2.$$

We select using

$$\mathcal{R}_n(s) = \widehat{b}_n(s)^2 + \frac{1}{|\mathcal{T}|}\widehat{v}_n(s) + \zeta \mathrm{CV}_{\mathrm{in}}\{\ell_\omega(\widehat{Q}_1^{s}, \widehat{Q}_2^{s})\}, \tag{4}$$

where $\zeta \geq 0$ is optional. The theoretical default is $\zeta = 0$, in which case the criterion targets the target-MSE scale: squared EIF drift plus an influence-function second-moment penalty. A small regression-loss component can improve finite-sample stability, but then the asymptotic argument requires the resulting combined risk to remain locally equivalent to the target remainder.

The selected configuration is

$$\widehat{s} = (\widehat{\theta}, \widehat{b}) \in \arg\min_{s \in \mathcal{S}_n} \mathcal{R}_n(s).$$

This step turns the representation dimension, regularization strengths, and computational budget into components of the estimator rather than externally fixed tuning constants. As in Super Learner and cross-validated TMLE, selection over a finite or slowly growing library can be absorbed into the asymptotic analysis by treating the selected candidate as a data-adaptive element of the candidate library [41,44,47]. A one-standard-error rule may be used as a conservative finite-sample variant, choosing the simpler candidate, smaller d_A, d_R, larger regularization, and smaller b, among candidates whose validation loss is statistically indistinguishable from the minimum.

Step 0: Baseline Candidate. For each $\theta \in \Theta_n$, begin by fitting initial outcome regressions on $\mathcal{T}$:

$$\widehat{Q}_1^0 \approx \mathbb{E}[Y \mid X, R = 1], \qquad \widehat{Q}_2^0 \approx \mathbb{E}[\widehat{Q}_1^0(X) \mid W, A].$$

We then set intercept-only propensity estimators

$$\widehat{\pi}_A^0(W) := \frac{1}{|\mathcal{T}|}\sum_{i \in \mathcal{T}} A_i, \qquad \widehat{\pi}_R^0(X) := \frac{1}{|\mathcal{T}|}\sum_{i \in \mathcal{T}} R_i.$$

Using $(\widehat{Q}_1^0, \widehat{Q}_2^0, \widehat{\pi}_A^0, \widehat{\pi}_R^0)$ as initial nuisance estimates, we apply the TMLE fluctuation step for the recovered ATE [10] and obtain

$$(\widehat{Q}_1^{\star 0}, \widehat{Q}_2^{\star 0}) \leftarrow \mathrm{TMLE}\Big[\widehat{Q}_1^0, \widehat{Q}_2^0, \widehat{\pi}_A^0, \widehat{\pi}_R^0; \mathcal{T}\Big]. \tag{5}$$

Although the baseline propensity estimators are constant, the associated clever covariates need not vanish, so this fluctuation step may still update the initial regressions. We initialize the budget path with either the targeted tuple $\widehat{\eta}^{\theta,0} = \left(\widehat{Q}_1^{\star 0}, \widehat{Q}_2^{\star 0}, \widehat{\pi}_A^0, \widehat{\pi}_R^0\right)$ or the untargeted tuple $\widehat{\eta}^{\theta,0} = \left(\widehat{Q}_1^0, \widehat{Q}_2^0, \widehat{\pi}_A^0, \widehat{\pi}_R^0\right)$. The targeted initialization may stabilize the first update by removing the drift captured by the initial propensity estimates, whereas the untargeted initialization keeps $b = 0$ closer to a plug-in starting point.

Budgeted Candidate Step $b = 1, \ldots, B$. For each candidate b and fixed hyperparameter value θ, proceed as follows.

1. Set the current working outcome regressions equal to the previous targeted candidate:
$$\widehat{Q}_1^b \leftarrow \widehat{Q}_1^{\star(b-1)}, \qquad \widehat{Q}_2^b \leftarrow \widehat{Q}_2^{\star(b-1)}.$$
2. Construct collaborative pseudo-outcomes on $\mathcal{T}$. For units with $R_i = 1$, define the direct attrition-drift proxy
$$e_{R,i}^b = \widehat{Q}_1^b(X_i) - Y_i^\dagger.$$
Next define the selection-corrected pseudo-outcome
$$\xi_i^b = \widehat{Q}_1^b(X_i) + \frac{R_i}{\widehat{\pi}_R^{b-1}(X_i)}\{Y_i^\dagger - \widehat{Q}_1^b(X_i)\},$$
where the residual term is set to zero when $R_i = 0$. Finally, for all units define the factual-arm second-stage drift proxy
$$e_{A,i}^b = \widehat{Q}_2^b(W_i, A_i) - \xi_i^b.$$
3. Fit the candidate attrition and treatment propensity models on $\mathcal{T}$
$$(\widehat{\beta}_R^b, \widehat{\gamma}_R^b, \widehat{\kappa}_R^b) \in \underset{\beta_R, \gamma_R, \kappa_R}{\arg\min} \left[\mathrm{CE}_R(\pi_{R,\beta_R,\gamma_R}) + \lambda_R^b \, \mathcal{C}_R(\beta_R, \kappa_R) + \tau_R^b \, \mathcal{B}_R(\beta_R)\right],$$
$$(\widehat{\beta}_A^b, \widehat{\gamma}_A^b, \widehat{\kappa}_A^b) \in \underset{\beta_A, \gamma_A, \kappa_A}{\arg\min} \left[\mathrm{CE}_A(\pi_{A,\beta_A,\gamma_A}) + \lambda_A^b \, \mathcal{C}_A(\beta_A, \kappa_A) + \tau_A^b \, \mathcal{B}_A(\beta_A)\right],$$
where $\mathcal{C}_R$ uses $e_{R,i}^b$, $\mathcal{C}_A$ uses $e_{A,i}^b$ with the fixed previous-level treatment weights
$$\omega_{A,i}^{(1),b-1} = \frac{A_i}{\widehat{\pi}_A^{b-1}(W_i)}, \qquad \omega_{A,i}^{(0),b-1} = \frac{1 - A_i}{1 - \widehat{\pi}_A^{b-1}(W_i)}.$$
4. Form the candidate propensity estimators
$$\widehat{\pi}_A^b(W_i) = \sigma\big(g_{A,\widehat{\gamma}_A^b}\{h_{A,\widehat{\beta}_A^b}(W_i)\}\big), \qquad \widehat{\pi}_R^b(X_i) = \sigma\big(g_{R,\widehat{\gamma}_R^b}\{W_i, A_i, h_{R,\widehat{\beta}_R^b}(X_i)\}\big).$$
In the implementation, we clip them below at the fixed level ϵ_{clip} and above at $1 - \epsilon_{\text{clip}}$; this clipping level is not a library coordinate.

5. Apply the TMLE targeting step for the recovered ATE, using $\widehat{Q}_1^b, \widehat{Q}_2^b$ as initial regressions and $\widehat{\pi}_A^b, \widehat{\pi}_R^b$ as candidate propensities:

$$(\widehat{Q}_1^{\star b}, \widehat{Q}_2^{\star b}) \leftarrow \mathrm{TMLE}\left[\widehat{Q}_1^b, \widehat{Q}_2^b, \widehat{\pi}_A^b, \widehat{\pi}_R^b; \mathcal{T}\right]. \tag{6}$$

6. Store the candidate $\widehat{\eta}^{\theta,b} = \left(\widehat{Q}_1^{\star b}, \widehat{Q}_2^{\star b}, \widehat{\pi}_A^b, \widehat{\pi}_R^b\right)$ and continue until $b = B$.

Final Estimator. The inner cross-validation step selects a joint hyperparameter–budget pair $\widehat{s} = (\widehat{\theta}, \widehat{b})$. After selection, the candidate construction procedure is rerun on the full outer training sample $\mathcal{T}$ with the selected pair, yielding training-fold nuisance estimates $\overline{\eta}^{\widehat{s}} = (\overline{Q}_1, \overline{Q}_2, \overline{\pi}_A, \overline{\pi}_R)$. To obtain the fold-specific estimator, we keep the selected representations and propensity scores fixed and apply a final low-dimensional TMLE fluctuation on the held-out evaluation fold $\mathcal{E}$:

$$(\widehat{Q}_1^{\sharp}, \widehat{Q}_2^{\sharp}) \leftarrow \mathrm{TMLE}\left[\overline{Q}_1, \overline{Q}_2, \overline{\pi}_A, \overline{\pi}_R; \mathcal{E}\right].$$

The fold-specific estimator is then

$$\widehat{\psi}_{\mathcal{E}}^{\sharp} = \frac{1}{|\mathcal{E}|} \sum_{i \in \mathcal{E}} \left\{\widehat{Q}_2^{\sharp}(W_i, 1) - \widehat{Q}_2^{\sharp}(W_i, 0)\right\}.$$

Outer cross-fitting averages $\widehat{\psi}_{\mathcal{E}_k}^{\sharp}$ across validation folds. This final validation-fold targeting step ensures that the empirical EIF equation is solved on the same observations used to evaluate the fold-specific plug-in estimate. Candidate construction, representation learning, and hyperparameter selection remain separated from $\mathcal{E}$, while the final targeting step estimates only a low-dimensional fluctuation parameter. If one instead targets only on $\mathcal{T}$ and evaluates a plug-in estimator on $\mathcal{E}$, the usual empirical EIF cancellation does not automatically hold on $\mathcal{E}$, and an additional stability argument is required.

For each fixed θ, the terminal candidate B coincides with the ordinary, non-collaborative propensity fit in that representation class. Including this endpoint allows the procedure to revert adaptively to the standard estimator when collaboration does not improve out-of-sample targeted fit. We emphasize that $b = B$ reduces to the ordinary TMLE of [10] only when the selected representation class is flexible enough to represent the full propensity mechanisms, for example with sufficiently large d_A, d_R and negligible bottleneck penalty. For moderate d_A, d_R, it is a representation-constrained TMLE, which is a deliberate regularization.

5 Asymptotic Validity

By the standard TMLE fluctuation argument, the targeting steps in equations (5) and (6) solve the empirical EIF equation on the sample used for targeting, up to numerical optimization error [10,42]. In the final estimator, this equation is solved on each outer validation fold after the hyperparameters have been selected on the corresponding training fold:

$$\mathbb{E}_{\mathcal{E}} D(\widehat{\eta}^{\widehat{s},\sharp}, \widehat{\psi}_{\mathcal{E}}^{\sharp}; O) = o_{P^\circ}(n^{-1/2}).$$

This validation-fold targeting is the CV-TMLE analogue of the usual empirical EIF-solving step [47].

Theorem 2 (High-level asymptotic validity). *Let $\psi^\circ = \Psi[P^\circ]$ be the true recovered ATE. Let $\mathcal{S}_n$ in (3) be the joint hyperparameter–budget library, and let $\widehat{s} \in \arg\min_{s\in\mathcal{S}_n} \mathcal{R}_n(s)$ be the inner-cross-validated selector based on (4). Let $\widehat{\eta}^{\widehat{s},\sharp}$ and $\widehat{\psi}^\sharp$ denote the outer validation-targeted nuisance tuple and the resulting cross-fitted plug-in estimator. Write $\bar{\eta}$ for the probability limit of the selected nuisance tuple; under collaborative robustness $\bar{\eta}$ need not equal η°. Assume:*

(A1) ***Sampling, positivity, and boundedness.*** *$O_1, \ldots, O_n$ are i.i.d. from P°. There exists $\epsilon_0 > 0$ such that*

$$\epsilon_0 \leq \pi_A^\circ(W) \leq 1 - \epsilon_0, \qquad \epsilon_0 \leq \pi_R^\circ(X) \leq 1$$

almost surely. The outcome, nuisance estimators after clipping, and EIFs induced by candidates in $\mathcal{S}_n$ are uniformly bounded.

(A2) ***Library-size and oracle-selection control.*** *The library is finite for each n and either N_n is fixed or grows slowly enough that the cross-validation oracle inequality applies. A sufficient condition for the empirical-process part of selection is $\log N_n = o(n^{1/2})$, together with the usual boundedness or sub-Gaussian envelope conditions. Equivalently, the selected risk satisfies*

$$\mathcal{R}_n(\widehat{s}) - \inf_{s\in\mathcal{S}_n} \mathcal{R}_n(s) = o_{P^\circ}(1),$$

up to numerical optimization error [41,44].

(A3) ***Existence of an asymptotically valid oracle configuration.*** *There exists a possibly data-dependent sequence $s_n^\dagger \in \mathcal{S}_n$ such that*

$$\left| Rem(\widehat{\eta}^{s_n^\dagger,\sharp}, \eta^\circ) \right| = o_{P^\circ}(1), \qquad Rem(\eta, \eta^\circ) := \mathbb{E}_{P^\circ}[D(\eta, \psi^\circ; O)].$$

This assumption holds when an oracle configuration satisfies one of the multiple-robustness regimes or the collaborative regimes of Theorem 1.

(A4) ***Selection-risk transfer and stability.*** *For any sequence $\widetilde{s}_n \subset \mathcal{S}_n$, if*

$$\mathcal{R}_n(\widetilde{s}_n) - \mathcal{R}_n(s_n^\dagger) = o_{P^\circ}(1),$$

then

$$\left| Rem(\widehat{\eta}^{\widetilde{s}_n,\sharp}, \eta^\circ) \right| - \left| Rem(\widehat{\eta}^{s_n^\dagger,\sharp}, \eta^\circ) \right| = o_{P^\circ}(1).$$

This condition is plausible when the leading part of $\mathcal{R}_n$ is the held-out EIF-drift criterion in (4), because the criterion targets the squared drift. If the optional regression-loss component dominates, or if the procedure is refitted after selection, the condition is a stability assumption transferring the oracle property from the selected library index to the final refitted estimator.

(A5) ***Cross-fitted empirical-process control.*** *With*

$$F(\widehat{\eta}, \bar{\eta}, \psi^\circ; O) = D(\widehat{\eta}, \psi^\circ; O) - D(\bar{\eta}, \psi^\circ; O),$$

the selected nuisance tuple satisfies, fold by fold,

$$(\mathbb{E}_{\mathcal{E}} - \mathbb{E}^\circ) F(\widehat{\eta}^{\widehat{s},\sharp}, \bar{\eta}, \psi^\circ; O) = o_{P^\circ}(n^{-1/2}).$$

Outer cross-fitting, together with the finite-dimensional validation-fold fluctuation, avoids Donsker restrictions for the initial nuisance learners; the selected-candidate version requires the same control uniformly over the finite library, with the usual $\sqrt{\log N_n}$ max-inequality factor.

Then the following hold.

(i) ***Consistency.*** *If assumptions* (A1)–(A5) *hold, then*

$$\widehat{\psi}^\sharp \xrightarrow{P^\circ} \psi^\circ.$$

(ii) ***Rate asymptotic linearity.*** *If, in addition, the oracle satisfies*

$$\left| Rem(\widehat{\eta}^{s_n^\dagger,\sharp}, \eta^\circ) \right| = o_{P^\circ}(n^{-1/2}),$$

and (A2)–(A4) *hold at the $o_{P^\circ}(n^{-1/2})$ scale, then*

$$\sqrt{n}\big(\widehat{\psi}^\sharp - \psi^\circ\big) = \frac{1}{\sqrt{n}} \sum_{i=1}^{n} D(\bar{\eta}, \psi^\circ; O_i) + o_{P^\circ}(1) \rightsquigarrow N\big(0, \mathrm{var}_{P^\circ}\big(D(\bar{\eta}, \psi^\circ; O)\big)\big).$$

Thus collaborative robustness can deliver $\sqrt{n}$-asymptotic normality even when $\bar{\eta} \neq \eta^\circ$, but the limiting influence function is then generally not the EIF.

(iii) ***Efficiency.*** *If, moreover, all nuisance components are consistent for the truth, $\bar{\eta} = \eta^\circ$, and the usual second-order product-rate conditions hold, then*

$$\sqrt{n}\big(\widehat{\psi}^\sharp - \psi^\circ\big) \rightsquigarrow N\big(0, \mathrm{var}_{P^\circ}\big(D(\eta^\circ, \psi^\circ; O)\big)\big),$$

and the estimator attains the semiparametric efficiency bound.

Proofs and a remark on the high-level oracle-transfer and stability assumptions are given in the supplementary material. The theorem treats d_A, d_R, b, ω, λ_A, λ_R, τ_A, τ_R, and ρ as selected over a finite or slowly growing library; it does not prove that the neural optimizer consistently discovers an oracle representation.

5.1 Variance Estimation

For a single outer cross-fitting split, we use the empirical variance of the EIF-form estimating function evaluated at the selected validation-targeted nuisance estimates:

$$\widehat{\mathrm{var}}_{\mathrm{IF}} = \frac{1}{n} \widehat{\mathrm{var}}_n \left[D(\widehat{\eta}^{\widehat{s},\sharp}, \widehat{\psi}^\sharp; O) \right].$$

If the whole procedure is repeated over M independent random split assignments, with estimates $\widehat{\psi}_m$, EIF-form variance $\widehat{\text{var}}_{\text{IF},m}$, and $\bar{\psi} = M^{-1} \sum_{m=1}^{M} \widehat{\psi}_m$, define

$$V_W = \frac{1}{M} \sum_{m=1}^{M} \widehat{\text{var}}_{\text{IF},m}, \qquad V_B = \frac{1}{M-1} \sum_{m=1}^{M} (\widehat{\psi}_m - \bar{\psi})^2.$$

If the reported point estimate is the average $\bar{\psi}$, the pure Monte Carlo contribution of split randomization is V_B/M. A conservative instability-aware interval may instead use $V_W + V_B$, treating split and configuration variability as part of the reported uncertainty.

6 Simulation Task

We evaluate the proposed collaborative representation-based TMLE in a simulation study for the recovered average treatment effect under outcome selection. The design is intentionally challenging. The sequential outcome regressions are deliberately misspecified, which creates a difficult setting for the plug-in estimator. At the same time, the treatment and missingness mechanisms include many strong treatment instruments and missingness instruments. These variables make the propensity scores highly predictable, but much of this predictive signal is not directly relevant for reducing target-parameter bias. As a result, standard one-step and TMLE estimators using aggressively predictive neural propensity scores can suffer from unstable inverse-probability corrections. The simulation therefore probes the central motivation of collaborative learning: propensity score models should be learned with respect to the target parameter, not only with respect to treatment or missingness prediction. Further details on the data-generating process, nuisance learners, collaborative path, and inner targeted selector are given in the supplementary material. Code is available at: https://github.com/johandh2o/cr-tmle-outcome-selection.

The collaborative candidates use two fixed representation/regularization settings $(d_A, d_R, \omega, \lambda_A, \lambda_R, \tau_A, \tau_R, \rho)$: $\theta_1 = (3, 3, 0.6, 2.00, 5.00, 0.015, 0.005, 1.0)$ and $\theta_2 = (4, 4, 0.8, 3.00, 3.00, 0.010, 0.010, 1.0)$. The library estimator selects between them over budgets $b \in \{1, \ldots, B\}$, with $b = 0$ used only to initialize the path.

Table 1 illustrates distinct failure modes induced by the simulation design. The plug-in estimator has a persistent positive bias, approximately 1.52 across all sample sizes, which is consistent with the deliberate misspecification of the sequential outcome regressions. The neural-propensity TMLE benchmark is also unstable in this design. It has negative bias at every sample size, with biases -2.055, -0.824, and -2.134, and it has the largest MSE in all three sample sizes. This behavior suggests that the targeting step can amplify instability when the propensity models devote substantial capacity to treatment instruments and missingness instruments that improve prediction but do not necessarily reduce the drift of the target estimator.

The one-step and ridge Riesz estimators achieve the lowest MSE in these experiments. The one-step estimator has the smallest MSE at $n = 3000$, with

Table 1. Simulation performance by estimator and sample size. Bias and MSE are rounded to three decimals. Within each sample size, the smallest absolute bias and smallest MSE are shown in bold (average values over 100 Monte Carlo repetitions).

Estimator	$n = 3000$		$n = 5000$		$n = 7000$	
	Bias	MSE	Bias	MSE	Bias	MSE
CR-TMLE, θ_1 only	**−0.477**	4.787	**0.004**	6.267	**0.146**	3.479
CR-TMLE, θ_2 only	−0.539	5.915	0.145	4.685	0.176	2.909
CR-TMLE library, θ_1 and θ_2	−0.871	6.228	−0.059	5.575	−0.183	4.403
One-step, neural propensities	1.044	**1.230**	0.271	4.433	0.714	0.932
TMLE, neural propensities	−2.055	11.492	−0.824	6.665	−2.134	10.819
Plug-in, linear outcome reg.	1.531	2.428	1.520	2.371	1.521	2.364
Ridge Riesz regression	1.078	1.295	0.628	**0.575**	0.849	**0.794**

MSE 1.230, while ridge Riesz has the smallest MSE at $n = 5000$ and $n = 7000$, with MSEs 0.575 and 0.794, respectively. However, these low-MSE results should be interpreted together with their remaining positive bias. The one-step estimator has biases 1.044, 0.271, and 0.714, while the ridge Riesz estimator has biases 1.078, 0.628, and 0.849 for $n = 3000$, 5000, and 7000, respectively. Thus, in this simulation, the favorable MSE of these benchmarks appears to be driven partly by lower variability rather than by uniformly accurate bias correction.

The collaborative estimators show a different pattern. The θ_1-only CR-TMLE has the smallest absolute bias at all three sample sizes, with biases −0.477, 0.004, and 0.146 for $n = 3000$, 5000, and 7000, respectively. The θ_2-only estimator is also substantially less biased than the plug-in, TMLE, one-step, and ridge Riesz benchmarks, and it attains the smallest MSE among the collaborative estimators at $n = 7000$. The library estimator remains less biased than the non-collaborative benchmarks, but it does not uniformly select the most bias-reducing or most stable candidate, illustrating a finite-sample bias–stability trade-off.

Overall, the results should not be read as showing uniform dominance of CR-TMLE over all benchmarks. Rather, they support the more specific claim targeted by this experiment: in a setting with misspecified outcome regressions and many propensity-relevant but target-irrelevant instruments, collaborative representation learning can substantially reduce bias relative to plug-in, one-step, TMLE, and direct Riesz alternatives. The price is that the bias-reducing collaborative fits can have larger MSE, reflecting a genuine bias–variance trade-off. These findings are consistent with the motivation for a targeted collaborative selector: nuisance learning should balance estimated drift and variability for the parameter of interest, rather than optimize for prediction.

7 Conclusion

We introduced a target-aware alternative to stepwise CTMLE for causal effects under outcome selection. The estimator learns low-dimensional treatment and selection representations from drift-oriented pseudo-outcomes, uses a finite collaborative library selected by targeted cross-validation, and performs final targeting on held-out folds to preserve the empirical EIF equation. Methodologically, the proposal replaces order-dependent covariate search with representation learning that is explicitly tied to the bias of the target parameter. The theory clarifies when collaboration, rather than full propensity consistency, is sufficient for valid estimation, and it sharpens the exposure-side robustness condition by showing that arm-specific drift information is needed. The simulations illustrate the intended behavior in a challenging design with misspecified outcome regressions and many target-irrelevant instruments: collaborative representations can substantially reduce bias relative to plug-in, one-step, TMLE, and Riesz alternatives, although the most aggressive bias reduction may increase variance. These results motivate richer collaborative libraries and more stable selectors in future work. Overall, the paper shows that propensity learning for targeted causal inference should be organized around the estimand, not around nuisance prediction alone.

References

1. Avagyan, V., Vansteelandt, S.: Stable inverse probability weighting estimation for longitudinal studies. Scand. J. Stat. **48**(3), 1046–1067 (2021)
2. Bareinboim, E., Pearl, J.: Controlling selection bias in causal inference. In: Lawrence, N., Girolami, M. (eds.) Proceedings of the Fifteenth International Conference on Artificial Intelligence and Statistics, AISTATS, vol. 22, pp. 100–108. PMLR, La Palma, Canary Islands (2012)
3. Bhattacharya, R., Nabi, R., Shpitser, I., Robins, J.: Identification in missing data models represented by directed acyclic graphs. In: Adams, R., Gogate, V. (eds.) Proceedings of the 35th Conference on Uncertainty in Artificial Intelligence. UAI, vol. 115, pp. 1149–1158. PMLR (2020)
4. Bia, M., Huber, M., Lafférs, L.: Double machine learning for sample selection models. J. Bus. Econ. Stat. **42**(3), 958–969 (2024)
5. Biele, G., et al.: Bias from self selection and loss to follow-up in prospective cohort studies. Eur. J. Epidemiol. **34**(10), 927–938 (2019)
6. Chernozhukov, V., et al.: Double/debiased machine learning for treatment and structural parameters. Economet. J. **21**(1), C1–C68 (2018)
7. Chernozhukov, V., et al.: RieszNet and ForestRiesz: automatic debiased machine learning with neural nets and random forests. In: Sabato, S. (ed.) Proceedings of the 39th International Conference on Machine Learning. ICML, vol. 162, pp. 3901–3914. PMLR (2022)
8. Chernozhukov, V., Newey, W., Singh, R.: Debiased machine learning of global and local parameters using regularized Riesz representers. Economet. J. **25**(3), 576–601 (2022)
9. Correa, J., Tian, J., Bareinboim, E.: Generalized adjustment under confounding and selection biases. In: Proceedings of the AAAI Conference on Artificial Intelligence, vol. 32, no. 1 (2018)
10. de Aguas, J., Pensar, J., Varnet Pérez, T., Biele, G.: Recovery and inference of causal effects with sequential adjustment for confounding and attrition. J. Causal Inference **13**(1), 20240009 (2025). https://doi.org/10.1515/jci-2024-0009

11. Díaz, I.: Machine learning in the estimation of causal effects: targeted minimum loss-based estimation and double/debiased machine learning. Biostatistics **21**(2), 353–358 (2019)
12. Gruber, S., van der Laan, M.: Targeted maximum likelihood estimation: a gentle introduction. Am. Stat. **63**(4), 1–38 (2009)
13. Guo, A., Zhao, J., Nabi, R.: Sufficient identification conditions and semiparametric estimation under missing not at random mechanisms. In: Evans, R., Shpitser, I. (eds.) Proceedings of the Thirty-Ninth Conference on Uncertainty in Artificial Intelligence. UAI, vol. 216, pp. 777–787. PMLR (2023)
14. Huber, M.: Identification of average treatment effects in social experiments under alternative forms of attrition. J. Educ. Behav. Stat. **37**(3), 443–474 (2012)
15. Johansson, F., Shalit, U., Kallus, N., Sontag, D.: Generalization bounds and representation learning for estimation of potential outcomes and causal effects. J. Mach. Learn. Res. **23**(166), 1–50 (2022)
16. Ju, C., et al.: Scalable collaborative targeted learning for high-dimensional data. Stat. Methods Med. Res. **28**(2), 532–554 (2019)
17. Kato, M.: Riesz representer fitting under Bregman divergence: a unified framework for debiased machine learning. arXiv preprint arXiv:2601.07752 (2026)
18. Kato, M., Teshima, T.: Non-negative Bregman divergence minimization for deep direct density ratio estimation. In: Meila, M., Zhang, T. (eds.) Proceedings of the 38th International Conference on Machine Learning. ICML, vol. 139, pp. 5320–5333. PMLR (2021)
19. Lewin, A., Brondeel, R., Benmarhnia, T., Thomas, F., Chaix, B.: Attrition bias related to missing outcome data: a longitudinal simulation study. Epidemiology **29**(1) (2018)
20. Luo, W., Zhu, Y., Ghosh, D.: On estimating regression-based causal effects using sufficient dimension reduction. Biometrika **104**(1), 51–65 (2017)
21. McIsaac, M., Cook, R.: Statistical methods for incomplete data: results on model misspecification. Stat. Methods Med. Res. **26**(1), 248–267 (2017)
22. Mohan, K., Pearl, J., Ghahramani, Z., Welling, M., Cortes, C., Lawrence, N.: Graphical models for recovering probabilistic and causal queries from missing data. In: Weinberger, K. (ed.) Advances in Neural Information Processing Systems. NeurIPS, vol. 27. Curran Associates, Inc. (2014)
23. Mohan, K., Pearl, J.: Graphical models for processing missing data. J. Am. Stat. Assoc. **116**(534), 1023–1037 (2021)
24. Mohan, K., et al.: Graphical models for inference with missing data. In: Weinberger, K. (ed.) Advances in Neural Information Processing Systems. NeurIPS, vol. 26. Curran Associates, Inc. (2013)
25. Moosavi, N., Häggström, J., de Luna, X.: The costs and benefits of uniformly valid causal inference with high-dimensional nuisance parameters. Stat. Sci. **38**(1), 1–12 (2023)
26. Nabi, R., Bhattacharya, R., Shpitser, I.: Full law identification in graphical models of missing data: completeness results. In: Proceedings of the 37th International Conference on Machine Learning, ICML, pp. 7153–7163. PMLR (2020)
27. Negi, A.: Doubly weighted m-estimation for nonrandom assignment and missing outcomes. J. Causal Inference **12**(1), 20230016 (2024)
28. Pearl, J.: Causality, 2nd edn. Cambridge University Press, Cambridge (2009)
29. Rhodes, B., Xu, K., Gutmann, M.: Telescoping density-ratio estimation. In: Proceedings of the 34th International Conference on Neural Information Processing Systems, NeurIPS. Curran Associates Inc., Red Hook, NY, USA (2020)

30. Robins, J., Sued, M., Lei-Gomez, Q., Rotnitzky, A.: Comment: performance of double-robust estimators when inverse probability weights are highly variable. Stat. Sci. **22**(4), 544–559 (2007)
31. Saadati, M., Tian, J.: Adjustment criteria for recovering causal effects from missing data. In: Joint European Conference on Machine Learning and Knowledge Discovery in Databases, pp. 561–577. ECML PKDD, Springer (2019)
32. Schnitzer, M., Lok, J., Gruber, S.: Variable selection for confounder control, flexible modeling and collaborative targeted minimum loss-based estimation in causal inference. Int. J. Biostat. **12**(1), 97–115 (2016)
33. Seaman, S., White, I.: Review of inverse probability weighting for dealing with missing data. Stat. Methods Med. Res. **22**(3), 278–295 (2013)
34. Shalit, U., Johansson, F., Sontag, D.: Estimating individual treatment effect: generalization bounds and algorithms. In: Proceedings of the 34th International Conference on Machine Learning. Proceedings of Machine Learning Research, vol. 70, pp. 3076–3085. PMLR (2017)
35. Shortreed, S., Ertefaie, A.: Outcome-adaptive lasso: variable selection for causal inference. Biometrics **73**(4), 1111–1122 (2017)
36. Sun, B., et al.: Inverse-probability-weighted estimation for monotone and nonmonotone missing data. Am. J. Epidemiol. **187**(3), 585–591 (2017)
37. Tikka, S., Hyttinen, A., Karvanen, J.: Causal effect identification from multiple incomplete data sources: a general search-based approach. J. Stat. Softw. **99**, 1–40 (2021)
38. van der Laan, L., Lin, Z., Carone, M., Luedtke, A.: Stabilized inverse probability weighting via isotonic calibration. In: Huang, B., Drton, M. (eds.) Proceedings of the Fourth Conference on Causal Learning and Reasoning. CLeaR, vol. 275, pp. 139–173. PMLR (2025)
39. van der Laan, L., Ulloa-Pérez, E., Carone, M., Luedtke, A.: Causal isotonic calibration for heterogeneous treatment effects. In: Krause, A., Brunskill, E., Cho, K., Engelhardt, B., Sabato, S., Scarlett, J. (eds.) Proceedings of the 40th International Conference on Machine Learning. ICML, vol. 202, pp. 34831–34854. PMLR (2023)
40. van der Laan, M., Gruber, S.: Collaborative double robust targeted maximum likelihood estimation. Int. J. Biostat. **6**(1) (2010)
41. van der Laan M., Polley, E., Hubbard, A.: Super learner. Stat. Appl. Genet. Mol. Biol. **6**(1) (2007)
42. van der Laan, M., Rose, S.: Targeted Learning: Causal Inference for Observational and Experimental Data. Springer Series in Statistics. Springer, New York (2011)
43. van der Laan, M., Rubin, D.: Targeted maximum likelihood learning. Int. J. Biostat. **2**(1) (2006)
44. van der Vaart, A., Dudoit, S., van der Laan, M.: Oracle inequalities for multi-fold cross validation. Stat. Decisions **24**(3), 351–371 (2006)
45. Wei, K., Qin, G., Zhang, J., Sui, X.: Doubly robust estimation in causal inference with missing outcomes: with an application to the aerobics center longitudinal study. Comput. Stat. Data Anal. **168**, 107399 (2022)
46. Wei, K., Qin, G., Zhang, J., Sui, X.: Multiply robust estimation of the average treatment effect with missing outcomes. J. Stat. Comput. Simul. **93**(10), 1479–1495 (2023)
47. Zheng, W., van der Laan, M.: Cross-validated targeted minimum-loss-based estimation. In: van der Laan, M., Rose, S. (eds.) Targeted Learning: Causal Inference for Observational and Experimental Data. Springer Series in Statistics, pp. 459–474. Springer, New York (2011)

MDL Meets Latent Confounders: LNML-Based Causal Discovery

Zhongyi Que[1(✉)], Shin Matsushima[2], and Kenji Yamanishi[1]

[1] Graduate School of Information Science and Technology, The University of Tokyo, Tokyo, Japan
{que-zhongyi,yamanishi}@g.ecc.u-tokyo.ac.jp

[2] Graduate School of Arts and Sciences, The University of Tokyo, Tokyo, Japan
smatsus@graco.c.u-tokyo.ac.jp

Abstract. Causal discovery with nonlinear mechanisms and latent confounders remains challenging. Existing methods often rely on either linear assumptions or causal sufficiency, limiting their applicability. We propose an MDL-based causal discovery framework that explicitly accounts for latent confounders while allowing flexible nonlinear mechanisms by minimizing the luckiness normalized maximum likelihood (LNML) code-length. The causal relationship between each variable pair is determined by selecting the shortest code-length of the causal model, and we introduce the notion of Δ-pseudo-collinearity to identify dependencies induced by latent confounders. Based on these ideas, we develop a greedy algorithm, termed Pseudo-Collinearity Guided Causal Discovery (PCG-CD). Experiments on synthetic and real-world datasets demonstrate that the proposed method accurately recovers directed causal relationships and effectively detects latent confounders.

Keywords: Minimum description length principle · Causal discovery · Latent confounder · LNML code-length

1 Introduction

1.1 Motivation

Understanding causation is a fundamental problem in science, as it enables the identification of underlying relationships among variables in complex systems.

Most existing causal discovery methods assume causal sufficiency, meaning that all relevant variables are observed and no latent confounders exist. However, confounding factors are ubiquitous in real-world systems and pose major challenges for causal estimation. When analyzing the relationship between two variables X and Y, the observed dependence may arise from a direct causal effect, or from a latent confounder Z acting as a common cause. Only a limited number of approaches relax the causal sufficiency assumption, yet failing to account for confounders can introduce substantial bias and lead to incorrect conclusions.

M. Ceci et al. (Eds.): ECML PKDD 2026, LNAI 16941, pp. 641–658, 2027.
https://doi.org/10.1007/978-3-032-37654-1_37

In addition, causal mechanisms in practical applications, such as biology, neuroscience, economics, and climate science, are rarely linear. Restricting models to linear relationships risks model misspecification and may further obscure causal structure, particularly in the presence of latent factors. Incorporating nonlinear mechanisms is therefore essential for improving identifiability and robustness in causal discovery.

(a) X causes Y. (b) Y causes X. (c) Latent confounder exists. (d) Independence.

Fig. 1. Four possible causal relationships between two variables X and Y.

Kaltenpoth and Vreeken [8] suggested that an information-theoretic approach can help mitigate overfitting when estimating causal models with confounders. For example, suppose $X \not\perp\!\!\!\perp Y$ is observed. If X causes Y and no confounder is present, the joint distribution follows $P(X, Y) = P(X)P(Y|X)$. Alternatively, if a confounder Z influences both X and Y, the joint distribution becomes $P(X, Y, Z) = P(Z)P(X|Z)P(Y|Z)$. A straightforward method to identify a confounder is to check whether we can construct $\hat{Z}$ such that $X \perp\!\!\!\perp Y \mid Z$. A trivial solution is to set $\hat{Z} = X$, which ensures conditional independence even in the absence of a true confounder. Therefore, it is necessary to consider both the complexity of $\hat{Z}$ and its effect on X and Y.

Motivated by this observation, we adopt the minimum description length (MDL) principle [4,20,26] for causal discovery. Under this framework, the causal relationship between any two variables, whether $X \to Y$, $X \leftarrow Y$, $X \leftarrow Z \to Y$, or independence, is determined by selecting the model with the shortest codelength, as illustrated in Fig. 1. We employ the luckiness normalized maximum likelihood (LNML) code-length [4,15], which avoids explicit parameter priors and naturally incorporates sparsity through the luckiness function.

In this work, we address causal discovery with latent confounders by estimating nonlinear causal models through LNML-based model selection under the MDL principle.

1.2 Related Work

Classical causal discovery methods include constraint-based and score-based approaches. Constraint-based methods such as PC [24] infer a causal graph by testing conditional independencies and applying orientation rules, while FCI extends PC to allow latent confounders. Score-based methods, such as GES [2] and its variants [18], employ greedy search with penalized likelihood criteria but may converge to local optima.

To achieve identifiability beyond Markov Equivalence Classes (MECs), functional causal models (FCMs) impose assumptions on structural equations and noise distributions, including LiNGAM [21] with linear non-Gaussian mechanisms and ANM [5] with nonlinear relationships. Within the LiNGAM framework, ICA-LiNGAM [21] and DirectLiNGAM [22] recover full causal orderings under causal sufficiency, while ParceLiNGAM [25] and RCD [12] address unmeasured confounding by identifying variable pairs influenced by latent common causes and producing partially directed graphs with bidirected edges. Other extensions consider post-nonlinear assumptions [28] or address latent confounding in restricted settings, including CoCa [8] for nonlinear pairwise relations, CLOUD [11] for discrete data, and NOCADILAC [10], which models latent factors under a post-nonlinear assumption.

Information-theoretic approaches formulate causal discovery as a model selection problem under the MDL principle. Early methods such as SLOPE [13] and ORIGO [1] focus on bivariate or local causal direction, while GLOBE [14] extends MDL-based scoring to multivariate graphs under causal sufficiency. To relax the causal sufficiency assumption, latent-variable extensions based on MDL have been explored in model selection and causal discovery. For example, the decomposed normalized maximum likelihood (DNML) code-length criterion was proposed for hierarchical latent variable models [27], while methods such as CDHC [9] introduce hidden variables when doing so reduces the overall description length, though existing results mainly focus on linear Gaussian mechanisms.

Unlike existing MDL-based approaches that primarily assume linear Gaussian mechanisms or focus on limited settings, our method performs multivariate causal graph discovery with latent confounders under nonlinear mechanisms in continuous data, using LNML code-lengths for principled model selection.

1.3 Significance and Novelty

- *LNML-based code-length for causal models with latent confounders.* We introduce an LNML-based code-length formulation for estimating causal graphs in the presence of latent confounders. By adopting a tractable approximation under mild assumptions on the causal equations, the proposed framework enables efficient model selection without restricting the form of the causal mechanisms. To the best of our knowledge, this is the first MDL-based method that estimates causal graphs with latent confounders in a mechanism-agnostic manner.
- *Identification of latent confounders via pseudo-collinearity.* We propose the notion of Δ-pseudo-collinearity to identify latent confounders through differences in code-length. We establish a theoretical result showing that this gap grows at most linearly with the sample size in linear settings, with the coefficient determined by the noise level and the similarity of the causal mechanisms. We also discuss extensions to nonlinear cases.
- *PCG-CD: an efficient causal discovery algorithm.* We develop the PCG-CD algorithm, a greedy causal discovery algorithm that explicitly handles

latent confounders. Compared to GES and related score-based methods with $O(|V|^3)$ complexity, PCG-CD reduces edge evaluation to $O(|V|^2)$.
- *Empirical validation.* Extensive experiments on both synthetic and real-world datasets demonstrate that PCG-CD accurately recovers directed causal relationships and effectively detects latent confounders.

Code and supplementary material are available at: https://github.com/ZYQue/PCG-CD.

2 Notation and Preliminaries

We introduce the notation and assumptions for causal models, first under causal sufficiency and then extending to settings with latent confounders. We also summarize the MDL-based code-length formulation used throughout the paper.

2.1 Causal Model

We begin with a setting with causal sufficiency. A causal model is defined as $M = (G, F)$, where $G = (\boldsymbol{V}, \boldsymbol{E})$ is a directed acyclic graph (DAG) over continuous variables $\boldsymbol{V} = \boldsymbol{X} \in \mathbb{R}^d$, and $F = \{f_i\}_{i=1}^d$ denotes the causal mechanisms. An edge $X_{(i)} \to X_{(j)}$ indicates that $X_{(i)}$ is a parent of $X_{(j)}$.

The causal relationships between variables are described by structural equation models (SEMs) [16]:

$$X_{(i)} = f_i(\mathrm{pa}_i) + \varepsilon_i, \quad \varepsilon_i \perp\!\!\!\perp \mathrm{pa}_i,$$

where pa_i denotes the parents of $X_{(i)}$ in G, f_i is the causal function, and ε_i represents noise.

We then relax causal sufficiency by allowing latent confounders. Let $\boldsymbol{Z}$ denote unobserved variables that may jointly influence observed variables. The DAG including the confounders is then represented as $G = (\boldsymbol{V}, \boldsymbol{E})$, where $\boldsymbol{V} = (\boldsymbol{X}, \boldsymbol{Z})$. The causal relationship for variable $X_{(i)}$ becomes:

$$X_{(i)} = f_i(\mathrm{pa}_i, \mathrm{pa}_i^Z) + \varepsilon_i, \quad \varepsilon_i \perp\!\!\!\perp (\mathrm{pa}_i, \mathrm{pa}_i^Z),$$

where pa_i denotes the set of observed parents of $X^{(i)}$ in G, and pa_i^Z denotes the set of latent parents of $X^{(i)}$.

2.2 Minimum Description Length Principle

According to the MDL principle, the optimal model is the one with the minimum normalized maximum likelihood (NML) code-length [23]. In this work, we adopt the luckiness normalized maximum likelihood (LNML) code-length [4] for causal model selection. LNML extends the original NML formulation by incorporating prior knowledge through a penalty term. This allows us to enforce sparsity in the causal DAG and to control the complexity of the causal mechanisms. In our framework, the LNML code-length is computed from the normalized maximum posterior distribution, incorporating a sparsity constraint.

The LNML distribution is defined over a model class $\mathcal{M}$, where $p(\boldsymbol{X}; M)$ denotes the probability density of data X under model M, and $g(M)$ is a penalty function that controls model complexity. It is given by

$$p_{\mathrm{LNML}}(\boldsymbol{X}) := \frac{\max_{M \in \mathcal{M}} p(\boldsymbol{X}; M) e^{-g(M)}}{C_n}, \tag{1}$$

where

$$C_n := \int \max_{M \in \mathcal{M}} p(\boldsymbol{X}; M) e^{-g(M)} d\boldsymbol{X},$$

also referred to as the parametric complexity, is evaluated over all possible data $\boldsymbol{X}$ of length n.

The LNML code-length is defined as the negative log-likelihood of (1):

$$\begin{aligned} \mathcal{L}_{\mathrm{LNML}}(\boldsymbol{X}) &= -\log p_{\mathrm{LNML}}(\boldsymbol{X}) \\ &= \min_{M \in \mathcal{M}} \{-\log p(\boldsymbol{X}; M) + g(M)\} + \log C_n. \end{aligned} \tag{2}$$

When the penalty term $g(\cdot)$ is omitted, (2) reduces to the original NML code-length. Computing the LNML code-length is intractable due to the parametric complexity term C_n, so an approximation is used. To preserve MDL properties, the approximation is constructed as an upper bound on C_n, whose form depends on the probability model $p(\cdot)$, the penalty function $g(\cdot)$, and the data assumptions.

3 Luckiness Normalized Maximum Likelihood Code-Length for Causal Model Discovery

To flexibly model nonlinear causal mechanisms and enable principled model selection in the presence of latent confounders, we assume Gaussian process models and develop an LNML-based code-length for scoring causal models.

3.1 Assumptions on the Causal Mechanism

We model causal mechanisms using Gaussian processes (GPs) [19]. A GP is a collection of random variables such that any finite subset follows a multivariate normal distribution, and the associated function satisfies

$$f(x) \sim \mathcal{GP}(m(x), \kappa(x, x')),$$

where $m(x) = \mathbb{E}[f(x)]$ is the mean function, with the expectation taken with respect to the Gaussian process prior over functions, and $\kappa(x, x')$ is the covariance (kernel) function.

Assuming GP mechanisms removes the restrictive linearity assumption between a variable and its parents. A GP can also be represented as a linear model in a (possibly infinite-dimensional) feature space: $f = \sum_i \alpha_i \phi_i$.

Given data $\{(x_i, y_i)\}_{i=1}^n$, we assume

$$y_i = f(x_i) + \varepsilon_i, \quad \varepsilon_i \sim \mathcal{N}(0, \sigma^2),$$

so that the outputs $\boldsymbol{y}$ follow a joint Gaussian distribution:

$$\boldsymbol{y} \sim \mathcal{N}(\boldsymbol{m}, \boldsymbol{K} + \sigma^2 \boldsymbol{I}),$$

where $\boldsymbol{m} = [m(x_1), \ldots, m(x_n)]^T$ and $\boldsymbol{K}_{ij} = \kappa(x_i, x_j)$.

For a given x, the mechanism can be estimated as:

$$\begin{aligned} f(x) &= [\kappa(x_1, x), \ldots, \kappa(x_n, x)]^T (\boldsymbol{K} + \sigma^2 \boldsymbol{I})^{-1} \boldsymbol{y} \\ &= \sum_{i=1}^{n} \alpha_i \kappa(x_i, x), \end{aligned} \tag{3}$$

where $\boldsymbol{\alpha} = (\boldsymbol{K} + \sigma^2 \boldsymbol{I})^{-1} \boldsymbol{y}$ and α_i is the ith value of this vector.

GPs are adopted for two reasons. First, the induced reproducing kernel Hilbert space (RKHS) $\mathcal{H}$ may be infinite-dimensional, enabling a nonparametric representation of causal mechanisms and their code-lengths. Second, as shown by Kakade et al. [7], GP-based learning minimizes penalized regret, which aligns with the minimax formulation underlying NML code-length [23]. Note that not all model classes admit a valid NML distribution.

We use the radial basis function (RBF) kernel

$$\kappa(x, x') = \sigma_f^2 \exp\left(-\tfrac{1}{2l} \|x - x'\|_2^2\right), \tag{4}$$

as it is widely used in practice.

3.2 Luckiness Normalized Maximum Likelihood Code-Length

We first define the MDL score without confounders based on Gaussian process (GP) mechanisms. For a target variable $X_{(i)}$ with parents $\text{pa}_i(G)$ in a causal graph G, we fit a GP regression $f_i : \text{pa}_i(G) \to X_{(i)}$. Let $p(X_{(i)}|\text{pa}_i(G))$ denote the conditional probability of $X_{(i)}$ given its parent variables $\text{pa}_i(G)$, as induced by the Gaussian process regression model. The corresponding Bayesian score is given by [6,7]

$$\begin{aligned} L(X_{(i)}|\text{pa}_i(G)) := \min_{f_i \in \mathcal{H}_\kappa} \big(&- \log p(X_{(i)}|\text{pa}_i(G)) \\ &+ \|f_i\|_\kappa^2 \big) + \tfrac{1}{2} \log \det \left(\sigma^{-2} \boldsymbol{K}_{\text{pa}_i(G)} + \boldsymbol{I} \right), \end{aligned} \tag{5}$$

where $\|f_i\|_\kappa^2$ penalizes the complexity of the mechanism. For GP models learned from finite data, this term can be computed as

$$\|f_i\|_\kappa^2 = \boldsymbol{\alpha}^T \boldsymbol{K}_{\text{pa}_i(G)} \boldsymbol{\alpha},$$

with kernel matrix $\boldsymbol{K}_{\mathrm{pa}_i(G)}$ constructed using the kernel function defined in (4) and vector $\boldsymbol{\alpha}$ defined in (3).

The score in (5) can be viewed as an upper bound on the negative log-likelihood under a Bayesian prior, assuming the model follows a Gaussian process [6]. As shown by Kakade et al. [7], this Bayesian prior distribution and the penalized NML density correspond to the same underlying distribution, where $\|f_i\|_\kappa^2$ acts as a luckiness function in the LNML framework [4].

The overall description length of a causal graph G is defined as

$$L(\boldsymbol{X}|G) := \sum_{i=1}^{d} L(X_{(i)}|\mathrm{pa}_i(G)),$$

and the optimal causal model $\hat{M} = (\hat{G}, \hat{F})$, where $\hat{G}$ denotes the estimated causal graph and $\hat{F}$ denotes the corresponding estimated causal mechanisms, is obtained by first solving

$$\hat{G} = \arg\min_G L(X|G),$$

after which $\hat{F}$ is estimated by Gaussian process regression.

We now extend this formulation to settings with latent confounders. Consider two variables X and Y and a confounder Z. Given a causal graph G with known relationships, we can infer the unknown relationship between X and Y by comparing the description lengths of four candidate models:

$$X \to Y, \quad Y \to X, \quad X \leftarrow Z \to Y, \quad X \nleftrightarrow Y.$$

The MDL score for this reduced system is

$$\begin{aligned} L(X, Y|\mathrm{pa}_X, \mathrm{pa}_Y, Z) := \min\{&L(X \to Y), L(Y \to X), \\ &L(X \leftarrow Z \to Y), L(X \nleftrightarrow Y)\}, \end{aligned} \tag{6}$$

where

$$\begin{aligned} L(X \to Y) &:= L(Y|\mathrm{pa}_Y, X) + L(X|\mathrm{pa}_X), \\ L(Y \to X) &:= L(X|\mathrm{pa}_X, Y) + L(Y|\mathrm{pa}_Y), \\ L(X \leftarrow Z \to Y) &:= L(X|\mathrm{pa}_X, Z) + L(Y|\mathrm{pa}_Y, Z), \\ L(X \nleftrightarrow Y) &:= L(X|\mathrm{pa}_X) + L(Y|\mathrm{pa}_Y). \end{aligned} \tag{7}$$

Since the MDL score in (5) penalizes the complexity of f, setting $\hat{Z} = X$ would maximize the likelihood but would fail to minimize the description length. This approach avoids the overfitting issue discussed by Kaltenpoth and Vreeken [8].

Finally, for a causal model $M = (G, F)$ with observed variables and latent confounders, the resulting computable LNML objective is

$$\begin{aligned} \bar{\mathcal{L}}_{\mathrm{LNML}}(\boldsymbol{X}) := \sum_{i=1}^{d} \Big\{ &-\log p(X_{(i)}|\mathrm{pa}_i(G)) \\ &+ \|f_i\|_\kappa^2 + \tfrac{1}{2}\log\det\left(\sigma^{-2}\boldsymbol{K}_{\mathrm{pa}_i(G)} + \boldsymbol{I}\right)\Big\}. \end{aligned} \tag{8}$$

The optimal graph is obtained by minimizing $\bar{\mathcal{L}}_{\mathrm{LNML}}(\boldsymbol{X}|G)$ over G.

4 Algorithm for Solving a Causal Model with Latent Confounders

While LNML code-length can be defined with latent confounders, its direct computation is challenging due to reliance on sampling over unobservable variables. To address this issue, we introduce a computable approximation of the latent-confounder-aware code-length that removes sampling dependence. Based on this approximation, we propose the notion of *pseudo-collinearity* to theoretically characterize and identify latent confounding. These ideas lead to a novel causal discovery algorithm, **Pseudo-Collinearity Guided Causal Discovery (PCG-CD)**, which departs from conventional score-based methods by explicitly incorporating latent confounder detection into model selection.

4.1 Reformulation of Code-Length

In this work, we assume the presence of latent confounders, under which statistical dependencies may need to be jointly explained by observable variables and unobservable variables (latent confounders). To simplify the exposition, we henceforth focus on the residual components of variables when considering a pair of nodes A and B.

The residual component of a node is defined as the original variable minus the part explained by its known parents in the causal graph G. We denote the residual component of A by A_{res}. Under this formulation, the causal relationship between A and B can be identified by examining A_{res} and B_{res}, without reference to other observed nodes in G.

Under this setting, we consider a reduced system consisting of A_{res}, B_{res}, and an unobserved variable Z. The four candidate models differ only in the assumed causal structure among these variables, while Z is treated as present in all candidate models. The corresponding code-lengths (7) can be rewritten as follows:

$$
\begin{aligned}
&L(A_{\text{res}}|\text{pa}_{A_{\text{res}}} = \emptyset) + L(B_{\text{res}}|\text{pa}_{B_{\text{res}}} = A_{\text{res}}) + L(Z),\\
&L(A_{\text{res}}|\text{pa}_{A_{\text{res}}} = B_{\text{res}}) + L(B_{\text{res}}|\text{pa}_{B_{\text{res}}} = \emptyset) + L(Z),\\
&L(A_{\text{res}}|\text{pa}_{A_{\text{res}}} = Z) + L(B_{\text{res}}|\text{pa}_{B_{\text{res}}} = Z) + L(Z),\\
&L(A_{\text{res}}|\text{pa}_{A_{\text{res}}} = \emptyset) + L(B_{\text{res}}|\text{pa}_{B_{\text{res}}} = \emptyset) + L(Z).
\end{aligned}
$$

Since $L(Z)$ can be treated as constant, we can ignore it when comparing the code-lengths of the four cases.

We can also reformulate the code-lengths of the four cases as follows:

$$
\begin{aligned}
L(A_{\text{res}} \rightarrow B_{\text{res}}) &= L(A_{\text{res}}|\text{pa}_{A_{\text{res}}} = \emptyset) + L(B_{\text{res}}|\text{pa}_{B_{\text{res}}} = A_{\text{res}}),\\
L(A_{\text{res}} \leftarrow B_{\text{res}}) &= L(A_{\text{res}}|\text{pa}_{A_{\text{res}}} = B_{\text{res}}) + L(B_{\text{res}}|\text{pa}_{B_{\text{res}}} = \emptyset),\\
L(A_{\text{res}} \leftrightarrow B_{\text{res}}) &= L(A_{\text{res}}|\text{pa}_{A_{\text{res}}} = B_{\text{res}}) + L(B_{\text{res}}|\text{pa}_{B_{\text{res}}} = A_{\text{res}}),\\
L(A_{\text{res}} \not\leftrightarrow B_{\text{res}}) &= L(A_{\text{res}}|\text{pa}_{A_{\text{res}}} = \emptyset) + L(B_{\text{res}}|\text{pa}_{B_{\text{res}}} = \emptyset),
\end{aligned}
$$

where $A_{\text{res}} \leftrightarrow B_{\text{res}}$ denotes the case where a latent confounder causes both A and B, and $A_{\text{res}} \not\leftrightarrow B_{\text{res}}$ denotes the case where no causal relationship exists between A and B. The code-length of the case with latent confounder $L(A_{\text{res}} \leftrightarrow B_{\text{res}})$ serves as an approximation to $L(A_{\text{res}}|\text{pa}_{A_{\text{res}}} = Z) + L(B_{\text{res}}|\text{pa}_{B_{\text{res}}} = Z)$ by replacing Z with A_{res} and B_{res}. This approximation is heuristic in nature. Intuitively, one may expect $L(A_{\text{res}}|\text{pa}_{A_{\text{res}}} = B_{\text{res}})$ to approach $L(A_{\text{res}}|\text{pa}_{A_{\text{res}}} = Z)$ when $B = f(Z) + \varepsilon_B$, provided that the function $f(\cdot)$ is simple and the noise term ε_B is small (e.g., $B = Z + \mathcal{N}(0, 0.0001)$).

Since the quality of this approximation may vary with the complexity of the causal mechanisms, we do not use it to determine causal relationship types under the MDL principle. Instead, it is introduced solely to make the overall code-length of causal graphs with latent confounders computable, eliminating the need for explicit sampling of latent confounder values. This intuition extends naturally to the original nodes A and B in the causal graph G.

4.2 Pseudo-collinearity

After accounting for observable influences, if residuals of two nodes remain similarly dependent in both directions, we infer a shared latent confounder. We call this property pseudo-collinearity.

Pseudo-collinearity holds if:

$$\begin{aligned} L(A_{\text{res}}|\text{pa}_{A_{\text{res}}} = B_{\text{res}}) + L(B_{\text{res}}|\text{pa}_{B_{\text{res}}} = \emptyset) \\ \approx L(A_{\text{res}}|\text{pa}_{A_{\text{res}}} = \emptyset) + L(B_{\text{res}}|\text{pa}_{B_{\text{res}}} = A_{\text{res}}). \end{aligned} \tag{9}$$

If the difference between the left-hand side and right-hand side of (9) is large, meaning that the code-length of either $A \to B$ or $A \leftarrow B$ is significantly smaller, then the causal relationship between A and B is unidirectional and no latent factor is present. More specifically, we say that a pair of variables A and B exhibits **Δ-pseudo-collinearity** if

$$\begin{aligned} \Delta = |L(A_{\text{res}}|\text{pa}_{A_{\text{res}}} = \emptyset) + L(B_{\text{res}}|\text{pa}_{B_{\text{res}}} = A_{\text{res}}) \\ - \Big(L(A_{\text{res}}|\text{pa}_{A_{\text{res}}} = B_{\text{res}}) + L(B_{\text{res}}|\text{pa}_{B_{\text{res}}} = \emptyset)\Big)| \le n\epsilon, \end{aligned} \tag{10}$$

where n denotes the sample size and ϵ is a predefined threshold. Δ captures the discrepancy between alternative explanatory directions, and we regard A and B as Δ-pseudo-collinear whenever this discrepancy falls below the threshold $n\epsilon$.

4.3 A Theoretical Evaluation on Pseudo-Collinearity

The Δ in (10) should be small when pseudo-collinearity exists between nodes A and B. We begin by assuming that the mechanisms between a latent confounder Z and the observed nodes A and B are linear.

Theorem 1 **(Δ-pseudo-collinearity of Linear Case).** *Let nodes A and B be influenced by a common latent confounder Z, where A and B have no additional parents and the mechanisms $Z \to A$ and $Z \to B$ are linear. Then*

$$\Delta = O\big(nC(|coef_A - coef_B|, \sigma_Z, \sigma_A, \sigma_B)\big),$$

where n denotes the sample size, $|coef_A - coef_B|$ denotes the difference between the coefficients of the two mechanisms $Z \to A$ and $Z \to B$, σ_Z denotes the noise level of the latent confounder, and σ_A, σ_B denote the noise levels of A and B, respectively. Moreover, $C(|coef_A - coef_B|, \sigma_Z, \sigma_A, \sigma_B)$ decreases as the noise level σ_Z increases and as $|coef_A - coef_B|$ decreases, while the effect of σ_A and σ_B depends on their interaction with the mechanism coefficients and other noise terms.

To prove this theorem, we rewrite the latent linear confounding model as an induced linear dependence between A and B, compare the corresponding LNML code-lengths, and show that $\Delta = O\big(nC(|\text{coef}_A - \text{coef}_B|, \sigma_Z, \sigma_A, \sigma_B)\big)$. This linear scaling motivates the thresholding rule $\Delta \leq n\epsilon$ used in the algorithm. Due to space limitations, the complete proof is available in the supplementary material.

Theorem 1 establishes that, under linear mechanisms, the pseudo-collinearity gap Δ grows at most linearly with the sample size, serving as a reference case for extending the analysis to nonlinear settings. Motivated by this insight, our algorithm uses a threshold on Δ as a heuristic signal: values satisfying $\Delta \leq$ threshold are suggestive of latent confounding, whereas values of $\Delta >$ threshold tend to be more consistent with a directed causal relationship. The practical usefulness of this criterion is empirically demonstrated in Sect. 5.2.

For nonlinear mechanisms, the evaluation of pseudo-collinearity becomes more complex. However, if the mechanism between observed nodes is approximately linear (e.g., $a = 1 + 0.005z + z^3 + \varepsilon_a$, $b = -1 - 2z^3 + \varepsilon_b$), or if the range of values is sufficiently small, the gap Δ can still be analyzed in the same manner.

4.4 The PCG-CD Algorithm

Based on our earlier formulation of code-lengths for the four types of causal relationships and the notion of pseudo-collinearity, we propose a novel greedy causal discovery algorithm, termed Pseudo-Collinearity Guided Causal Discovery (PCG-CD), which differs fundamentally from existing score-based methods. In contrast to GES-based approaches, which have a computational complexity of $O(|V|^3)$ for edge evaluation, the proposed method operates with a reduced complexity of $O(|V|^2)$. Our method follows a deletion-based strategy that starts from a complete graph and progressively removes edges according to the MDL principle. An edge is removed only when its contribution to explaining the causal structure or reducing the overall code-length is negligible, and removed edges are never reintroduced. As a result, the overall code-length decreases monotonically throughout the procedure.

Algorithm 1. PCG-CD

Input: Dataset $\{X_{(1)}, \ldots, X_{(d)}\}$
Parameter: Threshold $n\epsilon$, maximum iterations $T_{\max}$
Output: Causal graph G

```
Initialize graph G with bidirected edge X_(i) ↔ X_(j) for all i ≠ j.
Initialize t ← 0.
Stage 1: Skeleton Construction
while G is still changing and t < T_max do
    for all adjacent variable pairs (X_(i), X_(j)) do
        if L(X_(i) ↮ X_(j)) < min{L(X_(i) → X_(j)), L(X_(j) → X_(i))} then
            Replace X_(i) ↔ X_(j) by X_(i) ↮ X_(j).
        else if |L(X_(i) → X_(j)) − L(X_(j) → X_(i))| > nϵ then
            Keep the direction with a smaller code-length.
        else
            Keep X_(i) ↔ X_(j).
        end if
    end for
    t ← t + 1.
end while
Stage 2: Cycle Removal
while G contains a directed cycle do
    for all unidirectional edges → in a cycle do
        Compute the loss for deleting or replacing → with ↔.
    end for
    Modify the edge with the minimum loss.
end while
return G.
```

PCG-CD proceeds in two stages and is designed to account for latent confounders. It starts from a fully connected graph where all variable pairs are linked by bidirected edges, representing maximal uncertainty and allowing for unobserved common causes.

In the first stage, the algorithm iteratively refines the graph by comparing LNML-based code-lengths under edge configurations for each variable pair. Edges are removed when no direct relation yields a shorter code-length, oriented when one direction is clearly favored, or kept bidirected when the code-length difference is below a threshold. The latter case reflects pseudo-collinearity, suggesting that the association is better explained by a latent confounder rather than a direct causal effect. This stage produces a partially oriented graph that encodes potential latent confounding. In the second stage, the algorithm enforces acyclicity by detecting directed cycles and modifying the edge whose adjustment causes the smallest increase in code-length, either by removal or by converting it to a bidirected edge. The final output is a directed acyclic causal graph balancing model simplicity and goodness of fit. Bidirected edges representing latent confounders are ignored when detecting directed cycles.

In this greedy procedure, the causal mechanisms F are re-estimated at each iteration by fitting Gaussian process regressions according to the current parent sets in G. Through the iterative refinements in the first stage and the acyclicity adjustments in the second stage, the algorithm progressively reduces the overall code-length and returns the final causal model $\hat{M} = (\hat{G}, \hat{F})$.

Note that the time complexity of edge checking in this algorithm is $O(|V|^2)$. To capture nonlinear mechanisms, we adopt a Gaussian Process assumption in the code-length definition, making GP regression the main computational cost and increasing runtime with sample size. Nevertheless, the PCG-CD edge-searching framework remains advantageous if alternative code-length definitions are adopted in other scenarios.

5 Experiments

We use Gaussian process regression with a composite kernel consisting of an RBF kernel and a white-noise kernel. The kernel is initialized with a length scale of 1.0 and a noise level of 1.0, while all hyperparameters are optimized automatically during training using the `scikit-learn` implementation. The threshold parameter used in the pseudo-collinearity criterion is set to $\epsilon = 5$. This value was selected empirically through preliminary experiments on synthetic graphs with similar sparsity levels and varying sample sizes, and was kept fixed throughout all experiments.

5.1 Performance Metrics

We first investigate the existence of pseudo-collinearity between pairs of nodes by comparing the MDL-based code-lengths with those derived from the ground-truth causal structure. We then assess the accuracy of the estimated causal graphs in scenarios involving multiple nodes. Although Structural Hamming Distance (SHD) [2] and Structural Intervention Distance (SID) [17] are widely used metrics for evaluating causal discovery methods whose outputs are fully specified DAGs, methods designed to handle latent confounders (e.g., FCI) typically output Partial Ancestral Graphs (PAGs). In such graphs, both edge orientations and interventional effects are generally not uniquely identifiable. Consequently, SHD and SID are not well suited for evaluating these methods. We therefore adopt structure-aware and confounder-aware metrics that more accurately reflect the information encoded in causal graphs containing both directed causal edges and latent confounders.

We use **Z-hit**, **E-hit**, **Sim1**, and **Sim2** to evaluate performance in multi-node settings. **Z-hit** measures whether the algorithm correctly identifies the relationship between the unique confounded pair $A \leftrightarrow B$ in the causal graph. **E-hit** evaluates whether the directed relationship between any node pair $A \rightarrow B$ is correctly identified. **Sim1** quantifies the similarity between the ground-truth causal graph and the estimated causal graph in terms of adjacency matrices, where $A \leftrightarrow B$ is treated as the absence of an edge between nodes A and B. In contrast, **Sim2** measures the similarity between the ground-truth directed graph and the estimated causal graph by treating $A \leftrightarrow B$ as the presence of both edges $A \rightarrow B$ and $A \leftarrow B$.

5.2 Synthetic Data

First, we conduct experiments on pairwise nodes to verify the presence of pseudo-collinearity. Similar to the circumstances described in Sect. 4.2, we assume that nodes A and B are dependent and that there are no other observable parents of A or B. Without loss of generality, we randomly generate data for nodes A and B under two causal relationships: $A \rightarrow B$ and $A \leftrightarrow B$, each occurring with a probability of 50%.

We consider both linear and nonlinear cases. In the linear case, nodes without parents follow the mechanism

$$x = U(-5, 5) + \mathcal{N}(0, \sigma^2),$$

where $U(\cdot)$ denotes the uniform distribution and the latter term represents additive Gaussian noise. Nodes with parents pa_x are generated according to

$$x = \alpha_1 + \alpha_2 \mathrm{pa}_x + \mathcal{N}(0, \sigma^2),$$

where the coefficients α_1, α_2 are drawn from $U(-10, 10)$.

In the nonlinear case, we adopt a cubic polynomial mechanism. Specifically, nodes without parents follow

$$x = U(-3, 3) + \mathcal{N}(0, \sigma^2),$$

and nodes with parents are generated as

$$x = \beta_1 + \beta_2 \mathrm{pa}_x + \beta_3 \mathrm{pa}_x^2 + \beta_4 \mathrm{pa}_x^3 + \mathcal{N}(0, \sigma^2),$$

where the coefficients $\beta_1, \beta_2, \beta_3, \beta_4$ are sampled from $U(-2, 2)$.

To verify that pseudo-collinearity arises in practical scenarios, we compare the gap between the code-lengths of the two causal directions, denoted as Δ in (10), with the ground-truth causal relationships $A \rightarrow B$ and $A \leftrightarrow B$. A smaller gap Δ indicates a higher probability that A and B do not share a direct causal relationship but are instead influenced by a common latent confounder. The experiments are conducted under different settings of data size and noise magnitude σ. For each setting, we perform experiments on 20 independently generated datasets and report the area under the ROC curve (AUC) in Table 1.

From the results shown in Table 1, we make the following observations. Pseudo-collinearity emerges in both the linear and nonlinear cases. Its manifestation becomes more pronounced as σ increases and the data size decreases. A possible explanation is that a higher noise level amplifies the apparent dependency between two directly connected nodes. In contrast, with larger sample sizes, the Gaussian process can fit increasingly fine-scale patterns, causing part of the observational noise to be absorbed into the estimated causal mechanism. This weakens the pseudo-collinearity effect. The results also depend on the range of variable values, or equivalently, on the range of the coefficients. In the experiments presented in Table 1, pseudo-collinearity is more clearly observed in the

Table 1. AUC scores of the code-length gap Δ for distinguishing direct causal relationships from latent confounding under different noise levels σ and sample sizes.

Noise level	Linear cases			Nonlinear cases		
σ	200	500	1000	200	500	1000
0.2	0.9048	0.8462	0.5521	0.9670	0.9792	0.7188
0.5	0.8889	0.7980	0.6146	1.0000	0.9762	0.9167
1.0	0.9688	0.9610	0.8485	1.0000	1.0000	1.0000

Table 2. Performance comparison under different sample sizes in terms of latent confounder detection, directed edge recovery, and graph similarity metrics.

Size	Method	Z-hit	E-hit	Sim1	Sim2
200	PCG-CD	**0.90**	**1.00**	0.83	0.73
	FCI	0.15	0.11	0.90	0.84
	FCI (all)	0.60	0.34	**0.91**	**0.89**
500	PCG-CD	**0.80**	**0.95**	0.84	0.60
	FCI	0.00	0.15	**0.92**	0.84
	FCI (all)	0.40	0.33	0.91	**0.87**
1000	PCG-CD	**0.80**	**1.00**	0.82	0.69
	FCI	0.05	0.07	**0.90**	0.82
	FCI (all)	0.45	0.39	0.89	**0.85**

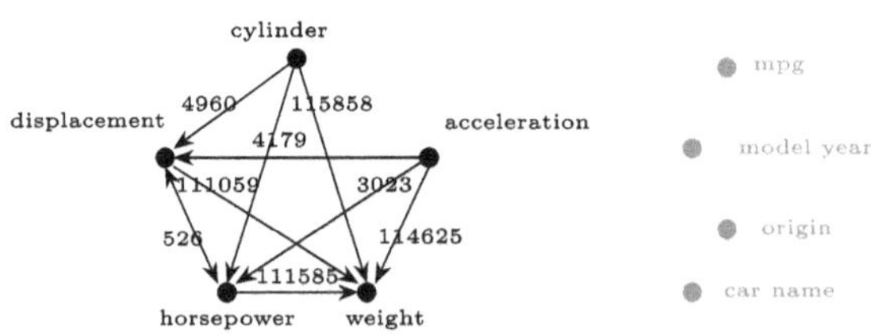

(a) Causal graph inferred by PCG-CD.

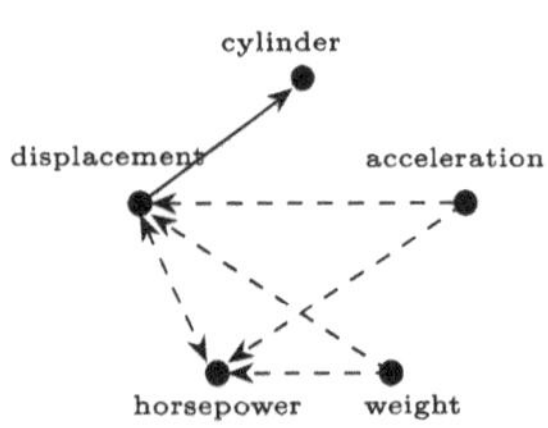

(b) Partial ancestral graph inferred by FCI. Dashed edges indicate partially oriented edges.

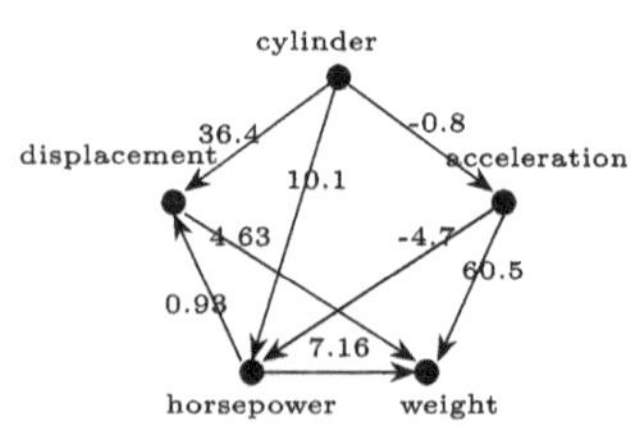

(c) Causal graph inferred by ICA-LiNGAM. The values indicate estimated edge strengths.

Fig. 2. Causal discovery results on the Auto MPG dataset.

nonlinear cases than in the linear ones, which can be attributed to the amplification of causal relationships by the higher-order terms of the polynomial mechanisms. If the interval of α_2 is increased, the results for the linear cases are expected to improve accordingly.

For datasets with multiple variables, we generate a random directed acyclic graph (DAG) G using the Erdős–Rényi model [3], and simulate data following the assumptions in Sect. 2.1. The graph contains six nodes, with an edge probability of 0.25. One node with at least two children is randomly selected as a latent confounder, and all remaining nodes are treated as observed variables. Nonlinear causal mechanisms are used, consistent with the previous experiment. For each setting, we generate 20 independent datasets.

Table 2 reports the average performance of the proposed PCG-CD method. We compare PCG-CD with FCI, a widely used constraint-based causal discovery algorithm that accommodates latent confounders and nonlinear causal mechanisms. Since FCI outputs a PAG with partially oriented edges, we consider two evaluation protocols: FCI, which evaluates only fully oriented edges ($\rightarrow$ and $\leftrightarrow$); and FCI (all), which resolves partially oriented edges by treating $\circ\!\!\rightarrow$ as $\rightarrow$ and $\circ\!\!-\!\!\circ$ as $\leftrightarrow$ for the purpose of computing evaluation metrics.

Table 2 summarizes the performance of different methods under varying sample sizes. Overall, PCG-CD consistently outperforms both FCI variants in Z-hit and E-hit, showing superior ability to identify latent-confounded pairs and directed causal relations. In contrast, standard FCI yields near-zero Z-hit and low E-hit across all sample sizes due to its conservative nature, while FCI (all) remains substantially inferior to PCG-CD, highlighting the difficulty of recovering both directed relations and latent confounders. Although FCI and FCI (all) achieve higher Sim1 and Sim2 scores, this mainly results from their preference for false negatives, producing extremely sparse graphs that artificially inflate similarity. Consequently, these higher similarity scores do not reflect accurate recovery of causal directions or latent confounding. Increasing sample size does not significantly improve the Z-hit or E-hit of FCI. In contrast, PCG-CD shows stable performance across all sample sizes, confirming its effectiveness in recovering informative causal structures beyond adjacency-level similarity.

5.3 Real-World Data

We evaluate the proposed method on the Auto MPG dataset[1], a widely used real-world benchmark for regression and causal analysis. After standard preprocessing, we remove six samples with missing values. We select *cylinders*, *displacement*, *horsepower*, *weight*, and *acceleration* as observable variables, and treat the remaining attributes (*mpg*, *model year*, *origin*, and *car name*) as unobservable.

We apply PCG-CD and FCI to the observable variables, and include ICA-LiNGAM as a reference method applied to the full dataset excluding *car name*. The causal relations and edge strengths inferred by ICA-LiNGAM among the selected variables are extracted for comparison.

[1] https://archive.ics.uci.edu/dataset/9/auto+mpg.

Figure 2 compares the causal graphs inferred by different methods. In PCG-CD, each edge is annotated with its Δ value. In score-based causal discovery, larger directional differences generally indicate higher confidence in edge orientation. The Δ values are almost qualitatively aligned with the edge strengths estimated by ICA-LiNGAM (Fig. 2c). The *displacement–horsepower* edge exhibits a Δ below the chosen threshold ($5\times$ size), suggesting latent confounding, similar to the assessment by FCI (Fig. 2b).

6 Conclusion

In this paper, we proposed an MDL-based framework for causal discovery that accommodates both nonlinear causal mechanisms and latent confounders. By leveraging LNML code-lengths, the proposed method evaluates causal relationships between variable pairs among four possible cases: $A \rightarrow B$, $A \leftarrow B$, $A \leftrightarrow B$, and $A \not\leftrightarrow B$, and reconstructs the causal graph by minimizing the overall description length.

A key component of our approach is the notion of Δ-pseudo-collinearity, which provides a principled criterion for identifying dependencies induced by latent confounders and is supported by theoretical analysis in linear settings. Building on these ideas, we developed PCG-CD, a greedy algorithm that achieves lower complexity than conventional score-based methods.

Experimental results on synthetic and real-world datasets demonstrate that PCG-CD consistently recovers informative causal structures, accurately identifies directed causal relationships, and effectively detects latent confounders. These results suggest that MDL-based causal discovery offers a promising direction for learning causal structure from partially observed data.

Acknowledgments. The research is partially supported by JSPS KAKENHI 24H00703.

References

1. Budhathoki, K., Vreeken, J.: Origo: causal inference by compression. Knowl. Inf. Syst. **56**(2), 285–307 (2018)
2. Chickering, D.M.: Optimal structure identification with greedy search. J. Mach. Learn. Res. **3**, 507–554 (2002)
3. Erdös, P., Rènyi, A.: On random graphs I. Publ. Math. Debrecen **6**(290–297), 18 (1959)
4. Grünwald, P.D.: The Minimum Description Length Principle. MIT Press, Cambridge (2007)
5. Hoyer, P., Janzing, D., Mooij, J.M., Peters, J., Schölkopf, B.: Nonlinear causal discovery with additive noise models. Adv. Neural. Inf. Process. Syst. **21** (2008)
6. Kakade, S.M., Ng, A.: Online bounds for Bayesian algorithms. Adv. Neural. Inf. Process. Syst. **17** (2004)

7. Kakade, S.M., Seeger, M.W., Foster, D.P.: Worst-case bounds for Gaussian process models. Adv. Neural. Inf. Process. Syst. **18** (2005)
8. Kaltenpoth, D., Vreeken, J.: We are not your real parents: telling causal from confounded using mdl. In: Proceedings of the 2019 SIAM International Conference on Data Mining, pp. 199–207. SIAM (2019)
9. Kaltenpoth, D., Vreeken, J.: Causal discovery with hidden confounders using the algorithmic Markov condition. In: Uncertainty in Artificial Intelligence, pp. 1016–1026. PMLR (2023)
10. Kaltenpoth, D., Vreeken, J.: Nonlinear causal discovery with latent confounders. In: Krause, A., Brunskill, E., Cho, K., Engelhardt, B., Sabato, S., Scarlett, J. (eds.) Proceedings of the 40th International Conference on Machine Learning. Proceedings of Machine Learning Research, vol. 202, pp. 15639–15654. PMLR (2023)
11. Kobayashi, M., Miyaguchi, K., Matsushima, S.: Detection of unobserved common cause in discrete data based on the MDL principle. In: 2022 IEEE International Conference on Big Data, pp. 45–54 (2022). https://doi.org/10.1109/BigData55660.2022.10020351
12. Maeda, T.N., Shimizu, S.: RCD: repetitive causal discovery of linear non-Gaussian acyclic models with latent confounders. In: International Conference on artificial intelligence and statistics, pp. 735–745. PMLR (2020)
13. Marx, A., Vreeken, J.: Telling cause from effect using MDL-based local and global regression. In: 2017 IEEE International Conference on Data Mining, pp. 307–316. IEEE (2017)
14. Mian, O.A., Marx, A., Vreeken, J.: Discovering fully oriented causal networks. In: Proceedings of the AAAI Conference on Artificial Intelligence, vol. 35, pp. 8975–8982 (2021)
15. Miyaguchi, K.: Normalized maximum likelihood with luckiness for multivariate normal distributions (2017). https://arxiv.org/abs/1708.01861
16. Pearl, J.: Causality: Models, Reasoning, and Inference, 1st edn. Cambridge University Press, Cambridge (2000)
17. Peters, J., Bühlmann, P.: Structural intervention distance for evaluating causal graphs. Neural Comput. **27**(3), 771–799 (2015)
18. Ramsey, J., Glymour, M., Sanchez-Romero, R., Glymour, C.: A million variables and more: the fast greedy equivalence search algorithm for learning high-dimensional graphical causal models, with an application to functional magnetic resonance images. Int. J. Data Sci. Anal. **3**, 121–129 (2017)
19. Rasmussen, C.E., Williams, C.K.I.: Gaussian Processes for Machine Learning. MIT Press, Cambridge (2006). http://www.gaussianprocess.org/gpml/
20. Rissanen, J.: Modeling by shortest data description. Automatica **14**(5), 465–471 (1978)
21. Shimizu, S., Hoyer, P.O., Hyvärinen, A., Kerminen, A., Jordan, M.: A linear non-Gaussian acyclic model for causal discovery. J. Mach. Learn. Res. **7**(10) (2006)
22. Shimizu, S., et al.: DirectLiNGAM: a direct method for learning a linear non-Gaussian structural equation model. J. Mach. Learn. Res. **12**(Apr), 1225–1248 (2011)
23. Shtar'kov, Y.M.: Universal sequential coding of single messages. Probl. Peredachi Inform. **23**(3), 3–17 (1987)
24. Spirtes, P., Glymour, C., Scheines, R.: Causation, Prediction, and Search, 2nd edn. MIT Press, Cambridge (2000)
25. Tashiro, T., Shimizu, S., Hyvärinen, A., Washio, T.: ParceLiNGAM: a causal ordering method robust against latent confounders. Neural Comput. **26**(1), 57–83 (2014)

26. Yamanishi, K.: Learning with the Minimum Description Length Principle. Springer, Heidelberg (2023)
27. Yamanishi, K., Wu, T., Sugawara, S., Okada, M.: The decomposed normalized maximum likelihood code-length criterion for selecting hierarchical latent variable models. Data Min. Knowl. Disc. **33**(4), 1017–1058 (2019)
28. Zhang, K., Hyvärinen, A.: On the identifiability of the post-nonlinear causal model. In: Proceedings of the Twenty-Fifth Conference on Uncertainty in Artificial Intelligence, UAI 2009, pp. 647–655 (2009)

Clustering and Pattern Mining

Composite Silhouette

Aggelos Semoglou[1,2(✉)], Aristidis Likas[3], and John Pavlopoulos[1,2]

[1] Athens University of Economics and Business, Athens, Greece
annis@aueb.gr
[2] Archimedes, Athena Research Center, Marousi, Greece
a.semoglou@athenarc.gr
[3] University of Ioannina, Ioannina, Greece
arly@cs.uoi.gr

Abstract. Determining the number of clusters is a central challenge in unsupervised learning, where ground-truth labels are unavailable. The Silhouette coefficient is a widely used internal validation metric for this task, yet its standard micro-averaged form tends to favor larger clusters under size imbalance. Macro-averaging mitigates this bias by weighting clusters equally, but may overemphasize noise from under-represented groups. We introduce Composite Silhouette, an internal criterion for cluster-count selection that aggregates evidence across repeated subsampled clusterings rather than relying on a single partition. For each subsample, micro- and macro-averaged Silhouette scores are combined through an adaptive convex weight determined by their normalized discrepancy and smoothed by a bounded nonlinearity; the final score is then obtained by averaging these subsample-level composites. We establish key properties of the criterion and derive finite-sample concentration guarantees for its subsampling estimate. Experiments on synthetic and real-world datasets show that Composite Silhouette effectively reconciles the strengths of micro- and macro-averaging, yielding more accurate recovery of the ground-truth number of clusters.

Keywords: Unsupervised learning · Clustering · Internal validation

1 Introduction

Clustering evaluation remains a crucial but challenging step in unsupervised learning, largely due to the inherent difficulty of assessing solutions without labeled data [11]. Among various internal clustering evaluation metrics, the Silhouette coefficient [17] is one of the most widely adopted, as it effectively quantifies the compactness and separation of clusters using only intrinsic dataset properties. Its ease of interpretation and widespread implementation in libraries such as `scikit-learn` [16] have made it a default choice in many practical applications. However, the traditional approach, micro-averaging Silhouette scores across all individual data points [2], is known to exhibit significant bias, particularly in datasets with imbalanced cluster sizes, frequently encountered in real-world applications. In such cases, larger clusters can disproportionately influence

M. Ceci et al. (Eds.): ECML PKDD 2026, LNAI 16941, pp. 661–678, 2027.
https://doi.org/10.1007/978-3-032-37654-1_38

the final score, potentially masking poor separation in minor clusters [15]. An alternative yet rarely utilized strategy, macro-averaging, aggregates Silhouette scores by first computing the mean Silhouette per cluster and then averaging across clusters. Although macro-averaging mitigates cluster-size bias by assigning equal weight to clusters irrespective of their sizes, it can overly emphasize smaller or under-represented clusters. This trade-off is especially evident in real-world settings. For instance, in medical clustering [25], where rare but clinically important patient subgroups must be identified, macro-averaging is often preferable because it ensures that these small clusters are not overshadowed. In contrast, in customer segmentation [12], where the business impact of large, well-defined customer groups dominates, micro-averaging tends to better reflect practical utility. Yet in other domains, such as topic clustering [26], where some themes are broad and frequent while others are niche but still valuable, it is often unclear which strategy should be preferred.

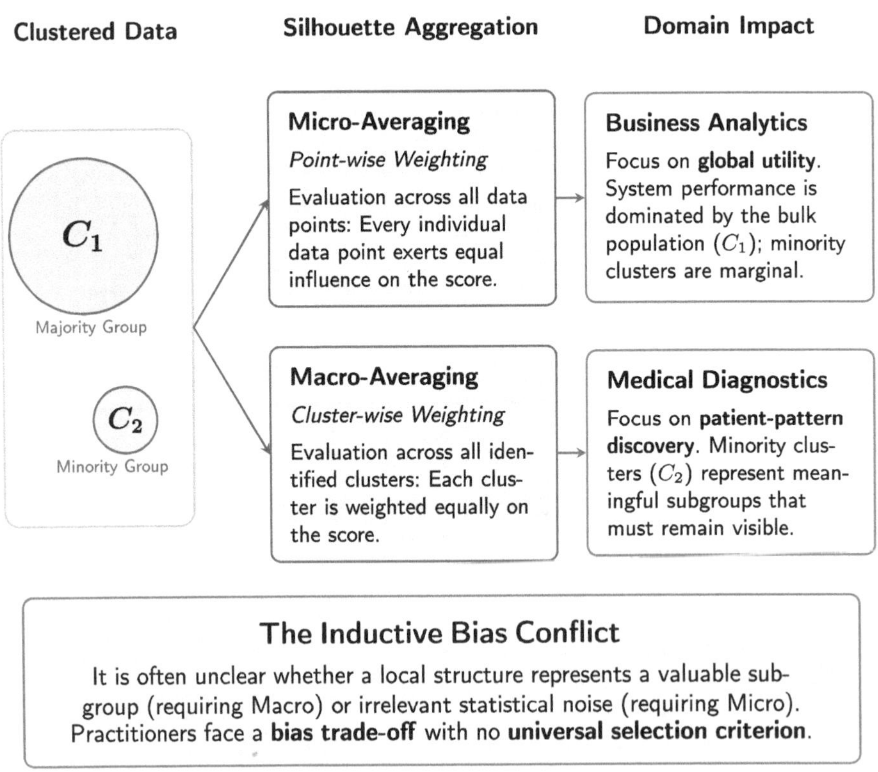

Fig. 1. Silhouette aggregation strategies: Global trends vs. local patterns.

Depending on the application, both majority coherence and minority representation may be important. Consequently, practitioners face a critical choice between two fundamentally different aggregation strategies, each having its own limitations, and with no clear rule for balancing them across datasets and clustering solutions (Fig. 1). Moreover, the disagreement between micro- and macro-averaging may itself carry useful information, as it can indicate whether clustering quality is driven primarily by majority structure or by the fidelity of smaller groups. This suggests that, rather than selecting one aggregation strategy globally, a more effective criterion should adapt to how these two perspectives agree or diverge across different views of the data. The absence of such a criterion is particularly problematic in practical settings, where internal validation metrics guide the choice of the optimal number of clusters. In such cases, inconsistent or biased metrics can lead to misleading evaluations and suboptimal clustering decisions. This raises a central question:

Could an internal criterion combine the strengths of micro- and macro-averaged Silhouette scores to guide cluster-count selection more accurately and reliably, without prior assumptions about which aggregation strategy is preferable?

To address this question, we introduce Composite Silhouette, a subsampling-based internal validation criterion that aggregates micro- and macro-averaged Silhouette scores over repeated subsampled clusterings. Instead of relying on a single partition or enforcing a fixed global preference between micro- and macro-averaging, our method computes the two scores on each subsampled clustering and combines them through a subsample-specific convex combination, whose mixing weight is determined by the normalized discrepancy between them and smoothed by a bounded nonlinearity. The final score is then obtained by averaging these per-subsample composite scores across subsampling trials, yielding a more stable and adaptive criterion for cluster-count selection. In this sense, Composite Silhouette performs discrepancy-driven adaptive aggregation: the relative weight assigned to the two Silhouette views is determined locally at the subsample level, rather than fixed in advance for the entire dataset. This allows the criterion to respond to heterogeneous structure without committing a priori to either majority-dominated or minority-sensitive evaluation. We show that this formulation enjoys useful deterministic properties and admits finite-sample concentration guarantees for its subsampling estimate. Across synthetic and real-world datasets, Composite Silhouette accurately identifies the number of clusters in regimes where either micro- or macro-averaging alone would be effective, without requiring prior knowledge of which aggregation strategy is better suited to the data, while remaining competitive in balanced settings. Against a broad range of internal validation baselines, including both averages over subsampled clustering runs and averages from repeated clustering runs on the full dataset, Composite Silhouette achieves the strongest overall performance in recovering the ground-truth number of clusters. Overall, this work offers a principled and practical alternative to existing internal validation metrics, enabling more reliable model selection in settings where traditional approaches may fail to capture the underlying cluster structure accurately.

The Composite Silhouette implementation and experimental code are publicly available at https://github.com/semoglou/compsil. The Python package is available on PyPI at https://pypi.org/project/compsil/.

2 Related Work

Internal Cluster Validity Indices. Internal validity indices provide a label-free way to evaluate clustering solutions by examining only the geometry and dispersion of the data [1,8,9]. Some indices focus on cluster separation, such as the Dunn index [7], which takes the ratio of the minimum inter-cluster distance to the maximum intra-cluster diameter to ensure worst-case separation. Other measures, like the Calinski–Harabasz criterion [4], compare between-cluster dispersion against within-cluster dispersion, favoring compact, well-separated groups. The Davies–Bouldin index [5] quantifies cluster similarity by averaging, for each cluster, the worst ratio of its scatter to its nearest neighbor's separation and selects the clustering that minimizes this average. Among these, the Silhouette Coefficient stands out for its interpretability: it assigns each point a score in $[-1, 1]$ that balances cohesion against separation. Aggregated as an overall metric or examined at the per-sample level, Silhouette offers both global validation and a diagnostic for potentially misassigned points, making it a versatile tool in practice [6]. Yet, despite its popularity, the Silhouette metric, like other internal indices, can be sensitive to dataset characteristics such as cluster shape, density variation, and especially cluster-size imbalance, which may distort aggregated scores and lead to suboptimal model selection [10,24]; similar challenges also arise for unsupervised cluster-count selection procedures such as the Elbow method [21,22] and the Gap Statistic [23].

Silhouette Aggregation Strategies. Most implementations of the Silhouette score rely solely on micro-averaging [20], which aggregates the Silhouette values of all data points, effectively giving greater influence to larger clusters. While this approach is intuitive and widely used, it can introduce bias when cluster sizes are highly imbalanced. Macro-averaging, which first computes the mean Silhouette per cluster and then averages across clusters, has been proposed as an alternative to mitigate this effect [15,18]. However, macro-averaging can overemphasize small or under-represented clusters, reducing the influence of majority groups. These two aggregation strategies therefore reflect different perspectives on clustering quality, and neither is uniformly preferable across datasets.

Sampling Approaches and Heuristics. Sampling-based strategies have also been explored as a way to stabilize internal validation or reduce the computational burden of repeated clustering evaluation. Uniform subsampling can make large-scale validation more tractable, while repeated runs and averaging can reduce sensitivity to random initialization or sampling variability [13]. In the context of Silhouette-based evaluation, such approaches may partially alleviate the dominance of large clusters or improve robustness, but they do not by themselves resolve the underlying tension between micro- and macro-aggregation. More generally, heuristic combinations of validation criteria or averaging schemes have been considered, though such approaches often rely on fixed design choices or manually selected weights that may not adapt well to the structure of a given dataset [14]. Unlike stability-based validation criteria, which use resampling to assess the reproducibility or predictability of clustering assignments [3,13], and recent ensemble approaches that fuse assignment stability with Silhouette-based geometry for confidence estimation [19], our use of subsampling targets the aggregation of micro- and macro-level Silhouette evidence for cluster-count selection.

Filling the Gap. Although a wide range of internal validation methods has been proposed, existing approaches do not directly address how micro- and macro-averaged Silhouette scores should be combined in a data-adaptive way for cluster-count selection. In particular, current methods typically rely on a single aggregation strategy, fixed averaging rules, or standalone internal indices, without exploiting how the discrepancy between micro- and macro-level evaluations evolves across repeated subsampled clusterings. This leaves a methodological gap in settings where cluster-size imbalance or heterogeneous structure makes either aggregation strategy alone insufficient. Our work addresses this gap by introducing a subsampling-based Composite Silhouette criterion that adaptively combines micro- and macro-averaged Silhouette scores at the subsample level through a discrepancy-sensitive weighting mechanism. The resulting score provides a principled and practical approach to internal cluster-count selection without requiring prior assumptions about which aggregation perspective is more appropriate.

3 Methodology

In this section, we formalize Composite Silhouette, denoted by S_{mM}, and introduce the notation used throughout the method. The proposed formulation evaluates clustering quality through repeated subsampled clusterings, allowing the relationship between micro- and macro-averaged Silhouette to be assessed across multiple views of the data rather than through a single partition. The resulting construction yields an adaptive composite criterion that captures the relative behavior of the two aggregation strategies while producing a single score for cluster-count selection.

3.1 Setup and Notation

Let $\mathcal{X} = \{x_i\}_{i\in\mathcal{I}} \subset \mathbb{R}^d$ be a dataset, where $\mathcal{I} = \{1, 2, \ldots, N\}$ indexes the N observations. Our goal is to evaluate candidate numbers of clusters by examining how clustering quality behaves across repeated subsampled views of the data, rather than relying on a single partition of the full dataset. To this end, let $\mathcal{K} \subset \mathbb{N}_{>1}$ denote the set of candidate cluster counts, and fix $k \in \mathcal{K}$. We also fix a subsampling fraction $\phi \in (0, 1]$, define the subsample size as $m = \lfloor \phi N \rfloor$, and let $B \in \mathbb{N}$ denote the number of subsamples. For each $b \in \{1, \ldots, B\}$, we draw independently a subset $I_b \subset \mathcal{I}$ of size m, uniformly at random without replacement from $\mathcal{I}$, and define the corresponding subsample by:

$$X^{(b)} = \{x_i \in \mathcal{X} : \ i \in I_b\} \subset \mathcal{X}.$$

These subsamples provide multiple partial views of the dataset, allowing us to study how internal validation behaves under repeated perturbations of the data.

Let $F(\cdot\,;\,k)$ denote a clustering algorithm that, given a dataset and a candidate number of clusters k, returns a partition into k distinct (non-empty) clusters. Applied to the subsample $X^{(b)}$, it yields the partition:

$$F(X^{(b)};k) = \{C_1^{(b)}, \dots, C_k^{(b)}\}, \tag{1}$$

where $\{C_r^{(b)}\}_{r=1}^k$ are the clusters obtained on the b-th subsample. In this way, each candidate k is associated with B subsampled clusterings, which provide repeated local views of the structure induced at that value of k.

3.2 Subsample Silhouette Scores

For a fixed number of clusters $k \in \mathcal{K}$ and a fixed subsample $X^{(b)}$, we now define the Silhouette quantities associated with the partition $F(X^{(b)};k)$. For each observation $x_i \in X^{(b)}$, let $C_i^{(b)}$ denote the cluster to which x_i is assigned. The Silhouette value of x_i is based on two quantities: its average dissimilarity to the points in its own cluster $a_i = a_i^{(b)}(k)$, and its average dissimilarity to the nearest competing cluster $b_i = b_i^{(b)}(k)$:

$$a_i = \frac{1}{|C_i^{(b)}| - 1} \sum_{\substack{x_j \in C_i^{(b)} \\ j \neq i}} \|x_i - x_j\|, \quad b_i = \min_{\ell \neq c_i^{(b)}} \frac{1}{|C_\ell^{(b)}|} \sum_{x_j \in C_\ell^{(b)}} \|x_i - x_j\| \tag{2}$$

Here, a_i measures how well x_i is embedded within its assigned cluster, while b_i measures its average dissimilarity to the closest alternative cluster. Smaller values of a_i indicate stronger within-cluster cohesion, whereas larger values of b_i indicate stronger separation from neighboring clusters. Using these two quantities, the Silhouette score of x_i, $s_i = s_i(k)$, on the b-th subsample is given by:

$$s_i^{(b)} = \frac{b_i - a_i}{\max\{a_i, b_i\}} \in [-1, 1]. \tag{3}$$

A value close to 1 indicates that the observation is well matched to its assigned cluster and well separated from competing clusters, a value near 0 indicates ambiguity, and a negative value suggests that the observation may fit better in another cluster.[1] We next aggregate these per-instance values in two different ways: micro-averaged ($S_{\mathrm{m}}^{(b)}$) and macro-averaged ($S_{\mathrm{M}}^{(b)}$) Silhouette scores:

$$S_{\mathrm{m}}^{(b)} = \frac{1}{m} \sum_{i \in I_b} s_i^{(b)}, \quad S_{\mathrm{M}}^{(b)} = \frac{1}{k} \sum_{r=1}^{k} \frac{1}{|C_r^{(b)}|} \sum_{x_i \in C_r^{(b)}} s_i^{(b)}. \tag{4}$$

[1] As in standard implementations of the Silhouette coefficient, singleton clusters are assigned a Silhouette value of zero, since the within-cluster average dissimilarity is not defined for clusters containing a single observation.

These correspond to two complementary ways of evaluating clustering quality on the same subsample. The micro-averaged score ($S_{\mathrm{m}} \in [-1, 1]$) assigns equal weight to all observations and is therefore more strongly influenced by the structure of larger clusters. In contrast, the macro-averaged score ($S_{\mathrm{M}} \in [-1, 1]$) first averages within clusters and then across clusters, so that each cluster contributes equally regardless of its size. As a result, it is more sensitive to the quality of smaller groups. These scores form the components of our composite criterion. In the next subsection, we compare these subsample-level quantities and use their relationship to define the weighting scheme underlying Composite Silhouette.

3.3 Subsample-Level Discrepancy and Weighting Scheme

For a fixed candidate number of clusters k, $S_{\mathrm{m}}^{(b)}$ and $S_{\mathrm{M}}^{(b)}$ may evaluate the same subsampled clustering differently. We quantify this difference on the b-th subsampled clustering through the discrepancy:

$$\Delta_b = S_{\mathrm{m}}^{(b)} - S_{\mathrm{M}}^{(b)}. \tag{5}$$

When $\Delta_b > 0$, micro-averaging assigns a higher score than macro-averaging, indicating that the clustering quality on that subsample is reflected more strongly by the observation-level, global view. Conversely, when $\Delta_b < 0$, macro-averaging assigns the higher score, indicating that the evaluation is driven more strongly by the cluster-level view. Thus, Δ_b captures both the direction and the magnitude of the disagreement between the two aggregation strategies. This discrepancy is not meant to declare one aggregation inherently correct. Rather, it serves as a local signal of how the clustering structure revealed by a given subsample is reflected by the two Silhouette aggregations. The larger of the two scores is not treated as an oracle, but as the aggregation view that is more favorable to the structure observed in that subsample; the combination therefore shifts only smoothly toward that view while still retaining information from the other one. Instead of imposing a fixed preference for either perspective, we use this local disagreement to balance micro- and macro-averaging adaptively within each subsampled clustering. Since the magnitude of Δ_b may vary across $b \in \{1, \ldots, B\}$, we normalize it relative to the largest absolute discrepancy observed across the B subsamples $\Delta_{\max} = \max_{1 \leq b \leq B} |\Delta_b|$:

$$\widetilde{\Delta}_b = \frac{\Delta_b}{\Delta_{\max} + \varepsilon} \in (-1, 1), \quad \varepsilon > 0 \text{ small for stability (default: } 10^{-12}). \tag{6}$$

This ensures that the discrepancy is interpreted relative to the range of disagreement observed across the current collection of subsampled clusterings, rather than through its raw scale. To obtain a smooth and stable transformation of the normalized difference, we pass $\widetilde{\Delta}_b$ through the hyperbolic tangent function:

$$z_b = \tanh(\widetilde{\Delta}_b). \tag{7}$$

This transformation is monotone and nearly linear around zero, so small values of $\widetilde{\Delta}_b$ are preserved almost proportionally, whereas larger ones are gradually compressed. Its smoothness, symmetry, and gradual saturation make $\tanh(\cdot)$ a natural choice for "encoding" local micro–macro disagreement in a stable and interpretable way (see Supplementary Material §B for an ablation over alternative transformations, including linear, nonlinear, and hard-threshold mappings).

For each subsample $b \in \{1, \ldots, B\}$, we use z_b to combine $S_{\mathrm{m}}^{(b)}$ and $S_{\mathrm{M}}^{(b)}$ in a way that reflects their relative behavior on that subsample; we map $z_b \in (-1, 1)$ to $(0, 1)$ and define the subsample-specific convex weight assigned to $S_{\mathrm{m}}^{(b)}$ as:

$$w_b = \frac{1 + z_b}{2} \in (0, 1), \tag{8}$$

so that the weight assigned to $S_{\mathrm{M}}^{(b)}$ is $1 - w_b$. By construction the weighting remains centered around $\frac{1}{2}$. In particular, when $\Delta_b > 0$, we have $w_b > \frac{1}{2}$, so the combination places greater emphasis on micro-averaging; when $\Delta_b < 0$, then $w_b < \frac{1}{2}$, so the emphasis shifts toward macro-averaging. If $\Delta_b \approx 0 \Rightarrow w_b \approx \frac{1}{2}$, meaning the two strategies are weighted equally. Thus, the sign of Δ_b determines which aggregation is favored on a given subsample, while its transformed magnitude determines how strongly that preference is expressed. This yields a subsample-specific balancing mechanism between the two Silhouette aggregations, favoring the aggregation view that is more strongly expressed in each subsampled clustering while still accounting for the other in proportion to the magnitude of their discrepancy, namely $w_b S_{\mathrm{m}}^{(b)} + (1 - w_b) S_{\mathrm{M}}^{(b)}$.

3.4 Composite Silhouette

For a fixed candidate number of clusters k, the Composite Silhouette score is obtained by averaging the B subsample-specific convex combinations induced by the weights w_b (Eq. 8):

$$S_{\mathrm{mM}} = \frac{1}{B} \sum_{b=1}^{B} \left[w_b S_{\mathrm{m}}^{(b)} + (1 - w_b) S_{\mathrm{M}}^{(b)} \right]. \tag{9}$$

This yields a single criterion that summarizes clustering quality across repeated subsampled views of the data while preserving how the relative support for micro- and macro-averaging varies from one subsample to another (Fig. 2).

Properties. For convenience, let $S_{\mathrm{mM}}^{(b)} := w_b S_{\mathrm{m}}^{(b)} + (1 - w_b) S_{\mathrm{M}}^{(b)}$ denote the composite score on the b-th subsample. Since $w_b \in (0, 1)$, each $S_{\mathrm{mM}}^{(b)}$ is a convex combination of $S_{\mathrm{m}}^{(b)}$ and $S_{\mathrm{M}}^{(b)}$, and therefore satisfies $\min\{S_{\mathrm{m}}^{(b)}, S_{\mathrm{M}}^{(b)}\} \le S_{\mathrm{mM}}^{(b)} \le \max\{S_{\mathrm{m}}^{(b)}, S_{\mathrm{M}}^{(b)}\}$. Substituting $w_b = \frac{1+z_b}{2}$ and $\Delta_b = S_{\mathrm{m}}^{(b)} - S_{\mathrm{M}}^{(b)}$ gives (see detailed analysis in Supplementary Material §A):

$$S_{\mathrm{mM}}^{(b)} = \frac{S_{\mathrm{m}}^{(b)} + S_{\mathrm{M}}^{(b)}}{2} + \frac{\Delta_b z_b}{2} = \frac{S_{\mathrm{m}}^{(b)} + S_{\mathrm{M}}^{(b)}}{2} + \frac{\Delta_b}{2} \tanh\left(\frac{\Delta_b}{\Delta_{\max} + \varepsilon} \right).$$

Thus, each subsample-level composite starts from the midpoint of the micro- and macro-averaged Silhouette scores and is then pulled toward the larger one

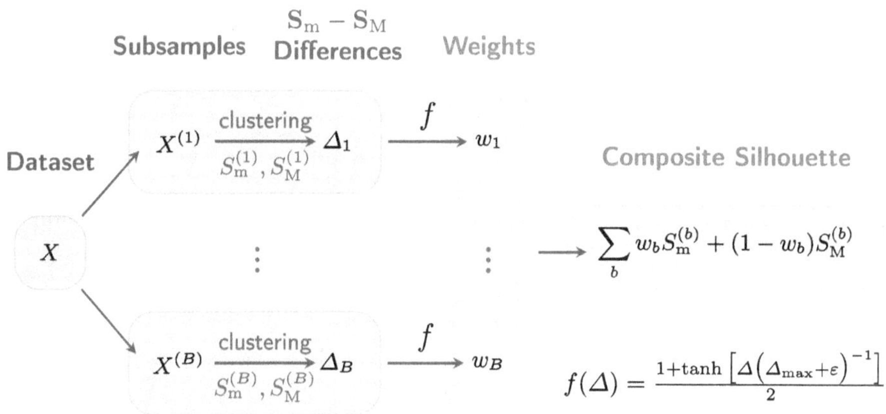

Fig. 2. Overview of the S_{mM} evaluation for a given number of clusters k.

by an amount controlled by the transformed discrepancy. Averaging over the B subsamples yields:

$$\frac{1}{B}\sum_{b=1}^{B}\min\{S_{\mathrm{m}}^{(b)}, S_{\mathrm{M}}^{(b)}\} \leq S_{\mathrm{mM}} \leq \frac{1}{B}\sum_{b=1}^{B}\max\{S_{\mathrm{m}}^{(b)}, S_{\mathrm{M}}^{(b)}\} \Rightarrow S_{\mathrm{mM}} \in [-1, 1].$$

Notably, although each $S_{\mathrm{mM}}^{(b)}$ lies between its corresponding micro- and macro-averaged components, the final score S_{mM} need not lie between the sample-averaged quantities

$$\overline{S}_{\mathrm{m}} = \frac{1}{B}\sum_{b=1}^{B} S_{\mathrm{m}}^{(b)}, \qquad \overline{S}_{\mathrm{M}} = \frac{1}{B}\sum_{b=1}^{B} S_{\mathrm{M}}^{(b)}, \tag{10}$$

since our proposed formulation averages subsample-specific convex combinations rather than applying a single global convex combination to $\overline{S}_{\mathrm{m}}$ and $\overline{S}_{\mathrm{M}}$ (illustrated in Figs. C.2(c), C.4(a) of the Supplementary Material). Indeed, using $w_b = \frac{1+z_b}{2}$ (Eq. 8) and $\Delta_b = S_{\mathrm{m}}^{(b)} - S_{\mathrm{M}}^{(b)}$ (Eq. 5), we obtain (detailed analysis in Supplementary Material §A):

$$S_{\mathrm{mM}} = \frac{\overline{S}_{\mathrm{m}} + \overline{S}_{\mathrm{M}}}{2} + \frac{1}{2B}\sum_{b=1}^{B}\Delta_b z_b.$$

Thus, S_{mM} is the midpoint of $\overline{S}_{\mathrm{m}}$ and $\overline{S}_{\mathrm{M}}$ plus a discrepancy-dependent correction term, rather than a single convex combination of the two sample-averaged scores.

$\mathbf{S_{\mathrm{mM}}}$ Cluster Count Selection. Evaluating S_{mM} over the candidate set $\mathcal{K}$, allows us to select the number of clusters as the value of k that maximizes the

Composite Silhouette score:[2]

$$k^\star = \arg\max_{k \in \mathcal{K}} S_{\mathrm{mM}}(k). \tag{11}$$

The proposed criterion is intended for selecting the number of clusters rather than directly producing a final clustering of the full dataset. After $k^\star$ is selected, a final partition can be obtained by applying the chosen clustering algorithm to the complete dataset with $k = k^\star$.

Complexity. Let $T_F(m, d, k)$ denote the cost of applying the clustering algorithm $F(\cdot; k)$ to a subsample of size m in dimension d. For a fixed candidate number of clusters k, clustering across the B subsamples costs $\mathcal{O}(B\, T_F(m, d, k))$, while computing the corresponding subsample-level micro- and macro-averaged Silhouette scores costs $\mathcal{O}(B\, m^2 d)$. The remaining operations specific to S_{mM} (namely the computation of discrepancies, transformations, weights, and the final averaging) are linear in B and therefore negligible. Hence, for a fixed k, the overall complexity is $\mathcal{O}\big(B\, T_F(m, d, k) + B\, m^2 d\big)$.

In the case of k-means: $T_F(m, d, k) = \mathcal{O}(kmd)$, yielding $\mathcal{O}(Bkmd + Bm^2 d)$. Thus, S_{mM} preserves the dominant computational profile of repeated subsampled Silhouette evaluation while adding only negligible discrepancy-aware overhead.

4 Theoretical Analysis

We briefly summarize the main probabilistic guarantee underlying Composite Silhouette; full statements, extensions, and proofs are deferred to the Supplementary Material (§A). For the analysis, we consider the candidate set $\mathcal{K}$ and assume that the subsamples are drawn independently according to the sampling scheme, while any randomness of the clustering algorithm is also independent across trials and independent of the subsampling. In our method, the normalizing quantity $\Delta_{\max} = \Delta_{\max}(k)$ is computed from the same subsamples used to form S_{mM}, which induces dependence across the resulting terms. To obtain concentration bounds with standard tools, we therefore analyze a closely related version in which $\Delta_{\max}$ is estimated from an independent set of subsamples and then used to form the final score. This preserves the form of the method while ensuring that the per-subsample composite scores used in the analysis are independent and identically distributed. In practice, this distinction is mainly technical: the independent estimation of $\Delta_{\max}$ is introduced to obtain clean concentration bounds, while the empirical behavior remains very similar to that of the implemented version for moderate to large values of B. Under this setup, each subsample composite $w_b S_{\mathrm{m}}^{(b)} + (1 - w_b) S_{\mathrm{M}}^{(b)}$ lies in $[-1, 1]$, so Hoeffding's inequality applies directly. In particular, when the candidate set $\mathcal{K}$ is finite, for any $\delta \in (0, 1)$, the estimate $\sup_{k \in \mathcal{K}} \left| S_{\mathrm{mM}}(k) - \mathbb{E}\left[S_{\mathrm{mM}}^{(b)}(k) \mid \Delta_{\max}(k) \right] \right| \le \sqrt{\frac{2 \ln(2|\mathcal{K}|/\delta)}{B}}$ holds with conditional

[2] A more conservative alternative (supported by our implementation) is to select k by maximizing a lower confidence bound (LCB) of $S_{\mathrm{mM}}(k)$, thus favoring candidates with both high score and low subsampling variability.

probability at least $1 - \delta$ (proof in Supplementary Material, §A.2). Thus, the entire curve $k \mapsto S_{\mathrm{mM}}(k)$ is uniformly estimated at rate $O(B^{-1/2})$, so the relative ordering of candidate cluster counts is increasingly stable as the number of subsamples grows. The corresponding fixed-k concentration bound is given in Supplementary Material (§A.1), while Supplementary Material (§A.3) shows that, under a standard positive-margin condition on the subsampling objective (i.e., the optimal candidate is separated from all others by a strictly positive gap in the subsampling expectation), the probability of selecting the optimal candidate approaches one as B increases. Together, these results show that increasing the number of subsamples improves both the accuracy of the estimated Composite Silhouette curve and the reliability of the resulting choice of $k^{\star}$.

5 Empirical Validation

5.1 Synthetic and Real-World Datasets

We evaluate Composite Silhouette on four synthetic datasets and twelve real-world datasets spanning balanced and imbalanced cluster structures, heterogeneous cluster scales, tabular data, image representations, and text embeddings.

The **synthetic datasets** (S1–S4, visualization in Fig. 3) are designed to probe different structural regimes, from clean and well-separated clusters to strongly imbalanced and heterogeneous mixtures: **S1** consists of 10,000 samples generated from 5 Gaussian clusters with standard deviation 0.5. This dataset provides a clean and nearly balanced benchmark with sharply separated groups, for which we expect both aggregation strategies to perform well (Eq. 4). **S2** consists of 10,000 samples generated from 6 Gaussian clusters with standard deviation 0.9. Relative to S1, the clusters are less sharply separated, yielding a balanced but more diffuse setting in which micro-averaging is expected to provide the stronger signal. **S3** contains 2,300 samples arranged in 5 clusters with pronounced size and scale imbalance: two large clusters of 1,000 samples each and three small clusters of 100 samples each. The two large clusters are placed relatively close to one another and have larger spread ($\sigma = 1.8$), whereas the three small clusters are more compact ($\sigma = 0.5$). This dataset is intended to highlight the tension between observation-level and cluster-level aggregation under imbalance, and we expect macro-averaging to be more informative in this setting. **S4** contains 4,090 samples distributed over 12 clusters with multiple size regimes: two large clusters (1,500 samples each), two medium clusters (300 each), five small clusters (80 each), and three tiny clusters (30 each). The cluster spreads vary across groups ($\sigma \in \{2.2, 1.2, 0.9, 0.6\}$), producing a challenging setting with substantial heterogeneity in both scale and cluster size, in which we do not expect either micro- or macro-averaging alone to perform consistently well.

The **real-world datasets** include binary and multiclass data from tabular, vision, and text domains:[3] **Parkinsons** (PKS) contains $n = 195$ voice recordings

[3] Available via `scikit-learn`, OpenML, UCI, and Hugging Face Datasets.

described by $d = 22$ features and forms $k = 2$ classes. **Wine** (WNE) contains $n = 178$ wine samples with $d = 13$ chemical attributes and $k = 3$ classes. **Blood Transfusion** (BLD) contains $n = 748$ donor records with $d = 4$ numerical features and $k = 2$ classes. **Digits** (DGT) contains $n = 1{,}797$ handwritten digit images with $d = 64$ and $k = 10$ classes. **BBC News** (BBC) contains $n = 2{,}225$ news articles across $k = 5$ topics; documents are embedded with `all-MiniLM-L6-v2` and reduced to $d = 50$ dimensions by PCA. **HTRU2** (HTR) contains $n = 17{,}898$ astrophysical signal instances described by $d = 8$ features and $k = 2$ classes, with strong class imbalance. **STL-10** (STL) contains $n = 5{,}000$ natural images from $k = 10$ classes; images are represented by pretrained ResNet-18 embeddings of dimension $d = 512$. **20 Newsgroups** (NSG) contains $n = 11{,}314$ training documents from $k = 20$ topic categories; we use TF–IDF representations, reduced to $d = 100$ dimensions via truncated SVD. **Spambase** (SPM) contains $n = 4{,}601$ email instances represented by $d = 57$ numerical features and $k = 2$ classes. **Minds-14** (MDS) contains $n = 2{,}797$ utterances from $k = 14$ intent classes; utterances are embedded with `all-MiniLM-L6-v2`, and reduced to $d = 85$ dimensions by PCA, and ℓ_2-normalized. **Bank Marketing** (BNK) contains $n = 45{,}211$ customer records with numerical dimension $d = 7$ and $k = 2$ classes. **Banking77** (B77) contains $n = 13{,}083$ utterances from $k = 77$ intent classes; utterances are embedded with `all-MiniLM-L6-v2`, reduced to $d = 50$ dimensions by PCA, and ℓ_2-normalized. For tabular datasets, we standardize numerical features before clustering. For representation-based datasets, we cluster the transformed feature spaces described above.

5.2 Experiments

We compare S_{mM} (Eq. 9) against a broad set of internal validation baselines under a common k-means evaluation protocol. The comparison includes subsample-averaged micro- and macro-averaged Silhouette scores $\overline{S}_{\text{m}}$, $\overline{S}_{\text{M}}$ (Eq. 10), computed on exactly the same subsamples used by S_{mM}, as well as repeated full-data averages of micro- and macro-averaged Silhouette (avg S_{m}, avg S_{M}), Calinski–Harabasz (avg CH), and Davies–Bouldin (avg DB), where the number of repeated runs matches the number of subsamples used by S_{mM}. Here, "full-data average" refers to averaging the corresponding index across repeated k-means runs on the full dataset under different random initializations. For completeness, we also report the number of clusters selected by the mean Elbow criterion (avg EL) and by the Gap statistic (GAPs).

For each dataset, we evaluate methods over a candidate set of cluster counts centered at the ground-truth value: $\mathcal{K} = \{k_{\text{GT}} - 5, \ldots, k_{\text{GT}} + 5\}$. When $k_{\text{GT}} < 5$, we instead use $\mathcal{K} = \{2, \ldots, k_{\text{GT}} + 5\}$, ensuring that the search range always begins at 2. For each score-based method, we report the selected number of clusters (Table 1) and the value attained at the ground-truth number of clusters k_{GT} (§5.1, Supplementary Material §C; Table C.1). Trend figures over candidate values of k for S_{mM}, $\overline{S}_{\text{m}}$, and $\overline{S}_{\text{M}}$, together with the corresponding results obtained using GMM, and Bisecting k-means are provided in the Supplementary Material §C (Figs. C.1–C.4; Tables C.2–C.3).

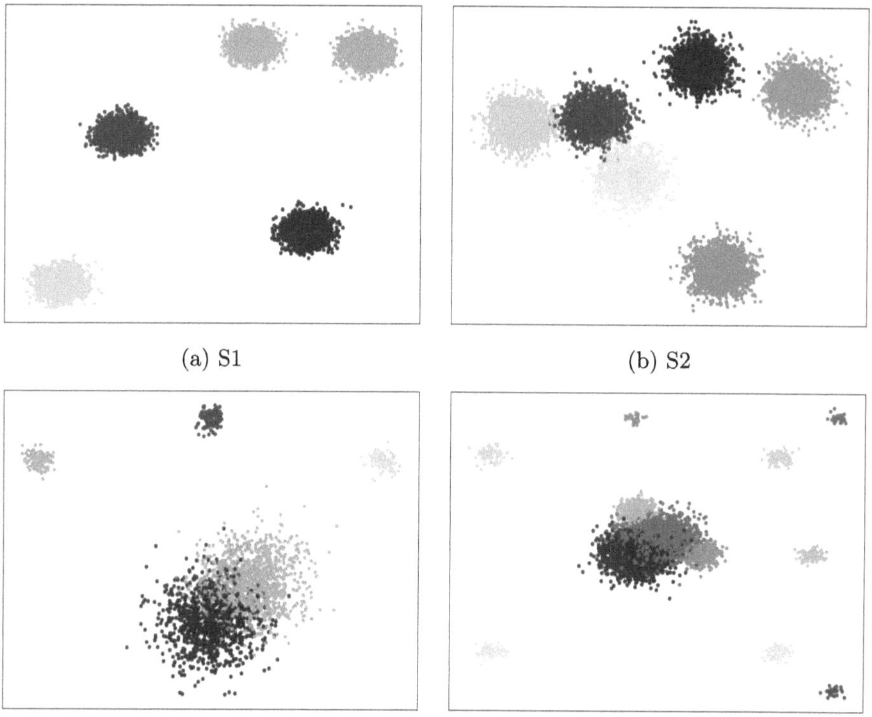

(a) S1 (b) S2

(c) S3 (d) S4

Fig. 3. Synthetic datasets (**S1-S4**), colored by ground-truth cluster labels.

S_{mM} **Parameters.** Across all experiments, we use $B = 20 - 30$ subsamples and the subsample size is selected automatically from the dataset size N and the largest candidate number of clusters $k_{\max}$. Specifically, the subsample size is chosen as the larger of two quantities: a fraction (ϕ) of the dataset size, and a minimum size of 30 observations per candidate cluster at $k_{\max}$. The fraction is set to 80% of the data for datasets with at most 2,000 samples, 60% for datasets with between 2,001 and 20,000 samples, and 40% for larger datasets. The resulting value is then capped at the full dataset size. In this way, the rule preserves sufficient cluster representation for large candidate values of k while keeping the computational cost manageable on larger datasets.

To examine how the Composite Silhouette estimate stabilizes as the number of subsamples B increases, we study its approximation error as a function of B at the ground-truth number of clusters k_{GT}. For each dataset, we first compute a reference estimate using $B_{\max} = 200$ subsamples under the same automatic subsample-size rule described above. We then treat this $B_{\max}$ estimate as a high-precision proxy and, for each smaller value $B \in \{10, 20, \ldots, 200\}$, approximate it by recomputing S_{mM} from only B subsamples drawn without replacement from the full pool of 200. This subsampling of subsamples is repeated 25 times

Table 1. Selected number of clusters for S_{mM}, $\overline{S}_{\mathrm{m}}$, $\overline{S}_{\mathrm{M}}$, avg S_{m}, avg S_{M}, avg CH, avg DB, avg EL, and GAPs, under the k-means protocol (values at the ground-truth number of clusters in Supplementary Material §C Table C.1). All score-based criteria are maximized over $\mathcal{K}$ except avg DB, which is minimized. **Bold** entries indicate that the selected k is the ground-truth k_{GT}.

Dataset	S_{mM}	$\overline{S}_{\mathrm{m}}$	$\overline{S}_{\mathrm{M}}$	avg S_{m}	avg S_{M}	avg CH	avg DB	avg EL	GAPs
S1	**5**	**5**	**5**	**5**	**5**	**5**	**5**	**5**	**5**
S2	**6**	**6**	3	**6**	3	**6**	**6**	3	**6**
S3	**5**	2	**5**	2	**5**	10	**5**	**5**	3
S4	**12**	8	13	9	9	16	9	9	14
PKS	**2**	**2**	**2**	**2**	**2**	3	**2**	3	7
WNE	**3**	**3**	**3**	**3**	**3**	**3**	**3**	**3**	**3**
BLD	**2**	**2**	6	**2**	6	6	4	4	5
DGT	**10**	**10**	**10**	**10**	9	3	9	3	**10**
BBC	**5**	6	**5**	**5**	**5**	2	7	**5**	9
HTR	**2**	**2**	**2**	**2**	**2**	4	3	4	7
STL	**10**	**10**	**10**	6	6	6	**10**	8	14
NSG	**20**	24	21	23	24	24	24	21	24
SPM	**2**	**2**	**2**	**2**	**2**	3	**2**	3	3
MDS	**14**	15	12	15	**14**	**14**	**14**	**14**	16
BNK	**2**	**2**	**2**	**2**	**2**	8	8	8	**2**
B77	**77**	82	**77**	81	**77**	72	81	81	75

for each value of B, producing a distribution of absolute errors relative to the $B_{\max}$ estimate. Figure 4 summarizes how this error decreases as the number of subsamples grows, shown separately for synthetic and real-world datasets.

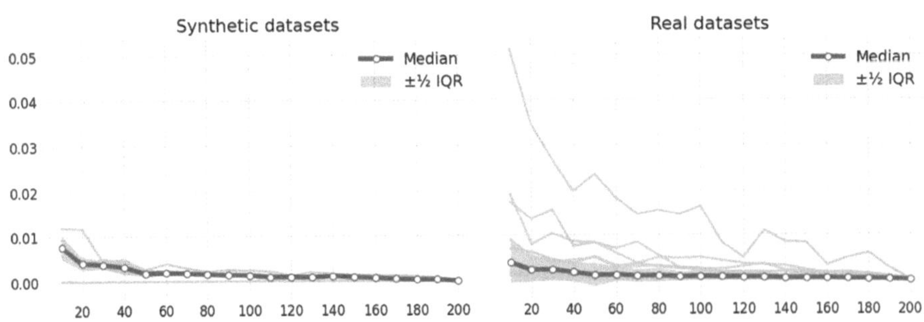

Fig. 4. Approximation error of S_{mM} as a function of the number of subsamples B (left: synthetic datasets, right: real-world datasets). Curves: gray: per-dataset median absolute error, blue: across-dataset median, shaded band: $\pm\frac{1}{2}$ IQR. (Color figure online)

Finally, to complement our complexity analysis (Sect. 3.4), we examine how the runtime of S_{mM} scales with dataset size. We generate synthetic Gaussian data with fixed cluster structure ($k = 5$, $d = 10$), and increasing sample size N (from 1,000 to 500,000), and compare a single-k evaluation of S_{mM} (using $B = 20$) with the standard (scikit-learn) Silhouette score computed on the full dataset.

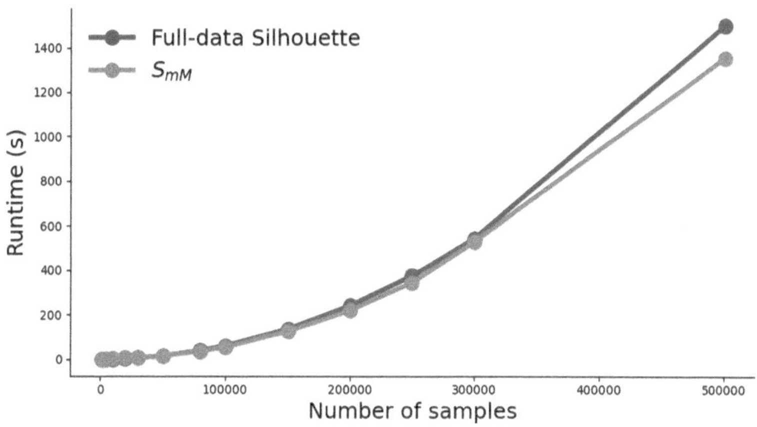

Fig. 5. Runtime as a function of the number of samples N for a single-k evaluation of S_{mM} and for the standard Silhouette score computed on the full dataset. (Color figure online)

5.3 Results

Table 1 shows that S_{mM} (Eqs. 9, 11) recovers the ground-truth number of clusters on all sixteen datasets considered (Sect. 5.1), making it the only criterion in our comparison to do so consistently. This holds across balanced synthetic data (S1, S2), strongly imbalanced and heterogeneous synthetic settings (S3, S4), tabular datasets, image embeddings, and text representations. Importantly, whenever one of the two subsample-averaged Silhouette views (Eq. 10) provides the stronger signal, S_{mM} follows it without requiring prior knowledge of whether micro- or macro-averaging should be preferred (Table 1, Supplementary Material §C); see, for example, S1, where both $\overline{S}_{\mathrm{m}}, \overline{S}_{\mathrm{M}}$ identify the ground-truth number of clusters, S2, where the micro view is more informative, and S3 and B77, where the macro view is more informative (Table 1, Supplementary Material §C; Table C.1, Figs. C.1–C.4). At the same time, S_{mM} remains effective in more ambiguous cases where neither view alone identifies k_{GT}, such as S4, NSG, and MDS. This behavior also extends beyond k-means, as shown by the corresponding GMM and Bisecting k-means results in Supplementary Material §C (Tables C.2–C.3). We further assess the final full-data k-means partitions obtained at the selected values of k using external clustering metrics, with ACC, ARI, NMI, and AMI results reported in Supplementary Material §C, Fig. C.5. Nevertheless, the selected value of k depends on the clustering algorithm used to generate the candidate partitions, and performance may degrade when the algorithm is poorly matched to the geometry of the data. These findings directly support our motivating question: S_{mM} is able to combine the strengths of micro- and macro-averaged Silhouette for cluster-count selection without assuming in advance which aggregation strategy is preferable. This remains the case even in settings where neither view alone aligns with the ground truth, suggesting that the composite captures a more informative signal than either aggregation strategy on its own.

A second observation is that the subsample-averaged baselines $\overline{S}_{\mathrm{m}}$ and $\overline{S}_{\mathrm{M}}$ are generally more reliable than the corresponding averages across repeated full-data runs, which supports the use of repeated subsampled views rather than repeated random initializations alone. The automatic subsample-size rule (Sect. 5.2) is sufficient across all datasets and does not require dataset-specific tuning. Figure 4 further shows that the approximation error of S_{mM} decreases rapidly with the number of subsamples: the across-dataset median error is already below 0.01 at $B = 10$ for both synthetic and real data, while even the most difficult real datasets remain within roughly 0.05 and improve steadily as B increases. Thus, moderate values such as $B = 20$–30 are adequate in practice. Table B.1 in Supplementary Material §B additionally shows that the tanh transformation yields the most reliable S_{mM} ground-truth recovery among the tested z_b transformations (Sect. 3.3; Eq. 7). Finally, Fig. 5 shows that S_{mM} remains computationally competitive: despite including repeated subsampling, clustering, and aggregation, its runtime stays competitive with the full-data Silhouette baseline and the advantage becomes more pronounced as the dataset size grows.

6 Conclusion

We introduced Composite Silhouette (S_{mM}), a discrepancy-aware internal validation criterion that combines micro- and macro-averaged Silhouette scores through repeated subsampled clusterings. By using subsample-specific convex weights derived from the local disagreement between the two aggregation views, S_{mM} adaptively favors the more informative perspective without discarding the other. At the same time, the method remains computationally practical, with modest additional overhead beyond repeated subsampled Silhouette evaluation and natural compatibility with parallel computation. Empirical results show that S_{mM} identifies the correct number of clusters more reliably than either subsample-averaged micro- or macro-averaged Silhouette alone, as well as standard internal baselines, across balanced, imbalanced, and structurally heterogeneous settings. These findings indicate that combining the two Silhouette views locally, rather than committing to one of them globally, yields a more robust basis for cluster-count selection. A natural direction for future work is a more systematic study of the regimes in which the composite remains informative even when both component views are individually misleading, in order to better characterize the structural conditions that favor discrepancy-aware aggregation. Overall, S_{mM} provides a practical and broadly applicable framework for cluster-count selection that is adaptive and effective across diverse data domains.

Acknowledgments. This work has been partially supported by project MIS 5154714 of the National Recovery and Resilience Plan Greece 2.0 funded by the European Union under the NextGenerationEU Program.

Disclosure of Interests. The authors declare that they have no competing interests.

Availability of Data and Code. The implementation, experimental code used to reproduce the results, scripts for generating the synthetic datasets, and supplementary material are publicly available at https://github.com/semoglou/compsil.

References

1. Arbelaitz, O., Gurrutxaga, I., Muguerza, J., Pérez, J.M., Perona, I.: An extensive comparative study of cluster validity indices. Pattern Recogn. **46**(1), 243–256 (2013). https://doi.org/10.1016/j.patcog.2012.07.021
2. Batool, F., Hennig, C.: Clustering with the average silhouette width. Comput. Stat. Data Anal. **158**, 107190 (2021). https://doi.org/10.1016/j.csda.2021.107190
3. Ben-Hur, A., Elisseeff, A., Guyon, I.: A stability based method for discovering structure in clustered data. In: Pacific Symposium on Biocomputing, pp. 6–17 (2002). https://doi.org/10.1142/9789812799623_0002
4. Caliński, T., Harabasz, J.: A dendrite method for cluster analysis. Commun. Stat.-Theory Methods **3**(1), 1–27 (1974). https://doi.org/10.1080/03610927408827101
5. Davies, D.L., Bouldin, D.W.: A cluster separation measure. IEEE Trans. Pattern Anal. Mach. Intell. **PAMI-1**(2), 224–227 (1979). https://doi.org/10.1109/TPAMI.1979.4766909
6. Dudek, A.: Silhouette index as clustering evaluation tool. In: Jajuga, K., Batóg, J., Walesiak, M. (eds.) Classification and Data Analysis, pp. 19–33. Springer, Cham (2020). https://doi.org/10.1007/978-3-030-52348-0_2
7. Dunn, J.C.: A fuzzy relative of the ISODATA process and its use in detecting compact well-separated clusters. J. Cybern. **3**(3), 32–57 (1973). https://doi.org/10.1080/01969727308546046
8. Halkidi, M., Batistakis, Y., Vazirgiannis, M.: Cluster validity methods: Part I. ACM SIGMOD Rec. **31**(2), 40–45 (2002). https://doi.org/10.1145/565117.565124
9. Halkidi, M., Batistakis, Y., Vazirgiannis, M.: Clustering validity checking methods: Part II. ACM SIGMOD Rec. **31**(3), 19–27 (2002). https://doi.org/10.1145/601858.601862
10. Hassan, B.A., Tayfor, N.B., Hassan, A.A., Ahmed, A.M., Rashid, T.A., Abdalla, N.N.: From A-to-Z review of clustering validation indices. Neurocomputing **601**, 128198 (2024). https://doi.org/10.1016/j.neucom.2024.128198
11. Jain, A.K., Murty, M.N., Flynn, P.J.: Data clustering: a review. ACM Comput. Surv. (CSUR) **31**(3), 264–323 (1999). https://doi.org/10.1145/331499.331504
12. John, J., Shobayo, O., Ogunleye, B.: An exploration of clustering algorithms for customer segmentation in the UK retail market. Analytics **2**(4), 809–823 (2023). https://doi.org/10.3390/analytics2040042

13. Lange, T., Roth, V., Braun, M.L., Buhmann, J.M.: Stability-based validation of clustering solutions. Neural Comput. **16**(6), 1299–1323 (2004). https://doi.org/10.1162/089976604773717621
14. Liu, Y., Li, Z., Xiong, H., Gao, X., Wu, J.: Understanding of internal clustering validation measures. In: 2010 IEEE International Conference on Data Mining, pp. 911–916. IEEE (2010). https://doi.org/10.1109/ICDM.2010.35
15. Pavlopoulos, J., Vardakas, G., Likas, A.: Revisiting Silhouette aggregation. In: Pedreschi, D., Monreale, A., Guidotti, R., Pellungrini, R., Naretto, F. (eds.) Discovery Science, pp. 354–368. Springer, Cham (2025). https://doi.org/10.1007/978-3-031-78977-9_23
16. Pedregosa, F., et al.: Scikit-learn: machine learning in python. J. Mach. Learn. Res. **12**, 2825–2830 (2011)
17. Rousseeuw, P.J.: Silhouettes: a graphical aid to the interpretation and validation of cluster analysis. J. Comput. Appl. Math. **20**, 53–65 (1987). https://doi.org/10.1016/0377-0427(87)90125-7
18. Semoglou, A., Likas, A., Pavlopoulos, J.: Silhouette-driven instance-weighted k-means (2026). https://arxiv.org/abs/2506.12878
19. Semoglou, A., Pavlopoulos, J.: CAKE: confidence in assignments via k-partition ensembles. Mach. Learn. Appl. **24**, 100915 (2026). https://doi.org/10.1016/j.mlwa.2026.100915
20. Shahapure, K.R., Nicholas, C.: Cluster quality analysis using silhouette score. In: 2020 IEEE 7th International Conference on Data Science and Advanced Analytics (DSAA), pp. 747–748. IEEE (2020). https://doi.org/10.1109/DSAA49011.2020.00096
21. Shi, C., Wei, B., Wei, S., Wang, W., Liu, H., Liu, J.: A quantitative discriminant method of elbow point for the optimal number of clusters in clustering algorithm. EURASIP J. Wirel. Commun. Network. **2021**(31) (2021). https://doi.org/10.1186/s13638-021-01910-w
22. Thorndike, R.L.: Who belongs in the family? Psychometrika **18**(4), 267–276 (1953). https://doi.org/10.1007/BF02289263
23. Tibshirani, R., Walther, G., Hastie, T.: Estimating the number of clusters in a data set via the gap statistic. J. Roy. Stat. Soc. Ser. B (Stat. Methodol.) **63**(2), 411–423 (2001). https://doi.org/10.1111/1467-9868.00293
24. Vendramin, L., Campello, R.J.G.B., Hruschka, E.R.: Relative clustering validity criteria: a comparative overview. Stat. Anal. Data Mining ASA Data Sci. J. **3**(4), 209–235 (2010). https://doi.org/10.1002/sam.10080
25. Wang, Y., et al.: Unsupervised machine learning for the discovery of latent disease clusters and patient subgroups using electronic health records. J. Biomed. Inform. **102**, 103364 (2020). https://doi.org/10.1016/j.jbi.2019.103364
26. Yuan, M., Zobel, J., Lin, P.: Measurement of clustering effectiveness for document collections. Inf. Retrieval J. **25**(3), 239–268 (2022). https://doi.org/10.1007/s10791-021-09401-8

Contrast Slice Discovery on Sequential Data

Daniel Bastos(✉), Renato Vimieiro, and Vitor Emanuel

Departamento de Ciência da Computação, Universidade Federal de Minas Gerais, Av. Antônio Carlos, 6627, Belo Horizonte, Minas Gerais 31270-901, Brazil
{danielbastos,rvimieiro,vitorvital}@dcc.ufmg.br

Abstract. Machine learning models rarely fail uniformly. Understanding where and why they fail is crucial for developing them responsibly. While existing debugging tools identify high-error regions, they ignore how those errors differ across classes. We propose a new framework for finding subgroups where a model performs well on one class but poorly on another. We call this task contrast slice discovery. Unlike ordinary slice discovery methods that ignore class distribution inside slices and mainly support tabular or image data, our approach aims at contrasting class failures in sequential models. We define interpretable contrast slices through sequential patterns and introduce ConSequence (Contrastive Sequential Slice Discovery), a Monte Carlo Tree Search algorithm for discovering them. The framework then enables post hoc and model-agnostic analysis. We conducted experiments on five datasets spanning sequential, spatiotemporal, and textual domains. The results show that ConSequence consistently identifies slices with high per-class performance contrast, while the baseline failed to identify relevant slices. We hope this work highlights the importance of analyzing model failures at the class level and provides a new tool for understanding sequential models.

Keywords: Slice Discovery · Sequential Data · Subgroup Discovery · Machine Learning · Monte Carlo Tree Search

1 Introduction

As current processes become increasingly more reliable in machine learning models, their fairness and understanding must be prioritized. Lack of auditing and debugging might result in deployments that have unknown biases to certain subgroups hidden by the overall good model performance. A well-known example is related to recidivism prediction instruments, which were found to assign higher risk for black offenders than for whites [2]. Furthermore, machine learning models have been shown to perform poorly on minority and marginalized populations in areas such as medical [5,18] and financial [1].

To aid practitioners, the framework slice discovery has emerged as an option. It focuses on finding slices, i.e. subgroups of data that share a pattern, where a model systematically underperforms. This is usually quantified by comparing a

M. Ceci et al. (Eds.): ECML PKDD 2026, LNAI 16941, pp. 679–696, 2027.
https://doi.org/10.1007/978-3-032-37654-1_39

global metric against the slice's, for example the absolute precision difference, where high deltas point to interesting subgroups. While slice discovery is not required to be post hoc or model-agnostic [7,12,30], designing it as such increases its applicability across the wide range of models used today, regardless if they are tree-based models, deep neural networks, or large language models, for example. Interpretability is also a relevant design choice. Slices that cannot be understood or acted upon offer little value.

In practice, however, when faced with a high-error slice, practitioners may ask why the model fails in that region, or more intuitively: it fails, but in contrast to what? Current slice discovery methods [3,7,23] typically answer only the *where*. For example, consider the aforementioned recidivism prediction instrument. Suppose a slice represents defendants with a history of petty crimes from impoverished neighborhoods. Within this slice the model assigns high error to the non-recidivism class but lower error to the recidivism class, suggesting that socioeconomic features are being interpreted as strong indicators of reoffending. This contrast between classes then exposes the source of confusion.

Sequential data classification is another setting where understanding model failures is particularly important. Models trained on sequential data are being deployed in high-stakes domains, such as patient health prediction from clinical events [19]. Yet, compared to tabular, image, or text-based classifiers, the tools available to audit and debug these models remain underdeveloped.

Nevertheless, the slice discovery approaches discussed above do not support sequential data. Although some works address NLP tasks, the same methods do not necessarily transfer to other sequential domains. This work addresses both gaps by introducing ConSequence[1], a Monte Carlo Tree Search (MCTS) algorithm that identifies subgroups where a model exhibits contrasting performance across classes and describes them through interpretable sequential patterns. The main contributions of this work are summarized in Subsect. 1.1.

1.1 Main Contributions

This work makes the following contributions:

1. We introduce contrast slice discovery, a framework that identifies slices where the model exhibits contrasting performance per class, e.g. high error for one class and low error for another;
2. We propose ConSequence (Contrastive Sequential Slice Discovery), an extension of MCTSExtent [16] for contrast slice discovery in sequential data;
3. We evaluate ConSequence on multiple sequential datasets, demonstrating its ability to find failure modes not detected by current slice discovery frameworks.

[1] https://github.com/danielSbastos/ConSequence.

2 Related Work

2.1 Slice Discovery

Slice discovery searches for subgroups of data, called slices, where a model systematically underperforms. In tabular data, these subgroups are usually described using conjunctions of attribute-value conditions, which keeps the resulting slices interpretable. SliceFinder [3] searches for slices that present differing performance from the overall model, while SliceLine [21] instead focuses on regions containing many high-loss predictions. SubROC [23] compares the ROC-AUC curve of a slice with the global ROC-AUC curve, while Conformalized EMM [9] uses conformal prediction to identify regions of high model uncertainty.

When dealing with high-dimensional data such as images or audio, slice discovery is often performed in representation space. Domino [10] follows this strategy by fitting a mixture model over cross-modal embeddings and then producing natural language descriptions of the discovered groups. GEORGE [24] clusters model representations to group similar failure cases, and Spotlight [7] learns a projection that exposes regions where model behavior differs. These approaches operate in representation space and therefore do not return symbolic slice descriptions, which can make the resulting groups harder for practitioners to interpret.

As for textual data, DEIm [12] finds slices and then generates explanations and model improvement steps. Zhang et al. [30] design slice discovery with LLMs as an active learning problem, where sampled examples are shown to practitioners, who verify whether they correspond to a shared error pattern.

Most of these approaches rely on static descriptions of the data, which can be restrictive in sequential domains where model behavior depends on the order of events rather than on individual attributes. Recent work identifies atypical performance regions in time-series classifiers using shapelet representations [22]. While effective for time-series data, this approach does not naturally extend to other types of sequential inputs, leaving other sequential domains without slice discovery tools.

2.2 Sequential Model Debugging and Analysis

Sequential models are widely used in tasks such as clinical risk prediction [19], time series anomaly detection [29], and natural language processing [8]. Diagnosing their failures, however, remains challenging. Errors may arise from interactions across time points, making them difficult to attribute to individual features or events.

Local interpretability methods focus on explaining individual predictions. Perturbation-based approaches identify subsequences that influence the model's prediction [17]. While useful for understanding specific decisions, these methods do not identify systematic model failures across the dataset.

Several tools support more global inspection of sequential models. LSTMVis [25] and DeepSeer [27] visualize hidden state dynamics to help identify recurring behaviors in RNNs. In NLP, CheckList [20] tests models against predefined linguistic capabilities, while Errudite [28] and LIT [26] provide interfaces for exploring model errors through an interactive analysis. These approaches rely on manual exploration and focus on overall error patterns.

However, none of the above approaches automatically identify subgroups where model performance differs across classes. Our work addresses this limitation by introducing contrast slice discovery, which defines slice quality in terms of class performance contrast within the slice. We use sequential patterns as the description language for slices, inspired by discriminative sequential pattern mining [16].

3 Contrast Slice Discovery

A contrast slice groups instances that share a common pattern. In this work, such slices are discovered using ConSequence. To find regions where the model's performance varies across classes, a quality score measures the divergence of the per-class soft error. The soft error is the absolute difference between the true label and the model's predicted probability. This divergence is measured both between the slice's classes and relative to each class's global baseline. A high score, then, indicates a subgroup where the model treats the classes differently from its overall behavior.

For sequential data, slice descriptions are represented as sequential patterns, i.e., ordered sequences of itemsets. Consecutive itemsets are separated by a gap controlled by a maximum gap parameter, ranging from zero to infinity (no gap constraint).

The remainder of this section describes the main components of ConSequence. Subsection 3.1 presents the search algorithm, Subsect. 3.2 defines the quality function, Subsect. 3.3 addresses pattern redundancy, Subsect. 3.4 describes the statistical validation procedure, and Subsect. 3.5 discusses the algorithm's complexity.

3.1 ConSequence

To navigate the high-dimensional space of sequential patterns, we propose ConSequence, a MCTS algorithm built upon MCTSExtent [16]. ConSequence adapts MCTSExtent for contrast slice discovery by replacing the quality function in the *select* and *rollout* policies while leaving the *expand* and *update* policies unchanged. Furthermore, it adds a statistical validation step in the pipeline.

The search is performed over the training set using the corresponding model soft error scores. The root node corresponds to the empty pattern and its extent contains all training instances. Each node represents a sequential pattern, and the search tree is expanded by progressively generalizing these patterns. The four original MCTSExtent policies, together with our adaptations, are briefly described below.

Select. Starting from the root node, the algorithm traverses the tree by repeatedly selecting the child with the highest UCT (Upper Confidence bounds applied to Trees) score, as shown in Eq. 1.

$$\mathrm{UCT}(\mathrm{parent}, \mathrm{node}) = \frac{\varphi_{\mathrm{node}}}{v_{\mathrm{node}}} + 0.5 \cdot \sqrt{\frac{2 \ln(v_{\mathrm{parent}})}{v_{\mathrm{node}}}} \quad (1)$$

where φ_{node} is the accumulated quality of the node, v_{node} its visit count, and v_{parent} the visit count of its parent node.

Expand. At the selected node, a child pattern is generated by sampling a candidate sequence from instances not covered by the current pattern. The child pattern is obtained as the longest common subsequence (LCS) between the current pattern and the sampled candidate, respecting the maximum gap between itemsets. The gap parameter limits how far apart matched itemsets may appear in a sequence.

Rollout. From the expanded node, a simulation is performed by removing a random number of itemsets from the beginning, the end, or both, from the pattern. The resulting pattern is evaluated, and its quality is used as the rollout reward.

Update. The rollout reward is backpropagated to all parent nodes, updating visit counts and cumulative quality. Patterns that meet the constraints of minimum support, minimum per-class count, and positive quality are inserted into the priority set, which is ordered by quality.

3.2 Quality Measure

To rank candidate slices, we define a raw quality score φ_{raw} that rewards slices where the two classes exhibit contrasting soft errors and at least one class deviates from its respective baseline. It also penalizes class imbalance and can apply a support penalty.

The soft error for an instance is defined as $|y_{\mathrm{true}} - \hat{y}_{\mathrm{true}}|$, where $y_{\mathrm{true}} \in \{0, 1\}$ is the true label and $\hat{y}_{\mathrm{true}}$ is the predicted probability of the true label. For example, an instance from class 1 predicted with probability 0.2 would have a soft error of $|1 - 0.2| = 0.8$.

The raw score decomposes into four components: (1) between-class contrast, s_g; (2) deviation regarding the baseline, $d_{g,B}$; (3) class balance; and (4) a support penalty. It is formally defined in Eq. 2. Here, g denotes a candidate *slice (group)* and B denotes the *baseline*, i.e., the model evaluated on the full dataset.

$$\varphi_{\mathrm{raw}} = (s_g \cdot d_{g,B}) \cdot (b_g \cdot p_{g,B}) \quad (2)$$

For numerical stability, the final quality score φ is obtained by applying a sigmoid transformation to φ_{raw}, as shown in Eq. 3.

$$\varphi = \frac{1}{1 + e^{-(\varphi_{\text{raw}} - \nu)}} \tag{3}$$

where $\nu = 2$ is a constant offset applied across all experiments.

We now formally define each component of our score.

Separation. s_g represents the standardized between-class contrast. The numerator corresponds to the absolute difference in mean soft error between the two classes, while the denominator normalizes this difference by the largest within-class standard deviation. As a result, slices with high variability receive lower scores, as defined in Eq. 4.

$$s_g = \frac{|\mu_0^g - \mu_1^g|}{\max(\sigma_0^g, \sigma_1^g)} \tag{4}$$

Deviation. Following a z-score-like deviation, $d_{g,B}$ measures how exceptional a slice is relative to the baseline B. A slice where both classes perform similarly to their baselines is not informative, even if the within slice contrast is high. This term rewards slices where at least one class deviates substantially from its global mean soft error μ_c^B, normalized by its baseline standard deviation σ_c^B, as presented in Eq. 5.

$$d_{g,B} = \max(d_{0,B}, d_{1,B}), \quad d_{c,B} = \frac{|\mu_c^g - \mu_c^B|}{\sigma_c^B} \tag{5}$$

Class Balance. In Eq. 6, b_g penalizes slices dominated by a single class. It corresponds to a scaled binary Gini impurity, ranging from 0 to 1, where 1 represents perfectly balanced classes and 0, complete imbalance.

$$b_g = 4 \cdot p_0 \cdot p_1, \quad p_c = \frac{n_c^g}{n_0^g + n_1^g} \tag{6}$$

Support Penalty. Similar to the Klösgen size weighting [14], $p_{g,B}$ applies a penalty relative to the slice size, as shown in Eq. 7. With $\gamma = 0$, all slices are treated equally regardless of size, while increasing γ favors larger sizes.

$$p_{g,B} = \left(\frac{|g|}{N}\right)^{\gamma}, \quad \gamma \geq 0 \tag{7}$$

where $|g|$ is the number of instances in the slice and N is the total number of instances in the dataset.

3.3 Similarity Filtering

Following the original MCTSExtent procedure, candidates are sorted by quality in descending order once all iterations are complete, and patterns are filtered to reduce redundancy. Two patterns are deemed similar if their Jaccard measure exceeds a user-defined threshold (θ). At most k' patterns are passed to statistical validation.

3.4 Significance Filtering

After similarity filtering, the remaining patterns are tested for statistical significance. For each candidate slice, k'' random subgroups with the same support and class balance are sampled from the same model training dataset. The contrast term $s_g \cdot d_{g,B}$ is computed for each random subgroup and compared with the value obtained for the original candidate slice. The p-value is the fraction of random subgroups whose contrast term exceeds that of the candidate slice. A hypothesis test is then performed at significance level $\alpha = 0.05$. Then, to control the false discovery rate, Benjamini-Hochberg correction is applied and only slices with adjusted p-values below α are returned.

3.5 Complexity

During T iterations, the execution time is dominated by the quality evaluations performed in the *expand* and *rollout* policies, each requiring a full dataset scan. Although introducing a maximum gap increases the LCS cost compared to the original MCTSExtent, the dataset scan cost remains dominant. Assuming a constant maximum gap, with N sequences, checking whether a pattern of length L_p is a subsequence of a sequence of length L_s requires $O(L_p L_s)$ operations. Therefore, the time complexity is $O(TNL_pL_s)$.

The memory complexity is determined by the dataset and the search tree. Storing the dataset requires $O(NL_s)$ in memory, where L_s is the average sequence length. After T iterations, the search tree contains T nodes, each storing an extent of size up to N in the worst case. Therefore, the memory complexity is $O(TN + NL_s)$.

4 Experiments

We evaluate ConSequence on five datasets spanning three domains: spatiotemporal, sequential, and textual data. The experiments aim to assess whether contrast slice discovery can identify subgroups where model performance diverges across classes, and whether the discovered slices remain statistically significant after filtering and validation.

4.1 Experimental Setup

Datasets. For *spatiotemporal* data, we use two drawing datasets. The **MNIST** dataset [6] provides handwritten digit images, which we convert into pen stroke sequences using the skeleton-based pipeline from [13]. We restrict the classification task to digits *8* and *3* due to their similar visual structure. The **Quick, Draw!** dataset [11] contains sketches sequences collected from an online drawing game. We filter the dataset to retain only single-stroke drawings and then select the *arm* and *leg* categories.

Table 1. Datasets summary statistics.

Dataset	N	n_0	n_1	μ_0^B	μ_1^B	μ^B	Avg. seq. len.	Vocab. size
MNIST	5,262	2,649	2,613	0.205	0.117	0.161	45.1	335
Quick, Draw!	4,320	2,155	2,165	0.183	0.151	0.167	108.0	160
Malware	1,647	1,111	536	0.238	0.169	0.216	200.0	208
Toxicity (Women)	6,785	3,392	3,393	0.291	0.194	0.243	78.4	30,522
Toxicity (Sexuality)	3,997	2,744	1,253	0.399	0.379	0.393	81.3	30,522

For *sequential* data, we use the **Malware** dataset from [15], which consists of Windows API call sequences extracted from executable programs. The classification task distinguishes malicious software (e.g., spyware, backdoors, and viruses) from benign software (e.g., internet, gaming, and business applications).

For *textual* data, we derive two datasets from the **Jigsaw Unintended Bias in Toxicity Classification** dataset [4], where the task is to classify whether a comment is toxic or not. We evaluate under two identity contexts, and filter comments annotated as 100% related to women and 100% related to sexual orientation (gay or lesbian).

Model Training. For the MNIST, Quick, Draw!, and Malware datasets, we train a Bidirectional LSTM classifier using the Adam optimizer with learning rate 1×10^{-3}. For MNIST and Quick, Draw!, a light architecture is used (2 layers, hidden size 6) and trained for 3 epochs. For the Malware dataset, the hidden size is increased to 32 with 2 layers and trained for 5 epochs.

For the toxicity datasets, we fine-tune `bert-base-uncased` [8] for binary toxicity classification over 2 epochs. Models were trained to achieve good to moderate predictive performance, targeting a mean soft error between 0.15 and 0.30. This allows the framework to operate in diverse settings.

Parametrization and Data Summary. Table 1 summarizes the dataset statistics, including class distribution, global soft error baselines, average sequence length and vocabulary size.

Table 2 lists the parameters used by ConSequence for each dataset. The parameters shown include the maximum gap constraint (*max_gap*), the support penalty coefficient γ, the similarity threshold θ and the number of *iterations*. The values were chosen empirically, and accounted for the trade-off further explained on Subsect. 5.1. Unless stated otherwise, all runs retrieve the top-k patterns with $k = 5$, parse the first non-redundant $k' = 100$ patterns, sample $k'' = 1000$ subgroups in the FDR test, use a minimum support of 60 instances, and require at least 10 instances per class.

For the toxicity datasets, the algorithm operates on BERT token identifiers rather than raw text. Tokens in the discovered patterns are mapped back to the BERT vocabulary to recover the textual representations shown in the analysis.

Table 2. Search parameters per dataset.

Dataset	max_gap	γ	θ	Iterations
MNIST	2	0.2	0.05	30,000
Quick, Draw!	5	0.0	0.1	70,000
Malware	5	0.1	0.1	30,000
Toxicity (Women)	1	0.0	0.5	50,000
Toxicity (Sexuality)	1	0.2	0.1	50,000

4.2 Experimental Results

Table 3 presents the top-5 slices from a sample execution for each dataset after similarity and significance filtering. Although 20 experiments were conducted for each dataset configuration, summarized in Table 6, only one representative sample is displayed.

For each slice we report the quality score (φ), the difference in mean soft error between classes (Δ_g), the per-class mean soft error within the slice ($\mu_c^g \pm \sigma_c^g$), and the slice support. Across datasets the slices cover only a small portion of the data (typically around 1–5%). Since φ is obtained by applying a sigmoid transformation to φ_{raw}, and parameter tuning differs across datasets, quality scores should be interpreted per dataset.

Figure 1 from MNIST, Malware, and Toxicity (Women) shows the cumulative distributions of soft error per class for the baseline and two selected slices. In the baseline distributions the class curves largely overlap, while in the slices they separate clearly.

For MNIST and Quick, Draw!, Fig. 2 shows example instances from two slices with the matching pattern highlighted in red. For the Toxicity (Women) dataset, Table 4 provides example comments from a discovered slice.

Table 6 reports the average algorithm metrics taken over 20 runs. The pattern validation pipeline (all patterns, after similarity filtering, after significance

Table 3. Top-5 slices per dataset ranked by quality (φ).

Dataset	Rank	φ	Δ_g	$\mu_0^g \pm \sigma_0^g$	$\mu_1^g \pm \sigma_1^g$	Support
MNIST	1	0.957	0.591	0.742 ± 0.123	0.151 ± 0.105	62 (1.18%)
	2	0.501	0.563	0.642 ± 0.143	0.079 ± 0.165	283 (5.38%)
	3	0.460	0.489	0.191 ± 0.163	0.680 ± 0.201	77 (1.46%)
	4	0.365	0.405	0.160 ± 0.144	0.565 ± 0.256	143 (2.72%)
	5	0.356	0.380	0.188 ± 0.167	0.568 ± 0.244	197 (3.74%)
	Avg.	**0.528**	**0.486**			**152 (2.89%)**
Quick, Draw!	1	0.754	0.580	0.676 ± 0.287	0.096 ± 0.147	60 (1.39%)
	2	0.591	0.517	0.603 ± 0.316	0.085 ± 0.123	62 (1.44%)
	3	0.479	0.447	0.144 ± 0.195	0.591 ± 0.301	73 (1.69%)
	4	0.438	0.408	0.532 ± 0.300	0.125 ± 0.209	64 (1.48%)
	5	0.413	0.343	0.128 ± 0.165	0.471 ± 0.296	82 (1.90%)
	Avg.	**0.535**	**0.459**			**68 (1.58%)**
Malware	1	0.960	0.348	0.465 ± 0.053	0.117 ± 0.028	91 (5.53%)
	2	0.919	0.338	0.460 ± 0.044	0.122 ± 0.063	83 (5.04%)
	3	0.739	0.415	0.570 ± 0.146	0.154 ± 0.081	67 (4.07%)
	4	0.630	0.311	0.502 ± 0.103	0.191 ± 0.112	76 (4.61%)
	5	0.586	0.336	0.508 ± 0.137	0.172 ± 0.073	71 (4.31%)
	Avg.	**0.767**	**0.350**			**78 (4.71%)**
Toxicity (Women)	1	0.921	0.615	0.740 ± 0.187	0.124 ± 0.091	67 (0.99%)
	2	0.837	0.632	0.750 ± 0.146	0.118 ± 0.073	135 (1.99%)
	3	0.776	0.544	0.675 ± 0.187	0.131 ± 0.081	71 (1.05%)
	4	0.573	0.490	0.634 ± 0.222	0.143 ± 0.108	146 (2.15%)
	5	0.539	0.450	0.599 ± 0.208	0.149 ± 0.111	60 (0.88%)
	Avg.	**0.729**	**0.546**			**96 (1.41%)**
Toxicity (Sexuality)	1	0.217	0.311	0.257 ± 0.085	0.567 ± 0.160	77 (1.93%)
	2	0.199	0.253	0.300 ± 0.124	0.553 ± 0.156	63 (1.58%)
	3	0.177	0.199	0.339 ± 0.118	0.537 ± 0.134	69 (1.73%)
	4	0.177	0.197	0.343 ± 0.139	0.540 ± 0.172	81 (2.03%)
	5	0.175	0.214	0.309 ± 0.092	0.523 ± 0.159	81 (2.03%)
	Avg.	**0.189**	**0.220**			**72 (1.80%)**

filtering) shows ConSequence's ability to retain genuinely contrasting slices while discarding spurious ones.

4.3 Benchmark

We evaluate ConSequence against Domino [10]. Domino searches for overall high-error slices rather than class-specific error slices. For MNIST and Quick, Draw!, we derive a set of numeric features from the stroke sequences, such as path statistics and movement proportions. Similarly, for the Malware dataset, numeric features were also derived but accounted for sequence token count (e.g. number of API calls from the system calls $Nt*$) and entropy. For the textual datasets, the raw text is provided directly to Domino without additional feature engineering. The default configuration[2] from Domino was used.

Table 5 reports the average metrics across 20 executions. For a fair comparison, the quality and pattern delta were calculated for each Domino slice using the respective dataset parameter values in Table 2. Domino obtained average quality scores of 0.097 ± 0.026 on MNIST and 0.130 ± 0.030 on Malware. ConSequence achieved 0.527 ± 0.019 and 0.719 ± 0.039 on the same datasets. Both methods returned lower quality scores on the Toxicity (Sexuality) dataset (0.193 ± 0.005 for ConSequence vs. 0.189 ± 0.032 for Domino), but ConSequence produced a higher class error contrast ($\Delta_g = 0.262 \pm 0.014$) compared to Domino ($0.141 \pm 0.016$).

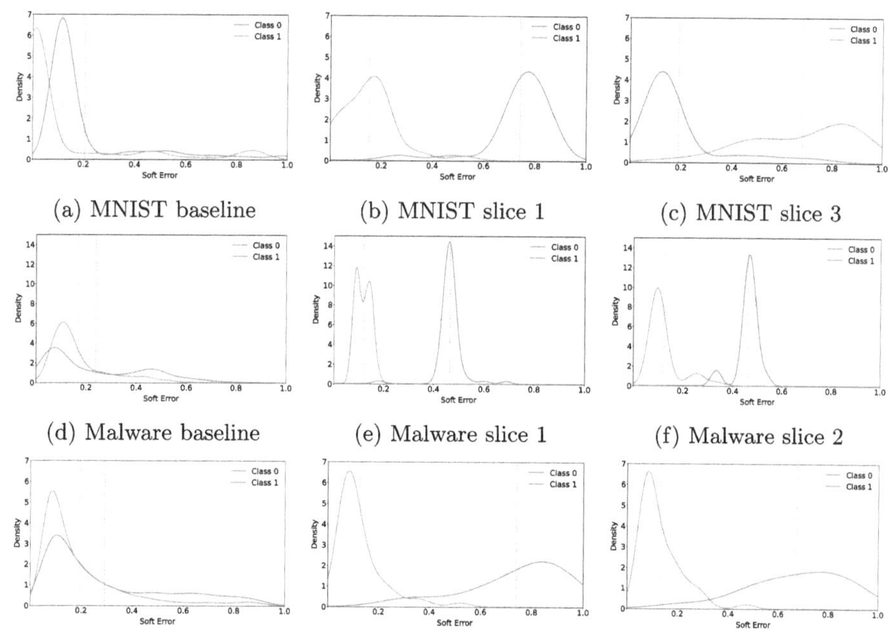

(a) MNIST baseline (b) MNIST slice 1 (c) MNIST slice 3

(d) Malware baseline (e) Malware slice 1 (f) Malware slice 2

(g) Tox. (Women) baseline (h) Tox. (Women) slice 1 (i) Tox. (Women) slice 3

Fig. 1. Per-class soft error distributions for the baseline model and selected slices across datasets. Rows correspond to MNIST, Malware, and Toxicity (Women).

[2] `n_slices = 5, n_mixture_components = 25, y_log_likelihood_weight = 1, y_hat_log_likelihood_weight = 1.`

Table 4. Example comments from the discovered ***racist*** slice in the Toxicity (Women) dataset.

Content warning: The following examples contain offensive or sensitive language.

Class	Text
Not toxic	Never seen this woman before but she looks kind of hot in that outfit. However if she wore a bikini patterned after the Confederate flag, that would be crossing the line. If she is a Fox News person, most likely she is a ***racist***. Should hot looking racists be less hated?
Not toxic	That's like saying a ***racist*** doesn't hate black people, he just hates the color of their skin. Or an anti-Semite doesn't hate Jews, he just hates their religion. Or a misogynist doesn't hate women, he just hates their gender.
Toxic	Criticize a black man and the left calls you a ***racist***. Criticize a woman and you are a sexist. Now I will criticize you as a fool and you can call me intolerant.
Toxic	As a white right wing nut deplorable gun owning ***racist*** conservative pig... I never "groped" a female who did not want... groping. We hang those people.

Toxic mean soft error = 0.144, Not toxic mean soft error = 0.634.

The results suggest that targeting overall error is insufficient for discovering contrasting slices. ConSequence handles this by explicitly using the performance gap between classes in the search objective.

5 Analysis

The most diverse behavior appears in MNIST and Quick, Draw!, where the top slices alternate between classes carrying the higher error (Table 3). In MNIST,

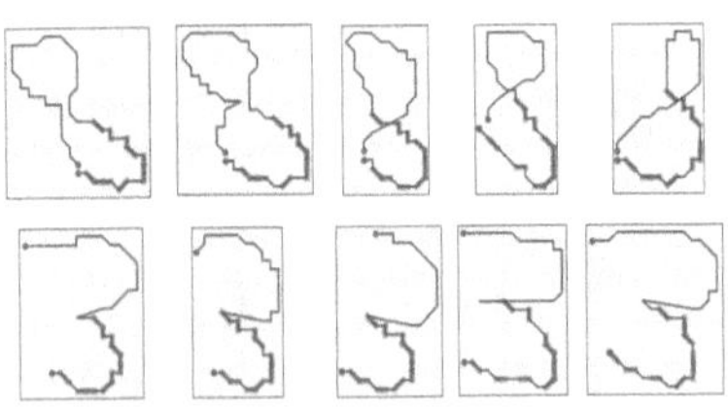

(a) MNIST slice 3. $\mu_1^g = 0.680$ (digit 8), $\mu_0^g = 0.191$ (digit 3).

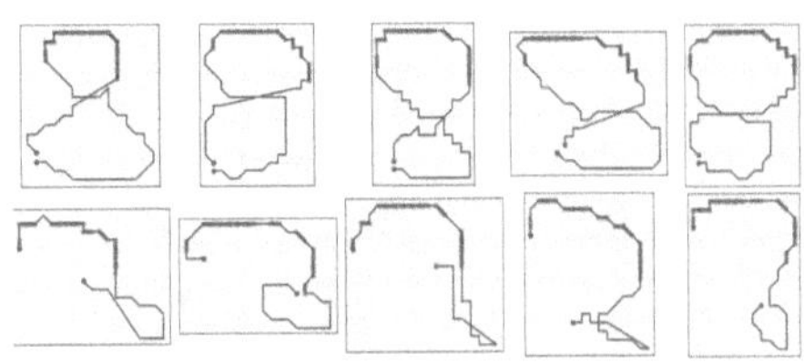

(b) MNIST slice 8. $\mu_1^g = 0.083$ (digit 8), $\mu_0^g = 0.740$ (digit 3).

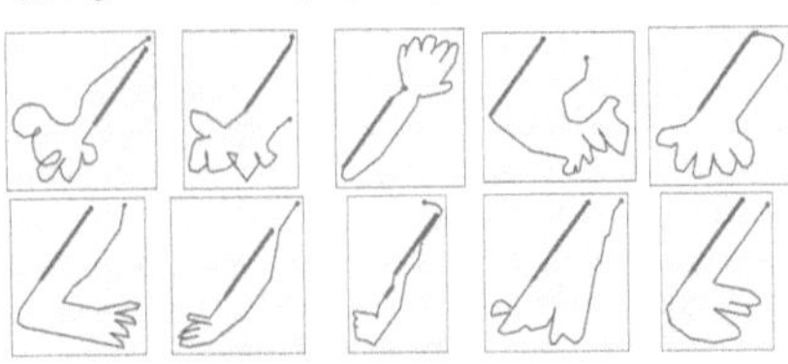

(c) Quick, Draw! slice 1. $\mu_1^g = 0.096$ (arm), $\mu_0^g = 0.676$ (leg).

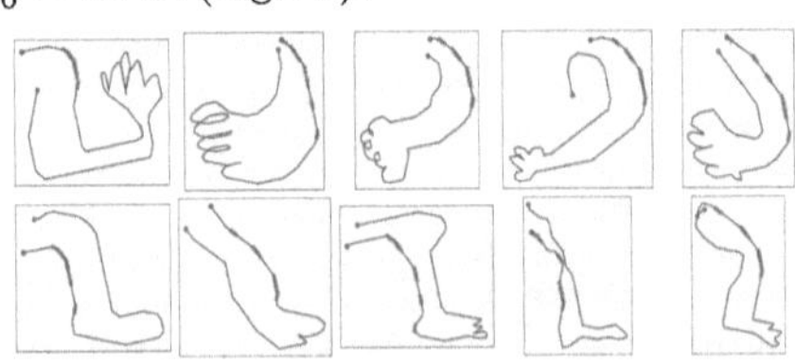

(d) Quick, Draw! slice 3. $\mu_1^g = 0.591$ (arm), $\mu_0^g = 0.144$ (leg).

Fig. 2. Example instances from discovered slices in MNIST and Quick, Draw!. The highlighted pattern in red indicates the matching subsequence in the stroke sequence. (Color figure online)

Table 5. Top-5 slice metrics (ConSequence vs. Domino, $\mu \pm \sigma$).

Dataset	Top-5 φ		Top-5 Δ_g	
	ConSequence	Domino	ConSequence	Domino
MNIST	$\mathbf{0.527 \pm 0.019}$	0.097 ± 0.026	$\mathbf{0.486 \pm 0.025}$	0.115 ± 0.044
Quick, Draw!	$\mathbf{0.566 \pm 0.036}$	0.118 ± 0.008	$\mathbf{0.455 \pm 0.022}$	0.048 ± 0.010
Malware	$\mathbf{0.719 \pm 0.039}$	0.130 ± 0.030	$\mathbf{0.351 \pm 0.014}$	0.091 ± 0.022
Toxicity (Women)	$\mathbf{0.726 \pm 0.061}$	0.129 ± 0.005	$\mathbf{0.542 \pm 0.026}$	0.086 ± 0.017
Toxicity (Sexuality)	$\mathbf{0.193 \pm 0.005}$	0.189 ± 0.032	$\mathbf{0.262 \pm 0.014}$	0.141 ± 0.016

slices 1 and 2 assign higher error to class 0, while slices 3–5 reverse this. In Quick, Draw!, slice 1, 2, and 4 assign higher error to class 0, e.g. $\mu_0^g = 0.676$ vs $\mu_1^g = 0.096$ for the top slice, while slices 3 and 5 reverse the contrast, e.g. $\mu_0^g = 0.144$ vs $\mu_1^g = 0.591$. The slices therefore capture multiple distinct failure modes.

It is observed that overall model error does not directly relate to slice quality. For example, the top MNIST slice has quality 0.957 with a model mean soft error of 0.161, while the top Toxicity (Sexuality) slice has quality 0.217 with a model mean soft error of 0.393. Higher overall model error therefore does not imply stronger contrast slices, since slice quality depends on localized differences in model behavior.

Table 6. ConSequence average search statistics ($\mu \pm \sigma$).

Dataset	All patterns	After similarity	Significant	Nodes explored
MNIST	$17,001 \pm 377$	86 ± 5	45 ± 3	$24,408 \pm 277$
Quick, Draw!	$13,518 \pm 182$	100 ± 0	75 ± 7	$33,396 \pm 371$
Malware	$4,931 \pm 63$	24 ± 2	18 ± 2	$10,347 \pm 61$
Toxicity (Women)	$1,589 \pm 29$	100 ± 0	99 ± 1	$9,805 \pm 87$
Toxicity (Sexuality)	$1,075 \pm 27$	100 ± 0	95 ± 2	$6,774 \pm 151$

In MNIST, the first plotted slice contains higher error on 8 s, meaning it is being confused with 3 s. The pattern in Fig. 2a appears on the bottom right side of both 3 s and 8 s. In this slice the mean soft error is $\mu_0^g = 0.191$ for 3 s and $\mu_1^g = 0.630$ for 8 s. The pattern in Fig. 2b matches the top of 3 s, which resembles the wide arc seen in some 8 s, with mean soft errors $\mu_0^g = 0.740$ for 3 s and $\mu_1^g = 0.083$ for 8 s.

In Quick, Draw!, the slices expose bias related to stroke direction in the model errors. In Fig. 2c, left-inclined legs exhibit higher error than visually similar arms ($\mu_0^g = 0.676$, $\mu_1^g = 0.096$). In Fig. 2d, arms with a specific top long curve instead contain higher error than visually similar legs ($\mu_0^g = 0.144$, $\mu_1^g = 0.591$).

The Malware dataset produces slices with smaller Δ_g values, but the per-class soft errors have low standard deviation, indicating stable model behavior within each slice. Across the top slices the model assigns higher error to benign samples, indicating a tendency to classify benign software as malware.

For the textual datasets, the vocabulary is large (over 30,000 tokens), and with varying sequence lengths. Most discovered patterns are short (1-3 tokens), and the maximum gap had to remain small to preserve textual coherence. The pattern *racist* in Table 4 forms a slice where non-toxic comments tend to use defensive and well-written language, while toxic comments are more aggressive. In this slice the model assigns higher error to the non-toxic class ($\mu_0^g = 0.634$) than to the toxic class ($\mu_1^g = 0.144$).

Table 6 also illustrates the efficiency of the search. For example, the MNIST dataset has a vocabulary of $|V| = 335$ tokens and an average sequence length of 45.1, resulting in an extremely large combinatorial pattern space. In contrast, the MCTS search evaluates approximately 24,408 nodes, showing that ConSequence can identify useful slices while exploring only a small portion of the search space.

These results show that contrast slice discovery can find class-specific failures that would be otherwise hidden when analyzing model performance via global metrics.

5.1 Parameter Sensitivity Analysis

A sensitivity analysis evaluated the four parameters: *max_gap*, γ, θ, and *iterations*. Each parameter was varied independently while keeping the others fixed. The evaluated ranges are shown in Table 7.

Preliminary experiments indicated that the support penalty (γ) had a substantially larger effect on quality than the remaining parameters. With $\gamma = 0.5$, varying *iterations*, *max_gap*, and θ changed the average top-5 quality by at most 0.150. To better isolate the effects of these parameters, the baseline configuration was adjusted to iterations $= 10,000$, $\theta = 0.5$, $\gamma = 0.1$, and *max_gap* $= 2$.

As shown in Fig. 3, increasing the number of iterations from 1,000 to 30,000 raises the average top-5 quality from 0.345 to 0.958. However, the gain beyond 15,000 iterations is modest (0.814 to 0.958) while doubling execution time. Increasing *max_gap* from 0 to 5 similarly improves quality (0.583 to 0.975), at the cost of reduced temporal coherence.

The parameter θ controls result diversity. Larger values improve quality (0.377 to 0.986) but increase overlap among slices. Likewise, reducing the support penalty improves quality (0.952 at $\gamma = 0$ vs 0.160 at $\gamma = 1$), though it favors smaller slices. Overall, parameter selection involves balancing quality, support, diversity, temporal coherence, and execution time.

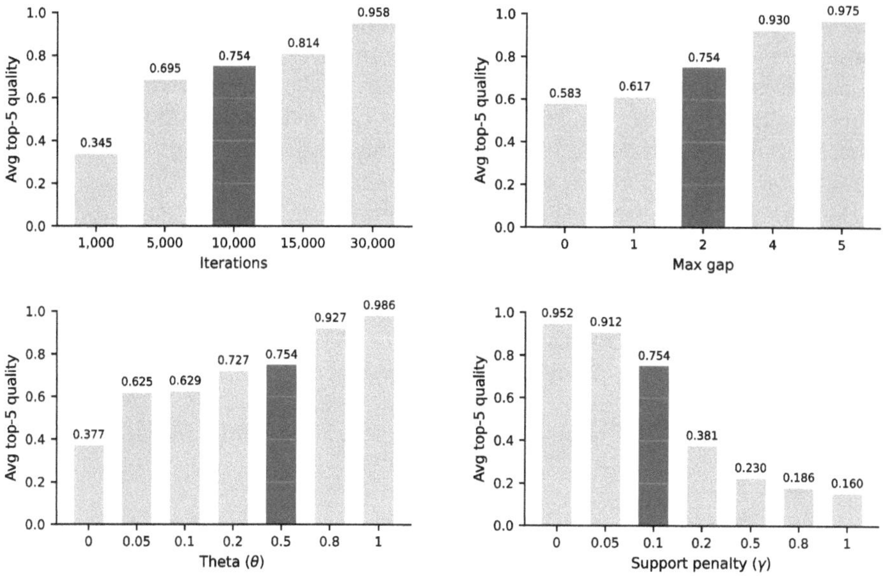

Fig. 3. Parameter sensitivity analysis for varying *iterations*, *max_gap*, θ and γ.

Table 7. Sensitivity analysis parameters values.

Parameter	Tested values	Baseline
Iterations	1,000, 5,000, 10,000, 15,000, 30000	10,000
max_gap	0, 1, 2, 4, 5	2
θ	0, 0.05, 0.1, 0.2, 0.5, 0.8, 1	0.5
γ	0, 0.05, 0.1, 0.2, 0.5, 0.8, 1	0.1

6 Conclusion

This work introduced contrast slice discovery, a framework for identifying subgroups where a model behaves differently across classes, and ConSequence, an extension of MCTSExtent for discovering such slices in sequential data. The approach reveals class-specific differences in model performance that are not visible through traditional slice discovery methods, and extends slice discovery to sequential domains.

Experiments on five datasets from spatiotemporal, sequential, and textual domains show that ConSequence consistently finds statistically significant slices with strong per-class contrast, while the baseline produced lower quality slices. Furthermore, the analysis shows that it is possible to identify model biases toward certain patterns, especially in the visual datasets, and understand why the model assigns higher errors to one class in those regions.

A sensitivity analysis revealed specific parameter trade-offs. Lowering the support penalty or increasing the maximum gap results in higher quality scores, but produces smaller and less temporally coherent slices, respectively. Likewise, higher similarity thresholds increase quality but reduce slice diversity. Altogether, the parameterization requires balancing pattern quality, slice support, diversity, temporal coherence, and execution time.

Despite the interesting results, the framework has known limitations. The MCTS approach creates a memory bottleneck on big datasets, and the algorithm requires careful parameter tuning. For future work, addressing these computational constraints and using adaptive tuning techniques are the main priorities. Furthermore, contrast slice discovery could be extended to tabular and image data and integrated with model debugging systems.

Acknowledgments. The authors would like to thank FAPEMIG for supporting this project.

Disclosure of Interests. The authors have no competing interests to declare that are relevant to the content of this article.

References

1. Bono, T., Croxson, K., Giles, A.: Algorithmic fairness in credit scoring. Oxf. Rev. Econ. Policy **37**(3), 585–617 (2021). https://doi.org/10.1093/oxrep/grab020
2. Chouldechova, A.: Fair prediction with disparate impact: a study of bias in recidivism prediction instruments. Big Data **5**(2), 153–163 (2017). https://doi.org/10.1089/big.2016.0047
3. Chung, Y., Kraska, T., Polyzotis, N., Tae, K.H., Whang, S.E.: Slice finder: automated data slicing for model validation. In: 2019 IEEE 35th International Conference on Data Engineering (ICDE), pp. 1550–1553 (2019). https://doi.org/10.1109/ICDE.2019.00139
4. Borkan, D., Sorensen, J., Dixon, L., Vasserman, L.: Jigsaw unintended bias in toxicity classification. Kaggle (2019). https://kaggle.com/competitions/jigsaw-unintended-bias-in-toxicity-classification
5. Colacci, M., et al.: Sociodemographic bias in clinical machine learning models: a scoping review of algorithmic bias instances and mechanisms. J. Clin. Epidemiol. **178**, 111606 (2025)
6. Deng, L.: The MNIST database of handwritten digit images for machine learning research. IEEE Signal Process. Mag. **29**(6), 141–142 (2012)
7. d'Eon, G., d'Eon, J., Wright, J.R., Leyton-Brown, K.: The spotlight: a general method for discovering systematic errors in deep learning models. In: Proceedings of the 2022 ACM Conference on Fairness, Accountability, and Transparency, FAccT 2022, pp. 1962–1981. Association for Computing Machinery, New York, NY, USA (2022). https://doi.org/10.1145/3531146.3533240
8. Devlin, J., Chang, M.W., Lee, K., Toutanova, K.: Bert: pre-training of deep bidirectional transformers for language understanding (2019). https://arxiv.org/abs/1810.04805

9. Du, X., Yang, S., Duivesteijn, W., Pechenizkiy, M.: Conformalized exceptional model mining: telling where your model performs (not) well. In: Ribeiro, R.P., et al. (eds.) Machine Learning and Knowledge Discovery in Databases. Research Track, pp. 528–544. Springer, Cham (2026)
10. Eyuboglu, S., et al.: Domino: discovering systematic errors with cross-modal embeddings (2022). https://arxiv.org/abs/2203.14960
11. Google Creative Lab: The quick, draw! dataset (2017). https://github.com/googlecreativelab/quickdraw-dataset, 50 million drawings across 345 categories collected from the Quick, Draw! game
12. Hua, W., Jin, L., Song, L., Mi, H., Zhang, Y., Yu, D.: Discover, explain, improve: an automatic slice detection benchmark for natural language processing. Trans. Assoc. Comput. Linguist. **11**, 1537–1552 (2023)
13. de Jong, E.D.: MNIST digits as stroke sequences (2016). https://github.com/edwin-de-jong/mnist-digits-as-stroke-sequences. Accessed 2026
14. Klösgen, W.: Explora: a multipattern and multistrategy discovery assistant, pp. 249–271. American Association for Artificial Intelligence, USA (1996)
15. Li, C., Lv, Q., Li, N., Wang, Y., Sun, D., Qiao, Y.: A novel deep framework for dynamic malware detection based on API sequence intrinsic features. Comput. Secur. **116**, 102686 (2022). https://doi.org/10.1016/j.cose.2022.102686. https://www.sciencedirect.com/science/article/pii/S0167404822000840
16. Mathonat, R., Nurbakova, D., Boulicaut, J.F., Kaytoue, M.: Anytime mining of sequential discriminative patterns in labeled sequences. Knowl. Inf. Syst. **63**(2), 439–476 (2020). https://doi.org/10.1007/s10115-020-01523-7
17. Meng, H., Wagner, C., Triguero, I.: Explaining time series classifiers through meaningful perturbation and optimisation. Inf. Sci. **645**, 119334 (2023)
18. Obermeyer, Z., Powers, B., Vogeli, C., Mullainathan, S.: Dissecting racial bias in an algorithm used to manage the health of populations. Science **366**(6464), 447–453 (2019)
19. Patharkar, A., Cai, F., Al-Hindawi, F., Wu, T.: Predictive modeling of biomedical temporal data in healthcare applications: review and future directions. Front. Physiol. **15** (2024). https://doi.org/10.3389/fphys.2024.1386760
20. Ribeiro, M.T., Wu, T., Guestrin, C., Singh, S.: Beyond accuracy: behavioral testing of NLP models with CheckList. In: Jurafsky, D., Chai, J., Schluter, N., Tetreault, J. (eds.) Proceedings of the 58th Annual Meeting of the Association for Computational Linguistics, pp. 4902–4912. Association for Computational Linguistics, Online (2020). https://doi.org/10.18653/v1/2020.acl-main.442. https://aclanthology.org/2020.acl-main.442/
21. Sagadeeva, S., Boehm, M.: Sliceline: fast, linear-algebra-based slice finding for ml model debugging. In: Proceedings of the 2021 International Conference on Management of Data, SIGMOD 2021, pp. 2290–2299. Association for Computing Machinery, New York, NY, USA (2021). https://doi.org/10.1145/3448016.3457323
22. Saliba, S., Vimieiro, R.: Explaining atypical performance regions for time series classifiers with shapelets (2025). https://ssrn.com/abstract=5963076, sSRN Working Paper
23. Siegl, T., Coşkun, K., Hiller, B.C., Mirzaei, A., Lemmerich, F., Becker, M.: Subroc: AUC-based discovery of exceptional subgroup performance for binary classifiers. arXiv preprint arXiv:2505.11283 (2025)
24. Sohoni, N., Dunnmon, J.A., Angus, G., Gu, A., Ré, C.: No subclass left behind: fine-grained robustness in coarse-grained classification problems. In: Proceedings of the 34th International Conference on Neural Information Processing Systems. NIPS 2020. Curran Associates Inc, Red Hook, NY, USA (2020)

25. Strobelt, H., Gehrmann, S., Pfister, H., Rush, A.M.: Lstmvis: a tool for visual analysis of hidden state dynamics in recurrent neural networks. IEEE Trans. Visual Comput. Graphics **24**(1), 667–676 (2018). https://doi.org/10.1109/TVCG.2017.2744158
26. Tenney, I., et al.: The language interpretability tool: extensible, interactive visualizations and analysis for NLP models. In: Liu, Q., Schlangen, D. (eds.) Proceedings of the 2020 Conference on Empirical Methods in Natural Language Processing: System Demonstrations, pp. 107–118. Association for Computational Linguistics, Online (2020). https://doi.org/10.18653/v1/2020.emnlp-demos.15. https://aclanthology.org/2020.emnlp-demos.15/
27. Wang, Z., Huang, Y., Song, D., Ma, L., Zhang, T.: Deepseer: interactive RNN explanation and debugging via state abstraction. In: Proceedings of the 2023 CHI Conference on Human Factors in Computing Systems. CHI 2023. Association for Computing Machinery, New York, NY, USA (2023). https://doi.org/10.1145/3544548.3580852
28. Wu, T., Ribeiro, M.T., Heer, J., Weld, D.: Errudite: scalable, reproducible, and testable error analysis. In: Korhonen, A., Traum, D., Màrquez, L. (eds.) Proceedings of the 57th Annual Meeting of the Association for Computational Linguistics, pp. 747–763. Association for Computational Linguistics, Florence, Italy (2019). https://doi.org/10.18653/v1/P19-1073. https://aclanthology.org/P19-1073/
29. Zamanzadeh Darban, Z., Webb, G.I., Pan, S., Aggarwal, C., Salehi, M.: Deep learning for time series anomaly detection: a survey. ACM Comput. Surv. **57**(1) (2024). https://doi.org/10.1145/3691338
30. Zhang, M., Ijner, P., Wald, Y., Creager, E.: Active slice discovery in large language models (2025). https://arxiv.org/abs/2511.20713

Imputation Meets Clustering: Exploiting Latent Subgroup Structure for Missing Data Recovery

Chuyao Zhang[1], E. Li[1], Taochen Chen[1], Yiqun Zhang[1(✉)], Yuzhu Ji[1], Shuping Zhao[1], Peng Liu[1], and Yiu-ming Cheung[2]

[1] School of Computer Science and Technology, Guangdong University of Technology, Guangzhou, China
{zhangchuyao,lie1,chentaochen1}@mails.gdut.edu.cn, {yqzhang,yuzhu.ji,shupingzhao,liupeng}@gdut.edu.cn

[2] Department of Computer Science, Hong Kong Baptist University, Kowloon, Hong Kong SAR, China
ymc@comp.hkbu.edu.hk

Abstract. Missing data is prevalent in practical applications, making effective imputation an essential preprocessing step for downstream analysis. Real-world datasets often exhibit complex latent structures composed of multiple subgroups with distinct distributions. However, existing methods often overlook such population heterogeneity. Without explicit structural guidance, these methods tend to produce generic estimates that blur subgroup boundaries and lack instance-level fidelity. While incorporating subgroup information offers a remedy, it faces a circular dependency: reliable subgroup identification requires complete data, while data completion is the imputation objective itself. To resolve this, we propose CAGI (Cluster-Aware Generative Imputation), a framework that reformulates clustering and imputation as a mutually reinforcing co-optimization process. CAGI employs a "Partition-Guide-Restore" strategy where dynamic cluster assignments act as local priors to condition a Generative Adversarial Network. An iterative feedback loop is established to progressively refine both cluster structures and imputed values toward faithful subgroup distributions. To ensure distributional stability, CAGI further employs a multi-level optimization objective combining instance-level reconstruction with distribution-level regularization. Extensive experiments on 14 benchmark datasets with 15 representative baselines demonstrate the superiority of CAGI. The source code is available at: https://github.com/supercocachii/CAGI.

Keywords: Missing values imputation · Clustering · Generative Adversarial Networks · Mixed-attribute data

1 Introduction

Missing values are pervasive in real-world datasets, arising from sensor failures [42], human entry errors, privacy protection mechanisms, and other factors [1]. Such incompleteness poses fundamental risks to downstream learning

M. Ceci et al. (Eds.): ECML PKDD 2026, LNAI 16941, pp. 697–715, 2027.
https://doi.org/10.1007/978-3-032-37654-1_40

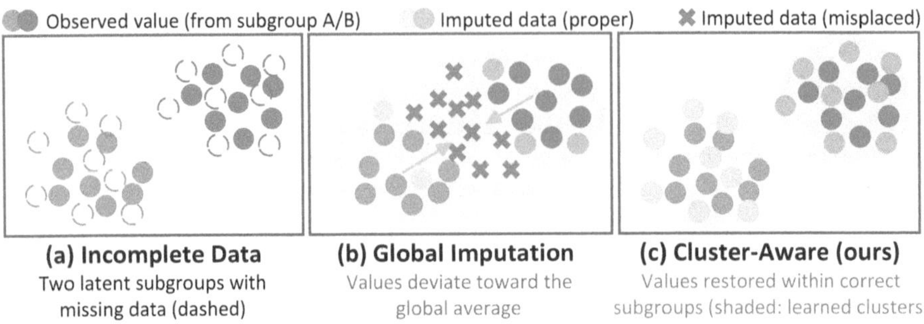

Fig. 1. Motivating example of imputation under subgroup heterogeneity in an unsupervised setting. Subgroup colors are shown only for illustration. (a) Incomplete data with two latent subgroups whose memberships are unknown. (b) Global imputation, agnostic to latent structure, deviates toward the global average and produces misplaced values. (c) CAGI discovers subgroup structure (shaded regions indicate learned cluster boundaries) and restores correct regions.

tasks, degrading classification accuracy, producing unreliable clustering, and introducing bias into automated decision systems [3]. To mitigate these risks, *imputation*, the process of estimating plausible values for unobserved entries based on available information, has been a widely used preprocessing step. Crucially, imputation is not merely about filling in blanks; its fundamental goal is to recover the true latent distribution from partially observed samples, thereby providing a reliable foundation for subsequent analysis.

Missing data mechanisms are typically categorized into three types [18]: (1) Missing Completely At Random (MCAR), where missingness is independent of all data; (2) Missing At Random (MAR), where missingness depends only on observed values; and (3) Missing Not At Random (MNAR), where missingness depends on the unobserved values themselves. Imputation methods have advanced substantially over the past decade. Following common practice in recent imputation benchmarks [10,34], this paper focuses on the MCAR setting.

Early statistical approaches such as Mean/Mode substitution [18] and EM algorithm [9] offer simple and interpretable solutions, but rely on parametric or linear assumptions that limit their expressiveness. Iterative conditional approaches such as MICE [32] and MissForest [29] estimate missing values through chained conditional models or Random Forests, but may face scalability challenges on high-dimensional data with complex inter-variable structures. More recently, deep generative models offer more expressive alternatives. GAN-based methods such as GAIN [33] model the data distribution through adversarial training, VAE-based methods such as MIWAE [20] learn latent representations via variational inference, and diffusion-based methods such as TabCSDI [48] and DiffPuter [35] reconstruct data through iterative denoising. These methods demonstrate a superior ability to capture complex feature correlations.

Despite their power, existing methods often treat the dataset as a monolithic entity, implicitly learning a smooth, unimodal manifold over all samples. This assumption overlooks the latent population heterogeneity prevalent in practice. Real-world datasets are typically composed of multiple subgroups with distinct statistical characteristics. For instance, patients in clinical diagnostics may belong to distinct disease subtypes, while customers in marketing databases fall into diverse demographic segments. When a unified model is trained on such distributionally heterogeneous data without explicit structural guidance, the learned distribution conflates multiple modes into a global average. As illustrated in Fig. 1, consider a dataset containing two subgroups with missing values (Fig. 1(a)). A global imputation model, agnostic to this latent structure, generates estimates reflecting the marginal distribution averaged across subgroups (Fig. 1(b)). These imputed values reside in regions of the feature space that are "plausible on average" but "incorrect for any specific subgroup". This leads to two key issues: *distributional shift* occurs when imputed values deviate from each subgroup's true conditional distribution, and *boundary violation* occurs when imputed values cross subgroup boundaries and distort the subgroup structure. Such errors are not merely theoretical concerns. For instance, in clinical applications, imputing biomarker values without accounting for disease subtypes can obscure important diagnostic signals.

A natural remedy is to first identify subgroups via clustering and then impute within each subgroup. However, this straightforward strategy encounters a fundamental circular dependency: reliable subgroup identification requires complete data, while complete data is the very objective of imputation. Prior two-stage approaches [13,27] adopt a cluster-then-impute pipeline that treats cluster assignments as one-off preprocessing outputs. Since errors in the initial cluster assignments are irreversibly fixed, such methods cannot correct the subgroup structure during the learning process.

This paper, therefore, proposes CAGI (Cluster-Aware Generative Imputation) to reformulate clustering and imputation as a coupled co-optimization process. The key insight lies in the fact that identifying latent structures and recovering missing entries are coupled objectives that enhance each other through iterative feedback. Following a "Partition-Guide-Restore" strategy, CAGI first bootstraps subgroup discovery via missing-tolerant clustering that provides initial cluster assignments even when data is substantially incomplete. Then an adversarial generator incorporates these assignments as conditioning signals, narrowing the generative search space to synthesize missing values that adhere to the statistical patterns of specific subgroups. Finally, it feeds refined imputations back to periodic reclustering, establishing an iterative imputation-reclustering-reimputation cycle that progressively improves both clustering and imputation. Accordingly, CAGI produces plausible imputed values that are in line with the specific subgroup structure (Fig. 1(c)). To guard against distributional fragmentation caused by inaccurate early clusters, CAGI further employs a multi-level optimization objective: instance-level constraints (adversarial training combined with reconstruction loss) ensure element-wise accuracy, while a distribution-level optimal transport regularization based on Sinkhorn divergence enforces global geometric consistency. The main contributions are:

- **Subgroup-Conditional Generative Strategy.** A cluster-conditioned generation approach that decomposes the complex global distribution into compact subgroup-specific manifolds, reducing generative uncertainty in high-dimensional regimes.
- **Alternating Optimization with Self-Correction.** We develop an iterative imputation-clustering loop that treats cluster assignments as tunable latent variables, anchored by reconstruction constraints on observed entries to progressively rectify early-stage clustering deviations.
- **Multi-Level Objective for High-Fidelity Recovery.** A composite objective combining instance-level reconstruction with distribution-level regularization is designed, preserving distinct local patterns while simultaneously maintaining a smooth global data topology.

2 Related Work

Deep learning-based imputation and unsupervised data analysis techniques that are highly relevant to CAGI and the targeted mixed data are discussed below.

2.1 Deep Learning Approaches for Imputation

Deep generative models address the limitations above by learning to approximate the underlying data distribution.

GAN-Based Methods. GAIN [33] adapts the GAN [11] framework to imputation by training a generator to fill missing entries and an element-wise discriminator to identify which components were imputed. MisGAN [16] extends this by jointly learning a data generator and a mask generator to model complex missingness patterns. While computationally efficient, GAN-based methods are susceptible to training instability [2,26].

VAE-Based Methods. Variational Autoencoder approaches optimize the evidence lower bound for probabilistic imputation [14]. MIWAE [20] employs importance-weighted autoencoders to tighten the bound for improved log-likelihood estimation, while HI-VAE [22] handles mixed-type data through heterogeneous likelihoods. However, these methods tend to produce over-smoothed estimates due to inference suboptimality [7], and the restrictive Gaussian prior limits their capacity to capture complex multi-modal distributions [30].

Graph and Transformer-Based Methods. GRAPE [34] and IGRM [49] represent the data matrix as a bipartite graph and recover missing entries via message passing between samples and feature nodes. ReMasker [10] adapts the masked autoencoding paradigm and learns to reconstruct randomly masked features via Transformer-based self-attention. These methods may incur overhead from graph construction and quadratic attention complexity [50].

Optimal Transport-Based Methods. OTImpute [21] aligns distributions by minimizing Sinkhorn divergence [8] between observed and imputed data, while TDM [43] further applies invertible transformations before distribution matching. Despite their sound theoretical foundation, these methods typically require solving expensive optimization subroutines for divergence computation, leading to substantial training costs [24].

Diffusion-Based Methods. TabCSDI [48] models data generation as a reverse stochastic process, gradually denoising random noise conditioned on observed values. DiffPuter [35] integrates denoising within an EM framework, NewImp [6] reformulates imputation via gradient flow, and SimpDM [19] stabilizes accuracy through self-supervised regularization. Although achieving superior fidelity, diffusion models suffer from high inference latency due to the need for hundreds of iterative sampling steps [17,28].

2.2 Unsupervised Pattern Analysis Techniques

Early approaches rely on parametric or linear assumptions, and thus struggle to capture complex non-linear dependencies. Accordingly, non-parametric approaches, such as K-Means [25], leverage group-level structure but are vulnerable to seed initialization and data heterogeneity, i.e., a mixed dataset composed of both numerical and categorical attributes.

In recent years, significant progress has been made in robust mixed data clustering. Recent advancements have developed novel distance metrics [38], hierarchical merging [4], multi-granular distributions [41], and homogeneous concept spaces [39] to accurately partition the complex mixed data [29,44]. Concurrently, exploring value orders [37], developing order-inspired metrics [40], learning order forests [45], as well as cluster-customized category relationships [46] have proven highly effective for categorical data clustering.

3 Proposed Method

To address the challenge of imputing missing values in data with complex latent structures, we propose the CAGI framework (Fig. 2). CAGI follows a "Partition–Guide–Restore" principle, and its imputation architecture consists of three key components: (1) a missing-tolerant clustering module that discovers subgroups from incomplete data, (2) a cluster-conditioned generator that performs subgroup-aware imputation, and (3) an adversarial mechanism that enforces element-wise realism. These components are integrated through a multi-level learning objective and a progressive alternating training procedure. In the following, we first introduce the problem formulation, then detail the imputation architecture, learning strategy, and alternating training loop.

3.1 Problem Formulation

Let $\mathbf{X} \in \mathbb{R}^{n \times d}$ denote a dataset with n samples and d features, partially observed under a binary mask matrix $\mathbf{M} \in \{0, 1\}^{n \times d}$, where $m_{ij} = 1$ indicates an observed entry. Each sample $\mathbf{x}_i$ is decomposed into observed components $\mathbf{x}_i^{obs}$ and missing components $\mathbf{x}_i^{mis}$. The imputation goal is to estimate $\mathbf{x}_i^{mis}$ by modeling $P(\mathbf{x}^{mis} \mid \mathbf{x}^{obs})$. CAGI leverages clustering to uncover latent subgroups $\{c_1, \ldots, c_K\}$ in real-world data. By incorporating the cluster assignment into the imputation process, CAGI targets the cluster-conditional distribution $P(\mathbf{x}^{mis} \mid \mathbf{x}^{obs}, c)$. Within a GAN [11] framework, the generator's raw output is:

$$\bar{\mathbf{x}} = G(\tilde{\mathbf{x}}, \mathbf{m}, c), \tag{1}$$

where $\tilde{\mathbf{x}}$ fills missing entries with noise, $\mathbf{m}$ is the mask, and c is the cluster assignment. The completed sample merges generated and observed values:

$$\hat{\mathbf{x}} = \mathbf{m} \odot \mathbf{x} + (1 - \mathbf{m}) \odot \bar{\mathbf{x}}, \tag{2}$$

where $\odot$ denotes element-wise multiplication. By conditioning on c, the model narrows the generation scope to the relevant subgroup, thereby ensuring that the imputed values reflect the characteristics of the specific underlying subgroup.

3.2 Cluster-Aware Generative Imputation

To resolve the circular dependency discussed in Sect. 1, CAGI unifies clustering and imputation into an alternating optimization process. The architecture is detailed below, organized around the "Partition-Guide-Restore" strategy.

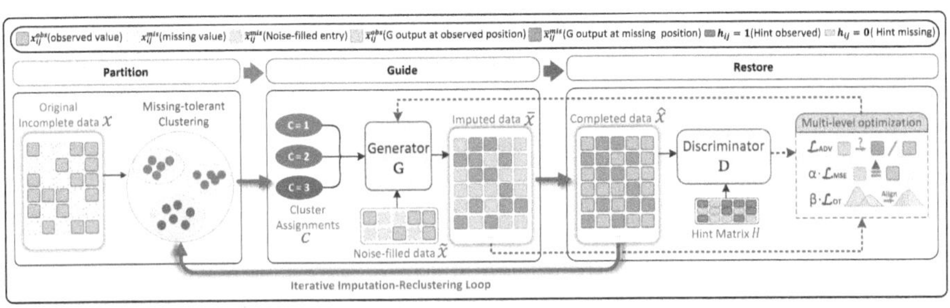

Fig. 2. The overall architecture of CAGI framework following a "Partition-Guide-Restore" design: the missing-tolerant clustering module first assigns the incomplete data into clusters and treats the labels as conditioning signals for generator G. Then G imputes all positions to produce $\bar{x}$, and the completed data $\hat{x}$ retains original observed values and replaces missing entries with $\bar{x}_{ij}^{mis}$, which is fed to discriminator D alongside the hint matrix. D and G engage in adversarial training where D distinguishes observed from imputed entries while G deceives D. An iterative imputation-reclustering process updates the assignments until convergence, yielding $\hat{x}$ as the final imputed output.

Partition: Missing-Tolerant Clustering. Standard clustering algorithms (e.g., K-Means) cannot operate on incomplete data, as the standard Euclidean distance cannot be computed when features are partially missing. To initiate the process, we employ a missing-tolerant clustering mechanism that computes partial distances based solely on shared observed features. This strategy follows the well-established practice of partial-distance clustering [23,36], which allows standard clustering algorithms to operate directly on incomplete data without requiring prior imputation. For any two samples $\mathbf{x}_i$ and $\mathbf{x}_j$, the set of commonly observed features is:

$$\mathcal{S}_{ij} = \{k : m_{ik} = 1 \wedge m_{jk} = 1\}. \tag{3}$$

The partial distance between two samples is computed as:

$$d(\mathbf{x}_i, \mathbf{x}_j) = \sqrt{\frac{d}{|\mathcal{S}_{ij}|} \sum_{k \in \mathcal{S}_{ij}} (x_{ik} - x_{jk})^2}, \tag{4}$$

where the scaling factor $\frac{d}{|\mathcal{S}_{ij}|}$ normalizes the partial sum to approximate the full-dimensional Euclidean distance, ensuring that sample pairs with different numbers of co-observed features remain comparable. When $\mathcal{S}_{ij} = \emptyset$, the distance is set to infinity and the sample is assigned to the nearest cluster with which it shares observed features. Based on this distance metric, we assign each sample to a cluster $c_i \in \{1, \ldots, K\}$, providing the initial subgroup guidance for the generator. Note that K need not match the true number of subgroups. Rather, the purpose of clustering is to constrain the generator within localized regions of the feature space, reducing the risk of cross-subgroup imputation illustrated in Fig. 1.

For purely numerical datasets, standard K-Means is used with the partial distance metric defined in Eq. (4). For datasets containing categorical features, we employ K-Prototypes [12], which combines Euclidean distance for numerical features with the simple matching distance for categorical features. Specifically, for two samples $\mathbf{x}_i$ and $\mathbf{x}_j$, the combined distance is defined as:

$$d_{\text{mix}}(\mathbf{x}_i, \mathbf{x}_j) = \sqrt{\frac{d_{num}}{|\mathcal{S}_{ij}^{num}|} \sum_{k \in \mathcal{S}_{ij}^{num}} (x_{ik} - x_{jk})^2 + \gamma \cdot \frac{d_{cat}}{|\mathcal{S}_{ij}^{cat}|} \sum_{k \in \mathcal{S}_{ij}^{cat}} \delta_{ij}^k}, \tag{5}$$

$$\delta_{ij}^k = \begin{cases} 0, & \text{if } x_{ik} = x_{jk}, \\ 1, & \text{if } x_{ik} \neq x_{jk}. \end{cases} \tag{6}$$

d_{num} and d_{cat} denote the total number of numerical and categorical features, $\mathcal{S}_{ij}^{num}$ and $\mathcal{S}_{ij}^{cat}$ are the sets of co-observed numerical and categorical features between samples $\mathbf{x}_i$ and $\mathbf{x}_j$, and γ is a balancing parameter that controls the relative contribution of categorical dissimilarity.

Guide: Cluster-Conditioned Generation. With the initial cluster assignments established, the generator G receives a composite input consisting of the noise-filled data $\tilde{\mathbf{x}}_i$, the mask $\mathbf{m}_i$, and the cluster assignment c_i. Missing positions are initialized with feature-wise noise $\mathbf{z}_i$ whose j-th entry is sampled as $z_{ij} \sim \mathcal{N}(\mu_j, (0.1 \cdot \sigma_j)^2)$:

$$\tilde{\mathbf{x}}_i = \mathbf{m}_i \odot \mathbf{x}_i + (1 - \mathbf{m}_i) \odot \mathbf{z}_i. \tag{7}$$

The mean μ_j anchors the initialization at the center of the observed distribution, while the small variance factor 0.1 keeps the initial perturbation mild, preventing the noise from dominating the early generator output. This initialization serves only as a starting point: as training proceeds, the generator progressively overwrites the initial values through the iterative loop (Sect. 3.4), so the final performance is not tightly coupled to this specific choice.

The raw generator output $\bar{\mathbf{x}}_i = G(\tilde{\mathbf{x}}_i, \mathbf{m}_i, c_i)$ is then combined with observed values to produce the completed sample:

$$\hat{\mathbf{x}}_i = \mathbf{m}_i \odot \mathbf{x}_i + (1 - \mathbf{m}_i) \odot \bar{\mathbf{x}}_i. \tag{8}$$

By conditioning on c_i, G learns a subgroup-specific mapping $G(\cdot \mid c = k)$, narrowing the generative search space and reducing generation uncertainty.

Restore: Adversarial Imputation. The restoration quality is enforced by an adversarial mechanism adapted from GAIN [33]. A discriminator D evaluates each completed sample $\hat{\mathbf{x}}_i$ in an element-wise manner, outputting the probability that each feature corresponds to an observed entry. Formally, $D : \mathbb{R}^d \times \{0,1\}^d \rightarrow [0,1]^d$, where the j-th output $D(\hat{\mathbf{x}}, \mathbf{h})_j$ estimates the probability that the j-th feature of $\hat{\mathbf{x}}$ is observed. To prevent the discriminator from trivially memorizing the mask pattern, a hint mechanism is incorporated. The hint matrix $\mathbf{h}_i \in \{0,1\}^d$ reveals partial information about which positions are observed:

$$\mathbf{h}_i = \mathbf{b}_i \odot \mathbf{m}_i, \tag{9}$$

where $\mathbf{b}_i \in \{0,1\}^d$ is sampled element-wise from Bernoulli(p_h). Entries with $h_{ij} = 1$ reveal observed positions, whereas entries with $h_{ij} = 0$ leave the status ambiguous. Through this adversarial structure, the generator is trained to produce imputations that are indistinguishable from real values at the element level, promoting convergence toward the true conditional distribution.

3.3 Multi-level Learning Objective

A potential challenge of cluster-conditioned generation is distributional fragmentation, particularly when early cluster assignments are inaccurate. CAGI addresses this through a composite objective operating at two complementary levels: instance-level fidelity and distribution-level consistency.

Instance-Level Fidelity. CAGI enforces element-wise accuracy through adversarial learning and reconstruction consistency. The discriminator D is trained to maximize correct identification of observed versus imputed entries:

$$\mathcal{L}_D = -\mathbb{E}_{\hat{\mathbf{x}},\mathbf{m},\mathbf{h}}\Big[\mathbf{m} \odot \log D(\hat{\mathbf{x}}, \mathbf{h}) + (1 - \mathbf{m}) \odot \log\big(1 - D(\hat{\mathbf{x}}, \mathbf{h})\big)\Big]. \tag{10}$$

The generator G aims to deceive D specifically on the missing components:

$$\mathcal{L}_{ADV} = -\mathbb{E}_{\hat{\mathbf{x}},\mathbf{m},\mathbf{h}}\Big[(1 - \mathbf{m}) \odot \log D(\hat{\mathbf{x}}, \mathbf{h})\Big]. \tag{11}$$

A reconstruction constraint on observed entries penalizes the generator for distorting positions where the ground truth is known, encouraging it to learn an identity mapping on observed features:

$$\mathcal{L}_{MSE} = \frac{1}{|\mathcal{O}|} \sum_{(i,j)\in\mathcal{O}} (x_{ij} - \bar{x}_{ij})^2, \tag{12}$$

where $\mathcal{O} = \{(i, j) : m_{ij} = 1\}$ denotes the set of observed entries, and $\bar{x}_{ij}$ is the raw generator output before combining with observed values.

Distribution-Level Consistency. While cluster conditioning guides the generator toward subgroup-specific subspaces, adversarial training on incomplete data may introduce distributional fragmentation. To promote a coherent manifold structure, a distribution-level regularizer based on Optimal Transport (OT) is incorporated. Specifically, the Sinkhorn divergence [8] is adopted to enforce self-consistency within the generated distribution. For a mini-batch of completed samples $\hat{\mathcal{B}} = \{\hat{\mathbf{x}}_1, \ldots, \hat{\mathbf{x}}_b\}$, CAGI randomly partitions them into two disjoint subsets $\hat{\mathcal{B}}_1$ and $\hat{\mathcal{B}}_2$ of equal size, then minimizes their transport cost:

$$\mathcal{L}_{OT} = Sinkhorn_\epsilon(\hat{\mathcal{B}}_1, \hat{\mathcal{B}}_2), \tag{13}$$

where $Sinkhorn_\epsilon$ denotes the optimal transport cost with regularization parameter ϵ. The entropy regularization smooths the transport plan so that the divergence reflects distributional structure rather than individual point positions, yielding reliable estimates even on mini-batch-sized subsets [8]. The underlying intuition is that two random subsets drawn from a stable distribution should be statistically indistinguishable. By minimizing the divergence between random partitions, CAGI penalizes geometric irregularities and encourages a compact manifold, complementing the element-wise reconstruction objective.

Composite Objective. The final generator objective balances instance-level fidelity and distribution-level consistency:

$$\mathcal{L}_G = \mathcal{L}_{ADV} + \alpha \cdot \mathcal{L}_{MSE} + \beta \cdot \mathcal{L}_{OT}, \tag{14}$$

where α controls the weight of the reconstruction constraint and β governs the strength of the distributional regularization. The three loss components serve complementary roles: $\mathcal{L}_{MSE}$ anchors instance-level fidelity by leveraging observed ground truth, $\mathcal{L}_{ADV}$ promotes statistical realism through adversarial signals, and $\mathcal{L}_{OT}$ enforces global distributional coherence to prevent fragmentation induced by cluster conditioning. Overall, the complete training procedure alternates between updating D via Eq. (10) and updating G via Eq. (14).

3.4 Progressive Alternating Training

A core proposition is the dynamic *imputation-clustering loop* that treats cluster assignments as continuously updated latent variables rather than fixed information. Every T iterations, the current generator $G^{(t)}$ completes the training set to obtain $\hat{\mathbf{X}}$, while standard K-Means is then applied to $\hat{\mathbf{X}}$ to update assignments $\mathcal{C}^{(t)}$ based on the currently available features, which can be summarized as:

Step 1 - **Impute.** Generate completed data using the current model:

$$\hat{\mathbf{x}}_i^{(t)} = \mathbf{m}_i \odot \mathbf{x}_i + (1 - \mathbf{m}_i) \odot G^{(t)}(\tilde{\mathbf{x}}_i, \mathbf{m}_i, c_i^{(t)}); \tag{15}$$

Step 2 - **Reclustering**. Re-apply clustering on the completed data:

$$\mathcal{C}^{(t+1)} = Clustering(\{\hat{\mathbf{x}}_1^{(t)}, \ldots, \hat{\mathbf{x}}_n^{(t)}\}, K). \tag{16}$$

This feedback loop creates mutually reinforcing trends: improved cluster guidance reduces generative uncertainty, while refined imputations correct early-stage assignment errors. Crucially, the $\mathcal{L}_{MSE}$ term anchors this process to observed ground-truth signals, preventing divergence. At inference time, a new incomplete sample is assigned to its nearest cluster via the missing-tolerant distance metric (Eq. 4), and then imputed by the trained generator conditioned on the identified cluster assignment.

It is also noteworthy that the per-epoch training cost of CAGI scales linearly with sample size n, achieving a favorable trade-off between imputation quality and computational efficiency.

4 Experiments

This section evaluates CAGI from four perspectives: (i) imputation fidelity against 15 state-of-the-art baselines across 14 datasets, (ii) the contribution of each design component through ablation, (iii) sensitivity to key hyperparameters and scalability, (iv) downstream utility on classification and clustering tasks.

4.1 Experimental Settings

Datasets. The evaluation uses 14 public real-world datasets. We consider six numerical datasets (*spam*, *breast*, *wine*, *yeast*, *blood*, *california*), three categorical datasets (*car*, *mushroom*, *letter*), and five mixed-type datasets (*credit*, *adult*, *shoppers*, *heart*, *news*). Numerical features are normalized to $[0, 1]$ via Min-Max scaling and categorical features are transformed via the Analog Bits encoding scheme [5]. Compared to one-hot encoding, Analog Bits yields a more compact representation that scales logarithmically with the number of categories, particularly beneficial for high-cardinality features.

Baselines. CAGI is compared against 15 representative imputation methods spanning statistical, machine learning, and deep learning paradigms: Mean/Mode [18], KNNImpute [31], MICE [32], MissForest [29], GAIN [33], MIWAE [20], MIRACLE [15], OTImpute [21], TDM [43], GCImpute [47], TabCSDI [48], GRAPE [34], ReMasker [10], IGRM [49], and DiffPuter [35].

Table 1. Comparison of imputation performance on numerical datasets (measured by RMSE). The best and second-best results are highlighted for each dataset.

Method	**spam**	**breast**	**wine**	**yeast**	**blood**	**california**
Mean/Mode	$.0559_{\pm.0025}$	$.1459_{\pm.0078}$	$.1059_{\pm.0016}$	$.1239_{\pm.0044}$	$.1660_{\pm.0153}$	$.1628_{\pm.0009}$
KNNImpute	$.0634_{\pm.0026}$	$.1182_{\pm.0046}$	$.1106_{\pm.0021}$	$.1283_{\pm.0047}$	$.1451_{\pm.0133}$	$.1645_{\pm.0011}$
MICE	$.0729_{\pm.0011}$	$.1038_{\pm.0044}$	$.1335_{\pm.0021}$	$.1638_{\pm.0062}$	$.1884_{\pm.0145}$	$.1945_{\pm.0009}$
MissForest	$.0604_{\pm.0037}$	$.0982_{\pm.0032}$	$.1087_{\pm.0023}$	$.1231_{\pm.0048}$	$.1270_{\pm.0044}$	$.1531_{\pm.0040}$
GAIN	$.0743_{\pm.0212}$	$.1239_{\pm.0189}$	$.1613_{\pm.0206}$	$.1369_{\pm.0123}$	$.1553_{\pm.0217}$	$.2120_{\pm.0310}$
MIWAE	$.0561_{\pm.0017}$	$.0916_{\pm.0028}$	$.1078_{\pm.0009}$	$.1298_{\pm.0057}$	$.1349_{\pm.0110}$	$.1410_{\pm.0016}$
MIRACLE	$.0560_{\pm.0026}$	$.1484_{\pm.0147}$	$.1116_{\pm.0022}$	$.1236_{\pm.0049}$	$.1445_{\pm.0149}$	$.1632_{\pm.0047}$
OTImpute	$.0654_{\pm.0014}$	$.0951_{\pm.0025}$	$.1129_{\pm.0023}$	$.1454_{\pm.0048}$	$.1751_{\pm.0101}$	$.1796_{\pm.0009}$
TDM	$.1073_{\pm.0008}$	$.1651_{\pm.0063}$	$.1320_{\pm.0018}$	$.2023_{\pm.0283}$	$.1969_{\pm.0033}$	$.2121_{\pm.0205}$
GCImpute	$.1442_{\pm.0017}$	$.0975_{\pm.0055}$	$.1045_{\pm.0016}$	$.1340_{\pm.0189}$	$.1508_{\pm.0135}$	$.1442_{\pm.0014}$
TabCSDI	$.0704_{\pm.0046}$	$.1103_{\pm.0056}$	$.1231_{\pm.0021}$	$.1452_{\pm.0017}$	$.1832_{\pm.0115}$	$.1551_{\pm.0011}$
GRAPE	$.0604_{\pm.0022}$	$.1062_{\pm.0065}$	$.1047_{\pm.0017}$	$.1205_{\pm.0057}$	$.1325_{\pm.0125}$	$.1441_{\pm.0027}$
ReMasker	$.0546_{\pm.0020}$	$.1227_{\pm.0037}$	$.1088_{\pm.0017}$	$.1396_{\pm.0035}$	$.1620_{\pm.0020}$	$.1455_{\pm.0028}$
IGRM	$.0571_{\pm.0019}$	$.1000_{\pm.0073}$	$.1111_{\pm.0016}$	$.1243_{\pm.0047}$	$.1557_{\pm.0146}$	$.1578_{\pm.0015}$
DiffPuter	$.0564_{\pm.0027}$	$.1032_{\pm.0031}$	$.1029_{\pm.0023}$	$.1195_{\pm.0025}$	$.1421_{\pm.0161}$	$.1415_{\pm.0006}$
CAGI (ours)	$.0532_{\pm.0016}$	$.0884_{\pm.0053}$	$.0997_{\pm.0014}$	$.1173_{\pm.0063}$	$.1539_{\pm.0144}$	$.1489_{\pm.0014}$

Metrics. Root Mean Square Error (RMSE) is adopted for numerical attributes and Proportion of Falsely Classified entries (PFC) [29] for categorical attributes, where imputed continuous values are decoded back to discrete categories before evaluation. Lower values indicate better performance for both. Downstream utility is assessed through two tasks: (1) *Classification*, where a Logistic Regression classifier is trained on imputed data and evaluated by Area Under the ROC Curve (AUROC), and (2) *Clustering*, where K-Means is applied to imputed data with the number of clusters matching the ground-truth class count, and Adjusted Rand Index (ARI) is reported. Following prior work [10,33–35], missing values are generated under the multivariate MCAR setting, where missingness is introduced independently across all features and samples. Unless otherwise stated, the missing rate is set to 0.6 to evaluate methods under challenging conditions. Each experiment is repeated five times with 5-fold cross-validation, and the average performance is reported. In each repetition, a new MCAR mask is independently generated, and imputation models are fitted on the training fold only, with imputation quality evaluated on the test fold.

Table 2. Comparison of imputation performance on categorical datasets (measured by PFC). The best and second-best results are highlighted for each dataset.

Method	**car**	**mushroom**	**letter**
Mean/Mode	$.6582_{\pm.0212}$	$.4101_{\pm.0070}$	$.7690_{\pm.0035}$
KNNImpute	$.6664_{\pm.0097}$	$.3399_{\pm.0037}$	$.7898_{\pm.0019}$
MICE	$.6684_{\pm.0128}$	$.3369_{\pm.0068}$	$.8245_{\pm.0022}$
MissForest	$.6887_{\pm.0136}$	$.2774_{\pm.0094}$	$.7742_{\pm.0134}$
GAIN	$.6665_{\pm.0121}$	$.4449_{\pm.0228}$	$.8487_{\pm.0164}$
MIWAE	$.6749_{\pm.0195}$	$.2720_{\pm.0080}$	$.7663_{\pm.0024}$
MIRACLE	$.6977_{\pm.0206}$	$.3161_{\pm.0259}$	$.8507_{\pm.0106}$
OTImpute	$.6814_{\pm.0128}$	$.3029_{\pm.0034}$	$.7489_{\pm.0019}$
TDM	$.6624_{\pm.0119}$	$.5135_{\pm.0099}$	$.8720_{\pm.0032}$
GCImpute	$.6611_{\pm.0104}$	$.3854_{\pm.0294}$	$.7438_{\pm.0026}$
TabCSDI	$.6675_{\pm.0140}$	$.3130_{\pm.0085}$	$.7770_{\pm.0039}$
GRAPE	$.6626_{\pm.0141}$	$.3898_{\pm.0303}$	$.7718_{\pm.0057}$
ReMasker	$.6986_{\pm.0129}$	$.2859_{\pm.0054}$	$.7524_{\pm.0032}$
IGRM	$.6747_{\pm.0160}$	$.3454_{\pm.0082}$	$.7793_{\pm.0040}$
DiffPuter	$.6684_{\pm.0155}$	$.2952_{\pm.0098}$	$.7521_{\pm.0037}$
CAGI (ours)	$.6539_{\pm.0126}$	$.2532_{\pm.0032}$	$.7333_{\pm.0027}$

4.2 Imputation Performance

Tables 1, 2 and Fig. 3 present imputation performance on single-type and mixed-type datasets, respectively. CAGI ranks first on 7 out of 9 single-type datasets and achieves the lowest combined error on 4 out of 5 mixed-type datasets. Although no single method dominates across every dataset due to varying data characteristics, CAGI's consistent superiority across diverse benchmarks supports the central hypothesis: by partitioning the generative search space via cluster conditioning, the imputation model approximates a collection of simpler subgroup-specific distributions rather than a single complex global one, yielding higher instance-level fidelity. CAGI also demonstrates strong performance on mixed data, as the subgroup-specific co-occurrence patterns between numerical and categorical features are captured by the combined distance metric.

4.3 Ablation Study

Table 3 validates the design of CAGI by removing key modules and loss terms.

Impact of Key Components. Removing cluster conditioning ("w/o *Clustering*") leads to degradation across all datasets, with the largest drop on *spam*. Without subgroup priors, the generator approximates the entire data distribution as a single manifold and loses the ability to capture subgroup-specific patterns. This directly validates CAGI's core design premise. Disabling periodic reclustering ("w/o *Updating*") reduces CAGI to a fixed cluster-then-impute pipeline. The consistent degradation confirms the value of iterative co-refinement over static assignments, even when initial clusters are imperfect.

Impact of Loss Functions. The reconstruction loss $\mathcal{L}_{\text{MSE}}$ proves to be the most critical component: its removal causes RMSE to increase dramatically, confirming that $\mathcal{L}_{\text{MSE}}$ serves as the primary anchor for instance-level fidelity. The Sinkhorn regularization $\mathcal{L}_{\text{OT}}$ has a strong impact on categorical data: removing

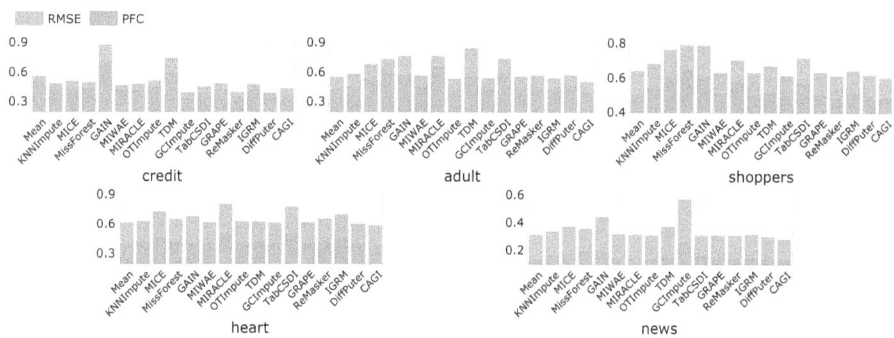

Fig. 3. Imputation performance comparison on mixed-type datasets. Each stacked bar shows RMSE (top) and PFC (bottom) simultaneously.

Table 3. Ablation study on key components and loss functions.

Method	spam	letter	adult	
	RMSE	PFC	RMSE	PFC
Full Model	**.0532**$\pm$.0016	**.7333**$\pm$.0027	**.1177**$\pm$.0011	**.4006**$\pm$.0040
• *Impact of Key Components*				
w/o *Clustering*	.0598$\pm$.0014	.7548$\pm$.0028	.1239$\pm$.0013	.4103$\pm$.0034
w/o *Updating*	.0580$\pm$.0029	.7369$\pm$.0036	.1193$\pm$.0013	.4022$\pm$.0035
• *Impact of Loss Functions*				
w/o $\mathcal{L}_{\text{MSE}}$	.1224$\pm$.0161	.7525$\pm$.0047	.1447$\pm$.0260	.4060$\pm$.0032
w/o $\mathcal{L}_{\text{ADV}}$	.0591$\pm$.0016	.7351$\pm$.0027	.1178$\pm$.0013	.4015$\pm$.0034
w/o $\mathcal{L}_{\text{OT}}$	.0586$\pm$.0014	.7731$\pm$.0030	.1187$\pm$.0013	.4242$\pm$.0050

it leads to a notable degradation in PFC. This aligns with the design rationale that distribution-level consistency is particularly important for categorical features, where small distributional shifts can flip discrete category assignments. Removing $\mathcal{L}_{\mathrm{ADV}}$ also degrades performance, confirming that adversarial training further improves the statistical quality and training stability of the imputation.

Training Loss Analysis. To further understand how the multi-level objectives interact during optimization, Fig. 4 visualizes the relative contribution of each loss term over training on the *spam* dataset. The optimization naturally progresses through three phases: **(1) Foundation (early phase):** $\mathcal{L}_{\mathrm{MSE}}$ dominates the total gradient, driving the generator to establish coarse fidelity. **(2) Transition (middle phase):** $\mathcal{L}_{\mathrm{ADV}}$ progressively increases as the generator shifts from pure reconstruction toward adversarial refinement, improving the statistical plausibility of imputed values. **(3) Refinement (late phase):** $\mathcal{L}_{\mathrm{ADV}}$ becomes the primary gradient driver, pushing the generated distribution toward statistical indistinguishability from the observed data. Throughout all phases, $\mathcal{L}_{\mathrm{OT}}$ maintains a consistent contribution, providing persistent geometric regularization. The convergence of all components to stable ratios indicates that the alternating optimization reaches a stable equilibrium.

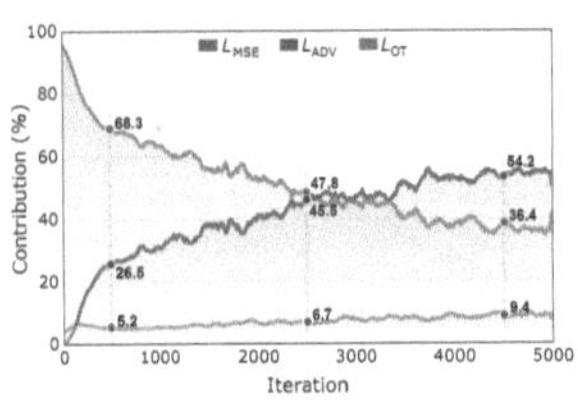

Fig. 4. The contribution ratio of each loss component ($\mathcal{L}_{\mathrm{MSE}}$, $\mathcal{L}_{\mathrm{ADV}}$, and $\mathcal{L}_{\mathrm{OT}}$).

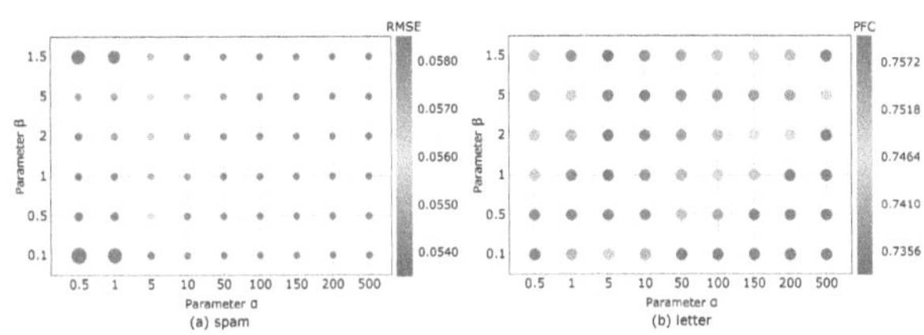

Fig. 5. Sensitivity to loss weights α ($\mathcal{L}_{\mathrm{MSE}}$) and β ($\mathcal{L}_{\mathrm{OT}}$) on datasets *spam* (a) and *letter* (b). Metric values are indicated by bubble size and color.

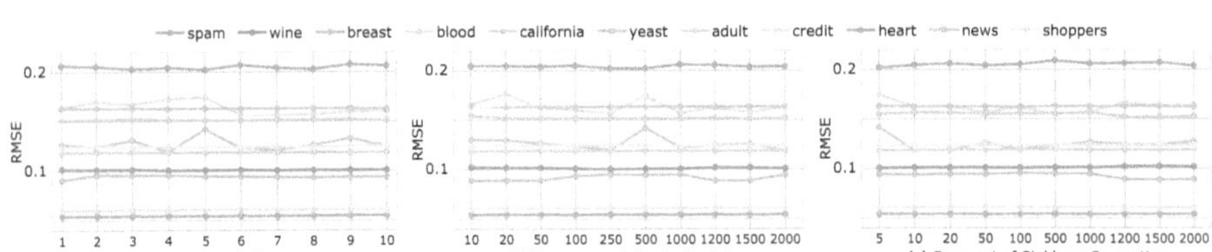

Fig. 6. Sensitivity to: (a) number of clusters K, (b) cluster update frequency, and (c) Sinkhorn computation frequency. Default setting: $K = 5$, cluster update frequency $= 500$, Sinkhorn frequency $= 5$.

4.4 Sensitivity Analysis

This subsection examines the sensitivity of CAGI to key hyperparameters (i.e., Loss Weights, Number of Clusters, and Update Frequencies).

Loss Weights. Figure 5 presents a grid search over $\alpha \in [0.5, 500]$ and $\beta \in [0.1, 5]$. RMSE on *spam* remains near-optimal across a broad region where $\alpha \geq 10$, with degradation occurring primarily when α is small and β simultaneously large; a similar pattern emerges on *letter*. Overall, α must maintain sufficient dominance to anchor instance-level fidelity, while β serves as a complementary regularizer whose exact value is not critical within a reasonable range.

Number of Clusters. As shown in Fig. 6(a), performance is remarkably stable across a wide range of K values. This empirically confirms the design choice discussed in Sect. 3.2: since cluster assignments serve as soft locality priors rather than strict subgroup identifiers, the model tolerates substantial variation in K without significant degradation.

Update Frequencies. The cluster update frequency (Fig. 6(b)) reveals a clear trade-off: very frequent updates introduce instability as the generator continuously adapts to rapidly shifting assignments, while very infrequent updates condition the generator on stale subgroup information. The optimal range of 50–500 iterations provides sufficient time for the generator to adapt to current assignments before receiving updated guidance. The Sinkhorn computation frequency (Fig. 6(c)) exhibits a similar trade-off.

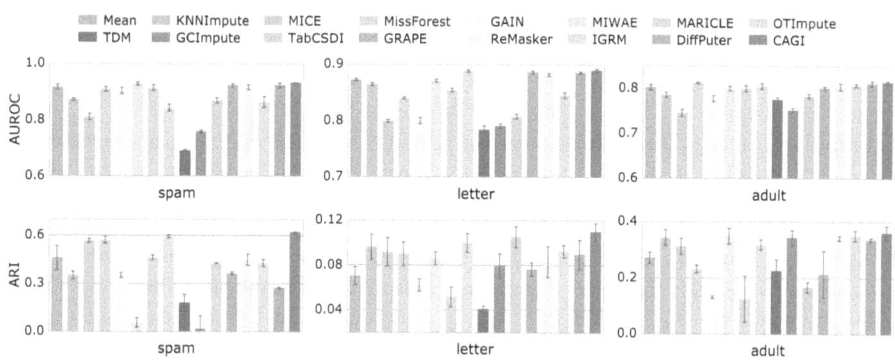

Fig. 7. Classification performance (top, measured by AUROC) and clustering performance (bottom, measured by ARI) on *spam*, *letter*, and *adult*. Higher values indicate better performance for both metrics.

4.5 Downstream Task Evaluation

This subsection evaluates whether CAGI's improved imputation fidelity translates into tangible gains for classification and clustering.

Classification Performance. As shown in Fig. 7(top), CAGI achieves competitive or superior AUROC scores across all datasets. This indicates that the improved imputation fidelity translates into downstream gains: higher-quality imputations preserve discriminative signals that benefit the classifier.

Clustering Performance. As shown in Fig. 7(bottom), CAGI achieves the highest or near-highest ARI on the majority of datasets. This is directly explained by CAGI's design: explicitly modeling subgroup structure during imputation naturally preserves inter-cluster separability. Such preservation is valuable for unsupervised downstream tasks where distributional fidelity matters more than pointwise accuracy.

5 Conclusion

In this paper, we propose CAGI to guide imputation via a "Partition-Guide-Restore" strategy. Cluster assignments and imputed values are jointly refined through an iterative feedback loop, where each progressively improves the others. To ensure both instance-level fidelity and distribution-level consistency, CAGI adopts a multi-level learning objective combining cluster-conditioned adversarial generation with optimal-transport regularization. Extensive experiments demonstrate CAGI's superiority in imputation fidelity and downstream tasks utility. While CAGI shows robust performance across a range of cluster counts K, automatically determining an appropriate K could further tailor the model to the intrinsic structures of different datasets and improve accuracy. Future work will explore data-driven cluster granularity selection, investigate the interplay between subgroup structure and non-random missingness mechanisms, and further generalize the framework to temporal data with sequential dependencies.

Acknowledgments. This work was supported in part by the National Natural Science Foundation of China under grants: 62476063, 62374047, and 62302104; in part by the Natural Science Foundation of Guangdong Province under grants: 2025A1515011293 and 2026A1515011337; in part by the General Research Fund of the Research Grants Council of Hong Kong under Grants: 12202025 and 12202924; in part by the State Key Lab of Processors, Institute of Computing Technology, CAS, under grant: CLQ 202407, in part by the Guangdong and Hong Kong Universities "1+1+1" Joint Research Collaboration Scheme with grant: 2025A0505000004, and in part by the HKBU Seed Funding for Collaborative Research Grants with grant: RC-SFCRG/23-24/R2/SCI/10.

Disclosure of Interests. The authors have no competing interests to declare that are relevant to the content of this article.

References

1. Alwateer, M., Atlam, E.S., Abd El-Raouf, M.M., et al.: Missing data imputation: a comprehensive review. J. Comput. Commun. **12**, 53–75 (2024)

2. Arjovsky, M., Chintala, S., Bottou, L.: Wasserstein generative adversarial networks. In: Proceedings of the 34th International Conference on Machine Learning, pp. 214–223. PMLR (2017)
3. Ayilara, O.F., Zhang, L., Sajobi, T.T., et al.: Impact of missing data on bias and precision when estimating change in patient-reported outcomes from a clinical registry. Health Qual. Life Outcomes **17**(1), 106 (2019)
4. Cai, S., Zhang, Y., Luo, X.: Robust categorical data clustering guided by multi-granular competitive learning. In: Proceedings of the 44th International Conference on Distributed Computing Systems, pp. 288–299. IEEE (2024)
5. Chen, T., Zhang, R., Hinton, G.: Analog bits: generating discrete data using diffusion models with self-conditioning. arXiv preprint arXiv:2208.04202 (2022)
6. Chen, Z., Li, H., Wang, F., et al.: Rethinking the diffusion models for missing data imputation: a gradient flow perspective. Adv. Neural. Inf. Process. Syst. **37**, 112050–112103 (2024)
7. Cremer, C., Li, X., Duvenaud, D.: Inference suboptimality in variational autoencoders. In: Proceedings of the 35th International Conference on Machine Learning, pp. 1078–1086. PMLR (2018)
8. Cuturi, M.: Sinkhorn distances: lightspeed computation of optimal transport. Adv. Neural. Inf. Process. Syst. **26** (2013)
9. Dempster, A.P., Laird, N.M., Rubin, D.B.: Maximum likelihood from incomplete data via the EM algorithm. J. Roy. Stat. Soc.: Ser. B (Methodol.) **39**(1), 1–22 (1977)
10. Du, T., Melis, L., Wang, T.: Remasker: imputing tabular data with masked autoencoding. In: Proceedings of the 12th International Conference on Learning Representations (2024)
11. Goodfellow, I.J., Pouget-Abadie, J., Mirza, M.: Generative adversarial nets. Adv. Neural. Inf. Process. Syst. **27** (2014)
12. Huang, Z.: Extensions to the k-means algorithm for clustering large data sets with categorical values. Data Min. Knowl. Disc. **2**(3), 283–304 (1998)
13. Hwang, J., Suh, D.: CC-gain: clustering and classification-based generative adversarial imputation network for missing electricity consumption data imputation. Expert Syst. Appl. **255**, 124507 (2024)
14. Kingma, D.P., Welling, M.: Auto-encoding variational bayes. arXiv preprint arXiv:1312.6114 (2013)
15. Kyono, T., Zhang, Y., Bellot, A., van der Schaar, M.: Miracle: causally-aware imputation via learning missing data mechanisms. Adv. Neural. Inf. Process. Syst. **34**, 23806–23817 (2021)
16. Li, S.C.X., Jiang, B., Marlin, B.: MisGAN: learning from incomplete data with generative adversarial networks. arXiv preprint arXiv:1902.09599 (2019)
17. Li, Z., Huang, Q., Yang, L.: Diffusion models for tabular data: challenges, current progress, and future directions. arXiv preprint arXiv:2502.17119 (2025)
18. Little, R.J., Rubin, D.B.: Statistical Analysis with Missing Data, 3rd edn. Wiley (2019)
19. Liu, Y., Ajanthan, T., Husain, H., Nguyen, V.: Self-supervision improves diffusion models for tabular data imputation. In: Proceedings of the 33rd ACM International Conference on Information and Knowledge Management, pp. 1513–1522 (2024)
20. Mattei, P.A., Frellsen, J.: MIWAE: deep generative modelling and imputation of incomplete data sets. In: Proceedings of the 36th International Conference on Machine Learning, pp. 4413–4423. PMLR (2019)

21. Muzellec, B., Josse, J., Boyer, C., Cuturi, M.: Missing data imputation using optimal transport. In: Proceedings of the 37th International Conference on Machine Learning, pp. 7130–7140. PMLR (2020)
22. Nazabal, A., Olmos, P.M., Ghahramani, Z., Valera, I.: Handling incomplete heterogeneous data using VAEs. Pattern Recogn. **107**, 107501 (2020)
23. Patil, B.M., Joshi, R.C., Toshniwal, D.: Missing value imputation based on k-mean clustering with weighted distance. In: Ranka, S., et al. (eds.) IC3 2010. CCIS, vol. 94, pp. 600–609. Springer, Heidelberg (2010). https://doi.org/10.1007/978-3-642-14834-7_56
24. Peyré, G., Cuturi, M.: Computational optimal transport: with applications to data science. Found. Trends® Mach. Learn. **11**(5-6), 355–607 (2019)
25. Raja, P., Thangavel, K.: Missing value imputation using unsupervised machine learning techniques. Soft. Comput. **24**(6), 4361–4392 (2020)
26. Salimans, T., Goodfellow, I., Zaremba, W.: Improved techniques for training GANs. Adv. Neural. Inf. Process. Syst. **29** (2016)
27. Samad, M.D., Abrar, S., Diawara, N.: Missing value estimation using clustering and deep learning within multiple imputation framework. Knowl.-Based Syst. **249**, 108968 (2022)
28. Song, J., Meng, C., Ermon, S.: Denoising diffusion implicit models. arXiv preprint arXiv:2010.02502 (2020)
29. Stekhoven, D.J., Bühlmann, P.: MissForest–non-parametric missing value imputation for mixed-type data. Bioinformatics **28**(1), 112–118 (2012)
30. Tomczak, J., Welling, M.: VAE with a VampPrior. In: Proceedings of the 2018 International Conference on Artificial Intelligence and Statistics, pp. 1214–1223. PMLR (2018)
31. Troyanskaya, O., Cantor, M., Sherlock, G.A.: Missing value estimation methods for DNA microarrays. Bioinformatics **17**(6), 520–525 (2001)
32. Van Buuren, S., Groothuis-Oudshoorn, K.: mice: multivariate imputation by chained equations in R. J. Stat. Softw. **45**, 1–67 (2011)
33. Yoon, J., Jordon, J., Schaar, M.: GAIN: missing data imputation using generative adversarial nets. In: Proceedings of the 35th International Conference on Machine Learning, pp. 5689–5698. PMLR (2018)
34. You, J., Ma, X., Ding, Y., et al.: Handling missing data with graph representation learning. Adv. Neural. Inf. Process. Syst. **33**, 19075–19087 (2020)
35. Zhang, H., Fang, L., Wu, Q., Yu, P.S.: DiffPuter: empowering diffusion models for missing data imputation. In: Proceedings of the the 13th International Conference on Learning Representations (2025)
36. Zhang, S., Zhang, J., Zhu, X., et al.: Missing value imputation based on data clustering. In: Transactions on Computational Science I, pp. 128–138. Springer (2008)
37. Zhang, Y., Cheung, Y.M.: An ordinal data clustering algorithm with automated distance learning. In: Proceedings of the 34th AAAI Conference on Artificial Intelligence, vol. 34, pp. 6869–6876 (2020)
38. Zhang, Y., Cheung, Y.M.: Graph-based dissimilarity measurement for cluster analysis of any-type-attributed data. IEEE Trans. Neural Netw. Learn. Syst. **34**(9), 6530–6544 (2022)
39. Zhang, Y., Cheung, Y.M., Zeng, A.: Het2Hom: representation of heterogeneous attributes into homogeneous concept spaces for categorical-and-numerical-attribute data clustering. In: Proceedings of the 31st International Joint Conference on Artificial Intelligence, pp. 3758–3765 (2022)

40. Zhang, Y., Zhao, M., Jia, H., et al.: Categorical data clustering via value order estimated distance metric learning. Proc. ACM Manage. Data **3**(6), 1–24 (2025)
41. Zou, R., Zhang, Y., Zhang, Y., et al.: Adaptive micro partition and hierarchical merging for accurate mixed data clustering. Complex Intell. Syst. **11**(1), 84 (2025)
42. Zhang, Z., Zhang, Y., Zeng, A., et al.: Time-series data imputation via realistic masking-guided tri-attention bi-GRU. In: Proceedings of the 26th European Conference on Artificial Intelligence, pp. 3074–3082 (2023)
43. Zhao, H., Sun, K., Dezfouli, A., Bonilla, E.V.: Transformed distribution matching for missing value imputation. In: Proceedings of the 40th International Conference on Machine Learning, pp. 42159–42186. PMLR (2023)
44. Zhao, L., Zhang, Y., Ji, Y.: Heterogeneous drift learning: classification of mix-attribute data with concept drifts. In: Proceedings of the 9th International Conference on Data Science and Advanced Analytics, pp. 1–10. IEEE (2022)
45. Zhao, M., Feng, S., Zhang, Y.: Learning order forest for qualitative-attribute data clustering. In: Proceedings of the 27th European Conference on Artificial Intelligence, pp. 1943–1950. IOS Press (2024)
46. Zhao, M., Huang, Z., Lu, Y.: Break the tie: learning cluster-customized category relationships for categorical data clustering. In: Proceedings of the 40th AAAI Conference on Artificial Intelligence, vol. 40, pp. 28715–28723 (2026)
47. Zhao, Y., Udell, M.: Missing value imputation for mixed data via gaussian copula. In: Proceedings of the 26th ACM SIGKDD International Conference on Knowledge Discovery & Data Mining, pp. 636–646 (2020)
48. Zheng, S., Charoenphakdee, N.: Diffusion models for missing value imputation in tabular data. arXiv preprint arXiv:2210.17128 (2022)
49. Zhong, J., Gui, N., Ye, W.: Data imputation with iterative graph reconstruction. In: Proceedings of the 37th AAAI Conference on Artificial Intelligence, vol. 37, pp. 11399–11407 (2023)
50. Zhuang, B., Liu, J., Pan, Z.: A survey on efficient training of transformers. arXiv preprint arXiv:2302.01107 (2023)

Author Index

M. Ceci et al. (Eds.): ECML PKDD 2026, LNAI 16941, pp. 717–719, 2027.
https://doi.org/10.1007/978-3-032-37654-1

FSC
www.fsc.org
MIX
Papier | Fördert gute Waldnutzung
FSC® C083411

Kolibri 360 GmbH
Ferdinand-Jühlke-Straße 7
99095 Erfurt, Deutschland
produktsicherheit@kolibri360.de